Descriptive Catalogue of Derbyshire Charters in Public and Private Libraries and Muniment Rooms

Descriptive Catalogue

OF

Derbyshire Charters

IN

Public and Private Libraries
and Muniment Rooms

DESCRIPTIVE CATALOGUE

OF

Derbyshire Charters

IN

Public and Private Libraries and

Muniment Rooms

COMPILED,

With Preface and Indexes.

FOR

SIR HENRY HOWE BEMROSE, KT.,

BY

ISAAC HERBERT JEAYES

Assistant-Keeper in the Department
of MSS., British Museum.

LONDON

BEMROSE & SONS LTD., 4, SNOW HILL, E.C.

AND DERBY

—

1906

PREFACE.

THE present volume of abstracts of ancient deeds relating to the County of Derby owes its publication to the following circumstances :—

The Derbyshire Library and Collection of Sir H. H. Bemrose includes an extensive and varied mass of manuscripts, among which are many original deeds of ancient and modern date. The services of an expert being sought to examine and catalogue these with a view to the possible publication of some of them, the present Editor undertook the work. While this was being done, a little enquiry soon elicited the fact that there were numerous other deeds, in private hands, scattered through the County, which would be placed at Sir Henry's disposal for so useful a purpose as the publication of a book of Derbyshire Charters. Moreover, the British Museum was known to be rich in Derbyshire deeds, having in its entirety the charters collected by Adam Wolley and bequeathed by him to the nation in 1828, as well as many others, and it was, therefore, decided to make short abstracts in English, which should embrace all the salient points of each document, of all the Derbyshire deeds, either in public archives or private muniment rooms, to which access could be had.

It will be seen from the appended list of owners, etc., that the 2,787 charters treated in this volume were derived from no less than thirty-four different sources. With very few exceptions, the charters are in actual existence, and have been examined by the Editor, whose object has been to include only those deeds which can themselves, if necessary, be referred to.

The earliest charter included is one to Calk Abbey, to which the date of *circ.* 1129-1139 has been assigned, and it was decided to include nothing later than A.D. 1550.

The twelfth century charters, of which there are fifty-six, have been printed in full (except one or two, the originals of which could not be seen).

The Editor would gladly have included, especially, the collections of the Duke of Devonshire, the Duke of Rutland, and Sir Francis Burdett, of Foremark, but though these owners expressed sympathy with the work, various circumstances prevented their collections being dealt with at this time. A few, however, of the last-named owner's very early charters have been taken from printed books and inserted, though the originals were not examined. There are ample materials in these three collections alone for another volume equal in bulk to the present one if its reception be such as to encourage a continuation of the enterprise.

The arrangement of the abstracts is as follows:—Where a deed refers to one place only, it will, naturally, be found under that place. Where, however, several places occur in one deed, the abstract will be found under the place which is mentioned *first* in the deed, and to that place cross references will be added under the other places mentioned.

There are added three separate Indices—viz., of Places, Persons, and Matters, whereby, it is hoped, the contents of the book will be easily accessible, not only to local antiquaries, genealogists, and others, but also to those who have the more serious end in view—namely, the compilation of original materials for the future history of Derbyshire. In the preparation of the Index the Editor has been much assisted by the careful work of Mr. E. E. Taylor, the Curator of Sir H. H. Bemrose's Library at Derby.

The Editor wishes to thank most cordially the following noblemen, gentlemen, and ladies, who have acceded so willingly to his applications for the use of their charters, viz.:—The Right Hon. Lord Scarsdale, of Kedleston; the Hon. Henry J. Coke, of Longford; the Right Hon. F. J. S. Foljambe, of Osberton, Notts.; Sir E. O. Every, Bart., and Godfrey Mosley, esq., of Derby, his trustee; Sir Ralph H. S. Wilmot, Bart., of Chaddesden, and Miss Wilmot; Gen. John Talbot Coke, of Trusley; Col. William Langton Coke, of Brookhill; C. E. B. Bowles, esq., of Wirksworth; Miss de Rodes (now Mrs. Locker-Lampson), of Barlborough Hall; Charles Drury, esq., of Sheffield; W. Drury Lowe, esq., of Locko; W. R. Holland, esq., of Ashbourne; Mrs. Mundy, of Markeaton; Haughton C. Okeover, esq., of Okeover; Mrs. Pole-Gell, of Hopton; R. R. Redmayne, esq., Chapter Clerk at Lichfield; G. Trevelyan Lee, esq., Town Clerk of Derby; and to Henry J. Ellis, esq., of the Manuscript Dept., British Museum, for valuable assistance in dating, etc., the twelfth century charters. Also to many others in the County who have aided him by their advice and suggestions in his efforts to find out the hiding-places of these manuscript treasures; the editors of printed books bearing on the subject; the owners of private catalogues; and to the writers of various articles in the *Journals* of the Derbyshire Archæological and Natural History Society, all of which works the Editor has ventured to make use of.

But chiefly are his thanks due and offered to Sir H. H. Bemrose, the instigator and promoter of the book, who has met all the Editor's suggestions in a most generous and public-spirited manner, and at whose expense the volume is published.   His devotion to all that concerns the County is well known, but if this publication should prove to be acceptable and useful at all, it will be chiefly owing to him, and he will have added one more to his many services to the Town and County of Derby.

I. H. JEAYES.

British Museum.
March, 1906.

Contents.

	PAGE
References after Abstracts, Explanation of · · · ·	ix
Corrigenda · · · · · · · · · ·	xi
Derbyshire Charters · · · · · · · ·	1
Indexes :—	
Places · · · · · · · · ·	355
Names. · · · · · · · ·	389
Matters · · · · · · · ·	481
Owners and Sources of Charters · · · · ·	485

Explanation of the References

AT THE END OF EACH ABSTRACT.

Add. = Additional Charters, British Museum.

Campb. = Campbell „ „ „

Cott. = Cotton „ „ „

Eg. = Egerton „ „ „

Harl. = Harley „ „ „

Lansd. = Lansdowne „ „ „

Stowe = Stowe „ „ „

Toph. = Topham „ „ „

Woll. = Wolley „ „ „

P. R. O. = Public Record Office. (Cal. of Ancient Charters.)

D. of L. = Duchy of Lancaster. (Taken from the Thirty-fifth Report of Public Records, Appendix I.)

*Bemrose = Deeds in the possession of Sir H. H. Bemrose.

Berkeley = Deeds at Berkeley Castle. (From the Printed Catalogue; Ed., I. H. Jeayes.)

*Bowles = Deeds in the possession of C. E. B. Bowles, Esq., of Wirksworth.

*Brookhill = Deeds in the possession of Colonel W. L. Coke, of Brookhill.

Burdett = Deeds in the possession of Sir F. Burdett,[1] at Foremark.

Chest. Mun. = The Muniments of Chesterfield Corporation. (From the Printed Catalogue, by J. Pym Yeatman, Esq.)

D. A. J. = *Derbyshire Archæological Journal.*

Debdale v. Trusley.

*Derby Mun. = The Muniments of Derby Corporation.

*de Rodes = Deeds of Miss de Rodes, of Barlborough Hall.

*Drury = The Beresford Charters, formerly in the possession of J. F. Lucas, Esq., of Bentley Hall, from whom they passed to Charles Drury, Esq., of Sheffield, their present owner.

---

[1] Taken from *The Topographer* (1790), Vol. II., pp. 264-285, and from Bigsby's *History of Repton.*

*Drury Lowe = Deeds of W. Drury Lowe, Esq., of Locko.

*Every = Deeds of Sir E. O. Every, Bart., at Egginton. (By permission of the Trustees.)

*Foljambe = Deeds of the Right Hon. F. J. S. Foljambe, of Osberton.

Gregory = "penes J. Gregory, of Overton." (Kerry Transcripts.)

Gresley = Deeds of Sir Robert Gresley, Bart., at Drakelowe. (From the Printed Catalogue; Ed., I. H. Jeayes.)

Hallowes = "Deeds of Rev. B. Hallowes, of Glapwell." (Kerry Transcripts.)

*Holland = Deeds in the possession of W. R. Holland, Esq., of Ashbourne.

Horton = The Horton Charters. (From Ussher's *History of Croxall.*)

*Kedleston = Deeds of the Right Hon. Lord Scarsdale, at Kedleston.

Kerry = The transcripts made by Rev. C. Kerry (now in the possession of Sir H. H. Bemrose) from various collections.

*Lichfield = The Muniments at Lichfield Cathedral.

*Longford = Deeds of Hon. H. J. Coke, at Longford.

*Mundy = Deeds of Mrs. Mundy, at Markeaton.

Ogston = "Ogston Hall Charters." (Kerry Transcripts.)

*Okeover = Deeds of H. C. Okeover, Esq., of Okeover.

*Pole-Gell = Deeds of the late H. Chandos-Pole-Gell, Esq., of Hopton Hall.

R. D. G. = Robinson's *Derbyshire Gatherings* (1866).

Reliquary = Jewitt's *Reliquary.*

Roper = A few Calk Abbey Charters taken from Harl. MS. 2044 (British Museum), and stated there to be in the possession of "S. Roper, of Monks Kirby."

*Trusley = Deeds of General J. T. Coke, of Trusley, late of Debdale.

*Wilmot = Deeds of Sir R. H. S. Wilmot, Bart., at Chaddesden.

CORRIGENDA.

P. 23 (No. 176, l. 3), *for* Cornhull *read* Cornhill.

P. 25 (No. 189, l. 10), *for circ.* 1254 *read ante* 1254.

P. 27 (No. 209, l. 5), *for* Amine *read* Avyne.

P. 31 (No. 238, l. 2), *for* Comton *read* Comtun.

P. 31 (No. 238, l. 11), *for* Ashenden *read* Ashdown.

P. 39 (No. 301), *after* Stenerdale *read* [? Stevordale].

P. 54 (No. 431, l. 2), *omit* to Robert fil. Rog. de la Grene.

P. 65 (No. 523, l. 3), *for* bailiff *read* bailiffs.

P. 66 (No. 528), *for circ.* 1129-1139 *read* [1132-1136].

P. 68 (No. 531, l. 9), *for* capiti *read* caput.

P. 75 (No. 578, l. 2), *for* ? co. Derby *read* co. Bedf.

P. 76 (No. 590, l. 2), *after* Nye *add* [? Nyke].

P. 85 (headline), *for* Chelardiston *read* Chellaston.

P. 86 (No. 677, l. 3), *for* Avery [daughter?] *read* Avine [wife].

P. 96 (No. 772), *for* Koryfsmythe *read* Knyfsmythe.

P. 102 (No. 827, l. 5), *for* Swaloc *read* Swaloe.

P. 112 (No. 912, l. 5), *for* Maweyswn *read* Maweysyn.

P. 121 (No. 985, l. 3), *for* de *read* le.

P. 135 (No. 1092, l. 1), *for* Hinkneshille *read* Hinkreshille.

P. 147 (No. 1198, l. 3), *for* Staverley *read* Beverley.

P. 147 (No. 1200, l. 8), *for* Mergawute *read* Mergawnte.

P. 148 (No. 1201, l. 4), *for* Flexhewere *read* Fleschewere.

P. 165 (N. 1349, l. 1), *after* Kyvetone *add* [? *for* Knyvetone].

P. 176 (No. 1431, l. 5), *for* Cornhull *read* Cornhill.

P. 181 (No. 1469, l. 9), *for* justa *read* juxta.

P. 212, No. 1700 should be under "Middleton, Stoney."

P. 218 (No. 1741, l. 2), *for* Philip *read* Philippa.

P. 220 (No. 1752, l. 3), *for* Hubert *read* Herbert.

P. 227 (No. 1813), *for* Oslaston *read* Osliston.

P. 230 (No. 1833, l. 4), *for* 170 *read* 1270.

P. 233 (No. 1868, l. 7), *for* 1399 *read* 1422.

P. 246 (No. 1954, l. 8), *for* Muligny *read* Suligny.

P. 255 (No. 2022, l. 7), *for* Humelun *read* Hamelun.

P. 255 (No. 2026, l. 5), *for* Masey *read* Mascy.

P. 278 (No. 2194, l. 3), *for* Richard *read* Robert.

P. 282 (No. 2227, l. 3), *for* Freynan *read* Freyman.

P. 283 (No. 2233, l. 6, 2235, l. 6), *for* Smetheby *read* Smetheley.

P. 285 (No. 2253, l. 2), *for* Hartbill *read* Harthill.

P. 290 (No. 2288, l. 5), *for* Waddeley *read* Waldeley.

P. 304 (No. 2396, l. 3), *for* Heles *read* Hales.

P. 306 (No. 2412, l. 4), *for* 1306 *read* 1366.

P. 310 (No. 2450, l. 2), *for* Ballok *read* Bullok.

P. 310 (No. 2455, l. 5), *for* Uwerthorp *read* Ulkerthorp.

P. 314 (l. 17), *for* Cubley *read* Sudbury.

P. 325 (No. 2580, l. 2), *for* Nulcrum *read* Hulcrume.

P. 329 (No. 2607, l. 4), *for* 4 Edw. II. [1310] *read* 4 Ric. II. [1380].

P. 329 (No. 2611, l. 8), *for* seriuens *read* seruiens.

P. 336 (No. 2660, l. 1, 5), *for* Cloptone Claptone *read* Hopton.

P. 336 (No. 2665, l. 4), *for* Daron *read* Baron.

P. 338 (No. 2681, line 4), *for* his *read* her.

P. 341 (No. 2712, l. 5), *for* Monseye *read* Monjoye.

P. 343 (No. 2720, l. 5), *for* Knyvete *read* Knyvet[on].

xi

DERBYSHIRE CHARTERS.

ABNEY, IN HOPE.

(ABBENAY, ABBENEY, ABBENEYE, ABNEYE.)

1. GRANT from William de Barkystun and Marjory, his wife, to Robert de Abbeneye, of a bovate of land in Abbeneye. Witn. Olyver de Langeford, Simon de Gonsyl, John de Bamforde, etc. *Temp.* Edw. I. (Woll. viii. 1.)

2. RELEASE from William fil. Joh. Fox, de Offerton, to Thomas del Cloughe of a messuage and a bovate of land in Abbeneye. Witn. Richard le Archer, Peter de Shatton, Richard Fox, etc. Dat. Offerton, W. in Pentecost [25 May], 10 Edw. II. [1317]. (Woll. viii. 4.)

3. GRANT from John fil. Rob. de Baggeschawe de Abbeney, to William de Baggeschawe, of a messuage and a bovate of land in Abbeney. Witn. John Larchere, Thomas Larchere, John Hebbe, etc. Dat. S. a. All Saints [1 Nov.], 4 Ric. II. [1380]. (Woll. viii. 8.)

4. RELEASE from John Abbenay, of Castelton, to John Wylde of Abbenay, of lands in Abbenay. Dat. Hope, S. b. F. of St. George [23 Apr.], 21 Ric. II. [1398]. (Woll. viii. 3.)

5. POWER of Attorney by John Alott, capellanus, to Thomas Woderove of Hope, to deliver seisin to Thomas Bagscha of Abnaye, of lands in Abneye. Dat. F. of St. Juliana [16 Feb.], 18 Hen. VI. [1440]. (Woll. viii. 9.)

6. LEASE for 86 years from the Abbot and Convent of the Blessed Virgin Mary of Rufford [Co. Notts.], to Ralph Eyre of Offirton, of the Grange of Abney. Dat. Rufford, 5 Feb., 1473[4]. (Woll. ii. 80.)

7. QUITCLAIM from Thurstan Hall of Overhurst to Roger Foliambe of Lynacre Hall, esquire, of all his lands, etc., within the vill and field of Abney. Witn. Richard Bouthe of Abney, Renald Bouthe, William Kede, William Bradscha of Lynacre Hall, Gilbard Schaw of Walton. Dat. at Lynacre-hall in the parish of Brampton, 14 Apr., 10 Hen. VIII. [1519]. (Bowles.)

ABNEY *v.* also under BRADWELL, CHESTERFIELD, OFFERTON.

ALDERCAR *v.* under CODNOR.

ALDERWASLEY.

(Alderwashele, Alderwaslegh, Alderwasleghe, Allerwaslegh.)

8. Extract of court held at Beaur [Beaurepair] on Th. b. F. of All Saints [1 Nov.], 12 Edw. IV. [1462], recording the surrender of a messuage and land in Alderwaslegh by John Patton to the use of John Valens and Katherine his wife, dau. of the said John Patton, who were thereupon admitted. (Pole-Gell.)

9. Extract of court held at Holand on Th. a. F. of St. Valentine [14 Feb.], 22 Edw. IV. [1483], recording the surrender by John Valence and Katherine his wife, of a messuage and land in Allerwaslegh and their re-admission. (Pole-Gell.)

10. Extract of court held at Duffeld on Th. b. F. of St. Gregory [12 Mar.], 5 Hen. VII. [1490], recording the surrender by Thomas Hervy, of Workesworth, of various enclosed lands in Alderwaslegh to the use of Thomas Wyggeley, of Callow, thereupon admitted. (Pole-Gell.)

11. Grant from Richard Norton of Alderwasleghe and Thomas, his son, to Richard Saucheverell, gent., of lands in Alderwasleghe, and appointing attorneys. Dat. 15 Dec., 19 Hen. VII. [1503]. (Woll. iii. 19.)

12. Extract of court held at Beaurepair, 2 Aug., 12 Henry VIII. [1520], recording the surrender by Richard Valance of a messuage and land in Alderwashele, which he held jointly with Katherine his mother, to the use of John Valance his brother. (Pole-Gell.)

13. Extract of court held 3 May, 38 Hen. VIII. [1546], recording the admission of Henry Sacheverell, esquire, son and heir of Ralph Sacheverell, to land in Alderwasley, and a cottage, etc., in Ashleyhey. (Pole-Gell.)

ALDWARK, in Bradborne.

(Aldewerk, Aldewerke, Aldwork, Audewerk.)

14. Lease, for 40 years, from Ranulph de Snetirton to William de Ibole, of land in Audewerk; rent 10s. Witn. Roger de Wedenisley, Henry de Cromforde, Henry, son of Thomas de Hopton, etc. Dat. F. of St. Michael [29 Sept.], 1289. (Woll. x. 5.)

15. Grant from Ranulph fil. Ran. de Snyterton to John fil. Ric. Knot de Bontessale, of a toft and lands in Aldwork; rent during 40 years, 8s., and after that time 10 marks. Witn. Ranulph de Snyterton, de Hopton, John le Porter, etc. Dat. Aldewerke, S. a. Michaelmas [29 Sept.], 3 Edw. II. [1309]. (Woll. x. 8.)

16. Grant from Ranulph fil. Ranulphi de Snyterton to William fil. Ade de Middelton, of lands in Aldewerk; rent for 40 years, 10s., and after that period 10 marks. Witn. Ranulph de Snyterton, sen., Henry de Hopton, William de Hopton, etc. Dat. F. of St. Edmund, Abp. [16 Nov.], 3 Edw. II. [1309]. (Woll. x. 11.)

17. GRANT from Ranulph fil. Ran. de Snuterton to William de Ibulle de Aldewerke and Agnes, his wife, of a messuage and lands in Aldewerke, for life or for 20 years; rent, during 20 years, 10s., and afterwards 100s. Witn. Dom. Robert de Ibull, perpetual vicar of Assheburne, Henry de Hoptone, John fil. Radulfi de Aldewerk, etc. Dat. Michaelmas, 1310. (Woll. x. 6.)

18. GRANT, for life, from Ranulph fil. Ranulfi junioris de Sniterton, to William de Ibulle de Aldewerke, and Agnes, his wife, and Nicholas, their son, of a messuage and lands in Aldewerke, their heirs to hold the same for 53 years in case of their decease within that period, at a rent during that time of 10s., and afterwards 100s. Witn. Dom. Robert de Ibul, perpetual vicar of Assheburne, Henry de Hopton, John fil Joh. de Aldewerke, etc. Dat. Sat. b. F. of SS. Philip and James [1 May], 1317. (Woll. x. 10.)

19. GRANT, in free marriage, from Ralph fil. Joh. de Bondissale of Aldewerke, to Roger Colte and Yngelesia, daughter of the said Ralph, of lands in Aldewerke; rent 1d. Witn. Robert de Wordisleye, Henry fil. Thome de Hopton, Henry de le How, in Aldewerke, etc. *Temp.* Edw. II. (Woll. x. 16.)

20. GRANT for life from William de Attelowe and Agnes, his wife, of two messuages and lands in Aldewerke; rent, 10s. 8d. Dat. Wirkesworthe, F. of Nat. of B. V. M. [8 Sept.], 42 Edw. III. [1368]. (Woll. x. 12.)

21. DEFEASANCE by John Leeke of Sutton-in-the-Dale, Esq., of a bond given by Thomas Saucheverell, of Kyrkby in Asshfeld, Co. Notts., etc., for delivery of title deeds of lands in Aldewerke, with waiver of claim upon two deeds specified at length. Dat. 20 Nov., 19 Hen. VII. [1503]. (Woll. x. 15.)

ALFRETON.

22. RELEASE from Thomas de Chawrthe, mil., to Simon fil. Petri de Grenhulle, of a rent of 21d., part of a rent of 5s. 9d., due from him for lands in Alfertone. Witn. Rob. Sautcheverel, mil., Ranulph de Wandesleya, mil., Rob. de Watenhow, etc. Dat. Nortone, T. bef. F. of B. V. M. [25 Mar.], 12 Edw. I. [1284]. (Woll. i. 21.)

23. CONFIRMATION by John Markham, Richard Byngham, Robert Clyfton, and others, as feoffees of Thomas Chaworth, to Henry Foliambe, esq., for life, of the stewardship of the manors of Alfreton, Norton and Williamthorp, and of all other lands, etc., in co. Derby which they hold to the use of the said Thomas, with a yearly fee of 40s. Dat. 15 Sept., 14 Edw. IV. [1474]. (Foljambe.)

24. LEASE, for 33 years, from Henry Wylloughby, Esq., to Robert Wilson and Agnes, his wife, for £18, in pursuance of an award made in a dispute between Cristofer Fitz-Randolph, of Westwood, Co. Notts., gent., and Jane, his wife, with the said Henry, of lands called Birchwood, in Alfreton; rent 4 marks. Dat. 24 Sept., 34 Hen. VIII. [1542]. (Woll. xii. 136.)

ALKMONTON.

25. LETTER from Rodbert de Bakepus, dominus de Alkemunton, whereby licence is granted to the Hospital of St. Leonard at Alkemunton to enclose a nook of land in le Horestone, and a place of land in the waste of le Fertewode, which John de Bakepuz, dominus de Barton, had given to the said Hospital. Witn. Dom. John de Longforde, mil., Dom. Giles de Memel, mil., Henry, dominus de Benteleye, etc. *Temp.* Hen. III. or Edw. I. (Woll. vi. 1.)

ALLESTREE *v.* under CASTLETON.

ALPORT, IN YOULGRAVE.

26. LETTER testimonial from Rauf Saucheverell, squier, and John Saucheverell, his son and heir apparent, that a yearly rent of 10s. and the suit to Aldeport mill, released by them to Henry Alyn and Nicholas, his son, were never 'entailed to them nor to any of their ancestors. Dat. Th. a. Michaelmas, 2 Ric. III. [1484]. (Woll. ii. 33.)

ALPORT *v.* also under BAKEWELL, HADDON.

ALSOP-LE-DALE.

(ALSHOP, ALSOPE.)

27. GRANT from Roger de Huncesdon to Thomas de Bradeford, of Richard and Adam, filii Walteri fil. Galfridi de Huncesdon, his nativi, with all their following, goods and chattels in Huncesdon [? Hanson Grange]. Witn. Robert de Thorp, John de Thorp, Adam de Thorp, Ralph Rufus, Ralph fil. Ranulfi, Richard fil. Nagge, Richard fil. Rad. de Thorp. Early Hen. III. (Okeover.)

28. GRANT from Henry fil. Ranulfi de Alsope to Thomas, his brother, of the land which Matilda de Sippele some time held in Alsope, to hold by service of one pair of gloves on the F. of St. James. Witn. Jurdin de Snuterton, Roger de Wentlesle, Robert de Thorp, Robert de Huncesdon, John de Cramphord, Rachenald de Karsint[on]. *Temp.* Hen. III. (Holland.)

29. GRANT from Richard fil. Petri de Huncedon to Henry fil. Thome de Alsop of three acres of land in Huncedon [? Hanson, nr. Alsop], lying between the land of Burton Abbey and of Roger Cokayn. Witn. Stephen de Irton, Geoffrey Martel, de Peverwiz, Hugh Bonseriant de Thorpe, etc. (?) *Temp.* Henry III. (Holland.)

30. GRANT from Henry fil. Thome de Alsop to John Morkoc de Esseburn of 20 acres of land and a croft in the fields of Alsop, with three buildings within his court in Alsop. Witn. Stephen de Irton, Henry de Kniveton, Roger de Bradeburn, Ranulph de Alsop, Thomas de Mapelton. Dat. Fr. aft. Epiphany [6 Jan.], 1287. (Holland.)

31. GRANT from Henry fil. Thome de Alsop to Dom. Walter de Lich', chaplain, " et duabus nutritis suis scilicet Avicie et Margarie juniori de filiabus suis," of a toft with buildings in Alsop, which toft extends from the King's highway to the croft of his own house; with other land at Le Rewestones, etc., in Alsop. Witn. Ranulf de Alsop, Richard de Morleye, Herbert fil. Herberti, Ralph Scherecroft, etc. [? late thirteenth century.] (Holland.)

32. GRANT from Henry Wilchar of Alsop with consent of Agnes, his wife, to Ranulph fil. Henrici de Alsop, of a house and six acres of land in the fields of Alsop. Witn. Ranulph de Alsop, John fil. Johannis de Alsop, Ralph Schercroft, of Eyton, etc. *Circ.* 1300. (Holland.)

33. GRANT from Ranulph de Alsop fil. Henrici de Alsop to Roger Chaumberleyn, parson of Rerisby [Rearsby, Co. Leic.], of all his land in Alsop. Witn. Ranulph de Alsop, John fil. Thome de Alsop, John fil. Simonis de Alsop, etc. Dat. T. aft. F. of St. Ambrose [4 Apr.], 1311. (Holland.)

34. GRANT from Ralph fil. Johannis de Alsop to Ranulph fil. Henrici de Alsop, of the third part of a messuage and land in Alsop, namely, that messuage which Henry fil. Herberti holds on le Rugweye, and the land lying on Le Pykestonlondes, Dalesyde, Hulliforlong, Oldeofne, and Pynhul, with the reversion of two roods in Alsop which Letitia, widow of John de Alsop, holds in dower. Witn. Ranulph fil. Ranulphi de Alsop, Henry fil. Roberti de Alsop, Henry Parsey, de Fennybentileye, etc. Dat. S. b. Inv. of H. Cross [3 May], 6 Edw. II. [1313]. (Holland.)

35. ATTORNEY from Margaret fil. Ranulphi fil. Henrici de Alsop to Thomas de Thurmeston, to receive seisin of the lands which her father gave her in Alsop. Dat. M. a. Pur. [2 Feb.], 1326[7], (Holland.)

36. QUITCLAIM from Beatrix que fuit uxor Ranulphi fil. Henrici de Alsop to Margaret dau. of the said Ranulph, her late husband, of all the latter's lands in Alsop. Witn. William Cordel, de Castre, William le Eyr, William Waryn, etc. Dat. M. a. F. of St. Peter in cathedra [22 Feb.], 1326[7]. (Holland.)

37. Similar QUITCLAIM from Dionisia fil. Henrici de Alsop to the said Margaret of the same lands. Witn. Ranulph de Alsop, Thomas de Estafford de Asschebourne en le Pek, Thomas Adam, etc. Dat. Th. a. F. of St. Matthias [24 Feb.], 1326[7]. (Holland.)

38. GRANT from Margaret fil. Ranulphi de Alsop to John de Kynardsey of all the lands, etc., which she had of the feoffment of her father in Alsop. Witn. Thomas Wythir, Dom. Hugh Mene[l], William de Byrchouyr, Roger de Tystyngton, Ranulph de Alsop. Dat. Stamford, Fr. a. F. of St. George [23 Apr.], 1 Edw. III. [1327]. (Holland.)

39. QUITCLAIM from Ranulph, dominus de Alsop, to John de Kynardesey of the tenements which the latter had from Margaret fil. Ranulphi de Alsop, his kinsman, in Alsop. Witn. John de Migners, William Brian, John de Kynardesey, jun. Dat. 1327. (Holland.)

40. GRANT from Richard Aleyn of Alsop to John de Kynardeseye of two messuages, etc., in Alsop. Witn. William de Bientelegh, Richard de la Pole, Robert Foucher, etc. Dat. Beh. of St. John B. [29 Aug.], 1 Edw. III. [1327]. (Holland.)

41. QUITCLAIM from Hugh de Kynardsaye to William fil. Johannis de Kynardesey, his brother, and Elizabeth, his wife, of all the lands which he had by grant from Dom. John de Kynardesseye in Alsop. Dat. F. of Circumcision [1 Jan.], 19 Edw. III. [1346]. (Holland.)

42. RELEASE from John Shepherd of Alshop *al.* John fil. Johannis fil. Willelmi de Stanshop to Robert Kynardeseye de Lokkeslegh of a messuage and two bovates of land in Alshop [Alsop] which John de Dale holds. Witn. Thomas Dethek de Uttoxhatr', Thomas Alshop, William Walkere, etc. Dat. Uttoxhatre [Uttoxeter], Vig. of SS. Peter and Paul [29 June], 9 Hen. IV. [1408]. (Holland.)

43. LEASE for 60 years from Sir Henry Sacheverell, of Morley, to Thomas Alsop, of Alsop-in-le-Dale, of a messuage in Alsop-lee-Dale, in which he now dwells, at a yearly rent; and to find the said Sir Henry "an able horse and harnes for oone man to do the kynge seruyce" when demanded. Dat. 24 March, 26 Hen. VIII. [1535]. (Drury.)

ALSOP *v.* also under PARWICH.

ALSTONLEIGH *v.* under COMBS, in Chapel-en-le-Frith.

ALVASTON.

(ALEWOLDESTONE, ALWALDESTON, ALWASTON, AYLLEWASTONE.)

44. GRANT from Oliver de Sautcheuerel to the Nuns of St. Mary de Pratis, Derbeye, of two messuages, which Richard Wildy and Simon Tinctor [Dyer] held in Alewoldestone. Witn. Dom. W[illiam] de Muschamp, Archdeacon of Derby, Mag. N——, "Officialis," Hugh de Ekyntone, etc. Early Hen. III. (Woll. viii. 62.)

45. GRANT from Roger fil. Galfridi le Chamberleng to the Canons of the Blessed Virgin de Parco Stanleye [Dale Abbey] of an acre of land in Alwaldeston. Witn. Thomas Hanselin, Robert de Haregeve, Stephen fil. Burge, etc. *Circ.* 1270. (Bemrose.)

46. ACKNOWLEDGMENT by John de Staunton of the receipt of 10 marks for rent of the manor of Alwaston from Ralph de Freschevile, dominus de . . . ouch. Dat. Derby, Fr. a. F. of St. Luke [18 Oct.]. 17 Edw. I. [1289]. (Harl. 86 I. 3.)

47. GRANT from John Griffyn, dominus de Ayllewaston, and Elizabeth, his wife, to Dom. Richard de Wylughby, mil. of the moiety of the manor, etc., of Ayllewaston, which fell to the said John and Elizabeth on the death of Dom. William Fawel, mil. Witn. William Rosel, William Chaddesden, milites, William Sawcheverel, Simon Pouger, de Willesthorp, William Michel, John Suet, etc. Dat. S. b. F. of St. Lucy [13 Dec.], 16 Edw. II. (1322.) (Add. 6,106 i.)

ALVASTON *v.* also under BOULTON.

APPERKNOWL *v.* under UNSTONE.

APPLEBY.

48. QUITCLAIM from Thomas, Rector of Appelby, to Laurence [de S. Edwardo], Abbot, and the Convent of Burthon [Burton-on-Trent] of tithes, Peter's pence, and other payments formerly claimed by him from the Abbey tenants in his parish, including fourpence for every marriage ceremony. Witn. Dom. Geoffrey de Appelby, Walter de Stretton, William, parson of Stretton, etc. [1229-1260.] (Stowe 48.)

APPLETREE HUNDRED.

49. ACQUITTANCE by Robert Belle, yeoman of the King's Chamber, to Ralph Illyngworth, Ralph Meynell, Piers Pole, William Coke, and William Huet, collectors of tenths in the hundred of Appultre, for £47 8*d.* Dat. 26 June, 4 Hen. VII. [1489]. (Woll. viii. 69.)

ASH, NEAR ETWALL.

50. QUITCLAIM from John de Rocheford, de comitatu de Derby to John Freman, of four acres of land abutting on Tulcroft in the fields of Assh, and other land there lying on Holeweye, with two selions in the same fields "apud Stantune Slade," and a rent in Assh. Witn. Dom. Robert de Tuiford, mil., John le Bek, Adam de Boutton. Dat. apud Assh, Th. aft. Christmas, 38 Edw. III. [1364]. Seal of arms, defaced. (Brookhill.)

ASHBOURNE.

(ASCHBURNE, ASCHEBURNE, ASHBOURN, ASHEBURN, ASHEBURNE, ASSCHEBORNE, ASSCHEBURN, ASSCHEBURNE, ASSEBURN, ASSHBURN, ASSHBURNE, ASSHEBOURNE, ASSHEBURN, ASSHEBURNE, ESBURNIA, ESSEBURN.)

51. CONFIRMATION by William de Ferrar [iis], Comes Dereb', to Ralph de Mungai of land in Hunderwude [Underwood] in the manor of Asseburn, which he held when the said William recovered the Wapentake of Wirk[sworth]; rent 4*s.* Witn. William de Rideware tunc senescallus, Robert fil. Walkel[in], Jordan de Touke, Herbert de Merlee, Robert de Bella fide, Thomas de Ednesoure, Robert de Aluithleg'. *Temp.* John. (Woll. ix. 5.)

52. GRANT from Serlo de Grendon to Walter fil. Humfridi of a toft in Campedene between the two tofts held by Geoffrey Hiepe. Witn. William, capellanus, Simon de Sancto Mauro, Robert and William, filii Joce, Richard Hokebroc, Robert Clericus, Geoffrey Hiepe, Robert Telar. *Temp.* John. (Woll. vi. 42.)

53. GRANT from Roger fil. Rob. de Underwod to Roger fil. Ran. de Mercinton, of half an acre of land in Winhul, extending towards Scolebroc; rent, a barbed arrow. Witn. Evo de Taddel', Richard fil. Rogeri de eadem, Richard fil. Ran. de Underwode, John de Offedecot, William fil. Inguses. *Temp.* Hen. III. (Woll. ix. 6.)

54. QUITCLAIM from John de Lea and Idonea his wife to Hugh de Acauere of a toft which they held sometime from the latter in Esseburn. Witn. Robert de Esseburn, Robert de Wennesleg, John de Offedecote, Henry de Alsop, Thomas de Esseburn, Roger de le Wodehus, William Puterel, etc. Late Hen. III. (Okeover.)

55. QUITCLAIM from Robert fil. Philippi de Esseburn to Nicholas de Clyfton of an acre and a half of land in Meyele in the territory of Esseburn, namely, that land which the said Robert obtained from Henry Fenekelspire, before the King's Justices at Westminster. Witn. Thomas de Tiddeswell, William de Bokestones, Symon de Tuttebyre, Robert de Tissinton, John Like. *Temp.* Edw. I. (Okeover.)

56. GRANT, in tail, by Richard de Marchinton, miles, to Thomas fil. Ade de Assheburn, of lands near Scolebrok, in Assheburn', in the fees of Bradeley and Underwode; rent, 5*s.* Witn. Will Cokeyn of Assheburn', Will de Knyveton' of the same, Roger de Marchinton, Richard Hervi, etc. *Temp.* Edw. I. (Woll. ix. 61.)

57. GRANT from Brian, carpentarius de Assheburn, to William his son and Agnes his wife, of a messuage and buildings in Assheburne lying between a tenement which Thomas de Stafford held, and a tenement of the said William. Witn. William Cokayn, William de Stafford, John his son, Geoffrey de Quickeshull. Dat. Assheburn, S. b. Conv. of St. Paul [25 Jan.], 6 Edw. II. [1313]. (Drury.)

58. COVENANT, whereby William fil. Hen. de Knyveton re-grants to William fil. Dom. Matthei de Knyvetone lands in Assheburne; rent, a rose. Witn. Dom. Roger de Bradeburne, Nicholas de Merchintone, Serlo de Mountejoye, etc. Dat. Bradel', F. of Conv. of St. Paul [25 Jan.], 6 Edw. II. [1313]. (Woll. vi. 32.)

59. GRANT from John fil. Dom. Rogeri de Bradeburn, mil., to Margery fil. Mathei de Knyveton de Bradeleye, of a messuage with buildings upon it, etc., in Assheburn. Witn. William Cokeyn, of Assheburn, Thomas fil. Ade, of the same, William de Kniveton, Roger de Marchinton, Robert de Cluware. Dat. F. of St. Peter ad vincula [1 Aug.], 1319. (Okeover.)

60. GRANT from Henry de Clifton de Assheburn to Thomas de la Phole de Assheburn, of a toft in Assheburn lying at the head of the town between the high road and the land which Roger de Bradeburn held, and extending from the high road leading to Offidecote up to the curtilages in Motterlone. Witn. William Cokeyn, bailiff of Assheburn, William de Knyveton, of Assheburn, Robert de Cloware, Richard Herui, Henry de Mapilton, Hugh fil. Roberti de Assheburn, Richard de Derleye, clericus. Dat. Assheburn, Mor. of Conv. of St. Paul [26 Jan.], 1326[7]. (Okeover.)

61. GRANT from Isabella que fuit uxor Willelmi de Stafford de Assheburn to Dom. Robert de Clifton de Assheburn, of a messuage, etc., in Assheburn, one head extending to the high road and the other to Scolbrok. Witn. Thomas fil. Ade de Assheburn, William de Knyveton, Richard Heruy, Laurence de Acouere, etc. Dat. M. b. F. of St. Gregory [12 Mar.], 1331. (Drury.)

62. RELEASE from William fil. Hen. de Mapultone to William fil. Matthei de Knyvetone, of Asscheburne, of a rent of 6*s.* 6*d.* from a tenement in Asscheburne. Witn. Thomas fil. Thome, Adam de Asscheburne, John de Holond, etc. Dat. M. a. F. of St. Michael [29 Sept.], 5 Edw. III. [1331]. (Woll. vi. 18.)

63. GRANT, for two lives, from William de Bradeleye and William de Hultone, chaplains, to William fil. Matthei de Knyvetone and Margery, his wife, of a messuage in Asscheburne, with remainder to Henry and others, their sons. Witn. William de Mapulton, of Asscheburne, John Cokayn, Thomas fil. Thome, etc. Dat. F. a. Exalt. of H. Cross [14 Sept.], 7 Edw. III. [1333]. (Woll. vi. 19.)

64. GRANT from William fil. Matthei de Knyvetone to Dom. William de Bradeleye and Dom. William de Hultone, chaplains, of a messuage in Asscheburne. Witn. William de Mapulton, of Asscheburne, John Cokayn, Thomas fil. Thome Adam, etc. Dat. Th. a. Nat. of the B.V.M. [8 Sept.], 7 Edw. III. [1333]. (Woll. vi. 20.)

65. GRANT from John de Holond, of Ashbourne, to Henry Ailmot and Alice his daughter of 100 shillingsworth of rent in Asshebourne from lands which belonged to Hugh fil. Rob. fil. Hugonis for the payment of which the said John binds himself, his heirs, executors, and all his tenements in Ashbourne. Witn. William de Knyveton, John Cokein, John de Lymistre, Robert de Clifton, Thomas Adam. Dat. M. a. F. of St. Barnabas [11 June], 8 Edw. III. [1334]. (Okeover.)

66. GRANT from William de Knyvetone, of Assheburne, to Robert, his son, of two places of land with edifices in Assheburne, with remainder to Nicholas and John, sons of the grantor. Witn. Ralph le Ken, Will de Eytone, Henry de Mapultone, etc. Dat. T. a. F. of St. Matthew [21 Sept.], 11 Edw. III. [1337]. (Woll. vi. 21.)

67. GRANT from Ralph de Shirley and Margaret, his wife, to Ralph de la Pole de Hertyndon of the lands, etc., which descended to the said Margaret on the death of Walter Waltesheff, her father, in Adgaresly, Co. Staff., and in Assheburn, Bradeley, Knyveton, Peuerwych, Bradburne, and La Lee, near Bradburn, Co. Derb., except those lands which the said Walter held for term of the life of William de Hopton. Witn. William de Mapelton, William de Knyueton, John de Lemystre, Thomas de Matherfeld, of Assheburn, Richard Hervy, of the same, William le Aviner, William de la Dale, both of the same. Dat. apud Assheburn, F. of St. John B. [24 June], 12 Edw. III. [1338]. (Okeover.)

68. LEASE for 8 years from John de Bretteby, of Burton-on-Trent, and Sibilla, his wife, to William de Waterfal, of eighteen pence annual rent from a "celda" in Assheburn lying between the "celda" of Adam Daird and the "celda" of Robert de Alstonefeld. Dat. S. b. F. of All Saints [1 Nov.], 18 Edw. III. [1344]. (Drury.)

69. GRANT from Dom. Alexander de Cobbeley, chaplain, to Lettice, relicta Johannis de Knyveton and the heirs of their bodies, of a messuage, etc., in Assheburne, one head of which extends to the high road and another on the water called Scolbrok. Witn. John Cokayn, of Assheburne, Thomas Adam, John de la Pole, etc. Dat. Assheburne, F. of St. Giles, Abbot [1 Sept.], 1351. (Drury.)

70. GRANT from John fil. Hugonis de Asheburn to William Sterre, of the same, of a plot of land in Asheburn, with buildings upon it, etc., between the plots of Thomas le Locsmyht and Emma le Cok. Witn. John Cokayn, Thomas Adam, Adam de Bylley. Dat. M. a. F. of St. Luke [Oct. 18], 26 Edw. III. [1352]. (Okeover.)

71. RELEASE from Johanna fil. Joh. Dounynge of Asscheborne to Nicholas de Knyvetone, of a messuage in Asscheburne. Witn. John Cokayne, John de Lemestre, Adam de Bylby, etc. Dat. Sat. a. F. of St. George [23 Apr.], 32 Edw. III. [1358]. (Woll. vi. 21a.)

72. RELEASE from Adam de Boleby, of Assheburne, and Alice, his wife, to Nicholas de Knyvetone, of the third part of a messuage and two cottages in Assheburne, which the said Nicholas had of the gift of John de Eyton, son of the said Alice. Witn. John Cokayne, of Assheburne, Thomas Adam, John de la Pole, of the same, etc. Dat. M. a. F. of St. Barnabas [11 June], 37 Edw. III. [1363], (Woll. vi. 25.)

73. GRANT from Thomas de Grattone fil. et her. Will. de Grattone to Nicholas de Knyvetone, of an annual rent of 8s. from tenements in Asshburne. Dat. F. of St. Peter "in cathedra" [22 Feb.], 45 Edw. III. [1371]. French. (Woll. vi. 61.)

74. POWER OF ATTORNEY by Richard Destafford, lord of Clyfton, to John de Astone, etc., to receive seisin of lands in Nedwode, Co. Staff., and Assheburne, and of the manor of Bredlawe [Broadlow Ash, in Thorpe], under a deed of feoffment made by Johan de la Pole. Dat. Westm. 47 Edw. III. [1373]. French. (Woll. vi. 59.)

75. QUITCLAIM from Henry le Waluour de Assheburn to Edmund Cokayn de Assheburn of a messuage in Assheburn in Le Bruge-strete between the water of Skolobrok and the said Edmund's land, and of a meadow called Paradis in Clifton. Dat. Assheburn, Th. a. F. of St. Michael [29 Sept.], 2 Ric. II. [1378]. (Okeover.)

76. GRANT from John Cokayn, of Assheburne, to Philip de Okore, Knt., Henry Wallour, and William Hayward, chaplains, of all his goods and chattels in Cos. Derby and Stafford or elsewhere. Witn. Nicholas de Stafford and John Basset, Knts., Roger de Bradburne, John de Bentley, Thomas Lymster, John de Eyton. Dat. Ashbourne, S. a. F. of St. Hilary [8 Jan.], 5 Ric. II. [1382]. (Okeover.)

77. GRANT from John de Okoure and Henry Wallour, chaplains, to John Crescy, rector of Longford, John Houbell, rector of Wynfeld, William de Monyash, vicar of Duffeld, John Fraunsoys, of Tykenale, and Thomas de Wombewell, of all the lands, etc., which John Cokayn, Knt., enfeoffed the said John and Henry with, in Asshebourne, Clyfton, Parwych, Kneueton, Irton, Styrton, Offtecote, and Underwod, Co. Derb., Malefeld and Snellefeld, Co. Staff. Witn. Nicholas de Longford, Knt., Oliver de Barton, William de Sallowe, etc. Dat. T. a. F. of St. Mark [25 Apr.], 7 Ric. II. [1384]. (Drury.)

78. GRANT from William de Knyveton de Bradelay to Thomas de Knyveton, of Asscheborne, of a messuage in Asschebourne lying between the messuage which John Pees holds from John Cokayn, Knt., and the messuage which William Barbour holds from the lord of Underwood. Witn. John Cokayn, Knt., of Asschebourne, Thomas Lymestre, Thomas Glover, ballivus de eadem, William Boturdon, and John Eyton. Dat. Asschebourne, F. of St. Laurence [2 Feb.], 5 Hen. IV. [1404]. (Okeover.)

79. GRANT from William Hebbe, rector of Edlaston, and William Boturdon to Richard Welbek, son and heir of John Welbek, of all their lands, in the fees of Compedon, Clufton, Bradelay, Offecote, and Underwode. Witn. Thomas Lymistre, Thomas Knyveton, Richard Spicer, and Thomas Glover, bailiffs. Dat. F. of St. Michael [29 Sept.], 11 Hen. IV. [1410]. (Drury.)

80. GRANT from William Auener, chaplain, to John de Okouere, fil. Philippi de Okouere, mil., of a messuage in Asscheburn which John de Derby late held, to hold for his life with remainder to Thomas de Okouere, his brother. Witn. John Cokayn, kt., John Cokayn, his son, Thomas de Knyventon, Nicholas de Lymestre, William de Boterdon, John de Elton. Dat. 20 July, 2 Hen. V. [1414]. (Okeover.)

81. QUITCLAIM from William Auener, chaplain, and Richard Spycer, of Assheburn, to John Smalley and Elena, his wife, of a tenement in the market place of Assheburn with an acre of land in the field of Offecote, which they had by feoffment from William Newenham, then vicar of Assheburn. Witn. William Boturdon, Nicholas de Lymestre, Thomas Poleson. Dat. M. b. F. of St. Bartholomew [24 Aug.], 2 Hen. V. [1414]. (Drury.)

82. LEASE, for 30 years, from Henry [Chichely], Archbp. of Canterbury, Henry [Beaufort], Bp. of Winchester, and Walter Hungerford, Knt., feoffees of the late King Henry V., of lands in the Duchy of Lancaster, to Henry Knyvetone, Esq., of a water-mill in Asshebourne, called le Newe Mylne; rent, 10 marks. Dat. 1 Apr., 17 Hen. VI. [1439]. (Woll. vi. 36.)

83. POWER of attorney from Margaret, widow of Thomas Knyvetone, to Nicholas Knyvetone, to deliver to John, her son, lands in Assheburne, Egyntone, and Hyltone. Dat. Myrcastone, 24 Mar., 25 Hen. VI. [1447]. (Woll. vi. 35.)

84. BOND from John Cokayn, of Ashbourn, Nicholas Mountgomery, jun., esquire, and Robert Jenkynson, of Hertyll, to Philip Okover, esquire, in thirteen marks payable at Michaelmas, 1456. Dat. 22 Apr., 30 Hen. VI. [1452]. (Okeover.)

85. LEASE, for 40 years, from Nicholas Mountegomery, squyer, to Willyam Gyte, of a tenement and land in Assheburne; rent, 5s., after the first five years. Dat. 15 Apr., 15 Edw. IV. [1475]. (Woll. x. 19.)

86. APPOINTMENT by Richard Welbeke, esquire, of Humfrey Okouer, esquire, to be chief seneschal, governor, and supervisor of all the said Richard's lands within the demesne of Asheburne in le Peke and elsewhere, Co. Derby, during the said Richard's life, with a yearly salary of 13s. 4d. Dat. 26 Nov., 15 Hen. VII. [1499]. (Okeover.)

87. FEOFFMENT from Henry Hudson, vicar of Asshburn, and Ralph Bersforde, of Asshburn, to John Mosley, of the same, of a messuage lying " in foristidio " de Asshburn, with attorney to Thomas Elton and Robert Crisha to deliver seisin. Witn. Robert Hassylhurst, Christopher Prince, clerks, John Barbur, marcer, etc. Dat. 2 June, 19 Hen. VII. [1504]. (Drury.)

88. QUITCLAIM from Anna Blakwall, widow of Richard Blakwall, to John Mosley, of Aschburne, mercer, of a messuage in the market place of Asshburne. Dat. 6 Feb., 5 Hen. VIII. [1514]. (Drury.)

89. GRANT from John Mosley, of Assheburne, to Thomas Blakwall, Thomas Hurte, etc., of a messuage in the market place of Assheburne. Dat. 7 May, 5 Hen. VIII. [1514]. (Drury.)

90. CONVEYANCE from Vincent Lowe, esq., to Anthony Fitzherbert, serjeant at law, German Pole, Nicholas Fitzherbert, esquires, Denis Lowe, Robert Lowe, and William Moreton, gentt., of his manors and lordships of Compteyn [? Compton in Ashbourne] and Denby, and all his lands in Assheburn, Bradley, Fenton, Eton [Cold Eaton], Sturston, Clyfton, Osmaston, and Merton, Co. Derby: to uses specified in indentures dated 2 July, 7 Hen. VIII., between Thomas Cokeyne, of Ashbourne, Knt., and the said Vincent. Dat. 8 July, 7 Hen. VIII. [1515]. Signed, Vyncent Lowe. (Drury-Lowe.)

91. INDENTURE between Sir Thomas Russell, "rood-prest," of Assheburne, on the one part, and John Knyvetone, of Myrcaston, gent., "patrone of the same servyce and chantre," and Sir Herre Hudson, vicar of Ascheburne, on the other part, witnessing the delivery, by the said vicar, to the said Sir Thomas, of certain mass-books, chalices, vestments, and other goods to the same chantry. Dat. 15 Jan., 7 Hen. VIII. [1516]. (Woll. vi. 38.)

ASHBOURNE *v.* also under ATLOW, CLIFTON, COLD EATON, DENBY, MAPPLETON, MATLOCK, WIRKSWORTH.

ASHFORD.

(ASSHEFORD, AYSSHEFORD, ESSEFORD.)

92. KING'S WRIT to the Sheriff for recovery of debts from William de Birchull, lessee of Ashford Manor. Dat. 1276. (Lichf. oo. i.)

93. COURT-ROLLS of the Manor of Ashford in the Peak on various days in 9th year of Edw. III. [1335]. (Okeover.)

94. RECORD of the surrender by Roger en la Dale at a court held at Esseford on Easter Eve, 28 Edw. III. [1354] of a messuage and land in Swyndale in Esseford to the use of John, his son. (Foljambe.)

95. GRANT from Otos [Otho] de Holand, Dom. de Assheford, to Godfrey Foliambe and his heirs of Hassope, of common of pasture in Longecelowe, in the lordship of Assheford. Dat. London, 23 Nov., 32 Edw. III. [1358]. Fr. (Woll. i. 16.)

96. QUITCLAIM from Felicia fil. Johannis Clerke de Longesdon to Nicholas Martyn, chaplain, of all the lands which were his father's in Ayssheford, Magna Longesdon, Mornesale, and Roland. Witn. Henry de la Pole, William de Addreley, John de Shirleye, Ralph de Baystowe. Dat. apud magna Longesdon, Fr. b. Nat. of St. John B. [24 June], 44 Edw. III. [1370]. (Bowles.)

97. EXTRACT of Court-roll of Ashford manor, recording the admission of Richard in-le-Dale and Thomas in-le-Dale, his son, to a messuage and 12 acres of land in Shelladon [Sheldon] on the surrender of John, son of Roger in-le-Dale, Joan his wife and John their son. Dat. Vig. of SS. Simon and Jude [27 Oct], 19 Ric. II. [1395]. (Foljambe.)

98. EXTRACT from the Court-roll of Assheford Manor, recording the surrender by Roger in the Dale of lands in "le Halle ende" called "Maykeberne," "Swyndalmedewe," etc., to the use of John his son in tail. Dat. Sat. a. F. of St. Martin [11 Nov.], 21 Ric. II. [1397]. (Foljambe.)

99. GRANT from John in-le-Dale of Assheford to William de Bagshawe, sen., and Nicholas in-le-Dale, son of the said John, of all his lands, etc., in Co. Derby. Witn. Roger Asser, Richard le Ebeter, Thomas Nicholson, etc. Dat. Assheford, S. b. F. of SS. Simon and Jude [28 Oct.], 6 Hen. IV. [1404]. (Foljambe.)

100. AWARD of John Lynacre, esq., and John Parker, of Norton Lees, and Robert Eyre, esq., and Edmund Levett, arbitrators between William Croft, sen., of Brampton, and William Croft, jun., of the same, adjudging that the former should have his choice whether or not to take 5 marks for his right to certain lands in the lordship of Asshford, and notifying to Henry Vernon, steward of Asshford, etc., his refusal. Dat. Chesterfield, 20 June, 16 Edw. IV. [1476]. (Foljambe.)

101. PARTICULARS of land, etc., held by William Croft, of Bromton, jun., of the gift of his father, viz., a "messe" and land in Assheford in the tenure of Robert Jonson, and a "messe" and land in Sheladon in the tenure of John White, with memorandum of the award as above (No. 100). [June, 1476.] (Foljambe.)

102. GRANT from William Staynton, of Peterboro', and Elizabeth his wife, dau. and heir of William Susanson, jun., to Henry Foliambe, of Walton, esq., Henry Vernon, esq., and John Dale, of all the lands, etc., in Ashford, inherited by the said Elizabeth from her father or John Susanson, her brother. Witn. Robert Schakersley, Ambrose Dedyke, esquires, etc. Dat. Walton, F. of Tr. of St. Edward the King [13 Oct.], 17 Edw. IV. [1477]. (Foljambe.)

103. POWER of attorney from William Staynton, of Peterboro', and Elizabeth his wife, dau. and heir of William Susanson, jun., to Richard Turner, of Brampton, and Robert Mellour to surrender in the court of Richard, Duke of Gloucester, at Asshford seisin to Henry Foliaumbe, Henry Vernon and John Dale, and the heirs and assigns of Henry Foliaumbe of all the lands, etc., inherited by the said Elizabeth from William her father and John her brother in Asshford. Witn. Robert Schakersley, Ambrose Dedyke, Christopher Baune, William Goeve, etc. Dat. Asshford, F. of Tr. of St. Edw. the King [13 Oct.], 17 Edw. IV. [1477]. (Foljambe.)

104. GRANT from Thomas Susanson, al. Bryggesende, of Peterboro', son and heir of John Susanson, son and heir of William Susanson, jun., formerly of Ashford, near Baqwell, to Henry Foliambe, of Walton, esq., Randolph Vernon, and others of all the messuages, lands, etc., which he inherited from Will. Susanson or any of his sisters in Ashford. Witn. John Northege, Thomas Balle, of Brampton, chaplain, etc. Dat. M. a. F. of St. Martin [11 Nov.], 18 Edw. IV. [1478]. (Foljambe.)

ASHFORD *v.* also under CHAPEL-EN-LE-FRITH, HADDON.

ASHLEYHAY.

(ASSHELEHEY, ASHLEYHEY.)

105. EXTRACT of court held at Peytyate on Th. a. F. of St. Edward [18 Mar.], 17 Hen. VII. [1502], recording the surrender by Richard Newton, of a close called Fysshepolehyll [in Ashleyhay] to the use of Thomas Wrygley. (Pole-Gell.)

106. EXTRACT of court held at Peytyate on Th. a. F. of St. Edward [18 Mar.], 17 Hen. VII. [1502], recording the surrender by Thomas Wrigley of a close called Alkokfyld and an enclosure called Littillwodfyld, etc. [in Ashleyhay] to the use of Geoffrey Wrygley. (Pole-Gell.)

107. EXTRACT of court held at Beaurep[aire], 8 Feb., 6 Hen. VIII. [1515], recording the surrender by Geoffrey W[r]igley of a cottage, close, etc., in Asshelehey to the use of Richard Sacheverell, Knt., thereupon admitted. (Pole-Gell.)

ASHLEYHAY *v.* also under ALDERWASLEY, DUFFIELD.

ASHOPE *v.* under CASTLETON.

ASHOVER.

(ASCHOVER, ASSHEOVER, ESSEOVERE, ESSHOURE, ESSHOVERE, ESSOVER, ESSOVERE, HASSCHOVERE.)

108. GRANT from Walter, Abbot, and the Convent "de Parco Stanle" [Dale] to Richard Venator, of the "landa in bosco de Morwde, ubi quondam heremite solebant habitare," and two acres of land between that "landa" and the dwelling-house of Walter Faber, with common of pasture in Stretton. Witn. Ralph, capellanus de Essouere, Dom. Roger de Stretton, Adam de Hanleia, William Clericus, John de Wakebrige, Robert de Oggedeston, William le Venur. [1204-1235.] (Woll. vii. 1.)

109. Confirmation of the preceding grant by Roger de Stretton to the said Richard Venator. Same witnesses and date. (Woll. vii. 2.)

110. Grant from Robert fil. Willelmi fil. Johannis de Ouerton to Symon Cadigan of the same, of land and tenement in Overton. Rent, 2s. and a pound of cumin. Witn. John Deyncurt, Robert Ribuf, Symon de Reresbi, Walter de Ogaston, Henry de Cnotinge, etc. Dat. F. of St. James [25 July], 1293. (Gregory.)

111. Grant from Simon Cadigan de Essouere to Richard Cadigan de Clatercotis his brother, of a bovate of land, etc., which Richard Fat formerly held in Overton, with a piece of land called Sywarde-parroc. Witn. Symon de Rerisby, William de Winefeld, William de la Grene, etc. Dat. Essouere, F. of St. Martin [11 Nov.], 24 Edw. I. [1296]. (Gregory.)

112. Grant from Robert fil. Willelmi fil. Johannis de Overton to Symon fil. Nicholai Catigon, living in Overton, of a croft called Caluecroft [in Overton]. Witn. William de Wynnefeld, Henry de Cnotting, William fil. Henrici de la Grene, Richard de Laffordia, clerk, etc. *Circ.* 1296. (Gregory.)

113. Grant from Henry de Mousters of Essovere to the Abbey "de Bello Capite" [Beauchief] of common of pasture and other privileges in Essovere. Witn. Dom. Henry de Braylisford, Dom. Robert de Deuetk', mil., Roger le Bretone, etc. *Temp.* Edw. I. (Woll. iii. 92.)

114. Release from Margery quondam uxor Rad. de Rerisby to Robert fil. Rad. de Rerisby of lands in Rerysby, Snellislund, Hengham, and Steyntone [Co. Linc.], of which she had impleaded the Abbot of Barlings [Co. Linc.], with freedom from all claims of dower of lands in Esseovere and Pleseley. Witn. Dom. Walter de Ryboyf, mil., Will de Steymsby, mil., Dom. Symon de Markam, Rector de Essovere, etc. *Temp.* Edw. I. (Woll. iii. 89.)

115. Grant and release from Margery de Rerysby quondam uxor Radulphi de Rerisby to Adam de Rerysby, her son, and Deugya, his wife, of the manor of Essovere called le Newehalle. Witn. Dom. Roger de Eincurt, rector ecclesie de Essovere, Will. le Bret, Roger le Breton, Ralph de Rerysby, etc. Dat. Essovere, F. of SS. Fabian and Sebastian [20 Jan.], 1302[3]. (Woll. iii. 90, 91.)

116. Grant from Robert fil. Dom. Roberti de Wylnebi to Alan fil. Radulphi Fat de Overton of the service which William fil. Johannis fil. Wymundi is accustomed to perform for all the land he holds of the said Robert in Overton, together with half an acre of land in Overton abutting on Serleparroc and the lane which leads to the moor. Rent, a pound of cumin and two shillings three times a year. Witn. Dom. Walter de Rybyf, Ralph de Rersby, Geoffrey de Dethic, Geoffrey de Monasteriis, Henry de Knotting, etc. *Temp.* Edw. I. (Gregory.)

117. Release from Ralph de Rerisby fil. Rob. de Rerisby to Godfrey del Stubbynges, in soka de Essovere, of lands called "le Hermite Ker," lying in the territory "del Stubbynge" in Esseovere; rent, 1d. Witn.

Adam de Rerisby, Robert de Winnefeld, William le Hunt, etc. Dat. S. a. F. of Ass. of B. V. M. [15 Aug.], 13 Edw. II. [1319]. (Woll. vii. 3.)

118. QUITCLAIM from Johanna quondam uxor Simonis fil. Godefridi del Stubbyng in soka de Essouere to William le Hunte de Overton, Richard le Huntte, his brother, and John le Huntte, his brother, of all the land which the said William, Richard, and John had by grant from the said Simon in Overton. Witn. Dom. Adam de Rerisby, Knt., Ralph de Rerisby, Walter de Oggaston, Robert de Winnefeld, Robert de Ubbestoft. Dat. Essouere, S. a. F. of the Ann. of the B.V.M. [25 March], 16 Edw. II. [1323]. (Gregory.)

119. GRANT from Hawisia quondam uxor Godefridi del Stubbynge de Essouer to William le Huntte and Richard, his brother, of a messuage and bovate of land in the fee of Essouer. Witn. Dom. Adam de Reresby, Ralph de Reresby, Robert de Praers, etc. Dat. Vig. of the Circumcision [31 Dec.], 18 Edw. II. [1325]. (Gregory.)

120. QUITCLAIM from John le Hunt de Essouer to Richard le Hunt, his brother, of two messuages and land called le Calvecroft and Sywardparrok in Essouer. Witn. Robert de Wynnefeld, Robert de Ubbestoft, Ralph de Cryche, Robert de la Stubbyng, etc. Dat. S. a. F. of St. Martin [11 Nov.], 20 Edw. II. [1326]. (Gregory.)

121. FINE from John fil. Ric. de Suttone de Averham and Johanna, his wife, to John de Musters and Alice, his wife, of the moiety of the fourth part of the manor of Esshoure. Dat. York, Michaelmas Term, 10 Edw. III. [1336]. (Woll. viii. 4.)

122. LEASE for 3 years from William de Musters, John de Musters, and Alice, his wife, of Tirswell, to Roger fil. Rob. de Wynfeld, of Essover, of a moiety of their manor in the vill of Essouer. Witn. Dom. Adam de Reresby, Ralph de Reresby, Robert de Wynfeld, etc. Dat. Essover, All Saints' Day [1 Nov.], 10 Edw. III. [1336]. (Cott. xxvii. 203.)

123. RELEASE from Roger fil. Rob. de Winfeld, of Esseovere, to Dom. Roger de Eyncourt, mil., Dominus de Parco, of 18s. rent from lands which Robert de Boterley held in Esshovere. Witn. Dom. Roger de Eyncourt, rector de Esshovere, Robert le Breton, Roger le Caus, etc. Dat. Sat. a. F. of St. Valentine [14 Feb.], 11 Edw. III. [1337]. (Woll. vii. 5.)

124. RELEASE from Margery quondam uxor Willelmi Knottyng de Hasschovere to Roger Deyncourt of lands "in villa et in soca de Hasschovere." Witn. Dom. Nicholas de Langtford, Henry de Bralesford, Robert Breton, Henry Bate, etc. Dat. apud le Parkehalle, F. of St. George [23 Apr.], 23 Edw. III. [1349]. (Woll. iii. 93.)

125. QUITCLAIM from Ralph Hunt of Topetun, son of Richard Hunt of Ashover, to John Hunt, his brother, of all the lands which belonged to Richard, their father, in Ashover. Witn. Dom. Thomas, rector of Asshover, Roger de Wynfeld, John fil. Simonis de Asshover, etc. Dat. F. of Nat. of B. V. M. [8 Sept.], 44 Edw. III. [1370], (Gregory.)

126. CERTIFICATE of Robert Ryboffe, Hugh Ulkerthorpe, Robert Barley, and others, all of Assheover, that their "neghbore" Ralph Hunte had made a grant to John Hunte, his brother, of various lands [in Ashover]. Dat. St. Andrew's Day [30 Nov.], 44 Edw. III. [1370]. (Foljambe.)

127. GRANT by William Cowlischaw to Thomas Cowlischawe, his son, of lands in Aschover; rent 3*s.*, to William Plumley. Witn. James Rolston, gen., Thomas Hunt, gen., Dom. Philip Eyre, rector de Aschovere, Dom. Walter Townerow, Dom. William Turner, capellani. Dat. 5 Sept., 1 Edw. IV. [1461]. (Woll. vii. 6.)

128. DEMISE from Thomas Babyngton of Dethicke, esquire, to Henry Hopkynson of Alton, in the parish of Assheover, husbandman, of a messuage and lands in Alton. Dat. 11 July, 1 Edw. VI. [1547] (P. R. O., c. 1217, i.)

ASHOVER *v.* also under IBLE, TUPTON.

ASTON-IN-HOPE. *v.* under SHATTON.

ASTON IN SUDBURY *v.* under CUBLEY, SUDBURY.

ASTON-ON-TRENT.

129. LETTERS of attorney from John Sawcheuerell, esquire, to Thomas Duffeld and William Cobyn to deliver seisin to Ralph Sawcheuerell, his son, and Elizabeth, his wife, of all his lands, etc., in the vill and fields of Aston on Trent. Dat. Th. b. F. of Nat. of St. John B. [24 June], 34 Hen. VI. [1450]. (Okeover.)

ASTON-ON-TRENT *v.* also under MORLEY.

ASTON, COAL.

(ASTON, COLD ASTON.)

130. GRANT from Thomas de Chaworth, mil., to John Harwye of Cold Aston of a toft and bovate of land in the vill and fields of Aston with a windmill there. Witn. Richard le Spari, Nicholas de Norton, Thomas del Wodhous, Peter de Bernis, Thomas de Thasilharst, etc. Late Hen. III. (D. A. J. ii. 10.)

131. GRANT from William de Chaword to William de Alnetona of all the land which Nicholas fil. Nicholai subtus le Klif sometime held of William [de Alnetona] in Aston. Witn. Roger, Abbot of Beauchief, Thomas de Leys, Peter de Wodehuses, Peter de Birchevend, William de Stobbeley. Late Hen. III. (?) (D. A. J. ii. 9.)

132. POWER of attorney from Henry Foljame of Walton, esq., to Roger Scryschlaw of Walton, to receive seisin from Thomas Fox of Cold Aston of lands, etc., in Cold Aston formerly belonging to John Fox of Dronfeld. Dat. F. of St. Luke [18 Oct.], 1 Henry VII. [1485]. (Foljambe.)

133. GRANT from John Fox of Drounfeld to Robert Fox and John Fox, his sons, Thomas Barley, and John Barley, of all his lands in Aston, Ekyngton, and Oneston, with a toft in Drounfeld. Witn. William Byngley, vicar of Dronfield, Christopher Barley, chaplain, etc. Dat. F. of Inv. of H. Cross [3 May], 1489. (Foljambe.)

COAL ASTON *v.* also under CHESTERFIELD, DRONFIELD.

ATLOW.

(Atlowe, Attelowe.)

134. Confirmation by Robert fil. Tholi to Sewall de Mungei of the tenement in "Winnedona," which his father and Serlo, his elder brother, held from the said Robert. Late twelfth century. (Woll. ix. 2.)

> Robertus filius Tholi omnibus hominibus et amicis suis presentibus et futuris salutem. Notum sit vobis quod ego R. concessi et hac presenti carta confirmavi Sewallo de Mungei tenementum in Winnedona quod pater suus et Serlo frater suus senior de me tenuerunt. In feudum et hereditatem sibi et heredibus suis tenendum de me et heredibus meis libere et quiete, pro omni servicio annuatim ii solidos reddendo ad festum sancti Jacobi, scilicet terram et moram a divisa Serlonis de Grend[on] usque ad terram Stephani de Longelega. Et si istam terram erburgare voluerit homines qui ibi manebunt habebunt omnes liberas communiones in bosco et in plano. Pro hac vero concessione predictus Sewalus devenit homo meus et dedit mihi dimidiam marcam et quoniam volo quod hec concessio firma et stabilis habeatur hac presenti carta confirmavi ei. His testibus Rogero Putrel, Galfrido de Esburnia, Radulfo filio Jordan, Henrico fil. Sewal', Ricardo de Pech, Gamello de Alesop, Radulfo de Peuerwic, Radulfo de Mung', Willelmo fratre eius, Ricardo de Cnivetun, Henrico filio Ailwini, Simun preposito, Adam fil. Galfridi, Roberto de Torp, Nicolao de Mapeltona, Galfrido fratre eius, Herberto de Ticintona, Henrico de Matlag, Swano de Yldresle, Roberto fratre eius et pluribus aliis et tota curia.

135. Deed by which Herebert de Merle and Margarita, his wife, release all right of common in the wood of the lord Hugh [de Okeover] called Winnedun, and in Mulneclif, and undertake that, if the said Hugh wishes to make a fishpond or park, they will not prevent him, according to the agreement made when they received the land of Attelawe by grant of the lord Hugh. Late twelfth century. (Okeover.)

> Sciant omnes presentes et futuri quod ego Herebertus de Merle et ego Margarita vxor eiusdem Hereberti de Merle et heredes nostri in bosco domini Hugonis quod vocatur Winnedun et in Mulneclif nullam omnino poterimus exigere communam, Neque tempore predicti Hugonis neque temporibus heredum suorum. Vivarium uero uel parcum faccre si voluerint idem Hugo vel heredes sui nos Herebertus scilicet et Margarita et heredes nostri eis nullo modo prohibere poterimus. Talis enim facta fuit Conventio quando terram de Attelawe de dono domini Hugonis recepimus. Et ut hoc firmum sit et stabile in perpetuum, Ego Herebertus de Merle hanc cartam sigilli mei munimine confirmaui.
>
> Hiis testibus, Geruasio capellano, Roberto de Ferrariis, Henrico de Brailesford, Roberto de Stantun, Gaufrido de Snelleston, Willelmo de Grendon, Radulfo de Bakepuz, Rogero de Wodnesle, Ranulfo de Alesop, Jordano de Snitterton, Roberto de Bradeburn, et Willelmo de Ticent', clerico, Roberto de Thorp et multis aliis.

136. Lease from Robert fil. Dom. Hugonis de Acouere to Warin fil. David de Attelowe of a bovate of land with croft adjacent in the vill and territory of Attelowe, which Jordan fil. Rogeri sometime held; to

2

hold for his life at a yearly rent of 9s. Witn. William de Hokenaston, clericus, John le Roc de Bradelg', Alexander de Holond, Adam, clericus de Hokenaston. Dat. F. of St. Bartholomew [24 Aug.], 1272. (Okeover.)

137. GRANT from Robert fil. Hugonis de Akouere to John, his brother, of two bovates of land, with buildings thereof, and toft, croft, and meadow in the fee of Attelowe, all of which Adam fil. Joh. de Attelowe sometime held of him; to hold at a rent of 6s. 8d., for all services " salvo tamen forinseco seruicio ad predictam terram pertinente preter francopleggiagium quod solebat ad eandem terram pertinere et salvis tamen . . . in ista donacione defensis in parco et le Mulneclif et alibi in locis consuetis " and suit at his mill of Attelow " ad vicesimum quartum granum de blado crescente super predictam terram." Witn. Matthew de Knyueton, Ralph de Munjoy, Robert de Fenton, Thomas de Mapilton, Thomas Heruy, John Blunt of Murkaston, Henry de Knyveton, William de Hulton. Dat. Morr. of St. Petronilla [31 May], 1278. (Okeover.)

138. QUITCLAIM from Henry fil. Henrici de Perton to Robert fil. Hugonis de Akouere of all the lands which belonged to his said father, Henry de Perton, in Attelowe. Witn. Roger de Wardington, Henry de Mapilton, Roger de Mercinton, Ralph de Munjoye, Robert de Wednisle, Roger de Mapilton, William de Hulton, clericus. *Temp.* Edw. I. (Okeover.)

139. COVENANT between Dom. William de Hamilton and Robert de Acouere, viz., that the former hold the manor of the latter, called Attelowe, for a term of twenty years, according to a deed in the possession of both, and that if either should contravene this covenant he shall give the other twenty pounds, to be levied by the Sheriff of Derby. Witn. Jordan de Sniterton, Walter de Aylisburi, Thomas Herui, Ralph Sparewater, William de Bentlg. Dat. apud London, mor. of St. Dunstan [? 20 May], 6 Edw. I. [1278]. (Okeover.)

140. QUITCLAIM from Leticia relicta Alexandri Mercatoris de Esseburn to Robert fil. Hugonis de Acouere of four bovates of land and three shillingsworth of annual rent in Attelowe, of which she was enfeoffed by the said Robert as pledge for three sacks of wool. Witn. Dom. William de Hamilton, clericus, Walter de Eylysburi, Matthew de Knyveton, Thomas de Mapilton, Robert de Fenton, John le Foun, Oliver le Foun, Oliver de Roulond, Henry de Roulond, Thomas Heruy. Dat. F. of St. Lawrence [2 Feb.], 1278[9]. (Okeover.)

141. GRANT from Roger de Acouere, dominus de Attelowe, to John de Attelowe, of a messuage and two bovates of land in Attelowe, at a rent of 12d. yearly, the said John to perform suit at his court of Attelowe and at his mill " et molabit ad vicesimum granum." Witn. Thomas de Esscheburne, William Wyldegos, John Wyldi, Robert de Strongeshul, tunc seneschallus. Dat. M. a. Ascension Day [31 May], 19 Edw. I. [1291]. (Okeover.)

142. QUITCLAIM from Roger de Wednesleye to Alexander le Parker de Attelowe of two shillings out of twelve shillings annual rent due from the latter in respect of lands in Attelowe. Witn. John fil. Thome de Mapulton, Roger de Derleye de Sturston, Henry de la Grene, John le Bercher, John de Tiddeswall. Dat. at Esseburn, M. b. All Saints' Day [1 Nov.], 1300. (Okeover.)

143. GRANT from Roger de Okouere, miles, to William le Parkere de Attelowe, Isolda, his wife, and John, his son, of a messuage and a bovate of land in Attelow which Hugh fil. Bate sometime held, and five acres in the same place lying in Le Underwode, to hold for their lives at a rent of 8s. 1d. Witn. John le Eyr de Attelowe, Richard de Ibull, John de Brassinton. Dat. F. of St. Barnabas [11 June], 1303. [Okeover.]

144. GRANT from Henry de Kneueton, miles, to Roger fil. Johannis de Acouere, of a culture of land in Attelowe, called Le Rouheloweflat. Witn. Dom. Roger de Bradebourne, knt., John le Sawvage, Ralph de Mounioie, Thomas Adam, Nicholas de Clifton. Dat. apud Esseburne, Vig. of St. Matthew [20 Sept.], 3 Edw. II. [1309]. (Okeover.)

145. SURRENDER from Henry de Kneueton, miles, to Roger fil. Johannis de Acouere, of a "cultura" of land in Attelowe which is called Le Rouheloweflat. Witn. Dom. Roger de Bradebourne, miles, John de Sawuage, Ralph de Munioie, Nicholas de Clifton, etc. Dat. at Ashbourne, Vig. of St. Matthew [20 Sept.], 3 Edw. II. [1309]. (Okeover.)

146. LETTERS of attorney from Henry de Kneueton, knt., to William de Kneueton, his brother, to deliver seisin to Roger fil. Johannis de Acouere, of a culture of land in Attelowe, called Rouheloweflat. Dat. apud Esseburne, Vig. of St. Matthew [20 Sept.], 3 Edw. II. [1309]. (Okeover.)

147. GRANT from Dom. Roger de Ocouere, Dominus de Attelowe, to William de Knyveton, Dominus de Bradeleye, that they may put to use one piece of waste in Attelowe called le Heyedewode, lying between le Rugebrok, le Ouleclough, le Skouteok, and the rivers which run under the mill of Attelowe, and may grub up, plough, and sow, or make a meadow of the same, as it may seem best to him, reserving to the said Roger common of pasture thereon after the hay and corn shall be carried. Witn. Dom. Roger de Bradeburn, knt., Mag. John de Bradeburn, clerk, William de Hopton, Ralph de Muntioye, etc. Dat. S. a. F. of St. Laurence [2 Feb.], 10 Edw. II. [1317]. (Okeover.)

148. GRANT from Roger [de Okover?] to Robert de Brocton of Attelowe of a plot of land in Attelowe which Hugh fil. Bate sometime held, on which the said Robert is to build a house at his own expense, except that the said Roger will supply the timber. Dat. T. bef. F. of St. Chad [2 Mar.], 1317[8]. (Okeover.)

149. GRANT from John fil. Alexandri de Attelowe, parcarius, to Dom. Roger de Acouere, knt., of a messuage, a bovate, and three acres of land in Attelowe which the said John had of the feoffment of Roger fil. Roberti de Wednesleye. Witn. Richard de Bradeburn of Hokenaston, Roger de Hopton, William le Parker de Attelowe, Robert de Brocton, William, clericus. Dat. Attelowe, Th. a. F. of St. Mark [25 Apr.], 2 Edw. III. [1328]. (Okeover.)

150. GRANT from Roger de Okouere, miles, to Richard Clifton of a bovate of land and an assart with buildings on it in the vill of Attelowe, at a rent of 10s. 2d. yearly with suit of court at his court and mill of Attelowe. Witn. John de Bradeburn, William Parker, John de Attelowe, Nicholas fil. Rogeri le Taillour. Dat. Attelowe, S. a Conv. of St. Paul [25 Jan.], 6 Edw. III. [1332]. Mutilated. (Okeover.)

151. GRANT from Isolda fil. et her. Engelard de Attelowe to Cristiana que fuit uxor Rogeri de Okouere, mil., of the lands and tenements in Attelowe which William le Parker of Attelowe had on lease from the said Engelard. Witn. John de Bradburne, William le Parker, John de Attelowe, William Bydel de Blore. Dat. apud Attelowe, M. a. F. of St. Hilary [13 Jan.], 14 Edw. III. [1341]. (Okeover.)

152. GRANT from Roger de Acouere, Dominus de Attelouwe, to Isolda fil. Edithe de Attelouwe and Eleanor, her daughter, of a messuage in Attelouwe which the said Isolda formerly held from him at will; to hold for their lives at a yearly rent of 12 pence. Witn. Thomas de Esseburne, William Wyldegos, Henry le Eyre, John Wildy, William le Parker, Robert de Strongeshull. Dat. M. a. Ascension Day [9 May], 19 Edw. [III.] [1345]. (Okeover.)

153. LEASE from Thomas, Dominus de Acouere, to William le Walyshe, of his mill of Attelowe with the watercourse, etc., for nine years, at a rent of a peppercorn the first year and 11s. for the remaining eight years. Dat. apud Acouere, S. a. Beh. of St. John B. [29 Aug.], 1359. (Okeover.)

154. PROCEEDINGS of various courts held at Attelowe, 49 Edw. III.-5 Ric. II. [1375-1382]. (Okeover.)

155. LEASE, for life, from Philip de Okere, knt., to Richard Parker and Margaret, his wife, of two places in Attelowe with two bovates of land and meadow adjacent, to hold at a rent of nine shillings and two pence. Witn. William de Wheston, Henry Schatergod, John Parker. Dat. Sat. a. F. of St. Luke [18 Oct.], 12 Ric. II. [1388]. (Okeover.)

156. CONVEYANCE from John Poole of Hertyngton and John Oker, feoffees of Thomas Oker, sen., to William Hondford, sen., Robert Hondford, and Thomas Alcrynton, chaplain, of all manors, lands, etc., of Oker [Okover], Castern, Ilom, Wodhous, Coldwall, Atlowe, Snelleston, Assheborn, Mapulton, and Hayfeld, in Cos. Staff. and Derby, which they had by feoffment from Thomas Oker. Witn. Christopher Dauemporte, Robert Smyth, Thomas Laurenson, William Itheryng, William Rowe. Dat. apud Oker, 1 Nov., 7 Hen. VI. [1428]. (Okeover.)

157. GRANT from John de Pole de Hertyngton and John Okor, sen., to Thomas de Okor, sen., of the manor of Okor with all their other messuages, etc., in the vills of Casterne, Ylum [Ilam], Wodhose [Woodhouse], and Coldwall, Co. Staff.; the manor of Atlow and all their other messuages, etc., in Snelleston Park and elsewhere in Co. Derb., and the reversion of lands which the said John Okor holds for his life in Mapulton, Snelleston, and Assheburne. Witn. Edmund Basset, William de Henford, John Meuerell, Thomas de Lymester, William Lymester, Henry Kneton, John de Bradburne. Dat. apud Okor, Th. a. Pur. of B. V. Mary [2 Feb.], 7 Hen. VI. [1429]. (Okeover.)

158. LETTERS of attorney from Thomas de Okor, sen., to William del Rawe to deliver seisin of his manors of Okor and vills of Casterne, Ylum, Wodhoses, Coldwall, and elsewhere, Co. Staff., and the manors of Atlow and Snelleston, Co. Derb., to John de Pole, de Hertynton, and to John de Okor, his brother. Dat. Okor, W. a. F. of St. Agatha [5 Feb.], 7 Hen. VI. [1429]. (Okeover.)

159. LEASE from John Pole of Hertyngton and John Okover, sen., esquires, to Thomas Okover, jun., of the manor of Okover, Co. Staff., the manors of Attelowe and Snelleston, Co. Derb., and all their other lands, rents., etc., which they had by feoffment from Thomas Okover, sen., and Thomas Okover, jun.; to hold for term of the lives of the said Thomas Okover, sen., and Thomas Okover, jun. Dat. Pur. of B. V. Mary [2 Feb.], 12 Hen. VI. [1434]. (Okeover.)

160. GRANT from Thomas de Okouere to John de Okouer, his son, of ten shillings annual rent due from Henry Bradburne in Atlowe. Witn. Philip de Acouer, " heres meus," Dom. John Brown, etc. Dat. F. of St. Edward, K. and M. [20 Nov.], 21 Hen. VI. [1442]. (Okeover.)

161. LETTERS of attorney from Thomas Okouere, esquire, to Thomas Duffeld to deliver seisin to John Gresley, knt., Walter Blount, Thomas Curson, John Curson, Henry de la Pole, and Nicholas Knyveton, esquires, of his manors of Okouere, Attelowe, and Snelston, with lands in the same. Dat. 6 Oct., 36 Hen. VI. [1457]. (Okeover.)

162. LEASE for four years from Philip Okouer, esquire, to Robert Knyveton, of Underwood, esquire, of a pasture called Urlewyke and " le Halfeld" in the fee of Atlowe, with all thorns growing within the said pasture to be cut and carried. Dat. Inv. of H. Cross [3 May], 1462. (Okeover.)

163. PROCEEDINGS of court of Philip Okouere, esquire, held at Atlowe, 12 Nov., 21 Edw. IV. [1481]. (Okeover.)

164. PROCEEDINGS of court of Humphrey Okeover, esquire, and Agnes, his mother, at Atlow, held 1 Dec., 16 Hen. VII., and 15 Nov., 17 Hen. VII. [1500, 1501]. (Okeover.)

165. PROCEEDINGS of various courts of Humphrey Oker, esquire, held for Atlow and Snelston on various days in 12-13 Hen. VIII. [1520-1521]. (Okeover.)

166. APPOINTMENT by Gervase Mark, prior of Dunstaple and the convent there, proprietors of the parish church of Bradburne with its chapels, of John Nyx, brother and canon of the Priory, to celebrate divine service at the chapel of Attlowe annexed to the said church of Bradburne. Dat. apud Dunstaple, 3 Nov., 1538. (Okeover.)

ATLOW *v.* also under CALLOW, SNELSTON.

BAGTHORPE, IN BRAMPTON.

167. POWER of attorney by William Wodhous, son and heir of John Wodhous of Brampton to Robert Heythcott of Callal [Calow] and Roger Crychelow of Dalton, appointing them to surrender at the Court of the Prior of St. John of Jerusalem, held at Normanton, a tenement called Bagthorpe in Brompton [Brampton] to Henry Foliambe, lord of Waltone. Witn. Oliver Scha, chaplain of Brampton, William Whythyll, Richard Turnor of the same. Dat. F. of Conv. of St. Paul [25 Jan.], 6 Hen. VII. [1490]. (Woll. iii. 77.)

168. EXTRACT of the Court of Normanton of William Weston, Prior of the Hospital of S. John of Jerusalem in England, held at Chesterfield, in the time of Ambrose Cave, knt., Preceptor of the same, of the surrender to Nicholas Wodhowse of London, pewterer, son of Richard Wodhowse of Brampton, of a messuage, etc., in Bagthorpe in the soke of Brampton. Dat. 22 Apr., 27 Hen. VIII. [1535]. (Woll. iii. 68.)

169. SIMILAR extract of the same Court, dated 1 Oct. [1535], whereat Richard Giles and Elizabeth, his wife, and Thomas Gyles, their son and heir, surrendered to the said Nicholas the said messuage, etc., in Bagthorpe, and received a moiety of the same. (Woll. iii. 69.)

BAKEWELL.

(BATHEKEWELLE, BATHEKWALLE, BATHEQUELLE, BAUCVELL, BAUCWELL, BAUKEWELL, BAUKQUELL, BAUQUELL, BAUQUEWELLE, BAUTHECWELL.)

170. GRANT from H[ugh de Nonant] Bishop, and the Dean and Chapter of Licheffeld to Matthew the canon, that he may continue to hold the third prebend in that church which he held at the time when John, Earl of Morton, granted the Church of Baucwell to Lichfield Church. [1192-1198.] (Lichf. B. 17.)

> Omnibus ad quos presentes littere peruenerint. H. miseratione diuina Couentr. Episcopus et Decanus de Licheffeld totumque euisdem Ecclesie capitulum, Salutem in vero Saluatore. Nouerit uniuersitas vestra quod dominus Johannes Comes Moriton' in perpetuam et puram elemosinam concessit uobis et Ecclesie uestre de Licheffeld ecclesiam de Baucwell cum omnibus ad eam pertinentibus. Et quoniam Mattheus canonicus tempore donationis illius in Ecclesia eadem tertiam possedit prebendam, sicut nec debuimus ita nec uoluimus eum benefitio suo priuare, Sed concessimus eī quod omnibus diebus uite sue benefitium illud integre possideat soluendo inde singulis annis in festo sancti Michaelis capitulo de Lichefeld unum aureum nomine pensionis.

171. Charter of King John, granting the church of Bathecwell to the church of St. Mary and St. Chad, Lichfield, and to Gaufridus [Geoffrey de Muschamp], Bishop of Coventry. (Lich. A 5.) The text (from a thirteenth century copy) is as follows:—

> Johannes, Dei gratia, etc. Sciatis nos pro amore Dei et pro salute anime nostre et animarum antecessorum et successorum nostrorum dedisse et concessisse et presenti carta nostra confirmasse Deo et ecclesie Beate Marie et sancti Cedde de Lichesfeld et venerabili patri nostro Gaufrido, Coventrensi episcopo et successoribus suis Ecclesiam de Bauthecwell cum prebendis et omnibus aliisad ecclesiam illam pertinentibus ut secundum ordinem et dispositionem quam Hugo, bone memorie Coventrensis episcopus super eadem ecclesia de Bathecwelle fecit ea cum omnibus pertinentiis suis in proprietatem ecclesie de Lichesf' libere conuertatur. Salvo tamen servicio trium presbyterorum qui in eadem ecclesia de Bathecwell deservient et iuxta arbitrium episcopi Diocesani rationabilem sustentationem habebunt. Ordinationem nuncque H. predicti episcopi quam super hoc fecit ratam habemus et futuris temporibus semper habebimus, Ecclesia autem de Lichefeld concessit nobis vnum presbyterum prebendarium in ecclesia de Lichefeld qui singulis diebus vite nostre missam cantabit pro sanitate et incolumitate nostra et post mortem nostram omnibus diebus missa pro salute anime nostre cantabitur imperpetuum. Quare volumus, etc. Testes, Willelmus Maresc[allus], Comes de Penbroc, Willelmus, Comes Sarum,

Johannes de Pratellis, Thomas Basset, Engelramus de Pratellis, Ricardus de Reueriis, Willelmus de Cantilupo.

Dat. per manum S. [Simonis fil. Roberti], Archidiaconi Wellensis, apud Valoyn', 3 Feb., anno 1 [1200].

172. CHARTER of King John granting to William Briewer lands in Bakewell, Meldesham, Thorpe, and elsewhere in Co. Derby. Dat. Westminster, 22 Mar., 1204. (D. of Lanc.)

173. QUITCLAIM from Robert fil. Johannis capellani to Robert Clid of a toft in Baukwell which he holds from the church of Baukwell on the north side of the church, to hold by service of 8*d.* per annum "et preterea semel metet in autumpno ad cibum Rectoris euisdem ecclesie." Witn. Luke de Begle, Richard de Ednesouer, Robert de Stanton, Robert de Kalueouer, William de Chatteswith, Nicholas de Ednesover, John de " Uueraddon pollard," Willot de Langesdon, William de Derlee, Thomas de eadem, Nicholas de Stancliue, Roger clericus. *Circ. temp.* John. (Lichf. B 6.)

174. QUITCLAIM from Wymarc' fil. Ric. Tannatoris de Baucwell to the Dean and Chapter of Lichfield and to the church of Baucwell of the toft which she holds there lying between the tofts of John clericus and Matthew le Sures. Witn. William le Wyne, William clericus, Roger Kask, Matthew Mercator, Hugh de Weston, Matthew Fullo, William de Oseburne, John clericus, Robert gener Huberti, etc. *Temp.* John (?). (Lichf. B 8.)

175. CONFIRMATION by William [de Cornhill], Bishop of Coventry and Lichfield, of the third part of the church of Bakewell, which Stepnen de Ridel had resigned to the Dean and Chapter. Witn. Mag. John Blundus, Mag. Nicholas de Weston, John de Ginges, William de Hadfeld, Richard de Chaucumb, Henry de Sancto Botulfo, Ralph, clericus de London, Simon Pinel, Robert de Marisco. [1215-1223.] (Lichf. B 3.)

176. BULL of Pope Honorius [III.] to the Dean and Chapter of Lichfield Church, confirming the grants of Bauqwell and Hope, with their chapels, etc., to W[illiam de Cornhull], Bishop of Coventry and Lichfield. Dat. Laterani, quarto Non. Maii [4 May], Pontif. a° 5 [1219]. (Lichf. B 22.)

177. QUITCLAIM from Thomas fil. et her. Wimarce vidue quondam vxoris Ade, mercatoris de Bauchuell to the Dean and Chapter of Lichfield and the church of Bauchwell, of the toft which his mother Wimarch held in that town. Witn. William le Wine, William, clericus, Roger Casken, Matthew, mercator, Hugh de Weston, Matthew Fullo, Matthew le Sureis, Alan Waket. *Circ.* 1220. (Lichf. B. 7.)

178. CONFIRMATION by Alexander [de Stavenby], Bishop of Coventry and Lichfield, to the church of Lichfield, of the churches of Baucwell with its chapels, and of the church of Hope with the chapel of Tidswell, with the churches of Kanoc [Cannock] and other churches in co. Staff., etc. Witn. William de Manec[ester], Dean of Lichfield, Richard de Stavenesby, Treasurer of Lichfield, Richard de Glovernia, Archdeacon of Coventry, William de Lucebi, Archdeacon of Derby, etc. *Circ.* 1230. (D. A. J. v. 134.)

179. CONFIRMATION by Alexander [de Stavensby], Bishop of Coventry and Lichfield, to " communa ecclesie Lichefeldenis," of the church of Bauchwell with its chapels, the church of Hope, with the chapel of Tidwell'; and also of the churches of " de Kanoco " [Cannock], Rugele, and Erlecg' [Arley], with pensions from the churches of Seneston [Shenstone] and Dunnelchurch [Dunchurch].

Witn. Mag. William de Manecestr', then Dean of Lichfield, Dom. Richard de Stauenesby, Treasurer, Mag. Richard de Glouernia, Archdeacon of Coventry, Mag. William de Luceby, Archdeacon of Derby, Dom. William de Hedfeld, Mag. Robert de Chebeleie, Dom. Robert, capellanus, Dom. Hugh, capellanus, Mag. Richard de Halton, Canons, Dom. Philip, Canon of Kenilw'rthe, " tunc capellanus noster," Mag. Ralph de Lacoc, Alexander Blundus, Symon Perdriz, Thomas de Luda, Clerks of the Bishop of Coventry and Lichfield, Ralph Elemozinarius, Walter de Halton, etc. Dat. 1232. (Lichf. B. 11.)

180. GRANT from Robert Child to Henry de Lexinton of the toft in Baucwell which he holds from Baucwell church by the service of 8*d*. per annum, " et metendo uno die in autumpno cum uno homine ad cibum Rectoris ecclesie." Witn. Richard de Marcham, Robert fil. Alexandri de Braiton, Ralph de Winnefeld, Robert de Trowell, Richard de Fenton, William Clericus, Roger Caskin, Hubert Mercator. *Temp.* Hen. III. (Lichf. B. 13.)

181. INDENTURE between Henry de Lexinton, the King's treasurer, and Ralph Vernon, whereby the former grants to the latter the right to plough and sow certain lands " que seminate fuerunt die et anno quo assisa nove dissaisine commune pasture in Baucvell capta fuit inter eos aput Notingeham " on Monday bef. F. of St. Luke [Oct. 18], 25 Hen. III. [1241], without exceeding or altering the extent tilled. Dat. 1243. (Lichf. D. 1.)

182. CONFIRMATION by Roger [de Weseham], Bishop of Coventry and Lichfield, of the charter of his predecessor, Alexander [de Stavensby] (B. 11). Witn. Mag. Ralph, Archdeacon of Chester, Mag. Henry de Wyshawe, "officialis noster," and Magistri R. de Lacoke, Th. Cumin, A. de Staunford, Walkelin and William, capellani, Roger de Thorton, William de Burgton, Thomas de Bradeford, clerici. Dat. apud Tachebrok, iii. Id. Apr. [11 Apr.], pontificatus nostri anno secundo [1246]. (Lichf. B. 14.)

183. COMPOSITION between the Dean and Chapter of Lichfield and Lenton Priory concerning tithes in Bakewell, Hope, and Tideswell. *Circ.* 1250. (D. A. J. v. 161.)

184. PARTICULARS of the estimated value of tithes received by Lenton Priory, Co. Notts., from lands in Bakewell, Hope, and Tideswell, and an account of the quarrel between the Priory and the Dean and Chapter of Lichfield concerning the tithes of Tideswell, the forcible seizure of sheep by the Prior's men in Tideswell Church, the damage done, etc. 1250-1251. (D. A. J. v. 142.)

185. DEPOSITIONS sworn at Bakewell, Tideswell, and Hope, touching Lenton tithe claims. 1251. (Lichf. M. M. 6.)

186. GRANT from H[enry de Lexinton], Dean of Lincoln, lessee under the Dean and Chapter of Lichfield of the churches of Baucwell [Bakewell] and Hope of 14 marks' worth of tithe to Lenton Priory, as taxed by Ralph de Cubbele, rector of Eyum [Eyam], J——, vicar of Esseburn [Ashbourne], and R——, vicar of Radford, in accordance with the award of the Warden of the Friars Minor of Leicester and the Archdeacon of Chester in a suit between the Chapter and the Priory. Dat. Lincoln xiiii. kal. Mar. [16 Feb.], 1252[3]. (D. A. J. v. 156.)

187. THE AWARD above quoted. Dat. Leicester, S. a. Pur. of B. V. Mary [2 Feb.], 1252[3]. (D. A. J. v. 156.)

188. SURRENDER by Henry de Lexinton, as Bishop of Lincoln, to the Dean and Chapter of Lichfield, of his farm in their churches of Bachewell and Hope, with their chapels, etc. Witn. Thomas, precentor, Ralph, treasurer of Lichfield, Mag. Henry de Wishawe, Canon of Lichfield, Roger de Foldon, John de Derbe, David de Sancta Frideswida, Canons of Lincoln, Roger de Caue, Hugh de Chaddesdon, James de Bakepuz. Dat. apud Parcum de Stowe, F. of St. Giles [1 Sept.], 1254. (Lichf. D. 3.)

189. ACKNOWLEDGMENT by William de Luceby, Archdeacon of Derby, of the exemption of the churches of Bathekwalle, Hope, and Tideswelle, from his jurisdiction, as decided by the Archdeacon of York "judice a domino papa delegato."
Witn. Mag. William de Manecestre, Dean, Mag. Thomas, precentor, Mag. Richard de Glovernia, treasurer, Mag. Peter de Radnoure, archdeacon of Salopesbir', Mag. William de Kilkenni, Hugh de Sotteby, Walter de Porton, Robert de Chebbeseie, Alexander Blund, William de Eccleshal, Simon de Norwis, John Francisc', Ralph de Terne, Canons of Lichfield. *Circ.* 1254. (Lichf. Y. 2.)

190. ROLL of parochial visitations of Bakewell. 1270. (Lichf. C.C. 1.)

191. DEED whereby William Folegambe of Wermenhull covenants not to alienate any of the lands in Baukewell that he holds under the Dean and Chapter of Lichfield. Witn. Dom. Robert de Herthull, knt., Thomas de Langesdon, Peter de Roland, Robert de Reyndon, Alan de Pickeworth. Late Hen. III. (Lichf. D. 4.)

192. LETTER from John [Peckham], Archbishop of Canterbury, to the Dean and Chapter of Lichfield, ordering, as Metropolitan, a revision of the stipends of the ministers of Bakewell and its chapelries, etc. Dat. apud Norwicum, xiii. Kal. Dec. [19 Nov.], 1280. (Lichf. Z. 1.)

193. LETTERS patent of Edward I. releasing to the Bishop of Coventry and Lichfield and the Dean and Chapter of Lichfield all claim in the advowson of the church of Bathekewelle. Dat. apud Rothelanum [Rhuddlan], 12 Nov., anno 10 [1282]. (Lichf. A. 10.)

194. QUITCLAIM from Hugo de Calfoure to Thomas fil. Johannis Elys de Langesdone, of a burgage in Bathequelle. Witn. Dom. W[illiam] de Gernun, tunc dominus de Bathequelle, Thomas le Raggede, Rob. Begum, etc. *Temp.* Edw. I. (Harl. 83 D. 57.)

195. TITHE roll of wool and lambs of the Jurisdiction of Bakewell. *Temp.* Edw. I. (Lichf. E. 7.)

196. TITHE roll of Bakewell. 1307. (Lichf. E. 10.)

197. RE-ORDINATION and modification of Archbishop Peckham's order concerning Bauquell and its chapelries, by Nicholas de Gore, Vicar-General of Canterbury, during vacancy of the See. Dat. Cantuar' xiii. Kal. Jul. [19 June], 1313. (Lichf. Z. 2.)

198. COMPOSITION between the Dean and Chapter of Lichfield and the parishioners of the various Bakewell chapelries as to payment of their curates. Dat. F. b. Nat. of B. V. M. [8 Sept.], 1315. (Lichf. T. 1.)

199. LETTERS patent, in duplicate, of Edward II. releasing all claim to the Bishop of Coventry and Lichfield and to the Dean and Chapter of Lichfield in the advowson of the church of Bathekewelle. Dat. Westminster, 25 Oct., anno 14 [1320]. (Lichf. A. 11, 12.)

200. DEED of William, fil. Dom. Will. Gernun, surrendering to his father the manor of Baukiswelle, with all beasts, goods, and other chattels, reserving only to himself two horses, one a bay, the other a gray, with a few other things. Dat. Esthorp, F. of St. Gregory [12 Mar.], 18 Edw. II. [1325]. (Harl. 50 G. 28.)

201. RECOGNISANCES entered into by Henry Corel of Bauquell, Robert Corel of the same, Walter de Arderne, Hugh le Sotheron, Richard Peck, and Richard de Burton, before John de Oxon', sheriff of Notts. and Derby, Hugh de Muscham, and Roger de Somervill, coroners of the county of Derby, for the good behaviour of Thomas Corel of Bauquell. Dat. Nottingham, Sat. b. Midsummer Day, 10 Edw. III. [1336]. (P. R. O. c. 2187.)

202. GRANT by Robert de Walleghe of Bauquewelle to Roger Bysshope of the same of a burgage and house in Bauquewelle. Witn. Henry de Suthrone, Rob. de Chepe, Gervase le Mercer, etc. Dat. Th. a. F. of St. Nicholas, Bishop [6 Dec.], 11 Edw. III. [1337]. (Woll. vii. 19.)

203. CONFIRMATION charter of King Edw. III. of the advowson of the church of Bathekewelle to the church of Lichfield. Dat. 10 Apr., anno 19 [1345]. (Lichf. A. 13.)

204. LEASE from Thomas de Gunston to Philip fil. Philippi de Stredleye and Alice, his wife, of lands in Baukewelle, Birchulles, Hassop, Parva, and Magna Longesdone and Aldeporte, for the lives of the lessees, with remainder in tail to James fil. Hugonis de Gunston and Joan, his wife. Dat. "in quinque septimanas Paschæ," 21 Edw. III. [1347]. (Harl. 83 F. 6.)

205. ACCOMPT-ROLL of Bakewell, returned by John Cokayne, Proctor for the Dean and Chapter of Lichfield. [1358-9.] (Lichf. F. 4.)

206. POWER of attorney by Alice, wife of Robert de Bakewell, to John de Burtone, chaplain, to deliver seisin to Robert le Bretener of a tenement in Bakewell. Dat. Derby, S. a. F. of St. John, a. p. l. [6 May], 17 Ric. II. [1394]. (Woll. ii. 73.)

207. GRANT from William de Monehase, parson of Bondessale, and Roger de Tibshylf, vicar of Baukquell, to Walter Blount, knt., Robert Foliambe, clerk, and Thomas Foliambe, of Hulme, with all its appurtenances. Witn. William Ferechfelde, knt., William Siliott, Robert Plumley, Roger de Hulm, etc. Dat. F. of St. Katharine [25 Nov.], 3 Hen. IV. [1401]. (Foljambe.)

208. LEASE for twenty-four years from Thomas de Stretton, Dean, and the Chapter of Lichfield, to Roger de Berdhalgh of a tenement at Bakewell on Flehill for twenty-four years. Dat. 12 Jan., 1402[3]. (Lichf. D. 9.)

209. DECLARATION by William de Moniasshe, chaplain, late rector of Bondessale [Bonsal], that a grant from him and Roger de Tybschelfe, vicar of Baukewell, to Walter Blount, knt., Robert Foliambe, clerk, and Thomas Foliambe, of Hulme, was made of their own free will for the souls of Godfrey Foliambe and Amine Foliambe, his father and mother. Witn. John Columbel, Richard Foliambe, and Henry de Mapulton, chaplain and rector of Bondesale. Dat. F. of All Saints [1 Nov.], 12 Hen. IV. [1410]. (Foljambe.)

210. GRANT from Richard Flecher of Baukewell to William Wostoncroft of a burgage, etc., lying on Flehyll between the land of the gild of the Holy Cross and the burgage of Richard Walker. Dat. Baukewell, F. of SS. Philip and James [1 May], 18 Edw. IV. [1478]. (Pole-Gell.)

211. ACQUITTANCE by . . . Mountgomery and Humfrey . . . to [Henry] Vernon, Esq., for £24, for rent of lands in Bakewell. Dat. F. of St. Michael [29 Sept.], 20 Edw. IV. [1480]. (Woll. x. 67.)

212. GRANT from Dom. John de Wolstoncroft, chaplain, to Robert Wolstoncroft, his brother, of a burgage in Bakewell and all those tenements, etc., there which came to him on the death of William Wolstoncroft, his father. Dat. 3 May, 4 Hen. VIII. [1512]. (Pole-Gell.)

213. FEOFFMENT from William Bowne of Holme, yeoman, to Godfrey Foliambe of Walton, knt., George Vernon of Haddon, esq., Thomas Rauson, clerk, "Gardianus de Tonge," Roger Bieston, vicar of Hareworthe, and others, of all his lands, etc., in Holme, Bakewell, and Assheforde. Dat. 1 Apr., 27 Hen. VIII. [1536]. Attached is the declaration of uses of the above, viz., to the use of the said William for his life, with remainder to his sons, etc. (Brookhill.)

214. GRANT from Henry Wyllyams, Dean, and the Chapter of Lichfield, as rectors of the proprietary parish churches of Baukewell, Hope, and Tyddeswall, to Ralph Gell of Hopton, of all the domains, manors, and liberties and sites of the rectories of Baukewell, Hope, and Tyddeswall, with lands in Holmesfeld and Ashford, Byrchyls, Monyashe, Haddon superior, and Capella in ly Fryth. Dat. 1 July, 1549. (Lichf. D. 26.)

BAKEWELL *v.* also under EYAM, HADDON, HOPE, MONYASH, TUNSTEAD.

BALLIDON.

(BALIDEN, BALIDENE, BALYDENE, BELIDENE).

215. GRANT from Ailwin fil. Swani and Robert and Henry, his "nepotes," to Adam Malet, and one life after him, of the land of Balidene, to be held of Richard de Herthul; rent, 3*d.* Late twelfth century. (Woll. vi. 2.)

Hec est conventio facta inter Ailwinum filium Swani et Rodbertum et Henricum nepotes suos et Adam Malet, Scilicet quod predictus

Ailwinus et nepotes sui concesserunt Ade Malet et cui de suis post decessum suum habere dignum duxerit totum rectum et hereditatem quod habent in terra illa de Balidene, scilicet quatuor bovates terre quas debent tenere de Ricardo de Herthul. Tenendam de eis et heredibus suis illi et cui placuerit de suis, reddendo inde annuatim iiid. ad festum sancti Martini. Pro hac autem concessione, predictus Adam dedit predicto Ailwino et nepotibus suis duas marcas argenti. Hiis Testibus, Rodberto de Ferariis, Henrico fratre suo, Rodberto filio Walchelini, Ricardo de Vernun, Willelmo fil. Hereberti, Nichola fil. Pagani, Willelmo de Rideware, Augustino fil. Milonis, Hugone de Greseleia, Rodberto de Sumerville et multis aliis.

216. GRANT, in fee, for two marks, from Richard de Heorthul to Adam Malet, of four bovates of land in Belidene; rent, 4s. Late twelfth century. (Woll. vi. 3.)

Sciant omnes qui sunt et qui venturi sunt quod ego Ricardus de Heorthul concessi et hac presenti carta mea confirmavi Ade Malet. et heredibus suis de me et heredibus meis in feudo et hereditate quatuor bovatas terre cum omnibus pertinentiis in Belidene. Hanc itaque terram prenominatam tenebit predictus A. et heredes sui de me et heredibus meis liberam et quietam ab omni servitio ad me pertinente salvo servitio forensi, reddendo annuatim quatuor solidos ad festum sancti Michahelis. Et sciendum est quod unus ex hominibus predicti A. in feudo manens erit ad omnes suos halimotz pro domino suo. Preterea predictus Ricardus non debet exigere aliquod auxilium a sepedicto A. nec ab hominibus suis. Pro ista concessione et hac carta facienda dedit predictus A. predicto R. duas marcas argenti et adhuc sciendum est quod sepedictus A. dedit dimidiam marcam argenti predicto R. pro quodam masuagio Torfini servicio predicto faciente et nullo alio exigente. Sciendum est adhuc quod istas quatuor bovatas prenominatas deresnavit predictus A. per preceptum domini Regis coram iusticiis apud Notingehan. Preterea predictus R. non exigebit a sepedicto A. vel ab hominibus suis aliquid iniuste vel aliqua mala causa.

His testibus, Thoma clerico de Badechewell, Rodberto de Fer[rariis], Henrico fratre suo, Hugone de Acoure, Rodberto de Grendon, Warnero de Beileie, Henrico de Bec, Ricardo de Bentl', Henrico de Heorth', Rodberto Malluuel cum pluribus aliis.

217. LEASE from John Cokayn, knt., to John Taylor of Balydene and Robert, his son, of the manor of Balydene, "dummodo eisdem tenere placuerit"; rent, 66s. 8d. Dat. Morrow of Annunc. B. V. M. [25 Mar.], 15 Hen. VI. [1437]. (Woll. vi. 4.)

218. COVENANT between Thomas Bate, esq., and Isabella, his wife, and John Cokayne, esq., whereby it is agreed that whenever the said John shall re-grant on demand to the said Thomas and Isabella, the manor of Middleton for the life of the said Isabella, he shall hold the manor of Baliden to himself and his heirs for ever. Dat. 16 Oct., 25 Hen. VI. [1446]. (Woll. vi. 5.)

BAMFORD.

(BAUMFORD, BAUMFORTH, BOWNFORD.)

219. GRANT from John fil. Oliveri de Baumford to John, the son of him and of Isabella Clement, of a messuage and a bovate of land which Rosa quondam uxor Petri de Baumford held in dower in Baumford. Witn. Tho. de Abbeney, Will. de Northleghes, Nich. de Baumford, etc. Dat. S. a. F. of Inven. of Holy Cross [3 May], 35 Edw. III. [1361]. (Add. 9237.)

220. QUITCLAIM from William fil. Joh. fil. Oliveri de Baumforth to William fil. Nich. de Baumforth, of lands in the same town; rent 4*d*. Witn. Robert le Ayr de Thornhyll, John Warde, John de Baumforth, etc. Dat. S. a. F. of St. Peter ad vincula [1 Aug.], 6 Ric. II. [1382]. (Add. 9240.)

221. GRAÑT from Robert Skynner de Baumforde and Rosa, his wife, to William Skynner, his son, of a messuage and land in Baumford; rent to the chief lord of the fee 4*d*. yearly. Witn. Oliver Hally de Schatton, William le Eyer de Hurst, Robert Foxe de Baumforde, etc. Dat. 1 Mar., 12 Hen. VI. [1434]. (Add. 9250.)

222. QUITCLAIM from John Skynner, son of Robert Skynnere de Baumforde, to William Skynnere, his brother, of a messuage and land in Baumforde. Dat. F. of Pur. of B. V. Mary [2 Feb.], 16 Hen. VI. [1438]. (Add. 7865.)

BAMFORD *v.* also under THORNHILL.

BARLBOROUGH.

(BARLBURGH.)

223. GRANT from Thomas de Hyll of Staley Wodthorp [Staveley Woodthorpe] to Thomas, Lord Clyfforth [Clifford], of all his lands, etc., within the demesne of Barlburgh and the demesne of Staley, with all his goods, etc. Witn. John Hard of Tharlsthorp, Stephen at Wode of Rowmley, William Stubbyng, etc. Dat. Th. in Easter Week [1 Apr.], 33 Hen. VI. [1455]. (Foljambe.)

BARLBOROUGH *v.* also under KILLAMARSH, SPINKHILL.

BARLOW.

(BARLEIA, BARLEY.)

224. CONFIRMATION by Adam de Lees to Allan Leham of all that land called Barley Woodsetts, between Le Roggwaygate and Waterfallgate. Witn. Thomas de Brampton, Peter de Dunston, Thomas de Woodhouse, Hugh de Linacre, etc. Undated. (Rel. xx. 109.)

225. GRANT from Jordan de Habetot to Robert Francus de Barleia of all that land which Thomas fil. Hardolf held between Lunbrok, the land of Orm, the carpenter, and Henganderidinge. Witn. Laurence de Burtona, Roger de Langleia, Hugh de Walltun, Hugh de Linacre, Thomas de Leyes, Nicholas le Dunne, William fil. Kalkin, Helyas de Bosco de Barleie, etc. Undated. (Rel. xx. 220.)

226. GRANT from Roger le Hem de Barley Wodsetis to William fil. Willelmi Fabri de eadem on his marriage with Margery, his daughter, and to their children, of the land which Nicholas Sub-monte sometime held in Barley Wodsetis, lying near Holbrok, Duntisburn, and Le Goldicroft. Witn. Jordan de Abetot, Thomas de Leys, Walter de Leys, Robert Edif. Undated. (Rel. xx. 220.)

227. GRANT from Walter le Caus de Brampton to William fil. Willelmi de Barley of all that land which Nicholas Sub-monte sometime held in Barley Wodsetis. Witn. Thomas de Leys, Walter de Leys, Robert Franceys, William le Hem, Roger le Hem. Undated. (Rel. xx. 220.)

228. GRANT from William de Abetot to the Hospitallers of Staveley of a bovate of land in Barleia lying between the land which was William Cronzun's and the land of Roger Le Eam which is called Langeleieker, for a term of twelve years from the Feast of St. Martin [11 Nov.], "anno postquam dominus Johannes rex Anglie cepit terdecimum denarium per Angliam" [sc. A.D. 1207]. Witn. Robert de Walet[on], Robert de Braminton, Nicholas de Langele, Roger filius suus, Walter de Heliun, Herbert de Hanl', Ralph filius suus, Alan, capellanus de Staveley, and many others. (Harl. 86 G 46.)

229. GRANT and quitclaim from Thomas Abtoft fil. et her. Roberti Abtoft de Barley, to Robert fil. Rob. de Hull de Barley Wodecetes of the reversion of a bovate of land called Hikelland on the death of his mother Mary. Witn. William de Wigley, William fil. Alani, Robert Mower, etc. Dat. F. of St. Peter [29 June], 1339. (Rel. xx. 164.)

230. GRANT from Robert de Barley, sen., Roger del More, Alan le Milner, sen., Alexander Bradschugh, and others, to Henry Nutte, of Castulton, of a messuage and bovate of land in Barley Wodesetes which Richard del Gorszes formerly held. Dat. Barley, S. a. F. of Corpus Christi [8 June], 1368. (Rel. xx. 110.)

231. GRANT from Thomas Gomfrey, clerk, and Robert Hykson, chaplain, to Joan, dau. of Richard G . . er, wife of Thomas del More, of all the lands, etc., in Barley which they had of the grant of Ralph Barker. Witn. William Grayne, John Hykson, etc. Dat. S. a. F. of St. Cedde [7 Jan.], 18 Ric. II. [1395]. (Foljambe.)

232. GRANT from Richard Hykson of Barley, chaplain, and Henry Fleccher, of Barleyleghes, to William Grayve of Barley and Matilda, his wife, of all the lands which they have of the said William in the fees of Barley and Dronfeld. Witn. Roger Johnson, Alan Milner, Robert Moldyng, etc. Dat. W. a. F. of SS. Simon and Jude [28 Oct.], 21 Ric. II. [1397]. (Foljambe.)

233. GRANT from William Barley, dominus de Barley, to James Maver, of a messuage, etc., extending between the common pasture, west, and the high road, leading from Homesfeld east, with a croft near the water of Dunsseburn on the south and the high road from Holmesfeld to Chastrefeld on the north, in the lordship of Barley in the fee of Staveley. Witn. William Coke of Holmesfeld, John Hasseland, Robert Willus, Robert Schemyld, etc. Dat. Th. b. F. of SS. Simon and Jude [28 Oct.], 1402. (Rel. xx. 110.)

234. GRANT from Robert Fleccher of Barlay to William de Neubolt of the same, and John Knutton, of a tenement in Barlay. Witn. John Elys of Whittyngton, Thomas Jamesson, etc. Dat. F. of St. Valentine [14 Feb.], 5 Hen. VI. [1427]. (Foljambe.)

235. CONFIRMATION by James Mouwer de Bradway to William Dorant of Barley and Joan Bentlay, his wife, dau. of William Bentlay, and to their children, of the lands, etc., in Barley Wodsetes, which descended to him on the death of Adam Mouwer, his father. Witn. John Barker, Robert Sergeant, Thomas Maynerd of Dronfield, etc. Dat. Barley, 1 June, 16 Hen. VI. [1438]. (Rel. xx. 112.)

236. GRANT from Agnes Fletcher of Barley, widow, to John Percy, vicar of Dronfeld, John Hordron, chaplain, and John Pare, of Notyngham, of a messuage and land in Barley which she had in conjunction with Robert Fletcher, her husband, by grant from William Newbolt and John Knotton. Witn. Robert Barley, sen., esq., Thomas Cokayn, gent., etc. Dat. F. of St. John B. [24 June], 37 Hen. VI. [1459]. (Foljambe.)

237. SALE from Robert Mower of Barley Woodesete to George, Earl of Shrewsbury, of the timber from the woods called Roweswood, Roweshagge, Alenhille, and two little hags called Depe Clough in the lordship of Barley. Dat. 18 Oct., 1526. (Rel. xx. 112.)

BARLOW *v.* also under DRONFIELD.

BARTON BLOUNT.

(BARTONA, BARTUN.)

238. *GRANT from Robert de Bachepus, with assent of Robert, his son and heir, to John, his son, of the whole land of " Comton " and " Aissendene " [West Compton and Ashdown, in E. Ilsley, Co. Berks.], to hold as freely as he himself held it of Earl Robert [de Ferrers] in the time of King Henry the elder by the service of one knight. [*Temp.* Hen. II., before 1166.] (Add. 21172.)

> Robertus de Bachep'. Omnibus hominibus totius Anglie tam presentibus quam futuris, Francis et Anglis salutem. Notum sit omnibus uobis me concessisse et dedisse Johanni filio meo pro seruitio suo totam terram de Comtun et de Aissendene [Compton and Ashenden, Co. Berks.] cum omnibus pertinentiis suis in Bosco et in plano, in pratis et in pascuis, in aquis et Molendinis, in viis et in semitis, tam libere et tam quiete quam ego melius eam tenui de Comite Roberto tempore Henrici Regis senioris per seruicium i militis de me tenendam et de heredibus meis ipse et heredes sui. Hanc donationem concessit Robertus filius et heres meus. Testes, Henricus presbyter, Hugo clericus de Cubeleia, Robertus de Piro, dapifer; Willelmus fil. Nigelli, Galfridus de Bachep', Rogerus Duredent, Radulfus de Gmelega, Radulfus de Mungumeri, Radulfus fil. Nicholai, Ricardus de Normantun et Robertus fil. eius, Willelmus fil. Terri, Robertus de Landa, Robertus de Trussele, Henricus fil. Roberti de Lega, Henricus de Barwa, Aluricus de Broctun, Reginaldus de Boslistun, Wimundus de Bartun, Robertus Rufus, Aluredus, Gillebertus fil. Cnihtwin et omnis Hallimot de Bartun.

239. GRANT and confirmation by Robert de Bakepuz to John, his brother, of the gift which his father made to the latter, of all his land of Barton and all his land of Benethleia [Hungry Bentley], for which the said John becomes his man in the court of his lord, Earl William de Ferrers, and gives to him, the said Robert, in acknowledgment a gold bezant. *Temp.* Hen. II., after 1166. (Harl. 45 F. 23.)

---

* This charter is included though the lands are in Berks, because it is manifestly a Derbyshire charter, as witness the concluding words "et omnis Hallimot de Bartun."

Robertus de Bakepuz, omnibus hominibus tocius Anglie Francis et Anglicis tam presentibus quam futuris salutem. Sciatis me dedisse et concessisse et hac presenti carta mea confirmasse Johanni fratri meo et heredibus suis in feudo et hereditate donacionem quam pater meus illi fecit pro seruicio suo scilicet totam terram de Bartona et totam terram de Benethleia cum omnibus pertinenciis, In villis et in agris et in boscis et in planis, In uiis et in semitis, In pratis et in pascuis, In aquis et in Molendinis, et in omnibus locis, Illi et heredibus suis pro homagio et seruicio suo dedi et quiete concessi, de me et heredibus meis tenendas, libere et quiete ab omni servicio ad me vel ad heredes meos pertinente per servicium unius militis, et sicut pater meus liberius et honorificencius ac quiecius ante ipsum terras predictas umquam tenuit. Pro hac vero donacione et concessione et confirmacione, Ipse Johannes deuenit homo meus in curia domini mei Comitis Willelmi de Ferers et ipse predictus Johannes dedit mihi in recognitione unum besantum aureum.

Teste Willelmo, Comite de Ferers, domino meo, Roberto de Perer, dapifero, Willelmo Pantun, Roberto de Ferers fratre Comitis, Roberto et Henrico de Ferers, awnculis Comitis, Sewalo filio Fulcheri, Roberto fil. Walchelini, Waltero de Sumetul, Gaufrido de Bachepuz, Humfrido de Thoke, Roberto de Hetford, Johanne de Turberuile, Roberto de Leia, Henrico filio suo, Ricardo de Normanton, Henrico fil. Walchelini, Petro fratre suo, Willelmo fratre suo et pluribus aliis. Apud Totesburiam.

BASLOW *v.* under BUBNALL, CHAPEL-EN-LE-FRITH.

BEARWARDCOTE, IN ETWALL.

(BEREWARDCOTE, BERVARDCOTE, BERWARDCOTE.)

240. GRANT, for six marks, by Nicholas de Chambres, to the nuns of St. Mary of Kynghesmedewe [King's Mead or De Pratis, Derby], of two acres of meadow in Bervardecote, with confirmation of four acres in the same, which they held of the gift of Nicholas de Fynderna. Witn. Nicholas de Henovere, Nicholas de Fynderna, William fil. Philippi, etc. *Temp.* Hen. III. (Woll. ix. 33.)

BEARWARDCOTE *v.* also under BURNASTON.

BEAUCHIEF.

(BEAUCHEF, BEAUCHIEFF, BEUCHEFF, DE BELLO CAPITE.)

241. GRANT from Hugh de Barkhowse to Ralph de Dore and William de Barkhowse of all the goods and chattels which he has in his tannery of Beauchief, with all dues belonging thereto. Witn. Adam Lawnder, Henry Barker of Beauchief, Thomas Barker of Dore. Dat. S. a. Nat. of St. John B. [24 June], 7 Ric. II. [1383]. (D. A. J. iii. 104.)

242. LEASE from John Swyffte, Abbot of Beauchief and the Convent of the same, to Nicholas Longford, squyer, of all lands, etc., within the precincts and bounds of the said Abbey in Beauchieff, for three years, at a yearly rent of a pair of gloves, certain lands, etc., being excepted as "Broode medow" and "Brekmedow," "a spryng that is called Hudclyff banke," the "walke mylne," the "smythees," "a barkhowse," a "Lawnderhowsse," the "kyrke yarde," etc. Dat. 1 May, 3 Edw. IV. [1463]. (Foljambe.)

243. Grant from John, Abbot of Beauchief, to Sir John Talbot, Earl of Shrewsbury, in return for his promised counsel, support, protection, and aid in every necessity, of a yearly fee for life of five marks at Beauchief. Dat. Scheafeld [Sheffield ?], 8 Aug., 6 Edw. IV. [1466]. Fine seal of the Abbot. (Foljambe.)

BEAUCHIEF *v.* also under Beeley, Chesterfield, Wirksworth.

BEELEY.

(Beghley, Belee, Beley, Bethley, Bethtley, Beyeleye, Beyleghe, Beyleye.)

244. Grant for five and a half silver marks with three bezants to his wife and three to Serlo, his son, and for admission of himself and his wife into spiritual fraternity with the house and the whole Præmonstratensian order, from Warnerius de Begalaia to the Abbey and Canons of Beauchef', of "totam harewdam" [Harewood Grange, in Beeley] and of land extending from the Cross of Wadescelf to Derley and of common of pasture for a specified number of cattle; rent, 10s. Witn. Ralph Basset, Canonicus de Rouecestre [Roucester, Co. Staff.], Hugh de Dronefeld, Robert, persona de Dereleia [Darley], Mag. Hugh de Cestrefeld, Geoffrey de Bramtona, Alan de Edelwaldeleia, etc. Early thirteenth century. (Woll. i. 13.)

245. Grant from Margery, domina de Bethtley, to Osbert de Chawortht of half a bovate of land in le Grevis, which Wydo de Bobinhul sometime held, and a meadow in Bethtley which the same Wydo bought from John de Bethtley. Witn. Robert Bojoun, Roger de Bobinhul, Richard de Basselowe, etc. *Temp.* Hen. III. (Woll. ii. 43.)

246. Grant from William fil. Osseberti de Chatiswortht to William fil. Hugonis de le Greves, of the lands named in the preceding charter. Witn. Richard de Crakemere, Robert de le Grevis, Robert de Frogcote, etc. *Temp.* Hen. III. or Edw. I. (Woll. ii. 43A.)

247. Grant from William fil. Osseberti de Chatiswortht to Aliscia fil. Rad. fil. Lescie de Edinsouere, of the moiety of that half-bovate of land which Ossebert, his father, sometime held in Le Grevis from Margaret, condam domina de Bethtleye, and the moiety of a meadow which Wydo de Bobinhull bought from John de Bethtleye in the field of Bethtleye. Witn. Richard de Crakemere, John de Roulisleye, Robert de Grevis, etc. *Temp.* Hen. III. or Edw. I. (Woll. ii. 44.)

248. Grant from the Abbot and Convent de Bello Capite [Beauchief] to William de le Grevis of half a bovate of land in le Grevis, which Osbert de Ore, Dominus de Beghley, gave to them; rent, 30d. Witn. Peter de Baumford, Adam de Ronnesley, William de Chatteswrth, Peter de Rolund. *Temp.* Hen. III. or Edw. I. (Woll. ii. 45.)

249. Copy of a grant from Robert del Greves of Beyleye to Robert, his son, of a messuage and a bovate of land in Beyleye; rent, 3s. ½d. Witn. John de Roulesley, Richard de Crakemere, John de Caltorp, etc. Dat. Beyleye, F. b. Pentecost [24 May], 31 Edw. I. [1303]. (Woll. ii. 52.)

3

250. GRANT from Robert fil. Steph. Attebrigge of Essovere to Giles del Greves and Leticia, his wife, of half a bovate of land in le Greves, near Beghley, which descended to him, with other land, at the death of Alice, his mother. Witn. Thomas de Beghley, Dominus de Beghley, John de Raunsley, Richard de Crakmersh, etc. Dat. Beghley, F. of St. Peter in Cathedra [22 Feb.], 1316[7]. (Woll. ii. 49.)

251. GRANT from Giles de Greves to Thomas, his son, of a half bovate of land and a messuage in the field of Greves. Witn. Thomas de Biley, Richard Crakemershe, Richard de Fallinghe, etc. Dat. Greves, Mor. of SS. Processus and Martinian [2 July], 1324. (Woll. ii. 48.)

252. GRANT from Thomas fil. Egidii de les Grevez to Thomas fil. Hen. de Chattesworthe of a place of land in Beley. Witn. Thomas de Beley, John de Caltone of Chattesworthe, William fil. Galfridi de Beley, etc. Dat. Beley, W. b. F. of St. Thomas [7 July], 31 Edw. III. [1357]. (Woll. ii. 46.)

253. GRANT from Thomas fil. Egidii de lez Greves to John, his son, of a messuage and land in lez Greves. Witn. Thomas de Beley, Thomas Attegate, and Roger Normone. Dat. Le Grevez, S. b. F. of St. Lawrence [2 Feb.], 33 Edw. III. [1359]. (Woll. ii. 47.)

254. GRANT from William de le Grewis to Giles fil. Matthei de Basselowe of half a bovate of land and a meadow in le Grewis, in the field of Beyeley; rent, 27d. Witn. John de Roulislegh, Richard de Crakemersh, Hugh de le Falling, etc. *Temp.* Edw. III. (Woll. ii. 50.)

255. GRANT from John Page and Alice, daughter of John Thomsone, of Chattesworthe, to William de Aderleye, Thomas de Aderleye, clerk, and William de Ulkerthorpe, of lands in Belee and Chattesworthe. Dat. Beeley, 10 Jan., 15 Ric. II. [1392]. (Woll. ii. 57.)

256. RELEASE from Thomas de Adarley, clerk, and William de Ulkerthorp, to Thomas, son of Giles del Greves, of lands in Beley and Chattesworth, which they held from John Page and Alice, his wife. Witn. Dionisius de Rollesley, Thomas, fil. Hugonis, and William Norman. Dat. Beley, W. a. F. of St. George [23 Apr.], 17 Ric. II. [1394]. (Woll. ii. 58.)

257. LICENSE by Robert, Abbas de Bello Capite [Beauchief], to Thomas Gylessone of le Greves, to alienate a messuage and half a bovate of land which he held of the same Abbot in le Greves. Dat. Beauchief, Kal. Maij [1 May], 21 Ric. II. [1398]. (Woll. ii. 51.)

258. LEASE for three lives from William Gresley, Abbas de Bello Capite [Beauchief], of the grange of Harewode, to William de Stone of Harewode, Johanna, his wife, and one son. Witn. William Ulkerthorppe, John Lynacre, Thomas Caus, etc. Dat. Beauchief Abbey, M. a. F. of St. Michael [29 Sept.], 10 Henry VI. [1431]. (Woll. i. 14.)

259. GRANT from John Greveys of Beley to William Greveys of Bramtone, his brother, of a tenement with lands in Beley, which belonged to Thomas Gylessone, his father, and John, his brother. Witn. Henry Stafford of Beley, Dionisius Norman of the same, Richard Thomlynsone of Greveys, etc. Dat. Beley, F. of Ann. of B. V. M. [25 Mar.], 16 Hen. VI. [1438]. (Woll. ii. 54.)

260. RELEASE from Thomas Greveys, son of Giles Greveys of Beley, to William Greves of Bramtone, of lands in Beley apud le Greveys. Witn. Henry Stafford of Beley, Dionisius Norman of the same, Richard Thomlynsone of Greveys, etc. Dat. Beley, 1 Apr., 16 Hen. VI. [1438]. (Woll. ii. 53.)

261. RELEASE from John Greveys of Beley and Marjory, his wife, to William Greveys of Bramtone, of lands at le Greveys in the fee of Beley. Witn. Henry Stafford of Beley, Dionisius Norman, Richard Thomlynsone of Greveys, etc. Dat. Beley, 1 Apr., 16 Hen. VI. [1438]. (Woll. ii. 55.)

262. WRITING by Henry Columbelle, squyer, Sir Richard Johnson, etc., requesting alms for the support of a priest in the chapel of St. Mary in Beley, in Derwentdale, recently founded by John Eyre, chapeleyn. Dat. 18 Mar., 13 Edw. IV. [1473]. (Woll. i. 12.)

263. Will of William Greves of Beyleghe. Dat. 12 Feb., 1497[8]. Proved 5 Mar. same year. (Woll. ii. 59.)

264. BOND by Nicolas Grevys of Bramptone, husbandman, to William Grevys of Beley and John Grevys, his son, in 100 marks, for the occupation of a messuage [in Beeley] during his life. Dat. Beley, 8 Apr., 19 Hen. VII. [1504]. (Woll. ii. 62.)

265. LEASE from John Norton, Abbot, and the Convent of Beucheff [Beauchief], to Sir John Blakiswalle, chauntry-priest, of Dronfeld [Dronfield], of the grange called Harwod, for eighty years, with remainder to Christofer and Robert Blackwalle, his brothers, to Thomas, son of Cristofer, and John the son of Robert, and to Elizabeth and Agnes, daughters respectively of the said Cristofer and Robert; rent 40s. Dat. Chapter House of Beucheff, F. of Pur. of B. V. M. [2 Feb.], 1506[7]. (Woll. i. 15.)

266. AGREEMENT between Roger Cowper and Roger Cocken and Johanna Grevis and George Held, all of Beley, for an exchange of lands in Beley. Dat. 1 April, 3 Edw. VI. [1549]. (Woll. ii. 61.)

BEELEY *v.* also under CHATSWORTH, CHELMORTON, CHESTERFIELD, SOMERSALL.

BEIGHTON.

(BECTHON, BECTON, BEGHTON.)

267. GRANT, for fourscore marks, from Dom. Walter de Furneaus, miles., to William de Furneaus, his brother, of the manor of Becton; rent, 1d., due on St. Radegund's Day in St. Radegund's Church, Becton. Witn. Dom. Thomas de Furnival, Dom. William de Cressi, Dom. Thomas de Eywyle, milites, etc. *Temp.* Edw. I. (Campb. iv. 11.)

268. GRANT from Robert de Fornaus, miles., Dominus de Becthon, with consent of William de Fornaus, his brother, to Geoffrey Bareth and Matilda, his wife, of lands in Becthon; rent, 13d. Witn. William Gere of Becthon, William de Parco of the same, William de Mauthone, jun., etc. Dat. F. of Nat. of St. John B. [24 June], 2 Edw. III. [1328]. (Campb. v. 16.)

269. GRANT from John fil. Rog. de Byrlay in Becthon to John Pye, of a messuage, etc., in the vill and territory of Byrlay in Becthon. Witn. Robert Waryn, William Gers, William de Pecco, etc. Dat. F. of St. Michael [29 Sept.], 2 Edw. III. [1328]. (Foljambe.)

270. GRANT in tail from Robert de Furneaux and William de Furneaux to William fil. Thom. de Sawere, of Beghton, of a garden in Beghton and land in Walterthorpe; rent, 8*s.* Witn. William Gere, of Beghtone, Gilbert de Somersdeby, William fil. Galfridi of the same. Dat. W. a. F. of St. Gregory [12 Mar.], 4 Edw. III. [1330]. (Campb. i. 1.)

271. GRANT from John Pye to Richard de Byrton of Treton and Alice, his wife, dau. of the said John, of a messuage, etc., in Byrley, in the fee of Beghton. Witn. William de Staynton, William de Hallenthorp, William de Cotyngham. Dat. S. a. F. of Inv. of H. Cross [3 May], 30 Edw. III. [1356]. (Foljambe.)

272. GRANT from Robert Pye of Tukysford in le Cley [Tuxford, Co. Notts.] to William Smyth of Morysburgh [Mosborough] and John Mymmòtt of the same, of a toft and croft in Byrley and fifteen acres of land in the fields of Byrley. Witn. William Smyth, jun., Robert Smyth, John Tomson, etc. Dat. Ekyngton, S. a. Michaelmas, 8 Hen. V. [1420]. (Foljambe.)

273. GRANT from Robert Pye of Tuxford in le Cley [Co. Notts.] to William Plomley of sixteen acres of land and meadow in the fields of Birley. Witn. William Tilley of Hakunthorpe, John Tomson of Rygeway, John Nelsthorpe, John Cade. Dat. Ekynton, F. of St. Matthias* [24 Feb.], 10 Hen. V. [1423]. (Foljambe.)

274. GRANT from William Plomleg to John Robert, jun., of sixteen acres of land and meadow in the fields of Birley. Witn. William Dolphyn, John Tomson of Rygeway, Giles Blount, etc. Dat. Plomley, 16 July, 11 Hen. V. [*sic* ? for 1 Hen. VI., 1423]. (Foljambe.)

275. GRANT from William Smyth of Mosburgh and John Mymmot of the same to John Robert of Byrley, of a toft and croft in Byrley and fifteen acres of land in the fields of the same. Witn. John Wylson, John Wendesley, Thomas Newbold. Dat. Ekynton, F. of Pur. of B. V. M. [2 Feb.], 32 Hen. VI. [1454]. (Foljambe.)

276. GRANT from John Robert of Birley, in the parish of Beghton, to Thomas Fryth of Gledles, John Newbolt of Hakynthorp, and Robert Mymot of Rygeway, of a toft and 15 acres of land in Birley. Witn. John Alston, William Wigfall, etc. Dat. Birley, F. of St. Andrew [30 Nov.], 2 Hen. VII. [1486]. (Foljambe.)

277. GRANT from John Robert to William Robert, his son, of a toft and croft in Byrley with other lands in Byrley and Oldefelde. Witn. John Newbold, Thomas Fryth, etc. Dat. F. of St. Cecilia [22 Nov.], 4 Hen. VII. [1488]. (Foljambe.)

278. QUITCLAIM from John Robartte and John Gyles of Birley, son of Giles Robarte, late of Birley, near Beghton, to Henry Foliambe,

---

*A mistake here, as 10 Hen. V. began 21 Mar., 1422, and he died 31 Aug., 1422. The Saint's day may be in error, or "10 Hen. V." should be "1 Hen. VI."

lord of Walton, of sixteen acres of land [in Birley]. Dat. W. a. Christmas, 1488. (Foljambe.)

BEIGHTON *v.* also under BRAMPTON, CHESTERFIELD.

BELPER.

(BEARPER, BEAUPER, BEAUREPER.)

279. GRANT from John Wyttyngtone of Derby, smythe, to John Bothe of Arlestone, esq., and John Fitzherbert of Etwelle, esq., of a messuage and croft in Beaureper. Witn. John Waundelle, Rob. Wyttyngtone, etc. Dat. 26 May, 15 Edw. IV. [1475]. (Woll. vii. 33.)

280. EXTRACT from court-roll of Belper Manor held at Duffield on Th. a. F. of the Epiphany [6 Jan.], 13 Hen. VII. [1498], recording the surrender by John Sowter of an acre of land and half a rood in Stanley, etc. (Trusley.)

281. RELEASE from Margaret, widow of John Brigge of Maperley, to Robert Tykhulle of le Stanley Graunge, gent., of lands in Beaureper. Witn. Robert Morten of le Parkhalle, gent., John Morten of Maperley, gent., Henry Fawconer of Schypley, etc. Dat. 10 July, 22 Hen. VII. [1507]. (Woll. viii. 66.)

282. RENTAL of lands in Belper. 1537. (Kerry xiv. 55.)

283. LEASE from Henry Sacheuerell of Ratclyff upon Sore, esq., to Thomas Sacheverell of Cheuerell Hall, Co. Notts., gent., of a moiety of all the "tithe cornes of all maner of greynes tythe hey and all other tythes" in the "toune hamelettes belonging to Beauper," parcel of the parsonage of Duffeld, "pryncipals tythe woll and lambe tythe eggs appuls and tythe wodd excepted and alweis reservid to ye said Henry." Dat. 20 Apr., 36 Hen. VIII. [1545]. (Trusley.)

BENTLEY, FENNY.

(BENETYLEE, BENTELEY, FYNNY BENTELEY.)

284. GRANT from Nicholas de Benetylee to John, his son, by Avice, his wife, of a moiety of the cultivated land held by him of Robert fil. Geraldi, at a yearly rent of five shillings and a pair of gloves worth one penny. Witn. Dom. R. "presbyter," Ralph de Tykenhal, Ralph, clericus de Stapenhill, etc. *Temp.* Hen. III. (Stowe 46.)

285. LEASE, for twelve years, from Henry Bradburne to John Whithed of his water-mill of Fynny Benteley, the tenant to keep the mill in good repair, but the lessor to supply the necessary timber. Dat. Michaelmas Day, 18 Hen. VI. [1439]. (Bemrose.)

286. LEASE from Cicelye Sandford of Cryche, widow, to John Beresford of Bradeley Ashe, of all her lands, etc., in the lordship of Fenny Bentley. Dat. 6 May, 14 Hen. VIII. [1522]. (Beresf. 72.)

BENTLEY, FENNY, *v.* also under BRADBURN.

BENTLEY, HUNGRY.

(BENETHLEIA, BENTELEYE.)

287. GRANT from John de Nedham of Benteley to Thomas fil. Amote de Benteleye, of lands in the fee of Benteleye; rent, 2*d*. Witn. Philip de Benteleye, John fil. Hen. de Benteleye, William Perfey of the same, etc. Dat. S. a. F. of SS. Simon and Jude [28 Oct.], 1 Ric. II. [1377]. (Woll. iii. 4.]

288. GRANT from William le Cook, vicar of Longeford, and Ralph de Alkemontone, chaplain, to William de le Halle of Bentley and Emma, his wife, of lands in Bentley. Witn. Tho. Coupere, Will. de Alkemontone, John Feirolet, etc. Dat. Bentley, S. a. F. of St. Thomas, Ap. [21 Dec.], 4 Ric. II. [1380]. (Woll. iii. 6.)

289. RELEASE from John Meynille, chaplain, to Oliver de Bertone, of the manor of Benteleye. Dat. London, S. a. Pur. of B. V. M. [2 Feb.], 5 Ric. II. [1382]. (Woll. iii. 5.)

BENTLEY, HUNGRY, *v.* also under BARTON BLOUNT.

BIRCHILL *v.* under BAKEWELL.

BIRCHOVER.

(BIRCHEOVERE, BIRCHOUER, BURCHORE, BYRCHEOR, BYRCHORE, BYRCHOUERE.)

290. GRANT from Henry fil. Willelmi Carpentarii de Birchouer to Richard fil. Maye of all his lands, etc., in the fields, etc., of Birchouer, which Ralph de Aula sometime held. Witn. John Selveyn of Winster, Ralph Gerart, Roger, dominus de Wendesleye, Robert Aubrey. *Circ.* 1270. (Kerry xix. 367.)

291. RELEASE from Henry fil. et her. Willelmi dicti Carpentarii de Birchovere to Thomas fil. Henrici de Stantoneleyes of lands in "le Romesey side" in Birchover; rent, one halfpenny. Witn. Thomas de Grattone, clericus, William de Longesd[on] in Yellegrave, Henry de Hotot', etc. *Temp.* Edw. I. (Woll. ii. 29.)

292. GRANT from Robert de Waddisley fil. Ade de Waddisl' to Thomas fil Henrici de Stantoneleyis of his demesne land, which Simon de Cromforde, William de Essebourne, etc., held of him, with the wood called Sabyneheye, etc., in Bircheovere; rent, 2*d*. Witn. Dom. Adam de Herthul, Thomas Folegambe, clericus, Henry de Otot, Hugh de Meynel in Wynstre, etc. *Temp.* Edw. I. (Woll. ii. 11.)

293. GRANT from William de Birchovere to Thomas, his son, and Cecilia, his son's wife, of the manor of Bircheouere; rent, £10 and a rose. Witn. Geoffrey de Dethek, Ranulph de Snittertone, John de Suttone, etc. Dat. Bircheovere, T. a. F. of St. Luke [18 Oct.], 10 Edw. III. [1336]. (Woll. ii. 66.)

294. GRANT from Thomas de Birchovere to Robert de Aldeport, capellanus, of the water-mill of Birchovere and of 5*s*. 10*d*. rent from William de Hulle, with homage of the same. Witn. Walter fil Ade de Bircheovere, Henry Faber, Walter le Reve, etc. Dat. Bircheovere, Vig. of Holy Trinity [6 June], 23 Edw. III. [1349]. (Woll. ii. 67.)

295. GRANT, in tail, from Robert de Aldeport, chaplain, to Thomas de Bircheovere and Cecilia, his wife, of the water-mill of Birchovere, with 5*s*. 10*d*. rent, and the homage of William de Hulle. Witn. Hugh Meignille of Wynster, Robert de Grattone, Robert de Knyvetone, etc. Dat. Birchover, Morr. of Holy Trinity [8 June], 23 Edw. III. [1349]. (Woll. ii. 24.)

296. GRANT from Thomas de Birchovere to Robert de Aldeporte, rector of Neutone, Robert de Wyrkesworthe, chaplain, of lands, etc., in Birchovere, and rent from lands in Stantone. Witn. Thomas Foliaumbe, Dominus de Eltone, John de Resintone, Thomas de Rideware, etc. Dat. Birchovere, W. a. F. of St. Valentine [14 Feb.], 1350 [1351]. (Woll. ii. 17.)

297. GRANT from William de Aldewerk of Birchovere to William Eleyn of Brasyngtone, chaplain, of lands in Birchovere. Witn. John de Shirley, Walter Aleyn of Birchovere, John le Smythe of the same. Dat. Birchovere, T. b. Pentecost [24 May], 2 Ric. II. [1379]. (Woll. ii. 28.)

298. INVENTORY of the lands of Henry de Aldwerk in Birchover. 1413. (D. A. J. xxii. 49.)

299. TERRIER of the lands of Henry de Aldewerk in Birchover. Dat. Aldewerk, F. of St. Peter in cathedra [22 Feb.], 1 Hen. V. [1414]. (Kerry xix. 368.)

300. QUITCLAIM from Nicholas Baxter of Derby and Margaret, his wife, widow of Richard del Hill, of the parish of Yolgrave, to John de Strelley fil. Nicholai de Strelley, knt., John Hunt of Asshover, William Boxon of Rokeston, co. Bedf., and William Aston of London, of all his lands in Le Hill, Birchover, and Stanton in Yolgrave, which were sometime Richard del Hill's. Dat. Derby, S. a. F. of the Assumption [15 Aug.], 4 Hen. V. [1416]. (Kerry xix. 370.)

301. GRANT from John Hyklyng of Lynbe, esquire, and Joan, his wife, to Richard Wayne of Herthill of his lands, etc., in the lordship of Birchover called Hill Place. Witn. Nicholas Gilbert, Richard Stenerdale, Thomas Aldwerk, etc. Dat. at Hill, F. of St. Martin [11 Nov.], 10 Hen. VI. [1431]. (Kerry xix. 371.)

302. GRANT from Robert Hyll of Asshebe de la Souche and Richard Hill, his son, to Richard Knollus of Netherhaddon, of a messuage and three bovates of land called le Hyll in Birchover. Witn. William Cantrell, John Sonyoure, Richard Aleyn. Dat. M. a. Michs. Day, 7 Edw. IV. [1467]. (Kerry xix. 371.)

303. QUITCLAIM from Roger Wayne of Alport to Henry Vernon, knt., Richard Vernon, and Thomas, sons of the said Henry, Robert Gylbert, sen., William Smethley, vicar of Youlgrave, and others, of all the lands which he acquired from the late John Aldwarke in Birchover and Normanton. Dat. 14 May, 7 Hen. VII. [1492]. (Kerry xix. 372.)

304. SALE, for £4, by Thomas Kenylmarche, lord of Byrchore, to Aden Beresford, of a wood called Medovclyffe, growing under Byrchore, "with free entre and ovtegate that ys most spedful to him his servaunts and caryage," up to Michaelmas, 1505. "Also the said Aden schalle leyffe ii^c weyvers in ordur wythin the seyd wode seche as are lycly to be tymburtrevs," etc. Dat. 13 Oct., 10 Hen. VII. [1502]. (Woll. ii. 68.)

305. LEASE, for thirty years, by John [Bourchier], Abbot of " our lady of the medowez of Leycester," to Henry Barth, husbandman, of the tithes of Burchore; rent, 33s. 4d. Dat. 1 Apr., 26 Hen. VIII. [1535]. (Woll. xi. 74.)

306. LEASE, for twenty-one years, from Denys Beresford, gent., to Raffe Gell of Hoptone, co. Derby, gent., of the lordship of Byrchovere [Birchover]; rent, £5 6s. 8d. Dat. 15 Oct., 33 Hen. VIII. [1541]. (Woll. xi. 66.)

307. GRANT, for £63 6s. 8d., from George Gyfford, esq., to Thomas Alen of Woodhouse, yeoman, of tithes called Byrcheor tithes in Yolgrave; rent, 3s. 4d. Dat. 18 Aug., 4 Edw. VI. [1550]. (Woll. xi. 78.)

BIRCHOVER *v.* also under YOULGRAVE.

BLACKWELL NR. ALFRETON *v.* under PINXTON.

BOLSOVER.

(BOLLESOUERE.)

308. LEASE from Margery fil. Ade de Venella of Cesterefeld, to Robert fil. Stephani de Newbold of the same of half an acre of land in the fee of Peverel, abutting on Ryhull and on the road to Bollesouere, for five years. Witn. William de Riggeway, Roger Lauerok, etc. Dat. F. of the Annunciation [25 Mar.], 10 Edw. II. [1317]. (Foljambe.)

309. EXTRACT from the Court-roll of the Manor of Bolsover, recording the admittance of Richard de Hyghege to a messuage [in Bolsover] as next heir to Roger Jeke, chaplain, his uncle. Dat. M. a. F. of St. Edward [5 Jan.], 3 Hen. V. [1416]. (Foljambe.)

BONSALL.

(BONDESALE, BONDESALL, BONDESHALL, BONDSALE,
BONTESHALE, BONTISAL, BONTISHAL,
BONTSALL, BOUNTESHALL.)

310. GRANT from Walter fil. Osbert de Bontisal to Nicholas fil. Galfridi de Ybol of a selion of land in Bontisal, on "le Daleside." Witn. Ralph Sele de Bontishale, Henry fil. Ric. de eadem, Richard fil. Joh. de eadem, etc. *Temp.* Hen. III. (Foljambe.)

311. GRANT from John de Calton, capellanus, to John, his son, of a messuage and eight acres of land in Bontishal. Witn. Robert de la Dale. John Hayle, etc. Dat. Octave of Epiphany [6 Jan.], 29 Edw. III. [1356]. (Foljambe.)

312. GRANT from Adam le Smyth of Bondishal to Alice, wife of Nicholas le Ward, of the same, of all the lands [in Bonsal] which he had from the said Nicholas, to hold for term of her life. Witn. William fil. Renald de Bontishal, John Hayle, John le Hyve. Dat. Bontishal, F. of All Saints [1 Nov.], 1361. (Foljambe.)

313. GRANT from Nicholas le Warde of Bondesale to Nicholas le Hayward, chaplain, of a messuage and three acres of land in Bondesale, lying beyond Ibulsty in Whitemareslak, Littellowe, etc. Witn. William fil. Reginaldi, John Hayle, William in le Dale, John le Souter. Dat. F. of SS. Simon and Jude [28 Oct.], 49 Edw. III. [1375]. (Foljambe.)

314. QUITCLAIM from Alice, widow of Nicholas Warde, of Bondsale, to Sir Nicholas Hayws of Brassyngton, chaplain, of a messuage and land in the vill and field of Bondsale. Witn. William Dale, John Hyve, William Bayle, etc. Dat. F. of St. Ambrose [4 Apr.], 1395. [Foljambe.]

315. GRANT from Nicholas le Hayward of Bondsale, chaplain, to Henry Mapulton, John Garard, and William Vade, chaplains, of a messuage and land in Bondsale, at a yearly rent of 2*d.*, to the heirs of Nicholas le Warde. Witn. John, son of Henry de Bondsale, Robert Smyth, etc. Dat. W. a. F. of St. Hilary [13 Jan.], 1402[3]. (Foljambe.)

316. GRANT from Henry de Mapulton, William Vade, and John Marard, chaplains, to Thomas de Eyton, "walker," and Joan, his wife, of a messuage and three acres of land in the town and fields of Bondesale, which they had of the feoffment of Nicholas Hayward, chaplain. Witn. Robert Smyth, William Barfot, William le Stones, etc. Dat. S. a. F. of All Saints [1 Nov.], 5 Hen. IV. [1403]. (Foljambe.)

317. GRANT from John Webster to John Guyte of Over Haddon and John, his son, of a messuage, etc., and 12 acres of land in the town and fields of Over Bondsale. Witn. Robert de Dale, William Herryson, Hugh Smyth, etc. Dat. Fr. a. Conc. of B. V. M. [8 Dec.], 3 Hen. VI. [1424]. (Foljambe.)

318. GRANT from the same to the same and Elena Guyte, his wife, of a messuage and 10 acres of land in the town and fields of Bondesale. Witn. Robert de Dale, William Herrison, Hugh Smyth, etc. Dat. Fr. a. Conc. of B. V. M. [8 Dec.], 3 Hen. VI. [1424]. At the back is the note, "This Deed was proved to have been forged." (Foljambe.)

319. EXTRACT of court-roll of Bondeshall manor held at Wirksworth, 5 Mar., 38 Hen. VI. [1460], recording the surrender by John Thomlynson into the hands of the Queen, of 18 acres of land, etc., in Staley [Staveley], late in the tenure of John Fletcher, to the use of John Gyte; Humphrey [Stafford], Duke of Buckingham, being then Steward. (Foljambe.)

320. RELEASE from Alice Jacson to Richard Eyre of Hogimaston of lands, tenements, etc., in the town and fields of Bondesall. Witn Richard Alsopp, John Hoght, John Eyre. Dat. F. of St. Michael, 1 Edw. IV. [1461]. (Foljambe.)

321. EXTRACT of court-roll of Bountesall Manor, recording the surrender by Thomas Wodde, as attorney for John Thomlynson of Medilton, near Yollegreve, of eight acres of land, etc., to the use of Henry Gretton and Agnes, his wife. Dat. W. a. F. of St. Bartholomew [24 Aug.], 2 Edw. IV. [1462]. (Foljambe.)

322. ATTORNEY from Richard Walker, vicar of Wybunbere, late rector of Bondesall, to William Walet and Henry Nedham, to surrender, in the court of Bondesall, to the use of Thomas Foliambe, esq., all his estate and term in Bondesall Mill. Dat. 9 Oct., 4 Edw. IV. [1464]. (Foljambe.)

323. CERTIFICATE from Henry Hylton of Bondsall, John Dawkyn, priest, John Adam, Robert Adam, Tho. Roos, John Chyldars, etc., that Henry Gratton and Agnes, his wife, have taken seisin of a "place" in Over Bondsall, after the death of Ellen Robynson, sometime wife of John Guylte, Henry Guylte releasing the same. Dat. 13 Oct., 12 Edw. IV. [1472]. (Foljambe.)

324. LEASE from Henry Gratton to Henry Gyte of a "plase with the Byggyng ther vppon," and all the land apperteining in Over Bontsall until the F. of Inv. of H. Cross [3 May], for 10s. Witn. Thomas Storer, Thomas Hervey, Will. Ballyden, etc. Dat. Wyrkesworth, 22 Dec., 12 Edw. IV. [1472]. (Foljambe.)

325. RELEASE from Henry Guyte or Quyte of Bonteshale to Henry Gretton and Agnes, his wife, of a messuage and 12 acres of land in Bonteshale and all the lands, etc., in the same, formerly John Webster's. Witn. William Leche, Henry Hilton, etc. Dat. Bonteshale, 2 Mar., 13 Edw. IV. [1474]. (Foljambe.)

BONSALL *v.* also under BRASSINGTON, CHESTERFIELD.

BOROWCOTE *v.* under CRICH.

BOROWE *v.* under WALTON-ON-TRENT.

BOULTON.

(BOLTON, BOLTONE.)

326. CONFIRMATION by Patrick de Bolton fil. Oliveri de Saucheverel to the church of St. Mary at Derley, in perpetuity, of all rents and lands which they had in the thirty-fourth year of King Henry, son of King John, in the fee of William fil. Ricardi de Boltone. Witn. Dom. Robert le Vavasour, Robert de Esseburna, milites, Ralph de Tikehale, etc. *Temp.* Edw. I. (Add. 5236.)

327. QUITCLAIM from Robert de Saucheverel, Dominus de Boltone, fil. Patricii de Saucheverel, to the church of St. Mary at Derlega [Darley Abbey], of all his lands and tenements which they had of his fee in the towns of Boltone and Alwastone, of the gift of William fil. Ric. de Boltone. Witn. Dom, Hugh de Stredlega, William de Chaddesdene, John Fauvel, milites, Ralph de Saucheverel, etc. Dat. Derby, Vig. of St. James [24 July], 1282. (Add. 5237.)

328. QUITCLAIM from the same Robert to the aforesaid church of all the arable land in the field of Bolton called Aukeput, near the marsh, which they have of the gift of Robert fil. Simonis de Boltone, formerly the "nativus" of the aforesaid Patrick, his father. Witn. Robert de Dethek, Hubert de Frechevile, Hugh de Hergreve, etc. Dat. Derley, F. of Pur. of B. V. M. [2 Feb.], 15 Edw. I. [1286]. (Add. 5238.)

329. CONVEYANCE from Reginald, quondam vicarius ecclesie beati Petri, Derby, to Ralph de [F]rechevile, of land in the territory and meadows of Boulton, which he had for a term of 18 years from Robert fil. Henrici de Boulton, reserving to himself a crop of wheat and rye standing on six acres of the above land, called Le Bottes. Dat. Derby, M. b. F. of St. Bartholomew [24 Aug.], 1294. (Harl. 86 G. 43.)

330. GRANT from William Saucheverel, Dominus de Hopwelle, to Robert Foucher of Osmundestone, of 13s. 4d., silver, in yearly rent for yearly participation for the whole term of his life in the chief messuage of the same Robert in Boltone. Dat. Boltone, Fr. a. F. of St. Cedde [2 Mar.], 18 Edw. III. [1344]. (Add. 5240.)

BOWDON.

(BAUDON, BAWDON, BOUDON, BOWDENE)

v. under CHAPEL-EN-LE-FRITH.

BOYLESTONE.

(BOILESTON, BOYLESTON, BOYLESTUNE, BOYLISTON, BOYLLESTON, BOYLSTON, BOYLSTONE.)

331. CERTIFICATE by Alexander [Stavenby], Bishop of Coventry and Lichfield, that at the presentation of Ralph de Grendon he has admitted Walter, son of William de Lichfield, preist, as rector of that moiety of Boylleston church which Master Roger de Grendon, called "Simple" (simplex), held by consolidating that moiety with the moiety to which he admitted him on the presentation of Walter de Ridewar'. Dat. Derby, xviii. Kal. Jan. [15 Dec.], 1238. (P. R. O., B. 3594.)

332. GRANT, in tail, from Matilda Peche to Roger de Rideware, her son, of all her land in the vill. of Boyliston, with the capital messuage and moiety of the advowson of the church, to be held of Dom. Will de Ferrar[iis], Comes Derb', capitalis dominus feodi illius, with reversion, to Walter and John, brothers of the grantee, and John de la Launde, his "nepos." Witn. Ralph fil. Nicholai, William de Montegomery, Hugh de Meynill, tunc senescallus predicti Comitis, Nygel de Langeford, Robert de Pyru, Henry de Braylesford, Robert de Mercinton, Robert capellanus, Rector ecclesie de Myldenhale, Roger capellanus, Rector ecclesie de Stapilford, Roger de Norton, *Circ.* 1254. (Eg. 441.)

333. INSPEXIMUS and confirmation by William de Ferrar[iis], Comes Derb', of the above charter of Matilda Peche [Eg. 441]. Dat. Hecham, first Sunday in Lent [1 Mar.], 38 Hen. III. [1254]. (Eg. 442.)

334. INQUISITION of the lands, etc., of Dom. Ralph de Grendona in Boilistona made by Richard Fitun, John Morel, Henry Spendeluue, Engelard de Makkelege, Thomas de Ibole, and other "legales et probi homines," who say that he holds nothing from the king "in capite," that he holds seventeen bovates of land from Dom. Andrew de Grendon, on which cottars are settled, that there is there half a mill, value 10s. per annum, that he holds a moiety of the advowson of Boiliston church "et valet ad personam v. marc," and a moiety of Boyliston, that Robert, his son, is his next heir, and is fourteen years old, and that when scutage runs, he, as attorney of Dom. Andrew de Grendon, is responsible to the Earl of Derby for the eighth part of a knight's fee. Dat. S. a. F. of St. Scholastica [10 Feb.], 40 Hen. III. [1256]. (Campb. xi. 10.)

335. LEASE from Roger de Rydeware, Dominus de Boyleston, fil. quondam Dom. Rog. de Rydeware, to John de Basingges, citizen of London, of Boyleston manor, with the advowson of the church and the new manor lately built in Boylestone wood, for 10½ years from the feast of the Annunciation, 22 Edw. I. [25 March, 1294]. Witn. Will. de Meynil, Hen. de Braylesford, Hen. de Knyveton, Hen. fil. Herberti, John de Langgeforde, Ralph de Monioye, milites, Ralph Sparewater, etc. (Stowe 47.)

336. FINAL CONCORD, whereby Roger de Rydeware and Philomena, his wife, grant to John de Basyngges the manor of Boylestone, with the advowson of the church; consideration money, £100 sterling. Westminster, Michaelmas Term, 23 Edw. I. [1295]. (Campb. xi. 11.)

337. QUITCLAIM from Hugh fil. et her. Will. de Grendon to John de Basingg, of the homage and service of Stephen de Grendon for tenements in Boyleston. Witn. John de Bakepuiz, Ralph de Schirley, knts., Ralph de Bakepuiz, etc. Dat. Mor. of St. Thomas, M. [29 Dec.], 28 Edw. I. [1299]. (Bemrose.)

338. GRANT and quitclaim from William fil. Hugonis de Grendon to Walter Waldeshef and Joan, his wife, dau. and heir of John de Basynges, of the homage and services of Stephen de Grendon in respect of the moiety of Boyleston manor and the advowson, which services, etc., his father, Hugh de Grendon, enfeoffed to Roger de Rydeware, by whom they were enfeoffed to John de Basynges. Witn. Dom. Walter de Monte Gomeri, Ralph de Shirlee, Roger de Bradebourne, Ralph de Rolleston, knights, etc. Dat. Mor. of F. of Pur. of B. V. M. [3 Feb.], 6 Edw. II. [1313]. (Bemrose.)

339. DEED of William de Wyklewode, rector of Bromlegh, Rochester dioc., Ralph Shirlee, knt., Thomas de Swanlond, and Thomas Halle, executors of the will of Walter Walderschef, late citizen of London, appointing Dom. John de Roucester (a co-executor), Dom. Richard de Douebrugge, and Thomas de Foston, chaplains of the three chantries in Boylestone church founded by the said Walter Walderschef in his will, for the support of which he bequeaths 18 marks of rent., viz., 13½ marks which the late king, Edward II., gave him from tenements late William Lychtfot's in Chepe Street, London, and 60s. from a "taberna depicta" held by Willam Gauger in Vintry, London. Dat. 1 May, 1334. (Okeover.)

340. GRANT from Walter fil. Walteri de Rideware, mil., to John Cokayne of Assheburne, of the manor of Boylestone. Witn. Nich. de Longeforde, mil., Henry de Brailsford, mil., John de la Pole of Assheburne, etc. Dat. Th. a. Easter [12 Apr.], 26 Edw. III. [1352]. (Woll. vi. 7.)

341. RELEASE from William le Fissher of Coton and Agnes, his wife, Roger de Mittone and Margaret, his wife, to Nicholas de Kent of Boilestone and Isabel, his wife, of a messuage and lands in Boilestone, which they held of the gift of Nicholas de Creswell of Boileston. Witn. Roger de Sapurtone, John de Sapurtone, Thomas Was, etc. Dat. M. a. Pur. of B. V. M. [2 Feb.], 50 Edw. III. [1376]. (Woll. vi. 9.)

342. RE-GRANT, in tail, from William de Sleford, Dean of the King's Chapel at Westminster, John Slore, Roger de Sapurtune, senr., and others, to Roger de Sapurtune, junr., and Elizabet, his wife, of the manor of Boylestune. Dat. Th. b. F. of St. George, Mart. [23 Apr.], 47 Edw. III. [1373]. (Woll. vi. 8.)

343. GRANT from Johanna Bakepuiz to John de Aston of all her lands in Boilestone for term of her life; rent, 5s. 2d. Dat. 6 Oct., 7 Ric. II. [1383]. Seal of arms. (Woll. vi. 10.)

344. RELEASE from Johanna, widow of William Bakepuz, to Sir Walter Blount, knt., of lands in Boylestone. Witn. Nich. de Mountegomery, Nich. de Longeford, knts., and John Fitzherbert. Dat. Bartone, M. b. F. of St. Nicholas [6 Dec.] 21 Ric. II. [1397]. (Woll. vi. 11.)

345. GRANT from William Prodhomme of Burton-upon-Trent to Henry de Tydnesore, chaplain, William de Chawmber of Falde, and Ralph Byschop of Hambury, of a messuage and lands near Margerelone in Boyleston; rent, 12*d*. Witn. Richard Walker, Robert Draper of Coten, John Durdant of Sudbury, Arthur de Rolleston. Dat. Boylestone, M. b. Nat. of St. John B. [24 June], 2 Hen. IV. [1401]. (Woll. vi. 12.)

346. RELEASE from Richard Draper and Johanna, his wife, to John le Carter, of lands in Boylestone. Witn. Thomas de Barlow, rector of Boylestone, John le Clerk, John Sany, etc. Dat. F. of St. Augustine [26 May], 17 Hen. VI. [1439]. (Woll. vi. 13.)

347. GRANT from Johanna, daughter of John Carter of Boylstone, to Thomas Crue of Wich Malbane [Nantwich] of a messuage and garden in Boylston, held of the gift of William Carter of Ettwalle. Witn. John Langley, chaplain, Roger Standiche, Thomas Eyre, etc. Dat. 7 Apr., 19 Edw. IV. [1479]. (Woll. vi. 14.)

348. POWER of attorney by Thomas Crue of Wich Malbanc [Nantwich] and Agnes, his wife, to Nicholas Sàpertone and Robert Sapertone, to deliver seisin to Hugh Venables of lands in Boylstone. Dat. 15 Aug., 8 Hen. VII. [1493]. (Woll. vi. 16.)

349. AWARD of Sir Edmund Latham, priest, and others, in a dispute between William Melbourne and his brother Rauff, respecting the possession of a cottage, etc., in "the Casey" in Boilstone, viz., that the two "shall from hensforth be lovers and frends like as brothern aught to be," that William shall keep possession of the cottage, etc., and pay the said Rauff £9. Dat. 16 Jan., 21 Hen. VII. [1505]. (Add. 4877.)

350. LEASE, for 40 years, for 10 marks, from William Blount, Lord Mountjoy, to Robert Palmer of Douuebrigge, yeoman, of his capital messuage and lands in Boylestone; rent, £3 3s. 4d. Dat. 28 Jan., 22 Hen. VII. [1507]. (Woll. vi. 15.)

BOYLESTONE *v.* also under MACKLEY.

BOYTHORPE.

(BOITHORP, BOYSORP, BOYTHORP, BOYTHORPP, BOYTORPH.)

351. LEASE from Peter de Tybethilf and Mary, his wife, to Walter de Linacre of Cestrefeld of land in Boythorp, for 9 years. Witn. Adam fil. Bonde, Richard fil. Ulnot, Robert fil. Edwini, etc. Dat. F. of St. Martin [11 Nov.], 36 Hen. III. [1251]. (Harl. 112 E. 23.)

352. GRANT from Albreia vidua de Boytorp to Reginald fil. Galfridi of an acre of land in Sudlegh [in Boythorpe]. Witn. John de Pecco, Robert de Boytorp, Richard fil. Wlnad, etc. *Temp.* Hen. III. (Foljambe.)

353. GRANT from Robert fil. Rob. de Boythorp to "parvus Henricus tannator" of a rood of land in Boythorp lying on Haspelund. Witn. Adam Blund, Robert de Dokemantun, Geoffrey Juvenis, etc. *Temp.* Hen. III. (Foljambe.)

354. GRANT from Richard de Haulee to John de Pecco of two acres of land in Boysorp which Walter de Cesterfeld, clericus, formerly held. Witn. Thomas de Legys, Thomas de Bramton, Peter, senescallus de Briminton, Adam fil. Bonde, etc. *Temp.* Hen. III. (Foljambe.)

355. GRANT from Richard de Hauley to Ralph Bugge fil. Radulfi de Notingham of all the lands which he acquired by feoffment from John Abselon in Boithorp, to hold by a rent of a pound of pepper and two pence on St. James's day [25 July]. Witn. Dom. Richard de Vernun, Dom. Matthew de Hathirsege, Dom. Roger de Eyncurt, Hugh de Pecco, etc. *Temp.* Hen. III. (Longford.)

356. GRANT from Edusa quondam vxor Ade de Cateclyue to John de Kalale fil. Roberti de Kalale of an acre of land in Boythorp in the place called Le Lowe, near the road from Kalale to Walton. Witn. Henry Cesterfeld, clerk, Alan de Lenne, Peter de Topton. *Temp.* Hen. III. (Longford.)

357. GRANT from Robert fil. Cristiane de Boythorp to Hugh de Peck of all his meadow in the territory of Boythorp. Witn. Peter fil. Hug. de Briminton, Hugh de Duckemanton, Peter Fox, etc. *Temp.* Hen. III. (Foljambe.)

358. GRANT from William fil. Rob. de Somersale to Ralph fil. Hug. de Boythorpe of half an acre of land in Boythorpe lying in Rogerflat on Hungerhill. Witn. Henry Clericus, John de Calahal, Robert Juvenis, etc. *Temp.* Hen. III. (Foljambe.)

359. QUITCLAIM from Adam fil. Hug. de Lincoln de Cestrefeld to Henry fil. Henrici clerici de Cestrefeld of land called Littilmor in the territory of Boythorp and in the fee of Dronfeld. Witn. Roger Laverok, Hugh de Neubolt, Richard Laveroc, etc. *Temp.* Edw. I. (Foljambe.)

360. GRANT from John fil. Herberti de Cholingham de Cestrefeld to Henry de Cestrefeld, clericus, of land in Boythorp. Witn. Peter de Briminton, Roger de Blye, Will. de Kattecliue, etc. Late thirteenth century. (Harl. 83, G. 39.)

361. GRANT from William fil. Henrici de Henovir to Roger fil. Joh. Laverok of Cestirfeld of all his right in 1½ acres of land in the fee of Boythorp, at a yearly rent of a clove of gilly-flowers [unum clavum gariofili] on the F. of St. John B. [24 June]. Witn. Robert de Len, John de Pecco, John Durant, etc. *Temp.* Edw. I. (Foljambe.)

362. GRANT from William fil. Hen. de Henouere in Chestrefeld to John de Calale in Cestrefeld of an acre and a rood of land in the fields of Boythorp on Stonforye. Witn. Robert de Len, Alan de Len, Peter de Tapton, etc. *Temp.* Edw. I. (Foljambe.)

363. GRANT from John de Calale to Roger de Maunisfeld in Cesterfeld of an acre and a rood of land in the fee of Boythorp. Witn. Michael de Hauersegg, Richard Scotard, Roger Laverok, etc. Dat. Cesterfeld, Vig. of the Assumption [14 Aug.], 25 Edw. I. [1297]. (Foljambe.)

364. GRANT from William de Rondithe quondam serviens Decani Lincolnie in Cesterfeld and Emma, his wife, to John fil. Ade Bonde, of half an acre of land in the fields of Boythorp in Hormisholm. Witn. Roger de Blida, Hugh fil. Durant. *Circ.* 1300. (Foljambe.)

365. GRANT from Ralph fil. Hugonis de Boythorp to Robert fil. Radulphi de Essouer de Cesterfeld of three roods of land in the fields and fee of Boythorp. Witn. Henry clericus de Cesterfeld, Roger Lauerock, Richard de Bateley, etc. Dat. Cesterfeld, S. a. Inv. of H. Cross [3 May], 30 Edw. I. [1302]. (Longford.)

366. GRANT from Thomas de Wyngerworth to Dom. Hugh le Cuper capellanus paroch[ie] tunc de Wyngerworth of a toft in Boytorph. Witn. Hugh de Neubold, Roger Laueroc, Ralph de Boytorp. *Temp.* Edw. I. (Foljambe.)

367. QUITCLAIM from Henry clericus de Cesterfeld to John Bonde of a yearly rent for lands in Boythorp. Witn. Roger Laveroke, Adam de Neubolde, John Durand, etc. Dat. S. a. F. of St. James [25 July], 34 Edw. I. [1305]. (Foljambe.)

368. GRANT from Dom. Richard de Bingham to Richard, his son, of all his messuages, lands, etc., in Boythorp. Witn. Richard de Whatton, John Bozoun, Hugh Buntyng, Roger Laveroc, John Deyncurt, etc. Dat. Bingham, W. a. F. of St. John of Beverley [7 May], 35 Edw. I. [1307]. (Longford.)

369. GRANT from Stephen Hacsmal of Cestrefeld to Henry de Wyngerworth in Chesterfield of land in the fields of Boythorp, on the road from Chesterfield to Nottingham. Witn. Adam de Neubolt, Nicholas Clappisale, Will de Rygeway, etc. Dat. Chesterfield, F. of St. John B. [24 June], 3 Edw. II. [1310]. (Harl. 83 F. 9.)

370. QUITCLAIM from Agnes, widow of Robert de Essovere, of her dower lands, namely, three acres in the fee of Boythorp, near the land of William Kydekas. Witn. William de Riggewaye, Roger Laueroc, Thomas Gyot, etc. Dat. Chesterfield, W. a. All Saints' Day [1 Nov.], 10 Edw. II. [1316]. (Longford.)

371. GRANT from John fil. Ric. Bonde to Roger de Maunnesfeld of 1½ acres of land in Boythorp. Witn. Roger Lauerok, John de Warsop, Roger de Glapwell, etc. Dat. Pentecost [15 May], 16 Edw. II. [1323]. (Foljambe.)

372. GRANT from Robert fil. Ric. de Bateley of Boythorp to John fil. Joh. Bonde of a yearly rent from land on the "Louwe," in the fee of Boythorp. Witn. John le Warsop, William Lorimer, Roger de Maunesfeld, etc. Dat. Sat. a. F. of St. Cuthbert [20 Mar.], 19 Edw. II. [1326]. (Foljambe.)

373. GRANT from Robert de Bateleye to Robert de Hampton of an acre of land in "le Ryches," in the fee of Boythorp. Witn. John fil. Joh. Bonde, John de Maunesfeld, William de Lorimer, etc. Dat. S. a. Pur. of B. V. M. [2 Feb.], 6 Edw. III. [1333]. (Foljambe.)

374. GRANT from Roger fil. Ade de Neubold to Robert le Lorimer and Cecily, his wife, of a rood of land in the fee of Boythorp, on the "Longelandys." Wit. Roger de Glapwelle, John Bonde, Walter Ketill, etc. Dat. M. b. F. of St. Margaret [20 July], 7 Edw. III. [1333]. (Foljambe.)

375. GRANT from John fil. Joh. Bonde of Cestrefeld to Robert Hampton of Chesterfield and John de Mannysfeld and Henry de Mannysfeld, "confratres gilde beate Marie de Cestrefeld," of six acres of land in the fields of Boythorp, for the payment of tenpence for ten masses to be said in the church of All Saints at Cestrefeld yearly, on the obit day of each, for the souls of John Bonde and Cecily, his wife, and eight others of the family. Dat. S. a. F. of St. Ambrose [4 Apr.], 11 Edw. III. [1337]. (Harl. 83 D. 33.)

376. LEASE, for 12 years, from Roger fil. Ranulphi de Chastrefeld to Joan, widow of Roger Lauerok, of lands in the fee of Boythorpp, near the king's highway leading from Chastrefeld towards Wyngerworth. Dat. S. a. F. of Exalt. of H. Cross [14 Sept.], 30 Edw. III. [1356]. (Longford.)

377. PRESENTMENT of jury that Ralph Longford held a moiety of the manor of Boythorp of Ralph, Dominus de Cromwell, but by what service they are ignorant, or whether it be held of the manor of Dronfield or of the manor of Elmeton; that Nicholas Longford is Ralph's next heir, aged 14; and that Thomas Longford's claim to a moiety of the manor by feoffment from the said Ralph Longford cannot be sustained. *Temp.* Edw. III. (Longford.)

378. GRANT from Henry fil. Henrici clerici de Cesterfeld to Dom. Richard de Byngham of the services of Richard de Dokemanton and other tenants (including the Guild of St. Mary, Chesterfield, the Guild of Holy Cross, Chesterfield, and the "Gilda Fabrorum" of Chester-field) for lands of the fee of the said Dom. Richard de Byngham in Boythorp. Witn. Dom. Roger de Brette, knt., Roger Breton, William le Brette, Hugh Saunfayle, etc. *Temp.* Edw. III. (Longford.)

379. GRANT from John de Mannsfeld of Chestrefeld to Roger fil. Nicholai de Longford, mil., of 2s. 6d., annual rent in Boythorpe. Witn. Roger Harecourte, John Wate of Thwathweyt, Henry de Mannsfeld, etc. Dat. Boythorpe, F. of SS. Simon and Jude [28 Oct.], 9 Ric. II. [1385]. (Woll. i. 86.)

380. QUITCLAIM from Elisabeth, widow of John Calall to Thomas Calcroft of all actions on account of two acres of land and a half in the demesne of Boythorp which he had of the grant of John Calall. Dat. third Saturday in Lent [1 Mar.], 12 Hen. VI. [1434]. (Foljambe.) .

381. EXTRACT from court-roll of Boythorpe, recording the surrender by John Calall of 2½ acres of land to the use of Thomas Calcrofte of Chestrefeld. Dat. M. b. F. of St. Matthias [24 Feb.], 13 Hen. VI. [1435]. (Foljambe.)

382. SALE from Rauf Longforth of Longforth, knt., to Sir Godfrey Foliambe of Walton, knt., of the manor of Boythorpe, with all appur-tenances in Boythorpe and Haseland, for £155. Dat. 18 Sept., 28 Hen. VIII. [1536]. (Longford.)

383. DEED whereby Edward Gryffen and Edward Bonne covenant, on behalf of Sir Rauf Longforth and Dorothy, his wife, to assure, by a common recovery, to Sir Godfrey Foliambe the manor of Boythorpe. Dat. 10 Sept., 31 Hen. VIII. [1539]. (Longford.)

BOYTHORPE *v.* also under CHESTERFIELD, KILLAMARSH.

BRACKENFIELD, IN MORTON.

(BRAKYNWHITH.)

384. LEASE, for 10 years, from Hugh Willughby, esq., to William Otwey, of a messuage and two bovates and a half of land, one cottage, one croft called Milnecroft, and a parcel of land called Bordeland in Brakynwhith. Dat. 6 Apr., 20 Edw. IV. [1480]. (Lansd. 168.)

BRADBORNE.

(BRAD' IN PECCO, BRADBURNE, BRADDEBURNE, BRADEBORNE, BRADEBURN.)

385. CONFIRMATION by William de Ferariis, Comes Dereb', to William fil. Roberti fil. Hallewardi, of the lands and tenements held by Robert, his father, of Comes William, father of the said Earl [William Ferrars, Earl of Derby, *ob.* 1190]. Witn. William de Rideware, tunc senescallus, Roger and Walter, his sons, Henry de Ferariis, Robert fil. Walkelini, Ranulf de Alesope, John de Mapilton, Hugh de Meleburn. *Temp.* John. Endorsed "Bradburn." (Campbell xi. 9.)

386. LEASE, for 20 years, from Robert fil. Rob. fil. Tholy, with the assent of Dionisia, his wife, to Dom. Robert fil. Hugonis de Acouere, of four bovates of land in Bradeburn, which Hugh de Acouere gave in free marriage with the said Dionisia, his sister; the said term to begin at Michaelmas, "anno eo decennonal[is] cicli quarto et dominicali littera F" [1275 ?]. Witn. Nicholas, persona de Esseburn, Hugh, capellanus de Acoure, Thomas de Curzeun, Roger fil. Josei, Geoffrey Blundus, Peter Blundus, Geoffrey, clericus, Matthew de Kniveton, Thomas Juvenis. (Okeover.)

387. AWARD made under a mandate from Pope Martin [IV.], dat. Id. Nov. aº 3 Pontif. [1283], by the Abbot of St. James without Northampton and the Priors of St. Alban's and St. Andrew's, Northampton, in composition between the Prior of St. Peter's, Dunstaple [co. Bedf.], and Lawrence, Abbot of La Dale, respecting tithes in Brad' in Pecco. Dat. Bedeford, Sat. a. Inv. of Holy Cross [3 May], 1286. Witn. Philip, Abbot of Lavend' [Lavinden, co. Bucks.], Master Robert Coreie, John Blundel, William de Cadindone, clerks, etc. (Woll. x. 33.)

388. GRANT from Henry fil. Henrici de Mapilton, "manens in feodo de Bradeleg'," to Simon Colle of Bradeborne and Lettice, his wife, of two messuages and four bovates of land with meadow adjacent, in Bradeborne. Witn. Dom. Henry fizHerberd, Henry de Kneveton, Roger de Bradeborne, knts., John de Bradeborne, Robert de Waddisleye in Brassington, Matthew de Flagg in la Lee. Dat. Assheburne, S. a. Beh. of St. John B. [29 Aug.], 1303. (Okeover.)

389. GRANT from John de le Thokes de Irton to Robert de le Thokes de Bradeburn, his brother, of two bovates of land in Bradeburn which the said John had by feoffment from Simon Colle. Witn. Nicholas Robyn de Bradeburn, Richard Parlebyne, John fil. Henrici, Nicholas, clericus, de Assheburn, John le Horsemon. Dat. apud Bradeburn, F. of St. Chad, Bp. [2 Mar.], 1329[30]. (Okeover.)

390. GRANT from William fil. Agnetis de Parua Bradeburne to William del Hegh, chaplain, living in Parva Bradeburne, of a messuage, two bovates of land, and a place called Wengebuttus, which he had by feoffment from Robert del Thocus in Parva Bradeburn. Witn. John le Eyr de Hokenaston, John fil. Joh. de eadem, William fil. Andree de Mapulton de eadem, John fil. Hugonis de Bradeburne, Hugh Balle, William Parlebien. Dat. Bradeburne, T. a. Pur. of B. V. M. [2 Feb.], 35 Edw. III. [1361]. (Okeover.)

391. GRANT from Robert del Tokes de Parva Bradburne to William fil. Agnetis de Parva Bradburne of a messuage and two bovates of land in Bradburne which he had of the feoffment of Simon Colle, and a

4

place and two bovates of land which he had of the feoffment of John
del Tokes, his father, in Bradburne. Witn. John le Eyr de Hokenaston,
John fil. Joh. fil. Alexandri de eadem, William fil. Andree de Mapleton,
John fil. Hugonis de Bradburne, William Parlebien. Dat. Bradburne,
F. of SS. Fabian and Sebastian [20 Jan.], 35 Edw. III. [1362].
(Okeover.)

392. GRANT from William del Hough de Brassinton, chaplain, to
William fil. Roberti de Tokes de Parva Bradeburn, of two bovates of
land and meadow in Parva Bradeburn. Witn. John de Bentelay, John
de Rossinton of Tissinton, Nicholas de Rossinton of Knyveton, etc. Dat.
S. b. Ann. of B. V. M. [25 Mar.], 1 Ric. II. [1378]. (Okeover.)

393. ASSIGNMENT by Matilda fil. Willelmi fil. Roberti del Thokies
de Braddeburne to Robert del Thokus de Braddeburne of her share of
the reversion of a messuage and two bovates of land in Braddeburne
which William de Braddeburne of Brassington granted to William del
Hogh of Brassington, chaplain, for his life, with reversion on the latter's
death to the said Matilda and her sister Margery. Witn. John fil.
Hugónis de Braddeburne, William fil. Johannis de eadem, John fil.
Johannis de Hokenaston, Henry le Hayuard de Brassington, Richard
Hebbe, John de Eyton, William Pokoc. Dat. Braddeburne, S. b. F. of
SS. Tiburtius and Valerian [14 Apr.], 6 Ric. II. [1383]. (Okeover.)

394. ATTORNEY from Richard Bagot, esq., John Lathbury, esq.,
William Purdhomme, merchant, John Forth, chaplain, to John Wygley
of Wyrkesworth and Roger Grenehall, to deliver to Henry Bradburn
and Margery, his wife, seisin of their manors of Bradburn and Legh,
the water-mills of Bradburn and Bentley [Fenny Bentley], Raunnesclyf
close in Bentley, Ryddyngpark close in Knyveton, and of all their lands
in Parwich, Bradburn, and Legh. Dat. 4 Jan., 30 Hen. VI. [1452].
(Bemrose.)

395. ATTORNEY from Laurence Lumhall and Laurence Parker to
Thomas Brewester and John Brewester to take seisin of lands, etc.,
called Molderigge and Cardelhay in Bradburne and Hertyngton which
they hold of the lease of John, Prior and the Priory of Dunstaple.
Dat. 6 Edw. IV. [1466-7]. (Okeover.)

BRADBURNE *v.* also under ASHBOURNE, ATLOW.

BRADLEY.

(BRADELE, BRADELEGE, BRADELEY, BRADLEGE.)

396. COPY (14th century) of a grant from Serlo de Grendone to Serlo
fil. Radulphi de Moungay of lands and wood between his fishpond at
Bradleye and the vill. of Gilderessege [Yeldersley] with common of
land in Bradele and Sturstone, for his own cattle and the cattle of
the men of Gildresle ; rent, a pair of white gloves or one penny. Witn.
Henry fil. Sewalli, Robert Britton, Henry de Braillesford, Leodegarius
de Oure, Walter de Montegomeri, Ralph le Bakeput, John Irton, William
de Burgenny, Robert de Morie. *Temp.* Ric. I.-John. (Woll. vi. 43.)

397. COPY (14th century) of a release from Ralph de Moungoye to
William fil. Henrici de Knyvetone, Augnes Salveyn, of lands in Bradele
and Knyvetone. Witn. Dom. Hugh de Meynel, Dom. Ralph de
Braillesford, Dom. Nicholas de Longeford, milites. Undated. (Woll. vi.
44.)

398. Grant from Henry d' Strton to Thomas, condam foristarius domini Willelmi de Strton, of five acres of land in the territory of Bradel' and an assart which he had from Robert de Okebroc in Bradel'. Witn. Dom. William de Strton, Henry de Osbaundist', Serlo de Munge, etc. *Temp.* Hen. III. (Woll. vi. 30.)

399. Covenant of grant made in presence of Dom. Gilbert de Preston and others, Justices Itinerant, from Agnes de Greslege, Prioress of Gratia Dei [Grace Dieu Priory in Belton], co. Leicester, to Matthew de Chynetone, of permission to hold lands belonging to the Priory in Bradlege and Surstant [Sturston]; rent, 20s. Witn. Dom. Henry de Bec, mil., Dom. Peter de Toc, mil., and Peter de Bakepus, mil., Haytrop de Osmunston, Richard fil. Hervy, Thomas fil. Herberti de Somersale, Richard frater suus. Dat. 53 Hen. III. [1268-9]. (Woll. vi. 28.)

400. Sale from William Coulbeard of Bradeley, clerk to John de Hodgnett, of all his goods within the manor of Bradley, as well as the trees growing on the lands there held by the said John. Witn. John de Whiterock, William de Wolseley, Richard de Mould of Bradley. Dat. Sat. a. F. of the Circumcision [1 Jan.], 14 Edw. I. [1286]. (R. D. G., f. 69.)

401. Grant from Henry de Knyvetone to Thomas de Reverewiche of lands in Bradelege and Sturstone; rent, 9s. Witn. Dom. Roger de Bradeburne, Roger Cokayn, Thomas de Mappiltone, etc. Dat. Th. a. F. of the Assump. of B. V. M. [15 Aug.], 21 Edw. I. [1293]. (Woll. vi. 29.)

402. Grant from William Trussebouz to Henry fil. Will. de Knyvetone, knt., of lands in Bradeley, Sturstone, and Holond. Witn. Edw. de Chaundoys, Henry de Braillesford, Thomas Peche, milites, etc. Dat. Bradley, S. b. F. of St. Cedde, Conf. [7 Jan.], 18 Edw. III. [1345]. (Woll. vi. 33.)

403. Grant from Sarra fil. Henrici fil. Herui de le Grene and Joan, her sister, to Thomas de Rosyngton of all their lands in the fee of Bradley. Witn. Edmund Cokayne of Assheburn, John de Pole, Thomas de Knyveton. Dat. F. of Ex. of H. Cross. [14 Sept.], 44 Edw. III. [1370]. (Drury.)

404. Grant from William de Grendon to Robert Textor of the land which James Textor held in Campeden in the fee of Bradele. Witn. Levenad Faber, Henry de Cruce, William fil. Luce, Nicholas de Derby, Roger, his son, Robert and Henry, sons of Leuenad, William Spendeloue. Late 14th cent. (Okeover.)

BRADLEY *v.* also under Ashbourne, Denby, Matlock.

BRADSHAW *v.* under Chapel-en-le-Frith.

(Bradesha, Bradschawe, Bradsha.)

BRADWELL.

(Bradewell, Bradwall.)

405. Grant from Robert de Bradewell, fil. Will. fil. Fabiani de Bradewell to Richard, his brother, of half a bovate of land in Bradewell: rent, a rose on the F. of SS. Peter and Paul [29 June]. Witn. John Flemink, ballivus de Pecco, Will. Hally, Robert Balgy, etc. *Temp.* Hen. III. or Edw. I. (Add. 7267.)

406. FINAL concord made in the Court of John, King of Castile and Leon, Duke of Lancaster, at Castelton, on W. b. F. of St. John [24 June], 50 Edw. III. [1376], before Ralph de Baystowe, "locum tenens," Thome de Wombewelle, "tunc ballivi de Alto Pecco," John Hublyn, "tunc receptor denariorum Castri et honoris," etc., whereby John de Wetton and Elena, his wife, release to Walter de Bradwalle a messuage and nine acres of land in Bradwall. (Woll. ii. 75.)

407. LEASE, for five years, from James Denton, Dean, and the Chapter of Lichfield to Nicholas Bagshawe of Capella de ly Fryth, of the tithes of hay and corn at Bradwell and of the mill of Brugh. Dat. 15 July, 1532. (Lichf. D. 22.)

408. LEASE, for 99 years, from Henry Wyllyams, Dean, and the Chapter of Lichfield, of the tithes of Bradwell, Brughmill, Offreton, Abney, and Abney Grange, Upper and Lower Shatton, Overton, and Hylowe, to Nicholas Bagshawe of Farewell, co. Staff. Dat. 1 Oct., 1551. (Lichf. D. 28.)

BRADWELL *v.* also under CASTLETON.

BRAILSFORD, NEAR N. WINGFIELD.

(BRAYLESFORD NEXT TUPTON.)

409. GRANT from Henry de Braylesford to William de Braylesford, near Tupton, and Agnes, his wife, of a messuage and a half bovate of land in Braylesford, next Tupton. Witn. Thomas de Bernehulle, Hen. Bate, John de Braylesford, etc. Dat. Wynnefeld, S. a. F. of St. Ambrose [4 Apr.], 30 Edw. III. [1356]. (Woll. vi. 65.)

BRAILSFORD *v.* also under OSMASTON.

BRAMPTON.

(BRAMT', BRAMTON, BRAMTONE, BROMTON.)

410. RELEASE from Hugh fil. Alani de Dukemanton to the Hospital of St. Leonard for Lepers at Cestrefeld of homages, wards, reliefs, etc., from land granted to the said Hospital by Ascer de Tapton, in the said Hugh's fee in Bramton. Witn. Peter, dictus senescallus de Brimington, Simon fil. Roberti de Wytington, Hugh de Pecco, etc. *Temp.* Hen. III. (Harl. 112 G. 39.)

411. GRANT from William fil. Hugonis de Cestrefeld to Gilbert fil. Walteri Cementarii [the Mason] of Cestrefeld, of lands in Brampton and Hulm, and rent from lands in Hulm and Neubald. Witn. Ralph de Rerisby, Thomas de Brampton, Peter de Briminton, etc. *Temp.* Hen. III. (Harl. 112 G. 54.)

412. GRANT from Hugh de Linacre to Geoffrey, clericus, de Bramton, of land in Brampton, at a rent of five shillings. Witn. Philip, decanus, Robert Avenel, Stephen, persona de Cestirfeld [Chesterfield], Robert de Ennecurt, Roger de Ennecurt, Ralph Bretun, etc. *Temp.* Hen. III. (Bemrose.)

413. GRANT from Hugh de Linacre to Adam de Esseburne of six acres of land in the field of Bramt', one head lying towards Smale and the other towards Morsike; rent, 18*d*. Witn. Robert Britone de Walet' [Walton], Ingilram de Bramt', Ralph de Bramt', Stephen Geg, etc. *Temp.* Henry III. (Woll. iii. 26.)

414. CONFIRMATION by Hugh de Linacre fil. Hugonis de Linacre to the Nuns and Brethren of Sempringham of all the land [in Brampton] which they hold from the said Hugh, his father, namely, a moiety of that land which Richard fil. Godwini granted to them, lying between the land of the Templars and the land which was Hugh fil. Godwini de Boithorp's, extending from the site of the old mill to Hipere river-bank, with common of pasture for six cows and two horses; to hold by rent of one pair of boots every second year on St. Martin's Day [11 Nov.]. Witn. Dom. Robert Britone, Robert de Briminton, Gilbert de Heslond, etc. *Temp.* Hen. III. (Woll. iii. 27.)

415. GRANT from Walter de Lynacre to Philip fil. Ricardi, clericus de Bramtona, of all the land which Richard de Cuwane formerly held in Bramtona. Witn. Thomas de Bramtune, Thomas de Leys, Robert de Welletune, Robert de Calehale, etc. *Temp.* Hen. III. (Foljambe.)

416. GRANT from Hugh fil. Rogeri servientis de Bramton to Alice fil. Emme Balle of three roods of land which he bought of Hugh fil. Thome de Calehal in the territory of Bramton "super le Brodestoy-thebuttis." Witn. Thomas de Bramton, Robert de Calehal, Robert Blund, etc. Late thirteenth cent. (Foljambe.)

417. QUITCLAIM from Robert le Caus of Brampton to Richard fil. Thom. de Wadeself of lands in Brampton. Witn. Nicholas de Hulm, John de la Hay, Hugh de Somersall, etc. *Temp.* Edw. I. (Foljambe.)

418. GRANT from Robert de le Frith to Roger fil. Henrici de Algerthorp of four acres of ground in the place called Pigotstorth between the land of Adam de Newbold and the common pasture [in Brampton]; rent, 12*d*. yearly. Witn. Robert le Caus, Hugh de Lenakir, Richard Gin, Will de Birley, etc. *Temp.* Edw. I. (Add. 9216.)

419. RELEASE from Robert fil. Rogeri de Thebirthis to Hugh de la Hay of land in Bramton. Witn. Thomas fil. Radulphi de Brampton, Thomas de Wadshelf, Nicholas de Algarethorp, etc. *Temp.* Edw. I. (Harl. 112 E. 8.)

420. GRANT from Thomas fil. Radulfi le Caus de Bramtone to Robert fil. Hugonis Baldwyn de Bramton, clericus, of the annual rent of 22½*d*. paid by Peter de Brimington and Ranulf, fil. Margarete de Bramtone for lands called Lambert-land, Timberhagge, Holley-croft, and Hasterildstorthe, in the vill of Bramton. Witn. Stephen vicarius de Bramton, Hugh de Lynacre, John de la Haye, etc. *Temp.* Edw. I. (Harl. 83 E. 9.)

421. GRANT from Walter le Caus to Richard fil. Thome de Wadesself of land, etc., in Bramton, at a yearly rent of 12*d*. Witn. John de la Hay, Nicholas de Hulm, Hugh de Monisale, etc. *Temp.* Edw. I. (Foljambe.)

422. GRANT from Richard "Bercarius Alti Decani quondam Lyncolniensis" to Roger fil. Lamberti de Houlekotis of land [in Brampton] extending from the road leading to Hathyrsege to Burley-sike, etc. Witn. Thomas fil. Rad. de Bramton, Thomas de Wadeself, Hugh de Somersale. *Temp.* Edw. I. (Foljambe.)

423. GRANT from William fil. Joh. fil. Emme de Cestrefeld to Richard le Porter of four acres of land with meadow adjacent in the fields of Brampton. Witn. John Durant, Roger Lauerok, Hugh de Neubolt. Dat. T. a. F. of St. Nicolas [6 Dec.], 5 Edw. II. [1311]. (Foljambe.)

424. GRANT, for 4s., from William fil. Lamberti de Linacre to Hugh de Pecco of 6d. rent from land in Heysale in Bramton; rent, an apple in autumn. Witn. Dom. Robert le Bretun of Walton, Dom. Thomas de Bramtoun, Richer. fil. Wolnat, etc. *Temp.* Edw. I. or II. (Woll. iii. 29.)

425. GRANT from Thomas le Caus of Brampton to John fil. Petri de Brimington of a rent of 14d. in Brampton; rent, ½d. Witn. Jordan de Abbetot, Robert le Graunt, Hugh de Linaker, etc. *Temp.* Edw. I. or II. (Woll. iii. 34.)

426. GRANT from Walter Chauz fil. et her Thome Chauz of Bramton to the Abbey de Bello Capite [Beauchief] of common of pasture in Bramton. Witn. Dom. Thomas de Chaworthe, Dom. William de Staynesby, Robert le Graunt, etc. *Temp.* Edw. I. or II. (Woll. iii. 35.)

427. GRANT, for 3s., from Thomas fil. Hugonis fil. Ingrami de Bramton to Hugh de Pecco of 4d. rent from land in Heysale [in Brampton]; rent, an apple in autumn. Witn. Robert le Bretone of Waletone, Thomas de Branton, Thomas de Lees, etc. *Temp.* Edw. I. or II. (Woll. iii. 30.)

428. RELEASE from Simon fil. Joh. del Folde de Ekynton to the Hospital of St. Leonard at Cestrefeld of land in the fee of Brampton. Witn. William le Bret, Roger le Bretoun, Roger de Dokemonton, etc. Dat. Cestrefeld, Tues. in Easter Week [21 Apr.], 3 Edw. II. [1310]. (Harl. 112 H. 33.)

429. GRANT, in tail, from Roger fil. Hugonis le Serjaunt de Brantun to Stephen fil. Hugonis Somersale of Brantun of land in Brantun. Witn. Hugh de Linacre, Roger de Vygley, John de eadem, etc. Dat. S. a. F. of St. Dunstan [21 Oct.], 4 Edw. II. [1310]. (Woll. iii. 41.)

430. QUITCLAIM from Adam fil. Will. Auburnehor de Cesterfeld to Richard le Porter of five acres of land with meadow adjacent in the fee of Brampton. Witn. Adam de Neubold, Roger Lauerok, William de Rygeway. Dat. S. b. Pentecost [26 May], 7 Edw. II. [1314]. (Foljambe.)

431. GRANT from Roger fil. Rob. le Caus of Bramton to Robert fil. Rog. de la Grene to Robert fil. Rog. de la Grene of all the land, etc., which Richard de Marton formerly held [in Brampton] at a yearly rent of 3s. Witn. Hugh de Linakyr, Thomas de Somersale, John de Neuport, etc. Dat. Bramton, Th. b. F. of St. Martin [11 Nov.], 1315. (Foljambe.)
    On the back are notes by Henry Foliambe touching a dispute as to a title with Philip Leche, with an oath to keep the peace towards him until Michaelmas.

432. GRANT from Augnes fil. Walteri le Caus of Bramton to William de Ekynton, in Cloune, of lands, tenements, etc., in Brampton. Witn. Roger le Caus, Roger de Linaker, Thomas de Somersale, etc. Dat. Bramton, S. a. F. of St. Ambrose [4 Apr.], 11 Edw. II. [1317]. (Harl. 112 G. 52.)

433. GRANT from Robert fil. Will. del Shahe of Brampton to Thomas fil. Roberti de Somersale of the same of lands in Brampton, which descended to him after the death of Adam del Shahe, his uncle. Witn. Robert fil. Rogeri Le Bretone, Dom. de Walton, Roger le Caus, Roger de Lynaker, etc. Dat. F. of Ass. of B. V. M. [15 Aug.], 17 Edw. II. [1323]. (Woll. iii. 42.)

434. SALE, for half a mark, by Nicolas fil. Stephani de Algarthorp to Hugh fil. Hugonis, clerici de Brantone, of Lambert fil. Willelmi de Schiremer, with all his suit. Witn. Roger de Abbetot de Barl', Thomas de Lees, Thomas de Bramton, etc. *Temp.* Edw. II. (Woll. iii. 32.)

435. RELEASE from William de Calale to Richard de le Frit of Bramton of land called Le Holm, in Bramton, with right of way in a road between West Wykegate and Colleforde. Witn. Dom. William, capellanus de Bramton, Hugh de Linaker, John de le Hay, etc. *Temp.* Edw. II. (Woll. iii. 40.)

436. LEASE from Adam fil. Roberti Haunche of Bramton to Thomas Glay of the same, for 12 years, of lands in Bramton. Witn. Robert de le Fruth, Roger de le Frith, Thomas de Calale, etc. Dat. Pentecost [23 May], 7 Edw. III. [1333]. (Woll. iii. 48.)

437. LEASE from William de Wygleye of Brampton to Thomas Glay of the same, for 42 years, of lands in Brampton; rent, 6s. Witn. John de Wygleye, Thomas fil. Roberti de Somersale, Robert del Fyth, etc. Dat. F. of St. Martin [11 Nov.], 7 Edw. III. [1333]. (Woll. xii. 46.)

438. GRANT from Alice, que fuit vxor Rogeri de Waltone to Robert del Fryh of Bramptone of land and meadow lying in Astrilstorh, in the fee of Brampton. Witn. Roger le Caus, Roger de Lynaker, Roger del Fryh. Dat. Chesterfield, 3 Jan., 11 Edw. III. [1338]. (Woll. iii. 43.)

439. GRANT from Robert del Fryh' of Brampton to Richard de Birley of the same of a rent of 12d. from lands in Brampton. Witn. John de Wygeley, Thomas fil. Roberti de Somersale, Thomas fil. Hugonis de Somersale, etc. Dat. S. a. F. of St. Barnabas [11 June], 12 Edw. III. [1338]. (Woll. iii. 44.)

440. GRANT from Richard fil. Nicholai de Schwatwayt to Richard fil. Rogeri del Fryth of Bramton of land in Bramton. Witn. Roger le Caus, John de Wiggelay, Robert de Fryth, etc. Dat. S. a. F. of St. Swithin [15 July], 12 Edw. III. [1338]. (Woll. iii. 45.)

441. GRANT from Alice, Johanna, and Agnes, fil. et her. Ricardi de Bryches de Brampton, to Robert Fryth fil. Ricardi Fryth of the same, of lands late in possession of the said Richard; rent, 50s. Witn. Ric. de Holb . . ., John de Hay, Roger Caus, etc. Dat. Brampton, F. of St. Martin [11 Nov.], 1339. (Woll. i. 87.)

442. POWER of attorney from Hugh fil. Stephani de Brampton to Hugh fil. Roberti de Brampton to deliver seisin to Dom. Richard Deyngeland, capellanus, of land called Morisfeld. Dat. S. b. F. of St. Katharine [25 Nov.], 39 Edw. III. [1365]. (Woll. iii. 51.)

443. RELEASE from Richard de Bramptone and John de Hynckurcelle of Chestrefeld, capellani, to Thomas de Hope of Bramptone, of

lands in Brampton to hold of the [Benedictine] Nunnery of Fosse
[co. Linc.], with reversion to Roger fil. Johannis dil Frithe and Katerine,
his wife, etc. Witn. Roger de Wygley, John de Whityngton, Nich. de
Bauqwell, etc. Dat. Chastrefeld, S. a. Exalt. of Holy Cross [14 Sept.],
41 Edw. III. [1367]. (Woll. iii. 50.)

444. Grant from Richard North and Joan, his wife, to Hugh
Balderton and Alice, his wife, of five acres of land in "Le Ledes" in
Brampton inherited from the said Joan's father, John del Frith. Witn.
Robert Caus, William de Lynnacre, William de Barley, etc. Dat. Fr.
a. F. of St. Margaret [20 July], 8 Ric. II. [1384]. (Foljambe.)

445. Lease from Roger fil. Avicie de Bramptone and Alice, his wife,
widow of William Glay of Brampton, to John in le Dale of Brampton,
of lands in Brampton, during the life of the said Alice; rent, 18d.
Dat. F. of St. Martin [11 Nov.], 21 Ric. II. [1397]. (Woll. iii. 39.)

446. Grant from John de Gos[ner] and Robert Shirbroke to William
de Schage of Wadsholf of a messuage and lands in Brampton. Witn.
John Bradshag', William Fryth, etc. Dat. F. of St. Lucy [13 Dec.],
6 Hen. IV. [1404]. (Woll. iii. 53.)

447. Grant from John de Gosner, chaplain, and Robert de Schirbroke of Walton to William de Schaghe, sen., of Wadscholf, of lands
in Wadscholf, lying between Bagthorpe and Horswod, in Brampton.
Witn. John Caws of Brampton, John son of Hugh, John Schaghe, etc.
Dat. Pur. of B. V. M. [2 Feb.], 6 Hen. IV. [1405]. (Woll. iii. 61.)

448. Memorandum that Thomas Cause, under age, holds of
Thomas Foliambe certain lands, etc., in Brampton for the rent of two
marks and military service, that the said Thomas Foliambe seised
his body on S. b. Martinmas [11 Nov.], 14 Hen. IV. [1412] at
Brampton, and offered him Margaret Taweran to wife at Walton, Sat.
a. Michaelmas, 2 Hen. V. [1414], and the said Thomas Cause refused
her. (Foljambe.)

449. Grant from Roger Stevenson of Brampton to William Ulker-
thorp, esq., and William Stevenson of Alfreton of lands in Brampton.
Witn. Thomas Cause, John Lynnacre, William Lynnacre, etc. Dat.
Th. a. F. of St. Martin [11 Nov.], 7 Hen. VI. [1428]. (Woll. iii. 55.)

450. Grant from John Raynburgh of Collowe [Calow] to John
Nayler son of John Nayler of Newark of three roods of land in the
fields of Brampton, upon "le Turnesthagh." Witn. Robert Leghe,
William del Wode, John Pety, etc. Dat. Collowe, F. of Conv. of
St. Paul [25 Jan.], 1434[5]. (Foljambe.)

451. Release from Thomas in le Dale son of John in le Dale of
Brampton to John Hereson of Chestrefeld of lands in Brampton which
he had at the death of John in le Dale, his grandfather, and Margote,
his wife. Witn. Peter de Kyndoyr, William Grevis, Thomas de Croftis,
etc. Dat. T. b. F. of the Circumcision [1 Jan.], 6 Hen. VI. [1437].
(Woll. iii. 59.)

452. Release from John Hereson of Chestrefeld to John Scha, son
of Richard Scha of Brampton, of lands in Brampton. Witn. Thomas
Hemmyng of Brampton, Nicholas Caskyn of the same, William Grevys
of the same, etc. Dat. Th. a. Ann. of B. V. M. [25 Mar.], 16 Hen. VI.
[1438]. (Woll. iii. 57.)

453. POWER of attorney by Thomas Hugate of Chestrefeld, esq., to Roger Shaugh of Brampton, to deliver seisin to John Stevenson, sen., of Brampton, of two messuages in Brampton. Dat. Morrow of St. Matthew [22 Sept.], 17 Hen. VI. [1438]. (Woll. iii. 52.)

454. LEASE from "Ion of Schagh yᵉ son of Richard of Schagh of Brampton," to Margery "of yᵉ Dale," wife of Robert "of the Dale," and to Richard, their son, of half the land which he purchased of "Jon" Henrison of Chestrefeld, formerly belonging to "old Jon of yᵉ Dale"; rent, 1*d.* Witn. John Lynacure, Thomas Cause, John Schagh of Somersall, etc. Dat. Brampton, F. of Pur. of B. V. M. [2 Feb.], 17 Hen. VI. [1439]. (Woll. iii. 56.)

455. POWER of attorney by Richard Wodhous, chaplain, to John Derton of Normanton, to receive seisin of lands surrendered by Richard Glover of Brampton. Dat. Aschover, M. a. Ann. of B. V. M. [25 Mar.], 18 Hen. VI. [1440]. (Woll. iii. 54.)

456. GRANT from John Shawe of Somersale to William Vernon, esq., Thomas Clarell, esq., Thomas Foliambe, jun., William Foliambe, and William Croft, of two messuages, etc., in Brampton. Witn. Thomas Foliambe, sen., John Shawe, John Turnour, etc. Dat. F. of St. Matthew [21 Sept.], 22 Hen. VI. [1443]. (Foljambe.)

457. ASSIGNMENT by William Cause of Brampton to Robert Cade of the same of a lease, for 12 years, of lands in Brampton held of Johanna Bate of Chestrefeld, dated F. of St. Gregory, Pope [12 Mar.], 37 Hen. VI. [1459]; rent, 12*s.* Witn. John Asche, John Cantrell, Roger Aschover of Bramptone. Dat. 20 Mar., 1459. (Woll. iii. 49.)

458. RELEASE from William Schae, son of John Schae, late of Chanderell, to Richard Asshe of Chestrefeld, of all his lands, etc., in Brampton, in a place called Chanderell, formerly belonging to Matilda de Heye, widow of Hugh de Heye. Witn. Thomas Foliambe, esq., Peter Freschevile of Staveley, John Lynnacher, etc. Dat. 17 July, 3 Edw. IV. [1463]. (Foljambe.)

459. LEASE, for 20 years, from John Assh of Chestrefeld, baker, and Isabel, his wife, one of the daughters and heirs of Thomas Cauce of Brampton, to Thomas Foliaumbe, lord of Walton, esq., of the fifth part of certain lands in Brampton; rent, 26*s.* 8*d.* Dat. 7 May, 4 Edw. IV. [1464]. (Woll. iii. 36.)

460. RELEASE from William Rawlynson of Hegate, next Heyfeld, in Bowdon, to Henry Foliambe, lord of Walton, esq., of all the lands, in Brampton, which he had jointly with Thomas Foliambe, esq., and Peter Kynder, of the feoffment of John Gaskyn of Brampton. Witn. Henry Vernon, Edm. Vernon, Peter Frecchevyle, Nich. Gansell, esquires, etc. Dat. Walton, F. of All Saints [1 Nov.], 8 Edw. IV. [1468]. (Foljambe.)

461. ACQUITTANCE from Nicholas Baguley and Johanna, his wife, dau. and heir of Thomas Cokee of Brampton, to Henry Folgeham, lord of Walton, esq., for 13*s.* 4*d.* for the farm of all their lands, etc., in Brampton. Dat. 28 Dec., 49 Hen. VI. [1470]. (Foljambe.)

462. ACQUITTANCE from Nicholas Baguley and Johanna, his wife, daughter and heir of Thomas Cauce of Brampton to Henry Foliambe, esq., Lord of Walton, for 13*s.* 4*d.* for rent of lands, etc., in Brampton. Dat. 14 July, 11 Edw. IV. [1471]. (Foljambe.)

463. SIMILAR acquittance, dated 18 July, 12 Edw. IV. [1472]. (Foljambe.)

464. POWER of attorney from Henry Stafford, rector of Treton [Treeton, co. York], formerly "preceptor" of Halomeshire, to John Asshe, jun., and James Ethcotte of Chestrefeld, to deliver seisin to Robert Powte of Chestrefeld and Alice, his wife, of a close called "Rygewey Rawe" in Brampton. Dat. Treton, F. of St. George [23 Apr.], 13 Edw. IV. [1473]. (Foljambe.)

465. POWER of attorney by Dionisia Wodhouse to John Ralston to surrender, in the Court of the Prior of the Hospital of St. John of Jerusalem of Normanton, a messuage with lands in Baggthorppe, in the soke of Brampton, to the use of Robert Gregory, etc. Dat. Sowth Wynfeld, 4 Apr., 17 Edw. IV. [1477]. (Woll. iii. 58.)

466. POWER of attorney from William Marschall, chaplain, to John Wortheye, chaplain, and John Schawe of Doghole, to give seisin to Richard Assch of Chestrefeld, Richard Heithcote of the same, Ralph Heithcote of the same, and John Pypes, chaplain, of a close in Pokenaye. Dat. Brampton, F. of Nat. of St. John B. [24 June], 22 Edw. IV. [1482]. (Foljambe.)

467. RENTAL of John Lynacre, sen., made at Brampton, and referring to lands at Plumley, Westwell, Swootall, Hackynthorp. Haselam, Begheton, etc. Dat. 28 Mar., 2 Hen. VII. [1487]. (Foljambe.)

468. WILL of William Croft of Brampton, sen., leaving all his lands, etc., in Brampton or elsewhere in trust to Henry Folgiam to grant the same to Mapota Crofte, his widow, for her life, and after her death to divide them between Nicholas Crofte and William Crofte, his sons. Witn. John Somersal, Richard Schaw, etc. Dat. 14 Apr., 1485. Endorsed with probate, 3 May, 1485. (Foljambe.)

469. LEASE, for 10 years, from Nicholas Bayguley and Jane, his wife, one of the daughters and heirs of Thomas Cause of Bromton, to Richard Eyre of Plumley, of the fifth part of certain lands in Bromton; rent, 26s. 8d. Dat. F. of St. John B. [24 June], 11 Hen. VII. [1496]. (Woll. iii. 67.)

470. POWER of attorney from William Hyll of Sowth Wynfeld and Thomas Kyrkland of Ripley, appointing William Bradscha of Wadchelf and Richard Sha of Bagthorpe, in the soke of Brampton, their attorneys, to surrender in the court of the Prior of the Hospital of St. John of Jerusalem at Normanton, a messuage and lands in Brampton to Richard Wodhause of Rypley, with reversion to William Wodhause, son and heir of John Wodhause of Brampton, his brother. Dat. 27 July, 16 Hen. VII. [1501]. (Woll. iii. 66.)

471. MORTGAGE, for 10s., from Robert Asshe to Christofer Midleton, of a parcel of land in Brampton. Dat. Corpus Christi, [10 Jun.], 4 Hen. VIII. [1512]. (Woll. iii. 78.)

472. LEASE, for 21 years, from Nicholas Woodhouse of London, "puterer," to Thomas Watson, husbandman, of lands in Bagthorpe, in the soke of Brampton; rent, 40s. Dat. F. of Ann. of B. V. M. [25 Mar.], 27 Hen. VIII. [1536]. (Woll. iii. 63.)

473. LEASE, for 30 years, from John Turnor of Chaundrell, co. Derby, yeoman, and Richard, his son and heir, and John Turner of Chasterfeld, fuller, to George Turner of Chaundrell, of lands at Chaundrell [Chander Hill], in Brampton; rent, 26s. 8d. Witn. "Mestre" Lynaker, Thomas Channer, Jhon Stevynson, etc. Dat. 2 Nov., 32 Hen. VIII. [1540]. (Woll. iii. 64.)

BRAMPTON, *v.* CHESTERFIELD, DERBY, TEMPLE NORMANTON,

WALTON.

BRASSINGTON.

(BRACENTONE, BRACINTON, BRACINGTON, BRACYNTON.)

474. CONFIRMATION by William de Ferrars, Comes Derbe, to the Abbot and monks of Buldewas [Buildwas, co. Salop] of two grants from Hugh fil. Dom. Will. quondam Comitis Derbe of common pasture for 500 sheep and for 340 sheep in the manors of Bracynton and Bonteshale. Dat. apud Beurepeyr, S. a. F. of St. Hilary [13 Jan.], 35 Hen. III. [1251]. Copy, fourteenth century. (Foljambe.)
On the back is a copy of grant from Fulcher fil. Fulcheri de Hirt to the same Abbey of all his land of Yvenbrok as Swain de Mapeldon and Hirald, his brother, granted it to him.

475. GRANT from William de Ferrars, Earl of Derby, to Adam le Wyne of the land which Hamo the clerk held of the Earl in Bracentone in the Peak, near Yuenbroc and Horburyhale, with lands in Hopton. Witn. Geoffrey de Gresele, then Steward, and seven others. Thirteenth century. (Pole-Gell.)*

476. GRANT from William de Ferrars, Earl of Derby, to William de Grendone, of 40 acres of land in Bracinton. (Pole-Gell.)*

477. GRANT and confirmation from Cecily, dau. and heir of Hugh de Ferrars, widow, to the Church and Canons of "St. Mary of Park Stanley" [Dale Abbey] of the gift which William son of Ingeram of Nottingham made to them in Bracington [Brassington], Kersington [Carsington], and Hopton. Witn. Dom. Thomas de Ferrars, her uncle, Master Hosbert, rector of Hegham, Dom. Robert, rector of Stowe, and others. Thirteenth century. (Pole-Gell.)*

478. INSPEXIMUS and confirmation by Robert de Ferrars, son and heir of William de Ferrars, formerly Earl of Derby, of the grant, etc., by Cecily, dau. and heir of Hugh de Ferrars. (Pole-Gell.)*

479. RELEASE from Henry, Duke of Lancaster, Earl of Derby, etc., to the Abbot and Convent "de la Dale," of the rent of 12s. which they paid for land granted to them by Cecily, dau. and heir of Hugh de Ferrars, and confirmed by Robert de Ferrars, in [Brassington, Hopton, and Carsington]. Dat. Th. a. Tr. of St. Thomas [7 July], 34 Edw. III. [1360]. French. (Pole-Gell.)

BRASSINGTON *v.* also under MATLOCK.

---

*On visiting Hopton in 1902 this charter could not be found. This abstract is taken from the Hist. Com. Report, IX, Part II, 402, 403.

BREADSALL.

(BRAYDSALE, BREYDESALE.)

480. GRANT from Nicholas fil. Nicholai Fabri of Breydesale to William fil. Thome de Chadesdene and Idonea, his wife, and the heirs of their bodies, of six selions of arable land "cum tota terra frisca adiacente" in Breydesale [Breadsall], which six selions lie at Southewode, near Chadesden fields. Witn. Dom. William le Herbeiour, mil., Geoffrey de Detheyek, William ad crucem, etc. Dat. Southewode, S. b. F. of St. Andrew [30 Nov.], 10 Edw. II. [1316]. (Wilmot.)

481. GRANT from Nicholas fil. Nicholai Fabri de Breydesale to William fil. Thome de Chadesdene and Idonya, his wife, and the heirs of their body, of sixteen selions and five butts of land in Breydesale at Southewode, in exchange for six acres and three-quarters of a rood in Horseley. Witn. Dom. William le Herbeiour, mil., Geoffrey de Detheyek, William ad Crucem, etc. Dat. Southewode, Fr. a. F. of St. Andrew [30 Nov.], 10 Edw. II. [1316]. (Wilmot.)

482. RELEASE from John Gotken of Wyndeley to the House of the Holy Trinity, Braydsale Park, of his right in land formerly in the possession of Peter de Wyndeley. Dat. Braydsalepark, Vig. of St. Peter, Ap., 8 Hen. VI. [1430]. (P. R. O., B. 661.)

BREADSALL *v.* also under LOCKO, NETHER.

BREASTON.

(BRAYSTONE, BREIDESTONE, BREYDISTON.)

483. GRANT from J——, Abbot "de Parco Stanl" [Dale Abbey], to John de Lokinton, for his homage and service, of two bovates of land in Breideston; rent, 10s. Witn. "the seal of our chapter." [1233-1253.] (D. A. J. xxiv. 150; *facsimile.*)

484. GENERAL release from William Halom of Braystone, "tayllour," and Lucy, his wife, dau. and co-heiress of Richard Cartare of Braystone, to John Reynare of Swanwyk and Cecily, his wife, dau. and co-heiress of the same. Dat. 6 Apr., 24 Hen. VIII. [1533]. (Woll. iv. 3.)

485. GRANT from Nicholas son of Hugh de Wermondisworth to John son of William son of Hauwis of Breydiston, of land, a toft, and croft; part of the land in "le Borim," part abutting on the road from Notingham, part abutting on Thorlirsike, and part upon Holewalhel. Witn. Hugh le Tenerey of Eyton, Elias de Riseley, etc. Undated (P. R. O. c. 2061.)

BRETBY.

(BRETTEBI.)

486. SALE from Philip de Kima to Dom. Ranulph, Earl of Chester, of the vill of Brettebi [Bretby]. Witn. Dom. Hugh, Abbot of Chester, P[hilip] de Orrebi, Justice of Chester, Guarin de Vernon, John de Arden, A. de Sulign', Mag. Hugh de Cestria, etc. [1208-1226.] (Berkeley, 151.)

487. GRANT from Ranulph, Earl of Chester and Lincoln, to Stephen de Segrave of the vill of Bretby, which Symon de Kymba sometime held. Witn. Philip de Orreby, Justice of Chester, Baldwin de Ver, William de Vernon, Nicholas de Litteris, etc. [1209-1228.] (Berkeley, 154.)

488. ACCOMPT-ROLL of Robert Myddelton, collector of rents for the manor of Lynton, Mich., 23 Hen. VI. to 24 Hen. VI. [1445]; with the accompt of Thomas Hanson, Steward of the Manor of Bretby, for the same period. (Bemrose.)

489. LETTERS of attorney by John [Mowbray, 3rd] Duke of Norfolk, Earl of Nottingham and Earl Marshal of England, to William Matthew, esq., William Gourley, Thomas Morys, and John Wylne, Prior of Repton, to deliver seisin to Humphrey [Stafford, 1st] Duke of Buckingham, Thomas [10th] Lord Roos, John [Talbot, 1st] Lord Lisle, Ralph [Boteler], Lord Sudeley, Sir Henry Inglose, knt., and Richard Wallere, esq., of his lordships of Gower and Kilvey, in South Wales, and his manors of Bretby [co. Derby] and Northpydill [North Piddle, co. Worc.]. Dat. 20 July, 26 Hen. VI. [1448]. (Add. 17740.)

490. ATTORNEY from John [Stafford], Archbishop of Canterbury, Thomas [Bouchier], Bishop of Ely, and others, to John Wylne, Prior of Repton, and three others, to deliver seisin to Humphrey, Duke of Buckingham, Thomas, Lord Roos, John, Lord Lisle, Ralph, Lord Sudely, Henry Inglose, knt., and Richard Wallet, esquire, of the manor of Bretby. Dat. 26 Nov., 27 Hen. VI. [1448]. With seals and signature of John Mowbray, Duke of Norfolk, Lord of Bretby Manor. (Berkeley 598.)

491. ARTICLES of agreement of Thomas, Lord Berkeley, and Sir Richard Sacheverell, with Marie, Lady Hungerford, for the bargain and exchange by the former of the manors of Bretby, Coton, Rosliston, Linton, and Repton, co. Derby, with others in co. Leic., for the manors of Aller, Newton, St. Loe, Pensford, Publon, and Wollard, co. Som. Dat. 30 June, 17 Hen. VIII. [1525]. (Berkeley 572.)

492. LEASE, for 20 years, from Thomas, Lord Berkeley, to Sir John Porte, knt., Justice of the Common Pleas, of two pools well stocked with fish at Bretby, whereof the said Sir John had the charge and care "unto such time as the said Sir John was made one of the king's justices." Dat. 25 Feb., 18 Hen. VIII. [1527]. (Berkeley 697.)

BRETBY *v.* also under LINTON, NEWTON SOLNEY, REPTON.

BRETTON IN EYAM *v.* under FOOLOW.

BRIERLY *v.* under TRUSLEY.

BRIMINGTON.

(BREMYNGTON, BRIMENTON, BRIMINTUN, BRIMYNGTON, BRYMMYNGTON, BRYMYNGTON.)

493. GRANT from William fil. Rog. de Brimenton, with assent of William his elder son, to Jordan his son, of land in Brimenton. Witn. Matthew fil. Willelmi, William de Tapeton, Akon de Witenton, etc. Early thirteenth century. (Foljambe.)

494. GRANT from Ralph fil. Galf. de Cimiterio de Brimintun to Swanus fil. Hug. de Witintun of a plot of meadow in the territory of Brimintun. Witn. Peter de Brimintun, Gilbert de Taptun, Richard fil. Wlnet. *Temp.* Hen. III. (Foljambe.)

495. GRANT from Thomas fil. Radulphi de Cimiterio de Brimington to John Scot of Brimington of a toft in Brimington. Witn. William le Bret, Peter de Brimington, John fil. Radulfi de Brimington. Dat. S. a. F. of St. John B. [24 June], 10 Edw. II. [1317]. (Foljambe.)

496. ACQUITTANCE from Thomas de Colby "custos feodorum domini Thome Wake" to Robert fil. et her. Rog. le Breton, for 40s. paid on the death of the said Roger, "pro duplicatione redditus" of the manor of Bremyngton held of the said Dom. Thomas Wake. Dat. S. a. F. of St. Laurence [10 Aug.], 1324. (Foljambe.)

497. GRANT from William fil. Joh. fil. Petri de Hallumschire of Brimington to William fil. Will. de la More, of a messuage and land lying on Brokelhill, Mokholme, etc., in Brimington. Witn. Peter de Brimington, Adam Seket, Simon Goderhil, etc. Dat. Sat. a. F. of St. Matthias [24 Feb.], 3 Edw. III. [1329]. (Foljambe.)

498. LEASE, for nine years, from Giles fil. Anote de Thwathweyt to Peter fil. Ade de Bosco de Bremyngton, of arable land in Kerrowe [in Brimington]. Dat. F. of St. Luke [18 Oct.], 13 Edw. III. [1339]. (Foljambe.)

499. QUITCLAIM from Elizabeth fil. Petri fil. Gilberti le Schepherde to Richard fil. Roberti de Bollesorwodehouses of all the lands of her father at Brimington. Witn. Richard Stuffyn, John de Tapton, John le Barker, etc. Dat. S. a. F. of St. Denis [9 Oct.], 15 Edw. III. [1341]. (Foljambe.)

500. GRANT and counterpart from John Barker to Roger fil. Ric. de Tapton and Emma dau. of the grantor, in tail, of a tenement and lands in Bremyngton, with remainder to Richard Stuffyn, Robert Duraunt, and John de Neubold. Witn. John de Maunesfeld, Robert Duraunt, etc. Dat. Th. a. Inv. of H. Cross [3 May], 18 Edw. III. [1344]. (Foljambe.)

501. BOND from Robert le Breton, Lord of Walton, to Robert his son, of land called Dobynholm, in the fee of Brymyngton, in the field of Tapton. Witn. Roger le Caus, Richard Stoffyn, Robert Duraunt, etc. Dat. Brymyngton, S. a. F. of the Assumption [15 Aug.], 21 Edw. III. [1347]. (Harl. 112 G. 37.)

502. GRANT from John fil. Rog. de Beghton to John fil. Ade Smyth of land lying on "Wippeleye," "le Wetelandes," etc., in Brimington. Witn. Roger fil. Ranulphi, John fil. Mariote. Dat. Sat. a. Beh. of St. John B. [29 Aug.], 25 Edw. III. [1351]. (Foljambe.)

503. LEASE from John de Loudham to Robert Wele and William Pertrikoure, of lands, etc., in Brimyngton and Whityngton for 14 years. Dat. M. a. Michs., 39 Edw. III. [1365]. (Foljambe.)

504. GRANT from Alice dau. of Roger Dobyn to Matilda, her sister, of all her lands, etc., in Brimington. Witn. John del Wode, Peter del Wode, etc. Dat. Chastrefeld, S. a. F. of St. Alphege [19 Apr.], 51 Edw. III. [1377]. (Foljambe.)

505. PARTITION of the manor of Brymyngton, specifying in great detail the portion assigned to Thomas Foljambe. Dat. Brymyngton, 29 Mar., 18 Ric. II. [1395]. (Foljambe.)

506. PARTICULARS of lands held by William Tapton of John Barleye at Tapton Bridge, in Swoddale, at Brymyngton, etc., and of other lands in the same places. *Circ.* 1400. (Foljambe.)

507. LEASE from Henry Hunte of Tupton to John Dewee of Brimyngton of a messuage in Brimyngton for 100 years, at a yearly rent of 5*s.* to the said Henry and 20*d.* to Richard de Bawkewell. Witn. John de More, John Bate, sen., etc. Dat. M. b. Pentecost [10 May], 12 Hen. VI. [1434]. (Foljambe.)

508. QUITCLAIM from William Higdon of Edinsower and Joan, his wife, to William Hunt of Tupton of a tenement and two acres of land in Brimyngton which John Dewe, latè husband of the said Joan, had of the grant of John Wode. Witn. Richard Lece, William Hygdon, William Hyne, etc. Dat. Edinsouer, Michaelmas Day, 39 Hen. VI. [1460]. (Foljambe.)

509. GRANT from Thomas Foliambe, lord of Walton, esq., to John Asshton, knt., Henry Foliambe, esq., William Foliambe, clerk, and John Cooke, of a moiety of the manor of Brymmyngton, with lands, etc., in Whytyngton, Tapton, Dunston, and Normanton, a messuage in Hulme, with land there and in Brampton, and Loudeham Manor in Riby, co. Linc. Witn. John Foliambe, gent., Thomas Fox of Walton, etc. Dat. 20 Nov., 3 Edw. IV. [1463]. (Foljambe.)

510. GRANT from Agnes, widow of William Maryotte of Brymyngton, dau. and heir of Henry Burchefeld, to Henry Foliambe, lord of Walton, of a croft in Brymyngton, called "Nicolzerde," with all the lands, etc., in Taddyngton, Burcheffeld, and Prestclyffe, or elsewhere, in co. Derby, which descended to her from her father. Witn. Henry Vernon, John Leek, esqq., John Skotte, etc. Dat. Brymyngton, F. of St. Bartholomew [24 Aug.], 3 Hen. VII. [1487]. (Foljambe.)

BRIMINGTON *v.* also under CHESTERFIELD, DERBY, TUPTON, WALTON.

BRINLASTON.

(BRYNLASTON.)

511. ATTORNEY from John Braylesford of Ettewall to William Scrivenere of Derby and another to give seisin to John . . . and Cecily, his wife, of eighteen acres of arable land in the fields of Brynlaston. Dat. Ettewall, 4 April, 22 Ric. II. [1399]. (Trusley.)

BRINLASTON *v.* also under WILLINGTON.

BROADLOW ASH.

(BRADELOW, BRADLOWE.)

512. GRANT from William fil. Henrici de Fennybenteley to John de la Pole de Assheburn of a meadow called Gamelesley in Bradelow; to hold at a rent, after the end of 20 years, of 20*s.* Witn. John fil. Joh. de Benteley, Henry le Ballif de eadem, John fil. eius. Dat. Assheburn, 12 Oct., 38 Edw. III. [1364]. Seal of arms. (Okeover.)

513. LEASE, for 20 years, from King Edward [IV.], with the advice of the council of the Duchy of Lancaster, to Ralph Oker, gent., of all the lands, etc., of Bradlowe, with herbage and pasture of the wood of Bradlowe, parcel of the Duchy; to hold at a yearly rent of £9 13s. 4d. Dated apud Castrum de Notyngham, 2 Apr., anno 14 [1474]. (Okeover.)

514. WARRANT of King Richard III., instructing Rauff Oker, gent., to give up possession to Sir Marmaduke Constable, Steward of the Honor of Tutbury, of all the lands, etc., in Bradlowe, in the Duchy of Lancaster, which he at present holds on lease, but which have now been leased to James Berdesley and Hugh Berdesley. Dat. 26 Apr., 2 Ric. III. [1485]. (Okeover.)

BROADLOW ASH *v.* also under ASHBOURNE.

BROUGH, IN HOPE.
(BURGH.)

515. GRANT from William fil. Willelmi Blaunchard of Castiltone to Peter de Shattone, forester, of a rent of 2s., with a day's reaping in autumn, price 2d., from a tenement in Burgh. Witn. Clement de la Ford, Ballivus de Pecco, William Halley, Robert le Eyr, etc. Dat. Castiltone, W. b. F. of Annunc. [25 Mar.], 33 Edw. I. [1305]. (Woll. iii. 11.)

BROUGH *v.* also under BRADWELL, CASTLETON, SHATTON.

BRUSHFIELD.
(BREITREICHFELD, BRIETHICEFELD, BRITREICHFELD, BURCHEFFELD.)

516. CONFIRMATION, for 3 marks, by Sewale fil. Fulcheri of a covenant made between the Abbey of Rucford [Rufford, co. Notts.], and Walthof de Morneshale, respecting lands in Briethicefeld on condition of payment to the said Sewale of an annual rent of one mark. Late twelfth century. (Woll. ix. 3.)

> Sewale filius Fulcheri omnibus filiis sancte matris ecclesie tam presentibus quam futuris salutem. Notum sit uobis me concessisse et carta mea confirmasse conuentionem illam que facta est inter fratres de Rucfordia et Walthef de Morneshale scilicet de terra de Briethicefeld parte Walthef quicquid ei pertinet et communem pasturam de tota terra sua cum omnibus aisiamentis per omnia sicut in cirographo eorum continetur. Tali conditione quod ipsi fratres uisu Walthef debent reddere mihi et heredibus meis unoquoque anno tantummodo unam marcham argenti de ferma propter omne seruitium terrenum in perpetuum. Sciatis etiam quod Walthef et heredes sui quieti sunt apud me et heredes meos de una marcha de ferma sua. Insuper debeo esse inter predictos fratres et omnes homines et omnes calupnias et omnia seruitia terrena. Propterea dederunt mihi iii marchas propter concessum. Testibus Ascet' sacerdote, Matilda femina Sewal', Rodberto filio Osm', Rodberto filio Chol, Hor' Bas', Willelmo de Mugei, Henrico filio Fulcher et Fulcher fratre eius, Serlo de Grendune, Willelmo le Burgin cum aliis pluribus.

BRUSHFIELD *v.* also under BRIMINGTON, LONGSTONE.

BURNASTON.

(BRUNALDESTON, BRUNNALDESTON, BRUNUFYSTONE, BRYNNALDSTONE, BYRNASTON.)

517. GRANT by Celestra, relicta Walteri de Ribef, to Nicholas fil. Henrici de Brunufystone, in free marriage with Ysabel, her daughter, of a toft in Brunufystone which Engelard held near the toft of Henry de Bruwys, and five acres of land near Brakincroft abutting on Breryafhedlond. Witn. Dom. Walter de Ribef, Henry de Chambreys, Henry de Bruwys, Richard fil. Orm de Brunufyston, etc. Late thirteenth century. (Woll. ix. 36.)

518. GRANT from Nicholas fil. Henrici de Brunnaldiston and Isabella, his wife, to Ossebert de Frithisby, clericus, of five acres of land in the territory of Brunnaldeston, in a culture called Brakencroft, which the said Nicholas had received from Celestra, widow of Walter de Riboef, in marriage with Isabel, her daughter; rent, 1*d.* Witn. Walter fil. Walteri de Riboef, Janne de Dersyth, Richard le Despenser, etc. Late thirteenth century. (Woll. ix. 37.)

519. GRANT and release, for 22*s.*, from Roger fil. et her. Walteri de Chambereys, Dominus de Berewardecote and of Brunnaldiston, to Walter Truttok, of Brunnaldiston, of a rent of two shillings and an arrow, which he paid for a tenement in the fee of Brunnaldistone; rent, a peppercorn, reserving only foreign service, viz., 3*d.* yearly "ad tolnetum de Tutteburi" and 3*d.* "ad le Schirrevestur et ad palefridum," and scutage "quando currit," viz., 2*s.* 6*d.* Witn. Walter de Ribef of Etewelle, Richard dictus Foliot, William Orm, Nigel de le Breres, etc. Dat. Christmas Eve, 1291. (Woll. ix. 34, 35.)

520. GRANT from Henry fil. Henrici de Trusselegh of Kyrkelongele [Kirk Langley] to John Truttok of Brunnaldeston, of a messuage and lands in the vill and territory of Brunnaldeston, excepting three acres, which the said John inherited at the death of Walter, his father. Witn. Dom. Hugh de Meignill, Dom. John de Twyford, milites, Richard de Rybuff, Dominus de Etwell, etc. Dat. Vigil of F. of Pur. of B. V. M. [1 Feb.], 9 Edw. II. [1316]. (Woll. ix. 39.)

521. GRANT from John Tructok of Brunnaldeston to Henry fil. Henrici de Trusseleghe of Kyrkelongele [Kirk Langley] of a rent of 6*s.* 8*d.* from a messuage and lands in Brunnaldeston. Witn. Dom. Hugh de Meignill and Dom. John de Twiford, milites, Richard de Rybuf, Dominus de Etwell, William Orm, William de le Burghes, etc. Dat. Sun. b. Inv. of Holy Cross [3 May], 9 Edw. II. [1316]. (Woll. ix. 38.)

522. GRANT and release from John Bozoun, Dominus de Ednes-over, to Isabel, que fuit uxor Henrici de Braylesford de Brunaldeston, of a rent of 6*s.* from lands which were William del Borwes' in Brunaldeston. Witn. John de Rocheford, William de Bakepuz, William Eyring, etc. Dat. Vigil and Feast of Pur. of B. V. M. [1, 2 Feb.], 27 Edw. III. [1353]. (Woll. ix. 40, 41.)

523. GRANT from Thomas Milner of Derby and Matilda, his wife, to John Stanley and William Stanley, knts., etc., of lands in Brynnald-stone. Witn. John Hoghton, John Godard, bailiff of Derby, Roger Orme, etc. Dat. Morr. of St. Michael [30 Sept.], 2 Hen. VI. [1423]. (Woll. iv. 39.)

5

524. GRANT from John Stathum of Horseley, son and heir of John Stathum of Horseley, and of Elizabeth, his wife, to Robert Leek and William Sherle, of all his lands in Byrnaston and Berwardcote. Witn. John Bothe, esquire, John Fyndern, esquire, John Donyngtone, esquire, etc. Dat. 10 July, 16 Edw. IV. [1476]. (Woll. ix. 42.)

525. GRANT from Henry Stathum of Nottingham, son and heir of John Stathum, late of Gonerton, co. Notts., deceased, to Thomas Mellours, Mayor of Nottingham, Richard Savage, esq., Thomas Harpham, and others, of all his lands, etc., in Burnaston and Berwardcote. Dat. 10 July, 22 Hen. VIII. [1530]. (Debdale.)

BURNASTON *v.* also under ETWALL.

BUXTON.

(BUXSTONIS, BUXSTONYS, BUXTONIS, BUXTONYS.)

526. GRANT from Thomas Mathewe of Buxstonys, yeoman, and Alice, his wife, one of the daughters and heirs of Owin Coterell, late of the same, and Margery Coterell of the same, "singlewoman," the other of the daughters and heirs of the said Owin, to Antony Lowe of Aldyrwasle [Alderwaslee], gent., of a messuage and lands in Buxstonys. Witn. Richard Sacheverelle, esquire, Thomas Revell, gent., Andrew Lowe, gent., etc. Dat. Buxstonys, 7 Sept., 1 Hen. VIII. [1509]. (Woll. i. 90.)

527. GRANT from Thomas Mathews of Buxtonys, yeoman, and Alice, his wife, one of the sisters and heirs of Nicholas Coterell, son and heir of Owin Coterell, late of Buxstonis, and Margery Coterell of the same, "synglewomane," the other sister and heir of the said Nicholas, to Anthony Lowe of Aldyrwasley, gent., of a messuage in Buxstonis. Witn. Richard Sacheverell, esq., Thomas Revell, gent., Thomas Netham, etc., of Buxtonis, yeomen. Dat. 7 Sept., 1 Hen. VIII. [1509]. (Woll. vii. 14.)

BUXTON *v.* also under EYAM.

CALDWELL *v.* under DRAKELOW, ROSLISTON.

CALK.

(CALC, CALCH, KALC.)

528. NOTIFICATION from William, Archbishop of Canterbury and legate of the Apostolic See, to Roger, Bishop of Chester, and Ranulph, the Earl, and all the faithful, that, since William, Abbot of Chester, in the presence of the Archbishops of York and Rouen, at the Council in London, celebrated on the Sunday when "I am the Good Shepherd" is sung [*sc.* 2nd S. a. Easter], has restored to the Canons of Calk the church of Calk, and promised to restore all things that had been taken away by him or his men, as well as the Earl's charter, which had been lost, the said William the Archbishop wishes that the said church remain free and quit to the said Canons for the service of God. *Circ.* 1129-1139. (Add. 7214.) The text is:—

Willelmus Dei gracia Cantuar[iensis] Archiepiscopus et sedis apostolice legatus, Rogero eadem gracia Cestrensi episcopo et Rannulfo Comiti et omnibus sancte Dei ecclesie fidelibus per Angliam salutem et Dei benedictionem. Notum omnium deuotioni sit quoniam Willelmus Abbas Cestrensis in presentia nostra et archiepiscoporum Eboracensis et Rotomagensis et aliorum episcoporum qui concilio Lundonie interfuerunt quod celebrauimus in dominica quando cantatur, ego sum pastor bonus, tempore Henrici regis, canonicis de Calc reddidit ecclesiam suam de Calc et quietam clamauit et omnia sua que per illum vel per suos ill[is] ablata fuerunt reddere uel restaurare de suo promisit et quod etiam cartam Comitis de eadem re quam habuerant quamque per ipsum perdiderant restitueret. Vnde uolo et firmiter precipio ut eadem ecclesia amodo ad opus predictorum canonicorum ad seruiendum Deo libera et quieta permaneat. Rogo etiam uos omnes ut pro amore Dei et nostro eandem ecclesiam consilio uestro et auxilio muniatis. Valete.

529. GRANT in soul-alms from Matthew de Preers to the church of St. Giles at Calch of land in Wilintune; and grant from his wife, the Lady Beatrice, of " sex denarios uel dimidiam modium seglei " yearly for the rest of her life. *Temp.* Steph.—Hen. II. (Stowe 139). The text is:—

Omnibus sancte Dei ecclesie filiis salutem. Notum uobis sit quod Matheus de Preers concessit et dedit ecclesie sancti Egidii de Calch dimidiam acram prati in Wilintun in magnum pratum ultra Fuledic in primam partem eiusdem prati in feudo et elemosina libere, quiete, ab illo et ab heredibus eius pro anima sua et pro animabus omnium parentum suorum et pro firmitate eiusdem ecclesie et Domina Beatrix uxor euisdem Mathei dedit sex denarios uel dimidiam modium seglei omni anno uite sue pro redempcione anime sue et parentum suorum in festuitatem sancti Egidii. Teste, Horm presbytero et Johanne et Nicholao fratre eius et Hosb[erto] et Simundo filio Toch.

530. NOTIFICATION from Agnes fil. Ricardi fil. Nigelli de Malpas to the Canons of Calk of the land of two cowherds in Cheguurthia [? Kegworth, co. Leic.], " cum una masura," at the end of the town, namely, 32 acres of land, in perpetual alms for the souls of her sons, Robert, Richard, and William, and of Nigel, her lord of Malpas. *Temp.* Steph.—Hen. II. (Bemrose.) The text is:—

Agnes filia Ricardi filii Nigelli de Malpas omnibus filiis sancte ecclesie salutem. Notum uobis sit me dedisse et concessisse ex patrimonio meo et hereditate mea Deo et sancte Marie et Sancto Egidio et canonicis de Calc terram duorum bibulcorum in Cheguurthia cum una masura que est ad introitum uille ex parte occidentali et ex meridiana parte uie, scilicet, triginta duas acras, sexdecim ex una parte uille et sexdecim ex alia parte in perpetuam elemosinam pro salute anime mee et domini mei et Rodberti filii mei et pro animabus patris et matris mee et Nigelli domini mei de Malpas et Ricardi et Willelmi filiorum meorum et omnium antecessorum meorum, liberam et quietam ab omni seruicio et consuetudine et ab omnibus querelis et placitis et ab omnibus rebus sicut ulla elemosina liberius dari potest, excepto seruicio regis quia de aliis seruitiis terra illa libera est. Illam uidelicet quam predictus Willelmus filius meus prefatis canonicis diuisit [? for dimisit].

Teste eodem domino meo Nigello des Puis, et Willelmo filio meo iuniore, et Herui sacerdote et Pichot sacerdote de Suttunia et Gilberto clerico del Malpas, et Rodberto clerico de eadem uilla, et Petro filio eiús, et Thoma et Fuca fratribus Rodberti et Umfrido milite de Boneburi, et Willelmo filio suo et Warino Maillard, et Henrico Ostricer de Aluredo et Nicholao, fratre suo et Ysaac armigero et Hugone Cochet, et Alberto clerico, et Rogero fratre suo et Willelmo clerico filio Wlurici et Rodberto fratre Gilberti de Malpas.

531. Notification from Matilda, Countess of Chester, to Walter, Bishop of Coventry, that she, with the consent of the Earl Hugh, her son, has granted to the Canons of Calc a "cultura quarerie" of "Rependon iuxta Trente," with the advowson of the church [1154-1160]. (Bemrose.) The text is:—

Waltero Dei Gratia Couentrensi Episcopo, vniuersisque sancte matris ecclesie filiis, Matillis Comitissa Cestrie, salutem, Vestra noscat sanctitas, me concessu Comitis Hugonis filii mei dedisse Deo et sancte Marie et canonicis de Calc in puram et perpetuam elemosinam culturam quarerie de Rependon iuxta Trente, simul cum aduocatione ecclesie Sancti Wicstani de Rependon cum omnibus eidem pertinentibus conditione hac quod conuentus ibi constet tanquam capiti cum oportunitas idonea hoc expetierit cui Calc subiciatur membrum eius etenim diocesis semper permansit. Prece igitur multimoda uestram exoro dulcedinem quatinus hanc elemosinam consilio uestro caritatiue inceptam permanere faciatis ratam. Teste ipso Comite Hugone filio meo, Willelmo Abbate Lileshill, Helia priore de Bredune, Rogero capellano, Turri clerico, Aluredo de Cumbrei, Luuel de Hesbi, Nicholao de Mealtun, multis aliis. Apud Rependon. Vale.

532. Confirmation by Robert, Earl of Ferrars, to St. Giles and the Canons of Calc of the carucate of land which Haraldus gave them in "leca" [? Leek, co. Staff.], and the chapel, for the soul of his brother Reinald, canon in the said House. Early Hen. II. (Bemrose.) The text is:—

R[obertus] Comes de Ferr[ariis] uniuersis Sancte ecclesie filiis et omnibus hominibus et amicis suis francis et anglis, salutem. Sciatis me concessisse et confirmasse Sancto Egydio et canonicis de Calc illam carru[c]atam terre quam Haraldus dedederat eis in leca [? Leek] et capellam pro anima fratris sui Reinaldi canonici in domo predicta in perpetuam elemosinam, solam et quietam ab omni seruicio et consuetudine que mihi pertinet et heredibus meis post me et prohibeo omnibus baill[i]u[i]s et ministris meis ne capiant pecunias in nam[io] pro ullo defectu alicuius seruitii quod Haraldus uel heredes sui debebunt mihi uel heredibus meis. Teste R. capellano et Gilleberto presbitero et Ricardo clerico et Johanne presbitero de Leca, et Roberto de Piro, dapifero, et R. de Seile, cunest [abulario], et Ricardo de Curzun et Reinaldo de Gresele et Ada de Tich' et aliis pluribus.

533. Notification from Hugh de Bellocampo that whereas he had given to the Canons of Calk the tithes of his mill of Meleburna [Melbourne], but that they proved to be useless to them and difficulty was often experienced in collecting the same, he hereby grants to them, in exchange, one virgate of land in Newton [King's Newton], namely, that which belonged to Ranulph fil. Toch, so that the tenant of the land shall have all common rights and liberties as one of his own men holding so much land in the same vill has, and if such man do an injury to any of the canons he shall give satisfaction in the Canons' Court. And this land and liberties he grants for the salvation of the souls of Henry fil. Matilde Imperatricis, etc. Early Hen. II. (Add. 7213.) The text is :—

> Uniuersis sancte matris ecclesie filiis Hugo de Bellocampo salutem. Notum uobis sit quod ego Hugo de Bellocampo dederam Deo et sancte Marie et Sancto Egidio de Calc canonicisque eiusdem loci decimas de molendinis meis de Meleburna in perpetuum. Sed quia eis utiles non erant et in recepcione illarum multotiens impediebantur concedo eis in excambiis predictarum decimarum unam uirgatam terre in Neutona illam scilicet que fuit Radulfi filii Tochi inperpetuum elemosinam liberam et quietam ab omnibus secularibus consuetudinibus et operibus et seruitiis sicut aliqua elemo[si]na liberius dari potest, ita quod ille qui predictam terram de predictis canonicis tenebit omnes communitates et libertates habebit quas unus ex hominibus meis in eadem uilla tantum tenentibus habet in bosco scilicet et plano in prato et pascuis et ceteris libertatibus ad terram pertinentibus. Si autem predictus homo canonicorum alicui meorum hominum iniuriam fecerit in curia predictorum canonicorum ei satisfaciat. Hanc autem terram et has libertates concedo eis pro salute Henrici filii Matildis imperatricis et liberorum suorum et pro salute mea liberorumque meorum meorumque beniuolentium. His testibus, Waltero clerico meo, Herberto presbitero de Aluualdestona, Roberto de Kakestona, Stephano clerico de Rependona, Samsone camerario, et Balduuino clerico de Meleburna, et multis aliis, Valete.

534. GRANT from Hugh de Bello Campo to the Canons of St. Mary and St. Giles of Kalc of two acres of meadow in Meleburne, for the souls of King Henry and his Queen, and their children, his own children, Hamo Peverel, etc. Early Hen. II. (Add. 7081.)

> Omnibus Sancte Matris ecclesie filiis Hugo de bellocampo salutem. Sciatis me dedisse et concessisse Deo et sancte Marie et sancto Egidio et canonicis de Kalc, duas acras prati mei de Meleburne in perpetuam elemosinam has acras assignaui eis in Kingesholme ut ibi eas de me et successoribus meis liberas et quietas ab omni seculari seruicio teneant imperpetuum pro salute anime domini mei regis Henrici et regine sue et omnium liberorum suorum et anime mee et uxoris mee et omnium filiorum filiarumque mearum et Hamonis Peuerel et omnium antecessorum meorum. His testibus Stephano sacerdote, Helia filio Galfridi et Radulpho de Northfolc, Waltero clerico meo, et Baldewino clerico et Sampsone Camerario meo, et Willelmo Pincerna, et Ricardo Locard, et pluribus aliis.

535. *NOTIFICATION from Hugh, Comes Cestrie, to Richard, Bishop of Coventry, of his confirmation of Countess Matilda's grant of Rapenduna church to the church and Canons of Calch (v. under Repton). Witn. the Countess Matilda, his mother, Richard, his uncle, Ralph, his chaplain, William and Herbert, his clerks, and Geoffrey and Constantine, Alured de Conbrai, William Patric, Gilbert fil. Picot, Richard Luvetot, Roger de Livet, Bertram Camerarius, Jordan Rasur. *Circ.* 1162. (Burdett.)

536. CONFIRMATION by Hugh, Earl of Chester, of all possessions and liberties of the church of St. Giles of Calc and the Canons there, in soul-alms for his father, mother, etc., as the charters of his father

---

* The copies of this charter given in Bigsby's *Description of Repton,* p. 58, and in *The Topographer* (1790), p. 251, are too imperfect to be introduced in full here. I have been unable to get a sight of the original charter at Foremark. (Ed.)

witness, viz., the wood between Sceggebroc and Aldreboc, and Little
Geilberga, a culture between Alrebroc and Sudmude, the little mill of
Rapendone, and four bovates of land in Tichehale. And of the gift of
Nicholas, sacerdos, two bovates in the same vill, and the chapel of
Smithesbi. And of the gift of Geva Ridel, one "mansura terre" in
Tamwurth. And of the gift of Earl Hugh's father one boat in the
fishery of Chester, for fishing where they will, and a "mansura terre"
for the use of their fisherman; the land of Loftescot, as the road descends
from Rapendone to the "fons" called Neuhalhewelle, and as the same
"fons" descends to the boundaries of Meeltone, etc. And all the land
of Eswin Esegar of Trengestona: with the land and services of Reginald
fil. Alfwini de Rapendona, and Nicholas "armiger patris mei"; with
court "tam plenariam quam habeo meam in Rapendona," etc. Witn.
Ralph de Meinilwarin, Alfred de Cumbrai, Alfred de Suleini, Richard de
Luvetot, Roger de Livet, Gilbert fil. Pigot, Robert fil. Giliberti, William,
clericus de Barva, Bortram, camerarius, Sewal, Alexander frater ejus,
Ralph de Brichesbard, Robert Pincerna, William Barba Aprilis clericus.
Dat. Apud Barvam. *Circ.* 1162. (Dugdale VI., Pt. I. 598.)

537. GRANT in soul-alms from Gregory de Diua to the church of
St. Giles of Kalc and the "religiosi viri" there of the "baptismalis
ecclesia Sancte Anne de Sutthona super Soram" [Sutton Bonnington,
Co. Notts.], the said men of Kalc to find a canon priest or secular priest
and a clerk to perform divine service there. Witn. Thomas capellanus
filius Radulphi de Duninton, Walter diaconus, Roger clericus filius
Rathnal de Derb', Stephen clericus de Rapendon, Stephen clericus, filius
Osberti de Ticheam, Reginald clericus filius Willelmi sacerdotis de
Thicheal, et Henry frater eius, William clericus de Stanton super
Threntam. Late Hen. II. (Roper.)

538. CONFIRMATION by Leodegarius de Diue to the Canons of Kalc
of the advowson of the church of St. Anne of Sutton super Soram [Sutton
Bonnington], which his father Gregory de Diue gave them. Witn.
William Testard, tunc archidiaconus, Robert de Torf, decanus, William
Picot, Gervase de Clifton, Thomas Patric, William de Leke, John his
son, William Maillard, Ralph and Thomas his brothers, John Roges,
Robert fil. Suani. *Circ. temp.* John. (Roper.)

539. GRANT from William Patric to the church of St. Giles and
Canons of Calc of a rent of six shillings yearly from his mill of Sutona
super Soram [Sutton Bonnington]. Witn. Thomas Patric, the grantor's
uncle, Robert frater eius [*sc.* Thome Patric], Gilbert clericus de Maupas
Roger clericus, Lambert de Bousrohart (?), Fulk Mailart, Richard
Gawarden, Robert Traine, Robert Patric, Robert de Hibernia, Henry
fil. Gilberti. Early thirteenth century (?). (Roper.)

540. GRANT from Henry de Hertishorn, fil. Domine Agathe de
Hertishorn to the church of St. Giles of Calc and the Canons there of
three acres of arable land in the territory of Hertishorn, with all appur-
tenances in the vill and without on Schuchawe towards the south. Witn.
John de Stapenhull, Richard fil. Bertrami de Hertishorn, Ralph de
Tykeh', John Wychard de Breslya, William Balle of Rapendon.
Undated. (Burdett.)

541. AGREEMENT between Simon [de Sutton], Prior, and the
Convent of Repyngdon [Repton], and John de Schepeye, lord of
Smythesby, and Agnes, his wife, as to an encroachment by the latter
on the cemetery of the church of St. Mary Magdalen at Smythesby

[Smisby]; as to a heriot seized by him on the death of Robert le Parker, tenant of the Priory; as to enclosure by him of "le Bondewode" in Calke and Smisby, wherein the Priory has common of pasture, and as to the road leading from the Priory to their cell at Calke. Witn. Giles de Meingill, Robert de Greseley, "chiualers," Robert Foucher, etc. Dat. at Repyngdon, W. b. F. of St. John Baptist [24 June], 21 Edw. III. [1347]. Fr. (Stowe 137.)

CALK, *v.* also under REPTON.

CALLOW *v.* under MAPPLETON.

(CALDELOWE.)

CALOW, NEAR CHESTERFIELD.

(CALALE, CALALL, CALEHALE, CALHALE, KALALH, KALHALE.)

542. GRANT from Peter fil. Rog. de Kalhale to Ralph le Choyfer de Cesterfeld of land, etc., in Kalhale. Witn. Robert Brito de Waletona, Robert fil. Willelmi, Ralph Selvein, Richard and John capellani de Cesterfeld, Robert de Ednessowe, etc. Early thirteenth century. (Foljambe.)

543. QUITCLAIM from John fil. Petri de Kalehal to John fil. Rob. de Calehal of a yearly rent of a halfpenny for a meadow lying near the water called Fulbrok [in Calow]. Witn. William le Brett de Briminton, John de Briminton, Henry fil. Hugonis de Kalehal, etc. Late Hen. III. (Foljambe.)

544. GRANT, for 16*s.*, from Reyner fil. Roth de Cesterfeld to Thomas fil. Roberti Kedloc of the same, of lands lying on Buggecroft in Calehale; rent, 12*d.* Witn. Hugh de Pecco, Reginald fil. Galfridi, Peter Fox, etc. *Temp.* Edw. I. (Woll. vii. 27.)

545. RELEASE, for one mark, from Thomas fil. Roberti Kedloc de Cestrefeld to Peter Fox of the same, of three acres of land which he bought of Reyner fil. Roth de Cestrefeld, in the territory of Calhale, lying on Bucgecroft; doing service, viz., 12*d.* yearly to the Hospital of St. Leonard of Cestrefeld. Witn. Hugh de Peke, Roger de Blythe, Ranulph de Garthorp, etc. *Temp.* Edw. I. (Woll. vii. 28.)

546. RELEASE from Matilda, quondam vxor Thome fil. Roberti Kedloc of Cesterfeld to Robert de Lenne of Cestrefeld of three acres of land, which Thomas dictus Kedeloc bought of Reyner fil. Roth de Cestrefeld, in the territory of Calale lying in Bucgecroft. Witn. Henry de Cesterfeld, clerk, Alan de Lenne, Peter de Toptone, Hugh de Tuxforde, etc. *Temp.* Edw. I. (Woll. vii. 29.)

547. GRANT from Henry fil. Petri Fox of Cestrefeld to Robert le Len of the same of three acres of land in Calale; rent, 12*d.* Witn. Hugh de Linakir, Robert de Gildeford, Robert fil. Galfridi de Boythorp, etc. *Temp.* Edw. I. (Woll. vii. 26.)

CALOW *v.* also under CHESTERFIELD, WADSHELF.

CALTON LEES *v.* under DARLEY.

CALVER.

(Calfour, Calfover, Caluour, Calvere, Calvore.)

548. Agreement between Reginald de Meudry and Isolda, his wife, on the one part, and Robert de Calfover on the other, that the same Robert shall lease to the said Reginald and Isolda two acres of meadow in Calfover, that is to say, at Calvere Croft and four parcels of meadow in Holewesike, and all his demesne field under Bromleye, and four half-acres at Welleflate, and three islands "inter duo vada," for ten years, for yearly rent of 4s. Witn. John, Abbas de la Dale, Robert de Muschamp, Hugh de Stapilford, Luke de Byleye, Ralph, capellanus, de Coddenovere, Peter de Funtenaye, etc. Dat. Pur. of B. V. M. [2 Feb.], 23 Hen. III. [1239]. (Lansd. 584.)

549. Grant from Godfrey de Roland to Thomas Gomfray, clerk, and Richard Gomfrey, clerk, of all his lands, etc., in Caluore and Midultoncliff, with housbote and heibote, meadows, pastures, etc., appertaining. Witn. Thomas de Wednesley, mil., John de Stafford, Thurstan del Boure, etc. Dat. Tu. a. F. of St. James [25 July], 19 Ric. II. [1395]. (Wol. vii. 54.)

550. Attorney from Henry son and heir of Thomas Eueryngham of Staynburgh, co. York, esquire, to Thomas Revell, to receive seisin of all the lands in Calvore and Bramelegh which his father had jointly with John, Earl of Shrewsbury, and John, his son and heir, of the feoffment of Robert Staforthe of Ayome [Eyam], etc. Dat. 21 Feb., 15 Edw. IV. [1476]. (Lichf. S. 50.)

CALVER *v.* also under Eyam, Middleton, Monyash,
N. Padley, Rowland.

CAMPDEN *v.* under Bradley, Clifton.

CARSINGTON *v.* under Ashbourne, Brassington.

CASTLETON.

(Castelton, Castilton, Le Castilton, Castylton.)

551. Grant from Richard fil. Ric. fil. Rogeri de Castelton to Robert, his son, of his land at Castelton. Witn. Richard Daniel, Thomas Molendinarius, Richard de Sutton, etc. *Temp.* Hen. III. (Bemrose.)

552. Grant from William le Jay de villa castri de Pecco [Castelton] to Nicholas le Conuers of the same of half a burgage in Castilton. Witn. Thomas le Raggede, German Pygot, William Pygot, etc. *Temp.* Edw. I. (Foljambe.)

553. Grant from Dionisia, quondam uxor Thome le Conuers, to John fil. Thome Foliaumbe de Tideswell, of a messuage, etc., in Castelton. Witn. John del Halle, Henry del Halle, Robert le Taylor. Dat. Sat. b. Pur. of B. V. M. [2 Feb.], 11 Edw. II. [1318]. (Foljambe.)

554. Grant from John, son and heir of Robert Balgy, jun., to William, his son, and Joan, dau. of John del Halle of Castilton, of all the messuages, etc., which were formerly Robert Balgy's in Le Castilton, with the lands which William Trayhot sometime held, and the land which Cecily, widow of William Pygot, holds as dower, and which, on her death, revert to the said John Balgy. Witn. William fil. Thom. Hally, William fil. Will. Norreys, etc. Dat. S. b. F. of St. Valentine [14 Feb.], 10 Edw. III. [1336]. (Bemrose.)

555. GRANT from William fil. Ric. Larcher of Hoklouwe and Dionisia que fuit uxor Thome fil. Nicholai le Conuers to Thomas fil. Thom. le Conuers of a messuage in Castilton. Witn. Robert Foleiaumbe, tunc ballivus de Pecco, Ralph Despayne, John del Halle, etc. Dat. S. a. F. of Inv. of H. Cross [3 May], 12 Edw. III. [1338]. (Foljambe.)

556. GRANT from Thomas fil. Thom. le Conuers to John fil. Thom. Foleiaumbe of Tideswell of a messuage in Castilton. Witn. John del Halle, Adam Withloc, William Rotur, clericus. Dat. S. a. F. of St. Andrew [30 Nov.], 14 Edw. III. [1340]. (Foljambe.)

557. GRANT from Hugh de Strenley to John Talbot, Lord Talbot and Furnival, Roger Stedeman, and Richard Worteley, of lands and tenements in Castleton, Burgh, Alestre, Hope, and Assheoppe, co. Derby. Witn. Nicholas de Eyer, Oliver Halle, John Staveley, etc. Dat. Burgh, F. of St. Hilary [13 Jan.], 2 Hen. VI. [1424]. (Harl. 84 A. 49.)

558. LEASE from William Abnay of Hope to Richard Dutton of the same, of a messuage, land, etc., in " le Casteton clyff " in Castleton. Dat. Hope, M. a. F. of Ann. of B. V. M. [25 Mar.], 10 Hen. VI. [1432]. (Foljambe.)

559. FEOFFMENT by Nicholas Eyre of Redseats, to Richard Gernon of Hasylbadge, Henry Columbell of Darley, Walter Holly, and Hugh Nedham, of all his lands in Redseats, Castylton, Bradwall, Herdikwall, and Sterndale in High Peak, in trust for the said Nicholas, with remainder to his sons, Nicholas and Martin, etc. Witn. John Marchinton, Ralph Downes, etc. Dat. Th. a. F. of St. Martin [11 Nov.], 1 Ric. III. [1483]. (Bemrose.)

560. GRANT from William Orme to Nicholas Eyere of a burgage in Castleton lying between the water-mill and the high road. Witn. Henry Hall, John Down, Richard Howe. Dat. F. of St. Barnabas [11 June], 1 Hen. VII. [1486]. (Bemrose.)

561. GRANT from Edmund Wodrofe, son of Oliver Wodrofe, to Nicholas Eyre, of a parcel of land called Le Redsettes, in Castelton, lying between the king's land called Kytlowegreves and Castelton field. Witn. Henry Hall, Robert Forneys, Thurstan Joll, etc. Dat. 13 Nov., 11 Hen. VII. [1495]. (Bemrose.)

562. GRANT from Thomas Balgye of Aston, sen., and Thomas, his son, to Martin Eyre, son of Nicholas Eyre, that he may take a yearly rent from their tenements in Castleton up to the value of £12 as a marriage portion for Agnes, dau. of the said Thomas Balgye, sen., wife of the said Martin. Dat. 22 Apr., 13 Hen. VII. [1498]. (Bemrose.)

563. GRANT from Henry Tym of Castleton to Oliver Tym, his son and heir, of a tenement and eight acres of land in Castleton. Witn. Nicholas Eyr of Reedseyts, Thomas Gardyner, Henry Hall, jun. Dat. Castleton, 10 Feb., 15 Hen. VII. [1500]. (Kerry xvi. 135.)

564. GRANT from Ralph Trykett to Elias Staley of a rood of land in Brod Car Hey and half an acre of land in Pedderflatt, in exchange for two roods in Le Hayes and part of a " hadlond " in Overmerstonys abutting on the water of Pekysars [in Castleton]. Witn. Thurston Townend, chaplain, Thomas Barbour, Roger Hethcott. Dat. Hope, 11 Jan., 11 Hen. VIII. [1520]. (Bemrose.)

565. GRANT from John Eyre, late of Redsettes, to Adam Barbur of Pyndall, John Marshall of Lytton, and Roger Wryght of Herdycwall, of all his lands in Castylton and elsewhere in co. Derby, in trust for the said John Eyre and his heirs, in tail male. Dat. 17 Nov., 28 Hen. VIII. [1536]. (Bemrose.)

566. EXEMPLIFICATION of plea brought by Elizeus Staley against William Nedham, son and heir of Otvel Nedham, respecting the title to lands, etc., in the possession of Robert Nedham in Castleton and other lands called Rydyngs, Foxhill, and Salford Yard, in the same place. Dat. 28 June, 1 Edw. VI. [1547]. (Bemrose.)

567. SALE by Thomas Savage "of the Spyttell," in Castleton to Elize Staley of Reidseates, in the same, of several pieces of land, the bounds of which are given in much detail, in the parish of Castleton. Dat. 4 Mar., 2 Edw. VI. [1548]. (Bemrose.)

568. GRANT from Thomas Savage de le Spytell, in Castleton, to Elizeus Staley of Readseats, of a piece of meadow described as "oon outfall of medoe," with four acres and three roods of meadow in Castleton. Dat. 6 Mar., 2 Edw. VI. [1548]. (Bemrose.)

569. BOND by Thomas Savage of Castilton [Castleton], gent., to William Bradshawe of Marple, co. Chest, gent., in £100, for the observance by Margaret, daughter of Roger Howe of Ashope, wife of Godfrey Bradshawe, son and heir of the said William, of an award. Dat. 20 Jan., 3 Edw. VI. [1550]. (Woll. xii. 65.)

570. ACQUITTANCE by Thomas Savage of Castleton, gent., to William Bradsha and Godfrey Bradsha of Merpull [Marple, co. Chester], yeoman, for £5 13s. 4d., to the use of Margaret How, dau. of Roger How of Asheop, in part payment of 40 marks. Dat. 1 May, 4 Edw. VI. [1550]. (Woll. xii. 49.)

CASTLETON *v.* also under CHESTERFIELD, EYAM, HOPE, HIGH PEAK.

CATTON.

(CATTON-SUPER-TRENTAM, CATTONE.)

571. GRANT from Hugh de Sancta Cruce and Isabel, his wife, to Dom. Almaric de Sancto Amando, of a messuage and the virgate of land in Cattone, which Ivo Prepositus held of them in villeinage, and the said Ivo with his following, etc., with several annual rents there. Witn. Dom. Robert de la Warde, Dom. Richard Corsun, milites, William de Coursun, Robert de Staunton, William de Herteshorn, William Elys, Robert le Rodman de Yoxhelle, Robert le Glovere, etc. *Temp.* Edw. I. (Horton.)

572. GRANT from Thomas fil. Willelmi quondam de Cattone capellani to John Legamer de Cattone, of land in the Liberty of

Cattone, severally abutting on Croxhale, Le Vendiles, Rowdicke, Sorrunhed, etc. Witn. William Geffrey, Robert le Glovere, John Helot, Richard Helot, Robert Elys. *Temp.* Edw. I. (Horton.)

573. GRANT from Thomas fil. Michaelis Geffrey de Cattone to Henry fil. Willelmi Geffrey de Cattone of a messuage, etc., in Cattone lying on Le Grene, with land lying in Catton fields on Tonghul, Caustede, etc. Witn. John le Glovere, Walter atte Grange, William Geffrey, John Helot. Dat. S. a. F. of St. John B. [24 June], 2 Edw. II. [1309]. (Horton.)

574. GRANT from Agnes, relicta Walteri Geffrey, to John Helot, her son, of a messuage and three acres of land in Catton. Witn. Thomas le Glovere, Henry de Grangia, Richard le Cursun, John Brekediche. Dat. Fr. a. F. of St. John B. [24 June], 7 Edw. II. [1314]. (Horton.)

575. GRANT from John de Sancto Amando, knt., Dominus de Cattone, to Henry fil. Will. Geffrey, of a messuage and virgate of land in Cattone. Witn. Richard Dispensarius, Dom. Geoffrey capellanus, John le Glover, Walter atte Grange, John Heylot, William Geffrey. Dat. Sat. b. F. of St. Margaret [13 July], 11 Edw. II. [1317]. (Horton.)

576. GRANT from William fil. Joh. le Glover of Cattone to Robert de Scheylle of Elleford of eleven acres of land in the fee of Cattone, lying in Le Brokforlonge, Les Blakebuttes, Le Claybuttes, Le Wallehulle, Milnewardesforlonge, Goteacre, Watergalle, Cokschutehul, Fullesmedowfurlonge, Le Holme, and Ruylonde. Witn. William le Corzon, John Oky, William Waleys of Walton, etc. Dat. S. a. F. of SS. Peter and Paul [29 June], 1 Edw. III. [1327]. (Horton.)

577. GRANT from John Helot, sen., of Cattone, to Thomas his son, of a messuage, land, and annual rent due from Thomas le Persun, in Cattone. Witn. John Oky, Richard le Cursun, John Helot, Henry Geffrey, etc. Dat. Sat. a. F. of St. Michael, 2 Edw. III. 1328. (Horton.)

578. GRANT from Ralph fil. Reginaldi Pyrot of Herlyngdon to Almaric de St. Amand, mil., of the manor of Herlyngdon [? co. Derby], in exchange for the manor of Catton. Witn. Domm. John de Handle, Nich. de la Beche, John de Morteyn, Peter de Lorynga, milites, Thomas de Stodle, etc. Dat. Herlyngdon, Th. a. Nat. of St. John B. [24 June], 10 Edw. III. [1336]. (Cott. xxviii. 109.)

579. GRANT from Joan fil. Will. fil. Walteri Geffrey de Cattone to Thomas fil. Nicholai le Fysshere, William fil. Henrici Geffrey, and Robert fil. Nicholai le Fysshere, of a messuage and croft in Cattone. Witn. John Oky de Lyntone, Henry Geffray, William le Glovere, etc. Dat. T. b. F. of St. George [23 Apr.], 23 Edw. III. [1349]. (Horton.)

580. GRANT from John Oky to John fil. Will. le Glovere of half an acre of land in the fee of Cattone lying "in le Brodemedwe super le Hurstes," in exchange for half an acre in Oxmonnemedwe. Witn. John le Glovere, Thomas le Fyshere, William Geffrey. Dat. F. of Ex. of H. Cross [14 Sept.], 29 Edw. III. [1355]. (Horton.)

581. GRANT from Margery Baylly to Ralph de Herteshorne, vicar of Croxhalle [Croxall], and John Pymme of Cattone, of all her possessions in Catton, except a cottage, etc., called Le Neweyerd. Witn.

William de Cursun, dominus de Croxhale, Richard de Ruggeley, sen., William Geffrey de Catton, etc. Dat. S. a. Pur. of B. V. M. [2 Feb.], 1 Hen. IV. [1400]. (Horton.)

582. RE-GRANT from Ralph de Herteshorn, vicar of Croxall, to Henry Pymme to Margery Bailly, of the above-named lands, for term of her life, with remainder to Henry Prust and Matilda, his wife, and their heirs. Witn. William Cursone, dominus de Croxhalle, William Gardiner de Waltone, John Prestessone, etc. Dat. S. a. F. of St. Valentine [14 Feb.], 1 Hen. IV. [1400]. (Horton.)

583. ATTORNEY from Alianora que fuit uxor Almarici de Sancto Amando to John Cherteseye, Richard Parker, and John Yoxhale, to take seisin of her manors in cos. Berks, Oxon., Wilts., Glouc., and the manor of Catton-super-Trentam, co. Derby, which were lately conveyed to her and the said Almaric by Henry Ingepenne, William Tuderley, and Philip Shepiere by fine. Dat. 31 July, 3 Hen. IV. [1402]. (Horton.)

584, 585. GRANT and QUITCLAIM from John Prustessone and Matilda, his wife, to John Hugge and Matilda, his wife, of a piece of land in Cattone called Le Orchard. Witn. John Pymme, Henry Prust, Thomas Nikes. Dat. Th. and S. a. Ann. of B. V. M. [26, 30, Mar.], 6 Hen. IV. [1405]. (Horton.)

586. AGREEMENT between the above-named parties as to the rent to be paid for the place called Le Orchard, with a clause permitting the said John Hugge to use the water in a certain well (puteus) in the upper part of Le Orchard. Dat. M. aft. F. of Inv. of H. Cross [4 May], 6 Hen. IV. [1405]. (Horton.)

587. QUITCLAIM from Thomas Peyure, Geoffrey Ingepenne, Henry Durnforde, clerk, and Edmund Daunvers, to Alianora, widow of Almaric de Sancto Amando, mil., of the manor of Cattone. Witn. John Hyde, Thomas Abburbury, John Coterone, William Coventre, William Dancastre. Dat. apud Wydehay, 12 July, 6 Hen. IV. [1405]. (Horton.)

588. ATTORNEY from Alianora, widow of Almaric de Sancto Amando, mil., to William Stokes and Roger de la Bache, to give seisin to Roger Horton of the manor of Cattone-super-Trentam. Dat. Th. a. F. of St. James [25 July], 6 Hen. IV. [1405]. (Horton.)

589. ATTORNEY from John de Cumberford, Joan, his wife, Roger Belzetter, and Alice, his wife, to John Usgathorp, to give seisin to Robert Usgathorp of a messuage in Catton. Dat. Lichfield, Tr. of St. Thomas [7 July], 9 Hen. IV. [1408]. (Horton.)

590. ATTORNEY from Roger de Horton to Henry Prust and Thomas Nye to deliver seisin to William fil. Rog. Starky of Northwich, John fil. Rog. Starky, Geoffrey fil. Joh. de Masty, Thomas le Brette, etc., of a tenement in Catton. Dat. 7 Mar., 10 Hen. IV. [1409]. (Horton.)

591. GRANT from Ralph Herteshorn, Vicar of Croxhale, to John Shepherde of Catton and Cecily, his wife, of a messuage and buildings in Cattone, with a garden, a croft called Shortcroft, and meadow-land in Upmore Medwe, which he lately acquired from William fil. Will. Fyssher. Witn. John Hopkinsone, Henry Preste, Thomas Nyke, John Hugge, etc. Dat. F. of St. Andrew [30 Nov.], 14 Hen. IV. [1412]. (Horton.)

592. GRANT from Ralph Herteshorne, vicar of Croxhale, to Roger Horton, dominus de Cattone, of a virgate of land, a croft called Longhayrowe, and an acre of meadow in Cattone, which he lately acquired from William fil. Will. Fysher. Witn. John Hopkynsone, Henry Preste, Thomas Nyke, John Whytynge, etc. Dat. F. of St. Michael [29 Sept.], 1 Hen. V. [1413]. (Horton.)

593. GRANT from William Fyssher to Richard Hugge of a messuage, land, and rent in Catton, the land lying on Siluresmedowe, Brokefurlong, Cockeshetĕhulle, Gotacre, Fernysende, Ruyland, and Brodemedowe. Witn. William Yrpe, John Preste, Richard Nycke, etc. Dat. Sat. a. F. of St. George [23 Apr.], 22 Hen. VI. [1444]. (Horton.)

594. GRANT from Margaret, relicta Henrici Ampe, to William Ampe, her son, of all the lands which fell to her in Cattone on the death of Agnes Geffrey, her mother, with remainder, on failure of male heir to the said William, to John Pant of Yoxhall, and on failure of heir to him, to Henry Vernon, esq., son of William Vernone of Harlastone, knt. Witn. William Vernon, knt., Thomas Stanley, esq., John Fraunceys of Alrewas, etc. Dat. 16 March, 35 Hen. VI. [1457]. (Horton.)

595. GRANT from John Hugge to Richard Hugge, his son, and Margaret, his wife, of a piece of land called Orcharde, in Cattone, near the high road. Witn. John Smyth, Roger Lee, Henry Whythynge. Dat. Pur. of B. V. M. [2 Feb.], 1 Edw. IV. [1462]. (Horton.)

596. BILL of delivery from William —— and Edmund Sterky of Stretton-on-Dunsmore to William Brenstone, Abbot of Burton-on-Trent. of a little coffer containing five "evidences" concerning the manor of Catton, to preserve till such time as the said William and Edmund, or their heirs, shall require them to prove their title to the said manor. Dat. 2 July, 8 Edw. IV. [1468]. (Horton.)

597. GRANT from Henry Irpe to Roger Horton of a messuage with croft, a croft called Baconscroft, and land in Sheldemedowe, in Cattone, as security for the payment by the said Henry to the said Roger on two stated days in the chapel of St. Nicholas de Cattone of a sum of money to the use of the wardens of the chapel of St. John Bapt., of Marchyngton. Witn. Willam Smythe, John Hugge, Richard Smyth. Dat. Th. a. F. of St. Dunstan [21 Oct.], 4 Hen. VII. [1488]. (Horton.)

598. GRANT from Henry Irpe to John Cursone de Croxsalle, esq., of a messuage with croft in Cattone which Henry Koucure formerly held, with other land there and a croft lying between Ruylonde and Vymoremedowe. Witn. Thomas Gresley, knt., John Stretehay, Edmund Alcok, vicar of Croxsalle, etc. Dat. F. of St. Vincent [22 Jan.], 5 Hen. VII. [1490]. (Horton.)

599. COVENANT between Margaret, Countess of Richmond, mother of Henry VII., and Roger Horton of Catton, esq., whereby the latter agrees that his son shall be married to such "gentilwoman as her grace or her assignes shall thynke convenient," and that he shall deliver him to the said Princess, "and to cause hym by the advice of the said princes to be founde at Scole or in Courte to lerne the kynges laws or th' other wyse as the seyd princes shall avice from tyme to tyme," in return for which the Princess agrees to support the said Roger's title to recover any manors, lands, etc., in the realm of England, either by "peticion, accion, sewte, entre, or otherwyes." Dat. 18 Oct., 18 Hen. VII. [1502]. (Horton.)

600. GRANT from Richard Prest of Catton to John Corsone of Croxsall, esq., of all messuages, lands, etc., in Catton, which fell to him on the death of his father, Thomas Prest. Witn. John Stretehay, William Cursone, sen., Edmund Alcok, vicar of Croxsalle, Thomas Stretehay, etc. Dat. 11 Apr., 24 Hen. VII. [1509]. (Horton.)

601. GRANT from Thomas Curson, son and heir of John Curson of Croxall, esquire, in performance of the last will and testament of the said John Curson, to John Horton, son and heir-apparent of Roger Horton of Catton and Anne, wife of the said John and sister of the said Thomas, of all messuages, lands, etc., in Cattone, which the said Thomas holds or which were held by his father; with attorney to John Urpe and Thomas Smyth to give seisin. Dat. 20 Sept., 8 Hen. VIII. [1516]. (Horton.)

602. DEED of sale from William Large of Newebold Verdune, co. Leic., to Thomas Sprott of Asshmerbroke of a messuage and land in Cattone, which fell to him on the death of Thomas Large, his father; with attorney to Robert Hylle and William Aston to give seisin. Witn. John Myners, Thomas Campdene, John Broke. Dat. apud Measham, 4 Sept., 21 Hen. VIII. [1529]. (Horton.)

CATTON *v.* also under WALTON-ON-TRENT.

CAULDWELL.

(CALDWALL, CALDEWALL, CALDEWELL.)

603. MEMORANDUM of claim by Thomas de Gresley, knt., from the cottar tenants of the Lord Abbot of Burton-on-Trent, from each tenant one day's work with the sickle. *Temp.* Ric. II. (Gresley.)

604. LEASE, for life, from Thomas de Greseley, mil., Dominus de Drakelowe, to Thomas Netbreyder, "Botyler de Drakelowe," of a rent of 13s. 4d. from a messuage and other lands adjacent in Caldwell, late belonging to Robert Glover, and from two acres in Walton lying in Brodholm. Witn. John Abell, Roger de Gresley, Walter Marreys. Dat. Drakelow, M. b. F. of St. Margaret [20 July], 1 Hen. IV. [1400]. (Gresley.)

CAULDWELL *v.* also under DRAKELOW, ROSLISTON, WALTON.

CHADDESDEN.

(CHADDESDON, CHADISDEN.)

605. GRANT from John de Loyac de Chadisden to Thomas fil. Galfridi de Chadisden of two selions of land in Chadisden lying on Le Wolputhul, abutting on le Tvenlesiche. Witn. Dom. William le Herbeiour de Chadisden, Nicholas de Derlegia, Nicholas le Wine, etc. Late thirteenth century. (Wilmot.)

606. APPLICATION of the inhabitants of Chaddesden for episcopal licence for a cemetery to their chapel; with depositions of witnesses attached. Dat. 1347. (Lichfield AA. 9.)

607. GRANT from Henry le Baylif of Spondon, chaplain, to Dom. William le Herbyiour, knt., and Isabella, his wife, of a toft and croft in Chaddesden. Witn. William Gilbert of Chaddesden, William Ysmay, William ad crucem, etc. Dat. F. of St. Andrew [30 Nov.], 17 Edw. III. [1343]. (Wilmot.)

608. QUITCLAIM from William fil. Willelmi le Clerc de Chaddesden to Henry de Chaddesden of a messuage and toft in Chaddesden. Dat. Sat. a. Easter [22 Apr.], 20 Edw. III. [1346]. (Wilmot.)

609. DEED of Henry Bayly, Warden of the Chantry in the chapel of the B. V. Mary of Chaddesden, and William Ketelby and Edmund Koc, chaplains of the same, with the consent of Robert, Bishop of Coventry and Lichfield, of Nicholas de Chaddesden, clerk, and Dom. Geoffrey de Chaddesden, rector of Long Whatton, executors of the will of Henry de Chaddesden, late Archdeacon of Leicester, who founded the said chantry for three chaplains, and appointed a house for the same and for the warden, and allotted lands in Cos. Derby and Leicester for their support, whereby they agree to appoint a fourth chaplain in the person of Dom. John Claypole to live with them in the same dwelling-house, etc. Late Edw. III. (Wilmot.)

610. CONFIRMATION by Ralph de la Pole, serjeant-at-law, and John Curson, esquire, to Margaret, widow of Walter Twyford, esquire, of the lands in Chaddesdon which the said Margaret holds for life with remainder to the said Ralph and John. Dat. Mor. of St. James [26 July], 22 Hen. VI. [1444]. (Kerry xix. 327.)

611. GRANT from Edmund Angers of Chaddesden and Anne, his wife, to Thomas Strete, warden, and Henry Boonde, chaplain, of Chaddesden Chantry, of an acre and a half of land in Warfen, within the territory of Chaddesden. Witn. Robert Tykhull, Thomas Otyngham, John Shepard, "sythesmyth," etc. Dat. 20 Sept., 37 Hen. VI. [1458]. (Wilmot.)

612. QUITCLAIM from Nicholas Angerz, son and heir of Edmund Angerz, to Thomas Strete, warden of the Chantry of Chaddesden, and Henry Bonde, chaplain of the same, of an acre and rood of land in Warfen, in Chaddesden. Dat. 24 Sept., 37 Hen. VI. [1458]. (Wilmot.)

613. LEASE from Thomas Ratclyff, knt., master of Burton St. Lazars and the Brethren there to Sir Henry Sacheverele, knt., of the tithes and parsonage, with the tithe barn and the glebe land of Chaddysden and a messuage there in the tenure of Nicholas Tonyclyff; to hold for term of 20 years at a yearly rent of sixteen pounds: the lessee to keep the parsonage in good repair as well as the "waterwark of the medow," and if either the said Sir Henry, Dame Isabel, his wife, or William, his son, die within the said term, the longest liver on leaving the premises shall give to the said House of Burton 6*s.* 8*d.* "in the name of an obbett [obit] to be prayed for." Dat. 4 Apr., 19 Hen. VIII. [1528]. Seal of the House of Burton, chipped. (Mundy.)

614. LEASE from Thomas Lyghe, Doctor of Law, master "of Burton Saynt Lazar Jerusalem in England," and the Brethren there, to Leonard Bardesey, gent., of the parsonage and tithes of Chaddesden, co. Derby, and all the glebe lands, etc., thereto belonging, and also all houses, buildings, etc., to the said parsonage or to the House of Burton "in the ryght off the house off Burton or churche off Spondon within the townshype and hamlet or feldes of Chaddesden," now in the holding of William Saycheuerell, gent.: to hold for term of 40 years to begin at the end of the latter's term, at a yearly rent of sixteen pounds. Dat. 8 Nov., 32 Hen. VIII. [1540]. (Mundy.)

CHADDESDEN *v.* also under SPONDON.

CHAPEL-EN-LE-FRITH.

(CAPELLA-DEL-FRITH, CAPELLA-DE-LY-FRYTHE, CHAPEL-EN-LE-FRYTH, CHAPELL-EN-LE-FRITH, LE CHAPPELLE-IN-LE-FRITHE.)

615. PAROCHIAL visitation schedule of courts held at Chapel-en-le-Frith, Ashford, Sheldon, and Baslow. 1292. (Lichfield C.C. 3.)

616. GRANT from Richard fil. Johannis de Bradeschawe to his father and mother, John de Bradeschawe and Mary, his wife, of five acres and three and a half roods of land in Boudon [Bowden], lying in Thornyleye, Le Whytehalufeld, one half-acre being called Percsacre, nr. Holumedue. Witn. William fil. Johannis, Robert fil. Ricardi del Clough, John Luckeson, John del Holerinchawe, etc. Dat. apud capellam del Frith, Th. a. F. of St. Michael [29 Sept.], 6 Edw. III. [1332]. (Bowles.)

617. GRANT from William de Mosse of Combs to Richard, his son, of two acres of land in Boudon [Bowdon] called the Lege Acres, near Hayleyebroke, and one half-acre in the Rydynges above the Hayleye; with remainder to his sons John and Henry in succession. Witn. Robert Foleiambe, Bailiff of the Peak, William de Baggeshaugh, John de Ollerenshaugh, etc. Dat. Chapel-en-le-Frith, Th. a. F. of St. Lawrence [2 Feb.], 13 Edw. III. [1339]. (Rel. xvii. 164.)

618. LEASE, for four years, from Henry Wythewolf and Alice, his wife, to John de Beere and Agnes, his wife, of a rent of 7*s.* from a tenement in Forde. Witn. John de Bromore, John Pyk, John le Englissh, etc. Dat. apud Forde, F. of St. Mark [25 Apr.], 17 Edw. III. [1343]. (Woll. iii. 7.)

619. GRANT from William Broun of Bagschag to William le Boler de Blacwell and Elena, his wife, of a moiety of his land, etc., in the field of Bagschag in villa de Boudon. Witn. Nicholas fil. Hug. de Bagschag, Robert Mold, Hugh del Kulk, etc. Dat. apud capellam dal Fryt [Chapel-en-le-Frith], Th. a. F. of St. Edmund, Bp. [16 Nov.], 19 Edw. III. [1345], "in presencia Hugonis de Stredley tunc ballivi de alto Pecco et Thome de Bradschag sub-ballivi." (Foljambe.)

620. COMMISSION from the Chapter of Lichfield to their official, Dom. Peter Scarleston, Canon of Lichfield, to aid in repelling the intrusion of Thomas del Clough, a nominee of the Queen, into the chaplaincy of Chapel-en-le-Frith, annexed to the Church of Hope. Dat. iiii Kal. Jul. [28 June], 1350. (Lichfield T. 3.)

621. GRANT, in tail from Nicholas le Boler to William, his son, of a messuage and 8½ acres of land in Bagshawe, with remainder successively in tail to Thomas, John, Nicholas, and Roger, brothers, and Cecilia, sister of the said William. Witn. Walter Hally, Hugh Hally, William de Bagshawe, etc. Dat. Chapel-le-Frith, Fr. a. F. of St. Katherine [25 Nov.], 11 Ric. II. [1387]. (Foljambe.)

622. LEASE, for 10 years, from John fil. Joh. de Bradshawe, sen., to William fil. Joh. de Bradshawe, jun., of seven acres of land in Turnecroft. Dat. Chapel-en-le-Frith, M. a. F. of St. James [25 July], 21 Ric. II. [1397]. (Bowles.)

623. GRANT from John de Bradshawe to Roger Leche, knt., John Stafford, esquire, and John Alot, chaplain, of all the lands in Baudon [Bowden] which he inherited from Cecily Foliambe. Witn. William de Bagshawe, Hugh Halle, Walter de Kirke, etc. Dat. Baudon, 6 May, 9 Hen. IV. [1408]. (Bowles.)

624. LEASE, for 10 years, from John Bradshaw of Bradshawe to William Bagshaw of Chapel del Fryth of a parcel of land called Bradmersh. Dat. F. of St. Luke [18 Oct.], 8 Hen. VI. [1429]. (Bowles.)

625. DEED of entail whereby William Brome and Geoffrey Bagshawe, chaplains, convey two messuages and forty acres of land at Bradshaw and Turncroft [in Bowden] to John de Bradshawe, for life, and on his death to William, his eldest son, and his other sons, John, Robert, and Henry, in succession. Witn. Nicholas Brown, William Bagshaw, Walter de Kyrke, etc. Dat. Bradshawe, F. of St. Mark [25 Apr.], 8 Hen. VI. [1430]. (Bowles.)

626. SIMILAR DEED for one messuage and 43 acres of land at Lightbyrches. Same witnesses and date. (Bowles.)

627. COUNTERPART of lease from the Dean and Chapter of Lichfield to Thomas Armytage, chaplain of Chapel-en-ly-Fryth, of the tithes and altar dues of Chapel-en-le-Fryth and Fernilee, at a rental of £8, to be paid to the Chapter's attorney at the church of Tideswell. Dat. Dec., 1434. (Lichfield D. 10.)

628. LEASE, for 18 years, from William Bradshaw of Bradshaw to Roger le Couper, tailor, of the land called Bradmershe in Bowdon. Witn. John Shalcros, Walter de Marchynton, James de Legh. Dat. Th. a. F. of St. Martin [11 Nov.], 23 Hen. VI. [1444]. (Bowles.)

629. GRANT from William Boler of Bagschawe to Sir Randulph Barlawe, chaplain, Thomas Greensmyth of Bagschawe, and William Robinson, of all his lands, etc., in Bagschawe, within the township of Baudon. Witn. Nicholas Broune, William Baudon, Nicholas Staley, etc. Dat. Chapel le Frith, F. of St. Andrew [30 Nov.], 29 Hen. VI. [1450]. (Foljambe.)

630. LEASE, for 20 years, from William Bradshawe of Bradshawe to Roger Couper, tailor, of land called Bradmersshe; with warranty against the chief lord and Jocesa [Joyce], his mother. Witn. Henry Bailye, Rand[ulph] Oliver, Nicholas Dixson, chaplain. Dat. Vigil of the Annunciation [24 March], 35 Hen. VI. [1457]. (Bowles.)

631. LEASE, for eight years, from William Bradshawe of Bradshaw to Roger Couper, of land called Holghmede, in Bowdon. Witn. Henry Baylye, Thomas Olyver, Dom. Nicholas Dicson, chaplain. Dat. F. of St. Cedde, Bp. and Conf. [7 Jan.], 36 Hen. VI. [1458]. (Bowles.)

632. LEASE, for 19 years, from Joesa [Joyce] Bradshaw, widow, and William Bradshawe, her son, to William Redfern and Emmot, his wife, of the land called Turnecroft. Witn. Walter Marchinton, Dom. Nicholas Dicson, etc. Dat. 4 Oct., 37 Hen. VI. [1458]. (Bowles.)

6

633. GRANT from Nicholas Bowdon to Henry Vernon, esquire, William Waynwright, vicar of Glossop, and Nicholas Dikson, parish chaplain of Chapel-in-le-Frith, of all his lands, tenements, and goods, in Bowdon and in the county of Derby. Dat. 8 Apr., 17 Edw. IV. [1477]. (P. R. O. c. 3661.)

634. LEASE and counterpart, for 21 years, from William Bradshaw to "Hare" Bradshaw, his son, of the place called "ye Bradesha," with all his land and meadow there, except the "Greyve Croft," the said "Hare" to keep his mother according to her degree, etc. Dat. T. a. the Assumption [15 Aug], 18 Edw. IV. [1478]. (Bowles.)

635. CERTIFICATE by Nicholas Dikson, parson of Claxbe [Claxby, co. Linc.], Henry Bagshaw of the Ridge, gent., etc., of a declaration made by William Bradshaw of the Bradshaw, yeoman, upon his death-bed, namely, that the Hoole meadow was never of the Lyghtbirches land, nor ever given to John Bradshaw, his brother. Dat. 2 Aug., 1483. (Woll. xii. 48, 74.)

636. POWER of attorney by Thomas Berdvile and Ralph Sherard to Oliver Kyrke and Henry Bradshawe to deliver seisin to Edward Bakshawe of lands in Alstonelegh, in le Combs, and in le Gyves, alias Hordron-in-Bowdon. Witn. William Bradshawe, Edward Cross-leghe, Edward Aleyne, etc. Dat. at Chapel-in-le-Frith, S. a. F. of St. Edmund, K. and M., 2 Ric. III. [1484]. (Woll. iii. 23.)

637. GRANT, in tail, by Richard Blakewall to Thomas, son of Henry Bagshawe, and Cecilia, his wife, of a close in Bowdon, in the parish of Chapel-en-le-Frith. Witn. William Clayton, Robert Bagshawe, Thurston Aleyn, etc. Dat. 24 Nov., 11 Hen. VII [1495]. (Woll. iii. 10.)

638. STATEMENT by Robert Worth, "Baile" of Crich, gent., Thomas Awby of King's Bromley, co. Staff., Hugh Bradshaw of Morebarn, co. Leic., and John Bradshaw, jun., of Lichfield, testifying that John Bradshaw, sen., of Lichfield, on his death-bed, had denied that he had sold to Raynold Legh of Blackbroke, co. Derby, any other land than the messuage called Lightbyrch in Bowden, and that he declares that Hoole meadow was not part of the Lightbirch land. Dat. 6 March, 13 Hen. VII. [1498]. (Bowles.)

639. PETITION of Henry Bradshawe of Bawdon, yeoman, to the King [Henry VII.], for a warrant against Raynald Leghe of Blake-broke, to answer for a trespass upon a meadow of the said Henry in Bawdon, called Holmedowe, on the 28th Aug., a° 14 [1498]. (Woll. xii. 42.)

640. ORDER to the sheriff of co. Derby to summon a jury to try before John Vavesour and John Feyssher [Justices of the Common Pleas] the right of Henry Bredsha to certain lands in Bowden which Reginald Legh de Blakbroke claims to have belonged to his family since the time of Hen. III. Dat. Westm., 1 May, 14 Hen. VII. [1499]. (Woll. xii. 66.)

641. GENERAL release by John Bachcroft, "grammatice doctor" to Henry Bagshaw of Le Rydge, gent. Dat. F. of St. Matthew [21 Sept.], 15 Hen. VII. [1499]. (Woll. iii. 22.)

642. BOND by Reginald Legh of Blakebrok, esq., to Henry Bradshawe in £20, to observe a decision of Sir Rauf Longford, knt., etc., respecting the title to lands in Bowdene. Dat. 2 March, 15 Hen. VII. [1500]. (Woll. xii. 53.)

643. CERTIFICATE to the King by Sir Rauf Longford, knt., and Thomas Meyverell, of a decision given by them at Asheburne, in a claim made by Reynolde Lee, to part of a meadowe called Holmedowe, in the Chapel in the Fryth, in the possession of Herry Bradshawe. [1500]. (Woll. xii. 75.)

644. COUNTERPART of lease of tithes in Chapel-en-le-Fryth and Fairfield from Mag. Ralph Colyngwood, S.T.D., Dean, and the Chapter of Lichfield, to Thomas Bagshawe of Ford, for five years, at a rental of £5 13s. Dat. 31 Oct., 1516. (Lichfield D. 15.)

645. POWER of attorney by Godfrey Foliambe of Walton, esq., Roger Foliambe of Lynnacre Halle, esq., and George Savage, clerk to Nicholas Bagschawe of Le Chappelle-in-le-Frithe, Robert Gee of Lizdeygate, and Walter Marchington, of the same, yeomen, to receive seisin of lands which they held of Henry Bradschawe of Bradschawe in Bawden. Dat. 17 Apr., 10 Henry VIII. [1519]. (Woll. xii. 69.)

646. WILL of Henry Bradsha of Bradshaw, bequeathing "to Sant Mare howse of Coventre iiii*d.* Item to Sant Chaddes howse of Lychf[ield] iiii*d.*, etc., his "fermes" of "Tonstyd Mylne," "Eyvys," "Turnecroft," "Bradmarchys," to members of his family. Witn. S*r.* Wylliam Bagshaw, Vykar of Hope, S*r.* Steuen Bagsha, Curatt of y*e* Chapell in y*e* Fryth, Sr. John Bredbery, "owre Lady prest," etc. Dat. 2 Mar., 1521. Proved at Youlgrave, 29 Apr., 1523. (Bowles.)

647. COUNTERPART of lease from James Denton, LL.D., Dean, and the Chapter of Lichfield, of the fee-farm of Chapel-en-le-Fryth to Nicholas Browne de ly Marsche and Edward Dean, chaplain. Dat. 18 July, 1523. (Lichfield D. 19.)

648. LEASE, for lives, from Richard Bradshaw to his uncle, Henry Bradshaw, and Elizabeth, his wife, of lands called Turncrofts, in reversion on the death of Elizabeth Bradshaw, grandmother of the said Richard. Dat. 1 Dec., 29 Hen. VIII. [1537]. (Bowles.)

649. LEASE and counterpart from the Dean and Chapter of Lichfield to Thomas Armitage, capellanus capelle in ly Frythe, of the tithes of Capella de ly Frythe and Fernyle, for five years; with bond of the lessee to perform covenants. Dat. 26 July, 1538. (Lichfield D. 23, 24.)

650. RE-ARRANGEMENT of the terms of a lease originally granted in 25 Hen. VIII. for 31 years by Richard Bradsha of Bradsha to his uncle, William Bradsha of Marpul of the place called "Bradsha," then in the tenure of Henry Bradshaw, his uncle, and Elizabeth Bradshaw. Witn. Ottewell Bridburi of Bauckehed, Nicholas Bridbury, etc. Dat. 20 Apr., 33 Hen. VIII. [1542]. (Bowles.)

651. MORTGAGE from Richard Bradshaw of Bradshaw to William Bradshaw of Marpull of the lands of the Bradshaw. Witn. William Davenport of Goytes Hall, Alexander Elcock, William Chirten, schoolmaster, Richard Holmes, etc. Dat. 3 Dec., 34 Hen. VIII. [1542]. (Bowles.)

652. GRANT from Richard Bradsha of Bradsha, yeoman, to William Bradsha of Marpull of lands in Bradsha and Turnecrofte, in Bawdon. Witn. William Davenport of Goittes Hall, gent., etc. Dat. 5 Dec., 34 Hen. VIII. [1542]. (Woll. xii. 57.)

653. FINAL concord whereby Richard Bradsha conveys to William Bradshaw two messuages and various lands in Bowden. Dat. Easter Term, 35 Hen. VIII. [1543]. (Bowles.)

654. COVENANT to assure an annuity to Katharine, wife of Richard Bradshaw of Bowden, in lieu of the lands [in Bowden] which were settled on her, but have now been disposed of by the said Richard to William Bradshaw of Marple. Dat. 5 July, 35 Hen. VIII. [1543]. (Bowles.)

655. COVENANT whereby Richard Bradsha of Bawdene, gent., acquits William Bradshae of Marpoole, gent., of a payment of 40*s.*, out of a sum of £16 13*s.* 4*d.*, on condition that he acquits the said Richard of a similar sum towards Thomas Savage and Elis Staleys, payable to them, for use of Katerine, his wife. Witn. George Witmisleye, Bachelor of Laws, Chancellor to John [Bird], Bishop of Chester, John Chatham, Notary Public. Dat. 5 July, 35 Hen. VIII. [1543]. (Woll. xii. 58.)

656. SALE, for 200 marks, by Richard Brasha of Marpull, yeoman, kinsman and next heir to Henry Bradsha of Bradsha, yeoman, to William Bradsha of Marpull, yeoman, of lands in Bradsha in Bawden. Dat. 25 Aug., 35 Hen. VIII. [1543]. (Woll. xii. 67.)

657. GRANT from William Bradsha of Marpull to Anthony Shalcrus of Shalcrus, gent., and Thomas Savage of Castylton, of lands in Bradsha. Witn. William Davenport of Bromhall, esq., William Davenport of Chadkyrke, Leonard Shalcrus of Shalcrus, etc. Dat. 15 Sept., 35 Hen. VIII. [1543]. (Woll. xii. 80.)

658. LEASE, for 20 years, from William Bradshaw of Marple to John Gee of Hole Meadow [in Bradshaw]. Dat. 5 Feb., 35 Hen. VIII. [1544]. (Bowles.)

659. SALE, for 200 marks and £3, by Richard Bradshaw of Marpul, yeoman, kinsman and next heir to Henry Bradshaw of Bradshaw, yeoman, to William Bradshaw of Marpul, yeoman, of lands in Bradshaw in Bowden. Witn. William Davenport of Goytez Hall, gent., etc. Dat. 26 June, 1 Edw. VI. [1547]. (Woll. xii. 70.)

CHATSWORTH.

(CHATESWORTH, CHATTESWORTHE.)

660. GRANT from William Furneux, capellanus de Beghton, to Sir Godfrey Foliaumbe, knt., of lands in Chatesworth, Belegh, Wilynton, and Cheilmardon. Witn. Thomas de Wombwell, Ralph le Leche, Ralph Fremon, etc. Dat. Belegh, M. a. F. of Nat. of B. V. M. [8 Sept.], 45 Edw. III. [1371]. (Foljambe.)

661. GRANT from John de Sandale to Thomas, son of Gylbart de Toturhurst, of land in Chattesworthe. Witn. Roger Leche, William Leche, William Selven, etc. Dat. Chattesworthe, W. b. F. of SS. Peter and Paul [29 June], 21 Ric. II. [1397]. (Woll. ii. 56.)

CHATSWORTH *v.* also under BEELEY.

CHELARDISTON.

(CHELARDESTON.)

662. GRANT from Nicholas fil. Hugonis de Strethleg to William Clarel of a toft with half a bovate of land in Chelardeston in exchange for a toft which was Will. de Weregrave's and three acres of land. Witn. Dom. Geoffrey de Bek, Geoffrey Maureward, Robert de Staunton, knts., etc. *Temp.* Hen. III. (Foljambe.)

663. GRANT from William Clarell to Robert de Aldewerke and Joan dau. of the grantor, for life, of his land, etc., in Chelardeston, with remainder to their heirs male. Witn. Thomas de Chedworth, William le Bretton of Trhiberg, Adam de Wodehus, etc. *Temp.* Edw. I. (Foljambe.)

664. GRANT from Peter Constapularius de Chelardiston to William Clarell of an acre of land in the fields of Chelardeston. Witn. Nicholas fil. Silvestri, Hugh de Meleburn, Walter Bonde. Early 14th cent. (Foljambe.)

CHELMORTON.

(CHEILMARDEN, CHEILMARDON, CHELMARDON, CHELMERDON, CHELMORDON, CHEYLMARDEN, SCHEILMARTON.)

665. INDENTURE from twelve principal residents of Chelmorton, wherein, on receipt of a grant of a Chantry Chaplain and burial rights for their chapel, they stipulate to present and maintain the Chaplain, to fence in the cemetery, and to pay a pension of 4*s.* to the Dean and Chapter as Rectors. Dat. 1273. (Lichfield KK. 1.)

666. GRANT from Ralph fil. Radulphi Coterel de Tadinton to William fil. Johannis de Cungisden of an acre of land in Flagge. Witn. Nich. de Cungisden, Hen. de Nedham, John de Bulstones, etc. Dat. T. a. Palm Sunday [2 Apr.], 12 Edw. I. [1284]. (Harl. 83 E. 17.)

667. GRANT from John fil. Nich. le Gynour to William fil. Joh. de Congesdon, of lands in Scheilmarton, Tadenton, etc. Witn. Henr. de Congesdon, etc. Dat. Scheilmardon, Sat. b. the Feast of St. Thomas [21 Dec.], 11 Edw. II. [1317]. (Harl. 83 F. 7.)

668. GRANT from Henry fil. Ricardi fil. Matilde de Chelmarden to Nicholas de Conegerdon and John, his brother, of land in the fields of Flagge and the fee of Cheilmardon, lying at le Dedknaueforlonge, le Thisteli, Crowsethuse, etc. Witn. Hen. de Conegerdon, Hen. de Eyam, Hen. fil. Simonis, etc. Dat. 1 Edw. III. [1327]. (Harl. 83 F. 10.)

669. RELEASE from John le Gynour of Chelmordon to Henry son of John de Cungesdon, of land in Chelmordon. Witn. Hen. de Eyum, Jordan Gamul, John de Benteley, etc. Dat. Chelmardon, Sat. b. F. of St. Michael "in monte" [16 Oct.], 1329. (Harl. 83 F. 8.)

670. GRANT from Henry fil. Henrici de Eyum to Nicholas fil. Radulphi de Conegusdon and John fil. Henrici de Monihasse, of lands, etc., in Flagge and Cheilmarden, at a rent of 4½*d.* Dat. St. Martin's Day, 19 Edw. III. [1345]. (Harl. 83 E. 31.)

671. DEED of sale from Henry son of Adam Kay of Prestclif to Nicholas de Conegesdon and John, his brother, of land, etc. [? in Flagge]. Dat. Flagge, Fr. b. F. of St. Vincent [22 Jan.], 1346. (Harl. 83 F. 38.)

672. GRANT from Henry fil. Ade Kay of Prestcliff to Nicholas de Congesdon and John, his brother, of land in Flagge. Witn. Hen. de Congesdon, Tho. de Bocstones, Henr. de Eyum, etc. Dat. Cheilmardon, S. a. F. of St. Michael [29 Sept.], 20 Edw. III. [1346]. (Harl. 83 F. 39.)

673. QUITCLAIM from Henry fil. Nicolai de Conegusdon to Henricus Cay de Tideswelle, concerning land in Chelmardon. Witn. John de Benteley, Ric. de Pigton, Henr. de Conegusdon, etc. Dat. Th. a. F. of St. Andrew [30 Nov.], 20 Edw. III. [1346]. (Harl. 83 E. 16.)

674. GRANT from Henry fil. Ade Kay de Prestclif to Nicholas de Conegusden and John, his brother, of an acre of land in the field of Flagg and the fee of Cheilmardon. Witn. Henry de Conegusdon, Thomas de Bocston, Henry de Eyum, etc. Dat. Cheilmardon, F. of St. Lawrence [10 Aug.], 20 Edw. III. [1346]. (Harl. 83 F. 40.)

675. GRANT from the same to the same of three acres of land in the field of Flagg in the fee of Cheilmardon lying in Le Tustedus and half an acre of arable land on Dedknaveforlong. Dat. S. a. Ex. of H. Cross [14 Sept.], 1347. (Harl. 83 F. 41.)

676. GRANT from William le Foune son of John de Congesdon of Cheylmarden to Nicholas son of Ralph de Congexton and John, his brother, of five acres of land in Flagge in Cheylmarden. Dat. F. of St. Faith [6 Oct.], 21 Edw. III. [1347]. (Harl. 83 E. 45.)

677. GRANT from John de Assewell, parson of Makwith, John, vicar of Spondon, William de Monyash, vicar of Duffeld, and others, to Avery [daughter ?] of Godefrey Foliaumb of the land which they had from the said Godfrey in Chelmerdon, Flag, Neubold, Steuerdale, Redeclyf, Wylyngton, and Le Greues in Beley, with remainder to the said Godfrey and Avyne, his wife. Witn. Richard Vernon, knt., Thomas de Wendesley, Richard de Wynfeld, etc. Dat. Chelmerdon, M. a. Lady Day, 50 Edw. III. [1376]. (Foljambe.)

678. "INSPEXIMUS" of King Henry VIII., confirming a grant from William [Arnold], Abbot of Miravalle [Merivale, co. Warr.], and the Convent of the same, to Robert Dawkyn of Chelmerdon, yeoman, and Humphrey Dawkyn of the Office of Bailiffs of the manors of Chelmerdon and Flagg, and Cronxton and Pillesbury [both in Hartington], with an annuity of 26s.; dat. 11 Nov., 27 Hen. VIII. [1535]. Witn. Rich. Ryche, knt., at Westminster, 9 Feb., a⁰ 34 [1543]. (Harl. 112 F. 27.)

CHELMORTON *v.* also under CHATSWORTH, MONYASH.

CHESTERFIELD.

(CESTEREFELD, CESTERFELD, CESTIRFELD, CESTREFELD, CESTREFEUD, CHASTREFELD, CHESTREFELD, CHESTREFELDE, CHESTREFEUD.)

679. CHARTER granting to Richard Briewer son of William Briewer and his heirs the manor of Chesterfield, with Brimington and Whittington and the soke, and the whole wapentake of Scarsdale, to hold in fee farm of the King and his heirs. The charter also creates Chesterfield a free borough, granting to it a market and fair and all the same liberties as the borough of Nottingham. Reading, 10 Dec., 1213. (D. of L.)

680. CHARTER of King Henry III., confirming "hominibus Willelmi Briwerre qui de eo tenent et tenebunt in villa de Cestrefeld libertatem quam idem Willelmus eis concessit scilicet quod sint liberi Burgenses," and that they may have the same liberties and free customs which King John granted to the same William. Witn. R[ichard] Mar[shal], Comes Penbr[ochie], Peter de Ryuall capicer[ius], Pict[aviensis], Ralph fil. Nicholai, Godfrey de Crancumb, Geoffrey Dispensator, Geoffrey de Cauz, Richard fil. Hugonis. Dat. apud Theokesbiriam, 28 Dec., anno 17 [1232]. (Chest. Mun.)

681. NOTIFICATION of Hugh Wak to his Bailiffs of Cestrefeud [Chesterfield] of his grant to Joan que fuit vxor Willelmi Briwer, his uncle, of £8 13s. 4d. yearly in the name of dower "de furnis et Mercato" of Chesterfield, in exchange for a similar sum which she has received from Peter fil. Roberti in Briminton and Wytinton. [*Circ.* 1232.] (Foljambe.)

682. AGREEMENT made before the King's Justices between Dom. William Briuerre [Brewer], jun., and the Burgesses of Cesterfeld in defence of their liberties. Witn. Dom. H[ugo] Lincoln, Episcopus, Stephen de Segrave, William fil. Wor[ini], R[obert] de Lexinton, William Basset, Ralph fil. Nicholai, tunc justiciarii Domini Regis "et aliis fidelibus Domini Regis tunc ad Notingham presentibus." [*Circ.* 1226.] (Chest. Mun.)

683. GRANT from Robert fil. Sussanne de Ronisleye to Walter, clericus de Cestirfeld, of five acres and a half of land lying "juxta pontem Aldwini." Witn. Thomas de Leys, Peter de Briminton, John de Pecco, Richard fil. Wlnat, Hugh de Pecco, etc. *Temp.* Hen. III. (Foljambe.)

684. GRANT from Robert fil. Galfridi de Boytorp to Adam Blundus of two acres and a half of land and "vnum hulmum ad Reynolfs pontem . . . ubi vetus hospitale quondam fuerat." Witn. Simon de Linacre, Roger de Linacre, Hugh fil. Ingeram. *Temp.* Hen. III. (Foljambe.)

685. FIRST three lines of a letter from H. Clerk of Esseburne to S——, rector of the church of Cesterf', thanking him for his assistance in obtaining from the Dean the office of Schoolmaster of Chesterfield, etc. *Temp.* Hen. III. (Woll. x. 69.)

686. GRANT from Richard fil. Willelmi Bercarii de Cesterfeld to Hugh fil. Roberti Lorinarii of half an acre of land in the fields of Cesterfeld "super Neddirhulle," abutting on "Kalehalegate." Witn. Robert Lorinarius, Peter dictus Foy, William de Katteclive, etc. Late Hen. III. (Foljambe.)

687. GRANT from William fil. Presbyteri de Cesterfeld to Henry le Brun of Cesterfeld of half an acre of land in the territory of Cesterfeld lying on Haspelond "de feoudo de Perci." Witn. Peter de Briminton, William de Chattecliue, William de Neubolt, etc. Late Hen. III. (Foljambe.)

688. GRANT from John fil. Herberti de Cholintham de Cesterfeld to Walter fil. Rob. de Ho of half a toft, etc., in the new market of Cesterfeld. Witn. Hugh de Pek, William de Kattecliue, Peter Fox, etc. Late Hen. III. (Foljambe.)

689. GRANT from Walter de Lydezate de Hyll to John Ruggeweye, capellanus, and Henry Maunesfeld, of all the lands lying "supra Hyll aput Lydezate," with a piece of land "super Marthehyll." Witn. John Hyne of Chesterfield, John Stubbyng, John Hyll del Hyll, etc. Dat. apud Hyll, M. a. Pur. of B. V. M. [2 Feb.], 5 Edw. [I.] [1277]. (Foljambe.)

690.. QUITCLAIM from Alice fil. Rumphate de Cesterfeld to Roger de Blida of half a toft in Cesterfeld which was once her father's, lying on Haliwellegate. Witn. Hugh de Peck, William de Cateclive, Herbert de Colingham, etc. *Temp.* Hen. III.—Edw. I. (Foljambe.)

691. QUITCLAIM from Beatrice fil. Petri de Houeston to William fil. Ricardi de Schefeld of her right of dower as widow of Robert fil. Ricardi de Schefeld in a house in Aliuellgate in Cesterfeld. Witn. Richard fil. Wolnot, Ralph Palmer, Adam de Hulebrok, etc. *Temp.* Hen. III.—Edw. I. (Foljambe.)

692. LIST of tenements and lands of John de Maursfeld in Chesterfield and in the fee of Walton, with their yearly values, "anno Edw. viii°" [1279-80]. (Foljambe.)

693. GRANT from John de Arcwryt de Cesterfeld to the Guild of St. Mary at Chesterfield of two stalls formerly Thomas Gerard's, in the new market [of Chesterfield], and an acre of land in the fee of Boythorp, at a yearly rent of 6*d.* to Dom. Nicholas Wake, and 4*d.* to the Preceptor de Eykil (?) and to Henry, clericus, 4*d.* Witn. John de Brimintona, Simon de Hospitali, Philip de Lenne, etc. Late Hen. III. (Foljambe.)

694. GRANT from Isabella quondam uxor Egidii de Bobinhull of Cesterfeld to Roger, her son, of that part of a messuage, etc., in Saltersgate [in Chesterfield] which she had by grant of Alice fil. Joh. Heron. Witn. Robert Durant, Robert Felleson, Richard de Thornworth, etc. Dat. T. a. F. of St. Michael [29 Sept.], 14 Edw. I. [1285]. (Foljambe.)

695. GRANT from Richer fil. Wlnat de Cestirfeld, to William, his son, of two messuages and lands in Cestirfeld, Brimintone, Wytintone, Tappeton, Neubold, and Dunstone; rent, 1*d.* Witn. Peter de Brimintone, Jordan de Hapetot of Barlege, Roger de Blida, etc. 13th cent. (Woll. ii. 17.)

696. RELEASE, for one mark, from Peter fil. Rogeri Coty de Kalalh [Calale ?] to Hugh fil. Alani de Dukemantona, of land and common of pasture lying on the high street from Chestrefeld up to Buckebrighe, etc. Witn. Dom. Robert de Harestan, Dom. Roger de Eyncurt, Dom. Roger Britone, Dom. Jurdan de Abbetot, etc. 13th cent. (Woll. i. 88.)

697. GRANT from Roger de Eyncurt de Parco to William de Eyncurt, his brother, of his land of Aluinewode, with the cultures called Hungstubbing and Gernuncroft, and the great culture which lies "ante portam de Aluinewod," as they lie between the boundaries of Greyhirst Wood and Gravadune Wood, between Williamthorp and the great road leading towards Cesterfeld. Witn. Dom. Walter de Rybef, Dom. Henry de Braylesford, Dom. John de Eyncurt, persona de Winnefeld, Jocelyn de Steynesby, Ralph de Reresby, etc. Late 13th cent. (Foljambe.)

698. GRANT from John Wake, dominus de Lidel [Liddell] and of Chestrefeud, to his men of Chestrefeud, holders of burgages, that they may enjoy the same liberties and free customs which they had by grant from William le Brewer, sen., his predecessor, confirmed by Henry III. and by William le Brewer, jun. Dat. Kyrkeby in Moresheued [Kirkby Moorside, co. York], 30 May, 22 Edw. I. [1294]. (Foljambe.)

699. MORTGAGE by John fil. Alex. de Tapton to William fil. Ric. le Rede of Wyngerworth, of a messuage in Cesterfeld, to secure the payment of 5s. 3d. and half a quarter of corn at Michaelmas, 24 Edw. I. [1296]. Witn. Adam de Celda, Thomas de Tapton, etc. (Foljambe.)

700. QUITCLAIM from Sarra quondam uxor Radulfi, clerici de Cestrefeld, to Adam de Venella of Cestrefeld of half an acre of land in the field of Rihill [in Chesterfield]. Witn. John Durant, Adam de Neubolt, Hugh de Neubolt, etc. Dat. Cestrefeld, Vig. of Pur. of B. V. M. [1 Feb.], 25 Edw. I. [1297]. (Foljambe.)

701. GRANT from Emma que fuit uxor Ade Bete to Stephen, her brother, of the custody of all the lands, etc., in Cesterfeld, Boythorp, Neubold, Wytinton, Briminton, Tappeton, Dranefeld, Dunston, and Langeley which she had in custody with Simon fil. Ade Bete, her husband. Witn. William le Bret, Hugh de Linaker, Robert le Caus, etc. Dat. Sat. a. F. of St. Martin [11 Nov.], 26 Edw. I. [1298]. (Foljambe.)

702. INSPEXIMUS by Hugh fil. Hug. de Dokemonton of a charter of confirmation from Hugh, his father, to John Bonde of Cestrefeld, of a meadow in the field of Walton called Baystonbuttis. Witn. Henry, clericus de Cestrefeld, Alan de Len, William Husbonde, etc. *Temp.* Edw. I. (Foljambe.)

703. GRANT from Robert fil. Hen. de la Lanebanck of Cestrefeld to Henry fil. Henrici, clerici de Cestrefeld, of 1½ acres of land in Walton, lying on "Le Milnemoreflate," with warranty against Alice, his mother. Witn. Michael de Haversege, Roger de Maunnesfeld, John fil. Joh. Bonde, etc. *Temp.* Edw. I. (Foljambe.)

704. RELEASE, for six marks, from Roger fil. Radulphi Lorimer of Cesterfeld to John Durant of the same, of lands in Cestirfeld, Bramtone, Wytingholmis, and Houlotholm, with an annual rent of 10d. Witn. Will. de Brecte, Roger le Bretone, Rob. le Graunt, etc. *Temp.* Edw. I. (Woll. vii. 12.)

705. GRANT from Thomas fil. Rogeri de Fraxinis to Roger fil. Roberti Albi of Bramton of a plot of land on Le Balleye, near the road leading from Cestrefeld towards Bayequelle, abutting on Le Bredinbrigge and Le Gosegrene; rent, a rose. Witn. Robert le Caus, Hugh de Linaker, Robert de Somersale, etc. *Temp.* Edw. I. (Woll. iii. 47.)

706. QUITCLAIM from Syyeryld quondam uxor Hugonis Ketil de Cestrefeld to Robert fil. Rob. le Lorimer and Cecilia, his wife, of her right of inheritance, after the death of Adam Hadde of Cestrefeld, chaplain, in the third part of two acres of land upon Nedderhyll in the fee of Percy [in Chesterfield]. Witn. Hugh de Lynakyr, Richard de Neubold, John Durand. Early 14th cent. (Foljambe.)

707. GRANT from Robert de Peck, living in Chesterfield, to Peter fil. Hug. de Briminton of two acres of land lying on "le Hordthorp" [in Chesterfield]. Witn. Nicholas de Torp, Roger de Blithe, William de Peck, etc. Early 14th cent. (Foljambe.)

708. GRANT from John fil. Joh. Bonde to Margery, his sister, of a messuage, etc., in Cesterfeld which she had by grant from their father. Witn. Robert de Lenne, Alan de Lenne, Geoffrey Durant, etc. Early 14th cent. (Foljambe.)

709. GRANT from Richard fil. Willelmi ad barram de Cesterfeld to Richard fil. Hen. de Taptona of his right in all the lands, etc., inherited from his father in Cesterfeld. Witn. Henry clericus, Roger de Blye, William Kat, etc. Early 14th cent. (Foljambe.)

710. GRANT from William fil. Will. Richir to Roger fil. Galfridi de Walton of a yearly rent of 14*d.* in Cesterfeld for a tenement in Glenmonlane. Witn. Roger Laverock, John Duraunt, Stephen le Eyr. Dat. F. a. F. of St. Nicholas [13 Nov.], 1301. (Foljambe.)

711. QUITCLAIM from the same to Ralph fil. Petri de Brimington of all the lands which he sold to him when under age in Chesterfield, Tapton, and Newbold. Witn. Peter de Donston, William Fraunceys, Roger de Parva Tappeton, etc. Dat. Cestrefeude, F. of St. Mary Magd. [22 July], 30 Edw. I. [1302]. (Foljambe.)

712. GRANT from Mary de Calale, vidua, to Robert, her son, of a yearly rent of 2*s.* 8*d.* from a toft [in Chesterfield] in the "Wykeday Market," a curtilage in "Taptonlane," and a shop in "Souter Rowe." Witn. William le Bret, John Duraunt, Roger Laveroc, etc. Dat. S. a. Michaelmas, 32 Edw. I. [1304]. (Foljambe.)

713. GRANT from Henry fil. Simonis de Hospital, junioris, de Cestrefeld, to Alan de Hulmo de Cestrefeld of a toft lying "retro manum" in Cestrefeld, abutting on the lane leading from Le Wykeday-marketht towards the mill of the Dean of Lincoln. Witn. Adam de Newbold, John Durant, Richard Scotard, etc. Dat. Cestrefeld, S. b. Michaelmas, 34 Edw. I. [1306]. (Harl. 112 I. 17.)

714. GRANT from Adam le Mazoun of Cestrefeld to Simon, his son, of a shop [celda] in Cestrefeld in le Draperrowe. Witn. Roger Laverokes, Adam de Neubold, Hugh de Neubold, etc. Dat. F. of Pentecost [18 May], 2 Edw. II. [1309]. (Woll. vii. 35.)

715. GRANT from John Bete fil. Rogeri Bete of Cestrefeld to Roger fil. Ade de Blyd, of land in the fields of Cestrefeld. Witn. Roger Laverok, John de Warsop, Hugh de Neubolt, etc. Dat. Cestrefeld, Vig. of F. of St. Barnabas [10 June], 3 Edw. II. [1310]. (Harl. 112 G. 11.)

716. GRANT from Robert de Hulme of Cestrefeld to Alice, his daughter, of land in Cestrefeld "by Hindehand." Witn. Roger Laveroc, Adam de Neubold, Robert Darant, etc. Dat. Cestrefeld, W. a. Michaelmas [29 Sept.], 8 Edw. II. [1314]. (Harl. 112 I. 19.)

717. GRANT from Roger de Maunnesfeld to William le Loriner of half an acre of land in the fields of Neubold, lying on Heghebrockhill. Witn. William de Ryggeway, Richard le Porter, Roger de Glapwell, etc. Dat. Cestrefeld, S. a. F. of St. Luke [18 Oct.], 8 Edw. II. [1314]. (Foljambe.)

718. GRANT from Alan de Hulm to Roger de Glapwelle of land at the Stondelf, in the field of Cestrefeld. Witn. Adam de Neubold, Roger Laverok, William de Ryerway, etc. Dat. Cestrefeld, S. b. F. of St. Gregory [12 Mar.], 8 Edw. [? II. 1315]. (Harl. 112 I. 20.)

719. GRANT from William fil. Petri de Tapton of Cesterefeld to Henry, his son and heir, of all his lands, etc., in Cesterfield, Brampton, and Hulm. Witn. Stephen le Eyr, John le Palmer, Roger le Caus, etc. Dat. M. a. F. of St. Gregory [12 Mar.], 9 Edw. II. [1316]. (Foljambe.)

720. GRANT from William fil. Ade Finian to Agnes . . . and her heirs in tail of a messuage and lands in Cestrefeld, at a rose rent. Witn. Stephen le Eyr, ballivus de Cestrefeld, Adam de Neubolt, etc. Dat. 11 Edw. II. [1317-8]. (Foljambe.)

721. RELEASE from William son of Robert le Couper of Cestrefeld to Avice daughter of William Choys of the same, of all his right in 2*d.* yearly rent out of two messuages in Cestrefeld, in Glenmon Lane. Dat. F. of St. Hilary [13 Jan.], 13 Edw. II. [1319]. (P. R. O. ii., C. 2739.)

722. GRANT from Adam son of Ralph de Newbold, living at Cestrefeld, to Adam de Blyd of Cestrefeld, of land in Cestrefeld. Witn. Roger Laveroke, Rog. de Mammefeld, John de Warsup, Rob. Duraunt, etc. Dat. Cestrefeld, Easter Eve [18 Apr.], 14 Edw. II. [1321]. (Cott. xxviii. 6.)

723. SALE by John fil. Will. fil. Edde de Cestrefeld to Richard le Archer Hokelou'e Magna "de Pecco" of all his goods, chattels, etc., in a messuage in Saltergate, Cestrefeld. Dat. S. a. Tr. of St. Thomas [7 July], 16 Edw. II. [1322]. (Foljambe.)

724. RELEASE from Magota fil. Ade de Venella de Cestrefeld to Agnes, her aunt [matertera], formerly wife of the aforesaid Adam, of tenements and lands in Cestrefeld, between the croft of Roger de Blida and the lane leading from Sowtergate to St. Leonard's Hospital. Witn. Rob. Durant, Ranulph fil. Reginaldi, Roger de Glappewell, etc. Dat. Cestrefeld, F. of St. Barthòl. [24 Aug.], 17 Edw. II. [1323]. (Harl. 84 B. 8.)

725. LETTER of attorney from Roger fil. Rogeri de Manisfelde de Cestrefeld to Robert Pelleson, to give seisin of lands and tenements in "Novo foro" of Cestrefeld to John de Dunston. Dat. Cestrefeld, M. a. F. of Tiburtius and Valerian [14 Apr.], 5 Edw. III. [1331]. (Harl. 83 G. 34.)

726. GRANT from John le Barker of Aston to John fil. Joh. Tannatoris de Cestrefeld of a messuage abutting on the road from "Soutergate" to the new market and on the water called "Hyper," in Cestrefeld. Witn. Robert Durant, Ranulph de Haliwel, John Bonde. Dat. Sat. a. F. of St. John, a.p.l. [6 May], 9 Edw. III. [1335]. (Foljambe.)

727. SALE by William fil. Ade Alkoc to John fil. Ric. clerici of all the goods and chattels in his house in the "Wykday marketh" in Cestrefeld. Dat. S. a. Pur. of B. V. M. [2 Feb.], 11 Edw. III. [1337]. (Foljambe.)

728. QUITCLAIM from Adam fil. Rob. fil. Stephani de Neubold to John fil. Ade de Neubold of a messuage, etc., in Soutergate, in Cestrefeld. Dat. S. a. F. of St. Nicholas [6 Dec.], 11 Edw. III. [1337]. (Foljambe.)

729. GRANT from Stephen le Cutiller to Henry fil. Philippi de Neubold of a plot of land in Cestrefeld and three acres of land in the fee of Neubold. Witn. Roger de Glapwell, Robert Durant, etc. Dat. Trinity Sunday [7 June], 12 Edw. III. [1338]. (Foljambe.)

730. GRANT from Richard fil. Ade Albeyn to Robert de Hampton of the site of a messuage in Cesterfeld in Soutergate. Witn. Robert Durant, Henry le Eyr, William Ketill, William Kydeas, Henry Pexi. Dat. S. a. F. of St. Hilary [13 Jan.], 12 Edw. III. [1339]. (Foljambe.)

731. GRANT from the same to the same of his share of a messuage in Soutergate which was formerly Adam Fynian's. Witn. Henry de Maunesfeld, John Bete, Henry Pexi, etc. Dat. T. b. Michs., 1340. (Foljambe.)

732. GRANT from Roger de Glappewell of Cestrefeld to Roger de Blid of a messuage in the New Market, and land in a place called Behyndhand in Cestrefeld, to hold for his life, with remainder in tail to Philip de Blid and Leticia, his wife, and in default to Agnes and Lucy, daughters of Roger de Blid. Witn. Rob. Durraunt, Ric. Stuffyn, Tho. de Skeggeby, etc. Dat. Cestrefeld, Th. a. Michaelmas, 17 Edw. III. [1343]. (Harl. 112 H. 46.)

733. GRANT from Ranulph fil. Regin. de Halywell to John fil. Marie de Longeleye of a messuage, etc., in Chastrefeld, in Halywelle-gate. Witn. Robert Durant, William de Cheu, Robert Proudfot, etc. Dat. Sat. a. Epiphany [6 Jan.], 18 Edw. III. [1345]. (Foljambe.)

734. RE-GRANT from the same John to the same Ranulph and Isabel, his wife, of a messuage in Chastrefeld, in Halywellgate. Same witnesses. Dat. S. a. F. of St. Hilary [13 Jan.], 18 Edw. III. [1345]. (Foljambe.)

735. RELEASE from Elena que fuit uxor Johannis fil. Ric. de Neubold to Robert fil. Will. de Hulme of her right of dower in 14s. yearly rent from a tenement in the new market of Chastrefeld. Witn. Henry de Maunesfeld, Jauin Stedeman, Roger de Riggeway, etc. Dat. F. of St. Edmund, Bp. [16 Nov.], 21 Edw. III. [1347]. (Foljambe.)

736. GRANT from Margery condam uxor Roberti fil. Roberti Beyser to Richard de Dalby of a plot of arable land in Neubold, at the "Hwytflat." Witn. Robert Duraunt, John de Whytinton, etc. Dat. T. a. Oct. of Pur. of B. V. M. [2 Feb.], 22 Edw. III. [1348]. (Foljambe.)

737. GRANT from Joan condam ux. Roberti Aurifabri de Chastre-feld, to Margaret, dau. of the said Robert, of the moiety of a messuage and lands in Chastrefeld and Neubold. Witn. Robert de Hampton, William de Cheu, Roger de Bokynhill, etc. Dat. Th. a. Trinity [7 June], 1349. (Foljambe.)

738. GRANT from Henry de Maunesfeld to Henry and Robert, his sons, and the heirs of their bodies, of two messuages and 18 acres of meadow in Chastrefeld, and in the fees of Boythorp and Walton. Witn. Robert Doraunt, John de Whytington, Richard Stuffyn, etc. Dat. Fr. b. Nat. of St. John B. [24 June], 23 Edw. III. [1349]. (Foljambe.)

739. GRANT from Richard fil. Joh. de Tapton to William de Kyrkeby for his life of a stall in the New Market of Chastrefeld in "Mercer Rouwe." Witn. Robert Doraunt, Richard Stuffyn, John Mazon. Dat. Vig. of St. James [24 July], 23 Edw. III. [1349]. (Foljambe.)

740. GRANT from Robertus fil. Fellicis de Chastrefelde to Margareta, his daughter, of a messuage in the New Market between Clerimont Lane and the messuage of John le Goldsmyth, in Chestrefeld. Witn. John de Wyttyngton, Roger fil. Ranulphi. Dat. Th. a. F. of St. James [25 July], 24 Edw. III. [1350]. (Harl. 83 E. 12.)

741. LEASE from William Lorimer, capellanus, to John de Whityngton and Roger fil. Ranulphi de Haliwell, brethren of the Gild of St. Mary, in Chesterfield, to Hugh le Porter and Agneta, his wife, for their lives, of a messuage in the new market at Chastrefeld adjoining "Steppestonlane," and abutting on the highway and on the water called "Hipere." Witn. John Locker, John Bete, Thomas de Warsoppe, etc. Dat. Th. a. Conc. of B. V. M. [8 Dec.], 24 Edw. III. [1350]. (Foljambe.)

742. GRANT from the Aldermen and Brethren of the Gild of St. Mary, Chesterfield, to John fil. Joh. Bete and Marjory, his wife, for life, of a messuage in Chesterfield. Witn. Roger de Whityngton, Thomas Laverok, John de Digby, etc. Dat. S. a. F. of St. Ceadd, Bp. [2 Mar], 25 Edw. III. [1351]. (Foljambe.)

743. RELEASE from Richard Foliaumb to Henry de Hampton of a messuage in Chasturfeld. Dat. Vig. of St. Luke [18 Oct.], 1351. (Foljambe.)

744. GRANT from Peter fil. Rog. de Tapton to Robert de Birchouere and Roger Bete, chaplains, of all his lands, goods, etc. [in Chesterfield]. Witn. William Lorimer, chaplain, John Bete, Adam Picard, etc. Dat. Wedn. in Whitsun week [30 May], 26 Edw. III. [1352]. (Foljambe.)

745. GRANT from John de Barley to Robert, his elder son, of a messuage in Cestrefeld in "le Wikedaymarketh," near the oven of the lord of Chesterfield, anciently called "Le Witeoven." Witn. John de Wytington, ballivus Domini, John Goldsmyth, John Bete, etc. Dat. S. a. F. of St. Bartholomew [24 Aug.], 26 Edw. III. [1352]. (Foljambe.)

746. GRANT from Robert fil. Joh. Bete sen. to Robert fil. Ade Alkoc, of a messuage and land in Chastrefeld and in the fee of Tapton abutting on the "olde market stede." Witn. John de Whityngton, Thomas Laverok, Roger Laverok, etc. Dat. M. a. F. of Ex. of H. Cross [14 Sept.], 26 Edw. III. [1352]. (Foljambe.)

747. LEASE, for 60 years, from John de Wytington, Alderman of St. Mary's Gild of Chesterfield, and the Brethren, to William Aleyn of a messuage in Soutergate in Chastrefeld. Dat. F. of St. Peter in cathedra [22 Feb.], 34 Edw. III. [1360]. (Foljambe.)

748. GRANT from Marjory fil. Rogeri del Graunge of Chastrefeld to Innocent fil. Henrici Stonthacker of Chastrefeld of part of a messuage in Soutergate, Chastrefeld. Witn. John de Whityngton, Roger Daudesan, John Lark, etc. Dat. Chastrefeld, W. a. F. of the Ann. [25 Mar.], 37 Edw. III. [1363]. (Harl. 112 H. 56.)

749. GRANT from Peter de Tapton to Robert Alcok of land in Newbold "milneholme" which he had by grant from John Palmer. Witn. John de Whitington, John Goldesmyth, William Beverage, etc. Dat. T. a. All Saints' Day [1 Nov.], 34 Edw. III. [1360]. (Foljambe.)

750. GRANT from William Bate of Neubold to Robert de Barley fil. Joh. de Barley of Chastrefeld of a messuage in the "Wikeday-market" in the street called the "Flescheharneles" [in Chesterfield]. Witn. John de Dikeby, ballivus, John de Wytington, John Laverok. Dat. T. a. F. of St. Agatha [5 Feb.], 39 Edw. III. [1365]. (Foljambe.)

751. GRANT from Matilda de Huntynton to John Bete, of a messuage in Soutergate in Chastrefeld. Witn. John Laverok, John Hyngerselle, presbyter, John Gowele, etc. Dat. S. a. Nat. of St. John B. [24 June], 39 Edw. III. [1365]. (Foljambe.)

752. GRANT from Alice, widow of Henry de Wynfeld, to William de Wakebrige of a messuage in the new market in Chastrefeld. Witn. John de Whityngtone, John Lark, John Bete, etc. Dat. M. a. Michaelmas Day, 39 Edw. III. [1365]. (Woll. vi. 55.)

753. GRANT from William Beverege to Dom. Richard Porter, chaplain, of two messuages in Chastrefeld, one in Saltergate, the other in Haliwellgate. Witn. John de Dygby, John Bete, John Lark, etc. Dat. Th. a. F. of St. Martin [11 Nov.], 39 Edw. III. [1365]. (Foljambe.)

754. GRANT from Robert de Birchovere, rector ecclesie Omnium Sanctorum de Rischeton [Rushton, co. Northt.], to John le Goldsmyth of Chastrefeld of two acres of land in the fee of Newbold "in le Overheye." Witn. John Larc, John Bete, John Hyne. Dat. Th. a. Pur. of B. V. M. [2 Feb.], 40 Edw. III. [1366]. (Foljambe.)

755. GRANT from Adam fil. Hausie de Essheouere to William Beveregge and Alice, his wife, of a messuage in "Soutterrowe" and two messuages in "Fischerrowe" in Chesterfield. Witn. Nicholas de Baukwell, John de Wytington, Thomas Durant, etc. Dat. T. b. F. of St. Matthew [21 Sept.], 42 Edw. III. [1368]. (Foljambe.)

756. LEASE, for 24 years, from Henry fil. et her. Joh. Clerk of Chastrefeld to Ralph Fleschewer of two messuages in Chastrefeld, one in the "Wykeday" market and the other "in veteri foro." Dat. Michaelmas, 42 Edw. III. [1368]. (Foljambe.)

757. GRANT from Roger fil. Joh. de Neubold to Godfrey Foliaumbe, knt., Nicholas del Weld, persona tertie partis ecclesie de Derley, William de Kirklyngton, vicarius ecclesie de Bauquell and Nicholas Martyn capellanus, of all his messuages, etc., in Neubold. Witn. Roger de Wygley, John Lark, Thomas de Wombewell. Dat. Hassop, T. a. F. of St. Wolfrid, Bp. [12 Oct.], 42 Edw. III. [1368]. (Foljambe.)

758. LEASE from William Wakebrigge, John de Maunsfeld, and Thomas Durant to Agnes relicta Ade Louot and Isabella, their daughter, of a messuage, etc., in Chastrefeld, at a rose rent. Witn. John de

Wytington, John Laverok, John de Cigby, etc. Dat. S. a. F. of St. Katharine [25 Nov.], 1368. (Foljambe.)

759. GRANT from John fil. Avicie de Grenhill and Isabella, his wife, to Ralph de Dore, John de Raddecliff, and Robert fil. Rogeri le Tailur, of a messuage, etc., in the Wykedaymarket in Cestrefeld. Witn. John de Wytington, Robert, his son, John Lark, etc. Dat. Cestrefeld, Sat. a. F. of St. Barnabas [11 June], 43 Edw. III. [1369]. (Harl. 112 H. 59.)

760. GRANT from Alice, relicta Ricardi le Rissch, of Basselowe, to Nicholas de Asschouere of the reversion of a messuage in Chastrefeld in the Wykedaymarket and land in Boythorpe, late belonging to Richard fil. Tho. de Calfouere, her uncle. Dat. Th. a. F. of Epiphany [6 Jan.], 43 Edw. III. [1370]. (Foljambe.)

761. GRANT from William Roper of Basselowe to Nicholas de Asscheovere, cobbler, of a messuage in the "Wykedaymarket" in Chastrefeld and land in Boythorpe lying on Aspeland. Witn. John de Wytington, John Lauerok, Henry de Maunsfeld, etc. Dat. T. a. Epiphany [6 Jan.], 43 Edw. III. [1370]. (Foljambe.)

762. QUITCLAIM from John de Hinkersell to John Done, perpetual vicar of Chastrefeld, of a messuage, etc., in Chastrefeld abutting on Soutergate. Dat. F. of Pur. of B. V. M. [2 Feb.], 44 Edw. III. [1370]. (Foljambe.)

763. GRANT from Richard Milner, chaplain, to Dom. William de Staveley, chaplain, of a burgage in Chastrefeld lying in the old market. Witn. John de Wytington, John Laverok, John de Baukquell. Dat. T. b. F. of St. Luke [18 Oct.], 44 Edw. III. [1370]. (Foljambe.)

764. QUITCLAIM from Alice, widow of Richard Risscher of Basse-lowe, to Nicholas de Aschovere, cobbler, of a messuage in the Wykedaymarketh and land in Boythorpe and Neubold. Witn. John de Whytinton, Robert Joly, John le Knyfsmyth, etc. Dat. W. a. Epiphany [6 Jan.], 44 Edw. III. [1371]. (Foljambe.)

765. LETTERS patent of Edward III., granting licence to Richard de Chesterfield and Thomas Durant to alienate to the chaplain of All Saints' Church, Chesterfield, a messuage in Chesterfield for saying masses for their souls. Dat. 22 June, 46 Edw. III. [1372]. (Chest. Mun.)

766. GRANT from Matilda, relicta Rogeri Daudeson, to Dom. John Bonde, perpetual vicar of Chesterfield, and John de Maunsfeld, of a yearly rent from an acre of land in the fee of Chestrefeld. Witn. Thomas Durant, Robert Alcok, John Knyfsmyth, etc. Dat. F. of Ex. of H. Cross [14 Sept.], 46 Edw. III. [1372]. (Foljambe.)

767. GRANT from Adam Horn of Chastrefeld, chaplain, to Dom. Roger Bete of Chastrefeld of land and a messuage in Chastrefeld, in le Wykeday market. Witn. John Laverok, John Hyne, Rob. Laverok, etc. Dat. Chesterfield, M. a. F. of St. Edmund [20 Nov.], 47 Edw. III. [1373]. (Harl. 83 F. 31.)

768. LEASE from Thomas Bonde, vicar of Chesterfield, alderman of the Gild of St. Mary, to Thomas le Wright of two tofts in Chestre-feld, for 80 years. Dat. Easter Monday [2 Apr.], 48 Edw. III. [1374]. (Foljambe.)

769. GRANT from Matilda, widow of Roger Daudson of Chastrefeld, to William de Boseley and Matilda, his wife, of a garden in Chastrefeld, next the lane from Soutergate to the Dean of Lincoln's mill. Dat. F. a. Pur. of B. V. M. [2 Feb.], 1374[5]. (Foljambe.)

770. GRANT from John Laverok of Chastrefeld and Isabella, his wife, to John de Hynkreshill and Richard de Southwell, chaplains, of all their lands, etc., in Chestrefeld, Boythorp, Brampton, Neubold, Donston, Langeley, Dronfeld, Whityngton, Brimington, Staveley, Tapton, and Calal. Witn. John de Asshes, John Hyne, William Lorimer, etc. Dat. F. of St. Guthlac [11 Apr.], 49 Edw. III. [1375]. (Foljambe.)

771. RELEASE from Richard Porter and Richard Couper of Chastrefeld, chaplains, to Thomas de Burtone of Chastrefeld, of lands and tenements in Chastrefeld. Dat. Chastrefeld, T. b. F. of All Saints [1 Nov.], 49 Edw. III. [1375]. (Harl. 84 A. 12.)

772. RELEASE from John Koryfsmythe of Chastrefeld to Cecilia, his wife, Agnes, widow of John de Barley, and Alice, widow of Henry Knyfsmythe, to Thomas Durant of Chastrefeld, of a messuage in Chastrefeld, lying in Halywelgate. Witn. Nicholas de Baukwelle, John Laveroke, Robert Laveroke, etc. Dat. W. a. Epiph. [6 Jan.], 49 Edw. III. [1376]. (Woll. vii. 36.)

773. GRANT from Thomas de Wombwell, Robert Laverok of Chestrefeld, to John fil. Joh. de Dygby and Johanna, his wife, in tail, of all the lands within and without the town of Chastrefeld. Witn. Thomas Duraunt, Nicholas de Baukwell, John Laverok, etc. Dat. Sat. b. F. of Epiphany [6 Jan.], 49 Edw. III. [1376]. (Foljambe.)

774. POWER of attorney from William Franceys of Ilkeston, chaplain, to Robert de Barley, clerk, to deliver seisin to John de Stubbyng of Ashover, chaplain, Henry de Foston, chaplain of the chantry of Chastrefeld, and others, of a tenement in Chastrefeld. Dat. S. b. Nat. of St. John B. [24 June], 1 Ric. II. [1377]. (Foljambe.)

775. GRANT from John de Tapton to Thomas de Derton of two parts of a stall in the new market in Chestrefeld, in the "Drapour rowe." Witn. John Lauerok, John Hyne, Henry de Maunsfeld, etc. Dat. T. a. F. of St. Dunstan [19 May], 3 Ric. II. [1380]. (Foljambe.)

776. LICENCE from Richard II. to Richard de Chesterfield and Robert de Derby, clerks, to hold certain lands in Chesterfield and Newbold, to be assigned to Roger de Lesbes, chaplain of the chantry at the altar of St. Michael, in the parish church of All Saints, Chesterfield, and to Henry de Foston, chaplain of the chantry at the altar of St. Mary Magdalene, in the same church. Dat. 1 May, 4 Ric. II. [1381]. (Chest. Mun.)

777. GRANT from Margery, widow of Roger Michelson of Chestrefeld, to Roger del Leghes, Henry de Foston, chaplains, and others of a plot of land and meadow next Neuboldmilne, between the water called Roder and land of the lord of Chestrefeld. Witn. Henry de Maunsfeld, John de Maunsfeld, etc. Dat. F. of St. Bartholomew [24 Aug.], 7 Ric. II. [1383]. (Foljambe.)

778. GRANT from John de Sutton of Nottingham, weaver, and Matilda Bonde, his wife, to Richard de Aston, chaplain, and John Fraunces of Hertestoft, of the lands which belonged to Sir John

Bonde in Cestrefeld, Neubold, and Boythorpe. Witn. John de Rigeway, chaplain, Roger de Baukewell. Dat. Nottingham, F. a. F. of St. James [25 July], 8 Ric. II. [1384]. (Foljambe.)

779. LEASE from Alice, relict of Henry son of Robert de Wynfeld, to Sir Ralph Freccheville, knt., of her interest in land in Chestrefeld, for the term of her life. Dat. Chestrefeld, W. b. F. of St. Michael [29 Sept.], 8 Ric. II. [1384]. (Harl. 86 H. 13.)

780. GRANT from William de Staveley, rector of Tetwick [Todwick, W. R., co. York], to Thomas del Birkenschagh and Margery, his wife, of a tenement lying in Wykdaymarketh, abutting on the road to Knyfsmithgate, in Chesterfield. Witn. Adam Brown, Thomas Baret, Robert Coke, etc. Dat. S. b. F. of St. Leonard [6 Nov.], 9 Ric. II. [1385]. (Foljambe.)

781. GRANT from John de Barley, clerk, to Sir William Fienles, knt., Sir Nicholas de Gaushull, knt., Richard Vernon, William Echyngham, William de Batelesford, Roger Leche, John Cokerell, parson of Cranford, Robert de Barley, and others, of all his lands in Chestrefeld, Boythorp, Brampton, Linacre, Neubold, Hulme, Dronfeld, Dunston, Langley, etc. Witn. Thomas Oxcroft, William Nickeson, Thomas Oxcroft, etc. Dat. Th. a. Nat. of B. V. M. [8 Sept.], 12 Ric. II. [1388]. (Foljambe.)

782. QUITCLAIM from Agnes, widow of John de Asshborn, to Thomas de Derton, of a shop in Chestrefeld lying in the " Drapier-rowe." Witn. William Bate, John Hanneson, John de Dogmanton, etc. Dat. S. a. Conv. of St. Paul [25 Jan.], 1390. (Foljambe.)

783. GRANT from Robert de Whitewell and John de Stowe, "bacster," to John del Merssh, chaplain, of a messuage in " Wykdaymarketh " in Chesterfield and land in Boythorp. Dat. M. a. F. of St. James [25 July], 14 Ric. II. [1390]. (Foljambe.)

784. GRANT from Henry son and heir of John Clerk to John Hynkershull, chaplain, and others, of an acre of land near the " Coteleghes," in Chestrefeld. Witn. William de Calall, John de Calall, William de Shawe, etc. Dat. 6 May, 1391. (Foljambe.)

785. LETTERS patent granting to William de Horbury, clerk, Richard Porter, vicar of Chesterfield, Robert Cause, Henry de Maunsefeld, Hugh Draper, William de Lowe, and John del Assh, that they be a fraternity and guild in the church of All Saints, in honour of the Holy Cross. Dat. 25 Sept., 16 Ric. II. [1392]. (Chest. Mun.)

786. GRANT from Cecilia, widow of Robert de Birkes, to William de Bromylegh and Matilda, his wife, of an acre of land in Chestrefeld. Witn. Henry de Maunsfeld, William Lane, John de Normanton. Dat. T. a. F. of St. Edward, K. and M. [18 Mar.], 16 Ric. II. [1393]. (Foljambe.)

787. QUITCLAIM from Agnes, widow of Roger Godesone of Chestrefeld, to Henry de Maunsffelde, John del Asshe, and Will. del Lowe of Chestrefeld, of a messuage, etc., in Chestrefeld. Dat. M. a. F. of SS. Peter and Paul [29 June], 17 Ric. II. [1393]. (Harl. 83 F. 1.)

788. GRANT from Hugh de Thorpe, Richard de Rippelay, and Henry Fyche, chaplain, to Robert de Waplod and Avice, his wife, of a messuage in Chesterfield in " Wykdaymarketh," two acres of land

7

in Boythorp field, and half an acre of land in " Le Heye " in Neubold fields. Witn. Adam Broun, Richard Baret, Robert Cock, etc. Dat. W. b. Ass. of B. V. M. [15 Aug.], 17 Ric. II. [1393]. (Foljambe.)

789. ATTORNEY from Thomas de Byrkynschawe of Newerk to William Longestaffe, chaplain, to deliver seisin to Robert de Whytyngton, John Mapplesden, goldsmith, etc., of a messuage, etc., in Chestrefeld. Dat. Newerk, S. a. F. of Ex. of H. Cross [14 Sept.], 17 Ric. II. [1393]. (Foljambe.)

790. GRANT from John de Maunsfeld to William Cotenes and " Edayn," his wife, of a yearly rent of 9*s.* from his holm called Cutholm ; to be void if the said William and Edayn be not disturbed by claim of dower on the part of Elizabeth, wife of the said John, in the possession of Waltonholm, granted to them by the same [nr. Chesterfield]. Dat. F. of St. Nicholas [6 Dec.], 17 Ric. II. [1393]. French. (Foljambe.)

791. GRANT from John de Riggeway of Chastrefeld, chaplain, to William Eckyngham, Robert de Barley, Thomas Goumfrey, parson of Dronfeld, William de Wynfeld, parson of Thorp Basset [co. York], John Cokerell, parson of St. John, of Cranford [co. Northt.], and Robert de Whytyngton, of a barn and croft formerly called John Laverok's, at the end of the new market of Chestrefeld. Witn. Thomas de Bauquell, Hugh Drapour, etc. Dat. 8 Apr., 19 Ric. II. [1396]. (Foljambe.)

792. LEASE, for 20 years, from Robert de Maunsfeld to Roger de Hilles and Sibilla, his wife, of a messuage, etc., in Chestrefeld, in the new market. Dat. Mich. Day, 21 Ric. II. [1397]. (Foljambe.)

793. GRANT from Henry de Maunsfeld to Robert de Maunsfeld, John Curson of Ketelleston, John Nayl, William de Brynaston, and Richard de Shardelawe, the last three, chaplains, of all his lands, etc., in the fees and vills of Chestrefeld, Boythorp, Dronfeld, and Walton. Witn. John Bate, sen., Roger Boler, etc. Dat. M. a. Michaelmas Day, 21 Ric. II. [1397]. (Foljambe.)

794. LETTERS of attorney from Thomas Hunt of Lyndeby to William de Lowe of Chestrefeld, to deliver seisin to John Hunt of Asshovere, the younger, of a messuage and garden in Chestrefeld and land in the fields of Chesterfield aforesaid. Dat. Th. a. Michaelmas, 21 Ric. II. [1397]. (P. R. O., c. 1708.)

795. QUITCLAIM from Thomas de Nevill, Lord Furnivale, Thomas Goumfrey, rector of Dronfeld, Richard Goumfrey, late rector of Hengham, John de Maples of Shefeld, sen., and others, to John de Maunsfeld, of all the lands which they had of the feoffment of the same in Chesterfeld, Walton, Dronfeld, Neubold, and Brampton. Witn. Nicholas de Gausehill, Robert Frechevile, knts., Bartholomew Mongomery, etc. Dat. Chestrefeld, Fr. in Whitsun week [31 May], 21 Ric. II. [1398]. (Foljambe.)

796. LEASE from the Aldermen, Brethren, and Sisters of the Guild of St. Mary, Chestrefeld, to John Marschall and Margaret, his wife, of a messuage, etc., in Chestrefeld in " Glemangate." Dat. T. a. F. of St. Peter in cathedra [22 Feb.], 1 Hen. IV. [1400]. (Foljambe.)

797. GRANT from Richard son of William de Horseley and of Alice de Beston of Chestrefeld, to John Barley, William de Wynfeld, parson of Thorpe Basset, William de Aston, John Cokerell, and Roger de Hulme, "masun," of two acres of land in the fields of Chestrefeld and Neubolt, lying near the cross called "Jonessecrossbrown" and elsewhere. Witn. Roger de Bakewell, Roger Nettelworth, Thomas Calcroft, etc. Dat. 10 Mar., 1 Hen. IV. [1400]. (Foljambe.)

798. QUITCLAIM from Herbert de Whytyngton, John Mapplesden, goldsmith, and Roger Pees, to Roger de Baukewell, Roger de Criche, clerk, and John Cokerell, clerk, of a messuage in Chestrefeld in the Wykeday market, which they had jointly of the feoffment of Thomas Byrkynschawe of Newerk. Witn. Thomas Durant, John Maunsfeld, John del Asshes, etc. Dat. 7 Apr., 1 Hen. IV. [1400]. (Foljambe.)

799. POWER of attorney from Isabella Bankoc to William Rigeway to deliver to John Mauger, jun., seisin of a messuage and croft [in or near Chesterfield]. Dat. Chestrefeld, F. of Tr. of St. Thomas, M. [7 July], 1 Hen. IV. [1400]. (Foljambe.)

800. PARTICULARS of "mieses" and lands in Soutergate [Chesterfield] in the fee of Walenton [Walton]. *Circ.* 1400. French. (Foljambe.)

801. EXTRACT of court-roll of the manor of Chestrefeld, recording that at a great court held on Wed. a. F. of St. Mark [25 Apr.], 2 Hen. IV. [1401], Roger de Rosyngton and William Trucok, chaplain, did homage, etc., for lands and tenements within the manor. (Foljambe.)

802. GRANT from Robert Nettiswrht to Thomas Meystour and William de Holme, chaplain, of a messuage, etc., in Chesterfeld, in the "Wykday marketh," between the lane from "Knyfsmythgatte" to the church, etc. Witn. Hugh Drapour, Roger Bauquell, Roger Poklynkton, etc. Dat. M. a. F. of SS. Philip and James [1 May], 2 Hen. IV. [1401]. (Foljambe.)

803. GRANT from Henry de Maunsfeld to Sir Nicholas de Longeford, Sir Thomas de Wendesley, Sir Nicholas de Gausehill, and Sir John Cokeyn, knts., Roger Leche, and Henry de Bothe, "scutiferi," William Ingram, and William Frele, chaplains, and John de Maunsfeld, of all his lands, etc., in Chestrefeld, Boythorpe, Dronfeld, Walton, Haseland, and Brampton. Witn. Sir Ralph Frecchevile, knt., Robert de Plumley, etc. Dat. Fr. a. F. of Tr. of St. Thomas, M. [7 July], 2 Hen. IV. [1401]. (Foljambe.)

804. LEASE, for 20 years, from William Aston, Adam Lister, and John de Barley to John Calcroft, of four acres of land lying upon Sprolezerde [in Chesterfield]. Witn. Robert Whityngton, Roger Baukewell, John Normanton, etc. Dat. Ann. of B. V. M. [25 Mar.], 3 Hen. IV. [1402]. (Foljambe.)

805. GRANT from Robert Michelson to Adam Lyster and John Barley of a messuage in Chestrefeld. Witn. John Calcroft, Richard Baret, Robert Coke, etc. Dat. 5 Dec., 4 Hen. IV. [1402]. (Foljambe.)

806. QUITCLAIM from Cecilia, widow of Henry de Manusfeld, and Joan, widow of Robert de Manusfeld, bro. of Henry, to Thomas Scharp and William Webbester, chaplains, of all the lands, etc., which

the said Thomas and William have in Chesterfeld and in the fee of
Walton, Dronfeld, and Boythorp, of the grant of William Tructok,
chaplain, and Roger Rossyngton. Dat. 13 Apr., 5 Hen. IV. [1404].
(Foljambe.)

807. LEASE by Dame Johanne, Countess de Kent et Dame de
Wake, from Thomas de Anneslee, William Calale, Roger Herdewyk,
Johan Calale, and Roger Wormehill, of the manor of Chesterfield, for
term of 20 years, at a yearly rent of 25 marks. Dat. Brune [co. Linc.],
F. of Nat. of Our Lady [8 Sept.], 5 Hen. IV. [1404]. French.
(Chest. Mun.)

808. LEASE, for 99 years, from Hugh Draper, Alderman of the
Guild of the Holy Cross in Chestrefeld, and the Brethren of the same,
to Thomas Baret, of a rood of land lying "behyndband" [in Chester-
field] between land of St. Mary's Guild and land of John Bromeholme.
Dat. Ann. of B. V. M. [25 Mar.], 1405. (Foljambe.)

809. GRANT from Ranulph Bocher, Thomas Skynner, and Roger
Asshe to William Hudson of Dronfield, chaplain, of a messuage,
etc., in "Halywelgate," in the "Wekedaymarketh," abutting on the
"olde markethstede," which he had of the grant of Robert Waplod.
Witn. John Dorand, John Calcroft, John Normanton, etc. Dat. Th.
a. F. of St. Laurence [10 Aug.], 6 Hen. IV. [1405]. (Foljambe.)

810. GRANT from John son of Robert the clerk of Somerlesowe
to the Alderman, etc., of St. Mary's Guild, Chesterfield, of a plot of
land in Chesterfield, at a yearly rent of a peppercorn. Witn. Roger de
Baukewell, John de Calcroft, etc. Dat. F. of Nat. of B. V. M. [8 Sept.],
5 Hen. IV. [1405]. (Foljambe.)

811. DEFEASANCE of a grant from Robert de Whityngton and
Robert de Barley to Hugh Draper and Roger Lech, knt., of lands, etc.,
which were formerly John Barley's, conditional upon the payment of
£34 9s. Witn. John Durant, John Calcroft, John Normanton, etc.
Dat. Sat. a. Easter [19 Apr.], 7 Hen. IV. [1405]. (Foljambe.)

812. GRANT from William Frely, chaplain, and Roger son of
William Hanson, chaplain, to Mag. Robert Foliambe, clerk, John
Mapples of Rotherham and William Webster, chaplain, of two acres
in the fee of Dronfeld, in Pesecroft, next Fulbrok, one acre and one
rood in Sayntemarymedowe, two acres one rood in the fields of
Chestrefeld at the Stongravell, three roods in the same fields on Goldewellfflatte, three roods on and under Little Brokhull, seven acres in
the fee of Brampton on the Moorflatte, and one and a half acres in
the fee of Neubold. Witn. Ralph Frechevile, knt., William de Dethek,
knt., John Foliambe, etc. Dat. W. b. F. of St. Mark [25 Apr.],
7 Hen. IV. [1406]. (Foljambe.)

813. GRANT from Hugh Draper of Chesterfield, Alderman of the
Guild of Holy Cross, and the Brethren of the same, to Roger del
Asshe of Chesterfield, of a tenement in the new market on the water
of Hypur. Witn. Thurstan del Bowre, Roger Boler, William Broun,
etc. Dat. Whitsunday [15 May], 8 Hen. IV. [1407]. (Bemrose.)

814. GRANT from John son of John Calall to William Calall and
William Webster, chaplain, of his lands, etc., in Chesterfield, etc.
Witn. Thomas Foliaumb, Ralph de Clapwell, Richard Cook, etc. Dat.
Chestrefeld, Th. a. F. of St. Vedast and St. Amandus [6 Feb.],
10 Hen. IV. [1409]. (Foljambe.)

815. RELEASE from William Porter son of Richard Porter, clerk, to Roger de Wyngreworth, of lands and tenements which formerly belonged to the said Richard in Chestrefeld, in a place called "Behynde the hand"; and also of a barn [orreus] which formerly belonged to Innocentius Stonethakker. Witn. Thurstan de Boure, John Durant, Thos. Barrett, John de Normanton. Dat. Chesterfield, Vig. of St. Laurence [10 Aug.], 10 Hen. IV. [1409]. (Cott. xxviii. 91.)

816. GRANT from John de Normanton to William Webster, Thomas de Roodes, and John de Couentre, chaplains, and others of all his lands, goods, and chattels, etc., in Chestrefeld. Witn. Richard Cook, John Calcroft, jun., Roger Boolar. Dat. F. of the Assumption [15 Aug.], 10 Hen. IV. [1409]. (Foljambe.)

817. GRANT from Ankerus de Norton of Staley to Richard Porter of Chesterfield and John, his son, of two burgages and two acres of land in the fee of Chesterfield and Newbold, which two burgages lie at the end of the new market of Chesterfield, and one acre of land lying at Goldwell on the road from Chesterfield to Barley, and the other between the lands of John Maunsefeld and Brampton Brigge and abutting on the water called Smale. Witn. Ralph Durand, Christian del Boure, Robert Whityngton, etc. Dat. F. of St. Gregory [12 Mar.], 1 Hen. V. [1414]. (Ogston.)

818. GRANT from Robert Tapton son and heir of Peter de Tapton to Thomas his son, for the term of his life, of a tenement in Chestrefeld in the new market, with remainder to Thomas Baret and Thomas Haukynman. Witn. Thurstan del Boure, Ralph Durand, John Marre, etc. Dat. F. of St. Mary Magd. [22 July], 2 Hen. V. [1414]. (Foljambe.)

819. LEASE from Thomas de Tapton, Thomas Baret, and Thomas Haukynman to the Alderman and Brethren of St. Mary's Guild, Chestrefeld, of a tenement in Chestrefeld in the new market. Dat. M. a. F. of St. Mary Magd. [22 July], 2 Hen. V. [1414]. (Foljambe.)

820. GRANT from John Calall son and heir of John Calall to Robert Whityngton, William Sutton, clerk, and Thomas Baret, of all his lands, etc., in the fee of Chestrefeld. Witn. Roger Bawckewell, Ralph Dorand, John Calcroft, etc. Dat. F. of H. Trinity [26 May], 3 Hen. V. [1415]. (Foljambe.)

821. RELEASE from William Foxe of Hasland to Richard Hethcote of a cottage at the head of the new market in Chesterfield. Dat. F. of St. Matthew [21 Sept.], 4 Hen. V. [1416]. (Foljambe.)

822. GRANT from Roger Asshe of Chestrefeld and William Flyntham son and heir of Robert Flyntham, to John Gonor, etc., of a tenement and burgage in Chestrefeld, lying in the fee of the Dean of Lincoln. Witn. Ralph Durand, Roger Bawckewelle, William Bramptone, etc. Dat. Chestrefeld, Annunc. of B. V. M., 7 Hen. V. [1419]. (Woll. i. 83.)

823. GRANT from Richard Hawson, perpetual vicar of Chestrefeld, William Webster, and William Dunham, chaplains, to John Okor, of a messuage and tenement in Chesterfield which they had of the feoffment of Dame Alice, widow of Sir Philip Okor, knt. Witn. Thomas Foliambe, Thurstan de la Boure, John Fayrechilde, etc. Dat. F. of St. John B. [24 June], 8 Hen. V. [1420]. (Foljambe.)

824. RELEASE from Isabella Broun dau. of Robert Porter, to Thomas Baret, John Baret, clerk, and Thomas Gaule, of lands and tenements in Chestrefelde, in a place called the Hynd Hand. Witn. Thurstan del Boure, Will. Brampton, Rob. Brampton, etc. Dat. Chestrefelde, F. of St. Andrew [30 Nov.], 9 Hen. V. [1421]. (Harl. 112 G. 38.)

825. EXTRACT from court-roll of the manor of Chestrefeld, recording that at a great court of the Countess of Kent [Lucy, widow of Edmund Holland, Earl of Kent, *d.* 1407], John Carre received seisin of a stall in the Drapery, to hold for 15 years at a yearly rent of 4*d.* Dat. W. b. F. of St. George [23 Apr.], 10 Hen. V. [1422]. (Foljambe.)

826. GRANT from Johanna Gowle dau. and heir of Richard Gowle to John Leche of two stalls in the "Fyssherow" [in Chesterfield]. Witn. William Brampton, Robert Brampton, Richard Koke, etc. Dat. 1 Aug., 10 Hen. V. [1422]. (Foljambe.)

827. RELEASE from Henry Bothe and William Pyrton, esq., to Richard Cook of Chestrefeld and William Webster, clerk, of all their lands, etc., which lately belonged to John Maweger of Chestrefeld, in Chesterfield, Boythorp, and Hasseland [Hasland]. Witn. Henry Perepount, knt., Thurstan del Boure, esquire, Thomas Swaloc, Thomas Brygge, etc. Dat. F. of St. Hilary [13 Jan.], 1 Hen. VI. [1423]. (Foljambe.)

828. GRANT from Richard Haweson, vicar of Chestrefeld, to Roger de Bawkewell and Margery, his wife, in tail of a messuage in Chestrefeld in "Halywellgate" and 22 acres of land in Newbolt, with remainder in tail successively to John, bastard son of Roger de Bawkewell, and to Robert Collynson of Chapell del Fryth. Witn. Ralph Durant, Thomas Baret. Dat. 1 June, 2 Hen. VI. [1424]. (Foljambe.)

829. GRANT from John Parkar, baker, of Chesturfeld, to Richard Hauson, vicar of Chesturfeld, of a curtilage beyond the bridge at the end of the Sowtergate [in Chesterfield]. Witn. William Marchall, Thomas Sudbery, Gilbert Castelton, etc. Dat. F. of St. Michael [29 Sept.], 1424. (Foljambe.)

830. RELEASE from Thomas Hampton of Marchynton to William Barbour, Thomas Fox, Henry Hervy, chaplain, and Thomas Saer, of three messuages in Chestrefeld, in Halewelgate, and all the lands, etc., which they lately had of the feoffment of Richard Haweson, vicar of Chestrefeld, Ralph Durand, and others. Witn. Robert Plumley, William Plumley, John Lynacre, etc. Dat. Th. b. F. of St. Denis, Bp. [9 Oct.], 3 Hen. VI. [1424]. (Foljambe.)

831. LETTERS patent of Henry VI. to John Cokayn and James Strangways to hold an assise of novel disseisin for the Alderman and Brethren of St. Mary's Guild in the church of All Saints, Chesterfield, against Johanna, widow of Robert Barley of Barleylees. Dat. Westminster, 20 Jan., anno 3 [1425]. (Foljambe.)

832. GRANT from Richard Mellers and Cristiana his wife to Thomas Baret, John Baret, clerk, and Roger Tapton, of a messuage with land called Blithecroft, in Chestrefeld. Witn. William Brampton, Richard Cooke, Thomas Brigge, etc. Dat. Fr. a. Michaelmas, 4 Hen. VI. [1425]. (Harl. 112 I. 60.)

833. GRANT from Thomas Baret, John Baret, clerk, and Thomas Goule to John Leche, of six stalls lying together in the new market of Chestrefeld on the "Fyssherowe." Witn. William Marshall, Thomas Salcroft, Richard Salcroft, etc. Dat. 1 Mar., 4 Hen. VI. [1426]. (Foljambe.)

834. POWER of attorney from the Prior and Convent of Newstead [co. Notts.] to William Chapman to deliver seisin to Thomas Gowle and Thomas Barley, clerk, of a waste tenement in Saltergate in Chestrefeld. Witn. Thomas Baret, William Brampton, Richard Cook, etc. Dat. Newested, 4 Dec., 1426. (Foljambe.)

835. EXTRACT of court-roll of Chestrefeld, recording the admission of John Lech to six burgages, one in "Fissherrowe" and the rest in "Sowterrowe" in Chestrefeld. Dat. W. a. F. of St. Martin [11 Nov.], 6 Hen. VI. [1427]. (Foljambe.)

836. GRANT from Thomas Baret of Chestrefeld to Richard Baret and Katerine, his wife, of lands in Whyngby, Chestrefeld, and Calall, near Haselond. Witn. Will. Bramptone, Ric. Cooke, Rob. Bayly, etc. Dat. Chestrefeld, 16 Jan., 8 Hen. VI. [1430]. (Woll. i. 82.)

837. STATEMENT of the accompt of William Webster, chaplain, collector of the rents of St. Mary the Virgin in the church of All Saints, Chestrefeld, from Michs., 10 [Hen. VI.] to Michs., 11 [Hen. VI.] [1431-1432]. (Foljambe.)

838. GRANT from William Hudson to Thomas Foliamb, esq., Ralph Wode, Thomas Bythewater, and Richard Hadfield, of all the lands, etc., which he had of the grant of William Webster, chaplain, in Halewelgate, in Chestrefeld. Witn. Adam Saer, Henry Smyth, Roger Regotte, etc. Dat. 20 Sept., 15 Hen. VI. [1436]. (Foljambe.)

839. GRANT from Thomas Fox, Richard Innocent, Richard Hawson, chaplain, and Thomas Barley, chaplain, and Roger Tapton, to Hugh Horsyngton and Joan, his wife, of all the lands, etc., which were John Calhall's in Glewmangate and Marketstede in Chestrefeld. Witn. Thomas Calcroft, William Bradeshawe, Thomas Swalowe. Dat. 15 Aug., 17 Hen. VI. [1439]. (Foljambe.)

840. LEASE from Henry Perpount, knt., and the Brethren of the Guild of H. Cross, Chesterfield, to Sir Richard Howson, chaplain, and Richard Howson, jun., his nephew, of half an acre of land by the road leading to Caloll [Calow]. Dat. F. of St. Valentine [14 Feb.]. 22 Hen. VI. [1444]. (Foljambe.)

841. QUITCLAIM from Margery, widow of William Porter, to Thomas Foliambe, Alderman of St. Mary's Guild, Chestrefeld, William Webster, and William Marshall, chaplains of the Guild, and all the members of the same, of all actions on account of her lands, etc., in Chestrefeld. Witn. Richard Hauson, chaplain, William Worsley, etc. Dat. Morr. of F. of Ass. of B. V. M. [15 Aug.], 23 Hen. VI. [1445]. (Foljambe.)

842. GRANT from Thomas Fox of Cold Aston to Thomas Barret in tail, of lands, tenements, etc., which he had of the grant of Thomas Barret, father of the same Thomas, in Chestrefeld, Drownfeld, Neubold, and Tapton, with certain exceptions. Witn. Robert Barley, esquire, John Quyxley, John Owtram, etc. Dat. 10 Sept., 24 Hen. VI. [1445]. (Foljamhe.)

843. GENERAL pardon under the great seal to the Brethren of the Guild of the Holy Cross in All Saints' Church, Chesterfield, for lands purchased in mortmain. Dat. 4 Nov., 25 Hen. VI. [1446]. (Chest. Mun.)

844. GRANT from Adam Saer of Chestrefeld to John Newton of three messuages in Chestrefeld in Haliwelgate, and all his lands, etc., which were formerly Adam Browne's in Chestrefeld, Newbold, and Tapton. Witn. John Fychett, Richard Carre, John Russell, etc. Dat. F. of St. Thomas, Ap. [21 Dec.], 27 Hen. VI. [1448]. (Foljambe.)

845. GRANT from Thomas Foliambe son and heir of Thomas Foliambe, esq., to Henry Foliambe, his brother, for life, of all the lands, etc., in Chestrefeld which he had of the grant of William Webster, chaplain. Witn. Ralph Calcroft, vicar of Chestrefeld, Richard Calcroft, William Bradshaw, etc. Dat. F. of H. Innocents [28 Dec.], 31 Hen. VI. [1452]. (Foljambe.)

846. GRANT from John Tapitur to John [Beaumont], Viscount Beaumont, Ralph Calcroft, vicar of Chesterfield, William Calcroft of Benyngton, and John son of the said John, of all the lands, etc., which he had of the grant of John Myln, chaplain, in Chestrefeld and Newbold. Witn. Richard Calcroft, John Calcroft, Robert Brettener, etc. Dat. Fr. b. Michaelmas, 32 Hen. VI. [1453]. (Foljambe.)

847. DEFEASANCE of a bond from William Owtrem to John Geyte of Thorne, co. York, in £20, conditional on the payment in two instalments of £8, the said John Geyte and Marget, his wife, being also bound in £20 to deliver to William Owtrem an estate "in a place in Betewelstrete," in Chestrefeld. Dat. Th. a. Tr. of St. Thomas [7 July], 34 Hen. VI. [1456]. (Foljambe.)

848. GRANT from Margaret Sympson, sister and heir of William Webster, formerly chaplain of St. Mary's Guild, Chestrefeld, to Thomas Foliambe and James Foliambe, chaplain, of all the lands, etc., in co. Derby which the said William had of the grant and feoffment of John Calall. Dat. Fr. a. F. of St. Gregory [12 Mar.], 36 Hen. VI. [1458]. (Foljambe.)

849. LEASE from Robert Barley, esq., Alderman of the Guild of the H. Cross of Chestrefeld, and the Brethren of the same, to Richard Wyntour and Joan, his wife, of three burgages in "Potterraw." Dat. 1460. (Foljambe.)

850. GRANT from Richard Carre of Chestrefeld, sen., to Henry Buntyng, of two messuages in Chestrefeld, in Knyfesmythgate. Witn. Richard Asche, James Masse, John Dale, etc. Dat. F. of St. Bartholomew [24 Aug.], 38 Hen. VI. [1460]. (Foljambe.)

851. LEASE from Ralph Hall to William Cley of Wynfeld of a tenement, etc. [in Chesterfield] which the said Ralph had of the demise of the Abbey of Beauchief, to hold for 96 years, paying after the first 10 years 8s. 6d. to the Abbey. Dat. 14 Mar., 2 Edw. IV. [1462]. (Foljambe.)

852. CHARTER of King Edward IV. to the Burgesses of Chesterfield confirming the charter of King Henry III. Dat. Westminster, 17 Aug., anno 4 [1464]. (Chest. Mun.)

853. INDENTURE by which Peter Burrell, sub-chanter, and the Company of Vicars covenant, in consideration of lands in Chesterfield and [Shenstone, co. Staff.], of a pension from Dale Abbey and other emoluments given them by Dean Heywood, to say a daily mass before the Image of Jesus. *Circa* 1472. (Lichfield K. 5.)

854. QUITCLAIM from John [Talbot], third Earl of Shrewsbury, to Master Thomas Heywode, Dean of Lichfield, and William Hukyns, chaplain, of a messuage in Chestrefeld and land in Shenston [Shenstone, co. Staff.]. Dat. Lichfield, 3 Feb., 12 Edw. IV. [1473]. (Stowe 48.)

855. POWER of attorney from Thomas Balle, chaplain, to John Foliambe of Walton, gent., and John Northege, chaplain, to deliver seisin to Henry Foliambe, lord of Walton, of a stall in Chastrefeld between Drapurrowe and Fleshamulz, of an acre of land in Boythorp on Ashland, and of all his lands in Boythorp, in the fee of Peersie and in Ekyngton. Dat. Walton, Fr. b. F. of Ann. of B. V. M. [25 Mar.], 13 Edw. IV. [1473]. (Foljambe.)

856. GRANT from John Ethcote of Chestrefeld, mercer, and William Whythyll of Brampton, smith, to Christopher Todd of Walton, yeoman, and Henry Cantrell of the same, husbandman, of their estate in lands, etc., in Chestrefeld and in the fees of Newbold, Brampton, and Boythorp, at a yearly rent of £3 16s. 8d. to the abbot of Beauchief. Dat. F. of St. George [23 Apr.], 17 Edw. IV. [1477]. (Foljambe.)

857. POWER of attorney from Thomas son and heir of Thrustan Blakwall and Johanna, his wife, late of Chesterfelde, to Henry Foliambe, esq., to receive seisin of all their lands, etc., in Chesterfelde and to deliver and answer for the same in the King's Court there held, for three years. Dat. Walton, Wed. b. F. of S. Laurence [10 Aug.], 18 Edw. IV. [1478]. (Foljambe.)

858. DEED of sale by Thomas Blackwall, late of Chestrefeld, to Henry Foliambe, of Walton, " suyer," of a tenement called " the Hartle " in Chesterfeld, in the market " on the northe partte yᵉ cros," the said Henry to pay for the same £19 13s. 4d. Dat. M. b. F. of Ex. of H. Cross [14 Sept.], 18 Edw. [1478]. (Foljambe.)

859. LETTERS of Thomas, Abbot of Beauchief, appointing Henry Foliambe, esq., to be receiver of rents and bailiff for the abbey in Chesterfeld, Brampton, and Hethe, for the life of the said abbot, paying yearly from the proceeds eight marks to the chaplain of the Holy Cross Gild at Chesterfeld, and rendering a yearly accompt. Dat. Dronfeld, 12 July, 19 Edw. IV. [1479]. (Foljambe.)

860. COMPOSITION made " be the avyse of Robert Gryssop then beyng Alderman of the Burgh of Chestrefeld " with the whole commonalty of the Borough, for the good government of the same. Dat. 3 Mar., 19 Edw. IV. [1480]. (Chest. Mun.)

861. LETTERS patent of King Edward IV. to the Burgesses of Chesterfield, confirming to them the privileges which they possessed as tenants " de antiquo dominio Corone Anglie." Dat. Westminster, 12 May, anno 20 [1480]. (Chest. Mun.)

862. GRANT from Richard Lostowe, late of Chestrefeld, " mylner," to Ralph, his son, and Alice, wife of the said Ralph, of a tenement in Chestrefeld on the western side of the New market. Witn. John Foliambe, gentilman, John Assh, Thomas Harvy, etc. Dat. Chestrefeld, F. of Corpus Christi [1 June], 20 Edw. IV. [1480]. (Foljambe.)

863. BOND from Thomas Hampton of Leycester, brother and heir of John Hampton, to Richard Hethcote, in £20, for warranty of a messuage and lands in Chesterfield, Tapton, and Neubold, lately belonging to John Hampton. Dat. 22 July, 20 Edw. IV. [1480]. (Foljambe.)

864. AWARD by William Attkynson, mercer, John Schentowe, and others, that Thomas Calcrofte, son of Richard Calcrofte, shall cause his feoffees to make an estate to himself and the heirs of his body of a messuage, etc., in Chestrefeld in the Newe Market, with remainder to Johanna, wife of Thomas White, and the heirs of their bodies; and that in the event of his having issue, "his said issue that shalbe his heire" shall pay to the said Johanna 20 marks. Dat. Chestrefeld, 30 May, 1 Edw. V. [1483]. (Foljambe.)

865. RELEASE from John Smale of Allerhampton, co. Staff., barber, Thomas Smale, yeoman, and William Smale, yeoman, to Richard Heithcote of Chestrefeld, brasier, of all lands, etc., which he had by grant from Thomas Hampton, their uncle. Witn. Sir Ralph Cantrell, perpet. vicar of Chesterfield, Ralph Vernon, etc. Dat. Chesterfield, 23 Mar., 1 Ric. III. [1484]. (Foljambe.)

866. RELEASE from John Fox of Cold Aston, near Dranefeld, to Henry Foliambe of Walton, sen., of lands, etc., in Chestrefeld, Newbold, Donston, Langley, etc., which Thomas Fox, his father, had of the grant of Tho. Barrett, sen., and which should descend to him after the death of Thomas Barrett, clerk, son of Tho. Barrett, jun., son of Thomas aforesaid. Witn. Henry Vernon, John Leyke, Ralph Vernon, esqq., etc. Dat. Walton, Th. a. F. of St. Andrew [30 Nov.], 2 Ric. III. [1484]. (Foljambe.)

867. DECLARATION by Sir Thomas Balle, "prest," that neither John Calcroft, "ne his brodur Sir Rauffe Calcroft, yᵗ was vycarr off Chesterfeld, ne Thomas Calcroft fadur off yᵉ forsayd John and Rauffe," ever bought any land of his father his mother or himself, but that when he "was yonge and went vnto yᵉ scole, my fadur and my moder were ryght pore and the sayd Rauffe Calcrofte vycarr dyd rewarde theym and me dyverrs tymes towarde my scole hyre and tuke apon hym and occupyed suche lyffelod as we hadde, some in the feldez and some in yᵉ towne. Bot I ne nodur of theym never gaffe ne sold one fote off lyfflod bot one plas to Sir Richard Fleycher preste and geff on to Henry Foliambe esquyer all myne odur landes and tenementes," etc. Dat. Chesterfeld, 13 Apr., 2 Ric. III. [1485]. (Foljambe.)

868. GRANT from Henry Foliambe to John Rollesley of Rollesley, jun., John Dethykke of Braydesall, John Rollesley, son of Will. Rollesley, and William Dethykke, rector of Braydesall, of a yearly rent of eight marks from lands, etc., late John Barley's of Chestrefeld, and had by the said Henry from John Rollesley first named (excepting one place called "le halle of stage"), to hold the same for the life of the survivor of Robert Barley, son of John Barley, and Alice, his wife. Dat. 23 Dec., 2 Hen. VII. [1486]. (Foljambe.)

869. GRANT from Philip Lech, esq., to Richard Borowes, late of Chestrefeld, of a yearly rent of 6s. 8d., with right of distraint on his lands, etc., in Chestrefeld. Witn. James Walker, Thurstan Folow, Tho. Fox, etc. Dat. F. of St. Wulstan, Conf. [19 Jan.], 2 Hen. VII. [1487]. (Foljambe.)

870. ACQUITTANCE from Robert Barley of Barley Lees, jun., son and heir of Robert Barley of Barley, sen., esq., to Henry Foliambe, esq., for £4 received by the hands of Thomas Foliambe in the parish church of Chestrefeld, in presence of Richard Asshe, alderman, and others, in part payment of £20 due by virtue of an arbitration of John Savage, jun., knt. Dat. Chestrefeld, F. of Pur. of B. V. M. [2 Feb.], 2 Hen. VII. [1487]. (Foljambe.)

871. ACQUITTANCE from Robert Barley of Barley, sen., esq., Elena, his wife, and Thomas, his son, to Henry Foliambe, esq., for 10 marks, paid in the parish church of Chestrefeld in presence of Richard Asshe, alderman, and others, in part payment of 110 marks due on an award of John Savage, jun., knt. Dat. Chestrefeld, F. of Nat. of St. John B. [24 June], 2 Hen. VII. [1487]. (Foljambe.)

872. GRANT from John Tomson, Alderman of the Gild of St. Mary in All Saints' Church, Chesterfield, and the Brethren and Sisters of the same, to Richard Oxle, chaplain, of a messuage opposite the church in Chesterfield, in which Laurence Pyper, late chaplain of the said Gild, formerly dwelt, together with a yearly rent or salary of 100s., with wine and light, to hold the same for life, on condition that he celebrate mass for the Gild and be present in the choir on Sundays and festivals, etc. Dat. Christmas Day, 1488. (Foljambe.)

873. CHARTER of King Henry VII., confirming to the Burgesses of Chesterfield the charters of King Henry III. and King Edward IV. Dat. Westminster, 28 Oct., anno 10 [1494]. (Chest. Mun.)

874. LEASE from the Aldermen, Brethren, and Sisters of the Guild of the Blessed Virgin at Chesterfield to William Hervy, son and heir of Thomas Hervy, bocher, of an enclosure called Saintmareleys, lying between Cuttholme-lane and Brampton More, and a half acre of land in Loundmedowe; to hold for 21 years at a yearly rent of 15s. Dat. Chesterfield, F. of St. Valentine [14 Feb.], 1495[6]. (Bemrose.)

875. CHARTER of King Henry VIII. confirming to the Burgesses of Chesterfield the charters of Kings Henry III., Edward IV., and Henry VII. Dat. Westminster, 24 May, anno 3 [1511]. (Chest. Mun.)

876. CHARTER of King Edward VI. confirming to the Burgesses of Chesterfield the charters of Kings Henry III., Edward IV., Henry VII., and Henry VIII. Dat. Westminster, 28 Nov., anno 2 [1548]. (Chest. Mun.)

877. LETTERS patent of King Henry VIII. confirming a charter (dated 25 Sept., 1392) of King Richard II. (accidentally lost), and now seen on the Chancery Rolls, whereby the latter granted licence to Thomas Durant, John de Mannfield, Richard de Chesterfield, clerk, and John Innocent, to be a fraternity and guild in the church of All Saints, Chesterfield, in honour of the Blessed Virgin Mary. Dat. 26 Nov., anno 32 [1540]. (Chest. Mun.)

878. FINE from Godfrey Foljambe to Humphrey Roe of a hundred messuages, etc., in Chesterfelde, Newbold, Langley, Wyngarworth, Thawthwyk [? Swathwick, nr. Wingerworth], Beley, Bradwey, Byrchett, Grenehyll, Norton, Ounston, Somerlees, Draunfelde, Haston [Coal Aston], Hanley, Woodhall, Ekyngton, Beghton, Derby, Norton Leys,

Wurkysworth, Bonsall, Over Haddon, Abney, Hawpe, Castelton, Brampton, Tapton, Wyttyngton, Bremyngton, and Matlok, co. Derby. Dat. Martinmas Term, 33 Hen. VIII. [1541]. (Woll. ii. 71.)

CHESTERFIELD *v.* also under BOYTHORPE, CALOW, DERBY, EYAM, TEMPLE NORMANTON, STAVELEY, TUPTON, WALTON.

CLIFTON, NEAR ASHBOURNE.

(CLIFFTONE, CLIFTONE, CLUFFTON.)

879. CONFIRMATION by Serlo fil. Serlonis de Grendone to Sara de Mungay of land which William, his brother, held from William de Cliftona in the territory of Cliftone. Witn. Robert de Bellafide, Geoffrey Selvein, Nigel de Prestewde, Richard de Okebroc, Ranulf de Shirleia, etc. Early 13th cent. (Woll. ix. 8.)

880. GRANT from Richard de Cubbeleg' to William de Cubbeleg' his son, of a toft in Parva Clifton, lying between the toft of Philip Sacerdos and the toft of William de la Launde. Witn. Simon de Clifftone, William de la Launde, Thomas fil. Heruici, Roger fil. Heruici, Richard fil. Heruici, Robert de Cubbeleg', Richard le Yeph, Alexander mercator, William de Esseburn'. Early Hen. III. (Drury.)

881. RELEASE from Matilda quondam uxor Hugonis de Aula de Wyardestone to Nicholas fil. . . . de Marchyntone, of a messuage in Parva Cliftone. Witn. Will. le Chapman, Henry de Cobbeleye, etc. *Temp.* Hen. III. (Woll. ix. 46.)

882. GRANT from Robert fil. Roberti fil. Willelmi de Parva Clifton capellanus, to Ralph de Derby of Bradeleye, baker, and the heirs of his body by Lettice, his wife, of a piece of meadow in Little Clifton near the highway leading from Assheburn to Clifton, called Parodys. Witn. John fil. Rudulfi de Bradeleye, baker, John de Roucestre, Henry Aleynknaue, Simon de Rossinton. Dat. apud Parva Clifton, Sat. b. Pur. of B. V. M. [2 Feb.], 11 Edw. III. [1337]. (Okeover.)

883. GRANT from Margery de Cluffton fil. Roberti de Coblay sister and heir of John fil. dicti Roberti to John Cokayn "le Uncle," Richard Welbek of Campeden, Henry Wallour of Asscheburn, Robert de Clufftone, and Henry Wallour, chaplains, of all her lands in Cluffton and Compeden, co. Derb. Witn. Richard Spicer of Assheburn, Richard de Makenay, John de Mapulton, etc. Dat. Compedenn, 28 Dec., 5 Ric. II. [1381]. (Drury.)

CLIFTON *v.* also under ASHBOURNE.

CLOWN.

884. MARRIAGE settlement between Robert Eyre son of Robert Eyre of Padley and Elizabeth daughter of Nicholas Hodelston, by which lands in Romley [in Clown], Stauely, Tadynton, and Hope are given by the said Robert Eyre, the father, in trust to Thomas Fitz-William, sen., and Thomas Fitzwilliam, jun., esquires, Roger Eyre, Richard Alestre, Thomas Wymbische, and Thomas Byngham. Dat. 30 Dec., 11 Edw. IV. [1471]. (Harl. 83 E. 32.)

COAL ASTON *v.* ASTON, COAL.

CODNOR.

(CODENORE, CODENOVERE, CODNORE.)

885. LEASE, for 20 years, from John fil. Jermani de Codenovere to Thomas fil. Henrici Columbel of the same, of lands in Codenovere, abutting on the wood of Denaby, etc. (other boundaries given at great length). Rent, an apple. Witn. Henry Columbel of Codenovere, Adam Haneby, John de Bosco, etc. Dat. Michaelmas, 1285. (Woll. iv. 7.)

886. GRANT from John fil. et her. Germani de Codenouere to Thomas fil. Henrici Columbel of the same, of land, with buildings upon it, in Codenovere; rent, 5*s.* Witn. William, dominus de Henouere, Henry Columb of Codenovere, Eudo de Henovere, etc. *Temp.* Edw. II. (Woll. iv. 6.)

887. GRANT from Henry Columbel of Codenovere to Aleyn Columbel, his brother, of a place of land called Patecroft [in Codnor]. Witn. Rob. de Henovere, Will de Findren, Will de Draycote, etc. Dat. 6 May, 3 Edw. III. [1329]. (Woll. iv. 9.)

888. AGREEMENT for reversion of the land granted in the preceding charter to the grantor, failing right heirs of the grantee. Dat. 7 May, 3 Edw. III. [1329]. French. (Woll. iv. 8.)

889. GRANT from Henry Columbel of Codenore to Aleyn Columbel, his brother, of an acre of land in Codenore at Lodhil in exchange for three roods called Hillok-leheia. Dat. Codnor, 20 May, 19 Edw. III. [1345]. French. (Woll. iv. 11.)

890. DEFEASANCE by Henry Chaumberleyn of a grant from Henry Columbel of Codenore of a place and thirty sellions of land, on payment of 15*s.* 6*d.* Dat. Codenore, S. a. F. of St. Peter ad-vincula [1 Aug.], 1349. (Woll. iv. 16.)

891. GRANT from Richard de Basyngs of Codenore to Henry, his son, of Margaret fil. Johanne fil. Willelmi le Warde, his "nativa," whom he had of the gift of Dom. Richard de Wilughby, sen., mil., together with the lands of John le Ward in Codenore. Witn. Henry de Grey, sen., Walter de Ros, clerk, Will. Ferrour of Neuthorp, etc. Dat. Henore, F. of St. Peter ad-vincula, 33 Edw. III. [1359]. (Woll. iv. 13.)

892. GRANT from Richard de Basing, "pistor quondam domini Johannis domini de Codnore," to Roger le Koc of the same and Cecily, his wife, daughter of the said Richard, of all the lands in Codenore, late John le Warde's; rent 10*s.* Witn. William de Draycote of Loschowe [Loscoe], Richard de Draycote, Adam Webster, etc. Dat. F. of St. Petronilla [31 May], 2 Hen. IV. [1401]. (Woll. iv. 18.)

893. GRANT from Thomas Columbell of Thorpe "in glebis," armiger, to Thomas Colville of Codenore, of lands in Codenore. Witn. John Lord de Grey, knt., Henry Grey, Ric. Newport, armigeri. Dat. 10 Mar., 7 Hen. VI. [1429]. (Woll. iv. 17.)

894. POWER of attorney by Roger Coke of Codnore and Cecily, his wife, to Henry Statham of Morley and Thomas Curtes of Codenore, to deliver to Henry Coke of Codnor, a messuage and three crofts there. Dat. Codnore, M. a. F. of St. Thomas, M. [29 Dec.], 17 Hen. VI. [1439]. (Woll. iv. 15.)

895. LEASE, for 18 years, from John Coke of Langley to Henry Coke, John son of Richard de Guallay, etc., of a messuage and two bovates of land in C[odenore ?] called Ward land; rent 12s. Dat. F. of St. Luke [18 Oct.], 1443. (Woll. iv. 14.)

896. MEMORANDUM of the Auditor of the deficit in the accounts of John Clerk, bailiff, collector of rents for the dower of Elizabeth, Lady de Grey, in the demesne of Codnore, for the year commencing F. of St. Martin [11 Nov.], 27 Hen. VI. [1448]. (Woll. iv. 34.)

897. POWER of attorney from John Combe and Elizabeth, his wife, to Roger de Parsones of Codnore, to deliver to John Clerk of the same a messuage and lands in Codnore. Dat. M. b. F. of St. Michael, 28 Hen. VI. [1449]. (Woll. iv. 23.)

898. EXCHANGE, for 20 years, by Henry Cook of Codnor with John Clerk, Parker of Codnor Park, of half an acre of land called " Blake ote acre " · and half an acre lying in the Park-furlong, on condition that " yf yᵉʳ be any myne of cole gate of yᵉ said half acre cald blake ote acre yᵗ then yᵉ said John Clerk schall deliver yerly vnto yᵉ said Henry or to his assignes iii roke cole duryng yᵉ myne of yᵉ said half acre." Witn. John Wawden, bailiff of Codnor, Roger Rage, John Tymborhill. Dat. 20 Jan., 28 Hen. VI. [1450]. (Woll. iv. 26.)

899. MEMORANDUM by the Auditors of the surplus in the accounts of John Clerk, bailiff, collector of rents for the dower of Elizabeth, Lady de Grey, in the demesne of Codnore, from the F. of St. Martin Bp. [11 Nov.] to 5 Aug., 29 Hen. VI. [1450-1]. (Woll. iv. 32.)

900. ORDER by Henry, Lord de Gray, to the bailiff of his manor of Codnor, after inspecting Letters Patent of Henry, Lord de Grey, his father, confirming to John Clarke of Strounsell the custody of his parks of Codnor and Aldecar, with a daily payment of 2d. Dat. Codnor, 20 Jan., 37 Hen. VI. [1459]. (Woll. iv. 31.)

901. QUITCLAIM from Henry, Dominus de Gray, to John Broke and Joan, his wife, and their heirs, of a messuage and bovate of land in Codnore, which they lately acquired from Henry, Dominus de Gray, his father. Witn. Richard Malore, constable of Codnor Castle, John Fonglay, rector of Henore, William Lacc, etc. Dat. 20 Feb., 37 Hen. VI. [1459]. (Reliquary xi. 51.)

902. SALE, for £17 10s., by Herry Grey, knt., Lord Grey [of Codnor], and Dame Margaret, his wife, to William Roodes of Notyngham of all trees, wood, underwood, etc., lying between Boterley Park and Codnor Park, to Michaelmas, 1478. Dat. 23 Apr., 14 Edw. IV. [1474]. (Woll. iv. 22.)

903. LEASE, for nine years, from Robert Rempstone, esq., to John Clerk of Codnor, of lands in Codnor; rent, 13s. 4d., in defeasance of a grant by the said John of the same lands to the said Robert for 10 marks. Dat. Decoll. of St. John B. [29 Aug.], 14 Edw. IV. [1474]. (Woll. iv. 20.)

904. POWER of attorney from Robert Rempstone, esq., to William Chadwyk and William Roodes, to receive lands in Codnore. Dat. 27 Aug., 14 Edw. IV. [1474]. (Woll. iv. 21.)

905. INDENTURE between Sir John St. John and Sir Henry Willoughby, knts., and Thomas Leeke and Roger Johnson, recoverers of divers lands, etc., of the late Henry, Lord Grey. A bargain was made between Lord Grey and John Zouche for sale and purchase of the manor and castle of Codnore and the manors and lordships of Henor, Losco, and Langley, and of Estwayte, co. Notts., all which Zouche was to have immediately on the decease of Lord Grey; and of the reversion of his lands in Bitame and Castle Bitame, co. Lincoln, and of lands in Essex and Kent worth £100 yearly, belonging to the said lord, which Zouche was to have on the decease of Katherine, wife of Lord Grey, paying therefor 600 marcs, of which £100 is paid to Dame Katherine, executrix and late wife to Lord Grey, and to the said Tho. Leek. Thomas and Roger now agree to make to Sir John and Sir Henry (at cost of latter) a sufficient and lawful estate of premises in cos. Derby and Notts. Dat. 18 Aug., 15 Hen. VII. [1500]. (P. R. O., A. 547, 548.)

906. LEASE, for 10 years, from Thomas Cooke of Codnor, yeoman, to Thomas Clerk of the same, yeoman, of lands in Codnor and Heighnor; rent, 19s. Dat. F. of St. Martin [11 Nov.], 8 Hen. VIII. [1516]. (Woll. iv. 25.)

907. DECREE in a suit between Sir Robert Peygden *al.* Pygden, priest, complainant, and George Zouche, esq., defendant, before the "King's Counsaille," by which it is determined that the said Robert Peygden is to retain possession of the Free Chapel called St. Nicholas' Chapel, within the castle of Codnor, with the "mancyon house" attached and the commodities attached to the said chapel, to which he was presented by the late John Zouche, knt., by his deed also subscribed by the same George, from which chapel the latter had deforced him. Dat. 11 Feb., 33 Hen. VIII. [1542]. (Bemrose.)

COMPTON *v.* under ASHBOURNE.

COTON-IN-THE-ELMS.

(COTES, COTHES, COTON.)

908. QUITCLAIM from Stephen de Bello Campo to Burton [on Trent] Abbey of the vill of Cotes, which he had unlawfully seized. Late 12th cent. (Stowe 49.) The text is:—

Uniuersis sancte matris ecclesie filiis ad quos presens scriptum peruenerit Stephanus de Bello Campo salutem. Nouerit uniuersitas uestra me reddidisse et quietam clamasse Deo et sancte Marie et sancte Modewenne uirgini de Burtona et monachis ibidem Deo seruientibus uillam de Cotes cum omnibus pertinenciis suis quam iniuste occupaueram in perpetuum pacifice et quiete tenendam et habendam absque omni reclamatione de me uel heredibus meis. Et ut hec quieta clamacio rata et inconcussa perseueret ego presentis scripti testimonio et sigilli mei appositione roboraui. Hiis testibus, Johanne de Cadomo, Galfrido de Wiuerdestan, Hugone clerico de Derebi, Michaele seruiente prioris de Tutesberia et multis aliis.

909. QUITCLAIM from William fil. Warini de Upton to Stephen de Segrave of the vill of Cotes (formerly belonging to Stephen de Bello Campo, who held it from the King), with the consent of the sisters of the said Stephen de Bello Campo, viz., Isolda, Matildis, Alina, and Idona. Witn. Walter de Besebosc, Richard, Abbot of Hales, Walter de Bello Campo, etc. Early Hen. III. (Gresley.)

910. GRANT from Ralph de Arderne, with consent of Alina, his wife (confirmed in presence of King Henry) to Stephen de Segrave, of the land and tenement in Cotes sometime belonging to Stephen de Bello Campo, brother to the said Alina. Witn. R[alph], Bishop of Chichester, Chancellor, R[ichard], Bishop of Durham, J[osceline], Bishop of Bath, W[alter], Bishop of Carlisle, Treasurer, Hugh le Dispenser, Robert de Lexinton. *Circ.* 1230-1235. (Gresley.)

911. GRANT (and confirmation in the king's presence) from Ysolda de Bello Campo to Stephen de Segrave, of the land and tenement in Cotes, sometime belonging to Stephen de Bello Campo, her brother. Same witnesses as in preceding charter, together with Henry de Braibroc. *Circ.* 1230-35. (Gresley.)

912. GRANT from Gilbert de Segrave to Adam fil. Ricardi Pistoris in free marriage with Amabilia fil. Philippi de Wythrne, of a virgate of land in Cothes, which Henry fil. Hoseberti, his naif, held, and a plot of meadow called Brouneshurst with his garden in Cotes; annual rent, 5s. Witn. Dom. Rich. de Mundevylle, Dom. Adam Maweyswn, Dom. Will. de Wasteneys, Ralph Camerarius, jun., etc. *Temp.* Hen. III. [1241-1254]. (Gresley.)

913. GRANT from Isolda, que fuit uxor Nicholai le Mulner de Coton, to William Scot de Rostelaston of land in the fields of Coton, lying on le Haystowe, Le Hascheforlong, and at Le Breche. Witn. Richard Isabel de Rostelaston, Ralph Mareys de eadem, William Talbot, etc. Dat. Coton, M. a. F. of Ann. of B. V. M. [25 Mar.], 21 Edw. III. [1347]. (Gresley.)

914. QUITCLAIM from Matilda, quondam uxor Thome Baron de Rostliston to Richard Heyne de Melborne of all the lands and tenements in Rosliston and Coton, which sometime belonged to Thomas, her husband. Dat. Yclyngton, 1 Jan., 1 Ric. II. [1378]. (Gresley.)

COTON-IN-THE-ELMS *v.* also under BRETBY, REPTON, ROSLISTON.

COWLEY.

(COLLEY.)

915. GRANT from Colleta, widow of Hugh de Mornsale, to Peter Mote and Margery, his wife, and Bawdwyn, their son and heir, of a moiety of all the lands which descended to her from her parents in Colley. Witn. William de Bontessale, William Bulneys, rector, Hugh Orenge. Dat. Derleye, M. a. F. of St. John, a.p.l. [6 May], 43 Edw. III. [1369]. (Hallowes.)

COWLEY *v.* also under WIGLEY.

CRICH.

(CROUCH, CRUCH, CRUCHE, CRYCH.)

916. COPY (16th cent.) of a confirmation, for 20s., by Hubert fil. Radulfi to Peter de Wakebrugg fil. Ranulfi of land which he held in the time of Peter, his uncle, except the dower which the said Hubert gave him with Emma, his daughter, in Cruch and Suth Kethorne; rent, a pound of pepper. Witn. Robert Daincurt, parson of Scardeclif, Geoffrey de Musters, Peter de Dethec, etc. Early 13th cent. (?). (Woll. vi. 49.)

917. ACKNOWLEDGMENT by Brian de Bromtone of the receipt of £120 from Richard son and heir of William de Grey, for the ward of the manor of Cruch which the king granted him during the minority of the heirs of Dom. Anker de Frecheuile. Dat. Warewic, F. of SS. Peter and Paul [29 June], 54 Hen. III. [1270]. (Harl. 86 G. 55.)

918. MEMORANDUM that on the F. of St. Stephen [26 Dec.], 22 Edw. I. [1293], Richard de Grey surrendered to Ralph de Frecheville, at Cruch, by the hands of William Karewalle, 23 charters and deeds, which had been kept in his custody. (Harl. 46 H. 20.)

919. SALE by Ralph de Frecheuuile of Cruch to Dom. John Giffard of Chilintone, mil., of the wardship and marriage of Ralph fil. et her. Radulfi de Latheberi, or, in case of his death, of Robert, his brother. For the performance of which the said Ralph binds himself in £200. Witn. Dom. Hugh de Meverel, Dom. Robert de Touke, Dom. John de Beufyis, etc. *Temp.* Edw. II. (Woll. ix. 31.)

920. COPY of an acquittance by Ralph de Frecheville to Peter de Wakebrugg, for 4s. 8d. and a pound of pepper, for certain reliefs and services. Witn. Geoffrey de Stanford, steward, Geoffrey de Plaustowe. Dat. Crouch, T. b. F. of SS. Philip and James [1 May], 9 Edw. II. [1316]. (Woll. vi. 50.)

921. LETTERS Patent of Edw. III., whereby, in consideration of 10 marks paid by William de Wakebrugge, licence is granted to the Prior and Convent of Thurgarton, co. Notts., to tax their manors of Thurgarton, Fyskertone, Morton, Houryngham, and Crophulle Botiler [Fiskerton, Hoveringham, Cropwell Butler, co. Notts.], in £6 of annual rent for the support of a chaplain to pray for the good estate of the King and of Philippa [of Hainault], the Queen, of Edward, Prince of Aquitaine [the Black Prince], and the said William and Elizabeth, his wife, in the church of Cruch; and in a like rent of 40s. to Richard David, chaplain of the chantry of SS. Nicholas and Katerine in the same church, founded by the said William, and in a like rent of 20s. to Richard Walesby, chaplain at the chapel of St. John the Baptist and St. John the Evangelist of Normanton next Southwell. Dat. Westm., 10 Feb., 42 Edw. III. [1368]. (Woll. iv. 58.)

922. GRANT from William de Kynardesey to William de Dethek, knt., of the manor of La Lee [in Crich], with its appurtenances in Schokthorn, Wetecroft, Plastowe, Wakebrug, and Holewaus; to hold by rent of a rose at Midsummer. Dat. Dethek, M. a. F. of St. Hilary [13 Jan.], 15 Ric. II. [1392]. (Holland.)

923. LEASE, for 60 years, from Elyzabeth, Prioress of the Nunnery of Derby, to John Pole, son and heir of Rauff Pole of Wakebruge of a field called Nunnefeld in Crych; rent, 4s. Dat. 30 May, 6 Hen. VIII. [1514]. (Woll. iv. 51.)

924. EXTRACT from a document containing particulars of a grant by Henry VIII. to John Bellowe and Robert Bygott of a close called Nonneclose or Nonnefeld, lying in Barrowcote or Borowcote, in Criche, late belonging to the Priory of De Pratis *al* Kyngesmedes. Dat. Westm., 22 Nov. aº. 38 [1546]. (Woll. x. 68.)

8

925. Court-roll of Wessington and Cruche. *Temp.* Hen. VIII. (Woll. x. 9*.)

CRICH *v.* also under Plaistow, Tansley, Wirksworth.

CROMFORD.

(Crumford.)

926. Release, for four marks, from Agnes, fil. Ranulfi de Crumforde, widow, to John, her son and heir, of two bovates of land in Crumford. Witn. Jurdan de Snitertone, Robert de Esseburne, John fil. Gamel, etc. *Temp.* Hen. III. (Woll. viii. 16.)

CROMFORD *v.* also under Wirksworth.

CROXALL.

(Croxhall)|

927. Lease from the Abbot and Convent of Welbeck to John, Duke of Lancaster, of the pasture of Croxhall [Crukhull] and all the buildings thereon, as fully and entirely as the charters of King John purport, for term of three years, at 10 marks rent per annum. Dat. F. of St. Bartholomew [Aug. 24], 17 Ric. II. [1393]. (D. of L.)

CROXALL *v.* also under Catton.

CUBLEY.

(Cobbelag, Cobele.)

928. Grant from Ralph Pyppard to Ralph de Lathebury, his chamberlain, of a rent of 10s. from Bussuns [in Cubley]. Witn. Dom. Henry de Braylesford, Giles de Meynill, John de Bakepuz, milites, etc. Dat. Rutherfeld Pippard [Rotherfield Peppard, co. Oxon], S. a. F. of SS. Philip and James [1 May], 31 Edw. I. [1303]. (Woll. ix. 28.)

929. Grant, for life, from Walter de Montegomery to Alan Molendinarius [Miller] of Cobele, of the mill of Cobele; rent, four marks. Witn. Richard le Foun, Ralph de Bakepus, Henry de Bentle, etc. Dat. Th. b. Nat. of B. V. M. [8 Sept.], 31 Edw. I. [1303]. (Woll. ix. 52.)

930. Grant from William Sapurton, capellanus, and John Roger to Walter Mountegomery in tail male of the manors of Cubley, Sudbury, and Aston, with all other the lands which they had of the grant of the said Walter in Hill Somersall and Potter Somersall. Witn. William de Waryngton, William Bochervyl of Sudbury, Nicholas Mountegomery. Dat. 10 May, 15 Edw. III [1341]. (Foljambe.)

931. Grant from Walter Mountegomery to William Akover, dominus de Snelleston, of the manors of Cobbelag, Marston Mountegomery, and all his lands at Snelleston, to the grantor's use for his life, with remainder in tail male to the use of Nicholas Mountegomery, his son and heir. Witn. William de Halis, Geoffrey de Mountegomery, Richard de Aula, etc. *Circ.* 1350. (Foljambe.)

DALBURY.

(DALEBIRE.)

932. GRANT, in free marriage, from Robert de Beaufei to Nicholas fil. Walkelini, with Avice, his daughter, of a meadow " inter gardinum de Dalebir' et Litlehul " which Robert fil. Walkel[ini] held from him. Witn. Henry fil. Walk[elini], Hugh, Decanus, Michael de Langeford, Ralph de Bakepuz, Simon de Sancto Mauro, etc. Early 13th cent. (Woll. x. 23.)

DALBURY *v.* also under TRUSLEY.

DALE ABBEY.

(DEPEDAL, DE PARCO STANLE, LA DALE, STANLEY PARK, PARK STANLEY.)

933. CONFIRMATION from Peter de Sandiacre to the House of St. Mary of Depedale of four acres of land which his ancestors gave to the said House, in soul-alms for his wife, his children, and his father; for which grant the Canons of St. Mary of Depedale gave him 12s. Late Hen. II. (Add. 47504.)

Omnibus sancte matris ecclesie filiis ad quos hoc scriptum peruenerit, Petrus de Sandiacre salutem. Nouerit uniuersitas uestra me concessisse et hac presenti carta mea confirmasse Deo et domui Sancte Marie de Depedal quatuor acras terre illas scilicet quas antecessores mei predicte domui dederunt in perpetuam elemosinam pro me et uxore mea et natis meis et pro anima patris mei et omnium antecessorum meorum, libere et quiete ab omnibus seruitiis. Pro hac autem concessione et confirmatione canonici sancte Marie de Depedal dederunt mihi duodecim solidos. His testibus, Roberto de Muscha[mp], et d[u]obus filiis suis scilicet Hugone et Roberto, Hugone de Muscha[mp], Waltero de Hali[n], Roberto de Hereford, Ricardo de Buirun, Willelmo de Grendun, Fucher de Grendun, Hugone del Haie, Willelmo de Egnesham, Roberto de Sallou, et multis aliis.

934. CONFIRMATION from Roger de Strettone to Richard Venator of a grant by Walter [de Senteney], Abbot, and Convent de Parco Stanl' [Dale Abbey] of a tenement held of the Canons there. Witn. Ralph, capellanus de Esseovere, Dom. Roger de Strettone, Adam de Hanley, John de Wakebrige, Robert de Oggediston, William le Venur. *Circ.* 1204-1235. (Woll. vii. 2.)

935. INSPEXIMUS by Alexander [de Stavenby], Bishop of Coventry and Lichfield, of the Bull of Pope Honorius III., confirming to the monks of the Premonstratensian Order certain privileges granted them by his predecessors in reference to the Abbey of Dale or Stanley Park. Dat. Laterani V. Id Maii [11 May], anno 1 Pontif. [1217]. (Woll. xi. 22.)

936. CONFIRMATION from Peter de Sandiacre to the Premonstraten-sian Canons de Parco Stanleie of lands in Sandiacre which Richard fil. Roberti de Stapleford and Philip de Touke gave them. Witn. William de Mucham, Archdeacon of Derby [1199-1231], William de Grendone, Robert persona de Morley, etc. *Temp.* Hen. III. (Woll. vi. 1.)

937. BULL of Pope Gregory [IX.], to the Archbishop of Canterbury and others commanding them to excommunicate those who have injured the Abbot and Brethren de Parco Stanley, if laity, publicly, "candelis accensis," and if clergy, by suspension from office. Dat. Laterani vii. Kal. Febr. [26 Jan.], a° 7 Pontif. [1234]. (Woll. xi. 24.)

938. * DEED by which Robert de Ferrars, son and heir of William de Ferrars, takes the Abbey of Park Stanley under his protection. Dat. Vig. of SS. Philip and James [30 Apr.], 47 Hen. III. [1263]. (Pole-Gell.)

939. BULL of Martin [IV.], Pope, confirming tne iiberties of the Abbey of La Dale, Ord. Præmonstr., Dioc. Lichf., beg. "Cum a nobis petitur." Dat. Citta Vecchia, v. Kal. Maii [27 Apr.], anno 3 Pontif. [1283]. (Woll. xi. 2.)

940. GRANT from Richard fil. Petri de Sandiacre to the Canons "de Parco Stanley" [Dale Abbey] of "totum Wersenape in territorio de Sandiacre" to their use and for common pasture. Witn. R——, Prior de Lenton, Geoffrey de Sallicosa Mara, Robert Le Vavasur, Hugh de Morleg', etc. *Temp.* Edw. I. (Add. 47506.)

941. COPY of charter whereby Richard fil. Petri de Sandiacre confirms to the church and the Canons of St. Mary of Stanley Park in frankalmoigne the whole of his wood of Drisco [in Sandiacre] with the land of the same; also he quitclaims all his right in the wood which is called Blithgare, with the whole of the land from the rivulet of "Bromesbroc" between the park of Chirchehalla and the park of Stanley as far as "in Wacellum," near the park of Chirchehalla, and from thence the whole wood with the land from the aforesaid "Wacellum" to the way dividing the woods of Chirchehalla and Westhala, [Kirk Hallam and West Hallam]. *Temp.* Edw. I. [?]. (Bodl. D.C. 11.)

942. GRANT from William de Bonay, Abbot, and the Convent of Dale to "their very honoured Lord," William la Zouche, "Seygneur de Toteneys et de Haryngworht," and to Dame Agnes la Zouche, his "compaygne," of participation in the privileges, prayers, masses, etc., of the said Abbey, with requiems on their anniversaries, and on those of William la Zouche, father of the said William, who died in A.D. 1385; for Elizabeth "sa compaigne," who died on ix. Kal. Jun.; for Sire Henry de la Grene, knt., father of the above-named Agnes, who died viii Id. August.; for the mother of the said Agnes, who died Prid. Id. Novembr.; for Sire William de Clynton, Earl of Huntingdon, who died ix. Kal. Sept.; and for Dame Juliana, the Countess of Huntingdon. Dat. "al Abbey del Dale," 13 Feb., 1385[6]. Seal of arms of William la Zouche. (Add. 47495.)

943. LEASE, for lives, from the Abbot and Convent of Dale to William Thuryff and Agnes his wife, and to John and Robert his sons, of a messuage in Lamcote juxta Radclyf [Lamcote in Radcliffe, co. Notts.], with meadows, pastures, etc., and a culture of land called Colgrenewong in the fields of Radclyf; rent, 20s., the lessees to keep the houses, etc., in good repair, but the timber to be supplied by the Abbey, who will carry it as far as Nottingham, from whence it is to be carried at the lessees' expense. Dat. Dale, Th. a. Ann. of B. V. M. [25 Mar.], 1404. (Add. 47780.)

---

* This and several other early charters referred to in Historical Commission Report ix, part II, 402, 403, could not be found on my visit to Hopton in August, 1902. I.H.J.

944. COMPOSITION between John Cheyne, Canon of Lichfield and Prebendary of Sandiacre, and Henry, Abbot, and the Convent of Dale, *al.* de parco Stanley, as to the tithes of Whithornedale, between the wood of Warsnapes and Crosflat, and extending from the said Abbey to Sallowe up to the high road from Sandyacre. Dat. 19 Oct., 6 Hen. IV. [1404]. (Lichf. C. 49.)

945. CONFIRMATION by the Bishop and by the Dean and Chapter of Lichfield of a certain composition entered into between the Prebendary of Sandiacre and the Abbot of Dale, concerning certain tithes pertaining to the church of Sandiacre. Dat. 12 June, 1404. (Lichf. C. 50.)

946. BOND from Richard Notingham, Abbot, and the Convent of Dale, to John Knyveton, son of Richard Knyveton of Bradley, esq., in 40 marks, to observe covenants. Dat. Chapter House of the Abbey, 10 Mar., 1 Hen. VIII. [1510]. (Woll. i. 78.)

947. REGISTER of Dale Abbey, containing copies of about five hundred charters of the Abbey. (Cotton MS., Vespasian E. xxvi.)

DALE ABBEY *v.* also under CHESTERFIELD, MAPPERLEY, OCKBROOK, STANTON.

DARLEY.

(DERLAGH, DERLEYE.)

948. GRANT from Ysabel fil. Will. Rupheint of Hackinhale and of Cecilia, quondam uxoris sue fil. Henrici fil. Emme of Derl[eye], to John Magot and Mariota, his wife, of lands in the vill and territory of Derl[eye] and Farnley [Farley, co. Derby], which fell to her on her mother's death; rent, an apple at Christmas. Witn. Ric. de Lancerchumbe, clericus, Hugh fil. Andree de Derl[eye], Rob. de Stanclif, tunc diaconus, etc. *Temp.* Hen. III. (Woll. i. 2.)

949. GRANT from Ranulf de Snutertone to Thomas, his son, of a messuage and land which Henry de Etewelle held in Derlagh and a meadow in Stanclif. Witn. Dom. Robert de Dethek, mil., Roger de Wednisl', John de Suttone, etc. Dat. Derleghe, F. of Ann. of B. V. M. [25 Mar.], 32 Edw. [I. 1304]. (Woll. i. 1.)

950. GRANT from John fil. Ricardi Gerlaund of Derleye to Cecily, que fuit uxor Ricardi Gerlaund, of the same, of a rent of 33s. 4d. from lands within the parish of Derley. Dat. Notingham, W. b. F. of St. Matthew [21 Sept.], 20 Edw. III. [1346]. (Woll. i. 3.)

951. GRANT from Henry de Mapultone, rector of the church of Bonesale [Bonsall], and Richard Wyttlome, chaplain, to Dom. James de Audley, dominus de Audley, John Columbelle of Derley, and Roger Columbelle, of lands in Derley which they held of the feoffment of Richard de Kymburley, clericus de Wynfeld. Witn. John de Rollesle, Roger Wormell, Roger Jacsone, etc. Dat. Derley, F. of St. Michael [29 Sept.], 6 Hen. VI. [1427]. (Woll. i. 4.)

952. MARRIAGE settlement of John, son and heir-apparent of Rauf Wether of Ilom, co. Staff., and Elizabeth Columbell, dau. of Roger Columbell of Derley, co. Derb. Dat. 20 Aug., 11 Hen. VIII. [1519]. (Drury.)

953. COPY of an indenture whereby Sir William Drurye, knt., and Dame Elizabeth, his wife, one of the cousins and heirs of William Plompton, esq., sell to William Nedham of Thornesett, gent., the moiety of the manors of Darley and Edynsoure, with lands in Stanton, Pyllysley, Calton, and Calton Lees, which had descended to the said Elizabeth and to Dame Jane, her sister, wife of Sir John Constable. Dat. 15 May, 1 Edw. VI. [1547]. (Woll. xi. 40.)

954. GRANT from William de Nedham of Thornsett to Elizabeth Nedham, his mother, of an annuity of £10, arising from a moiety of his manor of Derley and other lands in the county. Dat. 14 July, 2 Edw. VI. [1548]. (Hallowes.)

DARLEY ABBEY *v.* under DERBY.

DENBY.

955. GRANT from Richard fil. Gilberti de Kylburne to Richard Kaysse fil. Joh. Kaysse of Kylburne of three acres of land "in parco de Bol" [in Denby], with the wood growing thereon, the said three acres to be measured by the perch of twenty-four feet. Witn. William Weye, John Threesse, William Gourell, etc. Dat. M. a. Inv. of H. Cross [3 May], 8 Hen. VI. [1430]. (Woll. iv. 73.)

956. EXTRACT from court-roll of the Prior of Lenton recording that Margaret, relict of John Horseley, late of Denby, was admitted to a messuage, two bovates of land, etc., in Denby during the minority of her son and heir William de Horseley. Dat. Th. a. F. of St. Luke [18 Oct.], 9 Hen. VI. [1430]. (Drury-Lowe.)

957. GRANT from Laurence Lowe, Dominus de Denby, to George Lowe and Thomas Lowe, his brother, Oliver Blakwall, rector of Barton-in-le-Denys, Nicholas Blakwall, vicar of Beston, Otiwell Lowe, Brian Lowe, sons of the said Laurence, and others, of the manor and lordship of Denby, with lands in Denby and Kilburn. Witn. John, Abbot of Dale, Ralph Saucheverell, esq., John Saucheverell, his son, dominus de Morley, and others. Dat. 1 Apr., 23 Edw. IV. [1483]. (Drury-Lowe.)

958. AWARD by William Huse, knt., Chief Justice of King's Bench, and Sir Guy Fairfax, knt., Justice of King's Bench, in settlement of a dispute between Lord Henry Grey and Laurence Lowe, concerning an annual rent of £19 6s. 8d. out of the manor of Denby, viz., that the said Laurence retain possession of the manor, subject to the payment of the above rent to Lord Grey. Dat. 20 Sept., 5 Hen. VIII. [1513]. (Drury-Lowe.)

959. GRANT from Laurence Lowe, Humphrey Lowe, Ottiwell Low, sons of the said Laurence and George Lowe, his brother, to Henry Grey, Lord Grey, of the said annual rent during his life, reserving the right, if the said annuity be in arrear 40 days, to distrain on their lands in Ashburn, Ofcote, Underwood, Eyton, Stourston, and Bradley, or elsewhere in co. Derby. Dat. 9 Feb., 5 Hen. VIII. [1514]. (Drury-Lowe.)

960. FINE levied at Easter, 20 Hen. VIII. [1529], whereby Richard Paynell and Isabella his wife convey to Anthony Fitzherbert, knt., Justice "de communi Banco'," John Porte, knt., German Pole, Robert

Batley, Robert Lowe, Denis Lowe, and William Mourton, two messuages, 300 acres of land, etc., in Denby, Fenton, Sturston, and Bradley. (Drury-Lowe.)

961. COMMON recovery by Thomas Cokayn, knt., Francis Cokayn, esq., Anthony Lowe, Edmund Cokayn, and Andrew Lowe, against German Pole, esq., and Robert Lowe, gent., of the manor of Denby. Dat. 6 Feb., 24 Hen. VIII. [1533]. (Drury-Lowe.)

962. EXEMPLIFICATION of various records securing the manor of Denby, sometime held by Henry Lord Grey of Codnor, to Vincent Lowe, Anthony Lowe, and others. Dat. 4 July, 36 Hen. VIII. [1544]. (Drury-Lowe.)

963. SALE from Anthony Lowe of Allerwaslegh, esq., to Vincent Lowe of Denby, esq., of all his lands, etc., in Parkhall, Denby and Kylburn. Dat. 4 July, 37 Hen. VIII. [1545]. (Drury-Lowe.)

964. GRANT from Vincent Lowe of Denby, esq., to his second son Jasper of the manor of Parkehall [in Denby], which he acquired from Anthony Lowe of Allerwaslegh, who acquired it from Peter Frechewell of Staley; with power to Stephen, his third son, to give seisin. Dat. 1 Apr., 4 Edw. VI. [1550]. (Drury-Lowe.)

DERBY, COUNTY OF.

965. GRANT to William Ferrers, Earl of Derby, of free warren in all his demesne lands of certain manors in the counties of Lancaster, Derby, and Stafford, and of a market and fair at his manors of Bolton, Uttoxeter, and Haywood. Dat. Hadsock, 14 December, 1251. (D. of L.)

966. COPY (sixteenth century) of the Roll of Knights' fees held of the King *in capite*, in co. Derby, as appeared by an inquisition held before Philip de Wylyby, Chancellor of the Exchequer. [6-8 Edw. I., 1278-80.] (Woll. xi. 1.)

967. EXEMPLIFICATION of divers charters of liberties granted by Henry III. to Simon de Montfort, Earl of Leicester, and William de Ferrers, Earl of Derby, namely, 14 December, 36 Hen. III., 1251, grant to William de Ferrers, Earl of Derby, of free warren in all the demesne lands of his manors in the counties of Stafford, Derby, and Lancaster, and a market and fair at the manors of Bolton, Uttoxeter, and Heywode, etc. Windsor, 22 October, 1331. (D. of L.)

968. INDENTURE between Rondulf Eggerton, esquire, and Robert Woode of Kell, gentleman, by which the said Rondulf agrees to marry Isabella, daughter of Robert Hill, deceased, and of Alice, late his wife, then the said Robert Woode's wife, "before the Nativ. of St. John Bapt. next," if the "said Isabella thereto will be privy and agreeable," and the said Robert Woode and Alice his wife, covenant to settle on Rondulf and Isabella lands, etc., in the county of Derby to the yearly value of six marcs. Dat. 20 Jan., 18 Hen. VII. [1503]. (P. R. O. c. 303.)

DERBY.

969. LETTERS from R——, Prior of the Nunnery of St. Mary-without-Derby [Kingsmead or De Pratis], soliciting alms for the repairs of the edifice, and reciting certain indulgences, of 130 days in all, granted to those who assist. At the foot is a copy of a Bull of Pope Honorius [III. ?] granting an indulgence of 40 days on the same behalf. Dat. Laterani IV. Kal. Apr. [29 Mar.], aᵒ 2. Pontif. [1218]. (Woll. xi. 25.)

970. NOTIFICATION by William Seruelauedy of Derby, of a lease to him by the Abbot and Convent of Burton[-on-Trent] of land in Derby, formerly held by Walter son of William " tinctor," of Esseburn, which he, with consent of Ynga his wife and Symon his son wholly resigned on setting out to the Holy Land; the rent to be paid partly to the Chamberlain of the Abbey and partly to Ralph de Frescherevile, lord of Alwaldeston. Witn. Thomas "juvenis" of Derby, William "juvenis," William de Chaddesden, and Symon Kolle, "prepositi," of Derby, Thomas Chous, etc. *Temp.* Hen. III. (Stowe 50.)

971. LEASE, for life, from William de Exsovere, manens in Derb', to William Caym de Derb', of two acres of arable land in the territory of Derby lying "super Collisleye" near the fields of Chaddesden and of Little Chester. Witn. William Olearius, Robert de Notingham, tunc ballivi Derb', Hugh de Cestrefeld, Thomas Kaym, etc. *Temp.* Hen. III. (Woll. i. 19.)

972. GRANT from Henry fil. Thome de Derb', manens in Parva Cestria, to Ralph de Smallege, faber, manens in Derb' of a rood of arable land in the territory of Derbe lying "subtus Collyslege," which the said Henry had purchased of Juliana, his sister. Witn. Roger le Hostiler in parva Cestria, Roger fil. Radulfi de eadem, Hugh Rypun, etc. *Temp.* Edw. I. (Woll. i. 18.)

973. LEASE for eight years from Thomas fil. Radulfi de Chaddesden to John his brother of all the tenements, etc., in Derby which the said Thomas acquired as heir to his father on his death. Witn. John fil. Gilberti and William Page, bailiffs of Derby, John de Chaddesdon of Derby, William le Wyne of Chaddesdon, Simon de Cestre. Dat. Derby, Michaelmas Day, 1308. (Okeover.)

974. AGREEMENT between Sire William de Alssopp, Abbot, and the Convent of Derleye, Sire Robert de Stretleye, and Richard Martel, lords and parceners of Chilewelle [Chilwell, co. Notts.], and Sire Richard de Grey, Seigneur de Toueton [Toton, co. Notts.], in settlement of a dispute between them, respecting the repairing and cleansing of the mill-dam of Chilewelle, etc. Witn. Sire William le Fitz-Williame, Sire Walter de Gonshulle, Sire John de Mounteneye, Sire Rauf de Rolliston, chivalers, etc. Dat. Codnouere, F. of St. Nicholas [6 Dec.], 8 Edw. II. [1314]. French. (Woll. v. 22.)

975. QUITCLAIM from William fil. Willelmi de Kyrkelongeley to Nicholas de Trouwelle de Derby of a messuage in Derby lying "in vico Fabrorum." Witn. John fil. Gilberti, Coroner of Derby, Hugh Adam, Thomas de Tuttebury, Richard de Liuerpol, etc. Dat. Derby, F. of St. Michael [29 Sept.], 12 Edw. II. [1318]. (Pole-Gell.)

976. LEASE from Roger de Massy de Morleya and Lucy his wife to Pagan le Draper de Derby for six years of a toft, with belongings, lying in The Briggegate at Derby, called Morleyhalleyerd; rent, 5s. silver yearly. Witn. Simon de Cestr., tunc ballivus de Derby, etc. Dat. Derby, T. Vig. of Ann. of B. V. Mary [24 Mar.], 1331. (Add. 5239.)

977. GRANT from Ralph Chaffare de Derby to Thomas de Yerdeleye of a curtilage in Derby lying in Juddekynlone. Witn. William Laverok, John de Bredon, bailiffs of Derby, John de Shardelowe, etc. Dat. Sat. b. Nat. of St. John B. [24 June], 17 Edw. III. [1343]. (Wilmot.)

978. GRANT from Thomas de Yerdeleye de Derby to Simon de Horsseley of Derby of a curtilage in Derby in Juddekynlone. Witn. John de Bynyngton, Walter de Trowell, bailiffs of Derby, John Swanswyre, etc. Dat. S. a. St. Michael's Day [29 Sept.], 18 Edw. III. [1344]. (Wilmot.)

979. QUITCLAIM from Geoffrey fil. Willelmi de Normanton de Derby to John Bate of Derby, jun., of land in Derby lying in Le Parkfeld beyond " le Syk," near land belonging to All Saints' Church. Witn. Walter de Trowell, John de Bynynton, bailiffs of Derby, Peter le Prentys, etc. Dat. S. a. Epiphany [6 Jan.], 18 Edw. III. [1345]. (Wilmot.)

980. GRANT from Edward III. to Henry, Earl of Lancaster, of Derby and of Leicester, in support of the dignity of the earldom of Derby which he had lately assumed, of £40 per annum receivable out of the farm of the town of Derby, together with the Castle of Harestan, co. Derby, by the service of rendering yearly to the King one rose in June, to hold to the said Earl and the heirs male of his body for ever, with reversion to the crown in case of failure of such issue. Dat. Westminster, 10 Nov. [1347]. (D. of L.)

981. GRANT from John de Morleye of Derby to John de Bredon of the same of an acre and a half of arable land in Derby lying in Le Wallfield, namely, in Litteldale, and near the house of the Lepers. Witn. Thomas de Tuttebury, Robert Alibon, bailiffs of Derby, John de Busseby, etc. Dat. M. a. All Saints' Day [1 Nov.], 1352. (Wilmot.)

982. RE-GRANT, for life, from Henry de la Pole to Henry de Wettone of lands in Derby, Cotton [? Cotton Farm, nr. Derby], and Luttechirche [Litchurch]; rent, a rose. Dat. Derby, S. a. F. of St. Denis [9 Oct.], 27 Edw. III. [1353]. French. (Woll. x. 35.)

983. GRANT from John de Bredon of Derby to Walter de Holbrok of an acre and a half of land in Derby lying in le Wallfeld, namely, in Lyteldale and near the Lepers' House. Witn. John Hachet, William de Brayllesford, bailiffs of Derby, Thomas de Yerdeleye, etc. Dat. W. in Easter Week [24 Apr.], 33 Edw. III. [1359]. (Wilmot.)

984. GRANT from John son of Hugh son of Ralph Chapmon of Derby to Robert le Marchale of the same place of a messuage in St. Mary's Street, Derby. Dat. F. of the Concept. of B. V. M. [8 Sept.], 38 Edw. III. [1364]. (P. R. O. B. 1253.)

985. GRANT from William Joly de Derby to John de Stanleye of a tenement in Judkynlone in Derby. Witn. Henry de Bredon, John de Coltmon, bailiffs of Derby, Roger de Notingham, Richard Bunte, etc. Dat. F. of St. Peter in Cathedra [22 Feb.], 39 Edw. III. [1365]. (Wilmot.)

986. GRANT from Richard de Thurmeleye, vicar of Ashbourne, to Thomas Tochet, clerk, and Thomas Foliaumb, of a ' messuage in Derby " in seynte Marigate." Witn. Robert de Murcaston, Roger de Asshe, bailiffs of Derby, William Pakeman, Hugh Adam, John Gybon, etc. Dat. F. of St. Matthias [24 Feb.], 2 Ric. II. [1379]. (Pole-Gell.)

987. GRANT from John de Berde of Derby to Richard de Stathum and Richard de Denton of a messuage with buildings in Derby, opposite the bridge across the Odbroke called "St. Peter's Bridge." Witn. John del Hay and William Payn, bailiffs of Derby, and others. Dat. Derby, 20 Feb., 14 Hen. IV. [1413]. (P. R. O. b. 1250.)

988. QUITCLAIM from John Ive, chaplain, to Robert Jurdan of Asshe, of a tenement in Derby "apud albam crucem" extending from the King's highway to the close of the Friars Preachers of Derby; together with half an acre of arable land in le Parkefeld, near Hedlecrosse, sometime belonging to Thomas Halome of Derby, miller. Dat. Chaddesden, M. a. All Saints' Day [1 Nov.], 5 Hen. VI. [1426]. (Wilmot.)

989. RELEASE from John Bothe of Derby to William Lystere of Little Chester of lands in Bryggecroft, lying next the land of the prebend of All Saints, and between those of the Abbey of Derley and the Dean of Lincoln. Dat. Derby, 10 Mar., 6 Hen. VI. [1428]. (Woll. i. 20.)

990. GENERAL release from John de Taptone of Hemyngton to William Lyster of Little Chestre from all actions, etc. Dat. Derby, S. a. Easter [19 Apr.], 11 Hen. VI. [1433]. (Woll. i. 79.)

991. LETTER from the Prioress of Derby [St. Mary de Pratis] to John [Halse or Hales], Bishop of Lichfield and Coventry, presenting Nicholas Brodwod of the diocese of Lichfield, acolyte, for ordination. Dat. 11 Sept., 1461. (Woll. viii. 61.)

992. QUITCLAIM from Robert son and heir of Thomas Stoke, late merchant of Derby, of a piece of land in Derby at the end of "Bagelone." Dat. 12 Dec., 1 Edw. IV. [1461]. (Wilmot.)

993. ATTORNEY from Hugh Tildesley and Matilda, his wife, to John Tildesley to deliver seisin to William Walker of Derby and Agnes his wife, and Edmund their son, of a garden in Derby, near "Baglone." Dat. 4 Apr., 9 Edw. IV. [1469]. (Wilmot.)

994. GRANT from John Curson of Ketylston, esquire, son and heir of John Curson, to Gralam Roulee, of three acres of land in the fields of Derby lying beyond Derwent, in Sydale, and in le Dychefeld. Witn. John Neuton, bailiff of Derby, Richard Strynger, John Wodehouse. Dat. M. b. St. George's Day [23 Apr.], 12 Edw. IV. [1472]. (Wilmot.)

995. GRANT from Gralam Roulee to William Merlege of three acres of land in the fields of Derby, one acre lying beyond Derwent, extending to Lyneysiche, one acre in Sydale, with one acre in le Dychefeld called Le Coltesacre. Witn. John Newton, bailiff of Derby, John Brid, Roger Justes, etc. Dat. T. a. F. of S. Mark [25 Apr.], 12 Edw. IV. [1472]. (Wilmot.)

996. FRAGMENT from the beginning of a Roll of Courts held at Derby on Thursdays, 4 Febr., 4 March, and 1 Apr., 18-20 Edw. IV. [1479-80]. (Woll. xi. 12.)

997. FEOFFMENT from Henry Foliambe, esquire, to John Savage, jun., knt., John Leeke, sen., esquire, and Humphrey Heyosy, esq., of the site, etc., of the manor of Rodyche [Rowditch], nr. Derby, and of rents of lands in Walton, Brampton, and Normanton, of a tenement in Chesterfield and rent in Brimington, etc. Dat. F. of Nat. of B. V. M. [8 Sept.], 5 Hen. VII. [1489]. (Foljambe.)

998. SALE by Philip Leche of Chattesworth, squier, to William Merlage of Derby of 13 fother of lead, "bool weght and marchaundable," with undertaking to "blok and brend" the same; with bond by William Higden of Cromforth and John Coghen of Hoptone in 100 marks for due performances. Dat. 7 Nov., 7 Hen. VII. [1491]. (Woll. viii. 14.)

999. BOND, in £20, from Richard Stryngar of Derby, grocer, and John Stryngar of the same, mercer, to Roger Justes, Richard Mounford, Roger Robyn, and William Couper, for the payment of twenty marks to John Farynton son of Thomas Farynton, when he reaches the age of twenty-one years, which sum of twenty marks the same Richard "hath taken to his possession with yᵉ warde and kepyng of yᵉ seid John his apprentice"; and in case of the said John's death before he comes of age the said Richard shall "sauf kepe yᵉ seid xx marcs to yᵉ vse and behofe of Rauff Farynton" and of Margaret Farynton, brother and sister of the said John, or the longer liver of them, to Rauff at the age of 21, and to Margaret "hir part" at the time of her marriage or at the age of 21, and in case of the death of all, the money to go to the use of All Saints' Church, according to the terms of the will of Thomas Farynton the father. Dat. 11 July, 9 Hen. VII. [1494]. (Derby Mun.)

1000. LEASE for 16 years from John Clostones and Nicholas Orcherd, "Baylyes," and the Burgesses of Derby to Thomas Waundell, miller, of Derby, of two corn mills and a "sithemyll," with all streams, floodgates, meadows, etc., and a parcel of the weir to the said mills belonging; rent, 100s. Dat. 30 Sept., 3 Hen. VIII. [1511]. (Derby Mun.)

1001. GRANT from George Sely, kinsman and heir of Thomas P[orte ?], namely, son of Margery, sister of the said Thomas, to John Porte, gent., Robert Blagge, Baron of the Exchequer, Thomas Porte, Doctor of Laws, etc., of a tenement in the parish of St. Peter's, Derby, to the use of the said John Porte, with power of attorney. Dat. 5 July, 4 Hen. VIII. [1512]. (Woll. xii. 104.)

1002. GRANT from James Oxle, Richard Shakere, and Edmund Turnour, wardens of the parish church of All Saints, Derby, with consent of the parishioners to John Neuton of a tenement in Baglone in Derby, called "le Churche House." Dat. 6 June, 5 Hen. VIII. [1513]. (Wilmot.)

1003. BOND, in £100, from Edmund Bradshawe of Iderechehay [Idridgehay] to John Neuton, to convey four acres of land in Derby, namely, three acres in Stokkesbrokefeld and one acre in Castelfeld. Dat. 26 Apr., 6 Hen. VIII. [1514]. (Wilmot.)

1004. GRANT from Thomas Shypley, citizen and cordwainer of London, and Elizabeth, his wife, to John Porte of Etwall, esquire, of one messuage in the parish of St. Peter, Derby, between the tenement of the nuns of Derby and the lane called Baglone. Dat. 26 Feb., 10 Hen. VIII. [1519]. Attached is a memorandum that the said John Porte, at the instance of several neighbours, "freely gave unto the seid Thomas and Elizabeth for such necessity and nede as they were in xxs. Alle be it I the same John Porte shewed evydences that the same mesuage with th' appurtenaunces was gyvyn to Harry Punt and to his heirez whos interest in the seid mese I the same John Porte and other to myn use have." (Trusley.)

1005. LEASE, for six years, from John Chapmonn, Wylliam Yerlle, Edward Lentun, and John Watsun, "Chamberlensse of the borughe of Derbe," to Thomas Blakesea, burgess and baker, with consent of "M^r ballywes and theyre breder," and of the "commenallte and by a commen halle allso the same tyme callyd by the commaunde-ment of M^r ballywes for the townys grette nessessite," for the sum of £6 towards "the Reypryascon and makynge of the townys weyre," of a common pasture called "Bradseahay" lying in the fields and parish of St. Peter's, Derby, at a yearly rent of 40*s.* Dat. 28 Feb., 15 Hen. VIII. [1524]. (Derby Mun.)

1006. LEASE from Robert York and Helize Cowper, bayliffes of Derby, and the Burgesses, to John Jonson of Derby, "sherman," and Cristofer Thakker, mercer, of five water-mills, with all streams, flood-gates, meadows, pastures, etc., and also "the weeres to the seid milles belongyng, as Thomas Waundell and William Byngley before tyme held theym," for a term of 41 years, at a yearly rent of £10. Dat. 20 Oct., 1526. (Derby Mun.)

1007, 1008. GRANT (and counterpart) from Ralph Whalley of Bunney (?), co. Notts. (in fulfilment of covenants with William Glossop of Wirksworth, made 8 Aug., 24 Hen. VIII.) to Richard Blakwall of Wirksworth, Ralph Gell, Thomas Thomson, and Peter Wynstanley, of all his lands in Bradmer and Staunford, co. Notts., Kirkeby Bellers, and Markefeyld, co. Leic., and in the town of Derby. Dat. 20 Aug., 24 Henry VIII. [1532]. (Pole-Gell.)

1009. GRANT from William Glossop of Wirksworth to the same feoffees of all his lands, etc., in Wirksworth. Same date. (Pole-Gell.)

1010. LEASE, in perpetuity, from John Johnson and Robert Jepson, bailiffs, and the Burgesses of Derby, to Robert Yorke, of a parcel of ground in Derby late in the holding of Thomas Leez, between the highway on the south, the ground of "Meister Babyngton" on the north, the ground of "Meister Pole" on the east, and the ground of "Meister Babyngton" on the west; rent, 8*d.* Dat. 8 Jan., 25 Hen. VIII. [1534]. (Derby Mun.)

1011. LEASE, for 80 years, from Thomas the Abbot and the Convent of Darley to Richard Hey of Derby, of ten acres of land and two acres of meadow in Derby. Dat. 1 Oct., 30 Hen. VIII. [1538]. (Bodl. D.C. 2.)

1012. EXEMPLIFICATION by Henry VIII., made at the request of Thomas Thacker of Highege, gent., and Gilbert Thacker his son of a decree by the Court of Augmentations, respecting a grant to them from Thomas [Page], Abbot of Darleigh, dat. 25 Feb., 27 Hen. VIII. [1536], of an annuity of 40*s.* from lands in the same county. Witn. Sir Rich. Ryche, knt. [Chancellor of the Court of Augmentations and afterwards Lord High Chancellor]. Dat. 20 Mar., 30 Hen. VIII. [1539]. (Campb. xxix. 13.)

1013. COVENANT between John Tailer, D.D., Dean of Lincoln, and Denis Beresford of Gray's Inn, London, "fermor of the parsonage of Chesterfelde," that, whereas John Constable, formerly Dean of Lincoln, on 2 Sept., 1527, leased to Edward Beresford, esq., father of the said Denis, the rectory, tithes, etc., of Chesterfield (excepting the advowson and the woods) and the site of the manor of Little Chester, with all the demesne lands attached and one fishing in the

River Derwent (the rectory, etc., for 59 years, and the site of Little Chester manor for 69 years), with certain provisoes as to repairs; now it is agreed that the said Denis shall repair, uphold, etc., the houses and buildings of the said parsonage and of the said manor-site, at his own costs, and pay all charges concerning the same, in consideration of which the Dean shall allow yearly to the said Denis 26s. 8d., and shall sell to the latter all the "trees and wood growing ther in his wood called Dudmore" for the sum of £24 sterling, the said Denis to leave standing "such convenient number of Stallings, Wevers and Kinges in the said wood as the said Deane maie be saved harmelesse ageinst the late statute made for savinge of woods and springs." Dat. 1 June, 37 Hen. VIII. [1545]. (Derby Mun.)

1014. Lease from Olyver Thacker of Little Chester, gent., to Richard Lightlad of Derby, tiler, of two houses and gardens lying in the street called "ye Marledge" in Derby, and two little crofts, late held by Robert Cokkes, near the said garden, for a term of 21 years, at a rent of 12s. Dat. 25 Mar., 2, Edw. VI. [1548]. (Derby Mun.)

1015. Lease from the Bailiffs and Burgesses of Derby to Thomas Sutton "of the Kynge's medewe nighe Derby" of a parcel of ground in Derby "adioynyng vnto the Fladyate of a certeyn mylne called the Castell mylne," for a term of 60 years, at a rent of 12d., the lessee to make on the said ground "one able and convenient house for a Walke mylne with two stokkes the one called a Potyere and the other a Fallere and also to make or cause to be made one sufficient waye or Cawsey for the Kynge's subjects to come and go as well with horsse as on foote by the sayd house into the holmes theyr." Dat. 27 Sept., 3 Edw. VI. [1549]. (Derby Mun.)

1016. Register of Darley Abbey, containing copies of about nine hundred Charters. (Cotton MS. Titus C. ix.)

DERBY *v.* also under Chesterfield, Crich, Litchurch, Wirksworth.

DARLEY ABBEY *v.* also under Whatstandwell.

DONISTHORPE *v.* under Gresley.

DORE.

1017. Quitclaim from John de Stolbaley, clerk, to Richard fil. Ade de Totinley, living in Dore, of all those lands, etc., in Dore which formerly belonged to Ranulph de Dore. Witn. Thomas de Leys, Thomas de Wodehouse, clerk, Peter de Bernis. Late 13th cent. (D. A. J. iii. 103.)

1018. Lease, for lives, from Ralph de Wellewick, knt., to Richard Fullo of Dore and Cecily his wife of the messuage and land which William Blys, father of the said Richard, sometime held in Dore. Witn. John de le Wodehouses, Thomas de Gotham, Richard Gilly, Thomas de Birchehewed, etc. Dat. at Bernetby, T. a. F. of St. Mary Magdalene [22 July], 1325. (D. A. J. iii. 102.)

1019. Grant, in tail, from Ralph son and heir of Sir Ralph de Wellewek, knt., to Ralph Cissor [Tailor] of Dore and Matilda his wife of land in Dore. Witn. John Wathe, John Wygleye, Robert Selioke, John Hollowey, etc. Dat. Barnetbe, S. a. F. of St. Martin [11 Nov.] [*circ.* 1330]. (D. A. J. iii. 103.)

1020. LEASE, for twelve years, from Margery Gilly, widow, to William del Lym of the messuage, etc., which Emma fil. Joh. del Horlowe her mother sometime held in Dore. Witn. Robert de Seliock, John de Wodehow, Hugh le Barker. Dat. Mor. of Ann. of B. V. M. [26 Mar.], 1333. (D. A. J. iii. 105.)

1021. GRANT from Ralph fil. Radulphi de Wellewyk to John fil. Henrici fil. Simonis de Moniassche and Matilda his wife, of lands, tenements, etc., in the fee of Dore. Witn. John Bate, Richard le Walkerre de Dorre, Hugh le Barkerre, etc. Dat. Berneby, W. b. F. of St. Thomas [21 Dec.], 1341. (Harl. 84 B. 26.)

1022. GRANT from William de Skipwith and Margaret his wife to John fil. Henrici fil. Simonis de Moniasche and Matilda his wife, of land, tenements, etc., in Dore, for the term of the life of Sir Simeon de Wellewik and that of his brother Robert. Witn. John Bate, John de Horlowe, Hugh le Barber, etc. Dat. Bernetby, W. b. F. of St. Thomas [21 Dec.], 1341. (Harl. 84 A. 35.)

DORE *v.* also under STAVELEY.

DOVERIDGE.

(DOUUEBRUG, DOWBRYGE, DUBBRUGE.)

1023. GRANT from Robert fil. Roberti fil. Rogeri, chaplain of Uttokeshather [Uttoxeter, co. Staff.], to Thomas fil. Thome de Eyton of eight selions of land in Douuebrug, near Uttoxeter. Witn. Henry Goderiche, Henry de Duddeley, Robert de Waltone, etc. Dat. W. a. F. of St. Michael [29 Sept.], 22 Edw. III. [1348]. (Woll. x. 38.)

1024. GRANT from Richard del Grene de Dubbrugge to Robert Deye, chaplain of Dubbruge, of land in that neighbourhood in Monnesholme and Cubache. Witn. Dom. Rob. de Knyveton, vicar of Dubbruge, William Fisshere, and Henry Turkeys of the same, etc. Dat. at Dubbruge, Sat. b. F. of Assumption [15 Aug.], 19 Rich. II. [1395]. (Stowe 51.)

1025. WILL of Robert Milwart of Eyton, with bequests to the Church of St. Cuthbert of Dowbryge. Dat. 29 Oct., 1513. (Drury.)

DOVERIDGE *v.* also under SOMERSALL.

DRAKELOWE.

1026. MANUMISSION by John de Greseleye, mil., Dominus de Drakelowe, of Thomas Nettebreyder, "Botiler de Drakelowe," with all his suit and following, goods and chattels. Dat. Drakelowe, S. a F. of St. Augustine [26 May], 2 Ric. II. [1379]. (Gresley.)

1027. BOND by John Gresley, mil., in 200 marks, to abide by the award of George, Duke of Clarence, Lord of Richmond, in certain disputes between the said John and the Abbot and Convent of Burton, the latter claiming certain lands and rents in Burton, co. Staff., Drakelow, Caldewall, and Lynton, co. Derby, a fishery in the Trent from a certain boundary called Redebanke, within the lordship of Walton, up to a water-mill of the said Abbot called Overmill, and the said John claiming title to other rents and lands of the Abbey in Burton, Tetenall, and elsewhere in co. Staff. Dat. 24 Feb., 6 Edw. IV. [1467]. (Gresley.)

1028. Award by Thomas [Wolsey], Cardinal Archbishop of York, in a suit brought by Sir John Savage, knt., and Alice his wife, " late the wife " of Sir William Greysley, knt., and executrix of his last will, Anthony Greysley, Thomas Greysley, Humfrey Greysley, and Edward Greysley, on the one part, against Sir George Greisley and John Saunders, on the other part, to substantiate their right and title to the manors of Drakelowe, co. Derby; Osgathorpe, co. Leic.; Tutbury Woodhouse, Colton, Moreton, Kingston, co. Staff.; Lullington, Castle Gresley, and Lynton, co. Derby; Norton, co. Staff.; Braceborough, Carleby, Thirlby, Baston, co. Linc.; and Seton-in-Spaldingmoor, co. York; whereby it is decreed that the said Sir George is to have possession of the said manors as the rightful heir of his brother, Sir William Greysley, who died " without issue of his body begotten," subject to certain rent-charges to be paid to the said Alice, wife of Sir John Savage, and to the said Anthony, Thomas, Humphrey, and Edward. Dat. Trinity Term, 16 Hen. VIII. [1525]. Endorsed, " The decree agaynst Lady Savage and her Basterd Sonnes for all the Gresleyes lands." (Gresley.)

DRAYCOTT.

(Dracot, Draycote.)

1029. Grant from Robert fil. Willelmi de Draycote to William le Seriand and Cecilia his wife of one acre of land in Lyttelmed in Draycote. Witn. William de Jarpenuill, Robert de Pipe, William fil. clerici de Draycote, etc. Dat. S. a. F. of St. Andrew [30 Nov.], 10 Edw. II. [1316]. (Add. 4882.)

1030. Will of William Roselle of Dracot. Dat. F. of St. Dunstan [21 Oct.], 1502. (Woll. i. 81.)

DRONFIELD.

Draneffeld, Dranefeld, Dranfeld, Dronefeld, Dronfeld, Dronfild, Dronsfeld.)

1031. Grant from Richard de Streton fil. Heruici to John fil. Laisig " dishalis " and Rohard fil. Horn de Honistun of all the land of " Gruwis." Witn. Hugh fil. Noch' persona de Dronefeld, Thomas de Dronefeld, Walter Dun, etc. Early 13th cent. (Foljambe.)

1032. Grant from Ralph Salvain of Thorp, with consent of Marjory his wife, to Geoffrey son of Stephen de Aston, of land in Hallehes [Hallowes-in-Dronfield]. Witn. Stephen, Abbot of Beauchief, John Wascelin, John de Einecurt, Leonius Saluanus, Thomas, parsona de Dranefeld. Early Hen. III. (Foljambe.)

1033. Grant from William fil. Matanie de Dranefeld to Thomas fil. Thom. Caskin of all his right in the land " del Gruves " pledged to him by Thomas del Leys, etc. [? in Dronfield]. Witn. Thomas del Leys, Adam de Neubold, Peter de Doneston, etc. Late 13th cent. (Foljambe.)

1034. Grant from Agnes fil. Radulphi Selveyn to Robert Selveyn her brother of four bovates of land in Haleghys [Hallowes, nr. Dronfield], and a bovate in Aston [Coal Aston]. Witn. Dom. Roger de Eyncurt, Dom. Peter de Briminton, Jocelin de Steynisby, Roger de Somervil, etc. Late 13th cent. (Foljambe.)

1035. QUITCLAIM from Peter de Berneys of Dronfeld to John de Stobbeleye of 2*d.* of yearly rent for land in the territory of Dronfeld. Witn. Nicholas de Stobbeleye, Robert Lille, Richard de Wodehousis, etc. Late 13th cent. (Foljambe.)

1036. GRANT from Peter fil. Agnetis to John fil. Ade fil. Petri de Somerlesowe of four plots of land in the fields and fee of Dronefeld. Witn. John de Stubleye, Richard fil. Thome de le Wodehous, William Louecok, etc. Dat. S. a. F. of St. Valentine [14 Feb.], 6 Edw. II. [1313]. (Foljambe.)

1037. GRANT from Emma que fuit uxor quondam Petri fil. Agnetis de Dronefeld to William fil. Eduse junioris de Dronefeld of lands sold by her late husband to him in Dronfeld. Witn. John de Stubleye, William Louecok, William fil. Thome de College, etc. Dat. Pur. of B. V. M. [2 Feb.], 8 Edw. II. [1315]. (Foljambe.)

1038. GRANT from William fil. Eduse sen. de Dronefeld to Matilda his daughter of land in the "Stubbyng" in Dronefeld. Witn. Richard de le Wodehouses, William de Colley, etc. Dat. F. of Epiphany [6 Jan.], 16 Edw. II. [1323]. (Foljambe.)

1039. GRANT from Thomas Rich to Richard le Chapmon of a toft, etc., in Dronfeld. Witn. Thomas de Totynglay, Adam le Spenser, William Lowcok. Dat. Th. a. Ass. of B. V. M. [15 Aug.], . . . Edw. [II. or III.]. *Mutilated.* (Foljambe.)

1040. GRANT from William fil. Alani de Wodesmethis to John de Wath of his tenement at Wodesmethis in Dronfeld. Witn. Guy Louterel, John de Capella, Roger de Hapilknole, Davit de Wetenthon, etc. Dat. Tr. of St. Thomas [7 July], 3 Edw. III. [1329]. (Rel. xx. 219.)

1041. GRANT from Richard fil. Roberti "super Moram" to Dom. . . . . . of all his goods, etc., in Dronefeld and Barley. Dat. Brampton, Th. a. Michs., 1338. (Foljambe.)

1042. GRANT from Richard Broun of Ekynton and Hugh de Tybschelf, chaplains, to Robert fil. Thom. de Sellyok, of the moiety of lands in Sellyok and Le Halughys with remainder to John his son and Dionisia Frene and the heirs of their bodies. Witn. John de Grey, dominus de Onston, Robert Bryan de Ekynton, etc. Dat. Halughes, M. a. F. of St. Nicholas [6 Dec.], 16 Edw. III. [1342]. (Foljambe.)

1043. GRANT from William fil. Petri fil. Agnetis de Dronfeld to Roger Danyel of Colleye of two acres, etc., of land in Dronfeld. Witn. Richard dil Wodehouses, Thomas Cocus of Colleye, William Loukoc, etc. Dat. Morr. of Nat. of St. John B. [25 June], 18 Edw. III. [1344]. (Foljambe.)

1044. GRANT from Henry de Cresewyk to Robert le Breton, Dom. de Walton, Philippa his wife, and Robert their son, of lands, tenements, etc., in the fee of Dronefeld. Witn. William de Linacre, Roger de Caus, Thomas de Somersal, etc. Dat. Dronefeld, S. a. F. of SS. Philip and James [1 May], 23 Edw. III. [1349]. (Harl. 112 H. 4.)

1045. GRANT from John de Somerleso to Richard le Taillour fil. Joh. le Chapman of part of his messuage in Dronfield. Witn. John de Wodhous, Henry Loucok, William Loucok, etc. Dat. T. a. Palm Sunday [10 Apr.], 25 Edw. III. [1351]. (Foljambe.)

1046. QUITCLAIM from Adam Tetlowe and Matilda his wife to Roger Clerk of Chesterfelde of the lands, etc., which John fil. Ad. Haneley held from William Eyncourt, knt. [? in Dronfield]. Witn. William Barker of Aston, Adam Spencer of Dranfelde. Dat. apud Somurlesowe, M. a. F. of St. Michael [29 Sept.], 27 Edw. III. [1353]. (Rel. xx. 219.)

1047. GRANT from Robert fil. et her. Thome Abbetoft of Barley to Roger fil. Elie de Birley of a yearly rent from lands in the fees of Dronfeld and Staveley. Witn. Roger de Wygeley, Robert de Barley, etc. Dat. S. a. F. of St. Gregory [12 Mar.], 30 Edw. III. [1356]. (Foljambe.)

1048. GRANT from Henry fil. Joh. Smyth to William Maynard of an acre of land in the fee of Dronfeld. Witn. Adam le Wright, John de Aston, Henry Loucok, etc. Dat. S. a. F. of St. Augustine [26 May], 40 Edw. III. [1366]. (Foljambe.)

1049. QUITCLAIM from Thomas fil. Joh. Smith of Dronfeld to Henry Smith of Dore of land in Dronfeld which he had from his father. Witn. Henry Loukoc, William Maynard, etc. Dat. S. a. All Saints' Day, 1366. (Foljambe.)

1050. GRANT from Thomas Rycher of Dronfeld to John del Croftus of five acres of arable land in the fields of Dronfeld in a place called Mostylegh. Witn. William fil. Hen. Loucok, William Shemyld, etc. Dat. F. of Epiphany [6 Jan.], 9 Ric. II. [1386]. (Foljambe.)

1051. LEASE from Alice, widow of Roger Milner, to John Seriaunt of Bradway and Adam his son, of a messuage, etc., which she had of the grant of Christiana her mother in Overbirched [Birchett in Dronfield] for 12 years. Dat. Birchehed, F. of Pur. of B. V. M. [2 Feb.], 20 Ric. II. [1397]. (Foljambe.)

1052. GRANT from Thomas Baret of Chestrefeld to William Hunte of the same of an acre of land and meadow in the fee of Dronfild, lying on Neddurhull between Rylee Syke and land of John Vlley. Witn. John Barbour, Robert Tapton, John Spicer. Dat. F. of Exalt. of H. Cross [14 Sept.], 8 Hen. IV. [1407]. (Foljambe.)

1053. GRANT from Roger de Bradeway to Robert Knowt of a messuage and lands in Bradeway [nr. Dronfield]. Witn. Ralph Barker of Dore, James Mawer, John Parker, etc. Dat. F. of St. Matthew [21 Sept.], 10 Hen. IV. [1409]. (Foljambe.)

1054. EXTRACT of court-roll of Dronfeld Manor recording the admission of William Cook of Holmesfeld to lands, etc., in the fee of Dronfeld and Barley on the surrender of William son of William de Mora, who had inherited them from his father. Dat. 1 Apr., 4 Hen. V. [1415]. (Foljambe.)

1055. GRANT from William Cook of Holmesfeld to Thomas Cook his son of all the lands, etc., which he had of the grant of William, son of William de Mora in the fee of Dronfeld and Barley. Witn. John Gray, Ralph Barker, Robert Owtrem, etc. Dat. Palm Sunday [12 Apr.], 4 Hen. V. [1416]. (Foljambe.)

1056. EXTRACT of court-roll of Dronffeld, recording the admission of Dame Alice de Deyncourt, of Thomas Fox, and William Cook to lands, etc., in Dronffeld, on the surrender of William Holbrok and Emma his wife. Dat. 7 Hen. V. [1419-20]. (Foljambe.)

9

1057. EXTRACT of court-roll of Dronfeld Manor, recording the admission of Thomas Fox and William Cooke to a messuage, etc., and 12 acres of land in Dronfeld on the surrender of Thomas de Wodhouse and Cecilia his wife, dau. and heir of Matilda Rycher. Dat. Th. a. F. of St. James [25 July], 10 Hen. V. [1422]. (Foljambe.)

1058. EXTRACT of court-roll of Dranfeld Manor, recording the admission of Thomas Foxe to an acre of land called "Blake Acre" on the surrender of Thomas Maynard. Dat. Fr. a. F. of St. Edw. Conf. [5 Jan.], 3 Hen. VI. [1425]. (Foljambe.)

1059. POWER of attorney from William Brampton of Chestrefeld to Richard Godoson to deliver seisin in the court of Dronfeld to John Clerke and Robert Fleches of all his lands, etc., in the fee of Dronfeld and Barley. Witn. William Clerke, John Boton, William Neubold. Dat. 10 Dec., 9 Hen. VI. [1430]. (Foljambe.)

1060. EXTRACT of court-roll of Dronsfeld Manor, recording the admission of John Seriaunt, as son and heir of William Seriaunt of Bradwey, to 20 acres of land in Bradwey in the fee of Dronsfeld. Dat. at the Court of Ralph, Lord Cromwell, Sat. b. F. of "Clausum Pasche" [16 Apr.], 14 Hen. VI. [1435]. (Foljambe.)

1061. RELEASE from William Chaumbre of Barleburgh to Thomas Fox, of all the lands, etc. [in Dronfeld ?] formerly belonging to Walter Lufetson of Assheford. Witn. Robert Seriaunt, Thomas Meynard, William Shemyld, etc. Dat. Dronfeld, 10 Oct., 17 Hen. VI. [1438]. (Foljambe.)

1062. EXTRACT from Roll of the Court at Dronfield, whereby Adam Serjant surrenders to Robert Serjant and Alice his wife and the heirs of their body, certain lands in Dronfield lately held by Robert Schemeld. Dat. F. of S. George [23 Apr.], 17 Hen. VI. [1439]. (Harl. 111 C. 41.)

1063. QUITCLAIM from Robert Barle, dominus de Barle, to Robert Mawer of Barle Wodsetes of a bovate of land called Gorstelandes, in Dronfield. Witn. John Cooke of Morehaws, William Cartwryght, William Boton del Lees, etc. Dat. Pur. of B. V. M. [2 Feb.], 1447[8]. (Rel. xx. 164.)

1064. LEASE, for 40 years, from William Bolloke, Alderman of the Guild of St. Mary in the parish church of St. John Baptist [Dronfield] and John Hordryn, chaplain of the same, with consent of the Brethren of the Guild, to Thomas Welton, sen., and Joyce his wife, of a messuage and land in the tenure of John Taylyor in Dronfeld. Witn. John Barker of Dore, William Owtrem, Thomas Fox, William Shemyng, William Cuttlove. Dat. Dronfeld, F. of St. Michael [29 Sept.], 1449. (Rel. xx. 165.)

1065. LEASE, for 40 years, from William Bolloke, Alderman of the Gild of St. Mary in the parish of St. John Baptist [Dronfield] to Thomas Melton, sen., and Joyce his wife of a messuage, etc., in Dronfield. Witn. John Barker of Dore, William Owtrem, William Shemyng, William Cuttlufe, etc. Dat. Michaelmas Day, 1449. (D. A. J. iii. 76.)

1066. GRANT from Thomas Fox of Cold Aston to John Fox his son and the heirs of his body, of all his lands, etc., in the town and fields of Dronfeld. Witn. Thomas Coke, John Parkar, Thomas Parkar. Dat. F. of SS. Peter and Paul [29 June], 36 Hen. VI. [1458]. (Foljambe.)

1067. APPOINTMENT by Humfry Bourchier, Baron Cromwell, knt., of Sir John Bussy as Steward of his manor of Dranfeld for life. Dat. Tatteshale, 13 April, 9 Edw. IV. [1469]. (Add. 20,504.)

1068. GRANT from John Fox of Cold Aston to Thomas [Rotheram], Bishop of Lincoln, Chancellor of England, William Hastings, Lord Hastings, knt., Robert Fox of Whaphynborowe, jun., Thomas Fox of Chestrefeld, jun., Will. Fox of the same, jun., Henry Herry of Aston, Thomas Fox, Robert Fox, and John Fox, his sons, of all his lands, etc., in Dronfeld, called "Asshford lande." Dat. M. b. Michaelmas, 14 Edw. IV. [1474]. (Foljambe.)

1069. DECLARATION by Raufe Leche of Burley Leeyhes, John Barley, John Barker, Henry Weydurherd, vicar of Dronfield, and others, that they have examined John Roger of Onston, the tenant of certain land in Ramsawe-feld [? in Dronfield] in dispute between Henry Pole and Richard Bullok. Dat. F. of Epiphany [6 Jan.], 17 Edw. IV. [1478]. (Rel. xx. 165.)

1070. EXTRACT of court-roll of Dronfeld manor, recording the admission of John Fox of Cold Aston to lands, etc., in Dronfeld on the surrender of Ralph Leche, who had the same of the grant of William Atkynson and Thomas Seladon. Dat. 8 Oct., 21 Edw. IV. [1481]. (Foljambe.)

1071. EXTRACT of court-roll of Dronfeld Manor, recording the admission, at a court of the feoffees of William, Lord Hastings, of John Parker and Robert Gylberd to lands, etc., in Dronfeld on the surrender of John Fox of Cold Aston and Thomas Fox his son and heir, who had the same of the grant of Sir John Melton, knt. Dat. Th. b. F. of Inv. of H. Cross [3 May], 22 Edw. IV. [1482]. (Foljambe.)

1072. COVENANT by Thomas Fox son and heir of John Fox of Aston to make an estate to Henry Foliambe of Walton, esq., after the death of John Fox his father of a close lying near the "Kokplas" in Draneffeld. Witn. John Foliambe, gent., John Scha, etc. Dat. F. of S. James, Apost. [25 July], 22 Edw. IV. [1482]. (Foljambe.)

1073. COVENANT by Thomas Fox son and heir of John Fox of Aston to make an estate to Henry Foliambe, esq., of Walton, after the death of John Fox his father, of a messuage, lands, etc., in Draneffeld, which Thomas Fox his grandfather had of the grant of John Assheford, or which he, Thomas Fox the younger, or his father, had of Ralph Leche, the said Henry Foliambe paying 20 marks in hand, two instalments of 40s., and one of 4 marks. Witn. John Foliambe, etc. Dat. F. of Exalt. of H. Cross [14 Sept.], 1 Ric. III. [1483]. (Foljambe.)

1074. POWER of attorney from Thomas Foxe of Aston to Richard Bullok, Bailiff of Dronfeld, and John Carteleye, to surrender in the court of Dronfeld a messuage and cottage to the use of William Foxe of Haslande. Dat. 14 Aug., 3 Ric. III. [1485]. (Foljambe.)

1075. COVENANT by Thomas Fox, son and heir of John Fox of Aston, to make an estate to Henry Foliambe of Walton, esq., after the death of John Fox his father, of a tenement, with lands, etc., in Dronfeld, in the tenure of William Bromhead. Dat. F. of Pur. of B. V. M. [2 Feb.], 2 Hen. VII. [1487]. (Foljambe.)

1076. LIST of dues for burials, and legacies to be received for the use of the church at Dronfeld. Fifteenth century. (Woll. viii. 18a.)

1077. QUITCLAIM from George Mower of Barley Wodseets, son and heir of Robert Mower, deceased, to James Mower, his brother, of a messuage and bovate of land in Dronfeld called Gorsehouse, with a meadow called Care-medew which Nicholas Bagshawe inhabits. Dat. Tr. of St. Thomas [7 July], 26 Hen. VIII. [1534]. (Rel. xx. 218.)

DRONFIELD *v.* also under COAL ASTON, BARLOW, BOYTHORPE, HOPE, STAVELEY, TAPTON, UNSTONE.

DUCKMANTON.

(DOGMANTON, DOKEMANTON, DOKEMONTON, DOKMANTON, DUCEMANTUN, DUCHEMANETUNA, DUCKEMANTUNA, DUCMANTON, DUGMANTON, DUKEMANTUN, DUKEMANTUNE, DUKMANETON.)

1078. RE-GRANT from G[eoffrey] Ridel to Gervase fitz Richard of the latter's heritage of Duchemanetun, to hold of him and his heirs by one knight's service for Duchemanetun and for the land of Colestun [Colston-Basset, co. Notts.] which he holds of his (Geoffrey's) brother [*sc.* Ralph Basset], with a statement of the recognition in Geoffrey's court that W. fitz Richard had made over Duchemanetun in heritage to Gervase his brother and had surrendered it to Geoffrey [as lord] in order that he might re-grant it as above, which he had done, receiving homage for the same. *Circ.* 1155-1160. (Woll. i. 42.)

    G. Ridel. Omnibus hominibus suis clericis et laicis, Francis et Anglis salutem. Sciatis me reddidisse Geruasio filio Ricardi hereditatem suam videlicet Duchemanetun sibi et heredibus suis ad tenendum de me et de heredibus meis liberam et quietam per seruicium unius militis pro Duchemantuna et pro terra de Colestun quam de fratre meo tenet. Quia recognitum fuit in curia mea quod W. frater eius filius Ricardi fratrem suum G. in sua libera potestate inde hereditauit, et mihi eandem Duchemanetun reddidit et omnino de se et suis quietam dimisit, ut istum G. in hereditatem. Quapropter ei eandem terram reddidi et hommagium suum inde accepi. Quare uolo et firmiter precipio ut libere et quiete et honorifice teneat, sicut antecessores sui melius et liberius de antecessoribus meis tenuerunt. T[estibus] Radulfo, Priore de Landa [Laund], Radulfo Basset, W. Basset, Thoma de Sais, Bosone, G. de Sutton, Helia clerico, Vnfrido Pulein, Roberto de Weled[on], W. de Colestun, W. filio Hugonis, Roberto filio Lewine et aliis multis.

1079. GRANT, in soul-alms, from Geoffrey fil. Petri [afterwards Chief Justice of England] to the Premonstratensian Canons of the Abbey of Wellebec [Welbeck, co. Notts.], of the church of St. Peter of Ducemanetun. [1187-1188.] (Woll. i. 43.)

    Omnibus Sancte Matris Ecclesie filiis presentibus et futuris Galfridus filius Petri salutem, Sciatis me dedisse et hac carta mea confirmasse Deo et ecclesie Sancti Jacobi de Wellebec et Canonicis ibidem Deo seruientibus ordinis Premonstrati Ecclesiam Sancti Petri de Ducemanetun cum omnibus pertinentiis suis in puram et perpetuam Elemosinam pro salute anime mee et uxoris mee et heredum meorum. Testibus, Ranulfo de Glamuile, Justicia Domini Regis, Gerardo fratre suo, Willelmo filio Ranulfi, Roberto de Leistun, Henrico de Maudune, abbatibus, Ricardo del Pec, Willelmo fil. Roberti.

1080. LETTER from Ivo Cornubiensis, Archdeacon of Derby, to the clerks appointed by the Chapter of Scaruesdale, instituting the Abbot and Canons of Wellebeck in the church of St. Peter of Duchemanetun, on the presentation of Geoffrey fil. Petri, afterwards Chief Justice of England, which they had maintained their right to in the Court of King's Bench at Westminster, before Ranulph de Glanville and six other King's Justices. [1187-1188.] (Woll. i. 46 B.)

Magister Ivo Cornub[iensis] Archidiaconus Dereb' omnibus clericis per capitulum de Scaruesdale constitutis salutem. Nouerit uniuersitas uestra nos ad presentationem Galfridi fil. Petri instituisse abbatem et canonicos de Wellebech in ecclesia Sancti Petri de Duchemanetuna et eis personatum prefate ecclesie concessisse quam ipsi dirationauerunt in Curia Domini Regis apud Westmonasterium coram Justiciis Domini Regis, scilicet Rannulfo de Glanuill, Hugone Dunelmensi, Johanne Norwicensi, Galfrido Heliensi, episcopis, Godefrido de Luci, Gocelino Archidiacono Ricardo Thesaurario Domini Regis. Testibus, Magistro Ascelino, Hugone de Dranefeld, Stephano de Cestrefeld, Geruasio fil. Roberti, Ricardo de Stafeleg', Roberto de Aumeton, Gregorio de Scardecliue.

1081. GRANT from H[ugh Nonant], Bishop of Coventry, to the Abbey of Wellebec [Welbeck, co. Notts.], of the church of Duckemant[on], with condition for appointing a chaplain and celebrating an anniversary of the obits of the bishop and his successors. [1187-1188.] (Woll. i. 44.)

H. miseracione diuina Couentrensis Episcopus omnibus tam clericis quam laicis ad quos littere presentes peruenerint salutem ab autore salutis. Nouerit uniuersitas uestra nos attendentes paupertatem et religionem conuentus de Wellebec in remissionem peccatorum nostrorum et pro animabus predecessorum nostrorum et eorum qui nobis succedent concessisse, donasse et presenti carta confirmasse abbati et Conuentui de Wellebec ecclesiam de Duckemanton cuius aduocatio dinoscitur ad eos pertinere libere et quiete cum omnibus pertinenciis suis in perpetuam elemosinam possidendam ita ut liceat eis fructus et omnes conuentiones et possessiones in proprios usus conuertere, Abbas autem dicti monasterii capellanum honestum prouidebit qui, cum episcopo uel ei qui uicem eius gesserit fuerit presentatus, eidem Ecclesie deseruiet. Et abbas episcopo uel eius officialibus de episcopalibus per omnia respondebit salua nimirum episcopi canonica iusticia. Sepedictus etiam abbas firmiter in manu nostra promisit quod anniuersarium diem obitus nostri et successorum nostrorum pontificum sub ea ueneratione sub qua et abbatis euisdem loci faciet celebrari. Ut igitur hec donatio nostra perpetuis temporibus firma perseueret eam sigilli nostri munimine confirmamus. Testibus, Willelmo Duredent, Magistro Ricardo de Gnohushal, Magistro Acelino, Philippo decano de Derebi, Magistro Martino Lumbardo, Magistro Siluestro, Magistro Helia, Magistro Johanne Kenteis, Radulfo clerico et pluribus aliis.

1082. CONFIRMATION from Geoffrey [de Muschamp], Bishop of Coventry, to the Abbey of Wellebec, of the church of Dukmanton, granted to the abbey by his predecessor H[ugh Nonant]; also a pension of 3 marks and 3 shillings from the church of Ettewelle during the life of H—— nunc eiusdem ecclesie vicarius and at his death, two parts of the said church, and power to the Abbot of presenting a clerk to the remaining third part. Witn. Paul, Abbas de Leicestria, Mag. Robert, Archidiaconus de Salopesburi, Mag. Helyas de Chiueleia,

Mag. Simon de Derbi, Mag. Walter Malet, Walter et Matthew capellani, Richard de Scalt', Thomas de Beuerlaco, Nicholas Camerarius. [1196-1208.] (Woll. i. 45.)

1083. GRANT from Matildis de Wlveleia to the Abbey of St. James of Wellebec, with the assent of Geoffrey her heir, of a bovate and half-bovate of land in the vill of Dukemantune and the toft which was Edwin's, and the meadow "quod fuit messario eiusdem ville," paying a yearly rent of 2 *nummi* at Martinmas. Witn. Hugh fil. Leising, Robert fil. Ragenaldi, Henry fil. Roberti, Henry fil. Mabille, Robert de Aneslaia, William fil. Roberti le Frere, Robert clericus de Tibeschelf, Geoffrey clericus de Sulghl', Walter homo Roberti. *Temp.* Ric. 1—John. (Woll. i. 46a.)

1084. GRANT, for one mark, from Hamo fil. Walter de Dukemanton, to the Canons of Wellebec of his toft, etc., in Dukemanton, which he held of Hawisa fil. Roberti Torcard; rent, 14d. Witn. John de Orrebi, William fil. Gregorii de Scarleclive, William fil. Thome de Suttone, Henry de Pecco, Robert fil. Raghnardi, etc. Early Hen. III. (Woll. i. 54.)

1085. GRANT from Geoffrey fil. Simonis de Ducmanton, to the Abbey of Wellebec, "quod homines tenentes de feudo meo sequantur molendinum suum de Ducmanton et faciant molendinum et stagnum sicut solebant et sicut alii homines de predicta villa de Ducmanton." Witn. Alan de Ducmanton, Geoffrey fil. Hugonis, Peter de Peck, Roger de Ingham, etc. *Temp.* Hen. III. (Woll. i. 48.)

1086. COVENANT whereby Hugh fil. Alani de Duckemanton releases to William, Abbot, and to the Convent of Wellebeke, six bovates of land in Duckemanton and various other pieces of land near Kyrkelane, Pirlewellsike, etc., in exchange for lands in the same place, and 10 marks. Witn. Dom. Roger Briton, Dom. Peter de Brimington, Robert de Wyverton, and others. Dat. Annun. B. V. M., 1243. (Woll. i. 53.)

1087. GRANT from Wi[lliam], Abbot, and the Convent of Wellebeke, to Hugh fil. Alani de Duckmantone and Emma his wife, of full participation in all spiritual goods, with full and solemn service at their decease, and the enrolment of their names in the martyrology of the Abbey, in return for their benefactions to the Abbey, and especially for remission of a bond for 5 marks. Dat. Vigil of Annun. of B. V. M. [24 Mar.], 1243[4]. (Woll. i. 49.)

1088. GRANT from Geoffrey fil. Galfridi de Dukemaneton to Hugh fil. Galfridi de Dukmaneton his brother of lands in the vill of Dukemaneton; rent, two marks. Witn. Dom. Roger de Eyncurt, Dom. Roger Briton, Joscelin de Steinesby, Robert de Ockeston, Adam de Norton, Henry de Frowic, etc. Dat. First Sunday in Advent [2 Dec.], 32 Hen. III. [1247]. (Woll. i. 64.)

1089. GRANT from Geoffrey fil. et her. Galfridi fil. Hugonis de Ducmanton to the Abbey of Welbec, of four bovates of his demesne lands, together with his capital dwelling-house in Ducmanton; rent, half a mark. Witn. Dom. Roger Briton, Dom. Peter de Brimington, milites, Robert de Wyverton, Hugh fil. Alani de Ducmanton, and others. *Temp.* Hen. III. (Woll. i. 65.)

1090. GRANT, for 7 marks, from Hugh fil. Galfridi de Ducmantona, to Hugh fil. Alani de Ducmantona, of two bovates of land in the territory of Ducmantona; rent, one pound and a half of wax. Witn. Dom. Roger Briton de Waltona, Dom. Peter de Brinhingtona, Peter fil. Hugonis de eadem, Stephen fil. Petri de Calaal, etc. *Temp.* Hen. III. (Woll. i. 56.)

1091. GRANT from Peter fil. Willelmi de Pecc[o] and Matildis filia Henrici de Ducmantone, "sponsa mea," to the Canons of Wellebec, of the fifth part of the mill of Ducmantone; rent, 4s. With under-takings respecting the grinding of corn produced on the estate of the grantor at the said mill. *Temp.* Hen. III. (Woll. i. 55.)

1092. RELEASE from Martin fil. Radulfi de Hynkneshille to the Abbey of Wellebec of land called Presteridhing in the territory of Ducmanton, which was the "maritagium Susanne matris mee." Witn. Hugh, vicarius de Ducmantone, Ralph de Sydenhale, Alan de Briming-tone, etc. *Temp.* Hen. III. (Woll. i. 50.)

1093. RELEASE from Gwydo de Foresta, Master of the Temple, in England, to Thomas, Abbot of Wellebeke, of 12s. of rent from lands in Dugmanton; rent, 2s. Witn. John de Dugmantone, Prior of Wellebeke, Robert de Whattone, sub-prior, Nich. de Cumba, etc. Dat. Dynesl' [Temple Dynnesley, co. Heref.], F. of St. Barnabas [11 June], 1292. (Woll. i. 52.)

1094. GRANT from John [de Castrefeld], Abbot of Wellebeke, to Roger de Hinkereshul, of land in Dokemanton; rent, 2s. Witn. William le Bret of Brimington, Roger de Dokemanton, Thomas de Hinkereshal, etc. Dat. Welbeke, Vig. of Epiph. [5 Jan.], 1310[11]. (Woll. i. 51.)

1095. CONFIRMATION from John de Stoteville, Dominus de Ekynton, of a grant by Matildis de Duckmanton, to the Abbey of Wellebecke, of two bovates of land and a messuage in Dukmantone. Witn. Will. le Bret, Stephen Leyr, Roger de Dukmantone, William Dolfyn, etc. Dat. Ekyntone, F. of St. Ambrose [4 Apr.], 1314. (Woll. i. 47.)

1096. DEFEASANCE of a bond by Laurence fil. Ricardi fil. Rogeri de Dokmantone to William fil. Petri de Langwathe and Richard his brother, for £20, on condition that he ratifies a deed by Richard his father, by which the said William and Richard are enfeoffed in lands in Dokmanton. Dat. Dokmanton, Morr. of S. Bartholomew [25 Aug.], 14 Edw. II. [1320]. (Woll. i. 70.)

1097. BOND of Laurence fil. Ricardi de Dugmantone to Richard de Langewathe, clericus, to acquit him to the Abbot of Wellebecke, of 15d. rent of lands in Dugmantone. Witn. Roger de Hingkershille, Robert his brother, Hugh de Calhal, etc. Dat. Dugmantone, All Saints' Day [1 Nov.], 1326. (Woll. i. 69.)

1098. CONFIRMATION from Laurence fil. Ricardi de Dokemantone to Richard fil. Petri de Langwathe and William his brother of his grant made to them of lands in Dokemanton, together with a rent of 6d. Witn. William de Sancta Elena, John de Gayteford, John le Savage, coroner of Derby, etc. Dat. Netherlangwaht, Sun. b. Xmas. Day, 1 Edw. III. [1327]. (Woll. i. 71.)

1099. RELEASE from Laurence fil. Ricardi de Dukmantone to the Abbot of Welbeke, of a water-mill in Dukmantone, in exchange for permission to grind corn there, free of charge. Witn. Roger Dayncurt, mil., William de Uftone, John le Sauvage, etc. Dat. Derby, F. of St. Luke [18 Oct.], 4 Edw. III. [1330]. (Woll. i. 72.)

1100. RELEASE from Laurence fil. Riccardi de Dukemantone to Richard le Hunte of Essehovere [Ashover], of a capital messuage in Dukemantone. Witn. John de Wyggeleye, Roger fil. Rogeri de Dukmantone, Roger Gamel of Hynkersil, and others. Dat. Dukemantone, Morr. of Holy Trinity [27 May], 5 Edw. III. [1331]. (Woll. i. 67.)

1101. DEFEASANCE from Richard le Hunt of Essehovere to Laurence fil. Ricardi de Dukmanton, of a grant of a place of meadow land called Henneparke-medewe, in Dukmanton, in consideration of the payment of 70s. at Martinmas. Dat. Dukmantone, Sat. a. F. of St. Luke [18 Oct.], 6 Edw. III. [1332]. (Woll. i. 73.)

1102. RELEASE from Richard le Hunte of Essover to Dom. Roger Deyncourt, mil., of land called Henne Parke Medwe, in Dokemonton. Witn. Roger Somerville, Ralph de Reresby, Rob. de Vynfeld, etc. Dat. Parkshale, S. a. F. of St. Andrew [30 Nov.], 8 Edw. III. [1334]. (Woll. i. 59.)

1103. COPY of a final concord made at York, Michaelmas Term, 10 Edw. III. [1336], whereby Thomas de Ryther of Netherlangwathe and Idonia his wife surrender for 10 marks to Roger Deyncourt chiv^r lands and 8d. of rent in Dokemanton. (Woll. i. 57.)

1104. COPY of a final concord made at the same time and place, whereby William de Russhyndene and Alice his wife surrender, for 20 marks, to the same Roger, lands and a rent of 6d. in Dokemonton. (Woll. i. 57a.)

1105. GRANT from Laurence de Dokmantune fil. Ricardi de Dokmantone to Dom. Roger de Eyncourt, mil., dom. de Parco, of a rent of 7d. from lands in Dokmanton. Witn. Dom. William le Grey, mil., Dom. William de Byngham, mil., Robert Bryton, etc. Dat. Dokmanton, T. b. F. of SS. Simon and Jude [28 Oct.], 15 Edw. III. [1341]. (Woll. i. 68.)

1106. GRANT, in tail, from John de Wytyntone to Henry de Dukmantone and Matilda his wife of lands, with services of free-men and natives, in Dukmanton, together with the reversion of lands in the same place, held by Agnes, widow of Roger de Dukmantone, with reversion to John son of Matilda Laveroke, wife of Henry de Dukmantone, and to Alice, her daughter. Witn. Robert Frauncais, John de Plumley, etc. Dat. Dukmantone, M. b. F. of St. Margaret [20 July], 16 Edw. III. [1342]. (Woll. i. 66.)

1107. COVENANT between Alice, wife of Mons. Nicholas de Longeford, and Maude, wife of Sir Roger Deyncourt, for a marriage between Nicholas, son of the said Mons. Nicholas, and Alice, daughter of the said Roger, who agrees to enfeoff them with lands in Dugmanton and to grant the reversion of 100 marks to the said Maude at his death. Dat. Derby, M. a. Michaelmas Day, 20 Edw. III. [1346]. French. (Woll. x. 2.)

1108. GRANT in tail from Roger Deyncourt to Nicholas, son of Nicholas de Longfforde, and Alice, his wife, daughter of the said Roger, of lands in Dogmanton; rent, a rose. Witn. Henry Gate, Henry de Knyvetone, Walter Hapher, etc. Dat. Tues. in Easter week [3 Apr.], 21 Edw. III., 1347. (Woll. i. 58.)

1109. LEASE from Henry Noppe of Dugmanton and Edith his wife to John Grene of the same and Isabel his wife, of lands in Dugmanton, for 40 years. Witn. Roger de Hynkershulle, Roger son of Henry, John Coke, etc. Dat. F. of St. George [23 Apr.], 3 Ric. II. [1380]. (Woll. i. 60.)

1110. GRANT from John "bey^e Kyrk," chaplain, to Henry Laurance and Avice his wife of lands called Robcroft, in Dugmanton. Witn. John Watson, William Bochere, Anker Scorer, etc. Dat. F. of St. Silvester [31 Dec.], 17 Hen. VI. [1438]. (Woll. i. 63.)

1111. GRANT from John Stanley and Robert his son to John, Abbot of Welbec, of a water-course called "le Sought," running from a mine of sea-coal belonging to the said Abbot in Dugmanton, through or under the lands of the said John and Robert, as far as Reynaldbrigge. Dat. T. b. F. of SS. Simon and Jude [28 Oct.], 30 Hen. VI. [1451]. (Woll. i. 61.)

1112. GRANT from Thomas Laurans to Martin Laurans his son of lands lying between Pykmancroft and Dukmanton. Witn. Ralph Wryghte, chaplain of Dukmanton, Roger Wryght, Robert Downs, etc. Dat. F. of St. Blaise, Bp. [3 Feb.], 3 Hen. VII. [1488]. (Woll. i. 62.)

DUFFIELD.

(DUFFELD, DUFFELD-SUPER-AMBRE, DUFFEUD.)

1113. GRANT from William, Earl of Ferrars, son of William, Earl of Ferrars, to Gilbert de Horsseleye, of 24 acres of land, by the perch of 17 feet, in the forest of Duffeld-super-Ambre, at a rent of 20s. yearly. Late twelfth century. (Eg. 437.)

Willelmus Comes de Ferr[ariis] filius Willelmi Comitis de Ferr[ariis] omnibus hominibus suis et amicis clericis et laicis francis et Anglis tam futuris quam presentibus salutem. Sciatis omnes me dedisse et concessisse et hac presenti carta mea et sigillo nostro confirmasse Gileberto de Horsseleya quatuor uiginti acras terre per perticam xvii pedum in foresta mea de Duffeld super Ambre illi et heredibus suis tenendum de me et de meis heredibus in feudo et hereditate libere solute et quiete per xx solidos reddendo annuatim mihi uel heredibus meis pro omni seruicio ad me vel ad meos heredes pertinente, scilicet ad duos terminos medietatem ad annunciacionem beate Marie et alteram medietatem ad festum Sancti Michaelis et husbote et haibote de bosco iacente per uisum forestariorum meorum. Hanc uero donacionem dedi illi pro humagio et seruicio suo. Hii sunt testes, Robertus fil. Walkel[ini], Henricus eius frater, Johannes de Boscheuill, Willelmus de Rideware, tunc senescallus, Philippus clericus de Duffeld, Robertus de Grendon, Henricus fil. Hereberti, Hugo fil. Walteri, Radulfus de Wudeham, Hamo clericus, Robertus filius Gamel, et multis aliis.

1114. GRANT from Edmund son of Henry III. to Walter le Harpur of a toft in the vill of Duffeud to hold, for a yearly rent of 18d. Witn. Dom. Tho. de Bray, Hugh de Viene, Euger' de Hestriis, John Basset, etc. Dat. Tuttebure, 8 July, 11 Edw. I. [1283]. Seal of arms. (Add. 15774.)

1115. WRIT for assignment of dower to the Queen of Navarre, viz.:—Duffield Manor, with its members of Southwood, Holbrook, Heage, Belper, Alderwasley, Idridgehay, Newbiggin and Hulland,

Duffield Forest, Hertington Manor, Crondecote, Bonsall, Brassington, Spondon, Parwick, Appletree Hundred, Gresley Hundred, Newbold, etc. Brunton, 1298, 21 June. (D. of L.)

1116. RELEASE from Edmund Fasman to Cicely Fischer and John Bakelot, heirs of Henry Fischer, of all his right in the tenements in Duffeld which he had on the death of Thomas Fasman, his father. Witn. Sir Thomas Fraunceys, Sir William de Monyashe, vicar of Duffeld, etc. Dat. 2 Apr., 5 Ric. II. [1382]. (P. R. O. B. 3777.)

1117. RELEASE from Thomas Alibone, chaplain, to Cecilia Fisher and John Bakelot, heirs of Henry Fisher, of his right in tenements in the vill of Duffeld, which he had of the feoffment of Edmund Fasman of Derby. Witn. William de Meinasche, vicar of Duffeld, etc. Dat. 2 Apr., 5 Richard II. [1382]. (P. R. O. B. 1266.)

1118. DEED whereby Thomas Okour, esquire, farmer of the church of Duffeld, promises that he will pay to the Dean and Chapter of the new Collegiate Church of the Blessed Virgin at Leicester at Midsummer, 8 Hen. VI. [1430], for arrears of his farm of Duffeld Church, £6 17s. 3d. —and in part payment of the £42 for farm of the same for the 9th year of Henry VI. [1430], at Martinmas next, £13 6s. 8d.; at Christmas, £6 13s. 4d.; at Midsummer, £6 13s. 4d.; and at Martinmas following, £15 6s. 8d. Dat. 8 June, 8 Hen. VI. [1430]. (Okeover.)

1119. ATTORNEY from Edmund Bradshawe to Robert Rooper to surrender all his lands in Duffeld, Edrychey, and Asshleyhey, and elsewhere in the county within the demesne of Duffeld Frith, to the use of Robert Bradshawe, his son. Dat. 27 Aug., 3 Hen. VIII. [1511]. (Bemrose.)

1120. "NOTE of the Oxenyng lands in Duffeld," with the tenants' names. *Ante* 1536. (Kerry xiv. 47.)

DUFFIELD *v.* also under BEARWARDCOTE, BELPER, MERCASTON, MUGGINTON.

EATON, COLD.

(ETON.)

1121. DEED of sale from Humphrey Lowe, late of Denby, and Clement Lowe his son and heir-apparent, to Sir Henry Willoughby, knt., of the town of Eton, with all appurtenances, for £88 13s. 4d. Dat. 10 May, 14 Hen. VII. [1499]. (Drury-Lowe.)

EATON DOVEDALE.

(EYTON-SUPER-DOUUE.)

1122. LEASE, for 30 years, from Walter de Cokeseye, knt., and Isabella his wife to William Mareschal, of Seggeshale, of lands in Eyton-super-Douue; rent, 28s. Dat. Caldewell, M. a. F. of St. Valentine [14 Feb.], 4 Ric. II. [1381]. (Woll. ix. 68.)

EATON DOVEDALE *v.* also under ASHBOURNE.

EATON, LONG.

(EYTONE.)

1123. GRANT from Robert Teverey, esq., to John Babyngton, knt., Thomas Armestrong, esq., William Wentworth, esq., and John Crewker, gent., of lands in Stapleford, Thromptone [Thrumpton], and Estwhaite [Esthwaite], co. Notts., and in Eyton and Grenehill, co. Derby. Witn. Gervase Clyftone, knt., John Seyntandrew, esq., Hugh Annesley, esq., Robert Saucheuerell, etc. Dat. Stapleforde, 2 Sept., 11 Hen. VII. [1495]. (Woll. i. 22.)

1124. POWER of attorney from Robert Teverey, esq., to William Wentworth, jun., and Thomas Bromefeld, to deliver seisin of the above manors. Same date. (Woll. i. 23.)

EATON, LONG, *v.* also under STANTON-BY-DALE.

ECKINGTON.

(EKINTON, EKINTONE, EKKYNGTON, EKYNGTON, EKYNTON, EQUENTON, EQUINTONA, HEKENT', · HEKINTON.)

1125. PRESENTATION of John de Estoutevill, clericus, by his father, John de Estoutevilla, miles., to R[oger le Weseham], Bishop of Chester, for admission to the moiety of the church of Equintona. Dat. M. a. F. of St. Augustine [26 May], 1255. Seal. (Add. 20486.)

1126. LEASE from Thomas fil. Nicholai Mote of Equenton to Robert de Haselyngden, of land and buildings, etc. [in Equenton ?], for 20 years, commencing on the morrow of All Souls, 1314. Witn. Thos. de Bosco de Scheffeld, Lambert Dyer of Scheffeld, Adam Cook, etc. (Harl. 83 G. 52.)

1127. LETTERS of presentation from John Darcy, Dominus de Knayth, to Nicholas de Skargille, of the York diocese, to the living of Ekintone, in the diocese of Coventry and Lichfield. Dat. Hirste, 25 July, 1349. (Harl. 49 D. 2.)

1128. GRANT from Thomas Pereson, son and heir of John Pereson, late of Hanley, to Peter Fretchevyle, esq., of a toft and croft named Bramley, in Ekyngton. Witn. Joh. Both of Staveley, Rog. Turnour of the same, Rob. Rogger of Hanley. Dat. at Handley, 16 Feb., 20 Edw. IV. [1481]. (Add. 40, 156.)

1129. GRANT from Richard Bamby to John Plesaunce, vicar of Sheffeld, John Parker of Leess [Lees], and Richard Trippett of Atterclyffe, of lands, tenements, etc., in Sheffeld, Ecclysfeld, Roderham, Handsworth [co. York], and Ekkyngton [co. Derby]. Witn. John Baylze, clerk, Thomas Wryght, Richard Kylton, etc. Dat. Sheffeld, 23 July, 1 Ric. III. [1483]. (Harl. 112 G. 3.)

ECKINGTON *v.* also under COAL ASTON, HANDLEY, MOSBOROUGH, STAVELEY.

EDALE *v.* under SHATTON.

EDENSOR *v.* under DARLEY, PILSLEY.

EDLASTON-WITH-WYASTON.

(EDLUSTON; WEARDESTON, WIARDESTON, WYARDESTON,
WYARDISTON, WYARDSTON.)

1130. GRANT from Roger de Cobbeleye to Nicholas fil. Rog. de Marchynton of 2½ acres of land in Wyardeston, lying on Le Ouerefeld, etc. Witn. Hugh de Aula, William de Aula de Wyardeston, Richard de Hordreue. *Temp.* Edw. I. (Trusley.)

1131. GRANT from William de Aula to Nicholas fil. Rog. de Mercynton of an acre of land in Wyardeston, with the crop. Witn. Dom. Henry de Braylesford. Dom. Roger de Mercynton, milites, John Selueyn, etc. *Temp.* Edw. I. (Trusley.)

1132. QUITCLAIM from Avice and Margery filie Hen. fil. Thom. de Wyardeston to William their brother of all the lands which Henry their father and Emma the said Henry's mother held in the vill and fee of Wyardeston. Witn. Will de Longford, Roger de Cubbeleye, Roger le Hunte. Dat. M. a. F. of St. Barnabas [11 June], 1295. (Trusley.)

1133. GRANT from Thomas fil. et her. Hugonis de Aula de Wiardiston to John fil. Rog. Wildegos de Foston, of half-an-acre of land lying on Le Houshold in the fee of Wiardiston. Witn. Nicholas de Marchinton, John Selveyn, Richard de Horderne, etc. Dat. Sat. a. F. of St. Edmund, K. and M. [Nov. 20], 29 Edw. I. [1300]. (Trusley.)

1134. GRANT from John fil. Rog. Wyldegos to Robert le Ster de Calton of half-an-acre of land in Wyardiston lying on the "Houshold." Witn. Hugh de Aula, Thomas de la Grene, Thomas de Thorp. Dat. S. b. F. of St. Cuthbert [20 Mar.], 29 Edw. I. [1301]. (Trusley.)

1135. GRANT from Thomas de la Grene of Wiardiston to Henry fil. Will. de La Grene of half-an-acre of land in Wiardiston lying at Le Fennilache. Witn. Nicholas de Marcinton, William de Aula, Thomas de Winster, etc. Dat. F. of St. Laurence [2 Feb.], 1304[5]. (Trusley.)

1136. GRANT from John fil. Rog. Wyldegos de Foston to Henry fil. Will. de la Grene of an acre, etc., of land in the fee of Wyardeston. Dat. S. a. Michs. [29 Sept.], 34 Edw. I. [1306]. (Trusley.)

1137. GRANT from Richard de Aula de Wyardiston to Henry dictus Bonus of an acre, etc., of land in Wiardiston. Witn. Richard, clericus de Aulneton, Hugh de Aula, Richard de Hordrenne, etc. *Temp.* Edw. I. (Trusley.)

1138. QUITCLAIM from Margery fil. Hen. fil. Thom. de Wyardiston to William her brother of all the lands which Henry her father and Emma, the latter's mother, held in Wyarduston. Dat. M. a. F. of St. Barnabas [11 June], 1295. (Trusley.)

1139. QUITCLAIM from Thomas de la Grene de Wyardeston to Henry fil. Will. de la Grene of all his lands in Wyardeston. Dat. Fr. b. Nat. of B. V. M. [8 Sept.], 3 Edw. II. [1309]. (Trusley.)

1140. GRANT from William fil. Rog. de Cobeleye to Nicholas de Marchynton of four acres of land in Wyardeston. Witn. Thomas fil. Hug. de la Sale, Richard de Hordren, Thomas de la Grene. Dat. F. a. Ann. of B. V. M. [25 Mar.], 7 Edw. II. [1314]. (Trusley.)

1141. GRANT from Thomas fil. Nich. le Pottere to Nicholas de Marchinton of his messuage and land in Wyarduston. Witn. Robert de la Sale, Adam Hurt, Richard de Hordrene, etc. Dat. Vig. of St. Thomas, Ap. [21 Dec.], 10 Edw. II. [1316]. (Trusley.)

1142. GRANT from Richard de Horderne to Dom. Richard de Fillingleye, chaplain, of a messuage, etc., in Wyarduston. Dat. S. a. Pur. of B. V. M. [2 Feb.], 10 Edw. II. [1317]. (Trusley.)

1143. GRANT from Hugh fil. Will. de la Grene de Wyardeston to Henry his brother of a rood of land in Wyardeston lying "in le Hemrudyng super le Lymputford." Witn. William de Potloc, Richard de Hcrderne, Henry de Horderne. Dat. T. a. Trinity [31 May], 1317. (Trusley.)

1144. GRANT from Richard le Taillour fil. Joh. de Lek de Neuton to Nich. de Marchynton of 12*d.* annual rent from a messuage, etc., in Wyarduston. Witn. Adam le Gardiner, Nicholas fil. Leticie de Roddesleye, Richard de Horderne, etc. Dat. W. b. F. of Nat. of St. John B. [24 June], 10 Edw. II. [1317]. (Trusley.)

1145. QUITCLAIM from Thomas fil. Nicholai le Pottere to Nicholas de Marchinton of land and meadow in Wyarduston. Witn. Thomas fil. Reginaldi de Asscheburn, John de Pecco de Roddesley, Nicholas fil. Mich. de Roddesley. Dat. Roddesley, Th. a. Christmas, 13 Edw. II. [1319]. (Trusley.)

1146. GRANT from Thomas fil. Nich. le Porter to Nicholas de Marchinton of all his lands, etc., in Wyardeston. Witn. John de Pecco in Roddesley, Nicholas Horm, John de Roucestre, capellanus. Dat. T. b. F. of St. Mark [25 Apr.], 13 Edw. II. [1320]. (Trusley.)

1147. GRANT from Richard de Horderen to Reginald fil. Nich. de Marchinton of 2*s.* annual rent from all his lands in Wyardeston. Witn. Ralph de Marchinton, Nicholas Selveyn, John de la Peck, etc. Dat. Sat. b. Ascension Day [29 May], 14 Edw. II. [1321]. (Trusley.)

1148. GRANT from John de Coudrey to Reginald fil. Nicholai de Marchinton of six acres of land in the fee of Wyardeston lying in Schertwode and Stirkesmor. Witn. Ralph fil. Nich. de Marchinton, Nicholas Selveyn, Adam Hert, etc. Dat. Whitsunday [15 May], 1323. (Trusley.)

1149. QUITCLAIM from Adam de Wyndeston to Reginald de Marchenton of 22 acres of land in Schertwod and Stirkesmor in Wyardeston. Witn. Ralph de Marchenton, Nicholas Selueyn, Adam del Halle, etc. Dat. T. a. F. of St. Hilary [13 Jan.], 1323[4]. (Trusley.)

1150. GRANT from Reginald fil. Nich. de Marchinton to Ralph his brother of 10*d.* yearly rent in Wiardeston. Witn. John de Pecco de Roddesleye, Hugh Faber, Adam de Aula, etc. Dat. Sat. a. Pur. of B. V. M. [2 Feb.], 17 Edw. II. [1324]. (Trusley.)

1151. GRANT from William fil. Hen. fil. Emme de Wyardiston to Nicholas fil. Rog. de Mercynton of land in Wyardiston. Witn. Dom. Henry fil. Herberti, Roger de Bradeburn, mil., John Selvein. *Circ. temp.* Edw. II.

1152. GRANT from Richard de Hordrene to Nicholas de Marchinton of half an acre of land in Wyardiston. Dat. S. a. F. of St. James [25 July]. *Circ. temp.* Edw. II.

1153. GRANT from Henry de la Grene to Adam his son of all his lands in Wyardeston. Witn. Reginald de Marchynton, John Coudrey, Adam ad Aulam, etc. Dat. T. a. Trinity [28 May], 16 Edw. III. [1342]. (Trusley.)

1154. GRANT from John fil. Thom. de Wyardeston to Richard, ballivus de Yeveley, of half an acre and a rood of land in Wyardeston, near le Fennilachemarleput. Dat. T. b. F. of St. Hilary [13 Jan.], 26 Edw. III. [1353]. (Trusley.)

1155. GRANT from Cecily del Grene to Walter Tibbesone de Longeforde of all her lands, etc., in Wyardeston. Dat. T. a. Easter [7 Apr.], 29 Edw. III. [1355]. (Trusley.)

1156. QUITCLAIM from Henry fil. Joh. Coudrey to Thomas de Marchynton of Roddesley of 20*d.* annual rent in Wyardeston. Witn. Nicholas de Knyveton, Robert le Fower, Geoffrey de Salford, etc. Dat. Roddesley, M. a. Pur. of B. V. M. [2 Feb.], 45 Edw. III. [1371]. (Trusley.)

1157. GRANT from Walter Tibbesone to Dom. Will. de Clifton, rector of Edluston, and Dom. Richard Leche de Edluston, capellanus, of all the lands in Wyarduston which he had by grant from Cecily del Grene. Witn. Nicholas de Knyveton, Thomas de Marchinton, John Selven de Reggusley, etc. Dat. Morr. of Inv. of H. Cross [4 May], 50 Edw. III. [1376]. (Trusley.)

1158. GRANT from William Myners and Agnes his wife to William Myners his son of a messuage which they had by grant of William Cheyne in Wyardston. Witn. John Myners, esq., John Perkyn, William Hurt, etc. *Circ. temp.* Edw. III. (Trusley.)

EDNASTON.

(EADULMESTONE.)

1159. RELEASE from Roger Venator to Bartholomew, Prior, and the monks of Totesbure [Tutbury, co. Staff.], of lands in the manor of Semmeloia, towards Eadulmestone, in exchange for a confirmation of his old tenement held at 16*d.* rent, and a grant of 10 acres of land near the same, measured by the perch of 18½ feet; rent to the Prior, 12*d.* Witn. Sir William de Rideware, steward, Henry de Daneston, Ralph de Toruardeston, etc. *Temp.* Hen. III. (Woll. viii. 68.)

EGGINTON.

(EGGINGTON, EGINTON, EGKYNGESTON, EGKYNGTON, EGYNTON, EGYNTONE.)

1160. GRANT from Almaric de Gace to Ralph fil. Nicholai of all his land in Egkyngeston and Amboldeston [in Elvaston], "cum toto redditu meo de Dereby," which he inherited from his mother, to hold by tenure of one sparrow hawk or 12*d.* Witn. Stephen de Segrave, Justice of England, John fil. Philippi, Godfrey de Crawecrumb, Richard de Sandiacre, Oliver de Sautcheverel. Early Hen. III. (Every.)

1161. INSPEXIMUS and confirmation by Henry III. of the charter of Amauric de Gace (*v.* above). Witn. P. Wyntoniensis episcopus, S. de Segrave, Justicia Anglie, Walter de Clifford, Ralph Gernun, Geoffrey Dispensator, Geoffrey de Cauz. Dat. per manum venerabilis Patris R. Cycestrensis episcopi Cancellarii nostri apud Gloucestriam, 5 Jan., anno 18 [1234]. (Every.)

1162. SIMILAR confirmation by Henry III. of a similar but not identical charter, whereby Amauric de Gace sold to Ralph fil. Nicholai his land in Egkyngton and Amboldeston " cum toto redditu meo de Dereby," which he inherited from his mother, to hold to the said Ralph from Ralph de Frusenguill by doing service to the latter, " quantum pertinet ad octavam partem feodi unius militis." Same witnesses and date. (Every.)

1163. GRANT from John de Chandois, with the assent of Margery his wife to Richard fil. Willelmi de Eginton of all the land of Lappinge-haly with the meadow which Odo Winemer sometime held in the territory of Eginton and five selions lying near Horsmedwe and three other selions in the same vill. Witn. Thomas de Curzun, Fulcher de Yrton, mil., Nicholas de Finderne, Robert Ferbraz, Robert fil. Walkelini de Egington, etc. *Temp.* Hen. III. Fine seal of arms of John de " Chaundos." (Every.)

1164. GRANT from Margaret de Grendon to Richard fil. Will. de Eginton of a part of her land in the territory of Eginton, viz., three selions in Thacholm lying between the land of Geoffrey de Musters and the land of Godwin fil. Lefwini and two selions on Asphil. Witn. Robert fil. Fulcheri de Osmundeston, Ernald de Eston, Richard fil. Gileberti de Eston, Gilbert de Merston, Robert fil. Walkelini de Eginton. *Temp.* Hen. III. (Every.)

1165. GRANT from Margaret de Grendon, widow, to Richard fil. Will. de Eginton of a bovate of land in the vill of Eginton, with three selions near the road which leads to Tutesbire and a selion in Ambre-flat, three selions in Holme towards Neuton, a selion on Bruneshul, etc. Witn. Dom. Henry fil. Geroldi, Dom. John Talebot, Dom. Geoffrey de Musters, Dom. Henry fil. Walkelini, Dom. Hugh, persona de Eginton, Gilbert de Merston. *Temp.* Hen. III. (Every.)

1166. GRANT from Ralph fil. Nicholai to Richard fil. Will. de Eginton of a bovate of land which Godwin fil. Lefwyne sometime held in the said vill of Eginton. Witn. Dom. Robert de Duyn, Dom. Geoffrey de Bec, Dom. Robert de Esseburn, Dom. Nicholas de Sancto Mauro, Dom. Richard de Venables, Nicholas de Chadisden, clerk, Nicholas fil. Walclini, Robert fil. Walclini. Late Hen. III. (Every.)

1167. GRANT from Robert fil. Walkelini to Richard fil. Willelmi of a part of his land in the territory of Eggington, viz., three selions in Thacholm, two acres beyond Northbroc towards the heath, one acre on Asphil, one acre between Blachmere and the " divisa de Wilinton" which Ketel fil. Willelmi held, and half an acre in Flete. Witn. Dom. Geoffrey de Musters, Henry fil. Walkelini, Hugh decanus, Symon de Sancto Mauro, Gilbert de Merston, etc. Late Hen. III. (Every.)

1168. RELEASE from Margery que fuit uxor Johannis le Chaundois to Richard fil. Will. de Egynton of all the land of Lappingehaly with the meadow which Odo Wynemere held in the vill of Egynton, and five selions between Horsmedwe and the land of Godwin fil. Lewyn and three selions between Northbroc and the Heath. Witn. Thomas de Curzoun, Hugh le Meynel, Fulcher de Irton, mil., Nicholas de Fynderne, Robert Ferbraz, etc. Late Hen. III. (Every.)

1169. GRANT from Ralph fil. Hugonis de Gurney of Wylintune to Dom. Robert de Stafford and Gundreda his wife, of six acres of arable land in the territory of Egyntone lying in Egyntoneholm and Ryeflat. Witn. William de Muschamp, Robert Ferebras, Nicholas de Fynderne. *Temp.* Edw. I. (Every.)

1170. GRANT from Walter de Streton to John his first-born son and heir of twenty-six acres of arable land in the territory of Eginton lying in an assart called Le Newe Ruyding, between the assart of Dom. Robert de Stafford and the land of John de Chandoys. Witn. Dom. Robert de Tok, Ralph de Lattheburi, Richard le Seriant. Dat. Tu. a. F. of St. Martin [11 Nov.], 1301. (Every.)

1171. GRANT from Avice le Bonde of Egynton to Ralph de Lathebury of two acres of land in the territory of Egynton lying at Le Blakemere, Lombrekotedich, Potlocholm, and Barspol. Witn. Dom. Giles de Meygnyll, Robert le Touk, mil., Robert Ferbraz de Wylynton, William le Muschamp, Richard Foliot de Etewell. Dat. Tu. a. Michs. Day [29 Sept.], 31 Edw. I. [1303]. (Every.)

1172. RELEASE from Robert fil. Elie le Bonde de Egynton of the above lands to the said Ralph. Dat. F. of SS. Simon and Jude [28 Oct.], 31 Edw. I. [1303]. (Every.)

1173. GRANT from Thomas Cocus, manens in Eginton, to Robert his first-born son and heir, of a messuage with buildings thereon in the vill of Eginton, and forty-six acres of land in the same vill and territory. Witn. William le Sergant, William le Couper, Robert Caytewayte, Nicholas le Sergant. Dat. Fr. b. Nat. of St. John B. [24 June]. 1328. (Every.)

1174. GRANT, for life, from Thomas de Rolleston to William Phelip, chaplain, of a moiety of his land of Lappynghalugh in Egynton. Witn. Robert de Lathyngbury, John de Tyneworth, William de Pakynton, etc. Dat. Egynton, Th. a. F. of St. Katharine [25 Nov.], 11 Edw. III. [1337]. (Harl. 112 C. 40.)

1175. LEASE, for life, from Thomas de Rolleston to John fil. Johannis le Wrlyot of Egynton of a moiety of his land and meadow of Lappynghalugh in the vill of Egynton. Witn. Robert de Lathyngbury, John de Tymorth, William de Pakynton. Dat. Fr. a. F. of St. Katharine [25 Nov.], 11 Edw. III. [1337]. (Every.)

1176. GRANT from Theobald Trussell, mil., to William Tuttebury of Derby of all his lands, etc., with fishery and other rights in the vill of Egynton. Witn. Auered de Sulney, mil., John Frannceis, John Foucher, Ralph de Duffeld, John de Fyndern. Dat. Fr. in Whitsun Week [14 June], 33 Edw. III. [1359]. (Every.)

1177. QUITCLAIM from Richard de Tuttebury, Richard de Chedle, and William Andreu, chaplains, of all the lands with fisheries, etc., in the vill of Egynton lately held by William de Tuttebury of Derby. Witn. John Foucher, Ralph de Duffeld, John de Rolleston, etc. Dat. at Tuttebury, W. a. Conv. of St. Paul [25 Jan.], 34 Edw. III. [1360]. (Every.)

1178. CONVEYANCE from John de Rolleston to William fil. Nich. de Eginton of all that arable land which the latter had on lease from Richard de Mackeleye in Eginton, namely, at or near Omerflat, Smalmedewe, Lappinghalghdich, Asphull, Hethflat, and Tothebuttes. Witn. John Foucher, Richard de Rolleston, Henry de Lathebury. Dat. F. of St. Oswald [15 Apr.], 42 Edw. III. [1368]. (Every.)

1179. GRANT from John Fouch and Ermentrewe his wife to William Mareschal of Seggeshale, Margaret his wife, and others, of all their lands, etc., in Egynton, Ambaston [in Elvaston], Thurleston, Chaddesden, Rodburn, Potlok, Fyndern, Etewall, Berewardecote, Hethhouses, Horseleye, and Trusseleye. Dat. Inv. of H. Cross [3 May], 50 Edw. III. [1376]. French. (Every.)

1180. RE-CONVEYANCE from John fil. Joh. le Wryht of Egynton to Thomas de Rolleston, his lord, of all his land and meadow in Lappyn-halugh, which he held on lease. *Temp.* Edw. III. (Every.)

1181. GRANT from John de Brynnesley, rector of the church of Hoggesthorp, to Henry de Bothe of Norbury, esq., John de Bradley, vicar of Duffeld, Thomas Rypley, vicar of St. Michael, Derby, and Robert Smalley of Alwaston, of all the lands and tenements which he had of the feoffment of Robert Pole, parson of Colwyk, sometime parson of Swerkeston, and Robert de Walton, chaplain, in the vill of Egynton. Witn. John de Fynderne, John Lathbury, John de Bonyngton, Nicholas de Scheyl, Thomas de Makworth, esquires. Dat. 10 Nov., 5 Hen. ·V. [1417]. (Every.)

1182. GRANT from John Bothe, son and heir of Henry Bothe, to William Vernon, esquire, John Lawe, clerk, John Spycer, and Richard Buon, of an annual rent of six marks from the lands which Roger Wylson and others held in the vill of Egynton. Dat. 10 May, 7 Hen. VI. [1429]. (Every.)

1183. CONVEYANCE from John Bothe of Derby, Geoffrey de Hulme, Thomas Culcheth, and Nicholas Culcheth to Cecily le Gaunt and Elena, his daughter, of all those messuages in Egynton which Roger Willeson and others held and acquired by feoffment of John fil. Henrici Bothe. Witn. Thomas Bradshagh, Robert Smalley, Nicholas Dawson. Dat. 12 Sept., 8 Hen. VI. [1429]. (Every.)

1184. POWER of attorney from Nicholas Fyzherbert of Northbury, John Lathbury of Eggyngton, John Rolleston of Swerkeston, and John Saucheverell of Aston, esquires, to John Waundell of Eggyngton and John Clerk, to receive seisin of the manor and demesne of Eggyngton called Semereplace, with other lands, in the said town, which were lately Richard de Rolleston's, and two acres of lands in Hylton called Semereacres. Dat. 4 Feb., 14 Hen. VI. [1436]. (Every.)

1185. QUITCLAIM from Robert Lathbury filius junior Aluredi Lathbury, mil., to John Lathbury fil. Johannis Lathbury "nepotis mei," of all his lands in Egynton and Hethhouses which the said John fil. Johannis and Katherine hold of the feoffment of Henry Bradburne, esq., and William Lathbury. Dat. 11 June, 17 Hen. VI. [1439]. (Every.)

1186. GRANT from Margaret de Harley of Egynton to John Rogerson of a messuage and three roods of land in Egynton. Witn. John Lathbury, esq., John Rogers, William Bracley. Dat. M. b. F. of St. James [25 July], 32 Hen. VI. [1454]. (Every.)

10

1187. GRANT from William Vernon, knt., to John fil. Hen. Bothe, William son and heir of the said John, and Henry the son of the last-named William, of an annual rent of six marks from lands in Egynton. Dat. F. of Tr. of St. Thomas [7 July], 4 Edw. IV. [1464]. (Every.)

1188. GRANT from John Bothe of Erleston, esq., son and heir of Henry Bothe, to Henry de Rolleston, son of John Rolleston of Swerkeston, of a messuage in Egynton called Semereplace, and all other lands, meadows, fisheries, etc., which were sometime Richard Rolleston's in the same vill. Dat. 17 Aug., 5 Edw. IV. [1465]. (Every.)

1189. GRANT from Henry Rolleston, son and heir of John Rolleston of Swerkeston, to Thomas Stathum, knt., Henry Vernon, John Curson, John Both, Ralph Saucheverell, Henry Stathum, esquires, and others, of a messuage in Egynton called Semerplace, with fisheries, etc. Dat. 24 June, 8 Edw. IV. [1468]. (Every.)

1190. QUITCLAIM from Nicholas Agard of Newborough, co. Staff., esq., to William Mounyng, clerk, William Boylleston, John Agard, and eight others of two messuages and lands adjacent in the tenure of William Shorthose and a parcel of meadow in the tenure of the Prior of Tutbury, all in the fee of Eggington and Merston, co. Derby. Dat. F. of St. Bartholomew [24 Aug.], 18 Hen. VII. [1502]. (Every.)

EGGINTON *v.* also under ASHBOURNE, ROSTON, WILLINGTON.

ELMTON.

(ELMETON.)

1191. GRANT from John Bromale and Matilda his wife to William de Leek, John Oxton, and Edmund Cooke of Thurgarton, of all their lands in Elmeton. Witn. Dom. Nicholas de Gonsille, Dom. Ralph Frecchevyle, knt., William Marjory. Dat. Vig. of St. Matthew [20 Sept.], 20 Ric. II. [1396]. (de Rodes.)

1192. GRANT from John Regge de Walley and Joan his wife to Thomas Edeson of nine acres of land in the fields of Elmton. Witn. Robert Barker, John Scherston, Richard Kechyn. Dat. S. a. F. of St. Martin [11 Nov.], 3 Hen. VI. [1424]. (de Rodes.)

1193. GRANT, on petition, from King Henry [VIII.] to Sir William Tyler, knt., and Nicholas Carue, esq., of the manor of Elmeton and Holmesfield, co. Derb., and other manors in cos. Notts. and Salop, late belonging to Francis Lovell, Viscount Lovell [and forfeited to the Crown by Act of Attainder in 1489]. (Add. 22628.)

ELTON.

1194. LEASE from Godfrey Foliambe, custos Johannis fil. Thome Foliambe "Ward" domini Henrici Ducis Lancastrie to Richard Bon, of two messuages and three bovates of land in Elton, for 10 years. Dat. Morr. of Pur. of B. V. M. [3 Feb.], 31 Edw. III. [1357]. (Foljambe.)

1195. QUITCLAIM from William Pyrton, clerk, and Adam Nubyggyng, clerk, to Edward Foliambe, knt., John Staforth, sen., of Eyom, Roger Wormhyll and Thomas Waterhows, of the manors of Elton and Tyddeswall and 40 acres of land in Wormhyll, Lytton, Burton, and Abney. Dat. F. of Nativity [25 Dec.], 1424 [?]. (Foljambe.)

1196. ACQUITTANCE from Philip Leche, esq., to Henry Foljambe, esq., and Benedicta his wife, for 10 marks in full payment of 25 marks due to him by agreements touching the lordship of Elton. Dat. Vig. of SS. Simon and Jude [27 Oct.], 20 Edw. IV. [1480]. (Foljambe.)

ELTON *v.* also under BIRCHOVER, MELBOURNE.

ELVASTON *v.* under EGGINTON.

ETWALL.

(ETTEWALLE, ETTEWELLE, ETUUEL, ETWALLE.)

1197. LEASE from Bernard, Abbot, and the Convent of Burton-[-on-Trent], to Richard de Bersicote, of the land which his father John had held of them, and at the same rent, 10*s.*, with licence to make a mill in Bersicote [in Etwall]. [1160-1175.] (Stowe 77.)

Notum sit omnibus presentibus et futuris quod ego Bernardus dictus Abbas Burtonie totusque eiusdem loci conuentus concessimus et presenti carta confirmauimus huic Ricardo de Bersicote et heredibus suis terram patris sui Johannis quam tenuit die qua fuit uiuus et mortuus tenendam libere et quiete, sicut idem Johannes eam tenuit uidelicet pro decem solidis singulis annis reddendis videlicet ad festum Sancti Martini et ad festum sancti Johannis et pro suo libero seruicio. Concessimus etiam ei Molendinum faciendum et habendum in Bersicote sine detrimento et diminutione redditus Molendinorum nostrorum. His testibus, Primum ipso capitulo uidelicet Willelmo Priore, Audoeno suppriore, Martino, Willelmo cantore, tribus Ricardis et ceteris omnibus, Roberto de Stapenhell, Ailwino capellano, Reginaldo capellano, Radulfo de Chaldwell, Leisingo de Brontestune, Roberto de Hegworda, Ricardo filio Leising, Ernaldo filio Elfrici pistoris, Hereberto preposito, Waltero nepote Cutberti, Walarando Coco, Reginaldo filio Ailmeri, Hugone de Chalduuell, Humfrido de Herteshorne.

1198. GRANT from Malcolm Mosard fil. Radulfi Mosard and John Mosard fil. eiusdem Radulfi to Peter de Cestria, "prepositus de Staverle[y]," of land in the territory of Etuuel and Hinkershill which they had by grant of Hugh and Alice de Aldwark. Witn. William de Stotvile, Robert le Breton, Oliver de Langford, Ralph Cachehors, etc. [1282-1298]. (Harl. 86 H. 51.)

1199. GRANT from Hugh fil. Nicolai de Ettewalle and Selestria his wife, daughter of Fraunceys, with the consent of their children, Adam, William, and Matilda, to the Abbey of Wellebec of a ditch between their property and that of the Abbey, with stipulations as to building a wall. Witn. Walter le Rybef in Ettewelle, Richard Foliot of the same, Alexander de Morton in the same. Dat. Ettewelle, Palm Sunday, 1294. (Add. 26758.)

1200. GRANT from Peter fil. et her. Roberti de Herdewyk to Nicholas fil. Alexandri de Eginton of two acres and a half of land and half an acre of meadow in the field and meadow of Herdewyk [in Etwall], the land lying in the culture called Berneflat between the land of the Prior of Tutbury and that of Dom. Ralph de Meymur, and the meadow between the land of Walter, rector of Eginton, and that of Richard Folyot of Etewelle. Witn. Henry, rector of Eginton, William le Mergawute, William fil. Ermentrewe, John Chaundes, etc. Dat. T. a. F. of St. Barnabas [11 June], 29 Edw. I. [1301]. (Every.)

1201. GRANT from Robert fil. Rogeri de Eginton to John his son of an acre and a half of arable land in Hulton in a certain place called Le Herdewik. Witn. John Rowhe, John le Coupere, chaplains, Thomas le Flexhewere, William Caytewayte. Dat. S. a. Ann. of B. V. M. [25 Mar.], 8 Edw. III. [1334]. (Every.)

1202. QUITCLAIM from William Godladde of Hulton to Ralph de Lattheburi of the capital messuage of Heredwik which he had of the feoffment of William fil. Radulphi de Hulton. Dat. Sat. a. F. of St. Katharine [25 Nov.], 35 Edw. III. [1361]. (Every.)

1203. SALE by John Fitzherbert, King's Remembrancer, to John Port and Jehan, his wife, daughter of the said John, for 300 marks, of lands in Etwalle, Burnastone, Trusley, and Hylton, which the said John Fitzherbert had previously granted in trust to Water Odeby, John Chauntrell, clerks, etc., for his use. Dat. 21 May, 10 Hen. VII. [1495]. (Woll. xi. 48.)

1204. SALE by John Fytzherbert, King's Remembrancer of the Exchequer, to John Port, husband of Johane, daughter of the said John, of lands in Etwall, Burnaston, Trusley, and Hylton, with reversion to Eustace, son of the said John Fytzherbert, and John Fytzherbert of Norbury. Dat. 25 May, 10 Hen. VII. [1495]. (Woll. xii. 133.)

1205. RELEASE, for £160, from John Fitzherbert, Remembrancer of the Exchequer, to John Porte, husband of Johane, daughter of the said John Fitzherbert, of lands in Etwall, Burnaston, Trusley, and Hiltone. Dat. 28 Oct., 18 Hen. VII. [1502]. (Woll. xii. 103.)

1206. RELEASE from John Chaunterell, clerk, Ranulph Bylyngton, and John Copwode, gent., to John Porte of Etwall, gent., of lands in Etwall and elsewhere held of John Fitzherbert, Remembrancer of the Exchequer. Dat. 16 Mar., 19 Hen. VII. [1504]. (Woll. xii. 105.)

ETWALL *v.* also under BEARWARDCOTE.

EYAM.

(AIHUM, EIUM, EYHAM, EYOM, EYOME, EYOUM, EYUM.)

1207. GRANT from Eustace de Moreton to Richard de Staford of three bovates of land in Eium, one of which Richard, the latter's father, held; another Adam de Kileburn held; and the third, " quam ei perfeci de ipso dominico meo"; to hold by service of finding a lamp burning before the altar of St. Elena in the church of Eium during divine service. Witn. Serlo de Begele, Peter de Hassop, Robert de Calfhouera, Robert de Abeneya, Oliver de Saucheverel, etc. *Temp.* Hen. III. (Woll. vii. 37.)

1208. CONFIRMATION by Eustace fil. Eustachii de Moretain to Richard de Stafford of the preceding grant of land in Aihum, to hold by the same service. Witn. Serlo de Beeleg', Richard de Ednesor, Robert de Stanton, Robert de Calfor, etc. *Temp.* Hen. III. (Woll. vii. 38.)

1209. GRANT from Richard de Stafford to Roger his son of all that land which he had from Dom. Eustace de Mortein in the vill and territory of Eyum; the said Roger to hold by the same service of a lamp, etc. Witn. Robert le Archere, Matthew de Langisdon, Henry de Caluouere, John Bauquell, clericus, etc. *Temp.* Hen. III. (Woll. vii. 44.)

1210. RELEASE from William de Mortein of his claim to the services, following, and chattels of John fil. Nicholai de Eyum to Richard de Stafford, in consideration of 24*s.* Witn. William Maubuel, then Seneschal, Ralph de Eyincurt, Roger de Mortein, Roger de Stafford, Henry de Caluouere, William de Langisdon, Hugh de Hegelawe, Nicholas de Paddeley, William Albus de Grundelford, John clericus, etc. Dat. at Dunnisby, W. post clausum Pasca [29 Apr.], 32 Hen. III [1248]. Seal of arms. (Bowles.)

1211. GRANT from Roger fil. Rogeri de Staffordia to Richard de Stafford, his brother, of all that land in Eyum which Richard de Stafford, his grandfather, gave him. Witn. Thomas Foleiaumbe, William, his brother, William Hally, Thomas Foleiaumbe, etc. *Temp.* Hen. III. or Edw. I. (Woll. vii. 39.)

1212. GRANT from Roger de Morteyn dominus de Eyum to Roger le Rus and Agnes his wife of four messuages and six bovates of land in Eyum, held respectively by Thomas Attechirchestile, Roger Attecrosse, and others and four acres of waste land near Leyghumsti and common of pasture throughout the manor; rent, 40*s.* Witn. Dom. Richard de Herthulle, mil., and Dom. Thomas Foleiambe, mil., John Martyn, Peter de Roland, etc. Dat. Wed. b. Pur. of B. V. M., 28 Edw. I. [1300]. (Woll. vii. 40.)

1213. PROCEEDINGS taken in Winster Church relating to the divorce of Richard de Stafford and Isabella, his wife. Dat. Tu. a. All Saints' Day, 1308. (Bowles.)

1214. UNDERTAKING by Thomas de Furnival, sen., domimus de Hallumchire, to whom Agnes, "que fuit uxor Rogeri le Rous," and John her son have granted an annual rent of 20*s.* from four messuages and lands in Eyum, to hold the same Agnes and John acquitted in respect of the said rent "versus Dominum Rogerum . . . et Dominum Rogerum de Mortein." Witn. John Bozon, dominus de Edinsouere, Richard Foleiaumbe de Longisdon, Richard de la Pole, Richard le Archer, Robert de Caluoure, etc. Dat. Beauchef, Vig. of F. of Circumcision [31 Dec.], 1322. (Bowles.)

1215. GRANT from John fil. Roger le Rous to Gervase Rankel of a toft and bovate of land in Eyum, as in a deed of feoffment which the said Roger had from Dom. Roger de Morteyn, "condam domini de Eyum." Witn. Richard le Archer, Richard de Paddeley, etc. Dat. T. a. "Quasimodo" Sunday [3 Apr.], 16 Edw. II. [1323]. (Foljambe.)

1216. GRANT from Alexander de Leyum to Richard de Leyum, his brother, of lands in Eyum. Witn. Richard de Paddeley, William de Abbeney, Roger de Stafford, etc. Dat. F. of St. Peter ad Vincula [1 Aug.], 3 Edw. III. [1329]. (Woll. viii. 7.)

1217. RELEASE from James de Sulby to Gervase Rankelle of two bovates of land called Ryleghleyes in Eyum. Witn. Roger fil. Ricardi de Paudeley, Thos. Rankelle, William fil. Walteri de Eyum, etc. Dat. S. a. Nat. of St. John B. [24 June], 12 Edw. III. [1338]. (Woll. vii. 45.)

1218. GRANT from John fil. Gervasii Raunkell of Eyum to Agnes que fuit uxor Ricardi del Dale of Eyum of a messuage and two bovates of land in the vill of Eyum, in a place called Ryleye. Witn. John le Golert of Eyum, John fil. Rogeri de Stafford de eadem, William Note de eadem, etc. Dat. W. a. F. of St. John, a.p.l. [6 May], 25 Edw. III. [1351]. (Woll. vii. 42.)

1219. GRANT, in tail, from Agnes relicta Ricardi de Dale of Eyom to William fil. Willelmi de Stafford and Matilda, her daughter, in free marriage, of a messuage and two bovates of land in Ryleye in Eyom, with reversion to the grantor. Witn. John de Stafford of Eyom, William Note of the same, John le Chapman of Folowe, etc. Dat. T. a. Pur. of B. V. M. [2 Feb.], 28 Edw. III. [1354]. (Woll. vii. 61.)

1220. GRANT from Philip de Basselowe, chaplain, to John fil. Henrici de Moniassh and Matilda his wife and the heirs of their bodies, of two messuages, two bovates of land, and a place containing six acres " subtus Leyminsty " in the fee of Eyum, sometime held by Richard de Leyum; with remainder (on failure of heirs to the said John and Matilda) to Henry fil. Joh. fil. Henrici and his heirs born of Mariota, and on failure of heirs to them, to Nicholas Meuerell. Witn. John de Stafford, William Note, John le Chapmon, John de Bagschawe, John del Dale. Dat. Eyum, Sat. a. Octave of Easter [7 May], 29 Edw. III. [1356]. (Bowles.)

1221. GRANT from Joan and Matilda daughters of Richard del Dale de Eyum, widows, to John de Stafford of Eyum, of a plot of land lying between the high road and the common rivulet of the said town, and opposite his house. Witn. John fil. Henrici de Moniassh de Eyum, William de Hokelowe, John de Tonstedus del Fouwelowe. Dat. F. of Inv. of H. Cross [3 May], 44 Edw. III. [1370]. Endorsed " Carta de le Oxfold." (Bowles.)

1222. GRANT from Robert de Sulby to Roger Northe of Dobenehull and Dyonisia his wife, of a rent of 6s. from a tenement at Ryley in Eyum. Witn. Thomas de Wombewelle, John de Eyum, John de Stafford, etc. Dat. T. a. Easter [3 Apr.], 43 Edw. III. [1369]. (Woll vii. 43.)

1223. RELEASE from Robert fil. Rogeri Northe and Agnes his wife to John de Stafford of Eyom, of a rent of 6s. in Eyom. Dat. S. a. Exalt. of H. Cross [14 Sept.], 43 Edw. III. [1369]. (Woll. vii. 41.)

1224. GRANT from Thomas de Ouere, chaplain de Eyum, to John le Wright and Joan his wife, of a messuage and bovate of land in Eyum, which were sometime William Wysmon's. Witn. John Foliamb, John Nikbrother, John de Stafford, Nicholas de Wardelowe, Henry de Tiddeswell. Dat. Eyum, Th. a. F. of St. Cedda, Bp. [2 Mar.], 46 Edw. III. [1372]. (Bowles.)

1225. QUITCLAIM from Margery nuper uxor Johannis fil. Ricardi de Haddun to John de Stafford, sen., Thomas le Penne, chaplain, and Thomas Amote de Midulthun, of a messuage and nine acres of land and a half in Eyum which descended to her through Henry Gregory her brother. Witn. John le Archer del Heglowe, Nicholas de Wardelowe, John Cobyn. Dat. M. a. Pur. of B. V. M. [2 Feb.], 11 Ric. II. [1388]. (Bowles.)

1226. GRANT from John de Stafford de Eyoum and Thomas Amot de Midelton to John Rankell, chaplain, of two messuages and nine acres and a half of land in Eyoum. Witn. Nicholas del Leghes, Nicholas de Wardlowe, William Meverell, John del Mulne, Henry Gregory. Dat. F. of St. Laurence [2 Feb.], 16 Ric. II. [1393]. (Bowles.)

1227. ATTORNEY from Thomas Amot to John de Stafford to give seisin to John Rankell of the above lands. Same date. (Bowles.)

1228. GRANT from John Rankell to John Redser, rector of Eyum, Richard de Grendun, rector of Blore, and John Spondon, chaplain, of a messuage and nine and a half acres of land in Eyum. Witn. John de Stafford, William Meuerell, Stephen Marton, etc. Dat. S. a. F. of SS. Peter and Paul [29 June], 18 Ric. II. [1394]. (Bowles.)

1229. BOND from Matilda relicta Nicholai del Leghes de Eyoum and John del Leghes his son to John de Stafford, "in viginti plaustratis plumbi precii cuiusdam plaustrate quatuor libr' sex solid' et octo den," to be paid to the said John at Eyoum on S. a. Exalt. of H. Cross next, if the said Matilda and John do not pay the debts of the said Nicholas, and if the said John do not suffer any loss because of the said debts, or if the said Matilda or John sell "le Cluff plumbi" of the said John without his consent. Dat. W. a. F. of St. Martin [11 Nov.], 20 Ric. II. [1396]. (Bowles.)

1230. ATTORNEY from John Redser, rector of Eyum, and John Mappullus, sen., of Scheffeld, to John Rancekell, chaplain of Eyum to deliver seisin to John del Leghes of a messuage and two bovates of land in Eyum and a messuage with "duobus callis" in Chesturfield. Dat. Schefuld, W. b. All Saints' Day [1 Nov.], 22 Ric. II. [1398]. (Bowles.)

1231. GRANT from William Kalal de Normunthun and Randulph de Clapwell to Richard de Stafford and John Rankell, chaplain of Eyum, of a messuage and two bovates of land in Eyum, with a toft lying under Leghamsty, which they had by feoffment of John de Leghus. Witn. Thomas Foliambe, Thurstan de Beure, Roger Leche, etc. Dat. F. of St. Edward, K. and M. [18 Mar.], 1399 [1400]. (Bowles.)

1232. GRANT from Richard Stafford of Eyum and John Rankel, chaplain, of the same, to Alice, wife of John Stafford, esq., and Robert their son, of the messuage and lands in Eyum and the toft under Leghumsty which they had of the grant of William Kalal and Ralph de ·Clapwall. Witn. Nicholas de Wardelowe, John Cobyn, Stephen Martyn. Dat. F. of St. Peter and St. Paul [29 June], 1 Hen. IV. [1400]. (Bowles.)

1233. GRANT from John Redsyr, rector of Eyom, and John de Spondon, chaplain, to Dom. Thomas Nevyll, dominus de Hallumshire, and John de Wardelowe, of a messuage and nine and a half acres of land in Eyom which they had of the feoffment of John Rankell. Witn. Stephen Martyn, John Cobyn, Henry de Haselford, etc. Dat. apud Eyom, F. of St. Mathias [24 Feb.], 1 Hen. IV. [1400]. (Bowles.)

1234. ATTORNEY from John de Spondon to John Redsyr to deliver seisin of the above lands to the said Thomas and John. Dat. apud Barley, F. of St. Mathias [24 Feb.], 1 Hen. IV. [1400]. (Bowles.)

1235. ATTORNEY from Alice, wife of John Stafford, esq., and Robert their son to Richard de Knottesford of Neuton, co. Linc., to take seisin of a messuage, etc., in Eyum granted to them by Richard Stafford and John Rankell. Dat. apud Ketulesthorpe, S. a. Nat. of St. John B. [27 June], 1 Hen. IV. [1400]. (Bowles.)

1236. ATTORNEY from John Stafford of Eyum, esq., to John Rankell and Richard Stafford his brother to deliver seisin to Richard de Knottesforde, of all the lands in Folowe which the said John had of the grant of John Ranckell. Dat. apud Kettillesthorp, S. a. Nat. of St. John B. [27 June], 1 Hen. IV. [1400]. (Bowles.)

1237. GRANT from John Ranckell, chaplain, to Alice, wife of John Stafford, esq., and Robert, son of the said John Stafford and Alice, and the heirs of the said Robert in tail, of all the lands which he had by feoffment from John Stafford of Eyum, sen., father of the said John, in Eyum, Ryley, Folowe, Huclowe, Bawkwell, Yollgreve, and Castilton [Eyam, Riley, Foolow, Hucklow, Bakewell, Youlgrave, and Castleton, co. Derby]; to hold during the lifetime of the said Alice, with remainder to the said Robert, and on default of heirs to him then to John and Roger, the other sons of the said John Stafford. Witn. Thurstan de la Bowre de Tyddeswelle, Rob. de Middeltone of the same, Richard de Stafford of Highlowe, etc. Dat. F. of SS. Peter and Paul, 1 Hen. IV. [1400]. (Woll. vii. 46.)

1238. SALE from Geoffrey de Roulond, Nicholas Martyn, John Clerk, chaplain, John Andrew, chaplain, William fil. Johannis Smyth de Ascheford, and William Meuerell, to Nicholas de Wardelowe of Eyom and Thomas de Brischfeld, of all the oaks, ashes, and other trees growing in Festewod. Witn. John de Stafford, John Cobyn, Thomas Mascy. Dat. Eyum, Whitsunday, 4 Hen. IV. [1403]. (Bowles.)

1239. BOND from John Leghes, son and heir of Nicholas Leghes of Eyom, to John Stafford, esquire, for payment of £20. Dat. M. aft. F. of St. Peter ad vincula [1 Aug.], 6 Hen. IV. [1403]. (Bowles.)

1240. ACQUITTANCE from John Leghes son and heir of Nicholas Leghes to John Stafford, esq., for a sum of money for the reversion of a messuage and bovate of land in Eyum which Matilda, mother of the said John Leghes, held in dower, and, on her death, descended to the latter; and if the said messuage and land be entailed on the said John Leghes, the said John Stafford shall only hold it for his life. *Circ.* 1403. (Bowles.)

1241. ATTORNEY from John Leghes son and heir of Nicholas Leghes to John Cobyn to deliver to John Stafford, esq., seisin of a messuage and bovate of land in Eyom. Dat. M. a. F. of St. Peter ad vincula [1 Aug.], 6 Hen. IV. [1405]. (Bowles.)

1242. GRANT from John Leghes son and heir of Nicholas Leghes of Eyom to John Stafford, esq., of the reversion of a messuage and bovate of land in Eyom after the death of Matilda, his mother; to be held during life of the grantor. Witn. John Stafford, son of Henry Stafford of Eyam, John Cobyn of the same, Will. Bradshawe of the same, etc. Dat. M. a. F. of St. Peter ad vincula [1 Aug.], 6 Hen. IV. [1405]. (Woll. vii. 52.)

1243. GRANT from William Meverell of Eyom to Matilda de Gryndulforde, wife of Henry de Grundulforde, of Eyom, of a croft called Alencroft abutting on the road to Gryndulforde Bridge. Witn. Walter Meverell, John Meverell, Thomas de Bromhall. Dat. M. b. Pur. of B. V. M. [2 Feb.], 8 Hen. IV. [1407]. (Brookhill.)

1244. GRANT from John Meverell, sen., and Johanna his wife, and John their son and heir, to Thomas Martyn, of the moiety of the messuage called Ryleye which they had at the death of William de Stafford, father of the said Johanna. Witn. John de Stafford, esq., Nicholas Martyn, Richard de Stadone, etc. Dat. Eyam, 20 Aug., 11 Hen. IV. [1410]. (Woll. vii. 65.)

1245. GRANT from John son of Thomas Martin of Eyum to Nicholas Martin of Folowe of a messuage and two bovates of land in Eyum called Ryleye. Witn. John de Stafford, "squyer," Henry de Stafford of Myddelton Clyff, John de Leghum, etc. Dat. M. a. Pur. of B. V. M. [2 Feb.], 8 Hen. V. [1421]. (Woll. vii. 63.)

1246. POWER of attorney from John son of Thomas Martyn of Eyum to John de Holynworth of Mideltone to deliver seisin to Nicholas Martyn of Folowe of the same messuage, etc. Dat. Notyngham, Fri. a. Pur. of B. V. M., 8 Hen. V. [1421]. (Woll. vii. 64.)

1247. RELEASE from Robert Gerehard of Roddebume and Alice his wife to John Martyn her son of a toft and two bovates of land in Eyum called Ryleye. Witn. John de Stafford, "squyer," Henry de Stafford of Mydleton Clyff, John de Leghum, etc. Dat. M. a. Pur. of B. V. M. [2 Feb.], 8 Hen. V. [1421]. (Woll. vii. 62.)

1248. BOND from John Kyghley, knt., Richard Wallere, esq., and Robert Stafford, esq., and William Garner valettus, to Philip Braunche, knt., for payment of £350. Dat. 10 Oct., 1422. (Bowles.)

1249. GENERAL release from John Penyston, son and heir of William de Penyston de Basselowe, to John Stafford, jun., and Margaret his wife. Dat. Eyom, M. a. F. of St. Gregory [12 Mar.], 1 Hen. VI. [1423]. (Bowles.)

1250. GRANT from Richard Cobyn of Eyom to Richard Pygot, esq., and Ralphe Leche, esq., of all his goods and chattels in co. Derby, in return for £20. Witn. John Stafford of Mydelton, Richard Bawquell, Roger Milne. Dat. Eyom, F. of St. George [23 Apr.], 11 Hen. VI. [1433]. (Bowles.)

1251. GRANT from Roger Gerard of Rodburne and Alice his wife to Nicholas Martene of the same of lands in Ryley in Eyham. Witn. Peter de la Pole, Ralph and Henry, his sons, Walter Twyford, etc. Dat. 1 Aug., 14 Hen. VI. [1436]. (Woll. vii. 66.)

1252. GRANT from Nicholas Marten of Tiddeswalle to Henry Blackwalle of Blackwalle, John and William, sons of Roger Jonson of Tiddeswal Mylnehowse, of a messuage and two bovates of land in Eyum in Ryleye. Witn. John Stafford of Eyum, Walter Meverell of the same, Richard Bawkewelle of Mediltone Clyfe, etc. Dat. M. a. F. of St. Andrew [30 Nov.], 17 Hen. VI. [1438]. (Woll. vii. 67.)

1253. QUITCLAIM from John Wardlowe, son and heir of Nicholas Wardlowe, of Eyom, to Robert Stafford, of all the lands which descended to him on the death of his said father in Eyom. Witn. Roger Milne, Thomas Cobyn, Walter Meuerell. Dat. S. a. Exalt. of H. Cross [14 Sept.], 18 Hen. VI. [1439]. (Bowles.)

1254. RELEASE from Henry Blakwalle of Blakwalle and John and William, sons of Roger Jonson of Tiddeswal Mylnehowse, to Nicholas Marten of Tiddeswalle, of a messuage and two bovates of land in Eyum in Ryleye. Witn. Roger Jonson of Tiddeswal Mylnehowse, John Stafford of Eyum, John del Hylle of Folowe. Dat. 16 Jan., 20 Hen. VI. [1442]. (Woll. vii. 68.)

1255. DEED whereby the Prior and Convent of the Order of Mount Carmel of Doncaster acknowledge that they, with the consent of Nicholas Kerton, "noster pater prior provincialis," have received from

John Stafford of Eyum in the Peak a sum of money for the repair of their house and redemption of jewels pledged on account of their "intolerable debt," for which the Prior, etc., grant a mass with three collects to the said John and Margaret his wife. Dat. Stafford, at a general convocation, F. of St. Zacheus, 1444.

On the back is a memorandum by J. Stafford, enjoining his heirs to make certain grants to the "Priour of Newsted in Shyrewood" for a torch and for tapers to Eyam church, for which they shall have participation in the mass, etc., granted above. (Bowles.)

1256. SALE from Nicholas son of Robert Coterell to William son of Richard de Vernon, knt., and Ralph de Legh of all his goods and chattels in return for 20 marks. Witn. Christopher Nedham, Robert Radclyf, Henry Pylkynton. Dat. apud Thorshed, S. a. Nat. of B. V. M. [8 Sept.], 23 Hen. VI. [1444]. (Bowles.)

1257. GRANT from Nicholas Martyn of Tydeswall to Robert Stafford of Eyum of a messuage and two bovates of land in Eyum in Ryleye. Witn. Richard de Bawkwelle, John Byum, Roger Hasilford, etc. Dat. F. a. Nat. of B. V. M. [8 Sept.], 24 Hen. VI. [1445]. (Woll. vii. 69.)

1258. POWER of attorney from Nicholas Martyn of Tydyswalle to William Bothum of Stoke to deliver seisin to Robert Stafford of Eyum of a messuage and two bovates of land in Eyum in Ryleye. Same date. (Woll. vii. 70.)

1259. GRANT from Robert Stafford, esq., to Thomas Eyre and Richard Baukewell of all the lands in Eyam, Baukewell, Yolgreve, Tyddus[well], and Huclowe, on condition that they re-convey the same to the said Robert and Elizabeth his wife and their heirs in tail. Witn. John Grene of Bubbenhull, esq., Roger Mylne, sen., John de Leome. Dat. Eyome, 4 Jan., 24 Hen. VI. [1446]. (Bowles.)

1260. RE-CONVEYANCE of the above lands from the said Thomas and Richard to Robert Stafford, Elizabeth his wife, and their heirs. Dat. 6 Jan., 1446. (Bowles.)

1261. POWER of attorney from Margaret Stafford, widow of John Stafford, esq., to John Cook of Waltone and John Wylson of Calveovere, to deliver seisin to Richard Stafford, her son and heir, of lands in Eyam Clyf, alias Mydelton Clyf, together with two rents of 26s. 8d. and 5 marks. Dat. 4 Nov., 5 Edw. IV. [1465]. (Woll. vii. 60.)

1262. INDENTURE between Richard Stafford, gent., cousin and heir of Robert Stafford, esq., late of Eyam, and Thomas Foliambe, esq., enumerating the contents of a box of deeds delivered to the said Thomas Foliambe "to kepe to the behoofe and use of the said Richard and his heiress." Dat. 9 July, 7 Edw. IV. [1467]. (Foljambe.)

1263. AGREEMENT of Robert Barley of Barley, sen., esq., with Richard Bawkwell and Guy Grene, executors of the testament of Nicholas Stafford, late of Shroysbury, concerning the suits between the said Robert and the said Nicholas during his life, in accordance with the award of Robert Eyre, sen., esq., Roger Eyre, John Parker, and others, arbitrators. Dat. S. b. Pur. of B. V. M. [2 Feb.], 19 Edw. IV. [1480]. (Bowles.)

1264. DECLARATION by Richard Stafford, son and heir of John Stafford of Eyam, of the uses of an enfeoffment made 20 Oct., 6 Hen. VII. [1490], by him in trust to Robert Eyre of Padeley, jun.,

Philip Eyre, parson of Asshore, Roger Eyre of Hulme, Nicholas Stafford his brother, and Roger Eyre of Plumley, of lands in Eyam, Middiltone, Calvore, Rolond, Yolgreve, Tiddiswall, Longisdone, Huklow, Leom, and Bakewell. (Woll. vii. 48.)

1265. GRANT from William Milne of Wormyll and William his son to Peter, another son, of all his lands, etc., in Eyam. Dat. 24 Sept., 24 Hen. VII. [1508]. (Bemrose.)

1266. AWARD by Richard Suttone and John Porte, esquires, in a dispute between Humfrey Stafford, esq., to Rauff Martyn of Wynster, respecting the right to land named Ryley-in-Eyam. Dat. 11 Feb., 11 Hen. VIII. [1520]. (Woll. vii. 49.)

1267. LEASE, for 100 years, from Richard Bakewell, son of Henry Bakewell, to George Barley of Stoke, of all his lands, etc., in Eyam and Folowe (except one cottage). Dat. 1 Oct., 13 Hen. VIII. [1521]. (Bemrose.)

1268. GENERAL release from Thomas Bagshawe of Eyam, yeoman, and Humphrey Bagshawe, son and heir of the said Thomas, to Humphrey Stafford, esquire, Humphrey Stafford, Roland Stafford, and Anthony Stafford, sons of the said Humphrey, Michael Sele, and John Hardye. Dat. 22 Oct., 30 Hen. VIII. [1538]. (Bowles.)

1269. "PEDIGREE" of Peter de Lynford and his connection with the Stafford family. Sixteenth century. (Bowles.)

EYAM *v.* also under FOOLOW.

FAIRFIELD.

1270. SETTLEMENT of suit between the Dean and Chapter of Lichfield and Lenton Priory relating to the tithes of 500 acres of land in Fairfield in Hope. *Circ.* 1250. (Lichf. M.M. 16.)

1271. LETTERS patent of Edw. II., whereby licence is granted to William de Wikkilwod, parson of Boyleston, to re-enfeoff Walter Waldeshelf and Johanna his wife, in three messuages and lands in Fairefeld, Bukstones [Buxton], and Hope, and in the balliage of two forestries in Hopedale, with reversions to their daughters. Dat. York, 5 July, a° 15 [1322]. (Woll. iv. 59.)

1272. INDENTURE from eighteen residents of Fairfield, Woluelowe, and Pigktor, wherein, in recognition of leave from the Dean and Chapter of Lichfield to have a chantry chaplain and burial rights for their chapel, they bind themselves to present and maintain the chaplain, to reserve all rights of the mother church of Hope, and to pay a pension of £2 to the Dean and Chapter. Dat. 1 Feb., 1331[2]. (Lichf. KK. 2.)

FAIRFIELD *v.* also under TIDESWELL.

FARLEY.

(FARNLEYA, LE FARLEY.)

1273. GRANT from Thomas Rage of Codenore to Roger Rage and Alice his wife of a bake-house, a chamber, a pigstye, and lands in Le Farley; the said grant to be void should the said Alice survive her husband and marry again. Witn. John Clerke, Roger Coke, and Roger Gebbe. Dat. Codenore, 2 Sept., 5 Edw. IV. [1465]. (Woll. iv. 19.)

FARLEY *v.* also under DARLEY.

FERNILEE *v.* under CHAPEL-EN-LE-FRITH, HEAGE.

FINDERN.

(FINDERNA, FINDERNE, FINDIRNA, FYNDERNE.)

1274. LICENCE from Nicholas de Wilenton to Nicholas, Abbot, and the Convent of Burton [-on-Trent], to strengthen their fish-ponds at Finderne, promising never to build a mill there, and guaranteeing them against damage from the mills at Potlac. [1188-1197.] (Stowe 55.) The text is:—

> Uniuersis Sancte Matris Ecclesie filiis, Nicholaus de Wilentona salutem. Nouerit uniuersitas uestra me dedisse et concessisse et hac mea presenti carta confirmasse Domino N. abbati de Burtuna et conuentui eiusdem loci licenciam benigne uiuaria sua affirmare apud Finderne absque omni molestia et contradictione de me et de heredibus meis, ita quod numquam ibi fiat molendinum. Sed salua sit et integra tota secta de Finderne molendinis de Potlac in perpetuum. Et ut hec mea donatio rata sit et stabilis presentem cartam sigilli mei apposicione roboraui. Hiis testibus, Matheo capellano de Bauecwell, Willelmo de Vern', Roberto de Stokeport, Willelmo Gern', Roberto de Mideltona, Ada de Herthull, Roberto de Stantona, Roberto de Aluel', Rogero de Wodnesl', Henrico de Herthull, Ricardo de Ednesowra, Thoma fil. Ricardi, Hugone fil. Roberti de Waletona, et multis aliis.

1275. LICENCE from Robert de Toke to N[icholas], Abbot, and the Convent of Burton, to strengthen their fish-ponds at Finderne, promising never to build a mill there and to prevent the mills at Potlac from injuring their stews. [1188-1197.] (Stowe 56.)

N.B.—The text is identical with the preceding charter, excepting the substitution of name R. de Toke for that of N. de Wilentona.

1276. MEMORANDUM of lease held by Richard, "clericus" of Findern, from William [Melburne], Abbot, and the Convent of Burton, of land in Findern, and of his resignation to them of other lands therein. Witn., besides the whole Convent, Mag. Roger, "seniscallus," Philip de Wilinton, Ralph de Stapinhill, Hugh de Findern, Gervase de Kame, etc. [1197-1210]. (Stowe 53.)

1277. ACQUITTANCE from Ralph, clericus, fil. Mag. Ricardi de Finderna to Dom. Lawrence [de Sancto Edwardo], Abbot of Burtone [Burton-on-Trent], for seven years' rent in advance of all his land of Finderna, with the messuage adjoining. Witn. Nicholas fil. Hugonis de Finderna, John de Sala, Nicholas fil. Nicholai de Wylintone, John de Bersicote, etc. Dat. "post festum Annunciacionis dominice in Quadragesima" [25 Mar.], 1248. (Campb. iv. 15.)

1278. BOND given by Hugh de Gurney to the Abbot and Convent of Burton [-on-Trent] for his appearance with his wife Elizabeth before the Justices of the King's Bench or the Justices in Eyre for the execution of a conveyance of his land in Findirna, the Abbot and Convent paying his costs on the occasion; the bond to be executed by the Sheriff of Nottingham, with power to distrain on Hugh's goods in default of his appearance. Witn. Will. de Rolleston, sen., Ralph de la Bache, William de Muscampo, etc. *Circ.* 1275. (Stowe 52.)

1279. FINE from Hugh de Gurneye and Elizabeth his wife to John [Stafford], Abbot of Burton-on-Trent, of a messuage and land in Fynderne. Made before Mag. Roger de Seyton, Mag. Richard de Stanes, John de Cobbeham, and Thomas Welond, justices, in the octave of St. Hilary [20 Jan.], 3 Edw. I. [1275]. (Stowe 54.)

1280. CONVEYANCE from Joan de Fynderne, relicta Joh. de Fynderne, to John Makworth, Dean of Lincoln, Thomas Blount, Henry de Knyveton, Henry de Bothe, John de Irton, John Lathebury, and Thomas Bradeschawe, of her third part of the manor of Fynderne which she holds as dower, viz., all the chambers, with "le Parler, Norcere, Pantre, Botre, Wynceller," in the north part of the Hall, and a long house "under one roof," extending on the east towards "le Gaytehouse," and on the west towards the pool and several lands in the high field on "le Crow-nest," in "le middel forlonge," in "le Gores," on "le Foulthorne," in "le Gallemedowe," in "le Blakmeyre," in "le Ouerclose de Pottloke" called "Overhenmarshe," in "le Pottlokfeld" extending on the north towards "le Lytillwallehyll," which the said Joan holds in dower in Pottloke (except a part of the long house aforesaid which is called "le Werkhouse"); to hold in trust till Robert fil. et her. Joh. de Fynderne arrives at full age, or in case of his death, till the full age of the next heir, etc. Witn. Alvered de Lathebury, chev., Reginald de Lathebury, Henry Wychard, Thomas Makworth, John Crowker. Dat. Th. b. F. of St. Martin [11 Nov.], 8 Hen. V. [1420]. (Okeover.)

FINDERN *v.* also under REPTON.

FLAGG *v.* under CHELMERTON.

FOOLOW.
(FOLOW, FOLOWE, FOULOUE, LE FOULOWE.)

1281. RELEASE from Geoffrey, son of Richard de . . . arhis [?], to Richard Marmion, of lands in Fouloue and Eyam; rent, 3s. 1d. Witn. Henry de Malmeins [?], Thomas Vicarius, Robert de Akenei, etc. Late fourteenth century. (Woll. ii. 76.)

1282. GRANT from John Plummer and Robert de Hyndley to William Fox, William Cros, and John Ranckel, chaplains, of all the lands in the vill of Folowe and in the field of Bretton. Witn. John Foliamb de Teddeswell, Robert de Heghcote, John de Stafford, Stephen Martyn de Folowe, etc. Dat. Whitsun Tuesday [19 May], 51 Edw. III. [1377]. (Bowles.)

1283. QUITCLAIM from John Redser, rector of Eyum, and John Renkell, chaplain, to Alice, relicta Roberti le Taylur de Folowe, of a house and garden in le Foulowe. Witn. Stephen Martyn, John de Tunstedes, John de Foulowe, etc. Dat. Foulowe, T. a. F. of St. Martin [11 Nov.], 14 Ric. II. [1390]. (Bowles.)

1284. QUITCLAIM from John Rankell of Eyum, chaplain, to John de Stafford of the lands which he had of the feoffment of John Plumer and William Hendley, chaplains, in Folow and Bretton. Dat. Eyam, F. of Pur. of B. V. M. [2 Feb.], 1 Hen. IV. [1400]. (Bowles.)

1285. QUITCLAIM from Thomas Trote, son and heir of John Trote, late of Folowe, to Richard Stafford, kinsman and heir of Robert Stafford late of Eyham, of a messuage and five roods of land in Folowe which his said father had of the feoffment of the said Robert Stafford. Dat. 1 Feb., 2 Ric. III. [1485]. (Bowles.)

FOOLOW *v.* also under EYAM.

FOREMARK.

(FORNEWERK.)

1286. GRANT from Elys de Verdoun to Rowland Daneys of John atte Grene and Robert atte Grene, his "neifs," of Fornewerk, with their issue, goods, and chattels. Witn. Sire Emod [Edmund] de Apelby, Sir Averey de Solfuene, Robert de Sallowe, etc. Dat. Fornewerk, F. of St. Martin [11 Nov.], 25 Edw. III. [1351]. French. (P. R. O., B. 8005.)

1287. COVENANTS between Thomas Babyngton of Dethyk, esquire, and Ralph Fraunceys of Fornewerk, co. Derb., esq., for the marriage of Ralph Fraunceys with a sister, daughter, or other kinswoman of the said Thomas Babyngton. Dat. 1 July, 1489. (Foljambe.)

FOREMARK *v.* also under NEWTON SOLNEY.

FOSTON.

(FOSTONE, FOSTUN.)

1288. GRANT from Roger Wi[l]degos fil. Gerardi Wildegos to William Wi[l]degos of three selions of land in Foston and Scropton, in Coppelowe; rent to the lord of the fee, one rose yearly at the feast of St. John B. [24 June]. Witn. Dom. Will. le Herberiur, Henry fil. Herberti, Walter Akard, William le Mortimer, etc. *Temp.* Edw. I. (Add. 4842.)

1289. GRANT from Roger Wildegos de Fostun to William de Mortuo Mari de Scroptun and Alice his wife, of six acres of land in the vills of Scropton and Fostun lying in "Le Eyes," between the water of Dove and the high road leading to Sudbury. Witn. Thomas Morel, Walter Akard, William Coke of Scropton, etc. Dat. on the Vig. of SS. Philip and James [30 Apr.], 22 Edw. I. [1294]. (Add. 4837.)

1290. GRANT from the same to the same William "le Mertimer" and Alice his wife of one acre of arable land in "le Eyes." Witn. Will. Wildegos, Robert Scheret, Walter Acard, etc. Dat. Esseborn, Sat. b. F. of SS. Philip and James [1 May], 23 Edw. I. [1295]. (Add. 4838.)

1291. GRANT from Roger Wyldegos to Henry Mascori of three acres of land and meadow on the moor of Foston; yearly rent to the aforesaid Roger, one rose, and to the lord of the fee 2s. silver. Witn. Will. Wildegos, John Wildegos, Walter Hakard, etc. *Circ.* 1295. (Add. 4839.)

1292. GRANT from William fil. Gerardi Vildegos to John his son of a messuage with the buildings upon it in the vill of Foston; rent, a rose yearly. Witn. Dom. Thomas le Bray, sen., "Senescallus Tutteburie," Ralph, clericus de Rollustone, William de Tissinton, Walter Achard, etc. *Temp.* Edw. I. (Add. 4843.)

1293. GRANT from William fil. Roberti Wildgos to Dom. Henry fil. Herberti de Northbury [Norbury], of half an acre of land in the territory of Foston, lying in "le Hallemedue," and extending from the water of Swetebrok towards Le Spart. Witn. Richard de Kingesley, John Wace, Henry de Irton. *Temp.* Edw. I. (Add. 4840.)

1294. GRANT from Nicholas Wildegos fil. Roberti Wildegos to William Wildegos fil. et her. dicti Roberti Wildegos, of one acre of arable land in Fostone which he bought from Roger fil. Gerardi Wildegos. Witn. John Acard, Henry fil. Simonis de Foston, John de Crehton, etc. *Temp.* Edw. I. (Add. 4841.)

1295. GRANT from Engenulfus fil. Gilberti de Foston to Robert de Creterton of one acre of meadow in "le Allemedewe," in exchange for two selions of land "super Marewall." Witn. Will. Wildegos, Walter Acard, John fil. Simonis, etc. *Temp.* Edw. I. (Add. 4845.)

1296. GRANT from Robert de Creitton to Engenulfus fil. Gilberti de Fostone of two selions of land "super Marewall" in Foston, in exchange for one acre of land in "le Allemedewe." Witn. Will. Wildegos, Walter Acard, John fil. Simonis, etc. *Temp.* Edw. I. (Add. 4844.)

1297. GRANT from Henry fil. Johannis Symond de Fostone to William Wildegos of one selion in the fees of Foston and Scropton lying "super le Milneflat." Witn. John Wyldegos, Roger fil. Henrici Wildegos, Hugh de Asseborn, etc. Dat. Fostone, F. of St. Martin [11 Nov.], 1302. (Add. 1054.)

1298. GRANT from Robert fil. Roberti Shyret to John his brother of a messuage with the buildings standing above, and four selions of land in "le Longecroft," in Foston. Witn. John Wildegos, Roger Wildegos, John de Saperton, etc. Dat. S. a. F. of St. Mark [25 Apr.], 2 Edw. II. [1309]. (Add. 4846.)

1299. GRANT from Henry Symond de Fostone to Thomas Acard and Agnes his wife of a place of meadow lying in Smalmedewe in Fostone. Witn. John Wyldegos, Henry Mascory, etc. Dat. Fostone, S. b. Nat. of St. John B. [24 June], 1316. (Add. 1056.)

1300. GRANT from Matilda Wace of Foston to Walter de Cretton of a rood of land lying in the field and fee of Foston. Witn. John Wildegos, John de Cretton, Thomas Acard, Robert Wildegos. Dat. M. a. F. of the Ascension [17 May], 10 Edw. II. [1317]. (Mundy.)

1301. SURRENDER by Henry, capellanus, fil. Henrici clerici de Foston, to Dom. William de Foston, capellanus, of a messuage, with the houses built above it, in Scroptone and Fostone which the said Henry and Thomas his brother had by lease from the said William, for the term of their lives. Witn. John de Cregton, John de Colshull, Robert Mascory, etc. Dat. Foston, S. a. Ass. of B. V. M. [15 Aug.], 1326. (Add. 1057.)

1302. GRANT from Thomas Acard to John fil. Rogeri Wyldegos of three selions of land in Fostone. Witn. John de Kyngesleigh, John de Cregtone, etc. Dat. S. a. F. of Ann. of B. V. M. [25 Mar.], 1327. (Add. 3849.)

1303. GRANT from Henry fil. Johannis Symond de Fostone to Thomas fil. Johannis Acard de Fostone and Agnes his wife of a rood of land in the fee of Foston and Scropton, lying above Hareborowe. Witn. John Wildegos, Will. Wyldegos, John de Cretone, Henry, clericus de Foston, Thomas, clericus de eadem. *Temp.* Edw. II. (Add. 1055.)

1304. CHARTER from Henry, Earl of Lancaster and Leicester, granting to Janyn le Barber and Maud his wife three acres and a half of waste land in Foston. Witn. Will. le Blount, John de Freland, etc. Dat. the Castle of Tuttebury, 19 Oct., 9 Edw. III. [1335]. French. (Add. 4850.)

1305. GRANT from Elizabeth Shirret to Roger de Yrtone and Ysola his wife of a messuage and all his land in Foston and Scropton. Witn. John de Creghtone, Hugh Rodde, etc. Dat. F. of St. Mary Magd. [22 July], 12 Edw. III. [1338]. (Add. 4851.)

1306. GRANT from Henry fil. Willelmi fil. Engelard de Foston to Roger fil. Rogeri de Sapretone of two acres of arable land in the fee of Foston. Witn. John de Creighton de Foston, Robert Wildegos, Thomas Acard, etc. Dat. Vig. of St. Michael, "anno regni Regis Edwardi fil. Regis Edwardi tertii a conquestu quintodecimo" [? 1341]. (Add. 4847.)

1307. GRANT from William Fitzherbert to Thomas Acard of one selion and two butts of land in Foston. Witn. Ralph de Makeleye, etc. Dat. S. a. F. of SS. Peter and Paul [30 June], 20 Edw. III. [1347]. (Add. 4853.)

1308. QUITCLAIM from William fil. et her. Roberti Schyret de Foston of all his right in all the lands and tenements which the said John had of the gift of Elizabeth Schyret. Witn. Will. Fitzherbert, etc. Dat. S. a. Ass. of B. V. M. [15 Aug.], 22 Edw. iii. [1348]. (Add. 4854.)

1309. QUITCLAIM from the aforesaid William to Robert Wyldegos of one acre of land in Foston. Witn. John Creghtone, etc. Dat. W. a. F. of St. Katharine [25 Nov.], 22 Edw. III. [1349]. (Add. 4855.)

1310. QUITCLAIM from the aforesaid William to Thomas Acard of all his lands and tenements in Foston which formerly belonged to Robert Schyret, sen., or to Rob. Schyret, jun. Witn. John de Creghtone, etc. Dat. M. a. F. of St. Nicholas [6 Dec.], 22 Edw. III. [1349]. (Add. 4856.)

1311. GRANT from Henry fil. Enge de Fostone to Roger fil. Rogeri de Sapertone of a messuage and five acres of land in Fostone. Witn. John de Coleshulle, Robert Wildegos, John Wildegos, etc. Dat. F. of St. Cedda, Bishop [2 Mar.], 26 Edw. III. [1352]. (Add. 4857.)

1312. GRANT from Roger de Saperton to Robert Wildegos of the reversion of one built place with belongings in Foston. Witn. John de Coleshulle, etc. Dat. F. of St. Peter-in-Cathedra [22 Feb.], 33 Edw. III. [1359]. (Add. 4858.)

1313. CHARTER by which Johanna, relict of Thomas Acard, surrenders all her title and estate to Thomas, son and heir of the said Thomas Acard, in lands in Fostone and elsewhere. Witn. Godefroy Fuljambe, Walter de Caumpedone, Parson of the Church of Wygan, etc. Dat. 12 May, 39 Edw. III. [1365]. French. (Add. 4859.)

1314. INDENTURE by which William de Burton of Tuttebury grants to Henry Hichecocke of Foston and Enot his wife, for their lives, all his lands and tenements in Foston and Scropton. Witn. Rob. Wildegos, etc. Dat. 12 Mar., 41 Edw. III. [1367]. French. (Add. 4860.)

1315. LEASE, for seven years, from Alice, sometime wife of Thomas Rudde de Foston, to John Symond, of one place and three roods of arable land in the vill of Foston. Witn. Thomas Acard, etc. Dat. F. of Ann. of B. V. M. [25 Mar.], 1371. (Add. 4861.)

1316. LEASE from William Burton de Falde and Elizabeth his wife to William Rosyngtone de Foston of a messuage in Foston, for the term of 24 years; rent annually, 17*s.* Witn. Thos. Acard, John Hultone, etc. Dat. F. of St. Peter in Cathedra [22 Feb.], 34 Hen. VI. [1456]. (Add. 4863.)

GLAPWELL.

1317. GRANT from Thomas fil. Willelmi de Glapwelle to Dom. Thomas Beke, Bishop of St. David's, of his right in the tenement of Glapwell. Witn. Richard de Grey, "dapifer," Henry de Perepont, mil., Will. de Steynesby, mil., Hugh de Rodemarethyet, Robert le Grant, Hugh Stuffin, Simon de Glapwelle. [1280-1293.] (Harl. 52 G. 60.)

1318. GRANT from the same to the same Thomas Beke of a croft in Glapwell. Same witnesses. [1280-1293.] (Harl. 50 H. 1.)

1319. QUITCLAIM from the same to the same Thomas Beke of an acre of land and rent in Glapwell. Same witnesses. [1280-1293.] (Harl. 50 G. 59.)

GLAPWELL *v.* also under GREAT HAYFIELD.

GLOSSOP.

1320. GENERAL release from John Garlek of Glossop to Alice, widow of William del Rodes de Thurleston, and William and John her sons. Dat. Glossop, F. of St. Andrew [30 Nov.], 7 Hen. VI. [1428]. (Bemrose.)

GREENHILL.

1321. RELEASE from John Babyngtone, knt., Thomas Armestrong, esq., William Wentworth, esq., and John Crewker, gent., to Robert Teverey, esq., of a rent of 2*s.* 8*d.* from lands in Thrompton, co. Notts., and Grenehill, co. Derby. Dat. 5 Sept., 11 Hen. VII. [1495]. (Woll. i. 24.)

GREENHILL *v.* also under CHESTERFIELD, LONG EATON, NORTON.

GRESLEY.

1322. QUITCLAIM from Peter de Gresele to John de Segrave of three pieces of waste land in the fields of Gresley, Lynton, Rosliston, Cotene, and Lullington. Dat. Gresley, F. of Inv. of Holy Cross [3 May], 33 Edw. I. [1304]. French. (Gresley.)

GRESLEY *v.* also under DRAKELOW, DUFFIELD, REPTON.

GRINDLEFORD.

(GRINDULFORDE, GRYNDELFORD.)

1323. GRANT from William de Mortaigne to Roger de Leyun fil. Hamundi Carpuntarii of the land which Alan de Huckelowe had in Gryndelford. Witn. Richard Daniel, Henry de Tadigton, William de Heylone. *Temp.* Hen. III. (Brookhill.)

11

1324. GRANT from William Morton to Roger de Leyum fil. Hamundi Carpentarii of the land which Alan de Hucklowe, in the vill of Gryndelford, formerly held. Witn. Richard Daniel, Henry de Tadygton, Roger de Stafford, Robert le Arrecher, etc. *Temp.* Edw. I. (Brookhill.)

1325. GRANT from Richard de Grindulforde to Ralph de Grun of a messuage, etc., in Grindulforde. Dat. S. b. F. of St. Laurence [2 Feb.], 30 Edw. III. [1356]. (Brookhill.)

HACKENTHORPE.

(HAGENTHORP, HAKENETHORPE.)

1326. QUITCLAIM from Thomas Davy of Begheton to William Tylly of Hakenethorpe of five acres of land in Hakenethorpe in a field called Farmebregesfeld. Witn. Thomas Wilson, .John Newbold, John Birchete, etc. Dat. F. of St. Thomas [21 Dec.], 20 Edw. IV. [1480]. (Bemrose.)

1327. MORTGAGE by John Dave of Begheton and Jennett his wife to William Newbolt of four acres of land near Hagenthorp in a field called Hillfield. Witn. John Byrched of Swotall, Edmund Morton, Richard Lee. Dat. 18 Mar., 7 Hen. VIII. [1516]. (Bemrose.)

HADDON, OVER.

(ADDON SUPERIOR, HADDON SUPERIOR).

1328. GRANT from William fil. Willelmi fil. Radulfi to the Church of All Saints, Bakewell, of an acre and a half of land in Upper Haddon. Late twelfth century. (Lichf. B. 5.)

> Sciant tam presentes quam futuri quod ego Willelmus filius Willelmi fil. Radulfi de Superiori Hadd[on] dedi et concessi ac presenti carta mea confirmaui Ecclesie omnium sanctorum de Bauqll in puram et perpetuam elemosinam pro salute anime mee et animarum antecessorum meorum unam dimidiam acram terre in campo de Superiori Add[on] in loco qui uocatur Merefurlong. Preterea presenti carta mea confirmaui Eidem ecclesie illam acram terre quam pater meus dedit predicte ecclesie scilicet dimidiam acram que adiacet prope Costlaue et dimidiam acram supra Dicheclif et ut hec donacio et confirmacio mea rata permaneat eam sigilli mei impressione Roboraui. Hiis testibus, Serlone de Bechel', Ada de Hertil, Roberto fratre suo, Roberto de Caluoure, Willelmo de Chattiswrthe, Luca de Bechel', Johanne de Astun, et multis aliis.

1329. GRANT from John fil. Rogeri de Dale de Asshford to John de Burton of Bauquell and Richard Weluet, capellanus, of a messuage, etc., in Over Haddon. Dat. M. a. F. of St. Margaret [20 July], 17 Ric. II. [1393]. (Foljambe.)

1330. GRANT from William de Bagshagh, sen., to Emma, widow of John in le Dale, jun., for her life, of all the lands and tenements which he had jointly with Nicholas, son of the said John, in Over Haddon and Bauquell of the grant and feoffment of the said John. Witn. Roger Asser, Thomas Nicholson, William Jacson, etc. Dat. Asshford, 10 July, 12 Hen. IV. [1411]. (Foljambe.)

1331. GRANT from Robert Hasylhurst, "perpetual chaplain of the chantry of John Bradburne and Anne his wife in the parish church of Asshebume at the altar of St. Oswald in the south arch," to Thomas Sutton, gent., of a messuage, etc., in Over Haddon, now in the tenure of the said Thomas, with all appurtenances, liberties, profits, etc., in the same which the said Robert has "in iure cantarie predicte." To hold in fee farm at an annual rent to the said Robert of 15*s.* Dat. 20 Dec., 27 Hen. VIII. [1535]. (D. A. J. ix. 188.)

1332. CONFIRMATION of the above grant by Humphrey Bradbum of Hough, esquire, "true and undoubted patron of the said perpetual chantry." Dat. 26 Dec., 27 Hen. VIII. [1535]. (D. A. J. ix. 188, 189.)

HADDON, OVER, *v.* also under BAKEWELL, CHESTERFIELD, NETHER HADDON.

HADDON, NETHER.

1333. COUNTERPART of lease from Henry Williams, Dean, and the Chapter of Lichfield, to George Vernon of Haddon inferior, knt., of the tithes of Haddon inferior, Baukewell, Haddon superior, Rollesley, Alport, Moniashe, Tadington, Prestlyff, Sheldon, Hassilbache, and Asshford. Dat. 24 Jan., 4 Edw. VI. [1550]. (Lichf. D. 25.)

HALLAM, KIRK.

(CHIRCHEHALLA, CHIRCHEHALUM, CHIRKEHALUM, CHYRCHEHALAM, KIRKHALLOM, KIRKHALOM, KYRKHALUM.)

1334. GRANT from Richard de Sandiacre to Geoffrey le Parker of Kyrkhalum of the land which the same Geoffrey first held of the aforesaid Richard "in le Plumtrelege," and half an acre of land in "Syffonhil" which Robert le Blake held, reserving to the same Richard "le Blakegreue" and all his assarts. Witn. Robert de Muschamp, Ralph de Hereforde, William de Sand[iacre], William de Risele, Will. de Beghle, Matthew Cementarius, Ralph Halum, Hugh Barri, etc. *Temp.* Hen. III. (Lansd. 587.)

1335. GRANT from Henry fil. Galfridi Parcarii de Chirchehalum to Walter de Morle and Joan his wife for four silver marks of all that tenement in Chirchehalum which his father had of the gift of Dom. Richard de Sancdiacre, to hold of the said Dom. Richard at a yearly rent of one penny. Witn. Roberd de Muschamp, Hugh de Morle, William fil. Petri de Sancdiacre, Mathew de Sancdiacre, Nicholas Lupus de Morle, Ralph de Halum, Hugh Barri, etc. *Temp.* Hen. III. (Lansd. 588.)

1336. GRANT from Robert Bugge of Notingham to Walter de Morleg' and Joan his wife of two bovates of land in Kyrkehalum, which Beatrice, widow, sometime held. Rent, 16*s.* yearly. Witn. Hugh de Morleg', Nicholas fil. Johannis Henovere, Nicholas fil. Thome de eadem, Hugh de Muschaump, Ralph de Halum, Richard Bugge de Notingham, Richard Pek, etc. *Temp.* Hen. III. (Lansd. 589.)

1337. GRANT from William fil. Willelmi Noget de Draycote to William Ponger de Wyvelesthorpe and Alice his wife of all the right which he has in six virgates of land in the vill of Chyrchehalum which

Roger de Draytone his uncle formerly held of the gift of Dom. Richard de Grey. Witn. Martin fil. Nicholai de Wermundesworthe, Herbert de Ryseleghe, Michael de Breydeston, Henry fil. Roberti de Breydeston, Thomas le Power, etc. *Temp.* Edw. I. (Lansd. 595.)

1338. GRANT from William fil. Roberti Bugge of Notingham to Richard fil. Willelmi de Grey of an annual rent of 2*s.* in Chirkehalum for five silver marks. Witn. Roger de Saint Andrew, mil., Robert de Saucheverel, mil., Herbert de Wodehalle, William Ponger, William de Teverey, Robert de Muschamp, Geoffrey de Sandiakere, Richard de Brademere, Ralph de Barton, etc. *Temp.* Edw. I. (Lansd. 593.)

1339. FEOFFMENT from John Leeke, esq., to Henry Vernon, Henry Foliambe, and Ralph Oker of the manors of Kyrkhalum, co. Derby, and Collingham, co. Notts., in trust for uses specified. Dat. Sutton-in-the-Dale, 10 Sept., 5 Hen. VII. [1489]. (Foljambe.)

HALLAM, KIRK, *v.* also under DALE ABBEY, HUCKNALL, ILKESTON, SUTTON-IN-THE-DALE.)

HALLAM, WEST.
(HALUM.)

1340. GRANT from Matilda de Cromwell, Domina de Tateshale, to Johanna de Cromwell, now wife of Ralph de Cromwell, knt., dominus de Cromwell her son, of all her rents, profits, etc., in the lordship of Halum for the term of two · years in satisfaction of debt of the said Ralph. Dat. Tateshalle, F. of St. Martin [11 Nov.], 5 Hen. V. [1417]. (Harl. 49 A. 44.)

HANDLEY.
(HANDELEY, HANLEY.)

1341. GRANT from John Jordan, Rector ecclesie de Whystan [Whiston, co. York] to Ankerus Frechuille, dominus de Staveley, of lands in Hanley "in feodo de Stavely." Witn. Henry Bate, Roger de Wyggeley, Adam de Gotham, Will. Smyth de Ekyngton, John atte Parkezate de Hanley, etc. Dat. Handley, 15 Nov., 29 Edw. III. [1355]. (Add. 40145.)

1342. GRANT from Roger Lylly de Westhandeley to Peter Frecchevyle, dominus de Staveley, of lands in Handley lying in Westfeld, Parkefeld, Southfeld, and Northfeld and near "Westfeld Syk, Germyn Medowe, le Commyn, le Hady, Handley super le hill," and the lands of the Abbot of Bewchief, John Lylly, Tho. Calton, Rob. Pereson, etc. Witn. John Rodys de Staley Wodethorp, John Mercer de Staueley, Richard Whitehede, of the same, etc. Dat. Staveley, 4 Dec., 8 Edw. IV. [1468]. (Add. 40148.)

1343. GRANT from Peter Frecchevyle, esq., of Staveley, to Roger Lylly of Westhandeley, of eight acres of land in Handeley in exchange for six acres near Todepole in Staveley. Witn. John Rodys of Staveley Wodethorpe, John Mercer of Staveley, Richard Whitehede, etc. Dat. Staveley, 14 Jan., 8 Edw. IV. [1469]. (Harl. 86 H. 15.)

1344. RELEASE from John Roger of Hanley, "at parke gate," son and heir of Robert Roger of Walton, to Henry Foliambe of Walton, esq., of all the lands, etc., late his father's, in Hanley. Witn. Sir Nicholas Lankforth, Henry Perpound, knts., Henry Vernon, esq., etc. Dat. Hanley, 24 May, 17 Edw. IV. [1477]. (Foljambe.)

1345. GRANT from Robert Calton of Melton Mowbray, son and heir of Thomas Calton of the same, late of Chestrefeld, and formerly of Whittyngton, and of Margaret, wife of the said Thomas, dau. and heir of John Eyles, to Henry Foliambe, lord of Walton, of a tenement in Hanley in "le Hyetown" in the fee of Staveley, Stanley, and Ekyngton, and in "Heyffeld" in Bowdon. Witn. Ralph Cantrell, vicar of Chesterfield, etc. Dat. Hanley, 12 May, 20 Edw. IV. [1480]. (Foljambe.)

HANDLEY *v.* also under STAVELEY.

HARTINGTON.

(HARTYNGTON, HERTENDON, HERTINTON.)

1346. GRANT from William de Ferr[ers], Comes Derb', to Thomas fil. Fulcheri de Edenshouere, of all that land "a Kingestrete per Stamfridenmuth, ascendendo per uallem usque ad uiam de Peco et per uiam de Peco usque ad uiam de Midelton que uenit de Hertendon," etc., with 40 acres which the said Thomas formerly held of the manor of Hertendon, and pasture for 300 sheep, etc., yearly, at a rent of two pair of furred gloves or 12*d.* at Michaelmas. Witn. Reginald de Karleolo, tunc senescallus, Robert de Ferr[ers], "frater meus," Jurdan de Tonka, Robert fil. Walkelini, William de Vernone, Nigel de Prestwode. [1200-1225.] (Add. 24201.)

1347. GRANT from Roger de Brompton, parson of Bradley, and William Marsham, to William de Hertington and Margery, his wife, of all the lands in Hertinton which they lately had of the gift of the said William. Witn. John de Golbone, William de Cawardin, Nicholas de Penne, David de Malpas. Dat. S. b. F. of St. George [23 Apr.], 13 Ric. II. [1390]. (R. D. G. 69.)

1348. ACQUITTANCE by which Dorothea Comberford, Abbess of the Monastery of the Nuns Minoresses of the Order of St. Clare-without-Aldgate, London, and of the Convent of the same place, to Dom. George [Talbot], Earl of Shrewsbury, for the sum of xxvj*li.* xiij*s.* iv*d.* sterling from the farm of their rectory of Hertyngton for one year. Dat. 20 Oct., 18 Hen. VIII. [1526]. (Toph. 19.)

HARTINGTON *v.* also under BRADBURN, DUFFIELD, MATLOCK.

HARTSHORN.

(HERTESHORNE.)

1349. GRANT from Richard Kyvetone, John Iretone, and Robert Bradshaw to William Irelonde of a messuage with a croft and six butts of land in Herteshorne for the term of his life. Witn. John Wilne de Melburne, etc. Dat. 6 June, 10 Hen. VI. [1495]. (Add. 4878.)

1350. LETTERS of attorney from the aforesaid William Irelonde to Robert Rigby to enter and receive seisin of the aforesaid tenements in Herteshorne. Dat. 10 June, 10 Hen. VII. [1495]. (Add. 4879.)

HARTSHORNE *v.* also under CALK.

HARWOOD GRANGE *v.* under BEELEY.

HASLAND.

(HASELAND, HASELUND, HESELUND.)

1351. GRANT from Samson fil. Rog. de Haselund to Hugh de Linacre of a bovate of land in Heselund. Witn. Henry de Braylesford, John de Eyncurt, Roger de Eincurt, etc. Early Hen. III. (Foljambe.)

1352. LEASE from William de Lynacre to John fil. Ric. del Frith of four acres of land in the fields of Haseland, for 20 years. Dat. Chastrefeld, Michs. Day, 26 Edw. III. [1352]. (Foljambe.)

HASLAND *v.* also under CHESTERFIELD.

HASSOP.

(HASSOPP.)

1353. QUITCLAIM from Nicholas fil. et her. Petri Peverel of Hassop to Nicholas de Wakebrug of his homage and service in the fee of Hassop. Witn. Peter de Roland, Thomas de Langisdon, William de Kendale, etc. *Temp.* Edw. I. (Foljambe.)

1354. GRANT from John Steel, rector of Sudbury, John de Borton and William de Hampton, chaplain, to Avyne, widow of Sir Godfrey Foliambe, knt., of "housbote and haybote" and timber for her manor of Hassop in their wood of Lyndon and all the woods of their manor of Hednesouere. Dat. Bauquell, T. a. Michs., 5 Ric. II. [1381]. (Foljambe.)

HASSOP *v.* also under BAKEWELL, LITTON, MONYASH.

HATHERSAGE.

(ATHERSEGGE, HADERSICH, HATHERSEGE, HATHERSEGGE.)

1355. QUITCLAIM from John de Hallum de Bawnforth in Athersegge to Richard, son of William de Padelay, of a messuage and land in le Foorchys in Dungworth. Witn. John de Morwod, John de Leeston, Adam de Cowhalch, etc. Dat. S. b. F. of St. Edmund, K. and M. [20 Nov.], 1381. (Bemrose.)

1356. GRANT from Thomas, Prior, and the Convent of Landa [Laund], co. Leic., to the Dean and Chapter of Lichfield (for £60 paid by the latter towards the expenses of the appropriation of Hathersage Church to that Priory) of an annual rent of £40 out of the Rectory of Hathersage. Dat. 6 June, 1404. (Lichf. C. 30.)

1357. RENTAL of Hathersegge cum membris, in the time of Henry Pierpount, William Ryley, and other feoffees of Nicholas Langforth. Dat. Fr. b. F. of St. Anne, mother of the B. V. M. [26 July], 16 Edw. IV. [1476]. Vellum roll. (Longford.)

1358. LEASE from Ralph Longford, knt., to Thomas Wellys, John Wellys, and Margery Bouynton of his manor of Hathersegge, to uses mentioned in other indentures dated 10 Oct. previous. Dat. 23 Oct., 12 Hen. VII. [1496]. (Longford.)

1359. GRANT from Ralph Longford of Longford, knt., to John Fitzherbert of Norbury, Humfrey Bradburne, esquires, John Bradburne, Anthony Fitzherbert, serjeant-at-law, Nicholas Fitzherbert, and Edward Reddeferne, perpetual vicar of Longford, of all his manors, etc., in

Hadersich [Hathersage], and Newton Sulney, in trust for the said Ralph for his life, and on his death to his sons, Richard, Thomas, John, Henry, William, on failure of issue to any. Dat. 19 Sept., 2 Hen. VIII. [1510]. (Longford.)

HATHERSAGE *v.* also under MATLOCK.

HATTON.

(HETTON.)

1360. NOTIFICATION by Goyfred de Becco to his lord, William, Earl of Ferrers, of his grant to Gyllebert Calchon of a carucate of land at Hetton [Hatton], for 20s. and his service, and an annual payment of a red hawk and five shillings. *Temp.* Hen. II. [*circ.* 1170]. (Harl. 45 H. 5.)

> Domino suo W. Comiti de Ferrariis et omnibus baronibus suis, Goyfredus de Becco salutem. Sciatis me dedisse Gylleberto Calchoni in feedum et hereditatem ipsi et heredibus suis unam carrucatam terre apud Hettonam propter xx solidos quos mihi dedit et pro seruitio suo. Ipse uero in unoquoque anno pro ea mihi redditurus est unum nisum sorum et v. solidos et si forte euenerit quod hanc illi terram tueri non potero tantundem alibi tamque ualentem predicto modo de mea propria terra illi dabo. Teste, Ricárdo, priore Totesberie et Henrico de Achenuilla, capellano, et Ricardo de Campania et Ernulfo de Becco et Giralmo de Faleth et Thoma Dispensatore et Godfrido Larderario et Radulfo et Ricardo de Merstona et Osberno Cocc et Henrico filio eius et Siwardo Dogheafd. Ualete.

1361. GRANT from Alexander de Curtlinge to Roger fil. Rogeri de Braylisford of a messuage in Hatton; rent, 6d. Witn. Gilbert de Merston, William de Hog' fil. Radulfi, Richard Lacmon, etc. *Temp.* Hen. III. (Woll. ix. 47.)

1362. GRANT from Peter fil. Ricardi Wareyn of Hatton to Geoffrey Lawe of Tuttesbury [Tutbury], of land in Hatton. Witn. Hugh de Hatton, Simon Godrig of the same, Nicholas le Wite of the same, etc. Dat. M. b. F. of St. Dunstan [21 Oct.], 1297. (Add. 26093.)

1363. RELEASE from Geoffrey Lauwe of Tuttebury to Richard Russel and Alice his wife, daughter of the said Geoffrey, of land in Hatton. Witn. William de Hatton, Richard Courteys, Thomas de Leycestre of Tuttebur', etc. Dat. W. a. Ann. of B. V. M. [25 Mar.], 31 Edw. I. [1303]. (Add. 26094.)

1364. LEASE, for 20 years, from Richard fil. Petri de Hatton to William Broun of Swarkeston of a messuage in Hatton; rent, a rose. Witn. Geoffrey Roundel of Merston, Robert de Wylinton of the same, Nich. de Irreton, etc. Dat. F. of St. Michael [29 Sept.], 9 Edw. II. [1315]. (Woll. vi. 62.)

1365. GRANT from Nicholas le White of Hattone to John de Bollesover, chamberlain to Robert de Longdon, Prior of St. Mary's, Tuttebury, of land in Hatton. Witn. Thomas de Pilcote, Thomas le Ferrour of Hatton, Nicholas de Irton, etc. Dat. F. of Ann. of B. V. M. [25 Mar.], 14 Edw. II. [1321]. (Campb. xi. 15.)

1366. GRANT from Richard Russel of Tuttebure to William Shyngull, tanner, of lands in Hatton. Witn. Nicholas de Irton of Hatton, Adam Schingull, John Bette, etc. Dat. F. of St. Katharine [25 Nov.], 16 Edw. III. [1342]. (Add. 26095.)

1367. GRANT from Peter Passemer of Tuttebury to William Shyngull, tanner, of land in Hatton. Witn. William Rondel, William Burgeys, Robert Brese, etc. Dat. W. a. F. of St. Chad, Bp. [2 Mar.], 28 Edw. III. [1354]. (Add. 26096.)

1368. GRANT from William Shyngyl' of Tuttebury, tanner, to William de Burton of the same of land in Hatton. Witn. Rich. de Irton, Robert Brese, Hugh Roundel', etc. Dat. Fr. a. F. of St. Peter ad vincula [1 Aug.], 38 Edw. III. [1364]. (Add. 26098.)

1369. GRANT from John Chaundeler of Tuttebury to William de Burton of the same of land in Hatton. Witn. John de Duffeld, clerk, John de Losyngtone of Tuttebury, Robert Gybone of the same, etc. Dat. Sat. a. Sund. a. Easter [19 Apr.], 45 Edw. III. [1371]. (Add. 26097.)

HAYFIELD.

(HAYFFELDE.)

1370. GRANT from Margery de Berdhalgh to her sons William and Richard of six acres of land and a house in Great Hayfield in Berdechalghfeld. Dat. Chapel-en-le-Frith, S. a. F. of St. Andrew [30 Nov.], 12 Edw. III. [1338]. (Hallowes.)

1371. GRANT from Hugh fil. Willelmi de Berdhalugh to William de Berdhalugh his father and Edith his mother of a messuage and six acres of land in Great Hayfield [in Glapwell]. Witn. Nicholas Broun, John Cuterell, Robert Selby, Robert del Stryndes, etc. Dat. Berdhalugh, S. a. F. of Conc. of B. V. M. [8 Dec.], 24 Edw. III. [1350]. (Hallowes.)

1372. GRANT from William de Berdehalegh to Henry Schakelok of seven acres of land, etc., in le Wytehul in the vill of Magna Hayffelde. Witn. John Cotterell, Robert de Walkedene, Robert de Breddebere, etc. Dat. apud Capellam del Frith, F. of St. Peter in cathedra [22 Feb.], 29 Edw. III. [1355]. (Drury.)

1373. GRANT from Hugh fil. Ade Cissoris to William fil. Jacobi le Fyscher of five acres of land in Magna Hayffelde. Witn. Vincent de Haddefelde, Nicholas le Seriaunt, etc. Dat. Th. b. All Saints' Day [1 Nov.], 27 Edw. III. [1353]. (Foljambe.)

1374. GRANT from Roger de Berdhall, sen., to Robert de Nedham of three roods of land with buildings on it lying in the Whythull in Great Hayfield. Witn. Godfrey Foliambe, knt., bailiff, Robert de Boure, Robert de Bredbury, William de Melner. Dat. at Whithull, S. a. Easter [24 Apr.], 36 Edw. III. [1362]. (Hallowes.)

1375. GRANT from Henry Shakelock to Robert de Nedeham of seven acres of land with buildings on it in Whythull in Great Hayfield. Dat. Berdhalgh, S. a. Easter [24 Apr.], 36 Edw. III. [1362]. (Hallowes.)

HAYFIELD *v.* also under ATLOW, HANDLEY, OLLERSETT.

HAZLEBADGE *v.* under HADDON, NETHER.

HAZLEWOOD.

(HASELWOD.)

1376. CONVEYANCE from Walter Blount to Godfrey Foliaumbe, mil., and Auine his wife of the site of his manor of Haselwod, with all the buildings thereon within and without the moat, except the inferior [pejor] grange, the "Deyrye," and the great garden without the moat. Witn. Dom. John, Duke of Lancaster, William Croyser, Aldred Sulny, Edmund de Apelby, and Robert de Twyford, knts., etc. Dat. Hasilwode, S. a. Ascension Day [13 May], 43 Edw. III. [1369]. (Foljambe.)

HEAGE.

(HEEGGE, HEGHEYGG, HEYGHEGG.)

1377. WILL of Richard Spendlove, bequeathing lands in Alcokfeld, in le Fernelee, in Heegge, to Elen his wife. Witn. Will. Parker, Ralph Bradshawe, Hugh Dycons, etc. Dat. Heegge, F. of Ass. of B. V. M. [15 Aug.], 11 Edw. IV. [1471]. (Woll. vii. 31.)

1378. GRANT from Johanna, widow of John Spendlove, of Heegge, to Thurstan Wilde and Robert Freke, of four acres and a half of land in Alcokfeld in le Fernelee, in Heegge. Witn. William Parker, Ralph Bradshawe, Hugh Dykons, etc. Dat. F. of Ass. of B. V. M. [15 Aug.], 11 Edw. IV. [1471]. (Woll. vii. 79.)

1379. RELEASE from Thurstan Wilde and Robert Freke to Johanna, widow of John Spendlove, of Heegge, of 4½ acres of land in Alcokfeld, in le Fernelee, in Heegge, with remainder to Richard Spendlove and Elen, his wife, and in case of the re-marriage of the said Elen to John Spendlove, their son. Witn. Will. Parker, Ralph Bradshawe, Hugh Dykons, etc. Dat. Mor. of F. of Ass. of B. V. M. [16 Aug.], 11 Edw. IV. [1471]. (Woll. vii. 32.)

HEAGE *v.* also under DUFFIELD, TANSLEY, WAKEBRIDGE.

HEANOR.

(HEIGHNOR, HEYNORE.)

v. under CODNOR, LANGLEY.

HILTON.

(HULTON, HYLTON.)

1380. POWER of attorney from Alice dau. of John Fraunceys, esq., and wife of Henry, son and heir of John Rolleston, esq., to John Hareson of Hilton to receive seisin of a close in Hilton called Berkeshey, a piece of meadow called Le Halowes and two acres of land in Potloke meadow and other lands in the same vill of Hilton. Dat. 6 March, 27 Hen. VI. [1449]. (Every.)

HILTON *v.* also under ASHBOURNE, ETWALL, ROSTON.

HOGNASTON.

(HOGGIMASTONE, HOGGMASTON, HOKENASTON, HOKNASTON.)

1381. GRANT from John de Hoght' of Hognaston to Richard his son of a tenement and land in Hokenaston. Witn. Thomas Alsope, Hugh Heyre, Tho. Mason. Dat. Hokenaston, F. of St. Chad [2 Mar.], 24 Hen. VI. [1446]. (Woll. i. 33.)

1382. GRANT from John Hoght', sen., of Hoggimastone to Richard Hoght' his son of a cottage and land in Hoggimaston, and a croft called Mapulton, a portion of which abuts upon "the place" of the abbey of Rowset' [Rocester, co. Staff.], a rent of 2*d.* to be paid to John Hoght', brother of the said John. Witn. Richard Alsoppe, Tho. Mason, Ric. Eyre. Dat. 20 May, 34 Hen. VI. [1456]. (Woll. i. 34.)

1383. RELEASE from Henry Vernon, knt., Philip Leche, Thomas Babyngton, esquires, Robert Blakwalle, John Gell, Henry Stylton, etc., at the desire of Richard Blakwalle to Roger Anabulle of Asshlehey of lands in Hoknaston, with power of attorney for seisin. Dat. 10 Oct., 15 Hen. VII. [1499]. (Woll. i. 35.)

1384. RELEASE from John Shawe, late of Chesterfield, *al.* John Somersell, and Elizabeth, his wife, to Roger Annable of Hognaston of lands in Hognaston. Witn. Thomas Vicars of Chesterfield, teiliour, Ric. Pillesley, of the same, potter, and Ric. Prihe of the same, fletcher. Dat. 2 Sept., 27 Hen. VIII. [1535]. (Woll. i. 36.)

1385. LEASE, for four years, from George Anabull of Hoknastone, son of Roger Anabulle of co. Derby, labourer, to Robert Beynbryge of the same, husbandman, of lands in Hoknaston; rent, 2*d.* Witn. Hanken Berney and Hugh Lylee. Dat. 20 Mar., 30 Hen. VIII. [1539]. (Woll. i. 37.)

1386. GRANT from Roger Anabull of Hokenastone, co. Derby, yeoman, and George Anabul his son to Humfrey Kyrkland of Whettcroft, husbandman, of a messuage and lands in Hoknaston. Witn. William Sutton, clerk, John Allsoppe, Robert Allsoppe, Anthony Alsoppe, etc. Dat. 5 Mar., 31 Hen. VIII. [1540]. (Woll. i. 38.)

1387. QUITCLAIM from Johanna Anabull, wife of Roger Anabull of Hoknaston to Humfrey Kyrkeland of Whettecrofte, of land forming part of her dower in Hoknaston. Witn. Will. Suttone, clerk, John Alsope of Hoknaston, Hugh Lylee. Dat. 6 Mar., 31 Hen. VIII. [1540]. (Woll. i. 39.)

1388. RELEASE from Johanna Anabulle, widow of Roger Anabulle, of Hoknastone, to Humfrey Kyrkeland of Whetcroft, of a messuage and lands in Hoknaston which had been granted to him by Roger, her husband, and George, their son, on the previous 5 March. Witn. John Alsopp of Hoknaston, Robert and Anthony Allsoppe, his sons, and others. Dat. 27 Oct., 32 Hen. VIII. [1540]. (Woll. i. 40.)

1389. BOND, in £100, from Thomas Mason of Hognaston, yeoman, to Richard Blackwall, Robert Tunsted, and Rauf Gell of Hopton, to convey to George Mason his son and Jone Gell, and the heirs of their bodies, lands, etc., belonging to the said Thomas in Hognaston. Dat. Pur. of B. V. M. [2 Feb.], 33 Hen. VIII. [1542]. (Pole-Gell.)

HOGNASTON *v.* also under ASHBOURNE.

HOLBROOKE *v.* under DUFFIELD.

HOLLINGTON.

(HOLINTON, HOLYNGTON.)

1390. GRANT from Emelina fil. Roberti de Monte Gomerry widow to Robert fil. Roberti de Grendon of the third part of a bovate of land in the field of Holinton, and of all essarts there which she inherited from Walter de Monte Gomorry, her brother; to hold by rent of white gloves at Easter or one penny, at the option of the tenant. Witn. Dom. William de Monte Gomerry, G—— de Segissal, R—— de Piru, Gilbert de Merston, John de Tutesbir', etc. *Temp.* Hen. III. or Edw. I. (Woll. ix. 44.)

1391. GRANT from Alexander fil. Willelmi de Cortlingestone to Robert fil. Roberti de Grendon, of a bovate of land in Holinton which Symon fil. Anfredi formerly held, in exchange for lands in the fields of Hatton which Bridwaldus formerly held; rent, 12d. Witn. Dom. William de Monte Gomorry, G—— de Segissal', R—— de Piru, W—— Morel', Gilbert de Marston, etc. *Temp.* Hen. III. or Edw. I. (Woll. ix. 45.)

1392. GRANT from Edmund Foyne of Holynton to William de Huclow of a yearly rent of 22s. fom his lands, etc., in [Hollington ?] during the term of the grantor's wife Joan. Witn. Thomas Mongumbri, John Durdent. Dat. Vig. of F. of Inv. of H. Cross [3 May], 2 Ric. II. [1379]. (Foljambe.)

1393. GRANT from Dom. Thomas Blount, knt., to Alvered de Longeforde, esq., of all his lands, etc., in Holyngton, Folefort, and Ardesley which lately belonged to his father, Walter Blount, knt. Witn. Thomas Greseley, Nicholas Montgomery, knts., Peter de la Pole, John Curson, Robert Smalley, etc. Dat. apud Holyngton, 18 Nov., 11 Hen. VI. [1432]. (Longford.)

1394. GRANT from Alvered Longford to Nicholas Fitzherbert, esq., Laurence Caton, and Thomas Barlow, chaplains, of all his lands in Holyngton, Foleford, Ardesley, and Okemedow, in co. Derby, which he had by feoffment of Thomas Blount, knt., son and heir of Walter Blount, knt., deceased. Witn. Richard Vernon, John Cokayn, Thomas Gryseley, knts., etc. Dat. Holyngton, 1 Dec., 13 Hen. VI. [1434]. (Longford.)

1395. GRANT from Nicholas Fitzherbert, esquire, Laurence Caton, and Thomas Barlowe, chaplains, to Aluered Longford, esquire, of an annual rent of 20s. from the lands which they hold by feoffment of the said Aluered in Holyngton, Foldford, Ardesley, and Okemedow, co. Derby. Dat. 5 Dec., 13 Hen. VI. [1434]. (Longford.)

HOLME NR. BRAMPTON.

(HULM.)

1396. CONFIRMATION by Griffin fil. Wennuwini to Robert fil. Mathei de Reydon of all the land which Matthew his father gave him in Hulm. Witn. Dom. Richard de Stretton, Yvo, persona, Matthew de Langisdon, William le Wine, William de Langisdon, Nicholas de Winnefeld, Ralph Bugge, William de Esseburne, William, clericus, Hugh Penn, Ralph de Selladon, John de Bathequell, clericus, etc. *Temp.* Edw. I. Seal of arms. (Bowles.)

HOLME NR. BRAMPTON *v.* also under BRAMPTON, CHESTERFIELD.

HOLMESFIELD.

(HOLMESEFELD, HOLMESFELD, HOMSFELD.)

1397. COVENANT whereby Walter d'Aincurt and John his son release to Ralph fil. Rogeri d'Aincurt the service of a fourth knight, which was in dispute between them, in return for Holmesfeld. [1156-1165.] (Woll. x. 1.)

> Notum sit omnibus tam presentibus quam futuris tam francis quam anglicis me Walterum d'Aincurt et Johannem filium meum remisisse Radulfo filio Rogeri d'Aincurt et suis heredibus seruicium quarti militis quod fuit in calumnia, seruicium trium militum facientibus quietum de nobis et nostris heredibus illi et suis heredibus, et huius conuencionis causa relaxant predictus Radulfus et sui heredes mihi et meis heredibus calumniam de Holmesfeld. Huius conuentionis testes sunt hii, Rannulfus uic[ecomes] Robertus filius eius, Radulfus Anselin, Galfridus de Constentin, Willelmus d'Aubenni, Galfridus Ridel, Serlo de Pleselei, Geruasius Auenel, Paganus de Santa Maria, Hugo de Houringam, Helias de Fanolcurt, Radulfus de Grincurt, Eustachius de Bergete, Galfridus filius Pagani, Roger filius Suani, et totus comitatus Notingeham et Derbeie.

1398. GRANT from Roger de Bradway to Robert Knowt of land abutting on the demesne of Holmesfeld. Witn. Ralph Barker, James Mawer, John Parker, etc. Dat. Bradeway, F. of St. Matthew [21 Sept.], 10 Hen. IV. [1409]. (Harl. 112 A. 43.)

1399. EXTRACT from Roll of the great court of Lady Alice de Ayncourt of the manor of Holmesfeld, held on M. b. F. of St. George [23 Apr.], 5 Hen. V. [1417], recording the admission of Johanna, daughter of John Fauncher, sen., to a messuage and seven bovates of land. (Woll. viii. 19A.)

1400. EXTRACT from roll of court of the manor of Holmesfeld, held on T. a. F. of SS. Tiburtius and Valerian [14 Apr.], 9 Hen. VI. [1431], whereat John Faunchall paid fine for a messuage and a bovate of land which descended to him at the death of Johanna, his sister. (Woll. viii. 30.)

1401. SIMILAR extract, dated as above, recording the surrender by John Fanchalle of a messuage and bovate of land to the use of William Crofte, with licence to lease the said land to William his son for twenty years. (Woll. viii. 19.)

1402. EXTRACT from roll of court of the manor of Holmesfeld, held Sat. a. Easter [14 Apr.], 14 Hen. VI. [1436], at which John Wode surrendered a croft to the use of John Faunchelle. (Woll. viii. 20A.)

1403. EXTRACT from roll of court of the manor of Holmesefield, held on 15 Oct., 22 Hen. VI. [1443], at which Thomas Welton surrendered a messuage and a bovate of land in Holmesfeld to the use of William Croftes, who afterwards surrendered the same to the use of Thomas Welton. Rent during 10 years, 12*d.*, and after that time, 2*s.* (Woll. viii. 22.)

1404. GENERAL release from Johanna, wife of John Faunchall, sen., of Holmesfeld, to John, her husband. Witn. John Barker, Robert Grene, Nicholas Burton. Dat. Dronfeld, 3 Dec., 33 Hen. VI. [1454]. (Woll. viii. 21.)

1405. EXTRACT from roll of court of the manor of Holmesefield, held 2 June, 34 Hen. VI. [1456], at which John Faunchall, sen., surrendered a messuage and a bovate of land in le Faunchallegatehede and a rent of 5s. 11d. to the use of William Croft, cooper. (Woll. viii. 29A.)

1406. SIMILAR extract, dated 28 May, 6 Edw. IV. [1466], at which William Croft received a messuage and a bovate of land in Holmesfeld, lately held by Thomas Welton for term of life. (Woll. viii. 23.)

1407. SIMILAR extract, dated 6 June, 12 Edw. IV. [1472], at which William Crofte, son and heir of William Crofte, received three messuages and three bovates of land in Fawnchalle-gate. (Woll. viii. 24.)

1408. COURT-ROLLS of Holmesfield manor. [1480-1651.] (D. A. J. xx. 52.)

1409. EXTRACT from the roll of the great court of John Savage, jun., knt., for the manor of Holmesfeld, held 21 Nov., 7 Hen. VII. [1491], at which Nicoll Qwyt surrendered an annual rent of 12d. from a messuage and curtilage, for the support of the chaplain of St. Swithin of Holmesfeld. With a notice that this copy is written by the steward in a certain small missal, given to the monastery "de Bello Capite." [Beauchief Abbey.] (Woll. viii. 18.)

1410. EXTRACT from roll of court of Lady Margaret Savage, widow of John Savage, for the manor of Holmesfeld, held Th. a. F. of St. Katherine [25 Nov.], 10 Hen. VII. [1494], at which William Crofte, jun., surrendered three messuages and three bovates of land in Faunchalgate to the use of William Crofte his father. (Woll. viii. 24A.)

1411. EXTRACT from roll of the same court, at which William Crofte surrendered three messuages and three bovates of land in Fownchalgate to the use of William his son, with remainder to Roger, John, and Edward, brothers of the said William. (Woll. viii. 30.)

1412. GRANT from John Owtrem of Holmesfeld, sen., to William Croft and William Kyng of lands in Holmesfeld in trust for William Owtrem his son, with covenant that the said John and William Owtrem shall occupy "the hed howse with the parler and the chambre aboof," and the said William hold certain lands. For the due performance of which the said John binds himself in £20. Witn. William Kyng of Holmesfeld, John Kyng of the same, John Caltoon of Totteley. Dat. F. of Circumcision [1 Jan.], 19 Hen. VIII. [1528]. (Woll. viii. 25.)

1413. LEASE, for 12 years, from William Croft of Holmesfeld to William Doo of the same, of a messuage and lands lately held by the widow of Roger Croft, with a close called Avice Dooll; rent, 16s. Dat. F. of St. Peter in cathedra [22 Feb.], 1533. (Woll. viii. 26.)

1414. ACQUITTANCE from William Croft of Holmesfeld, son of William Croft deceased, to Katerine Croft, widow, his mother, for 9s., and to Michael Croft, his brother, for 5s., being his last payment, "puerilis partis sue," on account of goods which belonged to the said William Croft, sen., deceased. Witn. George Mower of Barley Wodsetes, George Hancoke of Barley Lees, and William Curtenall of the same. Dat. 31 Hen. VIII. [1539-40]. (Woll. viii. 27.)

1415. EXTRACT from roll of the court of Lady Elizabeth Savage widow, for the manor of Holmesfeld, held on Vig. of St. Laurence [9 Aug.], 32 Hen. VIII. [1541], at which Michael Crofte, son and heir of William Crofte deceased received three messuages and lands in Holmesfeld. (Woll. viii. 32.)

1416. EXTRACT from roll of great court of John Savage, knt., for the manor of Holmesfeld, held 18 April, 7 Edw. VI. [1553], at which Michael Croft, son and heir of William Croft deceased surrendered lands in Holmesfeld, to the use of Edward Eyre, esq., and John Fauneshawe, who surrendered two messuages and lands in the same place, in the tenure of Nicholas Newbold, to the use of the aforesaid Michael. (Woll. viii. 31.)

1417. A BREVIAT of the customs of the manor of Holmesfeld drawn up by the copyholders at the request of the lord. Sixteenth century. (Woll. xi. 30.)

1418. LIST of the copyholders of the manor of Homsfeld, with co-tenants of inheritance. Sixteenth century. (Woll. viii. 35.)

HOLMESFIELD *v.* also under BAKEWELL, ELMTON.

HOPE.

(HAWPE, HOPPE, HOWPE.)

1419. COPY of a grant from John, Earl of Morton, to Hugh, Bishop of Coventry, of the church of Hope with the chapel of Tideswell. Dat. 1192. (Lichf. B. 23.) The text is:—

Omnibus sancte matris ecclesie filiis ad quos presentes littere pervenerint, Johannes, Comes Morton, salutem. Noverit vniuersitas . . . Dei et pro salute anime mee et patris mei et matris et domini Regis fratris mei concessisse et donasse venerabili patri meo Hugoni Coventrensi episcopo et successoribus suis in perpetuam elemosinam ecclesiam de Hope cum capella de Tydd cum omnibus aliis ad ecclesiam vel capellam pertinentibus in decimis et oblacionibus et omnibus obvencionibus et in terris et pascuis et omnibus aliis scilicet cum iure aduocacionis et cum omni alio iure quod in ecclesia illa seu earum pertinenciis habebam et cum omni iure quod ad eas pertinebat, cum omni integritate et libertate imperpetuum possidenda et secundum disposicionem eiusdem episcopi et omnium successorum suorum omnibus futuris temporibus ecclesia illa et capella cui vel quibus voluerint personis debeant in perpetuum assignari vel in prebend[am] vel in honorem alicuius ecclesiarum suarum vel Coventrens' vel Lich' vel in alios usus pro voluntate ipsius Episcopi. Ut hec autem mea donacio predicta et concessio rata et inconcussa imperpetuum debeat obseruari sigilli mei impressione et proprii anuli apposicione roboraui et super altare dominicum ecclesie Coventrensis cartam illam posui et manu propria confirmavi. Testes Robertus, comes de Meuslet, Willelmus Briequerre, Gerardus de Canuill, Engeranus de Pratell[is], Reginaldus de Wassenuill, Hugo de Neuill, Willelmus de Hardredesh'. Dat. apud Coventr' anno secundo, ab incarnatione domini millesimo centesimo nonagesimo secundo per manum Stephani Ridel cancellarii nostri.

1420. CHARTER of Geoffrey [de Muschamp], Bishop of Coventry, granting to the "communa Licheffeldensis ecclesie" 20 marks yearly "ad cervisam habendam" out of the church of Hope and its chapelries, payable by the rector or rectors for the time being. [1199-1209.] (Lichf. B. 1.) The text is:—

Gaufridus Dei gratia Coventr. Ecclesie humilis minister. Uniuersis Christi fidelibus ad quos presens pagina peruenerit, Salutem in Domino. Quoniam ea potissimum merentur fauorem que ad multorum conferuntur subsidium, Vniuersitati uestre notum facimus nos diuine miseracionis intuitu dedisse et concessisse commune Licheffelden' Ecclesie que supra modum tenuis est et modica, viginti marcas annuas ad ceruisam habendam, Scilicet de Ecclesia de Hopa et de capellis suis, Ita videlicet quod cum eadem ecclesia cum suis capellis uacauerit, ille qui eas tenebit siue illi, si forte plures ibi fuerint rectores, predictas viginti marcas eidem commune secundum facultates portionum suarum annuatim persoluent, ad duos terminos, medietatem ad festum Sancti Michaelis, et medietatem ad Pascha. Si uero ipsa matrix ecclesia sine aliquibus capellis uel pertinentiis suis uacauerit, memorata communa partem predictarum viginti marcarum secundum valentiam rei uacantis habebit, donec tota ecclesia cum suis pertinentiis plene uacauerit. Ut igitur hec nostra donatio firmitatis vigorem obtineat imperpetuum eam presenti scripto et sigilli nostri appositione confirmariumus. Hiis testibus, magistro Erardo, canonico Eboracensi, Magistro Johanne de Newere, Magistro Nicholao de Weston', Osberto de Witinton, Michaele capellano, Willelmo de Damartin, Thoma de Beuerlaco.

1421. CONFIRMATION from William [de Cornhill], Bishop of Coventry, to the church and canons of Lichfield, of the church of Hope with the chapel of Tidewell. [1215-1221.] (Lichf. B. 4.)

1422. GRANT from Ralph Talebot to Henry de Grengel' of a half acre of land in Hope lying near Thornawe. Witn. Elias de Thornhill, Peter de Syatton, Elias and Robert, fratres de Aston, Geoffrey de Ouerton, Ranulph de Burgo, Elyas fil. Elye de Thornhill. Early Hen. III. (Lichf. B. 2A.)

1423. GRANT from same to Robert de Lexinton of a half acre of land in Hope, near Thornawe. Witn. Dom. Rouland de Sutton, John Burdun, Elyas de Thornhill, Elias his son, Peter de Syatton, etc. Early Hen. III. (Lichf. B. 2B.)

1424. GRANT from William Cassy to Henry de Grengel' of a half acre of land in Hope, namely, at Thornawe. Witn. Elias de Thornhill, Elias filius eius, William de Heylawe, Peter de Syatton, Robert Archer, Arnald de Heghlawe, Richard de Syerd, Walter clericus. Early Hen. III. (Lichf. B. 2C.)

1425. GRANT from the same to Robert de Lexinton of a half acre of land in Hope at Thornawe. Witn. Dom. Rouland de Sutton, John Burdun, Elyas de Thornhill, Elyas his son, Peter de Syatton, Elyas, Robert, fratres de Aston, Geoffrey de Offerton, Ranulph de Burg, Henry fil. Ricardi, Robert and Walter, clerici. Early Hen. III. (Lichf. B. 2D.)

1426. LEASE from W[illiam de Mancester], Dean, and the Chapter of Lichfield to Henry de Lexinton [Dean of Lincoln, 1243] for his life, of the reversion (on the death or resignation of Robert de Lexinton his brother) of the mother church of Hope (excepting the chapel of Tiddeswell with its appurtenances), "quas antiquitus percipere consuevit antequam W[illelmus] Comes de Ferrariis custodiam castri de Pecco habuit." [1222-1243.] (Lichf. D. 2.)

1427. BOND from Robert fil. Hugonis de Hope to the Dean and Chapter of Lichfield, covenanting not to divide, sell, or mortgage his holding of a manse and two bovates of land in Hope. Witn. Dom. Thomas de Wymundham, Precentor of Lichfield, Mag. William de Attelberge, William de Stanford, William de Neuton, and Walkelin de Houton, Canons of the same; William, Vicar of Hope, John Daniel, William Folegambe, Thomas his brother, Thomas le Archer, etc. [1254-1278.] (Lichf. D. 5.)

1428. INSPEXIMUS of Henry III. of the grant of his father John, when Earl of Morton, to Hugh, Bishop of Coventry, of the church of Hoppe, with the chapel of Tidewell (which John had sealed and laid "super altare dominicum ecclesie Coventrei" and which bore date 1192). Witn. W[alter], Bishop of Bath and Wells, Roger de Leybourne, Robert Aguillon, John de Verdun, William de Grey, William de Actte, Nicholas de Leukennore, William Belet, Ralph de Bakepuz, Bartholomew le Bygod. Dat. Kenilleworth, 7 Sept., anno 50 [1266]. Great seal, restored. (Lichf. A. 9.)

1429. GRANT from Richard de Wepur to Emma, wife of Oliver de Hope, of a burgage and fourth part of a burgage in the vill of Hope. Witn. Roger de Kelby, Gilbert le Wayte, Gilbert Balle, etc. *Temp.* Edw. I. (Add. 47497.)

1430. GRANT from William le Mareschalman de Burgo to William fil. Petri de Schatton, forestarius, of a piece of meadow in Hope lying "sub Okelis." Witn. Clement de la Fordye, ballivus de alto Pecco, Robert Balgi, jun., Elias de Thornehulle, William Halby, Robert le Eyr, Robert Wodereue, Geoffrey le Flemeng, clerk. Dat. Schatton, S. b. All Saints' Day [1 Nov.], 34 Edw. I. [1306]. (Bowles.)

1431. LETTERS PATENT of Edward III. confirming the inspeximus of Henry III. confirming (*a*) the grant by King John "dum fuit comes Morton" to Hugh, Bishop of Coventry, of the church of Hope with the chapel of Tidewelle (dated 1192); (*b*) the grant by William [de Cornhull] "dudum Coventrensis minister" to the church and canons of Lichfield of the same church and chapel; and (*c*) the confirmation by Edward II. his father of the church of Bathekewell to the Dean and Chapter. Dat. 10 Apr., anno 19 [1345]. (Lichf. A. 15.)

1432. ROLL of parochial visitations of Hope; 1345. Fourteenth century. (Lichf. CC. 7, 8.)

1433. GRANT from Richard fil. Joh. fil. Nale de Burgo to Dom. William Godwine, vicar of Hope, of five acres of land in Hope lying on "Ekles." Witn. Nicholas le Heyr, Gervase Woderowe, William, vicar of Castelton, etc. Dat. S. a. F. of St. Dunstan [19 May], 1359. (Foljambe.)

1434. GRANT from William fil. Will. de Haywode and Avissia, widow of Robert le Say, to John le Vikersson of five acres lying on "Eckeler" in Hope. Witn. Gervase Woderowe, Hugh Carles, William de Halle, etc. Dat. F. of Ann. of B. V. M. [25 Mar.], 35 Edw. III. [1361]. (Foljambe.)

1435. GRANT from John Vikeresson to Richard de Wetton, John his brother, and Helen, wife of the said John de Wetton, of five acres of land in Eckeler in the field of Hope. Witn. Nicholas Leyr, Gervase Woderove, etc. Dat. M. a. Tr. of St. Thomas [7 July], 50 Edw. III. [1376]. (Foljambe.)

1436. RELEASE from William fil. John de Vikerson to the same of the same land on Eckeler in Hope. Same witnesses. Dat. Tu. a. F. of Tr. of St. Swithun [15 July], 50 Edw. III. [1376]. (Foljambe.)

1437. RELEASE from John Wele of Cadyngton and William Clerk of Hope, chaplain, to John Bower of Hope and Rose his wife, of lands in Hope, with reversion to Thomas Swynok and Elen his wife, daughter of the said John Bower, and to the Guild of St. Mary of Dronfield. Witn. Ric. Forester, vicar of Hope, Robert Woderove, William Abney, and others. Dat. Hope, M. b. F. of St. Michael [29 Sept.], 18 Ric. II. [1394]. (Woll. iii. 13.)

1438. GRANT and counterpart from Richard de Hope, son and heir of Robert Magotessone de Hope to Mag. John Ondeby, Archdeacon of Derby, and Dom. John Cheyne, clerk, of the reversion of all lands which were sometime Anibilla's, his mother's, in Hope and Astonfeld, and which Robert Magottesone his father "per legem terre" holds for his life. Witn. Robert Eyr, William Woderoue, John Pedeler, etc. Dat. Hope, M. a. Michaelmas Day, 2 Hen. IV. [1400]. Endorsed: "Carta Ricardi de Hope de reversione terrarum et tenementorum Magotsone in Hope pro cantaria M. Ric. Bermyngham." (Lichf. B. 24.)

1439. POWER of attorney from Richard de Rouworth of Hope to John Wele, chaplain, and Richard Bockyng to give seisin to Anabilla his sister of a piece of land under Minley called Demryding [in Hope]. Witn. William Clerk, chaplain, Roger Bockyng, John le Herdeman. Dat. Hope, W. a. F. of St. Bartholomew [24 Aug.], 6 Hen. IV. [1405]. (Foljambe.)

1440. GRANT from William Abbenay of Hope to Ralph de Staueley, knt., Richard de Sudbery, rector of Crofton [W. R., co. York], Richard Pygot of Hokelowe, and Richard Abbenay his son of all his lands and tenements in Hope and elsewhere in the county. Witn. William Woderove of Hope, Robert Eyre, forester, John Kyrkeyerd, Richard de Baggeschawe, etc. Dat. M. a. F. of SS. Tiburtius and Valerian [14 Apr.], 10 Hen. IV. [1409]. (Foljambe.)

1441. CONFIRMATION from Thomas de Stretton, Dean of Lichfield, to Nicholas, son of William le Eyre of Hope, of the wardship of James, son of the same William, and of Anabella Clerk, his widow, heiress of William Clerk, chaplain, and of his lands in Hope, and in case of the death of the said James, then to have the wardship of Thomas, "frater germanus iunior dicti Jacobi"; rent, 3s. 4d. Dat. Lichfield, 31 May, 1409. (Woll. ii. 78.)

1442. GRANT from William Horderon and Annabella his wife to John de Staffelay of a piece of arable land called "Le Damrydyng" lying between "le Grenesyde" and "Le Nonneley" [in Hope]. Witn. Robert Eyer, Richard Abnay, Richard Warde, Richard Bagschagh, etc. Dat. Hope, Sat. b. F. of Ass. of B.V.M. [15 Aug.], 12 Hen. IV. [1411]. (Foljambe.)

1443. LEASE from the Prior and Convent "dez Preez" of Derby to Walter Halley, of Blakebroke, Henry Joye, Hugh son of the said Walter Hally, and William del Kyrk of Chapel, of the pasture of Byrstallegh in the parish of Hope. Dat. Derby, F. of SS. Philip and James [1 May], 8 [Hen. VI. ? 1430]. French. (Foljambe.)

1444. ACQUITTANCE from William Brome, vicar of Baukewell and receiver of the Dean and Chapter of Lichfield there, to James le Eyere, their Steward at Hope, for 100*s.* Dat. Hope, 10 Oct., 17 Hen. VI. [1438]. (Woll. iii. 24.)

1445. MANOR of Hope. Admission of Robert Eyre, esq., as tenant of a messuage and land on the surrender of John Sylverlok, at a court of the Dean and Chapter of Lichfield held Th. a. F. of St. Laurence [10 Aug.], 19 Edw. IV. [1479]. (Foljambe.)

1446. GRANT from Robert Eyre of Padley, sen., esq., and Robert Eyre of the same, jun., esq., to Nicholas Staley of Hope, and Agnes his wife of a forestry [or tract of forest land] and lands in Hope which they held of Christofer Staley his father, with remainder to brothers and sisters. Witn. Thomas Balge of Aston, Nicholas Eyre of Hope, Christopher Midiltone of Shattone. Dat. Padeley, 20 Aug., 11 Hen. VII. [1496]. (Woll. ii. 79.)

1447. GRANT from Thomas Wylde to Thomas Hawkysworth de Thorneseyt in Bradfeld and Robert Bunttyng, of all his lands in Hope. Dat. 12 Sept., 15 Hen. VII. [1499]. (Brookhill.)

1448. GRANT from Thomas Haukysworth of Thorneseyt in Bradfeld parish, and Robert Bunttyng of Hope, to Thomas Wilde of Offorton, in the parish of Hope, and Elizabeth his wife, of all the lands which they hold by feoffment of the said Thomas. Witn. Edward Hawkysworth, William Walkeden, Thomas Bacon. Dat. 24 Nov., 15 Hen. VII. [1499]. (Brookhill.)

1449. GRANT from John Bockyng of Hope to John Savage of Eidale and Elias Staley of Pindale, of a messuage and twenty acres of land in Hope. Dat. 6 July, 21 Hen. VIII. [1529]. (Bemrose.)

1450. LEASE, for 21 years, from John Eyre of Redsettes to Ellys Staley of Pyndall, of the messuage called Red Settes, with all appurtenances in the fields of Howpe and Castylton. Dat. 20 Mar., 27 Hen. VIII. [1536]. (Bemrose.)

1451. LEASE, for 40 years, from Henry Wyllyams, Dean, and the Chapter of Lichfield to Rauf Hethcote of Hope and William his son, of a croft called Hallcroft in Hope, with houses, etc., enclosed with "hays and dyches on bothe sydes Pekesarse," and land called "the Ruddyng" abutting upon the "water of Pekeserse." Dat. 10 May, 1544. (Pole-Gell.)

1452. BOND from William Hethcote of Leycestre, chaplain, to Henry Wyllyams, Dean, and the Chapter of Lichfield, for the sealing and delivery by Rauf Hethcote of Hope and William his son, Richard Barber and Henry Bagshawe, their sureties, of "a lease of Halcroft wth ii houses in Hope, a barne and the Rydding".let to the said Rauf and William by the said Dean and Chapter. Dat. 30 Oct., 1544. (Pole-Gell.)

HOPE *v.* also under BAKEWELL, CASTLETON, CHESTERFIELD, FAIRFIELD, ROMILEY.

HOPTON.

1453. LICENCE from King Edward III. to the Abbot and Abbey of Dale to receive seisin of sixty acres of moor in Hopton from Richard le Cursun, parson of the church of Breideshale, and William Shymmyng — and a toft, seven acres and a half of land and an acre of meadow in Stanton iuxta Dale from Robert de Sallowe, in accordance with the permission granted by the King's father (Edward II.) to Dale Abbey to acquire, notwithstanding the Statute of Mortmain, lands to the annual value of 100s. Dat. 5 July, anno. 17 [1343]. Great seal. (Add. 47514).

1454. BOND from Thomas Wylcokes of Coventry, fyshemonger, and Robert Smythe of the same, skynner, to Ralph Jell of Hopton, gent., for payment to the latter of £40. Dat. 12 Oct., 3 Edw. VI. [1549]. (Pole-Gell.)

HOPTON *v.* also under ASHBOURNE, BRASSINGTON, WIRKSWORTH.

HORSLEY.

(HORSELEY.)

1455. GRANT from Thomas, son of Thomas Purchas, of Langeley Mareys, to Gilbert Keys of Kylbourne, of lands in Horseley and Kilbourne. Witn. Will. de Tuttebury, Thomas de Tuttebury, William de Sellowe, etc. Dat. London, "in Fletestret, parish of St. Brigide," F. of St. Michael [29 Sept.], 34 Edw. III. [1360]. (Woll. iv. 71.)

1456. ACQUITTANCE from Thomas Boteler, knt., to Henry Balle, for £10 10s., purchase money for a messuage, croft, etc., in Horsley, formerly belonging to Thomas Trees. Dat. 1 May, 3 Hen. VII. [1488], (Foljambe.)

1457. EXTRACT of roll of court of Horston held at Horsley, M. b. F. of St. Anthony [11 May], 13 Hen. VII. [1498], recording the surrender by John Keys of a close called Pyllersych in the vill and fields of Kylborn to the use of Henry his son, Elizabeth his wife, and the heirs of their bodies. (Debdale.)

1458. EXTRACT of roll of court of Horston held at Horsley, M. b. F. of Nat. of B. V. M. [8 Sept.], 13 Hen. VII. [1498], recording the surrender by John Hogeson of part of a close of John Kais in the fields of Kilburn. (Debdale.)

1459. LEASE, for 31 years, from John Rossell of Draycote, yeoman, to Thomas Ashton of Horsley of a piece of herbage land in Horsley abutting on the lane called Vycar Lane, and a piece of meadow ground abutting on a "broke called Botell broke," near the land of Henry Statham. Dat. 21 Oct., 31 Hen. VIII. [1539]. (Wilmot.)

1460. SALE by Margarett Johnson, widow, and Henry Johnson, her son, of Horseley, gent., to Thomas Sacheverell of Kyrkby in Asshefeld [Kirkby-in-Ashfield, co. Notts.], gent., of seven score oaks and other wood in Horseley. Dat. 22 Mar., 2 Edw. VI. [1548]. (Woll. xii. 115.)

HORSLEY *v.* also under BREADSALL, KILBURN, STAVELEY.

HUCKLOW, GREAT and LITTLE.

(HOKELAWE, HOKELOWE, HOKLOWE, HUKLOWE.)

1461. GRANT from Richard Daniel of Tideswelle to Richard fil. Rankelli de Parva Hokelawe of the whole vill of Parva Hokelawe as he himself had it by grant from Henry de Laxinton, sometime Bishop of Lincoln [1253-58]. Witn. Dom. William de Morteyng, Gervase de Bernak, Richard de Herthul, Robert his brother, knts., Robert de Abbeneye, John Foleiambe, Robert Foleiambe, etc. Late Hen. III. (Foljambe.)

1462. GRANT from William [de Hales], Abbot of Lylleshulle [Lilleshall], and of the Convent of the same place, to Richard fil. Johannis Daniel de Tyddeswalle and Johanna his wife of 6d. silver or twelve "ciphos albos de pretio sex denariorum" of annual rent for a certain quitclaim and release which the said Richard made to the convent of one messuage and bovate of land in Magna Huckelowe. "Teste Deo et capitulo." Dat. apud Lylleshull, F. of St. Bartholomew [24 Aug.], 1301. (Add. 8443.)

1463. GRANT from Thomas fil. Ricardi Larcher de Hokelowe to Thomas fil. Johannis Larcher de Hokelowe of a messuage, with five houses and ten acres of land, in Magna Hokelowe. Witn. John Foliaumbe, James Coterell, Roger de Stafford, Alan le Archer, Andrew Larcher. Dat. Hokelowe, Sat. a. F. of St. Hilary [13 Jan.], 16 Edw. III. [1343]. (Bowles.)

1464. GRANT from Thomas fil. Ric. Larcher to Thomas fil. Johannis Larcher of a messuage and ten acres of land in Magna Hokelowe; rent, 20 marks "argenti vel auri" at Midsummer. Witn. Dom. William de Streddeley, mil., John Foleiamb, Henry de Tyddiswall, John de Stafford, William Note de Eyum. Dat. M. b. F. of St. Gregory [12 Mar.], 32 Edw. III. [1359]. (Bowles.)

1465. DEED whereby the said Thomas fil. Ric. Larcher releases to the said Thomas fil. Johannis the annual rent of 20 marks for a term of 70 years. Dat. Fr. a. Ann. of B. V. M. [25 Mar.], 32 Edw. III. [1359]. French. (Bowles.)

1466. GRANT from Thomas fil. Johannis Larcher to Nicholas fil. Johannis de Stafford of a messuage and 12 acres of land in Hoklowe which he had of the grant of Thomas fil. Ric. Larcher. Witn. John Foliamb, Thomas his son, Henry fil. Radulfi. Dat. apud Tidd', Sat. b. F. of St. Peter in cathedra [22 Feb.], 36 Edw. III. [1362]. (Bowles.)

1467. LEASE, for 56 years, from Nicholas, son of John de Stafford, to John de Stafford his father, of a messuage and 10 acres of land in Great Hoklowe which were devised to the said Nicholas by the will of the late Thomas son of John le Archer, who held them at the time of his death on a 70 years' lease from Thomas, son of Richard le Archer. Dat. F. b. F. of St. Margaret [20 July], 46 Edw. III. [1372]. French. (Bowles.)

1468. QUITCLAIM from Thomas fil. Ricardi Larcher, dominus de Magna Huklowe, to John de Stafford, of a messuage and 10 acres of land in Magna Huklowe which John Larcher formerly held; saving only a penny annual rent to the said Thomas. Witn. John Foliaumbe, John Larcher, Henry de Tiddeswell. Dat. W. b. F. of St. James [25 July], 46 Edw. III. [1372]. (Bowles.)

HUCKLOW *v.* also under EYAM, PADLEY, TIDESWELL.

HUCKNALL, AULT.

(HUKNALL.)

1469. RELEASE from John Benet to John Leek, son and heir of William Leek of Lanforth, of the manors of Lanforth, Hick[lyng], Estleek, and Saxendale [Langford, Hickling, East Leek, Saxondale, co. Notts.], with appurtenances in Wyverton and Carcolstone [Wiverton and Carlcaston], same county, the manor of Huknall [Ault Hucknall] and Sutton in la Dall [co. Derby], with advowson of the churches of Hicklyng at Sutton [co. Notts.], the manor of Sandeacre and Harstone [Sandiacre, co. Derby, Harston, co. Leic.], with lands in North Colyngham, Stockwith, Holme justa Newerk, Gedlyng, and Elstone [co. Notts.], Kirkhalome [Kirk Hallam, co. Derb.], and Dalderby, Craslound, and Gunthorpe, co. Linc. Witn. John You (?), Thomas White, John Mill, jun., of North Colyngham, etc. Dat. Eyleston, 5 Feb., 11 Edw. IV. [1472]. (Woll. i. 77.)

HULLAND.

(HOLAND.)

1470. GRANT from Robert de Ferr[ariis] fil. et her Dom. Willelmi de Ferr[ariis], Comitis Dereb', to Henry Shelford, of five score acres of land, viz., 40 acres sometime held by Symon de Tonk' in the ward of Holand and 60 acres lying "inter Hayam de le Neubigging et le Costlowe," with husebote and haybote in the same ward; rent, a sparrow hawk or 6*d.*, at the option of the said Henry, and suit to the two great Courts of Beurepayr, namely, those at Easter and Michaelmas. Witn. Will de Ferr[ariis], "frater meus," Dom. John de Soleny, William Haunselin, Stephen de Mineriis, tunc senescallus, Ralph Barry, Andrew de Jarpenuil, etc. Dat. Pillesbury, Fr. a. Conv. of St. Paul [25 Jan.], 46 Hen. III. [1262]. (Woll. vi. 48.)

1471. EXTRACT from court roll of Holand held at Idridgehay on 13 Nov., 14 Hen. VIII. [1522], whereat seisin was delivered to William Alsop of a close called Cotepyngull, in Holand, which Thomas Wilson had surrendered to his use at a court held at Shotill [Shottle] parke on the Eve of All Saints in the preceding year. (Woll. i. 84.)

HULLAND *v.* also under BRADLEY, DUFFIELD, MERCASTON.

HONDOW *v.* under UNSTONE.

HURDLOW, NR. EARL STERNDALE.

(HORDLAWE.)

1472. GRANT from John de Byroun, mil. [ob. 1295] to Henry his brother, for his homage and service, of all his land of Hordlawe, with men, "nativi," liberties, etc. To hold to the said Henry "et heredibus suis de corpore suo in facie ecclesie legitime procreatis" by service to the chief lord of the eighth part of the service of one knight, and two capons "in Mayo apud Salveyam" [Sawley]. Witn. Henry de Irton, Ralph le Wyne, Geoffrey de Bracebrigge, Adam de Prestwike, Jordan de Crompton, John de Buckstanis, Elias de Nedham "sergand," etc. Late 13th cent. (Harl. 111 E. 17.)

1473. BOND from John de Nedham to William Gudhyne of Hurdlow, jun., for the payment of ten marks. Dat. Hurdlow, F. of Pur. of B. V. M. [2 Feb.], 6 Hen. VI. [1428]. (Hallowes.)

IBLE.

(IBELL, IBOLE, IBUL, IBULLE, YBOLE, YBULL.)

1474. GRANT from Henry Forestarius of Ybole to Nicholas fil. Ricardi de Ybole of a croft in Ybole; rent, 1*d.* Witn. Richard le Porter of Caldelowe, Henry fil. Thome de Hopton, Henry fil. Henrici de Hopton, clericus, etc. *Temp.* Edw. I. (Woll. x. 17A.)

1475. GRANT from Robert fil. Nicholai de Ybole to Ranulph fil. Ranulphi de Sniterton of a rent of 1*d.* from lands in Ybole. Witn. Ranulph de Sniterton, sen., Henry de le Gruffe, Richard le Chapman, etc. Dat. Th. a. F. of St. Matthew [21 Sept.], 32 Edw. I. [1304]. (Woll. x. 42.)

1476. GRANT from John fil. Ranulphi de Snyterton, sen., to Ranulph de Snyterton, of 9*d.* rent from lands near the well of Ybull, etc. Witn. John Attewalle, Roger fil. Nicholai Chapmon of Ybulle, and William Preest of the same. Dat. Ybull, F. of St. Bartholomew [24 Aug.], 31 Edw. III. [1357]. (Woll. x. 7.)

1477. GRANT from Magota del Howe of Ibul to Adam del Stryt of lands in Ibul; rent, 8*s.* 5½*d.* Witn. John Atyswelle of Ibul, John del Stones of the same, William Prest, etc. Dat. Th. a. Pentecost [16 May], 11 Ric. II. [1388]. (Woll. x. 17.)

1478. GRANT from John Nedham of Ibulle to Robert Knyveton sen., esq., etc., of a messuage and lands in Ibulle which they had of the feoffment of John Sutton of Wynster. Witn. Ralph Gelle of Ibulle, John Beliden', and John Beghton. Dat. Pur. of B. V. M. [2 Feb.], 32 Hen. VI. [1454]. (Woll. x. 14.)

1479. GRANT from William Dale of Ibulle and Thomas Dale of Asshovere to Ralph Saucheverell, esq., of a messuage, etc., in Ibulle. Witn. Ralph Gelle of Ibulle, Richard Heywarde, and William Mowbrey of the same. Dat. Ex. of Holy Cross [14 Sept.], 1 Edw. IV. [1461]. (Woll. xi. 43.)

1480. POWER of attorney by the same to Richard Waller to deliver seisin to Ralph Saucheverelle, esq., of the above-named messuage, etc., in Ibulle. Same date. (Woll. x. 44.)

1481. DEED of sale from Thomas Sacheverell, son and heir of William Sacheverell late of Sneterton, to Sir Henry Vernon, knt., of all his lands, etc., in the towns and lordships of Ibell and Ashoure "negh vnto Wurkysworthe." Dat. 11 Sept., 24 Hen. VII. [1508]. (Trusley.)

IDRIDGEHAY.

(EDDRICHESHAY, EDRECHHAY, IDDURSHEY, IDRICHEHAY, IDRICHHAY, YDERYCHAY.)

1482. GRANT from Thomas Smyth and Agnes his wife, daughter and one of the heirs of Roger Bradshaw, late of Eddricheshey *al.* Iddurshey to Margaret Bradshawe, widow of the said Roger, of all the share of the said Agnes of her father's lands in Eddricheshey. Witn. John Curson of Kedilston, esq., John Verney of Eddricheshey, Henry Shakulton, Robert Cowhop. Dat. M. a. F. of St. Peter ad vincula [1 Aug.], 2 Ric. III. [1484]. (Bemrose.)

1483. LEASE, for five years, from Laurence of the Haye, of Derby, and Jone his wife, to Margaret Bradshawe, sister to the said Jone, of the land, etc., in Idrichhay which came to her on the death of her father, Roger Bradshawe. Dat. 31 Mar., 12 Hen. VII. [1497]. (Bemrose.)

1484. GRANT from Thomas Somer, son and heir of Christopher Somer of Yderychey to Margaret his mother for her life of an enclosure in Yderychay called Furnycottfeld, which the said Thomas acquired from Thomas Mellor. Witn. Thomas Alton, William Gambull, Thomas Storer. Dat. 23 June, 22 Hen. VIII. [1530]. (Bemrose.)

1485. QUITCLAIM from Robert Smythe of Kyrke Yreton, yeoman, to Margaret, wife of Christopher Somer, of all the lands in Yderychay which he had jointly with Margaret, lately wife of Roger Bradsha, by grant from the said Christopher and Margaret Somer. Witn. William Madocke, chaplain, Thomas Parker, Thomas Brammall. Dat. 23 June, 22 Hen. VIII. [1530]. (Bemrose.)

1486. QUITCLAIM from Richard Smythe, son and heir of Thomas Smythe and of Agnes, dau. and one of the heirs of Roger Bradshawe, to Thomas Somers of all the lands formerly Roger Bradshawe's in Edrechhey. Dat. F. of St. George [23 Apr.], 24 Hen. VIII. [1532]. (Bemrose.)

IDRIDGEHAY *v.* also under DUFFIELD, HULLAND.

ILKESTON.

(ELKESTON, HILKESD'.)

1487. COVENANT between Hugh fil. Radulfi and the Bailiffs and Burgesses of Nottingham to settle a dispute concerning freedom from toll in Nottingham, namely, that the Bailiffs and Burgesses grant that the whole land of the said Hugh " de baronia de Gant," viz., in Hilkesd' [Ilkeston], Stanton [Stanton in the Dale], Halum [West or Kirk Hallam], Schippeleg' [Shipley], and Breydest' [Breaston], be free of toll in respect of all things for food and clothing, both in the fair of Nottingham and outside, but they shall give toll " pro tinctura pannorum factorum et pro lana tincta, et postea si velint facient texere et fullare pannos faciendos de predicta lana tincta et refullare similiter si velint pannos tinctos sine tolneto." And for all merchandise they shall give toll all the year. And if any dispute arise among the burgesses concerning purchases, the seller or buyer shall acquit himself by his oath, but when any " villanus " buys sheep in summer to sell against the winter, or similarly pigs to sell after mast time, they shall give toll as for merchandise. For this concession the said Hugh shall pay the said Bailiffs, etc., 2s. yearly. Witn. John, Abbot of Dale, Roger, Prior of Lenton, Nigel de Lisurs, Ralph de Trehanton, Richard de Rybof, Roger de Cressy, Reginald de Meudry, Robert de Duyn, Robert le Vavassur, knts., Robert de Muschamp, and others. *Circ.* 1240-1250. (Add. 47498.)

1488. RELEASE from William la Zouche, 3rd Baron of Totness and Haringworth, to the Abbey of " La Dale," of the advowson of the church of Ilkeston, granted to the Abbey by Hugh de Willughby, clerk, John Pole of Nuburthe, William de Sallowe of Stanton, Henry Coton, Parson of Aston, Richard, Parson of Hauston, and John de Halom, Parson of Lamley, who held it from Henry, Parson of Braunstone [Braunston, co. Northt], John, Parson of Everdon, same county, and John Marchaunt, clerk. Witn. Sir John Clyntone, Sir Edmund de Appilby, Sir Will. Astley, knts., etc. Dat. 12 Oct., 10 Ric. II. [1388]. (Add. 26216.)

1489. RELEASE from Jocosa, widow of Roger del Schawe of Elkeston, and from Thomas de Shawe their son, to Thomas, Prior of Trentham and the convent of that place, of their right in lands in the vill of Elkeston, late the property of Matilda Basset. Dat. 1 July, 5 Hen. VI. [1427]. (P. R. O. B. 1490.)

INKERSALL *v.* under ETWALL, STAVELEY.

IVONBROOK GRANGE, NR. WIRKSWORTH.

(EUENBROKE, EVENBROKE, IUENBROC, IUENBROOK, YUENBROC, YUENEBROK.)

1490. * GRANT from Robert son of Adam le Wyne to Robert son of Ingelram of Nottingham, of the land in Yuenbroc, Horburghale, and Hopton, which was formerly held by Hamo the clerk, paying yearly 12*s.* to the Earl of Derby, etc. Thirteenth century. (Pole-Gell.)

1491. QUITCLAIM from Ranulph fil. Ranulphi de Sniterton, Dominus de Ibole [Ible in Wirksworth] to the Abbot, etc., of Buildwas of two watercourses within their grange of Iuenbroc. Witn. Hugh de Bocstones, Hugh le Meyne of Wynstre, Roger de Wodnesleye, etc. Dat. apud Stone, Whitsun Tuesday, 2 Edw. II. [1309]. (Foljambe.)

1492. QUITCLAIM from Richard Foliamb to Buildwas Abbey of the grange of Yuenebrok [Ivonbrook] and all their lands in the county of Derby. Witn. Dom. Godfrey Foliamb, knt., Robert Corbet, knt., John Cokayn, William Banastur, etc. Dat. Bildewas, Nat. of St. John B. [24 June], 40 Edw. III. [1366]. (Foljambe.)

1493. LEASE from Buildwas Abbey to Oliver de Barton and Alice his wife of the grange of " Euenbrooke en le haut Peck," with the profit of the mill, etc., for twenty-four years, at a yearly rent of eight marks. Dat. Ashebourne, Th. b. F. of St. George [23 Apr.], 2 Ric. II. [1379]. (Foljambe.)

1494. LEASE from Thomas Fuliambe, esq., of Walton, to Richard Vernon of Haddon, knt., of the grange called " Evenbroke Grange," with a water-mill, two "shepecotes," and all lands, etc., appertaining, as held by the said Thomas by lease from the Abbot of Buildwas, to hold the same for three years, paying the due rents, etc., to the Abbot of Buildwas, to Nicholas Gilbert, and to the King. Dat. London, 3 May, 14 Hen. VI. [1436]. (Foljambe.)

---

* On my visit to Hopton in 1902, this charter could not be found. The above abstract is from Hist. Comm. Report ix. ii. 402.

1495. GRANT from John, Abbot of Buldewas, to John Talbot, Lord Furnival [*cr.* Earl of Shrewsbury, 1442], Thomas Talbot, Nicholas Mountgomery, knt., Hugh Bourgh, esq., and Edmund Basset, esq., of eight marks of yearly farm from the grange of Iuenbrook for term of the life of John Dronfeld. Dat. Buldewas. *Circ.* 1440. (Foljambe.)

1496. LEASE from Thomas Foliambe to Sir Richard Vernon, knt., of the grange, etc., of Euenbroke for three years, at a yearly rent of eight marks to the Abbot of Buildwas. Dat. Inv. of H. Cross [3 May], 19 Hen. VI. [1441]. (Foljambe.)

IRETON, KIRK.

(IRTON, KIRKIRTON, YRTON.)

1497. GRANT from John Husbond of Kirkirton and Alice his wife to Thomas Okeovere, esq., and William Bagger, chaplain of Brassyngtone, of lands in Irton. Witn. Thomas Rappoke, William de Stapulle, John Baynay, etc. Dat. Ireton, S. a. F. of St. Ambrose [4 Apr.], 11 Hen. IV. [1410]. (Woll. vii. 17.)

1498. GRANT from Thomas Okeover, esq., to Walter de Wolley of Wirkesworth, of lands in Kirkirton which the said Thomas, together with William Bagger, chaplain, had of the gift of John Husbond and Alice his wife. Witn. Rob. Verney, John Parker, Thomas Dey, etc. Dat. Irton, M. a. Pur. of B. V. M. [2 Feb.], 5 Hen. VI. [1427]. (Woll. vii. 18.)

IRETON, KIRK, *v.* also under ASHBOURNE, KEDLESTON.

KEDLESTON.

(KETELESTUN, KETILSTONE, KETLESTONE.)

1499. GRANT from Richard de Curzun to Thomas fil. Thome de Curzun of the whole vill of Ketelestun, with the advowson of the church and mill, etc., to hold by service of a knight's fee. [1198-1199.] (Kedleston.) The text is :—

> Ric[ardus] de Curzun omnibus hominibus et amicis suis salutem. Sciatis me redd[id]isse et concessisse et recognouisse Thome fil. Thome de Curzun totam uillam de Ketelestun cum aduocacione Ecclesie et cum molendino et cum omnibus aliis pertinenciis que pertinent ad predictam villam de Ketelestun, tenendam de me et heredibus meis ille et heredes sui libere et quiete ab omni seruicio pro seruicio unius militis, saluo forinseco seruicio et inde homagium suum mihi fecit. His testibus, Hugone Bardolf, Magistro Rogero Arundel, Philippo fil. Roberti, Galfrido Haket, Justiciariis domini Regis apud Notingham anno decimo Regni Regis Ricardi et aliis baronibus et fidelibus domini Regis ibidem tunc presentibus, Willelmo filio Walkeline, Johanne de Boschuill, Willelmo de Rideware, Symone de Tuschet, Roberto fil. Walkeline, Willelmo de Godinton, Philippo de Derbi, Henrico Decano et pluribus aliis.

1500. QUITCLAIM from Richard de Curzun to Thomas de Curzun de Ketlestone of the aid which he owed him for the making of his first-born son a knight and for the marrying of his first-born daughter, in respect of the tenement he holds, on account of the aid which he made for making the first-born son of his lord the Earl of Ferrars a

knight, and for the marrying of the Earl's first-born daughter. *Circ.*
1200. (Kedleston.)

> Notum sit omnibus Christi fidelibus ad quos presens scriptum
> peruenerit quod ego Ric[ardus] de Curzun condonaui et quietum
> clamaui Thome de Curzun de Ketleston auxilium quod mihi debuit
> ad filium meum primogenitum militem faciendum et ad primo-
> genitam filiam meam maritandam de tenemento quod de me tenet,
> scilicet propter auxilium quod fecit mihi ad primogenitum filium
> domini mei Comitis de Ferrariis militem faciendum, et ad
> primogenitam filiam suam maritandam. Ut autem litere iste rate
> et inconcusse permaneant, sigilli mei impressione eas corroboraui.
> Hiis testibus, Rad[ulpho] filio Nicholai senescaldo domini Comitis
> tunc temporis, Rad[ulpho] de Bakepuz, Nicholao de Chambreis,
> Thoma persona de Croxhale, Roberto Forest[ario], Galfrido Albo,
> Thoma Bussun et multis aliis.

1501. LEASE from William le Burgelune to Thomas de Curzun of
his meadow of Osmundemedwe "una cum parte Marger[ie] matris mee,"
namely, the meadow lying between Aspineforde and Skitering up to
Oddebroc, for term of twelve years, that is, to take twelve crops; at
a rent of two pence; with warranty against all men "et insuper versus
matrem meam." Witn. Eustace de Luddam, Hugh le Bel, Fulcher de
Irton, Thomas Bussun, John de Turri, Robert de Schaldeford, Geoffrey
Blundus. Dat. Easter, 16 Hen. III. [1232]. (Kedleston.)

1502. LEASE, for term of 12 years, from Margery, quondam vxor
Willelmi le Burgelun, to Thomas de Curzun, of her share of Osmunde-
medwe which falls to her as dower. Same date and witnesses, with
William de Curzon, Thomas fil. Radulphi de Schobenhale. (Kedleston.)

1503. GRANT from William le Burgelun fil. Willelmi le Burgelun
of Weston to Thomas de Curzun of the meadow of Osmundemedwe,
between Yrton and Weston, as fully and entirely as William his father
held it. Witn. Eustace de Ludham, Sheriff of Nottingham, Roger le
Breton, knt., Geoffrey de Bakepuz, William de Picheford, William de
Menil, Engeluf de Braileford, Robert de Carleolo, Fucher de Yrton,
Geoffrey le Blund, Thomas Buyssun, etc. *Circ.* 1232. (Kedleston).

1504. QUITCLAIM from Margeria, quondam vxor Willelmi le
Burgmun (*sic*) to Dom. Thomas de Cursun of all the right she has
in the meadow of Osmundismedwe "nomine dotis." Witn. John, Abbas
de Parco, Fulcher de Irton, Hugh de Meynil, Henry Tuscheth, Thomas
Basun, etc. Dat. 26 Hen. III. [1241-2]. (Kedleston.)

1505. GRANT from Robert Twyford, Dominus de Longley, William
Arrosmythe, parson of Longley, John Brewode, parson of Rodburne, and
Roger de Wyngreworthe, to John Cursone fil. Johannis Cursone de
Ketilstone and Margaret his wife, dau. of Nicholas Mongomery, knt.,
and the heirs of their bodies, of the manor of Ketilstone, with the
advowson of the church and the reversion of a third part of the same
manor which Hugh Husee, knt., and Joan his wife hold in dower of
the said Joan, the reversion of a messuage called "le Stanley" place,
and four acres of land which John Repdone de Ketilstone holds, also
the whole lordship of Weston Undrewode. In case of the death of
the said John and Margaret without heirs, the said manors, etc., to
pass to Thomas, brother of the said John Curson, to Margaret Curson
their sister, and finally to the right heirs of the said John Cursone,
sen., father of the said John, Thomas, and Margaret. Witn. Roger

Bradshawe, Dominus de Meygnylle Longley, Thomas Makworth, John Irtone, John Burgulone. Dat. Morr. of St. Laurence [11 Aug.], 12 Hen. IV. [1411]. (Kedleston.)

1506. INQUISITION before Richard Blackwall, esq., Escheator after the death of John Curson of Kedleston, esq., showing the descent of the manor. Dat. Derby, 6 Sept., 2 Edw. VI. [1548]. (Woll. xi. 37.)

KILBURN.

(KILLEBURN, KYLBOURN, KYLBURN.)

1507. GRANT from Robert fil. Herberti de Killeburn to Gilbert fil. Roberti Keys of the same, of lands in Killeburn; rent, 5*d.* Witn. Will. de Parco de Dineby, Dom. Robert capellanus de Horseley, Richard Keys de Killeburn, etc. *Temp.* Edw. I. (Woll. iv. 68.)

1508. GRANT from William fil. Roberti de Ettewelle to John fil. Gilberti Keys of Kylbourn, of a messuage in Kylbourn. Witn. Gilbert Keys of Kylbourn, Hugh de Wynester, Richard fil. Willelmi, etc. Dat. F. of St. Michael [29 Sept.], 14 Edw. III. [1336]. (Woll. iv. 69.)

1509. GRANT from Robert, perpetual Vicar of Horssley, and Dom. William Normantone of the same, to Gilbert Keys of Kylburn, Johanna his wife, and John their son, of lands in Kylburn and Horsley. Witn. Hugh de Menyel of Kylburn, Henry de le Hewad, Ralph fil. Roberti of the same. Dat. Th. a. F. of St. James [25 July], 1349. (Woll. iv. 70.)

1510. RE-GRANT from John Forest, parson of Braydeshall, Thomas Waterhous of Duffeld, and William de Neuthorpe, chaplain, to John Kays of Kilburn, and Amice his wife, of lands in Kilburn, Horsley, and Horsley-parkes, with remainder to Henry, son of the said John. Witn. Will. Flaxman, John de Normanton, Henry de Hilton of Horsley, etc. Dat. Tu. a. Michaelmas Day [29 Sept.], 3 Hen. IV. [1401]. (Woll. iv. 72.)

KILBURN *v.* also under DENBY, HOPE, HORSLEY.

KILLAMARSH.

(KYNWALDEMERS, KYNWALMARCHE, KYNWALMERCH, KYNWOLMARSH.)

1511. CONFIRMATION for three marks from Robert de Menul' to Ralph fil. Nicholai of lands which the father of the said Ralph held in Kynwaldemers, with certain privileges at the mill; rent, half a mark. Witn. Roger de Pleslay, John, clericus de Wytwalle, John, persona de Barleburgh, etc. *Temp.* Edw. I. (Woll. vii. 78.)

1512. LEASE from Nicholas Longford, knt., to Thomas Foliambe, esq., of all his lands, etc., in Kylwalmerch, Barleburgh, and Boythorpe, co. Derby, and Basford, co. Notts. Witn. Thomas Meverell, John Longford, George Caryngton, Roger Foliambe, William Basset, etc., John, Vicar of Longford. Dat. 35 Hen. VI. [1456-1457]. (Foljambe.)

1513. GRANT from Nicholas Serlby, esq., Henry Ynce of Spynkhill, Henry Ellot of Kynwolmarsh, and Christopher Rodes de la Halgh in Staveley to Richard Hewet, of a messuage in Kynwolmarsh Netherthorp, called Wodhous-thing in the tenure of William Atkyn, which they

acquired from William Hewet, father of the said Richard; with
remainder to John Hewet, brother of the said Richard. Witn. Richard
Eyre of Plumley, gent., Richard Cade, William Hasilhirst, etc. Dat.
31 Mar., 20 Hen. VII. [1505]. (Rel. xx. 219.)

1514. DECLARATION of uses of a feoffment from John Huet of
Kynwalmarche to Henry Eliot and Isabel his wife of a messuage and
closes of pasture in Kynwalmarche. Dat. 12 Apr., 24 Hen. VII.
[1509]. (Rel. xx. 218.)

KNIVETON.

(KNYUENTON, KNYVETON.)

1515. PARDON from Edward III. to Thomas de Knyveton and
Nicholas his brother, for their complicity in the death of William
Spenser and acts of outlawry. Dat. Westm., 19 June, aº 27 [1353].
(Woll. vi. 31.)

1516. GRANT from Margery, widow of John de Knyveton, to Thomas
de Knyveton, of the manor of Knyveton, with the marriage of Nicholas,
son and heir of the said John, and in case of his death, within age,
the marriage of Emma his sister. Dat. Knyveton, M. a. F. of the
Ascension [10 May], 32 Edw. III. [1358]. (Woll. vi. 34.)

1517. LEASE, for 20 years, from Thomas Shanynton of Farley to
Thomas de Okeover of all his land called "Les Flates," near Knyuenton
[Kniveton], to hold at a yearly rent of 14s. Witn. John Wareyn, Adam
Lyghtwod, Richard Bromley. Dat. Christmas Day, 13 Hen. IV. [1411].
(Okeover.)

1518. COUNTERPART of lease from the Dean and Chapter of
Lichfield to Ralph Gell of Hopton of all the rents and emoluments of
the Chapel of Knyveton, with "Ly Parsonage place," for eight succes-
sive terms of five years, beginning in 1548, the lessee to provide a
fit and continuously resident Chaplain, and to repair all buildings.
Dat. 1 June, 1537. (Lichf. D. 21.)

1519. GRANT from Henry Wyllyams, Dean, and the Chapter of
Lichfield, to Thomas Gell, son of Ralph Gell of Hopton, of the rectory
house of the parish church of Knyveton, with the glebe lands, etc.
Dat. 1 July, 1549. (Lichf. D. 27.)

KNIVETON *v.* also under ASHBOURNE, BRADBURN, BRADLEY.

LANGLEY, KIRK, and MEYNELL.

(KYRKELONGELEYE, KYRKELONGLEY, LANGELYA,
LONGELAYMEYGNYLL, LONGELEMEYGNYLL, LONGELEY,
LONGELEYMEYGNYLL, LONGLEY.)

1520. GRANT from Roger de Bradel' to the "ecclesia beate Marie
de Kyngesmedewe juxta Derbeyam et monialibus ibidem" of all his
land and tenement in Langelya, with the mill, etc., which he held of
the gift of Mag. John de Weston, his uncle. Witn. Henry de Braylesford, Giles de Meynill, Oliver de Dodingesheles, Oliver de Rowlande,
Engyllard de Braylesford, Dom. Walter vicarius ecclesie Sancte
Werburge, Derb', etc. Thirteenth century. (Woll. viii. 52, 60.)

1521. GRANT from William Russel of Kyrkelongeleye to Robert fil. Ricardi de Makworthe of an acre of land in Kyrkelongeleye. Witn. Hugh de Meygnyll, Robert de Aulâ de Makworthe, John de Oddyngeseles, etc. Dat. Sat. b. F. of Ann. of B. V. M. [25 Mar.], 31 Edw. I. [1303]. (Woll. ix. 73.)

1522. GRANT from Adam Fythyon of Longelemeygnyll and Emma his wife to Juliana de Hundesworth of nine acres of arable land in the vill and fields of Kyrkelongeleye. Witn. Hugh de Meygnyll, William de Trusselege, William de Brascynton, John de Derleye, etc. Dat. apud Longelaymeygnyll. Dat. Morr. of Inv. of H. Cross [3 May], 32 Edw. I. [1304]. (Mundy.)

1523. GRANT from John de Derley of Kyrkelongeleye to John fil. Roberti Junioris de Westone, and Henry his brother, of a rent of 5s. from a messuage and meadow in Kyrkelongeleye. Witn. William de Trusseley, William de Brasynton, Henry de Bradelowe, etc. Dat. Fr. a. F. of St. Augustine [26 May], 1 Edw. II. [1308]. (Woll. iii. 3.)

1524. GRANT from Henry de Bredelowe of Kyrkelongeleye to Dom. Hugh de [Meinil], miles, Dominus de Longeleyemeygnyll, of three selions of land in the vill and territory of Kyrkelongeleye lying in the field of the wood at Le Fyxpol, between the land of John de Oddyngeseles and the land of Henry le Warde. Witn. William de Trusseley de Kyrkelongeleye, William de Brascynton, Henry le Warde, etc. Dat. Mor. of Pur. of B. V. M. [2 Feb.]. *Temp.* Edw. II. (Mundy.)

1525. QUITCLAIM from John de Longeley, clericus, to Nicholas de la Weld and William de Taryngton, chaplain, of a messuage, toft, and croft in Kirkelongley which formerly belonged to his brother, Henry de Longeley, chaplain, and descended by right of inheritance to the said John; with twenty acres of land in the same place. Witn. Hugh Slegh, Hugh Bate, Henry Mengnell, etc. Dat. at Duffeld, W. a. Michaelmas Day, 45 Edw. III. [1371]. (Mundy.)

1526. GRANT from Robert Twyford, armiger, to John Clement and Stephen Hykmons, chaplains, of all the lands, etc., which he had of the feoffment of Gerard Maynell in the vill and fields of Kyrkelongley. Witn. John Curson of Ketleston, arm., Thomas Bradfeld of Myrcaston, arm., Henry Pole of Mogenton. Dat. F. of SS. Peter and Paul [29 June], 20 Hen. VI. [1442]. (Mundy.)

1527. SALE from Thomas Twyford, son and heir of Walter Twyford of Langley, to Richard Knyveton of Bradley, sen., esq., of a pasture and close called Hakwood in the parish of Langley, late in the tenure of Robert Dawkyn. Dat. 3 Apr., 17 Hen. VII. [1502]. (Mundy.)

1528. GRANT from Thomas Twyford, son and heir of Walter Twyford, late of Longley, to Ralph Delves, esq., John Porte, John Knyveton, son of Richard Knyveton of Bradley, esq., and Henry Proctour, clerk, of a pasture or enclosure in the parish of Langley called Hakwood, with attorney to John Alsop of Spoundon and William Newbold of Bradley to give seisin. Dat. 6 Apr., 17 Hen. VII. [1502]. (Mundy.)

1529. RELEASE from Thomas Twyford, son and heir of Walter Twyford, late of Langley, to John Holme, Ralph Delves, John Porte, John Kniveton, Humphrey Kneveton, and Henry Proctour, of three pastures or enclosures in the parish of Langley, called "the lytyll launde," "Lytyll Hakwod," and "Wolley." Dat. 18 Sept., 18 Hen. VII. [1502]. (Mundy.)

1530. Lease, for three years, from Richard Knyveton, sen., esq., to Thomas Twyford, esq., John Alsope of Spoundon, of three closes in Kyrkelongley, whereof one is called Lytelhakwode, another called Woley, the third called Litell Launde; rent, 30*s.* Dat. 25 Mar., 18 Hen. VII. [1503]. (Mundy.)

1531. Exemplification of a recovery by Ralph Delues, esq., John Knyveton, John Porte, and Henry Proctour, clerk, against Thomas Twyford, esq., of 62 acres of land in Kyrkelongley. Dat. 24 May, 18 Hen. VII. [1503]. (Mundy.)

LANGLEY in Heanor.

1532. Lease, for 21 years, from Matthew Knyveton of Bradley, esq., and John Knyveton of Storeston, his uncle, to John Gents of Langley in Heynore and William Hunter of the same, of a close in Langley; rent, 31*s.* 8*d.* Dat. 20 Jan., 31 Hen. VIII. [1540]. (Woll. iv. 24.)

LANGLEY in Heanor *v.* also under Codnor, Shipley.

LANGLEY, nr. Chesterfield.

(Langele, Langeley, Langeleye, Longeley, Longley.)

1533. Release from Leticia fil. Galfridi de Brereleye to John fil. Rogeri de Langeleye of land which Roger de Langeleye gave to Walter de Doneston her grandfather at Langleye, lying on Brocholclif, near the road leading towards Neubolt. Witn. Thomas de Leyis, Roger le Albecot, Thomas de Bramton, Roger, clericus de Cestrefed, etc. *Temp.* Hen. III. (Harl. 112 G. 35.)

1534. Grant from John de Langeleye to William clericus de Witinton of land lying on Brocholclif, between the road from Langeley to Newbolt and land of Robert fil. Radulfi. Witn. Robert de Hedenishovere, Thomas de Hedenishovere, Thomas de Leyis, Robert de Witinton, etc. *Temp.* Hen. III. (Harl. 112 I. 43.)

1535. Grant from John fil. Rog. de Langeley to William Palmer of Langeley of lands in Langeley. Witn. Robert de Wytintona, Peter de Brimentona, Simon de Linacre, etc. *Temp.* Hen. III. (Foljambe.)

1536. Grant from Will. fil. Joh. de Longley to Thomas de Colle in Longeley of three and a half acres of land in the fields of Longeley. Witn. Thomas de Leys, Peter de Doneston, Jordan de Barlay, etc. *Temp.* Edw. I. (Foljambe.)

1537. Quitclaim from Leticia fil. Roberti fil. Bate de Langeleye to William fil. Galfridi de Langeleye of her right of inheritance after the death of Susanna her mother in lands, etc., held of the lord of Brimington in Langeleye. Witn. Richard Caskyn, Robert Caskyn, etc. Dat. F. of St. Martin [11 Nov.], 5 Edw. II. [1311]. (Foljambe.)

1538. Lease from John fil. Ranulphi of Whytinton to Robert fil. Rogeri Fox of Dunston of two acres of land in the fee of Langele for ten years. Witn. John fil. Will. de Dunston, William Caskyn, Richard Caskyn, etc. Dat. S. b. Michs. Day, 11 Edw. III. [1337]. (Foljambe.)

LANGLEY *v.* also under Chesterfield.

LEA *v.* under Crich.

LEAM *v.* under Eyam.

LINACRE.

(LINAKER.)

1539. GRANT from Garnar de Neapoli, Prior of the Brothers of the Hospital of Jerusalem in England, to John de Linacre of two bovates of land in Linacre which they acquired from Roger, son of Rauekel; yearly rent, 2*s.* Dat. 1189. (Add. 13932.) The text is:—

Notum sit omnibus tam presentibus quam futuris quod ego Garnarius de Neapol[i] prior fratrum Hospitalis Jer[usa]limitani in Anglia de communi assensu et uoluntate fratrum Capituli nostri concessi et presenti carta confirmaui Johanni de Linacra et heredibus suis duas bouatas terre in Linacra quas habemus ex donatione Rogeri fil. Rauekel cum pertinentiis suis. Tenendas et habendas de domo nostra iure hereditario libere et quiete, reddendo inde singulis annis domui nostre duos solidos ad festum sancti Bertelmi pro omni seruicio et consuetudine nobis inde pertinente. Ita tamen quod in obitu suo et successorum suorum similiter, tercia pars catallorum suorum que super predictam terram erunt pro salute anime sue domui nostre remanebit. Hiis testibus, Fratre Alano de Sancta Cruce, Fr. Matheo, Fr. Roberto Paruo, Fr. Osberto de Nordfolc, Fr. Briano de Lond', Fr. Hugone de Binford, Fr. Nicolao de Cadmel, tunc Magistro Eboraci, Fr. Simone de Scoth', Waltero clerico. Anno incarnationis dominice $M^o.C^c.lxxx^oix^o$

LINACRE *v.* also under CHESTERFIELD, WESTWELL.

LINTON.

(LYNTONE.)

1540. ACCOMPT-ROLL of Robert Myddelton, collector of rents for the manor of Lyntone, Mich., 23-24 Hen. VI. [1445], with the accompt of Thomas Hanson, Steward, of the Manor of Bretby for the same period. (Bemrose.)

LINTON *v.* also under DRAKELOW, GRESLEY, ROSLISTON.

LITCHURCH in DERBY.

(LUTCHURCH.)

1541. LEASE, for 44 years, from Thomas [Grevys], Abbot of Derley, to Antony Babyngton of Dedyke [Dethick], esquire, of a tenement in Lutchurch; rent, 73*s.* 4*d.* Dat. 10 Aug., 16 Hen. VIII. [1524]. (Woll. iv. 60.)

1542. SALE, for £10, by Humfrey Dugmanton, gent., to Rauf Sacheverell of Ratclif upon Sore [Ratcliff-upon-Soar, co. Notts.], of the lease of a tenement and "chefe place" in Lutchurch, which he held from Kateryn, Lady Babyngton, widow of Sir Antony Babyngton, knt. Dat. 11 June, 29 Hen. VIII. [1537]. (Woll. iv. 61.)

1543. LIST of freeholders owing suit at the court of Lutchurch. On the back is a rough draft of a grant by Thomas Pole of Wakbrigge to Ralph Pole, his son and heir apparent, of land in Boghwode, in the territory of Matlock. Sixteenth century. (Woll. xi. 11.)

LITCHURCH *v.* also under DERBY.

LITTLEOVER.

(PARVA OURE, PARVA OVERA.)

1544. DECLARATION by Philip Marci and Anna [Ser]affini his wife that they lease the village of Parva Oure of the Abbot and Convent of Burton[-on-Trent] for life only, and that they have delivered to the Abbot and Convent a copy of the charter by which they hold it, which shall be valid against any contrary contention by themselves or their heirs. Witn. Walter [de Senteney], Abbas de Dala, Bartholomew, Prior de Totesbiri [Tutbury, co. Staff.], William de Vernon, Mag. Stephen de Radecliue, Mag. Robert de Seka, Ralph Grim, etc. [1204-1235.] (Stowe 85.)

1545. GRANT from John de Cornera de Derby to the Abbot and Convent of Burton-on-Trent of a tenement which he held in fee of them in Parva Overa, together with the rent and service paid to him by Roger de Walton in respect of a tenement held of him in the same place. Witn. Dom. William and Dom. Giles de Meynil, mil., John de Chandos, Dom. de Rodburne, Mag. Will. fil. Roberti de Henovere, etc. *Temp.* Edw. I. (Stowe 62.)

LITTLEOVER *v.* also under MICKLEOVER.

LITTON.

(LYTTON.)

1546. GRANT from Ralph Wlvet de Litton to the Church of St. John at Tydeswelle and to Ralph, Dean, and the Chapter of Lichfield, as Rectors of that church, of a toft and lands at Litton, with half an acre of land in the same place extending from the head of the town to the stone cross towards Tudeswell. Witn. Thomas, Precentor of Lichfield, Roger Rusteng, Canon of the same, John de Uttokeshal, Thomas de Crawell, Succentor, Alan, Vicar of Tideswell, Ralph fil. Radulfi, presbiter, Henry de Lytton, Simon de Ascell, Hugo Martin, etc. [1214-1222.] (Lichf. B. 9.)

1547. SALE and release by Richard de Ednissouere to Nicholas de Blacquell of Robert fil. Reginaldi de Litton, with his homage and service, the said Nicholas to pay to the chief lord one penny rent or a pair of white gloves. Witn. Richard le Raggede, Henry de Caluouere, etc. Late thirteenth century. (Foljambe.)

1548. GRANT from Richard de Grey to William fil. Roberti de la Morhaghe of twelve acres three roods of land with half a toft in the vill and fields of Litton, lying on Backedale, Tydeswellisethis, Suclowe, Wythynewelle, etc. Witn. Jocelin de Steynisb' tunc temporis senescallus, Richard Danyll, Hugh de la Morhag', Thomas Folegaumbe, Roger Folegaumbe, etc. Early Edw. I. (Add. 26419.)

1549. QUITCLAIM from Thomas fil. Ricardi Willyson of Litton to Walter Gregory of land in Litton. Witn. John Figour, John de Benteleye, etc. Dat. S. a. F. of St. Matthew [21 Sept.], 21 Edw. III. [1347]. (Add. 7824.)

1550. GRANT from Nicholas fil. Walteri Gregore to John fil. Thome de Litton of four acres and a half of land in the fee of Litton lying on Hommuldon, Wylmeslowe, Borford, etc. Witn. Thomas fil. Ricardi, Henry de Toyneshende, Adam de Blakwall, etc. Dat. F. of SS. Simon and Jude [28 Oct.], 49 Edw. III. [1375]. (Add. 7842.)

1551. COUNTERPART of lease from Ralph Colyngwoode, Dean, and the Chapter, to Edmund Eyre, Vicar of Tideswell, and Roland Eyre his brother, of the fee-farm of Litton, with tithes of corn and hay of Hassopp, Longesdon maior [Great Longstone], Wardelowe [Wardlow], and Rowland [Roland], for five years. Dat. 5 Nov., 1516. (Lichf. D. 16.)

LITTON *v.* also under TIDESWELL, WALTON.

LOCKO.

(LOCHAY, NETHERLOKHAW.)

1552. QUITCLAIM from Nicholas fil. Rob. le Wyne to Alan de Pickworth of land with toft, etc., which Robert des Poer held from the said Alan on Palm Sunday, 1261, in the town and neighbourhood of Lochay [Locko]. Witn. William de Chaddesden, clerk, Roger de Draycott, clerk, John de Lozak, Elyas de Stretton, etc. *Circ.* 1261. (Rel. iii. 174.)

1553. AGREEMENT between Rauf Bridde [signs " Beyrd "] of Nether-lokhawe, gent., and Jane Dethike of Bredsall, widow, for the marriage of Richard Bridde, his son and heir, with Margaret, daughter of the said Jane. The said Rauffe to convey to Sir Wm. Saucheverell, knt., Nicholas Assheby, etc., the fee simple of lands and tenements of the yearly value of nine marks, in trust for the use of the said Richard and Margaret. The said Margaret to pay 40 marks. Dat. 22 Aug., 13 Hen. VIII. [1522]. (Woll. xii. 117, 118.)

LOCKO *v.* also under SPONDON, YELDERSLEY.

LONGFORD.

(LANGEFORD, LANGFORTH, LONGEFORD.)

1554. FINAL concord made at Notingham before William Briwerre, Sheriff, whereby John de Saucheuerel quitclaims to Oliver fil. Nigelli de Bubendona all his right in Bubendona, Longeford, Malmertona, in Turuerdestona [Thurvaston], co. Derby, and in Alaxton [Allexton], etc., co. Leic. Witn. Henry, subvice-comes, William de Leca, William de Rothomago, Hubert fil. Radulfi, Simon Tuschet, Robert de Muscampo, Thomas Dispensator, Sewale de Munjai, William de Verdun, Hugh de Acouer, etc. *Temp.* John. (Longford.)

1555. GRANT from King Henry III. to Nigel de Longford of free warren in Longeford, co. Derb., and Athelaxton [Allexton]. Witn. W[alter de Cantelupe], Bishop of Worcester, Simon de Montfort, Earl of Leicester, John de Plesset[is], Earl of Warwick, Peter de Sabaudia, John Maunsell, prepositus de Beuerlaco, Mag. William de Kilkenny, Archdeacon of Coventry, Ralph fil. Nicholai, Bertram de Crioyll, John de Lessington, Robert de Walerand, Robert le Noreys, Roger de Lokinton. Dat. Westminster, 9 June, anno 36 [1252]. (Rel. N.S., v. 108.)

1556. LEASE, for 30 years, from Dom. Nigel de Lanford to Robert Marescallus fil. Roberti Fabri de Wotton of nine selions on " le Stoniflat iuxta crucem Stephani," and a toft in Bobinton which Stephen le Blodletere sometime held. Witn. John de Langeford, William his brother, Micael de Langeford, Robert de Grendon, etc. Dat. All Saints' Day [1 Nov.], 37 Hen. III. [1252]. (Longford.)

13

1557. FINE levied in Hilary Term at Derby in 42 Hen. III. [1258], before John, Abbot de Burgo Sancti Petri, Roger de Thurkleby, Peter de Percy, and John de Wyuill, Justices itinerant, whereby Roger Durdent releases to Nigel de Langeford right of estover in the said Nigel's park, and in his other woods in Longford, and Nigel grants to Roger a "marcata" of annual rent from his water-mill in Langeford called Bubbedonmilne. (Longford.)

1558. COVENANT made at Derby before the Justices in Eyre between Dom. Nigel de Langeford and Roger de Mercinton and Elianor his wife, whereby the said Sir Nigel agrees not to make waste in or sell the wood of Langeford, called Brendewode, without licence from the said Roger, who undertakes to allow the said Sir Nigel free enjoyment of an assart called Limputruding, with cottages and land and a rent of 3*s.* from the same. Witn. Dom. Will. de Mungomery, Dom. Peter du Gant, Dom. Peter de Bakepuz, etc. Dat. Morr. of SS. Tiburtius and Valerian [15 Apr.], 53 Hen. III. [1269]. (Woll. ix. 59.)

1559. LEASE, for 41 years, from Dom. Nigel de Longeford to William de Longesdon, manens in Iueleg', of an assart which Matthew formerly servant of Roger de Mercenton sometime held; with common of pasture throughout the whole fee of Longeford, Malmarton [Mammerton], and Bobbedon [Bupton], except in the said Nigel's park, or corn, or meadows, and timber for building from Brendewode. Witn. Dom. William de Meynell, Giles de Meynill, William de Longeford, John de Benteleg', Robert le Fowyn, etc. Dat. Michaelmas, 1272. (Longford.)

1560. GRANT from Oliver fil. Ade de Kauelond to Emma his sister of a bovate of land with half an acre of meadow "in curto prato" [in Bobbedon], viz., the half-acre "prati Durdonis." Witn. Dom. Robert de Essebury, Dom. Nigel de Longeford, Dom. Ralph de Grendon, Dom. Robert de Perrer, etc. *Temp.* Hen. III. (Longford.)

1561. GRANT from Ralph le Foun fil. Henrici le Foun, with consent of Emma his wife, to Dom. Nigel de Longeford of an annual rent of 12 pence from land in Bubendone. Witn. Dom. Ralph de Grendon, Dom. Henry de Breylesford, Stephen de Yrton, Hamund de Sapurton, Michael de Longeford. *Temp.* Hen. III. (Longford.)

1562. GRANT from Michael de Langeford to Dom. Nigel fil. Nigelli de Langeford of three acres of land in Langeforde in the fields of La Wodehuse and four acres in Burleg', etc. Witn. Dom. Peter de Bakepuz, Dom. Robert de Ferrers, Henry de Irton, Henry de Mapelton, Roger Durdent, etc. *Temp.* Hen. III.-Edw. I. (Longford.)

1563. GRANT from Nigel fil. Nigelli de Langeford to Michael de Longeford of land in Langeford, viz., towards La Wodehuse in Burleg', etc. Witn. Dom. Peter de Bakepuz, Dom. Robert de Ferrers, Henry de Mapelton, Stephen de Irton, Henry le Foun, William de Longeford, Robert le Foun. *Temp.* Hen. III.-Edw. I. (Longford.)

1564. ACCORD of suit moved before Dom. John de Vallibus and his companions, itinerant Justices at Derby, whereby Roger Duredent releases to Oliver de Langeford, knt., all his right in estovers in two woods of the said Oliver called Le Brentewode and Le Parrok, in return for which the said Oliver grants to the said Roger 30 acres of land (by perch of 18½ feet) in the said wood of Brentewode. Witn. Dom. Henry de Braylesford, William de Meynill, Giles de Meynill, Henry fil. Herberti, Roger de Mercinton, knts., William de Langeford, etc. Dat. 9 Edw. I. [1280-1281]. (Longford.)

1565. FINAL CONCORD between Dom. Oliver de Longeford and Dom. Roger de Mercinton, whereby the said Oliver leases to Roger and Eleanor his wife 20 acres of land in le Brendewode extending from Berleyford, near the road leading to Le Wodehous, to be stubbed up and cultivated, common of pasture being reserved to the said Oliver after the hay and corn are carried; and the said Roger grants to Oliver "ut possint se approwiare . . . de toto vasto suo in le Brendewode et de quodam prato quod vocatur le Ruddemedwe," and releases to him all the tenements which Henry "Prepositus," Robert "Prepositus," and Richard Le Latour enclosed in Le Wodehous, common of pasture in le Brendewode and in le Ruddemedwe after the hay and corn are carried to the said Roger and Eleanor and their tenants of Malmarton. Witn. Dom. William de Meynil, Henry fil. Herberti, Ralph de Monioye, knts., John Moule, etc. Dat. "apud Derbe in itinere Justic[iarum]," S. a. Inv. of H. Cross [3 May], 9 Edw. I. [1281]. (Longford.)

1566. GRANT from John fil. Oliveri le Fown of Holinton' to Roger de Mercinton' and Elianor his wife, of twenty acres of land in le Brendewode of Longeford; rent, 1*d.* Witn. Dom. Henry de Braylisforde, Dom. Henry Fitz-Herbert, Dom. Ralph de Monjoy', milites, etc. *Temp.* Edw. I. (Woll. ix. 64.)

1567. GRANT from Richard fil. Rogeri Durdent to Roger de Mercinton of thirty acres of land in Longeford; rent, a rose. Witn. Dom. Henry de Braylesford, Dom. William de Meynil, Dom. Giles de Meynil, milites, etc. Dat. Roddesley, M. a. F. of St. Lucy [13 Dec.], 1282. (Woll. ix. 60.)

1568. QUITCLAIM from Robert fil. Michaelis Wethyr of Longeforde Wodehouses to Dom. John de Longeford and Joan his wife of an assart in the fee of Longeford called Berleyruding. Witn. Dom. Henry de Braylesford, Henry de Knyveton, Giles de Meynell, John de Bakepuz, Geoffrey, vicar of Longford, etc. Dat. S. b. F. of St. Andrew [30 Nov.], 23 Edw. I. [1294]. (Longford.)

1569. GRANT from William Carectarius de Bobedone to Roger Eflawe of a bovate of land in Bobedon which the said William holds on lease from Nicholas, Dominus de Longeford. Witn. Robert de Grendon, Robert de Esseburne, Robert le Taylur, etc. Dat. F. of St. Clement [17 Nov.], 1314. (Longford.)

1570. GRANT from Robert fil. Thome Otting de Longeford to Richard de Diluerene and Isabella his wife, of a toft, etc., in Longford. Witn. Ralph de Bakepuz, Hugh de Fulford, Gilbert Swift, clerk, etc. Dat. T. b. F. of St. Martin [11 Nov.], 1316. (Longford.)

1571. LEASE, for 18 years, from Nicholas, Dominus de Longeford, to Cecily, relict of Henry de Alkemonton, of a messuage, etc. [in Longford] which her late husband held for a term of years. Dat. F. of St. Martin [11 Nov.], 10 Edw. II. [1316]. (Longford.)

1572. GRANT from Richard de Pountfret to Dom. Nicholas de Longeforde, knt., of a messuage and piece of land in Longeford Wodehuses which he had by grant of Thomas fil. Edithe extending from Berleye to "le Schephouscroftus," and from the park of the said Nicholas to "le Wodehouses." Witn. Dom. Hugh de Meingneil, Dom. John de Twyford, Dom. Nicholas de Marchinton, etc. Dat. Mor. of St. Peter ad vincula [2 Aug.], 12 Edw. II. [1318]. (Longford.)

1573. GRANT from Roger Bissop of Longeford to Roger his son of land in Longeford lying in Le Schurthehul, etc. Witn. Robert de Aschebury, Oliver de Coulond, Robert de Grendon. Dat. S. a. F. of St. Gregory [12 Mar.], 1 Edw. III. [1327]. (Longford.)

1574. QUITCLAIM from William Wythur of Longeford Wodehousus to Dom. Nicholas de Longeford, knt., of all his lands in Longeford. Witn. Ralph de Marchinton, Ralph de Mountioe, Robert de Asschbourne, etc. Dat. F. b. F. of St. Dunstan [21 Oct.], 5 Edw. III. [1331]. (Longford.)

1575. DEFEASANCE of bond from Nicholas de Langeford, knt., to Fr. Philip de Thame, Prior of the Hospital of St. John of Jerusalem in England, in £10, for the repayment of a loan of 100s. (which he has received by the hand of Fr. William de Brex) at their house "Fontis Clericorum." Dat. "apud fontem Clericorum" [Clerkenwell], 13 March, 11 Edw. III. [1337]. (Longford.)

1576. GRANT from Nicholas de Longefforde, knt., to Walter le Harpere of Longeford, of four and a half acres of land in the fee of Longefford. Witn. Nicholas Selueyn, Oliver de Couland, Roger Duredent, Alexander de Hyde, Robert de Grendon. Dat. Longford, Vigil of St. James [24 July], 11 Edw. III. [1337]. (Longford.)

1577. COVENANT of grant from William fil. Ricardi de Pountefreit to Walter le Harpur of Shirleg' of a messuage and lands in the field of Longeford, and eight acres of land called Le Flytenflate in the fee of Alkemonton, etc. Witn. Nicholas Selueyn, Reginald de Marchington, Roger Duredent, etc. Dat. Th. a. Michaelmas Day, 13 Edw. III. [1339]. (Longford.)

1578. GRANT from Roger de Fulford to Adam fil. Radulfi de Assche of a messuage, etc., in Wodehouses, Burley, Bobbedon, and Longford. Witn. Dom. William de Falford, rector of Longeford, Robert de Asschebourne, Roger Durdent, William Jurdon, etc. Dat. Bobbedon, S. a. Pur. of B. V. M. [2 Feb.], 1347[8]. (Longford.)

1579. BALANCE SHEET of accompts of Longford Manor. 1360. (Lichf. N. 11.)

1580. GRANT from William de Salford, parson of Longford, Thomas de Longeford, parson of Wynfeld, and John Cressy, parson of Thorp, to Nicholas de Longeford, knt., of 200 "marcate" of annual rent. Dat. Longford, F. of H. Trinity [12 June], 36 Edw. III. [1362]. (Longford.)

1581. LEASE, for lives, from Nicholas de Longeforde, knt., to John Amysson and Matilda his wife, of a cottage near the Mill of Bubbdon. Dat. Longford, W. a. F. of St. Cedda, Bp. [7 Jan.], 3 Ric. II. [1380]. (Longford.)

1582. GRANT from William Dylreû de Longford to Oliver de Barton and Dom. John Cressy, rector of Longford, of all the lands which he holds in Longford. Witn. Thomas Mongomery de Couland, Robert Fowne, John Durdent, etc. Dat. Longford, M. a. Michaelmas Day, 5 Ric. II. [1381]. (Longford.)

1583. DEED whereby Nicholas de Longeford grants to William Fitzherbert of Northbury [Norbury] all his land "en le Milneholme" near Dovebrugpleos, between Ekkescroft and Theveholme, in exchange for the land called Alwaldesholme "del coulesue desques al ewe de Douue." Dat. Northbury, 26 Aug., 14 Ric. II. [1390]. Seal of arms of William Fitzherbert. (Longford.)

1584. LEASE from Dom. Nicholas de Longeford, knt., to ·John Amysson of Longeford of a cottage, garden, and croft near the mill of Longeford and Bubbedon, with remainder to Richard, son of the said John; the lessees to find the lord a man "ad levandum fenum" for a day, a man in the autumn for reaping for a day, and a man "ad opus molendini" for a day, and to make suit to the mill of Longford, and to the Court of Longford. Dat. Longford, M. b. F. of St. Dunstan [21 Oct.], 20 Ric. II. [1396]. (Longford.)

1585. GRANT from Robert de Dillereu to William Cook, vicar of Longford, Henry Jacson, chaplain, and others, of all his lands in Longford. Witn. Nicholas de Longeford, knt., Nicholas de Montegomery, knt., Thomas de Montegomery de Coland, John Durdent, etc. Dat. S. b. All Saints [1 Nov.], 3 Hen. IV. [1401]. (Longford.)

1586. PROCEEDINGS of the great court of Longeford held on Vigil of St. Barnabas [10 June], 3 Hen. IV. [1402]. Vellum roll, one membrane. (Longford.)

1587. PROCEEDINGS of the great court of Nicholas de Longeford, knt., Lord of Longford, 3 Hen. IV.-13 Hen. IV. [1402-1412]. Vellum roll, eight membranes. (Longford.)

1588. FEOFFMENT from Ralph de Longford, knt., to Thomas, Bishop of Durham, Ralph de Shirley, Nicholas de Mountgomery, Richard de Radclyf, knts., and Roger Venables, parson of Routhstorn, of his manors of Longford, Hathirsege, and Ellaston, and all other his lands in cos. Derby, Stafford, Notts., and Warwick, with the remainder of all the lands which Margery, que fuit uxor Nicholai de Longford, mil., holds for her life. Witn. John de Pole, Thomas de Oker, John de Bradburn. Dat. T. b. F. of St. Barnabas [11 June], 7 Hen. VI. [1429]. Seal of arms. (Longford.)

1589. ATTORNEY from the same Ralph to George de Longford and Nicholas de Clayton to deliver seisin of the same manors, etc. Dat. T. b. F. of St. Barnabas [11 June], 7 Hen. VI. [1429]. Seal of arms. (Longford.)

1590. LEASE, for life, from Ralph de Longeforde, knt., son and heir of Nicholas de Longeforde, mil., "quarti," to Thomas del Bouke of a messuage and two bovates of land in Bubton and a field called Orchardefeld, with common of pasture in Longeford and Bubton. Dat. Longeford, F. of St. Martin [11 Nov.], 8 Hen. VI. [1429]. (Longford.)

1591. LEASE, for twenty years, from Thomas, Bishop of Durham, Ralph de Shirley, Nicholas Mountgomery, Richard de Radclyf, knts., and Roger Venables, parson of Routhstorn, to Ralph de Longford, knt., of the manor of Longford, with all the lands in Longford, Bubton, Malmarton Woddehous, Bentley, Holynton, and Shirley which they hold by feoffment of the said Ralph. Dat. Wed. b. Easter [12 Apr.], 8 Hen. VI. [1430]. (Longford.)

1592. GRANT from Thomas, Bishop of Durham, Ralph Shirley, and other trustees, to whom the late Ralph Langeford, knt., enfeoffed the manor of Longford, to Thomas Longford, esq., brother of the said Ralph, that he may occupy the said manor and receive its revenues, to recompense him for the great charges he has been put to "circa prosecutionem et defensionem dicti manerii," until Nicholas, son of the said Ralph, arrive at full age. Dat. 12 Jan., 11 Hen. VI. [1433]. (Longford.)

1593. QUITCLAIM from Thomas Margetson of Shirley to Thomas Longford, esq., of all his lands in Longford which lately belonged to Matilda Hichecokkes, his aunt. Dat. 12 May, 13 Hen. VI. [1435]. (Longford.)

1594. LEASE from Ralph Shyrley to Ralph Holyngton, Prior of Callewyche, and Laurence Catton, Vicar of Maffelde [Mayfield] of all his manors, lands, etc., which he sometime held jointly with Thomas, Bishop of Durham, Nicholas Mountgomery, Richard Radclyff, knts., and Roger Venables, late parson of Routhstorne, all now deceased, in cos. Lanc., Derby, Staff., Linc., Notts., and Warwick, of the grant of Ralph Longford, now deceased. Witn. Thomas Blounte, Thomas Greseley, John le Byronne, Laurence Warenn, knts., etc. Dat. 24 Nov., 17 Hen. VI. [1438]. (Longford.)

1595. QUITCLAIM from Robert Holynton, Prior of Calwyche, to Laurence Caton, clerk, of all their manors, etc., which sometime belonged to Ralph Langford', knt. Dat. 10 Sept., 26 Hen. VI. [1447]. (Longford.)

1596. GRANT from Nicholas Longford, knt., to John Curson, esq., Nicholas Fitzherbert, esquire, John, Prior of Colwich, and William Bonyngton, esquire, of the manors of Longford and Hedersege. Witn. William Vernon, John Gresley, knts., Henry Knyveton, etc. Dat. Longford, 14 Jan., 38 Hen. VI. [1460]. (Longford.)

1597. CONVEYANCE from Henry Radissh, clerk, to Nicholas Longford, esq., son and heir of Nicholas Longford, knt., of the manors of Longford, Newton Sony, Parkhall, Pynkeston, Normanton, Blakwell, Barleburgh, Kynwalmerssh, and Hadersegge, co. Derby, and other manors, etc., in cos. Notts., Linc., Lanc., Staff., and Leic. Witn. Henry Vernon, Ralph Shirley, John Curson, Nicholas Fitzherbert, esquires. Dat. 1 June, 10 Edw. IV. [1470]. (Longford.)

1598. ATTORNEY from the same Henry Radissh to Henry Tykhill and others, to deliver seisin of the said manors to the said Nicholas. Dat. 1 June, 10 Edw. IV. [1470]. (Longford.)

1599. POWER of attorney from Nicholas Longford, esq., son and heir of Nicholas Longford, knt., to John FitzHerbert and William Ryley, to receive seisin from Henry Radissh, clerk, of the same manors, etc. Dat. 1 June, 10 Edw. IV. [1470]. (Longford.)

1600. QUITCLAIM from John Curson, esquire, and Nicholas Fitzharbert, esquire, to Nicholas Longford, esquire, son and heir of Nicholas Longford, knt., of the manors of Longford, Neuton Sulney, and Hethersege, with lands there and elsewhere in co. Derby, which he had of the feoffment of the said Nicholas Longford. Dat. 12 June, 10 Edw. IV. [1470]. (Longford.)

1601. ATTORNEY from Nicholas Longford, knt., to Thomas Fox and others, to deliver to John, Bishop of Coventry and Lichfield, Henry Pierpount, knt., John Trafford, knt., William Damport, Robert Calverley, and William Ryley, seisin of his manors of Longford, Park-hall, Pynkston, Normanton, Blakwell, Barleburgh, Kynwalmerssh, and Hadersege, co. Derby. Dat. 6 Apr., 15 Edw. IV. [1475]. (Longford.)

1602. RENTAL of Langforth-cum-membris in the time of Henry Pierpount and others, feoffees of Nicholas Langforth, knt., including Bubdon, Malmarton, Holyngton, Shirley, Roddesley. Dat. 16 Edw. IV. [1476-7]. Vellum roll. (Longford.)

1603. BOND from Ralph Longford, knt., and John Fitzherbert of Norbury, esquire, to Margaret Longford, widow, in 500 marks, to abide by the award of Thomas, Earl of Derby, arbitrator to settle disputes arising from the will of the late Nicholas Longford, knt., brother to the said Ralph. Dat. 20 Nov., 5 Hen. VII. [1489]. (Longford.)

1604. WILL of Rafe Longforde, knt., dated 13th Jan., 1510[1]. (Longford.)

1605. GRANT from Ralph Longford, knt., to Edmund Trafford, Thomas Jarrard, esquires, John Port, son and heir apparent of John Port, Thomas Fitzherbert, son and heir apparent of Anthony Fitz-herbert, knt., and others of all his manors, lands, etc., of Longford, Normanton, Pynkeston, Halwyngfeld, Morton, Blackewell, Whytewell, Pyllesley, Kynnewalmarch, and Hathersege, co. Derb., with other manors in cos. Lanc., Linc., Notts., Salop, Warwick, and in the Marches of Wales. Dat. 10 Apr., 26 Hen. VIII. [1535]. (Longford.)

1606. LEASE from William Cooke of Trusseley, gent., to Nicholas Longforth of Longforth, yeoman, of a close called Rough Moore in the parish of Longforth. Dat. 24 June, 28 Hen. VIII. [1536]. (Trusley.)

1607. INQUISITION before Richard Lucas, esq., Escheator, after the death of Ralph Langford, knt. [of Longford], which finds that he died on 23rd Sept. last past, and that Nicholas Langford, his son and heir, is twelve years of age, etc. With signature of the said Richard. Dat. Derby, 17 Nov., 35 Hen. VIII. [1543]. (Woll. xi. 36.)

LONGFORD *v.* also under MAMMERTON, YEAVELEY.

LONGSTONE, GREAT and LITTLE.

(LANGESDUNA, LANGISDON, LONGESDON, LONGISDON, LONGSTON.)

1608. COPY (fourteenth century) of a grant from Ralph de Monioye to Serlo de Monioye his son of a moiety of the vills of Parva Longesdon, Mornesale, and Brittrichisfield [Brushfield], to hold to him and his heirs in tail. Witn. Dom. William de Menyll, Henry de Kneveton, milites, Peter de Roland, Laurence de Acouere, etc. Early thirteenth century. (Foljambe.)

1609. GRANT from Serlo de Muniaie fil. Radulfi de Muniaye to Matthew fil. Thome de Bauqwell, of four bovates of land in Parua Longisdon and Breitreichfeld. Witn. Walter de Estewet', tunc vicecomes, Robert de Dun, Jordan de Sneterton, Robert de Muniaie, etc. Early Henry III. (Add. 19284.)

1610. GRANT from William fil. Waldeui de Langesduna to Thomas fil. Ric. de Pech of four acres of land in Langesdon, with the site of a "bercharia" and common pasture. Witn. Serlo de Beilea, Peter de Hashopa, William de Litton, William de Derlea, Adam de Stanton, etc. Early thirteenth century. (Foljambe.)

1611. GRANT from Robert Lutrell to Thomas fil. Ric. fil. Will. de Pec of land in the fields of Longesdon Parva. Witn. Richard de Herthill, Serlo de Beileg, Adam de Hertill, Thomas de Ednesover, etc. Early Hen. III. (Foljambe.)

1612. ATTORNEY from Richard de Edinshouer of Tyssinton to Frater John de Baucwelle, Canonicus de la Dale, and Magister William de Edinshouer, brother of the grantor, to make a covenant with Thomas Foleiambe, Ballivus de Pecco, concerning his rent in Langisdon, "prout interlocuti sumus apud Baucwelle, ultimo colloquium simul habentibus." Dat. apud Tyssinton, S. a. Conv. of St. Paul [25 Jan.], 1272[3]. (Foljambe.)

1613. GRANT from Richard Foliambe fil. Thom. Foliambe to Hugh fil. Joh. de Birchelif of a toft, etc., in Birchelif. Witn. Robert Bofton, Peter de Roland, John de Caluouere, etc. *Temp.* Edw. I. (Foljambe.)

1614. GRANT from Johanna de Rolande to Alan le Taillour of land in Magna Longesdon. Witn. William fil. Ricardi, Robert Huy, Thomas fil. Ade, etc. Dat. F. of St. Leonard [6 Nov.], 36 Edw. III. [1362]. (Woll. iii. 14.)

1615. BAILIFF'S ACCOMPT-ROLL of Longston Major and Minor. Fourteenth century. (Lichf. G. 6.)

1616. FEOFFMENT from James, Lord Audeley, knt., Edmund Trafford, knt., Henry Langley, and Geoffrey Shakersley to Richard Shakersley of the manor of Little Longesdon, with lands, etc., in Great and Little Longesdon, Mornesale, and Brightrichefeld [Brushfield], which they lately had of the feoffment of John Shakersley, deceased. Witn. William Vernon, knt., John de la Pole, esq., John Cokayn, esq., Walter Blount, esq. Dat. 20 June, 31 Hen. VI. [1453]. (Foljambe.)

1617. COUNTERPART of lease from John Yotton, Dean, and Chapter of Lichfield, to Robert Shacurley of Longsdon, of the tithes of Mornesale [in Little Longstone], for five years, at a rental of 12s. Dat. 7 May, 1493. (Lichf. D. 11.)

1618. COUNTERPART of lease from James Denton, LL.D., Dean, and the Chapter of Lichfield, to Christopher Jamys of Tyddeswall, of the tithes of corn and hay in Hardwykwall and Mornsall, for five years. Dat. 26 Feb., 1522[3]. (Lichf. D. 17.)

LONGSTONE *v.* also under ASHFORD, BAKEWELL, EYAM, LITTON, TIDESWELL.

LOSCOE.

(LOSCOWE.)

1619. GRANT in tail by Richard de Grey, Lord of Codenovere, to Rauf "le fiz Esteuene sur la Grene de Loscowe," and Juliana his wife, of a bovate of land in Loscowe. Witn. Robert de Henovere, Johan Benedicite, Adam de Pas, Thomas Columbell, etc. Dat. Codenovere, Th. a. F. of St. Ambrose [4 Apr.], 5 Edw. I. [1277]. French. (Woll. iv. 5.)

LOSCOE *v.* also under CODNOR.

LULLINGTON *v.* under DRAKELOW, GRESLEY.

MACKLEY.

(MACLEY, MAKELEY, MAKKELEY, MAKLEY.)

1620. LETTERS of attorney from John Tadyngton de Assheburne, chaplain, to John Kette of Foston, to deliver seisin of lands and tenements in Makley and Boilleston to Richard Vernon, knt., William Vernon, esq., and Nicholas Baker, Rector of the Church of Boilleston. Dat. Th. a. Easter, 17 Hen. VI. [1438]. (Add. 4875.)

1621. GRANT from Robert Wasse de Macley Wodhouses to Richard Vernoun, knight, and others, of all his lands and tenements in co. Derby. Witn. John Hilton of Foston, etc. Dat. F. of St. Michael [29 Sept.], 17 Hen. VI. [1438]. (Add. 4876.)

MACKLEY *v.* also under BOYLESTON, RODSLEY, SUDBURY.

MACKWORTH.

(MACWORTHE, MAKWORTHE.)

1622. GRANT from Roger fil. Henrici to Hugh fil. Willelmi Juvenis of half an acre of assart in Bikirwode [in Mackworth], near the assart of Walch[elin] fil. Petri. Witn. Hugh de Mora, Robert fil. Hugonis, Philip de Macwrh, William Cusin, Herbert Suan, Gilbert clericus, Peter Deleis, Hugh Lupus, Henry Juvenis, Simon de Mora. Early Hen. III. (Woll. vi. 66.)

1623. SALE by Hugh fil. Simonis de la More of Macworth to Robert fil. Willelmi le Vavasur of Scippeleg', of land in Macworthe lying on Hertyshevid. Witn. Dom. Thomas Anselin, Simon Chuschet, rector of the church of Macworth, John, "Scriptor," de Derby, etc. *Temp.* Hen. III. (P. R. O. c. 3757.)

1624. GRANT from Henry VIII. to Ralph Gell of Hopton, gent., of all the tithes "granorum et garbarum" in the parishes of Makworthe and Marton late belonging to the Monastery of Derlay [Darley], now dissolved. Dat. 2 March, anno 31 [1540]. (Pole-Gell.)

1625. GRANT from Robert Thorley of Leighes, co. Essex, and late of Cranebrook, co. Kent, to William Thorley *al.* Draper of Mackworth, of all the lands now or lately in the occupation of Thomas Shepard, in Mackworth, late belonging to the Monastery of Kingsmeade, co. Derby, now dissolved; which lands the said Robert had by feoffment of Walter Hendle, Clement Smyth, and John Mason, knts., to hold the same from the King "as of his manor of Charyng," co. Kent. Dat. 20 Jan., 2 Edw. VI. [1549]. Witn. to livery of seisin, Robert Thacker, vicar of Mackworth. (Mundy.)

MACKWORTH *v.* also under MARKEATON.

MAKENEY.

(MACKENEY, MAKKENEY, MAKNEY.)

1626. CONVEYANCE from Robert de Mackeney to William de Mackeney of a meadow in Mackeney called "Buricroft," to hold for five crops from Midsummer, 37 Hen. III. [1253]. Witn. John de Sottewell, etc. (P. R. O., c. 1949.)

1627. GRANT from Robert Rawlyn of Makkeney to William de Makkeneya, lord of Makkeney, and Alice his wife, of a messuage and land in Makkeneye, the land lying in tillages called "la Surlond," Costowe, "la Stonylonde," "Estforlong," "Morforlong," and in a tillage at "la Putlonde," an acre called "Wlfacre" in "la Westfeld," half an acre in "la Stonylonde," and land in Wetforlong, "la Ryforlong," Gorforlong, "la Westforlong," in "la Bottes," in "la Wetelonde," in Northforlang, and in a place called "Le Hasse." Dat. Fr. a. Tr. of St. Thomas [7 July], 33 Edw. I. [1305]. (P. R. O. c. 2479.)

1628. DEMISE by Dame Helen of Mackeneye to John Cokelstote and Joan his wife of two cottages, with lands, meadows, etc., in Makney, for her life. Dat. Mor. of Michaelmas [30 Sept.], 45 Edw. III. [1371]. (P. R. O. c. 91.)

MAMMERTON.

(MALMARTON, MALMERTON, MALUERTON.)

1629. GRANT from Nigel, Dominus de Longeford, to Roger de Mercinton and Eleanor his wife, of the whole vill of Malmerton [Mammerton, in Longford], for their lives; all their men "tam liberi quam villani, locaticii seu conducticii" to be quit of suits of court and mills unless they wish to grind at his mill "et tunc molent propinquiores illi cuius bladum invenerint super molendinum infra molas ad molendinum," giving the twenty-fourth grain for "moltura"; to be quit also of pannage, etc. Witn. Dom. Peter de Bakepuys, Henry de Braylusford, James de Scyrleye, knt., Roger Durdent, etc. *Temp.* Hen. III. or Edw. I. (Longford.)

1630. GRANT from Thomas fil. Ric. de Alkemunton to Richard de Pountfreyt of a culture of land called "le Flyteneflat," lying between Malmarton and Alkemunton field. Witn. Dom. Giles de Meynell, John de Bakepuz, knts., John Selueyn, Richard Durdent, etc. Dat. Malmarton, Tu. a. Trinity [4 June], 31 Edw. I. [1303]. (Longford.)

1631. LEASE from William le FitzRichart of Pountfreit to Nicholas de Longeforde of his tenements at Malmarton in the fee of Longford (except the hall and chamber adjoining thereto), for his life. Dat. M. b. Michaelmas [29 Sept.], 19 Edw. III. [1345]. (Longford.)

MAMMERTON *v.* also under LONGFORD.

MAPPERLEY.

(MAPERLAY, MAPERLEG', MAPERLEIGH, MAPERLEY, MAPIRLEYE.)

1632. QUITCLAIM and resignation by Ysabela relicta quondam Roberti de Lameleg' in Maperleg', into the hands of Simon, Abbas ecclesie de Stanleg' [Dale Abbey], of all the land with messuage which Robert de Lameleg', her late husband, held [in Mapperley] for his life "et non amplius." Witn. Hugh de Morley, Hugh de Gurney, Richard Rachel in Stanleg', Everard de eadem, Geoffrey de Herdilby. *Temp.* Hen. III.-Edw. I. (Add. 47499.)

1633. RELEASE from Richard fil. Ivonis de Maperley to Geoffrey de Herdeby and Isabella his wife of lands and houses which belonged to his father Ivo in Maperley. Witn. Nicholas de Henore, Thomas del Heued, William fil. Avicie de Maperley, Hugh de Lameley, etc. *Temp.* Hen. III.-Edw. I. (Woll. viii. 63.)

1634. GRANT from Isabella, quondam uxor Galfridi de Herdeby to William her son of her lands in the vill and territory of Mapirleye. Witn. Dom. Roger de Morteyn, tunc Dominus de Maperlay, Dom. William de Ros, Dominus de Ilkesdone, Dom. William tunc rector ecclesie de Ilkesdone, etc. *Temp.* Edw. I. (Woll. viii. 65.)

1635. GRANT from Roger de Billesdon of Herdby, "de comitatu Leycestrie," to William fil. Galfridi de Herdby, "de comitatu Derbeye," and Isabella his wife, of all his messuages, lands, etc., in the vill and fields of Maperley, with remainder to Johanna their daughter. Witn. Robert de Sallowe, Hugh Burdet of Kirkehalum, Walter Othehede of Maperley, Henry Othehed, etc. Dat. Th. a. F. of St. Hilary [13 Jan.], 1331. (Woll. viii. 64.)

MAPPLETON.

(MAPELTON, MAPILTON, MAPULTON.)

1636. GRANT from Hilbertus de Colleg' to Roger de Wednesley of his mill-pool between the rocks [inter rupes] of Calwelawe [Callow]; in return for which the said Roger grants to the said Hilbertus permission to grind his own corn at his mill of Wednesle' [Wensley, in Darley Dale], with free grinding rights from Christmas to Easter, and his own malt. Witn. Robert de Acavere, Robert de Thorp, Henry de Alsop, Henry de Mapelton, William de Derbe, William de Leya, etc. Early thirteenth century. (Kerry xix. 13.)

1637. GRANT from Henry fil. Rogeri de Mapilton to Geoffrey his son of two plots of land with buildings thereon in Mapilton and two acres and a half and fourteen selions of land in the same vill. Witn. Roger de Wednesleye, dominus de Mapilton, John frater eius, Robert Aliot, Nicholas Wyther de Thorp, Richard de Huncindon. Dat. at Mapilton, Th. a. F. of St. Chad [2 Mar.], 16 Edw. II. [1313]. (Okeover.)

1638. QUITCLAIM from Henry fil. Rog. de Mapelton to Geoffrey his son of eleven selions of land in Mapelton which the same Geoffrey held by lease from Petronilla que quondam fuit uxor predicti Rogeri de Mapelton quondam patris mei, and which the said Petronilla had in dower. Witn. Roger de Wednisleye, Robert fil. Hugonis de Mapelton, John de Wednisleye, Richard Scaiward. Dat. M. b. F. of St. Mark [25 Apr.], 1320. (Okeover.)

1639. GRANT from Geoffrey fil. Henrici fil. Rogeri de Mapelton to Rikewere his sister of his messuage, with buildings thereon, in Mapelton. Witn. Roger de Wednisleye, Dominus de Mapelton, Henry fil. Rogeri de eadem, Richard Meverel, etc. Dat. Fr. b. F. of St. Margaret [20 July], 1322. (Okeover.)

1640. LEASE, for life, from Roger de Wednesleye, dominus de Mapilton, to John de Stanclif, of the watercourse of Bradeburnebrok belonging to the said Roger's demesne of Mapilton, with a proviso that if the said John die within twenty years, his heirs may hold the same to the end of that term of twenty years; to hold by a yearly rent of a grain of pepper for twenty years, but if the said John live longer that he shall pay a yearly rent of 6s. 8d. Witn. Thomas de Mathelfeld of Assheburn, John fil. Roberti de Mapilton, John de Wednesleye, Richard Broun. Dat. S. a. F. of St. Denis [9 Oct.], 4 Edw. III. [1330]. (Okeover.)

1641. GRANT from Roger de Acouere, miles., to Richard Pecard of Mapulton and Rekewere his wife, of all the lands which he holds in the fee of Mapulton; to hold for their lives at a rent of a grain of pepper at Christmas. Witn. Roger de Wedenesley, dominus de Mapulton, John frater ejus, John Aliot, Roger fil. Rogeri de Mapulton, William Blak. Dat. at Mapulton, F. of St. James [25 July], 9 Edw. III. [1335]. (Okeover.)

1642. QUITCLAIM from John fil. Gilberti de Wednesleye to Margery de Alspade of all the lands, tenements, meadows, etc., in the vill and fee of Mapulton; to hold for her life with remainder, on her death, to Christiana que fuit uxor domini Rogeri de Acouere, militis. Witn. Roger de Wednesleye, dominus de Mapulton, John frater ejus, John Alyot. Dat. at Mapulton, Ascension Day [17 May], 15 Edw. III. [1341]. (Okeover.)

1643. GRANT from Hugh de Wednesleye de Mapilton to Margery de Alspade, for her life, of all the lands and tenements in the vill and fee of Mapilton, with remainder, on her death, to Christiana que fuit uxor dom. Rogeri de Acouere, militis. Witn. Roger de Wednesleye, dominus de Mapilton, John frater ejus, John Alyot, Richard Pykard, William de Clifton. Dat. at Mapilton, S. a. Ex. of H. Cross [14 Sept.], 14 Edw. III. [1341]. (Okeover.)

1644. GRANT from Thomas de Mapelton, manens in feodo de Bradeleye, to Adam Beleby de Asseburne, of all his arable land in the fee of Mapelton, except Heywode, with remainder on the said Adam's death, if it occurs within twenty years, to the said Adam's heirs. Witn. John Cokeyn, Thomas Adam, Henry de Auener. Dat. Tu. a. F. of St. Thomas M. [29 Dec.], 27 Edw. III. [1353]. (Okeover.)

1645. POWER of attorney from Philip de Okore, knt., for livery of seisin to Thomas de Marchinton, knt., John Crecy, rector of Longford, John Wade, rector of Legh, and Thomas de Schene, of certain lands, etc., in Caldelowe [Callow, in Mappleton], Attlowe, Snelleston, Mapulton, and Parwych, co. Derb., and in the vill of Okore, co. Staff., with all his goods and chattels in the same. Dat. Ashbourne, Vig. of Pur. of B. V. M. [1 Feb.], 5 Ric. II. [1382]. (Okeover.)

1646. GRANT from Thomas Okover of Okover, esquire, to John Okover his son, of all his lands, etc., within the fee of Mapulton, Assheburn, and Snelston, which John Okover his brother held for term of his life; together with a pasture called Heywodfeld, in the fee of Mapulton. Witn. John Waren, Richard Welbek, Richard Wirley, Thomas Laurenson, Henry Broun. Dat. Th. a. F. of St. Oswald, K. and M. [5 Aug.], 9 Hen. VI. [1429]. Seal of arms. (Okeover.)

1647. GRANT from Richard Irton fil. et her. Ric. Irton to Thomas Berseford of Newton Graunge, co. Derb., of all his tenements, etc., in the town and fields of Mapulton-by-Asshebourne. Witn. John Cursun, esquire, Henry Bradburne, esq., John de Berseford, John Toples of Tyssyngton, etc. Dat. Mapulton, M. a. F. of St. Barnabas [11 June], 23 Hen. VI. [1445]. (Drury.)

1648. GRANT from Thomas Okouer, esquire, to Richard Boys and Cecily his wife of a pasture called Hewodfeld in the fee of Mapulton extending from the waste of Mapulton to the meadow of Assheburn. Witn. William Ilum of Assheburne, Thomas Robert, Peter Lymster, Richard Wilson, Richard Madeley. Dat. Mapulton, 20 Sept., 35 Hen. VI. [1456]. (Okeover.)

1649. LETTERS of attorney from Thomas Okouer to Thomas Persaye to deliver seisin to Richard Boys and Cecily his wife, of a pasture called Hewodfeld in the fee of Mapulton. Dat. apud Mapulton, 20 Sept., 35 Hen. VI. [1456]. (Okeover.)

1650. LETTERS of attorney from Thomas Okouer to Thomas Parfaye to deliver seisin to Richard Boys and Cecily his wife of all his lands in the fee of Mapulton. Dat. 22 Sept., 35 Hen. VI. [1456]. Seal of arms. (Okeover.)

MAPPLETON *v.* also under ASHBOURNE, ATLOW, SNELSTON.

MARKEATON.

(MARKETON, MARTON.)

1651. LEASE, for her life, from Thomas de Derbe of Marketon to Margaret his daughter of a place and house standing upon it in Marketon. Witn. William Knox, Robert Bercarius Hugonis de Longele, Richard le Palmer. *Temp.* Edw. I. (Mundy.)

1652. GRANT from William Knug of Marketon to John fil. Henrici del Peek de Derby and Joan his wife of a messuage, etc., lying between the messuage of Margaret de Derby and John fil. Roberti de Hynton, and a piece of land called Le Holm, lying between Swetbrok and Ryecroft in Marketon. Witn. Henry de Flamsted, John Phelipot, Walter le Palmer, etc. Dat. M. b. F. of St. Denis [9 Oct.], 26 Edw. III. [1352]. (Mundy.)

1653. QUITCLAIM from Robert Cook, chaplain, John Shepherde of Marketon, and Henry Philyppot of the same, and John Cnogg, to Joan del Peek quondam uxor Johannis de Marketon of all the lands which they had by feoffment of the said Joan within the vill and territory of Marketun. Dat. M. a. Easter [8 Apr.], 21 Ric. II. [1398]. (Mundy.)

1654. POWER of attorney from John Brewode, parson of the church of Rodeburne, to Thomas Brewode of Rodeburne, to give seisin of lands in Mackeworthe and Marton [Markeaton], which the said John had jointly with Richard Befayse of Trusselay by feoffment of Henry Felepot and Matilda his wife, William de Brewod, Richard Fuche, and Margery his wife. Dat. apud Rodeburne, M. a. F. of St. Nicholas [6 Dec.], 10 Hen. IV. [1408]. (Mundy.)

1655. GRANT from William Fucher of Marton to Thomas Moniassh, clerk, Richard Sutton, and John Stevenson, of all lands, etc., in the vill and fields of Marton and Macworthe. Witn. John Agard of Marton, William Sondy, Henry Lambard. Dat. Sat. a. Pur. of B. V. M. [2 Feb.], 11 Edw. IV. [1472]. (Mundy.)

1656. POWER of attorney from William Fucher of Marton to John Tomas and John Fucher to give seisin of the above lands to Thomas Moniassh, clerk, Richard Sutton, and John Stevenson. Dat. Sat. a. Pur. of B. V. M. [2 Feb.], 11 Edw. IV. [1472]. (Mundy.)

1657. EXEMPLIFICATION of a recovery by John Mondy, Robert Brudenell, Justice of Common Pleas, Andrew Wyndesore, knt., and others, against William Goche, of the manors of Marketon, Makworth, and Alestre, with eight messuages, a water-mill, etc., in the same places and in Derby, and the advowson of the church of Makworth. Dat. 23 Nov., 8 Hen. VIII. [1516]. (Mundy.)

1658. WILL of Dame Julian Mundy, widow, late wife of Sir John Mundy, knight and Alderman of London. Dat. 20 Sept., 1537. Probate is attached, dated 26th September, 1537. (Mundy.)

1659. COURT-BOOK of "Merketon cum aliis villatis" [*sc.* Makworth and Alestre], of Thomas Audeley, knt., chancellor, and other feoffees of John Mondy and Juliana his wife, 21 Dec., 27 Hen. VIII. [1535]— 10 Aug., 30 Hen. VIII. [1538]; and subsequently of Vincent Mundy, esq., 9 Oct., 30 Hen. VIII.—Michaelmas, 33 Hen. VIII. [1541]. (Mundy.)

1660. EXTRACT of view of frank pledge with great court of Vincent Mundy, esquire, held 28 Oct., 37 Hen. VIII. [1545], for the manor of Marketon-cum-membris, giving list of persons at Marketon, Mackworth, and Alestre fined for non-appearance at courts, breaking the assize of bread and beer, etc. (Mundy.)

MARKEATON *v.* also under MACKWORTH.

MARSTON MONTGOMERY *v.* under CUBLEY, SUDBURY.

MARSTON-UPON-DOVE.

(MERSTON.)

1661. GRANT, in tail, from Robert de Ferr[ariis], fil. et her. Dom. Willelmi de Ferr[ariis] quondam Comitis Derb', to Henry fil. Henrici Ouwein of ten acres of land in Holmhay-in-Merston, which Ralph le Gater sometime held; to hold by suit at his two great courts of Mercinton and a rent of five shillings. Witn. William de Ferr[ariis], "frater meus," Dom. Richard de Herthull, Dom. Gerard de Sutton, Dom. John de Suleny, Andrew de Jarcunuill, etc. [1254-1278.] (Woll. ix. 67.)

1662. VALUATION of two parts of the Manor of Marston [-on-Dove], declared after inquisition. *Temp.* Edw. I. (Lichf. R. R. 7.)

MATLOCK.

(MATHLAC, MATLOK, MATLOKE, MATLOKKE, MATTELOCKE,
MATTLOK, MATTLOKE.)

1663. CONFIRMATION by Henry III. to Stephen de Sedgrave of
the grant made to him by William de Ferrariis, Earl of Derby, in
Mathlac [Matlock]. Dat. 2 Nov. anno 18 [1233]. (Berkeley 231.)

1664. LETTERS patent declaring that Matlock, Underwood, and
Bradley shall be deemed members of the manors of Ashborne and
Wirksworth, and the wapentake of Wirksworth, notwithstanding the non-
specification thereof in the charter of the King, granting to Edmund,
Earl of Lancaster, the said manor and hundred in exchange for the
castles and counties of Cardigan and Carmarthen; saving to the said
Earl all other the members and appurtenances of the premises, although
not specified either in the aforesaid charter or in the present letters
patent. Dat. Westminster, 10 June, 1280. (D. of L.)

1665. GRANT, in tail, from William de Matlok, clerk, to Robert fil.
Walteri de Sewardsithe, and Emma his wife, in free marriage, of the
moiety of his chief messuage and lands in Matloke. Witn. Ranulph
de Sniterton, John de Sutton, Rob. de Mackeworth, etc. Dat. F. of
St. Leonard [Nov. 6], 19 Edw. III. [1325]. (Woll. i. 8.)

1666. GRANT from Richard fil. Gilberti de Wednisleye of Matlok
to William his son, of 8s. yearly rent from lands, etc., which Robert
le Whilwright, Emma his wife, and Thomas fil. Sim. de Hethcote held
from him in Matlok. Witn. Thomas le Myners, John de Sutton, Henry
Bygge, etc. Dat. Matloke, Easter Day [12 Apr.], 23 Edw. III. [1349].
(Woll. i. 6.)

1667. RELEASE from Roger de Wednesleye to William fil. Ricardi
fil. Gilberti de Matlok of lands which were John Alkok's in Matlok.
Witn. Henry Bygge, Nicholas Tybbesone, Henry le Wodewarde, etc.
Dat. S. a. Michaelmas Day [29 Sept.], 23 Edw. III. [1349]. (Woll.
i. 7.)

1668. LICENCE to the Bishop of Lincoln, Richard, Earl of Arundel,
Robert de la Mare, and others, to grant to John, Earl of Lancaster
and Richmond, and Blanche his wife, the castle and park of Bolingbrook, the knight's fees and advowsons of churches, abbeys, and other
religious houses pertaining to the castle and soke (with the exception
of the manor, town, and soke of Bolingbrook, and the manors of Sutton,
Thoresby, Waith, and Ingoldmells); the castle, town, manor, and honor
of Tutbury, the towns of Scropton, Marchington, Challengewood,
Uttoxeter, Agardsley, and Newburgh, the hundred of Higham Ferrers,
the manors of Higham Ferrers, Rushden, and Raunds, and the towns
of Matlock, Brassington, and Hartington, to hold to them and the
heirs of their bodies for ever, with remainder to the right heirs of
Henry, Duke of Lancaster. Dat. Westminster, 18 Nov., 1361.
(D. of L.)

1669. RELEASE from John Heyle of Bontsale and Matilda his wife
to John Hemmynge of Brampton and Matilda his wife of all their
lands, etc., in the town and fields of Matlok. Witn. Henry Mapulton,
vicar of Bontsale, Henry Matlok, John Flynt, etc. Dat. M. a. Nat.
of St. John B. [24 June], 7 Hen. V. [1419]. (Foljambe.)

1670. RELEASE from Ralph Leche, John Saucheverelle, John Rollesley, esquires, and John Yve of Chaddesdene, chaplain, to Henry Matloke, of lands in Matlock and Hathersagge, co. Derby. Witn. John Cursoun, esq., Henry de la Role, esq., John Rollesley, jun., etc. Dat. Snytertone, 20 June, 30 Hen. VI. [1452]. (Woll. i. 9.)

1671. EXTRACT from view of frank-pledge of the manor of Matlok, held at Wirk[sworth], on W. b. F. of St. Luke [18 Oct.], 13 Edw. IV. [1473], of the receipt by Richard Held, brother of Thrust' [Thurstan] Held, and heir to Edward Held, son of the said Thurstan, of a cottage and fourteen acres of land within the manor. (Woll. iii. 16.)

1672. SIMILAR extract of a court of the same manor held at Wirkysworth, Tu. b. F. of St. Andrew [30 Nov.], 2 Hen. VII. [1487], by Sir John Savage, steward, wherein Ralph Saucheverell, esq., surrenders a cottage and lands in Matloke to the use of Sir William Bowne. (Woll. iii. 17.)

1673. BOND by William Tagge of Matlocke, John Alsop of Hoknaston and Ralph Gell of Carsyngton, yeomen, to Richard Wigley of Mydelton, in £30, to observe covenants. Dat. 15 Dec., 25 Hen. VIII. [1533]. (Woll. xi. 71.)

1674. POWER of attorney from John Hemmyngwey to Issabella Otys, widow, kinswoman and heir of Henry Mattloke, to Ralph Gell and Antony Cley of Mattloke, to deliver seisin to William Tagge of lands in Mattloke. Dat. 20 June, 26 Hen. VIII. [1534]. (Woll. xi. 69.)

1675. EXEMPLIFICATION of a recovery in the Common Pleas by Ralph Gell and William Glosop, against Richard Wygley, of a messuage and land in Matlok. Dat. Westm., 11 July, 28 Hen. VIII. [1536]. (Woll. xi. 72.)

1676. SALE, for 20 marks, by Wylliam Tagg of Mattloke, gent., to John Wyggeley of Meddletone, yeoman, of lands in Mattlok. Dat. 3 Sept., 32 Hen. VIII. [1540]. (Woll. xi. 70.)

1677. SALE by William Tagg of Mattlok, co. Derby, to John Wyggely of Middleton, of lands in Mattlok. Witn. Ralph Gell of Karsyngton, John Allsope of Hoknaston, William Wygely of Workesworth, etc. Dat. 20 Dec., 32 Hen. VIII. [1540]. (Woll. xi. 68.)

1678. EXTRACT from a View of Frank-pledge of the same manor held at Wyrkisworth, 8 Oct., 35 Hen. VIII. [1543], Thurstan Wodcok being Steward, wherein William Bowne receives a cottage and lands in Matlock on the death of Henry Bowne, his father. (Woll. iii. 18.)

1679. NOTE of an attestation made by Robert Fogge of the Bouhwod, in Matlock, yeoman, aged 86, before Jemys Launne of Cromfort, Rycard Abell of the same, and William Fogge, of the payment of the chief rent of the Brouniswodes to Thomas Polle, etc., Lords of Whakebrig, "in rest and pesse wythe oute troubell" during 66 years. Dat. 9 Apr., 35 Hen. VIII. [1544]. (Woll. xi. 8.)

1680. EXEMPLIFICATION in the Court of Common Pleas of the decision of William Shelley, knt., and Henry Bradshawe, Attorney-General, at an Assize held at Derby, Hilary Term, 37 Hen. VIII. [1546], in a suit between German Pole, gent., Anthony Els, and Henry

Buntyng, on the one part, and Thomas Alsop, on the other part, whereby the said Thomas recovered damages against them for the illegal seizure of his cattle at Matlokke. Dat. Westm., 26 Jan., 38 Hen. VIII. [1547]. (Woll. xi. 32.)

MATLOCK *v.* also under ASHBOURNE, CHESTERFIELD, LITCHURCH, SNITTERTON, WAKEBRIDGE.

MEASHAM.
(MEISHAM, MEYSAM.)

1681. REPORT by W[illiam] de Muscamp, Archdeacon of Derby, to W[illiam de Cornhill], Bishop of Coventry, of an inquiry held at Derby by him, assisted by Mag. R[obert] de Bosco [Archdeacon of Coventry], and Mag. Zacharias de Chebese [Chebsey, co. Staff.], regarding the chapel of Meysam, viz., that it is found to belong to the mother-church of Repedon *al.* Rependon, and to have been leased for life by N[icholas], Prior of Rependon, at the request of "M. Comitissa" [Matilda, widow of Ranulf de Gernon, Earl of Chester, who founded Repton Priory in 1172, and died in 1189, *v.* Stowe 153], to Richard, capellanus, who had held it before the institution of Rependon Priory, "de personis de Rependon," and that corpses were formerly brought from Measham to Repton for interment. [1215-1223.] (Stowe 132.)

1682. GRANT in duplicate from John de Meysham fil. Willelmi de Meysham to Richard fil. Rogeri de Nailiston of three half acres of land in the field of Meisham, lying on Redhul, Chul towards Fulsiche, Watermedwe, and elsewhere. Witn. Rob. de Crumbwelle de Meysham, William de Swepston, clericus, John de Nayliston, etc. Dat. Meisham, Morr. of F. of Nat. of St. John B. [25 June], .1 Edw. II. [1308]. (Gresley 170, 171.)

1683. QUITCLAIM from William fil. Johannis de Meisham to Richard fil. Rogeri de Naileston, of arable land in Meisham, on Chul towards Fulsiche, between the land of the Prior of Repton, and the land of Roger Henri de Appulby. Witn. William de Meisham, Thomas fil. Rogeri de Swarkeston, Nicholas Stake de eadem, etc. *Circ.* 1308. (Gresley 172.)

MEASHAM *v.* also under NEWTON SOLNEY.

MELBOURNE.
(MELBURN, MELBURNE.)

1684. GRANT to William le Estunir of Melburn of the land which belonged to William Fitz-Welneth in the manor of Melburn, by rendering 3*s.* yearly to the King's use by the hands of his bailiff of Melburn. Dat. Westminster, 1 Sept., 1256. (D. of L.)

1685. TWENTY-FOUR COURT-ROLLS of the manor of Melbourne, including Osmaston, Normanton, Cehllaston, Swarkeston, King's Newton, and Elton. 15 Edw. III.—end of Hen. VIII. [1341-1547]. (D. of L.)

1686. GRANT to Henry, Earl of Lancaster, of a market and fair at his manor of Melburn, in the county of Derby, the market on Wednesday, and the fair on Michaelmas Day and the two following days. Dat. York, 3 March, 1328. (D. of L.)

14

1687. LEASE granted to Matilda of Lancaster, Countess of Ulster, by Henry, Earl of Lancaster, Derby, and Leicester, Seneschal of England, of the castle and manor of Melburne, to hold at a rose rent. Dat. 18 Mar., 21 Edw. III. [1347]. French. (Harl. 43 c. 47.)

MELBOURNE *v.* also under CALK, KING'S NEWTON.

MERCASTON.

(MIRCASTON, MURCASTON, MURCHAMSTON, MURKALISTON, MYRCASTON, MYRKASTON.)

1688. GRANT, for six marks, from Amabilia de Murchamstona, quondam uxor Roberti de Seldeford, to Robert fil. Rogeri fil. Ordryz de Murchamston, of three bovates of lands in the vill of Murchamston; rent, 6s. 8d.; with clauses relating to the grinding of the corn grown on the lands. Witn. Magister Johannes, rector ecclesie de Mogintona, William le Burgillun de Weston, Thomas Buzun de Kettliston, Robert fil. Nicholai quondam rectoris medietatis ecclesie de Mogintona, William fil. Emme de Murchamstona, etc. Dat. W. b. Ann. of B. V. M. [25 Mar.], 1256. (Woll. vi. 47.)

1689. GRANT from William fil. Herberti de Northbyre to Stephen de Irtone of two shillings annual rent in Murkaliston, to be received from Dom. Anabilia quondam uxor Roberti de Shelford, for land sometime held by Thomas de Ednisouera; rent, an apple "in festo beati Barlacii." Witn. Dom. William de Mungomery, William, his son, James de Shirley, Matthew de Kniveton, Engelard de Cursun, etc. *Temp.* Edw. I. (Woll. vi. 39.)

1690. LEASE from Dom. John Gifford of Chilinton, miles, to Robert Sadeworthe of Murcaston of a messuage and lands which he held "per legem Anglie" in Murcaston by Moginton. Witn. Thomas de la Hide, John de Somerforde, Robert de Ouerton, Henry de Ilum. Dat. at Chilinton, co. Staff., W. a. Pur. of B. V. M. [2 Feb.], 12 Edw. III. [1338]. (Every.)

1691. GRANT from Ralph de Seynpere of Murcaston·to Thomas Scortred and Margery, his wife, of lands in Murcaston. Witn. Henry de Schelford of Murcastone, John le Wodeuard of the same, Thomas son of John, of the same. Dat. S. a. F. of St. Oswald, K. and M. [5 Aug.], 45 Edw. III. [1371]. (Woll. vi. 40.)

1692. GRANT from William Beke, vicar of Sallowe, John Fitz-Herbert, and Richard Spicer, to Johanna, widow of Nicholas de Knyveton, of the manor of Murcaston, with appurtenances in Murcaston and Mogynton, with reversion to Thomas, son of Nicholas de Knyveton, parson of Northbury [Norbury], and Robert de Knyveton, vicar of Dubbrugg' [Doveridge], and to others, and finally to the right heirs of Nicholas de Knyveton, father of the said Thomas. Witn. Nich. de Mountgomery, Walter Blount, John Bassett, John Cokayn, John de la Pole, knts., etc. Dat. Murcaston, F. of SS. Peter and Paul [29 June], 1391. (Woll. vi. 41.)

1693. GRANT from John Cokayn, knt., John de Knyveton of Bradley, Roger de Bradburne, and Richard Cokayn, to William de Hyde, chaplain of the church of St. Oswald at Asscheburn, of an annual rent of 100s. from the manor of Mircaston, in which they had been enfeoffed by Nicholas de Knyveton of Underwood, esq., to found a chantry there, and for prayers for the souls of Johanna, widow of the said Nicholas, Henry de Knyveton, Robert de Knyveton, Nicholas de Knyveton, William de Knyveton, and Margery his wife, and Thomas de Knyveton, also for John, Duke of Aquitaine and Lancaster, from whom the manor was held, and John de Schepye, Dean of Lincoln. Witn. Nicholas de Mountgomery, Walter Blount, Philip de Okore, Nicholas de Longeford, knts., etc. Dat. Asschburne, S. Nat. of B. V. M. [8 Sept.], 1392. At the foot are confirmations of the grant by the said John [de Schepeye], Dean of Lincoln, and John [Burghill], Bishop of Lichfield and Coventry, dated, respectively, Lincoln, 18 Mar., 1392, and Eccleshall, 10 July, 1404. (Woll. xi. 31.)

1694. GRANT from Robert Twyford of Longley to John Bradburne del Hogh of the moiety of a messuage which he had by feoffment from Henry Asceburst, parson of a moiety of the church of Mogynton, lately deceased, and of John Aschehurst, with all meadows, etc., and eighteen acres of land in Myrcaston [Mercaston], with the office of Forester in le Warde de Holande [Hulland]. Witn. Thomas Knyveton, Thomas Bradfeld, Thomas Kent, etc. Dat. M. a. Ann. of B. V. M. [25 Mar.], 2 Hen. VI. [1424]. (Bemrose.)

1695. QUITCLAIM from William Mere, son and heir of John Mere, brother of Thomas Mere, to John Bradburne, esq., of all his lands in Myrkaston, and of the "forestaria" of Holandward in Duffeldefryth, all of which the said John had jointly with the said Thomas by feoffment from Richard Grendon. Dat. Whit Monday [18 May], 12 Edw. IV. [1472]. (Bemrose.)

MICKLEOVER.

(MAGNA OURA, MAGNA OVERA, MAGNA OWRA, MAGNA UURE.)

1696. AWARD of the Priors of Wirksoph [Worksop, co. Notts.], Pontefract [co. York], and Blith [Blyth, co. Notts.], acting under authority from Pope Honorius [III.], by which the vicarage of Magna Owra is assigned to the Abbot and Convent of Burton[-on-Trent], on payment of seven marks to Mag. R—— de Burton, Vicar of Magna Owera. Witn. R[obert], Prior of Lenton [co. Notts.], H——, Dean of Ratford [Radford, co. Notts.], Mag. Godfrey de Rupill, Thomas, "capellanus" of Blyth, etc. Dat. 1226. (Stowe 58.)

1697. FINE from Richard [de Insula], Abbot of Burton[-on-Trent], to Roger le Breton, and his men of Rughedich, of rights of common pasture for their cattle, etc. (excepting their goats and pigs during the acorn season), in the manor of Magna Uure and in Parva Uure, and of land in Basingerys; in return for the right of clearing sixty acres of land in Syortegrave [near Mickleover], subject to certain rights of free entry and pasture. Made at Nottingham before Hugh [de Wells], Bishop of Lincoln, Stephen de Segrave, Robert de Lexinton, William Fitz-Warin, and William Basset, justices in Eyre, the Morrow of Michaelmas, 10 Hen. III. [30 Sept., 1226]. (Stowe 59.)

1698. NOTIFICATION from Nicholas fil. Walkelin de Henover of a lease to him by Richard de Insula, Abbot, and the Convent of Burton[-on-Trent], of land in Magna Oura, called Crosforlong, with rights of herbage in the wood called Merwineswode and of common pasture in Magna Oura. Witn. Rob. fil. Walkelin and Henry, his brother, Rob. de Tok, Rob. de Bella Fide [Beaufoy], Symon de Sancto Mauro, Nicholas de Breideshale, constable of Thuttesbiri [Tutbury], etc. [1223-1229.] (Stowe 61.)

1699. GRANT from Thomas de Maddelega to Laurence de St. Edwardo, Abbot, and the Convent of Burton[-on-Trent], of lands in Magna Overa which he had recovered from them at Nottingham before the Justices in Eyre by writ of *mort d'ancestor* in 16 Hen. III. [1231-32]; and quitclaim of other lands in the same place, which he had claimed at the same time. Witn. Dom. Ranulph de Ferrariis, Dom. Geoffrey de Gresel [Gresley], Dom. Rob. de Tok, Dom. Rob. de Warda, etc. [1231-1260.] (Stowe 60.)

1700. GRANT from Thomas de Furnivall, Dominus de Hallumschire, to Godfrey Foliaumbe and to his men and tenants of Hassop, of common of pasture in the manor of Midilton iuxta Eyum, with liberty to cut turf, etc. Dat. Sheffield, M. a. F. of St. John B. [24 June], 21 Edw. III. [1347]. (Woll. i. 17.)

MIDDLETON, STONEY.

(MIDDILTON, MIDDYLTON, MIDILTON-JUXTA-EYUM, MIDULTON, MIDYLTON, MYDELTON.)

1701. GRANT from Godfrey de Roland to Thomas Gomfray and Richard Gomfray, clerks, of lands in Caluore and Midultonclif, with housbote and heibote, etc. Witn. Thomas de Wednesley, knt., John de Stafford, Thurstan del Boure, etc. Dat. T. a. F. of St. James [25 July], 19 Ric. II. [1395]. (Woll. vii. 54.)

MIDDLETON, STONEY, *v.* also under EYAM.

MIDDLETON-BY-WIRKSWORTH.

(MIDDILTON.)

1702. GRANT from Symon fil. Henrici de Crumforde to Joan uxor Rob. fil. Ricardi de eadem, of a bovate of land with a toft in Middilton which the said Symon acquired from Henry fil. Ade de Erlesbure. Witn. William de Crumforde, Nicholas fil. Symonis de eadem, Henry Gamyl, John de Aula de Middelton, Alan de Bonteshale, etc. Dat. F. of St. Luke [Oct. 18], 31 Edw. I. [1303]. (Okeover.)

MIDDLETON-BY-WIRKSWORTH *v.* also under WIRKSWORTH.

MIDDLETON-BY-YOULGRAVE.

(MIDDELTON, MYDDLETON.)

1703. POWER of attorney from Richard de Herthulle, mil., to John Wodehous, clericus, and Richard de Leycestre, to deliver seisin to Giles, his son, and Katerine, his wife, daughter of John le Walsshe, lord of Sheldesleye, of his manor of Myddelton. Dat. Sheldon, Trin. Sun. [19 May], 38 Edw. III. [1364]. (Cott. xxvi. 23.)

MIDDLETON-BY-YOULGRAVE *v.* also under ASHBOURN, BONSALL.

MILTON, NR. REPTON.

(MELETON, MELTON.)

1704. LETTER from O[sbert] de Bereford to R[obert], Prior of Rependone [Repton], desiring him to recognise William fil. Willelmi fil. Symonis de Melton as heir of his father to a virgate of land in Melton, whereof he [Osbert] had formerly been "principalis et capitalis," but in which he had granted his interest, including a yearly rent of four shillings to the fabric of the Priory Church. *Temp.* Edw. I. (Stowe 133.)

MILTON *v.* also under REPTON.

MONSALL.

(MORNESALE.)

v. under LONGSTONE.

MONYASH.

(MANIAS, MANYASSHE, MONIAS, MONIASCH, MONIASCHE, MONIASH, MONIASSH, MONYASHE, MONYASSE, MONYASSH, MONYASSHE.)

1705. DEED whereby William fil. Alani undertakes to keep whole and indivisible a manse and bovate of land granted to him by Ralph [de Sempringham], Dean, and the Chapter of Lichfield at Manias [Monyash]. Witn. Ralph Decanus, Thomas de Wimudham, precentor, Mag. Peter de Radenouere, and Mag. William de Atteleberge, Dom. William de Staunford, William de Neuton, John de Sparham, Walkeline, "pretacte ecclesie canonicis" [1254-1257]. (Lichf. B. 15.)

1706. GRANT from John de Lyonis to He[nry] fil. Simon. fil. Roberti de Moniash of a tenement and land in Moniash. Witn. Robert le Wyne de Haddon, Matthew le Sergeant of Haddon, Ralph Coleret, etc. Late thirteenth century. (Harl. 83 G. 32.)

1707. GRANT from Henry fil. Simonis [fil. Roberti] de Moniasche to Henry fil. Roberti of an acre and a half of land in various places in the fields of Moniasche, namely, in Brockewall, Le Morlondes, Le Brounemore, etc. Witn. Ralph Coterel, jun., William Wyne, Ralph de Cungesdon, etc. Dat. Moniasche, S. b. F. of St. Peter in Cathedra [22 Feb], 1316[7]. (Harl. 83 G. 43.)

1708. GRANT from the same to the same of an acre of land in Moniasch lying in Knottelowe, Les Smalenithynges, Moniaschedale, and Doggesedslacke. Witn. Ralph Coterel, Ralph de Cungusdon, John de Stanedon, William Kyde, etc. Dat. Moniasche, M. b. Pur. of B. V. M. [2 Feb.], 1322[3]. (Harl. 83 G. 44.)

1709. GRANT from Roger de Neubold to Nicholas fil. Radulphi de Congesdon of a messuage and lands in Moniash. Witn. William Coterell, John de Benteley, Thomas de Bucstones, etc. Dat. Moniash, F. of St. Matthias [24 Febr.], 12 Edw. III. [1338]. (Harl. 84 A. 1.)

1710. INDENTURE from twenty-four residents of Moniasch, wherein, in recognition of grant of burial rights to their chapel, they covenant to pay a farthing to the Vicar of Bakewell for each corpse on the day of burial, and to present at the High Altar at Bakewell every All Saints' Day twelve pence for the Dean and Chapter. Dat. 5 June, 1345. (Lichf. KK. 3.)

1711. GRANT from Laurence Lynford to Thomas Partut of land, etc., at Cheselowe in Moniasch. Witn. John de Cotes of Moniasch, Henry de la More, and Will. Helys. Dat. Moniasch, F. of St. Andrew [30 Nov.], 35 Edw. III. [1361]. (Harl. 83 G. 31.)

1712. GRANT from Laurence de Lynford, knt., to William de Lynford and John de Stafford, "consanguineos meos," of all his lands, etc., "cum mineris plumbi," woods, turbary, etc., in Moniassh, Chelmerdon, Caluour, and elsewhere, co. Derby, Magna Lynford and Thorneburgh, etc., co. Bucks., and in Estharnam, co. Wilts. Witn. John de Ludlowe, knt., John de Aylisbure, knt., Hugh Chastleton, knt., John de Stafford, etc. Dat. Lynford, Morr. of St. Michael [30 Sept.], 38 Edw. III. [1364]. (Bowles.)

1713. GRANT from Henry fil. Simonis de Moniassch to John fil. Henrici de Moniassch of land and buildings in Moniassch. Witn. Will. Helys, John del Cotes, Simon de Ernesby de Moniassch, etc. Dat. Moniassch, Tu. a. Inv. of H. Cross [3 May], 40 Edw. III. [1366]. (Harl. 84 B. 35.)

1714. GRANT from William fil. Rogeri Kyde de Moniassch to John fil. Henrici de Moniassch of lands and a messuage in Moniassch. Witn. Henry fil. Simonis de Moniassch, Will. Helys, Hen. Attemore, etc. Dat. Tu. a. Conv. of St. Paul [25 Jan.], 41 Edw. III. [1367]. (Harl. 83 G. 1.)

1715. GRANT, for life, from William Elys of Monyassch, Henry Attemore of Monyassch, William Elys, etc., to Amicia, wife of Adam le Wryth of Monyassch, of land in the same. Witn. William fil. Rogeri fil. Dyot of Monyassch, Robert Mathew, John Smylter, etc. Dat. Sat. in Easter Week [12 Apr.], 45 Edw. III. [1371]. (Harl. 112 H. 26.).

1716. GRANT from Adam le Writh de Moniassch to Dom. Henry de Fayrfeld and Hugh fil. Henrici fil. Johannis, "capellanus," of land and tenements in Moniassch. Witn. Will Elys, Henry del Mere, Henry Bayart, etc. Dat. Moniassch, S. a. Octave of the Epiphany [6 Jan.], 48 Edw. III. [1375]. (Harl. 84 A. 38.)

1717. RELEASE from Alice, widow of John le Smythe de Moniasch, to John fil. Petri de Moniasch, of a messuage and land in Moniasch. Dat. Baseford, S. a. Nat. of St. John B. [24 June], 50 Edw. III. [1376]. (Harl. 84 A. 36.)

1718. CONVEYANCE from Nicholas Coterell and Roger de Gaddesby to Laurence de Lynford and Alice his wife, of all the lands which they have of the feoffment of the said Laurence in Monyasch, Chelmorden, Hassop, Caluoure, and Roulisley; with the reversion of the lands which Margery, widow of William de Lynford, holds in dower, which reversion they also have of the feoffment of the said Laurence. Witn. James Coterell, John Foleiambe, Roger North, Robert de Hethecote, etc. Late Edw. III. Copy. (Bowles.)

1719. GRANT from Thomas Odam de Moniassh and Margaret his wife to John Fox of Aldport of a messuage, etc., in Moniassh. Witn. Thomas Trech of Moniassh, John del More, William de Moniassh, etc. Dat. Moniassh, S. a. F. of St. Hilary [13 Jan.], 8 Hen. IV. [1407]. (Harl. 84 A. 7.)

1720. GRANT from William Mon, Chaplain of the Chantry of the B. V. Mary of Monyash, to the Dean and Chapter of Lichfield, of an acre of land, etc., in Monyassh, lying between the Hall of the Chantry and the land of Hugh fil. Henrici capellani. Witn. Dom. Robert Merford, succentor of Lichfield Church, Peter Halughton, vicarius chori eiusdem ecclesie, John Dean, Vicar of Hope in Pecco, and Robert Ouerton, literatus. Dat. Monyash, F. of St. Michael [29 Sept.], 1 Hen. V. [1413]. (Lichf. B. 25.)

1721. GRANT from John Asshely, chaplain, to Thomas Vernon, son of Sir Richard Vernon, John Stafford de Eyam, William Monyasshe, Thomas in le Dale, etc., of land in Monyasse. Dat. F. of Pur. of B. V. M. [2 Feb.], 15 Hen. VI. [1437]. (Harl. 83 D. 13.)

1722. ATTORNEY from John, Earl of Shrewsbury, John Talbot, knt., Thomas Eueryngham, sen., esquire, and Thomas Eueryngham, jun., esquire, to John Cobyn, their bailiff of Monyasshe and Chelmardon, to demand, levy, distrain, and receive the rents and services in the lands and demesnes of Monyasshe and Chelmardon due to them " cum officio berghmaistorii." Dat. 1 July, 30 Hen. VI. [1452]. (Bowles.)

1723. WRIT to Robert Stafford, esquire, ordering him not to make " vastum vel estrepamentum " in the 40 messuages, 400 acres of land, 40 acres of meadow, 1,000 acres of pasture, 100 acres of wood, and 10 pounds' worth of rent in Manyasshe, Chelmerdon, Camore, Bromley, and Oslaston, pending the hearing of a suit between the said Robert and Thomas Vernon, esquire. Dat. 4 Feb., 32 Hen. [VI.] [1454]. (Bowles.)

1724. ATTORNEY from John Barowe, esquire, to Richard Stafford, to take seisin of all the lands, meadows, "et mineram plumbi," in Manyassh, Chelmardon, and Caluore, and elsewhere, in co. Derby, which he has by feoffment of Thomas Lynford, esq., and deliver them to Robert Stafford, esq., William de la Pole, John Milne, and Thomas Wild. Dat. 3 Jan., 33 Hen. VI. [1455]. (Bowles.)

1725. LEASE, for twenty years, from Humfrey Stafford of Eyam, co. Derby, esq., to Hew Sheldon of Monyashe, jun., yeoman, of a messuage and lands in Monyashe; rent 21s. 4d. Dat. 1 Mar., 33 Hen. VIII. [1542]. (Woll. vii. 47.)

MONYASH *v.* also under BAKEWELL, HADDON.

MORLEY.

(MORLE.)

1726. COVENANT for the partition of lands in Eston [Aston], Sardelova [Shardlow], Wilne, Morley, Smalley, and Kidesleia [Kidsley-in-Smalley], Warenodbi [Wartnaby, co. Leic.], Angodestorp [Osgathorpe,

co. Leic.], Huberetorp and Trengeston [Thringston, co. Leic.], between
William de Verdun and Aliz his wife, Philip de Wasteneis and Amphelisa
his wife, and Simon de Sancto Mauro and Yseuda his wife, late
belonging to Dina, the mother of the said Aliz, Amphelisa, and
Yseuda. *Circ.* 1200. (Add. 5235.)

Hec est finalis concordia facta inter Willelmum de Verdun et
Aliz uxorem suam et Philippum de Wasteneys et Amphelisam
uxorem suam et Simonem de Sancto Mauro et Yseudam uxorem
suam de toto te[ne]mento quod tenuit Robertus filius Walteri et
de toto tenemento quod tenuit Dina mater predictarum Aliz et
Amfelise et Yseude, scilicet quod Willelmo de Verdun et uxori sue
A. in rationabili parte sua remanet totum tenementum cum
pertinentiis et libere tenentibus quod Robertus filius Walteri tenuit
in Eston et Sardeloua et Wilna excepto seruicio Jordani de Tocha
et exceptis vii denariis de seruicio Thome filii Willelmi et exceptis
octo Bouatis terre in Wilna quas tenent Reginaldus de Wilna et
Hawis uidua et Robertus frater Baldewini et exceptis xii denariis
de tofta quam Doda tenuit et excepta terra quam Roger pastor
tenet in Sardeloua et remanet eidem Willelmo tertia pars terre et
Molendini de Warenodbi que Robertus filius Walteri tenuit in
eadem uilla, et tertia pars bosci de Morle et Smalle et Kidesle
parco infra partem suam computato et totum jus quod P. de
Wasteneis et Amphelisa uxor eius et S. de Sancto Mauro et Y.
uxor eius habuerunt in terra quam tenet Willelmus filius Nigelli
ita scilicet quod venient in curiam Regis ad comodum Willelmi
et illud jus illi quietum clamabunt. Philippo uero de Wasteneis et
Amphelise uxori sue in rationabili parte sua de predictis tenementis
Roberti et Dine remanet totum tenementum quod Robertus filius
Walteri tenuit in Kirkebi cum pertinentiis et libere tenentibus preter
illud quod Juliana de Daiuill [? Damill] in curia domini Regis
recuperauit de illis et remanet illi tertia pars terre et Molendini de
Warenodbi que Robertus filius Walteri tenuit in eadem uilla et
totum tenementum cum pertinentiis et libere tenentibus quod
predicta Dina tenuit in Angodestorp et Huberetorp et Trengeston
tam in bosco quam in plano et due virgate terre in Hemminton
quas Hugo de Waldo et Brun tenuit et seruicium Willelmi de
Naileston, scilicet vi solidi. Simoni uero de Sancto Mauro et
Yseude uxori sue remanet totum tenementum cum pertinentiis et
libere tenentibus quod Robertus filius Walteri tenuit in Morle et
Smalle et Kidesleia preter tertiam partem bosci et remanent illi
octo Bonate terre in Wilna quas tenent Reginaldus et Hawis uidua
[et] Robertus supradicti et xii denarii de tofta quam Doda tenet
in Wilna et terra Rogeri Pastoris in Sardelova et remanent quatuor
virgate terre illi in Hemminton quas Reginaldus et Adam et Roger
et Matillis quondam uxor Bruning tenent et tertia pars terre et
Molendini de Warenodbi que predictus Robertus tenuit in eadem
uilla et totum seruicium Jordani de Tocha de toto tenemento
quod tenet de feudo quod fuit Roberti filii Walteri et totum
seruicium Jordani de Snitertona de eodem feudo et totum seruicium
Ricardi Marescalli de feudo illo et vii denarii de seruicio Thome
filii Willelmi in Sardeloua et Wilna. Et sciendum quod Willelmus
de Verdun debet reddere per annum, P. de Wasteneis et S. de
Sancto Mauro, xx denarios ad perficiendum seruicium Comitis
Leicestrie pro terra de Hemminton. Hanc autem conuentionem
fideliter obseruandam W. et P. et S. iurauerunt et sigillis suis
confirmauerunt. His testibus G. Abbate Cestrie, B. Decano

Cestrie, Helya de Dithiswrhe, Roberto de Trengeston, Roberto de Morle, Hugone fratre suo, Gaufrido de Sancto Mauro, Warino de Snipeston, Willelmo filio Rogeri, Henrico filio suo, Willelmo de Gardino, Gileberto de Lindeseia et aliis.

MOSBOROUGH.

(MORESBUR', MORESBURGHE, MORESBUROUGHE, MORESBURUGH,
MORISBURG, MORISBURICH, MORSBUR', MORYSBURG,
MOSBURGH, MURSBUR'.)

1727. QUITCLAIM from Simon frater Henrici, Domini de Morsbur', to the said Henry of land in the vill of Morsbur' which Edena, his aunt, held. "Necnon fide media insuper tactis et inspectis sacrosanctis in curia Domini Johannis de Stuteuill apud Hekent[on] integre prefatam terram abiuraui." Witn. Ralph and John, persone de Ekent[on], Roger, clericus, tunc senescallus, Ralph Briton, Mag. Geoffrey, Ralph Russel, etc. *Temp.* Hen. III. (Harl. 83 G. 46.)

1728. RELEASE from Richard fil. Simonis de Morsbur' to John fil. Petri de Morsbur' of all lands and tenements, etc., held by the said John in demesne in Morsbur'. Witn. Dom. William de Estutevilla, William Mandrel, William Dolfyn, Roger de Bectona, etc. *Temp.* Hen. III. (Harl. 83 G. 47.)

1729. GRANT from Henry fil. Roberti domini de Moresbur to Simon, his brother, of a bovate of land in the vill of Moresbur, which Ralph persona de Hekint[on] last held, "et quia prefate bovate terre due acre desunt in loco qui uocatur Harcherridding uersus austrum eidem perficiam cum uno prato quantum in manu mea habui tunc quod Robertus filius Fabiani assartauit iuxta locum qui uocatur Oxhefordheforthe." Witn. Ralph and John, persone de Hekint[on], Roger clericus tunc senescallus, Ralph Brito, Mag. Geoffrey, John Doufin, etc. *Temp.* Hen. III. (Harl. 83 G. 48.)

1730. GRANT from Richard de Morisborick fil. Radulfi fil. Jordani, quondam Rectoris medietatis ecclesie de Ekintona to Ralph fil. Henrici, domini de Morisburick, of a bovate of land in the fields of Morisburich, which his father formerly held, and which came to him on the death of Alice fil. Roberti "fratris mei." Rent, a rose and twelve pence. Witn. Philip Marescallus de Ekyntona, Robert de Bramlay, John Dolfin de Plomelay, etc. *Temp.* Hen. III. (Harl. 83 G. 49.)

1731. GRANT from Gilbert fil. Roberti de Morysburg to Ralph fil. Henrici "fratris mei" of two selions of land in the field called "Le Rysevey." Witn. Philip Marescallus de Ekynton, Will. Dolphyn, John Dolphyn, etc. *Temp.* Hen. III. (Harl. 83 G. 50.)

1732. GRANT from John fil. Petri de Morisburg to Ralph fil. Henrici de Morisburg of various lands in the fields, etc., of Morisburg. Witn. Geoffrey de Becthon, clericus, Philip de Ekinton, marescallus, Will. Martyn de Hanley, John Dolfyn de Plomelay, Walter Dolfyn, etc. *Temp.* Hen. III. (Harl. 83 G. 51.)

1733. GRANT from Robert de Morisburg' to Robert fil. Andree de Morisburg' of land in Morisburg'; rent, 1*d.* Witn. Philip Marescall', William Dolfin, John Dolfin, etc. *Temp.* Edw. I. (Cott. xxvii. 146.)

1734. GRANT from Robert fil. Andree de Moresburghe to Hugh his son of a messuage and lands in Moresburghe. Witn. John de Moresburghe, Will. Dolfyn of Plumley, John Dolfyn, etc. Dat. F. of St. Andrew [30 Nov.], 1315. (Cott. xxvii. 147.)

1735. GRANT from Robert fil. Andree de Moresburg' to John de Hacunthorpe of lands in Moresburgh'. Witn. Rob. Brian, William Gere of Begtone, Richard de Hacunthorpe, etc. Dat. 1 Feb., 10 Edw. II. [1317]. (Cott. xxvii. 148.)

1736. GRANT from Robert fil. Andree de Moresburgh' to John fil. Willelmi de Hacunthorp of land in Moresburgh. Witn. John le Mareschall, Robert Brian, William Gere of Beghton, etc. Dat. 11 Mar., 10 Edw. II. [1317]. (Cott. xxvii. 149.)

1737. GRANT from Avicia fil. Rogeri Badde to John de Hacunthorp and Joanna his wife of a messuage in Moresburgh. Witn. John de Moresburgh, John le Mareschall, Robert Brian, etc. Dat. Moresburgh, 20 June, 10 Edw. II. [1317]. (Harl. 112 F. 62.)

1738. RELEASE from Hugh fil. Roberti de Morisburg', clericus, to John de Hacunthorpe and Agnes his wife, of a messuage in Morisburg. Witn. Robert Brian, William fil. Radulfi de Kinwaldmershe, Giles de Roumelay, etc. Dat. Ekyntone, S. a. F. of St. Michael [29 Sept.], 8 Edw. III. [1334]. (Cott. xxvii. 150.)

1739. GRANT from Richard de Hacunthorpe, clerk, to John de Hacunthorpe his brother of a house with a chamber which Emma " que fuit uxor Johannis de Moresburough " held in dower in Moresburugh, to hold for term of the life of the said John at a yearly rent of one penny. Witn. John le Sauuage, Robert Brian, William fil. Radulphi de Kynwoldmersch, etc. Dat. Moresburugh, 8 Apr., 10 Edw. III. [1336]. (Lansd. 107.)

1740. SALE by Nicholas Clyff to Elizabethe Frechevyle, widow, for 20s., of a messuage and two oxgangs of lands in Mosburgh in the lordship of Ekyngton. Dat. 20 Oct., 21 Hen. VIII. [1529]. (Add. 40160.)

MUGGINTON.

(MOGINTONE, MOGYNTON.)

1741. GRANT from Henry de Irtone fil. Henrici de Irtone to William de Irtone his brother and Philip his wife of forty acres of land in Weston, viz., 34 acres in Mogintone field abutting on the road leading from Weston to Wynley and six acres of land in a place called Thisker, in exchange for certain lands and rents in Totinleye which the said William acquired by feoffment from Mag. Adam de Meygnelle, clerk. Witn. Dom. Hugh de Meygnelle, Roger de Bradeburne, knts., Richard le Cursun of Ketleston, William de Tissingtone, William de Stanley, etc. Dat. Irton, S. a. F. of St. Nicholas [6 Dec.], 6 Edw. II. [1312]. (Kedleston.)

1742. ROLL of pleas relating to the manors and advowsons of Muggyngton, Eggyngton, and Rodburne, on the occasion of a presentation to Muggington Church, now vacant, the right to which was claimed by Thomas Babyngton. Dat. Easter, 3 Hen. VIII. [1512]. (Woll. xi. 21.)

MUGGINTON *v.* also under MERCASTON, RADBOURNE, WESTON.

NETHERTHORPE *v.* under STAVELEY.

NEWBOLD, NR. CHESTERFIELD.

(NEUBOLD.)

1743. GRANT from Rog. fil. Nicholai de Langele to Walter de Duneston of land above "Brocholclif," between the road to Neubold and land of Robert fil. Radulfi. Witn. Walter Durs of Dronfield, Robert fil. Johannis de Neubold, Robert fil. Nicholai, etc. *Temp.* Hen. III. (Harl. 112 I. 42.)

1744. RELEASE from Thomas fil. Elie Tinctoris [Dyer] de Cesterfeld to Michael de Haversegge, burgensis de Cesterfeld, of five acres of land in the fee of Neubold, lying on Brochul, near the water called "Smale." Witn. Alan de Len de Cesterfeld, Rob. de Len, Joh. Durant, etc. *Temp.* Edw. I. (Harl. 84 A. 56.)

1745. GRANT from Stephen le Cueller of Cestrefeld to Henry fil. Philippi de Neubold of Chesterfield and to Matilda his wife, of two acres of land in the fee of Neubold, "apud Susane Welle." Dat. Trinity Sunday [7 June], 12 Edw. III. [1338]. (Harl. 83 E. 11.)

1746. GRANT from Robert fil. Philippi de Neubold, manens in Cestrefeld, to Robert le Breton, Dominus de Walton, Philippa his wife, and Robert their son, and his heirs, of six acres of land in the fee of Newbold, lying in "le Holmes" near Aldewynlane, etc. Witn. Roger Breton, John fil. Rogeri Bate of Chesterfield, John de Wytinton, etc. Dat. Newbold, Vig. of St. Laurence [10 Aug.], 13 Edw. III. [1339]. (Cott. xxviii. 8.)

NEWBOLD *v.* also under CHELMARTON, CHESTERFIELD. DUFFIELD.

NEWTON GRANGE.

1747. LEASE, for 81 years, from Robert Crystylton, Abbot, and the Monastery of Combermere, to Thomas Barsford, of their grange called Newton Graunge, at a yearly rent of £6 13s. 4d. Witn. Thomas Huw, Roger Spenser, etc. Dat. Combremere Chapter House, Vig. of St. Andrew [29 Nov.], 1472. (Drury.)

1748. ATTORNEY from Katherine, widow of Thomas Beresford, to Gervase Rolleston, gent., to "sue and folowe" all maner of actions concerning "the ferme of Newton Graunge." Dat. 12 Nov., 37 Hen. VIII. [1545]. (Drury.)

1749. BOND from Laurence Beresford and Edmund Beresford of Newton Graunge to Matthew Knyveton, esq., and Katharine Beresford, widow, to abide by the award of Thomas Powtrell of West Halome, James Rolston, Adam Eyre, and Richard Nedham, arbitrators to settle suits between them relating to Newton Grange. Dat. 21 Nov., 37 Hen. VIII. [1545]. (Drury.)

1750. AWARD of Thomas Powtrell, James Rolleston, Richard Nedham, and Adam Eyre, arbitrators to settle suits between Matthew Knyveton of Bradley and Katherine Baresford of Newton Graunge, widow, on the one part, and Edmund Baresforde and Laurence Baresford of Newton Graunge, of the other, respecting the title, use, and farm of Newton Graunge. Dat. 15 Dec., 37 Hen. VIII. [1545]. (Drury.)

1751. QUITCLAIM from Katharine Barysford, late of Newton Graunge, widow (in accordance with an award by Thomas Powtrell and others, arbitrators to settle suits between her and Matthew Kniveton of Bradley and Edmund Berysford and Laurence Berysforde), to the said Edmund, of the tenement known as Newton Grange. Dat. 30 Apr., 38 Hen. VIII. [1546]. (Drury.)

NEWTON, KING'S.

(NEUTONA.)

1752. GRANT from Hugo de Bellocampo to the Canons of St. Mary and St. Giles de Calc of a virgate of land in Neutona instead of the tithes of mills in Meleburna. Witn. Walter, his clerk, Hubert, priest of Alwardestona, Rob. de Rakestone, etc. *Temp.* Hen. II. (Add. 7213.)*

NEWTON, KING'S, *v.* also under CALK, MELBOURNE.

NEWTON SOLNEY.

(NEUTON, NEUTON SULNY, NEWTON SULNY, NUETONA.)

1753. FINAL concord made "in curia domini Regis apud Cadom' [Caen], in the sixth year of King John [1204-5], before William Crassus, tunc senescallus Normannie, Samson, abbas Cad[omi], John de Alencon, Ralph Labbe, Geoffrey de Cortona, Roger Talebot, and other Justices there, whereby Ralph de Argosis conveyed to Alured de Solenneio, his brother, a portion of his inheritance in the land which belonged to Alured his father and Joan his mother, namely, the manor of "Nuetona, in Anglia" [Newton Solney], with a meadow "apud Bawe" [Bayeux], keeping for himself the lands in Normandy. (Every.)

1754. RELEASE, for 40*s.*, from Robert Palefrey of Neutone to Dom. Norman de Sulene of land which sometime belonged to Ralph Palefrey, his father, in the vill of Newton. Witn. Dom. Nicholas de Seymor, John de Stapenhulle, Henry Mauweysin, etc. Early Hen. III. (Woll. x. 45.)

1755. RELEASE from Reginald, Prior, and the Convent of Repund' [Repton], to Norman de Solenei, Dominus de Neuton, of their claim in the Park of Neut' (saving their tithes), for a part of his wood of Swarthlighay; and of their tithes of a mill and fishery in the manor of Neuton, for 4*s.* yearly rent; and of their tithes of hay in the vill of Neuton, for land in Longedoles. Witn. John de Stapnhul, Geoffrey de Stant[on], Ralph de Tichenale, Walter de Boreford, William Balle. *Circ.* 1230. (Woll. x. 34.)

1756. AGREEMENT between Reginald, Prior of Rapendon, and the Convent, and Norman de Soleni, Dominus de Neuton, whereby the Priory quitclaims to the said Norman the park of Newton, common of pasture, cutting of trees, right of way, in return for which the latter grants to the Priory a part of Swarthlinghay wood; also the Priory grants to him the tithe of one mill belonging to the manor of Neuton, tithe of fishery within Neuton manor for an annual rent of 4*s.*; with

---

* The text of this charter is given under Calk.

the tithe of hay of his demesne of Neuton, for which the said Norman gave two perches in Longedoles and Scorthedoles. Witn. John de Stapenhull, Geoffrey de Stanton, Ralph de Tykenh', Walter de Bereford, William Balle of Rapendon. *Temp.* Hen. III. Fine Priory seal. (Every.)

1757. QUITCLAIM from John Pichard fil. Ade Pichard of Neuton to Norman de Soleni, mil., of a garden in the vill of Neuton, extending from the path leading to the church up to the River Trent, and half an acre lying on Derlestowe. Witn. John de Chandoos, Nicholas de Seymor, Robert de Stanton. *Temp.* Hen. III. (Every.)

1758. GRANT from Alured de Solny, miles., Dominus de Neuton super Trentam, to William de Solny, his son, clerk, of a messuage and a bovate of land in the vill and territory of Neuton super Trentam which Robert Broun held from him in villeinage in the vill of Neuton, with a messuage called "Le Holdelauton," lying between Le Schercesti and the messuage of John le Carter, whereof one head abuts on Brounuslowe and another head on Le Causey, with half an acre of meadow lying between [the meadow] of the Prior of Repindon and his own meadow; with seven acres of land in the field of Neuton [boundaries given in detail]; with all kinds of fishery through all his demesne water in Trent and Douue "cum omnimodis ingeniis," with an annual rent of 6s. 4d. from a messuage and bovate in the same vill. Rose rent. Witn. Robert Abel of Tykenhale, Peter de Melbon, William Pichard of Newton, Robert, clericus de Wynsul, Richard Someter de Neuton. Dat. M. a. F. of St. Barnabas [11 June], 32[?] Edw. I. [1304]. (Every.)

1759. GRANT from John fil. Rogeri Sauenay of Neuton Sulny to Robert fil. Dom. Aluredi de Sulney, knt., mil., of ten shillings' worth of rent from his lands in Neuton Sulny. Witn. Roger Saueney, Thomas Saueney, William Pichard, Robert Sulny, etc. Dat. Sat. a. F. of St. Laurence [10 Aug.], 21 Edw. III. [1347]. (Every.)

1760. GRANT from John de Bollehawe and Thomas de Bildeston, chaplains, to Alvred de Sulney, knight, of a rent issuing out of the manor of Newton Sulny. Dat. M. a. F. of St. Hilary [13 Jan.], 41 Edw. III. [1368]. (P. R. O. B. 2778.)

1761. POWER of attorney from Nicholas de Longeford to William atte Walle, chaplain, to deliver in his name to Richard Scrop, Bishop of Coventry and Lichfield, Philip de Okouere, John de Clynton, knts., Oliver de Barton, John de Aston, and John Shayle, to hold during the said Nicholas' life the fourth part of the manor of Neuton Sulny and the moiety of the manor of Blakwell, and also his portion of lands in Orby, co. Linc., and his share of rents in Wylyngham. Dat. 24 Aug., 14 Ric. II. [1390]. (Every.)

1762. PROCEEDINGS of courts of the manor of Newton Sulney, held Fr. bef. F. of St. Martin [11 Nov.], 15 Hen. VI. [1437]. Vellum roll. (Longford.)

1763. BOND from John Appylby, esquire, to Nicholas Longford, knt., in £100, to abide by the award of John Portyngton, one of the Justices of Common Bench, in a dispute concerning the title to a fourth part of the manor of Neuton Sulny. Dat. 22 July, 25 Hen. VI. [1447]. (Every.)

1764. GRANT from Nicholas Longforde, knt., to John Longford, rector of Northewynfeld, John Lathbury, esq., and John Bonyngton, esq., of all his lands, etc., in Newton Sulney, and in Hathersegge. Dat. F. of Pur. [2 Feb.], 13 Edw. IV. [1474]. (Longford.)

1765. LEASE from John, Prior, and the Convent of Repton, to William Dethyk of Newhall, esq., of the tithe-barn and yard, with all their tithe cornes of Newton Solney, for a term of twenty years, at a rent of £10. Dat. 4 Sept., 20 Hen. VIII. [1528]. (Every.)

NEWTON SOLNEY *v.* also under PINXTON.

NORBURY.

(NORBURI, NORTHBURY.)

1766. GRANT from Ranulf Seylyn of Rotinton to William Hert of Norbury, fil. Henrici Hert of Rotington, of lands in Norbury, near the little cross, and contiguous to the land which Jordan, rector of Norbury, formerly held. Witn. Dom. William de Montegomeri, Dom. William fil. Herberti de Norbury, Dom. Hugh de Okover, etc. *Temp.* Edw. I. (Woll. ix. 74.)

1767. GRANT, for 90 marks, and a brown horse, by Thomas de Wyvile of Stanton to William fil. Herberti de Norburi, of lands in Norburi and Rossyntone [Roston]; rent, 1d. Witn. Dom. Geoffrey de Bakepuz, Dom. Nigel de Langeford, Dom. William de Meysham, etc. Thirteenth century. (Woll. viii. 53.)

1768. DEFEASANCE of bond for £40 from Henry de Knyveton, parson of the church of Northbury [Norbury], to Thomas del Hull of Snelston, Robert del Hull, Walter Tyrry, and John Brown, all of Snelston, contingent on the payment to the said Henry by Philip de Okore or the said Thomas, Robert, Walter, and John, of 37s. 4d. at four terms in the year for three years. Dat. Northbury, S. a. Assumption of B. V. M. [15 Aug.], 6 Edw. III. [1332]. French. (Okeover.)

✓ **1769.** COVENANT whereby John Cokayn, knt., Thomas Okover, Aluered de Longeford, esquire, and Thomas Dawkyn, chaplain, agree with John de la Pole de Hertyngdon and Henry de Bothe, esquires, that if Nicholas fil. et her. Henrici Fitzherbert live till he come to full age or shall be married by the said John de la Pole and Henry de Bothe "infra etatem," that the two latter shall pay forty pounds to Alice, Joan, and Elizabeth, sisters of the said Nicholas, for which sum of money the said John, Thomas, Aluered, and Thomas have granted for a term of 15 years to the said John and Henry the manor of Norbury, with the advowson of the church and all the lands which they formerly held of the grant of William Avener and Richard Aunger, clerks; the said manor, etc., to revert at the end of the term to the said Nicholas Fitzherbert and his heirs for ever. Witn. Thomas Lymestre, Henry Knyveton, rector of Norbury, William Boturdon, William Lymestre, Henry Stere. Dat. at Norbury, Fr. b. F. of St. Michael [29 Sept.], 4 Hen. V. [1416]. (Okeover.)

✓ **1770.** WILL and deed of appointment of Elizabeth Fitzherbert, widow of Ralph Fitzherbert of Norbury. Dat. 20 Oct., 1490. (D. A. J. xx. 32.)

1771. RECORD of a suit brought by John Fitzherbert, esquire, against Henry Cotes of Snelston, labourer, and Thomas Fayrechild, late of Snelston, miller, for trespass and damage to trees and grass at Norbury. Dat. Hilary Term, 17 Hen. VII. [1502]. (Okeover.)

NORMANTON, TEMPLE.

(NORMANTON, NORTH NORMANTON.)

1772. EXTRACT of roll of the court of the Prior of the Hospital of St. John of Jerusalem, held at Normanton, at which Roger Herdwyke, son and heir of William Herdwyke of Herdwyke surrendered lands in Normanton which he held of the gift of William, his father, to William Herdwyke, his brother. Dat. F. of St. Luke [18 Oct.], 32 Hen. VI. [1453]. (Woll. iii. 67.)

1773. BOND from John Warwyk of Lanforth, co. Notts., and William Warwyk of Normanton, to Thomas Foliaumbe, esq., in £10, that at the next court of St. John of Jerusalem in England of the lordship of North Normanton, the said John Warwyk shall make an estate to such person as the said Thomas Foliaumbe shall appoint of all his lands, etc., in the said lordship. Dat. 19 July, 38 Hen. VI. [1460]. (Foljambe.)

1774. RECITAL "de quibus consuetudinibus tenuras manerii de Normanton . . . tangentibus sive spectantibus quod quidem manerium est et pertinet milicie templi Salomonis cum suis juribus libertatibus et consuetudinibus," consisting of rules for the free tenants, etc., "predicti manerii, vz. Normanton, Chesturfeld, Brampton, Denby, Pothloc [?], and Ryley." Followed by Proceedings of the Great Courts, with views of frank pledge of the Priors of the Hospital of St. John of Jerusalem, held at Chesterfeld and Normanton, 26 Hen. VI.—10 Hen. VIII. [1447-1518]. Vellum roll, 16 ft. long. (Mundy.)

NORMANTON, SOUTH, *v.* under PINXTON.

NORTON.

1775. GRANT from Thomas de Chaword to Alice fil. Agnetis Castelayn of Osberton and Rose, her daughter, of all that land at "le Heytridding" which William de le Heytridding sometime held in the soke of Norton, with other lands there. Witn. Dom. William de Folkingham, Abbot of Beauchief, John de Brimingtona, William Mateney of Dronfield, Thomas de Wodehuses, Peter de Leys, etc. *Temp.* Edw. II. (D. A. J. ii. 6.)

1776. GRANT from Thomas de Chauworth, knt., Dominus de Norton, to John Tynet and Isabella his wife, of all the lands which were sometimes Robert Louccok's, and a piece of land called Harecrofte in Norton. Witn. Adam de Gotham, Robert Seliok, Adam Parker, William Hervy, John Aleyn. Dat. 17 Sept., 26 Edw. III. [1352]. (D. A. J. ii. 7.)

1777. GRANT from William Chaworth, Lord of Norton, to John de Blithe, of land in "Le Lyes" in the parish of Norton. Witn. Tho. Parker, Robert Bleyn, etc. Dat. Norton, S. a. F. of St. Mark [25 Apr.], 51 Edw. III. [1377]. (Add. 27329.)

1778. GRANT from Adam Bate fil. Rogeri de Parva Norton to Hugh del Barkhous of Leghes, of all the lands which came to him on the death of Roger Bate, his father, in Little Norton and in the soke of Norton. Witn. William de Barkhous of Wodseates, William de Mora de Grenhul, Thomas de Jurdanthorp, etc. Dat. F. of Pur. of B. V. M. [2 Feb.], 7 Ric. II. [1384]. (D. A. J. ii. 8.)

1779. BOND from Thomas Flesshovere of Lincoln, formerly of Chesterfield, to Henry Foliambe, lord of Walton, esq., in £20, to perform covenants on a sale of lands, etc., in Norton Leez. Dat. Chesterfield, W. a. F. of St. James [25 July], 21 Edw. IV. [1481]. (Foljambe.)

1780. QUITCLAIM from Nicholas Bullok to Richard Bullok of Onston, of all messuages which he has in Jordenthorpe, within the parish of Norton. Witn. Dom. John Croke, vicar of Norton, John Selioke, Richard Blythe. Dat. Norton, 30 Jan., 17 Hen. VII. [1502]. (Rel. xx. 165.)

1781. CONFIRMATION by Will. Blythe of Berneby-super-Dune [Barnby-upon-Don], co. York, gent., of a grant in tail from William Blythe, his grandsire, to William Blythe of Norton, of lands and tenements in Norton and Grenyll [co. Derby], and Dynyngton and Crokes [Dinnington and Crookes, co. York], with remainder to the heirs male of Thomas Blythe, father of William Blythe of Barnby. Witn. John Blythe, clerk, Richard Strete, clerk, Nicholas Bagshawe, etc. Dat. Beaudesert, 30 Sept., 28 Hen. VIII. [1536]. (Harl. 112 G. 15.)

1782. AWARD of Sir John Chaworthe and Sir Phelype Draycot, knts., arbitrators to settle disputes between John Selioke of Hesil-barowe, co. Derb., gent., and John Parker of Norton Lees, respecting tenements at Gledelees, co. York, and that called Jurdanthorpe in the lordship of Norton Lees. Dat. 6 Aug., 35 Hen. VIII. [1543]. (Rel. v. 113.)

1783. DEED of sale, with condition of voidance, by Thomas Dynham of London, esq., to John Selyoke of Hasyllborough, co. Derby, of half the manor of Norton and other land in Norton and Colde Aston, for £400. Dat. 1 Dec., 38 Hen. VIII. [1546]. (Add. 27330.)

NORTON *v.* also under ALFRETON, CHESTERFIELD.

NORTON IN SCARSDALE HUNDRED *v.* under UNSTON.

OAKTHORPE.

(OCTHORP.)

1784. QUITCLAIM from Lesota, widow of Richard Wyley, dau. and heir of John fil. Nicholai de Octhorp, to Thomas Gresley, mil., John Gresley, mil., Thomas Astley, and William Arderne de Meysham, of all the lands she inherited from her father in Octhorpe, in cos. Derby and Leicester, or elsewhere, in the same counties. Witn. — Inggwerdeby, Dominus de Willesley, John Abell, John Baseby de Meysham, etc. Dat. Oakthorpe, Fr. a. Conc. of B. V. M. [8 Dec.], 1 Hen. V. [1413]. (Gresley 396.)

OCKBROOK.

(OKEBRO.)

1785. BULL of Honorius [III.], granting protection to the Abbot and Convent de Parco Stanleie, more especially as regards their possessions in Okebro, Stanle, and Depedale. Dat. 4 Non. Dec. [2 Dec.], aᵒ· Pontif. 9 [1224]. (Woll. x. 32.)

OFFCOTE, NR. ASHBOURNE.

(OFFIDECOTE.)

1786. GRANT from Roger de Mapilton, fil. Ricardi de Bredbur', to Roger fil. Ranulphi de Mercinton of half an acre of land in the meadow of Offidecot, "scilicet meliorem que spectabat ad vnam bovatam terre quam Ricardus de Alnetis aliquando tenuit"; rent, an arrow at Easter. Witn. John de Offidecote, William fil. Ingus of the same, Walter de Kniveton, Alexander Mercator de Esseburn, William de Bredlowe, etc. *Temp.* Hen. III. (Woll. ix. 63.)

1787. GRANT from Gerard de Sutton and Adelicia his wife, William de Aldewerick, and Agnes his wife, etc., to Roger fil. R——, of land in Offidecote; rent, one mark. Witn. Dom. Robert de Esseburne, Thomas his brother, Robert de Aldewerick', etc. *Temp.* Edw. I. (Woll. x. 3.)

OFFCOTE *v.* also under ASHBOURNE, COLD EATON, DERBY.

OFFERTON IN HOPE.

(HOFFNERTOUN, OFFERTONA, OFFIRTON, OFFIRTUN, OFFRETON.)

1788. DEED whereby Matilda and Elena "sorores de Offerton cum consensu boronum [? bonorum] nostrorum Eustachii et Roberti" withdraw from a suit against John Fox of Offerton. Witn. Robert le Eyr, William de Abbeney, etc. *Temp.* Hen. III. (Brookhill.)

1789. GRANT from Hugh fil. Will. de Offirtun to William fil. Philippi de Thornhyl, of all his land, etc., in Kenteney. Rent, a pair of white gloves. Witn. Peter de Hyrst, Elyas de Baumford, Elyas de Astun, Robert de Abeney, Peter le Hoare de Hope. *Temp.* Hen. III. (Brookhill.)

1790. GRANT from Hugh fil. Gerberti de Stoke to William fil. Philippi de Thornhyl of five acres of land in Kenteney in the field of Superior Offirtun. Witn. Elyas de Bamford, Peter de Hyrst, Robert de Abney, etc. Late Hen. III. (Brookhill.)

1791. GRANT from Hugh fil. Will. de Offirtun to William fil. Philippi de Thornhyl of all his land in Kenteney. Witn. Peter de Hayrsle, Nicholas de Paddelay, Robert de Abeney. Late Hen. III. (Brookhill.)

1792. GRANT from [?] Brustall . . . to Robert his son of all his land of Offertona, near the land of Robert de Hedenesouer. Witn. John Fox [?], Robert de Hedenesouere, William de Monte. Dat. at Offerton, xiii. kal. Sept. [20 Aug.], 10 Edw. I. [1282]. With seal of arms of "Robert Cocus." (Brookhill.)

15

1793. GRANT from Alice fil. Rog. de Lacy de Hassop to Eustace de Hofnerton of two acres of land on Le Stobbing in Hoffnertoun. Witn. Roger le Archer, Thomas de Bocstons, Elias de Baumford, etc. *Temp.* Edw. I. (Brookhill.)

1794. GRANT from Robert le Raggede fil. Ric. le Raggede to William Fox of Offerton, of all the lands which he holds in the name of Matilda, his wife, in the fee and territory of Over Offerton, Nether Offerton, " vel Kauereshegge." Witn. William Hally, William Foliambe, Thomas his brother, Thomas de Langedon, Robert de Abbeney, parson of Bampford, Peter le Hore, etc. *Temp.* Edw. I. (Brookhill.)

1795. GRANT from Robert le Raggedde fil. Ric. le Raggedde, jun., to William Fox of the land he had in the name of Matilda his wife, " in feodo solo," in Over and Nether Offerton. Witn. William Hally, William Foleiaumbe, Thomas his brother, etc. Late thirteenth century. (Brookhill.)

1796. QUITCLAIM from Alice fil. Rob. le Hore to John Fox of Offerton of all the lands which he holds and which William Fox his father held in Offerton. Witn. William de Abbeney, William Hally, Robert le Heyr. Dat. S. a. F. of St. Barnabas [11 June], 1314. (Brookhill.)

1797. GRANT from Robert fil. Eustachii de Offerton to William fil. Joh. Fox of those two acres of land which he had by grant of his father in Offerton. Witn. William Hally, William de Abbeney, Robert de Edinsour, etc. Dat. S. a. Nat. of B. V. M. [8 Sept.], 11 Edw. II. [1317]. (Brookhill.)

1798. QUITCLAIM from Richard del Strindes to William fil. Joh. Fox and Joan his wife of 16 acres of land in Offerton. Witn. John Foleiaumbe of Tiddiswelle, William de Abbeneye, Alexander de Abbeneye, etc. Dat. S. a. Michaelmas, 7 Edw. III. [1333]. (Brookhill.)

1799. GRANT from Richard Fox to Thomas Fox his son of a messuage and nine acres of land at Le Storthe in Over Offerton. Witn. Will. de Abbeneye, Thomas del Clogh, Richard del Clogh, etc. Dat. S. a. F. of St. Bartholomew [24 Aug.], 9 Edw. III. [1335]. (Brookhill.)

1800. GRANT from Thomas fil. Willelmi de Abney to William fil. Will. Fox de Offerton of a messuage, etc., on Le Storthe in Offerton. Dat. T. a. F. of St. Augustine [26 May], 17 Edw. III. [1343]. (Brookhill.)

1801. GRANT from Thomas fil. Joh. Gardyner de Castelton and Agnes his wife to Richard Wyld de Abnay of 16 acres, etc., of land in Offerton. Witn. William de Bagshaze, Richard de eodem, Thomas Dicher, etc. Dat. Ann. of B. V. M. [25 Mar.], 2 Ric. II. [1379]. (Brookhill.)

1802. GRANT from Joan and Agnes fil. Hug. de Bircheld to Richard Wyld of Abenay of a messuage, etc., in Over Offerton. Dat. Nat. of St. John B. [24 June], 16 Ric. II. [1392]. (Brookhill.)

1803. GRANT from Adam le Ward and Agnes his wife to William de Bradshawe of lands in Over and Nethur Offerton. Dat. S. a. F. of St. Peter in cathedra [22 Feb.], 21 Ric. II. [1398]. (Brookhill.)

1804. LEASE, for 12 years, from John, son of Nicholas Fox, jun., of Offerton, to Thomas Fox of Schatton, of a messuage with three houses and lands. Dat. S. b. F. of Nat. of St. John B. [24 June], 1399. (Woll. viii. 5.)

1805. QUITCLAIM from Margery fil. Rog. Barker of Hathersegg to John Wylde of Abneye of all the lands she inherited on the death of her mother in Offerton. Witn. Roger Massy of Hylowe, Richard Stafford, John Abney, etc. Dat. Ann. of B. V. M. [25 Mar.], 7 Hen. V. [1419]. (Brookhill.)

1806. FINE levied in Easter Term, 9 Hen. fil. Hen. [? Hen. V., 1421], before Robert Hull, John Cokayn, John Preston, William Babyngton, and John Martyn, Justices, whereby Thomas del Bank of Alkemonton and Joan his wife convey to John Wyld of Abbeney a messuage and sixteen acres of land in Offerton. (Brookhill.)

1807. LEASE from John Glossop of Wodesetys in Norton to Henry Foliaumbe of a messuage in Offerton called Le Storth, for 12 years. Dat. F. of St. Martin [11 Nov.], 5 Edw. IV. [1465]. (Brookhill.)

1808. GRANT from Thomas Hawkysworth of Thornsyt to Robert Buntyng of all his lands in Offerton. Dat. 24 Nov., 15 Hen. VII. [1499]. (Brookhill.)

1809. QUITCLAIM from Thomas Meverell, esq., to Thomas Wyld of Offerton in le Peke of two tenements in Offerton. Dat. 21 Apr., 17 Hen. VII. [1502]. (Brookhill.)

1810. GRANT from Thomas Wylde to Thomas Barley, esq., of all his lands, etc., in Offerton in Hope. Dat. 26 July, 18 Hen. VII. [1503]. (Brookhill.)

1811. COUNTERPART of lease from James Denton, LL.D., Dean, and the Chapter of Lichfield, to John Beresforde of Bradeley Asche of the tithes of Offerton, Abney, Abney Grange, Shatton Superior et Shatton Inferior, and Overton. Dat. 27 July, 1523. (Lichf. D. 18.)

OFFERTON *v.* also under BRADWELL.

OLLERSETT.

(OLLERSHEDDE.)

1812. INQUISITION made at Derby, 31 March, 3 Hen. VIII. [1512], before Henry Cokayn, escheator of the King in the said county, and a jury, concerning the title to lands in Ollershedde, Whytyll, Shydyerd, Hayfeld, Holywodhed, and Bothom, co. Derb., from John Doncalfe, vicar of Prestbury, and Richard Shead, who was seised of them by charter dated Michs., 28 Hen. VI. [1449] to John Berd, son of Nicholas Berd, the present owner. (Jewitt's " Reliquary.")

OSLASTON.

1813. SALE by William Coke, son and heir of William Coke of Trusley, gent., to Sir John Porte of Etwall, knt., Justice of the King's Bench, of a messuage and lands in Oslaston, Trusley, and Thurvastone. Dat. 18 Mar., 21 Hen. VIII. [1530]. (Woll. xii. 107.)

OSLASTON *v.* also under MONYASH.

OSMASTON.

(OSMUNDSTON.)

1814. TESTIMONY of various clerical witnesses (past and present Rural Deans), examined in the Chapel of Osmundston [Osmaston] in Brailsford parish, as to whether that chapel was in the Deanery of Ashbourn or "Castilar." Dat. Tu. a. F. of St. Kenelm [17 July], 1345. (Lichf. AA. 8.)

OSMASTON *v.* also under MELBOURNE.

OVERTON.

1815. GRANT from Margery quondam uxor Radulphi Rerisby to Richard de Northegge of a toft, croft and bovate of land in Overton, and four plots of land in Clatercotes. Witn. William de Wynfield, Peter Pecke, Henry Knottyng, etc. *Temp.* Edw. III. (Foljambe.)

OVERTON *v.* also under BRADWELL, OFFERTON.

PADLEY, NETHER.

1816. LEASE from Henry Wyllyams, Dean, and the Chapter of Lichfield, of the tithes in Nether Padley, Lyttle Huclowe, and Caluor-infra-Hope, to Thomas Fitzherbert, knt. Dat. 1 Feb., 1552[3]. (Lichf. D. 29.)

PAKNAGE IN BRAMPTON.

(POCKNEDGE.)

1817. POWER of attorney to Katerine, widow of William Harlaston, to Roger Shaghe, to deliver seisin to Richard Stevenson and Matilda, wife of John Stevenson, of two messuages in Paknage. Dat. 20 May, 23 Hen. VI. [1445]. (Woll. iii. 60.)

PAKNAGE *v.* also under BRAMPTON.

PARWICH.

(PERWICH, PEUERWICH, PEVERWICH, PEWERWICH.)

1818. GRANT from Henry fil. Reginaldi de Peverwich to the church and monks of St. Mary of Gerwedon [Garendon, co. Leic.], of half an acre of arable land in the field of Pewerwich, lying on "le Middelfur-long subtus le Ringes" and on Bleccheringes. Witn. Geoffrey fil. Randulfi, Henry fil. Rogeri, Henry fil. Galfridi, Adam de Leie, etc. *Temp.* Hen. III. (Eg. 454.)

1819. GRANT, in soul alms, from Emma fil. Roberti Hakkefot of Peuerwiche, widow, "post mortem Gaufridi," her husband, to the church and monks of Gerondon [Garendon, co. Leic.], of two roods of land in the territory of Peuerwich, one rood lying on Middilhil, and the other between Ringweye and Flaxdale. Witn. William, capellanus, Henry fil. Henrici, Geoffrey fil. Ranulfi de Peuerwich, Adam de Stan-lowe, etc. *Temp.* Hen. III. (Campb. xv. 13.)

1820. GRANT from Ralph fil. Petri fil. Haylwardi de Peuirwich to Robert de Acouere of a bovate of land in Peuirwich, which the said Peter his father held from Henry fil. Rogeri de Peuirwich. Witn. Robert de Esseburn, Jordan de Snitterton, Roger de Wednesle, Henry de Alsop, Robert de Thorp, Henry de Ylum, William de Leya. *Temp.* Edw. I. (Okeover.)

1821. GRANT from Henry fil. Galfridi de Peuirwich to Robert de Acauere of his toft on " le Halleclif," in which there is a spring before the gate nearest the toft of Roger fil. Joce [? in Parwich]. Witn. Robert de Esseburn, Jordan de Snitterton, Roger de Wednesle, Henry de Alsop, Robert de Thorp, Robert de Wednesl', William de Leya. *Temp.* Edw. I. (Okeover.)

1822. GRANT from Hugh del Wycheges to Dom. John de Dene, knt., of all the lands in Perwich and Alsop which he acquired on the death of Mag. Andrew de Esseburne, whose heir he is. Witn. Dom. Roger de Bradeburne, knt., Dom. Henry de Kneveton, knt., John de Bradeburne, etc. [? Fourteenth century.] (D. A. J. viii. 19.)

1823. QUITCLAIM from Edward Salysbery of Rythlond, son and heir of Ralph Salysbery, to Humphrey Bradbourn of Hough, of various lands in Parwich. Dat. 6 Oct., 16 Hen. VII. [1500]. (Bemrose.)

PARWICH *v.* also under ASHBOURNE, BRADBURN, CALLOW, DUFFIELD, SOMERSALL, WIRKSWORTH.

PEAK, THE

1824. MEMORANDUM from the Archdeacon of York to the Abbot of Burton, reciting that Pope Innocent had instructed him to adjudicate between the Archdeacon of Derby and the Dean and Chapter of Lichfield, in the dispute as to archidiaconal rights over churches within the peculiar jurisdiction of the Peak. Contending parties appeared at York. Decision given against the Archdeacon. Dat apud Rusmareis, Mor. of St. Laurence [11 Aug.], 1246. (Lichf. Y. 1.)

1825. INQUISITION taken at Bakewell before Proctors of the Dean and Chapter of Lichfield and of the Dean of Lincoln, as to the tithes in the Peak pertaining to Lenton Priory [co. Notts.]. *Circ.* 1250. (Lichf. MM. 1.)

1826. SHORT particulars as to the tithes of hay "spoiled" in the Peak district by Lenton Priory, with "nomina villarum parochie de Tideswell vnde prior spoliauit decimas vi et armis." *Circ.* 1250. (Lichf. MM. 2.)

1827. REPORT of the Archdeacon of St. Albans to the Pope as to the failure of different commissions to settle the dispute between the Dean and Chapter concerning the Peak churches and Lenton Priory. Dat. 1251. (Lichf. MM. 3.)

1828. INSPEXIMUS from Roger, Bishop of Coventry and Lichfield, of a sealed instrument of William, his predecessor, dated Whitsun Tuesday, setting forth the settlement of a dispute between Lenton Priory and the Dean and Chapter of Lichfield, viz., that the Prior, etc., " percipient duas partes omnium decimationum dominicorum W. Peverell tam cultorum quam colendorum . . . in cartis monachorum quas habuit de W. Peverell, capitulum vero Lychefeld tertiam partem omnium predictorum," etc., with a third part of the tithe of lead. Dat. Heywood, v. Id. Mart. [11 Mar.], 1251[2]. (Lichf. MM. 4.)

1829. COVENANT from Henry de Lexinton, Dean of Lincoln, and lessee of the Peak tithes, to pay fourteen marks per annum to Lenton Priory. Dat. Lincoln, xiiii. Mar., 1252[3]. (Lichf. MM. 7.)

1830. *AWARD of Papal Commissioners in the Lenton strife, given at St. Mary's, Leicester. Dat. 1252.

1831. COMPOSITION between the Dean and Chapter of Lichfield and Lenton Priory, as to the commuting of the Peak tithes due to Lenton Priory, according to the Leicester judgment. Made in the church of Bakewell by Ralph de Cubbel', Robert de Radeford, and John, Vicar of Ashbourne. Dat. 1253. (Lichf. MM. 10.)

1832. TITHE and mortuary rolls of the Peak jurisdiction; 1254-1476. (Lichf. E. 1-37.)

1833. INDENTURE between the Dean and Chapter and R——, Prior of Lenton, touching the tithes of Baucwell, Hopa, and Tideswell, "provenientium de dominicis que fuerunt Willelmi Peverelli." *Circ.* 170. (Lichf. MM. 12.)

1834. LIST of tithes in the Peak Jurisdiction payable to Lenton Priory according to an inquisition held on the F. of the Nativity of the B. V. M. [Sept. 8], 1272. (Lichf. MM. 13.)

1835. INQUISITION of Lenton tithes in Peak Jurisdiction, taken at Tideswell twenty-two years after the "spoliation." Dat. 1274. (Lichf. MM. 14.)

1836. A LONG roll concerning the renewed contention between the Dean and Chapter of Lichfield and Lenton Priory, wherein are recited five royal charters or letters of Edw. I. bearing on the dispute. Dat. 1278. (Lichf. MM. 15.)

1837. ACCOMPT-ROLLS of the Peak Jurisdiction. *Temp.* Edw. I. —[1524]. (Lichf. F. 5.)

1838. LIST of granges in the Peak Jurisdiction, apparently drawn up for purposes of national taxation. *Temp.* Edw. I. (Lichf. H. 1.)

1839. BAILIFFS' roll of the Peak Jurisdiction. *Temp.* Edw. I. (Lichf. F. 1.)

1840. †GRANT from Robert, son of Adam le Wyne, to Robert, son of Ingelram, of all his land at Leitegvil in the Peak. Thirteenth century. (Pole-Gell.)

1841. PROFIT roll of the Peak churches, pensions, mortuaries, etc., with names in full. Dat. 1340. (Lichf. E. 15.)

1842. SUMMARY of receipts from the Peak Jurisdiction. Dat. 1340. (Lichf. F. 6.)

1843. LETTERS patent of Queen Philippa, granting licence to William le Eyr, forester in fee of the Forest of High Peak, to perform his office of custody there by deputy. Dat. at Woodstock, 24 Dec., 19 Edw. III. [1345]. (Lansd. 114.)

---

* Printed in Derbyshire Arch. Journal, Vol. V., p. 157.

† Could not be found at Hopton : taken from Hist. Comm. Report IX., App. ii. 403.

1844. POWER of attorney from Thomas, son of Sir Richard de Byngham, knt., to Master Simon de Botelesford, master of the schools of Neuwerk [Newark, co. Notts.], to receive rents in the Peak from John Den of Stantonleyez, and Richard, Rector of Byngham [Bingham, co. Notts.]. Dat. Neuwerk, F. of St. Gregory [12 Mar.], 19 Edw. III. [1345]. (Woll. ii. 25.)

1845. GRANT in tail from King Edward III. to John his son, Duke of Lancaster [called] King of Castile and Leon, (in consideration of his surrender of the Earldom and honours of Richmond), of the castle, manor, and honour of Tykhill [co. York], and of the castle and manor of High Peak, with the knight's fee thereto belonging, and those granted to the King by Robert de Lisle, knt., besides various advowsons, manors, and honours in several counties. Witn. W[illiam Whittlesey], Abp. of Canterbury, and other members of the Council, John Knyvet, Will. de Francheden, John Moubray, Thomas de Ingelby, William de Wychyngham, Roger de Mells, John de Cauendissh. Dat. 25 June, 46 Edw. III. [1372]. Great seal. (Cott. xv. 1. and D. of L.)

1846. CONFIRMATION from King Richard II. of the above charter. Dat. Westminster, 15 Sept., 1377. (D. of L.)

1847. TERRIER-ROLLS of property in the Peak Jurisdiction. Fourteenth century.ˈ (Lichf. F. 2, 3.)

1848. ACCOUNT-ROLLS of the Peak Jurisdiction, with lists of mortuaries; 1400-1524. (Lichf. F. 8-14.)

1849. INQUISITION taken before Henry Vernon, esq., Steward, Master of the forests of George, Duke of Clarence, of the Forest of High Peak. Dat. 6 Nov., 11 Edw. IV. [1471]. (Woll. x. 66.)

1850. BOND given by William Bagshawe of Hope and his sureties of £200 to the Dean and Chapter of Lichfield, upon his being appointed Receiver-General of tithes, etc., in the Peak District. Dat. 17 May, 22 Hen. VII. [1507]. (Lichf. D. 12.)

1851. VALUATION of property of the Chapter of Lichfield, in the Peak Jurisdiction, made upon survey; 1523. (Lichf. F. 13.)

1852. COPY of "Valor Ecclesiasticus" as to Lenton tithes in the Peak. *Temp.* Hen. VIII. (Lichf. MM. 17.)

PEAK, HIGH, *v.* also under TIDESWELL.

PEVEREL, HONOUR OF.

1853. LETTERS patent directing the knights, freemen, foresters, and others on the honor and castle of [Peverel] and forest of High Peak to be respondent to John de Warenne, Earl of Surrey, to whom the King has granted the said honor, castle, and forest for life, as fully as they were held by William Peverel before they escheated to the crown, at a yearly rent of 437 marcs, 6s. 8d. Dat. 19 Edw. III. [1345]. (P. R. O. A. 210.)

1854. LEASE, for twenty-one years, from Harry Eland of Baseford [Basford, co. Notts.], esq., to Harry Foliaumbe of Waltone, esq., of the office of the "Bailliship" of the Honor of Peverell, in the Hundred of Scarsdale, at the death of Margaret, wife of Richard Prudhomme. Dat. 24 June, 20 Edw. IV. [1480]. (Woll. ii. 69.)

1855. ACQUITTANCE from Richard Purdon of Scleford to Henry Foliambe of Walton, esq., for 20*s.* due at Pentecost, for the farm of the Bailiff of the Honour of Peverel, by reason of the dower of his, the said Richard's, wife, and for 20*s.* due at Martinmas. Dat. F. of All Saints' [1 Nov.], 21 Edw. IV. [1481]. (Foljambe.)

1856. ACQUITTANCE from Henry Eland of Baseford [Basford, co. Notts.], to Henry Foliambe, lord of Walton, esq., for £20 in full payment of £40 due to him for the office of Bailiff of the Honour of Peverel in the Wapentake of Scaresdalle. Witn. John Page, gent., John Foliambe, gent., John Scha, etc. Dat. Baseford, F. of St. George [23 Apr.], 21 Edw. IV. [1481]. (Foljambe.)

1857. ACQUITTANCE from Richard Prudhome of Slefford, co. Linc., to Henry Foliambe of Waltone, esq., of 20*s.* for farm of the bailiwick of the honor of Peverell, being the dower of Margaret, his wife. Dat. F. of St. Leonard [6 Nov.], 22 Edw. IV. [1482]. (Woll. ii. 70.)

1858. ACQUITTANCE from Richard Prudhome of Sleforde [co. Linc.], and Margaret, his wife, to Henry Foliambe of Walton, esq., for 20*s.* due at Martinmas for the farm of the bailiwick of the Honour of Peverel. Dat. F. of St. Katherine [25 Nov.], 1 Rich. III. [1483]. (Foljambe.)

1859. GRANT from Henry Eylande of Basford, co. Notts., "squier," to Henry Foliambe of Walton, "squier," of the office of "Baillyship of yᵉ honour and fee of Peverell in Scarresdale" for forty years. Dat. 5 June, 3 Hen. VII. [1488]. (Foljambe.)

PILSBURY *v.* under CHELMORTON.

PILSLEY IN EDENSOR.

(PILLESLEY, PYLLESLEY.)

1860. GRANT from William, vicarius de Castleton, John de Longesden, clericus, and William le Meter, capellanus, to Godfrey Foliaumbe and Thomas his son of all their demesne in Pillesley which they had of the grant of Robert de Yrland and Laurence de Schryvenham, late vicar of Tiddeswell. Witn. John Foliaumbe of Longesdon, John de Stafford, etc. Dat. S. a. Ann. of B. V. M. [25 Mar.], 1360. (Foljambe.)

1861. GRANT from John de Assewell, parson of Makworth, John, vicar of Spondon, William Monyash, vicar of Duffeld, Roger Tippeshelf, chaplain, and William Michel, chaplain, to Thomas, son of Godfrey Foliaumbe, for life, of all the lands which they had of the grant of Godfrey Foliaumbe in Pillesley, with the mill of Edenessoure, with remainder to the said Godfrey and Avyne his wife. Witn. Richard Vernon, knt., Richard de Wynfeld, etc. Dat. Bauquell, M. a. F. of Annun. of B. V. M. [25 Mar.], 50 Edw. III. [1376]. (Foljambe.)

PILSLEY *v.* also under DARLEY.

PINXTON.

(PENCHISTON, PENCUSTON, PENKESTON, PENKESTON
NORMANTON, PYNKESTON, PYNKESTON AND NORMANTON,
PYNKSTON, PYNKSTONE.)

1862. GRANT from Robert fil. Will. de Aufertone to Ralph le Poher (with the consent of Ranulph, the latter's brother), of Normanton, to hold by one knight's fee, and Penchiston, to hold by a fourth part of a knight's fee. Witn. William, Abbas de bello capite [Beauchief], William de Leche, John de Leche, Robert de Leche, Robert de Waleton, Peter de Herthil, Roger de Alreton, Henry de Edwalton. Early Hen. III. (Woll. x. 46.)

1863. DEFEASANCE by Alverey de Sulney, chev., to Will. de Wine, chev., of a bond for 100 marks, on condition that he observes certain covenants entered into respecting the manors of Pencuston and Normonston, and the advowsons of the churches there. Dat. Sat. a. F. of St. Luke [18 Oct.], 30 Edw. III. [1356]. French. (Woll. x. 47.)

1864. GRANT from Alured de Sulney, knt., to William de Mielton, John de Bollehawe, and Adam Toralde, chaplains, of the manor of Penkeston, with the hamlet of Normanton and the advowsons of the churches there, also the manors of Blacwelle [nr. Alfreton], and Wylingham, with appurtenances in Orby, co. Linc., and the manor of Basford, co. Notts. Witn. Walter de Mungumry, John de Gresleie, Will. Bakepuz, knts., Robert Franceys, etc. Dat. Blacwelle, S. b. F. of St. Barnabas [11 June], 43 Edw. III. [1369]. (Woll. x. 48.)

1865. GRANT from William de Mielton, John de Bolhawe, and Adam Torald, chaplains, to Alured de Sulny, knt., of a rent of £100 from the manor of Penkeston, with the hamlet of Normanton and Blacwelle. Witn. Nicholas de Longeford, Henry de Braylesford, Robert Trusbutes, knts., etc. Dat. M. a. F. of St. Barnabas [11 June], 43 Edw. III. [1369]. (Woll. x. 51.)

1866. GRANT from Aluered de Sulne, knt., to John de Pynkeston of a messuage and lands in Holbroke, in the fields of Pynkeston and Kyrkeby [Kirkby, co. Notts.], which William, son of Hugh de Denby, held of Dionisia le Wyne, Lady of Pynkeston; rent, 6s. 10¾d.; the said John to pay in addition 6s. 8d. for heriot. Witn. Robert de Langetone, Robert de Brynnesley, John Cutte, etc. Dat. S. a. F. of St. Martin [11 Nov.], 49 Edw. III. [1375]. (Woll. x. 49.)

1867. RELEASE from Thomas Foliambe, of co. Derby, and Robert Longham, of co. Leicester, to Thomas Stafford, knt., and Alice, his wife, and Nicholas de Langford, knt., and Margery, his wife, of the manor of Penkeston and Normanton, excepting the advowson of the church of Normanton, and to the grantors and the heirs of the said Robert a rent of £12 from the said manor. Dat. M. b. Pentecost [8 May], 14 [Ric. II., 1391]. (Woll. x. 52.)

1868. GRANT in trust from Thomas [Langley], Bishop of Durham, Ralph Sy . . . , [Nicholas] Mountgomery, knts., and Roger Venables, parson of Rowstorne, to Thomas Chaworthe, knt., of rents after the death of Ralph Longford, knt., and Margaret his wife, and of George Longford, esq., until the majority of Nicholas, son and heir of the said Ralph, out of two parts of the manors of Pynkeston, Normanton, and Blakwelle. Dat. 12 Nov., 1 Hen. VI. [1399]. (Woll. xi. 47.)

1869. GRANT from Margery de Longford, widow of Nicholas de Longford, knt., to the Abbot of Welbek [Welbeck, co. Notts.], the Prior of Thurgartone [Thurgarton, co. Notts.], John B[el]lasys, parson of Halwynfeld, Thomas Chelastone, parson of Normanton, and William Smalley, parson of Morton, of a pourparty of the manor of Pynkeston and Normanton, excepting the advowson of the church of Normanton, and a rent of £6 (with a clause of distraint), for a chaplain to pray for the soul of Alured Sulny, knt., in the church of Neutone Sulny, conceded by Nicholas de Longford and his wife. Witn. John Dercy, Thomas Chaworthe, knts., Henry Perpunt, etc. Dat. M. a. F. of St. Martin [11 Nov.], 10 Hen. IV. [1408]. (Woll. x. 57.)

1870. FINE levied at Westminster on F. of Pur. of B. V. Mary [2 Feb.], 13 Hen. [IV. ? 1412], whereby Richard Cliderhowe, esq., and Margery his wife deliver, for 100 marks, to Richard Lassy, Thomas Grey, sen., and John, son of John Cliderhowe, a moiety of the manor of Penkeston Normanton, and a fourth part of the manors of Newton Solney and Blakwell. (Woll. x. 53.)

1871. RELEASE from John, son of John de Cliderhowe, to Richard Lassy, of the moiety of the manor of Penkeston Normanton, and the fourth part of the manor of Neweton Sulny and Blakewelle, and of lands in Baseford [Basford, co. Notts.], which the said John held with the aforesaid Richard, and Thomas Grey, sen., from Richard Cliderhowe, esq., and Margery, his wife. Dat. S. b. F. of St. Matthew [21 Sept.], 13 Hen. IV. [1412]. (Woll. x. 54.)

1872. CONFIRMATION by Alice, widow of Thomas de Stafford, knt., and sister and one of the heirs of John Sulney, knt., to William de Kirkeby, of a messuage and lands in Penkeston and four acres of land in Kirkeby in Asshefeld [Kirkby-in-Ashfield, co. Notts.], "pro quodam certo," to be paid yearly at her court of Penkeston ; rent, a rose. Dat. 10 Dec., 7 Hen. V. [1419]. (Woll. x. 55.)

1873. QUITCLAIM from Alice, sometime wife of Thomas Stafford, knt., to Nicholas Strelley, knt., Nicholas Wymbyssh, clerk, John Horspole, clerk, William Chilwell, chaplain, of half her manor of Pynkeston and Normanton, a fourth part of her manor of Blakwelle with appurtenances in Pynkeston and Normanton, Blakwelle, and Kyrkeby, with the advowsons of the churches of Pynkeston and Normanton. Witn. Henry Somers, Chancellor of the Exchequer, Thomas Chaworth, knt., Robert Beeston. Dat. 1 Feb., 8 Hen. V. [1421]. (Brookhill.)

1874. GRANT from Richard de Radclyf, rector of Longford, Nicholas de Clayton, and William del Byrches of Ryssheom, son of the fourth Nicholas de Longford, knt., to Ralph, son of the manors of Pynkeston and Norm[anton], Newton Sulny, and Blakewell, with lands in Baseford [Basford, co. Notts.]. Witn. Nicholas de Muntgomere, knt., Henry del Bothe, Richard Browne, etc. Dat. 28 June, 2 Hen. VI. [1424]. (Woll. x. 56.)

1875. GRANT from William Kirkeby of Pynkeston to John Kirkeby, his son, of a croft, etc., in Pynkeston called Normancroft. Witn. Jacobus Whitword, Richard Richardson, Roger Newton, etc. Dat. 26 Jan., 22 Edw. IV. [1483]. (Trusley.)

1876. QUITCLAIM from William Kirkeby of Pynkeston, jun., son and heir of William Kirkeby, to John Kirkeby of Pynkeston, of a croft in Pynkeston abutting on the common lane, and called Normancroft. Dat. 3 Feb., 22 Edw. IV. [1483]. (Trusley.)

1877. GRANT from John Kyrkeby of Selston, fil. Will. Kyrkby de Pynkeston to Ralph Savage de Novo Loco in Shirwod, Edmund Savage, clerk, and John Walker, of a croft in Pynkeston called Normancroft, abutting on the land of Ralph Longeforde. Witn. James Mason, Reginald Ratcliffe, Thomas Gyne. Dat. Tu. b. F. of St. Nicholas [6 Dec.], 3 Hen. VII. [1487]. Fine seal of Felley Priory is attached. (Brookhill.)

1878. QUITCLAIM from William Kyrkby de Pynkestona to Ralph Savage of Newsted, Edmund Savage, and John Walkere, of a croft in Pynkeston called Normancroft.. Witn. Thomas Gunthorp, Prior de Novo Loco in Shyrwod [Newstead-in-Sherwood], Jacobus Savage de Lyndeby, esquire, John Savage de Hakenall, esquire. Dat. apud Felleya, F. of St. Silvester, Pope [31 Dec.], 3 Hen. VII. [1487]. (Brookhill.)

1879, 1880. GRANT and release from William Kyrkby of Pynkston to John Leek, arm., of a messuage and bovate of land in the lordship of Pynkston, with all his lands, etc., in cos. Notts. and Derby. Witn. Roger Hardwyk of Hardwyk, John Leek of Steynesby, William Wryght of Stanley. Dat. apud Pynkston, 12 Nov., 5 Hen. VII. [1489]. The seal of Wm. Gunthorpe, Prior of Newstead, is attached to the release. (Brookhill.)

1881. QUITCLAIM from William Kyrkby of Pynkston, jun., son and heir of William Kyrkby of Pynkston, sen., to John Leeke, arm., of a messuage and bovate of land in the lordship of Pynkstone or in the parish of Kyrkeby, with all his lands in cos. Notts. and Derby. Witn. Thomas Leeke, bailiff of Chesterfield, Edward Savage, rector of Heth, William Bentte, rector of Sutton-in-lee-Dale. Dat. 1 June, 5 Hen. VII. [1490]. (Brookhill.)

1882. GRANT from Ralph Savage de Novo Loco in Shirwode [Newstead], Edmund Savage, clerk, and John Walker of Harstoft, to Thomas Saucheverell, son of William Saucheuerell, of the croft, etc., called Normancroft in Pynkeston. Witn. Thomas Langton, Robert Kyrkby, gent., John Mortram, etc. Dat. Pynkeston, 1 Oct., 12 Hen. VII. [1496]. (Brookhill.)

1883. PARTICULARS of suit brought at Derby by Christopher FitzRandolff against Thomas Saucheverell, lately of London, gent., Robert Whitworth, and other husbandmen of Pynkeston, for breaking the said Christopher's enclosure, killing two oxen, and doing other enormities at Pynkeston. A day is appointed for settling the case amicably. Dat. Easter Term, 18 Hen. VII. [1503]. (Brookhill.)

1884. GRANT from John Leeke of Sutton-in-le-Dale, sen., esquire, to Symon Dygby, esq., Thomas Saucheuerell, late of Kyrkby-in-Asshfeld, gent., William Clerkson, and Laurence Neweton of Pynkston, yeoman, of all his lands in Pynkston, co. Derby, and Kyrkby-in-Asshfeld, co. Notts.; with power of attorney to Robert Daubeney and Elias Rychardson to give seisin. Dat. at Sutton-in-le-Dale, 18 Dec., 19 Hen. VII. [1503]. (Brookhill.)

1885. Copy of grant from Thomas Sacheverell to Thomas Suthworth, rector of Normanton, John Pypys of Normanton, John Rechardson of Pynkeston, Geoffrey Cowper of Horsley Woodhous, of lands in Kirkby-in-Ashfield [co. Notts.], and Pynkeston, co. Derb. Dat. 16 Hen. VIII. [1524-5]. (Brookhill.)

1886. Covenant between Thomas Wodwarde of Horseley, co. Derby, yeoman, and Isabell his wife, and Thomas Sawcheuerell, son of the said Isabel and brother and heir of the late Henry Sawcheuerell, by the mediation of Henry Stathom, William Johnson, George Heythcote, Rauff Sawcheverell, and William Bulkar, concerning the inheritance of the said Thomas as to the jointure and dower of his said mother Isabel, widow of the late Thomas Saucheverell, sen., whereby it is agreed that the said Thomas Sacheverell, jun., shall execute a deed settling on his mother and her now husband the land called "Broke-hylle" (now held on lease from Rauf Langeforde, knt.), with all his lands lying in Penkeston field, to the yearly value of 12s., and "a litell howse calde Magge Howse," of the yearly value of 2s., for her life, subject to the yearly payment of 4s. to the said Thomas Saucheverell, etc. Dat. 4 Oct., 29 Hen. VIII. [1537]. (Brookhill.)

PLAISTOW.
(PLASTOWE.)

1887. Grant from William de Plastowe to Richard de Codintone of a messuage and land in Plastowe. Witn. Geoffrey de Dethek, Peter de Wakebrugge, Robert de Codyntone, etc. Dat. S. a. F. of St. James [25 July], 9 Edw. II. [1320]. (Woll. vi. 51.)

1888. Grant from Richard de Codintone to Nicholas Pistor [Baker] of Cruch, of lands which he had of William de Plastowe in Plastowe. Witn. Dom. William, vicar of Cruche [Crych], Geoffrey de Dethek, Peter de Wakebrugge, Geoffrey de Plastowe, etc. Dat. Cruch, F. of Nat. of B. V. M. [8 Sept.], 14 Edw. II. [1320]. (Woll. vi. 52.)

1889. Grant from Richard fil. Galfridi de Plastowe to William de Wakebrugge of a messuage and lands in Plastowe, in the fee of Shukthorne, in the parish of Cruche. Witn. Dom. William de Baliden, chaplain, Henry de Cotyngtone, John de Whetecroft, etc. Dat. Cruch, S. a. F. of St. Barnabas [11 June], 28 Edw. III. [1354]. (Woll. vi. 53.)

1890. Lease, for twelve years, from William de Kynardseye to William de Wakebrugge, Elizabeth his wife, and Richard Davys [?], chaplain, of the manor of [Plastowe ?] and lands in La Lee, Alveleye, Holdweye, Wetecroft, and Plastowe; rent, 52s. Dat. La Lee, Th. in Whitsun-week [1 June], 31 Edw. III. [1357]. (Woll. vi. 54.)

1891. Lease, for twenty-one years, from John, son of William Doule of Plastowe, to William de Wakbrugge, of a messuage and lands in Plastowe in Cruch; rent, a rose annually, and after the period of the lease, 20s. Witn. John fil. Roberti de Lee, Henry le Spenser, Robert Shepherd, etc. Dat. M. a. F. of St. Michael [29 Sept.], 32 Edw. III. [1358]. (Woll. vi. 56.)

1892. Grant from William Doule of Plastowe to Roger de Bradburne, William Blount, chaplain, John Deacone, and others, of a messuage and lands in Plastowe which belonged to John his brother. Witn. William de Rollestone of La Lee, Roger Cubbelle, Adam del Hulle, etc. Dat. Wakebrugge, 11 Nov., 5 Ric. II. [1381]. (Woll. vi. 57.)

PLEASLEY.

(PLESELE, PLESELEV, PLESELEYE, PLESILEG.)

1893. GRANT from Robert de Wilheby to William fil. Sanson of a toft and croft in the vill of Plesileg', with a bovate of land in the territory of Plesileg'; rent, 4s. Witn. Dom. Roger Deincurt, Dom. William, rector ecclesie de Plesileg', Hugh de Dukemonton, Roger de Sidenal, Alan fil. Hugonis, etc. Late Hen. III. (Lansd. 596.)

1894. GRANT from Thomas fil. Joh. de Schirebrok to Ralph fil. Willelmi Sampson de Pleseley of that bovate of land which Walter le Charetter formerly held of Nicholas de Bollesouer, grandfather of the said Thomas in Pleseley. Witn. Hugh Stuffyn, Thomas fil. Hugonis de Pleseley, Gilbert le Parker de eadem, Thomas super-grenam de eadem, Simon de Bateley. *Temp.* Edw. I. (Lansd. 597.)

1895. GRANT from Robert Sampson of Pleseleye to John his son of a messuage, croft, etc., and a bovate of land in the vill and fee of Pleseleye which were formerly held by Robert Sampson, his father. Witn. Hugh Stuffin of Schirebroc, Thomas fil. Johannis de Schirebroc, Richard Sampson, Gilbert le Warde, etc. *Temp.* Edw. I. (Lansd. 598.)

1896. DEED whereby Thomas [Beck], Menevensis Episcopus [Bishop of St. David's], grants that the Prior and Convent of Felley may hold certain lands and tenements in his fee of Pleseleya, for which the said Prior, etc., has been accustomed to perform customs and services according to their charters held from previous Bishops of St. David's, by performing personal service (viz., of the Prior or one of his Canons) at the Bishop's two great courts at Michaelmas and Easter, and by paying yearly 2s. 8d. for the tenement which the Priory holds of the grant of R. de la Bache; the said Prior being exempted from summons to the Bishop's Court for trial of thieves, etc., or other law business, and the said Bishop hereby takes the Priory under his protection like their other men and tenants "penes dominam Constanciam de Byerne et alios dominos de Tykehall capitales dominos feodi nostri predicti." For which privileges the Priory grants to the Bishop nine acres of land in Estefeld in the field of Pleseleya, lying on Ballehoue, and Langthwaytes. Witn. Dom. Henry de Perepount, Dom. William de Steynesby, milites, Hugh de Rodmerthwayt, Robert le Graunt, Hugh Stoffyn, William Pyte, Jordan de Sutton, Gilbert le Parker, Thomas le Breton. [1280-1293.] (Harl. 43 I. 16.)

1897. LETTERS patent of Edward I., granting permission to Thomas [Beck], Menevensis Episcopus [Bishop of St. David's], "quod mansum suum de Plesele in comitatu Derbeye muro de petra et calce firmare et kernellare et illud sic firmatum et karnellatum tenere possit sibi," etc. Dat. apud Bristoll, 1 Jan., anno 13 [1285]. Great seal. (Harl. 43 C. 52.)

1898. GRANT from Robert Trussebutte, knight, to Sir Ralph de Neville, lord of Raby, of a rent issuing out of lands and tenements in Pleselay and Rodmanthuayt. Dat. 28 April, 1359. (P. R. O., B. 2887.)

1899. CONVEYANCE from John fil. Dom. Johannis de Wylughby, militis, to Dom. William, Dominus de Huntyngfeld, Dom. William de Skypewith, Dom. William de Belesby, milites, Mag. Thomas de Friskenay, persona ecclesie de Wylughby, and Dom. Adam de Lymbergh, of six manors in co. Lincoln, other manors in cos. Northt. and Cambs., and the manor of Pleselay, co. Derby; to hold during the life of the said John at a yearly rent of a thousand marks. Witn. Dom. Walter de Hamby, Dom. William de Gyppeworth, Dom. Peter Chauant, milites, William de Stayne. Dat. apud Wylughby, F. of St. Thomas [21 Dec.], 35 Edw. III. [1361]. (Harl. 58 A. 48.)

PLEASLEY *v.* also under ASHOVER.

PLUMLEY *v.* under BRAMPTON, WESTWELL.

POSTERN IN DUFFIELD.

1900. COVENANT whereby Antony Lowe, gent., for the fee of 1*d.* per diem, grants to Roger Meynours, esq., "Serjaunt of the King's Celler," the custody of the Park of Postern, during the nonage of Henry Bradshaw, son and heir of John Bradshaw, deceased. Dat. 22 May, 15 Hen. VIII. [1523]. (Woll. iii. 95.)

POTLOK *v.* under DOVERIDGE, WILLINGTON.

PRIESTCLIFFE.

(PRESCLIF, PRESTCLEVE, PRESTCLIF, PRESTCLIFF, PRESTECLEF, PRESTECLEVE, PRESTECLIF, PRESTECLIFF, PRESTECLIFFE, PRESTECLYVE.)

1901. GRANT from Roger Coterel de Prestecleve to Roger fitzHenry of Schirley of an acre of land in Prestcleve. Witn. Hen. FitzYve, John le Clerke, etc. *Temp.* Edw. II. French. (Add. 8073.)

1902. GRANT from Adam fil. Rog. Coterel to Roger his son of a messuage, etc., in Presteclif. Witn. Roger fil. Ade Coterel, John Asser, John Hervy, etc. Dat. S. b. F. of St. Andrew [30 Nov.], 19 Edw. III. [1345]. (Foljambe.)

1903. GRANT from Robert fil. Thome en le Dale of Loggusdon to Roger fil. Ade Coturel of half an acre of land in Presteclif. Witn. John Asser, Adam Coturel, John Hervy, etc. Dat. S. b. F. of St. Peter [? 22 Feb.], 20 Edw. III. [1346]. (Foljambe.)

1904. GRANT from Henry fil. Ricardi atte Lydgate de Prestclif to John fil. Thome de Molendino, sen., of half an acre of land in Gratclifdale. Witn. John Hervy, Adam Coterel, William Andrea, etc. Dat. Easter Day [20 Apr.], 22 Edw. III. [1348]. (Bemrose.)

1905. GRANT from Dyota fil. Will. Hug. de Presteclif to Roger fil. Ade Coterel of an acre of land in Presteclef, lying in Le Brodewei. Witn. Roger Asser, Adam Coupemon, John le Knith, etc. Dat. S. a. F. of St. Cedda, Bp. [7 Jan.], 24 Edw. III. [1350]. (Foljambe.)

1906. GRANT from Thomas fil. Ade Coterell to Robert fil. Ade fil. Johannis of three roods of land in Presteclif lying on Lastenferlong. Witn. John Hervy, Thomas fil. Ricardi, William fil. Thome, etc. Dat. F. of St. Thomas, M. [29 Dec.], 27 Edw. III. [1353]. (Bemrose.)

1907. GRANT from Adam Coupmon of Presteclyve to Roger Coterel of half an acre of land in Presteclyve lying on "Lastonstorleg." Witn. Roger Asser, Henry Dycon, Adam Coterel, etc. Dat. Sat. b. Ass. of B. V. M. [15 Aug], 34 Edw. III. [1360]. (Foljambe.)

1908. GRANT from Ralph Coterell of Tadynton to John fil. Galfridi de Bryghtrichefeld of half an acre of land in the field of Prestecliffe lying upon Aldworthing. Witn. John Lumbard of Tadynton, John Hervy, Thomas Coterell, etc. Dat. S. b. F. of St. Cedda, Bp. ' [7 Jan.], 51 Edw. III. [1377]. (Foljambe.)

1909. GRANT from Nicholas Coterell of Tadynton to John de Brightrichefeld of land in Prestecliff lying in Grattecliffedale, Aldeworthinges, etc. Witn. Roger Asser, Robert le Mulner, Roger Hervy, etc. Dat. M. a. Pur. of B. V. M. [2 Feb.], 5 Ric. II. [1382]. (Foljambe.)

1910. GRANT from Cecilia, dau. of Henry Coterell, to Dom. Adam Coterell and Thomas Coterell of all her lands, etc., in Prestecliff. Witn. Henry Swannyld, Roger Asser, John Knyght, etc. Dat. W. b. Trinity [5 June], 7 Ric. II. [1384]. (Foljambe.)

1911. GRANT from Roger Hervy to John, son of Geoffrey de Brythrychefeld, of thirteen acres of land in Presclif which he had of the grant of John del Assher and Alice his wife. Witn. Thomas Coterel, John Hervy, John Dycon, etc. Dat. M. a. F. of St. Katherine [25 Nov.], 1390. (Foljambe.)

1912. GRANT from William fil. Roberti de Prestclif to Richard Wlfet and John de Cuggusden, chaplains, and Thomas de Rolond, of four tenements and nineteen acres of land in the fields and lordship of Prestclif. Witn. John Decon, Henry Coterel, John de Schath, etc. Dat. T. a. Michaelmas Day [29 Sept.], 22 Ric. II. [1398]. (Bemrose.)

1913. GRANT from Roger Knight of Prestcliff to William, son of Robert of the same, of an acre of land in Prestcliff lying in Gratclifdale. Witn. John Dykon, Roger de Saghe, etc. Dat. T. a. F. of St. Hilary [13 Jan.], 10 Hen. IV. [1409]. (Bemrose.)

PRIESTCLIFFE *v.* also under HADDON, TADDINGTON.

QUARNDON.

(QUARUNDON, QUERNEDON.)

1914. MORTGAGE from John Saucheverel, Lord of Hopwell, to Henry Fraunceys of Chaddesdeyn, Geoffrey Dawe, Rector of Cotegrave, William le Ward of Hopwell, and John de Shardlowe, of all his lands and tenements, with all his natives and with all their progeny and with all lands and tenements held by them in villeinage in the vill of Quarundon. Dat. Quarundon, F. of St. Stephen [26 Dec.], 8 Ric. II. [1384]. (Add 5241.)

1915. SURRENDER at Little Chester Manor Court by Thomas Potter and Elizabeth, his wife, of a messuage in Quernedon to the use of Robert Smyth. Dat. 13 Apr., 12 Edw. IV. [1472]. (Foljambe.)

1916. AWARD by Nicholas Mongombere, knight, and John, abbot of Derley, in a dispute between William Souch of Morley, "squier," and Joan, his wife, of the one part, and Elizabeth Saucheverell, widow, William Saucheverell, Robert Saucheverell, and Richard Saucheverell, her sons, of the other part, viz., the said William and Joan are to pay to the last named parties twelve marks, and to be quit and discharged of all other payments claimed by the same parties before the date of this award, also to deliver to Robert Saucheverell all such writings as they have of v marks of yearly rent in Quarndon granted by the said Joan in her widowhood to the said William, Robert, and Richard. Dat. 6 Apr., 5 Hen. VII. [1490]. (P. R. O., B. 2973.)

RADBOURNE.

(RODBOURNE, RODBURN, RODBURNE, RODDEBOURN, RODDEBURN, RODEBORN, RODEBURN, RODEBURNE.)

1917. QUITCLAIM from Elizabeth and Isabella de Staunton to Thomas de Staunton de Roddebourn of five shillings, which he is bound to pay according to the tenor of their charter. Dat. Th. in Easter Week [1 Apr.] [1350.] (Kerry xix. 288.)

1918. GRANT from Geoffrey Walleron of Lullington and Joan, his wife, and Elizabeth and Isabella, her sisters, to Thomas de Staunton, brother of the said Joan, Elizabeth and Isabella, of a toft and eight acres of land in Roddeburne which John de Murcaston and Margery his wife leased to the said Thomas for his life. Witn. John de Walton de Roddeburne, John de Rocheford, William Doddingeszeles, Henry Whytheued, etc.   Dat. S. a. F. of St. Matthew [21 Sept.], 1358. (Kerry xix. 287.)

1919. GRANT by Arthur de Rolleston and Margery his wife to Rouland de Waltun and Isabella his wife of a messuage and lands in Rodbourn which Henry Nayl formerly held, eight acres of land in Le Rudyngis field, and 26 acres in Portlokfeyld. Witn. Henry Meynell, Robert Tabbe, William de Drewode, etc.   Dat. S. b. the Purification [2 Feb.], 42 Edw. III. [1368].   (Kerry xix. 288.)

1920. GRANT from John de Staunton of Rodburn, chaplain, to Elizabeth Chaundoys of Rodbourn, Henry Fuche, chaplain, and John de Kent, of all his lands, tenements, rents, goods and chattels in Rodburne. Witn. Henry Naill, Richard Hall, Thomas Fox, etc.   Dat. S. a. F. of Nat. of B. V. Mary [8 Sept.], 10 Ric. II. [1386].   (Kerry xix. 290.)

1921. QUITCLAIM from John Morice of Lecchelade to Oliver de Barton, Henry de Kneueton, parson of Norbury, and John Curzon of Ketluston, of all the lands, etc., in Rodburne which were formerly John de Walton's.   Witn. Dom. Nicholas de Longford, Robert de Twyford, Philip de Okeouere, John Cokeyn, knts.   Dat. Th. a. F. of St. Barnabas [11 June], 10 Ric. II. [1386].   (Kerry xix. 289.)

1922. GRANT from John Morice of Lecchelade to Dom. John Staunton, chaplain, of Rodbourn, of all the lands, etc., in Co. Derby which came to him after the death of John Walton of Rodbourne.   Witn. Richard de Garston, mayor of Oxford, Walter Boldne, and John Bereford, bailiffs of Oxford, William Dagenyll, etc.   Dat. Oxford, 18 Apr. 12 Ric. II. [1388.]   (Kerry xix. 291.)

1923. QUITCLAIM from John de Walton of Lissyngton, co. Linc., to John Staunton of Rodeborn, chaplain, of all the lands which were formerly John Walton's of Rodeburne.   Witn. Robert de Ledes, Mayor of Lincoln, John de Carlton, Walter de Faldyngworth, William de Barkeworth, bailiffs of the same, etc.   Dat. F. of SS. Philip and James [1 May], 12 Ric. II. [1388].   (Kerry xix. 294.)

1924. QUITCLAIM from Ralph Meignell, John Dabrychcot, John de Foston, knights, John Curzon of Ketelston, Roger de Bradborne, Robert Martell, Thomas de Sutton, and John de Aston to Thomas de Wednesley, knt., Roger de Cryche, parson of Whityngton, William de Adderley, and others, of all the lands in Rodbourne, Mogynton and Egyngton, which they hold by feoffment of John de Staunton of Rodburne, chaplain. Witn. Robert de Twyford, John Basset, knts., Oliver de Barton, etc. Dat. M. b. F. of SS. Simon and Jude [28 Oct.], 12 Ric. II. [1388]. (Kerry xix. 297.)

1925. LEASE from John de Shyrwode and Alice his wife to Thomas de Wednesleye, knt., William de Adderley, and others, of all the lands, etc., which the said Alice had as dowry on the death of Rouland de Walton, her late husband, in Radbourne. Witn. Thomas de Dodding-zelles de Trusseleye, William de Brewode, Robert Jort, etc. Dat. Th. a. F. of St. James [25 July], 13 Ric. II. [1389]. (Kerry xix. 295.)

1926. GRANT from John de Kent and Emma his wife to Thomas de Wednesley, knt., William de Adderley, Roger Harecourt, Roger de Cryche, parson of Whytington, and William de Lowe of Chesterfield, of a messuage and two cottages in Rodburne which descended to the said Emma on the death of her father, Ralph Burgulun. Witn. John Curson of Ketelston, John Burgulon of Weston, William Crewker, etc. Dat. Th. a. F. of St. George [23 Apr.], 13 Ric. II. [1390]. (Kerry xix. 293.)

1927. GRANT from Elizabeth Chaundoys of Rodbourne, Henry Fuche, chaplain, and John de Kent to Thomas de Wednesley, knt., William de Adderley, Roger Harcourt, Roger de Cryche, parson of Whytington, and William del Lowe of Chesterfield, of all the lands which she acquired by feoffment from John de Staunton, chaplain, in Rodbourne. Witn. John Curson of Ketelston, John Burgylon, William Creuker, etc. Dat. Th. in the 2nd week after Easter [14 Apr.], 13 Ric. II. [1390]. (Kerry xix. 292.)

1928. QUITCLAIM from John de Stanton, chaplain, of Rodburne, to Thomas de Wednesley, knt., Roger de Cryche, parson of Whityngton, William de Adderley, Roger de Harecourt, and William de Lowe of Chesterfield, of all his lands, etc., in the fee of Rodborn. Witn. Robert de Twyford, John Basset, knts., John Curson, Thomas de Montgomery, etc. Dat. F. of Pur. [2 Feb.], 14 Ric. II. [1391]. (Kerry xix. 298.)

1929. GRANT from William Dethek, knt., to Reginald his son and his heirs in tail male of all his lands in the fee of Rodburn excepting two cottages, with reversion, if the said Reginald die without male issue, to his sons Thomas, Roger, William, and their heirs in tail male in succession. Witn. Dom. John Basset, knt., John Curson, Robert Twyford, Roger de Bradburn, etc. Dat. S. a. F. of SS. Peter and Paul [29 June], 4 Hen. IV. [1403]. (Kerry xix. 299.)

1930. GRANT from William de Dethek, knt., to Robert de Twyford, Dominus de Langley, Mag. John Brewode, rector of Rodeburne, Thomas Hunt de Lynby, Roger de Wyngurworthe, and Geoffrey de Detheck his son, of all his lands in Rodeburne and Mogynton. Witn. Edmund Basset, Roger Bradschawe, Henry Bothe, John Bradschawe. Dat. Morr. of Michaelmas Day [30 Sept.], 10 Hen. IV. [1408]. (Kerry xix. 301.)

1931. GRANT from Robert de Twyford, Dominus de Longley, John de Brewode, parson of Rodburn, and others, to Thomas de Dethek fil. Will. de Dethek, militis, of all the lands in Rodeburn which they hold by feoffment of the said William de Dethek, and were formerly Roland de Walton's, with remainder, if the said Thomas die without issue, to Roger his brother, and to John his brother if Roger die without issue. Witn. Nicholas Montgomery, Roger Leche, John Cokayn, knts., etc. Dat. 10 Oct., 12 Hen. IV. [1410]. (Kerry xix. 302.)

16

1932. GRANT from Thomas Dethek, of Uttoxhatre, esquire, to Dom. John Talbot, knt., William Marshall, esquire, Roger Dethic, esquire, and others, of all his lands in Rodburne. Witn. Thomas Grislee, knt., Henry Bothe, Dom. John Brewod, rector of Rodburne, etc. Dat. Nat. of St. John B. [24 June], 12 Hen. IV. [1411]. (Kerry xix. 302.)

1933. GRANT from Thomas Dethek to Robert Kynardysaye, esq., William Marshall, sen., and others, of all the lands which he acquired in Rodburn from William Dethek, knt., his father. Dat. Michs. Day, 13 Hen. IV. [1412]. (Kerry xix. 305.)

1934. GRANT from Auuredus de Lathbury, miles, to John Agulun, vicar of Merston, and Henry de Makkele, capellanus, of all his lands, etc., in the vill and fields of Roddeburne and Trusseley which Robert Gerard held of him. Witn. Peter de la Pole, Thomas Doddyngselz, Thomas de Brwode of Roddeburne, Robert Gerard, John Chapleyn of Trusley. Dat. at Cateby, 10 Sept., 1 Hen. VI. [1422]. (Every.)

1935. ABSTRACT of a Plea by Henry Pole and Alice, his wife, and John Babyngton, esq., against Robert Wode and Isabella, his wife, respecting lands in Rodborne, which had been granted by William Dethek, grandfather of the said Alice, and great-grandfather of the said John, to Reginald his son, with reversion to the aforesaid Alice and John. Dat. Hilary Term, 6 Edw. IV. [1467]. (Woll. xi. 6.)

1936. AWARD of Robert Brudenell in a dispute between Thomas Babyngton, esq., and Germyn Pole concerning the title to certain lands in Rodburne. Dat. 21 Nov., 1506. (Kerry xix. 306.)

RAVENSDALE *v.* under YELDERSLEY.

REPTON HUNDRED.

1937. PRECEPT from Queen Eleanor, consort of Henry II., to the Sheriff of Derbyshire, commanding that Matilda, Countess of Chester, may hold the hundred of Repton, with all liberties and customs. Dat. Salisbury [1174-1189]. (D. of L.)

REPTON.

(RAPANDUNE, RAPENDUN, RAPENDUNE, RAPPENDUN, REPEDON, REPENDON, REPENDONE, REPINDON, REPINGDON, REPPINDON, REPYNDEN, REPYNDON, REPYNDONE, REPYNGTON.)

1938. NOTIFICATION from Matilda, Countess of Chester, to Walter, Bishop of Coventry, that she, with consent of the Earl Hugh, her son, has granted to the Canons of Calc a "cultura quarrerie de Rependone iuxta Trente," with the advowson of the church. [1154-1160.]* (Bemrose.)

1939. NOTIFICATION from Matilda, Countess of Chester, to Walter, Bishop of Coventry, of her grant made with the permission of Earl Hugh, her son, to the Canons of Kalc, of the church of Rapendon, for the souls of King Henry, her grandfather, Ranulf, Earl of Chester,

---

* For the text of this charter *v.* under Calk.

her lord, Robert, Earl of Gloucester, her father, and of Mabel, his Countess, her mother, " on condition that the convent there stands as the Head to which Calk shall be subject." [1153-1160.] (Burdett.)

Waltero divina gratia Coventrensi Episcopo uniuersisque Sancte Matris Ecclesie filiis Matilda Comitissa Cestrie salutem, uestra noscat celsitas me concessu Hugonis Comitis filii mei dedisse Deo et Sancte Marie et Sancto Wistano et Canonicis de Kalc ecclesiam de Rapendon cum omnibus eidem pertinentibus liberam et quietam ab omni seculari servicio et ita liberam sicut aliqua ecclesia ad religionem liberius potest dari, pro salute anime mee et pro anima Henrici Regis avi mei, et Ranulfi Comitis Cestrie domini mei et Roberti Comitis Gloucestrie patris mei et Mabilie Comitisse sue matris mee, et pro animabus omnium antecessorum meorum, Conditione hac quod Conventus ibi constet tanquam caput, cui Calc subiiciatur. Illius tamen persone ecclesiam illam et eorum tenuram . . . comitante absque impedimento possideant . . . spontanea voluntate demissi' sibi sua largiti fuerint Prece ergo multimoda vestram exoro dulcidinem quatenus hanc elemosinam consilio vestro karitative inceptam permanere faciatis ratam. Teste ipso Comite Hugone filio meo, Nicholao, Galfrido, Turch' illius ecclesie personis, Willelmo, Abbate de Lilleshull, Helia Priore de Bredune, Aluredo de Cumbrei, Iuuel sacerdote de ——, Nicholao de Meltun, Magistro Adamo Ormo, Sacerdote de Wilinton, Roberto filio suo, Benedicto Hug[? onis] Com[? itis] avunculo, Roberto de Roppelei, Jordano de Rasur, Simone de Stanton. Tempore Roberti Prioris nobis data fuit hec Elemosina.

1940. GRANT from Matilda, Countess of Chester, wife of Ranulph the Earl, of the whole tithe of her manor of Rapendon and of all the adjacent parts, rents, etc., to the church of St. Wistan of Rapendon, as the charter of her lord witnesses. *Circ.* 1160. (Burdett.)

Matilda Comitissa Cestrie, uxor Ranulfi Comitis, omnibus Sancte Matris ecclesie filiis salutem. Sciatis me concessisse et hac carta mea confirmasse totam decimam de Manerio meo de Rapendon et de omnibus adjacentiis suis integre et de omnibus parcis meis Rapendon et . . . totam decimam meam de redditibus meis eiusdem ville et de placitis et querelis, Deo et Sancte Marie et ecclesie Sancti Wistani de Rapendon, sicut carta Domini mei testatur. Hiis testibus Willelmo capellano, Stephano clerico de Rapendon, Rogero Barbe d'Averil, Regin[aldo] pincerna, Simone nepote Comitisse, Henrico, et multis aliis.

1941. NOTIFICATION by Hugh, Comes Cestrie, to Richard, Bishop of Coventry, of his confirmation of Countess Matilda's grant of Rapenduna church to the Canons of Calch, with the same condition repeated [*v.* No. 1939]. Witn. the Countess Matilda his mother, Richard his uncle, Ralph his chaplain, William and Herbert his clerks, Geoffrey and Constantine, Alured de Combrai, William Patric, Gilbert fil. Picot, Richard Luvetot, Roger de Livet, Bertram Camerarius, Jordan Rasur. *Circ.* 1162. (Burdett.)

1942. PERMISSION from Hugh, Earl of Chester, for his mother, Countess Matilda [widow of Ranulf de Gernons, Earl of Chester] to give in soul-alms ten librates of land in Grantendune [Gransden, co. Hunt.] to the Canons of Rapendon. *Circ.* 1162-1167. (Stowe 158.)

Uniuersis sancte matris ecclesie filiis Hugo comes Cestrie salutem. Notum sit uobis me concessisse domine matri mee Matildi comitisse quod ipsa donet quando sibi placuerit in puram et

perpetuam elemosinam decem libratas terre in Grantendene deo
et Sancte Trinitati de Rapendona et canonicis ibidem deo seruientibus pro dei amore et salute patris mei Randulfi comitis Cestrie
et pro salute anime sue et mee et omnium antecessorum nostrorum.
Teste me ipso Ricardo de Luvetot, Gileberto filio Picot, Radulfo,
Vicecomite de Valle Vire, Rogero de Luvetot, Frembalt de Ridefort,
Seer de Stoke, Henrico Mansel, Radulfo Barbe de Aueril capellano
meo et Willelmo filio suo et pluribus aliis.

1943. GRANT in soul-alms from Matilda, Countess of Chester
[widow of Ranulf de Gernons, Earl of Chester], with consent of her
son Hugh, Earl of Chester, to the Canons of Rapendon, of all her
land of Grandendene [Gransden, co. Hunt.]. *Circ.* 1162-1167.
(Stowe 159.)

Matillis Comitissa Cestrie uniuersis sancte matris ecclesie filiis
et uniuersis hominibus Francis et Anglicis tam presentibus quam
futuris et omnibus ad quos presens carta peruenerit, salutem.
Sciatis me concessu filii mei Hugonis comitis Cestrie dedisse et
hac presenti carta mea confirmasse deo et ecclesie sancte Trinitatis
de Rapendona et canonicis ibidem deo seruientibus totam terram
meam de Grandendena cum omnibus pertinentiis in puram et
perpetuam elemosinam in bosco, et plano, in pratis et pascuis, in
uiis, et semitis, et siluis, in firmis, et redditibus, in auxiliis et
consuetudinibus, in seruitiis, et operibus et in omnibus rebus mihi et
heredibus meis pertinentibus liberam et quietam de omnibus rebus
que mihi et heredibus meis pertinent. Pro amore dei et pro salute
anime Henrici Regis et heredum suorum et matris eius imperatricis
amite mee et pro salute Roberti comitis Gloucestrie patris mei et
comitisse Mabillie matris mee, et pro salute comitis Ranulfi domini
mei, et pro salute anime mee, et Hugonis comitis Cestrie filii mei,
et omnium antecessorum et successorum nostrorum. Hiis testibus
Alano clerico, Rogero Barbe de Aueril, Stephano clerico de Rapendona, Reginaldo pincerna, Willelmo de Tilli, Thoma fratre Milonis.

1944. CONFIRMATION by Henry II. to Matilda, "cognata mea,"
Comitissa Cestrie, and to the Canons of Rappendona, of all reasonable
gifts and grants which Hugh, Comes Cestrie, made to them and confirmed by his charter. [1175 ?] (Burdett.)

Henricus Dei gratia Rex Anglie et Dux Normannie et Aquitanie
et Comes Andegavie Archiepiscopis, Episcopis, Abbatibus,
Comitibus, Baronibus, justiciariis, Vicecomitibus et omnibus
ministris fidelibus suis salutem. Sciatis me concessisse et presenti
carta mea confirmasse Matilde cognate mee comitisse Cestrie et
ecclesie sancte Trinitatis de Rappendona et canonicis ibidem Deo
servientibus omnes rationabiles donationes et concessiones quas
Hugo, Comes Cestrie eis fecit, et carta sua confirmavit. Quare
uolo et firmiter precipio quod prenominata Comitissa et prefata
ecclesia Sancte Trinitatis et Canonici eiusdem loci habeant et
teneant omnia tenementa que predictus comes eis concessit de feodo
suo bene et pacifice, libere, et quiete, plenarie, integre et honorifice
in bosco et plano, in pratis et pasturis, in aquis et molendinis, in
viis et semitis et in omnibus aliis locis cum omnibus libertatibus
et liberis consuetudinibus suis sicut carta predicti Comitis Hugonis
rationabiliter testatur. Testibus, Magistro Waltero de Const[antin],
Godefrido de Luci, Ranulpho de Glanvill, Thoma filio Bernardi,
Hugone de Morewich. Apud Lichisfeld.

1945. LETTER from Hugh, third Earl of Chester, to G[ilbert Foliot], Bishop of London, sending him a copy of his grant to Nicholas, Prior, and the Canons of Rapendon of the advowson of the church of Badewen [Gr. Baddow, co. Essex, dioc. Lond.], in confirmation of the grant by his mother, Matilda [widow of Ranulf de Gernons, second Earl of Chester]. [1172-1181.] (Stowe 153.)

G. dei gracia Londoniensi episcopo et omnibus sancte matris Ecclesie filiis Hugo Comes Cestrie salutem. Fidelis thesaurus memorie est scriptura que rerum seriem incommutabili loquitur ueritate, huius itaque prospectu rationis presenti pagine commendare decreui me concessisse Nicholao priori de Rapend' et canonicis eiusdem loci ibidem sancte Trinitati seruientibus in puram et perpetuam elemosinam jus aduocationis in Ecclesia de Badewen, sicut mater mea Matillis Comitissa concessit, et ne concessio ista in posterum uacillaret huius scripti munimine et sigilli mei appositione dignum duxi confirmare. Huic concessioni hii testes affuerunt, Radulfus barba aprilis, Vmfridus sacerdos de Rapend', Willelmus barba aprilis, Terricus Clericus, Thomas clericus de Luhteburht [Loughborough], Lamfram sacerdos de Stoke, Alanus Clericus, Richard Clericus, Willelmus sacerdos de Rapend', Stefanus frater eius, Jurdanus Rasur, Seer de Stoke, Gilebertus filius Picot, Willelmus de Aula, Milo, Haldanus, Hugo Basset, Jurdanus, Thomas Rasur, Odo Camerarius, Radulfus Clericus, Walterus filius Leuegar, Walter Corb, Gilebertus filius Ricardi, Eilwinus, Gilebertus de Heige, Alexander sacerdos.

1946. CONFIRMATION by Earl David, brother of the King of Scotland, to the Canons of Repton, of the church of Great Baddow, co. Essex, "as the charter of Countess Matilda, witnesses. [1189?] (Campb. xxx. 4.)

Comes David frater Regis Scotie omnibus hominibus suis tam presentibus quam futuris salutem. Sciatis me concessisse et carta mea confirmasse Deo et Sancte Marie et Sancto Wistano de Rependona et canonicis ibidem seruientibus ecclesiam de Bdewen in elemosinam sicut carta Matillis Comitisse testatur. His testibus, Roberto de Basigham, Bertolomeo monaco, Willelmo Reuel, Willelmo Burdet, Nicolao de Hanes, et multis aliis. Apud Wanntona, Valete.

1947. FINE by the Prior and Canons of Repedon from Richard de Berwa and Beatrice his wife, of a virgate of land in Repedon. Made at Nottingham, Sat. a. Exalt. of H. Cross [19 Sept.], 10 Ric. I. [1198]. (Stowe 135.)

Hec est finalis concordia facta in curia Domini Regis apud Noting[ham] sabbato proximo post exaltacionem sancte crucis anno x Regni Regis Ricardi coram Hugone Bard[olf] et Philippo fil. Roberti, Gaufrido Haget, Rogero Arundell, Justic[iariis] Domini Regis et aliis fidelibus Domini Regis ibidem tunc presentibus inter Ricardum de Berwa et Beatriciam uxorem eius petentes et Priorem et Canonicos de Repedon tenentes de i virgata terre cum pertinenciis in Repedon vnde placitum fuit inter eos in prefata curia scilicet quod predicti Ricardus et Beatricia quietum clamauerunt de se et heredibus suis totum jus et clamium suum quod habuerunt in predicta terra predictis priori et canonicis et eorum successoribus in perpetuum. Et pro hac quieta clamancia et concordia predicti prior et Canonici dederunt predictis Ricardo et Beatricie iii marcas argenti.

1948. CONFIRMATION by Ranulph, Comes Cestrie, of the exchange which Dom. Berta Comitissa, his mother, gave to the Canons of Rapundune, namely, the culture above the house of Sercehaia, where there is a quarry, in exchange for other land there between the road and the [water ?] " que descendit de Herteshorn," except the Court and the close of the chapel of St. Thomas, which remain to the said Canons and " de alneto sicut carta Domine matris mee testatur." Witn. Ralph de Maisnilwarin, Simon Tosch', Peter Ruane, Thomas Dispensator, Warin de Vernon, Robert Lancelin, and R. Lancelin his son, Roger de Camvile, Fulk fil. Warini, Peter clericus, Thomas clericus. *Circ. temp.* John. (Burdett.)

1949. GRANT from A——, Prior, and the Convent of Rappendon, with consent of W[illiam de Ecclesia S. Mariæ], Bishop of London, to Mag. Rannulph de Bisacia [Prebendary of St. Paul's], of the church of Badewe [Gt. Baddow, co. Essex], with all its revenues, except a yearly payment of half a mark to Sylvester, vicar of the said church. [1199-1218.] (Stowe 154.)

1950. GRANT from Simon Walensis of Grantinden to the Canons of Repton of his multure and of that of the men of his fee in Gransden, to be done at their mill in Gransden. Witn. William Gereb[aud], Alan de Werist——, Moses Le Tas, etc. Early thirteenth century. (Stowe 161.)

1951. GRANT from Simon fil. Simonis Walensis de Granteden [Gransden, co. Hunt.] to the Canons of Rapendon of the grinding of his own corn and of that of the men of his fee in Granteden, to be done at the mill of the said Canons in Gransden. Early thirteenth century. (Stowe 160.)

1952. CONFIRMATION by Robert [de Watford], Dean, and the Chapter of St. Paul's, London, of the grant by W[illiam de Ecclesia S. Mariæ], Bishop of London, to the Prior and Convent of Rappendon, to retain for their own sustenance the revenues of the church of " Badewe juxta Chilmeresford " [Gt. Baddow], which already belong to them " propter hospitum usus." [1218-1222.] (Stowe 155.)

1953. CONFIRMATION by Alexander [de Stavensby], Bishop of Coventry, to the Prior and Canons of Repindon, of the church of S. Wistan at Repindon, and the chapels of Neuton, Breteby, Melton, Forneworc, Engleby, Tikenhale, Smitesby, and Meysam, and of the church of St. Mary at Wilinton, which was granted by W[illiam de Cornhill], his predecessor [Bishop of Coventry 1215-23]. Witn. Dom. Richard de Stauenesby, the Bishop's brother; Mag. Richard de Glouernia, his official; Magg. W—— de Wygornia, Alexander " Blundus," Simon Perdriz, Philip, clericus, etc. Dat. London, S. Luke's Day, in the fifth year " pontificatus nostri " [18 Oct., 1228]. (Stowe 136.)

1954. GRANT, in soul-alms, from Ranulph, Comes Cestrie et Lincolnie, to the church of the Holy Trinity and the Canons of Repton, of " unam bigam cum unico equo semel in die in bosco meo de Tikenhall errantem ad focale ad usus suos proprios portandum per visum forestarii mei de Tikenhall," with licence to fish in the water of Trent below his house, where his lands extend towards Potlac, reserving, however, a right to fish there himself when necessary. Witn. William de Vernon, Justiciarius Cestrie, Ralph de Wray, Alured de Muligny, John de Lexinton, Geoffrey de Appelby, Norman de Suligny, Walter Findern, Mag. William de Wetton, Simon de Berford, Simon and John, clerks. *Circ.* 1230-1232. (Burdett.)

1955. QUITCLAIM from Ranulph, Comes Cestrie et Lincolnie, to Dom. Stephen de Sedgrave and his heirs, of all suits which they and their men of Bretby, Rosliston, and Cotes are accustomed to do at his wapentakes of Rapendon and Gresley. Witn. Will. de Vernon, Justiciarius Cestrie, William de Cantelupo, Fulk fil. Warini, Baldwin de Ver, etc. *Circ.* 1232. (Gresley 46.)

1956. GRANT from Robert fil. Roberti de Chateshale, miles, to the Canons of Reppindon of the land and tenement which he had by inheritance in the manors of Reppindon and Tykenhale, with all appurtenances within and without the said vills, except his wood of Tykenhale and Suthwode. Witn. Dom. Walter de Chateshale, "frater meus," Mag. Henry de Hertishorn, Roger de Somervile, Milo de Melton, Engellard de Corzun, William Balle, Robert Syminel de Reppindon, Philip Ótuere de Tykenhale. Dat. Morr. of Nat. of B. V. M. [8 Sept.], 44 Hen. III. [1260]. (Burdett.)

1957. INSPEXIMUS and confirmation by R—, Bishop of Coventry and Lichfield, of various charters of grants to the canons of Rependon since the first foundation of the Priory, namely, the church of St. Wistan, together with the chapels of Neuton, Bretby, Melton, Fornemerch, Engleby, Tykenhale, Smythesby, and Meysham, with all rights and privileges, save only to himself and his successors "pontifical and parochial rights"; granting also "quod in eorum ecclesia Sancti Wistani de Rependon in qua nunquam fuit vicaria ordinata, nec perpetuus vicarius constitutus possint sicut hactenus factum est per . . . presbyterum deservire, cum et videatur decentius et sic predicto monasterio magis tutum ut in predicta sua ecclesia per familiarem sibi presbyterum quam per extraneum serviatur." Witn. Mag. Ralph de Chaddesden, Thesaurarius Lych[field], Mag. William de Attlebye, Mag. Alan le Bretun, Canonici Lych[field], Mag. Adam de Walton, Mag. John de Kernyk, Mag. John de Craven, William de Mirley, clericus Domini Regis. Dat. London, Vig. of Ascension [14 May], 1271. (Burdett.)

1958. GRANT in soul-alms from Ralph de Hybernia, with the assent of Isabella his wife, to the Canons of Rependon, of about half a rood of land of his wood of Denewellehay annexed to their wood which they had by grant from William fil. Henrici de Hertishorn. Witn. William Pychard de Neuton, Peter de Melton, Hugh Walle de Rependon, Robert Muymenel de eadem, Henry Le Tanour de eadem. Undated. (Burdett.)

1959. GRANT from Ralph fil. Galfridi de Rependone to Ralph fil. Johannis fil. Radulphi of an acre of land in the fields of Rep' [Repton] abutting on Depedale and near the land of the Prior of Repton. Witn. Hugh Meye, John fil. Johannis, Nicholas Pikard, Warin the carpenter, John the baker. Late *temp.* Hen. III. (D. A. J. ix. 2.)

1960. QUITCLAIM from Ralph fil. Johannis fil. Radulfi de Rep' to Robert de Fornewerke, sissor [tailor], and Alice his wife, of half an acre which he had from Ralph fil. Galfridi lying in Depedale and extending to Le Croked Hayrowe [in Repton]. Witn. Robert le Snepston, William Balle, William le Mason, Hugh Meye, William Appleby. Dat. F. of St. Gregory [12 Mar.], 1 Edw. I. [1273]. (D. A. J. ix. 2.)

1961. AGREEMENT in settlement of a dispute between the Prior, etc., of Repton and the parishioners of Mesham, concerning the reparation of the chancel of that church, viz., that the Priory shall in future find a priest to perform divine service there, and that they should grant the parishioners free burial and all other liberties, and that in return the parishioners should new-build the church, and the Priory hereafter keep it in good repair. In testimony of which the following parishioners have affixed their seals: Dom. Adam de Monte-alto, Dominus de Meysham, Nicholas de Ynguareby, William fil. Domine de Meysham, William Hugelyn de Appleby, Philip de Snypeston, William le Marescall de Meysham, Richard Maunser de eadem, Richard Maunser de eadem, Robert de Crombwell de Meysham, Geoffrey de Hay de Pakinton, Ralph de Hay de eadem, John Godemere de Donasthorp, Richard Godemere de eadem, Adam Bercarius de Wyveleft. Witn. Henry Lovel, John de Weston, Simon de Waleden, Richard de Morley, Robert de Stanton, vicar of Melburn, Engellard de Curzon, Milo de Melton, etc. Dat. 1278. (Burdett.)

1962. GRANT in soul-alms from Bernard de Brus to the Canons of Rependon of all the land and tenement which he has in Rependon, Melton, and Tykynhale, with all appurtenances, liberties, and customs. Witn. Dom. Nicholas de Verdun, Engellard de Cursun, William Pichard, Geoffrey Wallarand, William de Stapenhull, John Vincent, Oliver de Linton, Hugh Walle de Rependon, Henry le Tanner de eadem. *Temp.* Edw. I. (Burdett.)

1963. CONFIRMATION by Robert de Brus to the Canons of Rependon of all the lands and tenements which belonged to Dom. Bernard de Brus, his "cognatus," of his fee in the manor of Rapendon. Witn. Dom. Nicholas de Verdun, Richard de Curzun, Alured Mulny, John de Meton, Walter de Corry, milites. Dat. Christmas Day, 13 Edw. I. [1284]. (Burdett.)

1964. COVENANT whereby William le Waleys de Magna Grauntesden promises to do suit at the mill of Robert, Prior of Rependon, in Gt. Gransden, and to allow his villeins of Gt. Gransden to do the same. Witn. William de Bereford, Nicholas de Warrewik, Roger de Hogham, etc. Dat. Westminster, W. b. F. of SS. Simon and Jude [28 Oct.], 17 Edw. I. [1289]. (Stowe 162.)

1965. QUITCLAIM from William Waleys de Magna Granteden to the Prior and Canons of Reppendon, of his "nativus," Nicholas "carpentarius," with all his following, goods, and chattels, etc. Witn. Thomas de Bassingbourn, miles, William de Stowe, Adam Gerebaud, etc. *Temp.* Edw. I. (Stowe 164.)

1966. COVENANT whereby William le Waleys of Magna Granteden exchanges with the Prior and Convent of Rapendona lands in Gransden. Witn. Adam Gerebaud, Nicholas fil. Godwyne, Henry Tranger, etc. *Temp.* Edw. I. (Stowe 165.)

1967. COVENANT whereby Simon le Waleys de Magna Grantesden exchanges with the Prior and Convent of Rependon lands in Grantesden. Witn. Adam Gerebaud, William Godwyn, John Catelyn, William Hopeldod, etc. Dat. Grantesden, F. of St. Margaret [20 July], 3 Edw. II. [1309]. (Stowe·166.)

1968. GRANT from Edmund, Earl of Arundel, to the Priory and Convent of Repindon, of all his "Wastum de Tikenale" called Schadhawe; rent, 20s. Witn. Dom. John Peche, miles, Dom. Henry de Appelby, miles, William de Corzoun, dominus de Croxhale, Robert Abel, William de Assewelle de Tikenale. Dat. Gloucester, Fr. a. Pur. of B. V. M. [2 Feb.], 5 Edw. II. [1312]. (Burdett.)

1969. GRANT from Ralph fil. Galfridi fil. Rogeri Carpentarii de Rep' to Robert le Taylur de Fornewerke, living in Repton, and Alice his wife, of a half acre of land in Repton lying on Honerbromhul, extending from the headland of the Prior up to Herdewiksiche. Witn. Dom. Hugh the chaplain, Robert de Snypeston, Hugh Meye, William Balle, etc. Dat. F. of St. Valentine [14 Feb.], 18 Edw. II. [1325]. (D. A. J. ix. 3.)

1970. GRANT from Ralph fil. Galfridi fil. Rogeri Carpentarii de Rep' to Robert le Taylur de Fornewerke and Alice his wife, of a half acre of land in Repton field towards Le Hay between Honerbromhul and Brasput. Witn. Dom. Hugh, the chaplain, Robert de Snipeston, William Appleby, Hugh Meye, William Balle. Dat. F. of St. Cedda [2 Mar.], 18 Edw. II. [1325]. (D. A. J. ix. 4.)

1971. GRANT from the same to the same of an acre of land lying in Le Mars between the lands of William super-le-hul and Matilda Agaz in Repton, and in the fields towards Neutone at Knavegrene. Same witnesses. Dat. S. b. F. of St. Gregory [12 Mar.], 18 Edw. II. [1325]. (D. A. J. ix. 5.)

1972. GRANT from Nicholas Pykard of Repingdon and Juliana his wife to Robert le Taylur of a half-acre of land in Repingdon lying at Kokthorn on Le Middelfurlong, between the lands of William Agaz and William Nike, and abutting on the land of Adam Gambone and of Robert Dousamour. Witn. Dom. Hugh le Barker, chaplain, William de Swarkeston, William Meye, etc. Dat. W. a. Epiphany [6 Jan.], 21 Edw. III. [1348]. (D. A. J. ix. 6.)

1973. CONFIRMATION by Ralph [Stratford], Bishop of London, to the Prior and Convent of Repyndon, of the church of Budwa Magna [Gt. Baddow, co. Essex]. Dat. at Stebbenhethe [Stepney, co. Midd.], 26 July, 1348. (Stowe 156.)

1974. MEMORANDUM that the Taxors and Collectors of tenth and fifteenth granted to the King for three years have received from the township of Repingdon 44s. 1¼d. in respect of the first term of the first year of the said grant. Dat. Derby, F. b. F. of St. Michael [29 Sept.], 22 [Edw. III.] [1348.] (D. A. J. ix. 7.)

1975. QUITCLAIM from John Cortel, vicar of Wylington, to John Cordy of Repindon, of a certain place with buildings upon it in Repindon, between the place of William de Herteshorn and the place called Le Steresplace. Dat. W. a. Ann. of B. V. M. [25 Mar.], 30 Edw. III. [1356]. (D. A. J. ix. 8.)

1976. GRANT from Alan Jonesson to Robert, son of Henry de Repindon, and Agnes his wife, of land in Repindon and lying at Collecros. Dat. M. a. Nat. of B. V. M. [8 Sept.], 35 Edw. III. [1361]. (P. R. O. c. 3363.)

1977. LEASE, for lives, from John de Mielton, chaplain, William
Botilere, Hugh de Engleby, and Nicholas Nyke, to Stephen Taylour
of Bretteby, Margery his wife, and Thomas their son, of. the third part
of a messuage in Repindon, and three butts of arable land lying on
Bromhul, half an acre towards Le Hay between Honourbromhull
and Barseputte, and half an acre on Kokethorn. Witn. Robert Wele,
John Wareyn, John Byshope, Robert Daubour, etc. Dat. Th. a. F.
of St. Gregory [12 Mar.], 14 Ric. II. [1391]. (D. A. J. ix. 9.)

1978. GRANT from John Cooke of Repindone, chaplain, to William
fil. Johannis de Engleby, of three selions of arable land "of Engleby"
lying together on Le Wyteflatte between the land of the Prior of
Repindone and John Fischere's land, which selions he had by feoffment
of Dom. William de Meiltone, chaplain, to hold by tenure of a rose
on St. John Baptist's Day, and sixteen pence each Michaelmas to the
"prepositus seu procuratur" of the altar lamp of the chapel of
St. Mary in the parish church of Repindon. Witn. John Frauceys
of Engleby, Symon Frauceys of Mieltone, Laurence Halm of Engleby,
etc. Dat. Engleby, Vig. of the Ascension [14 May], 16 Ric. II. [1393].
(D. A. J. ix. 10.)

1979. GRANT from Robert Dawbur and Alice Dawbur to Symon
Hauker, Robert Maynard, Henry Maysam, and William Neke of all
their goods and chattels, as security for a debt. Witn. John Bolt,
John Biscop, William Boteley, etc. Dat. Repyndon, F. of SS. Philip
and James [1 May], 5 Hen. IV. [1404]. (D. A. J. ix. 12.)

1980. QUITCLAIM from Peter de Melburn, William Marshall, Simon
Blackfordeby, Richard Bars, Vicar of Carolke-on-Trent, William
Colverdowse, vicar of Melburn, and John Burton, vicar of Ashby La
Zouche, to the Priory of Repton, of all their right to Estovers in the
woods of the said Priory called Lostoke, Shrubbe, Prestwoode, Calke-
woode, Knollewode, and Denewellhay. Witn. Simon, Abbat of Derley,
Thomas de Gressley, John Cokayne, Robert Frauceys, knts., John de
Shepey. Dat. 9 Hen. IV. [1407-8]. (Burdett.)

1981. GRANT from Robert Hanson of Repyndon and Thomas
Hether of Tuttebur' to Richard Piper and Alice his wife of half an
acre of arable land in the field of Repyndon, abutting on Hardewyksyche.
Witn. Thomas de Doddyngsels, John Bolte, Richard Nykke, etc. Dat.
Sat. a. Tr. of St. Edward, King [18 Feb.], 11 Hen. IV. [1410].
(D. A. J. ix. 12.)

1982. LETTERS of attorney from Mag. John Sudbury, custos Aule
de Valence Marie de Cantebrigg [Pembroke College, Cambridge], and
the Scholars there, to Mag. Thomas Lavenham, Mag. Richard Sutton,
and Mag. William Cros, to deliver seisin to William Maneysyn, Prior of
Repton and the Convent there, of a third part of a fourth part of the
manor of Repyndon which formerly belonged to John de Baliolo, and
which Mag. Thomas Bingham, late "Custos Aule predicte," had of
the gift and feoffment of Mary de Sancto Paulo, Comitissa Pembr[oke].
Dat. "in collegio nostro Aule predicte," 28 June, 12 Hen. IV. [1411].
(Burdett.)

1983. GRANT from John de Stranley, knt., and Joan his wife to
Henry de Knyveton, esq., Richard Lane of Hyde, William Fyndern
of co. Essex, Roger Normanton of Horseley, John Lever, citizen and
saddler of London, and John fil. Johannis de Fyndern, of their manor

of Repyngdon called "Stranley Espart," which lately belonged to Hugh de Stranley, knt., his father, with the appurtenances in Repyngdon, Meleton, Tykenhale, Twyford, and Wylington. Witn. Robert Fraunceys, Thomas Mawreward, Alvered de Lathbury, John Cokayn, knts., John de Irton, esquire. Dated 30 June, 13 Hen. IV. [1412]. (Kerry xix. 70.)

1984. FEOFFMENT from John de Fynderne to Peter de Melbourne, Robert Tillot, and John Draycott, chaplain of the same, of his manor of Repyndon, as also all the lands and tenements, which the aforesaid John, Richard de Longeforde, knt., John Cokayn, sometime Chief Baron of the Exchequer, and others had jointly with John Curson of Ketulston and John Foliambe now dead, of the feoffment of Robert [de Bray-brooke], Bishop of London, and Gerard de Braybroke, knt., in Repyndone, Meletone, and Tykenhale. Witn. Robert Fraunceys, Nicholas de Montgomery, Alvred de Lathbury, knights, etc. Dat. 22 May, 1 Hen. V. [1413]. (Add. 1537.)

1985. THE counterpart of the above (No. 1984). (Burdett.)

1986. RECOVERY by the Prior, etc., of Repton, against John Mackworth, clerk, Thomas Bradschawe, John Toke, etc., of "all the lands, meadows, waters, and pastures between Potlac broke and the village of Repton as two parts of the Manor of Potlac." Dat. 28 Feb., 9 Hen. V. [1422]. (Burdett.)

1987. "THE state of Repton Manor from the reign of Henry I. to that of Henry V.," drawn up in chronicle form, apparently to prove the title of Repton Priory to a "fourth part and a fourth part of a fourth part of the manor of Repton." *Temp.* Hen. V. (D. A. J. xxiv. 68-77.)

1988. LEASE from Dom. Thomas Beaumonde de Bakevile in Norman[nia], living in co. Leicester, William Cromwell, Thomas Comberworth, knts., of co. Linc., John Kyme of Fryskenay, John Hennage of Haynton, Henry de le Bothe, esquires, and others, to Margaret, late wife of William Handsacre, son and heir of William Handsacre, knt., of the fourth part of the manor of Repyngton, and lands in co. Stafford, with remainder on her death to the two daughters of the said William Handsacre. Witn. John Taylboys of Stalyngburgh, John Bradshagh of Derby, etc. Dated F. of the Nativity of the B. V. M. [8 Sept.], 7 Hen. VI. [1428]. (Kerry xix. 79.)

1989. GRANT from William Baker of Swartlingcote and Katharine his wife to Ambrose Fisher, chaplain, of all their lands, etc., in the towns and fields of Repyngton, Meleton, and Willyngton' holme. Witn. Richard Broune, William Warde of Coton, Robert Saveney, etc. Dat. Sat. a. F. of St. Denis [9 Oct.], 11 Hen. VI. [1432]. (D. A. J. ix. 14.)

1990. GRANT from the same to the same of an acre of land in Repyngton lying near Bromehil and Le More Syche. Witn. Richard Broune, Robert Dauber, Gilbert Ins. Dat. Sat. a. F. of St. Chad, Bp. [2 Mar.], 14 Hen. VI. [1436]. (D. A. J. ix. 15.)

1991. GRANT from Dom. John Wyllyngton of Repyngdon, chaplain, to Richard Huntte of a rood of land in the fields of Milton acquired from William Glede of Repyngdon. Witn. William Percy, Thomas Payne, etc. Dat. F. of St. Michael [29 Sept.], 25 Hen. VI. [1446]. (Bemrose.)

1992. POWER of attorney from John Bysshope to Robert Newton of Mylton and John Preste to deliver seisin to Edmund Vernon, esquire, and Richard Hunt, of all his lands in Repynden. Dat. F. of St. Katharine [25 Nov.], 35 Hen. VI. [1456]. (Bemrose.)

1993. GRANT from Ambrose Fisher, chaplain, to Ralph Fisher of an acre of land in Repingdon lying near Bromehill and Le More Syche. Witn. William Percy, William Hill, Richard Hunt, etc. Dat. M. a. F. of St. Dunstan [21 Oct.], 38 Hen. VI. [1459]. (D. A. J. ix. 15.)

1994. GRANT from Ralph Fisher of Repingdon to Roger Smythe, chaplain, to William Dawns [?] and John Clerk, of an acre of land near Bromehille and Le More Syche. Witn. William Percy, Richard Hunt, John Laurenson, etc. Dat. S. a. F. of St. John B. [24 June], 2 Edw. IV. [1462]. (D. A. J. ix. 16.)

1995. LEASE from John Yonge, Prior, and the Convent of Repyngdon, to Agnes Pratt, widow, and John her son, of a messuage and virgate of land in Repyngdon, to hold for their lives, at a yearly rent of 12s. Dat. Repingdon, 26 Sept., 1523. (Harl. 44 H. 57.)

1996. GRANT from Ralph Aleysaunder of Repingdon to John Fraunceis of Fornewarke [Foremark], jun., Richard Meysem, and George Smythe, of a piece of meadow containing half an acre lying in Leyholme within the lordship of Repingdon, namely, in "Repingdon-felde," abutting on "Potlock hege" on the north and "Quarell poole" on the south. Witn. William Meysem, John Smythe, John Pratt, etc. Dat. 1 Apr., 20 Hen. VIII. [1529]. (D. A. J. ix. 17.)

REPTON *v.* also under BRETBY, CALK, MEASHAM, NEWTON SOLNEY, ROSLISTON, WILLINGTON.

RISLEY.

(RYSLEY, RYSSELEY.)

1997. BOND from Alan in le Wylnes de Rysseley to Matilda que fuit vxor Hugonis Wyting de Rysseley in forty shillings to be paid to her by equal payments on the ensuing feasts of St. Martin [11 Nov.] and of the Purification of the B. V. M. [2 Feb.]. Dat. apud Rysseley, F. b. F. of St. Michael [29 Sept.], 8 Edw. II. [1314]. (Add. 47500.)

1998. LEASE from Hugh de Rysley, son of Hugh de Wyloby, deceased, to John, son of Thomas Marchall of Rysley, and Joanna his wife, of a messuage and lands in Rysley for term of thirty years, at yearly rent of 10s. Dat. Rysley, F. of St. Michael [29 Sept.], 10 Hen. IV. [1409]. (Harl. 85 F. 37.)

1999. ACQUITTANCE from Richard Willughby, Sheriff of Derby, to Hugh Willughby de Rysley for 10s. "de viride sera." Dat. 29 May, 28 Hen. VI. [1450]. (Harl. 58 B. 23.)

2000. LEASE from Thomas Molyneux, Thomas Willughby, sen., Robert Whitehede, and John Parc, to Thomas Willughby, son and heir of Hugh Willughby of Risley, esq., and Isabel his wife, daughter of John Bradburne, now of Hoghe, esq., of lands, etc., in Rysley. Witn. John Lucy de Rysley, Robert Sharman, etc. Dat. Rysley, Th. a. F. of St. Luke [18 Oct.], 7 Hen. VII. [1491]. (Harl. 83 E. 9.)

RODSLEY.

(REDDESLE, REDDISLE, REDISLE, REDISLEGE, REDISLEYE, RODDESLE, RODDESLEY, RODDESLEYE, RODDISLEE, RODDISLEGH, RODDISLEY, RODDUSLEY, RODESLE, RODESLEGE, RODESLEYE, RODISLE, RODISLEYA.)

2001. CONFIRMATION by Ralph de Boscherville to Reginald fil. Reginaldi de Roddesle of a bovate of land in Rodesle; rent, 10*d*. Witn. William de Vernon, Robert de Campania, John de Loke, Mikael, persona de Langeford, etc. Early thirteenth century. (Woll. ix. 18.)

2002. GRANT from Hugh fil. Will. de Shirle to Roger fil. Ranulfi de Mercinton of a bovate of land in Rodisle; rent, a pound of cummin. Witn. Dom. James de Shirle, Thomas de Menyl, William de Langeforde, etc. *Temp.* Hen. III. (Woll. ix. 21.)

2003. CONFIRMATION by William de Muntgomery to Philip de Gutinge of two bovates of land in Rodeslege which he held of the gift of Robert de Mulneton. Witn. Dom. William de Meisham, Dom. Nigel de Langeford, Dom. William FitzHerbert, Dom. Andrew de Grendon, milites, etc. *Temp.* Hen. III. (Woll. ix. 43.)

2004. GRANT by Robert fil. Odonis de Herberbure to Roger fil. Ranulfi de Mercinton of a chief messuage in Roddislee, with the moiety of the whole of that town; rent, 13*s.* 4*d*. Witn. Dom. Nigel de Longeford, Dom. William FitzHerbert, James de Schirlee, etc. *Temp.* Hen. III. (Woll. ix. 77.)

2005. GRANT from Robert fil. Odonis de Herbyrbure to Roger fil. Ranulfi de Mercinton for his homage and service of all the said Robert's capital messuage in Rodisleya and all his demesne there, with all lands, freemen, villeins, customs, etc. Witn. Peter de Touk, Henry de Braylisford, James fil. Sewalli de Shirli, John le Foun, etc. *Temp.* Hen. III. (Woll. ix. 78.)

2006. GRANT from Robert fil. Odonis de Herberbury to the same of a rent of one mark which he was accustomed to pay for lands in Redislege; rent, 12*d*. Witn. Dom. Henry de Bakepuz, Dom. James de Sirly, Dom. William de Meynil, milites, etc. *Temp.* Hen. III. (Woll. ix. 79.)

2007. GRANT from Robert de la Milneton to Philip de Guytingis of a bovate of land in the vill of Roddisley sometime held by Adam frater Roberti Warploc. Witn. Nigel de Langeford, Richard Fitun, Robert le Foun, etc. *Temp.* Hen. III. (Trusley.)

2008. GRANT from the same to the same of a bovate of land sometime held by Peter Bigarius in the vill of Roddisley. Witn. Nigel de Langeford, Richard Fitun, James, dominus de Sirley, etc. *Temp.* Hen. III. (Trusley.)

2009. CONFIRMATION, for four marks and 20*d*., by Robert de la Milneton to Philip de Guytingis of a bovate of land in Roddisley, which Adam fil. Roberti Warploc formerly held; rent, 1*d*. Witn. Dom. Nigel de Langeford, Richard Fitun of Bentley, William de Langeford, etc. Thirteenth century. (Woll. viii. 56.)

2010. RELEASE from Robert de Mulneton to Philip de Guttynges of a bovate of land in Redisle. Witn. Nigel de Langeford, James de Shirle, William de Langeford, etc. Thirteenth century. (Woll. viii. 57.)

2011. GRANT from Robert de la Mulneton to John Saule of Essebure of a bovate of land in Reddesle, together with Orme his "nativus"; rent, 6*d.* Witn. Stephen de Iretone, Richard Phytun, Roger Payn, etc. *Temp.* Hen. III.—Edw. I. (Woll. viii. 70.)

2012. GRANT from Robert de Mulneton to Roger de Mercinton of twenty-six acres of land in the fee of Redisle, in Redisley Clyf; rent, 1*d.* Witn. Robert de Duffeud, Richard de Coudrey, William de Langeford, etc. *Temp.* Hen. III. or Edw. I. (Woll. viii. 58.)

2013. COVENANT before John de Reygate and William de Norbury, Justices itinerant, whereby Robert de Mulneton and Robert de Mercynton grant common of pasture to Dom. William de Meynille and Robert le Faun in Redisleye, under certain conditions respecting the treatment and possession of the land. Witn. Dom. Geoffrey de Gresseley, Dom. Hugh de Streyleye, Dom. Geoffrey de Deyk', Dom. William de Schepe, milites, etc. Dat. Derby, S. a. Tr. of St. Thomas [7 July], 5 Edw. I. [1277]. (Woll. viii. 55.)

2014. LEASE, for forty years, from Nicholas de Marchinton to Robert Molendinarius de Rodesleye of all the land "que fuit de Wasto" in Heppeleymoor in the field of Rodesleye. Witn. Dom. John de Longeford, Robert de Schyrle, knts., John de Pecco in Rodesley. Dat. Martinmas, 1299. (Trusley.)

2015. GRANT from Adam Bercarius de Roddesley to Adam his son of a plot of land, with buildings, etc., in the fields of Roddesle and two selions lying on Yueleyrakes extending "a porta de Yueley usque le Wynyerd." Witn. Dom. Roger de Mercynton, Dom. Ralph de Munioye, knts., Henry de Knyveton, Geoffrey, perpetual vicar of Longeford, etc. *Temp.* Edw. I. (Trusley.)

2016. QUITCLAIM from Michael fil. Nich. de Roddesley to Nicholas his son of all his lands in Roddusley. Witn. Richard le Fowen of Yeveley, Nicholas de Marchington, John Selveyn, etc. Dat. W. a. F. of St. Lucy [13 Dec.], 3 Edw. II. [1309]. (Trusley.)

2017. GRANT from Geoffrey Oede of Herberbury to John de Beke of a rent "unius claui gilofre" [a clove of gillyflower], which Nicholas de Marchinton owed him for tenements in Roddesleye. Witn. Dom. Roger de Swynorton, Dom. John de Twyford, Dom. Richard de Perers, Dom. William de Chaddesdene, milites, etc. Dat. Kenilleworthe, W. a. Pentecost [29 May], 7 Edw. II. [1314]. (Woll. viii. 59.)

2018. GRANT from John fil. Thom. le Baillif of Clifton to Nicholas fil. Rog. de Roddisley of an acre of land in the fields of Roddesley lying on le Hekeclif. Dat. S. a. Michaelmas, 26 Edw. III. [1352]. (Trusley.)

2019. GRANT from William de Carriswall to Walter de Mounte Gomere, of Caverswall, Forsbrook, and Dilhorn manors, co. Staff., and Roddislegh manor, co. Derby. Witn. John Carriswall, Ralph Mountegomeri, Nicholas Fitzherbert, etc. Dat. F. of St. Peter [? 1 Aug.], 29 Edw. III. [1355]. (Foljambe.)

2020. GRANT from Thomas de Clifton, parson of the church of Yrton, John Wade, parson of the church of Legh, to Thomas de Marchinton of Rodesley of two parts of a messuage and bovate of land in Rodesley which were Thomas de Marchinton's, sen., with the reversion of the third part of the same on the death of Alice ux. Roger Michson, who holds it in dower. Witn. Henry de la Pole, Thomas de Wednesley, Ralph de Baystowe. Dat. Redesley, S. a. Tr. of St. Thomas, M. [7 July], 44 Edw. III. [1370]. (Brookhill.)

2021. AGREEMENT whereby Nicholas Mountgomery, squier, grants to Thomas Meverell, squier, the manor of Roddesley, in exchange for the lordship of Macley; and on the production by the said Thomas of a deed of confirmation of the said manor by Nicholas Mountgomery, father of the aforesaid Nicholas, he shall receive an annuity of four marks out of the same Makley; but in default of the production of such deed, then the said Nicholas is to pay an annuity of 40s. to Nicholas Meverell, son of the said Thomas, out of the manor of Roddesley. Dat. 18 Jan., 9 Edw. IV. [1470]. (Woll. ix. 22.)

RODSLEY *v.* also under YEAVELEY.

ROSLISTON.

(ROSLASTON, ROSTELASTON, ROSTELESTON, ROSTLASTON, ROSTLAVESTON, ROSTLAVESTONA, ROSTLAWESTON, ROSTLISTON, ROTHLASTON, ROXLAUESTON.)

2022. NOTIFICATION, with duplicate attached, by Robert, dapifer comitis Cestrie, of his grant to Ralph fil. Siwardi, "tenere totam terram suam de Rostlavestona hereditario iure . . . seruicio semi-militis, et ideo quod ipse sex uirgatas quas calumniabat in Burc mihi et meis heredibus concessit in pace, quare illa predicta seruicia sibi et heredibus concessi et concedo." Witn. Richard Paien, Richard de Maisam, Ralph Talebot, Walter de Dumuila, H. fil. Sturmi, Humelun Panton, etc. *Temp.* Rich. I. (Gresley 30, 31.)

2023. GRANT, in soul-alms, from Robert Maulovel fil. Stephani de Rampton to Merivale Abbey, of common pasture in his wood of Rosliston. Witn. William de Vernun, Geoffrey de Greseley, William persona de Seyla, Walter de Stratton, William persona, frater suus, Osbert Disert de Seyla, Peter de Lutterworth, William de Pethling. Early Hen. III. (Gresley 50.)

2024. GRANT from Robert Maulovel de Rostlaveston to Stephen de Sedgrave of his tenement in Rostlaveston. Witn. Robert de Lexinton, William de Martiwast, William de Wasteneys. Early Hen. III. (Gresley 51.)

2025. QUITCLAIM from Roger de Monte Alto, senescallus Cestrie, to Stephen de Segrave, of the service of one knight, which the latter was wont to perform to Roger de Monte Alto, his father, in respect of the vill of Rostlaweston; rent, a pair of gilt spurs at Easter or sixpence. Witn. Dom. Will. de Malo passu, Walkelin de Arden, William de Sancto Eadmundo. Early Hen. III. (Gresley 53.)

2026. GRANT from Roger de Mahaut, senescallus Cestrie, to Stephen de Segrave, for his service and homage, of eight virgates of land in Roxlaueston which Ralph Grim sometime held. To hold by performing service of half a knight. Witn. Dom. William de Insula, Robert de Colouill, Rob. de Masey, etc. Early Hen. III. (Gresley 54.)

2027. GRANT from Ralph Herlewin de Rostlaweston to Gilbert de Segrave of the moiety of a virgate of land in Rostlaweston, excepting four acres which Ralph clericus holds from him in fee; and a toft and croft for himself and his heirs. Witn. John de Stepenhull, Richard de Thamenhorne, Ralph de Claudewell, etc. [1241-1254.] (Gresley 71.)

2028. POWER of attorney by Nicholas de Segrave to John, his eldest son and heir, to affirm and confirm all the covenants between him and Merivale Abbey concerning an exchange of pasture in his wood of Grimswode and his wood of Rosliston. Witn. Dom. Geoffrey de Gresele, Dom. Theobald de Nevile, Thomas de Nevile, Robert de Malesouere, etc. [1254-1270.] (Gresley 102.)

2029. GRANT from Ralph Godefrey de Rostlaston, with the assent of William, his son and heir, to Ralph fil. Radulfi Talebot of Rosliston, his kinsman, in free marriage with Goda fil. Radulfi de Raueneston, of a curtilage in Rostlaston; rent, one halfpenny at Easter. Witn. Robert de Marisco, William de Caldewell, Thomas Lowell, etc. *Temp.* Hen. III.—Edw. I. (Gresley 110.)

2030. GRANT from Ralph Godefrey de Rostlaston to William fil. et her. Radulfi de Caldewell of three butts of land in the fields of Rosliston, lying in Chalwescroft, beneath the fish-pond of the said William, near the path leading to Rosliston. Rent, a rose on the F. of St. John Bapt. [24 June]. Witn. Milo de Meuton, Roger de Somervill, John de Stapenhull. *Temp.* Hen. III.—Edw. I. (Gresley 111.)

2031. GRANT from Cristiana, quondam uxor Radulfi Harlewine de Rostlaston, widow, to William fil. et her. Radulfi de Caldewell, of a selion of land in the field of Rostlaston in le Nether-Boym. Witn. Ralph Godefrey de Rostlaston, Ralph Talebot de eadem, Nicholas Hopper, etc. *Temp.* Hen. III.—Edw. I. (Gresley 112.)

2032. GRANT, for nine shillings, half a bushel of corn [frumentum], and half a bushel of fine wheat [siligo], by Nicholas de Hoppere de Rostlaston to Robert de Marey de Rostlaston, of an acre and a half of arable land in the fields of Rosliston lying in Ruschefurlong and in Kaldewellesunderlondes. Rent, a rose on the F. of SS. Peter and Paul [29 June]. Witn. Will. de Kaldewelle, Ralph Thaleboth de Rostlaston, Thomas Luvel, etc. *Temp.* Hen. III.—Edw. I. (Gresley 113.)

2033. QUITCLAIM from William de Wauere, Abbot, and the Convent of Merivale, to Nicholas de Segrave, of common of pasture for his cattle in Grymswode and Rosliston Wood, with a chace in Le Hautboys, so that the said Nicholas may enclose the said woods and have them "in suo separabili," in exchange for four acres of his wood in Le Hautboys in Seal. The said Nicholas also, with consent of John, his son and heir, grants to the said Abbey permission to enclose "et in separabili optinere" all that piece of land which they formerly acquired "ad fugacionem averiorum suorum ad pasturam suam de Grymswode et Rothlastonewode," with land called La Gore. Witn. Dom. Geoffrey de Gresele, Dom. Rob. de la Warde, milites, Dom. Hugh de Kaue, rector ecclesie de Clyfton, etc. *Temp.* Edw. I. (Gresley 159.)

2034. GRANT from William de Marisco de Rostelaston to William le Waleys de Walton and Agnes his wife of five acres in Rostliston field, lying at Drakelowemere, Grettenfurlong, Le Toftes, Hungerhill,

Le Peteputtes, and Oxfurlong (outside the priest's garden). Witn. Roger Adam de Walton, William Dunstan, Robert de Fynderne, etc. Dat. Rosliston, Th. in Whitsun Week [2 June], 1 Edw. II. [1308.] (Gresley 169.)

2035. LEASE from Stephen de Segrave, in the name of his lord and father, John, Lord of Segrave, to William le Warde de Cotene of the mill of Rosliston, with suit of court. Rent, twenty shillings and sixpence; the said William finding as surety to observe the conditions of the lease Richard Deveneshire de Cotene. Dat. Tu. a. F. of St. Chad [2 Mar.], 9 Edw. II. [1316]. (Gresley 177.)

2036. GRANT from Ralph Mechel de Roslaston to William Talbot, jun., de Roslaston, of land in Rosliston. Witn. Rob. Fabel, Stephen le Warde, Will. le Warde. Dat. Rosliston, Tu. a. F. of St. Luke [18 Oct.], 16 Edw. II. [1322]. (Gresley 201.)

2037. GRANT from Robert Nichol de Rostelaston to William Talebot, senior, de Rostelaston, of two parts of a messuage and of land in Rosliston, which he formerly held, as it was divided between him and Cecily, his late daughter. Witn. Richard Mareys, Robert Mareys, Ralph Michel, etc. Dat. F. of Ascension [5 May], 16 Edw. II. [1323]. (Gresley 203.)

2038. LEASE from Richard le Mareys de Rostelaston to William fil. Willelmi Talbot de eadem, and Cecily his wife, of three selions of arable land in the fields of Rosliston, lying on Sonderlondus, Southfield, and Gratterfurlong; rent, a rose at Midsummer. Witn. William Talbot, sen., Robert le Mareys, William le Warde de Coton, etc. Dat. Rosliston, M. a. F. of St. Thomas [21 Dec.], 10 Edw. III. [1336]. (Gresley 245.)

2039. GRANT from William Scot de Rostelaston to Dom. Adam Gould, capellanus, and Richard Austyn de Herlaston, of a messuage and land in Rosliston and Coton which the said William inherited on the death of Richard and Margery Scot, his father and mother, with the goods, chattels, and growing crops on the same land, and the reversion of three acres of land which Nicholas le Meleward holds for his life in Coton. Witn. Stephen le Warde, William Talbot, Richard Isbel, etc. Dat. Rosliston, F. of Ass. of B. V. M. [15 Aug.], 18 Edw. III. [1344]. (Gresley 262.)

2040. QUITCLAIM from William fil. Willelmi Talbot de Roslaston to Alice, que fuit uxor Willelmi Talbot, and to John her son, of all those lands and tenements which the said Alice and John held in Rosliston by grant from John atte Calengewode, capellanus, and which the latter acquired from William Talbot, father of the above-mentioned W. Talbot. Witn. Dom. Ralph de Rostlaston, capellanus, John Hoky, Stephen Warde de Coton, etc. Dat. W. b. F. of St. Bartholomew [24 Aug.], 21 Edw. III. [1349]. (Gresley 274.)

2041. GRANT from William Talbot de Rostlaston, senior, to William his son of a moiety of a virgate of land in Rosliston which sometime belonged to William Talbot, father of the grantor, lying on Apultre-furlong, Bruggefurlong, Le Mere, Grettenefurlong, Wethslade, Blake-londes, etc. Witn. Richard Marreys, Robert Marreys, Nicholas Isbel, etc. Dat. Rosliston, Mon. a. F. of Ann. of B. V. M. [25 Mar.], 25 Edw. III. [1361]. (Gresley 294.)

17

2042. GRANT from William le Glover de Calton to John fil. Stephani de Coton, capellanus, of arable land in Rosliston lying on Brokforlong, Bruggeforlong, etc. Witn. William Talbot, Richard Mareys, Nicholas Isbel, etc. Dat. Rosliston, F. of St. Katherine [25 Nov.], 39 Edw. III. [1365]. (Gresley 303.)

2043. QUITCLAIM from Ralph de Pareys and John de Coton, capellani, to Henry fil. Roberti Mareys, clericus, of all their lands and tenements in Rosliston and Walton-on-Trent, which they had by grant from Alice, que fuit relicta Willelmi Talbot, sen., de Rosteleston. Witn. Stephen Warde, Richard Mareys, Nicholas Isbel. Dat. Fr. b. Conv. of St. Paul [25 Jan.], 41 Edw. III. [1368]. (Gresley 307.)

2044. GRANT from John Canne de Rostelaston to Richard de Blaggreiv, manens in Rostelaston, of a messuage in Rosliston. Witn. Richard Mareys, William Talbot, Stephen le Warde, etc. Dat. Tu. a. Michaelmas Day [29 Sept.], 42 Edw. III. [1368]. (Gresley 308.)

2045. GRANT from Robert Mareys to Henry Mareys, clericus, of a messuage with garden near the messuage of William Humbreston, rector ecclesie de Walton, with all his goods in the town and fields of Rosliston. Witn. Richard Mareys, Nicholas Isbel, John Canne, etc. Dat. Rosliston, Sat. a F. of St. Andrew [30 Nov.], 42 Edw. III. [1368]. (Gresley 309.)

2046. GRANT from Robert fil. et her. Ricardi Isbel to John de Coton, capellanus, and others, of the reversion of all the tenements and lands in Rosliston which Joan his mother holds during life, and which will fall to him on her death. Witn. Richard Marreys, Nicholas Isbel, John Canne, etc. Dat. Easter Mond. [2 Apr.], 43 Edw. III. [1369]. (Gresley 312.)

2047. QUITCLAIM from the same of the reversion of same lands. Same witnesses. Dat. Wed. a. F. of St. Barnabas [11 June], 43 Edw. III. [1369]. (Gresley 313.)

2048. SIMILAR grant from the same to the same of the lands and tenements in Rosliston, which fell to him on the death of John Isbel, his uncle. Same witnesses and date. (Gresley 314.)

2049. GRANT from Richard Blagreue, manens in Caldewalle, to Walter fil. Ricardi Mareys, of a messuage in Rosliston. Witn. John Abel, Stephen Warde, William Talbot, etc. Dat. Rosliston, S. a. F. of St. John a.p.l. [6 May], 48 Edw. III. [1374]. (Gresley 326.)

2050. QUITCLAIM from Henry Mareys, capellanus de Rostlaston, to Walter Mareys, of a messuage and garden in Rosliston, lying between the messuage of Richard Mareys and the messuage of the late William Humbreston, rector ecclesie de Walton-super-Trent. Witn. Stephen Warde, William Canne, John Abell, etc. Dat. Rosliston, S. a. F. of Holy Trinity [22 May], 3 Ric. II. [1380]. (Gresley 343.)

2051. GRANT from Nicholas Isabel al. vocatus Nicholas Grene de Allerwas to Walter Marreys de Rostlaston of all his lands and tenements in Rosliston. Witn. John Abel, William Marreys, Stephen Warde, etc. Dat. Whitsun Tuesday [12 June], 9 Ric. II. [1386]. (Gresley 347.)

2052. POWER of attorney by Nicholas Isabel, al. Nicholas Grene de Allerwas, to William Hood de Coton, to deliver seisin to Walter Marreys de Rostlaston of all his lands in Rosliston. [1386.] (Gresley 348.)

2053. LEASE from Walter Mareys de Rostlaston to William Mareys of a messuage with garden, land, and meadow in Rosliston, for term of his life. Witn. John Abell de Caldewell, Richard Scot de Rostlaston, John at-Walle de eadem. Dat. Rosliston, F. of St. Thomas [21 Dec.], 5 Hen. IV. [1403]. (Gresley 369, 370.)

2054. QUITCLAIM from Henry Mareys de Rostlaston, capellanus, to Walter Mareis of all the lands and tenements which the former acquired in Rosliston from Ralph de Paris and John de Coton. Same witnesses and date. (Gresley 371.)

2055. GRANT from Walter Marreys de Rostlaston to John Marreys his son of all his possessions in Rosliston and Linton and elsewhere in co. Derby. Witn. Thomas Gresley, mil., John Abell de Caldewelle, William Warde de Coton, etc. Dat. Sat. a. F. of St. Hilary [13 Jan.], 14 Hen. IV. [1413]. (Gresley 395.)

2056. GENERAL release from John fil. Johannis Sheperd, *al.* dicti Johannis atte Walle de Rostlaston, to John Mareys fil. Walteri Mareys de Roslaston. Dat. Th. a. F. of St. Martin [11 Nov.], 4 Hen. V. [1416]. (Gresley 399.)

2057. QUITCLAIM from Henry Marreys, capellanus, to John Marreys de Rostlaston of all his lands, etc., in Rostliston, which were some-time Robert Isabell's, and were conveyed by him to the said Henry Marreys and feoffees now deceased. Witn. Thomas de Gresley, mil., John Dethik, armiger, John Abell, etc. Dat. Rosliston, Thurs. in Easter week [27 Mar.], 9 Hen. V. [1421]. (Gresley 403.)

2058. GRANT from John Marreys to his brother Nicholas Marreys of the reversion of a messuage and virgate of land lately held by John Dawson, which will fall to him on the death of his mother Alice, widow of Henry Marreys, sen. Witn. Henry Holond, William Ward de Coton, John Thurmond. Dat. Rosliston, W. a. F. of Epiphany [6 Jan.], 18 Hen. VI. [1440]. (Gresley 418.)

2059. GRANT and quitclaim from John Marreys to Thomas Smyth de Thorp and Joan his wife, of a cottage and croft, etc., in Rosliston. Dat. 27 Feb., 1 Mar., 20 Hen. VI. [1442]. (Gresley 419, 420.)

2060. GRANT from John Marreys fil. et her. Johannis Marreys to Nicholas his brother, "nunc manens in Sneynton iuxta Notyngham," of a messuage and virgate of land adjacent in Rosliston. Witn. Richard Calangewode, Thomas Wylkynson, Ralph Blacgreve, etc. Dat. M. a. F. of St. Vincent [22 Jan.], 22 Hen. VI. [1444]. (Gresley 421.)

2061. QUITCLAIM from John Marreys fil. et her. Joh. Marreys to William de Shepey, nunc manens in Caldewall, of that messuage and virgate in Rosliston which the said William lately acquired by grant from Nicholas Marreys, his brother, "manens in Sneynton iuxta Notyngham." Witn. John Broun, Robert Thirmond de Lynton, William Warde de Coton. Dat. S. a. Epiph. [6 Jan.], 23 Hen. VI. [1445]. (Gresley 426.)

2062. GRANT and quitclaim from John Marreys fil. et her Joh. Marreys and Margery his wife to Roger Gyldyrson, of all his lands, etc., in Rosliston. Witn. John Broune, Ralph Blacgreve de Lynton, Richard Calengewod de Caldewall. Dat. 9, 10 Dec., 27 Hen. VI. [1448]. (Gresley 427, 428.)

2063. QUITCLAIM from Alice Hyll, nuper uxor Johannis Marreys, sen., to John Marreys her son, of all the lands, etc., which she had from her said husband. Witn. John Broune, Ralph Blacgreve, Richard Chalengewod. Dat. 4 Dec., 27 Hen. VI. [1448]. (Gresley 429.)

2064. QUITCLAIM from William Babyngton, knt., to Roger Gyldreson, sen., of all those lands, etc., in Rosliston, which lately belonged to Walter Marys or John Marys his son. Witn. John Gresley, John Abney, John Cursun. Dat. Nottingham, F. of St. Agnes [21 Jan.], 27 Hen. VI. [1449]. (Gresley 430.)

2065. QUITCLAIM from William Wade de Coton and Alice his wife, John their son, and Agnes le Granger, que fuit uxor Ricardi Graunger, to Roger Gyldurson, of lands, tenements, etc., in Rosliston. Witn. John Dyson, Stephen Warde, Ralph Blakegreue, etc. Dat. F. of St. Michael [29 Sept.], 29 Hen. VI. [1450]. (Gresley 432.)

2066. GRANT and quitclaim from Roger Gylderson de Brynsley in com. Nottingham, Katharine his wife, and John his son, to John Paunton de Burton super Trent, of all his lands, etc., in Rosliston, Caldewall, and Lynton in co. Derby. Witn. Nicholas Chamber, Ralph Blakgreue, Richard Dawson, etc. Dat. 16 Apr., 30 Hen. VI. [1452]. (Gresley 433, 434.)

2067. GRANT from Thomas Smyth de Thorp and Joan his wife to William Smyth their son and Joan his wife, of a cottage and croft in Rosliston, the croft being that sometime belonging to John Marreys. Witn. Nicholas Chaumber de Caldewall, John Andrewe, and William Andrewe. Dat. 31 March, 36 Hen. VI. [1458]. (Gresley 435.)

2068. GRANT from John Pawnton de Burton super Trent, peyntour, to Mag. Thomas Pawnton, capellanus, his son, and others, of all his possessions in Rosliston. Witn. Nicholas Chawmber, Richard Chalengewood, Richard Irpe, and others. Dat. F. of St. George [23 Apr.], 5 Edw. IV. [1465]. (Gresley 439.)

2069. GRANT from John, Duke of Norfolk, the Archbishop of Canterbury, the Bishop of Winchester, and others, to Robert Bernard, esquire, for his good services to the said Duke, of an annuity of £10 from Rostlaston [Rosliston] Manor. Dat. 11 Dec., 1465. (Berkeley 613.)

2070. GRANT from John Broune de Roslaston to John Greysley, mil., and John Dawson, of all his lands and hereditaments in Rosliston, Coton, and Repingdon. Witn. Thomas Greysley, arm., Thomas Curson, arm., William Bromwich. Dat. F. of St. Andrew [30 Nov.], 11 Edw. IV. [1471]. (Gresley 441.)

2071. QUITCLAIM from John Dison of Walton-on-Trent to Thomas Paunton, clerk, S.T.P., son and heir of John Paunton, late of Burton-on-Trent, to Richard Broun de Roslaston and Elizabeth his wife, of all the lands and tenements in Rosliston, Caldwall, and Lynton, co. Derby, which the said John and Thomas, jointly with other feoffees, lately held from John Paunton. Dat. 7 May, 1 Hen. VII. [1486]. (Gresley 453.)

2072. GRANT from Mag. Thomas Paunton, clerk, S.T.P., to Richard Broun of Rosliston and Elizabeth his wife, of all the lands and tenements in Rosliston, Caldwall, and Lynton mentioned in the preceding deed. Witn. John Dyson, Richard Irpe, John Irpe, etc. Dat. 18 May, 1 Hen. VII. [1486]. (Gresley 454.)

2073. GRANT from Elena, widow of John Broune, late of Rostlaston, to William Dawson, son of John Dawson of Rostlaston, of a messuage, etc., in Rosliston, a wood and land in Coton, with other lands in Rosliston, Coton, and Repingdon which she acquired by grant from her late husband; with attorney to Thomas Cowper and Geoffrey Cowper to deliver seisin. Witn. Henry Vernon, knt., William Gresley, esq., Thomas Dethek, esq., etc. Dat. 20 July, 19 Hen. VII. [1504]. (Gresley 460.)

2074. QUITCLAIM from the same to Richard Broune of all her possessions in Rosliston, Coton, and Repingdon. Dat. 15 Apr., 20 Hen. VII. [1505]. (Gresley 461.)

2075. BOND, in £20, from William Broune of Uttoxator, co. Staff., yeoman, to Richard Wakelen, yeoman, to ensure to the latter and to Margery his wife peaceable possession of two messuages in Rosliston. Dat. 6 Mar., 2 Hen. VIII. [1511]. (Gresley 464.)

2076. ACQUITTANCE from William Browne of Uttoxeter, yeoman, to Richard Wakelyn of Rosliston, yeoman, for six pounds rent for two messuages in Rosliston which the latter holds on lease for his life, and for a parcel of land in Coton, now tenanted by Joan Swanne, widow, which the said Richard holds on lease for a term of ten years, with covenant by the said William, in case of the said Richard's death within the said term, to allow his heirs and assigns to possess the land till the expiry of the term. Dat. 6 Nov., 9 Hen. VIII. [1517]. (Gresley 469.)

2077. ACQUITTANCE from the same to the same for a rent of four pounds for a house in Rosliston, late in the holding of Walter Nowell, but which the said Richard now holds on lease for a term of ten years. Dat. 12 Sept., 11 Hen. VIII. [1520]. (Gresley 470.)

2078. GRANT and quitclaim from William Browne, son of Ralph Browne, and brother and heir of Richard Browne of Uttoxator, to William Wakelen, of Rostlaston, of all those messuages in Rosliston which the said Ralph sometime acquired from Thomas Paunton, clerk, son and heir of John Paunton. Witn. Richard Bratte, Richard Penyfader, William Rogers, and John Bratte. Dat. 20 May, 13 Hen. VIII. [1521]. (Gresley 471, 472.)

2079. QUITCLAIM from Anne Browne of Uttoxator, widow of William Browne, to William Wakelen of Rostlaston, of her dower lands in Rostliston. Dat. 1 Feb., 27 Hen. VIII. [1536]. (Gresley 477.)

ROSLISTON *v.* also under BRETBY, COTES, GRESLEY, REPTON.

ROSTON.

(ROSSYNGTON, ROTYNGTON.)

2080. GRANT from John Houlot, chaplain, and Roger persona ecclesie de Staueley to Robert Scot of Rotyngton [Roston] and Agnes his wife, of a messuage and bovate of land in Rotyngton. Dat. Rotyngton, F. of St. Andrew [30 Nov.], 23 Edw. III. [1346]. (? Every.)

2081. GRANT from Thomas fitz-Herbert of Rossyngton to Sir Nicholas Montegomery, knt., John de Fyndeme, Henry Bothe, John Fitz-Herbert of Rossyngton and John Vernay of lands in Rossyngton, Hultone, and Egynton. Witn. John Blount, John Cokayn, knts., William de Lemystre of Snelston, etc. Dat. S. b. F. of SS. Tiburtius and Valerian [14 Apr.], 5 Hen. IV. [1404]. (Woll. x. 18.)

ROSTON *v.* also under NORBURY.

ROWLAND IN BAKEWELL.

(ROLAND, ROLOND.)

2082. GRANT from Godfrey de Rolond to Nicholas Martyn, chaplain, of lands which descended to him at the death of John de Rolond, his father, in the vills of Roland, Caluore, and in a place called "Eyom Clife." Witn. Will. Wakebruge, John de Langesdone, clerk, John Follgeame of Little Langesdone, etc. Dat. Nat. of St. John B. [24 June], 39 Edw. III. [1365]. (Woll. vii. 53.)

2083. GRANT from Thomas de Bentley and Johanna his wife to John Andrew and John Clerk, chaplains, Godfrey de Rolond, Nicholas Martyn, etc., of lands which descended to the said Johanna at the death of Nicholas Martyn, chaplain, her uncle, in Rolond, Calvere, and Eyom Clyf. Witn. Roger Lethe, Henry de Longesdone, John Wryght of Ashford, etc. Dat. Rolond, Th. a. F. of St. John, a.p.l. [6 May], 4 Hen. IV. [1403]. (Woll. vii. 58.)

2084. GRANT in tail from Nicholas Martyn of Folowe, John Andrewe, and John Clerk, chaplains, and William Meverelle to Margaret, daughter and heir of Roger de Roland of the manor of Rolond, which they held from Thomas de Benteley and Johanna his wife, kinswoman and heir of Nicholas Martyn, chaplain, within the lordship of Eyom and Calvouere, with remainder to Margery, daughter of Godfrey de Rolond and Stephen de Rolond. Witn. Thomas Foliamb, John Stafford, James Cottrell, etc. Dat. T. a. F. of Epiph. [6 Jan.], 10 Hen. IV. [1409]. (Woll. i. 91; vii. 59.)

2085. RELEASE from Johanna, widow of Thomas de Bentley of Tyddiswell, to John Stafford of Eyam and Margaret his wife, daughter and heir of Roger de Roland, and to John, their son, of lands which formerly belonged to Richard Martyn, chaplain, uncle of the said Johanna, in Roland, Calvore, and Eyom Clyf. Witn. Roger Massey of Heghlowe, Richard Stafford of the same, Nicholas Martyn of Folowe, etc. Dat. Eyom, Fr. a. F. of St. Edmund [20 Nov.], 11 Hen. VI. [1432]. (Woll. vii. 57.)

2086. RELEASE from John Stafford of Eyom and Margaret his wife to John Stafford their son of lands which he holds conjointly with Robert Stafford, esq., in Roland, Calfoure, and Eyom Clyf, otherwise Midyltone Clyf, in Eyom. Witn. Thomas Babyngton of Leghe, Henry de Pole, Thomas Wodrofe, etc. Dat. Roland, Nat. of St. John B. [24 June], 23 Hen. VI. [1445]. (Woll. vii. 56.)

2087. GRANT from Dame Margaret Stafford, widow of John Stafford, esq., to Richard Stafford, their son and heir, of lands in Eyham Clyf, *alias* Midylton Clyf, and five marks annuity out of the manor of Roland; with proviso for the cessation of the annuity and provision for the unmarried daughters of the grantor at the discretion of Thomas Foliambe, esq. Witn. Thomas Foliambe, esq., Henry Foliambe, James Foliambe, chaplain, etc. Dat. 4 Nov., 5 Edw. IV. [1465]. (Woll. vii. 55.)

ROWLAND IN BAKEWELL *v.* also under ASHFORD, LITTON.

ROWSLEY.

(ROULESLEY, MECHELL ROLLESLEY, ROULISLEY.)

2088. COPY of a grant from Robert, son of Ralph de Stantona, to Robert Albus [White] of Roulesley, of a sart of land in Roulisley; rent, 3*s.* Witn. Sir Simon Basseth, John and William, his sons, Alexander, son of Robert de Stant[one], etc. Fifteenth century. (Woll. ii. 2.)

2089. GRANT from Thomas Sapertone, James Graver, rector of Sud[bury], T[homas], rector of Cubley, to . . . of Wennesley, gent., of a rent of two marks, from lands in Mechell Rollesley which they held of the gift of [Nic]holas Mountgomery, esq. Dat. 1 May, 1 Hen. VII. [1486]. (Woll. x. 37.)

ROWSLEY *v.* also under HADDON, MONYASH.

SANDIACRE.

(SANDIAKYR.)

2090. GRANT from P[eter] de Sandiacre, Athelina his wife, and Peter his son to Robert fil. Willelmi of seven bovates of land in Sandiacre free from all service; rent, 3*s.* For this grant the said Robert gave the said Peter 20*s.* Late twelfth century. (Add. 47502.)

> P. de Sandiacre omnibus hominibus suis francis et anglis presentibus et futuris salutem. Sciatis quod recognoui et concessi Roberto filio Willelmi vii bouatas terre in Sandiacre cum omnibus pertinenciis suis intus et foris libere et quiete ab omni seruicio quod ad me pertinet per iii solidos annuatim reddendos eidem Rodberto et heredibus suis Ex recognicione xx solidos mihi persoluit. Hoc concedit uxor mea Athelina et filius meus Petrus. His testibus (*sic*) Radulfus de Wildebuef, Herbertus de Broncote et frater eius Helyas, Galfridus de Triwelle, Anchetillus de Berges, Picot de Barre, Ricardus Crassus, Andreas de Wimundewald, Galfridus Putrel, Willelmus Britto, Hugo filius Walteri, Osmundus, Rodbertus de Pec, Robertus filius Radulfi, Osbertus de Salloe, Rogerus filius Osmundi, Valete.

2091. CONFIRMATION from P[eter] de Sandiacre to Robert fil. Willelmi of the seven bovates of land in Sandiacre granted to him by his father (*v.* preceding charter). Late twelfth century. (Add. 47503.)

> P. de Sandiacre. Omnibus hominibus suis francis et anglis presentibus et futuris salutem. Sciatis quod ego confirmaui Roberto filio Willelmi cartam patris mei de vii bovatis terre in Sandiacre et quod concessi eidem Roberto predictas bovatas cum omnibus pertinentiis et heredibus suis tenendas de me et heredibus meis libere et quiete intus et foris ab omni seruicio quod ad me pertinet per iii solidos annuatim reddendos ad festum Sancti

Michaelis. Pro hac confirmatione et recognitione dedit mihi predictus Robertus unam marcam. His testibus Radulpho de Wildebof, Gaufrido de Trewelle, Herberto de Bromcote, Anchet[illo] de Berges, Pichot de la Barre, Andrea de Wimunde-wold, Roberto filio Walterii, Patrico Rosel, Ricardo Mareschaldo, Helia de Eituna, Gaufrido de Esseburn et Henrico Decano, Roberto de Burgelega, Waltero de Sandiacre, Henrico de Tuschet, Simone de Tuschet, Radulpho Affete, Baldewino de Sandiacre, Osberto armigero, Roberto de Pec, Roberto armigero.

2092. GRANT from Robert fil. Willelmi de Stapelford to Adam his son of four bovates of land in the vill of Sandiacre, namely, those two which Stephen fil. Gileberti held, and those two which Galfridus vicinus predicti Stephani held, with all appurtenances and with the men holding the said lands; the said Adam to pay two shillings yearly rent. Witn. Hugh de Muschamp, Richard de Camera, Geoffrey de Trowelle, Philip de Touke, Robert de Brancote, Richard de Alardestre, David Burdet, Robert Marescallus de Stapelford, Thomas de Brikesard, German fil. presbiteri de Stap[el]ford. Seal (man in armour on horseback). Early thirteenth century. (Add. 47505.)

2093. GRANT from Richard fil. Petri de Sandiacre to the Canons "de Parco Stanleg" [Dale Abbey] and all the free men of Sandiacre, of "totum Wersenape in territorio de Sandiacre" of his fee to their own uses and for common pasture. Witn. R. Prior of Lenton, Geoffrey de Sallicosa mara, Walter de Esthewyt tunc vic[arius], Phelip de Stretleg', William de Biling, William de Ponynton, Thomas de Henowre, Robert le Vavasur, Hugh de Morleg', Hugh de Wuormodisworthe, Robert fil. Petri de Sandiacre, clericus, John de Eston. Early Hen. III. (Add. 47506.)

2094. GRANT from William de Bigheleghe to Reginald de Meaudre of a toft and croft in the vill of Sandiacre which belonged to Robert fil. Toky, in exchange for another toft lying between the toft of Alan fil. Walteri de Sandiacre and the toft of Geoffrey Engin of the same vill. Witn. Dom. Walter de Estweit, Thomas de Henovere, Richard de Sandiacre, William his brother, Robert le Vavaseur, Hugh de Rampestone, etc. *Temp.* Hen. III. or Edw. I. (Lansd. 600.)

2095. GRANT from John de Bromle, carpenter, to Nicholas le Coupar of Sandiakyr and Emma his wife of a toft at the head of the south vill of Sandiakyr, and lying between the toft of William Faber de Sandiakyr and the meadow called Formedue, and between the king's way and the water called Yrewas. Rent, a rose yearly. Witn. Dom. Richard le Gray, John de Stoke, John le Marescal, Will. le Bay, Will. Barnarde, Hugh fil. Nigel, Peter de Betegge, etc. *Temp.* Edw. I. (Lansd. 601.)

2096. GRANT from William de Grey de Sandiacre to William Hasard de Sandiacre and Alice his wife, and to one of the heirs of their bodies, of the moiety of the messuage formerly held by Emma le Deye, and nine acres and one rood of land, with three roods of meadow in the territory of Sandiacre. Rent, 10s. yearly. Dat. Sandiacre, F. of St. Michael [29 Sept.], 2 Edw. III. [1328], (Lansd. 602.)

SANDIACRE *v.* also under DALE ABBEY, SUTTON IN DALE.

SAWLEY.

(SALLOWE.)

2097. GRANT from Roland, Bishop of Coventry and Lichfield, to his servants, Edward Edmondson and Geoffrey Edmondson his son, of the site of his manor of Sallowe, with a dovecot, garden, etc., together with the ferry and fishery of the Trent there, and pastures called " Sandholme," " Begeford," " Conyngre Lays," " Haysekewylons," " Bondmanhall," " Lytyll Seke," " Lytell Hallowe," and " Wylnepyk," with other pastures called " le Lordes pastures," three mills for grain, and one fulling-mill called " Wylne myll," for their lives. Dat. Ecclesall, 10 Oct., 1536. (P. R. O. c. 1368.)

SAWLEY *v.* also under WILNE.

SCARCLIFF.

(SCARDCLIF, SCARDECLIVE.)

2098. CONFIRMATION by Pope Adrian IV. to Rufford Abbey of various grants of land in Rufford, Cratele [in Wellow, co. Notts.], Barton [Barton-on-Humber, co. Linc.], Wilgebi [Willoughby, co. Notts.], Eikering [Eakring, co. Notts.], Snape in Muscamp [Muskham, co. Notts.], Kelum [Kelham, co. Notts.], and other places in co. Notts.; and all that land which the Abbey has of the gift of Ralph de Ainecurt and Matilda his wife, cultivated and uncultivated, in the territory of Scardecliue [Scarcliff, co. Derby]. Dat. Laterani, Non. Nov. [5 Nov.], 1156. (Harl. 111 A. 2.)

2099. GRANT from Richard, son of John Henrison of Scardclif, to Thomas his son and Alice Pepir in tail, of all their lands, tenements, etc., in Scardeclif which he had of the grant of Robert Beregge, clerk, and which the same Robert lately recovered from Roger Somer, together with all the lands, etc., the wood of Scoulewode, and wastes in Thikclif which he had, of the grant of the same Robert, and which formerly belonged to Richard Hikson, chaplain, with remainder successively in tail to Richard, son of Peter Parker of Scardclif, and to Thomas his brother. Dat. 1 July, 1 Hen. V. [1413]. (Foljambe.)

SCROPTON.

2100. GRANT from Edmund fil. Henrici Regis Anglie to Robert de Creccon de Foston of ten acres of land of his waste of Scropton and Foston, of which three acres lie in the moor of Foston and Scropton, three acres near the mill of Mackeleye, three acres between le Witefeld and Copplowe, and one acre on Cleyenewitheges. Witn. Dom. William Withet, Dom. Roger Brabazon, Ralph de Rolleston, Robert Schiret, Roger Wildegos, Walter Acard, etc. Dat. apud Tutt' [? Tutbury], F. of Nat. of B. V. M. [8 Sept.], 14 Edw. I. [1286]. (Mundy.)

2101. GRANT from Henry Porteioye to John de Crectone of two acres of land in the territory of Scropton lying in Stoniacris, Scheteners, Plumtrefurlong, Hongindehul, and Bradefurlong. Witn. William de Mortimer, Thomas Morel, John de Pilkote, William Wildegos, etc. Dat. Scropton, W. a. Pentecost [17 May], 1296. (Mundy.)

2102. GRANT from William fil. Thome Morel of Scropton to John fil. Roberti de Cretton, living at Foston, and Elizabeth his wife, of four selions of land in the fee and territory of Scropton and Foston in Le Flecherusholm. Witn. William Wildegos of Foston, John Wildegos, William le Mortimer de Scropton. Dat. Scropton, S. a. F. of Ann. of B. V. M. [25 Mar.], 1305. (Mundy.)

2103. QUITCLAIM from Agnes quondam uxor Roberti de Creyton to John fil. Roberti de Creyton of her dower lands in Scropton and Foston. Witn. Henry clericus de Foston, Thomas Acard, Hugh Rudde, Henry Mascory. Dat. at Foston, F. b. F. of St. Cedda, Bp. [7 Jan.], 13 Edw. II. [1320]. (Mundy.)

2104. GRANT from William . . . . de Scroptone to Thomas Acard of all his land in a certain place called "le Newemedewe" in the fields of Scropton. Witn. Thomas de Mackary, etc. Dat. 16 Edw. II. [1322-3]. (Add. 4848.)

2105. GRANT from Henry Bonefaunt, chaplain, to John Rose de Scropton and Agnes his wife of two acres of land in the neighbourhood of Scropton and Farleston. Dat. M. b. F. of All Saints' [1 Nov.], 1331. (Add. 1058.)

2106. GRANT from Henry de Mershton, vicar of Tuttebury, and William de Lucy, chaplain, to Henry, son of Thomas Chaundeler of the same, of two burgages in Tuttebury and lands in Scroptone. Witn. William de Burton, John Davy, Henry Mason, etc. Dat. S. a. F. of St. Gregory [12 Mar.], 46 Edw. III. [1372]. (Add. 26104.)

2107. GRANT from Henry, son of Thomas le Chaundiler of Tutbury, to William de Burton of the same, of land in Scropton. Witn. John Took, Rob. Brese, Symon Godriche, etc. Dat. Th. b. F. of Inv. of Holy Cross [3 May], 46 Edw. III. [1372]. (Add. 26101.)

2108. RELEASE by Johanna, daughter of Thomas le Chaundeler of Tutbury, widow, to William de Burton of the same, of lands in Scropton held of Henry his brother. Witn. John Took, Robert Brese, Thomas Acard, etc. Dat. S. b. F. of St. John, a.p.l. [6 May], 46 Edw. III. [1372]. (Add. 26103.)

2109. RELEASE by Richard Pasmere of Tutbury to William de Boureton of the same, of lands in Scropton held of Henry le Chaundeler. Witn. John Took, Robert Brese, Thomas Acard, etc. Dat. S. b. F. of St. John, a.p.l. [6 May], 46 Edw. III. [1372]. (Add. 26102.)

2110. GRANT from John de Pulteney, Simon Broke, and John Skryven to Lawrence Fyton, Robert le Heuster, parson of the church of Bousworthe, and Stephen del Rowe, clerk, of all the lands, etc., in Annesley and Scropton, which they lately had of the feoffment of Thomas Greseley, John Kenling, Henry Ive, Laurence Braybon, clerk, and Catherine, late the wife of Henry le Wryght of Rolleston. Dat. F. of Pur. of B. V. M. [2 Feb.], 15 Hen. IV. (*sic*). (P. R. O. B. 80.)

2111. QUITCLAIM from Thomas Chedelle, formerly of Broghton, co. Derby, to William Burton de Tuttebury of his title to lands and tenements in the lands of Scropton. Witn. Thos. Acard, etc. Dat. "in vigilia carniprivii" [25 Feb.], 17 Hen. VI. [1438]. (Add. 4862.)

2112. EXTRACT from a view of frank-pledge held at Scropton on the F. of SS. Philip and James [1 May], 23 Hen. VII. [1508], of the admission of William Ayld and William his son to a tenement and land [in Scropton]. (Woll. vi. 17.)

2113. EXTRACT of roll of a court held at Scroptone, on Tuesday, F. of St. Luke [18 Oct.], 1 Hen. VIII. [1509]. (Add. 4865.)

SCROPTON *v.* also under FOSTON, MATLOCK.

SEDSALL.

(SEDDISSALL, SEGESALE, SEGESHALE, SEGGESALE, SEGGESHALE.)

2114. GRANT from William, son of Henry de Seggesale, to John Wymme de Uttokesathe and Walter his brother, of three acres of land in the fields of Seggesale. Witn. John le Mareschal, Ric. le Serjaunt, etc. Dat. S. a. Nat. of B. V. M. [8 Sept.], 13 Edw. III. [1340]. (Add. 4883.)

2115. GRANT from John Whyteheved de Assheborne to Nicholas de Beerd of a messuage and three acres of land in Segeshale. Witn. Will. de Montegomery, dominus de Segesale, John del Brugge, Andrew del Brugge, William Hankynsone, etc. Dat. T. a. F. of Beheading of St. John Bapt. [29 Aug.], 30 Edw. III. [1356]. (Add. 4884.)

SEDSALL *v.* also under THURVASTON.

SHARDLOW.

(SARDELOVA, SCHARDELOWE.)

2116. REMEMBRANCER'S Roll in the account of John ate Halle for the service of the Manor of Schardelowe at Coulynges from S. a. F. of Pur. of B. V. M. [2 Feb.] to Michaelmas [29 Sept.] following, 1331. (Add. 5245.)

SHARDLOW *v.* also under MORLEY.

SHATTON.

(SCHATTON, OVER SHATTON.)

2117. GRANT from Robert fil. Elie de Bradewell and Alice his wife to Dom. Thomas Foleiaumbe of Tediswell fil. Thome Foleiambe, mil., of a yearly rent of 12d. secured upon their lands in Schatton. Witn. Richard fil. Will. Foleiambe of Wormhull, Nicholas Foleiaumbe, Ralph Coterell. Dat. Tedeswell, S. a. F. of St. John a.p.l. [6 May], 26 Edw. I. [1298]. (Foljambe.)

2118. GRANT from Hugh de Streley to John Talbot, Lord Talbot and Fournyvall, Roger Stedman, and Richard Worteley, of a capital messuage and lands, etc., called "Over Shatton" in the Peak. Dat. Shatton, F. of Inv. of Holy Cross [3 May], 2 Hen. VI. [1424]. (P. R. O. c. 3362.)

2119. RELEASE by William del Bour', son of John del Bour' of Quytefeld to William del Brome, chaplain, of lands in Shatton, Burghe, Thornehulle, and Astone, and a forestry in Eydale. Witn. Richard le Vernoun, knt., John del Pole of Hertyngtone, Richard de Pylkyngton, etc. Dat. Shattone, Fr. a. F. of St. Matthew [21 Sept.], 7 Hen. VI. [1428]. (Woll. iii. 12.)

SHATTON *v.* also under BRADWELL.

SHELDON

(SHELADON, SHELLADON),

v. under ASHFORD, CHAPEL-EN-LE-FRITH, HADDON.

SHIPLEY.

(SHIPELEY.)

2120. GRANT from John Strelley, esq., to Henry Willoughby, Gervase Clifton, John Dygby, knts., Simon Dygby, Edward Stanop, and Roland Dygby, esquires, of all his lordship's manors, lands, etc., in Strelley, Billeborough, Trowell, Chilwell, Addenborough, Ratclyf-upon-Trent, South Leverton, Notyngham, Lenton, Muskeham, Oxton, Colson Basset, Bramcote, Codgrave, Stapulford, Wheteley, North Leverton, Hemsell and Baseforth, co. Notts., and Shipeley, Mapurley, and Langeley, co. Derby; with letter of attorney authorising Robert Strelley and Richard Baker to deliver seisin. Witn. John Babyngton, knt., Thomas Kebeell, one of the king's serjeants at law, and William Brett. Dat. 1 March, 11 Henry VII. [1496]. (P. R. O. c. 3270.)

SHIPLEY *v.* also under ILKESTON.

SHIREBROOK IN PLEASLEY.

(SCHIRBROK.)

2121. GRANT from John Bairg of Skardeclive to Richard de Dethek, capellanus, of all his lands, etc., in Schirbrok. Witn. Hugh Stuffyn, Thomas de Skyrbrok, John Salvage, etc. Dat. M. a. Tr. of St. Thomas [7 July], 13 Edw. II. [1319]. (Foljambe.)

SHIRLEY.

(SCHIRLEY.)

2122. GRANT from Ralph de Schirley, miles, to Nicholas de Marchyntone of a place of land in Schirley in exchange for other land there. Dat. Morr. of F. of Inv. of H. Cross [3 May], 4 Edw. II. [1311]. (Woll. ix. 20.)

SHIRLEY *v.* also under YEAVELEY.

SHUCKTHORN *v.* under PLAISTOW.

SMALLEY.

2123. DEMISE by Henry Rolleston, John Bradshawe, William Dethik, clerk, William Saucheverell, Henry Stathum, and Henry Reddeford, chaplain, to William Zouche and Joan, his wife, daughter and heiress of Henry Stathum, late lord of Morley, for their lives, of all the messuages and lands, etc., in Smalley, which they had of the grant of the said Joan, with remainder to her right heirs; also letter of attorney authorising Milo Blackwall and Thomas Mongombre to deliver seisin of the said premises. Dat. 18 May, 2 Hen. VII. [1487]. (P. R. O. B. 3360.)

SMALLEY *v.* also under MORLEY.

SMISBY.

(SMITHESBI, SMYTHESBY.)

2124. RELEASE from Ralph Payn of Caldewelle, chaplain, to John de Irland, son of Ralph de Irland of Horteshorn, of lands in Smythesby. Witn. Robert de Howe of Sekyntone, Thomas de Barlastone of Blacfordeby, John Pylle of Smythesby, etc. Dat. Smythesby, T. a. F. of St. Valentine [14 Feb.], 57 Edw. III. [1377]. (Woll. i. 89.)

SMISBY *v.* also under CALK.

SNELSTON.

(SNELLESDONE, SNELLESTON, SNELSTONE, SYLENESTON.)

2125. COVENANT between B[artholomew], Prior, and the Convent of Totesbir' [Tutbury], and Hugh de Aucoure and his heirs, that the Prior and Convent have granted to the said Hugh all their culture which is of their demesne beyond the bridge "hanging" towards Aucoure, between the road leading from Maafelt [Mayfield] to Aucoure and the Dove, with three selions besides, contiguous to the said culture in the part towards Aucoure; and the said Hugh has granted to the church of St. Mary and the monks serving there all his culture between the mill of Syleneston [Snelston, co. Derb.] and the fields of Maafelt on either side the Dove, which he retained in his own demesne of the land which he gave to Geoffrey his brother in Syleneston. Witn. Dom. William [de Ferrariis], Comes Derbe, Raginald de Kard', Dapifer, Stephen capellanus, John capellanus, Henry de Braillefort, William de Grendon, Geoffrey de Aucoure, Nicholas de Cauueland, Robert de Syrefort, Robert de Bec, Robert de Lee, Henry de Daneston, William de Ypestanes. Early thirteenth century [1200-1225]. Fragments of two seals. (Okeover.)

2126. GRANT from Matildis de Grendona to Roger de Accouere her son of all that land of his inheritance extending from the croft of Ralph fil. Willelmi tunc tenentis, to the ditch which divides the two cultures which extend from the king's way to Lutlewodebroc, with the meadow belonging to the said land; to hold by tenure of a pair of white gloves at Easter. Witn. Dom. Robert de Accouere, Dom. William de Mungomery, Dom. Robert de Esseburne, Dom. Thomas de Ednesouere, Dom. Richard de Ednesouere, Oliver le Foun, Ranulf de Westona, Henry le Foun. *Temp.* Edw. I. (Okeover.)

2127. LEASE from Adam Forestarius de Snelleston to William de le Hul in Snelleston of an acre of land in the fee of Snelleston, extending from the land of the late Adam Ody up to Littelwodebroc, to hold till the said William has had five crops from the land at the rent of a red rose on St. James' Day [25 July]. Witn. John Baule, William de Grendon, Henry de Thorp, Robert le Walour, Hugh de Thokeby, John le Ou, clericus. Dat. Michaelmas Day, 1285. (Okeover.)

2128. GRANT from William de Grendon fil. Serlonis de Grendon to Walter Mountegomery of messuages, etc., in Snelstone. Witn. Nicholas Herbert, John Terry, Henry Pees, etc. *Circ.* 1350. (Foljambe.)

2129. RELEASE from William Pachet, clericus, to Walter Mount-gomery and his heirs male in tail of a messuage and lands in Snelstone, with remainder in tail to William Mountgomery. Witn. William de Grendon, John Pachet, Henry Pees, etc. *Circ.* 1350. (Foljambe.)

2130. GRANT from Philip de Okoure, miles, to the Prior of Callewych, Thomas de Marchyngton, and Thomas de Shene, of all the lands and tenements, etc., which fell to the said Philip on the death of Thomas de Hoppewell in Snelleston of the inheritance of the late Robert de Stanton, and all his lands in Mapelton and Stanton. Witn. Nicholas de Longeford, John Cokayn, knts., Robert del Hull de Snellestun, John Broun, Adam Felcok de Mapelton. Dat. apud Snelleston, S. a. F. of St. Hilary [13 Jan.], 20 Ric. II. [1397]. (Okeover.)

2131. GRANT from Isabel, widow of Thomas del Hull de Snell-eston, to Henry de Knyveton, rector of the church of Norbury, and Henry Wallour, chaplain of lands in cos. Derby and Stafford inherited by her after the death of Isabel, widow of John Shaille and daughter and heiress of John de Hambury. Witn. Nicholas Mountegomery, John Cokayn, John Bagot, John de Ardern, milites, etc. Dat. at Snelston, M. a. Michaelmas, 7 Hen. IV. [1405]. (Stowe 64.)

2132. RENTAL of Okover lands in Calton [co. Staff.], Schene [Sheen, co. Staff.], and Snellesdone [Snelston]. Early fifteenth century. Imperfect. (Okeover.)

2133. GRANT from Thomas Okouere de Okouere to Henry, Abbot of Rocester, Richard Falthurst, parson of Kyngeley, Humphrey Walker of Casterne, and Thomas Lokwode of Thornebery, of a pasture called Coldewall, with a pasture called Brendewode in the demesne of Okouere, and all rents in Blore Woodhowse, with a piece of meadow in Wodehousse, and another pasture called Cokshuthull, in the demesne of Snelleston. Witn. Sampson Meverell, knt., John Curson, John Pole. Dat. Okeouer, 6 Sept., 18 Hen. VI. [1439]. (Okeover.)

2134. QUITCLAIM from Thomas Okouere of Okouere to Henry, Abbot of Rocestre, Richard Falthurst, parson of Kyngeley, Humphrey Walker of Casterne, and Thomas Locwod of Thornebery, of a pasture called Coldewall, and another pasture called Brendwode in the lord-ship of Okouere, with all appurtenances in Blore and Wodhowse, a piece of meadow in Blore and Wodhowse [co. Staff.], a pasture called Cokshuthill in the lordship of Snelleston, co. Derb. Witn. Samson Meverell, knt., John Curson, John Pole. Dat. Okouere, 9 Sept., 18 Hen. VI. [1439]. (Okeover.)

2135. COVENANT between Thomas Okouere and Raufe Basset for the marriage of Philip Okouere, cousin and heir of the said Thomas, with Thomasine, daughter of the said Rauf, and for the settling on the same, lands in Coldewall, Blore, Woodhouses, co. Staff., and in Snelleston, co. Derby. Dat. Okouere, 20 Sept., 18 Hen. VI. [1439]. (Okeover.)

2136. QUITCLAIM from John Broune of Snelston, clericus, to Thomas de Okouer, esquire, of all the manors, lands, etc., which he, the said John, held jointly with Ralph Basset, esquire, deceased, by grant from the said Thomas, in cos. Derby and Stafford. Dat. 28 Nov., 34 Hen. VI. [1455]. (Okeover.)

2137. GRANT from Thomas Lokwod to Philip Okouere of Okouere, esquire, and Thomasine his wife, of all his lands in Coldwalle, an enclosure called Brendwode, and a piece of land in Wodhows, near Blore, now in the tenure of Thomas Serle and Robert Lont, a rent of 20s. in Wodhows, land in Hyllemedowe, within the township of Wodhous, and in a pasture called Cokshuthill in Snelleston, co. Derby, which the said Thomas had of the Abbot of Rocester and Richard Faltehurst, rector of Kyngeley, of the feoffment of Thomas Okouere, esquire. Witn. John Curson of Ketelston, Nicholas Knyveton of Mircaston, William Basset of Blore, esquires, Humphrey Walker of Castern, gent., and William Tayllour of Meygnelongley. Dat. apud Longley, 20 Dec., 34 Hen. VI. [1455]. (Okeover.)

2138. POWER of attorney from Thomas Lokwod to William Sonde, rector of Blore, to deliver seisin to Philip Okouere of the lands described in preceding charter. Same date. (Okeover.)

2139. RENTAL of Richard Okover, esquire, for Snelston, viz., rents of assize of free tenants there, renewed 19 Jan., 4 Hen. VII. [1489], to be paid at the Feasts of Nat. of St. John Bapt. [24 June] and St. Martin-in-Hieme [11 Nov.] by equal portions; with rents of the farmers there and at Atlow, Mapulton, Ilom, Yeldersley, and Okover. (Okeover.)

2140. COVENANT for the marriage of Rondulf Eggerton, esq., with Isabel, dau. of Robert Hill, deceased, and of Alice his wife, now the wife of Rob. Woode, and the settlement on them of lands, etc., in Snelston of the yearly value of six marks. Dat. 20 Jan., 18 Hen. VII. [1503]. (P. R. O. c. 2751.)

2141. GRANT in trust from Humphrey Oker of Oker, esquire, to John Aston, knt., Thomas Cokkeyn, Humphrey Bradburne, esquires, John Blounte, Thomas Blounte, and William Hyll, chaplain, of his manor of Oker [Okeover], co. Staff., with all his lands, etc., in Oker, Wodhouse, Ilome [Ilam], and Castorne [Casterne], in the said county, with his manors of Snelston and Atlowe, with lands, etc., in Snelston, Atlowe, Mapulton, and Yeldersley, co. Derby; with attorney to Thurston Lance and William Trubsha to give seisin. Dat. 22 June, 23 Hen. VII. [1508]. (Okeover.)

2142. (*a*) RENTAL of Humphrey Okouer renewed 19 November, 6 Hen. VIII. [1514], in Snelston; (*b*) Rents of farmers paid quarterly for lands in Atlow; (*c*) Rents, as above, for Mapulton; (*d*) Rents, as above, for Yyldersley; (*e*) Rents, as above, for Wodhowse; (*f*) "Ilum and Castorne for chef Rentt"; (*g*) "Okover lordschype." (Okeover.)

2143. "THE Replicacion of Humfrey Okouer (*ob.* Apr., 30 Hen. VIII.) to the vnswere of John Fitzherbert," relating to an exchange of land called "the Morewalles," etc., in Snelston. *Temp.* Hen. VIII. (Okeover.)

SNELSTON *v.* also under ATLOW, CUBLEY, SUDBURY.

SNITTERTON.

2144. GRANT from Dom. Gerard de Suttone, miles, to William de Aldewerk of a selion of land lying between the lands of Dom. Robert de Marcham and Ralph fil. Gilberti de Snuterton at the west of the vill, in exchange for as much land in Snuterton lying near the land of Dunyig de Snuterton. Witn. Dom. Robert de Marcham, Ralph de Rerisby, Robert de Wednisleya, Henry de Matlac. *Temp.* Hen. III. (Woll. x. 4.)

2145. GRANT from Ranulph de Snyterton to John de Sutton of nine butts and a rood of land in exchange for half an acre and a rood in Snyterton. Witn. Roger de Wednslegh', John de Derlegh', Laurence Coterel, etc. Dat. F. of St. Gregory [12 Mar.], 1319[20]. (Woll. i. 1a, Woll. x. 64a.)

2146. RELEASE from Ranulph de Sniterton to John, fil. et her. Johannis de Sutton of an orchard and land in Sniterton, in exchange for other lands there. Witn. Roger de Wednesleye, Henry de Hopton, William de Hopton, etc. *Temp.* Edw. II. (Woll. x. 9.)

2147. GRANT from Richard de Dethek fil. Roberti de Dethek, knt., to John de Kynardeseye, jun., and Joan his wife of two parts of a moiety of the manor of Lee, near Dethek, together with the reversion of the third part of the said moiety (which Ranulph de Snitt[ert]on and Cecily his wife held by name of the said Cecily's dowry which she had from Thomas de Ferrariis, her late husband, on the said Cecily's death, with remainder, on failure of issue, to the said John and Jean, to Geoffrey fil. Roberti de Dethek. Witn. Dom. John de Heriz, Dom. Adam de Rerisby, Geoffrey de Dethek, etc. Dat. F. of St. Bartholomew [24 Aug.], 1 Edw. III. [1327]. (Holland.)

2148. GRANT from Henry de Suttone to Dom. Hugh fil. Alani de Ednessouere, chaplain, of all his lands, etc., in Snitterton and Matlock, which he inherited after the death of John and Thomas his brothers. Witn. John de Dethek, Roger de Wednesl', Ranulph de Snytertone, Gerard de Wednesl', etc. Dat. F. of St. Thomas [21 Dec.], 1350. (Woll. x. 13.)

SNITTERTON *v.* also under ASHBOURNE.

SOMERSALL IN BRAMPTON.

2149. BOND, in £40, from John Hygdon of Brimington to John Schawe of Somersall not to challenge the title of the latter to lands which were late Thomas Schawe's, father of the said John Schawe, in Somersall, Chesterfield, Walton, Brampton, Baslowe, Bubnell, Chatsworth, Hope, and Castelton. Dat. Tu. b. F. of St. Katharine [25 Nov.], 1 Hen. VII. [1485]. (Woll. iii. 72.)

2150. SIMILAR bond from Margaret Schawe, one of the daughters of Thomas Schawe, late of Somersall, to her brother John Schawe. Same date. (Woll. iii. 76.)

SOMERSALL HERBERT.

(CHERCHSOMERSALE, CHIRCHESOMERSALE, KIRKE SOMERSALE, SOMERSALE, SOMERSALE HERBERD'.)

2151. GRANT from Thomas fil. Willelmi Hereberti de Somersale to the church and canons of Rocester [co. Staff.] of four acres of land in Somersale which Richard fil. Symonis Bacun holds. Witn. Dom. Robert del Per', Hamo de Saperton, John Morel, Thomas de Mackelega, John fil. Symonis de Foston. *Temp.* Hen. III. (D. A. J. iv. 5.)

2152. QUITCLAIM from Hugh de Almunton to Thomas fil. Willelmi fil. Herberti de Somersale, his lord, of two bovates of land in Somersale. Witn. Dom. William de Montegomery, William de Meysam, knt., Dom. Peter de Bakepuz, Robert de Segeshale, Walter de Bosco, Richard fil. Herberti, clericus. *Temp.* Hen. III. (D. A. J. iv. 5.)

2153. LEASE for life from William de Mounttgomery to Thomas le Croweknaue of Conibruge, of land in Somersale to be held by his assigns for twenty years in the event of his death within that period; rent, 13*s.* Witn. Robert de la Mulnetone, Robert de Segishale, Ralph de Bosco of Douerebruge, etc. Dat. F. of Ann. of B. V. M. [25 Mar.], 15 Edw. I. [1287]. (Woll. ix. 55.)

2154. QUITCLAIM from Thomas fil. Herberti, Dominus de Somersale, to Walter fil. domini Willelmi de Saundeby, of three shillings annual rent [in Somersale], which the said Walter has purchased from William fil. Ricardi de Kyngistonleys, and which Alan Champeneys de Mercinton was accustomed to pay to the said William. Witn. Dom. William de Mongummery, Dom. Brian de Sancto Petro, Robert de Segisshal, etc. *Temp.* Edw. I. (D. A. J. iv. 7.)

2155. QUITCLAIM from William fil. Ricardi de Kyngestonlehees to Walter fil. dom. Will. de Saundeby of the homage and service (namely, an annual rent of three shillings) of Alan fil. Will. Champeneys, in respect of land in Somersale Herbert; and a grant of half an acre of meadow in Le Wytedoles in Somersale which Richard fil. Mathei de Schauynton held, paying an annual rent on the Feast of St. Blaise [3 Feb.] of one halfpenny. Witn. Dom. William de Montegomori, Richard de Kyngesley, Robert de Seggeshal. *Temp.* Edw. I. (D. A. J. iv. 7.)

2156. RELEASE from William fil. Ricardi de Kyngestonlehees to Walter de Saundeby of an annual rent of one halfpenny from half an acre of meadow in Somersale. Witn. William de Montegomore, Robert de Seggeshal, Richard de Kyngesley, John Wace, etc. *Temp.* Edw. I. (D. A. J. iv. 8.)

2157. LEASE from Alan de Denston to Elias del Lee de Nether Somersale of a messuage and lands in Uver Somersale, for forty years. Witn. Nicholas fitz-Herbert, Thomas fil. Margerie, John Erle, etc. Dat. apud Bretton, Vig. of St. Martin [10 Nov.], 11 Edw. II. [1317]. (Trusley.)

2158. RELEASE, for life, from Walter de Montegomery, mil., Dominus de Sudbury, to William fil. Alexandri de Somersale of the moiety of a messuage with land which Henry le Bercher held in Somersale Wodehousus; rent, 10*s.* Witn. Nicholas FitzHerbert de Somersale, Thomas Wace of Malkeley, Thomas fil. Margerie de Somersale. Dat. Murchinton Mongomery, Fr. a. F. of the Epiphany [6 Jan.], 11 Edw. II. [1318]. (Woll. ix. 56.)

2159. GRANT from Nicholas fil. Thome fil. Herberti de Somersale to Walter de Saundeby of a messuage and bovate of land which the latter had by grant from Alan fil. Will. Chaumpeneys in Somersale Herberd and a half-acre of meadow which Richard de Schauinton leased to him. Witn. Dom. Ralph de Munjoye, William de Mungomeri, Henry de Knyveton, Richard de Kyngesley. *Temp.* Edw. II. (D. A. J. iv. 9.)

18

2160. GRANT from Richard fil. Rob. de Mungomery to Henry fil. Thome fil. Herberti de Somersale and Roger his brother of land and meadow which he had from Henry fil. Thom. de Littlewode in Chirchesomersale. Witn. Nicholas fil. Herberti, John de Benteleye, Richard de Schauinton, etc. *Temp.* Edw. II. (D. A. J. iv. 10.)

2161. GRANT in tail from Thomas de le Lee de Somersale to William his son and Agnes fil. Benedicti de Shalcross his wife of the land in Lower Somersale which he purchased from Robert his brother and from William de Saundebi. Witn. Dom. Henry fiz Herebert, chaplain of Somersale, William ad-boscum de Doubregge, John de Schawenton. Dat. apud Scalecros, Vig. of St. James [24 July], 1325. (D. A. J. iv. 11.)

2162. LEASE, for sixteen years, from Walter de Mountegomery, knt., Lord of Sudbury, to John de Somery, chaplain, of a messuage and lands in Somersale, which Thomas, his brother, formerly held; rent, 11s. Witn. Henry de Delastone, Roger atte Yate, William atte Lone. Dat. Cubbeley, S. a. F. of St. James [25 July], 23 Edw. III. [1349]. (Woll. ix. 58.)

2163. GRANT from Edmund Hayward, chaplain, to John Edrech, jun., and Margery his wife, of all his lands in Somersale which he had by feoffment from the same John, with remainder to John Edrech fil. Walteri Edrech de Somersale. Witn. John Somersale, Thomas Boteler, Thomas Hardyng, etc. Dat. Sudbury, Whitsun Eve [21 May], 13 Hen. IV. [1412]. (D. A. J. iv. 14.)

2164. GRANT, in tail, from John Fitzherbert de Somersale to John Fitzherbert his son of a messuage and two bovates of land in Kirke Somersale, and the rent from a messuage and three bovates of land there which Henry by-ye-broke holds; with a messuage and bovate of land in Potter Somersale which he acquired from Thomas Okeyly, parson of Sudbury, Edward Bretby, and John Tadynton, chaplains, and a close called Dicheryddynge, in the fee of Dubbrige [Doveridge], and all those lands in Perwyche [Parwich] which he acquired from John in-le-Lene and Isabella his wife. Dat. F. of St. John B. [24 June], 1 Hen. VI. [1423]. (D. A. J. iv. 14.)

2165. GRANT from John Fyzherbert of Somursale to John Attebroke to William Fyzherbert, his uncle, John Myners of Uttoxeter, esquire, William Nodyon, chaplain, and Robert Attebrok, rector of Somersale, of all his lands in cos. Derby and Leicester. Witn. John Mydulton, William Perkyn, bailiff of Uttoxeter, etc. Dat. All Saints' Day, 18 Hen. VI. [1439]. (D. A. J. iv. 16.)

2166. GRANT from Robert Fraunces and Elizabeth his wife to John Fyzherbert of Somursale, son and heir of John Fyzherbert, deceased, of all the lands in Somersale which the said Elizabeth had jointly with her late husband, John Fyzherbert, of the grant of Adam Welton and Robert Brok, clerk. Witn. Robert de Aston, Richard Bagot, John Kynerdesley, John Myners, and William Perkyn, bailiff of Uttoxeter. Dat. 3 July, 38 Henry VI. [1460]. (D. A. J. iv. 17.)

2167. GRANT from Henry Kynerdesley of Uttoxather and Henry Mayster to John Fytzherbert of Cherchsomersale and Joan his wife of their manor of Church Somersale. Dat. 28 Aug., 38 Hen. VI. [1460]. (D. A. J. iv. 17.)

2168. GRANT from Joan Ade of Sudbury, widow, to John Fightharbart (*sic*) and Joan his wife, of all lands in Church Somersale, which late belonged to her father, John Edrich. Dat. Th. b. SS. Simon and Jude [28 Oct.], 4 Edw. IV. [1464]. (D. A. J. iv. 18.)

2169. BOND between John Madeley of Denston, co. Staff., to John Mountgomery of Cubley, knt., in £40 to ensure a conveyance to the latter of three closes in the lordship of Hyll Somersale. Dat. 6 June, 22 Hen. VII. [1507]. (Trusley.)

SOMERSALL HERBERT *v.* also under CUBLEY.

SOUTHWOOD *v.* under DUFFIELD.

SPINKHILL.

(SPYNKHILL.)

2170. GRANT, in tail, from John Spynkhill of Spynkhill to Richard Ince, his kinsman, of lands in Spynkhill, Barleburgh, and Staveley. Witn. Thomas Gansell of Barlburgh, sen., William Plumley of Plumley, esquires, John Rodys of Staveley Wodthorpe, etc. Dat. F. of St. Edm., Bp. [? 16 Nov.], 2 Edw. IV. [1462]. (Woll. vi. 58.)

SPONDON.

2171. GRANT from Henry fil. Nigelli de Spondon to Robert de Lousheby in Spondon of half an acre of land in Spondon lying on Le Morfurlong, etc. · Rent, a farthing; and for his soul's salvation and for the soul of Dom. Michael de Kirkeby, quondam vicarius de Spondon, one half-pound of wax for the altar of the B. V. Mary in Spondon church. Witn. Thomas la Poher, Hugh de Hereford, Henry de Morlege, etc. *Temp.* Hen. III. (Locko.)

2172. GRANT from Emma fil. Ricardi Mercatoris de Spondon to Robert de Lousheby in Spondon of an acre and a half rood of land in Spondon. Witn. Thomas le Poher, Hugh de Hereford, Henry de Morleg'. *Temp.* Hen. III. (Locko.)

2173. GRANT from the same Emma to the altar of the B. V. Mary, Spondon, "ad luminare eiusdem promouendum in ecclesia de Spondon per manus parochianorum," of one acre of land in the territory of Spondon lying on Godwich and on le Wetelondys. Witn. Robert de Karduyl, Henry de Morlege', Robert ad fraxinum, etc. *Temp.* Hen. III. (Locko.)

2174. GRANT from Henry fil. Nigelli de Morleye in Spondon in soul alms to the altar of the B. V. Mary for a lamp in the church of Spondon, of an acre of land in Spondon lying on Le Morfurlong. Witn. Robert de Karduyl, Hugh de Hereford, Robert ad fraxinum. *Temp.* Hen. III. (Locko.)

2175. LICENCE from the Bishop of Coventry and Lichfield for the appropriation of Spondon Church to the Hospital of Burton Lazars. Dat. apud Kynilleworth, xi. kal. Feb. [22 Jan.], 1286. (Lichf. AA. 1.)

2176. QUITCLAIM from Agnes fil. et her. Nicholai Averey de Spondon to William fil. Andree ad-le-Broc de Spondon and Agnes his wife, dau. of William de Kynston, of land in Spondon previously leased to the same for their lives. Witn. Thomas le Pouer, Robert de Cardoyl, Andrew ad fraxinum de Alwaston, etc. Dat. Michaelmas Day, 1296. (Kerry xix. 322.)

2177. GRANT from Hugh de Meinel of Winster to Simon fil. et her. Willelmi Ponger of Wyvelisthorp of a messuage in Spondon and a rent from three messuages in Le Wallemor. Witn. William le Herbeiour de Chaddesden, Thomas de Derleye, Thomas le Poer, etc. Dat. W. a. F. of St. Mark [25 Apr.], 4 Edw. III. [1311]. (Kerry xix. 323.)

2178. GRANT from Simon Ponger of Willesthorpe to Matilda his daughter of seven tofts and buildings in Spondon lying in Le Wallemor, which he had by feoffment from Hugh le Meynill of Winster. Witn. William de Chaddesden, knt., William le Wyne, William atte Crosse, William Cardoyle, etc. *Circ.* 1320. (Kerry xix. 324.)

2179. QUITCLAIM from Margery de Notyngham of Derby to John de Twyford and Margaret his wife of three acres of land in Spondon which she had by grant from Agnes Brok. Witn. William de Chaddesden, knt., William Wyn, William atte Cros, etc. Dat. M. a. F. of St. Luke [18 Oct.], 3 Edw. III. [1329]. (Kerry xix. 325.)

2180. ORDER by Edmund le Botiller to Thomas Broun to deliver to John de Twyford possession of the lands late Ralph Pipard's in Spondon. Dat. York, 1 Oct., . . . Edw. III. (Kerry xix. 325.)

2181. GRANT from Matildis Larcher of Nottingham to Robert de Lowesby of Spondon and Alice his wife of a messuage "ex opposito fontis" in the said vill, which she inherited on the death of Marjory Attebernes. Witn. John de Twyford, William Colman, Robert Baylli. Dat. F. of St. Gregory [12 March], 44 Edw. III. [1370]. (Locko.)

2182. GRANT from Robert Louseby of Spondon and Alice his wife to John le Carter of a messuage which they had by grant from Matildis le Archer. Witn. Dom. John de Twyford, vicar of Spondon, Richard Bayli, Robert Wildegos, etc. Dat. F. of St. George [23 Apr.], 44 Edw. III. [1370]. (Locko.)

2183. GRANT from Richard Botiler and Agnes his wife to John de Twyford, perpetual vicar of Spondon, and Henry Slayer of Chaddesden, chaplain (after their death and the death of their son) of a parcel of land in Alredholm in Spondon. Witn. Robert Louzeby, Richard Bayli, etc. Dat. F. of St. Leonard [6 Nov.], 5 Ric. II. [1381]. (Locko.)

2184. POWER of attorney from Nicholas de Stafford, "chivaler," and Elizabeth his wife, to John Turvey, to deliver seisin of the manors of Throwley and Frodeswall, co. Stafford, and of land in Spondon, to Mag. Edmund Destafford, clerk, Richard, vicar of Alstonefeld, Nicholas Rotour, and William Osmond, chaplains. Dat. Tu. b. F. of St. Barnabas [11 June], 16 Ric. II. [1393]. (Add. 27501.)

2185. POWER of attorney to the same from Edmund de Stafford, clerk, Richard, vicar of Astonefeld [Allstonefield, co. Staff.], Nicholas Rotour, chaplain, and William Osmond, chaplain, to deliver seisin of the same to Nicholas de Stafford, "Chivaler," and Elizabeth his wife. Dat. Th. a. F. of St. Barnabas [11 June], 16 Ric. II. [1393]. (Add. 27502.)

2186. POWER of attorney by John Grendone of Totone to Robert Whyte of Spondon, husbandman, and William Wedo, clerk of the Abbot of Dale, to deliver seisin to John Dracote and Agnes, his wife, of a tenement and lands which he had of the enfeoffment of Robert Halleswayne, senior. Dat. Spondon, Wednesday a. F. of St. Chad, Bp. [2 Mar.], 23 Hen. VI. [1445]. (Woll. i. 80.)

2187. ATTORNEY from Margaret nuper uxor Walteri Twyford to Henry Bradburne to take seisin of the lands of Robert Twyford of Chirche Longley, esquire, in Spondon and Chaddesdon. Dat. 16 Mar., 18 Hen. VI. [1440]. (Kerry xix. 326.)

2188. CONFIRMATION by Ralph de la Pole, serjeant-at-law, and John Curson, esquire, to Margaret, widow of Walter Twyford, esq., of the lands in Spondon, lately Robert Twyford's, which the said Margaret holds for life, with remainder to the said Ralph and John. Dat. Mor. of St. James [26 July], 22 Hen. VI. [1444]. (Kerry xix. 327.)

2189. LEASE, for twenty-one years, from Thomas Twyfort, esquire, to William Lokka of a house in Spondon, late in the holding of Thomas Butler, and "a meyne of land called Hobson thing." Dat. T. b. F. of St. Matthew [21 Sept.], 13 Hen. VII. [1497]. (Kerry xix. 327.)

2190. RENTAL of Spondon made in presence of Thomas Somercotes, auditor, Thomas Bothby, receiver, and Thomas Wade, deputy steward, by virtue of letters patent of the king dated 4 Feb., 2 Hen. fil. Henrici [sc. Hen. VIII., 1511]. (Locko.)

2191. GRANT from George Meverell of Thoroley, esq., to Philip Draycote, Arthur Eyre, Philip Okar, esquires, Thomas Babyngton, son and heir-apparent of Antony Babyngton, esq., James Denton, "utriusque juris doctor," Rich. Jernegan, John Gyfford, Edward Grey, knts., etc., and others, of the manor of Frodeswall, and land in Frodeswall and Thoroley [co. Staff.], and Spondon, to the use of a certain indenture made between him and Humphrey Boolande, on the marriage of his son and heir-apparent to Humphrey's daughter, 2 Sept., 15 Hen. VIII. [1523]. (Add. 27515.)

SPONDON *v.* also under DUFFIELD, TIDESWELL.

STAINSBY.

(STEYNISBY.)

2192. RELEASE from Richard, son of Roger Pite of Ridding, to William le Bret, of lands in Steynisby. Witn. Roger le Bret, John de Eynecourt, John de Brimintone, etc. Dat. Cestrefeld, F. of St. Luke [18 Oct.], 20 Edw. I. [1292]. (Woll. viii. 67.)

STANLEY.

2193. LEASE from Peter fil. Bate dicti Reve de Stanle to Thomas fil. Roberti de Halum of ten acres and a half of arable land in the territory of Stanley, lying severally in or abutting on Le Suthbreche, Lochaglisiche, Harland, Stanlebroke, Sporwell, Le Otherhalfrodes, Le Wychengrene, Le Grenewell, Morleybrigge furlong, Stanyrode under Morleyparke, Baliwelle, Le Sidyerd on the highway leading from Notingham to Morley, Le Endeland, Hundpittsike, Wythlandsike, Aspland, Dedemansgrene, etc., for a term of twelve years, at a rent of 14s. Witn. William fil. Will. de Stanle, Robert de Trowell, Geoffrey Rachel, Adam fil. Bate de Stanle. Dat. Trinity, 19 Edw. II. [1326]. (Woll. iv. i.)

STANLEY *v.* also under DALE ABBEY, HANDLEY, OCKBROOK.

STANTON-BY-DALE.
(STANTONA, STAUNTON.)

2194. GRANT from Ralph de Hereford to Robert fil. Walteri de Stanton of a bovate of land in the vill of Stanton which Walter fil. Achard, father of the said Richard, formerly held. Witn. Dom. John, Abbas de la Dale, Dom. Richard de Sandiacre, William de eadem frater suus, William de Risleya, Hugh de Wermundeswurh, Walter de Morleg', and others. *Circ.* 1240-1250. (Add. 47507.)

2195. GRANT from Walter de Morley and Joan his wife to the church of St. Mary de Parco Stanley and the Canons there, of the well called Wyhitlakeswelle, with a rood of land adjacent, in the territory of Stanton, "ad claudendum et fossandum et ad suum conductum ex illius fontis aque ductu faciendum," with right of way through the lands of the said Walter to the well. Witn. Dom. William de Gray, Dom. Robert le Vavasur, tunc vicecomes Nothingham, Hugh de Morley, Hugh de Duyn, Helyas de Ryseley, etc. *Circ.* 1245-1255. (Add. 47510.)

2196. GRANT from Hugh fil. Radulfi to Hugh de Muschamp of two bovates of land in the vill and fields of Stantona which William fil. Alexandri sometime held; to hold for the lives of the said Hugh and Ydonea his wife, at a yearly rent of one penny at Easter. Witn. Dom. Hugh, Abbas de parco de Stanley [Dale Abbey], Walter de Morley, Hugh de Morley, Nicholas de Henouere, William de Sandiacre, Elyas de Ryseley. *Circ.* 1250-60. (Add. 47509.)

2197. GRANT from Geoffrey de Detheke, for fifty marks received by the hand of Mag. William Juvenis de Derby, in the name of the Abbot, to the Abbey "de Parco Stanley" [Dale Abbey], for the support of one canon, of all his land and holding in Stanton, and for warranty of the same he has delivered to the said canons the charters which he had of the chief lords, and the charter of Helyas Fulcher of Osemundeston, by whom he was enfeoffed of the same. Witn. Mag. Richard de Morle, Robert de Muscamp, Hugh de Gurney, Will. de Sandiacre, Everard de Stanley, etc. [1272.] (Harl. 49 D. 51.)

2198. LETTERS of attorney from Geoffrey de Dethek to Robert his son to deliver seisin of all his lands in Stanton to the Abbey "de Parco Stanleye," according to a charter which they have from him. Dat. Notingham, Fr. b. F. of St. Edith [16 Sept.], 1272. (Harl. 49 D. 50.)

2199. QUITCLAIM from William de Morteyn, mil., to the church of the B. Mary de Parcho Stanley and the Canons there of all the land and tenement which they hold of his fee in Staunten of the grant of Geoffrey de Detheyk, at a yearly rent of 4*s.* silver. Witn. Hugh de Babington, tunc vicecomes de Notingham et Derbeye, William de Sancto Johanne, Dom. Walter, perpetual vicar of Waleshale, Robert de Muschamp, etc. Dat. 1272. (Harl. 53 E. 49, 50.)

2200. GRANT and quitclaim in soul-alms from Emicina de Morteyn to the church of St. Mary de Parco Stanley and the Canons there, of all the land and tenement which they hold of the grant of Geoffrey de Dethek of her fee in Stanton; yearly rent, 4*s.* Witn. Dom. Robert de Morteyn her son, Mag. Richard de Morley, Walter de Bakepuz, William de Teueray, etc. Dat. apud Nothing[ham], M. a. F. of St. Martin [11 Nov.], 1272. (Harl. 53 E. 48.)

2201. FINE levied at Westminster in Hilary Term, 21 Edw. I. [1293], whereby Philip de Stownesby and Isabella his wife convey to Robert de Sallowe a messuage and two bovates of land in Stanton by Sandiacre, for twenty marks. (Add. 47508.)

2202. QUITCLAIM from Ydonia relicta quondam Hugonis de Muschamp in Staunton to Serlo fil. Ricardi de Weledune, of a toft in Staunton which William fil. Alexandri sometime held and a plot of land called Le Chyricroft, and two acres and a half of arable land in the territory of the said vill, which the said Serlo acquired from the said Hugh. Witn. Dom. Laurence Teuren, Abbas de la Dale, Dom. William de Albiniaco, tunc rector ecclesie de Ylkystun, William Danvers, etc. *Temp.* Edw. I. (Add. 47511.)

2203. GRANT from . . . . Osmundeston to Geoffrey de Detheke of all his land and tenement in the vill and territory of Staunton. Witn. William de Chaddesden, Robert de Saucheverel, Robert de Cardoyl, Simon Spichfat, etc. *Temp.* Edw. I. (54 E. 24.)

2204. GRANT from William fil. Simonis Baret of Notingham to William Pouger of Wilkstorp of a tenement in the vill and territory of Stanton, to hold by rent of " unum semen piperis." Witn. Dom. Richard le Grey, Geoffrey de Saundiacre, Robert de Muschamp, Robert Turnepeny. *Temp.* Edw. I.-II. (Add. 47512.)

2205. GRANT, in tail, from William Pouger to Thomas Pouger his son of two messuages and lands in Staunton, near Sandiacre; yearly rent, during the life of the said William, 100*s.*, and after the death of the same, one clove of gillyflower at Christmas. Witn. Robert Saunzcheverel de Hopwelle, mil., Richard de Grey of Sandiacre, William le Herberour, etc. Dat. Staunton, W. a. Michaelmas, 2 Edw. II. [1308]. (Harl. 55 A. 6.)

2206. QUITCLAIM from William Pouger de Wilsthorp to Thomas Pouger his son of lands in Staunton, near Sandiacre. Witn. William Saucheuerell, Martin de Wermundesworth, Hugh Burdet, etc. Dat. Staunton, Mon. b. F. of Nat. of St. John Bapt., 8 Edw. II. [1315]. (Harl. 55 A. 7.)

2207. QUITCLAIM from William Pougier de Wylesthorpe to Thomas Pougier his son of lands in Staunton next to Sandiacre and Long Eyton. Witn. Robert de Sallowe, Hugh Bordet, William Michel, Robert Poutrel, etc. Dat. Wylesthorp, F. of St. Luke [18 Oct.], 16 Edw. II. [1322]. (Harl. 55 A. 8.)

2208. QUITCLAIM from Robert fil. Thome Pouger of Staunton next Sandiacre to William Danncroft [?] of the same, of three messuages, sixty-five acres of land, etc., in Stanton next Sandiacre. Dat. Stanton, S. a. F. of the Epiphany [6 Jan.], 12 Edw. III. [1338]. (Harl. 55 A. 9.)

2209. GRANT from William de Grey of Sandiacre, knt., to William Danvers of "Stanton pres del abbeye de la Dale" and to Joan his wife of all his lands, etc., in the vill of Stanton, which lands Robert de Sallowe formerly held on lease from Richard de Grey his father. Witn. Hugh Burdet of Halum, William de Muston of Morley, William Sautdecheuerel of Hopwell, Hugh de Muskham of Staunton, etc. Dat. 4 June, 13 Edw. III. [1339]. Seal of arms. (Add. 47513.)

2210. POWER of attorney by John Dreycote of Loscowe to William Burbage of Stanton next the Abbey of St. Mary of Dale, and Thomas Coghhen of the same, to deliver lands in Stanton to John Reynar of Swanwyke, son and heir of William Reynar and Cecily his wife, one of the daughters and heirs of Richard Cartar. Dat. 23 Mar., 24 Hen. VIII. [1533]. (Woll. iv. 2.)

2211. LEASE, for forty-one years, from John, Abbot of Dale, to John Dylke of Stanton in the Stones, co. Derby, of a close commonly called "the Condith felde" adjoining to "the Comyn More of Stanton aforesaid"; at a rent of 26s. 8d. Dat. 7 Apr., 29 Hen. VIII. [1538]. With seal of the Abbot. (Add. 47515.)

STANTON-BY-DALE *v.* also under DALE ABBEY, HOPTON, ILKESTON, LONG EATON.

STANTON, STANTON-LEYS, STANTON-WOODHOUSE.

(LEYS, STANTON IN ALTO PECCO, STANTON-IN-LE-PEAKE, STANTONELEAGHES, STANTONELEESSE, STANTONLEGE, STANTONLEYES, STANTONLEYS, STANTON WODEHOUSES, STAUNTON, STAUNTONELEYGH, STAUNTON WODEHOUSES.)

2212. GRANT, for fifty marks, from Robert fil. Ad. de Stantona to Adam his son, of lands which Walter de Bosco sometime held in Stanton, three bovates in Leys, and of Henry de Leys and Robert de Ker, and their homage and lands in Leys and Wodehuses, with pasture in the same places, and a yard for a sheepcot for five hundred sheep. Witn. Dom. Richard de Vernun, Dom. William de Mortain, Dom. Roger de Aynescurt, Dom. Richard de Hertil, Dom. Robert de Esseburne, milites, etc. *Temp.* Hen. III. (Woll. ii. 3.)

2213. GRANT, for twenty-four marks, from Adam fil. Rob. de Stauntona to Ralph fil. Rad. Bugge of Nottingham, of lands in Stanton-leys; rent, 1d. Witn. Dom. Richard de Vernun, Dom. Richard de Herthul, Dom. William Basset, milites, etc. *Temp.* Hen. III. (Woll. ii. 4.)

2214. GRANT from Richard de Stantone, clerk, to Robert Alais of Wynster of a messuage and lands in Stanton and Stantonleyes, paying a rent of 10s. to Henry de Gratton. Witn. Robert de Stanton, Robert de Wynnefeld, John de Condale, etc. Dat. Stanton, Vig. of Palm Sunday [20 Mar.], 5 Edw. I. [1277]. (Woll. ii. 15.)

2215. COVENANT dated* on the F. of St. Martin in Winter [11 Nov.], 1284, whereby Richard de Bingham, mil., leases for ten years to Thomas fil. Henrici ad Stantonleg a bovate of land in Stantonlege, at a rent of 10s. Witn. Adam de Rowleslege, Rob. de Woddeslege, etc. Dat. Bingham, F. of St. Bartholomew [24 Aug.], 12 Edw. I. [1284]. (Woll. ii. 10.)

2216. COPY (seventeenth century) of a bond by Richard fil. Ad. de Stanton to Dom. Thomas Foliambe, in 15s. annual rent for lands in Stanton. Witn. Richart Herthull, Richard Vernon, vicar of Yolgreave, Peter de Rouland, etc. Dat. Elton, Th. a. F. of the Assumption [15 Aug.], 22 Edw. I. [1294]. At the foot is a certificate of its agreement with the original deed, signed by Adam Slack, John Greaves, William Greaves, clerk, Edward Greaves, and John Leigh, "Ludimagister." (Woll. ii. 20.)

2217. GRANT from John del Lee fil. Ric. de Staunton to William de Crumford of a rent of 5s. 10d. from lands in Stauntonleyes. Witn. Ralph Coterel, William de Hopton, Henry de Gratton, etc. *Temp.* Edw. I. (Woll. ii. 13.)

2218. GRANT from Henry fil. Thome Foleiaumbe of Gratton to Robert le Fethelers of Wenster of a messuage and land in Stantonleyes; rent, 10s. Witn. Richard de Staunton, Ralph de Wennefelt, Robert de Wardelowe, etc. Dat. Vig. of All Saints' [1 Nov.], 28 Edw. I. [1300]. (Woll. ii. 12.)

2219. CONFIRMATION by Robert fil. Ric. de Dokinfeld, dominus de Staunton in Peeke, to Avice fil. et her. Thome fil. Hen. de Stauntoneleygh, condam domini de Birchovere, of all grants made to John fil. Rogeri de Birchovere by Robert fil. Ade and Adam fil. Mathei de Staunton, his ancestors, of lands in the fee of Staunton. Rent, one farthing in silver, to be paid yearly in the chapel of Birchovere on Michaelmas Day. Witn. Dom. Richard de Herthull, Ralph de Wynnefeld in Staunton, Henry de Gratton, etc. *Temp.* Edw. I.-II. (Woll. ii. 7.)

2220. GRANT from Robert, dictus le Fithelere, to Richard de Vernoun, clerk, living in Staunton, of the lands called Apiltremeduwe and Lytelmeduwe, in Staunton Wodehouses in the 'fee of Staunton, together with a wood called le Loverdes-Ker, which he held of the feoffment of Henry de Gratton. Witn. John de Roulesleye, Robert de Wardelowe, John de Coudale, etc. *Temp.* Edw. I.-II. (Woll. ii. 18.)

2221. CONFIRMATION from Henry Leygdfot of Stanton to William de Crumford of Birchover of grants of land in Stanton, made to him by Robert fil. Ric. de Staunton and Robert de Dokynfeld, of the site of mill-ponds and a water-mill there. Witn. Will. dil Hulle, Ralph Gerard, Adam de Colleye, etc. Dat. Tu. a. F. of SS. Simon and Jude [28 Oct.], 8 Edw. II. [1314]. (Woll. ii. 14.)

2222. RELEASE from Robert fil. Henrici de Gratton of Staunton to Robert Alcus of Wynster, dwelling in Le Wodehouses, in the fee of Staunton, of the lands in Staunton which he had by feoffment from Richard Glen of Stanton, clericus, reserving to himself an annual rent of 10s. Witn. Robert fil. Ric. de Staunton, Robert fil. Radulphi de Wynnefeld, John de Coudale, etc. Dat. S. a. Pur. of B. V. M. [2 Feb.], 1315[6]. (Woll. ii. 19.)

* Dated both at the beginning and the end. Possibly the original covenant dated 24 Aug. had been lost.—*Ed.*

2223. GRANT from Robert fil. Ric. de Staunton and Robert de Dokynfeld of Staunton to William de Crumford of Birchover, of sufficient land in Staunton to make a pond and build a water-mill. Witn. Thomas Foliaumbe, mil., Hugh de Meignell, William del Hulle, etc. *Temp.* Edw. II. (Woll. ii. 6.)

2224. GRANT from Richard fil. Ade de Staunton to Robert fil. Ric. de Dokonfeud, to Richard Fox of Birchover, Robert fil. Roberti de Winster of the same, Henry de Optone of the same, Alan fil. Regĩnaldi of the same, etc., of common of pasture upon the moor of Staunton. Dat. Tues. in Whitsun week [12 June], 30 Edw. I. [1302]. (Woll. ii. 8.)

2225. COPY (seventeenth century) of grant from William de Gratton, knt., to Henry de Aldham and Margate his wife, of the ward-ship and marriage of Hugh, son and heir of Robert de Stanton, and custody of his lands. Dat. Tu. a. F. of St. Mary Magd. [22 July], 5 Edw. III. [1331]. French. (Woll. ii. 9.)

2226. GRANT from Hugh, son of Robert de Staunton, to William de Birchover, of lands in Staunton and Birchover. Witn. Thomas Foliambe, knt., Robert de Knyvetone, Robert de Wynefeld, etc. Dat. Birchover, S. a. Ann. of B. V. M. [25 Mar.], 19 Edw. III. [1345]. (Woll. ii. 64.)

2227. GRANT from John Beard of Derby to Godfrey Foliambe, knt., of a messuage and lands in Stanton "in alto pecco." Witn. Ralph de Waystolke, Robert de Strandes, Ralph Freynan, etc. Dat. Stanton in le Peake, M. a. F. of St. Ambrose [4 Apr.], 46 Edw. III. [1372]. (Woll. ii. 22.)

2228. GRANT from Roger le Clerk of Worthington and Avice his wife to Godfrey Foliaumbe, knt., of a moiety of two plots of meadow in Stanton. Witn. Richard de Vernon, knt., John Foliaumbe, Thomas de Wednesleye, etc. Dat. F. of the Ass. of B. V. M. [15 Aug.], 47 Edw. III. [1373]. (Foljambe.)

2229. GRANT from Dame Alice de Langford to John de Horning-wold, Johanna his wife, and Johanna their daughter, of a messuage and lands in Stantoneleaghes, for twenty years; rent, 10s. 2d. Dat. Parkhall, F. of St. Martin [11 Nov.], 49 Edw. III. [1375]. (Woll. ii. 23.)

2230. DECLARATION by Thomas Reynalde and Isabell his wife that they have sold to Richarde Alyn, son of John Aleyne, "a place in Stanton." Witn. John Saucheverell, Henry Colombelle, John Dethyk, the parson of Derley, and the parson of Bonsale. Dat. 1 June, *circ.* 1452. (Woll. ii. 37.)

2231. RELEASE from Richard Aleyne, son of John Aleyne of Stanton Leghas, to John his father, of lands which the said John held in Stanton. Witn. John Knyveton, Richard Gylbert, Richard Bradbery of Grattone, etc. Dat. Morr. of F. of St. Bartholomew [24 Aug.], 30 Hen. VI. [1452]. (Woll. ii. 36.)

2232. GRANT from John Aleyn of Stanton Leghes to Henry Aleyn his son of lands in Stanton, with reversion of the same to Richard, son of the same John, and Thomas his brother. Witn. John Knyveton and Richard Gylbart, esquires, Richard Bradbery of Gratton, etc. Dat. Stanton Leghes, M. a. F. of St. Bartholomew [24 Aug.], 30 Hen. VI. [1452]. (Woll. ii. 39.)

2233. GRANT from John Steverdale, son and heir of William Steverdale, to Richard Vernon, esq., and Richard Crichelowe, vicar of Bakewell, of all the lands in Stanton and Steverdale which came to him on his father's death, and of lands that should revert to him at the death of Alice his mother. Witn. John Knyfton, Robert Gylbard, Nicholas Smetheby, etc. Dat. Stanton, M. a. Pur. of B. V. M. [2 Feb.], 11 Edw. IV. [1472]. (Woll. ii. 30.)

2234. BOND by Ralph Saucheverell, esq., and John Saucheverell, his son and heir, to Henry Alyn and Nicholas his son, for £20, for the observance of the conditions of the preceding release. Dat. Th. b. Michaelmas, 2 Ric. III. [1484]. (Woll. ii. 32.)

2235. RELEASE by Ralph Saucheverell of Snyterton, esq., and John Saucheverell of Morley, his son and heir, to Henry Alyn of Stanton Wodehouses and Nicholas Alyn, his son and heir apparent, of lands in Stanton Wodehouses, and also of an annual rent of 10s. and suit to the mill of Aldeport. Witn. Robert Gilbert, gent., Humfrey Knyvetone, gent., William Smetheby, vicar of Yolgreve, etc. Dat. Michaelmas Day, 2 Ric. III. [1484]. (Woll. ii. 31.)

2236. WRITING, whereby John Knyfton, gent., of Stanton, Nycholas Smetheley of the same, and Nycholas Bradbery of Gratton, testify that Henry Alyn of Stantoneleesse in Yolgreve is heir to lands [in Stanton?] given him by John his father, and that a claim to the same made by Richard his brother is unjust. Dat. 1 June, 2 Hen. VII. [1487]. (Woll. ii. 35.)

2237. LEASE, for sixty years, from Sir Henry Sawchev[er]ell of Morley, knt., to Thomas Alen of Wodhouse, yeoman, of lands in Stanton; rent, 10s. Dat. 16 May, 28 Hen. VIII. [1536]. (Woll. xi. 62.)

STANTON, ETC., *v.* also under BIRCHOVER, YOULGRAVE.

STAPENHILL.

(STAPENHULL, STAPUNHULL.)

2238. GRANT from John de Fereby of Covyntre, "Deyster," to John Colle of Burton-upon-Trent, of land in Stapenhull upon "le Mulnehurste," which he had of the gift of William Colle, father of the said John. Dat. Th. a. Exalt. of H. Cross [14 Sept.], 17 Ric. II. [1393]. (P. R. O. c. 3476.)

2239. QUITCLAIM from Richard Pollesworth, vicar of Stapenhull, Peter Gybun of Burton-on-Trent, and John Wryght, chaplain of the same place, to Walter Batell and William de Hoxale, chaplains, William Adamsone of Stapenhull, Richard Pavy of the same, and Henry Gunne of Hornynglowe, of land in Stapenhull. Witn. William Prodhom of Burton, Richard del Halle of Stapenhull, John Knyghtley de Wynshull. Dat. Stapenhull, Th. a. Trin. Sunday [25 May], 3 Hen. IV. [1402]. (Stowe 65.)

2240. CLAIM for acquitment by Nicholas Fitzherbert, lately Sheriff of Nottingham and Derby, for 36s. 8d., the rent of lands in Stapunhull. Dat. 37 Hen. VI. [1458-1459]. (Add. 27323.)

STAVELEY.

(STALEY, STALEY WODETHORP, STAUELYE, STAVELAY,
STAVELEY NETHERTHORPE OR NEYDURTHORPE, STAVELEY
WUDTHORPE, STAVELEYE, STAVELY.)

2241. GRANT from Hasculfus Musard to Robert de Thurneweit and
Herbert his brother of eight acres of land "de meo dominio," in
Stavele, for other eight acres "de hereditate sua." Witn. Dom.
Johannes, Fulcus de Muster, Ralph de Abetot, etc. (Harl. 86 H. 47.)
   (Attempted facsimile copy of a charter of *temp.* Ric. I., probably
made in thirteenth century.)

2242. LEASE, for eleven years, from William Abetot to the
Hospitallers of Stavele, of a bovate of land in Barley which Suein
held, lying between William Cronzun's land and Roger le Eam's land
called Langeleieker. "Hanc predictam terram tradidi et concessi
prenominatis Hospitalariis ad festum sancti Martini anno postquam
dominus Johannes rex Anglie cepit terdecimum denarium per Angliam
[*sc.* 1207]. Witn. Rob. de Walet', Robert de Braminton, Nicholas de
Langele, Roger his son, Walter de Heliun, Alan, capellanus de Stauele.
(Harl. 86 G. 46.)

2243. GRANT from Ralph Musard [ob. 1264] to William fil. Jordani
of a messuage which Wy held in Netherthorp, and land at Pikelovere,
Sutbrok, Lighull, Scrittendoles, etc. Witn. Richard, clericus, Robert
de Wynton, Walter de Heliun, etc. *Temp.* Hen. III. (Harl. 86 H. 48.)

2244. GRANT from Ralph Musard, in soul-alms for himself and
Isabel his wife to the Church of St. James of Wellebec [co. Notts.],
and the Canons there of a tithe of the pannage "de parcho et omnibus
boscis forinsecis de Stauele tam in denariis quam in porcis," to support
a lamp in the same church. Witn. Dom. William de Heriz, Dom.
Hacuil de Herdebereghe, Dom. Matthew de Hadhersegg, milites,
Hascuil Musard, persona de Witewell, etc. Early Hen. III. (Harl.
86 H. 49.)

2245. GRANT from Ralph Musard fil. et her. Dom. Radulfi Musard
to Robert Bote of a messuage, etc., in Staveleye, paying a yearly rent
to Dom. Cristiana, mother of the grantor, of 3*s.* for her life, and on her
death a pound of pepper to the grantor. Witn. Peter de Briminton,
Jurdan de Abbitot, William Musard, etc. *Circ.* 1265-70. (Foljambe.)

2246. QUITCLAIM from Nicholas le Vow to Henry de Lascy, Earl
of Lincoln, of messuages, lands, rents, etc., in Staveley juxta Cestrefeud. Witn. Milo de Stapelton, Richard de Sutton, James de Nevile,
etc. Dat. Potreton, co. York, 2 Dec., 28 Edw. I. [1299.] (Harl. 86
I. 7.)

2247. GRANT from Nicholas fil. Radulphi Musard to Peter de Cestria
[Provost of Beverley, 1282] of land in Stavely and Netherthorp, held
of him by Thomas Sway and Fulk fil. Normanni, together with the
person and property of the said Fulk. Witn. Dom. William de
Stuteville, Dom. Robert le Breton, Geoffrey de Detheck, etc. Early
Edw. I. (Harl. 86 H. 50.)

2248. GRANT from Richard, nepos Petri clerici de Stavely, to Dom. Peter de Cestria, prepositus Beverlaci [*circ.* 1282] of land called Le Steyward medeu, lying in "le Crombermere," in Stavely which Susan que fuit uxor Ricardi de Heliun held as dower. Witn. William le Breth, John de Brimington, William Martin, etc. *Temp.* Edw. I. (Harl. 86 I. 2.)

2249. LEASE, for ten years, from Ralph de Frechenvyll, sen., to Robert le Clerc and Adam fil. Johannis, both of Stavely, of two parts of the mills of Stavely; rent, six marks. Dat. Stavely, Fr. b. F. of SS. Philip and James [1 May], 9 Edw. II. [1316]. (Harl. 86 H. 12.)

2250. QUITCLAIM from Roger Musard to Robert de Middelton of all liveries, easements, housbote, and haybote, issuing from land belonging to him [? in Staveley]. Witn. Adam de Norton, Roger Cashors, Nicholas Lalinc. Dat. Stavely, F. of St. Michael [29 Sept.], 1320. (Harl. 86 H. 52.)

2251. FINAL concord whereby Ralph de Frecheuilla and Margaret his wife, by Robert de Whitwell, her proxy, received from Peter de Retherby, capellanus, two parts of the manor of Stauelye and the advowson of the church to them and their heirs male. Made before William de Bereford, John de Mutford, William de Herle, John de Stonore, and John de Bousser, Justices. Dat. 20 Oct., 18 Edw. II. [1324]. (Add. 40144.)

2252. GRANT from Edusa, widow of Roger fil. Elie de Barley Wodhous, to Giles fil. Sarre de Dronfeld, of all the lands which she inherited in the fee of Barley in the parishes of Staley and Dronfeld after the death of William de Wigley her father. Witn. Robert de Barley, etc. Dat. Th. b. F. of Circumcision [1 Jan.], 6 Ric. II. [1383]. (Foljambe.)

2253. GRANT from John Bakeqwell, chaplain, sometime of Staveley, to Anker Frechwell, late of Hartbill [Harthill, co. York], gent., Robert Roedes of Stavelay Wudthorpe, gent., and William Layche of Chastrefeld, yeoman, his feoffees, of lands, etc., in Stavelay and elsewhere in co. Derby. Witn. Ric. Frechwell, parson of Staveley, George Phelype, and Henry Oxlay. Dat. Staveley, 16 Apr., 13 Hen. IV. [1412]. (Add. 40146.)

2254. GRANT from Thomas Segrave to Geoffrey Segrave his son and Johanna his wife of the manor of Staley Wodethorp, with reversion on failure of issue to the heirs of the said Thomas and Margaret his wife. Witn. Nicholas, lord of Worteley, John de Keresforthe of Barnesley, Robert Hanson of Netherthorp, etc. Dat. Woodthorpe, 5 Oct., 19 Hen. VI. [1440]. (Add. 40147.)

2255. GRANT from Robert Flechar, sen., of Barley, to William Andrew, sen., and James Mawer of Barley Wodsetes, of a messuage and lands in the fee of Stavelay. Witn. Robert Barley, esq., John Hordryn, William Fentam, etc. Dat. Michs., 34 Hen. VI. [1455]. (Foljambe.)

2256. GRANT from William Andrew and James Mawer to William, son of Robert Flechar, of the messuage, etc., as above. Witn. as above. Dat. 4 Oct., 1455. (Foljambe.)

2257. GRANT from John Wodde of Staveley to Peter Frecchevile, lord of Staveley, esq., of a tenement in Staveley, near Lanewell, between Potterlane and the lands of the said Peter, which tenement he had acquired from Johanna Innocent, widow. Witn. John Both of Staveley, Richard Whitehed of the same, John Aleyn of the same, etc. Dat. at Staveley, 1 May, 19 Edw. IV. [1479]. (Add. 40149.)

2258. QUITCLAIM of John Lyly of Hanley, son and heir of Roger Lyly, to John Frechvyle of lands in Staveley, called Coldmuryan, late held by Thos. Lyly, grandfather of said John. Dat. 12 Oct., 2 Ric. III. [1484]. (Add. 40150.)

2259. RE-GRANT from Sir Thos. Wortteley, knt., Nicholas Gausell, John Sanford, esqs., Nicholas Worrteley, brother of Sir Thomas, Nicholas Serleby, jun., Roger Eyre, jun., and John Skyres, gentilmen, and Richard Witehed, chaplain, to Nicholas Fretchevyle, son of Peter Fretchvyle, of Staveley, of houses and lands in Staveley and Chestrefeld, Hannesworth Wodhouse, and Hertell [co. York.], (held by them as feoffees of said Peter), with remainder (1) to Ralph Fretchevyle, brother of the said Nicholas; (2) to Anker his brother; (3) to John, elder brother of the said Nicholas, Ralph, and Anker; and (4) to be sold and disposed of for the souls of the said Peter and his family. With power of attorney to John Bothe of Staveley, sen., and Richard Whitehede of the same, to give seisin. Witn. Thomas Hellgate of Chestrefeld, John Rodes of Nederthorp, Thomas Robyn of the same, etc. Dat. 19 May, 3 Hen. VII. [1488]. (Add. 40151.)

2260. RE-GRANT from the same to Ralph Fretchevyle, son of Peter Fretchvyle of Staveley, arm., of houses and lands in Staveley, Hyncersell, and West Handeley, and "molendinum falcatum vocatum a sythe mylne," near Holbroke (held by them as feoffees of the said Peter), with remainder (1) to Nicholas his brother; (2) to Anker his brother; (3) to John, elder brother of said Ralph, Nicholas, and Anker; (4) to be sold and disposed of for the souls of said Peter and his family. With power of attorney as above. Witn. Thomas Hellgate of Chestrefeld, Thomas Robyn of Nederthorp, Rogerus Turnour of Staveley, Richard Wryght, rector of Staveley, etc. Dat. 2 Jan., 4 Hen. VII. [1489]. (Add. 40152)

2261. GRANT from William Hoggyes of Hynkersall, son and heir of Robert Hoggyes, and Alice his wife, to John Fretchvile, son and heir of Peter Fretchvile of Staveley, esq., of land in Staveley called Button Ryddyng (lying between a close of Robert Eyre on the west and a common near Flyster lane on the east, a wood called Estwode on the north, and woods belonging to John Rodys and Robert Eyre on the south), which he had inherited from the said Robert and Alice; with attorney to John Carter and Thomas Turnour to give seisin. Witn. Will. Lowkok, chaplain, John Bothe of Staveley, Richard Whithed of the same. Dat. Hynkersall, 5 Nov., 11 Hen. VII. [1495]. (Add. 40154).

2262. GRANT from the same William Hoggyes and Alice his wife to John Fretchville, sen., of land in Staveley. Witn. William Lowkok, chaplain, John Bothe of Staveley, and Richard Whithed. Dat. Hynkersell, Th. b. F. of St. Leonard, Bp. [6 Nov.], 11 Hen. VII. [1495]. (Harl. 86 H. 27.)

2263. GRANT from Richard Ince of Spinkhull to John Frechevuyll of lands in Staveley in a place called Coldmurian (lying between Handley Wodde on the south, a common on the north, the Roder on the east, and a close belonging to Peter Frechvuyll on the west), inherited by him from his father, paying to Robert Linacre and his heirs 4*s.* yearly. Witn. Richard Whytehed of Staveley, Roger Turnour of the same, John Turnour of Wodthorpe, Christofer Rodd of Haghe, etc. Dat. Staveley, 3 May, 11 Hen. VII. [1496]. (Add. 40153.)

2264. SALE from Richard Whitehead of Staley, yeoman, to Rauff Frechwell, esquyer, of lands in Staley called Whiteleis, lying near the Roder, and "buttyng" on the bridge end called "kirke house bridge," for £8. Dat. 8 Feb., 18 Hen. VII. [1503]. (Add. 40155.)

2265. GRANT from Arthur Frechwell of Brymyngton, esquire, to Anker Frechwell and Richard Burcand, as feoffees, of lands in Staley, Ekyngton, Chesterfeld, Dronfeld, and Dawer, Newton by Folkingham [co. Linc.], Wales, Haneston, and Denyngton [co. York], late acquired by Ralph Frechwell, father of the said Arthur. With attorney to Rob. Rodes and Rob. Asshe to give seisin. Dat. Brimington, 6 Feb., 3 Hen. VIII. [1512]. (Add. 40157.)

2266, 2267. FEOFFMENT and counterpart from John Frechewell of Staley, esquire, to John Savage the younger, knt., John Leet, knt., Godfrey Fuliambe, Thomas Leek, esquires, George Lynacre, gent., and Elias Potter, of the manor of Nuthull [Nuthill in Burstwick, in Holderness, co. York], and lands in Nuthull and elsewhere in co. York, Stokholme, Incursell, Dronfeld, Horseley Stavely, Woodthorpe, and Netherthorpe, all in co. Derby, and Newton iuxta Falkyngham [co. Linc.], to the use of the said John Frechewell and Elizabeth his wife for their lives and for the execution of his will. With attorney to William Potter and Richard Smythe to give seisin. Dat. 22 Aug., 7 Hen. VIII. [1515]. (Add. 40158, 40159.)

2268, 2269. SALE, and counterpart, by the same George Lynacre of Plomeclay Hall, gent., to the same Peter Frecheviele of Stavelay, esquire, for £63 13*s.* 4*d.*, of the above lands and rent. Dat. 8 Dec., 31 Hen. VIII. [1539]. (Add. 40162, 40163.)

2270. BOND, in £100, by the same George Lynacre to the same Peter Frecheviell for performance of covenants in the above sale. Dat. 8 Dec., 31 Hen. VIII. [1539]. (Add. 40164.)

2271. CONVEYANCE from the same George Lynacre to the same Peter Frechviell of the same lands in Hanlay in Staveley, a close called Cloighfeld in Ekyngton, and a rent of 4*d.* in Over Hanlay [W. Handley]. Dat. 2 Jan., 13 Hen. VIII. [1540]. (Add. 40161.)

2272, 2273. SALE and conveyance by Sir Anker Carter of Newbottell [Newbottle, co. Northt.], priest, son and heir of John Carter, late of Staveley Neydurthorpe, to the above Peter Frechviell of Staveley, esq., of a messuage in Staveley Netherthorpe. Dat. 20 Oct., 3 Nov., 35 Hen. VIII. [1543]. (Add. 40165, 40167.)

2274, 2275. FINAL concord and counterpart, whereby Peter Frechevill receives from the same Anker Carter the same messuage in Staveley Netherthorpe. Consideration money, 40 marks. Dat. 27 Apr., 36 Hen. VIII. [1544]. (Add. 40168, 40169.)

2276. AWARD by Sir Wyllyam Inskyppe, parson of Clowne, Sir John Rey, vycar of Scartclyffe, John Townerow of Bolsover, and John Hoidgskynson of Sutton in Lee dayell, yeomen, arbitrators between the above Peter, now Sir Peter, Frechviell of Staveley, knt., of the one part, and Sir Richard Oxeley, priest, Henry Oxeley, and Nicholas Oxeley, son of the said Henry, of the other part, touching a moiety of the parsonage of Staveley acquired by the said Richard and Nicholas of Sir Ambrose Cave, knt., given at Bolsover 16 Oct., 1545; the said Nicholas and Richard to be undisturbed till 25 Apr. next; then to give up the said moiety for annuities of £3 and £1 3s. 4d. for 15 years, unless the said Richard shall first be preferred by the said Sir Peter to a better benefice, or the said Henry be granted a farm worth 40s. a year, in which cases other provisions apply. Dat. 16 Oct., 37 Hen. VIII. [1545]. (Add. 40170.)

2277. BOND in £40 by Robert Ynce of Spynkehill, yoman, Richard Ynce of Barlebrough, yoman, and Nicholas Hewite de Kynwaldmarshe, to the same Sir Peter Frechviell of Staveley, for the performance of a covenant between said Robert and Sir Peter bearing same date. Dat. 1 July, 1 Edw. VI. [1547]. (Add. 40174.)

2278. QUITCLAIM from Meriella Ynce of Spynkehill, in widowhood, to Richard her son of her interest by right of jointure in lands in Staveley. Dat. 12 Oct., 1 Edw. VI. [1547]. (Add. 40172.)

2279. SALE and conveyance by Richard Ynce of Beighton-felds, in the lordship of Barleburgh, and John, his son and heir, to Petur Frecheviell of Staveley, knt., of the reversion of their tofts and crofts and lands in Staveley, of the yearly value of 8s. 8d., the moiety of a close called High Breks, and a rent of 1d. on a close called Todepole, for £13 6s. 8d. Dat. 13 Jan., 1 Edw. VI. [1548]. (Add. 40171.)

2280. GRANT from Francis [Talbot, 5th] Earl of Shrewsbury, to Robert Swift of Beighton, esquire, of lands, etc., in Staley, late belonging to the college of Jesus of Rotheram, and granted to the said Earl by the Crown 11 Apr., 1549. With attorney to James Ashton and Edw. Jakeson, gents., to give seisin. Dat. 4 July, 3 Edw. VI. [1549]. (Add. 40175.)

STAVELEY *v.* also under BARLBOROUGH, BARLOW WOODSEATS, CHESTERFIELD, DRONFIELD, HANDLEY, ROMILEY, SPINK HILL, UNSTONE, WOODTHORPE IN STAVELEY.

STERNDALE *v.* under CASTLETON.

STENSON.

(STEYNESTON, STEYNSTON.)

2281. RELEASE from John del Bothe of Fyndern to Richard Elkesley of Steyneston of four acres of land in Steyneston which were granted to the said Richard by John Tonk. Dat. 16 Dec., 1 Hen. VI. [1422]. (Wilmot.)

STENSON *v.* also under TWYFORD.

STONEY HOUGHTON.

(HOCHTONE.)

2282. GRANT from Roger fil. Radulphi de la Bathe to Thomas, Bishop of St. David's, of his right in lands in Hochtone, which Roger de Sidenhale, grandfather of the said Ralph, gave to Alice his mother. Witn. Will. de Staynesby, mil., Robert le Graunte, Richard de Scodley, etc. Dat. Pleseley, 1280. (Harl. 45 G. 46.)

2283. GRANT from Richard Cocus and Amice his wife to John fil. Johannis le Sauvage of a messuage and four bovates of land in the vill of Hochtone. Witn. Hugh Stuffyn, Thomas de Schirebrok, Ralph Samsoun, etc. Dat. Pleseleye, S. b. Nat. of B. V. M. [8 Sept.], 4 Edw. II. [1310]. (Lansd. 599.)

STRETTON.

(STRATTON.)

2284. GRANT from Walter [de Senteney], Abbot of Stanle Park [Dale], to Richard Venator, of a "landa" in the wood of Morwde, "ubi quondam heremite solebant habitare," with pasture for six oxen, four cows, one sow, and a mare in the common pasture of Stretton, and husbote and haibote in Stretton Wood; rent, half a mark. Witn. Ralph, capellanus de Essovere [Ashover], Dom. Roger de Stretton, Adam de Hanleia, Robert de Oggedestun, William le Venur, etc. [1204-1235.] (Woll. vii. 1.)

2285. CONFIRMATION by Osbert fil. Walteri de Stretton to John fil. Roberti Dunelyn of a grant by Walter fil. Will. de Stretton, "quondam dominus de Stretton antecessor meus," to William Dunelyn, of two virgates of land in the same, which Pavia mater dicti Willelmi sometime held by service of a sparrow-hawk or 2*s.* yearly. Witn. William, Rector of Stretton, Simon de Norton, William de Stretton, "avunculus meus," etc. Dat. Stretton, M. b. F. of St. Michael [29 Sept.], 19 Edw. II. [1325]. (Add. 24206.)

STRETTON *v.* also under OFFERTON, TUPTON.

STURSTON

(STOURSTON, STURESTON, STYRTON, SURSTANT),

v. under ASHBOURNE, BRADLEY, DENBY.

SUDBURY.

2286. GRANT from Walter de Monte Gomery, mil., Dominus de Sudburi, to Hugh de Marchinton, chaplain, of nine acres of land in Sudbury; rent, 9*s.* Witn. Roger de Montegomery, Thomas Wace of Mackeley, John Wace of Sudbury, etc. Dat. Sudbury, Tu. F. of St. Scolastica [10 Feb.], 9 Edw. I. [1281]. (Woll. ix. 54.)

2287. POWER of attorney by Nicholas Mountgomery, knt., to John Foxlowe of Sudbury, chaplain, and John Tyrry of Cubley, to deliver seisin to Thomas Coton, esq., John Yeveley, parson of Cubley, and Laurence Braybon, chaplain, of a messuage and lands in Sudbury, part of the manor of Merston Mountgomery. Dat. 12 Apr., 6 Hen. VI. [1428]. (Woll. ix. 51.)

2288. AWARD by John Stanley, knt., Nicholas Fitz-Herberd, esq., etc., in a dispute between Nicholas Montgomere, esq., and Nicholas Agard of Sudbury, and Isabel Montgomere, mother of the said Nicholas, respecting title to the manors of Sudbury and Astone and lands in Makkeley-Campion, Okkes, Potter-Somersall, Waddeley, Somersall Herberts, and Snellaston, and Leegh [Leigh, co. Staff.]. Dat. Tuttebury, 17 July, 12 Edw. IV. [1472]. (Woll. ix. 49.)

SUDBURY *v.* also under CUBLEY.

SUTTON SCARSDALE.

(SOTON IN DAL, SUTTON IN DAL, SUTTON IN LE DALLE.)

2289. GRANT for life from Richard de Grey and Lucy, his wife, to Henry de Soton, of the manor of Soton in Dal, except the advowson of the church and warren, with reversion to the said Richard and Lucy after the expiration of sixteen years, in case of the death of the grantee within that period. Witn. Dom. Henry de Braylisford, Dom. Robert Saucheverel, Edmund de Aston, etc. Dat. Vig. of Holy Trinity [13 June], 22 Edw. I. [1294]. (Woll. i. 74.)

2290. GRANT from William fil. Rob. fil. Hen. de Dukemontone to Robert Glay de Calale of one acre and a half of land in the fee of Sutton in Dal. Dat. Sutton in Dal, F. of St. Cedde [7 Jan.], 6 Edw. III. [1333]. (Lansd. 603.)

2291. GRANT, in tail, from Thomas de Calale of Sutton in Dal to John fil. Joh. de Wiggeley and Johanna, daughter of the said Thomas, of lands in Sutton in Dal, which he held of the gift of Avice fil. Alani fil. Will. de Suttone in Dal. Witn. Dom. William, rector of Sutton in Dal, Adam de Pleseley, Richard Beverege, etc. Dat. Sutton in Dal, Fr. b. Conv. of St. Paul [25 Jan.], 6 Edw. III. [1333]. (Woll. i. 76.)

2292. GRANT from William de Grey of Saundiacre, knt., to Hugh fizWilliam, fizRandolf de Glapwell, and Emma his wife, of a cottage and curtilage in Sutton in Dal, for a rent of 4s. silver, and for suit at his two great courts of Sutton. Witn. Thomas de Calhale, Robert fizAlot, William fizThomas, etc. Dat. Sutton, 4 May, 11 Edw. III. [1337]. French. (Lansd. 604.)

2293. GRANT from William de Grey of Saundiacre, knt., to William de Hope and Eleyne his wife, with remainder to Alice their daughter, of a place of land in Sutton in Dal called Pokeneggezherd, and eight selions of land abutting on the said place, for a rent of 2s. of silver and service at the two great courts of the said William de Gray at Sutton. Dat. Sutton in Dal, 14 June, 12 Edw. III. [1338]. French. (Lansd. 605.)

2294. POWER of attorney from Alice, widow of John Leek of Landford, esq., to James Symsone, clerk, and Richard Shawe, to deliver seisin to John Leek of Halom [Hallam, co. Derby], and Thomas Leek of Newark, of the manors of Sutton in le Dalle, Sandiacre, and Kirkhalome. Dat. 6 Jan., 28 Hen. VI. [1450]. (Woll. i. 75.)

SUTTON SCARSDALE *v.* also under HUCKNALL.

SWARKESTONE.

(SWERKSTON.)

2295. GRANT from John de Saxton, clerk, John de Chelaston, Robert de Chelaston, chaplain, Geoffrey Fannell, chaplain, and John Baret of Weleston, to John de Driby and Margery his wife, of the rents and services of Thomas Grane, William Watte, John Dawe, Robert Ters, Richard Degge, and Margery Poule, all of Swarkeston, and of their tenements in the vill of Swerkeston; also the rents and services of Thomas Davy de Staunton and his tenements in Stonystaunton [co. Leic.], and of John Abel and his tenements in the vill of Tykenhale, and of Peter Passemere and others and their tenements in Tuttebury [co. Staff.]. Witn. Robert de Twyford, chivaler, Richard de Meygnill, chivaler, Robert Franceis, John Fyrbrace, etc. Dat. apud Bredon, Th. b. Nat. of St. John B. [24 June], 37 Edw. III. [1363]. (Lansd. 606.)

SWARKESTONE *v.* also under MELBOURNE.

TADDINGTON.

(TADINTON, TADYNGTON, TADYNTON, TATYNTON.)

2296. COURT-ROLLS of Thomas Ferrers, knt., and Anne his wife for the manor of "Worldeshend" in Tadynton, held on 3 May, 29 Nov., 2 Edw. IV. [1462]. (Bemrose.)

2297. COURT-ROLL of Tatyntone, taken before William Monyngtone, steward, 31, 37, 38 Hen. VI. [1452, 1458-60]. (Campb. xxiii. 17.)

2298. INDENTURE from twenty-three residents of Tadyngton, wherein, in recognition of grant of burial rights to their chapel, they covenant to maintain the cemetery, to reserve all rights of the Mother Church of Bakewell, and to pay a pension of 2*s.* to the Dean and Chapter of Lichfield. Dat. 15 June, 1345. (Lichf. KK. 4.)

2299. DEFEASANCE of grant from Henry fil. Ivonis de Tadinton of 100*s.* of rents in Tadinton and Presteclif to the Dean and Chapter of Lichfield, on condition that he enfeoffs Richard fil. Henrici de Schirleye and Joan fil. Henrici fil. Ivonis "cum ad nubiles annos peruenerit" and their children of a messuage and 28 acres of land in Presteclif, and other lands in Tadinton. Dat. Lichfield, Fr. a. F. of St. Valentine [14 Feb.], 14 Edw. III. [1340]. (Lichf. B. 19.)

2300. GRANT from Hugo de Gunston to the Dean and Chapter of lands in Taddington, Priestcliffe, and Tunstead. Dat. W. a. F. of St. Andrew [30 Nov.], 1342. (Lichf. B. 21.)

2301. TITHE roll of Taddington, Tunstead, and Bobenhull [Bubnell]. Dat. 1337. (Lichf. E. 12.)

TADDINGTON *v.* also under BRIMINGTON, CHELMORTON, HADDON.

TANSLEY.

(TANESLEY, TANNESLAY, TANNESLEY, TANNYSLEY, TANSELEY, TANYSLEG.)

2302. RELEASE from Thomas fil. Roberti, prepositi de Tanesley, to John fil. Galfridi de eadem, of half an acre of lands in the fields of Tanesley, lying on Raulinsford, Le Wetesford, etc. Witn. Henry "juxta aquam" de Tanesley, Sweyn fil. Radulphi de Harston, William Sweyn de Tanesley, Thomas del Croftis, etc. *Temp.* Edw. I. (Woll. i. 10.)

2303. GRANT from Richard fil. Roberti de Tanysleg to Thomas de Capella, faber de Tanysleg, of three roods of land in the territory of the same lying in Hennegrauestorht, etc., with all the "butts" he has on le Coppedelowe, and all the "butts" he has "iuxta scalam que vocatur Le Kyrke Styule," and two "butts" on Aylwynestorht. Rent, a halfpenny at Easter. Witn. Geoffrey de Tanysleg, Thomas fil. Roberti de eadem, Robert fil. Galfridi de eadem, Robert de Haddon, etc. *Temp.* Edw. I. (Woll. i. 11.)

2304. ROLL of Court of Edward de la Pole of Wakebridge Manor, held at Tanneslay, 3 Sept., 23 Hen. VI. [1444]. Nearly illegible. (Woll. xi. 2A.)

2305. RENTAL of the lands of German Pole of Wakbrygge in Tannysley, Hegheygg, and Cruche; signed by German Pole, 4 Oct., 30 Hen. VIII. [1538]. (Woll. xi. 19.)

2306. EXTENT of the lands of the same, viz., the manor of Wakbrugh in Matlock. Same date. (Woll. xi. 20.)

2307. COPIES of three Indictments against Roland Statham of Tanseley, John Statham, and German Statham of the same, husbandmen, for forcible entry upon the lands of Ralph Buntyng, Christopher Hanstock, German Pole, and William Johnson, at Tanseley. Dat. 5 Dec., 2 Edw. VI. [1548]. (Woll. xi. 7.)

TANSLEY *v.* also under WAKEBRIDGE, WIRKSWORTH.

TAPTON.

(TAPPETON, TAPTONA.)

2308. GRANT from William le Archer of Cesterffeld to Adam fil. Joh. Pistoris de Cesterfeld of half an acre of arable land in the territory of Tappeton, abutting on the land of the Hospital of St. Leonard at Chesterfield. Witn. John de Brimington, Ralph de Tapton, etc. Dat. Cestrefeld, S. a. Ex. of H. Cross [14 Sept.], 25 Edw. I. [1297]. (Foljambe.)

2309. GRANT from Richard Hacsmal of Cesterfeld to Adam fil. Joh. Pistoris de Cesterfeld of an acre of land in the territory of Tapton. Witn. Robert de Lenum, Richard le Heyr, etc. *Temp.* Edw. I. (Foljambe.)

2310. GRANT from Robert de Halues and Alice his wife to Robert Cissor of Cesterfeld and Agnes his wife of half an acre of land in the fields of Tapton. Witn. John de Brimpton, Robert de Tapton. *Temp.* Edw. I. (Foljambe.)

2311. GRANT from Adam fil. Gilberti de Taptona to William fil. Richeri of land in the territory of Taptona, including that which Richer fil. Wlnet held of Gilbert his father and the land which the same Richer formerly held from Agnes le Parminter, lying on Kaluecroft, Le Peselandis, Enedehul, and Longefurlong, a little "holm" near Neubold Mill, and the said Adam's share of five bovates of land on Le Brombyclif. Witn. Roger de Blida, Richard Hardi, Joh. fil. Cicelie, etc. *Temp.* Edw. I. (Add. 27184.)

2312. GRANT from Adam fil. Rog. de Parva Tapton to John fil. Ric. le Clerk of half an acre of land on the Castulfurlong in the fee of Tapton. Witn. John de Tapton, Robert Durant, John Bete, etc. Dat. Th. b. Circumcision [1 Jan.], 12 Edw. III. [1339]. (Foljambe.)

2313. GRANT from Adam fil. Thome de Tapton to John Clerk of land in the field of Tapton, lying in Sweddale, etc. Dat. Richard Stuffyn, Robert Durant, Adam Pycard, etc. Dat. F. of St. Gregory [12 Mar.], 17 Edw. III. [1343]. (Foljambe.)

2314. QUITCLAIM from Letiscia fil. Will. fil. Ade dil Bothe to John Goldesmyth of an acre of land in the fee of Tapton, next land of St. Leonard's Hospital, Chesterfield. Dat. Th. b. All Saints [1 Nov.], 1349. (Foljambe.)

2315. GRANT from Roger de Baukwell to John Barley of four roods of land in Tapton, abutting partly on the water called "Rodur." Witn. Robert de Whytyngton, Adam Broune, Robert Dandeson, etc. Dat. M. a. Ass. of B. V. M. [15 Aug.], 12 Ric. II. [1388]. (Foljambe.)

2316. POWER of attorney from Richard Havson, Thomas Brygge, Giles Redesir, and Thomas Swalo, sen., to John Fychette, to deliver seisin to Henry Pierpount, knt., Robert Wednesley, and others, of all the lands, etc., which they had of the grant of John del Wode in Great and Little Tapton. Dat. F. of St. Valentine [14 Feb.], 18 Hen. VI. [1440]. (Foljambe.)

2317. LEASE from Ralph [Cromwell], Lord "de Crowmbewell," Henry Pirpont, knt., Alderman of the Guild of H. Cross, Chesterfield, and others to John Wilson, of all the lands, etc., in the fields of Great and Little Tapton and in the fee of Dronfeld which they had of the feoffment of John del Wode. Witn. Thomas Bate, Steward of Chesterfield, William Bate, William Lynacre, etc. Dat. F. of St. Mark [25 Apr.], 23 Hen. VI. [1445]. (Foljambe.)

TAPTON *v.* also under BRIMINGTON, CHESTERFIELD.

THORNHILL IN HOPE.

(THORNEHULL, THORNHYLL.)

2318. GRANT from Humphrey Gulde de Grendon, chaplain, and Robert Leghes de Leghes to Robert Skynner de Thornhylle, in the parish of Hope, of messuages, lands, and tenements in Thornhyll and Bowmford [Bamford], which they had by feoffment from Robert Skynner. Witn. Nicholas Skynner of Boumford, Roger Skynner of the same, John Skynner, etc. Dat. M. a. F. of St. Andrew [30 Nov.], 21 Hen. VII. [1505].

THORNHILL *v.* also under SHATTON.

THORPE in HATHERSAGE.

2319. GRANT from Arthur Eyre of Padley to Edmund Eyre, perpetual vicar of Tyddyswall, and Stephen Eyre, son of Roland Eyre, of lands and tenements in Thorpe, in the parish of Hathersege. Dat. 12 Dec., 4 Hen. VIII. [1512]. (Add. 7193.)

2320. AWARD by Robert Fitzherbert, esq., Thomas Cokayne of Balidon, and John Flackett, arbitrators to settle disputes between William Stubbez and Thomas Stubbez, both of Thorpe, co. Derby, concerning their claims to a piece of land between Bentley Croft and the dwelling-house of the said William Stubbez. Dat. 4 Aug., 4 Edw. VI. [1550]. (Bemrose.)

THORPE *v.* also under ASHBOURNE, BAKEWELL.

THURVASTON.

(NETHERTHURUASTON, THURGHWESTON.)

2321. SETTLEMENT of dispute concerning 140 acres of land, eight acres of meadow, ten acres of pasture, etc., whereby John de Bakepuz of Barton, mil., conveys to Roger Durdent 50 acres of land, four acres of meadow, and the fourth part of a messuage, lying severally at Wache Grene, Le Batayleflat, Torlowe, Spinkes, Briddesgrene, etc., in Nether Thurvaston, which he held from Richard Durdent, father of the said Roger, in return for 90 acres of land, four acres of meadow, and ten acres of pasture in the same place. Witn. Dom. Nicholas de Longoford, Ralph de Breylisford, John de Twiford, milites, Ralph de Bakepuz, Richard de Pontfreynt. Dat. Barton, Pur. of B. V. M. [2 Feb.], 1330[1]. (Woll. ix. 75.)

2322. LEASE, for twenty years, from Nicholas de Longeforde to Matilda, wife of Adam Bate of Thurvaston, deceased, of two acres of land in Netherthuruaston, lying at Le Brodegapes, etc. Dat. F. of St. Martin [11 Nov.], 10 Edw. III. [1336]. (Longford.)

2323. RELEASE from Richard Bewofoy of Trusley and John del Lone of Oslaston to John ad-pontem de Thurvaston and Isabella his wife of lands in Thurvaston' and Sedirsalle, co. Derby, with a grant of lands in Rauseterr [Rocester] and elsewhere, co. Staff. Witn. John Chaplyn of Trusleye, Richard, son of William de Thurvastone, John del Grene of the same. Dat. S. b. F. of All Saints [1 Nov.], 16 Ric. II. [1392]. (Woll. x. 27.)

2324. NOTE of delivery by Nicholas Hasulhyrst and John Folowe on 19 Jan., 34 Hen. VI. [1456], to Robert Stafford, esq., of Eyham, of three deeds sealed with the seal of arms of Sir Laurens Lynford, an acquittance "betwyx Jhon Barow and John Stafford," a letter of attorney from Robert Stafford, and "xv dedys in a box inselyd" concerning the manor of Thurghweston. (Bowles.)

THURVASTON *v.* also under OSLASTON.

TIBSHELF.

(TIBBESCHELF, TIBBESELF, TIBSCHEF, TYBESCHELF, TYBESCHULFE, TYBSELFE.)

2325. GRANT from William Daniel of Tybeschelf to John de Weyteberhg of the site of a toft in Tybeschelf, with a grange lying next the little lane called "Smythistychil." Witn. Dom. John de

Eyncurt, William Cusin, Hugh de Dokemanton, Roger de Somirvile, etc. Dat. S. a. F. of St. Bartholomew [24 Aug.], 11 Edw. II. [1317]. (Foljambe.)

2326. GRANT from the same to the same of a moiety of a toft in Tybeschelf and all his lands in the vill and fee of Tybeschelf. Witn. Dom. John de Eyncurt, William Cosin, Hugh de Dokemanton. Dat. M. a. Michs., 15 Edw. II. [1321]. (Foljambe.)

2327. GRANT from the same to the same of land adjoining "Smythistwychil" and "Heliwelle-meduwe" in Tybeschelf. Same witnesses and date. (Foljambe.)

2328. GRANT from John de Whettebergh to Roger fil. Alani de Dukmanton of a messuage and a moiety of the lands which he had by grant from William Daniel in Tibbeschelf. Witn. Dom. Roger de Eynecourt, mil., Roger de Somervill, Thomas Barre, etc. Dat. Th. b. F. of St. Martin [11 Nov.], 11 Edw. III. [1337]. (Foljambe.)

2329. GRANT from Peter fil. Will. Daniel to Richard fil. Joh. Bozon quondam domini de Ednusore of a messuage and land in Tibschef. Witn. Dom. Roger Dayncurt, mil., Roger Somervile, John de Staynusby, William de Caltun. Dat. Ednusore, S. a. F. of St. Lucy [13 Dec.], 16 Edw. III. [1342]. (Foljambe.)

2330. GRANT and release from Robert fil. Will. Danyel to Richard Boson of all the lands which he inherited from his father in Tybeschulfe. Witn. Robert Fraunceys, John de Dogmanton, Henry Bryan, etc. Dat. F. of St. Stephen [26 Dec.], 16 Edw. III. [1342]. (Foljambe.)

2331. GRANT from John de Weyteburghe to Roger fil. Alani de Dukmonton and Agnes his wife, in tail, of a messuage and moiety of the lands which he had from William Danyel in Tibbeself. Witn. Richard Fraunceys, William his brother, John de Dukmanton. Dat. F. of St. Gregory [12 Mar.], 21 Edw. III. [1347]. (Foljambe.)

2332. GRANT from Symon de Tybeschelf, perpetual vicar of Tybeschelf, to William fil. Rogeri le Taylliour and Emmota fil. Joh. fil. Hen. Bate of Wingrewrth, and the heirs of their bodies, of lands in Tybeschelf. Witn. William Fraunceys, John de Dukmanton, etc. Dat. W. a. F. of Pur. of B. V. M. [2 Feb.], 44 Edw. III. [1370]. (Foljambe.)

2333. GRANT from Richard Tybschall, "weyfer," of York, to William Tybschall in Skegby, co. Notts., his brother, of "a house of *vis.* firme in Tybselfe," after the death of their father. Dat. York, 24 Feb., 5 Edw. IV. [1466]. (Foljambe.)

TIBSHELF *v.* also under TOTTINGLEY.

TICKNALL.

(TIKENHALL, TYKENHALE.)

2334. FINE to the prior of Rapindon from John "Coruisarius" and Alice his wife of two bovates of land in Tikenhall. Made at Nottingham, before Dom. J[ohn de Gray], Bishop of Norwich, Hugh de Bard[olf], Mag. Roger Arundell, John de Gestling, and Hugh de Bobi, Justices, on S. a. F. of St. Botolph [23 June], 4 John [1202]. (Stowe 138.)

TICKNALL *v.* also under REPTON, SWARKESTONE.

TIDESWELL.

(TIDDESWELL, TIDDESWELLE, TIDISWELL, TYDDESWALL,
TYDDESWALLE, TYDDESWELL, TYDDYSWELL, TYDESWELL,
TYDESWELLE, TYDISWELL, TYDYSWALL.)

2335. QUITCLAIM from Ralph Wlvet de Tydeswell to the Dean
and Chapter of Lichfield, as rectors of the Church of Tydeswell, of
four acres of land at Tideswell, one acre lying on Cockesbut, another
being called Clerkesburwes, and the rest in Oxebothem', between
Meddwedil and Vmfrey's Stontor, etc., one rood lying "Uppe the
Strupes"; for which grant Thomas, Precentor of Lichfield, gave him
20s. Witn. Magister William de Gudley, Ralph de Cubbel', Alan, Vicar
of Tideswell, William de Stanf', Ralph capellanus, Symon de Ascell,
Thomas le Archer, Hugo Martin, etc. [1214-1222.] (Lichf. B. 10.)

2336. INQUISITION roll as to the tithes due to Lenton Priory, with
account of spoliation of wool and lambs from Tideswell Church; 1251.
(Lichf. MM. 5.)

2337. DEPOSITIONS at Tideswell before Papal Commissioners as to
the parochiality of the Church; 1252. (Lichf. MM. 9.)

2338. PARTICULARS of the income, perquisites, etc., of Tideswell
Church on the entry of John Extraneus into the vicarage. *Circ.* 1250.
(D. A. J. v. 150.)

2339. DEPOSITIONS of witnesses examined by the Pope's Commissioners at Tideswell in a suit between the Dean and Chapter of
Lichfield with Lenton Priory, as to the former's claim that Tideswell
is a Parish Church, and not merely a chapelry to Hope; 1253.
(D. A. J. v. 150.)

2340. GRANT from John Daniel to Thomas fil. Joh. [Foljambe]
of ten acres, etc., of land in the culture of Kirkfurlong, Salteresford,
Littondale, etc. [in Tideswell], in exchange for 12 acres lying round
the stone cross of Tideswall, and a pair of white gloves yearly at Easter.
Witn. Dom. Richard de Vernon, William Franciscus, Gervase de
Bernak, Robert de Hertingtune, knts., William Foleiambe, Robert
Foleiambe, etc. *Temp.* Hen. III.-Edw. I. (Foljambe.)

2341. GRANT from Cicilia fil. et her. quondam Ric. de Herford
to Thomas Folegambe fil. Joh. Folegambe of ten acres of land which
she inherited from her father in Tydeswelle. Witn. Dom. Ralph de
Ecclessale, Richard le Ragget, William Folegambe, etc. *Temp.*
Edw. I. (Foljambe.)

2342. GRANT from Matilda quondam uxor Ric. de Herford to
Thomas fil. Joh. Folegambe of her right of dower in 20 acres of land
in Tydeswell. Witn. Dom. Ralph de Ecclesale, Richard le Ragged,
William Folegambe, etc. *Temp.* Edw. I. (Foljambe.)

2343. QUITCLAIM from Thomas fil. Ade de Herdewykewall to the
Dean and Chapter of Lichfield, of a certain "placia tofti vicarii de
Tidiswell" and of other lands, etc., in Tydeswell and Litton. Witn.
Dom. John Daniel, knt., William Folegambe, William Martin, John
Martyn, Ralph Coterel, etc. *Temp.* Edw. I. (Lichf. B. 16.)

2344. QUITCLAIM from Richard fil. et her. Joh. Danyel to Dom. Thomas Foleiaumbe, mil., of a plot of land lately enclosed by the latter, between his own "mansio" and that of John fil. et her. Hug. Pele. Witn. Dom. Richard de Herthull, Dom. Roger de Bradeburn, Richard fil. Will. Foleiaumbe, Nicholas le Conuers, Dom. Roger le Gode, vicarius de Tyddeswell, etc. Dat. Tyddeswell, Whit Monday [22 May], 1301. (Foljambe.)

2345. GRANT from Richard fil. Joh. Daniel de Tydiswell to William fil. Thome Andreu of three roods "in le Croftes" formerly John Louet's, and half an acre of land near "le Thornmedue" formerly Richard fil. Ric. Daniel's, in exchange for three roods "super le Worthingis." Witn. Tho. Foleiambe, mil., John fil. Will. Martin, William Redimon, John Quenild, etc. Dat. Fr. a. F. of St. Hilary [13 Jan.], 34 Edw. I. [1305]. (Add. 7788.)

2346. ROLLS of Parochial Visitations of Tideswell; 1345, 1347. (Lichf. cc. 5, 6.)

2347. GRANT from Thomas fil. Will. del Wheston and Alice his wife to Thomas fil. Thome Foleiambe of half an acre of land in Tydeswell. Witn. John Broun, Henry Alexander, William Andreu, clericus, etc. Early fourteenth century. (Foljambe.)

2348. GRANT from Thomas Broun of Wheston to Dom. Nicholas Martyn of Tyddeswell of an acre and a rood of land in Wheston [in Tideswell], lying near "Le Kirkegate," abutting on "le Neyercros." Witn. John Foliaumbe, Henry fil. Radulphi, William le Marschall, etc. Dat. F. of St. Matthew [21 Sept.], 36 Edw. III. [1362]. (Foljambe.)

2349. GRANT from Nicholas Martyn, capellanus, to Richard Botoun of an acre and rood of land in Wheston [in Tideswell], lying near the "Kirkegate," abutting on the lower cross. Witn. John Foliambe, William Rediman, etc. Dat. M. a. F. of St. Denis [9 Oct.], 37 Edw. III. [1363]. (Foljambe.)

2350. LEASE, for five years, from the Dean and Chapter of Lichfield to Roger de Northburgh [Prebendary of Lichfield], of the tithes of Tideswell, Lynton, Monshall [Monsall], Wardlow, Tunstede, Greatrakes, Wheston, Fairfield, etc., at an annual rent of £19. Dat. iiii. Non. Maij [5 May], 1364. (Lichf. D. 8.)

2351. GRANT from John fil. Radulphi de Haddon and Agnes his wife to Robert fil. Radulphi of a moiety of a messuage in Tyddiswell. Witn. William Marchal, William Andrew, clericus, etc. Dat. S. a. F. of St. Gregory [12 Mar.], 48 Edw. III. [1374]. (Foljambe.)

2352. GRANT from John Foliamb of Tiddeswell to William de Hockelowe of Tiddeswell of a plot of land in Tiddeswell. Witn. Robert de Hethkote, William Redymon, Nicholas Orme, etc. Dat. Fr. a. F. of St. Denis [9 Oct.], 49 Edw. III. [1375]. (Foljambe.)

2353. GRANT from John de Twyford, vicar of Spondon, Roger de Tybshelf, and Thomas Thachet, chaplains, to William de Hokelowe, of the fourth part of a messuage in Tyddeswell. Witn. Robert de Hethcote, John de Hethcote, William Alisaundre, etc. Dat. Fr. a. F. of St. Giles [1 Sept.], 2 Ric. II. [1378]. (Foljambe.)

2354. LICENCE from King Richard II., in confirmation of a similar licence from Edward III. now cancelled, to Nicholas de Stafford, chiv., James Foliaumbe, John Larcher of Heghlowe, William de Hokelowe, Robert Jowesone of Tunstides, Henry Alisaundre, chaplain, Robert Sharp, chaplain, Richard le Machon of Tiddeswelle, and Henry atte Tounesende de Lytton, and John fil. Henrici de Monyassh, in consideration of 20 marks received in the King's Hanaper, to convey for the support of two chaplains celebrating divine service at the altar of the Blessed Mary in the church of St. John Baptist, Tiddeswell, twelve messuages, and two hundred acres of land in Tiddeswelle, Litton, and Wormhulle. Dat. 20 Nov., anno 7 [1383]. (Woll. xi. 27.)

2355. LEASE, for life, from Mag. Edmund de Stafford, canon of Lichfield, afterwards Bishop of Exeter, Richard, vicar of Alstonefeld [Allstonefield, co. Staff.], Nicholas Rotour, chaplain, and William Osmund, chaplain, to Nicholas de Stafford, "chyvaler," and Elizabeth his wife, of the manors of Throwley and Frodeswall [Fradswell, co. Staff.], and Tyddeswell, with land in Tyddeswell, Wormhyll, and Spondon, and in the bailiwick of the Forest of High Peak, at a rose rent. Dat. Lycchefeld, 1 Oct., 12 Ric. II. [1388]. (Add. 27500.)

2356. LICENCE by Roger Foliaumbe to Nicholas de Stafford, knt., James Foliaumbe, and others to assign lands in Tiddeswell to support two chaplains, to pray for them and for the brethren of the guild of St. Mary in the church of St. John Baptist, Tiddeswell. Dat. 19 Sept., 16 Ric. II. [1392]. (Woll. iii. 15.)

2357. GRANT from Nicholas de Stafford, knt., James Foliaumbe, Robert Jewesone of Tunstede, Henry Alisaundre, Robert Sharpe, chaplains, Roger Machon of Tiddeswell, and Henry del Tounesende of Litton, to John Smyth and John Redymone, chaplains, of lands in Wormehull, Tiddeswell, and Litton, to found a chantry at the altar of the B. V. Mary in the church of St. John Baptist of Tiddeswell, for prayers for the souls of King Edward [III.], of King Richard II., of Anne, Queen of England [Anne of Bohemia], of John, Duke of Aquitaine and Lancaster [John of Gaunt], of William de Astone, his chancellor, of John Foliaumbe, John, son of Henry de Monyasshe, Henry de Tiddeswelle, John Alisaundre, Elizabeth, wife of the said Nicholas de Stafford, Roger Foliaumbe, Thomas, son of Godfrey Foliaumbe, knt., John de Stafford, sen., Thurstane de la Boure, and Margaret his wife, and Margaret his mother. Dat. Tiddeswelle, S. b. F. of St. Michael [29 Sept.], 16 Ric. II. [1392]. (Woll. xi. 26.)

2358. QUITCLAIM from William Alexander to Benedict de Asshton of a messuage and seven acres of land in Tyddeswall. Witn. Thomas Bentley, John Smyth, Thomas Whithalgh. Dat. Tyddeswall, Sat. a. F. of St. Katharine, [25 Nov.], 5 Hen. IV. [1403]. (Foljambe.)

2359. ACQUITTANCE from Richard Kooc of Chesterfelde to William Bradshawe of Tyddeswall for 60s. of his rent due to Edward Foliambe, knt., paid to him, the said Richard, as part of £7 due from the same Edward and William, with others, on a bond. Dat. 9 Aug., 6 Hen. V. [1418]. (Foljambe.)

2360. ATTORNEY from Hugh de Bradshawe to Hugh Willeson to deliver seisin of lands in Tyddeswell to William [la Zouche], Lord de Souche [Zouche], Thomas Roughton, William Purseglowes, vicar of Tyddeswell, and John Tunsted. Dat. W. b. F. of St. Cedda [7 Jan.], 19 Hen. VI. [1441]. (Foljambe.)

2361. ACQUITTANCE from William Brasier, chaplain, and Robert Nevell, executors of the will of Hugh Bradshawe, late of Coventry, to Roger Barton of Tyddeswall, for 5 marks. Dat. 19 Jan., 37 Hen. VI. [1459]. (Foljambe.)

2362. POWER of attorney from John Grysley and Thomas Stathum, knts., Will. Babyngton, Richard Willughby, John Casson, Nicholas Longford, Ralph Pole, and Nicholas Fitz-herbert, esqrs., and Thomas Babyngton, to John Stathum and John Coke of Walton, to deliver to Godith Foliambe, widow of Roger Foliambe, esq., seisin of the manor of Tyddeswall and of all other the lands, etc., in Tyddeswall, Huklow, Wormehyll, etc., which they had of the demise of John Spondon, abbot of Dale, and others, to the use of the said Godith for life. Dat. 5 Apr., 8 Edw. IV. [1468]. (Foljambe.)

2363. ACQUITTANCE from Henry Rolleston, esq., and Godith his wife, to Henry Foliambe, esq., for nine marks on account of rent for a farm in Tydyswall and elsewhere. Dat. 23 May, 9 [Edw. IV., 1469]. (Foljambe.)

2364. ACQUITTANCE from Henry Rolleston, esq., to Henry Foliambe, esq., for five marks for the farm of certain lands, etc., held of him by the said Henry in Tyddeswell and elsewhere "in Pecco." Dat. F. of Pentecost [5 June], 13 Edw. IV. [1473]. (Foljambe.)

2365. ACQUITTANCE from Thomas Odell, esq., to Henry Foliambe, esq., for 12 pounds of silver, for rent due on account of the dower of Margery his wife, late wife of Thomas Foliambe. Dat. 24 June, 13 Edw. IV. [1473]. (Foljambe.)

2366. POWER of attorney from Thomas Meverell, esq., to Henry Matlok and Alexander Fallus, to enter the manors of Throwsley [Throwley] and Frodeswalle [Fradswell], co. Staff., and his lands in Boterton [Butterton] and Stanshope in the same county, and his manor of Tyddeswalle and lands in Spondon, and half his manor of Stapley, co. Chest., and all estates in the said counties which belonged to his father, Sampson Meverell, miles, and to deliver seisin of the same to Nicholas Fitzherbert, esq., Richard Knyfton, esq., Edward Bageshagh, Thomas Taillour, vicar of Tyddeswall, and Richard Blaklach, chaplain. Dat. Throwley, 10 Sept., 13 Edw. IV. [1473]. (Add. 27513.)

2367. ACQUITTANCE from Thomas Wodell [*al.* Odell], esq., to Henry Foliambe, esq., for £12, due on account of the dower of Margery his wife. Dat. Vig. of F. of St. Andrew [29 Nov.], 14 Edw. IV. [1474]. (Foljambe.)

2368. ACQUITTANCE from Henry Rolleston, esq., to Henry Foliambe, esq., for nine marks, rent of land in Tyddeswell and elsewhere "in Pecco." Dat. F. of St. Martin [11 Nov.], 15 Edw. IV. [1475]. (Foljambe.)

2369. GRANT from Randolph Barton of Tyddeswell to John Knyveton, esq., Will. Stouerdale, chaplain, and others of all his lands, etc., in Tyddeswell or elsewhere, with his goods and chattels. Witn. Nicholas Barton, sen., John Barton, Richard Longden, etc. Dat. Sat. a. F. of St. Martin [11 Nov.], 18 Edw. IV. [1478]. (Foljambe.)

2370. ACQUITTANCE from Henry Rolleston, esq., to Henry Foliambe, esq., for nine marks for the farm of certain lands, etc., in Tyddyswell and elsewhere "in Pecco." Dat. F. of Pentecost [6 June], 1 Ric. III. [1484]. (Foljambe.)

2371. SIMILAR acquittance. Dat. F. of Pentecost [22 May], 2 Ric. III. [1485]. (Foljambe.)

2372. COUNTERPART of lease from James Denton, Dean, and the Chapter of Lichfield, to Christopher Jamys of Tyddeswall, yeoman, of "omnes domos" of the rectory farm of Tideswell, for 25 years. Dat. 1 March, 1525[6]. Attached to the above is a counterpart of another lease between the same, and of the same date, of the tithes of corn and hay at Hardwykwall and Hill. (Lichf. D. 20.)

TIDESWELL *v.* also under BAKEWELL, ELTON, EYAM, HOPE, HIGH PEAK.

TISSINGTON.
(TYSSINTON.)

2373. GRANT from William de Meinell to Walter de Mountegomery, knt., of a rent of £20 from the manor of Tyssinton, during the life of Robert, son of Richard Foleiambe. Dat. Longeleye Meinell, Easter Day [4 Apr.], 18 Edw. III. [1344]. (Woll. ix. 57.)

TOTLEY.
(TOTENLEY, TOTINLEY, TOTTELEY, TOTTYNLEY.)

2374. GRANT from John fil. Thome de Holm to Peter de Bernis of a place called Le Stord, "versus rivulum de Totinley" [Storth House, near Totley], with other lands there called Le Longecrofte, etc. Witn. Hugh de Linakir, Thomas de Leys, John de Birchevid, Thomas, clericus de Wodehuses, John, clericus de Stolbilley [Stubley]. Late thirteenth century. (D. A. J. iii. 100.)

2375. QUITCLAIM from John fil. Thome del Holm to Peter de Bernis of the place called le Storth [Storth House, near Totley], with land near Le Olrinwelle, and Le Longcrofte, etc. Witn. Jordan de Habetot, Thomas Leys, John de Bernes, etc. Late thirteenth century.

2376. LEASE from Ralph Barker of Dore to William del Croft, jun., and Alice his wife, of a messuage which Adam Milner sometime held in Totenley, with a moiety of Broune Croft there, to hold for their lives, with remainder successively to their sons, John, Robert, and William, in tail; the said Ralph to find timber for repairs and for making wheels and carts. Dat. S. a. F. of St. Bartholomew [24 Aug.], 8 Hen. IV. [1407]. (D. A. J. iii. 104.)

2377. LEASE, for lives, from Richard de Meygnill to Ralph le Barker and Joan his wife of a culture of land in Totenley called Becceley. Witn. William fil. Symonis, Roger le Walker, Robert fil. Rayneri, Thomas de Bircheved, etc. Dat. S. a. Inv. of H. Cross [3 May], 24 Edw. III. [1350]. (D. A. J. iii. 106.)

2378. COMMISSION to Sir John Nedeham and Sir Thomas Littelton, knts., to take an assise of novel disseisin on behalf of Ralph Fraunceys against John Barley, gent., and others concerning tenements in Tottynley, Herstofte, Biggyng, Tybshelf, and Little Stretton. Dat. Westminster, 10 June, 16 Edw. IV. [1476]. (Foljambe.)

2379. RELEASE from Ralph Fraunceys, esq., to John Fraunceys, his brother, of a yearly rent of 20s. from the manor of Totteley in Skaresdale, the reversion of which manor came to the said John after the death of John Barlowe. Dat. 8 Sept., 3 Hen. VII. [1487]. (Foljambe.)

TRUSLEY.

(TROSSELE, TRUSLEGH, TRUSLEH, TRUSLEYE, TRUSSELE, TRUSSELEGA, TRUSSELEIA, TRUSSELEIE, TRUSSELEY, TRUSSELEYE.)

2380. GRANT from Robert de Beufei to the Brethren of the Hospital of St. John of Jerusalem, of two bovates of land in Trusseleia which Paulinus held from him to the day of his death, for the souls of Robert, Earl of Ferrars, and of William, Earl of Ferrars [*ob.* 1191], his lord. *Temp.* Richard I. (Woll. x. 21.)

Notum sit omnibus sancte Matris ecclesie filiis tam presentibus quam futuris quod ego Robertus de Beufei dedi et concessi et presenti carta mea confirmaui Deo et sancte Marie et sancto Johanni Baptiste et beatis pauperibus sancte domus hospitalis ierosolimit' et fratribus eiusdem domus, duas bovatas terre in Trusseleia, illas scilicet quas Paulinus quondam de me tenuit cum omnibus pertinentiis suis et cum incrementis que predictus Paulinus de me tenuit in die illa qua mortuus fuit et uiuus ab omni seculari seruicio et exaccione mundana quietas et ita liberas ut qua elemosina melius uel liberius potest dari. Tenendas et habendas in puram et perpetuam elemosinam cum omnibus pertinentiis suis in bosco et plano, in pratis et pascuis, in moris et mariscis, in viis et semitis et in omnibus libertatibus et communitatibus que ad predictam villam pertinent. Ita quod ego et heredes mei hanc predictam terram contra omnes homines predictis fratribus warantizabimus. Hanc autem donationem feci predictis fratribus pro salute anime Roberti comitis de Fer[ariis] et Vill[elmi] Comitis de Fer[ariis] Domini mei et omnium antecessorum suorum et pro salute anime mee et omnium antecessorum et heredum meorum. Ita quod ego nec heredes mei in predictam terram nichil recuperare poterimus preter orationes et elemosinas. Hiis testibus Villelmo Comite de Fer[ariis], Roberto fratre eius, Roberto auunculo Comitis, Roberto de Bocheruilla, Radulfo de Gresseleia, Henrico de Mongoie, Reginaldo de Boileston et multis aliis.

2381. CONFIRMATION by Robert de Beufei to Livilde . . . of land in Breleia, co. Derby, which William fil. Serlonis, his grandfather, gave him, with the consent of Robert, father of the said Robert, to hold of the alms of Turmundel, where the bodies of his ancestors rest, by rent of twelve pence to be paid on the altar of the B. V. Mary of Turmundel; together with common of the vill in all liberties pertaining to the fee of Trusley. Late twelfth century. (Woll. x. 20.)

Sciant omnes tam presentes quam futuri tam clerici quam laici quod
ego Robertus de Beufei dedi et concessi et hac carta mea confirmavi Livilde et heredibus suis pro suo seruicio terram illam in
Breleiam quam Willelmus fil. Serlonis auus meus assensu patris
mei Roberti ei et heredibus suis dedit libere et quiete ab omni
seruicio de me et de heredibus meis, tenendam de elemosina
Turmundel ubi corpora meorum antecessorum requiescunt, reddendo
annuatim xii denarios quos ponere debet super altare sancte Marie
uirginis de Turmundel in die natiuitatis sue, Et concessi ei et
heredibus suis comune de willa in bosco et in plano et in omnibus
libertatibus pertinentibus ad feudum Trusseleie, et terra ista est
libera de comitatu et de Undredo et de tac et de tol, et de omnibus
seruiciis que pertinent ad me et ad heredibus meis (*sic*), preter
hos xii*d*. prenominatos. His testibus, Nicholao filio Pagani
dapifero comitis de Ferariis, Radulfo de Boschereuilla, Willelmo
filio Hereberti, Reginaldo filio Reginaldi de Gresele, Willelmo de
Trussel', presbitero, Henrico presbitero de sanctimonialibus,
Magistro Willelmo de Nestome, Magistro Ingeramo de Leis, et
Fulchero filio suo, et Petro suo fratre, Reginaldo filio Paullini,
Ricardo Martin, Radulfo Carpintario, Suano filio Brunmoni et
Willelmo fratre suo, Hulf de Ossauiston, Gilieberto eiusdem wille,
Ricardo de Findirne, Nicholao de Derbeia et Jocelino fratre suo
et multis aliis.

2382. QUITCLAIM from Emma, Prioress of St. Mary of Dereby, to
Robert de Belfai, their patron of Trossele, of land in Trussele, which
they held from Robert de Belfai, his father, namely, Pilateshul, with
a meadow lying between it and the stream which comes from Thormondeslee. Late twelfth century. (Woll. x. 22.)

Nouerint omnes sancte Matris ecclesie filii quod ego Emma
Priorissa sancte Marie de Derebi et totus eiusdem loci conuentus
reddidimus et quietam clamauimus inperpetuum Roberto de Belfai
patrono nostro de Trossele et heredibus suis quandam partem terre
in Trussele quam habuimus ex dono et confirmatione Roberti de
Belfai patris sui, scilicet totum Pilateshul cum prato quod est inter
ipsum Pilateshul et torrentem qui uenit de Thormondeslee pro
concessione et confirmatione quam fecit nobis de donationibus et
confirmationibus antecessorum suorum. Hiis testibus, Domino
Waltero, Abbate de Derlee, T. abbate de Crokesdon, Alexandro
canonico, H. de Breidesal, Simone de Tosch[et], H. filio Walkel[ini],
Johanne de Boschiervil, Matheo de Tosch[et], H. decano, T.
magistro, R. fratre eius et multis aliis.

2383. GRANT from Margaret, Prioress, and the nuns of Derby
[St. Mary de Pratis], with the assent " magistri nostri Willelmi prioris
Sancte Elene," to Robert de Beufei, of lands lying between Yelderis
and their meadow of Holtun and the bounds of Oslaueston, near
Trussele, in exchange for an assart near Brerleia. Witn. W[illiam],
Abbas de Derl', Thomas, Abbas de Crockesd' [Crokesden, co. Staff.],
W[illiam] de Muschamp, Archdeacon of Derby, Ralph fil. Nicholai,
Philip de Toc, Michael de Langeford, John de Saperton, Simon de
Sancto Mauro. Early thirteenth century. (Woll. viii. 51.)

2384. GRANT from Hugh de Hototh, with the consent of Ysabel
his wife, and of Geoffrey and Henry his brothers, to the nuns of Derby,
of part of his wood extending from the "mera" of William fil. Hugonis
to the "mera" of Trusselega, and from the "mera" of Dalenburi to

the assart of Gerard. Witn. William fil. Philippi, Henry and Robert, sacerdotes, Geoffrey de Hotot, Henry de Hototh, Peter fil. Mabille, Stephen de Longel', Gerard de Longel', Dorling de Ottun, William de Chent, Nicholas Ruffus, Hugh Cnaue, etc. Early thirteenth century. (Woll. x. 24.)

2385. LEASE from Raimon, Prioress, and the Convent of St. Mary de Kingesmedwe [Kingsmead, Derby], to Simon, rector de Trusleh', of two cultures of arable land in the fields of Truslegh, of which one lies near Hylderis, extending towards Oslaveston, and the other extends towards the meadow of the said nuns of Truslegh; to hold for his life at a yearly rent of two shillings. Witn. Mag. Alexander, Bishop of Coventry and Lichfield, Mag. William de Luteby, Archdeacon of Derby, Dom. Richard, tunc officialis Derbeiensis, Mag. Nicholas, rector of Cubbelegh, Dom. John, Dean of Derby, Thomas Juvenis, Nicholas fil. Aldred, Huron his brother, Hugh fil. Radulphi, Andrew fil. Petri, Nicholas Juvenis, Peter Col, Simon de Langhelegh. Early thirteenth century. (? Kedleston.)

2386. GRANT from Ralph Pippard to Ralph de Lathebury, "camerarius meus," of all his meadow of Trusseleye called "Ermite medewe." Witn. Dom. Henry de Braylesford, Giles de Meynill, John de Bakepuz, milites, Hugh de Meynil, Ralph de Rocheford, Robert de Sallowe. Dat. Rutherfeld Pippard, S. a. F. of St. Mark [25 Apr.], 31 Edw. I. [1303]. Seal of arms. (Woll. ix. 29.)

2387. POWER of attorney from Ralph Pippard, appointing Robert de Sallowe and Thomas de Thorp to deliver seisin to Ralph de Lathebury, his chamberlain, of a meadow in Trusseley called "Ermite medowe," and of 10s. rent in Bussouns. Dat. Rutherfeld Pippard, M. a. F. of SS. Philip and James [1 May], 31 Edw. I. [1303]. (Woll. ix. 30.)

2388. GRANT from John fil. Oliveri de Oddyngseles of Trusseleye to Robert de Beaufey of the same, and John his brother, of a messuage and a bovate of land in Trusseley, acquired from Margery, mother of the grantor. Witn. Dom. Giles de Meynil, Dom. John de Chundos, milites, William de Oddyngseles of Trusseleye, etc. Dat. Trusley, M. a. "Clausum Pasche" [22 Apr.], 1 Edw. II. [1308]. (Woll. x. 25.)

2389. GRANT from Robert fil. Willelmi de Trusseleye, capellanus, to Adam fil. Willelmi de Duffeld and Johanna, sister of the said Robert, and their heirs in tail, of a toft and bovate of land in Trusseley, late belonging to his father, William de Trusseleye. Witn. Dom. John de Beaufey, miles, William de Doddingzeles, Thomas de Beaufey, etc. Dat. F. of St. Michael [29 Sept.], 11 Edw. II. [1317]. (Woll. x. 26.)

2390. COPY (fifteenth century) of grant from John Orme of Brynalston to Arthur de Rolleston of an acre of meadow called La Balyacre in Trusleye. Witn. Thomas Mongomery de Coland, John Durdant, John Chapleyn de Trusleye, Edmund Fowen. Dat. Oslaston, S. b. Nat. of St. John B. [24 June], 7 Ric. II. [1383]. (Trusley.)

2391. COPY (fifteenth century) of grant from Arthur de Rolleston to John Cokayn of Berewardcote, William de Toturdon, and Henry Punt of Ashburn, of an acre of land called Balyacre in Trusley. Witn. Thomas Dodyngseles, Nicholas Irton, William Groos, John Roo, etc. Dat. Berewardcote, Th. a. F. of SS. Peter and Paul [29 June], 17 Ric. II. [1393]. (Trusley.)

2392. GRANT from John Cowdale and Elena his wife, daughter of Alice, daughter and one of the heirs of Thomas Dodingsels, Lord of . . . . to Humphrey [de Stafford, 7th] Earl of Stafford, Robert Grey, John Stanley, esquires, etc., of the manor of Trusseley, which descended to him at the death of Alice his mother. Witn. Walter Blount, John Cursone, Ralph Bassett, esquires, etc. Dat. F. of St. George [23 Apr.], . . . Hen. VI. [1422-1444]. (Woll. x. 29.)

2393. GRANT from Robert Fraunceys, esq., son and heir of Robert Fraunceys, knt., to John . . . ych, of all the lands in Trusseley, near Etwall, which fell to him on the death of his father. Witn. Richard Brown, Gilbert Ince, Richard Bulelogh. Dat. 19 Hen. VI. [1440-1]. Imperfect. (Woll. x. 28.)

2394. GRANT from Richard Vernon, knt., to John Vernon his son, of all his lands in Trusseley. Witn. Thomas Blounte, Sampson Meverell, knts., Nicholas Mountegomery, John Cokayn, Henry Bradborn, esquires, etc. Dat. Harlastone, 14 Sept., 26 Hen. VI. [1447]. Fine seal of arms. (Woll. x. 30.)

2395. GRANT from Henry Makworth, esq., to John Fitzherbert, son of Nicholas Fitzherbert of Norbury, esq., of a messuage, toft, and lands in Trusseley. Witn. William Coke of Trusseley, William Chapeleyn of the same, John Semper of Asshe, etc. Dat. Trusseley, 15 May, 6 Edw. IV. [1466]. (Woll. viii. 54.)

2396. NOTIFICATION by Sir Nicholas, Official of the Archdeacon of Derby, of the induction of Nicholas Brandewodde, priest, to the rectory of Trusley, to which he had been presented by John [Halse or Heles], Bishop of Lichfield and Coventry, at the death of Thomas Steynton, the last rector. Dat. Aston, 13 Apr., 1475. (Woll. x. 36.)

2397. QUITCLAIM from John Golde of Loghbergh, chaplain, son of John Golde of Parwich, to Henry Vernon, esq., of all his lands in Trusseley. Dat. 4 May, 18 Edw. IV. [1478.] (Trusley.)

2398. GRANT from John Vernon, esq., son of Richard Vernon, knt., to William Hastynges, knt., Lord of Hastyngs, John Ferrers, knt., Nicholas Mongombery, Humphrey Stanley, Edmund Vernon, esquires, Nicholas Agard, and William Vernon, the grantor's son, and the heirs of the body of the last-named William Vernon, of all his lands in Trusley, with remainder, on the death of the said William without issue, to the said John Ferrers and the heirs of his body and that of Matilda his wife. Dat. Trusley, 12 Apr., 20 Edw. IV. [1480]. (Trusley.)

2399. QUITCLAIM from John Vernon, son of Sir Richard Vernon, knt., to Henry Vernon, esquire, of all his lands in Trusseley. Dat. 10 Apr., 20 Edw. IV. [1480]. (Trusley.)

2400. GRANT from William Coke, sen., to Ralph Langforth, mil., Thomas Gresley, mil., Henry Derker, clerk, William Mascury, William Coke, jun., and John Yoman, of all his lands, etc., in Trusley. Witn. Henry Rowe, John Fowler, Thomas Semper, etc. Dat. 20 March, 6 Hen. VII. [1491]. (Trusley.)

2401. GRANT from William Coke of Trusseley to Thomas Toples, jun., of all his lands, etc., in Trusseley. Witn. William Pykryng of Thorneton, John Fowler of Salbery, Henry Roo, etc. Dat. Trusseley, 23 Oct., 11 Hen. VII. [1495]. (Trusley.)

2402. ACKNOWLEDGMENT by the Abbot, etc., of Beauchief, collector of the second moiety of a subsidy to the King "ad tuicionem et defencionem Ecclesie Anglicane juriumque et libertatum eiusdem per prelatos et clerum," of the receipt of 5s. 4d. from the Rector of Trusley. Dat. 31 May, 20 Hen. VII. [1505]. (Trusley.)

2403. GRANT from Godfrey Folgeambe, esq., Master William Masse, chaplain, John Stapull, and Martin Eyre, to Richard Vernon of Hasulbache, Thomas Chessyre, rector of Appulbe, William Braye, vicar of Hartington, and John Wellis, of the manor of Trusley, and of lands in Yolgrave. Dat. 20 May, 1 Hen. VIII. [1509]. (Woll. x. 31.)

TRUSLEY *v.* also under COLD EATON, ETWALL, OSLASTON.

TUNSTEAD.

(TONSTEDES, TOUNSTEDE, TUNSTEDE, TUNSTEDES.)

2404. GRANT from Reginald fil. Roberti de Shropschyre del Tunstedes and Alice his wife to Hugh de Gunston of a piece of land and house called Le Oldeberne in Tunstedes. Witn. Roger fil. Radulfi, jun., Roger fil. Radulfi, sen., Ralph fil. Jowe, Ralph de Wardelowe, etc. Dat. Baucquell, M. a. Tr. of St. Thomas [7 July], 1335. (Lichf. B. 28.)

2405. GRANT from John fil. Thome de Benteleye to Hugh de Gunston of one parcel of land and a house called Oldberne, as it stands on that tenement which Robert de Shropschire sometime held in Tonstedes, which he acquired by grant from Reginald fil. dicti Roberti de Shropschire. Witn. Roger fil. Rad. del Tonstedes, jun., Roger fil. Rad. senior, Ralph fil. Jowe, jun., William Jowe, etc. Dat. apud Tyddeswell, S. a. Ex. of H. Cross [14 Sept.], 1335. (Lichf. B. 18.)

2406. ATTACHED is quitclaim from Reginald fil. Roberti de Shropschire to Hugh de Gunston of the above land, etc. Same witnesses. Dat. S. a. Nat. of B. V. M. [8 Sept.], 1335. (Lichf. B. 18.)

2407. GENERAL pardon from Edward III. to Thomas fil. Thome fil. Ricardi de Wardelowe de Tounstede, for services in war "in partibus cismarinis" and also because he has found two sureties for his good behaviour and good services to the King, viz., John Warner of Elyngton and John fil. Johannis de Gymelyngeye, co. Bedf. Dat. "juxta civitatem Venet' in Britannia" [Vannes, in Brittany], 27 Dec., 16 Edw. III. [1342]. (? Foljambe.)

2408. LEASE, for five years, from the Canons of Lichfield to their "confrater," John Linderthorp, of the sheaf and hay tithes of their church of Baukwell, namely, in Tounstede, Gritrakes, Weston, etc., for five years, at a rent of £4 7s. 5d. Dat. xii. kal. Jun [21 May], 1344. (Lichf. D. 7.)

TUNSTEAD *v.* also under TIDESWELL.

TUPTON.

(THOPTON, TOPTON.)

2409. GRANT from Roger de Deyncurt, rector of Wynnefeld, to Mary his mother, for her life, and to William his brother, of all his land in Thopton, which William his father had of the feoffment of

20

Robert fil. Thome clerici de Thopton and William le Hil. Witn. John de Deyncurt, William le Bret, Roger le Bretun, John de Braylisford. Dat. apud Hallewynnefeld, S. b. F. of St. Gregory [12 Mar.], 25 Edw. I. [1297]. (Longford.)

2410. GRANT from Henry Hunte to Robert Wednesley and John Wodeward of all his lands, etc., in Topton, in the fee of Wyngreworth and Eggestowe [Egstow], in the fee of Stretton, Ashover, and Bryminton, in the parish of Chestrefeld. Witn. Thomas Glapewell, rector of Wynfeld, John Brailesford, etc. Dat. Tupton, F. of St. Denis [9 Oct.], 17 Hen. VI. [1438]. (Foljambe.)

TWYFORD.

2411. GRANT from William Mylnegate of Melbourn to Robert Fraunceys of Fornewerk, esquire, of all his lands, etc., in Twyford and Steynston, which came to him on the death of Emma, late wife of Roger Mylnegàte, late of Little Over, as son and heir of the said Emma. Witn. Henry del Both, John Lathbury, esquires, John Crewkere, etc. Dat. Twyford, 22 Oct., 22 Hen. VI. [1443]. (Wilmot.)

TWYFORD *v.* also under WILLINGTON.

UNDERWOOD IN ASHBOURNE.

(UNDERWODE, UNDREWODE.)

2412. GRANT from Thomas de Lemenstre of Assheburne to Thomas de Knyvetone of lands in Underwode lying between Baxtersiche and Assebecke. Witn. John Cokain, Edmund Cokayn, John de la Pole of Assheburne, etc. Dat. 5 Apr., 40 Edw. III. [1306]. (Woll. vi. 23.)

2413. LEASE from Maud, widow of William de Knyveton of Bradley to Thomas de Knyveton of a meadow in Undrewode during his life, with a payment of 13s. 4d. to him in case of her death within three years of the making of the lease. Witn. John Cokayn, Thomas Adam, John de la Pole, etc. Dat. Underwode, 31 May, 39 Edw. III. [1365]. French. (Woll. vi. 22.)

2414. GRANT from Giles Adam of Assheburne to Thomas de Knyveton, of all the "butts" of land which he held of Thomas Adam his father in Underwode. Witn. Edmund Cokayn of Assheburn, John de la Pole, Henry le Walour of the same. Dat. 10 Dec., 42 Edw. III. [1368]. (Woll. vi. 24.)

2415. GRANT from Alice Adam, daughter of Thomas Adam of Asshebourne, to Nicholas de Knyveton, of a meadow in Brodemedue and Skyrmaremedue in the fee of Undrewode. Witn. Nich. de Montegomery, John de la Pole, John Cokayn, knts., etc. Dat. Morr. of the Circumcision [2 Jan.], 14 Ric. II. [1391]. (Woll. vi. 27.)

2416. RELEASE from John de Cressy, parson of Longeford, John Houbelle, parson of Wynfeld, William de Monyasche, parson of Bondesale, and Thomas Wombewelle, to Nicholas de Knyvetone, of lands which he held of the feoffment of John Cokayn in Undrewode. Witn. Nichol de Montegomery, Philippe de Okere, John de la Pole, etc. Dat. F. of St. Mark [25 Apr.], 13 Ric. II. [1390]. French. (Woll. vi. 26.)

2417. BOND by John Bate of Assheburne and Richard Bate of the same to Lawrence Lowe, in £20, for the peaceable possession of lands in Underwode; with a clause setting forth that the bond is sealed with the seals of John Clerk, vicar of Assheburne, Richard Boys, and Thomas Metheley, Prior of Bella Valle [Beauvale], co. Notts. Dat. 12 May, 8 Edw. IV. [1468]. (Woll. vii. 15.)

UNDERWOOD *v.* also under ASHBOURNE, DENBY, COLD EATON, MATLOCK, METHLEY.

UNSTONE.

(HONSTON, HOUNSTON, ONESTON, ONESTONE, ONISTONE, ONSTON, ONSTONE, ONUSTON, OUENSTON, OUNSTON, OWNSTON, OWNSTONE.)

2418. GRANT from Richard de Stretote [Stretton ?], miles, dominus de Onestona, to Richard his son, of the manor of Onestone; rent, a pair of gilded spurs or 6*d.* at Christmas, and to Alina, "quondam uxor Hervei, filii mei," four pounds, silver, for her life "in nomine dotis." Witn. Dom. Walter de Rybof and Robert le Breton of Waleton, milites, Ralph de Rerisby, Roger de Someruile, Jordan de Apetote, etc. *Temp.* Hen. III. (Woll. vii. 71.)

2419. GRANT from Richard de Strettone, dominus de Onistone, to Adam fil. Willelmi de Newbold, of Peter fil. Hugonis de Somerbrige his "nativus." Witn. Thomas de Bramtone, Jordan de Dracote, Thomas de Leyes, etc. *Temp.* Edw. I. (Woll. vii. 74.)

2420. GRANT from Richard de Stratton, dominus de Oneston, to Adam fil. Willelmi de Neubolt, of two water mills, lands, and rent in Oneston in Scaruisdale. Rent, 1*d.* Witn. William le Bret, John de Bremington, Peter de Donston, etc. *Temp.* Edw. I. (Woll. viii. 36.)

2421. RELEASE from Richard de Streton, miles, dominus de Honeston, to Adam fil. Willelmi de Neubolt, of Richard fil. Jored and John fil. Henrici, his "nativi." Witn. John de Bremington, Nicholas de Hulm, Peter de Donston, etc. *Temp.* Edw. I. (Woll. viii. 37.)

2422. GRANT, for twenty pounds, silver, from Richard fil. Ricardi de Strettone, mil., to Sara, widow of Adam de Neubolt, and Adam her son, of the manor of Oneston; rent, 20*s.* Witn. Thomas de Leyes, Nich. de Hulm, Peter de Donston, etc. [*Temp.* Edw. I.] (Woll. vii. 72.)

2423. GRANT, for twenty pounds, silver, from Richard fil. Ricardi de Strettona, mil., to Sara, que fuit uxor Ade de Neubold, and Adam her son, of the manor of Onistone. Witn. Peter de Dunstona, Thomas de Leys, Nicholas de Hulm, John le Say, etc. *Temp.* Edw. I. (Woll. vii. 73.)

2424. GRANT from Alan de la Merche de Oneston to Sarra, widow of Adam de Neubolt, and to Adam her son, of two acres of land in Surmedue in the fee of Oneston, one acre lying in Heghfelt, and the other in Hunerfurlong. Witn. Peter de Dunston, Henry de Oneston, Ralph le Muner, Peter fil. Matilde, Adam de Somurlesue, Ralph de Bremington. Undated. (Rel. xx. 166.)

2425. GRANT from Dom. Richard de Stretton, knt., to William, clerk, son of Adam de Roard de Oneston, of the land which the said Adam sometime held in Oneston, with liberty to grind his corn at the said lord's mill, etc. Witn. Dom. Ancelm, rector of Dranefeud, William, clericus de Neubolt, Thomas de Ley, Jordan de Bailey, Nicholas de Hulme, William Matenie, John de Burcheued, Thomas, clericus de Apilcnol, etc. Undated. (Rel. xx. iii.)

2426. GRANT from Dom. Richard de Stretton to William fil. Ade de Oneston of a messuage, etc., in Oneston called Hundishon, with five acres of land in Oneston fields. Witn. Dom. Ancelm, parson of Dranefeld, Thomas de Leiis, Peter de Wodehousis, Peter de Bircheued, etc. Undated. (Rel. xx. 110.)

2427. GRANT from Adam de Over Neubold to Philip de Lemna in Cestrefeld of lands in Oneston; rent, 5*d.* Witn. Robert de Detheks, William le Foleiambe, John de Brimington, etc. *Temp.* Edw. I. (Woll. viii. 45.)

2428. GRANT from Jurdan de Lees to Roger Leham of his manor of Barley Woodsettes, between the waters of Hounston and Weanstons-sickes. Witn. Hugh Linacre, Thomas de Brampton, John de Mora, John de Stubley, Peter de Dranfield, William de Dunston, Adam Francis, Thomas de Woodhouse. Undated. (Rel. xx. 109.)

2429. GRANT from Robert fil. Joh. de Hundehowe to Richard fil. Ade de Neubold of lands in Onestone and in the fields of Wodethorppe. Witn. Peter de Brimingtone, Roger fil. Ade de Tapton, John de Dyggeleye, and others. Dat. M. b. F. of St. Matthew [21 Sept.], 9 Edw. II. [1315]. (Woll. viii. 39.)

2430. GRANT from Roger fil. Ade de Tapton de Cestrefeld to Peter de Apelknoll, Margaret his wife, and John their son, for their lives, of that arable land which Peter ad-pontem de Onston sometime held in the fee of Onston, with a curtilage, etc., in Apelknol. Witn. Richard de Neubold, Robert le Aptot, Roger Bate de Neubold, etc. Dat. W. in Easter Week [Apr. 6], 1317. (Rel. xx. iii.)

2431. GRANT from Allan, chaplain of Schoffeld [? Sheffield, co. York], to William fil. Philippi de Aston, of lands in the town of Apilknolle, in the fee of Wyngreworth. Witn. Roger de Apilknolle, Peter his brother, Adam de Hondhow, etc. Dat. S. a. Conv. of St. Paul [25 Jan.], 12 Edw. II. [1319]. (Woll. viii. 50.)

2432. QUITCLAIM from John Calfcroft of Onston, and John his son, to David fil. Simonis de Wthytinton, of a piece of land in Le Ryddinge in Onston. Dat. 16 Edw. II. [1322-3]. (Rel. xx. 221.)

2433. QUITCLAIM by Elena condam uxor Davyd de Whytinton to John dil Mersche of Onston, of three acres of land in the Wodthorp in the fee of Onston. Witn. John de Grey, dominus de Onston, John de Plumleye, Richard de Dronfeld Wodhouses, etc. Dat. S. a. Ass. of B. V. M. [15 Aug.], 16 Edw. III. [1342]. (Foljambe.)

2434. ACCOUNT of the descent of the manor of Onston from Sir Richard Strettone, knt., who sold it " to Sare off Neubolt and Adam her son," which Adam, dying without heir, was succeeded by his brother Richard, and on the latter's death by his brother Henry, who died in " a thowsand ccc. xl. ix.," leaving two daughters, who married John Grey and Richard Tetlow. Fifteenth century. (Woll. vii. 75.)

2435. GRANT from Nicholas Bisshop of Chapel in le Frith to Nicholas fil. Johannis de Somerlesou, of 3½ acres of land in Onstone. Witn. John Gray, Richard de Tetlowe, John le Taillour, etc. Dat. F. of St. Mary Magd. [22 July], 29 Edw. III. [1355]. (Woll. vii. 76.)

2436. GRANT from Robert . . . . de Hundehowe to William le Fytheler of Onstone, of lands in Onstone; rent, 2*d.* Witn. Thomas le Gray, Nicholas son of John de Somerleso, Thomas "ad-finem-ville," etc. Dat. Onstone, Sun. a. F. of St. Michael, Arch., 32 Edw. III. [1358]. (Woll. viii. 49.)

2437. QUITCLAIM from Angnes fil. Ricardi Broune of Whytyngton to William Fitheler of Onston of the lands which came to him on the death of William, clericus de Appulknoll, in Appulknoll, in the fee of Onston, called "le Norton Land" and "le Ker," lying between Somerslese and Apulknoll. Witn. Thomas Gray of Onston, Nicholas del Mersch, Ranulph de Whityngton, etc. Dat. S. a. Michs., 37 Edw. III. [1363]. (Rel. xx. 109.)

2438. GRANT from Thomas fil. Johannis Gray of Onestone, near Dronfeld, to Richard Gomfrey, clerk, of the manor of Onestone, with the moiety of a water-mill, excepting a rent of 7*s.* Witn. Nicholas de Bauqwelle, Nicholas de Onestone, John atte Tounehende, talior, etc. Dat. S. a. F. of St. James [25 July], 41 Edw. III. [1367]. (Woll. viii. 40.)

2439. LEASE from Richard Goumfrey to Thomas, son of John Grey de Ounston by Dronfield, and Joan his wife, of all his manor of Ounston for term of their lives, with remainder to John their son. Witn. Nicholas de Ounston, John atte Tounende, Adam Wryght de Aston. Dat. S. a. Michs., 42 Edw. III. [1368]. (Rel. xx. 109.)

2440. GRANT from Hugh Woulf, chaplain, and Peter del Wode of Briminton, to John Fleccher of Dronfeld, chaplain, of all the lands they had by feoffment from Robert fil. Egidii de Briminton in the fee of Oneston and in the fields of Brerlay. Witn. Nicholas de Oneston, John at Tounhend, Robert Dawson, etc. Dat. apud Chastourfeld, Vig. of Circumcision [31 Dec.], 8 Ric. II. [1384]. (Rel. xx. 219.)

2441. GRANT from Joan Vawsone, widow of Robert Vawsone of Appelknoll, to John Herwy, sen., John Herwy, jun., and John Metam of Astone, of all her lands, etc., in the vill of Appilknoll, in the territory of Ownstone and in the fee of Wyngreworth. Witn. John Gray, Nicholas de Ownston, and Roger Curtaysse. Dat. Pur. of B. V. M. [2 Feb.], 16 Ric. II. [1393]. (Rel. xx. 165.)

2442. QUITCLAIM from Thomas Grey of Ounston to John Grey his son, of the manor of Ounston, with the moiety of the mill there, etc. Witn. Thomas Comfrey, rector of Dronfield, Ralph Barker, Nicholas de Ounston, etc. Dat. 7 May, 1398. (Woll. xx. 221.)

2443. GRANT from Cecily, daughter of John Pereisson of Apulknoll, to William Hudsone, chaplain, of Dronfeld, of lands in Onuston. Witn. Nich. de Onuston, John Stubley of Wodsmythes, Will Rowmley of Apulknolle, etc. Dat. Trin. Sun. [29 May], 2 Hen. IV. [1401]. (Woll. viii. 46.)

2444. RELEASE by Richard de Chaterton, co. Lancs., to Nicholas de Oneston, of lands and tenements which he had of the gift of Roger de Chestrefeld, chaplain. Witn. Will de Dethek, Rob de Barley, Thurstan de Doure, etc. Dat. Chestrefeld, F. of St. Peter ad-vincula [1 Aug.], 6 Hen. IV. [1405]. (Woll. viii. 48.)

2445. GRANT from Richard de Chadirton to John Bullok, son of Thomas Bullok of Norton, of all his lands in Ounston, in the parish of Dronfeld. Witn. Nicholas de Ounston, John Gray, Thomas Maynard, etc. Dat. M. b. Christmas Day, 8 Hen. IV. [1406]. (Rel. xx. 166.)

2446. LEASE from John Talbot, Dóminus del Furnyvale, and Geoffrey Laucher to Thomas Bullok and John Bullok, of lands in Onston, at a yearly rent of an ounce of pepper. Witn. John Gray, William Wolhous, Ralph Povay. Dat. apud Roderham, F. of St. James [25 July], 12 Hen. IV. [1411]. (Rel. xx. 220.)

2447. QUITCLAIM from John Gray of Onston to William Aston, William Woderowe, and John Tunsted, of lands within the lordship of Oneston. Witn. Roger de Chestirfeld, William Hudson, chaplain, Robert Schemyld, etc. Dat. Dronfield, F. of St. Gregory [12 Mar.], 5 Hen. V. [1417]. (Rel. xx. 110.)

2448. GRANT from John Gray of Ouenston to John Leek, esq., John Acres, clerk, and Nicholas de Lowe, of lands in Ouenston; rent, a red rose at F. of St. John Bapt. [24 June]. Witn. Will Cook, Thos. Maynard, Roger Curteys, etc. Dat. F. of St. John B. [24 June], 6 Hen. V. [1418]. (Woll. viii. 47.)

2449. GRANT from John Gray de Oneston to William Aston, William Woderowe, and John Tunsted, of all his lands, etc., and the moiety of water-mill and all the lordship of Oneston " sub terra et extra terram." Witn. William Coke of Holmesfeld, Thomas Fox de Aston, Thomas Maynnarde, William Boton, etc. Dat. F. of St. Luke [18 Oct.], 1418. (Rel. xx. 218.)

2450. GRANT from Henry Hurryll of Wodesmethys to Roger his son of a piece of land with meadow in Oneston. Witn. John Ballok, Thomas Wodehalls, Thomas Benett. Dat. F. of St. Thomas, M. [29 Dec.], 9 Hen. VI. [1430]. (Rel. xx. 165.)

2451. GRANT from John Bullok of Norton to William Bullok his son and Elena his wife of all his lands in Onston, excepting those which were Christopher Belefeld's. Witn. John Percy, clerk, John Barker, Richard Selioke, Robert Outrem, Thomas Wodehouse. Dat. 1 Nov., 1431. (Rel. xx. 109.)

2452. RE-GRANT from William Aston and John Tunstede to John Gray of Onestone of lands in Onestone, lately held by the grantors conjointly with William Woderofe. Witn. Thomas Chaworth, Richard Vernone, knts., William Ulkerthorpe, esq., etc. Dat. 10 Nov., 10 Hen. VI. [1431]. (Woll. viii. 41.)

2453. ATTORNEY from William Aston and John Tunstede to John Bullock to deliver to John Gray of Oneston seisin of the lands which they held jointly with William Woderofe, now deceased. Dat. 10 Nov., 1431. (Rel. xx. iii.)

2454. RELEASE from William Aston and John Tunstede to John Gray of Onestone of lands in Onestone, which they held of the gift of the said John, conjointly with William Woderofe. Dat. 15 Nov., 10 Hen. VI. [1431]. (Woll. viii. 42.)

2455. GRANT from John Gray to Thomas, Bishop of Durham, John Radclyf, clerk, Henry de Longley, and John Bullok, of all the lands, etc., in Onston which he holds on lease from William Aston and John Tunstede. Witn. Thomas Chaworth, Richard Vernon, knts., William Uwerthorp, John Shakerley, etc. Dat. 15 Nov., 1431. (Rel. xx. iii.)

2456. ATTORNEY from Thomas, Bishop of Durham, John Radclyf, clerk, and others, to William Bullok, to take seisin of lands in Onston which John Gray gave them. Dat. 15 Nov., 1431. (Rel. xx. 109.)

2457. LETTERS patent of Henry VI., appointing James Strangways [Puisne Justice of the Common Pleas], and John Ellerker [Serjeant-at-Law], Justices, to hold an Assize "Nove disseisine," which John Bullok had arrayed against Christopher de Belfeld, respecting a tenement in Onestone. Dat. Westm., 8 Jan., aᵒ 11 [1433]. (Woll. vii. 77.)

2458. GRANT from Thomas Hurll of Kyrby, son and heir of Henry Hurll of Wodsmythes, to Robert Seriand of Dronfield, of all the lands which came to him on his said father's death, in Onston. Witn. Thomas Foxe of Aston, Richard de Cartlege, William Owtrem, etc. Dat. Dronfield, F. b. F. of St. Martin [Nov. 11.], 14 Hen. VI. [1435]. (Rel. xx. 109.)

2459. GRANT from John fil. Thome de Clogh to William Gray of Hanley and Peter Turner, of all the messuages, etc., he had of the grant of William Dowson, in Oneston, Norton in Scarsdale Hundred, etc. Witn. Richard Seliok of Norton, William Bullok, and Thomas Wodhous. Dat. Th. a. Trinity [12 June], 17 Hen. VI. [1438]. (Rel. xx. 165.)

2460. GRANT from Thomas Maynerd and John Clerke to Thomas Fox of Aston and Robert Sergeaunt, of all the lands, tenements, etc., in Oneston formerly belonging to Nicholas, son of John de Somerlese. Witn. Robert Schemeld, Richard Cartleg, Thomas Herve, etc. Dat. F. of St. James [25 July], . . . Hen. VI. [*circ.* 1439]. (Foljambe.)

2461. GRANT from John Clogh to Dom. William Pole, Earl of Suffolk, to Dom. Henry Grey, Richard Bingham, and John Cokfeld, of all his messuages, etc., in Oneston, Apulknol, and Norton. Witn. Adam Seriant, Robert Shemyld, William Gardener, William Moghson, etc. Dat. Sat. a. Nat. of B. V. M. [8 Sept.], 18 Hen. VI. [1439]. (Rel. xx. 219.)

2462. GRANT from Cecily Appurknoll of Ounston to John Leek of Sutton, esquire, Thomas Leeke, and John Dassenys of the same, of a tenement called Bryghouse in Ownston. Witn. Thomas Hanley of Hanley, Walter Glossok, Thomas Wodehus, etc. Dat. 20 Sept., 1439. (Rel. xx. 109.)

2463. INDENTURE whereby it is agreed that, for four marks, Nicholas Ganshill, esq., shall enfeoff John Clogh in lands in Oneston, Apulknoll, Norton, and Delmere, which he held of the gift of William Dowson. Dat. Barlburghe, Fr. a. F. of St. Cedde [7 Jan.], 18 Hen. VI. [1440]. (Woll. viii. 43.)

2464. ACQUITTANCE by the same to the same, for four marks, in pursuance of the agreement made in the preceding indenture. Dat. 20 Jan., 19 Hen. VI. [1441]. (Woll. viii. 44.)

2465. QUITCLAIM from Alice Hurl, relicta Henrici Hurl, to Robert Clerke of Somerleys, of the third part of her late husband's lands in Oneston, which third part was assigned to her as dower. Dat. Somerleys, "in festo Reliquiarum" [27 Jan.], 19 Hen. VI. [1440]. (Rel. xx. 222.)

2466. GRANT from Roger Hurrill to William Owtrem of a piece of land with meadow in Onston. Witn. Thomas Fox de Aston, Thomas Maynard, Adam Vnwyn. Dat. F. of St. Laurence [10 Aug.], 19 Hen. VI. [1441]. (Rel. xx. 166.)

2467. QUITCLAIM from William de la Pole, Marquis of Suffolk, Richard Bingham, Justice of King's Bench, and John Rockfield, to Richard Illyngworth, of all the lands which were sometime William Dawnson's or John Clough's in Appinknoll and Oneston. Dat. W. b. Epiphany [6 Jan.], 20 Hen. VI. [1442]. (Rel. xx. 220.)

2468. GRANT from Thomas Hervy, son and heir of John Hervy, to John de Holyngworth, of all his lands in Appulknoll and Oneston. Witn. John Selioke, John Bulloke, Thomas Fox. Dat. T. b. Michs. [29 Sept.], 21 Hen. VI. [1442]. (Rel. xx. 222.)

2469. QUITCLAIM from William Gray and Peter Tournor to John Holynworth of all the messuages, etc., which they lately acquired from John fil. Thomas Clogh in Appulknoll and Oneston. Witn. Richard Seliok, John Bullok, William Bullok. Dat. Th. b. F. of St. Michael [29 Sept.], 21 Hen. VI. [1442]. (Rel. xx. 219.)

2470. GRANT from John Holynworth to Richard Illingworth of all his lands in Onston and Appulknoll. Witn. Thomas Fox, Thomas Cooke, John Barker. Dat. S. a. Ex. of H. Cross [14 Sept.], 24 Hen. VI. [1445]. (Rel. xx. 222.)

2471. GRANT from William Harreson and Joan his wife of Dugmanton, to William Bullok, of the messuage in Apilknoll and Oneston which he had lately of the gift of John Shepherd. Witn. Thomas Seliok, Thomas Bullok, William Clerk, etc. Dat. Onston, 1 Apr., 31 Hen. VI. [1453]. (Rel. xx. 110.)

2472. QUITCLAIM from Robert, son of Ralph Tapton of Chesterfield, to William Bollock of Onston, of a messuage, etc., which Peter de Ponte sometime held, and John Appelknol held for his life [in Onston]. Dat. 1 June, 1454. (Rel. xx. 111.)

2473. GRANT from Ralph Illingworth, esq., to Thomas Hunt, of lands in Appurknoll, Dronfeld, and Staveley, late in the tenure of Richard Holden. Witn. Henry Foljambe, Peter Frechheuile, Robert Barley. Dat. 8 June, 7 Edw. IV. [1467]. (Rel. xx. 222.)

2474. GRANT from Roger de Ecclesale to Richard Bullok of a piece of wood in Canggull in the fee of Onston, abutting on Wyndhill lane and on Le Great Clough. Witn. Dom. Henry Wodhard, vicar of Dronfeld, John Parkar de Leys, Robert Barley of Barley, esquire, etc. Dat. Fr. "post finem [? festum] Beate Marie," 1471. (Rel. xx. 220.)

2475. LEASE from Henry Pierpount, knt., Thomas Pilkyngton, knt., and John Pierpount, esquire, to Richard Bullok, son of William Bullok, late of Oneston, and to Isabel his wife, dau. of Thomas Hunt, gent., of messuages and lands in Oneston and Apurknoll. Witn. Robert Barley, sen., Ralph Leche, and Henry Wedirhed, perpetual vicar of Dronfeld. Dat. 24 May, 16 Edw. IV. [1476]. (Rel. xx. 219.)

2476. COVENANT for sale by Raphe Clerke to Richard Bullok of a piece of land called Wodsmethys in Onston. Witn. Sir Thomas Boton, y⁰ preste, William Schaw, Robert Schemeld. Dat. Conv. of St. Paul [25 Jan.], 18 Edw. IV. [1479]. (Rel. xx. 166.)

2477. GRANT from Ralph Clerke to Richard Bullok of land called
"le Wodsmythys," in Oneston. Witn. John Selyok, Thomas Andrewe,
Robert Curtys, etc. Dat. Nat. of St. John B. [24 June], 19 Edw. IV.
[1479]. (Rel. xx. 222.)

2478. QUITCLAIM from Ralph Illyngworth, esquire, son and heir of
Richard Illingworth, knt., to Thomas Hunt, of a messuage and lands
in Oneston and Appurknoll, within the parishes of Dronfield and Staley.
(The Deed is sealed with the seal of John Hunt, Mayor of Nottingham.)
Dat. Onston, 12 Mar., 1483. (Rel. xx. 110.)

2479. GRANT from Edward Wodhouse of Retford, son and heir of
John Wodhouse, late of Onston, to Richard Bullok, of the reversion
of all the lands in Onston and Somurles which Isabella, now wife of
Ralph Estwode, his mother, holds for her life since the death of her
husband, John Wodhouse. Witn. William Byngley, vicar of Dronfield,
John Blakwall, chaplain, Robert Lowecok, etc. Dat. 24 Feb., 1487.
(Rel. xx. 111.)

2480. LEASE from Thomas Hunt to Richard Bullok and Isabella
his wife of a messuage and lands in Onston and Appurknoll, within
the parish of Dronfield, and lands in Stavely which he had from Ralph
Illingworth, esq., son and heir of Richard Illingworth, knt. Witn.
Robert Barley, sen., Roger Eyre, jun., John Barley. Dat. 24 June,
2 Hen. VII. [1487]. (Rel. xx. 221.)

2481. QUITCLAIM from Richard, son and heir of Ralph Illyngworth
of Stanford, co. Notts., to Richard Bullok of Onston, of all the messuages, etc., in Onston and Appurknoll which were the said Ralph's.
Dat. 9 June, 1503. (Rel. xx. 164.)

2482. GRANT from John Reyd of Hartyll to John Bolocke of a
close called "Le Preyst Closse" in Wodsmethe in Onston. Dat.
1 Apr., 1 Hen. VIII. [1510]. (Rel. xx. 220.)

2483. SALE from Robert Wuddus, son and heir of Thomas Wuddhus
of Honston, to John Bollokk and Henry Bollok, clerk, of lands in
Honston. Dat. 9 July, 1519. (Rel. xx. 109.)

2484. LEASE from Philip Bulloke of Ownstone to Richard Stevynsone
of land in Ownston, which the said Philip had of the lately-suppressed
Abbey of Beauchief. Dat. 1 May, 1538. (Rel. xx. 111.)

2485. QUITCLAIM (made in accordance with an award by William
Chainer of Brampton and others) between Elena Calcroft and Joan
Calcroft, daughters and co-heirs of Thomas Calcroft, late of Dronfield,
and William Bulloke) from the said Elena and Joan to the said William,
of the moiety of the said Thomas Calcroft's lands in Hundall and Appur-
knolle, in consideration of £10. Dat. 23 Mar., 1546[7]. (Rel. xx. 111.)

UNSTONE *v.* also under COAL ASTON, CHESTERFIELD.

WADSHELF.

(WADESELF.)

2486. ACQUITTANCE from Roger le Breton to William le Brette and
Mary his wife for five charters concerning lands, etc., which descended
to him after the death of Peter his brother in Wadeself, Calale, and
Walton. Dat. Chesterfield, Fr. a. Ass. of B. V. M. [15 Aug.],
18 Edw. I. [1290]. (Foljambe.)

2487. GRANT, for half a mark, from Roger fil. Rogeri Britone of Waletun, to Alan fil. Finiani de Waleton of a bovate of land in Wadeself; rent, 3s. 6d. Witn. Thomas fil. Radulphi de Bramton, Walter his son, Thomas de Wadeself, etc. *Temp.* Edw. I. or II. (Woll. iii. 31.)

WAKEBRIDGE.
(WAKEBRUGGE, WAKBRUG, WAKBRYGGE.)

2488. EXTENT of the manor of Wakebrugge. Dat. M. a. F. of St. John B. [24 June], 24 Edw. III. [1350]. (Woll. xi. 13.)

2489. EXTENTS of the lands and tenements of Rauf Pole of Wakbrug, in Wakbrug, Matloke, Tannesley, and Heegge. Dat. 6 May, 2 Ric. III. [1485]. (Woll. xi. 15-17.)

2490. EXTENT of the lands of John Pole of Wakbrygge in Wakbrygge, Matloke, and Tannysley, 6 June, 1 Hen. VIII. [1509]. (Woll. xi. 18.)

WAKEBRIDGE *v.* also under TANSLEY.

WALDLEY *v.* under CUBLEY.

WALTON-BY-CHESTERFIELD.
(WALLTON, WALETUN.)

2491. GRANT from Robert Baystan de Cestrefeld to Richard fil. Bond de Cesterfeld of all his meadow of Nevhalebarwe in Waleton, which Robert his father held of Laurence de Neubyghyng. Witn. Galfridus, vicarius de Cesterfeld, Adam Blundus, Thomas Gildkarman, etc. Late Hen. III. (Foljambe.)

2492. GRANT from Willam fil. Ranulphi de Waleton to Robert fil. Edwini de Cestrefeld of a rood of land in the territory of Waleton. Witn. Hugh de Dokemonton, Ralph de Sidenale, Robert de Ogedeston, etc. Late Hen. III. (Foljambe.)

2493. GRANT from William fil. Roberti de Ogediston to Nicholas fil. Joh. de Swathweyt of a culture of land in the territory of Waletun. Witn. Ralph de Sydenale, Thomas de Morton, Robert de Stubbinges, *Temp.* Hen. III.-Edw. I. (Foljambe.)

2494. LEASE from Matilda quondam uxor Nicholay de Swathuyt to Thomas Franceys of Cesterfeld, of land in Waletun, for six years, beginning at Martinmas, 55 Hen. III. [1270]. Witn. Thomas de Brampton, Robert Blund, Henry de Cesterfeld, etc. (Foljambe.)

2495. BAILIFF's accompt-rolls of Walton Manor. *Temp.* Edw. I.-II. (Lichf. N. 24-26.)

2496. GRANT from Roger le Breton, Dominus de Walton, to Robert de Calale, of two acres, etc., of land "super le Lauedy crofte" [in Walton]. Witn. Hugh de Lynaker, Roger de Dokemonton, William Beuerege. Dat. T. b. F. of St. Margaret [20 July], 33 Edw. I. [1305]. (Foljambe.)

2497. GRANT from Maria de Buxton to Roger her son of two acres and a plot of land called Wadeacre in the field of Walton. Witn. Roger Laverok, John de Warsope, Hugh de Neubolt, etc. Dat. S. a. F. of St. Valentine [14 Feb.], 5 Edw. II. [1312]. (Foljambe.)

2498. GRANT from John de Mora and Margery his wife to William their son of a toft and croft in Wengeby, in the fee of Walton. Witn. John de Wyggeleye, William de Wyggeleye, Thomas de Somersale. Dat. Walton, S. a. F. of St. Barnabas [11 June], 8 Edw. II. [1315]. (Foljambe.)

2499. GRANT from Alan fil. Galfridi de Hulm of Cestrefeld to Henry de Sutton, "magistro scolar[ium] de Cestrefeld," and Agnes, the said Alan's daughter, and their heirs in tail, of all his lands in Wengeby in the fee of Walton. Witn. Adam de Neubold, Roger Laueroc, Robert Durant, etc. Dat. S. b. F. of Inv. of H. Cross [3 May], 17 Edw. II. [1324]. (Foljambe.)

2500. GRANT from Elizabeth fil. Ric. clerici de Walton to John Parker, of all the lands, etc., which she inherited from her father in Walton. Witn. Roger Bretonn, sen., Thomas de Somersale, William de Wyggeley, etc. Dat. M. a. F. of Ex. of H. Cross [14 Sept.], 9 Edw. III. [1335]. (Foljambe.)

2501. GRANT from John Salmoun to John fil. Petri le Webbe of Caldham of half an acre of land at "le Hothe," in the tenure of Walton. Witn. John atte Hothe, Richard Palmere, Richard Taylour. Dat. 14 Edw. III. [1340]. (Foljambe.)

2502. GRANT from John de Maunsfeld and Elizabeth his wife to William de Cotenes and Edith his wife, of a certain holm called Waltonholm, in the fee of Walton. Witn. Henry de Maunsfeld, John del Asshe, Richard Beuerege, etc. Dat. S. a. F. of St. Nicholas [6 Dec.], 7 Ric. II. [1383]. (Foljambe.)

2503. QUITCLAIM from Henry fil. Hen. Bate of Thwathewait to William de Cotenes and Edith his wife, of a holm called Waltonholm in Walton. Witn. Henry de Maunsfeld, John del Ashe, Richard Beverege. Dat. F. of Ex. of H. Cross [14 Sept.], 9 Ric. II. [1386]. (Foljambe.)

2504. GRANT from John de Wyngeby, son and heir of Robert de Wyngby, to Richard Baret and Isabella his wife, of all his lands, etc., in Wingby or elsewhere in Walton. Witn. John Bate, John de Maunsfeld, Henry de Maunsfeld, etc. Dat. T. a. Tr. of St. Edw. Conf. [13 Oct.], 16 Ric. II. [1392]. (Foljambe.)

2505. GRANT from Alice de Wyngeby of Nottingham and John, son of Robert de Wyngeby, to Richard Baret, of all their wood growing in Wyngeby in Walton. Dat. W. a. F. of St. Luke [18 Oct.], 16 Ric. II. [1392]. (Foljambe.)

2506. GRANT from Isabella de Kerre of Walton, widow, to Thomas, son of John Parker of Walton, of the third part of all the lands which Richard Clerk, her father, had of the grant of the heirs of Roger de Wyggeley [in Walton]. Witn. Thomas de Brygge, Philip de Walesby, Robert de Wymby, etc. Dat. S. a. F. of St. Giles, abbot [1 Sept.], 17 Ric. II. [1393]. (Foljambe.)

2507. GRANT from Margery, widow of William Edison of Walton, to Thomas atte Brig and Robert Saunderson, of a messuage and half-bovate of land which came to her from William atte More, her father, in Walton. Witn. Henry Bate, John de Mannefeld, etc. Dat. Th. a. Epiphany [6 Jan.], 17 Ric. II. [1394]. (Foljambe.)

2508. GRANT from John Parker to Agnes Parker his mother, Elizabeth Parker his sister, and Agnes Parker his wife, of all his lands, etc., in Walton. Witn. Philip de Walesby, William del Hyll, John Graveler, etc. Dat. F. of St. Mary Magdalen [22 July], 20 Ric. II. [1395]. (Foljambe.)

2509. GRANT from William de Dryeholme, formerly dwelling in Walton, near Chestrefeld, to Walter Spenser of Walton Grange, of all his lands, etc., which he had by feoffment of Henry de Foston and Roger del Leghes, chaplains, in Walton. Witn. John Bate, Richard Bythebrok, Nicholas de Thwathewait, etc. Dat. M. b. F. of St. Dunstan [19 May], 20 Ric. II. [1397]. (Foljambe.)

2510. GRANT from Richard, son of John del Ker, to William Webbester and Henry Scotte, chaplains, and John de Maunsfeld, of all the lands, etc., in Walton which descended to him after the death of John del Ker, his father. Witn. Thurstan del Bowre, John Bate, Hugh Drapier, etc. Dat. 30 Sept., 5 Hen. IV. [1403]. (Foljambe.)

2511. LIST of tenants owing suit, with amounts, at the Court of the Manor of Walton. Mon. a. F. of St. Barnabas [11 June], 11 Hen. IV. [1410]—Easter [8 Apr.], 2 Hen. V. [1414]. (Foljambe.)

2512. PARTICULARS of land in and near Walton purchased from John Spenser on F. of Nativity of the B. Virgin [8 Sept.], 3 Hen. V. [1415]. (Foljambe.)

2513. GRANT from John Parker to Thomas Foliambe, sen., of all his lands, etc., in Walton. Witn. John de Hyll of Walton, William at ye Well, John Stabeler, Robert Mylner, etc. Dat. Walton, M. b. F. of St. Barnabas [11 June], 6 Hen. V. [1418]. (Foljambe.)

2514. GRANT from Roger Bawkewell of Dunston to Thomas Baret, John Baret, clerk, and Richard Baret, of all his lands, tenements, etc., in Wyngeby, in the fee of Walton. Witn. Ralph Durant, William Brampton, Richard Cook, etc. Dat. 4 May, 2 Hen. VI. [1424]. (Foljambe.)

2515. GRANT from Richard Innesand to Thomas Baret, Richard Tomes, and Roger Tapton, of all his lands and tenements in the town and fields of Walton and Wyngby, which he had of the grant of Thomas Baret. Witn. William Brampton, Richard Calcroft, John Marshall. Dat. Chestrefeld, 26 Oct., 8 Hen. VI. [1429]. (Foljambe.)

2516. POWER of attorney from Thomas Thirland of Notyngham, "marchand," Richard Hawson of Chestrefeld, chaplain, William Bradscha of the same, draper, and Richard Barbur, to John Deston of Normanton, clerk, to give seisin to John Turnour of Walton of a tenement and 15 acres of land, etc., in Walton. Dat. F. of St. Thomas, Ap. [21 Dec.], 18 Hen. VI. [1439]. (Foljambe.)

2517. GRANT from William Foliambe of Repham, co. Linc., gent., and John Holme, son and heir of Thomas Holme, late of Chestrefeld, to Thomas Foliambe, esq., of three roods of land in the territory of Walton. Witn. Ralph Calcroft, vicar of Chestrefeld, Robert Gryssop, etc. Dat. F. of Ann. of B. V. Mary [25 Mar.], 35 Hen. VI. [1457]. (Foljambe.)

2518. BOND from John Stubbyng and Giles Stubbyng of Hulme to Thomas Foliambe, esq., in five marks, to pay arrears of rent of lands late held by Thomas Cause, in the manor of Walton, the third part of which belonged in co-parceny to the said Thomas Foliambe, Elizabeth, wife of John Cheyny, esq., Dame Isabel, wife of Sir Bryan Stapleton, and Marget, wife of Richard Byngham, esq. Dat. F. of Ass. of B. V. M. [15 Aug.], 38 Hen. VI. [1460]. (Foljambe.)

2519. GRANT from John Scha, son and heir of John Scha of Somersale, and Agnes his wife, to John Turnour of Walton, of all the lands, etc., in Walton which they had of the grant of the same John Turnour, the same being now surrendered in exchange for ten acres in the fee of Brampton. Witn. Henry Foliaumbe, gent., Thomas Fox, Richard Assh, etc. Dat. 19 June, 1461. (Foljambe.)

2520. ACQUITTANCE from Robert Lacye of Stoke, near Newark, co. Notts., and Margaret his wife, to Henry Foliambe of Walton, esq., for £10 and two "togae," in payment for certain lands, etc., formerly belonging to Richard Abney of Hope, brother of the said Margaret, with general release. Dat. Walton, 18 May, 8 Edw. IV. [1468]. (Foljambe.)

2521. GRANT from Henry Foliambe, esq., to Thomas Odell, esq., and Margery his wife, of a yearly rent of £24 from his manors of Walton and Brymmyngton, and all his lands, etc., in Walton, Brymmyngton, Chestrefeld, Hulme, Brampton, and Lytton, and from his manor of Ryby, co. Linc., to hold the same for the life of the said Margery by way of dower out of the lands, etc., of Thomas Foliambe, esq., late her husband. Witn. Henry Vernon, Nich. Longford, Hen. Pierpoint, Rob. Barley, Peter Frecchevyle, esqq. Dat. 5 July, 8 Edw. IV. [1468]. (Foljambe.)

2522. LETTERS testimonial from Thomas Reynald, LL.B., Commissary of the Bishop of Coventry and Lichfield, granting to Henry Foliambe of Walton and John Foliambe administration of the goods of Thomas Foliambe of Walton, deceased intestate, the same having been appraised by James Hyton, Dean of Scarsdale, and others, and proclamations made at mass in Chesterfield Church. Dat. 27 May, 1469. (Foljambe.)

2523. ACQUITTANCE from Nicholas Baguley of Laynesholme, co. Lanc., yeoman, and Johanna his wife, to Henry Foliambe, lord of Walton, esq., for 40s. rent of lands, etc., late belonging to Thomas Cakee, father of the said Johanna; with release of all actions, etc., on account of debts due by Henry Foliambe, John Foliambe, or Thomas Foliambe. Dat. Walton, 10 June, 9 Edw. IV. [1469]. (Foljambe.)

2524. ACQUITTANCE from Thomas Odell, esq., to Henry Foliambe, esq., for 12 pounds of silver, for rent due on account of the dower of Margery his wife. Dat. 30 Nov., 9 Edw. IV. [1469]. (Foljambe.)

2525. ACQUITTANCE from Thomas Wodell [*al* Odell], esq., to Henry Foliambe, esq., for £12, due to him by reason of the dower of Margery his wife, late wife of Thomas Foliambe, esq. Dat. F. of St. Andrew [30 Nov.], 1470. (Foljambe.)

2526. LETTERS patent of Edward IV., granting a general pardon to Henry Foliambe of Walton. Dat. Westminster, 5 July, aᵒ 13 [1473]. (Foljambe.)

2527. ACQUITTANCE from Richard Malare, late Escheator for cos. Notts. and Derby, to Henry Foliambe, esq., of Walton, for £3, due to the Exchequer by the widow of Thomas Odell, on account of the third part of the Manor of Walton. Dat. Frid. F. of St. James [25 July], 17 Edw. IV. [1477]. (Foljambe.)

2528. ACQUITTANCE from Ralph Knyston, escheator for cos. Notts. and Derby, to Henry Foliambe of Walton, esq., for £3, due to the Exchequer by [Margery], widow of Thomas Foliambe, and wife of Thomas Odell, on account of her dower in the manor of Walton. Dat. 15 Oct., 18 Edw. IV. [1478]. (Foljambe.)

2529. ACQUITTANCE from Laurence Gaskyn, son and heir of John Gaskyn, late of Brampton, to Henry Foliambe, lord of Walton, for £3 13s. 4d., in part payment of 11 marks purchase money of certain lands, etc. Dat. Walton, F. of St. Luke [18 Oct.], 18 Edw. IV. [1478]. (Foljambe.)

2530. ACQUITTANCE from Isabel Nawbull to Henry Foliambe of Walton, esq., for 6s. 8d., in full payment of 15s. for a parcel of land called "Hovyerdes." Dat. Lady Day, 21 Edw. IV. [1481]. (Foljambe.)

2531. INDENTURE between Henry Foliambe of Walton, "swyer," and John Coterell of Walton, whereby the latter, having offended and trespassed "in takyng of certeyn corne fro Crystore Scha," covenants not to "come on thys syde yᵉ water off Derwentt" within 7 miles of Walton or 3 miles of Walton manor for 7 years on pain of forfeiting 20s. yearly of "yᵉ lyfflorde yᵗ was old Robert Coterell's." Dat. Lady Day, 23 Edw. IV. [1483]. (Foljambe.)

2532. LEASE by Thomas Durand, son and heir of Thomas Durand, to Henry Foliambe of Walton, sen., of three closes called "Wytyngholm," for 12 years after the decease of his "grandam Hellysabet Eyre." Dat. 25 July, 1488. (Foljambe.)

2533. COVENANTS between Henry Foliambe, sen., of Walton, "squier," and John Leeke, sen., of Sutton-in-le-Dale, squier, for the marriage of Godfrey Foliambe, son and heir of the said Henry (or in the event of his death to Thomas Foliambe, second son of the same), with Katherine, dau. of the said John Leeke, or (in the event of her death) with Muriel, second dau. of the same, and for the marriage of John Leeke, son and heir of the said John, with Jane, dau. of the said Henry Foliambe. Dat. 9 June, 4 Hen. VII. [1489]. (Foljambe.)

2534. BOND by Thomas Lucy of Charlecote and Godfrey Foljambe of Walton, knts., to John Heron and Thomas Bolayn, knts., for £100, to be paid to the king's use at Michaelmas next. Dat. 14 May, 13 Henry VIII. [1521]. Endorsed: Condition of above bond, witnessing that if the said Lucy and Foljambe shall pay 100 marks to the said Heron and Bolayn, for the king's use, at Easter, A.D. 1523, the said bond shall be void. (P. R. O. A. 4422.)

WALTON *v.* also under CHESTERFIELD, DERBY, WADSHELF.

WALTON-ON-TRENT.

2535. GRANT from William Gardiner de Burton-subtus-Needwood to Robert de Coton of Walton, of a messuage sometime held by John Durant in Walton-on-Trent. Witn. William Smyth, John Clerk, Stephen Gardiner. Dat. Th. in Easter Week [18 Apr.], 3 Edw. I. [1275]. (Bemrose)

2536. GRANT from Robert de Monte Alto de Com. Derb. sen[escallus] Cestrie, to Walter de Esturton and Juliana his wife, of the manor of Waleton-super-Trentam, with the advowson, etc.; yearly rent, one pair of gilt spurs. Witn. Dom. Hugh fil. Otonis, Richard de Bosco, Robert de Stokeport, John le Tyeys, John de Gurney, William le Lung, milites, Ralph de Burgo, miles, de Melton, etc. *Temp.* Edw. I. or Edw. II. [bet. 1296-1329]. (Harl. 53 E. 13.)

2537. LEASE, for thirty years, from Richard Durant de Walton-super-Trent, to William Talebot de Rostelaston, of land in Walton, lying on Le Breche, etc. Rent, a rose at midsummer. Witn. Will. Dunstan de Wallton, John Traynel de eadem, etc. Dat. Michaelmas, 14 Edw. II. [1320]. (Gresley.)

2538. GRANT from Stephen Gardiner of Walton-on-Trent to John de Fyndern of all the lands, etc., in Walton-on-Trent, which John fil. Johannis Dunston gave to Thomas Waleys. Witn. William Boghhey, rector of Walton, John de Yoxhale, William Ampe, etc. Dat. S. b. Ann. of B. V. M. [25 Mar.], 6 Hen. IV. [1405]. (Horton.)

2539. GRANT and quitclaim from John de Finderne to Roger Hortone of all his lands and possessions in Walton-on-Trent and Cattone. Witn. Thomas de Gresley, knt., Thomas Gruffythe, Richard Vernon de Horlastone, Thomas Stanley, and William Cursun, "scutiferi." Dat. 8 Apr., 4 Hen. V. [1416]. (Horton.)

2540. QUITCLAIM from Thomas Griffithe, esquire, to William Cheyne, Justice, Thomas Henster, Roger Cartwryhte, and others, of all the lands in Walton-on-Trent and Catton which they had by feoffment of Roger Horton. Witn. Thomas de Gresley, knt., Thomas Stanley, Hugh Erdeswyke, esquires, etc. Dat. apud Whychenore, Easter Day [23 Apr.], 2 Hen. VI. [1424]. (Horton.)

2541. QUITCLAIM from John Spencer fil. Ric. Spencer of Burton-on-Trent to William Horton, esq., son and heir of Roger Horton, of all the lands, etc., in Walton-on-Trent, Catton, and Borowe [co. Derby], which were lately Roger Horton's. Witn. Thomas Stanley, esquire, Richard Broune of Repton, Gilbert Ives. Dat. Walton, Th. a. F. of the Assumption [15 Aug.], 7 Hen. VI. [1429]. (Horton.)

2542. GRANT from John Abell de Stapenhill to Thomas Gresley, mil., Dominus de Drakelowe, of five acres of meadow in the meadow called Le Borough-holme, within the lordship of Walton-on-Trent, which five acres formerly belonged to William dict. Le Child de Calde-well, with power of attorney to Richard Penyston de Chattesworth to deliver seisin. Witn. John Dethek, Dom. de Neuhall, Henry Holand de Caldewall, Robert Thirmot de Lynton. Dat. Walton, M. of F. of Nat. of B. V. M. [8 Sept.], 9 Hen. VI. [1430]. (Gresley.)

WALTON-ON-TRENT *v.* also under CALDWALL.

WARDLOW *v.* under LITTON, TIDESWELL.

WATERTHORPE in BEIGHTON.

(WALTERTHORPE.)

2543. LEASE, for 20 years, from Robert de Forneus, knt., Lord of Becthon [Beighton], with the assent of William de Forneus, his brother, to Robert Jannel of Becthon, of a bovate of land in Walterthorp, in Becthon; rent, 8*s.* Witn. Will. Gere of Becthon, William de Pecco of the same, Will de Mauthon, jun., etc. Dat. Inv. of H. Cross [3 May], 2 Edw. III. [1328]. (Campb. viii. 17.)

WATERTHORPE *v.* also under BEIGHTON.

WENSLEY in DARLEY.

(WEDNESLEY.)

2544. ROYAL licence to Roger de Wednesley, jun., to enfeoff William de Bruggeton, chaplain, in the manor of Wednesley, held *in capite* as of the manor of Wikesworth [Wirksworth], by forfeiture of Thomas, Earl of Lancaster, for re-grant to the said Roger and Avice, his wife. Dat. Wynton, 2 May, 18 Edw. [II. 1325]. (Woll. i. 5.)

WESSINGTON *v.* under CRICH.

WESTON UNDERWOOD.

(WESTONA, WESTONE, WESTUNE.)

2545. NOTIFICATION to King Henry [II. ?] by Roger de Buron that he has quitclaimed Henry fil. Fulcheri and his heirs of five shillings annual rent of Weston, that he may pay the same to the Canons of St. Mary, Derby, and be as faithful to them as he has been to him. Undated. (Kedleston 21.)

> Benedicto Regi Anglorum H[enrico] et omnibus hominibus castellarie de Notingham et omnibus hominibus suis, francis et anglis, Rogerus de Buron, salutem. Sciatis me clamasse quietum Henricum filium Fulcheri et heredes suos a me et ab heredibus meis de quinque solidis singulis annis de redditu meo de Westona, ut ipse persoluat et heredes sui hos quinque solidos singulis annis Canonicis de Derbi. Et sicuti debet esse fidelis mihi de feudo meo, ita Canonicis Sancte Marie de Derbi sit fidelis et fidem faciat de his quinque solidis singulis annis soluendis. Testibus Alano et Henrico decanis, et Rogero de Cestr[ia], et Radulpho de Breidesh[ale], Petro de Sandiacre, et Patricio Rosel, et Alberto de Orsele, et David de Stantun, et Willelmo fil. Colling, et Walchel' monetario.

2546. GRANT from Henry fil. et her. Dom. Henrici de Irtona to Fulcher fil. Willelmi de Irtona, of a toft and croft in Weston, which Adam fil. Andree de Westone and Matildis, mother of the said Andrew, sometime held. Witn. Dom. William de Menylle, Henry Braylisforde, William le Burgyl[en], Robert de Scheldeforde, Robert fil. Ade de Westone. Early Hen. III. (Kedleston 20.)

2547. GRANT from William fil. Willelmi le Burgylon de Weston to William de Borley, brother of Henry de Borley and of Emma, eldest daughter of the grantor, of a toft and croft, etc., in Weston which Henry fil. Roberti sometime held from him in villeinage, together with the said Henry "cum tota sequela et catallis." Rent, 10 silver pence. Witn. Dom. Robert le Burgilon, rector of the moiety of the church of Moginton, Henry le Burgilon, Robert Campion, etc. Dat. apud Moginton, M. a. F. of St. Scholastica [10 Feb.], 1289[90]. (Kedleston 7.)

2548. LEASE, for life, from Richard fil. Roberti de Irtona to Mabel, relict of Robert Forestarius de Murkenistone, of two plots of land, with buildings, and eleven acres of arable land in the fields of Weston and Mogintone; paying rent to the heirs of Henry de Irtone, of William Burgilun, of "the son of Adam fil. Andree," and of William fil. Wakelin. Witn. William le Burgilun, Robert fil. Ade de Westone, Robert fil. Rogeri Freman de Mogintone, Robert Ordriche, etc. Late thirteenth cent. (Kedleston 11.)

2549. GRANT from Henry fil. Henrici, Dominus de Orton, to William his brother and Philippa his wife, dau. of Dom. Henry de Chaundoys, of a messuage, etc., in Westune, which John Cutts sometime held. Rent, a rose at midsummer. Witn. Henry de Braylisforde, Roger de Bradburne, knts., Richard de Curzone de Ketlistone, Henry de Querendone, etc. Dat. Sat. a. F. of St. Barnabas [11 June], 1 Edw. II. [1308]. (Kedleston 5.)

2550. GRANT from Henry fil. Henrici, Dominus de Parva Irtone, to William de Irtone, his brother, and Philippa, his wife, of 17½ acres of land in Weston, lying at Le Hallestudes, Piletlege, and Arthur-ruidinge. Witn. Henry de Querendone, Robert de Weston, Adam Cnotte, etc. Dat. F. of Exalt. of H. Cross [14 Sept.], 1310. (Kedleston 13.)

2551. MORTGAGE for £40 from Henry, Dominus de Parva Irton, to Richard le Cursoun of Ketliston, of all his lands in Weston (except the wood there and an assart called le Maney, Osmondegreue, and Le Longmore), with the lordship and services of the lands, etc., of his free tenants. Dat. Little Irton, Sat. a. F. of SS. Simon and Jude [28 Oct.], 15 Edw. II. [1321]. (Kedleston 17.)

2552. LEASE, for life, from Dom. Richard de Curzun de Ketles-tone, knt., to John de Hokenastone de Weston, of all the lands, etc., which Henry de Westone formerly held in Weston and Mogyntone, and all the lands which John Cut formerly held in the fee of Mogyntone. Witn. John le Burgylun of Westone, Henry fil. Roberti de eadem, William fil. Fulcheri de eadem. Dat. M. a. F. of St. Andrew [30 Nov.], 1326. (Kedleston 18.)

2553. GRANT from Richard le Curszon of Ketlestone, knt., to Robert fil. Ricardi de parva Irtone, of a messuage and land in the vill and fields of Weston. Witn. John Burguilone, Henry de Weston, John Officel, William fil. Rogeri, etc. Dat. Weston, W. a. F. of St. Ambrose [4 Apr.], 1333. (Kedleston 19.)

WESTON UNDERWOOD *v.* also under KEDLESTON.

21

WHALEY IN BOLSOVER.

(WALLEY.)

2554. LEASE from John Bryde, clerk, and Robert Bryde of Skegby, his brother, to Richard " of the Graunge," jun., of Walley, of a messuage and land in Walley, which they purchased from Adam " of Otley." Witn. Thomas Clerk, Robert Smyth of Warsop, etc. Dat. F. of St. Martin [11 Nov.], 23 Hen. VI. [1444]. (Foljambe.)

WHATSTANDWELL.

(WATSTANWELL.)

2555. SALE by John, Abbot of Derley, and the convent of the same, to James Beresforth and Laurense Beresforthe his brother, of all their wood growing in Watstanwell, between the bridge and William Wylde's tenement on the south, the lordship of Waekbrydge on the north, the water of Derwent on the west, and the moor on the east, except the wood growing in the Calfe Croft, etc., of the said tenement, with twelve years' " free entre and owt gayt " of the said woods; also grant of other wood near the abbot's well and the way to Crich, except Crabtree and Holyn, and except the trees adjoining the " Gape next benethe the lytyll Barne," the said James and Laurence granting that the abbot's tenant shall have " Tynsell " to repair the hedges; grant also to the said James and Laurence of twenty years to sell and carry away said woods, etc. Dat. 20 Feb., 1 Hen. VIII. [1510]. (P. R. O. C. 2476.)

WHATSTANDWELL *v.* also under DERBY.

WHEATCROFT

(WETECROFT),

v. under CRICH.

WHITTINGTON.

(WYTINTONA, WYTTINTONA.)

2556. CONFIRMATION from Thomas de Camera, filius Rogeri de Birley, of a grant to the Convent of Bellum Caput [Beauchief], of a rent of 21*d.* on land in Dunstorhes [? in Whittington]. Witn. Henry Wylte, Adam le Blunt, Robert de Brom, etc. Dat. 1280. (Harl. 83, E. 2.)

2557. GRANT from Ralph fil. Ric. de Hanley to Philip de Cesterfeld, gener Petri de Tappeton, of a bovate of land in Wytintona which the said Ralph acquired before the Justices Itinerant at Derby in Easter Term, 9 Edw. I. [1281]. Witn. John de Briminton, Peter de Dunston, Adam de Neubold, etc. (Foljambe.)

2558. GRANT from Thomas Rogger of Park gate, near Whittington, to Peter Frecchevile, esq., of all the lands, etc., at Parkegate, which he had of the grant of Robert Rogger his father. Witn. John Bothe of Staveley, Thomas Page, etc. Dat. Staveley, F. of St. Gregory [12 Mar.], 11 Edw. IV. [1471]. (Foljambe.)

WHITTINGTON *v.* also under BRIMINGTON, CHESTERFIELD.

WHITTLE

(WHYTYLL),

v. under OLLERSETT.

WHITWELL.

(WHITEWELL.)

2559. CERTIFICATE by John [Hales], Bishop of Coventry and Lichfield, that having examined the Register of Dom. William Heyworth, his predecessor, he finds that on the 12th of August, 1429, in his manor of Heywode, John Newerk was admitted to the parish church of Whitewell and canonically instituted, on the presentation of Ralph Cromwell, knt., Lord of Cromwell and Tateshale, the patron of the said church. Dat. in our manor of Beaudesert, 19 Feb., 1463[4]. (Add. 47516.)

WIGLEY.

(WIGGELAY, WIGGELEE, WIKELEY, WYGGELEY, WYGLEY.)

2560. GRANT from Walter de la Haye to Richard Mercator of the land which Robert Strangholf sometime held in Wiggelay. Witn. Ralph, persona de Heckinton, John Dolfin, Yvo de Burley, etc. Early Hen. III. (Foljambe.)

2561. GRANT from Ralph Dolfin to Richard Mercator of the same piece of land in Wikeley. Witn. Hugh de Linacre, Hugh fil. Ingerami, Yvo de Burley, etc. Early Hen. III. (Foljambe.)

2562. GRANT from Thomas fil. Radulfi de Bramton to Richard fil. Ade de Bosco of lands in Wiggelee and Bestril; rent, 5s. Witn. Dom. John, capellanus de Branton, Hugh de Linacre, Hugh fil. Ingelrami, etc. *Temp.* Edw. I. (Woll. iii. 38.)

2563. GRANT, for one mark, from Walter fil. Thome de Bramtone to Roger fil. Willelmi de Wiggeley, of lands in Wiggeley; rent, 2s. Witn. Hugh de Linaker, Nicholas de Holm, John de Brimingtone, etc. *Temp.* Edw. I. or II. (Woll. iii. 33.)

2564. GRANT, in tail, from Henry Perpound and Robert Barley to William Rollesby and Agnes, dau. of Robert Wigley, of the lands, etc., in Wigley, which they had of the grant of the said Robert Wigley. Witn. John Lenacre, Thomas Cause, Thomas Croft, etc. Dat. M. a. F. of St. Edmund [20 Nov.], 26 Hen. VI. [1447]. (Foljambe.)

2565. QUITCLAIM from Thomas Leeke of Beauchyff to' William Wylde of lands in Wygley and Barowcote in Cryche, which the said Thomas acquired from John Bellow and Robert Bygott, esquires, together with a cottage in Colley and a messuage in Cold Aston, all of which belonged to the lately-dissolved Abbey of Beauchief. Dat. 6 Apr., 1 Edw. VI. [1547]. (Woll. iv. 52.)

WIGWELL

(WIGGEWELL, WIGGEWELLE, WIGWALL, WYGEWALL, WYGEWELLE, WYGGEWALLE, WYGGEWELLE),

v. under WIRKSWORTH.

WILLIAMTHORPE.

2566. GRANT from Robert le Sauvage to William de Heryz of land near Williamthorpe and Normanton. Witn. Dom. Ingilran de Umuill, Dom. Roger de Eynecurt, Roger de Sydenhale, Jocelyn de Havermere, Nicholas de Meynill, etc. *Temp.* Hen. III.-Edw. I.

2567. LEASE from John Markham and Richard Byngham, knts., Justices of the King's Bench, Robert Clyfton, knt., William Gull, clerk, William Fitzwilliam, son and heir of John Fitzwilliam, esquire, William Babyngton, Richard Willughby, Thomas Foliambe, esq., and others, at the request of Thomas Chaworth, esq., to William Smyth of William-thorpe, of a messuage and land [in Williamthorpe]. Dat. 21 Jan., 5 Edw. IV. [1466]. (Foljambe.)

WILLIAMTHORPE *v.* also under ALFRETON.

WILLINGTON.

(WILENTON, WILENTONE, WILINTON, WILLINCTUN, WILLYNGTON, WILYNTON, WYLENTONE, WYLINGTON, WYLINTON, WYLLINTON, WYLLYNGTON.)

2568. COVENANT whereby the Abbot and Convent of Crokesden [Croxden, co. Staff.] grant to Richard de Hulcrombe and Margaret his wife free multure at the abbey mill at Wilinton of all corn acquired for the support of their household at Willington, and, if they wish, "facere tabernam de wainagio suo"; and they, in return, release their rights in Mainardesholm [in Willington], and pay twelve pence yearly to the abbey. Witn. Nicholas, "dominus de Wilinton," Richard de Etewele, Henry his brother, Oliver le Foun de Holinton, Mag. Simon, "persona de Trussele," Robert Ferbraz, etc. *Temp.* John-Hen. III. (Stowe 146.)

2569. GRANT, in soul-alms, from Nicholas, "miles dominus de Wilinton," to the church and canons of Rapendon, of land at Wilinton, including nine acres, "quas Johannes filius Symonis contulit cum corpore suo predictis canonicis in puram et perpetuam elemosinam de patrimonio suo in Wilinton." Witn. Dom. Geoffrey, "miles de Bec," Dom. William "miles de Verdon," Dom. Oliver, "miles Saucheverel," Robert, clericus, etc. *Temp.* John-Hen. III. (Stowe 140.)

2570. GRANT, in soul-alms, from John fil. Symonis de Wilinton to the Canons of Rapendon, of land at Wilinton. Witn. Dom. Nicholas, "miles de Wilinton," Dom. Geoffrey de Bec, Dom. William de Verdon, Dom. Oliver de Saucheuerel, Edwin de Rapendon, and Robert "clericus qui hoc scriptum scripsit." *Temp.* John-Hen. III. (Stowe 149.)

2571. GRANT, in soul-alms, from Hugh de Finderne, for himself and his wife Aline, to the Canons of Rapendon, of land in Wilinton. Witn. Dom. Bertram de Verdun, Robert Ferbraz, Reginald "capellanus de Rapendon," Robert, "clericus, qui scripsit hoc scriptum." *Temp.* John-Hen. III. (Stowe 147.)

2572. NOTIFICATION by Mag. Robert de Boscho, official of the Bishop of Coventry, of the induction of Dom. John, Prior, and the Convent of Rapendon, into the possession of the church of Wilenton, performed by him under the authority of P[andulf], Papal Legate, and of W[illiam de Cornhill], Bishop of Coventry. [1218-1221.] (Stowe 141.)

2573. INSPEXIMUS by Geoffrey, Prior, and the Convent of Coventry, of the confirmation by William [de Cornhill], Bishop of Coventry, of a grant from N[icholas] de Wilinton, "miles," formerly patron of Willington church, to the Prior and Canons of Rapendon, of a yearly pension of two besants to be paid by Ralph de Pointon, rector of the church of St. Mary at Wilinton; the church, on his death, to be appropriated by Repton Priory. Dat. "Mense Aprili, tercio die Pasche" [25 April], 1223. (Stowe 142.)

2574. LEASE by Richard de Hulecrombe and his wife to Ranulph [Blundeville], Earl of Chester and Lincoln, of land in Wylinton. Witn. William de Vernon [Justiciary of Chester 1229-1232], Robert de Tok, Robert de Warda, etc. [1217-1232.] (Stowe 66.)

2575. CONFIRMATION from R[ichard de Insula], Abbot of Burton [-upon-Trent, co. Staff.], of the grant by Dom. N[icholas] fil. Johannis de Wilinton to the church of the Holy Trinity and the Canons at Rapendon, of the advowson of the church of Wilinton. Witn. H[enry], Abbot of Derelega [Darley], B[artholomew], Prior of Tothesbire [Tutbury], Herbert, canon of Lichfield, Mag. William de Grafton, Mag. Robert de Chebbese, etc. [1222-1229.] (Stowe 143.)

2576. QUITCLAIM by Nicholas de Wilentun to Alexander de Corteligstoke, of John fil. Nicholai Le Bacheler. Witn. Dom. John, Prior de Rapendon, Robert Ferbraz, Roger, capellanus, Adam, capellanus, Thomas fil. Hugonis. Early Hen. III. (Stowe 148.)

2577. GRANT from Nicholas fil. Nicholai de Wylenton to Dom. Ralph fil. Nicholai, of the mills of Potloc, "cum molta et secta"; rent, a pair of white gloves or 1*d.* Witn. William de Vernun, William de Mongomeri, Sewale fil. Henrici, Geoffray de Beic, Geoffrey de Bakepuz, etc. *Temp.* Hen. III. (Woll. ix. 23.)

2578. GRANT from Nicholas fil. Nicholai de Wilenton to Ralph fil. Nicholai, of freedom from service for the mill of Potlac, formerly paid to the Abbot of Burtone, with right of entry into two bovates of land in Wilentone and Egenton, in case of distraint by the said Abbot. Witn. William de Vernun, Will. de Mongomery, Sewale fil. Henrici, Geoffrey de Beic, Geoffrey de Bakepuz, etc. *Temp.* Hen. III. [Woll. ix. 24.)

2579. GRANT from Nicholas, "dominus de Wylinton, fil. Nicholai de Wylinton," to the Canons of Repindon, of land in Wylinton, "cum corpore meo." Witn. Walter de Bereford, Ralph de Tikehale, and Peter "capellanus de Finderne." *Temp.* Hen. III. (Stowe 150.)

2580. GRANT from Ralph fil. Nicholai to Ralph de Bredona of land in Willinctun, which he bought of Richard de Nulcrume. Witn. Robert de Esburne, Geoffrey de Bakepuz, Roger le Bretun, Walter fil. domini Henrici del Beec, Robert fil. Waclin, etc. *Temp.* Hen. III. (Kerry xix. 61.)

2581. GRANT, in soul-alms, from Alexander de Kortlinstoke to the Canons of Rapendon of John "fil. Nicholai bachiler de Wilynton cum tota sequela sua." Witn. Adam, cappellanus, vicar of Wilynton, Walter de Bereford, Hugh, clericus, etc. *Temp.* Hen. III. (Stowe 144.)

2582. Fine, whereby Peter, Prior of Repindon, Milo de Repindon, "capellanus," and William Etebred, acknowledge certain lands in Wylington to be the property of Margery fil. Nicholai de Wylington; and she grants five acres thereof to the said prior and his successors, with permission to keep their mill-pond in its present state. Made at Nottingham, before Silvester [de Everdon], Bishop of Carlisle, Roger de Thurkelby, Gilbert de Preston, and Adam de Hilton, justices in Eyre. Dat. "a die Pasche [31 Mar.], in unum mensem," 36 Hen. III. [1252]. (Stowe 145.)

2583. Grant from Ralph de Bredona to John de Hull of all his lands, etc., in Wilinton, with his "nativi," Hugh de Brodeok and William his brother, with their chattels, etc. Witn. Peter de Tok, Henry de Becco, John de Chaundos, Hugh de Menill, William fil. Herberti, William de Muschamp, etc. *Circ.* 1255. (Kerry xix. 62.)

2584. Grant from Ralph de Gurney to Thomas fil. Galfridi de Potlock and Margaret his wife, and one heir of the same, of four selions of land in Wylinton, lying at Steymerebrugge, on Le Wyteflat, etc. Witn. William de Muschamp, Robert Ferbras, Nicholas de Fynderne, Robert de Fynderne, etc. Dat. Fr. a. F. of St. Ambrose [4 Apr.], 3 Edw. I. [1275]. (Kerry xix. 69.)

2585. Grant from Robert fil. Radulphi Ferebras of Willinton to Hugh de Verne of all the lands which the said Ralph his father held by feoffment from Dom. John de Hylle, in Wilinton. Witn. Dom. Robert de Stafford, Dom. Alured de Sulni, Dom. Nicholas de Verdun, knts., Robert de Mungoye, living in Twiford, Walter de Rubef de Etewelle, etc. [*Circ.* 1292.] (Kerry xix. 63.)

2586. Lease from Ralph de Gourney of Bolton to Thomas fil. Galfridi de Potlok and Margaret his wife, and to one heir of their bodies, of four acres of arable land in Wyllinton, lying in Potlockross, Harpefurlonge, le Morfurlong, le Neld at Staginnebrugge, extending to Findernewey, on Dunstall, etc. Witn. Robert Ferebraz, John de Notyngham, Nicholas de Fynderne, Henry de Camera in Twyford, etc. Dat. Derby "ad Pontechester," 1298. (Kerry xix. 64.)

2587. Grant and quitclaim from Nicholas de Wilinton to Hugh de Fynderne of seven shillingsworth of rent in Findern, in Wilinton, and in Potlac, which the said Hugh has hitherto paid yearly. Witn. Dom. Geoffrey de Gresele, Dom. William de Warda, John de Stapenhull, etc. *Circ.* 1302. (Kerry xix. 65.)

2588. Grant from William de Muschamp, jun., of Wylinton, to Thomas de Potlok fil. Galfridi and Margaret his wife, of two half-acres of land in the field of Wylinton, lying on Oldefeld Lancaans, beyond Normonweye, etc. Witn. Robert Furbras, Ralph le Gorney, Nicholas de Fynderne, etc. *Circ.* 1306. (Kerry xix. 67.)

2589. Grant from William de Muschamp to Thomas fil. Galfridi de Potlock and Margaret his wife, and to one heir of their bodies, of an acre of land in Wylinton lying on le Castelwaye and on le Helde. Witn. Robert Ferbraz, Ralph le Gourney, Nicholaus de Fynderne, etc. Dat. S. a. F. of St. Valentine [14 Feb.], 1306[7]. (Kerry xix. 66.)

2590. Lease from Ralph de Gourney to Thomas fil. Galfridi de Potlok and Margaret his wife, and to one heir of the same, of a half-acre of land in the fields of Wylinton, lying on Longedunstel, for their lives. Witn. Robert Ferbras, William de Muschamp, Nicholas de Fynderne, Robert de Fynderne, etc. Dat. the Mor. of St. Lucy [13 Dec.], 1309. (Kerry xix. 68.)

2591. GRANT from Ralph de Gurney to Thomas fil. Galfridi de Potlok and Margaret his wife, and to one heir born of the same, for their lives, of four bovates of land at Steymerebrugge in Wylinton. Witn. Dom. Robert de Tonk, knt., Robert Ferbraz, William de Muschamp, John Condy, etc. Dat. Th. a. F. of St. James [25 July], 4 Edw. II. [1310]. (Kerry xix. 70.)

2592. GRANT from Ralph de Gurney to Thomas fil. Galfridi de Potlock, Margaret his wife, and one male heir born of the same, for their lives, of two roods of arable land in Willington, lying near Le Thorpbreye, and on the Helm, etc. Dat. W. a. Epiphany [6 Jan.], 4 Edw. II. [1311]. (Kerry xix. 73.)

2593. GRANT from Ralph de Gurney to Thomas fil. Galfridi de Potlok, Margaret his wife, and to one boy born of the same, of two acres and a rood lying on Harpinfurlong and near the Brodewey, etc., in Wylenton. Dat. W. a. F. of St. Hilary [Jan. 13], 4 Edw. II. [1311]. (Kerry xix. 74.)

2594. GRANT from Ralph de Gurney to Thomas fil. Galfridi de Potlok and Margaret his wife, of an acre of land in the "cultura" called Helm, in the fields of Wylinton. Dat. Whitsuntide, 1311. (Kerry xix. 74.)

2595. GRANT from Ralph de Gurney to Thomas fil. Galfridi de Potlok and Margaret his wife, and one boy born of the same, for their lives, of half an acre of land in Wylinton, lying on le Wyteflat and on Piletcroft. Witn. Robert Ferbraz, Robert de Fynderne, William de Muschamp, John Cundy, etc. Dat. S. a. F. of the Annunciation [25 Mar.], 1312. (Kerry xix. 71.)

2596. GRANT from Ralph de Gurney of Wylinton to Thomas fil. Galfridi de Potloc and Margaret his wife and Richard their son, of half an acre of arable land in the fields of Wylinton, for their lives. Witn. Robert Ferbras, Robert de Finderne, William de Muschampe, John de Crottal, Robert Norman. Dat. Fr. in Whitsun week [16 May], 1312. (Kerry xix. 72.)

2597. GRANT from Ralph de Gurney to Thomas fil. Galfridi de Potloc and Margaret his wife, of half an acre of land on Dunstil, in the fields of Wylinton. Dat. F. of the B. V. M. [25 Mar.], 1313. (Kerry xix. 74.)

2598. GRANT, for three lives, from John Cheyne, parson of Hambury [Hanbury, co. Staff.], and Robert de Knyveton, vicar of Douvebrigg, to John de la Pole the elder, of an annual rent of £4 from lands in Potlok. Dat. 8 Sept., 7 Ric. II. [1383]. (Woll. iii. 1.)

2599. GRANT from John Milnere de Derby to Master John de Wodhouses, clerk, and Thomas Milner of Horsley, of all his lands, etc., in the vills and fields of Welyngton, Brynlaston, and Berrewardescote. Witn. William Mochaunde of Wyllyngton, John Orme of Brynlaston, Robert atte-Yate de Berwardecote. Dat. Brynlaston, F. of St. John, Ap. and Ev. [27 Dec.], 1 Hen. IV. [1399]. (Trusley.)

2600. Quitclaim from Margaret Fynderne, relict of Nicholas Fynderne, esquire, to John Fynderne her son, of all her dowry lands in Willyngton, Twyforde, and of the wood called Fynderne wood in Repton lordship. Dat. Christmas Day, 14 Edw. IV. [1474]. (Kerry xix. 79.)

WILLINGTON *v.* also under Calk, Chatsworth, Chelmorton, Newton Solney, Repton.

WILNE.

(Wilne, Kyrke Wyllne.)

2601. Will of William Rosell of Dracot, containing bequests to the church of Kyrke Wyllne [Wilne, co. Derby], and to the chapel of St. James of Dracot [Draycott in Wilne], etc. Witn. Robert Jamytyn, John Barne, Dom. John Tebald, chaplain. Dat. F. of St. Dunstan [21 Oct.], 1502. On the back is note of probate made in the presence of the Treasurer of Lichfield in the prebendal church of Sallow [Sawley]. (Woll. i. 81.)

WILNE *v.* also under Morley.

WINDLEY.

(Wyneley.)

2602. Re-grant from Henry Bradshaghe, Richard Bee, rector of a moiety of the church of Mogynton [Mugginton, co. Derby], and Thomas Bradshaghe, to Richard Prynce and Matilda his wife, of lands in Wyneley [Windley ?], Duffeld, and Mogyntone; and remainder to John Prynce, his brother, Johanna and Katerine, his sisters, Thomas Tykhulle, Alice Badeley, and Emma Thorpe. Witn. John Cursone, Thos. Knevetone, John Bradley, vicar of Duffeld, etc. Dat. Wyneley, 1 Oct., 10 Hen. VI. [1431]. (Woll. i. 85.)

WINDLEY *v.* also under Mugginton.

WINGERWORTH.

(Wyngarworth, Wyngreworth.)

2603. Rental of the manor of Wyngreworth, renewed in March, 5 Hen. VI. [1427]. (Woll. xi. 3.)

2604. Grant, in tail, from Robert de Wednesley, John Wodewarde, and Richard Bethebroke, to John del Stubbinge, of a messuage and lands [in Stubbing, nr. Wingerworth], which they had by grant from the same John. Witn. Thomas Saunderson of Twathewaith, Robert Wideson, Robert del Claye, etc. Dat. Stubbing, F. of St. Lucy [13 Dec.], 14 Hen. VI. [1435]. (Foljambe.)

WINGERWORTH *v.* also under Chesterfield, Tupton, Unstone.

WINGFIELD, ¡SOUTH.

(WINNEFEUD, WYNFELD, WYNFELDE.)

2605. GRANT from Walter fil. Will. de Hufton to Joanna fil. Dom. Johannis de Heriz, of the manor of Hufton. Witn. Robert, vicar of Winnefeud, Robert fil. Dom. Geoffrey de Dethek, John Deyncourt, Roger le Breton de Walton, etc. Dat. Hufton, Th. a. F. of SS. Tiburtius and Valerian [14 Apr.], 1292. (Harl. 112 I. 18 A.)

2606. RELEASE from the same Joanna to Dom. John de Heriz, her father, of the same manor. Witn. Henry de Knottyng, Henry de Codyngton, Walter de Oggaston, etc. Dat. Gonolston [Gonalston, co. Notts.], Morr. of Nat. of St. John B. [25 June], 21 Edw. I. [1293]. (Harl. 112 I. 18 B.)

2607. GRANT from John Whitehed, parson of Mogynton, and John Broune, clerk, to Dom. Robert de Swillyngton and Robert Gretehed, parson of Ekyngton, of their estate in the manor of Ufton, near Wynfeld, for the life of Robert Gretehed. Dat. Wynfeld, 1 Aug., 4 Edw. II. [1310]. (Harl. 112 F. 32.)

2608. LETTERS of attorney from John de Litton of Grymeston [Grimston, co. York], and Christiana his wife, to Nicholas de Stapleton and William Pamplyon, to give seisin to Dom. Robert de Swillyngton, of the manor of Ufton and lands in Ufton and Wynfeld. Dat. 3 Apr., 1 Ric. II. [1378]. (Harl. 112 I. 54.)

2609. LETTERS of attorney of Sir Robert de Swyllyngtone, knight, and Robert Gretehede, parson of Ekyntone, empowering William Parkere de Wynfelde and William de Halgtone, to receive seisin of the manor of Uftone, by virtue of a charter of Sir John Whitehede, parson of Mogyntone, and Sir John Broune, clerk. Dated at the manor of Wynfelde, 1 Aug., 4 Ric. II. [1380]. French. (Lansd. 135.)

WINSHILL.

(WINESHULL, WINISHULL, WINSUL, WYNCEL, WYNNUSHALE, WYNSELL, WYNSHUL, WYNSHULL, WYNSULL.)

2610. LEASE from John fil. Hen. fil. Gode de Tutesbiri to Rich. fil. Swain de Winsul of lands in Winsul, the rent to be paid partly to the said John and partly to the Abbot of Burton-on-Trent. Witn. Robert de Bursicot, Robert de Lucy, Rob. fil. Ernald, etc. *Temp.* John. (Stowe 68.)

2611. GRANT from Robert de Rolueston, "capellanus," to Ambrose fil. Eugenulfi de Wineshull, in marriage with his daughter Agnes, of the land which he bought from William fil. Willelmi Palmerii de Wineshull, of a messuage "in eadem villa" [Winshill in Burton-upon-Trent] and of a messuage "in villa Burthon," with reversion in case of failure of issue to the grantor. Witn. Dom. Geoffrey de Bec, John de Stape-hull, seneschal of Burton, Ralph fil. Willelmi clerici de Stapehull, Richard de Egenton, "seriuens," etc. *Temp.* Hen. III. (Stowe 151.)

2612. GRANT from William fil. Roberti de Wynnushule to Adam his son of land "in territorio de Wynnushule." Witn. Ralph de la Bache, seneschal of Burton, William de Hertishorn, Ralph "ad finem ville de Winnushule," etc. *Temp.* Hen. III. (Stowe 152.)

2613. AGREEMENT between William de Wyneshul and his son Henry, deacon of Wynshul, by which the latter, for four marks, resigns all claim on his father for support or assistance, Dom. John, chaplain, son of [the above William], John "faber" of Burton-on-Trent, John fil. Roger de Horninglowe, and John Hemining of Burton, being appointed sureties for the payment. Witn. Stephen de Wynshul and his brother Adam, Reginald Brun of Herninglowe, etc. Dat. Trin. Sun. [3 June], 1268. (Stowe 67.)

2614. QUITCLAIM by Matthew fil. William le Knist de Tatinhul [co. Staff.] to Thomas [de Pakinton], Abbot, and the Convent of Burton-on-Trent, of land in co. Staff. and in Winishull [co. Derby], with various services thereto annexed. Witn. Ralph de Burgo, Robert de Pipe, Richard de Barton, "clericus," Robert fil. Hen. de Vttokishath, Will. de Bosco-calumpniato, etc. [1281-1305.] (Stowe 70.)

2615. LEASE from Symon de Worthinton to Dom. John fil. Will. de Meleburn of land in Wynshull, formerly held by Robert fil. Rob. de Subbosco de Wynshull. Witn. William de Esseburn, Matthew de Scobenhal, Adam "vinetarius" de Burthon, etc. *Temp.* Edw. II. (Stowe 69.)

2616. INSPEXIMUS, by the "officialis jurisdictionis spiritualis," of Burton Abbey, of a grant by Nicholas fil. Robert le Clerk of Wynsull to William Gerard of Burton-on-Trent, of land in Wynsull. Witn. to grant, John del Warde and Maurice le Irenmonger of Wynsull, and Robert Lucy of Stapenhill, etc. Dat. at Wynsull, F. of St. Gregory [12 Mar.], 18 Edw. III. [1344]. Witn. to inspeximus, Dom. Richard de Assheburn, Dom. John de Felde, Dom. Rob. Flygh, chaplains, etc. Dat. in the conventual church of Burton, S. a. F. of St. Gregory [14 Mar.], 1343[4]. (Stowe 71.)

2617. QUITCLAIM by John de Kynttoley, al. Knyteley, sen., residing at Ascheby, to John Knytoley, junr., and Richard de Rudyngh, of lands in Wyncel. Witn. John de Wrhynton, Reginald Store, Richard Knyte, etc. Dat. at Burton[-on-Trent], F. of St. Katherine [25 Nov.], 49 Edw. III. [1375]. (Stowe 72.)

2618. LEASE, for lives, from Geoffrey Gresley, arm., with the consent of his co-feoffees, to William de Howeton, "Kever et Peyntour," of Burton-on-Trent, and Alice his wife, of all the lands, etc., in Wynshull, co. Derby, which sometime belonged to John Broun, fil. Willelmi Broun de Pontefracto. Rent, a red rose at Midsummer. Witn. John Abell, Henry de Caldwell, Reginald Roundell de Stapenhill. Dat. Tu. a. Decoll. of St. John B. [29 Aug.], 17 Hen. VI. [1439]. (Gresley.)

2619. AWARD of Sir Walter Gryffyth, knight, and John Wystowe, gent., arbiters between William [Bone], Abbot of Burton-upon-Trent, and William Schenette of Pakynton, labourer, concerning land in Wynsell, by which the latter is required to release the land to Thomas Cromewell of Burton-upon-Trent, receiving from the Abbot 40*s.* Dat. 8 July, 13 Hen. VIII. [1521]. Signed by the arbiters. (Stowe 73.)

WINSTER.
(WINESTERE, WYNSTER.)

2620. GRANT from Robert Fitz Col to William de Mungai, of his farm of Winster, paying 6*s.* (?) rent and a red hawk, and in addition the said William has given the said Robert a horse and 40*s.* Late Hen. II. Imperfect. (Woll. ix. 1.)

Omnibus dominanciis suis et amicis suis et hominibus suis
Robertus fil. Col. salutem Notum sit uobis me . . . dedisse
et concessisse huic Willelmo de Mungai propter seruicium suum
hominancium meam firmam de Winster . . . [s]ex solidos in
anno et propter seruicium quod ipse fecit patri meo et mihi in
feudo et in hereditate et . . . heredibus suis tenere de me
et de heredibus meis propter unum ruffum nisum in anno in
seisone reddit . . . pro omnibus serviciis illo et heredibus suis
et heredibus meis et adhuc dedit mihi propter donacionem unum
ecum et xl. solidos nummorum. Huius donacionis Testes sunt
Sawallus fil. Fulcheri, Fulcher frater eius et Serlo de Grendon et
Jurdanus filius eius Simund de Beirchouer et Rogerus filius eius et
Adam de Widele, Robertus clericus et Hanricus sacerdos, et Rogerus
clericus, Levenad Dihul et Gosi . . . Lefwinus de . . .
Ricardus de Leres . . . Willelmus nepos Willelmi de Mungai.
Valete.

2621. GRANT from William, Earl of Ferrars, to William de Mungai,
of the third part of a lead mine in Winestere; rent, a pair of boots
of Cordovan leather (duas ocreas cordewaninas). Late twelfth cent.
(Woll. ix. 4.)

Willelmus Comes de Ferr[ariis] omnibus hominibus suis et amicis
francis utque anglicis clericis et laicis tam presentibus quam futuris
salutem. Sciatis me dedisse Willelmo de Mungai in feudo et
hereditate tertiam partem mine mee plumbi quam habeo in campis
Winestere ubicunque fuerit inuenta in territorio predicte uille scilicet
Winester et quicunque eam foderit uel de terra eam eicerit aliquo
modo et quicquid ad opus meum dominicum solebit euenire, vel
aliquo modo accidere siue in Mina siue in consuetudinibus siue in
placitis et forifactis et escaetis omnibus et in omnibus vtilitatibus
et prouentibus que ex predicta mina potuit aliquo quocunque modo
uel aliquo tempore prouenire. Totam terciam partem illi plenarie
et integre donaui. Illi et heredibus suis de me tenendo et heredibus
meis libere, solute et quiete ab omni servicio, per duas ocreas
cordewaninas ad pentecosten annuatim reddendo pro omni Servicio.
Hanc uero donationem feci ego predicto Willelmo et eius heredibus·
pro homagio suo et servicio quod Willelmus mihi fecit antequam
ipse Willelmus deuenisset homo meus, Et ego inde recepi homagium
eiusdem Willelmi et ipse inde est homo meus et heredum meorum
et heredes sui erunt inde homines mei et heredum meorum
sicut de feudo et hereditate per seruicium predictum et libertatem
omnem sicut superius dictum est. Testibus Roberto et Henrico
de Ferr[ariis], patruis comitis, Roberto fil. Walcel[ini], Radulpho
de Seil, constabulario, Nicholao fil. Pagani tunc Dapifero, Henrico
fil. Wale[clini], Petro fratre suo, Sewallo fil. Henrici, Johanne fil.
Godefridi, Johanne le Fohun, Roberto fil. . . ., Henrico fil.
Gileberti, R . . . de Birchehoure, Johanne de Aldewerc, Johanne
de Mungai, Radulpho fil. Ohini, Hugone de Winestre, Petro fil.
Radulphi, Nicholao fil. Leuenod et pluribus aliis.

2622. GRANT, in tail, from Ralph de Munjoy to Robert de Munjoy,
his brother, of all his land of Wynster; rent, 12*d.* Witn. Robert de
Herthul, Adam de Herthul, Richard le Raggide, Thomas Folegaumbe,
etc. *Temp.* Hen. III. or Edw. I. (Woll. ix. 13.)

2623. RELEASE by Thomas fil. Roberti de Mountjoye to Ralph Gerard of Wynster of three messuages and lands in Wynster, with release from all actions by reason of any grants by Robert de Mountjoy, his father, for the observance of which he binds himself in £40. Witn. Gilbert Gerard of Wynster, Robert Mariote, Lodewyc de Wynster, etc. Dat. Sun. a. F. of St. Cedde [7 Jan.], 6 Edw. II. [1313].

2624. GRANT from Nicholas, son of John Selveyn, to Robert Marioth of Wynster, of a messuage in Wynster; rent, 12*d*. Witn. Hugh de Meignel of Wynster, Ralph Gerard of the same, Robert fil. Henrici of the same. Dat. Assheburne, Sat. a. Tr. of St. Thomas [7 July], 1315. (Woll. ii. 76A.)

2625. GRANT from Richard Gerard to William de Birchover of three messuages and land in Winster. Dat. F. of Beh. of St. John B. [29 Aug.], 8 Edw. III. [1334]. (Bodl. D.C. 10.)

2626. LEASE of the same to Richard and Agnes Gerard from William de Birchover. Dat. Th. a. F. of Beh. of St. John B. [1 Sept.], 1334. (Bodl. D. C. 9.)

2627. GRANT from Robert Gerrard of Wynstre and Alice his wife to Walter Gerard of the same, of all the lands, etc., which they had by feoffment from Dom. Thomas Meygnell, vicar of Glossop, in the vill of Wynstre. Witn. Hugh Meignell, Robert Gerard, Roger fil. Thome. Dat. T. a. F. of the Circumcision [1 Jan.], 25 Edw. III. [1352]. (Bemrose.)

WIRKSWORTH.

(WERKESWORTH, WERKUSWORTH, WIRK', WIRKESWORTHE, WORKESWORTH, WORSWORTH, WYRCUSWORTHE, WYRKES, WYRKESWORTH, WYRKISWORTHE, WYRKYSWORTH.)

2628. CONFIRMATION from Henry Braund of Wirksworth to the church and canons of the B. V. Mary of Derley of a fourteenth part of two cultures of land in Wyggewelle, which Vincent capellanus, his brother, gave with his body to them. Witn. Dom. Robert de Esseburne, Jordan de Snitterton, Hugh de Meynil, knts., Henry de Carduill, William le Liu, John de Plaustowe, Jordan de Ibul, William de Normanton, Thomas Coquus, Richard le Toller. *Temp.* Hen. III. (Rel. xvii. 66.)

2629. GRANT from Robert fil. Ric. Arkel to the church and canons of Derley of a fourteenth part of two cultures of land in Wyggewalle, which Robert le Wyne sometime held of him. Witn. Dom. Robert de Esseburne, Jordan de Snitterton, Hugh de Meynil, knts., Robert de Aldewerc, Ranulph de Wakebrugge, Peter de Vlkerthorpe, William le Liu, Alexander de Lowes, John de Plaustowe. *Temp.* Hen. III. (Rel. xvii. 67.)

2630. GRANT from William le Sureis de Wyrkesworth to the church and canons of Derley, of a seventh part of two cultures of land in Wiggewell, which Robert le Wyne sometime held of him. Witn. Dom. Robert de Esseburne, Jordan de Snitterton, Hugh de Meynil, knts., Henry de Carduil, William le Liu, Jordan de Ibul, John de Plaustowe, William de Normanton, Thomas Cocus. *Temp.* Hen. III. (Rel. xvii. 67.)

2631. GRANT from Robert fil. Gilberti de Wyrkesworth to the church and canons of Derley, of a seventh part of two cultures of land in Wyggewell, which Robert le Wyne sometime held of him. Witn. Dom. Robert de Esseburne, Jordan de Snittertone, Hugh de Meynil, knts., Henry de Carduil, John de Plaustowe, Jordan de Ibul, William de Normanton, Thomas Cocus. *Temp.* Hen. III. (Rel. xvii. 68.)

2632. GRANT from Ranulph fil. Walteri presbyteri de Wyrkesworthe to the church and canons of Darley of the fourteenth part of two cultures of land in Wiggewalle, which Robert le Wyne sometime held of him. Witn. Dom. Robert de Esseburne, Jordan de Snitterton, Hugh de Meynil, knts., Robert de Aldewerc, Ranulph de Wakebrugge, Peter de Vlkerthorp, William le Liu, Alexander de Lowes, John de Plaustowe. *Temp.* Hen. III. (Rel. xvii. 69.)

2633. GRANT from William de Ferr[ariis], Comes Derb', to the church and canons of Derle of five acres of land at Wiggewell, and a confirmation of all his land of Wiggewell which they held of his fee, namely, two cultures "sicut carte donatorum testantur." Witn. Dom. Hugh de Meynil, tunc senescallus, Dom. Robert de Esseburne, Dom. Robert le Vavassur, milites, etc. *Ante* 1247. (Woll. ii. 1.)

2634. SETTLEMENT of suit between the Abbot and Canons of Darley and the Dean and Chapter of Lincoln, relating to the tithes of land which was given to the canons by Vincent, formerly chaplain, and by William, Earl of Ferrers, in the parish of Wirksworth. Witn. R——, Precentor, and Ralph [de Leicester], Treasurer, of Lincoln, Mag. Simon de London, R—— de Belleston, Richard de Wisbech, canons of Lincoln, Mag. J. de Derby, S—— de Farewell, clerk, etc. Dat. Lincoln, W. a. Ass. of B. V. M. [15 Aug.], 1249. (Rel. xvii. 69.)

2635. GRANT from Henry fil. Ranulfi de Crumford and Adam fil. Roberti fil. Gilberti and Robert Faber de Wirkeswrth, to the Church and Canons of Derl' [Darley] of a fourteenth part of two cultures of land in Wiggewall, which Robert Le Wine sometime held. Witn. Dom. Robert de Esseburne, Jordan de Snutertona, Hugh de Meynil, knts., Robert de Aldewerhc, Ranulf de Wakebrugge, William Lelin, Alexander de Lowes, John de Plaustow, Thomas Cocus. *Temp.* Hen. III. (Holland.)

2636. GRANT from Ranulf de Petris de Wyrkesworthe to the Abbey of Derle, of the seventh part of two cultures of land in Wiggewelle. Witn. Rob. de Esbum, Jordan de Snuterton, Hugh de Meynil, milites, Henry de Cardul, William le Luy, Jordan de Ybul, etc. *Temp.* Hen. III. (Woll. i. 27.)

2637. GRANT from William fil. Radulphi le Fong to the church and canons of Derley of the lands which he and his father held in Haselhaye, nr. Wyggewelle. Witn. Robert le Vavassur, Robert de Esseburne, Hugh de Meynil, knts., Ranulph de Audewerc, Henry de Herlaston. Dat. F. a. F. of St. Cedde, Bp. [7 Jan.], 1252[3]. (Rel. xvii. 70.)

2638. QUITCLAIM, for 35s., by Johanna fil. Nicholai de Breydeshale, clerici, relicta quondam Roberti le Wyne, to the Abbot of Derleya [Darley, co. Derby], of all the lands of Wygewelle, which she held as her dower, together with one mark rent for the land, and surrender of the charter of settlement dated in full chapter on M. b. F. of St. Barnabas [11 June], 1260. Witn. Mag. Robert "Officialis" of Derby, William de Chaddesdene, Robert Olear', Laurence de Esseby, etc. *Temp.* Hen. III. (Woll. i. 26.)

2639. BOND by Peter le Sureys of Wyrkeswrth to Aaron, son of Jacob, the Jew, for 10 marks, to be paid at the quinzaine of Midsummer next. Dat. 15 Jan., 53 Hen. III. [1269]. (P. R. O. D. 47.)

2640. GRANT from Nicholas fil. Galteri de Wirkeswrth to the Abbey of Derle of the seventh part of two cultures of land in Wiggewell. Witn. Robert de Esseburne, Jordan de Snutertone, Hugh de Meynil, milites, etc. *Temp.* Hen. III. (Woll. i. 28.)

2641. QUITCLAIM by Peter le Norreys, dictus serviens de Wyrkesworth, to Robert de Derleya, of certain land which the former bought from William le Norreys, lying between land of the Canons of Darley at Wyggewell, and extending from Haselhay towards Wyggewellbrok. Witn. Geoffrey de Deth[ick], William de Aldwerke, Jordan de Snutertone, etc. *Temp.* Hen. III. (Woll. i. 29.)

2642. COMPOSITION of suits between Mag. Nicholas de Oxton, perpetual vicar of Wirksworth, and Henry, Abbot, and the Convent of Derley, respecting the small tithes arising from lands which the said abbot, etc., had in Wirksworth. Witn. Mag. John de Weston, Robert de St. Petro, Richard de Morley, William de Henouer, etc. Dat. Esseburn, F. of St. Gregory [12 Mar.], 1275. (Rel. xvii. 71.)

2643. CONFIRMATION by William Godman, perpetual vicar of Wirksworth, of the composition made in 1275 between N. de Oxton and Derley Abbey, respecting the small tithes of lands in Wirksworth. Witn. Mag. Robert de St°· Petro, Philip de Wyrkesworth, Peter de Mackworth, etc. Dat. F. of Pentecost [5 June], 1278. (Rel. xvii. 72.)

2644. GRANT to the King's brother, Edmund, Earl of Lancaster, of the manors of Wirksworth and Ashborne, and the wapentake of Wirksworth, in the county of Derby, in exchange for the counties and castles of Cardigan and Carmarthen. Dat. Westminster, 10 Nov., 1279. (D. of L.)

2645. BAILIFF's accompt-roll of Wirksworth; 1280. (Lichf. S. 4.)

2646. RATIFICATION by Roger, Bishop of Coventry and Lichfield (on an inspeximus by Oliver, Dean, and the Chapter of Lincoln), of the composition concerning small tithes from lands in Wirksworth, between the Vicar of Wirksworth and Derley Abbey. Dat. Heywoode, Pur. of B. V. M. [2 Feb.], 1285[6]. (Rel. xvii. 72.)

2647. CONFIRMATION of the same composition by John, Dean, and the Chapter of Lichfield. Dat. xvi. Kal. Apr. [17 Mar.], 1285[6] (Rel. xvii. 163.)

2648. CONFIRMATION of the same composition by Thomas, Prior of Coventry. Dat. xiii. Kal. Apr. [20 Mar.], 1285[6]. (Rel. xvii. 161.)

2649. QUITCLAIM from Matilda quondam vxor Johannis Palkocke de Eyhsbury to Dom. Philip de Eyhsbury, rector of Braundiston [? Braunstone, co. Leic.], of all lands which she holds in dower or which the said Philip and William his brother purchased from John Palkocke, her late husband, in Wyrkisworthe [Wirksworth], Middilton [Middleton], Hopton, Crumforde [Cromford], and Stepul [Steeple, in Wirksworth]. Witn. Dom. William dictus Godmon, vicar of Wirksworth, William fil. Bate de Wyrk', Nicholas Trusseloue, Roger fil. Nicholai, etc. Dat. All Saints' Day [1 Nov.], 1287. (D. A. J. iv. 2.)

2650. GRANT and quitclaim from Thomas fil. et her. Hugonis de Stanton et Clemencie de Herlaston, quondam vxoris sue, to Darley Abbey, of a bovate of land in Wyrkesworth called Boreoxgong. Witn. Elias de Schirleg, carpenter, Philip de la Rode, plaisterer, Henry de Pentriz, granger, etc. Dat. F. of St. Thomas, Ap. [21 Dec.], 1289. (Kerry xix. 308.)

2651. GRANT and quitclaim from " Thomas fil. et her. Hugonis de Stanton et Clemencie de Herlaston quondam uxoris sue," with the consent of Hugh his father, to the Abbot and Convent of Darley, of a bovate of land in Wyrkesworth, called Boreoxgong. Witn. Elias de Schirleg, carpenter, Philip de la Rode, plaisterer, Henry de Pentriz, granger, Geoffrey le Burgulon, etc. Dat. F. of St. Thomas, Ap. [21 Dec.], 1289. (Kerry xix. 308.)

2652. LEASE, for six years, from Adam ad fontem de Wyrkesworthe to William dictus Bate, of a croft in Wyrkesworthe. Witn. Dom. William Godman, vicar of Wirksworth, William de Crumforde, Robert Kesteven, John Trosseloue, etc. Dat. Nat. of B. V. M. [8 Sept.], 1295. (D. A. J. iv. 3.)

2653. GRANT from Peter fil. Willelmi le Sureys de Wirk' to Matilda his sister of a half acre and a half rood of land in the field of Wirke [Wirksworth], viz., the half acre in Hopton Dale and the half rood in Dale. Witn. Robert fil. Herwici de Wirk', Nicholas fil. Walteri de Wirk', Robert fil. Gilberti de Wirk', Ranulph super-petras . de Wirk', William Godmon, clerk. *Temp.* Edw. I. (D. A. J. iv. 2.)

2654. GRANT from Robert, son of Adam le Wyne, to Robert, son of Ingelram, of 60 acres of land between Leuenwelles and the way leading from Wirkesworthe and Bachewelle, which he had by grant from Dom. Robert de Staunthone, knt. Thirteenth cent. (Pole-Gell.)*

2655. RELEASE from Ran[ulf] fil. Henrici de Melnehovse to William fil. Bathe de Wirk' of a toft in Wirksworth, extending from the King's road to a certain ash tree placed there for a boundary. Witn. Dom. William Godmon, vicar of Wirksworth, Mag. Philip clericus de eadem, Henry fil. Thome de Hoptone. *Temp.* Edw. I. (Woll. i. 30.)

2656. CHARTER of Edward I., granting to his nephew, Thomas, Earl of Lancaster, a market and fair at his manor of Wirksworth. Dat. Dorchester, 2 Feb., 1306. (D. of L.)

2657. GRANT from Gilbert de Bradbury to Thomas fil. Henrici de Rodeheyth and Alice his wife, of a messuage in Wyrkes', near Le Daleweye. Witn. Nicholas de Cromford, John le Porter of Caldelowe, William fil. Bate of Wyrkes', etc. Dat. Tu. a. All Souls' Day [2 Nov.], 1315. (Woll. vii. 20.)

2658. GRANT from William le Wyne fil. Roberti le Wyne to William fil. Henrici de Hoptone, of lands in Wirkesworthe. Witn. Simon de Hoptone, Nicholas de Crumforde, Nicholas de Midelton in Wirkesworthe, etc. *Temp.* Edw. II. (Woll. i. 25.)

2659. GRANT from William de Hoptone to Dom. Milo, vicar of Wyrkesworthe, of land in Wyrkesworthe for life; rent, 26s. 8d. Witn. William de Kersyngtone, Nicholas de Cromford, William de Bradbury, etc. Dat. Wyrkesworthe, Fr. b. Ex. of H. Cross [14 Sept.], 19 Edw. II. [1325]. (Woll. i. 31.)

---

* Could not be found on my visit to Hopton ; taken from Historical Commission Report IX., App. ii., 402.

2660. GRANT from William de Cloptone to Nicholas de Roulisleye and Johanna his wife, of the reversion of lands in Wyrcusworthe, with the rents and services of William de Tokes and Alice his wife, of Nicholas de Assheburne, and of William le Chaloner of Wyrcusworthe, with reversion to Thomas, son of the said William de Claptone. Witn. Nich. Bate, Will. Bethebroke, Will. de Bredbare, etc. Dat. Wirkesworth, F. of St. Laurence [10 Aug.], 21 Edw. III. [1347]. French. (Woll. vi. 63.)

2661. GRANT, in fee, from William fil. Willelmi de Kersintone to John Arnald of Wyrkesworthe, chaplain, of lands and 6s. rent in Wyrkesworthe. Witn. Will. Bithebroke, Will. le Porter, Ric. le Porter, etc. Dat. F. of St. Machutus [15 Nov.], 23 Edw. III. [1349]. (Woll. vii. 21.)

2662. ACKNOWLEDGMENT before William Wyght de Hopton, Public Notary, by Robert de Yrton, vicar of Wirksworth, of the composition made between Nicholas de Oxton, a former vicar, and Darley Abbey, respecting the small tithes of certain lands in Wigwell (*v. supra*). Dat. 13 May, 1359. (Rel. xvii. 165.)

2663. GRANT from Margery, widow of John de Welde of Asshelehay, to William de Welde of Wyrkes[worth], Johanna his wife, and Matilda their daughter, of a messuage and cottage and four acres of land in Wyrkes'. Witn. Thomas de Castultone, vicar of Wyrkes', Nicholas Porter, Thomas Porter of the same, etc. Dat. Tu. a. F. of St. Edmund, Archbp. [26 Nov.], 5 Ric. II. [1381]. (Woll. vii. 22, 30.)

2664. GRANT from Johanna Arnald of Wyrkesworthe to Richard, son of Roger de Wygleye, of lands in Wyrkesworthe and Stephulle. Witn. William Porter of Wyrkesworthe, John Baron, John de Stepul, etc. Dat. Wyrkesworthe, S. b. F. of St. Margaret [20 July], 7 Ric. II. [1383]. (Woll. i. 32.)

2665. GRANT from Robert le Smyth of Wyrkesworth to William de Asschebourne and William de Wychelles, chaplains, of a messuage with buildings upon it in Wyrkesworth, near the King's highway. Witn. William le Porter de Wyrkesworth, John Daron, John Moll, etc. Dat. S. a. F. of St. Andrew [30 Nov.], 9 Ric. II. [1385]. (Kerry xix. 309.)

2666. FEOFFMENT by William Helyn of Brassington, chaplain, to John Brown, of two gardens in Wyrkesworth in "la Dale." Dat. Th. b. F. of Pur. of B. V. M. [2 Feb.], 14 Ric. II. [1391]. (P. R. O., A. 9140.)

2667. GRANT from John Tochet, son of John Tochet, to Thomas Foliambe, of a yearly rent of four marks from all his lands in Werkesworth and a "roba competens" at Christmas. Dat. Marketon, Michs. Day, 16 Ric. II. [1392]. (Foljambe.)

2668. GRANT from Thomas le Porter of Wyrkesworthe to William de Wynfeld, of land under Nortclyfe, abutting upon le Wassiche. Witn. Will. Wytur, sen., of Wyrkesworth, John Broun, John Barun, etc. Dat. F. of St. George [23 Apr.], 21 Ric. II. [1398]. (Woll. vii. 13.)

2669. GRANT from John Marchaunt and Marragdus Shorthose to the Prior and Convent of Burcestre of all their estate in lands and tenements in Wyrkesworth. Dat. Vigil of St. Matthias [24 Feb.], 6 Hen. IV. [1405]. (P. R. O. D. 963.)

2670. RELEASE from William de Alfertone, vicar of Radford, John Alot, and Thomas (?) Goytone, chaplain, to William de Wynfeld of Wyrkesworthe and Matilda his wife, of a cottage and lands in Wyrkesworthe. Dat. M. a. Nat. of St. John B. [24 June], 6 Hen. IV. [1405]. (Woll. vii. 23.)

2671. ATTORNEY from Walter Wolley of Wyrkesworth to John Snow for livery of seisin to Thomas Cobyn of Allerwaslegh and William Foceun of the same, of all his lands and possessions in Wyrkesworth. Witn. William Storar, William Wynfeld, John Forth. Dat. 10 Oct., 1 Hen. V. [1413]. (Kerry xix. 309.)

2672. EXTRACT of court-roll of Wyrkesworth held at Matlok, recording the admission of Walter Wolley of Wyrkesworth of a toft, etc., near the cemetery wall, lately in the tenure of William Wether. Dat. 6 June, 3 Hen. VI. [1425]. (Kerry xix. 310.)

2673. EXTRACT from the court-roll of the manor of [Wirks]worth, held 28 Jan., 6 Hen. VI. [1428], Nicholas Mountgomery being steward, at which John Ford surrendered three rods of land to the use of William Barker. (Woll. x. 65.)

2674. ATTORNEY from Walter Wulley, yeoman, to Robert Ayer of Padley, esquire, Richard Crowther of Wyrkesworth, and John Hassulwode of Callow, to dispose of all his lands in Wyrkesworth to the use of Margery his wife and of his sons. Dat. F. of St. Laurence [10 Aug.], 6 Hen. VI. [1428]. (Kerry xix. 311.)

2675. EXTRACT of court-roll of Wyrkesworth held 17 Nov., 7 Hen. VI. [1428], recording the admission of Walter Wolley to a piece of land called Les Bothes, lying near the cemetery of Wirksworth. (Kerry xix. 311.)

2676. QUITCLAIM from John Bee to Oliver Bee his father of a close near Wirksworth mill which they acquired jointly from Thomas Kneveton. Dat. 5 March, 12 Hen. VI. [1434]. (Kerry xix. 312.)

2677. EXTRACT of court-roll of Wyrkesworth, held 3 March, 16 Hen. VI. [1438], recording the surrender by Walter Wolley of all his lands in Wyrkesworth to the use of William Eton, chaplain; and the surrender by the latter, on the following day, of the same lands to the use of the said Walter and Margery his wife, and Roger their son, with reversion, if the said Roger die without heir of his body, to Elizabeth, Joan, Elena, and Agnes, daughters of the said Walter and Margery. (Kerry xix. 313.)

2678. ATTORNEY from John Lathbury, Richard Bagot, William Purdon, and John Forthe, vicar of the church of Longforth, to Thomas Alsop and Roger Greenhalwe, to deliver seisin to John Bradborne, son and heir of Henry Bradborne and Anne his wife, of the water-mill called Workesworth Milne. Witn. Thomas Blounte and Sampson Meverell, knts., Fulk Vernon, John Cokayne, Nicholas Fitzherbert, esquires. Dat. 12 July, 24 Hen. VI. [1446]. (Kerry xix. 314.)

2679. SURRENDER, at Wirksworth manor court, by William Alson of a cottage in Wirksworth, to the use of John Wigley and Ralph his son thereupon admitted. Dat. 21 Jan., 29 Hen. VI. [1451]. (Rel. xvii. 167.]

22

2680. BOND by John Wygley of Wyrkesworthe, co. Derby, yeoman, and Henry Lowe of Asshoure, husbandman, to John Wastnes, in £20, to answer to a plea of debt. Dat. 20 Sept., 36 Hen. VI. [1457]. (Woll. x. 64.)

2681. SALE from Elizabeth, widow of Thomas Mylne, sometime of Nottingham, to Nicholas Blakwall, vicar of Beston, and Rauf Cantrell, priest, of all her lands in Werkusworth, which formerly belonged to Walter Wolley his father. Witn. Thomas Codemon, Thomas Reedus, Richard Blakwal, William Hoghkynson, etc. Dat. 16 Nov., 5 Edw. IV. [1465]. (Kerry xix. 315.)

2682. EXTRACT of court of the Hundred of Worsworth held Wed. b. F. of the Purif. [2 Feb.], 6 Edw. IV. [1467], recording the admission of Thomas Caubrell of Alfeld to a messuage in Eyton. (Kerry xix. 316.)

2683. EXTRACT of court of the Hundred of Worsworth held Wed. b. F. of the Pur. [2 Feb.], 6 Edw. IV. [1467], recording the admission of Thomas Cantrell of Alfeld to a messuage in Eyton. (Kerry xix. 316.)

2684. GRANT from Richard Blackwalle of Wyrkesworthe and Thomas Harry to William Wynfeld of the same and Cecilia his wife, of a cottage and lands in Lee Breyche. Witn. Thomas Storer of Wyrkesworthe, John Smythe, Geoffrey Wodde, etc. Dat. Wyrkesworthe, 20 Apr., 12 Edw. IV. [1472]. (Woll. vii. 25.)

2685. EXTRACT from the Roll of the Little Court of the manor of Wirkesworth, held on Nat. of B. V. Mary [8 Sept.], 13 Edw. IV. [1473], at which Nicholas Scortred received in reveralty a parcell of land called Topsor, which he formerly held conjointly with his father; rent, 8*d*. (Woll. vii. 24.)

2686. EXTRACT of court-roll of the Hundred of Wyrksworth held 9 Feb., 12 Edw. IV. [1473], recording the admission of Thomas Cantrill to lands in Eyton lately held by Thomas Cantrell his father, now dead. (Kerry xix. 316.)

2687. EXTRACT of court-roll of Wirksworth held on Whitsun Tuesday [27 May], 17 Edw. IV. [1477], recording the surrender into the hands of the King by Thomas fil. Tho. Cantrell of a messuage in Eyton "de bondagio," with the adjacent lands, to the use of Laurence Lowe, thereupon admitted. (Kerry xix. 318.)

2688. ADMISSION of Robert Wilcokson to a piece of waste land in the Dale at Wirksworth for the enlargement of his tenement. Dat. Tu. a. F. of St. Thomas, M. [29 Dec.], 21 Edw. IV. [1481]. (Rel. xvii. 167.)

2689. GRANT from King Edward IV. to John Bowsefeld of the office of bailiff of the town and soke of Wirkesworth and the Beremaistership of the same, parcell of the Duchy of Lancaster, in such manner as Henry Wynter and others had held the same. Dat. London, 7 March, anno 22 [1482]. (Woll. viii. 15.)

2690. RELEASE by Ralph Saucheverell, esq., Sir Richard Smythe, rector of Yrton, and Roger Wudde of Matlok, to Robert Smythe of Wyrkesworth, of lands in Wyrkysworth, which they had of the grant of John Smythe, father of the said Robert. Witn. Robert Storor of Wyrkysworth, Robert Glossoppe of the same, Robert Wylkokson, etc. Dat. F. of St. Cuthbert [20 Mar.], 1 Hen. VII. [1485]. (Woll. vi. 64.)

2691. SURRENDER by Roger Wilkokson at Wirksworth Manor Court of lands late belonging to Robert Wilkokson in Wirksworth, to the use of John Wilkokson of Frytcheley, Thomas Alsybroke, Roger Hellott, Thomas Smyth of Medilton, and Ralph Ryley, thereupon admitted. Dat. 30 July, 8 Hen. VII. [1493]. (Rel. xvii. 167.)

2692. EXTRACT of court-roll of Wyrkysworth, held 19 Feb., 13 Hen. VII. [1498], recording the surrender by William Hervy of a house called "A Barkhouse" in Wirksworth, abutting on Walkmyln-lane, to the use of Henry Vernon, knt., thereupon admitted. (Kerry xix. 319.)

2693. COPY of a release by Henry Stortrede of Mogyntone, chaplain, Thomas Allsop of Bradburne, and John Wygley of Wyrkysworth, of a messuage and lands in Kirk Yretone. Witn. Roger Vernon, bailiff of Wyrkysworthe, Thomas Hervy of the same, John Gelle of Hopton, etc. Dat. 27 Dec. Fifteenth century. (Woll. viii. 12.)

2694. ATTORNEY from William fil. et her. Willelmi Harve to John Gell and William Rage, to deliver to the lord of Wirksworth Manor a messuage now in the tenure of Richard Peghell, to the use of Henry Vernon, knt. *Circ.* 1500. (Kerry xix. 320.)

2695. LEASE, for 44 years, from John, Abbot, and the Convent of Derley, to Thomas Babyngton of Dethyk, esquire, of their tenement and chief place at Wygewall, at a yearly rent of £3 6s. 8d. Dat. 30 Sept., 17 Hen. VII. [1501]. (Rel. xvii. 168.)

2696. RENEWAL of the above lease for a further term of 44 years from the same to the same. Dat. 10 Aug., 16 Hen. VIII. [1524]. (Rel. xvii. 225.)

2697. GRANT from William Glopsop of Wirkesworth to John Vernon, esq., of lands in Wirkesworthe, which he had of the gift of Thomas, son and heir of Thomas Smyth of the same, and appointing attorneys. Dat. 10 July, 7 Hen. VIII. [1515]. (Woll. iii. 21.)

2698. EXTRACT of court of George Hennage, Dean of Lincoln, held at Wirksworth, recording the surrender by Roger More of Derby, draper (by Ralph Gell of Hopton and another, his attorneys), of the fourth part of all his lands within the lordship of Wyrkesworth and Parwych or elsewhere in Wyrkesworth parish, late belonging to Henry Hylton, and afterwards to Margaret de Brampton, the latter's kinswoman, to the use of Richard Wygley of Midleton, thereupon admitted. Dat. 6 Nov., 24 Hen. VIII. [1532]. (Rel. xvii. 226.)

2699. LEASE, for 14 years, from Wyllyam Glosop of Graunge Felde, co. Derby, and Thomas Whalley, to Rauffe Gell of Hopton, gent., of a barn and close called the Halle close, in the parish of Wyrkysworth. Dat. Ann. of B. V. M. [25 March], 29 Hen. VIII. [1538]. (Pole-Gell.)

2700. LETTERS patent of Henry VIII., granting to Thomas Babington and John Hyde (for £603 1s. 6d.) various lands, etc., in cos. Lincoln, Chester, Hertford, Buckingham, Middlesex, and Nottingham, and in the following places in co. Derby, viz., Wigwall in Wirksworth, Lutchurch in St. Peter's parish, Derby, tithes in Tanesley, and Whitcroft parcel of Cruch rectory, all of which lands, etc., were sometime parcel of the possessions of the late dissolved Abbey of Darley. Dat. 20 June, 36 Hen. VIII. [1544]. (Rel. xvii. 226.)

2701. BOND from Thomas Babyngton of Dethyke, esq., to Humphrey Bradborne, knt., to abide by the award of Richard Curzon, William Legh, Anthony Lowe, John Francis, and William Sacheverell, in a dispute concerning a water-mill and water-course of Ludwell, in the lordship of Wirksworth. Dat. 4 Sept., 36 Hen. VIII. [1544]. (? Bemrose.)

WIRKSWORTH *v.* also under ASHBOURNE, CHESTERFIELD, IBLE, MATLOCK.

WOODTHORPE IN N. WINGFIELD.

(WODETHORPE IN SCHARVISDALE.)

2702. GRANT from Matthew de Knyvetone to Henry, his first-born son, of the manor of Wodethorpe in Scharvisdale; rent, 20s. sterl. yearly. Witn. Dom. John Deyncorte, then rector of the church of Wynnefelde, Roger Deyncorte, Jocelin de Steynisby, Ralph de Rerisby, Thomas, clerk, Robert, son of the same, William Basshet, Stephen de Yrtone, John le Ro de Bradale, William de Knyvetone, clerk, etc. *Temp.* Edw. I. (Lansd. 607.)

2703. GRANT from Matthew de Knyvetone to Henry, his son and heir, and Ysabella, daughter of Nicholas Meverel de Gaytone, of the whole manor of Wodethorp. Annual rent, one pair of white gloves. Witn. Dom. Robert le Bretone, Walter de Ribef', Stephen de Irtone, Jordan de Sottone, Thomas Meverel, Roger de Mercintone, Ralph de Munjoye, etc. [1287-1288.] (Lansd. 608.)

WOODTHORPE, NR. DRONFIELD.

2704. EXTRACT from roll of a court held at Holmesfeld, Mon. n. a. Easter, 30 Hen. VI. [1452], whereat William Croftes claims a messuage and bovate of land in Woodthorpe, as son and heir of William Croftes. (Woll. viii. 70.)

WOODTHORPE IN STAVELEY.

2705. INDENTURE, testifying to the right of Robert Maretoll to lands, tenements, etc., in Stavely Woodthorp, to whom they were granted by John, son of Ralph Frechevill, who had inherited them from his father, Ralph, son of Ralph Frechevill, who, after receiving them from his father, had become a Franciscan Friar at Nottingham, and confirming the same to Margaret, Amicia, and Isabella, grand-daughters of the said John. Witn. John de Purley, William de Neuylworth, Robert Robynson, etc. Dat. Thurs. a. F. of Transl. of St. Thomas [7 July], 19 Ric. II. [1395]. (Harl. 86 H. 14.)

WOODTHORPE IN STAVELEY *v.* also under STAVELEY.

WORMHILL.

(WORMEHUL, WORMELLE, WORMHULL.)

2706. GRANT from Thomas fil. Tho. Foleiambe, with the assent of Katerine his wife, to Thomas fil. Joh. Foleiambe, of a messuage, etc., and 15 acres of land in Wormehul, granted to him by Hugh de Morhage in free marriage with the said Katerine. Witn. Dom. William de Mortayn, Gervase de Bernak, knts., William Foleiambe, Thomas fil. Roger Foleiambe, etc. Early Edw. I. (Foljambe.)

2707. QUITCLAIM from Adam Cadas de Wormhull to Richard fil. Ade Forestarius de Wormhull of a messuage and an acre and a half in Wormhull. Witn. Richard Foliamb, Alan del Hull, Ralph fil. Nicholai de Tidd[eswall], Roger fil. Radulfi, Henry fil. Radulfi. Dat. Tideswall, S. b. Assumption of B. V. M. [15 Aug.], 11 Edw. III. [1337]. (Okeover.)

2708. GRANT from Richard Foliamb of Wormhull to John fil. Ricardi Foliamb, etc., of 32 acres of land in Wormhull. Witn. Simon del Halle, Robert fil. Willelmi del Tunstedes, Robert de Hope, etc. Dat. F. of Ass. of B. V. M. [15 Aug.], 20 Edw. III. [1346]. (Woll. viii. 10.)

2709. GRANT from Thomas Alynson of Herdwyckewalle, within the township of Wormelle, to Roger Alynson his brother, called Thomas, of land in " le Ware Slacke," adjoining land of St. Mary of Tyddeswalle, within the said township of Wormhill. Dat. F. of Tr. of St. Thomas [7 July], 3 Hen. IV. [1402]. (P. R. O. c. 606.)

WORMHILL *v.* also under TIDESWELL.

WYASTON.

(WYARDESTON.)

2710. LEASE, for life, from Hugh de Meignille, knt., to Richard de Yeveley, his bailiff, of a curtilage and lands in Wyardeston; rent, a rose. Dat. Tu. a. F. of St. Martin [11 Nov.], 26 Edw. III. [1352]. (Woll. ix. 66.)

WYASTON *v.* also under EDLASTON.

YEAVELEY.

(YEVELEY, YEVESLEY, YVELEE, YVELEYE.)

2711. RELEASE from William de Longeford to Roger de Mercinton of common of pasture, with permission to enclose lands, between Yvelee, Redislege, and Longeford. Witn. Dom. James de Schirle, Dom. Peter de Touke, Dom. Stephen de Irtone, etc. Dat. F. of St. Margaret [20 July], 53 Hen. III. [1269]. (Woll. ix. 19.)

2712. GRANT from William de Longeforde fil. et her. Willelmi de Longeforde to William de Meygnill, Dominus de Yveleye, of the homage and service of Thomas Golding and Johanna his wife, who served the said William for a certain tenement in Yeveleye. Witn. Hen. de Braylisforde, Ralph de Monseye, Giles de Meygnill, milites, etc. *Temp.* Edw. I. (Add. 4873.)

2713. GRANT from Henry de la Coudreye to William de Meynille of all his land in Wilmyshay, in the territory of Yueleye, which Richard de la Coudray had by grant from William de Langeford; rent, to the aforesaid Henry, one halfpenny silver, and to William de Langeforde, one penny silver. Witn. Dom. Thomas de Bray, Henry de Brayn, Ralph de Munjoye, Henry fil. Herberti, Roger de Mercintone, milites, Stephen de Irton, William de Bentleye. Dat. Th. b. Palm Sunday [3 Apr.], 1281. (Add. 4874.)

2714. GRANT from William de Shirley, chaplain, to Robert de Denstones, William Hebbe, etc., of a messuage and land in Yevesley. Witn. Robert Fraunces, Nicholas Mountgomery, John Cokayn, milites, etc. Dat. M. a. F. of Ass. of B. V. M. [15 Aug.], 8 Hen. IV. [1407]. (Campb. i. 10.)

2715. SALE from Thomas Charde "of the household of the Right honorable Lady Anne of Cleves, gentilman," to Vincent Mundy of Marketon, esq., of the site and chief messuage of the manor or late "Commaundrye of Yeveley otherwyse called Stede," in the county of Derby, parcel of the lands, and possession of the late Hospital of St. John Jerusalem in England lately dissolved, with the lands in Yeveley and Stede, a common called Darley More, the herbage of Oxwood in Stede and Yeveley, and all other lands there which the said Thomas had from the King by letters patent under the seal of the Court of Augmentations. Dat. 1 Mar., 33 Hen. VIII. [1542]. (Mundy.)

YELDERSLEY.

(THYLDRESLEGE, TILDERESSEG, TILDESSLEYE, TILDRESLEY, YELDERESLEYE, YELDURSLEY, YHILDERESLE, YHILDIRSLEY, YILDERSLEY, YLDERESLEY, YLDERSLEE, YLDERUSLEYE, YLDIRISLE, YLDIRSLI, YLDRISLEYE.)

2716. RELEASE by Hugh fil. Radulfi to William de Mungay his brother of land in Yldreslee, to be held of Sewale fil. Fulcheri, in exchange for land in Cratle, and part of the mill of Alretun, with ratification by William, son of the said Hugh, and Serlo de Mungay, his nephew. Late twelfth cent. (Woll. ix. 7.)

> Omnibus hominibus et amicis suis tam presentibus quam futuris Hugo fil. Radulfi salutem. Sciatis me quietum clamasse totum ius et Rectum meum quod habui in terra de Yldreslee et in omnibus eius pertinenciis Willelmo de Mungay fratri meo illi et heredibus suis tenendam de Sewallo filio Fulcheri et suis heredibus omnino quietam tam mei quam heredum meorum in perpetuum. Pro hac autem quieta clamacione reddidit mihi Willelmus frater meus totam terram suam quam habuit in Cratle et partem suam molendini de Alretun quietam de se et eius heredibus in perpetuum. Hanc autem quietam clamacionem Willelmus filius meus iurauit tenendam in perpetuum et Serlo de Mungay nepos meus ex parte sua similiter et vt hec quietancia rata permaneat et firma in perpetuum eam sigillo meo et presenti scripto confirmaui. Hiis testibus Willelmo, Comite de Ferr[ariis], Willelmo fil. Walkelini, Fulchero fil. Henrici, Sewallo fil. Henrici, Petro fil. Walkelini, Jordano de Toc, Willelmo de Menil, Adam de Hednessoure et pluribus aliis.

2717. GRANT from Serlo de Grendon to Serlo fil. Radulfi de Moungay of all the land with the wood which lies between the grantor's fish-pond of Bradeley and the vill of Tilderesseg and the spring at the head of the said fish-pond near the road to Ashbourne, "per quercus mercatas usque ad viam Domini Regis," with four acres beyond Le Brademers, measured by the perch of 20 feet, near the boundaries of Tilderessleye towards Rucroft, and common in all his land of Bradele and Stureston. Rent, a pair of white gloves. Witn. Henry fil. Sewalli, Robert Britton, Leodegarius de Bure, Walter de Montegomeri, etc. Early thirteenth cent. (Woll. vi. 43.)

2718. GRANT from Nicholas, Prior of Tutesbire [Tutbury], to Serlo de Mungay, of 10 acres of land in Thyldreslege and right to essart 10 acres in Littilhalyn, etc., for certain privileges, namely, that they may make a ditch between Ethnadeston wood and another wood which the Priory gave him, from Bradelegbroc to Wyttelegsiche, and may essart the land lying between Ethnadeston field and the high road from Derby to Ashbourne, and may construct a fish-pond and mill in Rauenesdal'. Witn. Dom. Robert de Esseburne, tunc senescallus, Geoffrey de Greselege, William de Mungumbry, Engonulf de Braylesford, Geoffrey de Bec, Oliver le Foun, etc. *Circ.* 1230. (Woll. ix. 76.)

2719. COVENANT whereby Serlo de Munjoye grants to Roger de Hordern and Matilda his wife a place of land in Yhildirsley called Hadeleye croft, to hold during the life of the said Matilda, at a rent of 6¼d., and after her death to the said Roger, at a rent of 2s. 7½d. Witn. Henry de Horderne, Richard de Horderne, William fil. Willelmi de Aula de Wyardestone, etc. *Temp.* Hen. III. (Woll. ix. 9.)

2720. COVENANT whereby Ralph de Munjay leases to William Thorsmon of Yldirsle and Isabel his wife, and Richard, Robert, and William their sons, a toft with buildings in Yldirsle, for 20 years, and nine acres of land in the same for 10 years; rent, 12s. 1d. Witn. Dom. James de Shirle, Roger de Mercinton, Matthew de Knyvete, etc. Dat. Michaelmas, 1273. (Woll. ix. 11.)

2721. LEASE by Dom. Ralph de Munioye, dominus de Ylderusleye, to Robert fil. Willelmi prepositi de eadem and Ing' his wife, filia Heruici de Sturstone, for their lives, of a piece of land with barn and cottage at Orlewic, in the fee of Taddeleye, lying between the road leading from Taddeleye towards Cornleye and the water called Askebec, at the yearly rent of half a mark. Witn. Henry de Knyueton, Matthew his brother, Hervey de Sturston, Richard de Mapilton, Robert clericus. Dat. W. a. Michaelmas, 1286. (Brookhill.)

2722. COVENANT whereby Dom. Ralph de Munjoye grants to Richard Attewelle and Alice his wife 16½ acres of land in Yldrisleye, which Richard fil. Willelmi prepositi formerly held; rent, 13s. 9d. Witn. John de Moretone, Henry Attegrene, etc. *Temp.* Edw. I. (Woll. ix. 12.)

2723. RELEASE by Robert fil. Serlonis de Munjoy to Ralph de Munjoy his brother, of a rent of 40s. in Yldirisle, and of 12 acres of land in Urlewike, also of a rent of half a mark from lands in Modinor, in the fee of Mercintone [Marchington, co. Staff.]. Witn. Dom. James de Shirle, Dom. Peter de Touke, Dom. Matthew de Knyvetone, etc. *Temp.* Edw. I. (Woll. ix. 14.)

2724. ACQUITTANCE by Peter de Peterstowe, prior et procurator domus de Deulacresse [Dieulacres Abbey, co. Staff.], to Serlo le Mountjoye fil. et her. quondam domini Radulphi de Mountjoye, late Sheriff of Lancaster, for an exchequer tally for 60s., which had been levied for the King's use upon the goods of the said Abbey by the said Ralph, "dum fuerat vicecomes Lancastrie." Dat. Yildirsely, near Esseburne, Vigil of St. Denis, Martyr [3 Oct.], 1316. (Woll. ix. 80.)

2725. SALE by Rauf de Mountjoye and Agneys Bagot to Serlo de Mountjoye, for 25 marks and 8d., of the crop growing upon a place of land in Yeldresleye, in which he had enfeoffed them. Dat. Lokhaye, Sat. a. Annun. of B. V. M. [25 Mar.], 10 Edw. II. [1317]. French. (Woll. ix. 16.)

2726. LEASE, for 20 years, by Margery, widow of Serlo de Mungjoye, to Robert de Irlande, of her dower in Yhilderesle and Urlewyke; rent, 5 marks and 10s. Witn. Roger de Bradeburne, Nicholas de Marchentone, milites, etc. Dat. F. of St. Clement [? 17 Nov.], 11 Edw. II. [1317]. (Woll. ix. 81.)

2727. SPECIFICATION of dower in lands and rents assigned for life by William Yrlond of Yeldursley, esq., to Dulcissa, widow of Robert Yrlond of the same, in Yeldursley and Lokhawe. Witn. Henry Knyventone, Robert Knyventone, Will. Lymester, etc. Dat. 1 Nov., 14 Hen. VI. [1435]. (Woll. ix. 70.)

2728. BOND by William Ireland of Ylderesley, gent., to William Babyngton, knt., William Babyngtone, esq., and John Brydde, in £40. Dat. 10 Mar., 20 Hen. VI. [1442]. (Woll. ix. 72.)

2729. EXEMPLIFICATION of recovery by Ralph Oker, esquire, against John Ireland, son and heir of Robert Ireland, of two messuages and various lands in Yeldersley. Dat. 11 Nov., 5 Hen. VII. [1489]. (Okeover.)

2730. GRANT from John Irelond fil. et her. Roberti Irelond of Yeldersley to Ralph Oker, that he may have sufficient wood for housbote and heybote from all his woods in Yeldersley for his two houses and lands in Yeldersley. Witn. Henry Vernon, knt., William Basset of Blore, John Fitzherbert of Norbury, esquires, Thomas Babyngton de Dethyk. Dat. 2 Sept., 7 Hen. VII. [1491]. (Okeover.)

2731. SETTLEMENT by John Ireland of Yeldresley, esq., of lands in Yeldresley, in the event of a marriage between William, his son and heir, or Robert, his second son, and Dorothy, daughter of Nicholas Agard, esq., with provision for Cecile and Margarete, daughters of the said Nicholas. Dat. 15 June, 12 Hen. VII. [1497]. (Woll. ix. 71.)

YELDERSLEY *v.* also under SNELSTON.

YOULGRAVE.

(YOLEG', YOLEGRAVE, YOLGRAVE, YOLGREFF, YOLGREVE, YOLGREYVA, YOLLGREVE, YOULGREVE, ZOLGREFF.)

2732. LEASE from Henricus Albus [White] de Yolegraue to Willelmus fil. Eliæ de Parva Longisdon, of two acres and three roods of land in Yolegraue, for 24 years. Witn. Dom. William, vicarius de Yolegraue, Will de Hoco, Rob. de Dokenfeld, etc. Dat. St. Martin's Day [11 Nov.], 44 Hen. III. [1260]. (Harl. 83 D. 10.)

2733. GRANT from Henry Niger [Black] de Yoleg' to William de Lang', of Adam le bey, his native, together with all his land and property, for the term of 40 years, to begin at the F. of St. John B. [24 June], 40 Hen. III. [1256]. Witn. William Grym, Vicar of Yolegreve, Will de Hoco, Adam de Stantun, etc. (Harl. 84 A. 5.)

2734. GRANT from Nicholas de Sterelley and William de Mounford to Robert fil. Roberti le Breton, Joanna fil. Philippi de Strelley, and their heirs in tail, of tenements and lands in Yolgreve. Witn. Will de Strelley, Roger le Breton, Thomas le Archere, etc. Dat. Yolgreve, S. b. Pur. of B. V. M. [2 Feb.], 23 Edw. III. [1349]. (Harl. 84 A. 47.)

2735. GRANT from Robert de Stanton to Roger fil. Huntredi of land in Stanton Wudhowses, to hold of the church of All Saints' of Yolgreff, for a rent of 3*s.*, which sum the said Robert had been accustomed to pay for the support of three lamps there. *Temp.* Edw. III. (Woll. ii. 27.)

2736. GRANT from John Stafford, esq., to John de Asshelay, chaplain of the chauntry of St. Mary's de Moniassh, of land and tenements in Yollgreve. Witn. John Foy de Yollgreve, Thomas Troche de Moniassh, Thomas in le Dale de Moniassh. Dat. Yollgreve, 10 Mar., 3 Hen. VI. [1425]. (Harl. 84 A. 39.)

2737. WILL of Agnes Alyn, wife of Henry Alyn. Witn. Wylliam Weyley, chaplain of Zolgreff, Richard Bargh, Richard Halle, jun. Dat. 4 Id. [10] Feb., 1507. Proved 9 Mar., same year. (Woll. ii. 38.)

2738. GRANT from Edward Pease and James Wilsone to Randall Wryght, of a messuage and lands late belonging to the Chantry of the Blessed Virgin of Yolgreyve in Byrcheovere, which they held of the gift of King Edward VI. Dat. 21 Sept., 3 Edw. VI. [1549]. (Woll. xi. 67.)

YOULGRAVE *v.* also under BIRCHOVER, EYAM, STANTON LEES, TRUSLEY.

ADDENDA.

ALLESTREE.
(ATHELARDESTRE.)

2739. FINE at Derby dated S. a. F. of St. Martin [16 Nov.], 10 John [1208], whereby Richard fil. Roberti acknowledges that three acres and a half in question at Athelardestre are the right of Robert Maunilwerd and Matilda his wife, in return for which the said Robert and Matilda quitclaim to the said Richard an acre and a half of the said land. (P. R. O., Hunter's *Fines*, p. 30.)

ASHBOURNE.

2740. GRANT by Richard fil. Henrici fil. Simonis de Taddeleg' to John fil. Elie de Essebourne, clericus, of two half-acres of land in Taddeleg'; to hold by rent of a peppercorn, on the F. of St. Oswald, King [5 Aug.]. Witn. Nicholas de Mercintone, Robert fil. Alexandri de Esseburne, Robert fil. Roberti de Tydeswelle, Ivo de Taddeleg', etc. *Temp.* Edward I. (Woll. iii. 8.)

ASHFORD.
(ESSEFORD.)

2741. COVENANT by Robert de Sallowe and Ralph de Lathbury, attorneys of Dom. Ralph Pypard to pay to Thomas de Macclesfeud £29 11s., the assessed value of the crops, farm implements, etc., upon the manor of Esseford, of which the said Thomas was formerly farmer; finding security for the said payment in the persons of Richard in-le-Dale, John in-le-Graue, Simon de Crumford, Thomas le Roo, Henry Bouryng, Elias fil. Ric. de Longesdon, and others. Dat. W. b. F of St. Lucy [13 Dec.], 31 Edw. I. [1302]. (Add. 37250.)

ASTON-ON-TRENT.
(ESTON.)

2742. FINE at Nottingham dated Fr. a. F. of St. Botulph [21 June], 4 John [1202], whereby Alan fil. Jordani quitclaims to Gilbert de Lindesia and Emma his wife, Richard . . . and Agnes his wife, two virgates of land, etc., in Eston, in return for which the said Gilbert, Emma, Richard and Agnes grant to the said Alan a messuage in Eston lying between two messuages of William Malmesert. (P. R. O., Hunter's *Fines*, p. 18.)

BARLBOROUGH.
(BARLEBRUG.)

2743. FINE at Nottingham dated the Octave of F. of SS. Peter and Paul [6 July], 4 John [1202], whereby William de Streton quitclaims to Sewale fil. Henrici a bovate of land in Barleburg'. (P. R. O., Hunter's *Fines*, p. 24.)

BARROW-ON-TRENT.
(BAREWE.)

2744. FINE at Westminster on Fr. a. Conv. of St. Paul [31 Jan.], 8 Ric. I. [1197], whereby the Hospitallers of St. John of Jerusalem released to Robert de Bakepuz the advowson of the church of Barewe, in return for which the latter, in the presence of Hugh [de Nonant] Bishop of Coventry, granted to the Hospitallers 100s. yearly to be paid by the parson, or in case of there being a vacancy, to be paid from the goods of the church. (P. R. O., Pipe R. S. Pub., Vol. XX., p. 64.)

BEAUCHIEF.
(BEUCHEF.)

2745. FINE at Derby on W. b. F. of St. Edmund [19 Nov.], 10 John [1208], whereby Serlo de Begelei and Robert Briton grant 60 acres of land in Wallton to the Church of St. Thomas M., of Beuchef, and the canons there. (P. R. O., Hunter's *Fines*, p. 32.)

BRADBORNE.
(BRADEBURNE.)

2746. FINE at Westminster dated five weeks after Easter, 9 John [1208], whereby Nicholas de Limeseie grants to Jordan de Toke a carucate of land in Hulton and ten bovates of land in Bradeburne to hold by free service of 50s. yearly. (P. R. O., Hunter's *Fines*, p. 27.)

BRETBY.
(BRETTEBY.)

2747. FINE at Nottingham dated Fr. a. Nat. of St. John B. [28 June], 4 John [1202], whereby Nicholas Suyenell quitclaims to Simon de Knyb' two virgates of land in Bretteby. (P. R. O., Hunter's *Fines*, p. 22.)

BROUGHTON WEST *v.* under DOVERIDGE.

CALLOW
(CALDELAWE),
v. under MAPPLETON.

CHESTERFIELD.

(Cestrefeld.)

2748. FINE at Westminster, F. of St. Cecilia [22 Nov.], 8 Ric. I. [1196], whereby John fil. Willelmi de Kelm releases to Michael de Ednesofre an acre of land at Haliwell in Cestrefeld for a silver mark. (P. R. O., Pipe Roll. Soc. Pub., Vol. XX., p. 28.)

2749. FINE at Nottingham dated Tu a. Nat. of St. John B. [25 June], 4 John [1202], whereby Alan fr. Simonis Palmer quitclaims to Herbert Carecarius and Isabella his wife a messuage in Cestrefeld. (P. R. O., Hunter's *Fines*, p. 22.)

CROXALL

(Croxhale),

v. under KEDLESTON.

DERBY.

(Derbi.)

2750. FINE at Nottingham dated Sat. a. F. of St. [Botulph, 22 June], 4 John [1202], whereby William fil. Hugonis quitclaims to Walter de . . . tebi and Bruning de Derb' and Agnes, widow, three tofts and four acres of land in Derby. (P. R. O., Hunter's *Fines*, p. 20.)

2751. FINE at same place and on same day whereby Richard Parmentar, Emma his wife, and Matilda sister to Emma, quitclaim to William fil. Lewin' a messuage in Derbi. (P. R. O., Hunter's *Fines*, p. 20.)

2752. FINE at same place and date, whereby Edwin fil. Aghemundi and Agnes his wife, quitclaim to Raghenald fil. Thore a messuage in Derb'. (*Ibid.*, p. 20.)

2753. FINE at Nottingham dated Sund. a. F. of St. Botulph [23 June], 4 John [1202], whereby Ingeram de Waldewich and Quenilda his wife acknowledge that a messuage in question in Derby is the right of Hawise fil. Walkelini and Letitia her sister, who shall hold it at a yearly rent of eightpence during the said Quenilda's life, and at her death they shall hold it free of the said rent. (*Ibid.*, pp. 20, 21.)

DOVERIDGE.

(Dubrig'.)

2754. FINE at Derby dated . . . F. of St. Martin [11 Nov.], 10 John [1208], whereby Henry de Penesion' acknowledges a certain acre of meadow in question in Brocton' to be the free alms of the church of Dubrig', and quitclaims the same to Richard, persona de Dubrig'. (P. R. O., Hunter's *Fines*, p. 31.)

DRAYCOTT.

(Draycot.)

2755. FINE at Derby dated S. a. F. of St. Edmund [23 Nov.], 10 John [1208], whereby Richard fil. Roberti grants to William Burgunun two bovates of land in Draycot, and acquits him of two shillings yearly to the chief lord. (P. R. O., Hunter's *Fines*, p. 33.)

EDINGALE

(EDELINGHALE, EDLINGHALL),

v. under KEDLESTON.

FINDERN.

2756. FINE at St. Bridget's, London, dated 15 days after Michaelmas, 6 John [1204], whereby Nicholas de Wilinton acknowledges that the free tenement, viz., 12 bovates, six acres and a mill in Finderne, and a mill in Potlac, which he holds, are the fee of William, Abbot of Burton, in return for which acknowledgment the latter grants the same to the said Nicholas to hold by service of 43*s*. 6*d*. yearly. (P. R. O., Hunter's *Fines*, p. 26.)

2757. FINE at [Derby] dated S. a. F. of St. Martin [16 Nov.], 10 John [1208], whereby Robert de Al . . . el quitclaims to Hugh de Findern and Nicholas de Wilinton four bovates of land in Finderne, for which quitclaim Hugh gave the said Robert three marks, and the same Nicholas granted to him two acres and a half of meadow and two acres of land in Findern, namely, in Heppelemead and Hurimandole. (P. R. O., Hunter's *Fines*, p. 30.)

2758. FINE at Derby dated the F. of St. Edmund [20 Nov.], 10 John [1208], whereby Nicholas de Wilinc' conveys to Robert de Alvel' two bovates of land in Finderne. (P. R. O., Hunter's *Fines*, p. 32.)

HARTSHORN.

(HERTESHORN, HERTISHORN.)

2759. FINE levied at Westminster on Thursd. a. F. of St. John B. [24 June], 7 Ric. I. [1196], whereby Bertram fil. Willelmi de Herteshorn and Alice fil. Roberti, his wife, acquire from Richard de Verdun four virgates of land in Herteshorn and convey to Richard the messuages of Symon fil. Basilie and of Ralph Le Melim in Herteshorn, with 60 acres of land there in the tenement of Fulesfenshiche, near the river towards Denevellhaie, and 30 acres near the land of the Templars, near the river towards Motlhaue. (P. R. O., Pipe Roll. Soc. Publ., Vol. XVII., p. 157.)

2760. FINE at Derby dated Fr. a. F. of St. Edmund [21 Nov.], 10 John [1208], to end a suit concerning a wood in Herteshorn, whereby Bertram de Caldun and Alice his wife quitclaim to Lucian de Seille and Agatha his wife a moiety of Danewallhei towards Danewall, and all the wood outside Danewallhei shall remain common to the said Lucian, Agatha, Bertram and Alice. (P. R. O., Hunter's *Fines*, p. 33.)

HEAGE. (?)

2761. FINE at Nottingham dated Fr. a. F. of SS. Peter and Paul [5 July], 4 John [1202], whereby Robert de Alveleg' leases to Peter de Dereth' and Alice his wife, his tenants, 36 acres of land in Stevenethornehaie at a yearly rental of 2*s*. 6*d*., the said tenants undertaking to strengthen his millpool on their land at Bedebroc, and they quitclaim to the said Robert 36 acres in Leheg' and in Riecroft and the said millpool. (P. R. O., Hunter's *Fines*, p. 24.)

HOLME by Bakewell.

2762. GRANT by Roger de Esseburn fil. Will. de Esseburn, dwelling in Bauquell, to Roger le Wyne and William le Wyne his brother, of 12½ acres of land, etc., in the territory of Holm by Bauquell: for his life, at a rent of 10s. to the lord of the fee and a rose to the grantor. Witn. William Hally, Peter de Roland, William, clericus, de Bauquell, Matthew de Reyndon, Matthew Brabyl, Philip de Esseburn.   Early fourteenth cent. (Add. 37,333.)

KEDLESTON.

(KETELESTON.)

2763. FINE at Nottingham dated the morr. of F. of St. Giles [17 Sept.], 10 John [1208], whereby Thomas de Curzon acknowledges the whole vill of Keteleston to be, by right of dower, Alice de Sumerville's (claiming by Richard de Curzun her son) for her life time, in return for which the said Richard grants to the said Thomas land in Twiford, Steineston, Croxhale, and Edelinghale, to the value of £9 7s. 6d., with the homages and services due therefrom: the said vill on the death of the said Alice to revert to the said Thomas to be held of the said Richard by service of one knight's fee.   Witn. Robert fil. Roberti, William de Curzon, Robert Hare, Roger fil. Willelmi, Eudo Pincerna, and Geoffrey de Edelingehale. (P. R. O., Hunter's *Fines*, p. 28.)

2764. FINE at Lichfield dated 5 May, 10 John [1209], between the same parties concerning the same vill of Ketelestun and lands of Twiford, Steineston, Croxhall, and Edlinghall. (P. R. O., Hunter's *Fines*, p. 34.)

MAPPLETON.

2765. FINE at Westminster dated 15 days after Easter [21 Apr.], 4 John [1203], whereby Peter fil. Radulphi and Alice his wife, by William de Dustun her attorney, convey to Hugh de Akovre sixteen bovates of land in the vill of Caldelawe, to hold at a rent of a sparrow hawk or two shillings for all services due to the manor of Wirkewrde. (P. R. O., Hunter's *Fines*, p. 25.)

2766. FINE at Derby dated M. a. F. of St. Edmund [20 Nov.], 10 John [1208], whereby Simon fil. Rogeri quitclaims to Felix de Hurst twelve acres of land in Caldelawe.   (P. R. O., Hunter's *Fines*, p. 32.)

MICKLEOVER.

2767. FINE at Nottingham dated Tu. aft. Nat. of St. John B. [25 June], 4 John [1202], whereby Roger fil. Willelmi quitclaims to the Abbot of Burton four bovates of land in Over.   (P. R. O., Hunter's *Fines*, p. 22.)

NORBURY.

(NORBIRI.)

2768. FINE at Westminster dated one month after Easter, 5 John [1204], whereby Wiliam fil. Roberti quitclaims to John fil. Wilelmi four carucates of land in Norbiri and in Rounton [? Roston]. (P. R. O., Hunter's *Fines*, p. 26.)

REPTON *v.* under TICKNALL.

RILEY *v.* under SCARCLIFFE.

ROSTON
(ROUNTON),

v. under NORBURY

SANDIACRE.
(SENDIACRE.)

2769. FINE at Westminster dated the octave of F. of St. John B. [1 July], — John [1199-1216], whereby Robert de Burun acknowledges that the two bovates of land which he holds in Sendiacre belong to John [de Grey], Bishop of Norwich, who now both grant the same to William fil. Roberti to hold from the said Robert by free service of 2 *lb.* of cummin yearly, for which grant the said Bishop and William grant to the same Robert this year's crops on the said land. (P. R. O., Hunter's *Fines*, p. 39.)

2770. FINE dated in the 3rd year of King John [1201-2], whereby John [de Grey], Bishop of Norwich, and Richard fil. . . . . convey to William fil. Roberti three bovates of land in Sendiacre, in return for which the latter grants to the said Richard the autumn's crop which he has sown on the said land. (Mutilated.) (P. R. O., Hunter's *Fines* (1844), p. 17.)

SCARCLIFFE.

2771. FINE dated 14 July, 11 John [1209], concerning one knight's fee with appurtenances in Danby de Wauz [Dalby on the Wolds], co. Leic., whereby Hubert fil. Radulphi (by Robert de Eincurt, his attorney) acknowledges the said fee to be the right of the Prior and Brethren of the Hosital of St. John of Jerusalem, who acquit the said Hubert of the service pertaining to that fee. In return for which acquittance the said Hubert grants to the said Prior, etc., the tenement which Pain fil. Swain holds in Riele with the said Pain himself and his following, a bovate of land held by Geoffrey fil. Herward in the same vill, with other lands in Sudstubbinges, Glappewellgrif, Strethelbuc, Dalewang, Poldlandesich; together with eight acres of land in Snaidhinges which Roger fil. Steinulf held at Riele. (P. R. O., Hunter's *Fines*, p. 35.)

SHARDLOW.
(SERDELAW.)

2772. FINE at Nottingham dated Fr. a. F. of St. Botulph [21 June], 4 John [1202], whereby Alan fil. Rogeri quitclaims to Alan fil. Jordani and Mary his wife, half a carucate of land in Serdelaw. (P. R. O., Hunter's *Fines*, p. 19.)

SHIREBROOK in Pleasley.

(Scirebroc.)

2773. Fine at Nottingham dated M. a. F. of SS. Peter and Paul [1 July], 4 John [1202], whereby William fil. Rolland quitclaims to John Dainoter and Matilda his wife, and Hugh de Stiveton and Sara his wife, two bovates of land in Scirebroc. (P. R. O., Hunter's *Fines*, p. 23.)

STANLEY.

(Stanleg'.)

2774. Fine at Nottingham on Th. a. F. of St. Botulf [20 June], 4 John [1202], whereby Cecily que fuit uxor Warini quitclaims to Richard fil. Muriell' one bovate of land in Stanleg', and receives the same again on lease at a yearly rent of sixpence. (P. R. O., Hunter's *Fines* [1844], p. 18.)

STANTON WOODHOUSE.

(Staunton.)

2775. Fine at Nottingham dated Fr. a. F. of SS. Peter and Paul [5 July], 4 John [1202], whereby Aline fil. Roberti quitclaims (by Matthew her son), to Adam de Staunton, 52 acres of land and a fourth part of a bovate and of two mills, etc., in Staunton, in return for which the said Adam grants to the said Aline two acres of meadow in the same vill lying near the ford of Haddon westward, and a fourth part of the said mills. (P. R. O., Hunter's *Fines*, p. 24.)

STENSON

(Steineston),

v. under Kedleston.

STOKE by Stoney Middleton.

(Stok.)

2776. Fine at Nottingham dated the Octave of the Purification [9 Feb.], 5 John [1204], whereby Gerebert de Stok' and Avice his wife quitclaim to Maurice de Andely and Isabel his wife four acres of land in Stok'. (P. R. O., Hunter's *Fines*, p. 25.)

SWADLINCOTE.

(Suartlincot.)

2777. Fine at Derby dated S. a. F. of St. Martin [16 Nov.], 10 John [1208], whereby Henry de Verdon and Hawise his wife, Robert de Sugkenhull and Petronilla his wife, and Dionisia, sister of the said Hawise and Petronilla, acknowledge a certain five acres of wood in Suartlincot to be the right of William de Gresle, who grants to the same Robert and Petronilla the moiety of the said five acres, which extends from Leverichegrave to Blackepit, and from Blackepit to Brockeholes, to hold by service of a sparrow-hawk. (P. R. O., Hunter's *Fines*, p. 31.)

TICKNALL.

(Tikenhall.)

2778. Fine at Nottingham dated S. a. F. of St. Botulph [23 June], 4 John [1202], whereby Alan de Tikenhall conveys to Matilda fil. Willelmi two virgates of land in Tikenhall, to hold at a yearly rent of 34*d.*, and "per liberum servicium sequendi wapintach' de Rapindon per annum ad custum suum." (P. R. O., Hunter's *Fines*, p. 21.)

2779. Fine at same place and date, whereby John Corvisarius and Alice his wife quitclaim to the Prior of Repton two bovates of land in Tikenhall. (P. R. O., Hunter's *Fines*, p. 21.)

TWYFORD

(Twiford),

v. under KEDLESTON.

WAKEBRIDGE.

(Wakebruge.)

2780. Fine dated . . . F. of Ascension [— May], 12 John [1211], whereby it is agreed that the bovate of land in question in [Wakebridge ?] shall remain to Hubert fil. Radulphi quit from Robert . . . and that certain other lands and services held or due from [William de Alneto], and Emma de Wakbrig in Watecroft, Done, Lefsihay and Wakebridge, William de Suckthorn, Robert de Buterlee, Ranulph de Wakebridge, Henry de Camera, Henry de Wakebrig, Robert de Watecroft, William de Buterdon, etc., are to be held by the said Robert . . . from the said Hubert at a yearly rent of 40*d.* (Mutilated.) (P. R. O., Hunter's *Fines*, p. 37.)

WALTON *v.* under BEAUCHIEF.

WHEATCROFT

(Watecrofte),

v. under WAKEBRIDGE.

WILLINGTON.

(Wilinton.)

2781. Fine at Derby dated . . . 10 John [1208-9], whereby Henry fil. —, quitclaims to Nicholas de Wilinton two bovates of land in Wilinton. (P. R. O., Hunter's *Fines*, p. 35.)

23

WILLESLEY.

(WIUESLEIA, WIVELESLE.)

2782. FINE at Westminster Tu. a. F. of St. Luke [21 Oct.], [9 Ric. I.], [1197], concerning twelve virgates of land at Wiuesleia and five virgates in Pakinton, whereby Alan de Sumeruille grants to Amabilia de Pakinton four virgates of land in Pakinton [Co. Leic.] to hold for her life at a yearly rent of eightpence. (P. R. O., Pipe R. S. Pub., Vol. XXIII., p. 39.)

2783. FINE at Derby dated Sat. a. F. of St. Martin [15 Nov.], 10 John [1208], whereby Christina fil. Roberti quitclaims to Alan de Sumervill five virgates of land and a third part of two virgates of land in Wivelesle and Pakinton. (P. R. O., Hunter's *Fines*, p. 29.)

WILNE.

2784. FINE at Leicester dated Tu. a. F. of St. Andrew [2 Dec.], 10 John [1208], whereby Nicholas de Wilinton quitclaims to Philip de Draycot eight bovates of land in Wilne. (P. R. O., Hunter's *Fines*, p. 34.)

WINSTER *v.* under YELDERSLEY.

WIRKSWORTH *v.* under MAPPLETON.

YELDERSLEY.

(GILDERLEG'.)

2785. FINE at York dated 15 days after Hilary [22 Jan.], 13 John [1212], whereby Philip de Ulecote and Joan his wife release to Ralph de Muniay and Avice his mother all claims which the said Joan has, by right of dower, in a third part of the vill of Gildreleg' and of Winster, in return for which the said Ralph and Avice grant to the said Philip and Joan four acres of land in Kineton lying in Winesdon field. (P. R. O., Hunter's *Fines*, p. 38.)

YOULGRAVE.

(HYOLEGRAVE.)

2786. FINE at Derby dated Sat. a. F. of St. Martin [15 Nov.], 10 John [1208], whereby Henry de Herthull and Hawise his wife quitclaim to Henry de Hotot a bovate of land and the fourth part of a mill in Hyolegrave. (P. R. O., Hunter's *Fines*, p. 29.)

INDEX OF PLACES.

N.B.—The figures in Clarendon type denote the main headings.

A.

Abbenay, Abbeney, Abbeneye, v. Abney.
Abenay, v. Abney.
Abnay, v. Abney.
Abney, 1-7, 408, 878, 1195, 1801, 1802, 1805, 1806, 1811.
Abney Grange, 408, 1811.
Abneye, v. Abney.
Acouere, Acoure, v. Okeover.
Addenborough, co. Notts., 2120.
Addon Superior, v. Haddon, Over.
Adgaresly, v. Agardsley.
Agardsley, co. Staff., 67.
Aihum, v. Eyam.
Aissendene, v. Ashdown.
Akouere, v. Okeover.
Alaxton, v. Allexton.
Alcokfeld, in Heage, 1377, 1378, 1379.
Aldecar Park, 900.
Aldeport, Aldeporte, v. Alport.
Alderwashele, Alderwaslegh, Alderwasleghe, v. Alderwasley.
Alderwasley, 8-13, 526, 527, 963, 964, 1115.
Aldewerk, Aldewerke, v. Aldwark.
Aldeworthinges, in Priestcliffe, 1909.
Aldewynlane, in Newbold, 1746.
Aldport, v. Alport.
Aldreboc, Alrebroc, 536.
Aldwark, 14-21, 299.
Aldwork, v. Aldwark.
Aldworthing, in Priestcliffe, 1908.
Aldyrwasle, Aldyrwasley, v. Alderwasley.
Alencroft, in Eyam, 1243.
Alenhille, in Barlow, 237.
Alestre, v. Allestree.
Alewoldestone, v. Alvaston.
Alfertone, v. Alfreton.
Alfreton, 22-24, 449.

Aliuellgate, in Chesterfield, 691.
Alkemonton, Alkemunton, v. Alkmonton.
Alkmonton, 25, 1577, 1630, 1806.
Alkokfyld, in Ashleyhay, 106.
Allemedewe, in Foston, 1295, 1296.
Aller, co. Som., 491.
Allerhampton, co. Staff., 865.
Allerwaslegh, v. Alderwasley.
Allestree, 557, 1657, 1659, 1660, 2739.
Allexton, co. Leic., 1554, 1555.
Allstonefield, co. Staff., 2184, 2185.
———Vicar. Richard [1388], 2355.
Allston Lee, 636.
Alport, in Youlgrave, 26, 204, 303, 1333, 1719, 2235.
Alredholm, in Spondon, 2183.
Alretun Mill, nr. Yeldersley, 2717.
Alrewas, co. Staff., 594.
Alshop, v. Alsop-le-Dale.
Alsop-le-Dale, 27-43, 1822.
Alsope, v. Alsop-le-Dale.
Alstonefeld, v. Allstonefield.
Alstonelegh, v. Allston Lee.
Alton, in Ashover, 128.
Aluinewod, in Chesterfield, 697.
Aluualdestona, v. Alvaston.
Alvaston, 44-47, 327, 970, 1181.
———Lord. Ralph de Frescherevile [temp. Hen. III.], 970.
———Presbyter. Herbert, early Hen. II., 533.
Alveleye, nr. Plaistow, 1890.
Alwaldesholme, nr. Longford, 1583.
Alwaldeston, v. Alvaston.
Alwaston, Alwastone, v. Alvaston.
Ambaston, in Elvaston, 1160, 1162, 1179.
Amboldeston, v. Ambaston.
Ambreflat, in Egginton, 1165.
Angodestorp, v. Osgathorpe.
Annesley, co. Notts., 2110.
Apelknol, v. Apperknowl.

Apilcnol, Apilknoll, etc., v. Apperknowl.
Appelby, v. Appleby.
Apperknowl, in Unstone, 2430, 2431, 2437, 2461, 2463, 2467-2471, 2473, 2475, 2480, 2481, 2485.
————Clerks. Thomas, 13th cent., 2425; William [1363], 2437.
Appilknoll, Appinknoll, v. Apperknowl.
Appleby, **48**, 1683.
————Rectors. Thomas [*circ.* 1229-1260], 48; Tho. Chessyre [1509], 2403.
Appletree Hundred, **49**, 1115.
Appulby, v. Appleby.
Appulknoll, etc., v. Apperknowl.
Appultre, v. Appletree.
Apulknol, v. Apperknowl.
Apultrefurlong, in Rosliston, 2041.
Apurknoll, v. Apperknowl.
Ardesley, 1393-1395.
Arley, co. Staff., 179.
Aschburne, Ascheburne, v. Ashbourne.
Ascheford, v. Ashford.
Aschover, v. Ashover.
Ash, near Etwall, **50**.
Ashborne, Ashbourn, v. Ashbourne.
Ashbourne, 37, **51-91**, 156, 157, 340, 386, 388, 389, 403, 512, 643, 685, 882, 883, 959, 970, 1290, 1493, 1620, 1640, 1644-1648, 1664, 1693, 1786, 2644, 2717, 2718, **2740**.
————Bailiffs. Will. Cokeyn [1326-7], 60; Tho. Glover [1404, 1410], 78, 79; Ric. Spicer [1410], 79.
————Chaplain. Will. de Hyde [1404], 1693.
————Clerk. Nicholas [1329-30], 389.
————Parson. Nicholas [(?) 1275], 386.
————"Rood-Prest." Sir Tho. Russell [1516], 91.
————Vicars. J—— [1252], 186; John [1253], 1831; Ric. de Thurmeleye [1379], 986; Wil. Newenham [1414], 81; John Clerk [1468], 2417; Hen. Hudson [1504], 87; Sir Herre Hudson [1516], 91.
Ashbourne, Deanery of, 1814.
Ashburn, v. Ashbourne.
Ashby-de-la-Zouch, co. Leic., 302.
————Vicar. John Burton [1408], 1980.
Ashdown, co. Berks., 238.
Ashebourne, v. Ashbourne.
Asheburn, Asheburne, v. Ashbourne.
Asheop, v. Ashope.
Ashford, **92-104**, 213, 214, 615, 1061, 1238, 1329, 1330, 1333, **2741**.
————Lord. Otos [Otho] de Holand [1358], 95.
————Steward. Hen. Vernon [1476], 100.
Ashland, in Boythorp, 855.
Ashleyhay, 13, **105-107**, 1119, 1383.

Ashope, in Hope, 557, 569, 570.
Ashoure, v. Ashover.
Ashover, **108-128**, 250, 300, 455, 774, 794, 934, 1100-1102, 1264, 1479, 1481, 2410.
————Rectors. Symon de Markham [*temp.* Edw. I.], 114; Rog. de Eincurt [1303], 115; Rog. de Eyncourt [1337], 123; Thomas [1370], 125; Philip Eyre [1461, 1490], 127, 1264.
————Chaplain. Ralph [*circ.* 1204-1235], 108, 934, 2284.
Askebec Water, nr. Yeldersley, 2721.
Aspeland, in Boythorpe, 761.
Asphil, Asphull, in Egginton, 1164, 1167, 1178.
Aspineforde, in Kedleston, 1501.
Asscheborne, Asschebourne, Asscheburn, Asscheburne, v. Ashbourne.
Assebecke, in Underwood, 2412.
Asseburn, v. Ashbourne.
Assh, v. Ash.
Asshburn, Asshburne, v. Ashbourne.
Asshe, v. Ash.
Asshebe de la Souche, v. Ashby-de-la-Zouch.
Asshebourne, Assheburn, Assheburne, v. Ashbourne.
Assheford, v. Ashford.
Asshelehey, v. Ashleyhay.
Assheoppe, v. Ashope.
Assheover, v. Ashover.
Asshford, v. Ashford.
Asshlehey, Asshleyhey, v. Ashleyhay.
Asshmerbroke, 602.
Asshore, v. Ashover.
Asshover, Asshovere, v. Ashover.
Aston, Coal, **130-133**, 842, 866, 878, 1034, 1046, 1066, 1068, 1070-1075, 1783, 2565.
————Parson. Hen. Coton [1388], 1488.
Aston-in-Hope, 1438, 1446, 2119.
Aston-in-Sudbury, 930, 2288.
Aston-on-Trent, **129**, 1726, **2742**.
Astonefeld v. Allstonefield.
Astonfeld, in Hope, 1438.
Astrilstorh, in Brampton, 438.
Athelardestre, v. Allestree.
Athelaxton, v. Allexton.
Athersegge, v. Hathersage.
Atlow, **134-166**, 1645, 2139, 2141, 2142.
————Lords. Rog. de Acouere [1291, 1317], 141, 147; Rog. de Acouere [1345], 152.
Atlowe, v. Atlow.
Attelow, etc., v. Atlow.
Attercliffe, co. York, 1129.
Atterclyffe, v. Attercliffe.
Attlowe, v. Atlow.
Aucoure, v. Okeover.
Audewerk, v. Aldwark.
Aukeput, in Boulton, 328.
Averham, 121.
Avice Dool, in Holmesfield, 1413.
Ayllewastone, v. Alvaston.

Aylwynestorht, in Tansley, 2303.
Ayome, *v.* Eyam.
Ayssheford, *v.* Ashford.

B.

Bachewell, *v.* Bakewell.
Backedale, in Litton, 1548.
Baconscroft, in Catton, 597.
Baddow, Gt., co. Essex, 1945, 1946,
    1949, 1952, 1973.
————Vicar. Sylvester [1199-1218],
    1949.
Badechewell, *v.* Bakewell.
Badewen, *v.* Baddow, Gt.
Bagelone, Baglone, in Derby, 992, 993,
    1002, 1004.
Baggthorpe, *v.* Bagthorpe.
Bagschag, Bagschawe, *v.* Bagshawe.
Bagshawe, 619, 621, 629.
Bagthorpe, in Brampton, 167-169,
    447, 465, 470, 472.
Bakewell, 104, 170-214, 705, 757,
    1237, 1259, 1264, 1329, 1330, 1333,
    1354, 1431, 1612, 1710, 1825, 1833,
    1861, 2408, 2654.
————Church of, 170, 171, 173-175,
    178-180, 186, 188, 189,
    199, 203, 214, 1328, 1431,
    1710, 1831, 2298, 2408.
————Chapelries of, 197, 198.
————Chaplain. Matthew [1188-97],
    1274.
————Clerk. Thomas [late 12th
    cent.], 216.
————Lord. Will. de Gernun [*temp.*
    Edw. I.], 194.
————Manor of, 200.
————Vicars. Will le Kirklyngton
    [1368], 757; Rog. de
    Tibshylf *al.* Tybschelfe
    [1401, 1410], 207, 209;
    Will. Brome [1438], 1444;
    Ric. Crichelowe [1472],
    2233.
Baliden, Balidene, *v.* Ballidon.
Ballehoue, in Pleasley, 1896.
Balleye, Le, in Chesterfield, 705.
Ballidon, 215-218.
Balydene, *v.* Ballidon.
Bamford, 219-222, 1794, 2318.
————Parson. Rob. de Abbeney
    [*temp.* Edw. I.], 1794.
Bampford, *v.* Bamford.
Baqwel, *v.* Bakewell.
Barewe, *v.* Barrow-on-Trent.
Barlay, *v.* Barlow.
Barlborough, 223, 1061, 1511, 1512,
    1597-1599, 1601, 2170, 2277, 2279,
    2463, 2743.
————Parson. John [*temp.* Edw.
    I.], 1511.
Barlburgh, Barlburghe, *v.* Barlborough.
Barle, Barlege, Barleia, *v.* Barlow.
Barlebrug, Barleburgh, *v.* Barlborough.
Barle Wodsetes, *v.* Barlow Woodseats.
Barley, *v.* Barlow.
Barleylees, Barleyleghes, *v.* Barlow Lees.

Barlings, co. Linc., 114.
Barlow, 224-237, 695, 817, 870, 871,
    1041, 1047, 1054, 1055, 1059, 1063,
    1263, 2242, 2252, 2255.
————Lords. Will. Barley [1402],
    233; Rob. Barle [1447-8],
    1063.
Barlow Lees, 232, 831, 870, 1414.
Barlow Woodseats, 224, 226, 227, 229,
    230, 235, 237, 1063, 1077, 1414,
    2255, 2428.
Barnby-upon-Don, co. York, 1781.
Barnetbe, *v.* Barnetby-le-Wold.
Barnetby-le-Wold, co. Linc., 1018,
    1019, 1021, 1022.
Barrow-on-Trent, 2541, 2744.
Barrowcote, in Crich, 924, 2565.
Barseputte, in Repton, 1977.
Barspol, in Egginton, 1171, 1172.
Barton Blount, 25, 238, 239, 344, 2321.
Barton-on-Humber, co. Linc., 2098.
Bartona, Bartone, Bartun, *v.* Barton
    Blount.
Baseford, *v.* Basford.
Basford, co. Notts., 1512, 1854, 1856,
    1859, 1864, 1871, 1874, 2120.
Basingerys, in Mickleover, 1697.
Baslow, 615, 760, 761, 764, 1249, 2149,
    2150.
Basselowe, *v.* Baslow.
Baston, co. Linc., 1028.
Batayleflat, Le, in Thurvaston, 2321.
Bath, co. Som., 910, 1428.
————Bishops of, *v.* Josceline;
    Giffard, Walter.
Bathecwell, Bathekewell, Bathekwalle,
    Bathequelle, *v.* Bakewell.
Bauchwell, Baucvell, Baucwel, *v.* Bake-
    well.
Bauckebed, 650.
Baudon, *v.* Bowdon.
Baukewell, Baukiswille, Baukquell, *v.*
    Bakewell.
Baumford, Baumforde, Baumforth, *v.*
    Bamford.
Bauquell, Bauqll, *v.* Bakewell.
Bauthecwall, *v.* Bakewell.
Bawden, Bawdon, *v.* Bowdon.
Bawe, *v.* Bayeux.
Bawkwell, *v.* Bakewell.
Baxtersiche, in Underwood, 2412.
Bayequelle, *v.* Bakewell.
Bayeux, 1753.
Baystonbuttis, in Walton, 702.
Beard Hall, nr. Hayfield, 1371, 1375.
Bearper, *v.* Belper.
Bearwardcote, in Etwall, 240, 519,
    524, 525, 1179, 2599.
Beauchef, *v.* Beauchief.
Beauchief, 241-243, 244, 248, 257, 258,
    265, 1032, 1214, 1342, 1775, 1862,
    2745.
————Abbey. 113, 242, 244, 248,
    258, 265, 426, 851, 856,
    859, 1342, 1409, 2484,
    2556, 2565, 2745.
————Abbots. Stephen, early Hen.
    III., 1032, William, early
    Hen. III., 1862; Roger,

late Hen. III., 131; Will.
de Folkingham, *t.* Edw. II.,
1775; Robert [1398], 257;
Will. Gresley [1431], 258;
John Swyffte [1463], 242;
John [1466], 243; Thomas
[1479], 859; John Norton
[1507], 265.
Beauchieff, *v.* Beauchief.
Beaudesert, co. Warw., 2559.
Beauper, *v.* Belper.
Beaur, Beaure, Beaurepair, Beaureper,
v. Belper.
Beauvale Priory, co. Notts., 2417.
————Prior. Thos. Metheley [1468],
2417.
Becceley, in Totley, 2377.
Becthon, Becton, *v.* Beighton.
Beeley, **244-266**, 660, 677, 878.
————Chapel of St. Mary in, 262.
————Lords. Osbert de Ore, late 13th
cent., 248; Tho. de Begh-
ley [1316-7], 250.
Beeston, co. Notts., 957.
————Vicar. Nicholas Blakwall
[1465-1483], 957, 2681.
Begheton, Beghton, *v.* Beighton.
Beghley, *v.* Beeley.
Begtone, *v.* Beighton.
"Behyndhand," in Chesterfield, 732,
808, 815.
Beighton, **267-278**, 467, 660, 878, 1326,
1327, 1735, 1736, 2279, 2280.
————Lord. Rob. de Fornaus
[1328], 268.
Belee, Belegh, Beley, *v.* Beeley.
Belidene, *v.* Ballidon.
Bella Valle, *v.* Beauvale.
Bello capite, de, *v.* Beauchief.
Belper, 8, 12, 107, **279-283**, 474, 1115,
1470.
Belton, co. Leic., 399.
Benethleia, *v.* Bentley, Hungry.
Benetylee, *v.* Bentley, Fenny.
Benteleye, *v.* Bentley, Hungry.
Bentley Croft, nr. Thorpe, 2320.
Bentley, Fenny, 34, **284-286**, 394.
Bentley, Hungry, 239, **287-289**, 1591.
Berdechalghfeld, in Hayfield, 1370.
Berdhalgh, Berdhalugh, *v.* Beard Hall.
Berewardcote, *v.* Bearwardcote.
Berkeshey, in Hilton, 1380.
Berks. co., 583.
Berleye, in Longford, 1572.
Berleyford, in Longford, 1565.
Berleyruding, in Longford, 1568.
Berneby, *v.* Barnetby-le-Wold.
Berneby-super-Dune, *v.* Barnby-upon-
Don.
Berneflat, in Etwall, 1200.
Bernetby, *v.* Barnetby-le-Wold.
Berrwardescote, *v.* Bearwardcote.
Bersicote Mill, in Etwall, 1197.
Bervardcote, Berwardcote, *v.* Bearward-
cote.
Beston, *v.* Beeston.
Bestril, (?) nr. Wigley, 2562.
Betewelstrete, in Chesterfield, 847.
Bethley, Bethtley, *v.* Beeley.

Beucheff, *v.* Beauchief.
Beurepayr, Beurepeyr, *v.* Belper.
Beverley. Provost. Peter de Cestria
[1282-1298], 1198, 2248.
Bewchief, *v.* Beauchief.
Beyeleye, Beyleghe, Beyleye, *v.* Beeley.
Biggyng, 2378.
Bikirwode, in Mackworth, 1622.
Bilborough, co. Notts., 2120.
Bildewas, *v.* Buildwas.
Bingham, co. Notts., 368, 2215.
————Rector. Richard [1345], 1844.
Birchehed, *v.* Birchett.
Birchelif, in Longstone, 1613.
Bircheouere, *v.* Birchover.
Birchett, in Dronfield, 878, 1051.
Birchill, 204.
Birchover, **290-307**, 2226, 2738.
————Lord. Tho. Kenylmarche
[1502], 304.
Birchulles, *v.* Birchill.
Birley, in Beighton, 269, 271-278.
Birrchwood, in Alfreton, 24.
Bitame, *v.* Bytham.
Bitham, *v.* Bytham.
Blachmere, in Egginton, 1167.
Blackewell, Blackwalle, *v.* Blackwell.
Blackwell, nr. Alfreton, 619, 1252, 1254,
1597-1599, 1601, 1605, 1761, 1864,
1865, 1868, 1870, 1871, 1873, 1874.
Blacwell, Blacwelle, *v.* Blackwell.
Blakebuttes, Les, in Catton, 576.
Blakegreue, Le, in Kirk Hallam, 1334.
Blakelondes, in Rosliston, 2041.
Blakemere, Le, in Egginton, 1171,
1172.
Blakewell, Blakewelle, *v.* Blackwell.
Blakmeyre, Le, in Findern, 1280.
Blakwalle, Blakwell, *v.* Blackwell.
Bleccheringes, in Parwich, 1818.
Blith, *v.* Blyth.
Blithecroft, in Chesterfield, 832.
Blithgare Wood, in Dale, 941.
Blore, co. Staff., 151, 1228, 1696, 2133-
2135, 2137.
————Prior [1226], 1696.
————Rector [1394]. Ric. de Gren-
dun, 1228.
Blyth, co. Notts., 1696.
————Capellanus, Thomas, [1226],
1696.
Bobbedon, Bobedon, Bobedone, *v.*
Bupton.
Bobenhull, *v.* Bubnell.
Bobinton, *v.* Bupton.
Boghwode, *v.* Boughwood.
Boileston, Boilestone, Boilistona, Boil-
leston, Boilstone, *v.* Boylestone.
Boithorp, *v.* Boythorpe.
Bolingbroke, co. Linc., 1668.
Bolingbrook, *v.* Bolingbroke.
Bollesouere, *v.* Bolsover.
Bol Park, in Denby, 955.
Bolsover, **308, 309**, 2276.
Bolton, Boltone, *v.* Boulton.
Bolton, co. Lanc., 965, 967.
Bondesale, Bondesall, Bondeshall, Bon-
dessale, *v.* Bonsall.

Bondewode, Le, in Calke and Smisby, 541.
Bondishal, Bondsale, Bonesale, *v.* Bonsall.
Bonsall, **310-325**, 474, 878, 951, 1115, 1669, 2230.
———Rectors. Will. de Monyasche, *al.* Moniasshe, *al.* Monehase [1401, 1410], 207, 209; Hen. de Mapulton [1410-1427], 209, 951, 1669; Ric. Walker [bef. 1464], 322.
Bonteshale, Bontisal, Bontishal, Bontsale, Bontsall, *v.* Bonsall.
Bordeland, in Brackenfield, 384.
Boreoxgong, in Wirksworth, 2650, 2651.
Borford, in Litton, 1550.
Borim, Le, in Breaston, 485.
Borowcote, *v.* Barrowcote.
Borowe, *v.* Barrow-on-Trent.
Botell broke, in Horsley, 1459.
Boterley Park, *v.* Butterley Park.
Boterton, *v.* Butterton.
Bothom, *v.* Bottam.
Bottam, 1812.
Boudon, *v.* Bowden.
Boughwood, in Matlock, 1543.
Boulton, **326-330**.
———Lord. Rob. de Saucheverel [1282], 327.
Bounteshall, *v.* Bonsall.
Bowden, Bowdene, *v.* Bowdon.
Bowdon, 460, 616, 617, 619, 623, 628, 629, 631, 633, 638-640, 642, 645, 652-656, 659.
Bowmford, Bownford, *v.* Bamford.
Boylestone, **331-350**, 1271, 1620.
———Lord. Rog. de Rydeware [1294], 335.
———Rectors. Will de Wikkilwod [1322], 1271; Nich. Baker [1438], 1620; Tho. de Barlow [1439], 346.
Boylestune, Boyliston, Boylleston, *v.* Boylestone.
Boylston, Boylstone, *v.* Boylestone.
Boysorp, Boythorp, *v.* Boythorpe.
Boythorpe, **351-383**, 693, 701, 738, 760, 761, 764, 770, 778, 781, 783, 793, 803, 806, 827, 855, 856, 1512.
Boythorpp, Boytorph, *v.* Boythorpe.
Braceborough, co. Linc., 1028.
Bracentone, Bracington, Bracinton, *v.* Brassington.
Brackenfield, in Morton, **384**.
Bracynton, *v.* Brassington.
Brad', in Pecco, *v.* Bradborne.
Bradborne, 67, 166, **385-395**.
Bradburne, Braddeburne, Bradeborne, Bradeburn, *v.* Bradborne.
Bradeburnebrok, in Mappleton, 1640.
Bradelay, Bradele, Bradelege, Bradeley, *v.* Bradley.
Bradeley Ashe, *v.* Broadlow Ash.
Bradelow, *v.* Broadlow Ash.
Brademers, Le, in Yeldersley, 2717.
Bradesha, *v.* Bradshaw.
Bradeway, *v.* Bradway.

Bradewell, *v.* Bradwell.
Bradfield, in Hope, 1447, 1448.
Bradlege, *v.* Bradley.
Bradley, 56, 58, 59, 67, 79, 90, 147, 388, **396-404**, 882, 959, 960, 1347, 1527, 1528, 1532, 1644, 1664, 1693, 1750, 1751, 2717.
Bradlowe, *v.* Broadlow Ash.
Bradmarchys, *v.* Bradmersh.
Bradmer, *v.* Bradmore.
Bradmersh, in Bowdon, 624, 630, 646.
Bradmersshe, *v.* Bradmersh.
Bradmore, co. Notts., 1008.
Bradschawe, *v.* Bradshaw.
Bradseahay, in Derby, 1005.
Bradsha, *v.* Bradshaw.
Bradshaw, 624-626, 628, 630, 631, 634, 635, 645, 646, 650, 651, 652, 656, 657, 659.
Bradshawe, *v.* Bradshaw.
Bradwall, *v.* Bradwell.
Bradway, in Dronfield, 235, 878, 1051, 1053, 1060, 1398.
Bradwell, **406-408**, 559.
Bradwey, *v.* Bradway.
Brailsford, nr. Derby, 1814.
Brailsford, near N. Wingfield, **409**.
Brakencroft, Brakincroft, in Burnaston, 517, 518.
Brakynwhith, *v.* Brackenfield.
Bramcote, co. Notts., 2120.
Bramelegh, *v.* Bramley.
Bramley, in Baslow, 548, 550, 1723.
Bramley, in Eckington, 1128.
Brampton, 7, 100, 101, 103, 104, 167, 168, 227, 259-261, 204, **410-473**, 509, 704, 705, 719, 770, 781, 795, 803, 812, 817, 856, 859, 878, 997, 1041, 1669, 1774, 2149, 2150, 2521, 2562.
———Chaplains. John [*temp.* Edw. I.], 2563; William [*temp.* Edw. II.], 435; Oliver Scha [1490], 167.
———Clerks. Geoffrey [*temp.* Hen. III.], 412; Philip fil. Ricardi [*temp.* Hen. III.], 415.
———Vicars. Stephen [*temp.* Edw. I.], 420.
Bramptone, Bramt', Bramton, Bramtone, *v.* Brampton.
Brantone, Brantun, *v.* Brampton.
Brassington, 297, 314, 388, 392, 393, **474-479**, 1115, 1497, 1668.
———Chaplain. Will Bagger [1410], 1497.
Brassinton, Brassyngton, Brasyngtone, *v.* Brassington.
Braundiston [? Braunstone, co. Leic.], Rector. Philip de Eyhsbury [1287], 2649.
Braunston, co. Northt., 1488.
———Parson. Henry [1388], 1488.
Braunstone, *v.* Braunston.
Braydesall, Braydeshall, Braydsale, *v.* Breadsall.
Braylesford, *v.* Brailsford.
Braystone, *v.* Breaston.

Breadsall, **480-482**, 868, 1453, 1510, 1553.
————Rectors. Ric. le Cursun [1343], 1453; John Forest [1401], 1510; Will. Dethykke [1486], 868.
Breadsall Park, House of the Holy Trinity at, 482.
Breaston, **483-486**, 1487.
Breche, Le, in Coton-in-the-Elms, 913.
Bredinbrigge, Le, in Chesterfield, 705.
Bredlawe, *v.* Broadlow Ash.
Bredon, *v.* Breedon-on-the-Hill.
Bredsall, *v.* Breadsall.
Bredune, *v.* Breedon-on-the-Hill.
Breedon-on-the-Hill, co. Leic., 2295.
————Prior. Helias [1153-60], 531, 1939.
Breideshale, *v.* Breadsall.
Breidestone, *v.* Breaston.
Breitreichfeld, *v.* Brushfield.
Brekmedow, in Beauchief, 242.
Bremyngton, *v.* Brimington.
Brendewode, Brentewode, in Longford, 1558, 1559, 1564-1566.
Brendewode-in-Okeover, 2133, 2134.
Brerleia, Brerlay, *v.* Brierly.
Breryafhedlond, in Burnaston, 517.
Bretby, **486-492**, 1540, 1953, 1955, 1957.
————Manor. Lord. John Mowbray, Duke of Norfolk [1448], 490.
Brettebi, *v.* Bretby.
Bretton, 1282, 1284, 2157.
Breydesale, *v.* Breadsall.
Breydest', Breydiston, *v.* Breaston.
Briddesgrene, in Thurvaston, 2321.
Brierly, 2383, 2440.
Briethicefeld, *v.* Brushfield.
Briggegate, The, in Derby, 976.
Brightrichefeld, *v.* Brushfield.
Brimenton, *v.* Brimington.
Brimington, **493-510**, 543, 679, 681, 695, 701, 770, 878, 997, 1094, 2265, 2410, 2521.
Briminton, Brimintone, Brimintun, Brimyngton, *v.* Brimington.
Brinlaston, **511**, 2599.
Bristol, co. Glouc., 1897.
Britreichfeld, *v.* Brushfield.
Brittrichisfield, *v.* Brushfield.
Broadlow Ash, 74, 286, **512-514**, 1811.
Brocholclif, Brochul, in Newbold, 1533, 1743.
Brockewall, in Monyash, 1707.
Brod Car Hey, in Castleton, 564.
Brodegapes, Le, in Thurvaston, 2322.
Brodemedowe, in Catton, 580, 593.
Brodestoythebuttis, in Brampton, 416.
Brodewei, Le, in Priestcliffe, 1905.
Brodholm, in Walton, 604.
Brokefurlong, in Catton, 593.
Brokehylle, *v.* Brookhill.
Brokelhill, in Brimington, 497.
Brokforlong, in Rosliston, 2042.
Brokforlonge, in Catton, 576.
Brokhull, Little, in Chesterfield, 812.
Brombyclif, Le, in Tapton, 2311.

Bromesbroc, in Dale, 941.
Bromhul, in Repton, 1977.
Bromlegh, *v.* Bromley.
Bromley, *v.* Bramley, in Baslow.
Bromley, co. Kent, 339.
————Rector. Will. de Wyklewode [1334], 339.
Brompton, Bromton, *v.* Brampton.
Brookhill, 1886.
Brough, in Hope, 407, 408, **515**, 557, 2119.
Broune Croft, in Totley, 2376.
Brounemore, Le, in Monyash, 1707.
Brouneshurst, in Coton-in-the-Elms, 912.
Brouniswodes, The, in Matlock, 1679.
Brounuslowe, in Newton Solney, 1758.
Bruggefurlong, in Rosliston, 2041, 2042.
Brugh, *v.* Brough.
Brughmill, *v.* Brough.
Brunaldeston, *v.* Burnaston.
Brune, co. Linc., 807.
Bruneshul, in Egginton, 1165.
Brunnaldeston, *v.* Burnaston.
Brunufystone, *v.* Burnaston.
Brushfield, 510, **516**, 1608, 1609, 1616.
Bryggecroft, in Derby, 989.
Bryghouse, in Unstone, 2462.
Bryminton, Brymmyngton, Brymyngton. *v.* Brimington.
Brynlaston, *v.* Brinlaston.
Brynnaldstone, *v.* Burnaston.
Bubbdon, Bubbedon, *v.* Bupton.
Bubdon, Bubendona, Bubendone, Bubton, *v.* Bupton.
Bubnell, 2149, 2150, 2301.
Bucgecroft, Buggecroft, in Calow, 544-546.
Buckebrighe, in Chesterfield, 696.
Budwa Magna, *v.* Baddow, Great.
Buggecroft, *v.* Bucgecroft.
Buildwas Abbey, co. Salop, 474, 1491-1496.
————Abbot. John [*circ.* 1440], 1495.
Bukstones, *v.* Buxton.
Buldewas, *v.* Buildwas.
Bunney, co. Notts., 1008.
Bupton, 1554, 1556, 1559-1561, 1569, 1581, 1584, 1590, 1591, 1602.
Burc, 2022.
Burchefeld, Burcheffeld, *v.* Brushfield.
Burchore, *v.* Birchover.
Burgh, *v.* Brough, in Hope.
Buricroft, in Makeney, 1626.
Burleg', *v.* Burley.
Burley, 1562, 1563, 1578.
Burleysike, 422.
Burnaston, **517-525**, 1203-1205.
Burnastone, *v.* Burnaston.
Burton [? near Bakewell], 1195.
Burton-on-Trent, co. Staff., 68, 345, 2611.
————Abbey. 48, 596, 603, 908, 970, 1027, 1197, 1274, 1276, 1278, 1279, 1544, 1545, 1696-1699, 1824, 2576, 2579, 2610, 2614, 2616, 2619.

Burton-on-Trent, Abbots. Bernard [1160-75], 1197; Nicholas [1188-1197], 1274; Will. Melburne [1197-1210], 1276; Ric. de Insula [1222-1229], 1697, 1698, 2575; Laur. de S. Edwardo [1229-1260], 48, 1277, 1699; John Stafford [1275], 1279; Tho. de Pakinton [1281-1305], 2615; Will. Brenstone [1468], 596; Will. Bone [1521], 2619.

Burton St. Lazar's Hospital, co. Leic., 613, 614, 2175.

———Masters. Tho. Ratclyff, Knt. [1528], 613; Tho. Lyghe [1540], 614.

Burtone, *v.* Burton-on-Trent.

Bussouns, Bussuns, in Cubley, 928, 2387.

Butterley Park, 902.

Butterton, co. Staff., 2366.

Button Ryddyng, in Staveley, 2261.

Buxton, 526-527, 1271.

Buxtonis, Buxtonys, *v.* Buxton.

Byngham, *v.* Bingham.

Byrcheor, Byrcheovere, *v.* Birchover.

Byrchett, *v.* Birchett.

Byrchore, Byrchouere, *v.* Birchover.

Byrchyls, 214.

———*v.* also Birchell.

Byrlay, Byrley, *v.* Birley.

Byrnaston, *v.* Burnaston.

Byrstallegh, in Hope, 1443.

Bytham, Castle, co. Linc., 905.

C.

Cadom', *v.* Caen.

Caen, 1753.

Calal, Calale, Calall, *v.* Calow.

Calc, Calch, *v.* Calk.

Caldelawe, Caldelowe, *v.* Callow.

Caldewall, Caldewell, *v.* Cauldwell.

Calehale, *v.* Calow.

Calfore, Calfour, Calfover, *v.* Calver.

Calhale, *v.* Calow.

Calk and Calk Abbey, 528-541, 1752, 1938, 1939, 1941.

Calkewoode, in Repton, 1980.

Callal, *v.* Calow.

Callewych, Callewyche, *v.* Calwich.

Callow, in Mappleton, 1474, 1636, 1645, 2765, 2766.

Caloll, *v.* Calow.

Calow, near Chesterfield, 167, 356, 450, 542-547, 696, 770, 836, 840, 2486.

Calton, co. Staff., 2132.

Calton, in Bakewell, 953.

Calton Lees, in Bakewell, 953.

Caluore, Caluour, Caluoure, *v.* Calver.

Calvecroft, in Ashover, 112, 120.

Calveovere, *v.* Calver.

Calver, 548-550, 1261, 1264, 1701, 1712, 1718, 1724, 1816, 2082-2086.

Calvere, *v.* Calver.

Calvor, Calvore, Calvouere, *v.* Calver.

Calwelawe, *v.* Callow.

Calwich Priory, co. Staff., 1594-1596, 2130.

———Parson. Rob. Pole [1417], 1181.

———Priors. Ralph Holyngton [1438-1447], 1594, 1595; John [1460], 1596.

Calwyche, *v.* Calwich.

Camore, 1723.

Campeden, *v.* Compton.

Canggull, in Unstone, 2474.

Cannock, co. Staff., 178, 179.

Canterbury, Archbishops of, *v.* Chichely (Henry); Peckham (John); Stafford (John); Whittlesey (William); William.

Capella del Frith, in ly Fryth, etc., *v.* Chapel-en-le-Frith.

Carcolstone, *v.* Carlcaston.

Cardelhay, in Bradborne, 395.

Cardigan, County and Castle of, 1664, 2644.

Care-medew, in Dronfield, 1077.

Carlby, co. Linc., 1028.

Carlcaston, co. Notts., 1469.

Carleby, *v.* Carlby.

Carlisle, Bishops of, *v.* Everdon, Silvester de; Mauclerc, Walter.

Carmarthen, County and Castle of, 1664, 2644.

Carolke-on-Trent, 1980.

———Vicar. Ric. Bars [1407-8], 1980.

Carsington, 477, 479, 1673, 1677.

Carsyngton, *v.* Carsington.

Casey, The, in Boylestone, 349.

Castelton, *v.* Castleton.

Castelwaye, Le, in Willington, 2589.

Casterne, co. Staff., 156-158, 2141, 2142.

Castilar, Deanery of, 1814.

Castilton, Castiltone, *v.* Castleton.

Castleton, 230, 406, 515, 551-570, 657, 878, 1237, 1433, 1450, 1801, 1860, 2149, 2150.

———Vicar. William [1359, 1360], 1433, 1860.

Castulfurlong, in Tapton, 2312.

Castulton, Castylton, *v.* Castleton.

Cateby, 1934.

Catton, 571-602, 2539-2541.

———Chapel of St. Nicholas at, 597.

———Lords. John de Sancto Amando, knt. [1317], 575; Roger Horton [1413], 592.

Cauldwell, 603, 604, 1027, 1122, 2066, 2067, 2071, 2072.

Causey, Le, in Newton Solney, 1758.

Caustede, in Catton, 573.

Cesterefeld, Cesterfeld, Cestirfeld, *v.* Chesterfield.

Cestrefeld, Cestrefeud, Cestrefeude, *v.* Chesterfield.

Chaddesden, 480, **605-614**, 971, 973, 988, 1179, 1670, 1914, 2177, 2187.
———Chantry of, 609, 611, 612.
———Chaplains of the Chantry. John Claypole, Will. Ketelby, Edm. Koc [*t.* Edw. III.], 609; Hen. Bonde, *al.* Boonde [1458], 611, 612.
———St. Mary's Chapel at, 606, 609.
Chaddesdene, Chaddesdeyn, Chaddesdon, *v.* Chaddesden.
Chaddysden, Chadesden, Chadisden, *v.* Chaddesden.
Challengewood, 1668.
Chalwescroft, in Rosliston, 2030.
Chanderell, *v.* Chander Hill.
Chander Hill, in Brampton, 458, 473.
Chapel-en-le-Frith, 214, 407, **615-659**, 828, 1370, 1372, 1443.
———Chaplains. Tho. Armytage [1434], 627; Nich. Dikson [1477], 633; Thos. Armytage [1538], 649.
———Curate. Sir Steuen Bagsha [1521], 646.
Chapel-en-le-Fryth, etc., *v.* Chapel-en-le-Frith.
Charing, co. Kent, 1625.
Charyng, *v.* Charing.
Chasterfeld, Chastourfeld, Chastrefeld, Chasturfeld, *v.* Chesterfield.
Chatesworth, *v.* Chatsworth.
Chatsworth, 252, 255, 256, **660, 661**, 998, 2149, 2150.
Chattesworth, Chattesworthe, *v.* Chatsworth.
Chaundrell, *v.* Chander Hill.
Chebese, *v.* Chebsey.
Chebsey, co. Staff., 1681.
Cheguurthia, *v.* Kegworth.
Cheilmarden, Cheilmardon, *v.* Chelmorton.
Chelardeston, Chelardiston, *v.* Chellaston.
Chellaston, **662-664**, 1685.
Chelmardon, Chelmerden, Chelmerdon, Chelmorden, *v.* Chelmorton.
Chelmorton, 660, **665-678**, 1712, 1718, 1722-1724.
Cheselowe, in Monyash, 1711.
Chester, 486, 536, 655.
———Abbots. G—— [*circ.* 1200], 1726; Hugh [1208-1226], 486.
———Archdeacon. Ralph [1246], 182.
———Bishops, *v.* Bird, John; Clinton, Roger de; Weseham, Rog. de.
———Dean. B—— [*circ.* 1200], 1726.
Chester, Little, 971, 972, 989, 990, 1013, 1014, 1915.
Chesterfield, 100, 168, 233, 308, 351, 359-365, 367, 369, 370, 375, 376, 378, 379, 381, 410-412, 428, 430, 438, 443, 451-454, 457-459, 464, 466, 473, 504, 542, 544-547, **679-878**, 997, 1013, 1046, 1052, 1059,

1068, 1230, 1345, 1352, 1384, 1533, 1744-1746, 1774, 1779, 1881, 2149, 2150, 2192, 2259, 2265, 2410, 2428, 2440, 2444, 2486, 2521, **2748, 2749**.
Chesterfield, Alderman. Rob. Gryssop [1480], 860.
———Bailiffs. Stephen le Eyr [1317-18], 720; J. de Dikeby [1365], 750; Tho. Leeke [1490], 1881.
———Chaplains. Richard, John [early thirteenth cent.], 542.
———Chantry of St. Mary Magdalene at, 776.
———Chaplain, Henry de Foston [1381, 1383], 776, 777.
———Chantry of St. Michael at, 776.
———Chaplain. Roger de Lesbes, *al.* del Leghes [1381, 1383], 776, 777.
———Church. 375, 685, 765, 776, 785, 802, 831, 837, 843, 870-872, 877, 2522.
———Clerks. Roger [*t.* Hen. III.], 1533; Walter [*t.* Hen. III.], 683; Henry [*t.* Edw. I.], 702, 703; Henry [1302], 365; Henry [1305], 367.
———"Gilda Fabrorum" at, 378.
———Guild of the B. V. Mary at, 375, 378, 693, 741, 742, 747, 768, 796, 808, 810, 819, 831, 837, 841, 848, 872, 874, 877.
———Chaplains. Will. Marshall, Will. Webster [1445], 841.
———Guild of the Holy Cross at, 378, 785, 808, 813, 840, 843, 849, 859, 2317.
———Lords of. Will. le Brewer [*t.* Hen. III.], 698; John Wake [1294], 698.
———Persona. Stephen [*t.* Hen. III.], 412.
———Rector. S—— [*t.* Hen. III.], 685.
———Steward. Thos. Bate [1445], 2317.
———St. Leonard's Hospital at, 410, 428, 545, 724, 2308, 2314.
———Vicars. Geoffrey [late Hen. III.], 2491; John Done [1370], 762; John Bonde [1372], 766; Tho. Bonde [1374], 768; Ric. Porter [1392], 785; Ric. Hauson, *al.* Haweson, *al.* Hawson [1420-1424], 823, 828-830; Ralph Calcroft [1452-1453], 845, 846, 867; Ralph Cantrell [1480-1484], 865, 1345.
Chestrefeld, Chestrefeud, Chesturfeld, *v.* Chesterfield.
Cheuerell Hall, co. Notts., 283.
Cheylmarden, *v.* Chelmorton.

Chichester, Bishops of, *v.* Neville, Ralph de.
Chilewelle, *v.* Chilwell.
Chilwell, co. Notts., 974, 2120.
————Lords. Ric. Martel and Rob. de Stretleye [1314], 974.
Chirchehalla, Chirchehalum, Chirkehalum, *v.* Hallam, Kirk.
Chul, in Measham, 1682, 1683.
Chyrchehalam, *v.* Hallam, Kirk.
Chyricroft, Le, in Stanton-by-Dale, 2202.
Clatercotes, in Overton, 1815.
Claxbe, *v.* Claxby.
Claxby, co. Linc., 635.
————Parson. Nich. Dikson [1483], 635.
Claybuttes, Le, in Catton, 576.
Clerkenwell, Co. Midd., 1575.
Clerkesburwes, in Tideswell, 2335.
Clifftone, *v.* Clifton.
Clifton, nr. Ashbourne, 77, 79, 90, **879-883.**
————Lord. Ric. Destafford [1373], 74.
————Rector. Hugh de Kaue [*t.* Edw. I.], 2033.
Clough, Le Great, in Unstone, 2474.
Cloune, *v.* Clown.
Clown, 432, **884.**
Cluffton, Clufton, Clyfton, *v.* Clifton.
Coal Aston, *v.* Aston, Coal.
Cobbelag, Cobbeleye, Cobele, *v.* Cubley.
Cockesbut, in Tideswell, 2335.
Cockeshetehulle, in Catton, 593.
Coddenovere, Codenore, Codenovere, *v.* Codnor.
Codgrave, *v.* Cotgrave.
Codnor, 548, **885-907,** 962, 974, 1273, 1619.
————Bailiff. John Wawden [1450], 898.
————Castle, 901, 905, 907.
————————Constable. Ric. Malore [1459], 901.
————Lords. Ric. de Grey [1277], 1619; John [1401], 892.
————Park, 898, 900, 902.
Codnore, Codnoure, *v.* Codnor.
Cokshutehul, in Catton, 576.
Cokshuthill, in Snelston, 2134, 2137.
Coland, *v.* Culland.
Cold Aston, *v.* Aston, Coal.
Cold Eaton, *v.* Eaton, Cold.
Cold Muryan, in Staveley, 2258, 2263.
Coldwall, co. Staff., 156, 157, 158, 2133, 2135.
Colestun, *v.* Colston Basset.
Colgrenewong, in Radclyf, 943.
Collecros, in Repton, 1976.
Colleforde, 435.
Colley, Colleye, *v.* Cowley.
Collingham, co. Notts., 1339.
Collingham, North, co. Notts., 1469.
Collisleye, *al.* Collyslege, in Derby, 971, 972.
Collowe, *v.* Calow.
Colston Basset, co. Notts., 1078.
Coltesacre, Le, in Derby, 995.

Colton, co. Staff., 1028.
Colwick, Colwyk, *v.* Calwich.
Colyngham, *v.* Collingham.
Combermere Abbey, co. Chest., 1747.
————Abbot. Rob. Crystylton [1472], 1747.
Combs, 617, 636.
Commyn, Le, in Handley, 1342.
Compeden, Compedenn, Compedon, Compteyn, *v.* Compton.
Compton-in-Ashbourne, 52, 79, 90, 404, 883.
Compton, West, co. Berks., 238.
Comtun, *v.* Compton, West.
Coppedelowe, in Tansley, 2303.
Coppelowe, in Foston, 1288.
Cornleye, nr. Yeldersley, 2721.
Costlaue, in Bakewell, 1328.
Costlowe, Le, in Hulland, 1470.
Costowe, in Makeney, 1627.
Cotegrave, *v.* Cotgrave.
Coteleghes, in Chesterfield, 784.
Coten, Cotene, *v.* Coton-in-the-Elms.
Cotepyngull, in Hulland, 1471.
Cotes, *v.* Coton-in-the-Elms.
Cotgrave, co. Notts., 1914, 2120.
————Rector. Geoffrey Dawe [1384], 1914.
Cothes, *v.* Coton-in-the-Elms.
Coton, *v.* Coton-in-the-Elms.
Coton Farm, nr. Derby, 982.
Coton-in-the-Elms, 341, 345, 491, **908-914,** 1322, 1955, 2035, 2038-2040, 2070, 2073, 2074, 2076.
Couland, *v.* Culland.
Coulynges, in Shardlow, 2116.
Coventry and Lichfield, See of, 193, 199.
————Archdeacons. Rob. de Bosco [1215-1223], 1681; Ric. de Glovernia [*c.* 1230, 1232], 178, 179; Will. de Kilkenny [1252], 1555.
————Bishops of, *v.* Burghill, John; Cornhill, Will. de; Durdent, Walter; Hales, John; Heyworth, Will.; Lee, Roland; Longespee, Roger; Muschamp, Geoffrey de; Nonant, Hugh de; Peche, Richard; Scrop, Richard; Stavensby, Alex. de; Stretton, Robert; Weseham, Rog. de.
————Priors. Geoffrey [1223], 2573; Thomas [1286], 2648.
Coventry, co. Warw., 646, 2361.
Cowley, **915,** 1043, 2565.
Crabtre Wood, in Whatstandwell, 2555.
Cranbrook, co. Kent, 1625.
Cranebrook, *v.* Cranbrook.
Cranford, co. Northt., 781, 791.
————Parsons. John Cokerell [1388-1396], 781, 791.
Crankston, in Hartington, 678.
Craslound, co. Linc., 1469.
Cratele, Cratle, in Wellow, co. Notts., 2098, 2716.
Crich, 286, 638, **916-925,** 1888, 1889, 1891, 2305, 2555.

Crich, Bailiff. Rob. Worth [1498], 638.
————Chantry of St. Nicholas and St. Katherine at, 921.
————Chaplain. Ric. David [1368], 921.
————Vicar. William [1320], 1888.
Criche, *v.* Crich.
Crofton, co. York., W.R., 1440.
————Rector. Ric. de Sudbery [1409], 1440.
Croked Hayrowe, Le, in Repton, 1960.
Crokes, *v.* Crookes.
Crokesdon, *v.* Croxden.
Crombermere, Le, in Staveley, 2248.
Cromford, **926**, 998, 1679, 2649.
Cromfort, Cromforth, *v.* Cromford.
Cromwell, co. Notts., 1340.
Crondecote, *v.* Crowdecote.
Cronxton, *v.* Crankston.
Crookes, co. York., 1781.
Crophulle Botiler, *v.* Cropwell Butler.
Cropwell Butler, co. Notts., 921.
Crosflat, in Dale, 944.
Crosforlong, in Mickleover, 1698.
Crouch, *v.* Crich.
Crowdecote, 1115.
"Crow-nest," Le, in Findern, 1280.
Crowsethuse, in Chelmorton, 668.
Croxall, 572, 581, 582, 591, 598, 600, **927**, 1968, 2763, 2764.
————Lord. Will. de Cursun [1400], 581, 582.
————Vicar. Ralph de Herteshorne [1400-1413], 581, 582, 591 ; Edm. Alcok [1490-1509], 598, 600.
Croxden Abbey, co. Staff., 2568.
————Abbot. T—— [late 12th cent.], 2382 ; Thomas [early 13th cent.], 2383.
Croxhale, Croxhall, Croxhalle, Croxsall, *v.* Croxhall.
Cruch, Cruche, *v.* Crich.
Crukhull, *v.* Croxall.
Crumford, *v.* Cromford.
Crych, Cryche, *v.* Crich.
Cubache, in Doveridge, 1024.
Cubbelegh, *v.* Cubley.
Cubley, 881, **928-931**, 2162.
————Rectors. Nicholas [early 13th cent.], 2385 ; Thomas [1486], 2089.
Culland, 1582, 1585.
Cutholm, Cuttholme, in Chesterfield, 790, 874.

D.

Dala, *v.* Dale Abbey.
Dalbury, **932**, 2384.
Dalby-on-the-Wolds, co. Leic., 2771.
Dalderby, co. Linc., 1469.
Dale, La, *v.* Dale Abbey.
Dale Abbey, 45, 108, 477, 479, 483, 548, 853, 933-**947**, 957, 1453, 1487, 1488, 1544, 1612, 1632, 1785, 2093, 2195, 2197-2200, 2202, 2211, 2284.

Dale Abbey, Abbots. Walter de Senteney [1204-1235], 934, 1544, 2284 ; John [*c.* 1233-1253], 483, 548, 1487, 1504, 2194 ; Hugh [1250-1260], 2196 ; Simon [*t.* Hen. III.-Edw. I.], 1632 ; Laurence Teuren [1286, etc.], 387, 2202 ; Will. de Bonay [1385-6], 942 ; Henry [1404], 944 ; John [1483], 957 ; Ric. Notingham [1510], 946 ; John [1538], 2211.
Dale, by Wirksworth, 2653, 2666.
Dalebire, Dalenburi, *v.* Dalbury.
Daleside, in Bonsall, 310.
Dalesyde, in Alsop-le-Dale, 34.
Dalewang-in-Scarcliffe, 2771.
Daleweye, Le, in Wirksworth, 2657.
Damrydyng, Demryding, in Hope, 1439, 1442.
Danby de Wauz, *v.* Dalby-on-the-Wolds.
Danewall, in Hartshorn, 2760.
Danewallhei *al.* Denevellhaie, in Hartshorn, 2759, 2760.
Darleigh, *v.* Darley.
Darley, 244, 757, 915, **948-954**, 2230.
————Parsons. Robert [early 13th century], 244 ; Nich. del Weld [1368], 757.
Darley Abbey, in Derby, 326-328, 974, 989, 1011, 1012, 1016, 1541, 1624, 1916, 2628, 2630-2633, 2635-2638, 2640-2643, 2646, 2650, 2651, 2662, 2695, 2696, 2700.
————Abbots. Walter [late 12th cent.], 2382 ; William [early 13th cent.], 2383 ; Henry [1222-9], 2575 ; Henry [1275], 2642 ; Will. de Alsopp [1314], 974 ; Simon [1407-8], 1980 ; John [1490], 1916 ; John [1501], 2695 ; John [1510], 2555 ; Tho. Grevys [1524], 1541 ; Tho. Page [1538-9], 1011, 1012.
Darley Moor, nr. Yeaveley, 2715.
Dawer, *v.* Dore.
Dedemansgrene, in Stanley, 2193.
Dedknaveforlong, in Chelmorton, 668, 675.
Dedyke, *v.* Dethick.
Delmere, 2463.
Demryding, *v.* Damrydyng.
Denby, 90, 885, 955-**964**, 1121, 1774.
————Lord. Laurence Lowe [1483], 957.
Denewellehay, in Repton, 1958, 1980.
Denyngton, co. York, 2265.
Depe Clough, in Barley, 237.
Depedal, Depedale, *v.* Dale Abbey.
Depedale, in Repton, 1959, 1960.
Derby, County of, **965-968**.
————Sheriffs. H. de Babington [1272], 2199 ; John de Oxon' [1336], 201 ; *v.* also under Notts.

Derby, County of. Coroners. Hugh de Muscham, Rog. de Somervil [1336], 201.

Derby, 206, 240, 279, 300, 327, 331, 511, 523, 878, 923, 969-1016, 1099, 1107, 1117, 1160, 1162, 1176, 1177, 1181, 1183, 1438, 1443, 1483, 1506, 1520, 1557, 1558, 1564, 1565, 1607, 1623, 1657, 1680, 1681, 1812, 1824, 1882, 1988, 2013, 2586, 2599, 2700, 2739, 2745, 2750-2755, 2757, 2758, 2760, 2766, 2777, 2781, 2783, 2786.

——All Saints' Church, 979, 989, 999, 1002.

———Churchwardens. James Oxle, Ric. Shakere, Edmund Turnour [1513], 1002.

——Archdeacons. Ivo Cornubiensis [1188], 1080; Will. de Mucham, *al.* Muscamp [1199-1231], 44, 936, 1681, 2383; Will. de Luceby [1232, *c.* 1254], 179, 189, 2385; John Ondeby [1400], 1438.

——Bailiffs. Will. Olearius, Rob. de Notingham [*t.* Hen. III.], 971; John fil. Gilberti, Will. Page [1308], 973; Simon de Cestr' [1331], 976; John de Bredon, Will. Laverok [1343], 977; John de Bynyngton, Walter de Trowell [1344-1345], 978, 979; Rob. Alibon, Thos. de Tuttebury [1352], 981; Will. de Brayllesford, John Hachet [1359], 983; Hen. de Bredon, John de Coltman [1365], 985; Rog. de Asshe, Rob. de Murcaston [1379], 986; Thomas Glover, Ric. Spicer [1410], 79; John del Hay, Will. Payn [1413], 987; John Hoghton, John Godard [1423], 523; John Neuton [1472], 994, 995; Nich. Orcherd, John Clostones [1511], 1000; Helize Cowper, Rob. York [1526], 1006; Rob. Jepson, John Johnson [1534], 1010.

——Chamberlains. John Chapmon, Wylliam Yerlle, Edward Lentun, John Watson [1524], 1005.

——Clerk. Hugh [late 12th cent.], 908.

——Coroners. John f. Gilberti [1318], 975; John le Savage [1327], 1098.

——Dean. Philip [1187-8], 1081; John [early 13th cent.], 2385.

——Friar Preachers of, 988.

Derby, Leper's House, 981, 983.

——Priory of St. Mary de Pratis, *al.* King's Mead, 44, 240, 923, 991, 1004, 1443, 1520, 1625, 2382-2385, 2545.

——Prior. R— [1218], 969.

——Prioresses. Margaret [early 13th cent.], 2383; Raimon [early 13th cent.], 2385; Elizabeth [1514], 923.

——St. Helen's Priory. Prior. William [early 13th cent.], 2383.

——St. Michael's Church, 1181.

———Vicar. Tho. Rypley [1417], 1181.

——St. Peter's Church and Parish, 329, 1001, 1004, 1005, 2700.

——Vicar Reginald [1294], 329.

——St. Werburgh's Church, 1520.

———Vicar. Walter [13th cent.], 1520.

——Streets, Bridges, Crosses, etc. Baglone, 992, 993, 1004; Bradseahay, 1005; Briggegate, 976; Bryggecroft, 989; "Churche House," le, in Baglone, 1002; Castelfeld, 1003; "Castel Mylne," 1015; Collislege, Collisleye, 971, 972; Coltesacre, Le, 995; the White Cross, 988; Dychefeld, 994; Hedlecrosse, 988; Juddekynlone, Judkynlone, 977, 978, 985; "Kynge's medewe," 1015; Littledale, Lyteldale, 981, 983; Lyneysiche, 995; Le Marledge, 1014; St. Marygate, 986; St. Mary's Street, 984; Morleyhalleyerd, 976; Odbroke, R., 987; Parkfeld, le, 979, 988; St. Peter's Bridge, 987; Stokkesbrokefeld, 1003; Sydale, 994, 995; Le Syk, 979; Vicus Fabrorum, 975; Le Wallfield, 981, 983.

Dereby, *v.* Derby.

Dereleia, Derlagh, Derlay, Derlega, Derleghe, *v.* Darley.

Derlestowe, in Newton Solney, 1757.

Derley, Derleye, *v.* Darley.

Derwentdale, 262.

Derwent, River, 994, 995, 1013.

Dethek, *v.* Dethick.

Dethick, 128, 922, 1287, 1541.

Dethicke, Dethyk, *v.* Dethick.

Deulacresse, *v.* Dieulacres.

Dicheclif, in Bakewell, 1328.

Dicheryddynge, in Doveridge, 2164.

Dieulacres Abbey, co. Staff. Prior et Procurator. Peter de Peterstowe [1316], 2724.

Dinnington, co. York, 1781.

Dobynholm, in Brimington, 501.

Doggesedslacke, in Monyash, 1708.
Doghole, 466.
Dogmanton, Dokemanton, Dokmanton, *v.* Duckmanton.
Doncaster, Convent of the Order of Mount Carmel of, 1255.
————Prior. Nich. Kerton [1444], 1255.
Done, 2780.
Donston, *v.* Dunston.
Dore, 241, 1017-1022, 1049, 1053, 1064, 1065, 2265.
Dorre, *v.* Dore.
Doubrigge, *v.* Doveridge.
Douue, *v.* Dove.
Douuebrigge, Douuebrug, Douvebrigg, *v.* Doveridge.
Dove, R., 1289, 1583, 1758, 2125.
Dovebrugpleos, 1583.
Doveridge, 350, 1023-1025, 1692, 2164, 2754.
————Chaplain. Rob. Deye [1395], 1024.
————Church of St. Cuthbert at, 1025.
————Persona. Richard [1208], 275*.
————Vicar. Rob. de Knyveton [1383-1395], 1024, 1692, 2598.
Dowbryge, *v.* Doveridge.
Dracot, *v.* Draycott.
Drakelow, 604, 1026-1028, 2542.
————Lords. John de Greseleye [1379], 1026; Tho. de Greseley [1400, 1430], 604, 2542.
Drakelowemere, in Rosliston, 2034.
Dranefeld, Draneffeld, Dranfeld, Dranfelde, Draunfelde, *v.* Dronfeld.
Draycote, *v.* Draycott.
Draycott, 1029, 1030, 1337, 1459, 2601, 2755.
————St. James's Chapel at, 2601.
Drisco, Wood of, in Sandiacre, 941.
Dronefeld, Dronfeld, Dronffeld, *v.* Dronfield.
Dronfield, 132, 133, 232, 235, 265, 359, 377, 701, 770, 781, 791, 793, 795, 803, 806, 809, 812, 842, 859, 866, 878, 1031-1077, 1404, 1437, 1743, 1775, 2252, 2265-2270, 2317, 2438, 2440, 2443, 2445, 2447, 2458, 2473, 2478.
————Alderman of St. Mary's Guild. Will. Bolloke [1449], 1064, 1065.
————Bailiff. Ric. Bullok [1485], 1074.
————Chaplain of St. Mary's Guild. John Hordryn [1449], 1064.
————Church of St. John the Baptist at, 1064, 1065, 1076.
————Guild of St. Mary at, 1064, 1065, 1437.
————Manor, 1054, 1057, 1058, 1060, 1067, 1070, 1071.
————Steward. Sir John Bussy [1469], 1067.

Dronfield, Personæ. Hugh f. Noch [early 13th cent.], 1031; Ancelm [13th cent.], 2425, 2426; Thomas [early Hen. III.], 1032.
————Rector. Tho. Goumfrey [1396, 1398], 791, 795.
————Vicars. John Percy [1459], 236; Hen. Wedirhed, *al.* Weydurherd *al.* Wodhard [1471-1478], 1069, 2474, 2475; Will. Byngley [1487], 2479.
Dronfield, Dronsfeld, Drounfeld, Drownfeld, *v.* Dronfield.
Dubbrige, *v.* Doveridge.
Dubbruge, Dubbrugg, *v.* Doveridge.
Ducemanetun, Duchemanetuna, Duckemantuna, *v.* Duckmanton.
Duckmanton, 1078-1112.
————Chaplain. Ralph Wryghte [1488], 1112.
————Church of St. Peter at, 1079, 1080.
————Vicar. Hugh [*temp.* Hen. III.], 1092.
Ducmanton, *v.* Duckmanton.
Dudmore Wood, in Little Chester, 1013.
Duffeld, Duffeud, *v.* Duffield.
Duffield, 10, 280, 283, 677, 1113-1120, 1181, 1510, 1525, 1861, 2602.
————Church, 1118.
————Clerk. Philip [late 12th cent.], 1113.
————Frith, 1115, 1119, 1695.
————Manor, 1115.
————Vicars. Will. de Monyash, *al.* Meinasche, *al.* Monyashe [1376-1384], 77, 677, 1116, 1117, 1861; John de Bradley [1417], 1181; John Bradley [1431], 2602.
Dugmanton, Dugmantone, Dukemantun, Dukemantune, *v.* Duckmanton.
Dukmaneton, Dukmantone, *v.* Duckmanton.
Dunchurch, co. Warw., 179.
Dungworth, 1355.
Dunnelchurch, *v.* Dunchurch.
Dunnisby, *v.* Dunsby.
Dunsby, co. Linc., 1210.
Dunsseburn, Water of, 233.
Dunstable Priory, co. Bedf., 166, 387, 395.
————Priors. John [1466-7], 395; Gervase Mark [1538], 166.
Dunstall, Dunstil, nr. Willington, 2586, 2597.
Dunstaple, *v.* Dunstable.
Dunston, 509, 695, 701, 770, 781, 866, 1538.
Dunstone, *v.* Dunston.
Dunstorhes [? in Whittington], 2556.
Duntisburn, in Barlow, 226.
Durham, Bishops of, *v.* Langley, Thomas; Poore, Ric le.

Dychefeld, Le, in Derby, 994, 995.
Dynesl', *v.* Temple Dynnesley.
Dynyngton, *v.* Dinnington.

E.

Eadulmestone, *v.* Ednaston.
Eakring, co. Notts., 2098.
East Leek, co. Notts., 1469.
Eaton, Cold, 90, 959, **1121**, 2683, 2687.
Eaton Dovedale, 1025. **1122.**
Eaton, Long, **1123, 1124,** 2207.
Ecclesfield, co. York., 1129.
Eccleshall, co. Staff., 1693, 2097.
Ecclysfeld, *v.* Ecclesfield.
Eckeler, in Hope, 1434-1436.
Eckington, 133, 272, 273, 275, 855, 878,
    1042, 1095, **1125-1129,** 1341, 1345,
    1731, 1738, 1740, 2265, 2271.
——Church, 1125.
——Lord. John de Stoteville
    [1314], 1095.
——Rector. Jordan [*t.* Hen. III],
    1730.
Eckington. Personæ. Ralph [early Hen.
    III.], 2560; Ralph and
    John [*t.* Hen. III.], 1727,
    1729; Rob. Gretehed
    [1380], 2607, 2609.
Edale, 1449, 2119.
Eddrichesey, Eddricheshay, *v.* Idridge-
    hay.
Edelinghale, *v.* Edingale.
Edenessoure, *v.* Edensor.
Edensor, 508, 522, 953, 1214, 1354, 1861,
    2329.
——Lords. John Bozon [1322],
    1214; John Bozoun [1353],
    522.
Edingale, 2763, 2764.
Edinsouer, Edinsouere, Edinsower, *v.*
    Edensor.
Edlaston, **1130-1158.**
——Rectors. Dom. Will. de Clifton
    [1376], 1157; Will. Hebbe
    [1410], 79.
Edlinghall, *v.* Edingale.
Edluston, *v.* Edlaston.
Ednaston, **1159.**
Ednesover, Ednusore, *v.* Edensor.
Edrechhay, Edrechhey, Edrychey, *v.*
    Idridgehay.
Edynsoure, *v.* Edensor.
Eggestow, *v.* Egstow.
Eggington, Eggyngton, Eginton, *v.*
    Egginton.
Egginton, 83, **1160-1190,** 1200, 1742,
    1924, 2081, 2578.
——Lord. Thos. de Rolleston
    [*t.* Edw. III.], 1180.
——Persona. Hugh [*temp.* Hen.
    III.], 1165.
——Rectors. Henry and Walter
    [1301], 1200.
Egkyngeston, Egkyngton, *v.* Egginton.
Egstow, 2410.
Egyngton, Egynton, Egyntone, *v.*
    Egginton.

Eidale, *v.* Edale.
Eikering, *v.* Eakring.
Eium, *v.* Eyam.
Ekinton, Ekintone, *v.* Eckington.
Ekkescroft, 1583.
Ekkyngton, *v.* Eckington.
"Ekles," in Hope, 1433.
Ekyngton, Ekynton, *v.* Eckington.
Elford, co. Staff., 576.
Elkeston, *v.* Ilkeston.
Ellaston, *v.* Ellastone.
Ellastone, co. Staff., 1588, 1589.
Elleford, *v.* Elford.
Elmeton, *v.* Elmton.
Elmton, **377, 1191-1193.**
Elston, co. Notts., 1469.
Elstone, *v.* Elston.
Elton, **1194-1196,** 1685.
——Lord. Tho. Foliaumbe [1351],
    296.
Eltone, *v.* Elton.
Elvaston, 1160, 1179.
Ely, Bishop of, *v.* Bourchier, Thos.
Engleby, *v.* Ingleby.
Equenton, Equintona, *v.* Eckington.
Erewash, River, 2095.
Erlecg', *v.* Arley.
Erleston, *v.* Arleston.
Ermite Medewe, in Trusley, 2386.
Esburnia, *v.* Ashbourne.
Esseborn, Esseburn, Esseburne, *v.* Ash-
    bourne.
Esseford, *v.* Ashford.
Essehovere, Esseovere, *v.* Ashover.
Esshoure, Esshovere, Essover, Essovere,
    v. Ashover.
Estefeld, in Pleasley, 1896.
Estharnam, *v.* Harnham, East.
Esthorp, 200.
Esthwaite, co. Notts., 905, 1123.
Estleek, *v.* East Leek.
Eston, *v.* Aston.
Estwayte, Estwhaite, *v.* Esthwaite.
Etewall, Etewell, Etewelle, *v.* Etwall.
Ethnadeston Wood, in Yeldersley, 2718.
Eton, *v.* Eaton, Cold.
Ettewall, Ettewalle, Ettewelle, *v.* Etwall.
Ettwalle, Etuuel, *v.* Etwall.
Etwall, 279, 347, 511, 519, 520, 521,
    1004, 1082, 1171, 1179, **1197-1206,**
    1813, 2393.
——Lord. Ric. de Rybuff [1316],
    520, 521.
——Vicar. [1196-1208], H——,
    1082.
Etwalle, Etwell, Etwelle, *v.* Etwall.
Euenbroke, *v.* Ivonbrook Grange.
Everdon, co. Northt., 1488.
——Parson. John [1388], 1488.
Eyam, 550, 1195, **1207-1269,** 1281, 1283,
    1285, 1464, 1721, 1725, 2082-2087.
——Church, 1207, 1255.
——Lord. Rog. de Morteyn [1300],
    1212.
——Rectors. Ralph de Cubbele
    [1252], 186; John Redser
    al. Redsyr [1390-1400],
    1228, 1230, 1233, 1283.

Eyam, Chaplains. Tho. de Ouere [1372], 1224 ; John Rancekell, *al.* Rankell [1398-1400], 1230-1232.
Eydale, *v.* Edale.
" Eyes," le, in Foston, 1289, 1290.
Eyham, *v.* Eyam.
Eyom, Eyome, Eyoum, *v.* Eyam.
Eyton, *v.* Eaton, Cold.
Eyton, *v.* Eaton-Dovedale.
Eyton, Eytone, *v.* Eaton, Long.
Eyton-super-Douue, *v.* Eaton Dovedale.
Eyum, *v.* Eyam.
" Eyvys," in Bowden, 646.

F.

Fairefeld, *v.* Fairfield.
Fairfield, 644, **1270-1272**, 2350.
Farewell, co. Staff., 408.
Farleston, in Scropton, 2105.
Farley, 948, **1273**, 1517.
Farnley, Farnleya, *v.* Farley.
Faunchalgate, Fownchalgate, etc., in Holmesfield, 1405, 1407, 1410, 1411.
Felley Priory, co. Notts., 1877, 1878, 1896.
Fennilache, Le, in Wyaston, 1135, 1154.
Fennybentileye, *v.* Bentley, Fenny.
Fenton, co. Staff., 90, 960.
Fernelee, Le, *v.* Fernilee.
Fernilee, 627, 649, **1377-1379**.
Fernyle, *v.* Fernilee.
Fernysende, in Catton, 593.
Fertewode, le, in Alkmonton, 25.
Festewod, in Eyam, 1238.
Findern, 1179, **1274-1280**, 2587, **2756-2758**.
——————Chaplain. Peter [*t.* Hen. III.], 2579.
——————Clerk. Richard [1197-1210], 1276.
Finderne, Findirna, *v.* Findern.
Fiskerton, co. Notts., 921.
Flag, *v.* Flagg.
Flagg, 666, 668, 670-672, 674 678.
Flagge, *v.* Flagg.
Flates, Les, nr. Kniveton, 1517.
Flaxdale, in Parwich, 1819.
Flehill, Flehyll, in Bakewell, 208, 210.
Flete, nr. Egginton, 1167.
Flyster Lane, in Staveley, 2261.
Flytenflate, Le, in Alkmanton, 1577, 1630.
Foldford, Foleford, Folefort, nr. Hollington, 1393-1395.
Folow, Folowe, *v.* Foolow.
Foolow, 1219, 1221, 1236, 1245, 1246, 1254, 1267, **1281-1285**.
Foorchys, le, in Dungworth, 1355.
Ford, in Chapel-en-le-Frith, 618, 644.
Forde, *v.* Ford.
Foremark, **1286, 1287**, 1953, 1957.
Formedue, in Sandiacre, 2095.
Fornemerch, Fornewerk, Forneworc, *v.* Foremark.

Fosse Priory, co. Linc., 443.
Foston, 1133, 1136, **1288-1316**, 1620, 1621, 2100, 2102, 2103.
——————Clerks. Henry [1320-1326], 1301, 1303, 2103 ; Thomas [*t.* Edw. II.], 1303.
Fostone, Fostun, *v.* Foston.
Fouloue, Foulowe, *v.* Foolow.
Foulthorne, Le, in Findern, 1280.
Fouwelowe, *v.* Foolow.
Fownchalgate, *v.* Faunchalgate.
Foxhill, in Castleton, 566.
Fradswell, co. Staff., 2184, 2185, 2191, 2355, 2366.
Frodeswall, *v.* Fradswell.
Fulbrok, in Calow, 543.
Fulbrok, in Dronfield, 812.
Fuledic, in Willington, 529.
Fulesfenshiche, in Hartshorn, 2759.
Fullesmedowfurlonge, in Catton, 576.
Furnycottfeld, in Idridgehay, 1484.
Fyndern, Fynderne, *v.* Findern.
Fyndernwood, in Repton, 2600.
Fynny Benteley, *v.* Bentley, Fenny.
Fyskertone, *v.* Fiskerton.
Fysshepolehyll, in Ashleyhay, 105.
Fyxpol, Le, in Kirk Langley, 1524.

G.

Gamelesley, in Broadlow Ash, 512.
Garendon Abbey, co. Leic., 1818, 1819.
Gaytehouse, Le, in Findern, 1280.
Gedling, co. Notts., 1469.
Gedlyng, *v.* Gedling.
Geilberga, Little, 536.
Gernuncroft, in Chesterfield, 697.
Gerondon, Gerwedon, *v.* Garendon.
Gilderessege, Gildersley, Gildresle, *v.* Yeldersley.
Glappewellgrif, in Scarcliffe, 2771.
Glapwell, **1317-1319**, 1371.
Gleadless, co. York., 1782.
Gledelees, *v.* Gleadless.
Glemangate, in Chesterfield, 796.
Glossop, 633, **1320**.
——————Vicars. Thos. Meygnell [1352], 2628 ; Will. Waynwright [1477], 633.
Gloucester, co., 583.
Gloucester, 1161, 1162, 1968.
Godwich, in Spondon, 2173.
Goldewellfflatte, in Chesterfield, 812.
Goldicroft, Le, in Barlow, 226.
Goldwell, 817.
Gonalston, co. Notts., 2606.
Gonerton, co. Notts., 525.
Gonolston, *v.* Gonalston.
Gore, La, in Rosliston, 2033.
Gores, Le, in Findern, 1280.
Gorforlong, in Makeney, 1627.
Gorsehouse, in Dronfield, 1077.
Gorstelandes, in Dronfield, 1063.
Gosegrene, Le, in Chesterfield, 705.
Gotacre, Goteacre, in Catton, 576, 593.
Gower, S. Wales, 489.

Goytes, Goytez, Hall, *v.* Goyt Hall.
Goyt Hall, co. Ches., 651, 659.
Grace Dieu Priory, in Belton, co. Leic., 399.
————Prioress. Agnes de Greslege [1268-9], 399.
Grandendena, *v.* Gransden.
Gransden, co. Hunt., 1942, 1943, 1950, 1951, 1964-1967.
Grantendune, Grantinden, etc., *v.* Gransden, co. Hunt.
Gratclifdale, Grattecliffedale, in Priest-cliffe, 1904, 1913.
Gratia dei, *v.* Grace Dieu Priory.
Grattenfurlong, Grettenfurlong, in Rosliston, 2034, 2038, 2041.
Grauntesden, *v.* Gransden.
Gravadune Wood, Chesterfield, 697.
Greatrakes, Gritrakes, 2350, 2408.
Greaves, *al.* Greves, The, in Beeley, *v.* under Beeley.
Greenhill, 878, 1123, **1321**, 1778, 1781.
Grenehill, Grenehyll, *v.* Greenhill.
Grenesyde, Le, in Hope, 1442.
Grenhul, Grenyll, *v.* Greenhill.
Gresley, 1028, **1322**, 1955.
Gresley Hundred, 1115.
Greves, Greveys, Grevis, Greaves, The, *v.* Greaves.
Greyhirst Wood, Chesterfield, 697.
Greyve Croft, in Bradshaw, 634.
Grimswode, Grymswode, nr. Rosliston, 2028, 2033.
Grindleford, 1210, **1323-1325**.
Grindleford Bridge, 1243.
Grindulforde, *v.* Grindleford.
Gritrakes, *v.* Greatrakes.
Grundelford, *v.* Grindleford.
Gruves, Gruwis, in Dronfield, 1031, 1033.
Gryndelford, Gryndulforde, *v.* Grindleford.
Gunthorpe, co. Linc., 1469.
Gyves, le, *al.* Hordron-in-Bowdon, 636.

H.

Hackenthorpe, 273, 276, 467, **1326**, **1327**.
Hackynthorp, *v.* Hackenthorpe.
Hadersege, Hadersegge, Hadersich, *v.* Hathersage.
Haddon, Nether, 302, **1333**.
Haddon, Over, 214, 317, 878, **1328-1332**, 1333, 2775.
Hady, Le, in Handley, 1342.
Hagenthorp, *v.* Hackenthorpe.
Hakenethorpe, Hakunthorpe, *v.* Hackenthorpe.
Hakwood, in Kirk Langley, 1527-1529.
Hakynthorp, *v.* Hackenthorpe.
Halcroft, *v.* Hallcroft.
Haleghys, *v.* Hallowes.
Hales Abbey. Abbot. Richard [early Hen. III.], 909.
Halgh, in Staveley, 1513.
Hallam, Kirk, 941, **1334-1339**, 1469, 1487, 1635, 2294.
Hallam, West, 941, **1340**, 1749.

Hallamshire, co. York, 464, 1214, 1233.
————Lords. Tho. de Furnival, senr. [1322], 1214; Tho. de Furnivall [1347], 1700; Tho. Nevyll [1400], 1233.
Hallcroft in Hope, 1451, 1452.
Halleclif, Le, in Parwich, 1821.
Hallehes, *v.* Hallowes-in-Dronfield.
Hallewynnefeld, Halwynfeld, Halwyng-field, *v.* Wingfield, N. or S.
Hallowes-in-Dronfield, 1032, 1034, 1042.
Halome, West, *v.* Hallam, West.
Halomeshire, Hallumshire, etc., *v.* Hallamshire.
Halowes, Le, in Hilton, 1380.
Halughes, Halughys, *v.* Hallowes.
Halum, *v.* Hallam.
Hambury, *v.* Hanbury.
Hanbury, co. Staff. Parson. John Cheyne [1383], 2598.
Handeley, *v.* Handley.
Handley, 878, 1128, **1341-1345**, 1732, 2260, 2263, 2271.
Handsworth, co. York, 1129, 2259.
Haneston, co. York, 2265.
Hanlay, Hanley, *v.* Handley.
Hannesworth, *v.* Handsworth.
Hanson, nr. Alsop, 27, 29.
Hardewyksyche, in Repton, 1969, 1981.
Hardstoft, nr. Tibshelf, 2378.
Hardwick, 1772, 1879, 1880.
Hardwyk, *v.* Hardwick.
Hardwykwall, 1618, 2372.
Hareborowe, in Foston, 1303.
Harecrofte, in Norton, 1776.
Harestan Castle, 980.
Harewode, Harewood, *v.* Harwood.
Hareworthe, *v.* Harworth.
Harland, in Stanley, 2193.
Harlington, co. Bedf., 578.
Harnham, East, co. Wilt., 1712.
Harringworth, co. Northt., 942.
Harston, co. Leic., 1469.
Harthill, co. York, 84, 301, 2259.
Hartington, 156-159, 395, 678, 1115, **1346-1348**, 1668, 1769.
————Vicar. Will. Braye [1509], 2403.
Hartle, The, in Chestrefeld, 858.
Hartshorn, 540, **1349**, **1350**, 1948, **2759**, **2760**.
Hartyngton, *v.* Hartington.
Harwod, *v.* Harwood.
Harwood Grange, in Beeley, 244, 258, 265.
Harworth, co. Notts. Vicar. Rog. Bieston [1536], 213.
Haryngworht, *v.* Harringworth.
Haselam, 467.
Haseland, *v.* Hasland.
Haselhay, Haselhaye, nr. Wigwell, 2637, 2641.
Haselond, Haselund, *v.* Hasland.
Haselwod, Hasilwode, *v.* Hazlewood.
Hasland, Haslande, 382, 803, 821, 827, 836, 1074, **1351**, **1352**.
Haspelond, Haspelund, in Boythorpe, 353, 687.

24

Hasschovere, *v.* Ashover.
Hasse, Le, in Makeney, 1627.
Hasseland, *v.* Hasland.
Hassilbache, *v.* Hazlebadge.
Hassop, 95, 204, 757, **1353, 1354,** 1551, 1700, 1718, 1793.
Hassope, Hassopp, *v.* Hassop.
Hasterildstorthe, in Brampton, 420.
Haston, *v.* Aston, Coal.
Hasylbadge, *v.* Hazlebadge.
Hasyllborough, *v.* Hazlebarrow.
Hathersage, 422, **1355-1359,** 1588, 1589, 1596-1601, 1605, 1670, 1764, 1805, 2319.
Hathersagge, Hathersege, Hattersegg, *v.* Hathersage.
Hathirsege, Hathyrsege, *v.* Hathersage.
Hatton, **1360-1369.**
Hauston. Parson. Richard [1388], 1488.
Hautboys, Le, in Seal, co. Leic., 2033.
Hawpe, *v.* Hope.
Hay, Le, in Repton, 1977.
Hayes, Le, in Castleton, 564.
Hayfeld, Hayffelde, *v.* Hayfield.
Hayfield, 156, 460, 1345, **1370-1375,** 1812.
Hayleye, The, in Bowden, 617.
Hayleyebroke, in Bowden, 617.
Haystowe, Le, in Coton-in-the-Elms, 913.
Haywood, in Mappleton, 965, 967, 1644, 1648, 1649.
Hazlebadge, 559, 1333.
Hazlebarrow, 1782, 1783.
Hazlewood, **1376.**
Heage, or High Edge, 1012, 1115, **1377, 1379,** 2305, **2761.**
Heanor, 886, 891, 905, 906, 1532.
———Rector. John Fonglay [1459], 901.
Heath, nr. Chesterfield, 859, 1881.
———Rector. Edward Savage [1490], 1881.
Heath, The, in Egginton, 1168.
Heckinton, *v.* Eckington.
Hedersege, *v.* Hathersage.
Hedlecrosse, in Derby, 988.
Hednesouere, *v.* Edensor.
Heegge, *v.* Heage.
Hegham, *v.* Higham Ferrers.
Heghebrock-hill, in Newbold, 717.
Hegheygg, *v.* Hepere.
Heglowe, *v.* Highlow.
Heighnor, *v.* Heanor.
Hekeclif, Le, in Rodsley, 2018.
Hakent', Hekinton, *v.* Eckington.
Helde, Le, in Willington, 2589.
Helm, in Willington, 2592, 2594.
Hemington, co. Leic., 1726.
Hempshill, co. Notts., 2120.
Hemsell, *v.* Hempshill.
Henganderidinge, in Barlow, 225.
Hengham, *v.* Ingham.
Hennegrauestorht, in Tansley, 2303.
Henneparke-medewe, in Duckmanton, 1101, 1102.
Henor, Henore, Henouere, *v.* Heanor.

Heppelemead, in Finderne, 2757.
Heppeleymore, in Rodsley, 2014.
Herdewik, Herdewyk, in Hilton, 1200-1202.
Herdewiksiche, *v.* Hardewyksyche.
Herdikwall, Herdycwall, nr. Castleton, 559, 565.
Herdwyke, *v.* Hardwick.
Herlyngdon, *v.* Harlington.
Hermite Ker, Le, in Ashover, 117.
Herstofte, *v.* Hardstoft.
Hertell, *v.* Harthill.
Hertendon, *v.* Hartington.
Herteshorne, *v.* Hartshorn.
Herthill, *v.* Harthill.
Hertinton, *v.* Hartington.
Hertishorn, *v.* Hartshorn.
Hertyll, *v.* Harthill.
Hertyngdon, Hertyngton, Hertynton, *v.* Hartington.
Hertyshevid, in Mackworth, 1623.
Heselund, *v.* Hasland.
Hesilbarowe, *v.* Hazlebarrow.
Heth, Hethe, *v.* Heath.
Hethersege, *v.* Hathersage.
Hethflat, in Egginton, 1178.
Hethhouses, in Egginton, 1179, 1185.
Hetton, *v.* Hatton.
Hewodfield, *v.* Haywood.
Heyedewode, in Atlow, 147.
Heyfeld, *v.* Hayfield.
Heyghegg, *v.* Heage.
Heynore, *v.* Heanor.
Heysale, in Brampton, 424, 427.
"Heytridding," Le, in Norton, 1775.
Heywode, *v.* Haywood.
Heywood, Heywode, 1828, 2559.
Hickling, co. Notts., 1469.
Hicklyng, *v.* Hickling.
Higham Ferrers, co. Northt., 1668.
———Rector. Hosbert [13th cent.], 477.
High Edge, *v.* Heage.
Highege, *v.* Heage.
Highlow, 408, 1225, 1237, 1805.
Hikelland, in Barlow, 229.
Hilkesd', *v.* Ilkeston.
Hill, in Birchover, 300-302, 2372.
Hilton, 83, 1184, 1201-1205, **1380,** 2081, 2746.
Hindeband, *v.* under Chesterfield.
Hinkershill, *v.* Inkersall.
"Hipere" Water, in Chesterfield, *v.* Hipper, R.
Hipper, R., 414, 726, 741, 813.
Hochtone, *v.* Stoney Houghton.
Hoffnertoun, *v.* Offerton.
Hoggesthorp, *v.* Hogsthorpe.
Hoggimastone, Hoggmaston, Hoginaston, *v.* Hognaston.
Hognaston, 136, 149, 320, 390, 391, **1381-1389,** 1673, 1677.
———Clerk. Adam [1272], 136.
Hogsthorpe, co. Linc., 1181.
———Rector. John de Brynnesley [1417], 1181.
Hokelawe, Hokelowe, *v.* Hucklow.
Hokenaston, *v.* Hognaston.

Hoklouwe, Hoklowe, v. Hucklow.
Hoknastone, v. Hognaston.
Holand, Holande, Holandward, v. Hulland.
Holbrok, in Barlow, 226.
Holbroke, in Pinxton, 1866.
Holbroke, nr. Staveley, 2260.
Holbrook, nr. Duffield, 1115.
Holdelauton, Le, in Newton Solney, 1758.
Holdweye, nr. Plaistow, 1890.
Hole Meadow, v. Holmedowe.
Holewalhel, in Breaston, 485.
Holewaus, in Crich, 922.
Holewesike, in Calver, 548.
Holeweye, in Ash, 50.
Holghmede, v. Holmedowe.
Holinton, v. Hollington.
Holleycroft, in Brampton, 420.
Hollington, 1390-1396, 1566, 1591, 1602.
Holm, Le, in Markeaton, 1652.
Holme, by Bakewell, 207, 209, 213, 2762.
Holmedowe, Holumedue, in Bowden, 616, 631, 639, 643, 658.
Holme, Le, in Catton, 576.
Holme, near Brampton, 411, 435, 509, 719, 781, 1396, 2521.
Holme, near Newton Solney, 1165.
Holme, near Newark, co. Notts., 1469.
Holmes, Le, in Newbold, 1746.
Holmesefeld, Holmesfeld, v. Holmesfield.
Holmesfield, 214, 233, 1054, 1055, 1193, 1397-1418, 2704.
————St. Swithin's Chapel at, 1409.
Holmhay, in Marston-on-Dove, 1661.
Holond, v. Hulland.
Holyngton, Holynton, v. Hollington.
Holyn Wood, in Whatstandwell, 2555.
Holywodhed, 1812.
Homesfeld, Homesfeld, v. Holmesfield.
Hommuldon, in Litton, 1550.
Homsfeld, v. Holmesfield.
Honerbromhul, Honourbromhull, in Repton, 1969, 1970, 1977.
Honston, v. Unstone.
Hopa, v. Hope.
Hope, 4, 176, 183-185, 557, 558, 564, 620, 646, 878, 884, 1270, 1271, 1419-1452, 1720, 1789, 1810, 1833, 1850, 2149, 2150, 2318, 2339.
————Church. 178, 179, 186, 188, 189, 214, 620, 1272, 1419, 1421, 1426, 1428, 1431.
————Vicars. William [1254-1278], 1427; Will. Godwine [1359], 1433; Ric. Forester [1394], 1437, John Dean [1413], 1720; Will. Bagshaw [1521], 646.
Hopedale, 1271.
Hoppe, v. Hope.
Hopton, 214, 306, 475, 477, 479, 998, 1389, 1453, 1454, 1490, 1518, 1519, 1624, 2649, 2653.
Hoptone, v. Hopton.

Hopwell. Lords. Will Saucheverel [1344], 330; John Saucheverel [1384]; 1914.
Horburghhale, Horburyhale, nr. Wirksworth, 475, 1490.
Hordlawe, v. Hurdlow.
Hordron, in Bowdon, 636.
Hordthorp, Le, in Chesterfield, 707.
Horestone, Le, v. Horston.
Hormisholm, in Boythorpe, 364.
Horseley, Horseleye, v. Horsley.
Horsley, 481, 524, 1179, 1455-1460, 1507, 1509, 1510, 1886, 2266-2270.
————Chaplain. Robert [temp. Edw. I.], 1507.
————Vicar. Robert [1349], 1509,
Horsley Woodhouse, 1885.
Horssley, v. Horsley.
Horston, 25, 1457, 1458.
Horswood, in Brampton, 447.
Hothe, Le, in Walton, 2501.
Houlotholm, near Chesterfield, 704.
Hounston, v. Unstone.
Houryngham, v. Hoveringham.
Houshold, Le, in Wyaston, 1133, 1134.
Hoveringham, co. Notts., 921.
Hovyerdes, in Walton, 2530.
Howpe, v. Hope.
Huberetorp, 1726.
Hucklow, Great and Little, 555, 1237, 1259, 1264, 1440, 1461-1468, 1816, 2362.
————Lord. Tho. f. Ric. Larcher [1372], 1468.
Hucknall, Ault, 1469.
Huclowe, v. Hucklow.
Hudclyff Banke, in Beauchief, 242.
Hufton, v. Ufton.
Huklow, Huklowe, v. Hucklow.
Huknall, v. Hucknall, Ault.
Hulland and Hulland Ward, 9, 402, 1470, 1471, 1694, 1695.
Hulliforlong, in Alsop-le-Dale, 34.
Hulm, v. Holme, nr. Brampton.
Hulme, v. Holme.
Hulton, Hultone, v. Hilton.
Huncedon, Huncesdon, v. Hanson, near Alsop.
Hundall, 2485.
Hunderwude, v. Underwood.
Hundishon, in Unstone, 2426.
Hungerhil, in Rosliston, 2034.
Hungerhill, in Boythorpe, 358.
Hungstubbing, nr. Chesterfield, 697.
Hurdlow, nr. Earl Sterndale, 1472, 1473.
Hurimandole, in Finderne, 2757.
Hwytflat, in Newbold, 736.
Hyetown, Le, in Handley, 1345.
Hylderis, in Trusley, 2385.
Hvlowe, v. Highlow.
Hylton, Hyltone, v. Hilton.
Hyncersell, Hynkersell, Hynkersil, v. Inkersall.
Hyolegrave, v. Youlgrave.
Hyper, Hypur, v. Hipper, R.

I.

Ibell, Ibole, Ibul, Ibulle, *v.* Ible.
Ible, **1474-1481**, 1491.
————Lord. Ranulph f. Ranulphi de Sniterton [1309], 1491.
Ibulsty, in Bonsall, 313.
Iddurshey, Iderechehay, Idrichehay, Idrichhay, *v.* Idridgehay.
Idridgehay, 1003, 1115, 1119, 1471, **1482-1488.**
Ilam, co. Staff., 156-158, 952, 2139, 2141, 2142.
Ilkesdone, *v.* Ilkeston.
Ilkeston, 774, **1487-1489**, 1634.
————Lord. Will. de Ros [*temp.* Edw. I.], 1634.
————Rectors. William [*t.* Edw. I.], 1634; Will. de Albiniaco [*t.* Edw. I.], 2202.
Ilom, *v.* Ilam.
Ingham, co. Linc., 114, 795.
————Rector. Ric. Goumfrey [1398], 795.
Ingleby, 1953, 1957, 1978.
Ingoldmells, co. Linc., 1668.
Inkersall, 1100, 1198.
Ireton, Kirk, 77, 389, 1485, **1497, 1498,** 1503, 1741, 2693.
————Persona. Thos. de Clifton [1370], 2020.
————Rector. R. Smythe [1485], 2690.
Ireton, Little, 2551.
Irton, *v.* Ireton, Kirk.
Irton Parva, *v.* Ireton, Little.
Iuenbroc, Iuenbrook, *v.* Ivonbrook Grange.
Ivonbrook Grange, nr. Wirksworth, 474, 475, **1490-1496.**

J.

Jonessecrossbrown, in Chesterfield, 797.
Jordanthorpe, 1780, 1782.
Jordenthorpe, *v.* Jordanthorpe.
Juddekynlone, in Derby, 977, 978, 985.
Jurdanthorpe, *v.* Jordanthorpe.

K.

Kalalh, *v.* Calow.
Kalc, *v.* Calk.
Kaldewellesunderlondes, in Rosliston, 2032.
Kalehalegate, in Chesterfield, 686.
Kalhale, *v.* Calow.
Kanoc, *v.* Cannock.
Karsyngton, *v.* Carsington.
Kaaureshegge, in Offerton, 1794.
Kedleston, 793, 994, 1482, **1499-1506,** 1526, 1688, 1741, **2763, 2764.**
Kelham, co. Notts., 2098.
Kelum, *v.* Kelham.
Kenilworth, co. Warw., 1428, 2017.
————Canon of. Philip [1232], 179.

Kenilleworth, *v.* Kenilworth.
Kent, co., 905.
Kenteney, 1789-1791.
Kerrowe, in Brimington, 498.
Kersington, *v.* Carsington.
Ketelestun, Ketelleston, Ketilstone, Ketleston, *v.* Kedleston.
Kethorne, South, 916.
Kettillesthorp, *v.* Kettlethorpe.
Kettlethorpe, co. Linc., 1235, 1236.
Kettliston, *v.* Kedleston.
Ketulesthorpe, *v.* Kettlethorpe.
Ketylston, *v.* Kedleston.
Kidsley, in Smalley, 1726.
Kilbourne, *v.* Kilburn.
Kilburn, 955, 957, 963, 1455, 1457, 1458, **1507-1510.**
Killamarsh, **1511-1514,** 1597-1599, 1601, 1605.
Killeburn, *v.* Kilburn.
Kilvey, in S. Wales, 489.
Kingestrete, nr. Hartington, 1346.
King's Bromley, co. Staff., 638.
Kingsley, co. Staff. Parson. Ric. Falthurst [1439-1455], 2133, 2134, 2137.
Kingsmead, *v.* under Derby.
Kingston, co. Staff., 1028.
Kirby Bellars, co. Leic., 1008, 1726.
Kirkby-in-Ashfield, co. Notts., 1460, 1866, 1872, 1873, 1881, 1884, 1885.
Kirkby Moorside, co. York, 698.
Kirkebi, Kirkeby, *v.* Kirkby.
Kirkeby Bellars, *v.* Kirby Bellars.
Kirkehalum, *v.* Hallam, Kirk.
Kirke Somersale, *v.* Somersall Herbert.
Kirkhallom, Kirkhalom, Kirkhalome, *v.* Hallam, Kirk.
Kirkirton, *v.* Ireton, Kirk.
Knaith, co. Linc., 1127.
————Lord. John Darcy [1349], 1127.
Knavegrene, nr. Repton, 1971.
Knayth, *v.* Knaith.
Kneveton, *v.* Kniveton.
Kniveton, 67, 77, 392, 394, 397, **1515-1519.**
Knollewode, in Repton, 1980.
Knottelowe, in Monyash, 1708.
Knyfsmithgate, in Chesterfield, 780, 802, 850.
Knyuenton, Knyveton, etc., *v.* Kniveton.
Kokplas, in Dronfield, 1072.
Kokthorn, in Repton, 1972.
Kylborn, Kylbourn, Kylbourne, Kylburn, *v.* Kilburn.
Kylwalmerch, *v.* Killamarsh.
Kyngeley, *v.* Kingsley.
Kynghesmedewe, *v.* Kingsmead.
Kynnewalmarch, Kynwaldemers, Kynwalmarche, *v.* Killamarsh.
Kynwalmerch, Kynwalmerssh, Kynwolmarsh, *v.* Killamarsh.
Kyrkby in Asshefeld, *v.* Kirkby-in-Ashfield.
Kyrkeby, *v.* Kirkby.
Kyrkeby in Moresheued, *v.* Kirkby Moorside.

Kyrkehalum, *v.* Hallam, Kirk.
Kyrkelane, in Duckmanton, 1086.
Kyrkelongele, Kyrkelongley, *v.* Langley, Kirk.
Kyrke Wyllne, *v.* Wilne.
Kyrke Yreton, *v.* Ireton, Kirk.
Kyrkhalum, *v.* Hallam, Kirk.
Kytlowegreves, in Castleton, 561.

L.

Lamcote, in Radcliffe, co. Notts., 943.
Lamley. Parson. John de Halom [1388], 1488.
Lancaster, County of, 965, 967, 1594, 1597, 1605.
Landa, *v.* Laund.
Lanewell, in Staveley, 2257.
Langeford, *v.* Longford.
Langele, *v.* Langley.
Langeleieker, in Barlow, 228.
Langeley, Langeleye, Langelya, *v.* Langley.
Langesdon, Langesdone, Langesduna, *v.* Longstone.
Langforth, *v.* Longford.
Langisdon, *v.* Longstone.
Langley, in Heanor, 905, **1532**, 2120.
Langley, Kirk and Meynell, **1520-1531**.
Langley, Kirk, 520, 521.
———Lord. Rob. Twyford [1408-1411], 1505, 1930, 1931.
———Parson. Will. Arrosmythe [1411], 1505.
Langley, Meynell, 1505, 2137, 2373.
———Lords. Hugh de Meinil *temp.* Edw. II., 1524; Rog. Bradshawe [1411], 1505.
Langley, nr. Chesterfield, 701, 770, 781, 866, 878, **1533-1538**.
Langthwaytes, in Pleasley, 1896.
Lappingehaly, Lappynghalugh, etc., in Egginton, 1163, 1168, 1174, 1175, 1178, 1180.
Laund Priory, co. Leic., 1356.
———Priors. Ralph [1155-60], 1078; Thomas [1404], 1356.
Lavinden Abbey, co. Bucks. Abbot. Philip [1286], 387.
Lea, by Dethick, 922, 1890, 1892.
Lea, in Bradborne, 67, 394.
Lee Breyche, nr. Wirksworth, 2684.
Lee, La, *v.* Lea.
Leegh, *v.* Leigh.
Leek, co. Staff., 532.
———Presbyter. John, early Hen. II., 532.
Lees, co. Lanc., 1129.
Lefsihay, 2780.
Legh, *v.* Lea, in Bradborne.
Legh, *v.* Leigh.
Leghamsty, Leghumsty, Leyghumsti, Leyminsty, in Eyam, 1212, 1220, 1231, 1232.

Leheg, *v.* Heage (?).
Leicester, County of, 609, 1597, 1784, 1867.
Leicester, 187, 609, 863, 1452, 1830, 1831.
———Archdeacon. Hen. de Chaddesden *t.* Edw. III., 609.
———Collegiate Church of, 1118.
———St. Mary de Pré Abbey. Abbotts. Paul [1196-1208], 1082; John Bowchier [1535], 305.
Leigh, co. Staff., 1645, 2288.
———Rector. John Wade [1382], 1645.
Leighes, co. Essex, 1625.
Leiston Abbey, co. Staff. Abbot. Robert [1187-1188], 1079.
Leitegvil, in the Peak, 1840.
Lenton, co. Notts., 2120.
———Priory, 183-186, 956, 1270, 1825-1836, 1852, 2336, 2339.
———Priors. R— early Hen. III., 2093; Robert [1226], 1696; Roger [1240-50], 1487; R—[circ. 1270], 1833 R— *temp.* Edw. I., 940.
Leuenwelles, nr. Wirksworth, 2654.
Leverichegrave in Swadlincote, 2777.
Leverton, N., co. Notts., 2120.
Leverton, S., co. Notts., 2120.
Leyholme in Repton, 1996.
Leys, *v.* Stanton.
Lichfield, co. Staff., 2765.
———Bishops, *v.* under Coventry.
———Church and See of. 170, 171, 178, 179, 203, 646, 945, 991, 1420, 1421, 1431.
———Dean and Chapter. 208, 214, 407, 408, 620, 627, 644, 647, 649, 945, 1333, 1356, 1426, 1427, 1444, 1445, 1451, 1452, 1519, 1546, 1551, 1617, 1618, 1705, 1720, 1811, 1816, 1824, 1828, 1831, 1833, 1836, 2335, 2339, 2343, 2350, 2372, 2647.
———Deans. Ralph [1214-1222], 1546; Will. de Mancester [1222-*circ.* 1254], 178, 179, 189, 1426; Ralph de Sempringham [1254-57], 1705; — John [1286], 2647; Tho. de Stretton [1402-1409], 208, 1441; Tho. Heywode [1473], 854; John Yotton [1493], 1617; Ralph Colyngwood [1516], 644, 1551; Jas. Denton [1523-32], 407, 647, 1618, 1811, 2372; Henry Williams [1544-53], 214, 408, 1333, 1451, 1452, 1519, 1816.
Lichfield. Canons. Matthew [1192-1198], 170; Rog. Rusteng [1214-22], 1546; Herbert [1222-

29], 2576; W. de Hedfield, R. de Chebeleie, Robert, Capellanus, Hugh, Capellanus, R. de Halton [1232], 179; Will de Kilkenni, Hugh de Sotteby, Walter de Porton, Robert de Chebbeseie, Alexander Blund, Will de Eccleshal, Simon de Norwis, John Francisc', Ralph de Terne [*circ.* 1254], 189; Hen. de Wishawe [1254], 188; P. de Radenovere, W. de Attleberge, W. de Staunford, W. de Neuton, J. de Sparham, Walkeline [1254-7], 1705; Will de Attelberge, Will de Stanford, Will de Neuton, Walkelin de Houton [1254-1278], 1427; W. de Attlebye, Alan le Bretun [1271], 1957; Peter Scarleston [1350], 620; Rog. de Northburgh [1364], 2350; Edm. de Stafford [1388], 2355; John Cheyne [1404], 944.

——Precentors. Thomas [1214-1222], 1546, 2335; Thomas [1254], 188, 189; Tho. de Wymundham [1254-1278], 1427, 1705.

——Succentors. Tho. de Crawell [1214-1222], 1546; Rob. Merford [1413], 1720.

——Treasurers. Ric. de Stavenesby [*circ.* 1230-1232], 178, 179; Richard de Glovernia [*ante* 1254], 189; Ralph de Chaddesden [1254, 1271], 188, 1957.

Lightbirch, Lightbyrches, Lyghtbirches, in Bowden, 626, 635, 638.
Lighull, in Staveley, 2243.
Lilleshall Abbey, co. Salop, 1462.

——Abbots. William [1153-1160], 531, 1939; Will. de Hales [1301], 1462.

Linacre, in Brampton, 7, 645, 781, **1539**.
Linaker, *v.* Linacre.
Lincoln, County of, 1594, 1597, 1605, 1899.
Lincoln, Mayor. Rob. de Ledes [1388], 1923.
Lincoln. Bailiffs. J. de Carlton, W. de Faldyngworth W. de Barkworth [1388], 1923.

——Deans Hen. de Lexinton [1243-1253], 186, 1426, 1829; Oliver [1286], 2646; John de Schepeye [1404], 1693; John Mackworth [1420], 1280; John Constable [1527], 1013; George Hennage [1532], 2698; John Tailer [1545], 1013.

Lincoln. Canons. Sim. de London; R. de Belleston; Ric. de Wisbech [1249], 2634; Rog. de Foldon, John de Derbe, David de Sancta Fridewida [1254], 188.

——Precentor. R— [1249], 2634.

——Treasurer. Ralph [de Leicester, 1249], 2634.

Linford, Great, co. Buck., 1712.
Linton, 488, 491, 579, 1027, 1028, 1322, **1540**, 2055, 2350.
Litchurch, in Derby, 982, **1541-1543**, 2700.
Litlehul, nr. Dalbury, 932.
Litteldale, Lyteldale, in Derby, 981, 983.
Littellowe, nr. Bonsall, 313.
Littelwodebroc, in Snelston, 2126, 2127.
Littilhalyn, in Yeldersley, 2718.
Littilmor, in Boythorpe, 359.
Littillwodfyld, in Ashleyhay, 106.
Littleover, **1544, 1545**, 1697.
Litton, 565, 1195, **1546-1551**, 2343, 2354, 2357, 2521.
Littondale, in Tideswell, 2340.
Lizdeygate, *v.* Lydgate.
Lochay, *v.* Locko.
Locko, **1552, 1553**.
Lodhil, in Codnor, 889.
Loftescot, nr. Repton, 536.
Lombrekotedich, in Egginton, 1171, 1172.
London (Chepe Street), 339.

——Dean and Chapter. 1952.

——Dean. Robert [de Watford] [1218-22], 1952.

——Monastery of Nuns Minoresses of St. Clare without Aldgate, 1348.

——Abbess. Dorothea Cumberford [1526], 1348.

Longecelowe, in Ashford, 95.
Longedoles, in Newton Solney, 1755, 1756.
Longedunastel, in Willington, 2590.
Longeford, *v.* Longford.
Longelaymeygnyll, Longelemeygnyll, etc., *v.* Langley, Meynell.
Longeley, *v.* Langley.
Longesdon, *v.* Longstone.
Longford, 382, 1155, 1359, 1512, **1554-1607**, 1629, 1631, 1645, 1874, 2711.

——Lords. Nigel [*temp.* Hen. III. or Edw. I.], 1629; Nicholas [1314-1316], 1569, 1571.

——Parsons. Mikael [early 13th cent.], 2001; Will. de Falford or Salford [1348-1362], 1578, 1580; John de Cressy [1390], 2416.

——Rectors. Will. de Falford [1348], 1578; John Cressy *al.* Crecy *al.* Cressy [1381-4], 77, 1582, 1645; Ric de Radclyf [1424], 1874.

Longford. Vicars. Geoffrey [1294],
1568, 2015; Will. le Cook [1380-
1401], 288, 1585; John Forthe
[1446], 2678; John [1456-7], 1512;
Edw. Reddeferne [1510], 1359.
Longford Woodhouses, 1568, 1572, 1574.
Longforth, *v.* Longford.
Longhayrowe, in Catton, 592.
Longisdon, *v.* Longstone.
Longley, *v.* Langley.
Longston, *v.* Longstone.
Longstone, Great and Little, 96, 194,
204, 1214, 1264, 1551, 1608-1618,
1860.
Loschowe, Losco, *v.* Loscoe.
Loscoe, 892, 905, 1619.
Loscowe, *v.* Loscoe.
Lostoke Wood, in Repton, 1980.
Loudeham Manor, in Riby, co. Linc.,
509.
Loughborough, co. Leic., Clerk.
Thomas [1172-81], 1945.
Loundmedowe, in Chesterfield, 874.
Louwe, The, Lowe, Le, in Boythorpe,
356, 372.
Ludwell in Wirksworth, Watercourse
of, 2701.
Luhteburht, *v.* Loughborough.
Lullington, 1028, 1322.
Lunbrok, in Barlow, 225.
Lutchurch, Luttechirche, *v.* Litchurch.
Lutlewodebroc, *v.* Littelwodebroc.
Lychefeld, Lychfield, *v.* Lichfield.
Lydgate, in Chesterfield, 645, 689.
Lyes, Le, in Norton, 1777.
Lylleshulle, *v.* Lilleshall.
Lyndon Wood, in Hassop, 1354.
Lyneysiche, in Derby, 995.
Lynford, *v.* Linford.
Lynnacre, *v.* Linacre.
Lynton, Lyntone, *v.* Linton.
Lyteldale, *v.* Litteldale.
Lytelhakwode, in Kirk Langley, 1530.
Lytillwallehyll, le, in Findern, 1280.
Lytton, *v.* Litton.

M.

Maafelt, *v.* Mayfield.
Mackeney, *v.* Makeney.
Mackeworth, *v.* Mackworth.
Mackley, 1620, 1621, ·2021, 2100.
Mackley Campion, 2288.
Mackley Wodhouses, 1621.
Mackworth, 677, 1521, 1622-1625, 1654,
1655, 1657, 1659, 1660, 1861.
————Parson. John de Assewell
[1376], 677, 1861.
————Rector. Simon Chuschet [*temp.*
Hen. III.], 1623.
————Vicar. Rob. Thacker [1549],
1625.
Macley, *v.* Mackley.
Macworth, *v.* Mackworth.
Maffelde, *v.* Mayfield.
Magge Howse, in Pinxton, 1886.

Mainardesholm, in Willington, 2568.
Makeley, *v.* Mackley.
Makeney, 1626-1628.
Makkeley, *v.* Mackley.
Makkeney, *v.* Makeney.
Makley, *v.* Mackley.
Makney, *v.* Makeney.
Makwith, Makworth, *v.* Mackworth.
Maldon Abbey, co. Essex. Abbot.
Henry [1187-8], 1079.
Malefeld, co. Staff., 77.
Malmarton, Malmerton, *v.* Mammerton.
Malpas, co. Ches., 530, 539.
————Clerks. Gilbert and Robert
[*t.* Steph.-Hen. II.], 530;
Gilbert [early 13th cent.],
539.
Maluerton, *v.* Mammerton.
Mammerton, 1554, 1559, 1565, 1602,
1629-1631.
Mammerton Woodhouses, 1591.
Manias, Manyasshe, *v.* Monyash.
Mapelton, Mapilton, *v.* Mappleton.
Maperlay, Maperleg', Maperleigh,
Maperley, *v.* Mapperley.
Mapirleye, *v.* Mapperley.
Mapperley, 281, 1632-1635, 2120.
————Lord. Rog. de Morteyn [*temp.*
Edw. I.], 1634.
Mappleton, 156, 157, 1636-1650, 2130,
2139, 2141, 2142, 2765, 2766.
————Lord. Rog. de Wednesleye
[1313-1341], 1637, 1639-
1643.
Mapulton, *v.* Mappleton.
Mapulton Croft, in Hognaston, 1382.
Mapurley, *v.* Mapperley.
Marchington, co. Staff., 596, 830, 1661,
1668, 2723.
————Chapel of St. John Baptist at,
597.
Marchyngton, Marchynton, *v.* Marching-
ton.
Marewall, in Foston, 1295, 1296.
Margerelone, in Boylestone, 345.
Markeaton, 1624, 1651-1660, 2667.
Markefeyld, *v.* Markfield.
Marketon, Marketun, *v.* Markeaton.
Markfield, co. Leic., 1008.
"Marledge," The, in Derby, 1014.
Mars, Le, in Repton, 1971.
Marsche, Ly, in Chapel-en-le-Frith, 647.
Marston Montgomery, 931, 2158, 2287.
Marston-upon-Dove, 1190, 1661, 1662-
1934.
————Vicar. John Agulun [1422],
1934.
Marthehyll, in Chesterfield, 689.
Marton, *v.* Markeaton.
Mathlac, *v.* Matlock.
Matlock, 878, 1543, 1663-1680, 2148,
2306, 2489, 2490, 2672.
Matlok, Matloke, Matlokhe, Mattlok,
etc., *v.* Matlock.
Maudune, *v.* Maldon.
Maupas, *v.* Malpas.
Mayfield, co. Staff., 1594, 2125.
————Vicar. Laurence Catton [1438],
1594.

Maykeberne, in Ashford, 98.
Measham, 602, **1681-1683**, 1784, 1953, 1957, 1961.
———Lord. Adam de Montealto [1278], 1961.
Mechell Rollesley, *v.* Rowsley.
Meddletone, Medilton, *v.* Middleton.
Meddwedil, in Tideswell, 2335.
Medovclyffe, in Birchover, 304.
Meeltone, *v.* Milton.
Meisham, *v.* Measham.
Melborne, *v.* Melbourne.
Melbourne, 533, 534, 914, 1349, **1684-1687**, 1752.
———Castle, 1687.
———Clerk. Baldwin [early Hen. II.], 534.
———Vicars. Rob. de Stanton [1278], 1961 ; W. Colverdowse [1408], 1980.
Melburn, Melburne, *v.* Melbourne.
Meldesham, 172.
Meleburna, *v.* Melbourne.
Meleton, Melton, *v.* Milton.
Melton Mowbray, co. Leic., 1345.
Mercaston, 83, 91, 137, 1526, **1688-1695**.
Mercinton, *v.* Marchington.
Mere, Le, in Rosliston, 2041.
Merivale Abbey, co. Warw., 678, 2023, 2028, 2033.
———Abbots. Will. de Wavere [*t.* Edw. I.], 2033 ; Will. Arnold [1535], 678.
Merketon, *v.* Markeaton.
Merston, *v.* Marston.
Merton [? Markeaton], 90.
Merwineswode, in Mickleover, 1698.
Mesham, *v.* Measham.
Meyele, in Ashbourne, 55.
Meygnylle Longley, *v.* Langley, Meynell.
Meysam, Meysham, Meysum, *v.* Measham.
Mickleover, **1696-1700**, **2767**, 1696.
———Vicar. R— de Burton [1226], 1696.
Middelton, *v.* Middleton.
Middilhil, in Parwich, 1819.
Middilton, *v.* Middleton.
Middleton, Stoney, 549, 1225, 1226, 1245-1247, 1250, 1252, 1261, 1264, **1701**, 2087.
Middleton-by-Wirksworth, 218, 1346, 1673, 1676, 1677, **1702**, 2649.
Middleton-by-Youlgreave, 321, **1703**.
Middleyton, Middylton, Midelton, etc., *v.* Middleton.
Mildenhall. Rector. Robert, Capellanus [*c.* 1254], 332.
Milton, nr. Repton, 536, **1704**, 1953, 1957, 1962, 1963, 1983-1985, 1989, 1991.
Minley, in Hope, 1439.
Miravalle, *v.* Merivale.
Mircaston, *v.* Mercaston.
Modinor, in Marchington, 2723.
Mogenton, Moginton, Mogynton, etc., *v.* Mugginton.
Mokholme, in Brimington, 497.

Molderigge, in Bradborne and Hartington, 395.
Monias, Moniasch, Moniash, Moniassch, etc., *v.* Monyash.
Monnesholme, in Doveridge, 1024.
Monsal Dale, 96, 1608, 1616-1618, 2350.
Monyash, 214, 1333, **1705-1725**.
———Chantry of the B. V. Mary at, 1720, 2736.
Monyashe, Monyassch, Monyasse, Monyassh, etc., *v.* Monyash.
Moorflatte, The, in Brampton, 812.
Morebarn, co. Leic., 638.
Moresbur', Moresburgh, Moresburoughe, Moresburugh, *v.* Mosborough.
More Syche, Le, in Repton, 1990, 1993, 1994.
Moreton, co. Staff., 1028.
Morewalles, in Snelston, 2143.
Morisburg, Morisburich, *v.* Mosborough.
Morisfeld, in Brampton, 442.
Morle, Morleg', *v.* Morley.
Morley, 894, 936, 957, 976, 1335, **1726**, 1916, 2123, 2193.
———Lord. John Saucheverell [1483], 957 ; Hen. Statham [*ante* 1487], 2123.
———Parson. Robert [*temp.* Hen. III.], 936.
Morleya, *v.* Morley.
Morleyhalleyerd, in Derby, 976.
Morlondes, Le, in Monyash, 1707.
Mornesale, Mornsall, *v.* Monsal Dale.
Morsbur', *v.* Mosborough.
Morton, 1605, 1869.
———Parson. Will. Smalley [1408], 1869.
Morton, co. Notts., 921.
Morwde, in Dale, 108.
Morwde, in Stretton, 2284.
Morysburg, Morysburgh, *v.* Mosborough.
Mosborough, 272, 275, **1727-1740**.
Mosburgh, *v.* Mosborough.
Mostylegh, in Dronfield, 1050.
Motlhaue, nr. Hartshorn, 2759.
Motterlone, in Ashbourne, 60.
Mugginton, 1526, 1688, 1690, 1692, **1741**, **1742**, 1924, 2547, 2548, 2552, 2602.
———Rectors. John [1256], 1688 ; Rob. le Burgilon [1290], 2547 ; John Whitehed [1380], 2607, 2609 ; Richard Bee [1431], 2602.
Muggyngton, *v.* Mugginton.
Mulneclif, in Atlow, 135, 137.
Murcaston, Murchamston, *v.* Mercaston.
Murchington Mongomery, *v.* Marston Montgomery.
Murkaliston, Murkaston, *v.* Mercaston.
Mursbur', *v.* Mosborough.
Muskham, Muscamp, co. Notts., 2098, 2120.
Myddelton, Mydelton, Mydleton, *v.* Middleton.
Myldenhale, *v.* Mildenhall.
Myrcaston, Myrkaston, *v.* Mercaston.

N.

Neddirhulle, Nedderhyll, in Chesterfield, 686, 706.
Neddurhull, in Dronfield, 1052.
Needwood, co. Staff., 74.
Nether-Boym, Le, in Rosliston, 2031.
Nethercross, at Tideswell, 2348.
Netherhaddon, *v.* Haddon, Nether.
Netherlokhaw, *v.* Locko.
Netherthorpe, *v.* Staveley.
Netherthurvaston, *v.* Thurvaston.
Neubald, *v.* Newbold.
Neubigging, *v.* Newbiggin.
Neubold, Neubolt, *v.* Newbold.
Neuhalhewelle, nr. Repton, 536.
Neut', *v.* Newton Solney.
Neuthorp, *v.* Newthorpe.
Neuton, *v.* Newton.
Neuton Sulny, *v.* Newton Solney.
Neuton - super - Trentam, *v.* Newton Solney.
Neuwerk, *v.* Newark.
Nevhalebarwe, in Walton, 2491.
Newark, co. Notts., 450, 789, 798, 1469, 1844.
Newbiggin and Hulland, 1115, 1470.
Newbold, 411, 695, 701, 711, 717, 729, 736, 737, 749, 750, 754, 757, 764, 770, 776-778, 788, 795, 797, 812, 817, 828, 842, 844, 846, 856, 863, 866, 878, 1115, 1533, 1534, **1743-1746**.
————Clerk. William [13th cent.], 2425.
Newbold Verdun, co. Leic., 602.
Newbolt, *v.* Newbold.
Newborough, co. Staff., 1190, 1668.
Newburgh, *v.* Newborough.
Newebold Verdune, *v.* Newbold Verdun.
Newerk, *v.* Newark.
Newested, *v.* Newstead.
Neweton Sulny, *v.* Newton Solney.
Newstead Abbey, co. Notts., 834, 1255, 1878-1880, 1882.
————Prior. Tho. Gunthorpe [1487-1489], 1878-1880.
Newsted, *v.* Newstead.
Newthorpe, co. Notts., 891.
Newton Grange, 1647, **1747-1751**.
Newton, King's, 533, 1685, **1752**.
Newton Solney, 1165, 1359, 1597-1600, **1753-1768**, 1869-1871, 1874, 1953, 1957, 1971.
————Lords. Norman de Solenei [*circ.* 1230], 1755, 1756; Alured de Solny [1304], 1758.
————Rector. Rob. de Aldeporte [1350-1], 296.
Newton Sony, *v.* Newton Solney.
Newton, co. Linc., 1235, 2265-2270.
Newton, co. Som., 491.
Nicolzerde, in Brimington, 510.
Nonneclose, *al.* Nonnefeld, *v.* Nunnefeld, in Crich.
Nonneley, Le, in Hope, 1442.

Norburi, *v.* Norbury.
Norbury, 1181, 1184, 1293, 1359, 1583, 1603, 1692, **1766-1771, 2768**.
————Rectors. Jordan [*temp.* Edw. I.], 1766; Hen. de Knyveton [1332], 1768; Tho. f. Nich. de Knyveton [1391], 1692; Hen. Knyveton [1416], 1769.
Normancroft, in Pinxton, 1875-1878, 1882.
Normandy, 1753.
Normanthun, *v.* Normanton.
Normanton, *v.* Normanton, Temple.
Normanton, 303, 1685, 2566.
Normanton next Southwell, co. Notts., 921.
————Chaplain of the Chapel of St. John B. and St. John Ev. [1368], 921.
Normanton, North, or Temple, 167-169, 465, 470, 509, 997, **1772-1774**.
Normanton, South, 1597-1599, 1605, 1863-1865, 1867-1871, 1873, 1885.
————Parson. Tho. Chelastone [1408], 1869.
————Rector. Tho. Suthworth [1524-5], 1885.
Normonston, *v.* Normanton, South.
Normonweye, nr. Willington, 2588.
Nortclyfe, in Wirksworth, 2668.
Northampton, co. of, 1899.
Northbroc, in Egginton, 1167, 1168.
Northbury, *v.* Norbury.
Northewynfeld, *v.* Wingfield, North.
Northpydill, *v.* Piddle, North.
Norton, 22, 23, 878, **1775-1783**, 2459, 2461, 2463.
————Lords. Tho. de Chauworth, Knt. [1352], 1776; Will. Chaworth [1377], 1777.
————Vicar. John Croke [1502], 1780.
Norton, co. Staff., 1028.
Norton, Little, 1778.
Norton Lees, 100, 878, 1779, 1782.
Notingeham, Notingham, *v.* Nottingham.
Nottingham, County of, 1193, 1278, 1588, 1594, 1597, 1605, 1879-1881.
————and Derby. Sheriffs. Will. Briwerre [*temp.* John] 1554; Eustace de Ludham [*c.* 1232], 1503; Rob. le Vavasur [*c.* 1245-55], 2195; Hugh de Babington [1272], 2199; John de Oxon' [1336], 201; Nich. Fitz-herbert [1458], 2240.
Nottingham Town, 181, 236, 369, 477, 485, 513, 525, 679, 682, 778, 902, 943, 950, 1246, 1336, 1338, 1487, 1490, 1503, 1554, 1697, 1699, 1947, 2064, 2120, 2193, 2198, 2334, 2742, 2743, 2747, 2749-2753, 2761, 2763, 2767, 2772-2776, 2778, 2779.
————Mayor. Tho. Mellours [1530], 525.

Notyngham, *v.* Nottingham.
Novus Locus, in Shirwood, *v.* Newstead.
Nuetona, *v.* Newton Solney.
Nunnefeld, in Crych, 923, 924.

O.

Oak Green, in Sudbury, 2288.
Oakthorpe, **1784.**
Ockbrook, **1785.**
Ockthorpe, *v.* Oakthorpe.
Odbroke, Oddebroc, 987, 1501.
Ofcote, *v.* Offcote.
Offcote, 60, 77, 79, 959, **1786, 1787.**
Offecote, *v.* Offcote.
Offerton, in Hope, 2, 408, 1448, **1788-1811.**
Offerton, Nether, "vel Kauereshegge," 1794.
Offertona, *v.* Offerton.
Offidecote, *v.* Offcote.
Offirton, Offirtun, Offorton, Offreton, *v.* Offerton.
Offtecote, *v.* Offcote.
Okebro, *v.* Ockbrook.
Okemedow, 1394, 1395.
Okeover, co. Staff., 136, 137, 153, 156-159, 161, 386, 1645, 1646, 2125, 2132, 2139, 2141, 2142.
———Chaplain. Hugh [1275 ?], 386.
Oker, *v.* Okeover.
Okkes, *v.* Oak Green.
Okor, Okore, Okouere, Okover, *v.* Okeover.
Oldefelde, 277.
Oldefeld Lancaans, in Willington, 2588.
Oldeofne, in Alsop-le-Dale, 34.
Ollersett, **1812.**
Ollershedde, *v.* Ollersett.
Olrinwelle, Le, in Totley, 2375.
Omerflat, in Egginton, 1178.
Oneston, Onestone, Onistone, *v.* Unstone.
Onston, Onstone, Onuston, *v.* Unstone.
Orby, co. Linc., 1761, 1864.
Orlewic, in Tadley, 2721.
Osberton, 1775.
Osgathorpe, co. Leic., 1028, 1726.
Oslaston, Oslaueston, *v.* Osliston.
Osliston, 1723, **1813,** 2383, 2385, 2390.
Osmaston-by-Derby, 90, 330, 1685, **1814,** 2197.
Osmondegreve, in Weston Underwood, 2551.
Osmundemedwe, Osmundismedwe, in Kedleston, 1501-1504.
Osmundestone, Osmundston, *v.* Osmaston.
Ouenston, Ounston, *v.* Unstone.
Ouerton, *v.* Overton.
Ouleclough, Le, in Atlow, 147.
Over, *v.* Mickleover.
Overbirched, *v.* Birchett.
Overhenmarshe, in Findern, 1280.

Overmill, in Drakelowe, 1027.
Overton, 110-112, 116, 118, 408, 1811, **1815.**
Ownwston, Ownstone, *v.* Unstone.
Oxebothem, in Tideswell, 2335.
Oxenyglands, in Duffield, 1120.
Oxford, County of, 583.
Oxford. Mayor. Richard de Garston [1388], 1922.
———Bailiffs. Walter Boldne, John Bereford [1388], 1922.
Oxfurlong, in Rosliston, 2034.
Oxmonnmedwe, in Catton, 580.
Oxton, co. Notts., 2120.
Oxwood, in Yeaveley, 2715.

P.

Packington, co. Leic., 2782, 2783.
Padeley, *v.* Padley.
Padley, 884, 1264, 1446.
Padley, Nether, **1816.**
Pakinton, *v.* Packington.
Paknage, in Brampton, 466, **1817.**
Paradis, Parodys, in Clifton, 75, 882.
Parco Stanle, de, *v.* Dale Abbey.
Parkefeld, in Handley, 1342.
Parkfeld, Le, in Derby, 979, 988.
Park Gate, nr. Whittington, 2558.
Parkehall, *v.* Parkhall.
Parkhall, in Ashover, 124, 1102, 1597-1599, 1601.
Parkhall, in Denby, 963, 964.
Parkshale, *v.* Parkhall.
Park Stanley, *v.* Dale Abbey.
Parodys, *v.* Paradis.
Parwich, 67, 77, 394, 1115, 1645, **1818-1823,** 2164, 2698.
Parwick, Parwych, *v.* Parwich.
Patecroft, in Codnor, 887.
Peak, The High, 515, 617, 619, 1346, 1426, 1493, **1824-1842.**
———Bailiffs. John Flemink [*t.* Hen. II. or Ed. I.], 405; Tho. Foleiambe [1273], 1612; Clement de la Ford [1305-1306], 515, 1430; Rob. Foleiaumbe [1338-1339], 555, 617; Hugh de Stredley [1345], 619; Thomas de Wombewelle [1376], 406.
———Forest. 1843, 1849, 1853.
———Foresters. Will le Eyr [1345], 1843; Hen. Vernon [1471], 1849.
Pecco, Villa castri de, *v.* Castleton.
Peck, Le haut, *v.* Peak, The.
Pedderflatt, in Castleton, 564.
Pekesarse, Pekeserse, Pekysars, Water of, 564, 1451.
Penchiston, Pencuston, Penkeston, *v.* Pinxton.
Pensford, co. Som., 491.
Percsacre, nr. Holumedue, in Bowden, 616.

Percy, Fee of, in Chesterfield, 687, 706, 855.
Perwich, Perwyche, *v.* Parwich.
Peteputtes, Le, in Rosliston, 2034.
Peuerwich, Peuirwich, Peuerwych, *v.* Parwich.
Peverel, Honour of, 308, 1853-1859.
Peverwich, *v.* Parwich.
Peytyate, nr. Ashleyhay, 105, 106.
Piddle, North, co. Worc., 489.
Pigktor, nr. Fairfield, 1272.
Pigotstorth, in Brampton, 418.
Pikelovere, in Staveley, 2243.
Pilateshul, in Trusley, 2382.
Piletlege, in Weston Underwood, 2551.
Pillesbury, *v.* Pilsbury.
Pillesley, *v.* Pilsley.
Pilsbury, 678, 1470.
Pilsley, in Edensor, 953, 1605, 1860, 1861.
Pinxton, 1597-1599, 1601, 1605, 1882-1886.
————Lady of. Dionisia le Wyne [1375], 1866.
Plaistow, 922, 1887-1892.
Plastowe, *v.* Plaistow.
Pleasley, 114, 1893-1899, 2283.
————Rector. William [late Hen. III.], 1893.
Pleselay, Plesele, Pleseley, Plesieleg, *v.* Pleasley.
Plomelay, Plomley, Plumbley, *v.* Plumley.
Plumley, 274, 467, 469, 1264, 1513, 1732, 1734.
Pocknedge, Pokenaye, *v.* Paknage.
Pokeneggezherd, in Sutton Scarsdale, 2293.
Pons Aldwini, in Chesterfield, 683.
Pontechester, at Derby, 2586.
Pontefract, co. York, 1696.
Portlokfeyld, in Radburne, 1919.
Postern, in Duffield, 1900.
Pothloc, Potlac, *v.* Potlock.
Potlocholm, in Egginton, 1171, 1172.
Potlock, in Willington, 1179, 1180, 1954, 1986, 2577, 2587, 2598, 2756.
Potlock Brook, in Repton, 1986.
Potlock, nr. Chesterfield (?), 1774.
Potlockross, in Willington, 2586.
Potloke meadow, in Hilton, 1380.
Potterlane, in Staveley, 2257.
Potterraw, in Chesterfield, 849.
Potter Somersale, *v.* Somersall, Potter.
Pottloke, *v.* Potlock.
Preez, Dez, Priory of, *v.* under Derby.
Presclif, *v.* Priestcliffe.
Prestbury, co. Ches. Vicar. John Doncalfe [1512], 1812.
Prestcleve, Prestclif, Prestcliff, Prestclyffe, *v.* Priestcliffe.
Presteclef, Prestecleve, Prestclif, Prestecliff, Presteclyve, *v.* Priestcliffe.
Presteridhing, in Duckmanton, 1092.
Prestlyff, *v.* Priestcliffe.
Prestwoode, in Repton, 1980.
Priestcliffe, 510, 671, 672, 674, 1333, 1901-1913, 2299, 2300.

Publon, *v.* Publow.
Publow, co. Som., 491.
Pykestonlondes, Le, in Alsop-le-Dale, 34.
Pykmancroft, nr. Duckmanton, 1112.
Pyllesley, Pyllysley, *v.* Pilsley.
Pynhul, in Alsop-le-Dale, 34.
Pynkeston, Pynkston, *v.* Pinxton.

Q.

Quarell Poole, in Repton, 1996.
Quarndon, 1914-1916.
Quarundon, Quernedon, *v.* Quarndon.

R.

Radbourne, 1179, 1247, 1505, 1545, 1654, 1742, 1917-1936.
————Lord. John de Chandos [*temp.* Edw. I.], 1545.
————Rector. John Brewode [1408-11], 1505, 1654, 1930-1932.
Radcliffe, Radclyf, *v.* Ratcliffe.
Radford, co. Notts. Dean. H—[1226], 1696.
————Vicars. R— [1252], 186; Will. de Alfertone [1405], 2670.
Radmanthuayt, in Pleasley, 1898.
Rapandune, Rapendon, Rapendun, etc., *v.* Repton.
Ratcliffe-on-Soar, 283, 1542.
Ratcliff-on-Trent, co. Notts., 2120.
Ratford, *v.* Radford.
Rauenesdal, in Yeldersley, 2718.
Raulinsford, in Tansley, 2302.
Raunds, co. Northt., 1668.
Rauseterr, *v.* Rocester.
Readseats, *v.* Redseats.
Rearsby, co. Leic., 114.
————Persona. Roger Chaumberleyn [1311], 33.
Reddesle, Reddisle, *v.* Rodsley.
Redebanke, in Walton, 1027.
Redeclyf, 677.
Redhul, in Measham, 1682.
Redisle, Redislege, Redisleye, *v.* Rodsley.
Redseats, in Castleton, 559, 561, 563, 565, 567, 568, 1450.
Redsettes, Reedseyts, Reidseates, *v.* Redseats.
Repedon, Rependon, Rependone, *v.* Repton.
Repindon, Repingdon, Reppingdon, *v.* Repton.
Repton Hundred, 1937.
Repton, 491, 531, 1938-1996, 2070, 2073, 2778.
————Chapel of St. Mary at, 1978.
————Chapel of St. Thomas at, 1948.
————Chaplain. Reginald [*t.* John-Hen. III.], 2571.
————Church and Priory, 535, 536, 541, 1681, 1683, 1704, 1755, 1756, 1758, 1765, 1938-1940, 1942-1954, 1956-

1973, 2334, 2569-2573, 2575, 2579, 2581, 2583, 2779.
Repton. Clerk. Stephen [early Hen. II.], 537, 1940.
———Personæ. Nicholas, Geoffrey, Turch [1153-60], 1939.
———Priors. Robert [1153·60], 1939; Nicholas [1172-81], 1945; A— [1199-1218], 1949; John [1218-21], 2572; Nicholas [1215-23], 1681; Reginald [c. 1230], 1755, 1756; John [early Hen. III.], 2576; Peter [1252], 2583; Robert [1289, t. Edw. I.], 1704, 1964; S. de Sutton [1347], 541; W. Maneysyn [1411], 1982; J. Wylne [1448], 489, 490; J. Yonge [1523], 1995; John [1528], 1765.
———Sacerdotes. Stephen [t. Hen. II.], 534; Humphrey, William [1172-81], 1945.
Repund', Repynden, Repyndon, Repyngdon, Repyngton, v. Repton.
Rerisby, Rerysby, v. Rearsby, co. Leic.
Rewestones, Le, in Alsop-le-Dale, 31.
Reynaldbrigge, Revnolf's Bridge, in Duckmanton, 684, 1111.
Rhuddlan, co. Flint, 193.
Riby, co. Linc., 2521.
Ridge Hall, Chapel-en-le-Frith, 635, 641.
Ridge, The; v. Ridge Hall.
Riecroft (?), in Heage, 2761.
Riele, v. Riley.
Rihill, in Chesterfield, 700.
Riley, in Scarcliffe, 1237, 1774, 2771.
Ringweye, in Parwich, 1819.
Rischeton, v. Rushton.
Risley, 1997-2000.
Robcroft, in Duckmanton, 1110.
Rocester, co. Staff., 2323.
———Abbey, 1382, 2133, 2134, 2137, 2151.
———Abbot. Henry [1439], 2133, 2134.
———Canon. Ralph Basset [early 13th cent.], 244.
Rodbourne, Rodburn, Roddebourn, Roddeburn, Roddeburne, v. Radbourne.
Roddesle, Roddesley, Roddesleye, v. Rodsley.
Roddislee, Roddislegh, Roddisley, Roddusley, v. Rodsley.
Rodeborn, Rodeburn, v. Radbourne.
Roderham, v. Rotherham.
Roder, River, 777, 2263, 2264, 2315.
Rodesle, Rodeslege, Rodesleye, Rodisle, Rodisleya, v. Rodsley.
Rodmanthuayt, v. Radmanthuayt.
Rodsley, 1145, 1146, 1150, 1156, 1567, 1602, 2001-2021, 2711.
Rodur, R., v. Roder.
Rodyche, v. Rowditch.
Rogerflat, in Boythorpe, 358.
Roggwaygate, Le, in Barlow, 224.

Roland, v. Rowland.
Rollesley, v. Rowsley.
Rolleston, co. Staff., Clerk. Ralph [t. Edw. I.], 1292.
Rolond, v. Rowland.
Rolston, v. Rolleston.
Romley Hall, in Clown, 223, 884.
Roslaston, Rosleston, v. Rosliston.
Rosliston, 913, 914, 1322, 1955, 2022-2079.
———Chaplain. Henry Mareys [1380], 2050.
Rossyngton, Rossynton, v. Roston.
Rostelaston, Rosteleston, v. Rosliston.
Rostherne, co. Chest., 1588, 1591, 1594, 1868.
———Parson. Rog. Venables [1429-1430], 1588, 1591, 1594.
Rostlaston, Rostlaveston, Rostlavestona, Rostlaweston, v. Rosliston.
Rostliston, v. Rosliston.
Roston, 1766, 1767, 2080, 2081, 2768.
Rothelanum, v. Rhuddlan.
Rotherham, co. York, 812, 1129, 2446.
———College of Jesus at, 2280.
Rotherfield Peppard, co. Oxon., 928, 2387.
Rothlaston, v. Rosliston.
Rotington, Rotyngton, v. Roston.
Rough Moore, in Longford, 1606.
Rouheloweflat, Le, in Atlow, 144-146.
Roulesley, Roulisley, v. Rowsley.
Rounton, v. Roston.
Routhstorne, v. Rostherne.
Rowdicke, in Catton, 572.
Rowditch, in Derby, 997, 1697.
Roweshagge, in Barlow, 237.
Roweswood, in Barlow, 237.
Rowland, 96, 1264, 1551, 2082-2087.
Rowmly, v. Romley Hall.
Rowset', v. Rocester.
Rowsley, 868, 1333, 1718, 2088, 2089.
Rowstorne, v. Rosthern.
Roxlaueston, v. Rosliston.
Rucfordia, v. Rufford.
Rufford, co. Notts., 2098.
———Abbey, 6, 516, 2098.
Rugebrok, le, in Atlow, 147.
Rugeley, co. Staff., 179.
Rughedich, v. Rowditch.
Rugweye, Le, in Alsop-le-Dale, 34.
Rushden, co. Northt., 754, 1668.
———Rector. Rob. de Birchovere [1366], 754.
Rusmareis, 1824.
Rutherfeld Pippard, v. Rotherfield Peppard.
Ruyland, Ruylonde, in Catton, 576, 592, 593, 597, 598.
Ryby, v. Riby.
Ryches, Le, in Boythorpe, 373.
Ryddyngpark Close, in Knyveton, 394.
Rydge, Le, v. Ridge Hall.
Ryecroft, in Markeaton, 1652.
Rygewey Rawe, in Brampton, 464.
Ryhull, nr. Bolsover, 308.
Rylee Syke, in Dronfield, 1052.
Ryleghleyes, in Eyam, 1217.

Ryley, in Eyam, 1218, 1219, 1222, 1244, 1245, 1247, 1251, 1252, 1254, 1257, 1258, 1266.
Ryley, Ryleye, *v.* Riley.
Rysevey, Le, in Mosborough, 1731.
Rysley, Ryssley, *v.* Risley.

S.

Sabyneheye Wood, in Birchover, 292.
St. Loe, co. Som., 491.
Saintmareleys, in Chesterfield, 874.
Salford Yard, in Castleton, 566.
Sallo, Sallowe, *v.* Sawley.
Salop, County of, 1193, 1605.
Salopesbir', *v.* Shrewsbury.
Salteresford, in Tideswell, 2340.
Saltergate, in Chesterfield, *v.* under Chesterfield.
Sandeacre, *v.* Sandiacre.
Sandiacre, 936, 940, 941, 944, 945, 1469, 2090-2096, 2294, 2769, 2770.
————Prebendary of. John Cheyne [1404], 944.
Sandiakyr, Sandyacre, *v.* Sandiacre.
Sardelova, *v.* Shardlow.
Sawley, 944, 1692, 2097, 2601.
————Vicar. Will. Beke [1391], 1692.
Saxondale, co. Notts., 1469.
Scalecros, *v.* Shalcross.
Scarcliff, 916, 2098, 2099, 2771.
————Persona. Rob. Daincurt, early 13th cent., 916.
————Vicar. John Rey [1545], 2276.
Scardclif, Scardeclif, Scardeclive, *v.* Scarcliff.
Scaresdalle, Scarresdall, *v.* Scarsdale.
Scarsdale, 1080, 1859.
Scarsdale, Hundred of, 1854.
————Wapentake of, 679, 1856.
Scartclyffe, *v.* Scarcliffe.
Scaruesdale, *v.* Scarsdale.
Sceggebroc, 536.
Schadhawe, in Ticknall, 1968.
Schardelowe, *v.* Shardlow.
Schatton, *v.* Shatton.
Scheafeld, Scheffeld, Schefuld, *v.* Sheffield.
Scheilmarton, *v.* Chelmorton.
Schene, *v.* Sheen.
Schephouscroftus, Le, in Longford, 1572.
Schercesti, Le, in Newton Solney, 1758.
Schertwod, in Wyaston, 1148, 1149.
Schippeleg', *v.* Shipley.
Schirebroc, Schirbrok, *v.* Shirebrook.
Schirley, *v.* Shirley.
Schokthorn, *v.* Shuckthorne.
Schuchawe, in Hartshorn, 540.
Schurthehul, Le, in Longford, 1573.
Schypley, *v.* Shipley.
Scippeleg', *v.* Shipley.
Scirebroc, *v.* Shirebrook.
Scleford, *v.* Sleaford.
Scolbrok, 53, 56, 61, 69, 75.
Scorthedoles, in Newton Solney, 1756.
Scoulewode, in Scarcliff, 2099.
Scrittendoles, in Staveley, 2243.

Scropton, 1288, 1289, 1297, 1301, 1303, 1305, 2100-2113.
Scroptone, Scroptun, *v.* Scropton.
Seal, co. Leic. Parson. William, early Hen. III., 2023.
Sedirsalle, *v.* Sedsall.
Sedsall, 1122, 1179, 2114, 2115, 2323.
Segeshale, Seggesale, Seggeshale, *v.* Sedsall.
Sellyok, 1042.
Semerplace, in Egginton, 1184, 1188, 1189.
Semmeloia Manor, nr. Ednaston, 1159.
Sempringham Priory, co. Lincs., 414.
Sendiacre, *v.* Sandiacre.
Seneston, *v.* Shenstone.
Sercehaia, in Repton, 1948.
Serdelaw, *v.* Shardlow.
Serleparroc, in Overton, 116.
Seton-in-Spaldingmoor, co. York, 1028.
Seyla, *v.* Seal.
Shalcross, 657, 2161.
Shalcrus, *v.* Shalcross.
Shardlow, 1726, 2116, 2772.
Shatton, 221, 408, 1430, 1446, 1804, 1811, 2117-2119.
Sheen, co. Staff., 2132.
Sheffield, co. York, 243, 795, 1126, 1129, 1230.
————Vicar. John Plesaunce [1483], 1129.
Sheladon, *v.* Sheldon.
Sheldesley, *v.* Shelsley.
Sheldon, 97, 101, 615, 1333, 1703.
Shelladon, *v.* Sheldon.
Shelsley, co. Worc. Lord. John le Walsshe [1354], 1703.
Shenston, *v.* Shenstone.
Shenstone, co. Staff., 179, 853, 854.
Shipeley, *v.* Shipley.
Shipley, 281, 1487, 1623, 2120.
Shirebrook, 1895, 2121, 2773.
Shirleg', *v.* Shirley.
Shirley, 1602, 2122.
Shrewsbury. Archdeacons. Robert [1196-1208], 1082; Peter de Radnoure [*c.* 1254], 189.
Shrubbe Wood, in Repton, 1980.
Shuckthorne, in Crich, 922, 1889.
Shydyerd, 1812.
Skitering, in Kedleston, 1501.
Skolobrok, *v.* Scolbrok.
Smalenithynges, Les, in Monyash, 1708.
Smale Water, in Chesterfield, 413, 817, 1744.
Smalley, 1726, 2123.
Smisby, 541, 1953, 1957, 2124.
————Chapel of, 536.
————Church of St. Mary Magdalen at, 541.
————Lord. John de Schepeye [1347], 541.
Smitesby, Smithesbi, *v.* Smisby.
Smithistychil, Smythistychil Lane, in Tibshelf, 2325, 2327.
Smythesby, *v.* Smisby.
Snaidhinges, in Scarcliffe, 2771.
Snape, in Muskham, co. Notts., 2098.
Snellaston, *v.* Snelston.

Snellefeld, co. Staff., 77.
Snellesdone, Snelleston, v. Snelston.
Snellislund, co. Linc., 114.
Snelston, 156-159, 161, 165, 931, 1645, 1646, 1768, 2125-2143, 2288.
————Lord. Will. Akover [*circ.* 1350], 931.
Sneterton, v. Snitterton.
Sneynton-juxta-Notyngham, 2060, 2061.
Snitterton, 949, 1481, 1670, 2144-2143.
Snuterton, Snyterton, v. Snitterton.
Somerlees, Somerlese, Somerleys, Somurles, v. Summerley, in Unstone.
Somersall, in Brampton, 2149, 2150.
Somersall Herbert, 2151-2169.
————Rector. Rob. Attebrok [1439], 2165.
Somersall, Hill, 930.
Somersall, Potter, 930, 2164, 2288.
Somersall Wodehousus, 2158.
Sorrunhed, in Catton, 572.
Soton in Dal, v. Sutton Scarsdale.
Soutergate, Souter Row, etc., in Chesterfield, v. under Chesterfield.
Southwood, in Breadsall, 480, 481.
Southwood, in Duffield, 1115.
Southwood, in Repton, 1956.
Spart, Le, in Foston, 1293.
Spinkes, in Thurvaston, 2321.
Spinkhill, 1513, 2170, 2277.
Spondon, 607, 614, 677, 1115, 1528, 1530, 1861, 2171-2191, 2355, 2366.
————Vicars. M. de Kirkeby [*t.* Hen. III.], 2171; J. de Twyford, 677, 1861, 2182, 2183, 2352.
Sporwell, in Stanley, 2193.
Spoundon, v. Spondon.
Sprolezerde, in Chesterfield, 804.
Spynkhill, etc., v. Spinkhill.
Spytell, The, in Castleton, 567, 568.
Stafford, County of, 965, 967, 1588, 1594, 1597, 1645.
Staginnebrugge, in Willington, 2586.
Stainborough, co. York., 550.
Stainsby, 2192.
Stainton, co. Linc., 114.
Stainton, v. Stanton.
Staley, Staley Woodthorp, v. Staveley.
Stamfridenmuth, nr. Hartington, 1346.
Stanclif, v. Stancliffe.
Stancliffe, in Darley, 949.
Stanford, co. Notts., 1008.
Stanle, Stanley, Stanley Park, v. Stanley.
Stanley, 280, 941, 1345, 1785, 1879, 1880, 2193, 2774.
————v. also Dale Abbey.
Stanshope, co. Staff., 2366.
Stanton-by-Dale, 1453, 1487, 2194-2211.
Stanton, co. Staff., 2130.
Stantoneleaghes, Stantoneleesse, Stantonlege, Stantonleyes, etc., v. Stanton-in-the-Peak.
Stanton-in-the-Peak, Stanton Lees, Stanton Woodhouse, 296, 300, 953, 1844, 2212-2237, 2735, 2775.
Stanton in Youlgrave, 300.

Stanton-on-Trent. Clerk. William [late Hen. II.], 537.
Stanton, Stoney, co. Leic., 2295.
Stantune Slade, in Ash, 50.
Stapenhill, 2238-2240.
————Vicar. Ri. Pollesworth [1402], 2239.
Stapenhull, v. Stapenhill.
Stapilford, v. Stapleford.
Stapleford, co. Notts., 1123, 2120.
————Rector. Roger, capellanus, [*c.* 1254], 332.
Stapley, co. Chest., 2366.
Stapunhull, v. Stapenhill.
Stauely, v. Staveley.
Staunford, v. Stanford, co. Notts.
Staunton, v. Stanton-by-Dale.
Stauntoneleygh, v. Stanton-in-the-Peak.
Stavelay, v. Staveley.
Staveley, 223, 228, 233, 319, 458, 770, 817, 884, 964, 1047, 1128, 1198, 1341-1343, 1345, 1513, 2170, 2241-2280, 2473, 2478, 2480, 2558.
————Chaplain. Alan [1207], 228, 2242.
————Lords. Ankerus Frechuille [1355], 1341; Peter Freccheuyle [1468], 1342.
————Parsons. Roger [1346], 2080; Ric. Frechwell [1412], 2253.
————Prepositus. Peter de Cestria [1282-98], 1198.
————Rector. Ri. Wryght [1489], 2260.
Staveley Woodthorpe, v. Woodthorpe.
Staverley, v. Staveley.
Staynburgh, v. Stainborough.
Stede, v. Stydd.
Steeple, in Wirksworth, 2649.
Steineston, v. Stenson.
Stenson, 2281, 2411, 2764.
Steppestonlane, in Chesterfield, 741.
Stepul, v. Steeple.
Steresplace, Le, in Repton, 1975.
Sterndale, in High Peak, 559.
Stevenethornehaie, (?) in Heage, 2762.
Steverdale, 677, 2233.
Steymerebrugge, in Willington, 2584, 2591.
Steynesby, v. Stainsby.
Steyneston, Steynston, v. Stenson.
Steynisby, v. Stainsby.
Steyntone, v. Stainton.
Stirkesmor, in Wyaston, 1148, 1149.
Stobbing, Le, in Offerton, 1793.
Stockwith, co. Notts., 1469.
Stoke, by Stony Middleton, 2776.
Stoke. Clericus. Lamfram [1172-81], 1945.
Stokholme, 2266-2270.
Stokkesbrokefeld, in Derby, 1003.
Stolbilley, v. Stubley.
Stondelf, The, in Chesterfield, 718.
Stone, co. Staff., 1491.
Stoney Houghton, 2282, 2283.
Stonforye, in Boythorpe, 362.
Stoniflat, in Longford, 1556.
Storeston, v. Sturston.

Storth House, nr. Totley, 2374, 2375.
Storth, Le, in Offerton, 1799, 1800, 1807.
Stourston, *v.* Sturston.
Stowe. Rector. Robert, 13th cent., 477.
Stranley Espart Manor, in Repton, 1983.
Strelley, co. Notts., 2120.
Strethelbuc, in Scarcliffe, 2771.
Stretton, 108, **2284, 2285,** 2410.
————Persona. William [*circ.* 1229-1260], 48.
Stretton, Little, 2378.
Stretton-on-Dunsmore, co. Warw., 596.
Stubbing, nr. Wingerworth, 2604.
Stubbyng, in Ashover, 117.
Stubbyng, in Dronefeld, 1038.
Stubley. Clerk. John, late 13th cent., 2374.
Sturston, 77, 90, 142, 396, 399, 401, 402, 959, 960, 1532, 2717.
Stydd, in Yeaveley, 2715.
Styrton, *v.* Sturston.
Suartlincot, *v.* Swadlincote.
Suclowe, in Litton, 1548.
Sudbury, 345, 930, 1289, 1354, 2158, 2162-2164, **2286-2288.**
————Lord. Walt. de Montegomery [1318, 1349], 2158, 2162.
————Parson. Thos. Okeyly [1423], 2164.
————Rectors. John Steel [1381], 1354; James Graver [1486], 2089.
Sudlegh, in Boythorpe, 352.
Sudstubbinges, in Scarcliffe, 2772.
Sulghl'. Clerk. Geoffrey [*temp.* Ric. I.-John], 1083.
Summerley, in Unstone, 2437, 2465, 2479.
Surstant, *v.* Sturston.
Susane Welle, in Newbold, 1745.
Sutbrok, in Staveley, 2243.
Suthwode, *v.* Southwood.
Sutona, or Sutthona, super Soram, *v.* Sutton Bonnington.
Sutton, co. Linc., 1668.
Sutton, co. Notts., 1469.
Sutton Bonnington, co. Notts., 537-539.
Sutton in Dal, *v.* Sutton Scarsdale.
Sutton Scarsdale, 1339, 1469, 1881, 1884, **2289-2294.**
————Rectors. William [1333], 2291; Will. Bentte [1490], 1881.
Sutton-super-Soram, *v.* Sutton Bonnington.
Swadlincote, **2777.**
Swarkestone, 1181, 1184, 1188, 1189, 1364, 1683, 1685, **2295.**
————Parson. Rob. Pole [*ante* 1417], 1181.
Swarthlinghay Wood, in Newton Solney, 1755, 1756.
Swathwick, nr. Wingerworth, 878.
Swerkeston, Swerkston, *v.* Swarkestone.
Swetbroke, in Markeaton, 1293, 1652.
Swoddale, Swootall, nr. Hackenthorpe, 467, 506.

Swyndale, in Ashford, 94, 98.
Sydale, in Derby, 994, 995.
Syffonhil, in Kirk Hallam, 1334.
Syortegrave, near Mickleover, 1697.
Syk, Le, in Derby, 979.
Syleneston, *v.* Snelston.
Sywardeparroc, in Ashover, 111, 120.

T.

Taddington, 510, 884, 1333, 1908, 1909, **2296-2301.**
Taddyngton, Tadenton, Tadington, Tadinton, *v.* Taddington.
Tadley, in Ashbourne, 2721.
Tadyngton, Tadynton, *v.* Taddington.
Tamworth, co. Staff., 536.
Tanesley, Tannesley, Tanselay, Tannysley, *v.* Tansley.
Tansley, **2302-2307,** 2489, 2490, 2700.
Tanysley, *v.* Tansley.
Tappeton, *v.* Tapton.
Tapton, 501, 506, 509, 695, 701, 711, 746, 770, 842, 844, 863, 878, **2308-2317.**
Taptonlane, in Chesterfield, 712.
Tateshalle, *v.* Tattershall.
Tatteshall, co. Linc., 1067, 1340.
————Lord of. Matilda de Cromwell [1417], 1340.
Tatteshale, *v.* Tattershall.
Tatynton, *v.* Taddington.
Teddeswell, Tediswell, *v.* Tideswell.
Temple Dynnesley, co. Hertf., 1093.
Tetenall, *v.* Tetenhall.
Tetenhall, co. Staff., 1027.
Tetwick, *v.* Todwick.
Thacholm, in Egginton, 1164, 1167.
Thawthwyk, *v.* Swathwick.
Theveholme, in Longford, 1583.
Thikclif, in Scarcliff, 2099.
Thirlby, *v.* Thurlby.
Thisker, in Mugginton, 1741.
Thopton, *v.* Tupton.
Thoresby, co. Linc., 1668.
Thormondeslee, *v.* Turmundel.
Thornawe, in Hope, 1422-1425.
Thornborough, co. Buck., 1712.
Thorneburgh, *v.* Thornborough.
Thorne, co. York, 847.
Thornesett, Thorneseyt, *v.* Thornsett.
Thornhill, in Hope, 220, **2318.**
Thornhyll, *v.* Thornhill.
Thornsett, 953, 954, 1447, 1448, 1808.
Thornsyt, *v.* Thornsett.
Thoroley, *v.* Throwley.
Thorpe, 172.
————Parson. John Cressy [1362], 1580.
Thorpe, in Hathersage, **2319, 2320.**
Thorpe-Bassett, co. York. Parson. Will. de Wynfeld [1396-1400], 791, 797.
Thrompton, Thromptone, *v.* Thrumpton.
Throwley, co. Staff., 2184, 2185, 2191, 2355, 2366.
Throwsley, *v.* Throwley.

Thrumpton, co. Notts., 1123, 1321.
Thurgarton Manor, co. Notts., 921.
———Priory. 921, 1869.
Thurghaveston, *v.* Thurvaston.
Thurlby, co. Linc., 1028.
Thurleston, *v.* Thurlston.
Thurlston, 1179, 1320.
Thurvaston, 1554, 1813, **2321-2324.**
Thuttesbiri, *v.* Tutbury.
Thyldreslege, *v.* Yeldersley.
Tibbeschelf, Tibbeshelf, Tibeschelf, Tibschef, *v.* Tibshelf.
Tibshelf, 1083, **2325-2333,** 2378.
———Clerk. Robert, *temp.* Ric. I.-John, 1083.
———Vicar. Symon de Tybeschelf [1370], 2332.
Tichehale, 536.
Tickhill, co. York, 1845.
Ticknall, 77, 1758, 1953, 1956, 1957, 1962, 1968, 1983-1985, 2295, **2334, 2778, 2779.**
Tiddeswalle, Tiddeswell, Tiddiswall, *v.* Tideswell.
Tideswell, 183-185, 553, 556, 627, 673, 1195, 1237, 1252, 1254, 1257-1259, 1264, 1282, 1419, 1428, 1431, 1461, 1462, 1466, 1546, 1551, 1618, 1798, 1826, 1833, 1835, 1860, 2117, **2335-2372,** 2405.
———Chapel and Church of. 178, 179, 184, 189, 214, 627, 1419, 1421, 1426, 1428, 1431, 1546, 2335, 2337-2339, 2346, 2354, 2357.
———Vicars. Alan [1214-1222], 1546; John Extraneus [*c.* 1250], 2338; Rog. le Gode, [1301], 2344; L. de Schryvenham [*ante* 1360], 1860; W. Purseglowes [1441], 2360; T. Taillour [1473], 2366; Edm. Eyre [1512-1516], 1551, 2319.
———St. Mary's Guild, 2356.
Tideswelle, Tidewell, Tidiswell, Tidwell, Tidswell, *v.* Tideswell.
Tikenhale, Tikenhall, *v.* Ticknall.
Tilderesseg', Tildessleye, Tildresley, *v.* Yeldersley.
Tissington, 38, 392, 1612, 1647, **2373.**
Tissinton, *v.* Tissington.
Todepole, in Staveley, 1343.
Todick, co. York. Rector. Will. de Staveley [1385], 780.
Tonghul, in Catton, 573.
Tonstyd Mylne, in Bowden, 646.
Topsor, in Wirksworth, 2685.
Topton, *v.* Tupton.
Torlowe, in Thurvaston, 2321.
Totenley, Totinley, *v.* Totley.
Totesbere, Totesbiri, Totesbure, *v.* Tutbury.
Tothebuttes, in Egginton, 1178.
Tothesbire, *v.* Tutbury.
Totley, 1412, 1741, **2374-2379.**
Totteley, Tottynley, *v.* Totley.
Tounstede, *v.* Tunstead.

Treeton, co. York. Rector. Hen. Stafford [1473], 464.
Trengeston, *v.* Thringston.
Trent, R. 1027, 1757, 1758.
Trentham Priory, co. Staff. Prior. Thomas [1427], 1489.
Treton, *v.* Treeton.
Trossele, *v.* Trusley.
Trowell, co. Notts., 2120.
Truslegh, Trusleh, Trusleye, *v.* Trusley.
Trusley, 1179, 1203-1205, 1606, 1654, 1813, 1925, 1934, **2380-2403.**
———Rectors. Simon, early 13th cent., 2385, 2569; T. Steynton [*ante* 1475], 2396; Nich. Brandewodde [1475], 2396.
Trusselay, Trussele, Trusselega, *v.* Trusley.
Trusseleia, Trusseleie, Trusseley, Trusseleye, *v.* Trusley.
Tudeswell, *v.* Tideswell.
Tukysford in le Cley, *v.* Tuxford.
Tulcroft, in Ash, 50.
Tunstead, 2300, 2301, 2350, **2404-2408.**
Tunstede, Tunstedes, *v.* Tunstead.
Tupton, 409, 507, 508, **2409, 2410.**
Turmundel, nr. Trusley, 2381, 2382.
Tunecroft, in Bowden, 622, 625, 626, 632, 646, 648, 652.
Turnesthagh, Le, in Brampton, 450.
Turuerdestona, *v.* Thurvaston.
Tustedus, Le, in Chelmorton, 675.
Tutbury, co. Staff., 239, 1114, 1159, 1165, 1177, 1190, 1200, 1292, 1314, 1362, 1363, 1365-1369, 1544, 1668, 1698, 2100, 2106, 2295.
———Castle, 1304, 1668.
———Constable. Nich. de Breideshale [1223-1229], 1698.
———Honor of. 514, 1668.
———Priors. Richard [*circ.* 1170], 1360; Bartholomew [1200-35], 1159, 1544, 2125, 2575; Nicholas [*c.* 1230], 2718; Rob. de Longdon [1321], 1365.
———Priory. 1159, 1190, 1200, 2125.
———Stewards. Tho. le Bray [*temp.* Edw. I.], 1292; Sir Marmaduke Constable [1485], 514.
———Vicar. Hen. de Mershton [1372], 2106.
Tutbury Woodhouse, co. Staff., 1028.
Tutesbire, Tuttebure, Tuttebury, Tuttesbury, *v.* Tutbury.
Tuxford, co. Notts., 272, 273.
Twiford, *v.* Twyford.
Twyford, 1083, **2411,** 2600, 2763, 2764.
Tybeschelf, Tybeschulfe, Tybeself, *v.* Tibshelf.
Tydd', Tyddeswall, Tyddeswalle, Tyddeswell, *v.* Tideswell.
Tydduswell, Tyddyswell, *v.* Tideswell.
Tydeswel, Tydeswelle, Tydiswell, Tydyswall, etc., *v.* Tideswell.
Tykehall, 1896.

Tykenale, Tykenhale, *v.* Ticknall.
Tykhill, *v.* Tickhill.
Tykynhale, *v.* Ticknall.
Tyssinton, Tyssyngton, Tystyngton, *v.* Tissington.

U.

Ufton, nr. N. Wingfield, 2605-2609.
Underwode, *v.* Underwood.
Underwood, in Ashbourne, 51, 56, 77-79, 143, 162, 959, 1664, 1693, **2412-2417**.
Undrewode, *v.* Underwood.
Unstone, 133, 878, 1042, 1069, 1780, **2418-2485**.
————Lord. John de Grey [1342], 1042.
Urlewyke, in Ashbourne, 162, 2723, 2726.
Uttokeshather, *v.* Uttoxeter.
Uttoxeter, co. Staff., 42, 965, 967, 1023, 1668.
————Bailiff. Will. Perkyn [1439-1460], 2165, 2166.
————Chaplain of. Rob. f. Rob. f. Rogeri [1348], 1023.

V.

Vannes, in Britanny, 2407.
Vendiles, Le, in Catton, 572.
Vycar Lane, in Horsley, 1459.
Vymoremedowe, in Catton, 597.

W.

"Wacellum," in Dale, 941.
Wache Grene, in Thurvaston, 2321.
Wackbrydge, *v.* Wakebridge.
Wadchelf, *v.* Wadshelf.
Waddeley, *v.* Waldley.
Wadescelf, Wadscholf, *v.* Wadshelf.
Wadshelf, 244, 446, 447, 470, **2486, 2487**.
Wadsholf, *v.* Wadshelf.
Waith, co. Linc., 1668.
Wakebridge, 922, 923, 1543, 1679, 1892, 2304-2306, **2488-2490**, 2555, **2780**.
Wakbrigge, Wakbrug, Wakbrygge, *v.* Wakebridge.
Wakebrug, Wakebruge, Wakebrugge, *v.* Wakebridge.
Waldley, in Marston Montgomery, 2288.
Walenton, *v.* Walton.
Wales, co. York, 2265.
Waleshale, *v.* Walsall.
Wales, Marches of, 1605.
Walet', Waletona, Waletone, Waletun, *v.* Walton.
Walkmylnlane, in Wirksworth, 2692.
Wallehulle, Le, in Catton, 576.
Wallemor, Le, in Spondon, 2177, 2178.
Walley, *v.* Whaley.
Wallfield, Le, in Derby, 981, 983.
Wallton, *v.* Walton.
Walsall, co. Staff. Vicar. Walter [1272], 2199.
Walterthorpe, *v.* Waterthorpe.
Walton, by Chesterfield, 356, 448, 692, 702, 703, 738, 793, 795, 800, 803,

806, 997, 2149, 2150, **2491-2534**, 2745.
Walton. Lords. Rob. f. Rog. Le Bretone [1323-1349], 433, 501, 1044, 1746; Tho. Foliambe [1463, 1464], 459, 509; Hen. Foliambe [1468-1490], 167, 278, 460-462, 510, 855, 1345, 1779, 1856.
Walton-on-Trent, 604, 1027, 2043, **2535-2542**.
————Rectors. Will. Humbreston [1368], 2045, 2050; Will. Boghhey [1405], 2538.
Waltonholm, in Walton, 790, 2502, 2503.
Wardeloe, *v.* Wardlow.
Wardlow, 1551, 2350.
Warenodbi, *v.* Wartnaby.
Ware Slacke, Le, in Wormhill, 2709.
Warewic, *v.* Warwick.
Warfen, in Chaddesden, 611, 612.
Warsnapes Wood, in Dale, 940, 944.
Wartnaby, co. Leic., 1726.
Warwick, County of, 1588, 1594, 1605.
Wassiche, Le, in Wirksworth, 2668.
Watecroft, *v.* Wheatcroft.
Waterfallgate, in Barlow, 224.
Watergalle, in Catton, 576.
Waterthorpe, in Beighton, 270, **2543**.
Watstanwell, *v.* Whatstandwell.
Weanstonssickes Water, in Barlow, 2428.
Weardeston, *v.* Wyaston.
Wednesle', Wednesley, *v.* Wensley.
Welbec, *v.* Welbeck.
Welbeck Abbey, co. Notts., 927, 1079-1087, 1089, 1091-1095, 1097, 1099, 1111, 1199, 1869, 2244.
————Abbots. William [1243], 1086, 1087; Thomas [1292], 1093; John de Castrefeld [1310-11], 1094; John [1451], 1111.
————Prior. John de Dugmantone [1292], 1093.
————Sub-prior. Rob. de Whattone [1292], 1093.
Welbek, Welbeke, Wellebec, Wellebecke, Wellebeke, *v.* Welbeck.
Welleflat, in Calver, 548.
Wells, co. Somer., 1428.
Welyngton, *v.* Willington.
Wendesleye, *v.* Wensley.
Wengebuttus, in Bradborne, 390.
Wengeby, *v.* Wingby.
Wensley, in Darley, 1636, **2544**.
Werkesworth, Werkusworth, *v.* Wirksworth.
"Werkhouse," le, in Findern, 1280.
Wermenhull, *v.* Wormhill.
Wersenape, *v.* Warsnapes.
Wessington, 925.
Westhala, *v.* Hallam, West.
Westhandeley, *v.* Handley, West.
Weston, *v.* Wheston.
Weston Underwood, 1503, 1505, 1741, **2545-2553**.
Westwell, 467.
West Wykegate, in Brampton, 435.

Wetecroft, v. Wheatcroft.
Wetesford, Le, in Tansley, 2302.
Wethslade, in Rosliston, 2041.
Whakebrig, v. Wakebridge.
Whaley, **2554**.
Whatstandwell, **2555**.
Whatton, Long, co. Leic., 609.
————Rector. Geoffrey de Chaddes-
　　　den, late Edw. III., 609.
Wheatcroft, 922, 1386-1388, 1890, 2781.
Wheatley, co. Notts., 2120.
Wheston, in Tideswell, 2348-2350.
Whetcroft, v. Wheatcroft.
Wheteley, v. Wheatley.
Whettcroft, Whettecrofte, v. Wheatcroft.
Whiston, co. York. Rector. John Jor-
　　　dan [1355], 1341.
Whitcroft, nr. Crych, 2700.
Whiteleis, in Staveley, 2264.
Whitewell, v. Whitwell.
Whithornedale, in Dale, 944.
Whithull, v. Whittle.
Whittington, 234, 503, 509, 679, 681,
　　　695, 701, 770, 878, 1345, 1534, 1538,
　　　2556-2558.
————Clerk. William, *temp.* Hen.
　　　　III., 1534.
————Parson. Rog. de Cryche
　　　　[1388-90], 1924, 1926-1928.
Whittle, in Gt. Hayfield, 1372, 1374,
　　　1375, 1812.
Whittyngton, v. Whittington.
Whitwell, 1511, 1605, **2559**.
————Clerk. John, *temp.* Edw. I.,
　　　　1511.
————Persona. Hascuil. Musard,
　　　　early Hen. III., 2244.
————Vicar. John Newerk [1464],
　　　　2559.
Whityngton, v. Whittington.
Whyngby, v. Wingby.
Whystan, v. Whiston.
Whytewell, v. Whitwell.
Whytinton, v. Whittington.
Whythull, Whytyll, v. Whittle.
Whytyngton, v. Whittington.
Wiardeston, Wiardiston, v. Wyaston.
Wich Malbane, v. Nantwich.
Wigan, co. Lanc., 1313.
————Parson. Walter de Caumpe-
　　　　done [1365], 1313.
Wiggelny, Wiggelee, v. Wigley.
Wiggewell, Wiggewelle, v. Wigwell.
Wigley, **2560-2565**.
Wigwall, v. Wigwell.
Wigwell, 2628-2633, 2635-2638, 2640,
　　　2641, 2662, 2695, 2696, 2700.
Wigwellbrok, 2641.
Wikedaymarketh, Le, v. Chesterfield.
Wikeley, v. Wigley.
Wikesworth, v. Wirksworth.
Wilenton, Wilentone, v. Willington.
Wilgebi, v. Willoughby.
Wilinton, Wilintune, v. Willington.
Willesley, 1784, **2782, 2783**.
————Lord. — Inggwerdeby [1413],
　　　　1784.
Williamthorp, v. Williamsthorp.

Williamsthorp, 23, 697, **2566, 2567**.
Willinctun, v. Willington.
Willingham, co. Linc., 1761, 1864.
Willington, 660, 677, 1167, 1169, 1171,
　　　1953, 1983, 1989, **2568-2601**, 2781.
————Rector. Ralph de Pointon
　　　　[1223], 2573.
————Sacerdos. Adam Orm [1153-
　　　　1160], 1939.
————Vicars. Adam, *t.* Hen. III.,
　　　　2582; John Cortel [1356],
　　　　1975.
Willoughby, co. Linc. Parson. Tho.
　　　de Friskenay [1361], 1899.
Willoughby, co. Notts., 2098.
Willyngton, v. Willington.
Wilmyshay, in Yeaveley, 2713.
Wilne, 1726, **2601, 2784**.
Wilts., County of, 583.
Wilynton, v. Willington.
Windley, 482, 1741, **2602**.
Wineshull, v. Winshill.
Winestere, v. Winster.
Wingby, in Walton, 836, 2499, 2504,
　　　2514.
Wingerworth, 366, 376, 699, 878, 2410,
　　　2431, 2441, **2603, 2604**.
————Chaplain. Hugh le Cuper,
　　　　temp. Edw. I., 366.
Wingfield, North, 409.
————Rectors. John de Deyncurt,
　　　　t. Edw. I., 697, 2702;
　　　　Roger de Deyncurt [1297],
　　　　2409; Tho. Glapewell
　　　　[1438], 2410; John Long-
　　　　ford [1474], 1764.
Wingfield, South, 465, 470, **2605-2609**.
————Vicar. Robert [1292], 2605.
Wingfield, N. or S., 1605, 1869, 2409.
————Parsons. Tho. de Longford,
　　　　parson of Wynfeld [1362],
　　　　1580; John Houbelle, par-
　　　　son of Wynfeld [1390],
　　　　2416; John Bellasys, par-
　　　　son of Halwynfeld [1408],
　　　　1869.
Winhul, in Ashbourne, 53.
Winishull, v. Winshill.
Winnedona, Winnedun, in Atlow, 134, 135.
Winnefeld, Winnefeud, v. Wingfield.
Winshill, **2610-2619**.
————Clerk. Robert [1304], 1758.
Winster, 1213, **2620-2627**, 2785.
Winsul, v. Winshill.
Wippeleye, in Brimington, 502.
Wirke, Wirkesworth, v. Wirksworth.
Wirkewrde, v. Wirksworth.
Wirksworth Town, 20, 319, 324, 394,
　　　878, 1008, 1009, 1481, 1498, 1664,
　　　1671, 1672, 1677, 1678, 2544, **2628**,
　　　2701, 2765.
————Vicars. Nich de Oxton [1275],
　　　　2642; Will. Godman *al.*
　　　　Godmon [1278-1295], 2044,
　　　　2649, 2652, 2653, 2655;
　　　　Milo [1325], 2659; Rob. de
　　　　Yrton [1359], 2662; Tho.
　　　　de Castultone [1381], 2663.

Wirksworth Town. Clerk. Phillip, *t.* Edw. I., 2655.

Wirksworth, Wapentake of, 51, 1664, 2644.

Wirkysworth, *v.* Wirksworth.

Witeoven, Le, in Chesterfield, 745.

Witewell, *v.* Whitwell.

Witinton, *v.* Whittington.

Wiuesleia, Wivelesle, *v.* Willesley.

Wiverton, co. Notts., 1469.

Wodehouses, in Longford, 1562, 1563, 1565, 1572, 1578.

Wodesetys, *v.* Woodseats.

Wodesmethis, Wodsmethys, Wodsmythys, in Dronfeld, 1040, 2476, 2477.

Wodethorpe, *v.* Woodthorpe.

Wodhose, Wodhuses, Wodhous, *v.* Woodhouse.

Wodhous-thing, in Killamarsh, 1513.

Woley, Wolley, in Kirk Langley, 1529, 1530..

Wolfacre, in Makeney, 1627.

Wollard, co. Som., 491.

Wolputhul, Le, in Chaddesden, 605.

Woluelow, 1272.

Woodhall, 878.

Woodhouse, co. Staff., 156-158, 307, 2133-2135, 2137, 2141, 2142.

Woodthorpe, nr. Dronfield, 2429, 2433, **2704.**

Woodthorpe, in N. Wingfield, **2702, 2703.**

Woodthorpe, in Staveley, 223, 1342, 1343, 2266-2270, **2705.**

Workesworth, *v.* Wirksworth.

Worldeshend Manor, in Taddington, 2296.

Wormehul, Wormelle, *v.* Wormhill.

Wormhill, 191, 1195, 1265, 2354, 2355, 2357, 2362, **2706-2709.**

Wormhull, Wormhyll, Wormyll, *v.* Wormhill.

Worsworth, *v.* Wirksworth.

Worthingis, Le, in Tideswell, 2345.

Wudthorpe, *v.* Woodthorpe.

Wurkysworth, *v.* Wirksworth.

Wyardeston, Wyardiston, Wyardston, Wyarduston, *v.* Wyaston.

Wyaston, **1130-1158, 2710.**

Wybunbury, co. Chest. Vicar. Ric. Walker [1464], 322.

Wygan, *v.* Wigan.

Wygewall, Wygewelle, *v.* Wigwell.

Wyggeley, Wygley, *v.* Wigley.

Wyggewall, Wyggewelle, *v.* Wigwell.

Wykeday Market, *v.* under Chesterfield.

Wylentone, *v.* Willington.

Wylingham, *v.* Willingham.

Wylington, Wylinton, Wylintune, Wyllinton, Wyllyngton, *v.* Willington.

Wylmeslowe, in Litton, 1550.

Wylughby, *v.* Willoughby.

Wylyngham, *v.* Willingham.

Wylynton, Wylyngton, *v.* Willington.

Wyncel, *v.* Winshill.

Wyndeley, *v.* Windley.

Wyndhill Lane, in Unstone, 2474.

Wyneley, *v.* Windley.

Wynfeld, Wynfelde, *v.* Wingfield.

Wyngarworth, Wyngerworth, Wyngreworth, *v.* Wingerworth.

Wyngeby, *v.* Wingby.

Wynley, *v.* Windley.

Wynnefeld, *v.* Wingfield.

Wynnushale, Wynsell, *v.* Winshill.

Wynshul, Wynshull, Wynsull, *v.* Winshill.

Wynster, *v.* Winster.

Wynstre, *v.* Winster.

Wynsul, *v.* Winshill.

Wynyerd, Le, in Rodsley, 2015.

Wyrkesworth, etc., *v.* Wirksworth.

Wytehul, *v.* Whittle.

Wytingholmis, Wytyngholm, in Walton, 704, 2532.

Wytinton, Wytintone, Wyttintona, Wyttyngton, *v.* Whittington.

Wytwalle, *v.* Whitwell.

Wyverton, *v.* Wiverton.

Y.

Ybole, Ybull, *v.* Ible.

Yderychay, *v.* Idridgehay.

Yeaveley, 2015, **2711-2715.**

Yelderesleye, *v.* Yeldersley.

Yelderis, nr. Trusley, 2383.

Yeldersley, 396, 2139, 2141, 2142, **2716-2731, 2785.**

Yeldursley, *v.* Yeldersley.

Yellegrave, *v.* Youlgreave.

Yeveley, Yevesley, *v.* Yeaveley.

Yhilderesle, Yhildersley, *v.* Yeldersley.

Yildersley, Yldirisle, Yldrusleye, etc., *v.* Yeldersley.

Ylkystun, *v.* Ilkeston.

Ylum, *v.* Ilam.

Yoleg', Yolegrave, *v.* Youlgrave.

Yolgrave, Yolgreff, Yolgreve, Yolgreyva, *v.* Youlgrave.

Yollegreve, Yollgreve, *v.* Youlgrave.

York, 1103, 1104, 1271, 1824, 2785.

Youlgrave, 307, 646, 1237, 1259, 1264, 2236, 2403, **2732-2738, 2786.**

————Vicars. Will. Grym [1256], 2734; William [1260], 2733; R. Vernon [1294], 2216; Will. Smetheby *al.* Smethley [1484-1492], 303, 2235.

————Chaplain. Will. Weyley [1507], 2737.

Youlgreave, Youlgreve, v. Youlgrave.

Yrewas, *v.* Erewash.

Yrton, *v.* Ireton, Kirk.

Yueleyrakes, in Rodsley, 2015.

Yuenbroc, Yuenebrok, Yvenbrook, *v.* Ivonbrook Grange.

Yvelee, Yveley, *v.* Yeaveley.

Z.

Zolgreff, *v.* Youlgrave.

INDEX OF NAMES.

A.

Aaron, son of Jacob, the Jew, 2639.
Abbenay, Abbeney, etc., v. Abney.
Abbetoft, Abbetot, Abbitot, Abetot, Abtoft, Apetot, Aptot, Habetot, Hapetot.
———Jordan de, 225, 226, 425, 695, 696, 2245, 2375, 2418.
———Ralph de, 2241.
———Rob. de, 2430.
———Rob. f. et heir Tho., 1047.
———Roger de, 434.
———Tho. f. Rob. de, 229.
———Will de, 228, 2242.
Abburbury, Tho., 587.
Abel, Abell, John, of Cauldwell, 604, 1784, 2049-2051, 2053, 2055, 2057, 2295.
———John, of Stapenhill, 2542, 2618.
———Rob., of Tykenhale, 1758, 1968.
———Rycard, of Cromfort, 1679.
Abney, Abbenay, Abbeney, Abbeneye.
———Alexander de, 1798.
———John, of Castelton, 4, 1805, 2064.
———Richard, 1440, 1442, 2520.
———Rob. de, 1, 1207, 1461, 1789-1791.
———Rob. de, parson of Bampford, 1794.
———Tho. de, 219.
———Tho. f. Will de, 1800.
———William de, 558, 1216, 1437, 1440, 1788, 1796-1799.
Abselon, John, 355.
Acard, Achard, Akard, Hakard.
———Agnes, w. of Tho., 1299, 1303.
———Johanna, wid. of Tho., 1313.
———John, 1294.
———Tho., 1299, 1300, 1302, 1306, 1307, 1310, 2103, 2104, 2108, 2109, 2111.
———Tho. f. Joh., de Fostone, 1303.
———Tho. s. and heir of Tho., 1313, 1315, 1316.
———Walter, 1288-1292, 1295, 1296, 2100.

Acauere, Accouere, Acouer, Acouere, etc., v. Okeover.
Acelinus, Ascelinus, magister, 1080, 1081.
Achard, v. Acard.
Achenuilla, Henry de, capellanus, 1360.
Acres, John, clerk, 2448.
Actte, Will. de, 1428.
Adam, capellanus, 2576.
Adam, vicar of Willington, 2581.
Adam, Alice, d. of Thos., 2415.
———Giles, of Ashbourne, 2414.
———Hugh, 975, 986.
———John, 323.
———Rob., 323.
———Rog., of Walton, 2034.
———Tho., of Ashbourne, 37, 65, 69, 70, 72, 144, 1644, 2413-2415.
———Tho. fil. Thome, 64.
Adamsone, Will., 2239.
Adderley, Addreley, Aderleye.
———Tho. de, clerk, 255, 256.
———Will. de, 96, 255, 1924-1928.
Ade, Joan, of Sudbury, 2168.
Ad-finem-ville, v. Tounesende.
Ad-pontem, de Onston, Peter, 2430.
Affete, Ralph, 2091.
Agard, Dorothy, Cecily, Margaret, daughters of Nich., 2731.
———John, 1190.
———John, of Marton, 1655.
———Nicholas, 2398.
———Nich., of Newborough, 1190.
———Nich., of Sudbury, 2288.
Agaz, Matilda, 1971.
———Will., 1972.
Aguillon, Rob., 1428.
Agulun, John, vicar of Merston, 1934.
Ailmont, Alice, d. of Hen., 65.
———Henry, 65.
Ailwin, capellanus, 1197.
Ainecurt, v. Deyncourt.
Akard, v. Acard.
Akenei, Rob. de., 1281.
Alais, Rob., of Wynster, 2214.
Alan, capellanus de Staveley, 228, 2242.
———clericus, 1945.
———decanus, 2545.
———vicar of Tideswell, 1546, 2335.

Alardestre, Richard de, 2092.
Albecot, Rog. le, 1533.
Albert, clericus, 530.
Albeyn, Ric. f. Ade, 730, 731.
Albi, Rog. f. Rob., of Brampton, 705.
Albiniaco, Will. de, rector of Ilkeston, 2202.
Albus, Geoffrey, 1500.
———Robert, 2088.
———Will., de Grundelford, 1210.
Alcok, Alkoc, Alkok.
———Edmund, vicar of Croxall, 598, 600.
———John, 1667.
———Rob. f. Ade, 746, 749, 766.
———Will. f. Ade, 727.
Alcrynton, Tho., chaplain, 156.
Alcus, Rob., 2222.
Aldeport, Rob. de, capellanus, 294, 295.
Aldeporte, Rob. de, rector of Neutone, 296.
Aldewerc, Aldewerhc, Aldewerck, Aldewerk, v. Aldwark.
Aldham, Hen. de, 2225.
———Margate de, 2225.
Aldwark, Aldewerc, Aldewerk, Aldewerick, Aldewerhc, *Audewerc, etc.
———Agnes, w. of Will. de, 1787.
———Alice, 1198.
———Hen. de, 298, 299.
———Hugh de, 1198.
———John, 303, 2621.
———John f. Joh. de, 18.
———John f. Rad. de, 17.
———Ranulph de, 2637.
———Rob. de, 663, 1787, 2629, 2632, 2635.
———Tho., 301.
———Will. de, 1787, 2144, 2641.
———Will. de, of Birchovere, 297.
Alencon, John de, 1753.
Alesop, v. Alsop.
Alestre, Ric., 884.
Alexander, canonicus, 2382.
———frater Sewalli, 536.
———mercator, 880.
———sacerdos, 1945.
Alexander, Aleysaunder, Alisaundre.
———Henry, chaplain, 2347, 2354, 2357.
———John, 2357.
———Ralph, 1996.
———William, 2352, 2353, 2358.
Aleyn, Aleyne, Alen, Alyn.
———Agnes, w. of Henry, 2737.
———Edward, 636.
———Henry, 26, 2234-2236.
———Henry, f. Joh., 2232.
———John, 1776, 2230-2232.
———John, of Staveley, 2257.
———Nich., f. Hen., 26, 2234, 2235.
———Rich., 302.
———Rich., of Alsop, 40.
———Richard, f. Joh., 2230-2232, 2236.
———Thos., 307, 2232, 2237.
———Thurston, 637.
———Walter, of Birchover, 297.

Aleyn, etc., William, 747.
Aleynknaue, Hen., 882.
Aleysaunder, v. Alexander.
Alfertone, Will., vicar of Radford, 2670.
Algarethorp, Algarthorp, Algerthorp.
————————Nicholas de, 419, 434.
————————Rog. f. Hen. de, 418.
Alibon, Rob., bailiff of Derby, 981.
Alibone, Tho., chaplain, 1117.
Aliot, Alyot.
———John, 1641-1643.
———Robert, 1637.
Alisaundre, v. Alexander.
Alkemonton, Alkemunton.
———Cecily, relict of Hen. de, 1571.
———Ralph de, chaplain, 288.
————Tho. f. Ric. de, 1630.
———Will. de, 288.
Allan, chaplain of Schoffeld [? Sheffield], 2431.
Allsope, Allsoppe, v. Alsop.
Almunton, Hugh de, 2152.
Alnetis, Rich. de, 1786.
Alneto, Will. de, 2780.
Alnetona, Will. de, 131.
Alot, John, chaplain, 5, 623, 2670.
Alreton, Rog. de, 1862.
Alson, Will., 2679.
Alsop, Alesop, Allsope, Alsope, etc.
———Anthony, 1386, 1388.
———Beatrix, wid. of Ranulph f. Henrici de, 36.
———Dionisia f. Henrici de, 37.
———Gamel de, 134.
————Hen. de, 54, 1636, 1820, 1821.
———Hen. f. Ran. de, 28.
———Hen. f. Rob. de, 34.
———Hen. f. Thome de, 29-31.
———John, 1386.
———John f. Joh. de, 32.
———John f. Simonis de, 33.
———John f. Thome de, 33.
———John, of Hoknaston, 1387, 1388, 1673, 1677.
———John, of Spondon, 1528, 1530.
———Letitia, wid. of John de, 34.
———Margaret f. Ran. f. Hen. de, 35, 36.
———Ralph f. Johannis de, 34.
———Ranulf de, 30-33, 37-39, 135, 385.
————Ranulph f. Hen. de, 32-34.
———Ranulph f. Ran. de, 34.
———Richard, 320, 1382.
———Robert, 1386, 1388.
———Thomas, 42, 43, 1381, 1680, 2678.
———Thomas f. Ranulfi de, 28.
———Thomas, of Bradburne, 2693.
———William, 1471.
———Will. de, Abbot of Darley, 974.
Alspade, Margery de, 1642, 1643.
Alston, John, 276.
Alstonefeld, Rob. de, 68.
Alsybroke, Thomas, 2691.
Alton, Tho., 1484.
Aluithleg', Rob. de, 51.
Aluredus, 238.

Alvel', Rob. de, 1274, 2757, 2758.
Alynson, Roger, 2709.
————Thomas, of Herdwyckewalle, 2709.
Alyot, *v.* Aliot.
Amot, Amote, Tho., 1225-1227.
Ampe, Margaret, relicta Hen., 594.
————William, 594, 2538.
Amysson, John, of Longeford, 1581, 1584.
————Matilda, w. of John, 1581.
————Ric., s. of John, of Longeford, 1584.
Anabull, Anabulle, Annable.
————George, of Hoknaston, 1385, 1386, 1388.
————Johanna, w. of Rog., of Hoknaston, 1387, 1388.
————Rog., of Asshlehey, 1383.
————Rog., of Hokenaston, 1384-1386, 1388.
Ancelm, rector of Dronfield, 2425, 2426.
Andely, Isabel de, 2776.
————Maurice de, 2776.
Andrew, Andrea, Andreu, Andrewe.
————John, 2067.
————John, chaplain, 1238, 2083, 2084.
————Thomas, 2477.
————William, 1904, 2067, 2255, 2256, 2347.
————William, chaplain, 1177.
————William, clericus, 2351.
————Will. f. Tho., 2345.
Aneslaia, *v.* Annessley.
Angers, Angerz.
————Anne, w. of Edmund, of Chaddesden, 611.
————Edmund, of Chaddesden, 611.
————Nich., s. and h. of Edmund, 612.
Annable, *v.* Anabull.
Annesley, Aneslai, Anneslee.
————Hugh, 1123.
————Robert de, 1083.
————Thomas de, 807.
Anselin, Ralph, 1397.
————Thomas, 1623.
Apelby, *v.* Appleby.
Apelknoll, Apilknoll, Apilknolle, Appelknoll, Appurknoll, Hapilknole.
————Cecily, 2462.
————John, 2472.
————John f. Pet. de, 2430.
————Marg., w. of Peter de, 2430.
————Peter de, 2430, 2431.
————Rog. de, 1040, 2431.
Apetot, Aptot, *v.* Abbetoft.
Apilknoll, *v.* Apelknoll.
Appleby, Apelby, Appelby, Appylby.
————Sir Edm. de, 1286, 1376, 1488.
————Dom. Geoffrey de, 48, 1954.
————Henry de, mil., 1968.
————John, 1763.
————William, 1960, 1970, 1971.
Appurknoll, *v.* Apelknoll.
Aptot, *v.* Abbetoft.
Aquitaine and Lancaster, John, Duke of, *v.* Lancaster, John, Duke of.

Archer, Archere, Le Archer, Arrecher, Larcher.
————Alan le, 1463.
————Andrew, 1463.
————John, 3, 1468.
————John, of Heghlowe, 1225, 2354.
————Matilda, of Nottingham, 2181, 2182.
————Ric. le, 2, 723, 1214, 1215.
————Rob., 1209, 1324, 1424.
————Rog. le, 1793.
————Thomas, 3, 1427, 2335, 2734.
————Tho., s. of John, 1467.
————Tho., s. of Ric., 1467.
————Tho. f. Joh., de Hokelowe, 1463-1466.
————Tho. f. Ric., de Magna Huklowe, 1463-1468.
————William le, 2308.
————Will. f. Ric., 555.
Arcwryt, John de, de Cesterfeld, 693.
Arden, John de, 486.
————Walkelin de, 2025.
Ardern, Arderne.
————Alina, w. of Ralph de, 910.
————John de, mil., 2131.
————Ralph de, 910.
————Walter de, 201.
————Will., de Meysham, 1784.
Argosis, Ralph f. Aluredi de, 1753.
Arkel, Rob. f. Ric., 2629.
Armestrong, Tho., 1123, 1321.
Armitage, Tho., capellanus Capelle-in-ly-Frythe, 627, 649.
Arnald, Arnold.
————Joan, 2664.
————John, chaplain, 2661.
————Will., Abbot of Merivale, 678.
Arrecher, *v.* Archer.
Arrosmythe, Will., parson of Longley, 1505.
Arundel, Earl of, *v.* Fitzalan, Rich.
————Rog., King's Justice, 1499, 1947, 2334.
Ascehurst, Hen., parson of Mugginton, 1694.
Ascelinus, *v.* Acelinus.
Ascell, Simon de, 1546, 2335.
Ascet', sacerdos, 516.
Asche, *v.* Ash.
Aschebury, Rob. de, 1573.
Aschehurst, John, 1694.
Ash, Asche, Assch, Assche, etc.
————Adam f. Rad. de, 1578.
————Isabel, w. of John, of Chestrefeld, 459.
————John, of Chestrefeld, 457, 459, 785, 787, 862.
————John, jun., 464.
————John del., 2502, 2503.
————Ric., Alderman of Chesterfield, 870, 871.
————Ric., of Chesterfield, 458, 466.
————Richard, 850, 2519.
————Robert, 471, 2265.
————Rog. de, bailiff of Derby, 986.
————Rog. del, of Chesterfield, 809, 813, 822.

Ashbourne, Asheburn, Asschbourne, Asscheburn, Asseborn, Asshborn, Assheburn, Esburn, Esburne, Esburnia, Esscheburne, Essebourne, Esseburn, Esseburna, Esseburne.
——Adam de, 62, 413.
——Agnes, wid. of John de, 782.
——Mag. Andrew de, 1822.
——Geoffrey de, 134, 2091.
——Hugh de, 1297.
——Hugh f. Rob. de, 60.
——John f. Elie, clericus, 2740.
——John f. Hug. de, 70.
——Nich. de, 2660.
——Philip de, 2762.
——Rich. de, chaplain, 2616.
——Rob. f. Alex. de, 2740.
——Rob. fil. Philippi de, 55.
——Rob. de, Knt., 2212, 2628-2633, 2635-2637, 2640.
——Rob. de, Senescallus, 2718.
——Robert de, 54, 326, 926, 1166, 1569, 1574, 1578, 1787, 1820, 1821, 2126, 2580.
——Rog. f. Will. de, 2762.
——Tho. fil. Ade de, 56, 59, 61.
——Tho. f. Regin. de, 1145.
——Tho. de, 54, 141, 152, 1787.
——Will. de, 292, 880, 1396, 2615.
——Will. de, chaplain, 2665.
Ashby, Assheby, Esseby.
——Laurence de, 2638.
——Nicholas, 1553.
Ashope, Peter de, 1610.
Ashover, Aschovere, Asscheover, Asshover, Essheouere, Esseouere, Essovere, Exsovere, etc.
——Adam f. Hausie, 755.
——Agnes, wid. of Rob. de, 370.
——John f. Sim. de, 125.
——Nich. de, 760, 761, 764.
——Rob. f. Rad. de, de Cesterfeld, 365.
——Rog., of Brampton, 457.
——Will. de, 971.
Ashton, Asshton.
——Benedict de, 2358.
——James, 2280.
——John, Knt., 509.
——Tho., of Horsley, 1459.
Asser, John, 1902, 1903.
——Rog., 99, 1330, 1905, 1907, 1909, 1910.
Assewell, John de, parson of Mackworth, 677, 1861.
——Will. de, of Ticknall, 1968.
Assheby, v. Ashby.
Assheford, John, 1073.
Asshelay, Asshely, John de, chaplain at Monyash, 1721, 2736.
Assher, Alice, w. of John del, 1911.
——John del., 1911.
Asshes, John del., 770, 798.
Astley, Tho., 1784.
——Sir Will., Knt., 1488.

Aston, Astone, Astun.
——Edm. de, 2289.
——Elias de, 1422, 1425, 1789.
——Geoffrey, s. of Stephen de, 1032.
——John de, 74, 343, 1048, 1328, 1761, 1924.
——John, Knt., 2141.
——Ric. de, chaplain, 778.
——Rob. de, 1422, 1425, 2166.
——Will., of London, 300.
——William, 602, 804, 2447, 2449, 2452-2455.
——Will. de, 797, 2357.
——Will. f. Phil. de, 2431.
Atkyn, Will., 1513.
Atkynson, Will., 864, 1070.
Atlow, Attelouwe, Attelowe.
——Adam f. Joh. de, 137.
——Agnes, w. of Will. de, 20.
——Eleanor, f. Isolde f. Edithe de, 152.
——Engelard de, 151.
——Isolda f. et h. Engelardi de, 151, 152.
——John de, 141.
——John f. Alex. de, 149-151.
——Warin f. David de, 136.
——Will. de, 20.
Attebernes, Marjory, 2181.
Attebrigge, Rob. f. Steph., of Ashover, 250.
——v. also Ad-pontem.
Attebrok, Rob., rector of Somersall, 2165.
Attebroke, John, 2165.
Attechirchestile, Tho., 1212.
Attecrosse, Rog., 1212.
Attegate, Tho., 253.
Attegrene, Henry, 2722.
Attelberge, Attlebye, Mag. Will. de, canon of Lichfield, 1427, 1957.
Attemore, Hen., of Monyassch, 1714, 1715.
Attewalle, John, 1476.
Attewelle, Alice, w. of Rich. 2722.
——Richard, 2722.
Attkynson, v. Atkynson.
Attlebye, v. Attelberge.
Atyswelle, John, of Ibul, 1477.
Aubenni, William d', 1397.
Aubrey, Rob., 290.
Auburnehor, Adam f. Will., de Cesterfeld, 430.
Audeley, v. Audley.
Audewerc, Rob. de, v. Aldwark.
Audley, Lord, v. Touchet, James.
——Tho., Knt., chancellor, 1659.
Audoenus, subprior of Burton Abbey, 1197.
Aufertone, Rob. f. Will de, 1862.
Aula, Adam de, 1150.
——Hugh de, 1130, 1134, 1137.
——John de, of Middleton, 1702.
——Ralph de, 290.
——Ric. de, 931.
——Ric. de, of Wyardiston, 1137.
——Rob. de, of Makworthe, 1521.

Aula, Tho. f. et h. Hug. de, de Wiardiston, 1133.
————William de, 1945.
————Will. de, of Wyardeston, 1130, 1131, 1135.
————Will. f. Will. de, of Wyardestone, 2719.
Aulam, Adam ad, 1153.
Aumeton, Rob. de, 1080.
Aunger, Ric., clerk, 1769.
Aurifaber, Joan, w. of Rob., de Chastrefeld, 737.
————Margaret, d. of Rob., 737.
Austyn, Rich., de Herleston, 2039.
Avenel, Gervase, 1397.
————Robert, 412.
Avener, Auener, Aviner.
————Henry de, 1644.
————Will., chaplain, 80, 81.
————Will., clerk, 1769.
————Will. le, of Ashbourne, 67.
Averey, Agnes f. et h. Nich., 2176.
Awby, Tho., of King's Bromley, 638.
Ayer, Robert, of Padley, 2674.
Ayld, Will., 2112.
————Will., s. of Will., 2112.
Aylisbure, John de, Knt., 1712.
Aylisburi, Walter de, 139.
Ayncourt, v. Deyncourt.
Ayr, Rob. le, de Thornhyll, 220.

B.

B——, Decanus Cestrie, 1726.
Babington, Babyngton.
————Antony, of Dethick, 1010, 1541.
————Hugh de, Sheriff of Notts. and Derby, 2199.
————John, esquire, 1935.
————John, Knt., 1123, 1321, 2120.
————Kateryn, wid. of Sir Anth., 1542.
————Thomas I., 2362.
————Thomas II., of Dethick, 1287, 1383, 1742, 1936, 2695, 2696, 2730.
————Thomas III., s. of Anthony, of Dethicke, 128, 2191, 2700, 2701.
————Thomas, of Leghe, 2086.
————William I., Knt., King's Justice, 1806, 2728.
————William II., 2064, 2362, 2567, 2728.
Bachcroft, John, 641.
Bache, Ralph de la, seneschal of Burton, 1278, 1896, 2612.
Bache, Rog. de le, 588.
Bacheler, Bachiler, John fil. Nich. le, 2576, 2581.
Bachepus, Bachepuz, v. Bakepuz.
Bacon, Tho., 1448.
Bacun, Ric. f. Sym., 2151.
Badde, Avicia f. Rog., 1737.
Badeley, Alice, 2602.

Bageshagh, v. Bagshaw.
Bagger, Will, chaplain of Brassyngtone, 1497, 1498.
Bagot, Agnes, 2725.
————John, Knt., 2131.
————Richard, 394, 2166, 2678.
Bagshaw, Bageshagh, Baggeschawe, Baggeshaugh, Bagscha, Bagschag, Bagschagh, Bagschawe, Bagsha, Bagshagh, Bagshaze, Bakshawe.
————Cecily, w. of Tho. s. of Hen., 637.
————Edward, 636, 2366.
————Geoffrey, chaplain, 625, 626.
————Henry, of the Ridge, 635, 641, 1452.
————Humphrey, s. and h. of Tho., 1268.
————John, f. Rob. de, of Abbenaye, 3.
————John de, 1220.
————Nich. f. Hug. de, 619.
————Nich., of Chapel-en-le-Frith, 407, 645.
————Nich., of Farewell, co. Staff., 408.
————Nicholas, 1077, 1781.
————Richard, 1440, 1442, 1801.
————Robert, 637.
————Steuen, curatt of the Chapell in ye Fryth, 646.
————Thomas, of Abnaye, 5.
————Tho., of Eyam, 1268.
————Tho., of Ford, 644.
————Tho., s. of Hen., 637.
————William de, 3, 99, 617, 1330, 1801.
————Will. de, of Chapel-en-le-Frith, 621, 623-626.
————Will., of Hope, 1850.
————Sir Wyll., Vykar of Hope, 646.
Baguley, Bayguley.
————Jane, w. of Nich., 461, 462, 469, 2524.
————Nicholas, 461, 462, 469, 2523.
Bailey, Baillif, Bailly, Bailye, Ballif, Bayli, Bayiif, Baylli, Bayly, Baylye.
————Hen. le, of Spondon, chaplain, 607.
————Hen., Warden of the Chantry of Chaddesden, 609.
————Henry, 512.
————Hen., 630, 631.
————John f. Hen., 512.
————John f. Tho. le, of Clifton, 2018.
————Jordan de, 2425.
————Margery, 581, 582.
————Richard, 2182, 2183.
————Robert, 836, 2181.
Baillif, Bailly, Bailye, v. Bailey.
Bairg, John, of Skardeclive, 2121.
Bakelot, John, 1116, 1117.
Bakepuz, Bachepus, Bachepuz, Bakeput, Bakepuiz, Bakepuys.
————Geoffrey I. de, 238, 239.
————Geoffrey II. de, 1503, 1767, 2577, 2578, 2580.

Bakepuz, etc., Dom. Hen. de, Knt., 2005.
———James de, 188.
———Johanna, w. of Will., 343, 344.
———John f. Rob., 239.
———John de, Knt., Dom. de Barton, 25, 337, 928, 1568, 1630, 2321.
———Dom. Peter de., 399, 1558, 1562, 1563, 1629, 2152.
———Ralph I. de, 135, 396, 932, 1500.
———Ralph II. de, 1428.
———Ralph III. de, 337, 929, 1570, 2321.
———Robert I. de, 238.
———Rob. f. et h. Rob., 238, 239, 2744.
———Rodbert de, dom. de Alkemunton, 25.
———Walter de, 2200.
———Will. de, 522.
———Will., Knt., 1864.
Baker, John, 1959.
———Katharine, of Swartlingcote, 1989, 1990.
———Nich., rector of Boyleston, 1620.
———Richard, 2120.
———Will., of Swartlingcote, 1989, 1990.
Bakewell, Bakequell, Bathequell, Baucwelle, Baukewell, Baukquell, Baukwell, Bauquell, Bauqwell, Bawckewell, Bawkewell, Bawkuell, Bawquell, etc.
———Alice, w. of Rob. de, 206.
———John, clericus, 1209, 1396.
———John, chaplain, 2253.
———John de, 763.
———Fr. John de, Canonicus de la Dale, 1612.
———John, bastard s. of Rog. de, 828.
———Margery, w. of Rog. de, 828.
———Matthew, son of Tho. de, 1609.
———Nich. de, 443, 755, 772, 773, 2438.
———Ric. de, 507, 1250, 1252, 1257, 1259, 1260, 1263.
———Ric., s. of Hen., 1267.
———Roger de, 778, 797, 798, 802, 804, 810, 820, 822, 828, 2315.
———Rog., of Dunston, 2514.
———Thomas de, 791.
Bakshawe, v. Bagshaw.
Balderton, Alice, w. of Hugh, 444.
———Hugh, 444.
Baldwin, clericus de Meleburna, 534.
Baldwyn, Rob. f. Hug., de Bramton, clericus, 420.
Balgy, Balge, Balgi, Balgye.
———Agnes, d. of Tho., of Aston, 562.
———John, s. and h. of Rob., 554.
———Robert, 405, 554, 1430.
———Tho., of Aston, senr., 562, 1446.

Balgy, etc., Tho., s. of Tho., of Aston, 562.
———Will., s. of John, 554.
Baliden, Dom. Will. de, chaplain, 1889.
Baliolo, John de, 1982.
Balle, Alice, f. Emme, 416.
———Gilbert, 1429.
———Henry, 1456.
———Hugh, 390.
———Tho., chaplain, 104, 855, 867.
———Will., of Repton, 540, 1755, 1756, 1956, 1960, 1969-1971.
Ballyden, Will., 324.
Bamford, Baumford, Baumforth.
———Elyas de, 1789, 1790, 1793.
———John de, 1.
———John f. Oliveri de, 219, 220.
———John f. Joh. f. Oliveri de, 219.
———Nich. de, 219.
———Peter de, 248.
———Rosa quondam ux. Petri de, 219.
———Will. f. Joh. f. Oliveri de, 220.
———Will. f. Nich. de, 220.
Banastur, Will., 1492.
Bank, Joan, w. of Tho. del, of Alkemonton, 1806.
———Tho. del, of Alkemonton, 1806.
Bankoc, Isabella, 799.
Barba Aprilis, Barbe d'Averil.
———Ralph, 1945.
———Ralph, capellanus Hug. Comitis, 1942.
———Roger, 1940.
———William, clericus, 536.
———Will. f. Rad., 1942, 1945.
Barber, Barbour, Barbur.
———Adam, of Pyndall, 565.
———Hugh le, 1022.
———Janyn le, 1304.
———John, 1052.
———John, mercer, 87.
———Maud, w. of Janyn le, 1304.
———Richard, 1452, 2516.
———Thomas, 564.
———William, 78, 830.
Bardesey, Leonard, 614.
Bardolf, Hugh, Justiciarius Regis, 1499, 1947, 2334.
Baresford, v. Beresford.
Baret, Isabella, w. of Rich., 2504.
———John, clerk, 824, 832, 833, 2514.
———John, of Weleston, 2295.
———Katerine, w. of Ric., 836.
———Richard, 788, 805, 836, 2504, 2505, 2514.
———Thomas, of Chesterfield, 780, 808, 818-820, 824, 828, 832-834, 836, 1052, 2514, 2515.
———Will. f. Sim., 2204.
Bareth, Geoffrey, 268.
———Matilda, w. of Geoffrey, 268.
Barfot, Will., 316.
Bargh, Richard, 2737.
Barker, Barkerre, Bercarius, Bercher.
———Adam, de Roddesley, 2015.
———Adam, de Wyveleft, 1961.

Barker, etc., Adam f. Ad., 2015.
———Emma, d. of John, 500.
———Hen., of Beauchief, 241.
———Henry le, 2158.
———Hugh le, 1020, 1021.
———Hugh le, chaplain, 1972.
———Joan, w. of Ralph le, 2377.
———John, 142, 235, 499, 500, 1404,
    2451, 2470.
———John le, of Aston, 726.
———John, of Dore, 1064, 1065,
    1069.
———Margery f. Rog., of Hather-
    segg, 1805.
———Ralph, 231, 1398, 2442.
———Ralph, of Dore, 1053, 1055,
    2376, 2377.
———Robert, 1192.
———Tho., of Dore, 241.
———William, 2673.
———Will., of Aston, 1046.
Barkeworth, Will. de, bailiff of Lincoln,
    1923.
Barkhous, Barkhowse.
———Hugh del, of Leghes, 1778.
———Hugh de, 241.
———Will. de, 241.
———Will. de, of Wodseates, 1778.
Barkystun, Margaret, w. of Will. de, 1.
———William de, 1.
Barlastone, Thos. de, of Blackfordby,
    2124.
Barlawe, Randulph, chaplain, 629.
Barley, Agnes, w. of John de, 772.
———Alice, w. of Rob., 868.
———Christopher, chaplain, 133.
———Elena, w. of Rob., 871.
———George, of Stoke, 1267.
———Johanna, wid. of Rob., 831.
———John de, 133, 506, 745, 797,
    804, 805, 811, 1069, 2315,
    2378, 2480.
———John de, clerk, 781.
———John, of Chestrefeld, 868.
———Jordan de, 1536.
———Rob., Alderman of H. Cross
    Guild, Chesterfield, 849.
———Rob., dominus de Barle, 1063.
———Rob. de, 230, 236, 781, 791,
    811, 842, 870, 871, 1047,
    1263, 2252, 2255, 2256,
    2444, 2473-2475, 2480,
    2521, 2564.
———Rob de, clerk, 774.
———Rob., of Assheover, 126.
———Rob., of Barley Lees, junr.,
    870.
———Rob., s. of John de, 745, 750,
    868.
———Thomas, 133, 1810.
———Thomas, chaplain, 839.
———Thomas, clerk, 834.
———Will. de, 444.
———Will., dominus de Barley, 233.
———Will. f. Will de, 227.
Barley Wodhous, Edusa, w. of Rog. f.
    Élie de, 2252.

Barlow, Tho. de, rector of Boylestone,
    346.
———Tho., chaplain, 1394, 1395.
Barlowe, John, 2379.
Barnarde, Will., 2095.
Barnby, Ric., 1129.
Barne, John, 2601.
Baron, John, 2664, 2665.
Barowe, John, 1724.
Barre, Picot de, 2090, 2091.
———Thomas, 2328.
Barrett, Thomas, sen., 815, 842, 866.
———Thomas, jun., 842, 866.
———Tho. s. of Tho. jun., clerk,
    866.
Barri, Hugh, 1334, 1335.
Bars, Richard, vicar of Carolke-on-Trent,
    1980.
Barsford, Tho., 1747.
Barth, Hen., husbandman, 305.
Bartholomew, Monachus, 1946.
———Prior of Tutbury, 2575.
Barton, Bartun.
———Alice, w. of Oliver de, 1493.
———John, 2369.
———Nich., sen., 2369.
———Oliver de, 77, 1493, 1582, 1761,
    1924.
———Ralph de, 1338.
———Randolph, 2369.
———Rich. de, clericus, 2614.
———Roger, 2361.
———Wimund de, 238.
Barun, John, 2668.
Barwa, Hen. de, 238.
Barysford, v. Beresford.
Bas', Hor', 516.
Baseby, John, de Meysham, 1784.
Basigham, Robert de, 1946.
Basing, Basingg, Basingges, Basynges,
    Basyngges, Basyngs.
———Cecily, d. of Ric. de, 892.
———Hen., s. of Ric. de, of Codnor,
    891.
———John de, 335-338.
———Ric. de, of Codnor, 891, 892.
Basselowe, Giles f. Matthei de, 254.
———Philip de, chaplain, 1220.
———Ric. de, 245.
Basset, Basseth, Bassett.
———Edmund, 157, 1495, 1930.
———Hugh, 1945.
———John, Knt., 76, 1692, 1924,
    1928, 1929.
———John, 1114.
———John, s. of Sir Simon, 2088.
———Matilda, 1489.
———Ralph, Canonicus de Roue-
    cestre, 244.
———Ralph, 1078, 2135, 2136, 2392.
———Sir Simon, 2088.
———Thomas, 171.
———Thomasine, d. of Ralph, 2135,
    2137.
———W—, 1078.
———William, 682, 1512.
———William, mil., 2213.
———William, justice in Eyre, 1697.

Basset, etc., William, of Blore, 2137, 2730.
———Will., s. of Sir Simon, 2088.
Basshet, William, 2702.
Basun, Tho., 1504.
Bate, Adam, f. Rog., de Parva Norton, 1778.
———Emmota f. Joh. f. Hen., of Wingerworth, 2332.
———Henry, 124, 409, 1341, 2507.
———Hugh, 1525.
———Isabella, w. of Tho., 218.
———Johanna, of Chestrefeld, 457.
———John, 1021, 1022.
———John, 507, 793, 2504, 2509, 2510.
———John, of Ashbourne, 2417.
———John, of Derby, jun., 979.
——— ——John f. Rog., of Chesterfield, 1746.
———Matilda, w. of Adam, 2322.
———Nicholas, 2660.
———Rich., of Ashbourne, 2417.
———Roger, 1778.
———Rog., de Neubold, 2430.
———Thomas, 218.
———Thos., steward of Chesterfield, 2317.
———William, 750, 782, 2317, 2652.
Batelesford, Will de, 781.
Batell, Walter, 2239.
Bathe, Rog. f. Rad. de la, 2282.
Bathequell, v. Bakewell.
Batley, Bateley
———Ric. de, 365.
———Rob. f. Ric. de, of Boythorp, 372.
———Robert, 373, 960.
———Simon de, 1894.
Baucwelle, Baukewell, Baukquell, Baukwell, Bauquell, Bauqwell, v. Bakewell.
Baudon, Will., 629.
Baule, John, 2127.
Baumford, Baumforth, v. Bamford.
Baune, Christopher, 103.
Bawckewell, Bawkewell, Bawkuell, Bawquell, v. Bakewell.
Baxter, Margaret, w. of Nich., 300.
———Nich., of Derby, 300.
Bay, Will. le, 2095.
Bayart, Hen., 1716.
Bayguley, v. Baguley.
Bayle, Will., 314.
Bayli, Baylif, Baylli, Bayly, Baylye, v. Bailey.
Baylze, John, clerk, 1129.
Baynay, John, 1497.
Baystan, Rob., of Chesterfield, 2491.
Baystowe, Ralph de, 406, 2020.
Beard, John, 2227.
Beatrice, widow, 1336.
Beaufei, Beaufey, Belfai, Beufei, Bella Fide.
———John de, mil., 2388, 2389.
———Robert I., 932, 2380, 2382.
———Robert II., de., 51, 879, 1698, 2381-2383.
———Thomas de, 2389.

Beaufort, Hen., Bp. of Winchester, 82.
Beaumonde, Dom. Thomas, de Bakevile, 1988.
Beaumont, John, Viscount, 846.
Bec, Becco, Beec, Beic, Bek.
———Ernald de, 1360.
———Dom. Geoffrey de, miles, 662, 1166, 2569, 2570, 2611.
———Geoffrey de, 2577, 2578, 2718.
———Goyfred de, 1360.
———Dom. Hen. de, 216, 399, 2583.
———John le, 50.
———Robert de, 2125.
———Walter f. dom. Hen. del, 2580.
Beche, Dom. Nich. de la, 578.
Bechel, v. Beeley.
Beck, v. Beke.
Bee, John, 2676.
———Oliver, 2676.
———Ric., rector of Mugginton, 2602.
Beeley, Bechel, Beeleg, Begelaia, Begele, Begelei, Beghle, Beghley, Begle, Beilea, Beileg, Beilie, Beley, Bethtley.
———John de, 245, 247.
———Marg. dom. de, 245, 247.
———Luke de, 173, 1328.
———Serlo, f. Warneri de, 244, 1207, 1208, 1328, 1610, 1611, 2745.
———Tho. de, Dominus de Beghley, 250, 252, 253.
———Warnerius de, 216, 244.
———Will. de, 1334.
———Will. f. Galfridi de, 252.
Beerd, Nich de, 2115.
Beere, Agnes, w. of John de, 618.
———John de, 618.
Beeston, Robert, 1873.
Befayse, Ric., of Trusselay, 1654.
Begalaia, Begele, Begelei, Beghle, Beghley, Begle, v. Beeley.
Begum, Rob., 194.
Beighton, Bectona, Becthon, Beghton.
———Geoffrey de, clericus, 1732.
———John, 1478.
———John, f. Rog. de, 502.
———Rog. de, 1728.
Beilea, Beileg, Beilie, v. Beeley.
Beirchover, v. Birchover.
Bek, v. Bec.
Beke, John de, 2017.
———Thomas, Bishop of St. David's, 1317-1319, 1896, 1897.
———Will., vicar of Sallowe, 1692.
Bel, Hugh le, 1501, 1502.
Beleby, Adam, de Asseburne, 1644.
Belefeld, Christopher, 2451.
Belesby, Dom. Will. de, 1899.
Belet, William, 1428.
Belfai, v. Beaufey.
Belfeld, Christopher de, 2457.
Beliden', John, 1478.
Bella Fide, v. Beaufey.
Bellasvs, John, parson of Halwynfeld, 1869.
Belle, Robert, 49.
Belleston, R— de, 2634.

Bello Campo, Alina, s. of Stephen de, 909.
———Hugh de, 533, 534, 1752.
———Idona, s. of Stephen de, 909.
———Isolda, s. of Steph. de, 909, 911.
———Matildis, s. of Stephen de, 909.
———Stephen de, 908-911.
———Walter de, 909.
Bellow, Bellowe, John, 924, 2565.
Belzetter, Alice, w. of Rog., 589.
———Rog., 589.
Benedicite, Johan, 1619.
Benedict, avunculus Hug. Comitis, 1939.
Benet, John, 1469.
Benett, Thos., 2450.
Bentley, Benetylee, Bentelay, Benteleg, Benteley, Benteleye, Bentl', Bentlay, Bentle', Bentlg.
———Avice, w. of Nic. de, 284.
———Henry, Dom. de, 25.
———Hen. le Ballif de, 512.
———Hen. de, 929.
———Joan, d. of Will., 235.
———Johanna, w. of Thomas, 2083-2085.
———John de, 76, 392, 669, 673, 1549, 1559, 1709, 2160.
———John, f. Hen. de, 287.
———John, f. Joh. de, 512.
———John, s. of Nic. de, 284.
———John, f. Tho., 2405.
———Nic. de, 284.
———Philip de, 287.
———Richard de, 216.
———Thomas, 2083, 2084, 2358.
———Tho. f. Amote de, 287.
———William de, 139, 2714.
Bentte, Will., rector of Sutton-in-lee-Dale, 1881.
Bercarius, Bercher, Le, v. Barker.
Berd, John, s. of Nich., 1812.
Berde, John de, of Derby, 987.
Berdesley, Hugh, 514.
———James, 514.
Berdhalgh, Berdehalegh, Berdhall, Berd-halugh.
———Edith, w. of Will. de, 1371.
———Hugh, f. Will. de, 1371.
———Margery de, 1370.
———Ric., s. of Margery de, 1370.
———Rog. de, sen., 1374.
———Roger de, 208.
———Will., s. of Margery de, 1370.
———Will. de, 1371, 1372.
Berdvile, Tho., 636.
Bereford, John, bailiff of Oxford, 1922.
———Osbert de, 1704.
———Walter de, 1756, 2579, 2581.
———Will. de, 1064.
———Will. de, King's Justice, 2251.
Beregge, Rob., 2099.
Beresford, Baresford, Beresforthe, Berse-ford, Bersforde, Berysford, etc.
———Aden, 304.
———Denys, 306, 1013.
———Edmund, of Newton Graunge, 1749-1751.

Beresford, etc., Edward, 1013.
———James, 2555.
———John de, 1047.
———John, of Bradley Ash, 286, 1811.
———Katherine, of Newton Graunge, 1748-1751.
———Laurence, of Newton Graunge, 1749-1751, 2555.
———Ralph, of Asshburn, 87.
———Tho., of Newton Graunge, 1647.
Berford, Simon de, 1954.
Berges, Anchetillus de, 2090, 2091.
Bergete, Eustace de, 1397.
Berkeley, Tho., Lord Berkeley, 491, 492.
Bermyngham, Master Richard, 1438.
Bernak, Gervase de, Knt., 1461, 2340, 2706.
Bernard, Robert, 2069.
Bernehulle, Tho. de, 409.
Bernes, John de, 2375.
Berney, Hanken, 1385.
Berneys, al. Bernis, Peter de, 130, 1017, 1035, 2374, 2375.
Berseford, Bersforde, v. Beresford.
Bersicote, Bursicot, John de, 1197, 1277.
———Richard de, 1197.
———Robert de, 2610.
Berta, Comitissa Cestrie, v. Chester, Earls of.
Bertolomeus, v. Bartholomew.
Bertone, Oliver de, 289.
Bertram, camerarius, 535, 536.
Berwa, Beatrice de, 1947.
———Richard de, 1947.
Berysford, v. Beresford.
Besebosc, Walter de, 909.
Beston, Alice de, of Chestrefield, 797.
Bete, Emma que fuit uxor Ade, 701.
———John, f. Rog., of Cestrefeld, 715.
———John, 731, 741-745, 751-754, 2312.
———Marjory, w. of John, f. Joh., 742.
———Rob., f. John, sen., 746.
———Rog., chaplain, 744.
———Dom. Rog. of Chastrefeld, 767.
———Simon, f. Ade, 701.
Betegge, Peter de, 2095.
Bethebroke, v. Bythebroke.
Bethtleye, v. Beeley.
Bette, John, 1366.
Beufei, v. Beaufey.
Beufyis, Dom. John de, 919.
Beure, Thurston de, 1231.
Beverage, Beuerege, Beverege, Bever-egge.
———Alice, w. of Will, 755.
———Richard, 2291, 2502, 2503.
———William, 749, 753, 755, 2496.
Beverlaco, Thomas de, 1082, 1420.
Bewofoy, Richard, of Trusley, 2323.
Bey, Adam le, 2733.
Beynbryge, Rob., of Hoknastone, 1385.
Beyser, Margery, condam ux. Rob. f. Rob., 736.
Bientelegh, Will de, 40.

Bieston, Rog., vicar of Hareworthe, 213.
Bigarius, Peter, 2008.
Bigheleghe, Will de, 2094.
Bildeston, Tho. de, chaplain, 1760.
Biley, Tho. de, 251.
Biling, Will. de, 2093.
Billesdon, Rog. de, of Herdby, 1635.
Binford, Fr. Hugh de, 1539.
Bingham, Byngham, Byngeham.
———Marget, w. of Rich., 2518.
———Richard, 23, 2461.
———Richard de, Knt., 2215, 2567.
———Anna, wid. of Ric., 88.
———Dom. Ric. de, 368, 378.
———Rich., Justice of King's Bench, 2467.
———Ric., s. of Dom. Ric. de, 368.
———Thomas, 884.
———Mag. Thos., late Warden of Pembroke Coll., Cambridge, 1982.
———Tho., s. of Sir Ric. de, 1844.
———Dom. Will. de, 1105.
Birchehoure, v. Birchover.
Bircheld, Agnes f. Hug. de, 1802.
———Joan f. Hug. de, 1802.
Birchelif, Hugh f. Joh. de, 1613.
Birchete, John, 1326.
Bircheved, Birchevend, Berchevid, Birchehewed, Burcheved, Byrched.
———John de, 2374, 2425.
———John, of Swotall, 1327.
———Peter de, 131, 2426.
———Tho. de, 1018, 2377.
Birchover, Beirchover, Birchehoure, Bircheoure, Birchouere, Bircheover, Byrchouyr.
———Cecilia, w. of Tho. de, 293, 295.
———R— de, 2621.
———Rob. de, chaplain, 744.
———Rob. de, rector of Rushton, 754.
———Roger fil. Simund de, 2620.
———Simund de, 2621.
———Tho. s. of Will. de, 293-296.
———Walter, f. Ade de, 294.
———Will de, 38, 293, 2226, 2625, 2626.
Birchull, Will. de, 92.
Bird, John, Bishop of Chester, 655.
Birkenschagh, Byrkynschawe.
———Margery, w. of Tho. del, 780.
———Tho., of Newerk, 780, 789, 798.
Birkes, Cecilia, wid. of Rob. de, 786.
Birley, Byrlay.
———John f. Rog. de, 269.
———Ric. de, of Brampton, 439.
———Rog. f. Elie de, 1047.
———Thos. f. Rog. de, 2556.
———Will de, 418.
Bisacia, Ranulph de, 1949.
Bishop, Biscop, Bisshop, Bissop, Byschop, Byshope, Bysshope.
———John, 1977, 1979, 1992.
———Nich., of Chapel-en-le-Frith, 2435.
———Ralph, of Hambury, 345.
———Rog., of Bakewell, 202.

Bishop, etc., Rog., of Longeford, 1573.
———Rog. s. of Rog., of Longeford, 1573.
———v. Bythebroke.
Bithebroke, v. Bythebroke.
Blacgreve, v. Blagreve.
Black, Henry, 2733.
Blackfordeby, Simon, 1980.
Blackwall, Blacquell, Blakewall, Blakwal, Blakwall, Blakwalle.
———Adam de, 1550.
———Agnes, d. of Rob., 265.
———Anna, wid. of Ric., 88.
———Christofer, 265.
———Elizabeth, d. of Cristofer, 265.
———Hen., of Blakwalle, 1252, 1254.
———Johanna, w. of Thrustan, 857.
———John, chaplain, 2479.
———John, s. of Rob., 265.
———Milo, 2123.
———Nich. de, 1547.
———Nich., vicar of Beston, 957, 2682.
———Oliver, rector of Barton-in-le-Denys, 957.
———Richard, 637, 1383, 1389, 1506, 2681, 2684.
———Ric., of Wirksworth, 1008, 1009.
———Rob., 265, 1383.
———Thomas, 89.
———Tho., s. of Crist., 265.
———Tho., s. and heir of Thrustan, 857, 858.
Blagge, Rob., Baron of the Exchequer, 1001.
Blagreve, Blacgreve, Blaggriev, Blakegreve, Blakgreve.
———Ralph, 2060, 2062, 2063, 2065, 2066.
———Richard de, 2044, 2049.
Blaggreiv, v. Blagreve.
Blak, Will., 1641.
Blake, Rob. le, 1334.
Blakegreve. Blakgreve, v. Blagreve.
Blakesea, Tho., 1005.
Blakewall, Blakwall, etc., v. Blackwall.
Blakiswalle, Sir John, chauntry-priest of Dronfield, 265.
Blaklach, Richard, chaplain, 2366.
Blaunchard, Will. f. Will., of Castiltone, 515.
Bleyn, Rob., 1777.
Blid, Blida, v. Blythe.
Blithe, v. Blythe.
Blodletere, Stephen le, 1556.
Blount, Blounte, Blund, Blundus, Blunt.
———Adam, 353, 684, 2491, 2556.
———Alexander, canon of Lichfield, 179, 189, 1953.
———Geoffrey, 386, 1501-1503.
———Giles, 274.
———Mag. John, 175.
———John, Knt., 2081.
———John, of Murkaston, 137.
———John, 2141.
———Peter, 386.
———Robert, 416, 2494.
———Thomas, 1280, 2394.

Blount, etc., Dom. Tho., Knt., 1393, 1394, 1594, 2678.
————Walter, 161, 1376, 1616, 2392.
————Walter, Knt., 207, 209, 344, 1393, 1692, 1693.
————Will., Lord Mountjoy, 350.
————William, 1304.
————Will., chaplain, 1892.
Blund, Blundus, *v.* Blount.
Blundel, John, 387.
Blundeville, Ranulph, *v.* Chester, Earls of.
Blunt, *v.* Blount.
Blye, Rog. de, 360, 709.
Blys, William, 1018.
Blythe, Blid, Blida, Blithe, Blyd.
————Adam de, 722.
————Agnes, d. of Rog. de, 732.
————John de, 1777.
————John, clerk, 1781.
————Leticia, w. of Philip de, 732.
————Lucy, d. of Rog. de, 732.
————Philip de, 732.
————Ric., 1780.
————Roger de, 364, 545, 690, 695, 707, 715, 724, 732, 2311.
————Tho. f. Will., of Barnby, 1781.
————Will, of Barnby, 1781.
————Will, of Norton, 1781.
Bobi, Hugh de, Justice at Nottingham, 2334.
Bobinhull, Isabella quondam uxo Egidii de, 694.
————Roger de, 245.
————Rog., s. of Isabella, 694.
————Wydo de, 245, 247.
Bocher, Ranulph, 809.
————William, 1110.
Bocheruilla, Rob. de, 2380.
Bocheryvl, Will., of Sudbury, 930.
Bockyng, John, of Hope, 1449.
————Richard, 1439.
————Roger, 1439.
Bocstones, *v.* Buxton.
Bofton, Robert, 1613.
Boghhey, Will., rector of Walton, 2538.
Boileston, *v.* Boyleston.
Boithorp, *v.* Boythorpe.
Bojoun, Robert, 245.
Bokestones, *v.* Buxton.
Bokynhill, Rog. de, 737.
Bolayn, Thos., knt., 2534.
Boldne, Walter, Bailiff of Oxford, 1922.
Boleby, Adam de, of Assheburne, 72.
————Alice, w. of Adam de, 72.
Boler, Cecilia, d. of Nich. le, 621.
————Elena, w. of Will. le, 619.
————John, s. of Nich. le, 621.
————Nicholas le, 621.
————Nich. s. of Nich. le, 621.
————Rog. s. of Nich. le, 621.
————Roger, 793, 813.
————Tho. s. of Nich. le, 621.
————Will. le, de Blacwell, 619.
————Will. s. of Nich. le, 621.
————Will. of Bagschawe, 629.
Bolhawe, Bollehawe, John de, chaplain, 1760, 1864, 1865.

Bollesorwodehouses, Ric. f. Rob. de, 499.
Bollesouer, Nich. de, 1894.
Bollesover, John de, chamberlain to the Prior of Tuttebury, 1365.
Bollock, Bollok, Bollokk, Bolocke, *v.* Bullock.
Bolt, Bolte, John, 1979, 1981.
Bolton, Boltone.
————Patrick de, 326, 328.
————Rob. f. Simonis de, 328.
————Will. f. Ric. de, 326, 327.
Bon, Ric., 1194.
Bonay, Will. de, Abbot of Dale, 942.
Bonde, Adam fil, 351, 354.
————Avice le, of Egynton, 1171.
————Cecily, w. of John, 375.
————Hen. chaplain of Chaddesden Chantry, 611, 612.
————John, 367, 374, 375, 702, 726.
————Sir John, 778.
————Dom. John, perpetual vicar of Chesterfield, 766.
————John f. Aue, 364.
————John f. Joh., 372, 373, 375, 703, 708.
————John f. Ric., 371.
————Margery f. Joh., 708.
————Matilda, w. of John de Sutton, 778.
————Rob. f. Elie le, de Egynton, 1172.
————Tho., vicar, and Alderman of St. Mary's Guild, Chesterfield, 768.
————Walter, 664.
Bondissale, Bondsale, *v.* Bonsall.
Bone, Will., Abbot of Burton, 2619.
Bonefaunt, Henry, chaplain, 2105.
Bonne, Edward, 383.
Bonsall, Bondissale, Bondsale, Bonteshale, Bontessale, Bontisal, Bontishal, Bontishalc.
————Alan de, 1702.
————Hen. f. Ric. de, 310.
————John, s. of Hen. de, 315.
————Ralph f. Joh. de, of Aldewerke, 19.
————Ric. f. Joh. de, 310.
————Walter f. Osberti de, 310.
————William de, 915.
————Will. f. Renald de, 312.
————Yngelesia f. Rad. f. Joh. de, 19.
Bonseriant, Hugh, de Thorpe, 29.
Bonteshale, Bontessale, Bontisal, Bontishall, *v.* Bonsall.
Bonus, Hen. dictus, 1137.
Bonyngton, John, 1181, 1764.
————William, 1596.
Boolande, Humphrey, 2191.
Boolar, Roger, 816.
Boonde, *v.* Bonde.
Bordet, *v.* Burdet.
Boreford, Walter de, 1755.
Borley, Henry de, 2547.
————Will. de, 2547.

Borowes, Borwes.
———Ric. late of Chestrefeld, 869.
———Will. del, 522.
Borton, *v.* Burton.
Boscheuill, Boscherville, Boschiervill, Boschereuilla, Boschuill.
———John de, 1113, 1499, 2382.
———Ralph de, 2001, 2381.
Bosco, De, Boscum, Ad.
———Helyas, de Barleia, 225.
———John, 885.
———Peter f. Ade, de Bremyngton, 498.
———Richard, mil., 2536.
———Rich. f. Ade, 2562.
———Mag. Rob., Archdeacon of Coventry, 1681, 2572.
———Tho., de Scheffeld, 1126.
———Walter, 2152, 2212.
———William, de Doubrigge, 2161.
Bosco-calumpniato, Will. de, 2614.
Boseley, Matilda, w. of Will. de, 769.
———William de, 769.
Boslistun, Reginald de, 238.
Boso, 1078.
Bote, Rob., 2245.
Boteler, Botiler, Botiller, Butler.
———Agnes, w. of Ric., 2183.
———Edm. le, 2180.
———Ralph, 489.
———Richard, 2183.
———Thomas, knt., 1456.
———Thomas, 2163, 2189.
———William, 1977.
Botelesford, Simon de, master of Newark Schools, 1844.
Boteley, Will., 1979.
Boterdon, Boturdon, William, 78-81, 1769.
Boterley, Rob. de, 123.
Bothby, Thos., 2190.
Bothe, Both, Bouthe.
———Henry de, 803, 827, 1280, 1769, 1874, 1930, 1932, 1988, 2081, 2411.
———Hen. de, of Norbury, 1181.
———Hen. s. of Will., 1187, 1188.
———John, 524, 1189, 2257, 2259-2262.
———John, of Arlistone, 279, 1188.
———John, of Derby, 989, 1183.
———John del, of Findern, 2281.
———John, of Staveley, 1128, 2558.
———John f. Hen., 1182, 1183, 1187.
———Letiscia f. Will. f. Ade dil, 2314.
———Richard, of Abney, 7.
———Will. s. and heir of John, 1187.
Bothum, Will. of Stoke, 1258.
Botiler, *v.* Boteler.
Boton, Botoun.
———John, 1059.
———Richard, 2349.
———Sir Thomas, priest, 2476.
———William, 2449.
Boton del Lees, Will., 1063.
Boturdon, *v.* Boterdon.
Bouchier, Tho., Bishop of Ely, 490.
Bouke, Tho. del, 1590.

Boulton, Rob. f. Hen. de, 329.
Bourchier, Humfry, Baron Cromwell, 1067.
———John, Abbot of "our lady of the medowez of Leycester," 305.
Boure, *v.* Bower.
Boureton, Will de, 2109.
Bourgh, Hugh, 1495.
Bouryng, Henry, 2741.
Bousrohart, Lambert de, 539.
Bousser, John de, Justice, 2251.
Bouthe, *v.* Bothe.
Boutton, Adam de, 50.
Bouynton, Margery, 1358.
Bowdon, Nich., 633.
Bower, Boure, Bowre.
———Christian del, 817.
———Elen, d. of John, 1437.
———John, of Hope, 1437.
———Mar. w. of Thurst. de la, 2357.
———Marg. m. of Thurst. de la, 2357.
———Robert de, 1374.
———Rose, w. of John, 1437.
———Thurstan de, 549, 813, 815, 818, 823, 824, 827, 1237, 1701, 2357, 2510.
———Will. f. Joh. del, of Quytefeld, 2119.
Bowne, Henry, 1678.
———Sir William, 1672.
———William, 1678.
———Will., of Holme, 213.
Bowre, *v.* Bower.
Bowsefeld, John, 2690.
Boxon, Will., of Rokeston, 300.
Boylestone, Boileston, Boylleston.
———Reginald de, 2380.
———William, 1190.
Boys, Cecily, w. of Ric., 1648-1650.
———Richard, 1648-1650, 2417.
Boythorp, Boythorpe, Boithorp.
———Albreia, vidua, de, 352.
———Hugh f. Godwini de, 414.
———Ralph f. Hug. de, 358, 365, 366.
———Robert de, 352.
———Rob. f. Christiane de, 357.
———Rob. f. Galfridi de, 547, 684.
———Rob. f. Rob. de, 353.
Bozon, Bozoun.
———John, 368.
———John, dominus de Edlinsouere, 522, 1214, 2329.
———Rich. f. Joh., 2329, 2330.
Brabazon, Dom. Roger, 2100.
Brabyl, Matthew, 2762.
Bracebrigge, Geoffrey de, 1472.
Bracley, Will., 1186.
Bradbery, *v.* Bradbury.
Bradborne, Bradbourn, Bradburn, Bradburne, Braddeburn, Bradebourne, Bradeburn.
———Anne, 2678.
———Henry, 160, 285, 394, 1185, 1647, 2187, 2394.
———Humphrey, of Hough, 1332, 1359, 1823, 2141.

Bradborne, etc., Humphrey, Knt., 2701.
——Mag. John de, clerk, 147.
——John de, 150, 151, 157, 388, 1359, 1588, 1822, 2000.
——John, del Hogh, 1694, 1695.
——John, s. and h. of Henry, 2678.
——John f. Hugonis de, 390, 391, 393.
——John f. Dom. Rog. de, 59.
——Margery, w. of Hen., 394.
——Ric. de, of Hokenaston, 149.
——Rob. de, 135.
——Dom. Rog. de, Knt., 58, 144, 145, 147, 338, 388, 401, 1741, 1822, 2549, 2726.
——Roger de, 30, 60, 76, 1151, 1693, 1892, 1924, 1929, 2344.
——Will. de, of Brassington, 393.
——Will. f. Joh. de, 393.
Bradbury, Bradbery, Bredbare, Bredbery, Bredbury, Breddebere.
——Gilbert de, 2657.
——Sr. John, "Lady prest" at Bradshaw, 646.
——Nicholas, of Gratton, 2236.
——Rich., of Gratton, 2231, 2232.
——Robert de, 1372, 1374.
——Roger f. Ric. de, 1786.
——William de, 2659, 2660.
Bradebourne, Bradeburne, v. Bradborne.
Bradeford, Thos. de, 27.
——Tho. de, clericus, 182.
Bradelowe, Hen. de, 1523.
Brademere, Ric. de, 1338.
Bradeschawe, v. Bradshaw.
Bradeway, v. Bradway.
Bradfeld, Tho., of Mercaston, 1526, 1694.
Bradley, Bradeley, Bradeleye.
——John de, vicar of Duffeld, 1181, 2602.
——John f. Rudulfi de, 882.
——Roger de, 1520.
——Dom. Will. de, chaplain, 63, 64.
Bradshaw, Bradeschawe, Bradscha, Bradschag, Bradsha, Bradshag, Bradshaghe, Brasha, Bredsha, etc.
——Agnes, d. of Rog., 1482, 1486.
——Alexander, 230.
——Edmund, of Iderechehay, 1003, 1119.
——Elizabeth, 648, 650.
——Elizabeth, w. of Hen., 648.
——Godfrey, s. and h. of Will., of Marple, 569, 570.
——Henry, 634, 636, 639, 640, 642, 643, 645, 646, 648, 650, 656, 659, 2602.
——Henry, s. and h. of John, 625, 626, 1900.
——Henry, Attorney - General, 1680.
——Hugh, late of Coventry, 2360, 2361.
——Hugh, of Morebarn, 638.

26

Bradshaw, etc., Joesa, 632.
——John, 446, 616, 622-626, 635, 1930, 2123.
——John, of Derby, 1988.
——John, senr., of Lichfield, 638.
——John, junr., of Lichfield, 638.
——Katharine, w. of Ric., 654, 655.
——Margaret, w. of Rog., 1482, 1483, 1485.
——Mary, w. of John de, 616.
——Ralph, 1377, 1378.
——Ric. f. Joh. de, 616.
——Richard, 648, 653.
——Ric., of Bowden, 655.
——Ric., of Bradshaw, 650-652.
——Ric., of Marpul, 656, 659.
——Robert, 1119, 1349.
——Rob. s. of John de, 625, 626.
——Rog., Dominus de Meygnylle Longley, 1505.
——Rog., 1930.
——Rog., of Idridgehay, 1482, 1483.
——Thomas, 1183, 1280, 1986, 2602.
——Tho. de, sub-ballivus de Alto Pecco, 619.
——William, 839, 845, 1803, 2359, 2516.
——Will. f. Joh. de, jun., 622, 625, 626.
——Will., of Bradshaw, 628, 630-632, 634-636.
——Will., of Eyam, 1242.
——Will., of Marple, 569, 570, 650-659.
——Will., of Lynacre Hall, 7.
——Will., of Wadchelf, 470.
Bradway, Bradeway, Rog. de, 1053, 1398.
Bradwell, Bradewell, Bradwalle.
——Alice, w. of Rob. de, 2117.
——Ric. f. Will. f. Fabiani de, 405.
——Rob. f. Elie de, 2117.
——Rob. f. Will. f. Fabiani de, 405.
——Walter de, 406.
Braileford, v. Brailsford.
Brailsford, Braileford, Brailesford, Braillefort, Braillesford, Bralesford, Braylesford, Braylisford, Brayllesford, Braylusford, Breylesford, Breylisford.
——Agnes, w. of Will. de, 409.
——Engonulf de, 1503, 2718.
——Engyllard de, 1520.
——Henry de, 124, 135, 332, 335, 340, 396, 402, 409, 1351, 1520, 1629, 2005, 2125, 2712.
——Dom. Hen. de, knt., 113, 697, 928, 1131, 1561, 1564, 1566-1568, 1865, 2289, 2546, 2549.
——Isabel, wid. of Hen. de, 522.
——John de, 409, 2409, 2410.
——John, of Etwall, 511.

Brailsford, etc., Dom. Ralph de, knt., 397, 2321.
———Rog. f. Rog. de, 1361.
———Will. de, 409.
———Will. de, bailiff of Derby, 983.
Braiton, Rob. f. Alexandri de, 180.
Bralesford, v. Brailsford.
Braminton, Rob. de, 228, 2242.
Brammall, Thomas, 1485.
Brampton, Bramptone, Bramptune, Bramton, etc.
———Alice, w. of Rog. f. Avicie de, 445.
———Geoffrey de, 244.
———Hugh f. Rob. de, 442.
———Hugh f. Stephani de, 442.
———Ingiram de, 413.
———Margaret de, 2698.
———Ralph de, 413.
———Ranulf f. Margarete de, 420.
———Ric. de, capellanus, 443.
———Robert, 824, 826.
———Rog. f. Avicie de, 445.
———Thomas de, 224, 354, 411, 415, 416, 424, 427, 434, 1533, 2419, 2428, 2494.
———The. f. Hugonis f. Ingrami de, 427.
———The. f. Rad. de, 419, 422, 2487, 2562.
———Walter f. Thome de, 2487, 2564.
———William, 822, 824, 826, 832, 834, 836, 2514, 2515.
———Will., of Chestrefeld, 1059.
Brancote, Robert de, 2092.
Brandewodde, Nich., priest, vicar of Trusley, 2396.
Branton, v. Brampton.
Brascynton, v. Brassington.
Brasha, v. Bradshaw.
Brasier, Will., chaplain, 2361.
Brassington, Brascynton, Brasynton.
———John de, 143.
———William de, 1522-1524.
Bratte, John and Richard, 2078.
Braunche, Philip, knt., 1248.
Braund, Henry, 2628.
Bray, Braye.
———Dom. Tho. de, 1114, 2714.
———Dom. Tho. le, senr., Senescallus Tutteburie, 1292.
———Will., vicar of Hartington, 2403.
Braybon, Laurence, chaplain, 2110, 2287.
Braybrooke, Braibroc, Braybroke.
———Gerard de, knt., 1984, 1985.
———Henry de, 911.
———Rob. de, Bishop of London, 1984, 1985.
Braylesford, Braylisford, Brayllesford, Braylusford, v. Brailsford.
Brayn, Henry de, 2714.
Brecte, v. Brett.
Bredbare, Bredbery, Bredbury, Breddebere, v. Bradbury.
Bredelowe, Hen. de, of Kyrkelongeleye, 1524.

Bredlowe, Will. de, 1786.
Bredon, Bredona.
———Henry de, bailiff of Derby, 985.
———John de, bailiff of Derby, 977, 981, 983.
———Ralph de, 2580, 2583.
Bredsha, v. Bradshaw.
Breidesal, Breideshale, Breydeshale.
———H— de, 2382.
———Joan f. Nich. de, 2638.
———Nich. de, constable of Tutbury, 1698.
———Ralph de, 2546.
Brekediche, John, 574.
Bremington, John de, 2420, 2421.
———Ralph de, 2424.
Brenstone, Will., Abbot of Burton-on-Trent, 596.
Brereleye, Leticia f. Galfridi de, 1533.
Breres, Nigel de le, 519.
Brese, Robert, 1367, 1368, 2107, 2108.
Bret, Breth, v. Brett.
Bretby, Bretteby.
———Edw., chaplain, 2164.
———John de, of Burton-on-Trent, 68.
———Sibilla, w. of John de, 68.
Bretener, Brettener, Rob., 206, 846.
Breton, Bretone, Bretoun, Bretton, Bretun, v. Briton.
Brett, Brecte, Bret, Breth.
———Mary, w. of Will. le, 2486.
———Dom. Rog. de, knt., 378.
———Roger le, 2192.
———Thomas le, 590.
———William le, 115, 378, 428, 495, 543, 701, 704, 712, 1094, 1095, 2120, 2192, 2248, 2409, 2420, 2486.
Bretteby, v. Bretby.
Brettener, v. Bretener.
Bretun, v. Briton.
Brewer, Briewer, Briuerre, Briwer, Briwerre.
———Joan que fuit uxor Will., 681.
———Ric. s. of Will., 679.
———William, 172, 680.
———Will. le, senr., 698.
———Will. le, junr., 682, 698.
———Will., Sheriff of Nottingham, 1554.
Brewester, John, 395.
———Thomas, 395.
Brewod, Brewode.
———John, rector of Rodburne, 1505, 1654, 1930-1932.
———Tho., of Rodeburne, 1654.
———Will. de, 1654, 1925.
Brex, Fr. Will. de, 1575.
Breydeshale, Breydishale, v. Breidesal.
Breydeston, etc., Hen. f. Rob. de, 1337.
———John, s. of Will., s. of Hauwis de, 485.
———Michael de, 1337.
Breylesford, v. Brailsford.
Brian, v. Bryan.
Bricheshard, Ralph de, 536.
Brid, Bridde, v. Bryde.

Bridburi, Ottewell, of Bauckehed, 650.
Bridbury, Nicholas, 650.
Bridwaldus, 1391.
Briequerre, Will., 1419.
Briewer, *v.* Brewer.
Brig, Brigge, Brygge, atte Brig.
————Margaret, wid. of John, of
      Maperley, 281.
————Thomas, 827, 832, 2316.
————Thomas, 2506, 2507.
Brightrichefeld, Bryghtrichefeld, John f.
      Galfridi de, 1908, 1909, 1911.
Brikesard, Thos. de, 2092.
Brimington, Brimenton, Brimentona,
      Brimingtona, Brimingtone, Brimin-
      ton, Brimintona, Brimintone, Brin-
      hingtona.
————Alan de, 1092.
————John de, 543, 693, 1775, 2192,
        2248, 2308, 2427, 2557,
        2563.
————John f. Petri de, 425.
————John f. Radulfi de, 495.
————Jordan f. Will. f. Rog. de, 493.
————Peter de, 360, 410, 411, 420,
        494, 495, 497, 683, 687,
        695, 1535, 2245, 2429.
————Dom. Peter de, 1034, 1086,
        1089, 1090.
————Peter f. Hug., 357, 707, 1090.
————Ralph f. Galf. de Cimiterio
        de, 494.
————Ralph f. Petri de, 711.
————Rob. de, 414.
————Rob. f. Egidii de, 2440.
————Tho. f. Rad. de Cimiterio de, 495.
————Will. f. Rog. de, 493.
————Will. s. of Will. de, 493.
Brimpton, John de, 2310.
Brinhingtona, *v.* Brimington.
Brischfeld, Tho. de, 1238.
Briton, Breton, Bretonn, Bretoun,
      Bretton, Bretun, Brito, Briton,
      Brittun, Bryton.
————Alan le, Canon of Lichfield,
        1957.
————Peter le, 2486.
————Philippa, w. of Rob. le, 1044,
        1746.
————Ralph, 412, 1727, 1729.
————Rob. le, Lord of Walton, 414,
        424, 501, 1044, 1746, 2418,
        2703.
————Rob., de Waletona, 413, 542.
————Rob. s. of Rob. le, 1044, 2734.
————Rob. s. of Rob. le, Dom. de
        Walton, 1746.
————Rob. f. Rog. le, Dom. de
        Walton, 433.
————Rob. f. et h. Rog. le, 496.
————Nich. f. Will. ad le, 496.
————Robert le, 123, 124, 427, 1198,
        2247.
————Rog. le, Dominus de Walton,
        696, 1086, 1088, 1089,
        1090, 2496.
————Rog. le, knt., 1503.
————Roger, 113, 115, 378, 428, 704,
        1697, 1746, 2409, 2486,
        2500, 2580, 2605, 2734.

Briton, etc., Rog. f. Rog., of Walton,
      2487.
————Thomas le, 1896.
————Will. le, of Trhiberg, 663.
————William, 2090.
Briuerre, Briwer, Briwerre, *v.* Brewer.
Broc, Brok, Broke.
————Agnes, w. of Will. ad le, 2176,
        2179.
————Joan, w. of John, 901.
————John, 602, 901.
————Robert, clerk, 2166.
————Will. f. Andr. ad le, 2176.
Brocton, Rob. de, of Attelowe, 148, 149.
Broctun, Aluric de, 238.
Brodeok, Hug de, 2583.
————Will. de, 2583.
Brodwod, Nich., 991.
Bromale, John, 1191.
————Matilda, w. of John, 1191.
Bromcote, Broncote.
————Helyas de, 2090.
————Herbert de, 2090, 2091.
Brom, Brome.
————Robert de, 2556.
————Will., chaplain, 625, 626, 2119.
————Will., vicar of Baukewell, 1444.
Bromefeld, Tho., 1124.
Bromeholme, John, 808.
Bromhall, Tho. de, 1243.
Bromhead, Will., 1075.
Bromle, John de, carpenter, 2095.
Bromley, Richard, 1517.
Bromore, John de, 618.
Brompton, Rog. de, parson of Bradley,
      1347.
Bromtone, Brian de, 917.
Bromwich, William, 2070.
Bromylegh, Matilda, w. of Will. de, 786.
————Will. de, 786.
Broncote, *v.* Bromcote.
Brontestune, Leising de, 1197.
Brown, Broun, Broune, Browne.
————Adam, 780, 788, 844, 2315.
————Anne, wid. of Will., 2079.
————Augnes f. Ric., of Whytyngton,
        2437.
————Elena, wid. of John, 2073.
————Eliz. w. of Rich., 2071, 2072.
————Henry, 1646.
————Isabella, 824.
————Dom. John, 160.
————John, 2061-2063, 2070, 2347,
        2666, 2668.
————John, of Snelston, 1768, 2136.
————John, clerk, 2607, 2609.
————John f. Will., of Pontefract,
        2618.
————Nich., de ly Marsche, 647.
————Nich., 625, 626, 629, 1371.
————Ric., of Ekynton, chaplain,
        1042.
————Rich. of Repton, 2541.
————Richard, of Uttoxeter, 2078.
————Richard, 1640, 1874, 1989, 1990,
        2071, 2072, 2074, 2393.
————Robert, 1758.
————Thomas, 2180.
————Thomas, of Wheston, 2348.

Brown, etc., Will., of Bagschag, 619.
———Will., of Swarkeston, 1364.
———Will., of Uttoxeter, 2075, 2079.
———Will., 813.
Brudenell, Rob., Justice of Common Pleas, 1657.
———Robert, 1936.
Brugge, Andrew del, 2115.
———John del, 2115.
Bruggeton, Will. de, chaplain, 2545.
Brun, Hen. le, of Cesterfeld, 687.
———Reginald, of Herninglow, 2613.
Brunnaldiston, Brunufystone.
———Isabella, w. of Nich. f. Hen. de, 518.
———Nich. f. Hen. de, 517, 518.
———Ric. f. Orm de, 517.
Brus, Bernard de, 1962, 1963.
———Robert de, 1963.
Brustall, Robert, 1792.
Bruwys, Hen. de, 517.
Brwode, Thomas de, of Radbourne, 1934.
Bryan, Brian.
———Henry, 2330.
———Rob., de Ekynton, 1042, 1735-1739.
———William, 39.
Bryches, Agnes f. et her. Ric. de, 441.
———Alice f. et her. Ric. de, 441.
———Johanna f. et her. Ric. de, 441.
———Richard de, 441.
Bryde, Brid, Bridde, Brydde.
———John, 995, 2728.
———John, clerk, 2554.
———Rauf, of Netherlokhawe, 1553.
———Richard, 1553.
———Rob., of Skegby, 2555.
Brygge, *v.* Brig.
Bryghtrichefeld, *v.* Brightrichefeld.
Brynaston, Will. de, chaplain, 793.
Brynnesley, John de, Rector of Hoggesthorp, 1181.
———Rob. de, 1866.
Bubendona, Oliver f. Nigelli de, 1554.
Buckingham, Duke of, *v.* Stafford, Humphrey.
Buckstanis, Bucstones, *v.* Buxton.
Bugge, Ralph, 1396.
———Ralph f. Rad., 355, 2213.
———Ric., de Notingham, 1336.
———Rob., of Notingham, 1336.
———Will. f. Rob., of Notingham, 1338.
Buirun, *v.* Burun.
Bulelogh, Rich., 2393.
Bulkar, Will., 1886.
Bullock, Bollokk, Bolocke, Bullok, Bulloke.
———Elena, w. of Will., 2451.
———Isabel, w. of Rich., 2475, 2480.
———John f. Tho., of Norton, 2445, 2446, 2450, 2451.
———John, 2457, 2468, 2469, 2482, 2483.
———Nicholas, 1780.
———Philip, 2484.
———Ric., Bailiff of Dronfeld, 1074.
———Ric., of Onston, 1780.

Bullock, etc., Richard, 1069.
———Rich., s. of Will., 2474-2477, 2479-2481.
———Thomas, 2446, 2471.
———Will., Alderman of the Guild of St. Mary, Dronfield, 1064, 1065.
———Will., 2459, 2469, 2471, 2472, 2485.
———Will., s. of John, 2451.
Bulneys, Will., rector [of Darley?], 915.
Bulstones, John de, 666.
Bunte, Ric., 985.
Buntyng, Bunttyng.
———Hen., 850, 1680.
———Hugh, 368.
———Ralph, 2307.
———Rob., 1447, 1448, 1808.
Buon, Richard, 1182.
Burbage, Will., 2210.
Burcand, Richard, 2265.
Burchefeld, Agnes, d. and heir of Hen., 510.
Burcheved, *v.* Bircheved.
Burdet, Bordet.
———David, 2092.
———Hugh, of Kirkehalum, 1635, 2206, 2207, 2209.
———William, 1946.
Burdon, John, 1423, 1425.
Bure, Leodegarius de, 2717.
Burg, Ranulph de, 1425.
Burgelega, Rob. de, 2091.
Burgelun, Burgelune, Burgillun, Burgilon, Burguilone, Burgulon, Burgulone, Burgulun, Burgunun, Burgylen, Burgylon.
———Emma f. Will. f. Will. le, 2547.
———Geoffrey le, 2651.
———Henry de, 2547.
———John le, 2552, 2553.
———John, of Weston, 1505, 1926, 1927.
———Margery, quondam ux. Will. le, 1501, 1502.
———Ralph, 1926.
———Rob. le, rector of Mugginton, 2547.
———Will. le, 1501, 1503, 1688, 2546, 2548, 2755.
———Will. f. Will. le, 1503, 2547.
Burgenny, Will. de, 396.
Burgeys, Will., 1367.
Burghes, Will. de le, 521.
Burghill, John, Bishop of Lichfield and Coventry, 1693.
Burgillun, *v.* Burgelun.
Burgilun, *v.* Burgelun.
Burgin, Will. le, 516.
Burgmun, Margeria, quondam ux. Will. le, 1504.
Burgo, Ralph de, 2614.
———Ralph de, de Melton, mil., 2536.
———Ranulph de, 1422.
———Ric. f. Joh. f. Naie de, 1433.
Burgton, Will. de, clericus, 182.
Burguilone, Burgulon, Burgulun, etc., *v.* Burgelun.

Burley, Ivo de, 2560, 2561.
Buron, *v.* Burun.
Burrell, Peter, sub-chanter of Lichfield, 853.
Bursicot, *v.* Bersicot.
Burton Abbey, the Prior and Chapter, 1197.
Burton, Borton, Burtone.
———Elizabeth, w. of Will., de Falde, 1316.
———John, vicar of Ashby-de-la-Zouch, 1980.
———John de, chaplain, 206.
———John de, of Bauquell, 1329, 1354.
———Laurence de, 225.
———Mag. R— de, Vicar of Mickle-over, 1696.
———Nicholas, 1404.
———Richard de, 201.
———Tho. de, of Chastrefeld, 771.
———Will., de Falde, 1316.
———William I. de, of Tuttebury, 1314, 1368, 1369, 2106, 2107.
———William II., of Tutbury, 2111.
Burun, Buirun, Buron.
———Richard de, 933.
———Robert de, 2769.
———Roger de, 2545.
Burwys, *v.* Borowes.
Busseby, John de, 981.
Bussun, Buyssun, Buzun, Thomas, 1500-1503, 1688.
Bussy, Sir John, Steward of the Manor of Dronfeld, 1067.
Buterdon, Will. de, 2780.
Buterlee, Rob. de, 2780.
Butler, *v.* Boteler.
Buxton, Bocston, Bocstones, Bocstons, Bokestones, Buckstanis, Bucstones.
———Hugh de, 1491.
———John de, 1472.
———Maria de, 2496.
———Roger f. Marie de, 2496.
———Thomas de, 672, 674, 1709, 1793.
———William de, 55.
Buyssun, *v.* Busson.
Buzun, *v.* Busson.
Bydel, Will., de Blore, 151.
Byerne, Constancia de, 1896.
Bygge, Henry, 1666, 1667.
Bygod, Bartholomew le, 1428.
Bygott, Robert, 924, 2565.
Bylby, Adam de, 71.
Byleye, Luke de, 548.
Bylley, Adam de, 70.
Bylyngton, Ranulph, 1206.
Byngeham, Byngham, *v.* Bingham.
Byngley, William, 1006.
———Will., Vicar of Dronfield, 133.
Bynyngton, Bynynton, John de, bailiff of Derby, 978, 979.
Byrched, *v.* Birchevid.
Byrches, Will. del, of Ryssheom, 1874.
Byrchouer, *v.* Birchover.
Byrkynschawe, *v.* Birkenschagh.
Byrlay, *v.* Birley.
Byronne, John le, Knt., 1594.

Byroun, Hen., b. of John de, 1472.
———John de, knt., 1472.
Byrton, Alice, w. of Ric. de, of Treton, 271.
———Ric. de, of Treton, 271.
Byschop, Byshope, etc., *v.* Bishop.
Bythebroke, Bethebroke, Bithebroke.
———Henry, 2164.
———Richard, 2509, 2604.
———William, 2660, 2661.
Bythewater, Thomas, 838.
Byum, John, 1257.

C.

Cachehors, Ralph, 1198.
Cadas, Adam, 2707.
Cade, John, 273.
———Richard, 1513.
———Rob., of Brampton, 457.
Cadigan, Catigon.
———Ric., de Clatercotis, 111.
———Simon, of Essouere, 110-112.
Cadindone, Will. de, 387.
Cadmel, Fr. Nicholas de, Magister Eboraci, 1539.
Cadomo, John de, 908.
Cakee, Thos., 2523.
Calall, Calaai, Calahal, Calale, Calow, Calehall, Calhal, Calhall, Kalal, Kalale, Kalehal.
———Elizabeth, wid. of John, 380.
———Hen. f. Hug. de, 543.
———Hugh de, 1097.
———Hugh f. Thome de, 416.
———Joan, d. of Tho. de, 2291.
———John de, in Cestrefeld, 358, 362, 363, 380, 381, 784, 807, 839, 848.
———John f. Petri de, 543.
———John f. Rob. de, 356, 543.
———John, s. of John, 814, 820.
———Mary de, 712.
———Peter f. Rog. de, 542.
———Robert de, 415, 416, 2496.
———Rob., s. of Mary de, 712.
———Stephen f. Petri de, 1090.
———Thomas de, 436, 2291, 2292.
———William de, 435, 784, 807, 814.
———William, 1232.
———Will., de Normanthun, 1231, 1232.
Calangewode, Calengewode, Chalenge-wod, etc.
———John atte, capellanus, 2040.
———Richard, 2060, 2062, 2063, 2068.
Calchon, Gyllebert, 1360.
Calcroft, Elena, d. of Thos., 2485.
———Joan, d. of Thos., 2485.
———John I., 804, 805, 809-811.
———John II., 816, 820.
———John III., 846, 867.
———Ralph, vicar of Chesterfield, 845, 846, 867, 2517.
———Richard, 845, 846, 2515.
———Thomas, 380, 381, 797, 839, 2485.
———Tho., s. of Ric., 864, 867.
———Will., of Benyngton, 846.

Caldewell, Will. f. et h. Rad. de, 2029-2032.
Caldun, Alice, w. of Bertram, 2760.
———Bertram de, 2760.
Caldwell, Hen. de, 2618.
Calfcroft, John, of Onston, 2432.
———John f. Joh., 2432.
Calk, Canons of, 528-541, 1938, 1939, 1941.
Calton, Caltone, Caltoon, Caltun.
———John de, of Chattesworthe, 252.
———John de, capellanus, 311.
———John, of Totteley, 1412.
———John, s. of John de, 311.
———Margaret, w. of Tho., of Melton Mowbray, 1345.
———Rob., of Melton Mowbray, 1345.
———Thomas, 1342, 1345.
———William de, 2329.
Caltorp, John de, 249.
Calver, Calfhouera, Calfor, Calfoure, Calfover, Caluouere, Caluoure, Kalueouer.
———Hen. de, 1209, 1210, 1547.
———Hugh de, 194.
———John de, 1613.
———Ric. f. Tho. de, 760.
———Robert de, 173, 548, 1207, 1208, 1214, 1328.
Calverley, Robert, 1601.
Camera, Henry de, 2780.
———Hen. de, of Twyford, 2586.
———Richard de, 2092.
———Thomas de, 2556.
———*v.* also Chambers.
Camerarius, Nicholas, 1082.
———Ralph, junr., 912.
———*v.* also Chamberlain.
Campania, Richard de, 1360.
———Robert de, 2001.
Campdene, Thomas, 602.
Campion, Robert, 2547.
Camvile, Rog. de, 1948.
Canne, John, 2044-2048.
Cantelupe, Walter de, Bishop of Worcester, 1555.
Cantelupo, Will. de, 1955.
Cantilupo, Will. de, 171.
Cantrell, Hen., of Walton, 856.
———John, 457.
———Ralph, vicar of Chesterfield, 865, 1345.
———Rauf, priest, 2681.
———Thomas, of Alfeld, 2683.
———Thomas, s. of Thos., 2686, 2687.
———William, 302.
Canuill, Gerard de, 1419.
Capella, John de, 1040.
———Thos. de, faber de Tansley, 2303.
Cardoyl, Carduill, Cardul, Karduyl, etc.
———Henry de, 2628, 2630, 2631, 2636.
———Rob. de, 2173, 2174, 2176, 2203.
———William, 2178.
Carecarius, Herbert, 2749.
———Isabel, w. of Herb., 2749.

Carectarius, Will., de Bobedone, 1569.
Carleolo, Kareolo.
———Reginald de, senescallus, 1346.
———Robert de, 1503.
Carles, Hugh, 1434.
Carlton, John de, bailiff of Lincoln, 1923.
Carpenter, Carpentarius, Carpinter, Carpuntarius.
———Brian, of Ashbourne, 57.
———Nicholas, 1965.
———Ralph, 2381.
———Ralph f. Galf. f. Rog. de Repton, 1969-1971.
———Rog. f. Hamundi, 1323.
———Warin, 1959.
Carre, John, 825.
———Ric., of Chestrefeld, 844, 850.
Carriswall, John, 2019.
———Will. de, 2019.
Carsington, Karsinton, Kersintone, Kersyngtone.
———Rachenald de, 28.
———William de, 2659.
———Will. f. Will. de, 2661.
Carteleye, John, 1074.
Carter, Cartar, le Carter.
———Anker, of Newbottle, priest, 2272-2275.
———Cecily, d. and co-heir of Ric., of Braystone, 484.
———Johanna, d. of John, of Boylstone, 347.
———John le, 346, 1758, 2182, 2261.
———Lucy, d. and co-heir of Ric., of Braystone, 484.
———Richard, 2210.
———Will., of Ettwalle, 347.
Cartleg, Cartlege, Rich. de, 2458, 2460.
Cartwryght, Will., 1063.
Cartwryhte, Rog., 2540.
Carue, Nich., 1193.
Caryngton, George, 1512.
Cashors, Roger, 2250.
Caskyn, Casken, Caskin.
———Nich., of Brampton, 452.
———Richard, 1537, 1538.
———Robert, 1537.
———Roger, 177, 180.
———Tho. f. Tho., 1033.
———William, 1538.
Casson, John, 2362.
Cassy, William, 1424, 1425.
Castelayn, Alice f. Agnetis, of Osberton, 1775.
———Rose, d. of Alice, of Osberton, 1775.
Castleton, Casteltone, Castultone.
———Gilbert, 829.
———Ric. f. Ric. de, 551.
———Rob. s. of Ric. de, 551.
———Thos. de, vicar of Wirksworth, 2663.
Castrefeld *v.* Chesterfield.
Cateclive, Cateclyve, Chatteclive, Katteclive, etc.
———Edusa quond. vx. Ade de, 356.
———William de, 360, 686, 687, 688, 690.
Catelyn, John, 1967.

Catigon, *v.* Cadigan.
Caton, Laur., chaplain, 1394, 1595.
Catton, Laurence, vicar of Maffelde, 1594.
Cattone, Tho. f. Will. de, 572.
Cauendissh, John de, 1845.
Caumpedone, Walter de, parson of Wygan, 1313.
Caus, Cauz, Cauce, Cause, Caws, Chauz.
———Augnes f. Walteri le, of Bramton, 432.
———Geoffrey de, 680, 1161, 1162.
———Isabel, d. and h. of Tho. of Brampton, 459.
———Jane, d. and h. of Tho. of Bromton, 462, 469.
———John, of Brampton, 447.
———Robert le, 417, 418, 444, 701, 705, 785.
———Rog. le, 123, 431-433, 438, 440, 441, 501, 719, 1044.
———Thomas, 258, 425, 448, 449, 454, 459, 2518, 2564.
———Tho. f. Radulfi le, de Bramtone, 420.
———Walter le, de Brampton, 227, 421, 426.
———Will., of Brampton, 457.
Cauueland, Kauelond.
———Emma f. Ade de, 1560.
———Nicholas de, 2125.
———Oliver f. Ade de, 1560.
Cave, Kaue.
———Ambrose, Knt., 168, 2276.
———Dom. Hugh de, rector of Clifton, 2033.
———Roger de, 188.
Cawardin, Will. de, 1347.
Cay *v.* Kay.
Caym, Kaym, Thomas, 971.
———Will., de Derby, 971.
Caytewayte, Robert, 1173.
———William, 1201.
Celda, Adam de, 699.
Cementarius, Gilbert f. Walt., 411.
———Matthew, 1334.
Cesterfield, Cestrefeld, etc., *v.* Chesterfield.
Cestr', Simon de, ballivus de Derby, 976.
Cestria, Mag. Hugh de, 486.
———Peter de, "prepositus de Beverley," 1198, 2247.
———Roger de, 2545.
Chaddesden, Chaddesdene, Chadisden, etc.
———Geoffrey de, rector of Long Whatton, 609.
———Hen. de, 608.
———Hen. de, Archdeacon of Leicester, 609.
———Hugh de, 188.
———Idonea, w. of Will. f. Thom. de, 480, 481.
———John f. Radulfi de, 973.
———John de, of Derby, 973.
———Nich. de, clerk, 609, 1166.
———Ralph de, treasurer of Lichfield, 188, 1957.

Chaddesden, etc., Tho. f. Galfridi de, 605.
———Tho. f. Radulfi de, 973.
———Will. de, Knt., 47, 327, 2017, 2178, 2179.
———Will. de, clerk, 1552.
———Will. de, "prepositus," of Derby, 970.
———William, 2203, 2638.
———Will. f. Thome de, 480, 481.
———Will. f. Will le Clerc de, 608.
Chadirton, Rich de, 2445.
Chadwyk, Will., 904.
Chaffare, Ralph, de Derby, 977.
Chalduuell, Hugh de, 1197.
Chaldwell, Ralph de, 1197.
Chalengewod, *v.* Calangewode.
Chalner, Will., of Brampton, 2485.
Chaloner, Will. le, 2660.
Chamberlain, Chamberleng, Chaumberleyn.
———Hen., 890.
———Rog. parson of Rerisby, 33.
———Rog. f. Galfridi le, 45.
———*v.* also Camerarius.
Chambers, Chamber, Chambereys, Chambreis, Chambres, Chambreys, Chaumber, Chaumbre, Chawmber.
———Hen. de, 517.
———Nicholas de, 240, 1500, 2066-2068.
———Rog. f. et her. Walteri de, Dom. de Berewardecote, 519.
———Will. de, of Falde, 345.
———Will. of Barleburgh, 1061.
Champeneys, etc., Alan fil. Will. de Mercinton, 2154, 2155, 2159.
Chandos, Chandois, Chandoos, Chaundes, Chaundois, Chaundos, Chaundoys, Chundos.
———Edward de, 402.
———Eliz. of Radbourne, 1920, 1927.
———Dom. Hen. de, 2549.
———John de, Dom. de Rodburne, 1545.
———John de, mil., 2388.
———John de, 1163, 1170, 1200, 1757, 2583.
———Margery, w. of John de, 1163, 1168.
Channer, Tho., 473.
Chapeleyn, Chapleyn.
———John, of Trusley, 1934, 2323, 2391.
———Will., of Truslay, 2395.
Chapman, Chapmon, Chapmonn.
———John, Chamberlain of Derby, 1005.
———John le, of Folowe, 1219.
———John le, 1220.
———John, s. of Hugh s. of Ralph, of Derby, 984.
———Richard le, 1039.
———Ric. le Taillour f. Joh. le, 1045.
———Ric. le, 1475.
———Rog. f. Nich., of Ybulle, 1476.
———Will, 834, 881.
Charde, Thos., gent. of Qu. Anne of Cleves's Household, 2715.

Charetter, Walter le, 1894.
Chastleton, Hugh, knt., 1712.
Chaterton, Rich. de, 2444.
Chateshale, Rob. f. Rob. de, Miles, 1956.
———Walter f. Rob. de, 1956.
Chatham, John, Notary Public, 655.
Chatsworth, Chatiswortht, Chatteswith, Chattesworthe, Chatteswrth, etc.
———Ossebert de, 247.
———Tho. f. Hen. de, 252.
———Will. de, 173.
———Will f. Osseberti de, 246-248.
———Will. de, 1328.
Chattecliue, *v.* Catecliue.
Chauant, Dom. Peter, 1899.
Chaucumb, Ric. de, 175.
Chaumber, Chaumbre, *v.* Chambers.
Chaumpeneys, *v.* Champeneys.
Chaundeler, *al* Chaundiler, Hen. s. of Thom., 2106, 2107, 2109.
———John, of Tuttebury, 1369.
Chaunterell, Chauntrell, John, clerk, 1203, 1206.
Chauz, *v.* Caus.
Chawmber, *v.* Chambers.
Chaworth, Chaword, Chaworth, Chaworthe, Chaworth, Chawrthe, etc.
——Sir John, knt., 1782.
———Osbert de, 245.
———Thomas, 23, 1775, 2567.
———Tho., knt., 22, 130, 1868, 1869, 1873, 2452, 2455.
———Tho. de, knt., Dom. de Norton, 1776.
——Dom. Tho. de, 426.
———William de, 131.
———Will., Lord of Norton, 1777.
Chebbescie. Chebbese, Chebese, Chebeleia.
———Rob. de, canon of Lichfield, 179, 189, 2575.
———Mag. Zacharias de, 1681.
Chedelle, Thos., of Broughton, 2111.
Chedle, Ric. de, chaplain, 1177.
Chedworth, Tho. de, 663.
Chelaston, John de, 2295.
———Rob. de, chaplain, 2295.
Chelastone, Tho., parson of Normanton, 1869.
Chelmardon, Hen. f. Ric. de, 668.
Chent, Will. de, 2384.
Chepe, Rob. de, 202.
Cherteseye, John, 583.
Chessyre, Thos., rector of Appulby, 2403.
Chester, Earls of.
——Berta, w. of Hugh, 1948.
———Hugh de Kyveliok, 531, 535, 536, 1938, 1939, 1941-1945.
———Matilda, comitissa, 531, 1681, 1937-1944.
———Ranulph de Blundeville, 1948, 1954, 1955, 2574.
———Ranulph de Gernons, 528, 1939, 1942.
Chesterfield, Cesterfeld, Cestirfeld, Cestrefeld, Chastrefeld, Chestirfeld.
———Alice f. Rumphate de, 690.
———Hen., clericus de, 702.

Chesterfield, etc., Hen. de, clericus, 356, 360, 546.
———Hen. f. Hen. cler. de, 359, 378, 703.
———Hen. f. et her. Joh., cler. de, 756, 784.
———Henry de, 2494.
———Hugh de, of Derby, 971.
———Mag. Hugh de, 244.
———John de, Abbott of Wellebeke, 1094.
———John f. Will. f. Edde de, 723.
———Margareta f. Rob. f. Fellicis de, 740.
———Philip de, 2557.
———Reyner f. Roth de, 544-546.
———Ric. de, clerk, 776, 877.
———Ric. f. Bond de, 2491.
———Ric. f. Will. ad barram de, 709.
———Richard de, 765.
———Richer f. Wlnat de, 695.
———Rob. f. Edwini de, 2492.
———Rob. f. Fellicis de, 740.
———Rog., clericus de, 1533.
———Rog. de, 2447.
———Rog. f. Ranulphi de, 376.
———Sarra quondam uxor Radulfi, cler. de, 700.
———Stephen de, 1080.
———Walter de, clericus, 354.
———Will. f. Hugonis de, 411.
———Will. f. Joh. f. Emme de, 423.
———Will f. Presbyteri de, 687.
———Will. f. Richeri f. Wlnat de, 695.
Cheu, Will. de, 733, 734, 737.
Cheyne, John, canon of Lichfield and prebendary of Sandiacre, 944.
———John, parson of Hanbury, 2598.
———Dom. John, clerk, 1438.
———Will., justice, 2540.
———Will., 1158.
Cheyny, Eliz., w. of John, 2319.
Chichely, Hen., Archbishop of Canterbury, 82.
Child, Robert, 180.
———Will. le, of Caldwall, 2542.
Chilwell, Will., chaplain, 1873.
Chirten, Will., of Chapel-en-le-Frith, schoolmaster, 651.
Chiueleia, Mag. Helias de, 1082.
Cholingham, Cholintham, John f. Herberti de, de Cestrefeld, 360, 688.
Chous, Thomas, 970.
Choyfer, Ralph le, de Cesterfeld, 542.
Choys, Avice, d. of Will., of Cestrefeld, 721.
Chuschet, Simon, rector of Mackworth, 1623.
Chyldars, John, 323.
Chynetone, Mathew de, 399.
Cigby, John de, 758.
Cissor, Agnes, w. of Rob., 2310.
———Hugh f. Ade, 1373.
———Matilda, w. of Ralph, of Dore, 1019.
———Ralph, of Dore, 1019.
———Robert, 2310.
Clappisale, Nicholas, 369.
Clapwell, Ralph de, 814, 1231, 1232.

Clarell, Clarel, Joan, d. of Will., 663.
——Thomas, 456.
——William, 662-664.
Clarence, Geo., Duke of, 1027, 1849.
Claudewell, Ralph de, 2027.
Claye, Rob. del., 2604.
Claypole, John, chaplain of Chaddesden Chantry, 609.
Clayton, Nich. de, 1589, 1874.
——Will., 637.
Clement, Isabella, 219.
——John, chaplain, 1526.
Clerk, Clarke, Clerke, Clericus, le Clerk.
——Anabella, 1441.
——Avice w. of Rog. le, 2228.
——Felicia, f. Johannis, de Longesdon, 96.
——H., of Esseburne, 685.
——Henry, 358.
——John, 346, 1059, 1184, 1273, 1901, 1994, 2460, 2535.
——John, vicar of Ashbourne, 2417.
——John, chaplain, 1238, 2083, 2084.
——John, bailiff, etc., of Codnor, 896-900.
——John, of Codnor, 903.
——John, of Strounsell, 900.
——John f. Ric. le, 2312, 2313.
——Raphe, 2476, 2477.
——Rich., 2506.
——Robert, 52, 2249.
——Rob. of Somerleys, 2465.
——Rog., of Chesterfelde, 1046.
——Rog. le, of Worthington, 2228.
——Thomas, 2554.
——Tho., of Codnor, 906.
——William, 108, 180, 1059, 2471.
——Will., of Hope, chaplain, 1437, 1439, 1441.
Clerkson, William, 1884.
Cley, Antony, of Matlock, 16⁻⅓.
——Will., of Wynfeld, 851.
Clid, Robert, 173.
Cliderhowe, John, s. of John, 1870, 1871.
——Margery, w. of Ric., 1870, 1871.
——Richard, 1870, 1871.
Clifford, Tho., Lord, 223.
——Walter de, 1161, 1162.
Clifton, Clifftone, Cluffton, Clyftone.
——Gervase de, 538.
——Gervase, knt., 1123, 2120.
——Hen. de, de Assheburn, 60.
——Margery de, 883.
——Nich. de, 55, 144, 145.
——Richard, 150.
——Robert, 23, 65.
——Dom. Rob. de, of Ashbourne, 61.
——Rob. de, chaplain, 883.
——Simon de, 880.
——Thos. de, parson of Kirk Ireton, 2020.
——Will. de, 879, 1643.
——Will. de, rector of Edluston, 1157.
Clinton, Clynton, Clyntone.
——Sir John, knt., 1488, 1761.

Clinton, etc., Rog. de, Bp. of Chester, 528.
——Will. de, Earl of Huntingdon, 942.
Clogh, Clough, Cloughe.
——John f. Tho. del, 2459, 2461, 2463, 2464, 2467, 2469.
——Richard del, 1799.
——Rob. f. Ric. del, 616.
——Tho. del, 2, 620, 1799.
Clostones, John, bailiff of Derby, 1000.
Cloware, Cluware, Rob. de, 59, 60.
Cluffton, Clufftone, v. Clifton.
Clyff, Nicholas, 1740.
Clyfforth, v. Clifford.
Clyftone, v. Clifton.
Cnave, Hugh, 2384.
Cnivetun, v. Knyveton.
Cnotinge, v. Knotting.
Cnotte, v. Knot.
Cobbeham, John de, King's Justice, 1279.
Cobbeleye, Cobeleye, Coblay, v. Cubley.
Cobyn, John, of Eyam, 1225, 1232, 1233, 1238, 1241, 1242.
——John, bailiff of Monyash, 1722.
——Ric., of Eyam, 1250.
——Thomas, 1253.
——Thomas, of Allerwaslegh, 2671.
——Will., 129.
Cocc, Cock, Cok, v. Coke.
Cochet, Hugh, 530.
Cocken, Rog., of Beley, 266.
Cocus, v. Coke.
Coddington, Codintone, Codyngton, Codyntone.
——Henry de, 2606.
——Richard de, 1887, 1888.
——Robert de, 1887.
Codemon, Thomas, 2681.
Codnor, Lords of, v. Grey.
Codnor, Codenouere, John f. et her. Germani de, 885, 886.
Coghen, John, of Hopton, 998.
Coghhen, Thomas, 2210.
Cokayn, Cokayne, Cokein, Cokeyne, etc.
——Edmund, de Assheburn, 75, 403, 961, 2412, 2414.
——Francis, 961.
——Hen., escheator of the King in co. Derby, 1812.
——John, 831, 1492, 1616, 1644, 2131, 2394, 2412, 2413, 2461, 2678.
——John, knt., 77, 78, 80, 217, 803, 1394, 1692, 1693, 1769, 1931, 1980, 1983, 2081, 2130, 2415, 2416, 2714.
——John, King's Justice, 1806.
——John, "le Uncle," 883.
——John, of Ashbourne, 63-65, 69-72, 76, 84, 218, 340.
——John, of Berewardcote, 2391.
——John, Proctor for the Dean and Chapter of Lichfield, 205.
——John, s. of John, 80.
——Richard, 1693.

Cokayn, etc., Roger, 29, 401.
———Tho., 236, 2141.
———Tho., knt., 90, 961.
———Thos., of Balidon, 2320.
———Will. of Ashbourne, 56, 57, 59.
———Will., bailiff of Ashbourn, 60.
Coke, Cocc, Cock, Cocus, Cok, Cook, Cooke, Coquus, Koc, Koke, Kooc.
———Adam, 1126.
———Cecily, w. of Rog., of Codnore, 892, 894.
———Edmund, chaplain of Chaddesden Chantry, 609.
———Edmund, of Thurgarton, 1191.
———Emma le, 70.
———Henry fil. Osberni, 1360.
———Hen., of Codnor, 894, 895, 898.
———John, 509, 1109.
———John, of Langley, 895.
———John, of Morehaws, 1063.
———John, of Repton, chaplain, 1978.
— ———John, of Walton, 1261, 2362.
———Osbern, 1360.
———Ric. of Chesterfield, 814, 816, 826, 827, 832, 834, 836, 2359, 2514.
———Robert, 780, 788, 805, 1792.
———Rob., chaplain, 1653.
———Rob. s. and heir of Tho., of Eginton, 1173.
———Rog., of Codnore, 892, 894.
———Roger, 1273.
———Thomas, 1055, 1066, 2470, 2628, 2630, 2631, 2635.
———Tho., of Codnor, 906.
———Tho., of Colleye, 1043.
———Tho., of Eginton, 1173.
———Walarand, 1197.
———William, 49, 1056, 1057, 2447, 2448.
———Will. le, vicar of Longford, 288, 1585.
———Will., of Holmesfeld, 233, 1054, 1055, 2449.
———Will., of Scropton, 1289.
———Will., of Trusley, 1606, 2395, 2400, 2401.
———Will., jun., of Trusley, 2400.
———Will., s. and h. of Will., of Trusley, 1813.
Cokee, Johanna, d. and h. of Tho., of Brampton, 461.
Cokelstote, Joan, w. of John, 1628.
———John, 1628.
Cokerell, John, parson of Cranford, 781, 791.
———John, 797.
———John, clerk, 798.
Cokeseye, Isabella, w. of Walter de, knt., 1122.
———Walter de, knt., 1122.
Cokkes, Robert, 1014.
Colby, Tho. de, 496.
Coleret, Ralph, 1706.
Coleshulle, Colshull.
———John de, 1301, 1311, 1312.
Colestun, W. de, 1078.
Colingham, Herbert de, 690.

Colle, John f. Will., of Burton-on-Trent, 2238.
———Lettice, w. of Simon, 388.
———Simon, of Bradeborne, 388, 389, 391.
———Tho. de, of Longley, 1536.
Colleg, Hilbertus de, 1636.
College, Will. f. Tho. de, 1037.
Colley, Will. de, 1038.
Colleye, Adam de, 2221.
Collynson, Rob., of Chapell del Fryth, 828.
Colman, Will., 2181.
Colouill, Rob. de, 2026.
Colte, Rog., 19.
———Yngelesia, w. of Rog., 19.
Coltmon, John le, bailiff of Derby, 985.
Columbel, Columb, Colombelle, Columbell, Columbelle.
———Aleyn, 887, 889.
———Elizabeth, d. of Rog., 952.
———Henry, 262, 2230.
———Hen., of Codenovere, 885-887, 889, 890.
———Hen., of Darley, 559.
———John, 209.
———John, of Darley, 951.
———Roger, 951.
———Thomas, 1619.
———Tho., f. Hen. of Codnor, 885, 886.
———Tho., of Thorpe "in glebis," 893.
Colverdowse, Will., vicar of Melburn, 1980.
Colville, Tho., of Codnor, 893.
Colyngwood, Ralph, Dean of Lichfield, 644, 1551.
Combe, Elizabeth, w. of John, 897.
———John, 897.
Comberford, Dorothea, Abbess of the Nuns Minoresses, Aldgate, London, 1348.
Comberworth, Tho., knt., 1988.
Comfrey, Thos., rector of Dronfield, 2442.
Conbrai, Alured de, 535.
Condale, John de, 2214, 2220, 2222.
Condy, John, 2591.
Congesdon, Conegerdon, Congesden, Conegusdon, Congesdon, Congexton, Cuggesdon, Cungesdon, Cungisden, Cungusdon.
———Henry de, 667-668, 672-674.
———Hen. f. Nich. de, 673.
———John de, chaplain, 1912.
———John, br. of Nich. de, 668, 671, 672, 674, 675, 676.
———John de, of Cheylmarden, 676.
———Nich. f. Radulphi de, 666, 668, 670-672, 674-676, 1709.
———Ralph de, 1707, 1708.
———Will. f. Joh. de, 666, 667.
Constable, Jane, w. of Sir John, 953.
———John, Dean of Lincoln, 1013.
———Sir John, 953.
———Sir Marmaduke, Steward of the Honor of Tutbury, 514.

Constantine, 535.
Constapularius, Peter, de Chelardiston, 664.
Constentin, Geoffrey de, 1397. .
Conuers, Dionisia, quondam ux. Tho. le, 553, 555.
————Nicholas, 2344.
————Nich. le, de villa castri de Pecco, 552.
————Tho. f. Thom. le, 555, 556.
Cook, Cooke, *v.* Coke.
Copwode, John, 1206.
Coquus, *v.* Coke.
Corb, Walter, 1945.
Corbet, Rob., knt., 1492.
Cordel, Will., de Castre, 36.
Cordy, John, 1975.
Coreie, Master Rob., 387.
Corel, Henry, of Bauquell, 201.
————Rob., of Bauquell, 201.
————Tho., of Bauquell, 201.
Cornera, John de, de Derby, 1545.
Cornhill, Will. de, Bishop of Coventry, 175, 176, 1421, 1431, 1681, 1953, 2572, 2573.
Cornubiensis, Ivo, 1080.
Corry, Walter, mill., 1963.
Corson, Corsun, *v.* Curzon.
Cortel, John, vicar of Willington, 1975.
Corteligstoke, Cortlingestone, Alex. de, 1391, 2576.
Cortona, Geoffrey de, 1753.
Corvisarius, Alice, w. of John, 2780.
————John, 2334, 2779.
Corzon, Corzoun, Corzun, *v.* Curzon.
Cosin *al* Cusin, Will., 2325, 2326, 2327.
Cotenes, Edayn, w. of Will., 790.
————Edith, w. of Will. de, 2503.
————Will. de, 790, 2503.
Coterel, Coterell, Cotterell, Coturel.
————Adam f. Rog., 1902-1904, 1907, 1910.
————Cecilia, d. of Hen., 1910.
————Henry, 1912.
————James, 1463, 1718.
————John, 1372, 2531.
————Laurence, 2145.
————Margery, of Buxton, 526, 527.
————Nicholas, 1718.
————Nich., s. and h. of Owin, late of Buxton, 527.
————Nich. s. of Rob., 1256.
————Nich., of Tadynton, 1909.
————Owin, of Buxton, 526.
————Ralph f. Rad., de Tadinton, 666.
————Ralph, 1707, 1708, 1908, 2117, 2217, 2343.
————Robert, 2531.
————Rog. de Prestecleve, 1901.
————Rog. f. Ade, 1902, 1903, 1905, 1907.
————Tho. f. Ade, 1906, 1908, 1910, 1911.
————William, 1709.
Coterone, John, 587.
Cotes, Hen., of Snelston, 1771.
————John de, of Moniasch, 1711, 1713.
Coton, Hen., parson of Aston, 1488.

Coton, John de, 2054.
————John f. Steph. de, capellanus, 2042, 2043, 2046-2048.
————Robert de, 2535.
————Thomas, 2287.
Coty, Peter f. Rog., de Kalalh, 696.
Cotyngham, William de, 271.
Cotyngtone, Hen. de, 1889.
Coudray, Coudrey, Coudreye.
————Henry de la, 2713.
————Hen. f. Joh., 1156.
————John, 1148, 1153.
————Rich. de, 2012, 2713.
Coulbeard, Will., of Bradeley, clerk, 400.
Coulond, Couland, Oliver de, 1573, 1576.
Coupmon, Coupemon, Adam, of Presteclyve, 1905, 1907.
Courteys, *v.* Curteys.
Coventre, John de, chaplain, 816.
————Will., 587.
Cowdale, Elena, w. of John, 2392.
————John, 2392.
Cowhalch, Adam de, 1355.
Cowlischawe, Thomas, 127.
————Will, 127.
Cowper, Coupar, Couper, Coupere.
————Emma w. of Nich. le, 2095.
————Geoffrey, 2073.
————Geoffrey, of Horsley Woodhous, 1885.
————Helize, bayliff of Derby, 1006.
————John le, chaplain, 1201.
————Nich. le, of Sandiakyr, 2095.
————Ric., of Chastrefeld, chaplain, 771.
————Roger le, 628, 630, 631.
————Rog., of Beley, 266.
————Thomas, 288, 2073.
————William, 999, 1173.
————Will. s. of Rob. le, of Cestrefeld, 721.
Crakemere, Crakmersh.
————Ric. de, 246, 247, 249-251, 254.
Cramphord, John de, 28.
Crassus, Richard, 2090.
————Will., senescallus Normannie, 1753.
Craucumb, Crawecrumb.
————Godfrey de, 680, 1160.
Craven, John de, 1957.
Crawell, Tho. de, Succentor of Lichfield, 1546.
Creighton, Creccon, Crecton, Creghtone, Cregton, Cregtone, Crehton, Creitton, Creterton, Cretone, Cretton, Creyton.
————Agnes, quond. ux. Rob. de, 2103.
————John de, 1294, 1300-1303, 1305, 1306, 1309, 1310, 2101.
————John f. Rob. de, 2102, 2103.
————Rob. de, 1295, 1296, 2100.
————Walter de, 1300.
Cresewyk, Henry de, 1044.
Cressy, Crecy, Crescy, Cressi.
————John, rector of Longford, 77, 1582, 1645, 2417.
————John, parson of Thorp, 1580.

Cressy, etc., Rog. de, knt., 1487.
———Dom. Will. de, 267.
Creswell, Nich. de, of Boileston, 341.
Creterton, Cretton, *v.* Creighton.
Crewker, Creuker, John, 1123, 1321, 2411.
———Will., 1926, 1927.
Crich, Criche, Cryche.
———Ralph de, 120.
———Rog. de, clerk, 798.
———Rog. de, parson of Whittington, 1924, 1926-1928.
Crichelowe, Crychelow.
———Richard, vicar of Bakewell, 2233.
———Rog., of Dalton, 167.
Crioyll, Bertram de, 1555.
Crisha, Rob., 87.
Croft, Crofte, Croftes, Croftis, Croftus.
———Alice, w. of Will., 2376.
———Edward, 1411.
———John del, 1050.
———John, br. of Will., 1411.
———Katerine, 1414.
———Mapota, 468.
———Michael, s. and h. of Will., 1414-1416.
———Nicholas, 468.
———Roger s. of Will., 1411, 1413.
———Thomas de, 451, 2302, 2564.
———Will, .456, 1401, 1403, 1405, 1406, 1410-1412, 2376, 2704.
———Will., s. of Will., 1401, 1407, 1410, 1411.
———Will., sen., of Brampton, 100, 468.
———Will., jun., of Brampton, 100, 101, 468.
———Will., of Holmesfeld, 1413, 1414.
Croke, Dom. John, vicar of Norton, 1786.
Cromford, Cromforde, Crumford.
———Agnes f. Ranulfi de, 926.
———Hen. de, 14.
———Hen. f. Ran. de, 2635.
———Joan ux. Rob. f. Ric. de, 1702.
———John, s. and h. of Agnes f. Ran. de, 926.
———Nicholas de, 2657-2659.
———Nich. f. Symon de, 1702.
———Simon de, 292, 2741.
———Symon f. Hen. de, 1702.
———Will de, 1702, 2217, 2652.
———Will. de, of Birchover, 2221, 2223.
Crompton, Jordan de, 1472.
Cromwell, Baron, *v.* Bourchier, Humfry.
Cromwell, Crombwell, Cromewell, Croumbewell, Crumbwell.
———Johanna de, 1340.
———Matilda de, Domina de Tateshale, 1340.
———Ralph, Dominus de, 377, 1060, 1340, 2317, 2559.
———Rob. de, de Meysham, 1682, 1961.
———Thos., of Burton, 2619.
———Will., knt., 1988.

Cronzun, William, 228, 2242.
Cros *al.* Crosse, Will. atte, 2178, 2179.
———Will., chaplain, 1282.
———Mag. Will., 1982.
Crossleghe, Edward, 636.
Crottal, John de, 2596.
Croweknaue, Thos. le, of Conibruge, 2153.
Crowker, John, 1280.
Crowther, Richard, 2674.
Croyser, Will., knt., 1376.
Cruce, Hen. de, 404.
Crucem, Will. ad, 480, 481.
Crue, Tho., of Wich Malbane, 347, 348.
———Agnes, w. of Tho., of Wich Malbane, 348.
Crystylton, Rob., Abbot of Combermere, 1747.
Cubley, Cobbeleye, Cobeleye, Coblay, Cubbele, Cubbeleg', Cubbeley, etc.
———Dom. Alexander de, chaplain, 69.
———John f. Rob. de, 883.
———Ralph de, rector of Eyum, 186.
———Ralph de, 1831, 2335.
———Richard de, 880.
———Robert de, 880, 883.
———Rog. de, 1130, 1132, 1892.
———William de, 880.
———Will. f. Rog. de, 1140.
Cueller, Stephen le, of Cestrefeld, 1745.
Culcheth, Nich. 1183.
———Thomas, 1183.
Cumba, Nich. de, 1093.
Cumberford, Joan, w. of John de, 589.
———John de, 589.
Cumbrei, Cumbrai, Alured de, 531, 536, 1939.
Cumin, Mag. Thomas, 182.
Cundy, John, 2595.
Cuper, Dom. Hugh le, capellanus de Wyngerworth, 366.
Curson, Cursoun, *v.* Curzon.
Curtenall, Will., of Barley Lees, 1414.
Curteys, Courteys, Curtaysse, Curtes, Curtys.
———Richard, 1363.
———Robert, 2477.
———Roger, 2441, 2448.
———Tho., of Codnor, 894.
Curtlinge, Alexander de, 1361.
Curzon, Corsun, Corzon, Corzoun, Coursun, Curson, Cursone, Cursun, Curzeon, Curzun, etc.
———Engelard de, 1689, 1956, 1961, 1962.
———John, senr., 1505.
———John, 161, 610, 1189, 1393, 1596, 1597, 1600, 1647, 1670, 2064, 2133, 2134, 2188, 2392, 2602.
———John, of Ketelleston, 793, 1482, 1506, 1526, 1924, 1926-1929, 1984, 1985, 2137.
———John f. Joh., de Ketilstone, 994, 1505.
———John, de Croxsalle, 598, 600.
———Margaret, w. of John f. Joh., de Ketilstone, 1505.

Curzon, etc., Richard I. de, 532.
————Richard II. de, 1499, 1500, 2763, 2764.
————Richard III. de, 574, 577, 1741, 2549, 2551-2553.
————Dom. Richard, miles, 571, 1963.
————Rich. le, parson of Breadsall, 1453.
————Richard, 2701.
————Thomas de, 161, 386, 1163, 1168, 2070, 2763, 2764.
————Tho. de, of Kedleston, 1500-1505.
————Tho., s. and heir of John, of Croxall, 600.
————Thomas f. Tho. de, 1499.
————Will. de, dominus de Croxhale, 571, 576, 581, 582, 1968.
————Will., senr., 600.
————Will. de, 1502.
————Will., scutifer, 2539.
Cusin, Will., 1622.
Cut, Cutte, Cutts, John, 1866, 2549, 2552.
Cuterell, John, 1371.
Cutiller, Stephen le, 729.
Cuttlove, Cuttlufe, Will., 1064, 1065.
Cuwane, Ric. de, 415.

D.

Dabrychcot, John, knt., 1924.
Dagenyll, Will., 1922.
Dainoter, John, 2773.
————Matilda, 2773.
Daird, Adam, 68.
Daiuill, Juliana de, 1726.
Dalby, Ric. de, 736.
Dale, Abbots of, *v.* Index of Places.
Dale, Agnes, relicta Ric. de, of Eyom, 1218, 1219.
————Emma, wid. of John in le, junr., 1330.
————Joan, w. of John in le, 97.
————Joan, d. of Ric. del, de Eyum, 1221.
————John del, 42, 850, 1220.
————"Old Jon of ye," 454.
————John in le, junr., 1330.
————John, in le, of Assheford, 99, 102, 103.
————John in le, of Brampton, 445.
————John, s. of John in le, 97.
————John, s. of Rog. en la, 94, 97, 98, 1329.
————Margery, w. of Rob. of the, 454.
————Margote, w. of John in le, 451.
————Matilda, d. of Ric. del, de Eyum, 1221.
————Nich., s. of John in le, 99.
————Nich., s. of John in le, junr., 1330.
————Richard in le, 97, 2741.
————Ric., s. of Rob. and Margery of the, 454.

Dale, etc., Rob. de la, 311, 317, 318.
————Rog. in the, 94, 98.
————Thomas in le, 97, 1721, 2736.
————Tho., s. of John in le, of Brampton, 451.
————Tho., of Asshovere, 1479, 1480.
————Will. de la, of Ashbourne, 67.
————Will. in le, 313, 314.
————Will., of Ibulle, 1479, 1480.
Damartin, Will. de, 1420.
Damport, Will., 1601.
Dancastre, Will., 587.
Dandeson, Robert, 2315.
Daneston, Hen. de, 1150, 2125.
Daneys, Rowland, 1286.
Daniel, Danyel, Danyll.
————Johanna, w. of Ric. f. Joh., de Tyddeswalle, 1462.
————John, 1427, 2340.
————John, knt., 2343.
————Peter f. Will., 2329.
————Richard, 551, 1323, 1324, 1548.
————Ric., of Tideswelle, 1461.
————Ric. f. Joh., de Tyddeswelle, 1462, 2344, 2345.
————Ric. f. Rich., 2345.
————Rob. f. Will., 2330.
————Rog., of Colleye, 1043.
————William, 2325-2328, 2331.
Danncroft, Will., 2208.
Danvers, Daunvers.
————Edmund, 587.
————Joan, w. of Will., 2209.
————William, 2202, 2209.
Danyel, Danyll, *v.* Daniel.
Darant, Rob., 716.
Darcy, Dercy.
————John, Dominus de Knayth, 1127.
————John, knt., 1869.
Darley, Abbots of, *v.* Index of Places.
Darley, Derlea, Derlee, Derlegia, Derlegh, Derleye, Derlya, Derlye, etc.
————Hugh f. Andree de, 948.
————John de, of Kirk Langley, 1522, 1523, 2145.
————Nich. de, 605.
————Ric. de, clericus, 60.
————Robert de, 2641.
————Rog. de, de Sturston, 142.
————Thomas de, 173, 2177.
————William de, 173, 1610.
Dassenys, John, 2462.
Daubeney, Robert, 1884.
Dauber, Daubour, Dawbur.
————Alice, 1979.
————Rob., 1977, 1979, 1990.
Daudeson, Daudson, Matilda, relicta Rog., 766, 769.
————Roger, 748.
Daunvers, *v.* Danvers.
Dave, Jennett, w. of John, of Begheton, 1327.
————John, of Begheton, 1327.
Davenport, Dauemporte.
————Christopher, 156.
————Will., of Bromhall, 657.
————Will., of Chadkyrke, 657.
————Will., of Goytes Hall, 651, 652, 659.

David, Earl, br. of the King of Scot-
land, 1946.
——Ric., chaplain of Crich
Chantry, 921.
Davy, John, 2106.
——Tho., of Begheton, 1326.
——Thos., of Staunton, 2295.
Davys, Ric., chaplain, 1890.
Dawbur, *v.* Dauber.
Dawe, Geoffrey, rector of Cotegrave,
1914.
——John, 2295.
Dawkyn, Humphrey, 678.
——John, priest, 323.
——Robert, 1527.
——Rob., of Chelmerdon, 678.
——Tho., chaplain, 1769.
Dawns, Will., 1994.
Dawnson, Will., 2467.
Dawson, John, 2058, 2070.
——Nicholas, 1183.
——Richard, 2066.
——Robert, 2440.
——Will., s. of John, 2073.
Dayncurt, *v.* Deyncurt.
Deacone, John, 1892.
Dean, Edward, chaplain, 647.
——John, vicar of Hope, 1720.
Decanus, Henry, 2091.
Decon, John, 1912.
Dedyke, *v.* Dethic.
Degge, Richard, 2295.
Delastone, Henry de, 2162.
Deleis, Peter, 1622.
Delues, Ralph, 1528, 1529, 1531.
Den, John, of Stantonleyez, 1844.
Denby, Will., s. of Hugh de, 1866.
Dene, Dom. John de, knt., 1822.
Denston, Alan de, 2157.
Denstones, Rob. de, 2714.
Denton, James, Dean of Lichfield, 407,
647, 1618, 1811, 2191, 2372.
——Richard de, 987.
Derby, Earls of, *v.* Ferrariis.
Derby, Derb', Derbe, Derbeia, Derbi.
——Bruning de, 2750.
——Mag. J., de, 2634.
——Jocelin de, 2381.
——John de, canon of Lincoln, 188.
——John de, 80.
——Lettice, w. of Ralph de, of
Bradeleye, 882.
——Margaret d. of Tho. de, of
Marketon, 1651, 1652.
——Nicholas de, 404, 2381.
——Philip de, 1499.
——Ralph de, of Bradeleye, 882.
——Rob. de, clerk, 776.
——Rog. s. of Nich. de, 404.
——Mag. Simon de, 1082.
——Tho. de, of Marketon, 1651.
——William de, 1636.
Dercy, *v.* Darcy.
Dereth, Alice, w. of Peter, 2761.
——Peter de, 2761.
Derker, Henry, clerk, 2400.
Dersyth, Janne de, 518.
Derton, John, of Normanton, 455.
——Tho. de, 775, 782.
Despayne, Ralph, 555.

Despencer, Dispensarius, Dispensator,
Dispenser.
——Hugh le, 910, 911.
——Geoffrey, 680, 1161, 1162.
——Richard, 518, 575.
——Thomas, 1360, 1554, 1948.
Destafford, *v.* Stafford.
Deston, John, of Normanton, clerk,
2516.
Dethic, Dedyke, Dethec, Detheck,
Dethek, Detheyck, Detheyek,
Dethick, Dethik, Dethike, Dethyk,
Dethykke, etc.
——Ambrose, 102, 103.
——Geoffrey de, 116, 293, 480, 481,
1887, 1888, 2197-2200,
2203, 2247, 2641.
——Geoffrey f. Rob. de, 2147.
——Geoff. s. of Will. de, 1930.
——Jane, of Bredsall, 1553.
——John, 2148, 2230.
——John, arm., 2057.
——John, of Braydesall, 868.
——John s. of Will. de, 1931.
——Margaret d. of Jane, 1553.
——Peter de, 916.
——Reg. s. of Will., 1929, 1935.
——Richard de, capellanus, 2121.
——Ric. f. Rob. de, 2147.
——Dom. Robert de, mil., 949.
——Robert de, 328, 2427.
——Rob. f. Dom. Geoff. de, 2605.
——Rog. s. of Will., 1929, 1931,
1932.
——Thomas, 2073.
——Thomas, of Uttoxeter, 42,
1932, 1933.
——Tho. s. of Will., 1929, 1931.
——Will. de, 2444.
——Will. de, knt., 812, 922, 1929,
1931, 1935.
——Will., rector of Braydesall, 868.
——Will., of Newhall, 1765.
——Will., clerk, 2123.
——Will. s. of Will., 1929.
Deuetk', Dom. Rob. de, 113.
Deveneshire, Richard, de Cotene, 2035.
Dewe, Dewee, John, 507, 508.
Dey, Deye, Emma le, 2096.
——Rob., chaplain of Doveridge,
1024.
——Thomas, 1498.
Deyk, Dom. Geoffrey de, knt., 2013.
Deyncourt, Ayncourt, Aynescurt, Aynes-
cart, D'Aincurt, Einecurt, Eyin-
curt, Eyncourt, Eyncurt, etc.
——Alice d. of Sir Rog., 1107.
——Dame Alice de, 1056, 1399.
——John, 110, 368, 1032, 1351,
2192, 2409, 2605.
——Dom. John de, 2325, 2326,
2327.
——Dom. John de, persona de
Winnefeld, 697, 2702.
——John f. Walt., 1397.
——Mary de, 2409.
——Matilda w. of Ralph de, 2098.
——Maude w. of Sir Rog., 1107.
——Ralph de, 1210, 2098.
——Ralph f. Rog., 1397.

Deyncourt, etc., Robert de, 412, 2771.
———Robert, parson of Scarcliff, 916.
———Roger, 124, 412, 1099, 1351.
———Dom. Roger de, 355, 1102-
    1104, 1108, 1893, 2212,
    2328, 2566.
———Dom. Rog. de, rector de
    Essovere, 115, 123.
———Roger, rector of Wynnefeld,
    2409.
———Rog. de, Dom. de Parco, 123,
    696, 697, 1034, 1088, 1105.
———Walter, 1397.
———Will. de, 697, 2409.
———Will. f. Will. de, 2409.
———William, knt., 1046.
Deyngeland, Dom. Ric., capellanus,
    442.
Dicher, Thomas, 1801.
Dicson, Dikson, Dixson, Dom. Nich.,
    chaplain, parson of Claxby, 630-633,
    635.
Digby, Dygby.
———Johanna w. of John f. Joh. de,
    773.
———John de, 742, 753.
———John, knt., 2120.
———John f. John de, 773.
———Roland, 2120.
———Simon, 1884, 2120.
Dihul, 2621.
Dikeby, John de, ballivus of Chester-
    field, 750.
Dikson, v. Dicson.
Dillereu, Dylreu.
———Rob. de, 1585.
———Will., de Longford, 1582.
Diluerene, Isabella, w. of Ric. de, 1570.
———Richard de, 1570.
Dina, 1726.
Disert, Osbert, of Seal, 2023.
Dison, John, of Walton-on-Trent, 2071.
Dispensarius, Dispensator, Dispenser,
    v. Despencer.
Dithiswrhe, Helyas de, 1726.
Diua, Diue, Gregory de, 537, 538.
———Leodegarius de, 538.
Dobyn, Alice, d. of Rog., 504.
———Matilda d. of Rog., 504.
Doda, 1726.
Doddingeszeles, Doddingzelles, Dod-
    dyngsels, Doddyngselz, Dodinge-
    sheles, Dodingsels, etc.
———Alice d. of Thos., 2392.
———Oliver de, 1520.
———Thomas de, de Trusselay, 1925,
    1934, 1981, 2391.
———William, 1918, 2389.
Dogheafd, Siward, 1360.
Dogmanton, v. Duckmanton.
Dokemanton, Dokmanton, v. Duckman-
    ton.
Dokenfeld, Dokenfeud, Dokonfeud,
    Dokynfeld.
———Rob. de, 2221, 2223, 2732.
———Rob. f. Ric. de, 2224.
Dolfin, Dolfyn, Dolphyn, Doufin.
———John, 1729-1734.
———Ralph, 2561.
———Walter, 1732.

Dolfin, etc., William, 274, 1095, 1728,
    1731, 1733, 1734.
Doncalfe, John, vicar of Prestbury,
    1812.
Done, John, perpetual vicar of Chastre-
    feld, 762.
Donestan, Doneston, Donston, v. Duns-
    ton.
Donyngtone, John, 524.
Doo, Will., of Holmesfeld, 1413.
Dorant, Dorand, Doraunt.
———Joan w. of Will., 235.
———John, 809.
———Ralph, 820.
———Rob., 738, 739.
———Will., of Barley, 235.
Dore, Ralph de, 241, 759.
———Ranulph de, 1017.
Douebrugge, Dom. Ric. de, 339.
Doufin, v. Dolfin.
Doule, John s. of Will., of Plastowe,
    1891.
———John br. of Will., of Plastowe,
    1892.
———Will., of Plastowe, 1892.
Dounynge, Johanna f. Joh. of Assche-
    borne, 71.
Doure, Thurstan de, 2444.
Dousamour, Robert, 1972.
Down, John, 560.
Downes, Ralph, 559.
Downs, Rob., 1112.
Dowson, Will., 2459, 2463.
Dracote, v. Draycote.
Dranefeld, etc., v. Dronfield.
Draper, Drapier, Drapour.
———Hugh, Alderman of the Guild
    of the Holy Cross, Chester-
    field, 785, 791, 802, 808,
    811, 813, 2510.
———Johanna w. of Ric., 346.
———Pagan le, de Derby, 976.
———Richard, 346.
———Robert of Coten, 345.
Draycote, Dracote, Dracott, Draycot,
    Draycott, Dreycote.
———Agnes w. of John, 2186.
———John, 2186.
———John, chaplain, 1984, 1985.
———John, of Loscowe, 2210.
———Jordan de, 2419.
———Sir Phelype, knt., 1782.
———Philip, 2191, 2784.
———Richard de, 892.
———Rob. f. Will. de, 1029.
———Roger de, clerk, 1552.
———William de, 887.
———Will. de, of Loschowe, 892.
———Will. f. cler. de, 1029.
Draytone, Rog. de, 1337.
Drewode, William de, 1919.
Driby, John de, 2295.
———Margery de, 2295.
Dronffeld Wodhouses, Rich. de, 2433.
Dronfield, Dranefeld, Dranfeld, Dran-
    field, Dronefeld, Dronfeld.
———Emma, que fuit ux. quondam
    Petri de, 1037.
———Giles f. Sarre de, 2252.
———Hugh de, 244, 1080.

Dronfield, etc., John, 1495.
———Matilda d. of Will. f. Eduse de, 1038.
———Peter de, 2428.
———Thomas de, 1031.
———Will. f. Eduse de, 1037, 1038.
———Will. f. Matanie, 1033.
———Will. f. Petri de, 1043.
Drurye, Elizabeth, w. of Sir Will., 953.
———Sir Will., knt., 953.
Dryeholme, Will. de, 2509.
Duckmanton, Dogmanton, Dokeman- ton, Dokemantun, Dokemonton, Dokmanton, Duchemanton, Ducke- manton, Duckmantone, Ducmanton, Dugmanton, Dukemaneton, Duke- manton, Dukemonton, Dukmane- ton, Dukmanton, Dukmonton, etc.
———Agnes w. of Rog. de, 1106, 2331.
———Alan de, 1085.
———Emma w. of Hugh de, 1087.
———Geoffrey f. Sim. de, 1085.
———Geoffrey f. Galfr. de, 1088, 1089.
———Hamo f. Walteri de, 1084.
———Henry de, 1106.
———Hugh de, 357, 702, 1893, 2326, 2327, 2492.
———Hugh f. Alani de, 410, 696, 1086, 1087, 1089, 1090.
———Hugh f. Galfridi de, 1088, 1090.
———Hugh f. Hug. de, 702.
———Humfrey, 1542.
———John de, 782, 2330-2332.
———John de, Prior of Welbeck, 1093.
———Laurence f. Ric. f. Rog. de, 1096-1101, 1105.
———Matilda, w. of Hen. de, 1106.
———Matildis f. Hen. de, 1091, 1095.
———Richard de, 378.
———Robert de, 353.
———Roger de, 428, 1094, 1095, 2496.
———Rog. f. Alani de, 2328, 2331.
———Rog. f. Rog. de, 1100.
———Will. f. Rob. de, 2289.
Duddeley, Hen. de, 1023.
Duffeld, Duffeud.
———Adam f. Will. de, 2389.
———John de, clerk, 1369.
———Ralph de, 1176, 1177.
———Robert de, 2012.
———Tho., 129, 161.
Dumuila, Walter de, 2022.
Dun, Robert de, 1609.
———Walter, 1031.
Dunelyn, John f. Rob., 2285.
———William, 2285.
Dunham, Will., chaplain, 823.
Dunne, Nich. le, 225.
Dunston, Donestan, Doneston, Dons- ton, Duneston, Dunstan.
———John de, 725.
———John f. Joh., 2538.
———John f. Will. de, 1538.
———Peter de, 224, 711, 1033, 1536, 2420-2424, 2557.

Dunston, etc., Walter de, 1533, 1743.
———William, 2034, 2428, 2537.
Durand, Durant, Duraunt, Durraunt.
———Geoffrey, 708.
———John, 361, 367, 423, 700, 704, 706, 710, 712, 713, 811, 815, 1744, 2535.
———Ralph, 817, 818, 822, 828, 830, 2514.
———Richard, 2537.
———Robert, 500, 501, 694, 722, 724, 726, 729, 730, 732, 733, 734, 736, 2312, 2313, 2499.
———Thomas, 755, 758, 765, 766, 772, 773, 798, 877.
———Thos. s. and h. of Tho., 2532.
Durdant, Durdent, Duredent.
———John, of Sudbury, 345.
———John, 1392, 1582, 1585, 2390.
———Richard, 1567, 1630, 2321.
———Roger, 238, 1557, 1562, 1564, 1576-1578, 1629, 2321.
———Walt., Bp. of Coventry, 531, 1938, 1939.
———William, 1081.
Durdo, 1560.
Durnforde, Hen., clerk, 587.
Durraunt, v. Durand.
Durs, Walter, of Dronfield, 1743.
Dustun, Will. de, 2765.
Dutton, Ric., of Hope, 558.
Duyn, Hugh de, 2195.
———Dom. Rob. de, 1166, 1487.
Dykon, Dycon, Dycons, Dykons.
———Henry, 1907.
———Hugh, 1377, 1378.
———John, 1911, 1913.
Dyer, Lambert, of Scheffeld, 1126.
Dygby, v. Digby.
Dyggeleye, John de, 2429.
Dylke, John, of Stanton-in-the-Stones, 2211.
Dylreu, v. Dillereu.
Dynham, Tho., of London, 1783.
Dyson, John, 2065, 2072.

E.

Eam, Rog. le, 228, 2242.
Ebeter, Ric. le, 99.
Ecclesale, Eccleshal.
———Ralph de, 2341, 2342.
———Roger de, 2474.
———Will. de, canon of Lichfield, 189.
Echyngham, Eckyngham, Will., 781, 791.
Edelwaldeleia, Alan de, 244.
Edensor, Edenshouere, Edinshouer, Edinsouere, Edinsour, Ednesofre, Ednesor, Ednesover, Ednesowra, Ednessowe, Ednisowra, Ednis- soure, Hedenesouer, Hadenishovere, Hednessoure.
———Adam de, 2716.
———Aliscia f. Rad. de, 247.

Edensor, etc., Hugh f. Alani de, chaplain, 2148.
——Michael de, 2748.
——Nicholas de, 173.
——Dom. Ric. de, 2126.
——Richard de, 173, 1208, 1274, 1547.
——Ric. de, of Tyssinton, 1612.
——Robert de, 542, 1534, 1792, 1797.
——Thomas de, 51, 1534, 1611, 1689, 2126.
——Tho. f. Fulcheri de, 1346.
——Mag. Will. de, 1612.
Edeson, Thomas, 1192.
Edif, Robert, 226.
Edison, Margery, wid. of Will., 2507.
Edmondson, Edward, 1536, 2097.
——Geoffrey, son of Edw., 2097.
Edmund, s. of Henry III., 2100.
Ednesoure, etc., *v.* Edensor.
Edrech, Edrich.
——Joan w. of John Fitzherbert, 2168.
——John f. Walt., 2163.
——John, junr., 2163.
——Margery w. of John, 2163.
Edwalton, Hen. de, 1862.
Edward I., IV., VI., *v.* England, Kings of.
Edwin, 1083.
Eflawe, Roger, 1569.
Eggerton, Alice, w. of Rondulf, 2140.
——Rondulf, 968, 2140.
Eginton, Egenton, Egington, Egynton, Ekyntone.
——John f. Rob. de, 1201.
——Nich. f. Alex. de, 1200.
——Ric. f. Will. de, 1163-1166, 1168.
——Rich. de, serviens, 2611.
——Rob. f. Rog. de, 1201.
——Rob. f. Walkelini de, 1163, 1164.
——Will. f. Nich. de, 1178.
Egnesham, William de, 933.
Eilwinus, 1945.
Eincurt, *v.* Deyncourt.
Eitune, *v.* Eyton.
Ekinton, Ekynton, Hugh de, 44.
——Philip de, marescallus, 1731-1733.
——Will. de, in Cloune, 432.
Eland, Hen., of Baseford, 1854, 1856.
Elcock, Alexander, 651.
Eleanor, Queen of Henry II., *v.* England, Kings of, Henry II.
Elemozinarius, Ralph, 179.
Eleyn, Will., of Brasyngton, chaplain, 297.
Eliot, Henry, 1514.
——Isabel, w. of Hen., 1514.
Elkesley, Richard, 2281.
Ellerker, John, Serjeant-at-law, 2457.
Ellot, Hen., of Kynwolmarsh, 1513.
Els, Anthony, 1680.
Elton, John de, 80.
——Thomas, 87.
Elys, Helys.
——John, of Whittyngton, 234.

Elys, etc., Robert, 572.
——Tho. fil. Joh., de Langesdone, 194.
——William, 571, 1711, 1713-1716.
——Will., of Monyassch, 1715.
Emma, Prioress of St. Mary, Derby, 2382.
Engelard, 517.
Engin, Geoffrey, 2094.
England, Kings of—
Edward I., 193, 1836, 1897, 2656.
Edward II., 339, 1271, 1431, 1453.
Edward III., 203, 765, 921, 980, 1431, 1453, 1515, 1845, 2354, 2357, 2407.
——Philippa, w. of, 921.
——Edward, son of, 921.
Edward IV., 513, 852, 861, 873, 875, 2526, 2689.
Edward VI., 876, 2738.
Henry II., 534, 1944, 2545.
——Eleanor, wife of, 1937.
Henry III., 326, 640, 680, 698, 852, 873, 875, 876, 910, 967, 1161, 1162, 1428, 1431, 1555, 1663, 1684.
——Edmund, son of, 1114.
Henry V., 82.
Henry VI., 831, 2457.
Henry VII., 599, 639, 873, 875, 876.
Henry VIII., 678, 875-877, 924, 1012, 1193, 1624, 2700.
John, 170-172, 228, 680, 997, 1419, 1428, 1431.
Richard II., 2354, 2357.
——Anne, w. of, 2357.
Engleby, Hugh de, 1977.
——Will. f. Joh. de, 1978.
Englissh, John le, 618.
Erdeswyke, Hugh, 2540.
Erlesbure, Hen. f. Ade de, 1702.
Ernesby, Simon de, de Moniassch, 1713.
Esburn, Esburne, Esburnia, *v.* Ashbourne.
Esegar, Eswin, 536.
Esscheburne, *v.* Ashbourne.
Essebourne, Esseburn, Esseburne, *v.* Ashbourne.
Essebury, Dom. Rob. de, 1560.
Esseovere, Essheouere, Essovere, *v.* Ashover.
Estafford, *v.* Stafford.
Estewet, Esthewyt, Estweet, Walter de, vice-comes, 1609, 2093, 2094.
Eston, Ernald de, 1164.
——John de, 2093.
——Ric. f. Gilberti de, 1164.
Estoutevilla, John de, miles, 1125.
——John de, clericus, 1125.
Estunir, Will. le, of Melburn, 1684.
Esturton, Juliana, w. of Walt. de, 2536.
——Walter de, 2536.
Estutevilla, Dom. Will. de, 1728.
Estwode, Isabella, w. of Ralph, 2479.
Etebred, William, 2582.
Ethcotte, James, of Chestrefeld, 464.
——John, of Chestrefeld, 856.
Eton, Will., chaplain, 2677.
Etwall, Etewele, Etewelle, Ettewalle, Ettewelle.

Etwall. etc., Adam, s. of Hugh, 1199.
———Henry de, 949, 2568.
———Hugh f. Nich. de, 1199.
———Matilda, d. of Hugh de, 1199.
———Richard de, 2568.
———Selestria, w. of Hugh de, 1199.
———Will., s. of Hugh, 1199.
———Will. f. Rob. de, 1508.
Everdon, Silvester de, Bp. of Carlisle, 2582.
Everyngham, Hen., s. and h. of Tho., of Staynburgh, 550.
———Thomas, senr., 1722.
———Thomas, junr., 1722.
Exsovere, v. Ashover.
Extraneus, John, 2338.
Eyam, Eyum.
———Henry de, 668, 669.
———Hen. f. Hen. de, 670, 672, 674.
———John de, 1222.
———John f. Nich. de, 1210.
———Will. f. Walt. de, 1217.
Eyhsbury, Dom. Philip de, rector of Braundiston, 2649.
———Will. de, 2649.
Eylande, Hen., of Basford, 1859.
Eyles, Margaret, d. and h. of John, 1345.
Eylysburi, Walter de, 140.
Eyncurt, v. Deyncourt.
Eyre, Eyer, Eyere, Eyr, Heyr, Heyre.
———Adam, 1749, 1750.
———Agnes w. of Martin, 562.
———Arthur, 2191, 2319.
———Edmund, vicar of Tideswell, 1331, 2319.
———Edward, 1316.
———Elizabeth, 2330.
———Henry le, 172, 730.
———Hugh, 1381.
———James s. of Will. le, of Hope, 1444.
———James le, steward of the Lichfield Chapter at Hope, 1444.
———John, 320, 2259.
———John, chapeleyn, 262.
———John le, de Attelowe, 143.
———John le, de Hokenaston, 390, 391.
———John, of Redsettes, 565, 1456.
———Martin, s. of Nich., of Redseats, 559, 562.
———Nicholas de, 557.
———Nich., of Redseats, 559.
———Nich., s. of Nich., of Redseats, 559, 564.
———Nich., of Hope, 1433, 1441, 1446.
———Philip, rector de Aschovere, 127, 1264.
———Ralph, of Offerton, 6.
———Richard, 1382, 2309.
———Ric., of Hogimaston, 316.
———Ric., of Plumley 469, 1513.
———Robert, 100, 515, 1456, 1435, 1443, 1445, 1788, 1796, 2261.
- - -Robert, Forester, 1446.
———Rob., senr., 1463.

Evre, etc., Rob., of Padley, senr., 1446.
———Rob. s. of Rob., of Padley, 884, 1364, 1446.
———Roger, 884, 1263.
———Roger, junr., 2480.
———Rog., of Hulme, 1264.
———Rog., of Plumley, 1264.
———Roland, 1551.
———Stephen le, ballivus de Cestrefeld, 716, 719, 720.
———Steph. s. of Roland, 2319.
———Thomas, 347, 1259, 1260.
———Tho., s. of Will. le, of Hope, 1441.
———William le, 36.
———Will. le, de Hurst, 221.
———Will. le, Forester in the fee of High Peak, 1843.
Eyring, Will., 522.
Eyton, Eytone, Eituna, Eitune.
———Helias de, 2091.
———Joan w. of Tho. de, 316.
———John, 72, 76, 78, 393.
———Thomas de, 316.
———William de, 66.
Eywyle, Dom. Tho. de, 267.

F.

Fabel, Robert, 2036.
Faber, Henry, 294.
———Hugh, 1150.
———John, of Burton-on-Trent, 2613.
———Levenad, 404.
———Nich. f. Nich., de Breydesale, 480, 481.
———Rob., de Wirkesworth, 2635.
———Walter, 108.
———Will, de Sandiacre, 2095.
———Will. f. Will., de Barley Woodsetis, 226.
Fairfax, Sir Guy, Justice of King's Bench, 958.
Faldyngworth, Walter de, bailiff of Lincoln, 1923.
Faleth, Giralmus de, 1360.
Falford, Will. de, rector of Longford, 1578.
Falling, Hugh de le, 254.
Fallinghe, Ric. de, 251.
Fallus, Alex., 2366.
Falthurst, Faltehurst, Richard, parson of Kingsley, 2133, 2134, 2137.
Fannell, Geoffrey, chaplain, 2295.
Fanolcurt, Helias de, 1397.
Farewell, S——— de, 2634.
Farynton, John s. of Tho., 999.
———Margaret, 999.
———Rauf, 999.
———Thomas, 999.
Fasman, Edmund, of Derby, 1116, 1117.
———Thomas, 1116.
Fat, Alan f. Rad., de Overton, 116.
———Richard, 111.

Faunchall, Faunchell, Fauncher.
———Joan d. of John, senr., 1399.
———Johanna, sister of John, 1400.
———Johanna, w. of John, senr., of
    Holmesfeld, 1404.
———John, 1400-1402, 1404, 1405.
Fauneshawe, John, 1416.
Fauvel, John, 327.
Fawconer, Hen., of Schypley, 281.
Fawel, Dom. William, 47.
Fayrechilde, John, 823.
———Tho., of Snelston, 1771.
Fayrfeld, Dom. Hen. de, 1716.
Feirolet, John, 288.
Felde, John de, chaplain, 2616.
Felepot, Hen., 1654.
———Matilda, w. of Hen., 1654.
Felleson, Robert, 694.
Fenekelspire, Henry, 55.
Fennybenteley, Will. f. Hen. de, 512.
Fentam, William, 2255, 2256.
Fenton, Richard de, 180.
———Robert de, 137, 140.
Ferbraz, Ferebras, Ferebraz, Furbras,
    Fyrbrace.
———John, 2295.
———Ralph, 2585.
———Robert, 1163, 1168, 1169, 1171,
    2571, 2576, 2584-2586,
    2587-2591.
Fereby, John de, of Coventry, 2238.
Ferechfelde, Will., knt., 207.
Ferrars, Ferrers, De Ferrariis, etc.
———Anne, w. of Thomas, 2296.
———Cecily, d. and h. of Hugh,
    477-479.
———Cecily, wid. of Thos., wife of
    R. de Snitterton, 2147.
———Henry fr. Rob. de, 215, 216,
    385.
———Henry de, patruus Comitis
    [Willelmi I.] de Ferers,
    239, 2621.
———Hugh f. Will. II. Com. Derbe,
    474.
———John, knt., 2398.
———Dom. Ranulph de, 1699.
———Robert I., Earl Ferrers [*ob.*
    1139], 238.
———Robert II., Earl Ferrers [*ob.*
    1158?], 238, 532, 2380.
———Robert III. de, Earl of Derby
    [*ob.* 1279], 334, 478, 938,
    1470, 1661.
———Rob. de, frater Comitis [Wil-
    lelmi I.], 239, 1346, 2380.
———Robert de, patruus [Willelmi I.],
    Comitis [de Ferers], 239,
    2621.
———Robert de, 135, 215, 216.
———Rob. f. et h. Will. Com. de
    Derby. *v. supra* Robert
    III., E. of Derby.
———Dom. Robert de [late thir-
    teenth century], 1562,
    1563.
———Robert de [1360], 479.
———Dom. Thomas de, 477.
———Thomas, knt., 2296.

Ferrars, etc., William I., Comes de
    Ferers [*ob.* 1190], 239, 385,
    1360, 2380.
———William II., Earl of Derby
    [*ob.* 1247], 51, 385, 1113,
    1346, 1426, 1500, 1663,
    2125, 2621, 2633, 2716.
———William III. de, Comes Derb',
    332, 333, 474-476, 965,
    967, 2634.
———William, s. of William quond.
    Com. Derby [1262], 1470,
    1661.
Ferrour, Tho. le, of Hatton, 1365.
———Will., of Neuthorp, 891.
Fethelers, Rob. le, of Winster, 2218.
Feyssher, *v.* Fisher.
Fienles, Sir Will., Knt., 781.
Figour, John, 1549.
Filius, *al.* Fitz.
———Achard, Walter, 2194.
———Ade, Hugh, 1373.
———Richard, Forestarius de Worm-
    hull, 2707.
———Thomas, 1614.
———Aghemundi, Agnes, w. of Edwin,
    2752.
———Edwin, 2752.
———Agnetis, Peter, 1036.
———Ailmeri, Reginald, 1197.
———Ailwini, Henry, 134.
———Alani, Richard, Earl of Arundel,
    1668.
———William, 229, 1705.
———Aldred, Huron, 2385.
———Nicholas, 2385.
———Alexandri, Will., 2196, 2202.
———Alfwini, Reginald, 536.
———Alot, Robert, 2292.
———Andree, Adam, 2548.
———Anfredi, Symon, 1391.
———Basilie, Symon, 2759.
———Bate, Adam, 2193.
———Hugh, 143, 148.
———Peter, 2193.
———Brunmoni, Suan, 2381.
———Will., 2381.
———Burge, Stephen, 45.
———Chol, *al.* Col. Robert, 516, 2620.
———Cicelie, John, 2311.
———Cnihtwin, Gilbert, 238.
———Colling, William, 2545.
———Durant, Hugh, 364.
———Dyot, Will. f. Rog., 1715.
———Edithe, Thomas, 1572.
———Elfrici, Ernald, 1197.
———Elie, Will., de Parva Longisdon,
    2732.
———Ermentrewe, Will., 1200.
———Ernald, Robert, 2610.
———Fulcher, Fulcher, 516, 2620.
———Henry, 516, 2545.
———Sewal, 239, 516, 2620, 2716.
———Galfridi, Adam, 134.
———Helias, 534.
———Henry, 1818.
———Reginald, 352, 544.
———Will., of Beighton, 270.
———Gamel, John, 926.

Fil. Gamel, Robert, 1113.
——Geraldi, Robert, 284.
——Geroldi, Dom. Henry, 1165.
——Gilberti, Adam f. Rob., 2635.
————Henry, 539, 2621.
————John, Bailiff of Derby, 973.
————John, Coroner of Derby, 975.
————Stephen, 2092.
——Godefridi, John, 2621.
——Godwini, Richard, 414.
——Godwyne, Nicholas, 1966.
——Hallewardi, Robert, 385.
————Will. f. Rob., 385.
——Hardolf, Thomas, 225.
——Henrici, Fulcher, 2716.
————Henry, 1819.
————Hen., Dom. de Irton, 2549-2551.
————capellani, Hugh, 1720.
————John, 389, 2421.
————Mariota, w. of Hen. f. Joh., 1220.
————Philippa, w. of Will., 2549.
————domini de Morisburick, Ralph, 1730, 1731.
————Roger, 1109.
————Roger, 1622.
————Rog., of Schirley, 1901.
————Sewale, 2577, 2578, 2621, 2716, 2743.
————ad Stantonleg, Thos., 2215.
Fil. Herberti, Fitzherbert, Fytzherbert, etc.
————Alice d. of Hen., 1769.
————Anthony, knt., Justice "de communi Banco," 96, 960, 1339.
————Elizabeth, d. of Hen., 1769.
————Eliz. wid. of John, 2066.
————Elizabeth wid. of Ralph, of Norbury, 1930.
————Eustace s. of John, 1204.
————Henry, 347, 355, 1119, 1288.
————Dom. Hen., knt., 388, 1451, 1564-1566, 2713.
————Dom. Hen., de Norbury, 1092.
————Henry, chaplain of Somersale, 2161.
————Hen. f. Th., of Somersale, 2160.
————Herbert, 91.
————Joan d. of Hen., 1769.
————Joan d. of John, 1203-1205.
————Joan w. of John, 2167, 2168.
————John, 844, 1500, 1602, 1772, 2449, 2464, 2465, 2768.
————John, Remembrancer, of the Exchequer, 1205, 1206.
————John, of Etwelle, 279.
————John, of Norbury, 1804, 1959, 1603, 2730.
————John, of Roston, 2084.
————John f. John, 2164-2168.
————John f. Nich., of Norbury, 2995.
————Nicholas, 90, 1959, 1394, 1395, 1596, 1597, 1600, 1769, 2019, 2160, 2188, 2367, 2366, 2676.
————Nich., of Norbury, 1784.

Fil. Herberti, etc., Nich., Sheriff of Notts., 2246.
————Nich. f. Hen., 1769.
————Nich. f. Tho., 2157-2159.
————Richard, clericus, 2155.
————Robert, 2300.
————Rog. f. Tho., 2160.
————Thomas, knt., 1816.
————Thomas, Dom. de Somersale, 2154.
————Thomas, of Roston, 2082.
————Tho. s. and h. of Sir Anthony, 1605.
————Thos. f. Will., 2151, 2152.
————William, 215, 1307, 1308, 2381, 2582.
————Will., knt., 2003, 2004.
————Will., of Norbury, 1589, 1689.
——Heruici, Richard, 399, 880.
————Roger, 880.
————Thomas, 880.
——Herward, Geoffrey, 2771.
——Hoseberti, Henry, 912.
——Hugonis, Alan, 1893.
————Geoffrey, 1085.
————Hugh, de Brantone, 434.
————John, 447.
————Richard, 680.
————Robert, 1622.
————Rog., de Brantun, 429.
————Thomas, 256, 2576.
————W——, 1078.
————William, 2384, 2750.
——Humfridi, Walter, 52.
——Huntredi, Roger, 2735.
——Ingeram, al. Ingelram, Hugh, 684, 2561, 2562.
————Robert, 1490, 1840.
————William, 477.
——Ingus, Will., of Offcote, 53, 1786.
——Joce, Robert, 52.
————Roger, 1821.
————William, 52.
——Johannis, Adam, 2249.
————Hugh f. Hen., capellanus, 1716.
————John, 1959.
————Robert, 173.
————Rob. f. Ade, 1906.
————William, 616.
——Jordani, Alan, 2742, 2772.
————Mary w. of Alan, 2772.
————Ralph, 134.
————William, 2243.
——Jored, Richard, 2421.
——Josei, Roger, 386.
——Jowe, Ralph, 2404, 2405.
——Kalkin, William, 225.
——Lefwyne, al. Lewin, Godwin, 1164, 1166, 1168.
————Robert, 1078.
————William, 2751.
——Leising, Hugh, 1083.
————Richard, 1197.
——Leuegar, Walter, 1945.
——Leuenan, Hen., 404.
————Rob., 404.
——Leuenod, Nicholas, 2621.
——Luce, William, 404.
——Mabille, Hen., 1083.
————Peter, 2384.

Fil. Mariote, John, 502.
——Matilde, Peter, 2424.
——Maye, Richard, 290.
——Milonis, Augustine, 215.
——Murielle, Richard, 2774.
——Nagge, Richard, 27.
——Nicholai, Ralph, 238, 332, 680, 682, 1160, 1162, 1166, 1511, 1555, 2383, 2577, 2578, 2580.
————Ralph, senesc. Comitis de Ferrara, 1500.
————Robert, 1743.
————Roger, 2849.
————quond. rectoris de Mogintona, Rob., 1688.
——subtus le Klif, Nich., 131.
——Nigelli, Hugh, 2095.
——Will., 238.
——Noch, Hugh, persona de Dronefeld, 1031.
——Normanni, Fulk, 2247.
——Ohini, Ralph, 2621.
——Osm', Robert, 516.
——Osmundi Roger, 2090.
——Otonis, Hugh, mil., 2536.
——Pagani, Geoffrey, 1397.
————Nicholas, dapifer Com. de Ferrariis, 215, 2381, 2621.
——Paullini, Reginald, 2381.
——Petri, Andrew, 2385.
————Geoffrey, 1079, 1080.
————Walchelin, 1622.
——Philippi, John, 1160.
————William, 240, 2384.
——Picot, al. Pigot, Gilbert, 535, 536, 1942, 1945.
——Presbiteri de Stapelford, German, 2092.
——Radulphi, Alice, w. of Peter, 2765.
————Emma, d. of Hubert, 916.
————Henry, 1466, 2348.
————Hubert, 916, 1554, 2771, 2780.
————Hugh, 1487, 2196, 2385, 2716.
————Peter, 2621, 2765.
————Ralph f. Joh., 1959, 1960.
————Robert, 1534, 1743, 2090, 2351.
————Roger, in parva Cestria, 972.
————Roger, sen., 2404, 2405.
————Will. f. Hug., 2716.
————Will. f. Will., 1328.
——Ragenaldi, al. Raghnardi, Robert, 1083, 1084.
——Randolfi, Christopher, 24, 1883.
————Geoffrey, 1818.
————Jane, w. of Cristofer, 24.
——Rankelli, Ric., of Little Hucklow, 1461.
——Ranulphi, John, of Whytinton, 1538.
————Ralph, 27.
————Vice-comitis, Robert, 1397.
————Roger, 502, 740.
————William, 1079.
——Rathnal, Roger, clericus, 537.
——Rauekel, Roger, 1539.
——Rayneri, Robert, 2377.
——Reginaldi, Ranulph, 724.
————William, 313.
——Ricardi de ...arhis, Geoffrey, 1281.

Fil. Ricardi, Gervase, 1078.
————Gilbert, 1945.
————Henry, 1425.
————clerici, John, 727.
————Philip, clericus de Bramtona, 415.
————Thomas, 1274, 1550, 1906.
————W—, 1078.
————William, 1614.
————Will., of Pountfreit, 1631.
——Richeri, Will., 2311.
——Roberti, Alice, 1730, 2759.
————Aline, 2775.
————Christina, 2783.
————Gervase, 1080.
————Henry, 1083, 2547.
————domini de Moresbur', Henry, 1729.
————Matthew f. Aline, 2775.
————Peter, 681.
————Philip, King's Justice, 1499, 1947.
————Richard, 2739, 2755.
————Simon, Archdeacon of Wells, 171.
————prepositi de Tansley, Thos., 2302, 2303.
————William, 1079, 2768-2770.
——Rogeri, Alan, 2772.
————Henry, 1818.
————Jordan, 136.
————Rob. f. Rob., chaplain of Uttoxeter, 1023.
————Simon, 2766.
————William, 1726, 2553.
——Rolland, William, 2773.
——Sanson, William, 1893.
——Serlonis, Will., 2381.
——Sewalli, Henry, 134, 396, 2717.
——Silvestri, Nicholas, 664.
——Simonis, Henry, 668.
————John, 1295, 1296, 2569.
————William, 2377.
——Siwardi, Ralph, 2022.
——Steinulf, Roger, 2771.
——Sturmi, H—, 2022.
——Swani, Ailwin, 215.
————Pain, 2771.
————Robert, 538.
————Roger, 1397.
——Terri, William, 238.
——Tholi, Robert, 134.
————Serlo, 134.
——Thome, Thomas, 62, 63.
————clerici, Robert, 2702.
————Roger, 2627.
————William, 1906, 2292.
——Thore, Raghenald, 2752.
——Toch, Ranulph, 533.
————Simund, 529.
——Toky, Robert, 2094.
——Walkelini, Avice, d. of Nich., 932.
——Walkelini, al. Walchelini, etc., H—, 2382.
————Hawise, 2753.
————Henry, 239, 932, 1113, 1165, 1167, 1698, 2621.
————Letitia, 2753.
————Nicholas, 932, 1166.

Fil. Walkelini, etc., Peter, 239, 2621, 2716.
——— Robert, 215, 239, 385, 932, 1113, 1166, 1167, 1346, 1499, 1698, 2580, 2621.
——— William, 239, 1499, 2548, 2716.
—— Walteri, Gilbert, of Cestrefeld, 411.
——— Hugh, 1113, 2090.
——— presbyteri de Wyrkesworthe, Ranulph, 2632.
——— Robert, 1726, 2091.
—— Warini, Fulk, 1948, 1955.
——— William, 682.
——— Will., justice in Eyre, 1697.
—— Wennuwini, Griffin, 1396.
—— Willelmi, Henry, 290, 291.
——— Henry f. Rog., 1726.
——— Inga f. of Rob., 2721.
——— John, 2768.
——— Ketel, 1167.
——— Matilda, 2778.
——— Matthew, 493.
——— Ralph, 2126.
——— sacerd. de Thicheal, Regin., cler, 537.
——— Richard, 1167, 1508.
——— prepositi, Ric., 2722.
——— prepositi de Ylderusleye, Robert, 2721.
——— Robert, 542, 2090, 2091.
——— Roger, 2767.
——— Thomas, 1726.
——— Thomas, jun., 884.
——— Thomas, sen., 884.
——— Sire Will. le, 974.
——— Will., s. and h. of John, 2567.
—— Wimarce, Thomas, 177.
—— Wlurici, William, clericus, 530.
—— Wolnot, al. Wlnat, al. Wlnet, al. Wolnat, Richer, 424, 683, 691, 2311.
—— Wymundi, Will. f. Joh., 116.
Fillingleye, Ric. de, chaplain, 1142.
Findern, Finderne, Findirne, Findren, Fyndern, Fynderne.
——— Aline w. of Hugh de, 2571.
——— Hugh de, 1276, 2571, 2587, 2757.
——— Joan, relicta Joh. de, 1280.
——— John de, 524, 1176, 1181, 1984, 1985, 2081, 2538, 2539.
——— John s. of Margaret, 2600.
——— Margaret, relict of Nich., 2600.
——— Nicholas de, 240, 1163, 1168, 1169, 2584, 2586, 2588-2590.
——— Nich. f. Hugonis de, 1277.
——— Ralph f. Ric. de, cler., 1277.
——— Richard de, 2381.
——— Robert de, 2034, 2584, 2590, 2595, 2596.
——— Rob. f. et h. Joh. de, 1280.
——— Walter, 1954.
——— William de, 887, 1983.
Finian, Fynian.
——— Adam, 731.
——— Will. f. Ade, 720.
Fisher, Feyssher, Fischer, Fissher, Fyscher, Fyshere, Fysshere, etc.
——— Agnes w. of Will. le, 341.

Fisher, etc., Ambrose, chaplain, 1989, 1990, 1993.
——— Cecilia, 1116, 1117.
——— Henry, 1116, 1117.
——— John, 1978.
——— John, Justice of the Common Pleas, 640.
——— Ralph, 1993, 1994.
——— Rob. f. Nich. le, 579.
——— Thomas le, 579, 580.
——— William, 593.
——— Will. le, of Coton, 341.
——— Will., of Dubbruge, 1024.
——— Will. f. Jacobi le, 1373.
——— Will. f. Will., 591, 592.
Fitheler al. Fytheler, Will. le, 2436, 2437.
Fitun, Fyton, Phytun.
——— Laurence, 2110.
——— Richard, 334.
——— Richard, of Bentley, 2007-2009, 2011.
Fitz, v. Filius.
Fitz-Welneth, Will., 1684.
Fitz-Yve, Henry, 1901.
Flackett, John, 2320.
Flagg in la Lee, Matthew de, 388.
Flamsted, Henry de, 1652.
Flaxman, William, 1510.
Fleches, Robert, 1059.
Flemeng, Geoffrey le, clerk, 1430.
Flemink, John, ballivus de Pecco, 405.
Fleschewer, Ralph, 756.
——— Tho. le, 1201.
Flesshovere, Tho., of Lincoln, 1779.
Fletcher, Fleccher, Flechar, Fleycher.
——— Agnes, of Barley, 236.
——— Hen. of Barleyleghes, 232.
——— John, 319.
——— John, of Dronfield, chaplain, 2440.
——— Sir Richard, preste, 867.
——— Ric., of Baukewell, 210.
——— Rob., of Barlay, 234, 236, 2255.
——— Will. s. of Rob., 2256.
Flygh, Rob., chaplain, 2616.
Flynt, John, 1669.
Flyntham, Will. s. and h. of Rob., 822.
Focenn, William, 2671.
Fogge, Robert, 1679.
——— William, 1679.
Fohun, John le, 2621.
Folde, Simon f. Joh. del., 428.
Foldon, Rog. de, canon of Lincoln, 188.
Foliot, Gilbert, Bishop of London, 1945.
——— Richard, 519.
——— Ric., of Ettewelle, 1171, 1199, 1200.
Foljambe, Foleambe, Foleaumbe, Folgeham, Folgiam, Folisambe, Foliaumbe, Foljaumbe, Follgeame, Fuliambe, etc.
——— Avyne w. of Godfrey, 209, 677, 1354, 1376, 1861.
——— Benedicta w. of Hen., 1196.
——— Cecily, 623.
——— Edward, knt., 1195, 2359.
——— Sir Godfrey I., knt., 95, 209, 660, 677, 1194, 1374, 1376, 1492, 1700, 1860, 1861, 2227, 2228.

Foljambe, etc., Sir Godfrey II., of Walton, knt., 213, 382, 383, 645, 878, 2266, 2267, 2403, 2533, 2534.
———Godith wid. of Rog., 2362.
———Henry f. Tho., of Gratton, 2218.
———Henry, of Walton [1452-1490], 23, 102-104, 132, 167, 278, 431, 460-462, 468, 509, 510, 845, 855, 857-859, 866-868, 870, 871, 997, 1072, 1073, 1075, 1196, 1339, 1344-1345, 1779, 1807, 1854-1859, 2087, 2363-2365, 2367, 2368, 2370, 2371, 2473, 2519-2533.
———James, 2354, 2356, 2357.
———James, chaplain, 848, 2087.
———Jane d. of Hen., 2533.
———John I., 812, 1224, 1461, 1463, 1464, 1466, 1468, 1718, 1984, 1985, 2228, 2348, 2349, 2352, 2357.
———John II. f. Thom., 553, 556.
———John III. f. Tho., 1194.
———John IV., of Longstone, 1860, 2082.
———John V. de Tiddeswell, 1282, 1798.
———John VI., 509, 855, 862, 1072, 1073, 1856, 2522, 2523.
———Katharine w. of Tho., 2706.
———Margery wid. of Thos., 2365, 2525.
———Nicholas, 2117.
———Richard I., 743, 1492, 2707, 2708.
———Richard II., 209.
———Ric., of Longstone, 1214.
———Ric. f. Tho., 1613.
———Richard f. Will., of Wormhill, 2117, 2344.
———Robert, 1461, 2340.
———Rob. f. Ric., 2373.
———Rob., Bailiff of the Peak, 555, 617.
———Rob., clerk, 207, 209, 812.
———Rog., 1512, 1548.
———Roger, of Lynacre Hall, Esq., 7, 645, 2356, 2357.
———Thomas I. miles, 1211, 1212, 1548, 2216, 2344, 2345, 2622.
———Thomas II. miles, s. of Thomas I., 2223, 2226.
———Thomas III. s. of Godfrey, of Walton, 448, 456, 505, 814, 823, 986, 1231, 1860, 1861, 1867, 2084, 2357, 2513, 2667.
———Thomas IV. s. of Thomas III., of Walton, 322, 456, 458-460, 509, 838, 845, 848, 870, 1262, 1494, 1496, 1512, 1773, 2087, 2117, 2347, 2517, 2518, 2521, 2522, 2567, 2706.

Foljambe, etc., Tho., Alderman of St. Mary's Guild, Chesterfield, 841.
———Tho., Ballivus de Pecco, 1612.
———Tho., Dominus de Eltone, 296.
———Tho., of Hulme, 207, 209.
———Tho., clericus, 292.
———Tho. 2nd son of Hen., 2533.
———Tho. f. John, 1466, 2340-2342, 2706.
———Tho. f. Rog., 2706.
———Tho. br. of Will., 1427, 1794, 1795.
———William I., 1211, 1427, 1794, 1795, 2340-2343, 2427, 2706.
———William II., 456.
———Will., clerk, 509.
———Will., of Repham, 2517.
———Will., of Wormhill, 191.
Folkingham, Will. de., Abbot of Beauchief, 1775.
Folow, Thurstan, 869.
Folowe, John, 2324.
Fong, Will. f. Rad. le, 2637.
Fonglay, John, rector of Henore, 901.
Fontem de Wyrkesworthe, Adam ad, 2652.
Ford, Clement de la, Ballivus de Pecco, 515.
———John, 2673.
Fordye, Clement de la, ballivus de alto Pecco, 1430.
Forest, John, parson of Breadsall, 1510.
Foresta, Gwydo de, Master of the Temple, in England, 1093.
Forestarius, Adam, 2127.
———Hen., of Ybole, 1474.
———Mabel relict of Robert, 2548.
———Robert, 1500.
Forester, Ric., vicar of Hope, 1437.
Fornaus, Forneaus, Forneus, Forneys, v. Furneaux.
Forth, John, chaplain, 394.
———John, 2761.
Forthe, John, Vicar of Longford, 2678.
Foston, Fostone, Engenulfus f. Gilberti de, 1295, 1296.
———Hen. de, chaplain at Chesterfield, 774, 776, 777, 2509.
———Hen. f. Eng. de, 1311.
———Hen. f. Hen. de, capellanus, 1301.
———Hen. f. Simonis de, 1294.
———Hen. f. Will. f. Engelard de, 1306.
———John de, knt., 1924.
———John f. Sym. de, 2151.
———Thomas de, chaplain, 339.
———Tho. f. Hen. de, 1301.
———Will., capellanus, 1301.
Fouch, Fouche, Foucher, Fuche, Fucher.
———Ermentrewe w. of John, 1179.
———Henry, chaplain, 1920, 1927.
———John, 1176-1179, 1656.
———Margery w. of Ric., 1654.
———Richard, 1654.
———Robert, 40, 330, 541.
———Will., of Marton, 1655, 1656.
Foulowe, John de, 1283.

Foun, Fowen, Fowyn, Foyne.
———Edmund, 1392, 2390.
———Emma, w. of Ralph f. Hen. le, 1561.
———Henry le, 1563, 2126.
———Joan w. of Edmund, 1392.
———John le, 140, 2005.
———John f. Oliveri le, of Holinton', 1566.
———Oliver le, 140, 2126, 2568, 2718.
———Ralph f. Hen. le, 1561.
———Richard le, 929, 2016.
———Robert le, 1559, 1563, 1582, 2007, 2013.
———William le, 676.
Fower, Rob. le, 1156.
Fowler, John, of Salbery, 2400, 2401.
Fox, Foxe, Hen. f. Petri, of Cestrefeld, 547.
———Joan, w. of Will f. Joh., 1798.
———John, of Aldport, 1719.
———John, of Cold Aston, 133, 866, 1066, 1068, 1070-1073, 1075, 1792.
———John, of Dronfeld, 132, 133.
———John, of Offerton, 1788, 1796.
———v. also Ash.
———John s. of Nich., jun., of Offerton, 1804.
———Peter, 357, 544, 545, 688.
———Richard, 2, 1799.
———Ric., of Birchover, 2224.
———Robert, 133, 1068.
———Rob., de Baumforde, 221.
———Rob., of Whaphynborowe, jun., 1068.
———Rob. f. Rog., of Dunston, 1538.
———Thomas, 830, 839, 869, 1601, 1799, 1920, 2519.
———Tho., of Cold Aston, 132, 842, 1056-1058, 1061, 1064, 1066, 1068, 1071, 1073, 1074, 2449, 2458, 2460, 2466, 2470.
———Tho., of Chestrefeld, jun., 1068.
———Tho., of Walton, 509.
———Tho. s. and h. of John, of Aston, 1072, 1073, 1075.
———Tho., of Schatton, 1804.
———William, chaplain, 1282.
———Will., of Chestrefeld, jun., 1068.
———Will., of Hasland, 821, 1074.
———Will., of Offerton, 1794-1796.
———Will. f. Joh., 2, 1797, 1798.
———Will. f. Will., de Offerton, 1800.
Foxlowe, John, chaplain, 2287.
Foy, John, 2736.
———Peter, 686.
Foyne, v. Foun.
Francheden, Will de, 1845.
Francis, Franceis, Franceys, Franciscus, Frauncais, Fraunceis, Fraunces, Fraunceys, Fraunsoys.
———Adam, 2428.
———Alice d. of John, 1380.
———Eliz. w. of Rob., 2166.
———Hen., of Chaddesdeyn, 1914.
———John, 1176, 2379, 2701.

Francis, etc., John, canon of Lichfield, 189.
———John, of Alrewas, 594.
———John, of Engleby, 1978.
———John, of Foremark, 1996.
———John, of Hertestoft, 778.
———John, of Tykenale, 77.
———Ralph, 2378, 2379.
———Ralph, of Fornewerk, 1287.
———Richard, 2331.
———Robert, 227, 1106, 1984, 1985, 2166, 2295, 2330.
———Rob., knt., 1980, 1983, 2714.
———Robert s. of Sir Rob., 2393.
———Rob., de Barleia, 225.
———Rob., of Fornewerk, 2411.
———Simon, of Milton, 1978.
———Sir Thomas, 1116.
———Thomas, 2494.
———William, knt., 2340.
———William, 711, 2331, 2332.
———Will., of Ilkeston, chaplain, 774.
Fraxinum, ad, Fraxinis, de.
———Andrew, de Alwaston, 2176.
———Robert, 2173, 2174.
———Tho. f. Rog. de, 705.
———v. also Ash.
Freccheville, Frecchevyle, Frechenvyll, Frechevile, Frechevilla, Frechevyll, Frechheuile, Frechhevyle, Frecheviell, Frechville, Frechvuyll, Frechvyle, Frechwell, Freschevile, Fretchvile, Fretchevyle, etc.
———Dom. Anker de, 917, 1341, 2253, 2265.
———Anker s. of Pet., 2259, 2260.
———Arthur, of Brymyngton, 2265.
———Eliz. w. of John, 1740, 2266-2270.
———Hubert de, 328.
———John, 2258.
———Joh. f. Pet., 2259-2263, 2266.
———John s. of Ralph, 2705.
———Marg. w. of Ralph de, 2251.
———Nicholas f. Pet., 2259, 2260.
———Peter, 458, 460, 1128, 2473, 2521, 2558.
———Peter, Lord of Staveley, 964, 1342, 1343, 2257, 2263, 2268-2277, 2279.
———Sir Ralph, knt., 779, 803, 812, 1191.
———Ralph de, 46, 329, 918-920, 2249, 2251, 2259, 2260, 2264, 2265.
———Ralph de, Lord of Alwaldeston, 970.
———Richard, parson of Staveley, 2253.
———Robert, knt., 795.
Freke, Rob., 1378, 1379.
Freland, John de, 1304.
Frele, Frely, Will., chaplain, 803, 812.
Freman, Fremon, Freyman.
———John, 50.
———Ralph, 660, 2227.
———Rob. f. Rog., 2548.
Frene, Dionisia, 1042.
Frere, Will. f. Rob. le, 1083.

Friskenay, Tho. de, persona de Wylughby, 1899.
Frith, Frit, Frithe, Fruth, Fryh, Fryth, Frythe.
————John del, 444.
————John f. Ric. del, 1352.
————Katerine, w. of Rog. dil, 443.
————Ric. de le, of Bramton, 435.
————Ric. f. Rog. del, of Bramton, 440.
————Rob. de, 418, 436-440.
————Rob. f. Ric., of Brampton, 441.
————Rog. del, 436, 438.
————Rog. f. Joh. dil, 443.
————Tho., of Gledles, 276, 277.
————William, 446.
Frithisby, Ossebert de, clericus, 518.
Frogcote, Rob. de, 246.
Frowic, Henry de, 1088.
Frusenguill, Ralph de, 1162.
Fuca fr. Rodberti, 530.
Fuche, Fucher, v. Fouch, etc.
Fulcher, Helyas, 2197.
Fulford, Hugh de, 1570.
————Roger de, 1578.
Fullo, Cecily, w. of Ric., of Dore, 1018.
————Matthew, 174, 177.
————Richard, of Dore, 1018.
Funtenaye, Peter de, 548.
Furbras, v. Ferbraz.
Furneaux, Fornaus, Forneaus, Forneus, Forneys, Furneaus, Furneux.
————Robert de, 270, 561.
————Rob. de knt., Lord of Beighton, 268, 2543.
————Dom. Walter de, 267.
————William de, 267, 268, 270, 2543.
————Will., capellanus de Beghton, 660.
Furnival, Lords, v. Nevill, Tho. de; Talbot, John.
————Dom. Tho. de, knt., 267.
————Tho. de, senr., dominus de Hallumchire, 1214, 1700.
Fyche, Hen., chaplain, 788.
Fychett, Fychette, John, 844, 2316.
Fyndern, Fynderne, v. Findern.
Fyrbrace, v. Ferbraz.
Fysher, Fysshere, v. Fisher.
Fythyon, Adam, of Longelemeygnyll, 1522.
————Emma, w. of Adam, of Longelemeygnyll, 1522.
Fyton, v. Fitun.

G.

G——, Abbas Cestrie, 1726.
Gace, Amauric de, 1160-1162.
Gaddesby, Roger de, 1718.
Gambone, Adam, 1972.
Gambull, William, 1484.
Gamel, Rog., of Hynkersil, 1100.
Gamul, Jordan, 669.
Gamyl, Henry, 1702.
Gant, Dom. Peter du, 1558.

Garard, John, chaplain, 315.
Gardiner, Gardener, Gardyner.
————Adam le, 1144.
————Agnes w. of Tho. f. Joh., de Castelton, 1801.
————Stephen, 2535, 2538.
————Thomas, 563.
————Tho. f. Joh., de Castelton, 1801.
————William, 2461.
————Will., of Burton-subtus-Needwood, 2535.
————Will., de Waltone, 582.
Gardino, Will. de, 1726.
Garlek, John, of Glossop, 1320.
Garner, Will., valettus, 1248.
Garston, Richard de, Mayor of Oxford, 1922.
Garthorp, Ranulph de, 545.
Gaskyn, John, of Brampton, 460.
————Laurence s. and h. of John, 2529.
Gate, Henry, 1108.
Gater, Ralph le, 1661.
Gauger, William, 339.
Gaule, Thomas, 824.
Gaunt, Cecily le, 1183.
————John of, D. of Lancaster, 2357.
Gausell, Gausehill, Gaushill, Gaushull, Gonshulle, Gonsille, Gonsyl, etc.
————Nicholas, 460, 2259, 2463, 2464.
————Sir Nich. de, knt., 781, 795, 803, 1191.
————Sim. de, 1.
————Thos., of Barlburgh, 2170.
————Sire Walter de, 974.
Gawarden, Richard, 539.
Gayteford, John de, 1098.
Gebbe, Roger, 1273.
Gee, John, 658.
————Rob., of Lizdeygate, 645.
Geffrey, Geffray, Agnes relicta Walteri, 574.
————Agnes, 594.
————Hen. f. Will., 573, 575, 577, 579.
————Joan f. Will., de Catton, 579.
————Tho. f. Mich., de Catton, 573.
————William, 572, 573, 575, 579-581.
Geg, Stephen, 413.
Gell, Gelle, Jell.
————John, of Hopton, 1383, 2693, 2694.
————Jone, 1389.
————Ralph, of Hopton, 214, 306, 1008, 1009, 1389, 1454, 1518, 1519, 1624, 1673, 1674, 1675, 1677, 2698, 2699.
————Ralph, of Ibulle, 1478, 1479.
————Tho. s. of Ralph, 1519.
Gentz, John, of Langley, 1532.
Geoffrey, 535.
————Mag., 1727, 1729.
————capellanus, 575.
————clericus, 386.
————clericus de Bramton, 412.
————Prior of Coventry, 2573.
————Vicar of Chesterfield, 2491.
————Vicar of Longford, 2015.
————persona de Repton, 1939.

Gerard, Gerart, Gerrard.
————Agnes w. of Rich., 2626.
————Alice w. of Rob., 2627.
————Alice w. of Rog., 1251.
————Gilbert, 2623.
————Ralph, 290, 2221, 2623, 2624.
————Richard, 2625, 2626.
————Robert, 1934, 2627.
————Rog., of Rodburne, 1251.
————Thomas, 693.
————Walter, 2627.
————Will., of Burton, 2616.
Gere, Will., of Beghton, 268, 270, 1735, 1736, 2543.
Gerebaud, Adam, 1965-1967.
————William, 1950.
Gerehard, Alice w. of Rob., of Radbourne, 1247.
————Rob., of Radbourne, 1247.
Gerlaund, Cecily, que fuit ux. Ric., 950.
————John f. Ric., 950.
Gernon, Gern', Gernun.
————Ralph, 1161, 1162.
————Ric., of Hasylbadge, 559.
————William, 1274.
————Dom. Will. de, Lord of Bakewell, 194.
————Will. f. Dom. Will., 200.
Gers, Will., 269.
Gervase, capellanus, 135.
Gestling, John de, Justice at Nottingham, 2334.
Geyte, John, of Thorne, 847.
————Marget w. of John, 847.
Giffard, Gifford, Gyfford.
————George, 307.
————Dom. John, of Chilinton, 919, 1690.
————John, knt., 2191.
————Walter, Bp. of Bath, 1428.
Gilbert, clericus, 1622.
————clericus de Maupas, 530, 539.
————presbyter, 532.
Gilbert, Gylbart, Gylberd, Gylbert.
————Nicholas, 301, 1494.
————Richard, 2231, 2232.
————Rob., senr., 303.
————Robert, 1071, 2233, 2235.
————Will., of Chaddesden, 607.
Gildeford, Robert de, 547.
Gildkarman, Thos., 2491.
Giles, Gyles.
————Elizabeth w. of Ric., 169.
————John, of Birley, 278.
————Richard, 169.
————Thomas, 169.
Gilly, Margery, 1020.
————Richard, 1018.
Ginges, John de, 175.
Gin, Richard, 418.
Glamuile, Gerard de, 1079.
Glanuile, Ranulf de, Justic. Regis, 1079, 1080.
Glapwell, Glapewell, Glappewell.
————Emma w. of Hugh, 2292.
————Hugh f. Will. de, 2292.
————Roger de, 371, 374, 717, 718, 724, 729, 732.
————Simon de, 1317-1319.

Glapwell, etc., Thos., Rector of Wingfield, 2410.
————Tho. f. Will. de, 1317-1319.
Glay, Rob. of Calale, 2290.
————Tho., of Bramton, 436, 437.
————Will., of Brampton, 445.
Glede, William, 1991.
Glen, Ric., clericus, 2222.
Glossok, Walter, 2462.
Glossop, Glopsop, Glosop, Glossope.
————John, of Wodesetys in Norton, 1807.
————Robert, 2690.
————Will., 1675, 2697.
————Will., of Wirksworth, 1008, 1009, 2699.
Gloucester, Richard, Duke of, 103.
————Mabel, Countess of, 1939, 1943.
————Robert, Earl of, 1939, 1943.
Glover, John le 573, 575, 580.
————John f. Will. le, 580.
————Ric., of Brampton, 455.
————Robert le, 571, 572, 604.
————Tho., Bailiff of Ashbourne, 78, 79.
————Thomas le, 574.
————William le, 579.
————Will f. Joh. le, 576.
————Will. le, de Calton, 2042.
Glovernia, Ric. de, Archdeacon of Coventry, etc., 178, 179, 189, 1953.
Gmelega, Ralph de, 238.
Gnohushal, Mag. Ric. de, 1081.
Gocelinus, Archidiaconus, 1080.
Goche, William, 1657.
Godard, John, bailiff of Derby, 523.
Gode, Rog. le, vicar of Tideswell, 2344.
Godefrey, Ralph, 2029-2031.
————Will. f. Rad., 2029.
Godemere, John, de Donasthorp, 1961.
————Richard, de Donasthorp, 1961.
Goderhil, Simon, 497.
Goderiche, Hen., 1023.
Godesone, Agnes, wid. of Rog., of Chestrefeld, 787.
Godinton, Will de, 1499.
Godladde, Will., of Hulton, 1202.
Godman, Godmon, Will., Vicar of Wirksworth, 2643, 2649, 2652, 2653, 2655.
Godoson, Richard, 1059.
Godrig, Simon, of Hatton, 1362.
Godwine, Dom. Will., Vicar of Hope, 1433.
Godwyn, William, 1967.
Goeve, Will., 103.
Golbone, John de, 1347.
Golde, John s. of John, of Loghbergh, chaplain, 2397.
————John, of Parwich, 2397.
Golding, Joan w. of Tho., 2712.
————Thomas, 2712.
Goldsmyth, Goldesmyth, John, 740, 745, 749, 754, 2314.
Golert, John le, of Eyum, 1218.
Gomfray, Gomfrey, Goumfrey.
————Richard, clerk, 549, 1701, 2438, 2439.
————Ric., late rector of Hengham, 795.

Gomfray, etc., Tho., clerk, 231, 549, 1701.
————Tho., rector of Dronfeld, 791, 795.
Gonor, John, 822.
Gonshulle, Gonsille, Gonsyl, *v.* Gausell.
Gore, Nich., de, Vicar-General of Canterbury, 197.
Gorszes, Ric. del, 230.
Gosi, 2620.
Gosner, John de, chaplain, 446, 447.
Gotham, Adam de, 1341, 1776.
————Thomas de, 1018.
Gotken, John, of Wyndeley, 482.
Gould, Dom. Adam, capellanus, 2039.
Goule, Gowele, Gowle.
————Johanna d. and h. of Ric., 826.
————John, 751.
————Thomas, 833, 834.
Gourell, Will., 955.
Gourley, Will., 489.
Gournay, Gourney, *v.* Gurney.
Goytone, Thomas, chaplain, 2670.
Grafton, Mag., Will. de, 2575.
Grane, Thomas, 2295.
Grange, Graunge, Grangia.
————Henry de, 574.
————Marjory f. Rog. del., of Chastrefeld, 748.
————Ric. of the, 2554.
————Walter atte, 573, 575.
Granger *al.* Graunger, Agnes wid. of Ric. le, 2065.
Grant, Graunt, Graunte.
————Rob le, 425, 426, 704, 1317-1319, 1896, 2282.
Gratton, *v.* Gretton.
Graue, John in le, 2741.
Graveler, John, 2508.
Graver, James, rector of Sudbury, 2089.
Gray, *v.* Grey.
Grayve, Grayne.
————Matilda, w. of Will., 232.
————Will., of Barley, 231, 232.
Greaves, Edward, 2216.
————John, 2216.
————Will., clerk, 2216.
Greenhalwe, Roger, 2678.
Greensmyth, Tho., of Bagschawe, 629.
Gregory IX., Pope, 937.
Gregory, Gregore.
————Henry, 1225, 1226.
————Nich. f. Walteri, 1550.
————Robert, 465.
————Walter, 1549.
Greisley, *v.* Gresley.
Grendon, Grendone, Grendun, Grendune.
————Dom. Andrew de, knt., 334, 2003.
————Fucher de, 933.
————Hugh f. et h. Will. de, 337, 338.
————John, of Totone, 2186.
————Jurdan f. Serlonis de, 2620.
————Margaret de, 1164, 1165.
————Matilda, de, 2126.
————Dom. Ralph de, 331, 334, 1560, 1561.
————Richard, 1695.
————Ric. de, rector of Blore, 1228.

Grendon, etc., Robert de, 216, 1113, 1556, 1569, 1573, 1576.
————Rob. s. of Dom. Ralph de, 334.
————Rob. f. Rob de., 1390, 1391.
————Master Rog. de, called "Simple," 331.
————Serlo de, 52, 134, 396, 516, 2620, 2717.
————Serlo f. Serlonis de, 879.
————Stephen de, 337, 338.
————William de, 135, 404, 476, 933, 936, 2125, 2127.
————Will. f. Hug. de, 338.
————Will. f. Serlonis de, 879, 2128.
Grene, Adam s. of Hen. de la, 1153.
————Cecily del., 1155, 1157.
————Guy, 1263.
————Hen. de la, 142, 1153.
————Hen. de la, knt., 942.
————Hen. f. Will. de la, 1135, 1136, 1139, 1143.
————Hugh f. Will de la, 1143.
————Isabel w. of John, of Dugmanton, 1109.
————Joan f. Hen. de le, 403.
————John del, 2323.
————John, of Bubbenhull, 1259.
————John, of Dugmanton, 1109.
————John atte, of Fornewerk, 1286.
————Nicholas, de Allerwas, 2051.
————Ric. del, de Dubbrugge, 1024.
————Robert, 1404.
————Rob. atte, of Fornewerk, 1286.
————Rob. f. Rog. de la, 431.
————Sarra f. Hen. de le, 403.
————Tho. de la, of Wiardiston, 1134, 1135, 1139, 1140.
————Will f. Hen. de la, 111, 112.
Grenehall, Roger, 394.
Grengel', Henry de, 1422, 1424.
Grenhill, Isabella w. of John de, 759.
————John f. Avicie de, 759.
Grenhulle, Simon f. Petri de, 22.
Gresley, Greisley, Gresel, Gresele, Greseleia, Gresle, Greslege, Gresselege, Gresseley, Gressley, Greysley, Grislee, Gryseley, Grysley, etc.
————Agnes de, Prioress of Grace Dieu, 399.
————Anthony, 1028.
————Edward, 1028.
————Geoffrey I. de, Senescallus Comitis Derby, 475, 1699, 2023, 2718.
————Dom. Geoffrey II. de, knt., 2013, 2028, 2033, 2587.
————Geoffrey III., 2618.
————Sir George, 1028.
————Hugh de, 215.
————Humfrey, 1028.
————John I., Dominus de Drakelowe, 1026, 1864.
————John II., 1784, 2064.
————John III., knt., 161, 1027, 1596, 2070, 2362.
————Peter de, 1322.
————Ralph de, 2380.
————Reginald f. Regin., 2381.
————Reinald de, 532.

Gresley, etc., Robert de, 541.
———Roger de, 604.
———Thomas I., knt. Dominus de Drakelowe, 604, 1393, 1394, 1784, 1932, 1980, 2055, 2057, 2110, 2539, 2540, 2542.
———Thomas II. de, knt., 598, 603, 2070, 2400.
———Will., Abbot of Beauchief, 258.
———William I. de, 2777.
———William II., knt., 1028, 2073.
Gretehed, Rob., parson of Ekyngton, 2607, 2609.
Gretton, Gratton.
———Agnes w. of Hen., 321, 323, 325.
———Henry, 321, 323-325, 2214, 2217.
———Robert de, 295.
———Rob. f. Hen. de, 2222.
———Tho. de, clericus, 291.
———Tho. f. and h. Will., 73.
———Will. de, knt., 2225.
Greves, Greveys, Grevez, Grevis, Grevys.
———Giles de, 250, 251, 260.
———Johanna, 266.
———John, 253, 259, 261, 264.
———Leticia w. of Giles del, 250.
———Marjory w. of John, 261.
———Nic., of Bramptone, 264.
———Robert de, 246, 247, 249.
———Rob. s. of Rob. del, 249.
———Tho., Abbot of Darley, 1541.
———Tho., s. of Giles de, 251-253, 256, 260.
———Will. de le, of Beeley, 248, 254, 263, 264.
———Will., of Brampton, 259, 260, 261, 451, 452.
———Will. f. Hug. de le, 246.
Grey, Gray.
———Edward, knt., 2191.
———Elizabeth, Lady de, 896, 899.
———Henry I. de, senr., 891.
———Henry II., 893.
———Henry III., Lord Grey of Codnor, 900-902, 905.
———Henry IV., Lord Grey, 958, 959.
———Henry V., Lord Grey of Codnor, 962.
———Dom. Henry VI., 2461.
———Joan w. of Tho., 2439.
———John de, Bishop of Norwich, 2334, 2769.
———John, Lord Grey of Codnor, 892, 893.
———John de, dominus de Unstone, 1042, 2433-2435.
———John, of Unstone, 2441, 2445-2449.
———John, 1055.
———John f. Tho. f. Joh., 2439, 2442.
———Katharine wid. of Henry, Lord Grey of Codnor, 905.
———Lucy w. of Ric. de, of Sutton, 2289.
———Marg., w. of Henry, Lord Grey of Codnor, 902.

Grey, etc., Richard de, Lord of Codnor, 1619.
———Dom. Richard le, 1337, 1338, 1548, 2095, 2204, 2205, 2209.
———Richard de, of Sutton, 2289.
———Ric. de, "dapifer," 1317-1319.
———Ric. de, Lord of Toton, 974.
———Ric. s. and h. of Will. de, 917, 918.
———Robert, 2392.
———Thomas, sen., 1870, 1871.
———Thomas, of Unstone, 2437-2439, 2442.
———William I. de, 1428.
———Dom. William II. de, 2195.
———Dom. William III. de, knt., 1105.
———Will. of Hanley, 2459.
———Will. de, of Sandiacre, knt., 2209, 2292, 2293.
———Will. de, of Sandiacre, 2096.
———Will. of Unstone, 2469.
Greysley, v. Gresley.
Griffin, Griffyn, Gryffen, Edward, 383.
———Elizabeth w. of John, 47.
———John, Dom. de Ayllewaston, 47.
Griffith, Griffithe, Gruffythe, Gryffyth.
———Thomas, scutifer, 2539, 2540.
———Sir Walter, knt., 2619.
Grim, Grym.
———Ralph, 1544, 2026.
———Will., vicar of Youlgrave, 2733.
Grincurt, Ralph de, 1397.
Grindleford, Grundulforde, Gryndulford, etc.
———Matilda w. of Hen. de, of Eyom, 1243.
———Richard de, 1325.
Grislee, v. Gresley.
Groos, Will., 2391.
Gruffe, Hen. de le, 1475.
Gruffythe, v. Griffith.
Grun, Ralph de, 1325.
Grundulford v. Grindleford.
Gryffin, v. Griffin.
Gryffyth, v. Griffith.
Gryndulford, v. Grindleford.
Gryseley, Grysley, v. Gresley.
Gryssop, Rob., Alderman of Chestrefeld, 860, 2517.
Guallay, John s. of Ric. de, 895.
Gudhyne, Will., of Hurdlow, junr, 1473.
Gudley, Mag. Will. de, 2335.
Gulde, Humphrey, de Grendon, chaplain, 2318.
Gull, Will., clerk, 2567.
Gunne, Henry, of Horninglow, 2239.
Gunston, Hugh de, 2300, 2404-2406.
———James f. Hugonis de, 204.
———Joan w. of James de, 204.
———Thomas de, 204.
Gunthorp, Tho., Prior of Newstead, 1878-1880.
Gurney, Gorney, Gourney, Gurneye.
———Elizabeth w. of Hugh de, 1278, 1279.
———Hugh de, 1278, 1279, 1632, 2197.

Gurney, etc., John de, mil., 2537.
————Ralph f. Hugonis de, 1169.
————Ralph de, of Bolton, 2584, 2586, 2588-2597.
Gutinge, Guttynges, *v.* Guytingis.
Guyte, Guylte, Gyte, Quyte.
————Elena, 318.
————Henry, 323-325.
————John, 319, 323.
————John, of Over Haddon, 317.
————John, s. of John, 317.
————Will., 85.
Guytingis, Gutinge, Guttynges, Philip de, 2003, 2007, 2009, 2010.
Gybon, Gybone, Gybun.
————John, 986.
————Peter, of Burton-on-Trent, 2239.
————Rob., of Tuttebury, 1369.
Gylderson, Gyldreson, Gyldurson, Gyldyrson.
————John f. Rog., 2066.
————Katharine, 2066.
————Roger, de Brynsley, 2062, 2064-2066.
Gylessone, John br. of Tho., 259.
————Tho., of le Greves, 257, 259.
Gymelyngeye, John f. Joh. de, 2407.
Gyne, Tho., 1877.
Gynour, John le, of Chelmordon, 667, 669.
Gyot, Tho., 370.
Gyppeworth, Dom. Will. de, 1899.
Gyte, *v* Guyte.

H.

H——, Decanus, 2382.
Habetot, *v.* Abbetoft.
Hachet, John, bailiff of Derby, 983.
Hacsmal, Stephen, of Cestrefeld, 369.
Hacsmall, Richard, 2309.
Hacunthorpe, Agnes, w. of John de, 1738.
————Joanna, w. of John de, 1737.
————John f. Will. de, 1735-1739.
————Richard de, 1735.
————Richard de, clerk, 1739.
Hadde, Adam, of Cestrefeld, 706.
Haddon, Haddun, Agnes, w. of John, 2351.
————John f. Rad. de, 2351.
————Margery, wid. of John de, 1225.
————Robert de, 2303.
Hadfield, Haddefelde, Hadfeld.
————Richard, 838.
————Vincent de, 1373.
————William de, 175.
Haie, Hugh del, 933.
Hakard, *v.* Acard.
Haket, *al.* Haget, Geoffrey, Justiciarius Regis, 1499, 1947.
Hakkefot, Emma, f. Rob., of Peuerwiche, 1819.
Halby, Will., 1430.
Haldanus, 1945.

Hales, *al.* Halse, Joh., Bp. of Coventry and Lichfield, 991, 2396, 2559.
————Will. de, Abbot of Lilleshall, 1462.
Halgtone, Will. de, 2609.
Halin, Walter de, 933.
Halis, Will. de, 931.
Haliwell, Halywell.
————Isabel, w. of Ranulph de, 734.
————Ranulph de, 726.
————Ranulph f. Regin, de, 733, 734.
————Rog. f. Ran. de, 741.
Hall, Halle.
————Adam del, 1149.
————Emma w. of Will. de le, 288.
————Henry, 553, 560, 561, 563.
————Hugh, 623.
————Joan d. of John del, of Castleton, 554.
————John del, 553, 555, 556, 2116.
————Oliver, 557.
————Ralph, 851.
————Richard, 1920, 2239, 2737.
————Simon del, 2708.
————Thomas, 339.
————Thurstan, of Overhurst, 7.
————William de, 1434.
————Will. de le, of Bentley, 288.
Hallam, Hallum, Halom, Halomey, Halum.
————John de, de Bawnforth, 1355.
————John de, Parson of Lamley, 1488.
————Lucy w. of Will., of Braystone, 484.
————Ralph de, 1334-1336.
————Tho., of Derby, 988.
————Thos. f. Rob. de, 2193.
————Will., of Braystone, 484.
Hallenthorp, Will. de, 271.
Halleswayne, Rob., sen., 2186.
Halley, Hally.
————Hugh, 621.
————Hugh s. of Walter, 1443.
————Oliver, de Schatton, 221.
————Walter, 621.
————Walter, of Blakebroke, 1443.
————William, 405, 515, 1211, 1794-1797, 2762.
————Will. f. Thom., 554.
Hallumschire, Will. f. Joh. de, 497.
Halm, Laurence, of Engleby, 1978.
Halse, *v.* Hales.
Halton, Mag. Richard de, Canon of Lichfield, 179.
————Walter de, 179.
Halues, Alice, w. of Rob. de, 2310.
————Rob. de, 2310.
Halughton, Peter, vicarius chori de Lichfield, 1720.
Hambury, Isabel, d. of John de, 2131.
————John de, 2131.
Hamby, Dom. Walter de, 1899.
Hamilton, Dom. Will. de, cler., 139, 140.
Hamo, clericus, 475, 1113, 1490.
Hampton, Henry de, 743.
————John, 863.
————Rob., 373, 375, 730, 731, 737.

Hampton, Tho., of Leicester, 863, 865.
——Tho., of Marchynton, 830.
——Will. de, chaplain, 1354.
Hancoke, George, of Barley Lees, 1414.
Handle, Dom. John de, 578.
Handsacre, Margaret, wid. of Will., 1988.
——Will., knt., 1988.
Haneby, Adam, 885.
Hanes, Nicholas de, 1946.
Hankynsone, Will., 2115.
Hanley, Haneley, Hanl', Hanleia.
——Adam de, 108, 934, 2284.
——Herbert de, 228.
——John f. Ad., 1046.
——Ralph s. of Herbert de, 228.
——Ralph f. Ric. de, 2557.
——Thos., of Hanley, 2462.
Hanselin, Haunselin.
——Thomas, 45.
——William, 1470.
Hanson, Hanneson.
——John, 782.
——Robert, of Netherthorpe, 2254.
——Rob., of Repton, 1981.
——Rog. s. of Will., chaplain, 812.
——Tho., Steward of Bretby Manor, 488, 1540.
Hanstock, Christopher, 2307.
Hapetot, v. Abbetoft.
Hapher, Walter, 1108.
Hapilknole, v. Apeknoll.
Haraldus, 532.
Hard, John, of Tharlsthorp, 223.
Hardi, Richard, 2311.
Hardredesh', Will. de, 1419.
Hardwyk, Herdewyk, Herdwyke.
——Peter f. et her. Rob. de, 1200.
——Roger, 807, 1879.
——Rog. s. and heir of Will., 1772.
——William, 1772.
——Will. f. Will., 1772.
Hardye, John, 1268.
Hardyng, Thos., 2163.
Harecourt, Harcourt, Roger, 379, 1926-1928.
Haregeve, Rob. de, 45.
Hareson, v. Harreson.
Harestan, Dom. Rob. de, 696.
Harlaston, Katerine, wid. of Will., 1817.
Harlewine, Cristiana quond. ux. Rad., 2031.
Harley, Margaret de, of Egynton, 1186.
Harpham, Thomas, 525.
Harpur, Harpere, Walter le, 1114.
——Walter le, of Longeford, 1576.
——Walter le, of Shirleg', 1577.
Harreson, Hareson.
——Joan w. of Will., 2471.
——John, of Hilton, 1380.
——Will., of Dugmanton, 2471.
Harry, Thomas, 2684.
Harston, Sweyn f. Rad. de, 2302.
Harwye, John, of Cold Aston, 130.
Hasard, Alice, 2096.
——Will., 2096.
Haselford, Hasilford.
——Henry de, 1233.
——Roger, 1257

Haselund, Samson f. Rog. de, 1351.
Haselyngden, Rob. de, 1126.
Hashope, v. Ashope.
Hasilhirst, Hassylhurst, Hasulhyrst, Hasylhurst.
——Nicholas, 2324.
——Rob., clerk, 87.
——Rob., chaplain at St. Oswald's altar, Ashbourne, 1331.
——Will., 1513.
Hasseland, John, 233.
Hassop, Peter de, 1207.
Hassulwode, John, of Callow, 2674.
——Margery w. of John, 2674.
Hastings, Will., Lord, 1068, 1071, 2398.
Hasulhyrst, Hasylhurst, v. Hasilhirst.
Hathirsege, Dom. Matt. de, 355.
Hatton, Hugh de, 1362.
——Ric. f. Petri de, 1364.
——Will. de, 1363.
Hauker, Symon, 1979.
Haukynman, Tho., 818, 819.
Haulee, Ric. de, 354.
Hauley, Ric. de, 355.
Haunche, Adam f. Rob., of Bramton, 436.
Haunselin, v. Hanselin.
Havermere, Jocelyn de, 2566.
Haversege, Hauersegg, Haversegge.
——Michael de, 363, 703, 1744.
Hawise, vidua, 1726.
Hawkysworth, Haukysworth, Edward, 1448.
——Tho., of Thornsyt, 1447, 1448, 1808.
Hawson, Hauson, Haweson.
——Ric., perpetual vicar of Chestre-feld, 823, 828-830, 839, 841, 2316, 2516.
Hay, Have.
——Geoffr. de, of Pakinton, 1961.
——Hugh de la, 419.
——John de la, 417, 420, 421, 435, 441.
——John del, bailiff of Derby, 987.
——Jone w. of Laurence of the, 1483.
——Laurence of the, of Derby, 1483.
——Ralph de, de Pakinton, 1961.
——Walt. de la, 2560.
Hayle, Heyle.
——John, of Bonsal, 311-313, 1669.
——Matilda, w. of John, 1669.
Hayrsle, Peter de, 1791.
Hayward, Edm., chaplain, 2163.
——Hen. le, de Brassington, 393.
——Nic. le, of Bonsal, chaplain, 313, 315, 316.
——Will., chaplain, 76.
Haywode, Will. f. Will. de, 1434.
Hayws, Sir Nic., of Brassyngton, chaplain, 314.
Hebbe, John, 3.
——Richard, 393.
——Will., 2714.
——Will., rector of Edlaston, 79.
Hedfeld, Dom. Will. de, Canon of Lichfield, 179.

Hegelawe, Hugh de, 1210.
Hegh, Will. del, chaplain, 390.
Heghcote, Robert de, 1282.
Heghlawe, Arnald de, 1424.
Hegworda, Rob. de, 1197.
Heige, Gilbert de, 1945.
Held, Edward, 1671.
Held, George, of Beley, 266.
————Richard, 1671.
————Thrust', 1671.
Helias, clericus, 1078.
————Magister, 1081.
————Prior de Bredune, 1939.
Heliun, Susan, q. f. ux. Ric. de, 2248.
————Walter de, 228, 2242, 2243.
Hellgate, Thomas, 2259, 2260.
Helot, Hellot, Hellott, Heylot.
————John, 572-575, 577.
————Richard, 572.
————Roger, 2691.
————Tho. s. of John, 577.
Helyn, Will. of Brassington, chaplain, 2666.
Helys, *v.* Elys.
Hem, Margery d. of Rog. le, 226.
————Rog. le, de Barley Wodsetis, 226, 227.
————Will. le, 227.
Heminming, John, of Burton, 2613.
Hemmynge, John, of Brampton, 1669.
————Matilda w. of John, 1669.
————Tho., of Brampton, 452.
Hemmyngwey, John, 1674.
Hendle, Walter, knt., 1625.
Hendley, Will., chaplain, 1284.
Henford, Will. de, 157.
Hennage, Geo., Dean of Lincoln, 2698.
————John, of Haynton, 1988.
Henover, Henouer, Henore, Henovere, Henowre, etc.
————Eudo de, 886.
————Mag. Will. f. Rob. de, 1545.
————Nicholas de, 240, 1633, 2196.
————Nich. f. Joh., 1336.
————Nich. f. Tho., 1336.
————Nich. f. Walkelin de, 1698.
————Robert de, 887, 1619.
————Thomas de, 2093, 2094.
————Will., dominus de, 886.
————Will. de, 2643.
————Will. f. Hen. de, 361, 362.
Henri, Rog., de Appulby, 1683.
Henricus, 1940.
Henrison, John, of Chestrefeld, 454.
————Rich. f. Joh., of Scarcliff, 2099.
————Thomas f. Ric., 2099.
Henry II., III., V.-VIII., *v.* England, Kings of.
Henry, Abbot of Darley, 2575.
————clericus, 693, 709.
————clericus de Cesterfeld, 365, 367.
————clericus de Foston, 2103.
————Decanus, 1499, 2545.
————Dominus de Morsbur', 1727.
————frater Reginaldi clerici, 537.
————nepos Ailwani f. Swani, 215.
————prepositus, 1565.
————presbyter, 238.

Henry, presbyter de sanctimonialibus, 2381.
————sacerdos, 2384, 2620.
————subvicecomes, 1554.
Henster, Thomas, 2540.
Heorthul, Hen. de, 216.
————Ric. de, 216.
Herberbure, Herberbury, Herbyrburi, Rob. f. Odon de, 2004-2006.
Herberour, Herbeiour, Herberiur, Herberour, Herbyiour.
————Isabella w. of Dom. Will. le, knt., 607.
————Dom. Will. le, 480, 481, 605, 607, 1288, 2177, 2205.
Herbert, Canon of Lichfield, 2575.
————Clerk of Hugh, E. of Chester, 535.
————presbiter de Aluualdestona, 533, 1752.
————Nicholas, 2128.
Herdby, Herdeby, Herdilby.
————Geoffrey de, 1632, 1633.
————Isabella w. of Geoffrey de, 1633, 1634.
————Isabella w. of Will. f. Galf. de, 1635.
————Joan d. of Will. de, 1635.
————Will. s. of Isabella, 1634,1635.
Herdebereghe, Hacuil de, mil., 2244.
Herdeman, John le, 1439.
Herdewyk, Herdwyke, *v.* Hardwyk.
Herdewykewall, Thos. f. Ade de, 2343.
Herebert, prepositus, 1197.
Hereford, Hugh de, 2171, 2172, 2174.
————Ralph de, 1334, 2194.
————Robert de, 933.
Herford, Cecily f. et h. Ric. de, 2341.
————Matilda qu. ux. Ric. de, 2342.
Hergreve, Hugh de, 328.
Heriz, Heryz.
————Joanna f. Joh. de, 2605, 2606.
————Dom. John de, 2147, 2606.
————Will. de, mil., 2244.
————Will. de, 2566.
Herlaston, Hen. de, 2637.
Herle, Will. de, Justice, 2251.
Herlewin, Ralph, 2027.
Heron, Alice f. Joh., 694.
————John, knt., 2534.
Herrison, Herryson, William, 317, 318.
Herry, Hen., of Aston, 1068.
Hert, Adam, 1148.
————Hen., of Rotington, 1766.
————Will., of Norbury, 1766.
Herteshorn, Hertishorn.
————Bertram f. Will. de, 2759.
————Hen. de, 1956.
————Hen. f. Dom. Agathe de, 540.
————Humphrey de, 1197.
————Ralph de, vicar of Croxall, 581, 582, 591, 592.
————Ric. f. Bertram de, 540.
————William de, 571, 1975, 2612.
————Will. f. Hen. de, 1958.
Herthill, Herthul, Herthull, Hertil.
————Adam de, 292, 1274, 1328, 1611, 2622.
————Giles s. of Ric. de, 1703.

Herthill, etc., Hawise de, 2786.
———Henry de, 1274, 2786.
———Katerine w. of Giles de, 1703.
———Peter de, 1862.
———Dom. Ric. de, 215, 1212, 1461, 1611, 1661, 1703, 2212, 2213, 2216, 2344.
———Dom. Rob. de, knt., 191, 1461.
———Robert de, 1328, 2622.
Hertington, Hertingtune.
———Margery w. of Will. de, 1347.
———Rob. de, knt., 2340.
———William de, 1347.
Hervi, sacerdos de Suttunia, 530.
Hervy, Harvy, Herui, Heruie, etc.
———Henry, chaplain, 830.
———John, 1902-1904, 1906, 1908, 1911.
———Richard, 56, 60, 61, 67.
———Roger, 1909, 1911.
———Thomas, 137, 139, 140, 324, 862, 2460, 2693.
———Thos. s. and h. of John, 2468.
———Tho., of Workesworth, 10.
———William, 1776, 2692.
———Will. s. and h. of. Tho., 874.
Herwy, John, sen., 2441.
———John, jun., 2441.
Hesbi, Luvel de, 531.
Heslond, Gilbert de, 414.
Hestriis, Euger' de, 1114.
Hetford, Robert de, 239.
Hethcote, Heithcote, Hethcott, Hethe-cote, Hethkote, Heythcote.
———George, 1886.
———John de, 2353.
———Ralph, of Chesterfield, 466.
———Rauf, of Hope, 1451, 1452.
———Richard, 466, 821, 863, 865.
———Robert de, 1718, 2352, 2353.
———Rob., of Callal, 167.
———Roger, 564.
———Tho. f. Sim. de, 1666.
———Will., of Leicester, chaplain, 1452.
———Will. s. of Rauf, of Hope, 1451, 1452.
Hether, Thomas, of Tutbury, 1981.
Heued, Tho. del, 1633.
Heuster, Robert le, parson of Bous-worthe, 2110.
Hewad, Hen. de le, 1509.
Hewet, Hewite, Huet.
———John, 1513, 1514.
———Nicholas, of Killamarsh, 2277.
———Richard, 1513.
———William, 49, 1513.
Hey, Ric., of Derby, 1011.
Heye, Matilda, wid. of Hugh de, 458.
Heyle, v. Hayle.
Heylone, Will. de, 1323.
Heyne, Ric., de Melborne, 914.
Heyosy, Humphrey, 997.
Heyr, Heyre, v. Eyre.
Heytridding, Will. de le, 1775.
Heywarde, Ric., of Ibulle, 1479.
Heywode, Tho., Dean of Lichfield, 853, 854.
Heyworth, Will., late Bp. of Coventry, etc., 2559.

Hibernia, Hybernia, Isabella de, 1958.
———Ralph de, 1958.
———Robert de, 539.
Hichecocke, Enot, w. of Hen., of Foston, 1314.
———Hen., of Foston, 1314.
Hichecokkes, Matilda, 1593.
Hiepe, Geoffrey, 52.
Higdon, Hygdon.
———Joan w. of Will., of Edinsower, 508.
———John, of Brimington, 2149.
———Will., of Cromforth, 998.
———Will., of Edinsower, 508.
Hikson, Hykson.
———John, 231.
———Richard, chaplain, 232, 2099.
———Rob., chaplain, 231.
Hill, Hyll, Hylle.
———Alice w. of Rob., 968, 2140.
———Alice, nuper ux. Joh. Marreys, 2063.
———Isabella d. of Rob., 968, 2140.
———John de, 2513, 2585.
———John, del Hyll, 689.
———John del, of Folowe, 1254.
———Margaret, wid. of Ric. del, 300.
———Richard, 300, 302.
———Robert, 602, 2140.
———Rob., of Ashby-de-la-Zouch, 302.
———Tho. de, of Staley Wodthorp, 223.
———Will., 1993, 2409, 2508.
———William, chaplain, 2141.
———Will., of South Wynfeld, 470.
Hilles, Rog. de, 792.
———Sibilla w. of Rog. de, 792.
Hilton, Hylton.
———Adam de, Justice in Eyre, 2582.
———Henry, 2698.
———Hen., of Bonsall, 323, 325.
———Hen. de, of Horsley, 1510.
———John, of Foston, 1621.
Hinkersell, etc., v. Inkersall.
Hirt, Fulcher f. Fulcheri de, 474.
Ho, Walter f. Rob. de, 688.
Hoare, Peter le, de Hope, 1789.
Hockelowe, v. Hucklow.
Hoco, Will. de, 2732, 2733.
Hodelston, Elizabeth d. of Nich., 884.
Hodgnett, John de, 400.
Hofnerton, Eustace de, 1793.
Hog', Will. f. Rad. de, 1361.
Hogeson, John, 1458.
Hoggyes, Alice w. of Will., 2261, 2262.
———Will. f. et h. Rob., 2261, 2262.
Hogh, Will. del, of Brassington, chap-lain, 393.
Hogham, Rog. de, 1964.
Hoghkynson, Will., 2681.
Hoght', John de, of Hognaston, 320, 1381.
———John, sen., 1382.
———John, jun., 1382.
———Richard, 1381, 1382.
Hoghton, John, Bailiff of Derby, 523.
Hoidgskynson, John, of Sutton-in-le-Dale, 2276.

Hokebroc, Richard, 52.
Hokelowe, *v.* Hucklow.
Hokenaston, Adam, clericus de, 136.
——————John de, 2552.
——————John f. Joh. de, 390, 391, 393.
——————Will. de, clericus, 136.
Hoky, John, 2040.
Holand, Otos [Otho] de, Dom. de Assheford, 95.
Holb. . . , Ric. de, 441.
Holbrok, Emma w. of Will., 1056.
——————Walter de, 983.
——————William, 1056.
Holden, Richard, 2473.
Holerinchawe, John del, 616.
Holland, Joan, Countess of Kent, 807.
——————Lucy, Countess of Kent, 825.
Hollowey, John, 1019.
Holly, Walter, 559.
Holm, Holme, Holmes.
——————John, 1529.
——————John f. Tho. de, 2374, 2375, 2517.
——————Nich. de, 2564.
——————Richard, 651.
——————Will. de, chaplain, 802.
Holond, Alexander de, 136.
——————Henry, 2058.
——————John de, of Ashbourne, 62, 65.
Holyngton, Ralph, Prior of Calwich, 1594.
Holyngworthe, Holynworth.
——————John de, 1246, 2468-2470.
Holynton, Rob., Prior of Calwich, 1595.
Hondford, Robert, 156.
——————Will., sen., 156.
Hondhow, Adam de, 2431.
Honistun, Rohard f. Horn de, 1031.
Honorius III., Pope, 176, 935, 969, 1696, 1785.
Hood, William, 2052.
Hope, Alice d. of Will. de, 2293.
——————Eleyne w. of Will. de, 2293.
——————Emma w. of Oliver de, 1429.
——————Richard de, 1438.
——————Robert de, 2708.
——————Rob. f. Hugonis de, 1427.
——————Tho. de, of Brampton, 443.
——————Will. de, 2293.
Hopeldod, Will., 1967.
Hopkinson, Hopkynson, Hopkynsone.
——————Hen., of Alton, 128.
——————John, 591, 592.
Hopper, Hoppere, Nicholas, 2031, 2032.
Hoppewelle, Thos. de, 2130.
Hopton, Hoptone, Hen. de, 2146.
——————Hen. f. Hen. de, clericus, 1474.
———————Hen. s. of Tho. de, 14, 16-19, 1474, 2655.
——————Roger de, 149.
——————Simon de, 2658.
——————Tho. s. of Will. de, 2660.
——————William de, 16, 67, 147, 2146, 2217, 2659.
——————Will. f. Hen. de, 2658.
Horbury, Will. de, clerk, 785.
Horderne, Horderen, Horderon, Hordrenne, Hordreue, Hordron, Hordryn, etc.
28

Horderne, etc., Annabella w. of Will., 1442.
——————Henry de, 1143, 2719.
——————John, 2255, 2256.
——————John, chaplain of St. Mary's Guild at Dronfield, 236, 1064.
——————Matilda w. of Rog. de, 2719.
——————Richard de, 1130, 1133, 1137, 1140-1144, 1147, 1152, 2719.
——————Roger de, 2719.
——————William, 1442.
Hore, Alice f. Rob. le, 1796.
——————Peter le, 1794.
Horlowe, Emma f. Joh. del, 1020.
——————John de, 1022.
Horm, presbyter, 529.
——————Nicholas, 1146.
——————*v.* also Orm.
Horn, Adam, of Chesterfield, chaplain, 767.
Horninglowe, John f. Rog. de, 2613.
Horningwold, John de, 2229.
——————Joan w. of John de, 2229.
——————Joan d. of John de, 2229.
Horseley, Horsseleye.
——————Gilbert de, 1113.
——————Margaret, relict of John, of Denby, 956.
——————Ric. s. of Will. de, 797.
——————Simon de, of Derby, 978.
——————William de, 956.
Horsemon, John le, 389.
Horspole, John, clerk, 1873.
Horsyngton, Hugh, 839.
——————Joan w. of Hugh, 839.
Horton, Anne w. of John, 601.
——————John s. and h. of Rog., 601.
——————Rog., dominus de Cattone, 592.
——————Rog., 588, 590, 597, 599, 2539-2541.
——————Will. s. and h. of Rog., 2541.
Hosbert, 529.
——————rector of Hegham, 477.
Hospital, Hen. f. Sim. de, jun., de Cestrefeld, 713.
——————Simon de, 693.
Hostiler, Rog. le, in parva Cestria, 972.
Hothe, John atte, 2501.
Hotot, Hototh.
——————Geoffrey de, 2384.
——————Henry de, 291, 2384, 2786.
——————Hugh de, 2384.
——————Ysabel w. of Hugh de, 2384.
Houbell, *al.* Houbelle, John, rector of Wynfeld, 77, 2416.
Houeston, Beatrice f. Petri de, 691.
Hough, Will. del, de Brassinton, chaplain, 392.
Houlekotis, Rog. f. Lamberti de, 422.
Houlot, John, chaplain, 2080.
Houringam, Hugh de, 1397.
Houton, Walkelin de, Canon of Lichfield, 1427.
How, Howe.
——————Hen. de le, 19.
——————Magota del, of Ibul, 1477.
——————Margaret d. of Rog., of Ashope, 569, 570.

How, etc., Richard, 560.
———Rob. de, of Sekyntone, 2124.
Howeton, Alice w. of Will. de, 2618.
———Will. de, " Kever et Peyntour," of Burton, 2618.
Howson, Sir Ric., chaplain, 840.
———Ric., jun., 840.
Hoxale, Will. de, chaplain, 2239.
Hublyn, John, receptor denariorum castri et honoris de Alto Pecco, 406.
Hucklow, Hucklowe, Hockelowe, Hoke-lowe, Huckelow, Huclow.
———Alan de, 1323, 1324.
———William de, 1221, 1392, 2352-2354.
Hudson, Hen., vicar of Ashbourne, 87, 91.
———Will., of Dronfield, chaplain, 809, 838, 2443, 2447.
Huet, v. Hewet.
Hufton, Walter f. Will. de, 2605.
Hug, Dyota f. Will., 1905.
Hugate, Tho., of Chestrefeld, 453.
Hugelyn, Will. de Appleby, 1961.
Hugge, John, 584-586, 591, 595, 597.
———Margaret w. of Ric., 595.
———Matilda w. of John, 584, 585.
———Richard, 593, 595.
Hugh, Abbot of Chester, 486.
———Canon of Lichfield, 179.
———capellanus de Acoure, 386.
———chaplain, 1969-1971.
———clericus, 2582.
———clericus de Cubeleia, 238.
———clericus de Derebi, 908.
———Comes, v. Chester, Earls of.
———Decanus, 932, 1167.
Hukyns, Will., chaplain, 854.
Hulcrombe, Hulcrume, Hulecrombe.
———Margaret w. of Ric. de, 2568.
———Richard de, 2568, 2574, 2580.
Hulebrok, Adam de, 691.
Hull, Hulle.
———Adam del, 1892.
———Isabel w. of Thos., 2131.
———John de, 2583.
———Robert, Justice, 1806.
———Robert del, 2130.
———Rob. del, of Snelston, 1768.
———Rob. f. Rob. de, of Barley Wodecetes, 229.
———Tho. del, of Snelston, 1768.
———William de, 294, 295, 2127, 2221, 2223.
Hulm, Hulme, Hulmo.
———Agnes f. Al. f. Galfr. de, 2499.
———Alan de, 713, 718.
———Alan f. Galfr. de, 2499.
———Alice d. of Rob. de, 716.
———Geoffrey de, 1183.
———Nicholas de, 417, 421, 2421-2423, 2425.
———Rob. de, of Cestrefeld, 716.
———Rob. f. Will. de, 735.
———Roger de, 207, 797.
Hulton, Hultone.
———John, 1316.
———Dom. Will. de, chaplain, 63, 64.
———Will. de, clericus, 137, 138.
———Will. f. Rad. de, 1202.

Humbreston, Will., rector de Walton, 2045, 2050.
Humfrey, 211.
Humphrey, sacerdos de Repton, 1945.
Huncesdon, Huncedon, Huncindon.
———Adam f. Walt. de, 27.
———Richard de, 1637.
———Ric. fil. Petri de, 29.
———Ric. f. Walt. de, 27.
———Robert de, 28.
———Roger de, 27.
Hundehowe, Rob. f. Joh. de, 2429.
Hundesworth, Juliana de, 1522.
Hungerford, Marie, Lady, 491.
———Walter, knt., 82.
Hunt, Hunte, Huntte.
———Hen., of Tupton, 507, 2410.
———Isabel w. of R. Bullok, 2475.
———John, Mayor of Nottingham, 2478.
———John, 118, 120, 125, 126.
———John, of Asshover, 300, 794.
———Ralph, 125, 126.
———Richard, 1991-1994.
———Ric. le, of Ashover, 118-120, 125, 1100, 1102.
———Rog. le, 1132.
———Thomas, 127, 2473, 2478, 2480.
———Tho., of Lynby, 794, 1930.
———William le, 117-119.
———Will., of Chesterfield, 1052.
———Will., of Tupton, 508.
Hunter, Will., of Langley, 1532.
Huntingdon, Earl of, v. Clynton, Will. de.
Huntyngfeld, Will., Dom. de, 1899.
Huntynton, Matilda de, 751.
Hurrill, Hurl, Hurll, Hurryl, Hurryll.
———Alice, relict. Hen., 2465.
———Henry, of Wodesmethys, 2450.
———Roger, 2466.
———Rog. s. of Hen., 2450.
———Thos. s. and h. of Hen., 2458.
Hurst, Felix de, 2766.
Hurt, Adam, 1141.
———Thomas, 89.
———William, 1158.
Husbond, Alice w. of John, 1497, 1498.
———John, of Kirkirton, 1497, 1498.
———William, 702.
Huse, Will., knt., Chief Justice of King's Bench, 958.
Husee, Hugh, knt., 1505.
———Joan w. of Hugh, knt., 1505.
Huw, Thomas, 1747.
Huy, Robert, 1614.
Hybernia, v. Hibernia.
Hyde, Hide.
———Alexander de, 1576.
———John, 587, 2700.
———Tho. de la, 1690.
———Will. de, chaplain of St. Oswald's Church at Ashbourne, 1693.
Hygdon, v. Higdon.
Hyghege, Richard de, 309.
Hyklyng, Joan w. of John, of Lynbe, 301.
———John, of Lynbe, 301.

Hykmons, Stephen, chaplain, 1526.
Hyll, *v.* Hill.
Hylton, *v.* Hilton.
Hyndley, Rob. de, 1282.
Hyne, John, of Chesterfield, 689, 754, 767, 770.
————William, 508.
Hynton, John f. Rob. de, 1652.
Hyrst, Peter de, 1789, 1790.
Hyton, Jas., Dean of Scarsdale, 2522.
Hyve, John, 312, 314.

I.

Ibole, Ibul, Ibull, Ibulle, Ybul.
————Agnes w. of Will. de, 17, 18.
————Jordan de, 2628, 2630, 2631, 2636.
————Nich. s. of Will. de, 18.
————Richard de, 143.
————Rob. de, vicar of Assheburne, 17, 18.
————Tho. de, 334.
————Will. de, 14.
————Will. de, de Aldewerke, 17, 18.
Illingworth, Illyngworth, Ralph, 49, 2473.
————Ralph s. and h. of Rich., 2478, 2480.
————Richard de, 2467, 2470.
————Ric. s. and h. of Ralph, 2481.
Ilum, Ylum, Henry de, 1690, 1820.
————Will., of Assheburne, 1648.
Ince, Ins.
————Gilbert, 1990, 2393.
————Richard, 2170.
————Richard, of Spinkhull, 2263.
Ingelby, Thomas de, 1845.
Ingepenne, Geoffrey, 587.
————Henry, 583.
Inggwerdeby, Dominus de Willesley, 1784.
Ingham, Roger de, 1085.
Inglose, Sir Henry, knt., 489, 490.
Ingram, Will., chaplain, 803.
Inkersall, Hingkershille, Hinkereshal, Hinkereshul, Hinkersell, Hynckurcelle, Hyngerselle, Hynkershull, Hynkreshille, Hynkreshill, etc.
————John de, 762.
————John, chaplain, 443, 770, 784.
————John, presbyter, 751.
————Martin f. Rad. de, 1092.
————Rob. de, 1097.
————Roger de, 1094, 1097, 1109.
————Susanna, 1092.
————Thomas de, 1094.
Innocent IV., Pope, 1824.
Innocent, Innesand.
————Joan, 2257.
————John, 877.
————Richard, 839, 2515.
Inskyppe, Will., parson of Clown, 2276.
Insula, Ric. de, Abbot of Burton, 1697, 1698, 2575.
————Dom. Will. de, 2026.
Ireland, Irland, Irelonde, Yrland.
————John s. of Ralph de, 2124.

Ireland, etc., John s. and h. of Rob., 2729-2731.
————Robert de, 1860, 2726.
————Robert s. of John, 2731.
————Will., 1349, 1350, 2727, 2728.
————Will. s. and h. of John, 2731.
Irenmonger, Maurice le, 2616.
Ireton, Irreton, Irton, Irtona, Orton, Yrton.
————Fulcher de, 1163, 1168, 1501, 1502, 1504.
————Fulcher f. Will. de, 2546.
————Henry de, 1293, 1472, 1562, 2548.
————Hen. f. Hen. de, 1741, 2550.
————Henry f. et h. Dom. Hen. de, 2546.
————John, 396, 1280, 1349, 1505, 1983.
————Nicholas de, 1364-1366, 2391.
————Philip w. of Will. de, 1741.
—-————Richard de, 1368.
————Ric. f. et her. Ric., 1647.
————Ric. f. Rob. de, 2548.
————Rob. f. Ric. de parva, 2553.
————Stephen de, 29, 30, 1561, 1563, 1689, 2011, 2702, 2703, 2711, 2713.
————William de, 1741, 2550.
Irpe, Henry, 597, 598.
————John, 2072.
————Richard, 2068, 2072.
Isbel, Isabell.
————Joan, 2046-2048.
————John, 2048.
————Nicholas, 2041-2043, 2045-2048.
————*al.* Grene, Nicholas, 2051.
————Richard, 2039.
————Robert, 2057.
————Robert f. et h. Ric., 2046-2048.
Itheryng, William, 156.
Iuuel, sacerdos, 1939.
Ive, Henry, 2110.
————John, chaplain, 988.
Ives, Gilbert, 2541.
Ivo Cornubiensis, Archdeacon of Derby, 1080.

J.

J————, Abbot "de Parco Stanle," 483.
————vicar of Esseburn, 186.
Jacson, Jacsone, Jakeson.
————Alice, 320.
————Edward, 2280.
————Hen., chaplain, 1585.
————Rog., 951.
————William, 1330.
Jamesson, Thomas, 234.
Jamys, Christopher, of Tyddeswall, 1618, 2372.
Jamytyn, Robert, 2601.
Jannel, Robert, 2543.
Jarpenuil, Jarpenuill, Jarcunuill.
————Andrew de, 1470, 1661.
————Will. de, 1029.
Jarrard, Tho., 1605.
Jay, Will. le, de villa castri de Pecco, 552.

Jeke, Rog., chaplain, 309.
Jell, *v.* Gell.
Jenkynson, Rob., of Hertyll, 84.
Jepson, Rob., bailiff of Derby, 1010.
Jernegan, Rich., knt., 2191.
Johannes, Dom., 2241.
John, King of England, *v.* England, Kings of.
John, Abbot of Beauchief, 243.
————Abbot of Derley, 2555.
————capellanus, 2125.
————capellanus de Bramton, 2562.
————capellanus de Cesterfeld, 542.
————clericus, 174, 1210, 1954.
————clericus de Stolbilley, 2374.
————Dean of Derby, 2385.
————Dean of Lichfield, 2647.
————frater Horm, 529.
————parson of Everdon, 1488.
————persona de Ekenton, 1727, 1729.
————presbyter de Leca, 532.
————prior of Colwich, 1596.
————prior of Dunstable, 395.
————vicar of Spondon, 677.
Johnson, Jonesson, Jonson.
————Alan, 1976.
————Henry, 1460.
————John, of Derby, 1006.
————John, bailiff of Derby, 1010.
————John s. of Rog., of Tiddeswal, 1252, 1254.
————Margaret, 1460.
————Sir Richard, 262.
————Robert, 101.
————Roger, 232, 905.
————Rog., of Tiddeswal, 1254.
————William, 1886, 2307.
————Will. s. of Rog., of Tiddeswal, 1252, 1254.
Joll, Thurstan, 561.
Joly, Robert, 764.
————Will., de Derby, 985.
Jordan, rector of Norbury, 1766.
Jordan, Jurdan, Jurdon.
————John, rector of Whystan, 1341.
————Rob., of Asshe, 988.
————William, 1578.
Jort, Robert, 1925.
Josceline, Bp. of Bath, 910.
Jowesone, *al.* Jewesone, Rob., of Tunstides, 2354, 2357.
Joyce, 630.
Joye, Henry, 1443.
Jurdan, Jurdon, *v.* Jordan.
Jurdanthorp, Tho. de, 1778.
Jurdanus, 1945.
Justes, Roger, 995, 999.
Juvenis, Geoffrey, 353.
————Henry, 1622.
————Hugh f. Will., 1622.
————Nicholas, 2385.
————Robert, 358.
————Thomas, 386, 2385.
————Tho., of Derby, prepositus, 970.
————Mag. Will., of Derby, 2197.
————Will., prepositus, 970.
Juxta-aquam de Tanesly, Henry, 2302.

K.

Kais, *v.* Keys.
Kakestona, Rob. de, 533.
Kalal, Kalale, Kalehal, *v.* Calow.
Kaldewelle, *v.* Caldewell.
Kame, Gervase de, 1276.
Kard', Reginald de, Dapifer, 2125.
Karewalle, Will., 918.
Karleolo, *v.* Carleolo.
Karsinton, *v.* Carsington.
Kask, Rog., 174.
Kat, Will., 709.
Katteclive, *v.* Cateclive.
Kaue, *v.* Caue.
Kay, Cay.
————Henry, de Tideswelle, 673.
————Hen. f. Ade, of Prestcliff, 671, 672, 674, 675.
Kaym, *v.* Caym.
Kays, Kaysse, *v.* Keys.
Kebeel, Thos., Sergeant-at-law, 2120.
Kechyn, Richard, 1192.
Kede, William, 7.
Kedloc, Kedeloc.
————Matilda, quondam ux. Thome, 546.
————Tho. f. Rob., of Cesterfeld, 544-546.
————Thomas, 546.
Kelby, Roger de, 1429.
Kelm, John f. Will. de, 2748.
Ken, Ralph le, 66.
Kendale, Will. de, 1353.
Kenling, John, 2110.
Kent, Countesses of, *v.* Holland.
————Emma de, 1926.
————Isabel w. of Nich. de, 341.
————John de, 1920, 1926, 1927.
————Nich. de, of Boilestone, 341.
————Thomas, 1694.
Kenteis, Mag. John, 1081.
Kenylmarche, Tho., lord of Byrchore, 304.
Ker, Kerre.
————Isabella de, 2506.
————John del, 2510.
————Rich. s. of John del, 2510.
————Robert, 2212.
Keresforthe, John de, of Barnesley, 2254.
Kernyk, Mag. John de, 1957.
Kersintone, Kersyngtone, *v.* Carsington.
Kerton, Nich., "prior provincialis" of the Priory of Mount Carmel, Doncaster, 1255.
Kesteven, Robert, 2652.
Ketelby, Will., chantry chaplain at Chaddesden, 609.
Ketil, Ketell, Ketill.
————Syyeryld quondam ux. Hug., 706.
————Walter, 374.
————William, 730.
Kette, John, of Foston, 1620.
Keys, Kais, Kays, Kayss, Kaysse.
————Amice w. of John, of Kilburn, 1510.

Keys, etc., Elizabeth w. of John, 1457.
———Gilbert, of Kilburn, 1455, 1507-1509.
———Hen. s. of John, 1457, 1510.
———Johanna w. of Gilbert, 1509.
———John, 1457, 1458, 1508-1510.
———Ric., de Killeburn, 1507.
———Ric. f. Joh., of Kylburne, 955.
Kilburn, Kileburn, Killeburn, Kylburn, Kylburne.
———Adam de, 1207.
———Ralph f. Rob. of, 1509.
———Ric. f. Gilberti de, 955.
———Rob. f. Herberti de, 1507.
Kilkenni, Will. de, canon of Lichfield, 189.
Kilkenny, Will. de, Archdeacon of Coventry, 1555.
Kima, *v.* Kyme.
Kingesley, Kyngesley, Kyngesleigh.
———John de, 1302.
———Richard de, 1293, 2156, 2159.
Kinwaldmershe, Kynwoldmersch.
———Will. f. Rad. de, 1738, 1739.
Kirke, Kyrk, Kyrke.
———Oliver, 636.
———Walter de, 623, 625, 626.
———Will. del, of Chapel, 1443.
Kirkeby, Kyrkby, Kyrkeby.
———John, of Pinxton, 1875, 1876.
———John, of Selston, 1877.
———Michael, vicar of Spondon, 2171.
———Robert, 1882.
———William de, 739, 1872.
———Will., of Pinxton, 1875-1881.
———Will., of Pinxton, jun., 1876, 1881.
Kirklyngton, Will. de, vicarius de Bauquell, 757.
Kneton, Hen., 157.
Knight, Knith, Knist, Knyght, Knyte.
———John, 1905, 1910.
———Matthew f. Will. le, de Tatinhul, 2614.
———Richard, 2617.
———Rog., of Prestcliff, 1913.
Kniveton, Cnivetun, Kneveton, Knyfton, Knyventone, Knyveton, Knyvetone, etc.
———Emma d. of John de, 1516.
———Johanna wid. of Nich. de, 1692, 1693.
———Henry de, 30, 82, 137, 335, 401, 1108, 1280, 1568, 1596, 1608, 1693, 1983, 2015, 2159, 2721, 2727.
———Hen. de, knt., 144-146, 388, 1822.
———Hen. de, rectory of Norbury, 1768, 1769, 2131.
———Hen. s. of Matth. de, 2702, 2703.
———Hen. s. of Will. de, 63.
———Hen. f. Will. de, knt., 402.
———Humphrey, 1529, 2235.
———John, 1516, 1529, 1531, 2231-2233, 2236, 2369.
———John de, of Bradley, 1693.

Kniveton, etc., John, of Storeston, 1532.
———John, of Myrceston, 91.
———John s. of Margaret, 83.
———John s. of Ric., of Bradley, 946, 1528.
———John s. of Will. de, 66.
———Lettice wid. of John de, 69.
———Margaret wid. of Thomas, 83.
———Margery f. Mathei de, 59.
———Margery w. of Will. de, 63.
———Margery wid. of John de, 1516, 1693.
———Matthew de, 137, 140, 386, 1532, 1689, 1749-1751, 2702, 2703, 2720, 2721, 2723.
———Maud wid. of Will., 2413.
———Nicholas, 71-73, 83, 161, 1156, 1157, 1515, 1516, 1692, 1693, 2416.
———Nich. of Mercaston, 2137.
———Nich. de, of Underwood, 1693.
———Nich. s. of Will. de, 66.
———Richard de, 134, 1349, 2366.
———Ric., sen., 1527, 1530.
———Robert, sen., 1478.
———Rob. de, 295, 1693, 2226, 2727.
———Rob. de, vicar of Doveridge, 1024, 1692, 2598.
———Rob., of Underwood, 162.
———Rob. s. of Will. de, 66.
———Thomas de, 79, 80, 403, 1515, 1516, 1693, 1694, 2412-2414, 2602, 2676.
———Tho. s. of Nich. de, parson of Norbury, 1692.
———Walter de, 1786.
———William de, 146, 1693.
———Will. de, of Ashbourne, 56, 59-61, 65-67.
———Will. de, of Bradley, 78.
———Will. de, Dom. de Bradeleye, 147.
———Will. de, clerk, 2702.
———Will. f. Hen. de, 58, 397.
———Will. f. Matthei de, 58, 62-64.
Knollus, Ric., of Netherhaddon, 302.
Knot, Cnotte.
———Adam, 2550.
———John f. Ric., de Bontessale, 15.
Knottesford, Knottesforde, Ric. de, 1235, 1236.
Knotting, Cnotinge, Cnotting, Knottyng.
———Henry de, 110, 112, 116, 1815, 2606.
———Margery quondam ux. Will., 124.
Knotton, John, 236.
Knowt, Robert, 1053, 1398.
Knox, William, 1651.
Knug, Will., of Marketon, 1652.
Knutton, John, 234.
Knyb', Simon de, 2747.
Knyfsmyth, Knyfsmythe, John, 764, 766, 772.
———Alice wid. of Hen., 772.
———Cecilia w. of John, 772.
Knyfton, *v.* Kniveton.
Knyght, Knyte, *v.* Knight.

Knyghtley, John, of Wynshull, 2239.
Knyston, Ralph, Escheator for Notts., etc., 2528.
Knyttoley, *al.* Knyteley, John, sen., 2617.
————John, jun., 2617.
Knyvet, John, 1845.
Knyvetone, *v.* Kniveton.
Koc, *v.* Coke.
Kolle, Symon, "prepositus," 970.
Kortlinstoke, Alex. de, 2582.
Koucure, Hen., 598.
Kulk, Hugh del, 619.
Kyde, Will., 1708.
————Will. f. Rog., de Moniassch, 1714.
Kydeas, William, 730.
Kydekas, Will., 370.
Kyghley, John, knt., 1248.
Kylton, Ric., 1129.
Kymba, *v.* Kyme.
Kymburley, Ric. de, clericus de Wynfeld, 951.
Kyme, Kima, Kymba.
————John, of Fryskenay, 1988.
————Philip de, 486.
————Symon de, 487.
Kynardsey, Kynardesey, Kynardessey, Kynardseye, Kynardysaye.
————Elizabeth w. of Wm. de, 41.
————Hugh de, 41.
————Joan w. of John de, 2147.
————John de, 38-41.
————John de, jun., 39, 2147.
————Robert, 1933.
————Rob., de Lokkeslegh, 42.
————Will. de, 922, 1890.
————Will. f. Johannis de, 41.
Kynder, Kyndoyr, Peter, 451, 460.
Kynerdesley, Hen., of Uttoxeter, 2167.
————John, 2166.
Kyng, John, of Holmesfeld, 1412.
————Will., of Holmesfeld, 1412.
Kyngesley, Kyngesleigh, *v.* Kingesley.
Kyngistonleys, Will. f. Ric. de, 2154-2156.
Kynston, Will. de, 2176.
Kynttoley, *al.* Knyteley, John, sen., 2617.
Kynwoldmersch, *v.* Kinwaldmershe.
"Kyrk, John beye," chaplain, 1110.
Kyrkby, Kyrkebv, *v.* Kirkeby.
Kyrkelongeley, Will. f. Will. de, 975.
Kyrkeyerd, John, 1440.
Kyrkland, Kyrkeland.
————Humfrev, of Whetcroft, 1386-1388.
————Tho., of Ripley, 470.
Kyveton, Richard, 1349.

L.

Labbe, Ralph, 1753.
Lacc, William, 901.
Lacmon, Richard, 1361.
Lacoc, Lacoke, Mag. Ralph de, 179, 182.

Lacy, Lacye.
————Alice f. Rog. de, de Hassop, 1793.
————Margaret w. of Rob., 2520.
————Robert, of Stoke, 2520.
Laffordia, Ric. de, clerk, 112.
Lalinc, Nich., 2250.
Lambard, Henry, 1655.
Lameley, Lameleg'.
————Hugh de, 1633.
————Robert de, 1632.
————Ysabela relicta Rob. de, 1632.
Lamfram, sacerdos de Stoke, 1945.
Lancaster, Earls and Dukes of.
————Edmund, 1664, 2644.
————Henry [*ob.* 1345], 1304, 1686.
————Henry [*ob.* 1361], 479, 980, 1194, 1668, 1687.
————John, 406, 927, 1376, 1668, 1693, 1845.
————Blanche w. of John, 1668.
————Thomas, 2544, 2656.
Lancaster, Matilda of, Countess of Ulster, 1687.
Lance, Thurstan, 2141.
Lancelin, R—— f. Rob., 1948.
————Robert, 1948.
Lancerchumbe, Ric. de, clericus, 948.
Landa, Rob. de, 238.
Lane, Richard, of Hyde, 1983.
————William, 786.
Lanebanck, Alice w. of Hen. de la, 703.
————Rob. f. Hen. de la, 703.
Lanford, *v.* Longford.
Lang', Will. de, 2733.
Langesdon, Langesdone, Langisdon, Langesduna.
————John de, clerk, 2082.
————Matthew de, 1209, 1396.
————Thomas de, 191, 1353.
————William de, 1210, 1396.
————Will. f. Waldeui de, 1610.
————Willot de, 173.
Langford, etc., *v.* Longford.
Langley, Langele, Langeleia, Langeleye, Longele, Longeley, Longelege, Longeleye, Longhelegh, Longley, etc.
————Gerard de, 2384.
————Henry, 1616, 2455.
————Hen. de, chaplain, 1525.
————Hugh de, 1651.
————John de, 1534.
————John, chaplain, 347.
————John de, clericus, 1525.
————John f. Marie de, 733, 734.
————John f. Rog. de, 1533, 1535.
————Leticia f. Rob. f. Bate de, 1537.
————Nicholas de, 228, 2242.
————Roger de, 225, 1533.
————Rog. f. Nich. de, 1743, 2242.
————Simon de, 2385.
————Stephen de, 134, 2384.
————Susanna, w. of Rob. de, 1537.
————Thomas, Bishop of Durham, 1588, 1591, 1592, 1868.
————Will. f. Galfridi de, 1537.
————Will. f. Joh. de, 1536.

Langton, Langedon, Langetone.
——Rob. de, 1866.
——Thomas, 1794, 1882.
Langwath, Langewathe.
——Ric. de, clericus, 1097.
——Ric. f. Petri de, 1096, 1098.
——Will. f. Petri de, 1096, 1098.
Lankforth, *v.* Longford.
Larcher, *v.* Archer.
Larderarius, Godfrey, 1360.
Large, Thomas, 602.
——Will., of Newebold Verdune, 602.
Lark, *al.* Larc, John, 748, 752-754, 759.
Lascy, Hen. de, Earl of Lincoln, 2246.
Lassy, Richard, 1870, 1871.
Latham, Sir Edmund, priest, 349.
Lathbury, Latheberi, Lathebury, Lath-yngbury, Lattheburi, Latthebury.
——Alvered de, knt., 1280, 1934, 1983-1985.
——Henry de, 1178.
——John, 394, 1181, 1184, 1280, 1764, 2411, 2678.
——John f. Joh., 1185, 1186.
——Katherine, 1185.
——Ralph de, 928, 1170-1172, 1202, 2387, 2741.
——Ralph f. et her. Rad. de, 919.
——Reginald de, 1280.
——Robert de, 1174, 1175.
——Rob. fil. jun. Aluredi, 1185.
——Rob. f. Radulfi de, 919.
——William, 1185.
Latour, Richard le, 1565.
Laucher, Geoffrey, 2446.
Launde, John de la, 332.
——Will. de la, 880.
Launne, Jemys, of Cromfort, 1679.
Laurance, Avice w. of Hen., 1110.
——Henry, 1110.
Laurans, Martin, 1112.
——Thomas, 1112.
Laurence [de S. Edwardo], Abbot of Burton, 48.
Laurenson, John, 1994.
——Thomas, 156, 1646.
Lauwe, Alice d. of Geoffrey, 1363.
——Geoffrey, of Tutebury, 1363.
Lavenham, Mag. Thos., 1982.
Laverock, Laueroc, Lauerok, Laveroc, Laverok, Laveroke, Laverokes.
——Alice d. of Matilda, 1106.
——Isabella w. of John, 770.
——Joan wid. of Rog., 376.
——John, 750, 751, 758, 761, 763, 767, 770, 772, 773, 791.
——John s. of Matilda, 1106.
——Robert, 767, 772, 773.
——Roger, 308, 359, 361, 363, 365-368, 370, 371, 423, 430, 710, 712, 714-716, 718, 722, 746, 2497, 2499.
——Thomas, 742, 746.
——Will., bailiff of Derby, 977.
Lawe, Geoffrey, of Tutbury, 1362.
——John, clerk, 1182.
Lawnder, Adam, 241.
Lawrence, Abbot of La Dale, 387.
Laxinton, *v.* Lexinton.

Layche, Will. of Chesterfield, 2253.
Lea, Idonea w. of John de, 54.
——John de, 54.
Leca, William de, 1554.
Le Carter, *v.* Carter.
Lece, Richard, 508.
Lech, Leche.
——John de, 826, 833, 835, 1862.
——Philip, 431, 869, 998, 1196, 1383.
——Ralph, 660, 1069, 1070, 1073, 1250, 1670, 2475.
——Ric., de Edlaston, capellanus, 1157.
——Robert de, 1862.
——Rog., knt., 623, 811, 1931.
——Roger, 661, 781, 803, 1231.
——Will., 325, 661, 1862.
Ledes, Rob. de, mayor of Lincoln, 1923.
Lee, Agnes w. of Will. de le, 2161.
——Elias del, de Nether Somersale, 2157.
——John del, 2217.
——John f. Rob. de, 1891.
——Reynolde, 643.
——Richard, 1327.
——Robert de, 2125, 2161.
——Roger, 594.
——Roland, Bp. of Coventry, 2097.
——Thos. de le, 2161.
——Will. f. Tho. de le, 2161.
Leek, Leeke, Lek, Leke, Leyke.
——Alice wid. of John, 2294.
——John, 510, 866, 997, 1339, 1879-1881, 2448.
——John, of Hallam, 2294.
——John, of Steynesby, 1879, 1880.
——John, of Sutton-in-le-Dale, 21, 1884, 2462, 2533.
——John s. and h. of John, 2533.
——John s. of Will. de, 538.
——John s. and heir of Will., 1469.
——Katharine, 2533.
——Muriel, 2533.
——Robert, 524.
——Thomas, 905, 2266, 2267, 2462.
——Tho., bailiff of Chesterfield, 1881.
——Thos., of Beauchief, 2565.
——Thos., of Newark, 2294.
——William de, 538, 1191.
Lees, Adam de, 224.
——Jurdan de, 2428.
——Thomas de, 427, 434.
Leeston, John de, 1355.
Leet, John, knt., 2266, 2267.
Leez, Thomas, 1010.
Lefwinus, 2620.
Lega, Hen. f. Rob. de, 238.
Legamer, John, de Catton, 572.
Leges, *v.* Leghes.
Legh, Leghe.
——James de, 628.
——Ralph de, 1256.
——Raynold, *al.* Reginald, of Blackbroke, 638-640, 642.
——Robert, 450.
——William, 2701.
Leghes, Leges, Leghus, Leyghes.
——John del, 1229-1231.

Leghes, etc., John s. and heir of Nich., 1239, 1240-1242.
————Matilda relicta Nich. de, 1229, 1240, 1242.
————Nicholas del, 1226, 1229.
————Robert de, 2318.
————Roger del, chaplain, 777, 2509.
Leghum, John de, 1245, 1247.
Legys, Thomas de, 354.
Leham, Allan, 224.
————Roger, 2428.
Leia, Leie, Leya.
————Adam de, 1818.
————Henry f. Rob. de, 239.
————Robert de, 239.
————William de, 1636, 1820, 1821.
Leicester, Earl of, v. Montfort, Simon de.
Leicester, Warden of the Friars Minor at, 186.
Leigh, John, Ludimagister, 2216.
Leis, Leiis, Leys, Leyes, Leyis.
————Fulcher f. Ingerami de, 2381.
————Henry de, 2212.
————Mag. Ingeram de, 2381.
————Peter de, 1775.
————Peter f. Ingerami de, 2381.
————Thomas de, 131, 225-227, 415, 683, 1017, 1033, 1533, 1534, 1536, 2374, 2375, 2419, 2422, 2423, 2426.
————Walter de, 226, 227.
Lelin, Le Liu, William, 2628-2630, 2632, 2635.
Lemestre, Lemenstre, Lemystre, Lymester, Lymestre, Lymistre, Lymster.
————John de, 65, 67, 71.
————Nicholas de, 80, 81.
————Thomas, 76, 78, 79, 157, 1769, 2412.
————William, 157, 1769, 2727.
————Will. de, of Snelston, 2081.
Lemna, Philip de, 2427.
Len, Lene, Lenne.
————Alan de, 356, 362, 546, 702, 708, 1744.
————Isabella w. of John in le, 2164.
————John in le, 2164.
————Philip de, 693.
————Robert de, 361, 362, 546, 547, 708, 1744.
Lenton, Priors of, v. Index of Places.
Lentun, Edward, Chamberlain of Derby, 1005.
Lenum, Rob. de, 2309.
Leome, John de, 1259.
Leres, Richard de, 2621.
Lesbes, Rog. de, chaplain of St. Michael's Chantry, Chesterfield, 776.
Lessington, John de, 1555.
Lethe, Roger, 2083.
Leukennore, Nich. de, 1428.
Levenad, 2620.
Lever, John, of London, saddler, 1983.
Levett, Edmund, 100.
Lexinton, Henry de, Dean and aft. Bishop of Lincoln, 180, 181, 186, 188, 1426, 1461, 1829.

Lexinton, John de, 1954.
————Robert de, 682, 910, 911, 1423, 1426, 1697, 2024.
Ley, Thomas de, 2425.
Leybourne, Roger de, 1428.
Leycestre, Richard de, 1703.
————Tho. de, of Tutbury, 1363.
Leygdfot, Henry, 2221.
Leyr, Nicholas, 1435, 1436.
————Stephen, 1095.
Leyum, Leyun, Alexander de, 1216.
————Richard de, 1216, 1220.
————Roger de, 1323, 1324.
Lich', Avice f. Walt. de, 31.
————Margery f. Walt. de, 31.
————Dom. Walter de, chaplain, 31.
Lichfield, Bishop of, v. Nonant, Hugh de.
————Canons of, 1421, 1431, 2408.
————Dean and Chapter of, 170, 174-177, 183-186, 188, 191-193, 198, 199, 208, 214, 407, 408, 644, 647, 649, 945, 1270, 1272, 1333, 1356, 1426, 1427, 1431, 1444, 1445, 1451, 1452, 1518, 1519, 1546, 1551, 1617, 1618, 1705, 1710, 1720, 1816, 1824, 1825, 1827, 1828, 1831, 1833, 1836, 1850, 1851, 2298-2300, 2335, 2339, 2343, 2350, 2372.
————Walter s. of Will. de, priest, 331.
Lightlad, Ric., of Derby, 1014.
Like, John, 55.
Lille, Robert, 1035.
Limeseie, Nicholas de, 2746.
Linacre, Lenacre, Lenakir, Linaker, Linakyr, Lynacre, Lynacure, Linaker, Lynaker, Lynnacher, Lynnacure, etc.
————George, 2266-2271.
————Hugh de, 224, 225, 412-414, 418, 420, 425, 431, 435, 547, 701, 705, 706, 1351, 2374, 2428, 2496, 2561-2563.
————John, 100, 258, 449, 454, 458, 467, 830, 1539, 2564.
————"Mestre," 473.
————Robert, 2263.
————Roger de, 432, 433, 438, 684.
————Simon de, 684, 1535.
————Walter de, 351, 415.
————William de, 444, 449, 1044, 1352, 2317.
————Will. f. Lamberti de, 424.
Lincoln, Adam f. Hug. de, 359.
————Bishops of, v. Hugo; Lexinton, Hen. de; Rotheram, Will.; Wells, Hugh de.
————Dean of, 713, 769, 822, 989, 1825.
————Dean and Chapter of, 2634.
————Earl of, v. Lascy.
Linderthorp, John, 2408.
Lindeseia, Lindesia.
————Emma w. of Gilb. de, 2742.

Lindeseia, etc., Gilbert de, 1726, 2742.
Linton, Oliver de, 1962.
Lisle, Lord, v. Talbot, John.
————Rob. de, knt., 1845.
Lister, Lyster, Lystere, Adam, 804, 805.
————Will., of Little Chester, 989, 990.
Lisurs, Nigel de, knt., 1487.
Litteris, Nicholas de, 487.
Littleton, Sir Thos., knt., 2378.
Littlewode, Hen. f. Th. de, 2160.
Litton, Lytton.
————Christiana w. of John de, 2608.
————Henry de, 1546.
————John f. Thos. de, 1550.
————John de, of Grimston, 2608.
————Rob. f. Reg. de, 1547.
————William de, 1610.
Liu, Will. le, v. Lelin.
Liuerpol, Richard de, 975.
Livet, Roger de, 535, 536.
Livilda, 2381.
Locard, Richard, 534.
Locker, John, 741.
Locsmyht, Thomas le, 70.
Loke, John de, 2001.
Lokinton, John de, 483.
————Roger de, 1555.
Lokka, William, 2189.
Lokwode, Lokwod, Locwod, Thomas, of Thornebery, 2133, 2134, 2137, 2138.
Lond', Fr. Brian de, 1539.
London, Bishop of, v. William de Ecclesia S. Marie.
London, Simon de, Canon of Lincoln, 2635.
Lone, John del, of Oslaston, 2323.
————Will. atte, 2162.
Longden, Richard, 2369.
Longdon, Rob. de, Prior of Tutbury, 1365.
Longeley, v. Langley.
Longesdon, Longesdone, Longisdon.
————Elias f. Ric. de, 2741.
————Henry de, 2083.
————John de, clericus, 1860.
————Will. de, in Iueleg', 1559.
————Will. f. Elie de, 2732.
Longespee, Rog., Bp. of Coventry, 2646.
————Will. de, Comes Sarum, 171.
Longestaffe, Will., chaplain, 789.
Longford, Lanford, Langeford, Langford, Langforth, Langgeforth, Langtford, Lankforth, Longeford, Longeforde, Longfford, Longforth, etc.
————Alice de, 2229.
————Alice w. of Nich. de, 1107, 1108.
————Aluered, 1393-1395, 1769.
————Dorothy w. of Sir Rauf, 383.
————George de, 1589, 1868.
————Hen. s. of Ralph, knt., 1359.
————Joan w. of Dom. John de, 1568.
————Dom. John de, knt., 25, 2014.
————John de, 335, 1512, 1556, 1568.
————John s. of Ralph, knt., 1359.
————John, rector of Northewynfeld, 1764.

Longford, etc., Margaret, 1603.
————Margaret w. of Ralph, 1868.
————Margery wid. of Nich. de, knt., 1588, 1867, 1869.
————Michael de, 932, 1556, 1561-1563, 2383.
————Nich. de, knt., 77, 124, 242, 340, 344, 377, 397, 803, 1344, 1357, 1512, 1569, 1571, 1572, 1574, 1575, 1576, 1580, 1581, 1583-1585, 1587, 1590, 1592, 1596-1603, 1606, 1607, 1631, 1693, 1761, 1763, 1764, 1865, 1867-1869, 2130, 2321, 2322, 2362, 2521.
————Nich. s. of Nich. de, 1107, 1108.
————Nigel de, 332, 1555-1561, 1629, 1767, 2003, 2007-2010.
————Dom. Nigel f. Nigelli de, 1562, 1563.
————Oliver de, 1, 1198.
————Oliver de, knt., 1564, 1565.
————Rauf, of Longford, knt., 377, 382, 383, 643, 1358, 1359, 1588-1592, 1594, 1595, 1603-1605, 1607, 1868, 1874, 1877, 1886, 2400.
————Richard de, knt., 1359, 1984, 1985.
————Rog. f. Nich. de, 379.
————Thomas, 377, 1592, 1593.
————Thomas de, parson of Wynfeld, 1580.
————Tho. s. of Ralph, of Longford, knt., 1359.
————William de, 1132, 1556, 1559, 1563, 1564, 2002, 2012, 2711, 2713.
————Will. s. of Ralph, knt., 1359.
————Will. f. et h. Will. de, 2711.
Longham, Rob., of co. Leicester, 1867.
Longley, etc., v. Langley.
Lont, Robert, 2137.
Lorimer, Lorinarius, Loriner.
————Cecily w. of Rob. le, 374, 706.
————Hugh f. Roberti, 686.
————Robert le, 374, 686.
————Rob. f. Rob. le, 706.
————Rog. f. Rad., 704.
————William de, 372, 373, 717, 770.
————Will., capellanus, 741, 744.
Lorynga, Dom. Peter de, 578.
Loscowe,' Lostowe.
————Alice w. of Ralph, 862.
————Juliana w. of Rauf, 1619.
————Ralph s. of Ric., 862.
————Rauf s. of Stephen, 1619.
————Ric., late of Chestrefeld, 862.
Losyngtone, John de, of Tuttebury, 1369.
Loucok, Louecok, Louccok, Loukoc, Lowecok, Lowcok, Lowkok.
————Henry, 1045, 1048, 1049.
————Robert, 1776, 2479.
————William, 1036, 1037, 1039, 1043, 1045.
————Will., chaplain, 2261, 2262.

Loucok, etc., Will. f. Hen., 1050.
Loudham, John de, 503.
Louet, John, 2345.
Louot, Agnes relicta Ade, 758.
————Isabella d. of Adam, 758.
Louseby, Lousheby, Lowesby, Lowseby, Louzeby.
————Alice w. of Rob. de, 2181, 2182.
————Robert de, 2171, 2172, 2181-2183.
Louterel, Guy, 1040.
Lovel, Lovell, Luvel.
————Francis, Viscount Lovell, 1193.
————Henry, 1961.
————Thomas, 2032.
Lowe, Andrew, 526, 961.
————Anthony, 526, 527, 961-964, 1900, 2701.
————Brian, 957.
————Clement, 1121.
————Denis, 90, 960.
————George, 957, 959.
————Henry, of Ashover, 2680.
————Humphrey, of Denby, 959, 1121.
————Jasper, s. of Vincent, of Denby, 964.
————Laurence, Dominus de Denby, 957-959, 2417, 2687.
————Nicholas de, 2448.
————Ottiwell, 957, 959.
————Robert, 90, 960, 961.
————Stephen s. of Vincent, 964.
————Thomas, 957.
————Vincent, of Denby, 90, 962,964.
————William de, 785, 787, 794, 1926-1928.
Lowell, Thomas, 2029.
Lowes, Alex. de, 2629, 2632, 2635.
Loyac, Lozac, John de, de Chadisden, 605, 1552.
Lucas, Rich., Escheator, 1607.
Lucebi, Luceby, Luteby, Will. de, Archdeacon of Derby, 178, 179, 189, 2385.
Luckeson, John, 616.
Lucy, John, 2000.
————Robert de, 2610.
————Rob. of Stapenhill, 2616.
————Thos., of Charlcote, 2535.
————Will. de, chaplain, 2106.
Luda, Thomas de, clerk of the Bishop of Coventry and Lichfield, 179.
Ludham, Luddam, Eustace de, Sheriff of Nottingham, 1501-1503.
Ludlowe, John de, knt., 1712.
Lufetson, Walter, of Assheford, 1061.
Lumbard, John, of Tadynton, 1908.
————Mag. Martin, 1081.
Lumhall, Laurence, 395.
Lung, Will. le, mil., 2536.
Lupus, Hugh, 1622.
————Nich., de Morley, 1335.
Luteby, v. Luceby.
Lutrell, Robert, 1611.
Lutterworth, Peter de, 2023.
Luvel, v. Lovel.
Luvetot, Richard, 535, 536, 1942.
————Roger de, 1942.

Lychtfot, William, 339.
Lydezate, Walter de, de Hyll, 689.
Lydgate, Hen. f. Ric. atte, de Prestclif, 1904.
Lyghe, Tho., Doctor of Law, master of Burton Saynt Lazar's Hospital, 614.
Lyghtwod, Adam, 1517.
Lylee, Lylly, Lyly.
————Hugh, 1385, 1387.
————John, 1342.
————John s. of Rog., of Hanley, 2258.
————Rog., de Westhandeley, 1342, 1343.
————Thomas, 2258.
Lym, Will. del, 1020.
Lymbergh, Dom. Adam de, 1899.
Lymester, etc., v. Lemestre.
Lynford, Alice w. of Laurence de, 1718.
————Laurence de, knt., 1711, 1712, 1718, 2324.
————Margery wid. of Will. de, 1718.
————Peter de, 1269.
————Thomas, 1724.
————William de, 1712.
Lyonis, John de, 1706.
Lyster, v. Lister.

M.

Macclesfeud, Tho. de, 2741.
Machon, Rich. le, 2354.
————Roger, 2357.
Mackary, Thomas de, 2104.
Mackley, Mackelega, Makeleye, Makkelega, etc.
————Engelard de, 334.
————Henry de, chaplain, 1934.
————Ralph de, 1307.
————Richard de, 1178.
————Thomas de, 2151.
Mackney, Mackeney, Mackeneye, Makenay, Makkeneya.
————Alice w. of Will. de, 1627.
————Dame Helen, 1628.
————Richard de, 883.
————Robert de, 1626.
————William de, 1626.
————Will. de, lord of, 1627.
Mackworth, Mackeworth, Macwrth, Makworth, Makworthe.
————Henry, 2395.
————John, Dean of Lincoln, 1280.
————John, clerk, 1986.
————Peter de, 2643.
————Philip de, 1622.
————Robert de, 1665.
————Rob. f. Ric. de, 1521.
————Thomas de, 1181, 1280, 1505.
Madeley, Maddelega.
————John, of Denston, 2169.
————Richard, 1648.
————Thomas de, 1699.
Madocke, Will., chaplain, 1485.
Magot, John, 948.
————Mariota w. of John, 948.

Magotesonne, Magottesone.
————Anibilla w. of Rob., 1438.
————Robert, 1438.
————Robert, de Hope, 1438.
Mahaut, Roger de, *v.* Monte Alto, Rog. de.
Mailart, Maillard.
————Fulk, 539.
————Ralph b. of Will., 538.
————Thomas, 538.
————Warin, 530.
————William, 538.
Mainwaring, Maisnilwarin, Meinilwarin, Ralph de, 536, 1948.
Maisam, Richard de, 2022.
Malare, Richard, Escheator for Notts., etc., 2527.
Malesouere, Robert de, 2028.
Malet, Adam, 215, 216.
————Mag. Walter, 1082.
Malluuel, Robert, 216.
Malmeins, Henry de, 1281.
Malmesert, William, 2742.
Malo Passu, De, *v.* Malpas.
Malore, Ric., constable of Codnor Castle, 901.
Malpas, Agnes f. Ric. f. Nig. de, 530.
————David de, 1347.
————Nigel, dominus de, 530.
————Richard f. Agn., 530.
————Rob. f. Agn., 530.
————Rodbert fr. Gilb. de, 530.
————Dom. Will. de, 2025.
————Will. f. Agn. de, 530.
Mammefeld, Rog. de, 722.
Mancester, Will. de, Dean of Lichfield, 179, 1426.
Mandrel, William, 1728.
Maneysyn, Will., Prior of Repton, 1982.
Mannefeld, John de, 2507.
Mannfield, John de, 877.
Mansel, Henry, 1942.
Mansfield, Manisfelde, Mannsfeld, Mannysfeld, Manusfeld, Manysfeld, Maunesfeld, Maunisfeld, Maunnesfeld, Maunsefeld, Maunsfeld, Maunsffelde.
————Cecilia wid. of Hen. de, 806.
————Elizabeth w. of John de, 790, 2502.
————Henry, 379, 689, 731, 735, 738, 761, 777, 785-787, 793, 803, 2502-2504.
————Hen. s. of Hen. de, 738.
————Joan wid. of Rob. de, 806.
————John de, 373, 375, 379, 500, 758, 766, 777, 790, 795, 798, 803, 817, 2502, 2504, 2510.
————Robert de, 792, 793.
————Rob. s. of Hen. de, 738.
————Roger de, in Cesterfeld, 363, 371, 372, 703, 717.
————Rog. f. Rog. de, 725.
Mapeldon, Hirald de, 474.
————Swain de, 474.
Maperley, Ivo de, 1633.
————Ric. f. Ivonis de, 1633.
————Will. f. Avicie de, 1633.

Maples, Mapples, Mappullus.
————John de, of Shefeld, sen., 795, 1230.
————John, of Rotherham, 812.
Mapplesden, John, 789, 798.
Mappleton, Mapelton, Mapeltona, Mapilton, Mapleton, Mappiltone, Mapulton, Mapultone.
————Geoff. de, 134.
————Geoffrey f. Hen. de, 1637-1639.
————Henry de, 60, 66, 138, 1562, 1563, 1636.
————Hen. de, chaplain, 315, 316.
————Hen. de, rector of Bonsall, 209, 951, 1669.
————Hen. f. Hen. de, 388.
————Hen. f. Rog. de, 1637-1639.
————John de, 385, 883.
————John f. Rob. de, 1640.
————John f. Thome de, 142.
————Nicholas de, 134.
————Petronilla, que quondam fuit ux. Rog. de, 1638.
————Richard de, 2721.
————Rikewere f. Hen., 1639.
————Rob. f. Hug. de, 1638.
————Roger de, 138.
————Rog. f. Rog. de, 1641.
————Thomas de, 30, 137, 140, 401, 1644.
————William de, 63, 64, 67.
————Will. f. Andree, 390, 391.
————Will. f. Hen. de, 62.
Mappullus, *v.* Maples.
Marard, John, chaplain, 316.
Marcham, Richard ce, 180.
————Robert de, 2144.
Marchaunt, John, 2669.
————John, clerk, 1488.
Marchington, Marchenton, Marchentone, Marchinton, Marchynton, Marchyntone, Marcinton, Mercenton, Merchintone, Mercinton, Mercintone, Mercynton.
————Eleanor w. of Dom. Rog. de, 1558, 1565, 1566, 1629.
————Hugh de, chaplain, 2286.
————John, 559.
————Nich. de, miles., 2726.
————Nich. f. Rog. de, 1130, 1131, 1133, 1135, 1140, 1141, 1144-1146, 1151, 1152.
————Nicholas de, 58, 881, 1572, 2014, 2016, 2017, 2122, 2740.
————Ralph f. Nich. de, 1147-1150, 1574.
————Reginald f. Nich. de, 1147-1150, 1153, 1577.
————Richard de, 56.
————Robert de, 332.
————Dom. Rog. de, knt., 1131, 1558, 1565-1567, 1629, 2015, 2703, 2711, 2713, 2720.
————Roger de, 53, 56, 59, 138.
————Rog. f. Ranulphi de, 1786, 2002, 2004, 2005, 2012.
————Thomas de, knt., 1645.

Marchington, etc., Thomas de, 1156, 1157, 2020, 2130.
————Walter, 628, 632, 645.
Marci, Anna Seraffini w. of Philip, 1544.
————Philip, 1544.
Mare, Rob. de la, 1668.
Mareschalman, Will. le, de Burgo, 1430.
Maretoll, Rob., 2706.
Mareys, Marreys, Marey, Marys.
————Alice wid. of John, 2058, 2063.
————Henry f. Rob., cler., 2043, 2045.
————Henry, capellanus de Rostlaston, 2050, 2054, 2057.
————John f. Joh., 2058-2063.
————John f. Walt., 2055-2057, 2064.
————Margery ux. Joh., 2062.
————Nich. f. John, 2058, 2060, 2061.
————Ralph, de Rostelaston, 913.
————Richard, 2038, 2041-2048, 2050.
————Robert de, 2032, 2038, 2041, 2045.
————Walter, 604, 2049-2055, 2064.
————William, 2051, 2053.
Margetson, Tho., of Shirley, 1593.
Mariote, Marioth, Maryotte.
————Agnes wid. of Will., of Brymyngton, 510.
————Robert, 2623, 2624.
Marisco, Robert de, 175, 2029.
————William de, 2034.
Marjory, William, 1191.
Mark, Gervase, prior of Dunstable, 166.
Markam, Symon de, Rector de Ashover, 114.
Markeaton, John de, 1653.
Markham, John, knt., 2567.
————John, 23.
Marmion, Richard, 1281.
Marre, John, 818.
Marshall, Marchale, Marchall, Marechal, Marescal, Marescaldus, Marescallus, Mareschall, Mareschaldus, Marschall, etc.
————Joanna w. of John, 1998.
————John, 796, 1998.
————John le, 1736, 1737, 2095, 2114, 2515.
————John, of Lytton, 565.
————Margaret w. of John, 796.
————Margaret w. of Will., of Seggeshale, 1179.
————Phil., de Ekinton, 1730-1733.
————Richard, Comes Penbrochie, 680.
————Richard, 1726, 2091.
————Robert le, of Derby, 984.
————Robert, de Stapelford, 2092.
————Will., Comes de Penbrok, 171.
————Will., chaplain of St. Mary's Guild, Chesterfield, 466, 841.
————William, 829, 833, 1932, 1933, 1980, 2348, 2351.
————Will. le, de Meysham, 1961.
————Will., of Seggeshale, 1122, 1179.
Marsham, William, 1347.

Marston, Mershton, Merston, Merstona.
————Gilbert de, 1164, 1165, 1167, 1361, 1390, 1391.
————Henry de, vicar of Tutbury, 2106.
————Richard de, 1360.
Martel, Martell.
————Geoffrey, de Peverwiz, 29.
————Ric., lord of Chilwell, 974.
————Robert, 1924.
Martin IV., Pope, 387, 939.
Martin, Marten, Martene, Marton, Martyn.
————Hugo, 1546, 2335.
————John, Justice, 1806.
————John, 1212, 2343.
————John s. of Tho., of Eyum, 1245-1247.
————John f. Will., 2345.
————Nich., chaplain, 96, 757, 2082-2084, 2349.
————Nicholas, 1238, 1244, 2083, 2348.
————Nich., of Folowe, 1245, 1246, 2084, 2085.
————Nich., of Radbourne, 1251.
————Nich., of Tiddeswalle, 1252, 1254, 1257, 1258.
————Rauff, of Wynster, 1266.
————Richard, chaplain, 2085.
————Richard, 431, 2381.
————Stephen, 1228, 1232, 1233.
————Stephen, de Folowe, 1282, 1283.
————Thomas, 1244.
————Will., 2248, 2343.
————Will., de Hanley, 1732.
Martiwast, Will. de, 2024.
Mascori, Mascory, Mascury.
————Henry, 1291, 1299, 2103.
————Robert, 1301.
————William, 2400.
Mason, George, 1389.
————Henry, 2106.
————James, 1877.
————John, knt., 1625.
————Thomas, 1381, 1382.
————Tho., of Hognaston, 1389.
————Will. le, 1960.
Massey, Mascy, Masey, Masse, Massy.
————James, 850.
————Lucy w. of Rog. de, de Morley, 976.
————Robert de, 2026.
————Rog., of Hylowe, 1805, 2085.
————Rog. de, de Morley, 976.
————Thomas, 1238.
————Will., chaplain, 2403.
Masty, Geoffrey f. Joh., de, 590.
Mateney, Will., of Dronfield, 1775.
Matenie, William, 2425.
Matherfeld, Mathelfeld, Tho. de, of Ashbourne, 67, 1640.
Matilda, Empress, 1943.
————Comitissa Cestrie, 531, 535, 1681, 1937-1946.
————femina Sewel', 516.
————quond. ux. Bruning, 1726.
Matlock, Matlag, Matlac, Matlok, Matloke, Mattloke.

Matlock, etc., Henry de, 134, 1669, 1670, 1674, 2144, 2366.
———Will. de, clerk, 1665.
———Will. f. Ric. de, 1667.
Matthew, Fr., 1539.
———canon of Lichfield, 170.
———capellanus, 1082.
———capellanus de Bakewell, 1274.
Matthew, Mathuse, Mathewe, Mathews.
———Alice w. of Tho., of Buxton, 526, 527.
———Robert, 1715.
———Tho., of Buxton, 526, 527.
———William, 489.
Maubuel, Will., seneschal, 1210.
Mauger, John, jun., 799.
Maulovel, Robert, 2023, 2024.
Maunilwerd, Matilda, 2739.
———Rob., 2739.
Maunsell, John, prepositus de Beuerlaco, 1555.
Maunser, Richard, 1961.
Maureward, Mawreward.
———Geoffrey, 662.
———Thomas, knt., 1983.
Maursfeld, John de, 692.
Mauthon, Will de, jun., 268, 2544.
Mauweysin, Maweysin.
———Dom. Adam, 912.
———Henry, 1754.
Maweger, John, of Chesterfield, 827.
Mawer, Maver.
———James, 233, 1053, 1398.
———Jas., of Barley Woodsetes, 2255, 2256.
———Rob., of Barley Wodsetes, 1063.
Maynard, Maynerd, Meynard.
———Robert, 1979.
———Thomas, 1058, 1061, 2445, 2448, 2449, 2460, 2466.
———Tho., of Dronfield, 235.
———William, 1048, 1049.
Mayster, Henry, 2167.
Mazon, Mazoun.
———Adam le, of Cestrefeld, 714.
———John, 739.
———Simon s. of Adam le, of Cestrefeld, 714.
Measham, Maysam, Meisham, Meysam, Meysem, Meysham.
———Henry, 1979.
———John f. Will. de, 1682.
———Richard, 1996.
———Dom. Will. de, 1767, 2003.
———Will. de, knt., 2152.
———Will. de, 1683, 1996.
———Will. f. Domine de, 1961.
———Will. f. Joh. de, 1683.
Mechel, Ralph, 2036.
Meinasche, Will. de, v. Monyash.
Meinilwarin, v. Mainwaring.
Melbourne, Meleburn, Melbon, Melburn, Melburne.
———Hugh de, 385, 664.
———John f. Will. de, 2615.
———Peter de, 1758, 1980, 1984, 1985.
———Rauff, 349.
———William, 349.

Melbourne, etc., Will., Abbot of Burton, 1276.
Meleward, Nich. le, 2039.
Melim, Ralph le, 2759.
Mellers, Cristiana w. of Ric., 832.
———Richard, 832.
Mellor, Mellour.
———Robert, 103.
———Thomas, 1484.
Mellours, Tho., Mayor of Nottingham, 525.
Mells, Roger de, 1845.
Melnehouse, Ranulf f. Hen., 2655.
Melner, v. Milner.
Melton, Mealtun, Meiltone.
———Sir John, 1071.
———Joyce w. of Tho., 1065.
———Milo de, 1956, 1961.
———Nicholas de, 531, 1939.
———Thomas, sen., 1065.
———Dom. Will. de, chaplain, 1978.
———Will. f. Will. de, 1704.
Mercator, Alex., de Esseburn, 1786.
———Emma f. Ric., de Spondon, 2172, 2173.
———Hubert, 180.
———Leticia relicta Alex., 140.
———Matthew, 174, 177.
———Richard, 2560, 2561.
———Wimarca wid. Ad., of Bakewell, 177.
Mercenton, Merchinton, Mercinton, Mercynton, v. Marchington.
Mercer, Gervase le, 202.
———John, de Staueley, 1342, 1343.
Merche, v. Mersch.
Mere, Henry del, 1716.
———Thomas, 1695.
———Will. s. and h. of John, 1695.
Merford, Rob., succentor of Lichfield, 1720.
Mergawnte, William le, 1200.
Merlage, Merlege, Will., of Derby, 995, 998.
Merle, Merlee, Herbert de, 51, 135.
———Margarita de, 135.
Mersch, Merche, Merssh.
———Alan de la, de Oneston, 2424.
———John del, chaplain, 783.
———John dil, of Onston, 2433.
———Nicholas del, 2437.
Merston, v. Marston.
Mertimer, v. Mortimer.
Metam, John, of Aston, 2441.
Meter, Will. le, capellanus, 1860.
Metheley, Thomas, Prior of Beauvale, 2417.
Meton, John, mil., 1963.
Meudry, Meaudre.
———Isolda w. of Reginald de, 548.
———Reginald de, 548, 2094.
———Reginald de, Knt., 1487.
Meuslet, Robert, Comes de, 1419.
Meuton, Milo de, 2030.
Meverel, Meverell, Meyverell.
———George, of Thoroley, 2191.
———Dom. Hugh de, 919.
———Isabella d. of Nich., 2703.
———Johanna w. of John, sen., 1244.
———John, 157, 1243, 1244.

Meverel, etc., John s. and h. of John, sen., 1244.
————Nicholas, 1220.
————Nich. f. Tho., 2021.
————Richard, 1639.
————Samson, knt., 2133, 2134, 2366, 2394, 2678.
————Thomas, 643, 1512, 1809, 2021, 2366, 2703.
————Walter, of Eyam, 1243, 1252, 1253.
————William, 1226, 1228, 1238, 1243, 2084.
Meye, Hugh, 1959, 1960, 1969-1971.
————William, 1972.
Meymur, Dom. Ralph de, 1200.
Meyne, Hugh le, of Wynstre, 1491.
Meynell, Maynell, Meignel, Meignill, Meignille, Meinel, Meingill, Meingneil, Menel, Menil, Mengnell, Menill, Menyel, Menul, Menyl, Menylle, Meynel, Meygnell, Meygnill, Meynil, Meynill, Meygnyll, etc.
————Mag. Adam de, clerk, 1741.
————Gerard, 1526.
————Giles de, 25, 541, 928, 1520, 1559, 1568.
————Dom. Giles de, knt., 1171, 1545, 1564, 1567, 1630, 2388, 2712.
————Henry, 1525, 1919.
————Hugh de, Dominus of Longeleyemeygnyll, 1524.
————Hugh, 38, 1504, 1521, 1522, 1572, 2223, 2583.
————Dom. Hugh I., mil., 1168, 2628 - 2632, 2635 - 2637, 2640.
————Dom. Hugh II., mil., 397, 520, 521, 1741.
————Dom. Hugh III., mil., 2710.
————Hugh de, senescallus comitis Derbe, 332, 2633.
————Hugh de, of Kylburn, 1509.
————Hugh, of Winster, 292, 295, 2177, 2178, 2624, 2627.
————John, chaplain, 289.
————Nicholas de, 2566.
————Ralph, knt., 1924.
————Ralph, 49.
————Richard de, chev., 2295.
————Richard de, 2377.
————Robert le, 1511.
————Thomas de, 2002.
————Thomas, vicar of Glossop, 2627.
————Will. de, knt., 1545, 1559, 1564, 1565, 1567, 1608, 2006, 2013.
————Will de, Dom. de Yveleye, 2712.
————William de, 335, 1503, 2373, 2546, 2713, 2716.
Meynours, Rog., "Serjaunt of the King's Celler," 1900.
Meystour, Tho., 802.
Michael, capellanus, 1420.
————persona de Langeford, 2001.
————serviens prioris de Tutesberia, 908.

Michael, Will., chaplain, 1861.
————William, 47, 2207.
Michelson, Margery wid. of Rog., of Chestrefeld, 777.
————Rob., 805.
Michson, Alice ux. Rog., 2020.
Middleton, Midelton, Midiltone, Midleton, Myddelton, Mydulton.
————Christofer, 471, 1446.
————John, 2165.
————Nicholas de, 2658.
————Robert, 488, 1274, 1540, 2250.
————Rob. de, de Tyddeswelle, 1237.
————Will. f. Ade de, 16.
Mielton, John de, chaplain, 1977.
————Will. de, chaplain, 1864, 1865.
Migners, John de, 39.
Mill, John, jun., of North Colyngham, 1469.
Milne, Mulne, Myln, Mylne, de Molendino.
————Eliz. wid. of Thos., 2681.
————John, chaplain, 846.
————John, 1226, 1724.
————John f. Tho., 1904.
————Peter s. of Will., of Wormyll, 1265.
————Roger, 1250, 1253, 1259.
————Will., of Wormyll, 1265.
————Will. s. of Will., of Wormyll, 1265.
Milner, Melner, Mulner, Mylner, Molendinarius.
————Adam, 2376.
————Alan, 230, 232.
————Alan, of Cobele, 929.
————Alice wid. of Rog., 1051.
————Isolda, que fuit ux. Nich le, 913.
————John, of Derby, 2599.
————Matilda w. of Tho., of Derby, 523.
————Ric., chaplain, 763.
————Robert, 1909, 2014, 2513.
————Thomas, 551.
————Tho., of Derby, 523.
————Thos., of Horsley, 2599.
————William, 1374.
Milneton, Mulneton, Rob. de la, 2003, 2007-2013, 2153.
Milo, 1945.
————vicar of Wirksworth, 2659.
Milwart, Rob., of Eyton, 1025.
Mineriis, Stephen de, senescallus, 1470.
Mirley, Will. de, clericus Dom. Regis, 1957.
Mittone, Margaret w. of Rog. de, 341.
————Roger de, 341.
Mochaunde, William, 2599.
Moghson, William, 2461.
Mold, v. Mould.
Moldyng, Robert, 232.
Molendinarius, v. Milner.
Molendino, De, v. Milne.
Moll, John, 2665.
Molyneux, Tho., 2000.
Mon, Will., chaplain of St. Mary's Chantry, Monyash, 1720.
Monasteriis, Geoffrey de, v. Musters.
Mondy, v. Mundy.

Monsall, Monisale, Morneshale, Mornsale.
————Colleta w. of Hugh de, 915.
————Hugh de, 421.
————Walthef de, 516.
Monte Alto, Adam de, Dom. de Meysham, 1961.
————Robert, 2536.
————Rog. de, 2025.
————Rog. f. Rog. de, senescallus Cestrie, 2025, 2026.
Monte, William de, 1792.
Montfort, Simon de, Earl of Leicester, 967, 1555.
Montgomery, Mongomberi, Mongombre, Mongomery, Mongumbery, Mongumbri, Mongumri, Monte Gomerry, Montegomeri, Montegomery, Monte Gomorry, Montgomere, Mountegomeri, Mountegomery, Mountgomery, Mungomery, Mungumbry, Mungumeri, Mungumri, Muntgomeri.
————w . . ., 211.
————Bartholomew, 795.
————Emelina f. Rob. de, 1390.
————Geoffrey de, 931.
————Isabel, 2288.
————John, of Cubley, knt., 2169.
————Margaret d. of Nich., knt., 1505.
————Nicholas de, knt., 344, 1393, 1495, 1505, 1585, 1588, 1591, 1594, 1692, 1693, 1868, 1874, 1916, 1931, 1984, 1985, 2131, 2287, 2415, 2416, 2714.
————Nicholas, 84, 85, 930, 931, 2021, 2089, 2288, 2394, 2398, 2673.
————Nich. f. Nich., 2021.
————Ralph de, 238, 2019.
————Ric. f. Rob. de, 2160.
————Roger de, 2286.
————Thomas, 1392, 1928, 2123, 2162.
————Tho., de Couland, 1582, 1585, 2390.
————Walter de, knt., 338, 1864, 2373.
————Walter de, knt., Dom. de Sudbury, 2158, 2162, 2286.
————Walter de, 396, 929-931, 1390, 2128, 2129, 2717.
————Dom. Will. de, 1390, 1391, 1558, 1689, 1766, 2126, 2152, 2154-2156.
————Will. de, Dom. de Segesale, 2115.
————Will. s. of Dom. Will. de, 1689.
————William de, 332, 2003, 2129, 2153, 2159, 2577, 2578, 2718.
Monyash, Meinasche, Monehase, Moniasche, Moniassch, Moniash, Moniassh, Moniasshe, Monihasse, Monyasche, Monyashe, Monyassh.
————Hen. f. Joh. f. Hen., 1220.

Monyash, etc., Hen. f. Simon de, 1706-1708, 1713, 1714.
————John f. Hen. de, 670, 1021, 1022, 1220, 1221, 1713, 1714, 2354, 2357.
————John f. Petri de, 1717.
————Matilda w. of John, 1021, 1022, 1220.
————Tho., clerk, 1655, 1656.
————William, 1719, 1721.
————Will. de, parson of Bonsall, 207, 209.
————Will. de, vicar of Duffeld, 77, 677, 1116, 1117, 1861.
Monyngtone, Will., 2297.
More, Mora, super Moram.
————Henry de la, 1711.
————Hugh de, 1622.
————Hugh f. Sim. de la, of Macworth, 1623.
————Joan w. of Tho. del, 231.
————John del, 507, 1719, 2428, 2498.
————Margery w. of John, 2498.
————Ric. f. Rob. super, 1041.
————Roger del, 230.
————Roger, of Derby, 2698.
————Simon de, 1622.
————Will. atte, 2507.
————Will. de, de Grenhul, 1778.
————William s. of John, 2498.
————Will. f. Will. de la, 497, 1054, 1055.
Morel, John, 334, 2151.
————Thomas, 1289, 2101.
————W . . ., 1391.
————Will. f. Tho., 2102.
Moresburgh, Moresburghe, Moresburough, Morisborick, Morisburg, Morsbur', Morysburg.
————Emma que fuit ux. Joh. de, 1739.
————Gilbert f. Rob. de, 1731.
————Henry, dominus de, 1727.
————Hugh f. Rob. de, clericus, 1734, 1738.
————John f. Petri de, 1728, 1732, 1734, 1737.
————Ralph f. Hen. de, 1732.
————Ric. f. Simon de, 1728, 1730.
————Robert de, 1733.
————Rob. f. Andree de, 1733-1736.
————Simon de, 1727-1729.
Morhage, Hugh de la, 1548, 2706.
————Will. f. Rob. de la, 1548.
Morice, John, of Lechlade, 1922.
Morie, Rob. de, 396.
Morkoc, John, de Esseburn, 30.
Morley, Morle, Morlege, Morleye.
————Henry de, 2171-2173.
————Hugh de, 940, 1335, 1336, 1632, 1726, 2093, 2195, 2196.
————Joan w. of Walter de, 1335, 1336, 2195.
————John de, of Derby, 981.
————Richard de, 31, 1961, 2197, 2200, 2642.
————Robert de, 1726.

Morley, etc., Walter de, 1335, 1336, 2194-2196.
Mornesale, etc., *v.* Monsall.
Morsbur', *v.* Moresburgh.
Morton, Moretain, Moreton, Mortaigne, Mortein, Morten, Morteyn, Morteyng, Mourton.
———Alexander de, in Ettewelle, 1199.
———Edmund, 1327.
———Emicina de, 2200.
———Eustace de, 1207, 1209.
———Eustace f. Eustachii, 1208.
———John, Earl of, 170, 1428, 1431, *v.* also England, Kings of, John.
———Dom. John de, 578.
———John de, 2722.
———John, of Maperley, 281.
———Rob., of le Parkhalle, 281.
———Rob. f. Emicine de, 2200.
———Dom. Rog. de, dom. de Eyum, 1210, 1212, 1214, 1215.
———Dom. Rog. de, Dominus de Maperlay, 1634.
———Thomas de, 2493.
———Dom. Will. de, knt., 1461, 2199, 2212, 2706.
———William, 90, 960, 1210, 1323, 1324.
Mortimer, Mertimer, de Mortuo Mari.
———Alice w. of Will. le, 1289, 1290.
———Will. le, 1288-1290, 2101, 2102.
Mortram, John, 1882.
Mortuo Mari, De, *v.* Mortimer.
Morwod, John de, 1355.
Morys, Tho., 489.
Morysburg, *v.* Moresburgh.
Mosard, John f. Rad., 1198.
———Malcolm f. Rad., 1198.
Mosley, John, of Assheburne, 87-89.
Mosse, John s. of Will. de, of Combs, 617.
———Hen. s. of Will. de, of Combs, 617.
———Ric. s. of Will. de, of Combs, 617.
———Will. de, of Combs, 617.
Mote, Bawdwyn s. and h. of Peter, 915.
———Margery w. of Peter, 915.
———Peter, 915.
———Tho. f. Nich., of Equenton, 1126.
Mould, Mold.
———Ric. de, of Bradley, 400.
———Robert, 619.
Moule, John, 1565.
Mounford, Richard, 999.
———Will. de, 2734.
Mounteneye, Sir John de, 974.
Mountjoy, Lord, *v.* Blount, Will.
Mountjoy, Mongoie, Monioye, Monjoye, Moungav, Moungoye, Mounioie, Mountejoye, Mountioe, Mountjoye, Mungai, Munge, Mungei, Mungjoye, Mungoye, Muniay, Munioie, Munjoy, Munjoye, Muntioye.
———Avice de, 2785.
———Henry de, 2380.

Mountjoy, etc., Hugh f. Rad. de, 2716.
———John de, 2621.
———Margery wid. of Serlo de, 2726.
———Dom. Ralph de, knt., 335, 1565, 1566, 2015, 2159, 2713.
———Ralph de, dom. de Ylderuslye, 2720-2723.
———Ralph de, 51, 134, 137, 138, 144, 145, 147, 397, 1574, 1608, 2622, 2703, 2712, 2725, 2785.
———Robert de, 1609, 2622, 2623.
———Rob. de, of Twiford, 2585.
———Rob. f. Serlonis de, 2723.
———Sara de, 879.
———Serlo de, 58, 134, 396, 398, 1608, 1609, 2716-2718, 2719, 2724, 2725.
———Sewall de, 134, 1554.
———Thos. f. Rob. de, 2623.
———William de, 134, 516, 2620.
———Will. nepos Will. de, 2620.
Mounyng, Will., clerk, 1190.
Mousters, *v.* Musters.
Mowbray, Moubray, Moubrey.
———John, third Duke of Norfolk, Earl Marshal, 489, 490, 2069.
———John, 1845.
———Will., of Ibulle, 1479.
Mower, Mouwer.
———Adam, 235.
———George, of Barley Wodsetes, 1077, 1414.
———James, 1077.
———James, de Bradway, 235.
———Robert, 229, 1077.
———Rob., of Barley Woodesete, 237.
Mucham, *v.* Muschamp.
Mulne, *v.* Milne.
Mulneton, *v.* Milneton.
Mulny, Alured, mil., 1963.
Mundevylle, Dom. Ric. de, 912.
Mundy, Mondy.
———Sir John, Alderman of London, 1657-1659.
———Dame Julian, 1658, 1659.
———Vincent, 1659, 1660, 2715.
Muner, Ralph le, 2424.
Mung', Ralph de, 134.
———Will. de, 134.
Mungomery, Muntgomeri, etc., *v.* Montgomery.
Murcaston, Murchamstona.
———Amabilia de, 1688.
———John de, 1918.
———Margery de, 1918.
———Rob. de, bailiff of Derby, 986.
———Rob. f. Rog. f. Ordryz de, 1688.
———Tho. s. of John, 1691.
———Will. f. Emme de, 1688.
Musard, Christiana w. of Ralph, 2245.
———Hascuil, persona de Witewell, 2244.
———Hasculfus, 2241.
———Isabel w. of Ralph, 2244.
———Nich. f. Rad., 2247.

Musard, Ralph, 2243, 2244.
———Ralph f. Rad., 2245.
———Roger, 2250.
———William, 2245.
Muschamp, Mucham, Muscamp, De Muscampo, Muscham, Muschaump, Muskham.
———Geoffrey de, Bp. of Coventry, 171, 1082, 1420.
———Hugh de, coroner for co. Derby, 201.
———Hugh de, 933, 1336, 2092, 2196, 2209.
———Hugh f. Rob. de, 933.
———Robert de, 548, 933, 1334, 1335, 1338, 1487, 1554, 2197, 2199, 2204.
———Rob. f. Rob. de, 933.
———Will. de, Archdeacon of Derby, 44, 936, 1169, 1681, 2383.
———William le, 1169, 1171, 1278, 2583, 2584, 2590, 2591, 2595, 2596.
———Will. de, jun., 2588, 2589.
———Ydonea w. of Hugh, 2196, 2202.
Musters, Mousters, Monasteriis.
———Alice w. of John de, 121, 122.
———Fulk de, 2241.
———Geoffrey de, 116, 916, 1164, 1165, 1167.
———Hen. de, of Essovere, 113.
———John de, of Tirswell, 121, 122.
———Will. de, of Tirswell, 122.
Muston, Will. de, of Morley, 2209.
Mutford, John de, Justice, 2251.
Muymenel, Rob., de Rependon, 1958.
Myln, Mylne, v. Milne.
Mylnegate, Emma wife of Roger, 2411.
———Will., of Melbourn, 2411.
Mymmot, Mymmott, Mymot.
———John, of Morysburgh, 272, 275.
———Rob., of Rygeway, 276.
Myners, Agnes w. of Will., 1158.
———John, 602, 1158.
———John, of Uttoxeter, 2165, 2166.
———Thomas le, 1666.
———William, 1158.
———Will. s. of Will., 1158.

N.

Naileston, Nailiston, Nayliston.
———John de, 1682.
———Ric. f. Rog. de, 1682, 1683.
———William de, 1726.
Nawbull, Isabel, 2530.
Nayl, Naill, Henry, 1919, 1920.
———John, chaplain, 793.
Nayler, John, s. of John, of Newark, 450.
Neapoli, Garnar de, Prior of the Hospitallers of St. John of Jerusalem in England, 1539.
Nedham, Nedeham, Netham.
———Christopher, 1256.
———Elias de, 1472.
———Elizabeth, 954.
29

Nedham, etc., Henry de, 322, 666.
———Hugh, 559.
———Sir John, knt., 2378.
———John de, 1473.
———John de, of Benteley, 287.
———John, of Ibulle, 1478.
———Richard, 1749, 1750.
———Robert, 566, 1374, 1375.
———Thomas, of Buxton, 527.
———Will., of Thornsett, 953, 954.
———Will. s. and h. of Otvel, 566.
Nelsthorpe, John, 273.
Nestome, Mag. Will. de, 2381.
Netbreyder, Nettebreyder, Tho., "Botyler de Drakelowe," 604, 1026.
Nettelworth, Roger, 797.
Nettiswrht, Robert, 802.
Neubyghyng, Nubyggyng, Adam, clerk, 1195.
———Laurence de, 2491.
Neuport, John de, 431.
———Richard, 893.
Neuthorpe, Will. de, chaplain, 1510.
Neuton, Neweton, Newton, John, 844, 1002, 1003.
———John, bailiff of Derby, 994, 995.
———Laurence, of Pynkston, 1884.
———Richard, 105.
———Robert, of Milton, 1992.
———Roger, 1875.
———Will. de, canon of Lichfield, 1427.
Neuylworth, Will. de, 2705.
Nevill, Nevile, Neville, Nevyll.
———Hugh de, 1419.
———James de, 2246.
———Sir Ralph de, lord of Raby, 1898.
———Robert, 2361.
———Dom. Theobald de, 2028.
———Tho. de, Lord Furnivale, 795.
———Dom. Tho., Dom. de Hallumshire, 1233, 1234.
———Thomas de, 2028.
Newbold, Neubold, Neubolt, Newbolt.
———Adam de, 367, 369, 418, 430, 700, 713, 714, 716, 718, 720, 1033, 2499, 2557.
———Adam fil. Ad. de, 2422-2424.
———Adam s. of Ralph de, 722.
———Adam f. Rob. de, 728.
———Adam f. Sare de, 2434.
———Adam f. Will de, 2419-2421.
———Elena que fuit uxor Joh. de, 735.
———Hen. f. Philippi de, 729, 1745.
———Henry s. of Sara de, 2434.
———Hugh de, 359, 366, 423, 700, 714, 715, 2497.
———John de, 277, 500, 1326.
———John f. Ade de, 728.
———John, of Hakynthorp, 276.
———Matilda w. of Hen. f. Phil. de, of Chesterfield, 1745.
———Nicholas, 1416.
———Richard de, 706.
———Rich. f. Ade de, 2429, 2430, 2434.
———Rob. f. Joh. de, 1743.

Newbold, etc., Rob. f. Phil. de, 1746.
———Rob. f. Stephani de, 308.
———Roger de, 1709.
———Roger f. Ade de, 374.
———Rog. f. Joh. de, 757.
———Sara wid. of Adam de, 2422-2424, 2434.
———Thomas, 275.
———William de, 234, 236, 687, 1059, 1327, 1528.
Newenham, Will., vicar of Assheburn, 81.
Newere, John de, 1420.
Newerk, John, vicar of Whitwell, 2559.
Nichol, Rob., 2037.
Nicholas, armiger patris Hugonis, Comitis, 536.
———clericus de Assheburn, 389.
———frater Horm, 529.
———fr. Hen. Ostricer, 530.
———miles, dom de Wilinton, 2568-2570, 2573.
———official of the Archdeacon of Derby, 44, 2396.
———persona de Esseburn, 386.
———persona de Repton, 1939.
———prior of Tutbury, 2718.
———rector of Cubley, 2385.
———sacerdos, 536.
Nicholson, Thomas, 99, 1330.
Niger, Henry, 2733.
Nikbrother, John, 1224.
Nike, Nikes, Neke, Nycke, Nyke, Nykke.
———Nicholas, 1977.
———Richard, 592, 1981.
———Thomas, 584, 590, 591.
———William, 1972, 1979.
Noget, Will. f. Willelmi, de Draycote, 1337.
Nonant, Hugh de, Bp. of Coventry, 170, 1081, 1082, 1419, 1428, 1431, 2744.
Noppe, Edith, w. of Hen., 1109.
———Hen., of Dugmanton, 1109.
Norbury, Will. de., Justice Itinerant, 2013.
———Dom. Will. f. Herberti de, 1766, 1767.
Norfolk, Duke of, *v.* Mowbray.
Norman, Normone.
———Dionisius, of Beley, 259-261.
———Robert, 2596.
———Roger, 253.
———William, 256.
Normanton, Geoffrey f. Will. de, de Derby, 979.
———John de, 786, 804, 809, 811, 815, 816, 1510.
———Richard de, 238, 239.
———Rob. f. Ric. de, 238.
———Roger, of Horseley, 1983.
———William de, 2628, 2630, 2631.
———Dom. Will., of Horssley, 1509.
Norreys, Noreys.
———Peter le, serviens de Wyrkesworth, 2641.
———Robert le, 1555.
———Will. f. Will., 554.

North, Northe.
———Agnes w. of Rob., 1223.
———Dyonisia w. of Rog., 1222.
———Joan w. of Ric., 444.
———Richard, 444.
———Rob. f. Rog., 1223.
———Roger, 1718.
———Rog., of Dobenehull, 1222.
Northburgh, Rog. de, Prebendary of Lichfield, 2350.
Northbyre, Will. f. Herberti de, 1689.
Northege, Northegge.
———John, 104.
———John, chaplain, 855.
———Ric. de, 1815.
Northfolc, Nordfolc.
———fr. Osbert de, 1539.
———Ralph de, 534.
Northleghes, Will. de, 219.
Norton, Adam de, 1088, 2250.
———Ankerus de, of Staley, 817.
———John, Abbot of Beucheff, 265.
———Nicholas de, 130.
———Ric., of Alderwasleghe, 11.
———Roger de, 332.
———Simon de, 2285.
———Tho. s. of Ric., 11.
Norwich, Bishop of, *v.* Gray, John de.
Norwis, Simon de, canon of Lichfield, 189.
Note, Will., of Eyam, 1218, 1220, 1464.
Nottingham, Notingham, Notyngham.
———John de, 2586.
———Margery de, of Derby, 2179.
———Ralph f. Rad. de, 355.
———Ric., Abbot of Dale, 946.
———Rob. de, bailiff of Derby, 971.
———Roger de, 985.
Nowell, Walter, 2077.
Nutte, Hen., of Castulton, 230.
Nye, Thomas, 590.
Nyx, John, canon of Dunstaple, 166.

O.

Ockeston, Robert de, 1088.
Octhorp, Lesota d. and heir of John de, 1784.
Odam, Margaret w. of Tho., de Moniassh, 1719.
———Tho., de Moniassh, 1719.
Oddyngeseles, John de, 1521, 1524.
———John f. Oliveri de, 2388.
———Margery de, 2388.
———Will. de, 2388.
Odeby, Walter, clerk, 1203.
Odell *al.* Wodell, Margery w. of Thos., 2521, 2524, 2525, 2527, 2528.
———Thos., 2365, 2367, 2521, 2524, 2525, 2527, 2528.
Odo, camerarius, 1945.
Ody, Adam, 2127.
Oede, Geoffr., of Herberbury, 2017.
Offedecote, John de, 53, 54, 1786.
Offerton, Offirton.
———Elena de, 1788.
———Eustachius de, 1788.

Offerton, etc., Hugh f. Will. de, 1789, 1791.
———Matilda de, 1788.
———Robert de, 1788.
———Rob. f. Eustachii de, 1797.
Officel, John, 2553.
Ogaston, Oggaston, Ogedeston, Oggedeston, Oggediston.
———Rob. de, 108, 934, 2284, 2492.
———Walter de, 110, 118, 2606.
———Will. f. Rob. de, 2493.
Okebroc, Richard de, 879.
———Robert de, 398.
Okeover, Acavere, Accouere, Acouer, Acouere, Acoure, Akouere, Akover, Akovre, Aucoure, Okar, Oker, Okere, Okor, Okore, Okouer, Okouere, Okour, Okoure, Okover.
———Alice wid. of Sir Philip, knt., 823.
———Agnes, 164.
———Cristiana w. of Rog. de, 151, 1642, 1643.
———Geoffrey de, 2125.
———Hugh I. de, 135, 216, 1554, 1766, 2125, 2765.
———Hugh II. de, 54, 386.
———Humphrey, 86, 164, 165, 2141-2143.
———John de, chaplain, 77.
———John f. Hugonis de, 137.
———John f. Philippi de, 80, 156-159, 823, 1646.
———John s. of Tho., 160, 1646.
———Laurence de, 61, 1608.
———Philip I. de, knt., 76, 155, 1645, 1693, 1761, 1768, 2130, 2416.
———Philip II., 2135, 2137, 2138.
———Philip III., 2191.
———Ralph, 513, 514, 1339, 2729, 2730.
———Richard, 2139.
———Robert de, 1636.
———Rob. f. Dom. Hugonis de, 136-139, 140, 386, 1820, 1821, 2126.
———Rog. de, miles, dominus de Attelowe, 141, 143-150, 152, 1641.
———Rog. de, fil. Matild. de Grendon, 2126.
———Thomas, senr., 80, 153, 156-161, 1497, 1498, 1517, 1646, 1648-1650, 1769, 2133-2135, 2136.
———Thomas, jun., 159.
———Thomasine w. of Philip, 2135, 2137.
———Will., dominus de Snelleston, 931.
Okeyly, Thos., parson of Sudbury, 2164.
Oky, John, 576, 577, 579, 580.
Olear', Robert, 2638.
Olearius, Will., bailiff of Derby, 971.
Oliver, Randulph, 630.
Ollerenshaugh, John de, 617.
Olyver, Thomas, 631.
Ondeby, John, Archdeacon of Derby, 1438.
Oneston, Onestone, Ounston.

Oneston, etc., Henry de, 2424.
———Nicholas de, 2438-2441, 2443-2445.
———Will. f. Ade de, 2426.
Optone, Henry de, 2224.
Orcherd, Nich., "Baylye" of Derby, 1000.
Ordriche, Robert, 2548.
Ore, Osbert de, Dominus de Beghley, 248.
Orenge, Hugh, 915.
Orm, the carpenter, 225.
Orm, Orme.
———Adam, sacerdos de Wilinton, 1939.
———John, of Brynlaston, 2390, 2599.
———Nicholas, 2352.
———Robert fil. Ad., 1939.
———Roger, 523.
———William, 519, 521, 560.
———v. also Horm.
Orme, nativus, 2011.
Orrebi, Orreby.
———John de, 1084.
———Philip de, Justice of Chester, 486, 487.
Orsele, Albert de, 2545.
Osbaundist', Henry de, 398.
Osbert, armiger, 2091.
Oseburne, William de, 174.
Osmond, Osmund, Will., chaplain, 2184, 2185, 2355.
Osmundeston, Rob. f. Fulcheri de, 1164.
Osmundus, 2090.
Osmunston, Haytrop de, 399.
Ossauiston, Hulf de, 2381.
———Gilbert, 2381.
Ostricer, Henry, 530.
Othehed, Henry, 1635.
Othehede, Walter, of Maperley, 1635.
Otley, Adam of, 2554.
Otot, Hen. de, 292.
Otting, Rob. f. Tho., de Longeford, 1570.
Ottun, Dorling de, 2384.
Otuere, Philip, de Tykenhale, 1956.
Otwey, Will., 384.
Otyngham, Thomas, 611.
Otys, Issabella, 1674.
Ou, John le, clericus, 2127.
Ouere, Tho. de, chaplain de Eyum, 1224.
Oure, Leodegarius de, 396.
Ouwein, Hen. f. Hen., 1661.
Over Neubold, Adam de, 2427.
Overton, Ouerton.
———Geoffrey de, 1422.
———Robert de, 1690.
———Rob., literatus, 1720.
———Rob. f. Will. de, 110, 112.
Owtram, Owtrem, Outrem.
———John, 842.
———John, of Holmesfeld, 1412.
———Robert, 1055, 2451.
———William, 847, 1064, 1065, 1412, 2458, 2466.
Oxcroft, Thomas, 781.
Oxlay, Oxle, Oxeley.
———Henry, 2253, 2276.
———James, warden of All Saints', Derby, 1002.

Oxlay, etc., Nicholas s. of Hen., 2276.
———Richard, chaplain, 872.
———Richard, priest, 2276.
Oxon', John de, Sheriff of Notts. and Derby, 201.
Oxton, John, 1191.
———Nicholas de, perpet. vicar of Wirksworth, 2642, 2643, 2662.

P.

Pachet, John, 2129.
———Will., clericus, 2129.
Paddelay, Padelay, Paudeley.
———Nicholas de, 1210, 1791.
———Richard de, 1215, 1216.
———Ric., s. of Will de, 1355.
———Rog. f. Ric. de, 1217.
Page, Alice w. of John, 255, 256.
———John, 255, 256, 1856.
———Tho., Abbot of Darley, 1012.
———Thomas, 2558.
———Will., bailiff of Derby, 973.
Paien, Richard, 2022.
Pakeman, William, 986.
Pakinton, Thos. de, Abbot of Burton, 2614.
Pakynton, Will. de, 1174, 1175.
Palefrey, Ralph, 1754.
———Rob. of Neutone, 1754.
Palkocke, John, 2649.
———Matilda, quond. ux. Joh., 2649.
Palmer, Alan fr. Sim. de, 2749.
———John, 719, 749.
———Ralph, 691.
———Richard le, 1651.
———Rich., 2501.
———Rob., of Douuebrigge, 350.
———Walter le, 1652.
———Will., of Langeley, 1535.
———Will. f. Will., 2611.
Pamplyon, William, 2608.
Pandulf, Papal legate, 2572.
Pant, John, of Yoxhall, 594.
Panton, Pantun, Paunton, Pawnton.
———Hamelun, 2022.
———John, of Burton-on-Trent, 2066, 2068, 2071, 2072.
———Thos. s. of John, capellanus, 2068, 2071, 2072, 2078.
———William, 239.
Parc, Isabel, 2000.
———John, 2000.
Parco, Will. de, of Becthon, 268.
———Will. de, of Dineby, 1507.
Pare, John, of Notyngham, 236.
Pareys, Ralph de, capellanus, 2043.
Parfaye, Thomas, 1650.
Paris, Ralph de, 2054.
Parker, Parkar, Parkere.
———Adam, 1776.
———Agnes, 2508.
———Alexander le, de Attelowe, 142.
———Elizabeth, 2508.
———Geoffrey le, 1334.
———Gilbert le, 1894, 1896.

Parker, etc., Isolda w. of Will. le, 143.
———John, 155, 1053, 1066, 1071, 1263, 1398, 1498, 2508, 2513.
———John, of Chesturfeld, 829.
———John, of Norton Lees, 100, 1129, 1782, 2474.
———John s. of Will. le, de Attelowe, 143.
———Laurence, 395.
———Margaret w. of Ric., 155.
———Richard, 155, 583.
———Rich. s. of Peter, 2099.
———Robert le, 541.
———Thomas, 1066, 1485, 1777.
———Thomas s. of John, 2506.
———Thos. s. of Peter, 2099.
———Will. le, 143, 149-152, 1377, 1378, 2609.
Parkezate, John atte, de Hanley, 1341.
Parlebien, Parlebyne.
———Richard, 389.
———William, 390, 391.
Parmentar, Parminter.
———Agnes le, 2311.
———Emma, 2751.
———Richard, 2751.
Parsey, Hen. de Fennybentileye, 34.
Parsones, Rog. de, of Codnor, 897.
Partut, Thomas, 1711.
Parva Bradburne, Will. f. Agnetis de, 390, 391.
Parva Clifton, Rob. f. Rob. de, 882.
Parva Tappeton, Rog. de, 711.
Parvus, Fr. Robert, 1539.
Pas, Adam de, 1619.
Passemer, Pasmer, Passemere.
———Peter, of Tutbury, 1367, 2295.
———Richard, of Tutbury, 2109.
Pastor, Roger, 1726.
Patric, Robert, 539.
———Rob. b. of Tho., 539.
———Thomas, 538, 539.
———William, 535, 539.
Patton, John, 8.
Paul, Abbot of Leicester, 1082.
Paulinus, 2380.
Paunton, Pawnton, v. Panton.
Payn, Payne.
———Ralph, of Caldwell, chaplain, 2124.
———Roger, 2011.
———Thomas, 1991.
———Will., bailiff of Derby, 987.
Paynell, Isabella w. of Ric., 960.
———Richard, 960.
Pease, Pees.
———Edward, 2738.
———Henry, 2128.
———John, 78.
———Roger, 798.
Pecard, v. Picard.
Pech, Peche.
———John, mil., 1968.
———Matilda, 332, 333.
———Ric., Bp. of Coventry, 535, 1941.
———Richard de, 134.
———Thomas, mil., 402.
———Tho. f. Ric. de, 1610.

Peck, Pec, de Pecco, Peeke, Peek, Pek.
——Henry de, 1084.
——Hugh de, 355, 357, 410, 424, 427, 544, 545, 683, 688, 690.
——Joan w. of John del., 1652, 1653.
——John de, 352, 354, 361, 683, 2014.
——John de la, of Rodsley, 1145-1147, 1150.
——John f. Hen. del., 1652.
——Peter, 1085, 1815.
——Peter f. Will de, 1091.
——Richard, 201, 1079, 1336.
——Robert de, 707, 2090, 2091.
——Tho. f. Ric. de, 1611.
——William de, 269, 707, 2543.
Peckham, John, Archbishop of Canterbury, 192, 197.
Pedeler, John, 1438.
Peghell, Richard, 2694.
Pele, John f. et h. Hug., 2344.
Pelleson, Rob., 725.
Pembroke, Earls of, *v.* Marshal.
Penesion', Hen. de, 2754.
Penn, Penne.
——Hugh, 1396.
——Nicholas de, 1347.
——Tho. le, chaplain, 1225.
Pentriz, Hen. de, granger, 2650, 2651.
Penyfader, Richard, 2078.
Penyston, John, s. and heir of Will. de, de Basselowe, 1249.
Pepir, Alice, 2099.
Per', Rob. del, 2151.
Percy, John, vicar of Dronfield, 236.
——John, clerk, 2451.
——Peter de, Justice Itinerant, 1557.
——William, 1991, 1993, 1994.
Perdriz, Symon, clerk of the Bp. of Coventry and Lichfield, 179, 1953.
Perepont, Perepount, *v.* Pierpount.
Perer, Perers, Perrer.
——Dom. Rich. de, knt., 2017.
——Robert de, dapifer, 239.
——Dom. Robert de, 1560.
Pereson, Pereisson, John, 2443.
——Robert, 1342.
——Tho. s. and h. of John, of Hanley, 1128.
Perfey, Will., of Benteleye, 287.
Perkyn, John, 1158.
——Will., bailiff of Uttoxeter, 2165, 2166.
Perpunt, *v.* Pierpount.
Persaye, Thomas, 1649.
Persun, Thomas le, 577.
Perton, Henry de, 138.
——Hen. f. Hen. de, 138.
Pertrikoure, Will., 503.
Peter, capellanus de Finderne, 2579.
——clericus, 1948.
——senescallus de Briminton, 354.
——f. Rodb. cler. de Malpas, 530.
Peterstowe, Peter de, prior of Dieulacres Abbey, 2724.
Pethling, Will. de, 2023.
Petras, Ranulph super, 2653.
Petris, Ranulph de, 2636.

Pety, John, 450.
Peverel, Peverell.
——Hamo, 534.
——Nich. f. et h. Petri, of Hassop, 1353.
——William, 1828, 1833, 1853.
Peverwich, Peuerwic, Peuerwich.
——Geoffrey f. Ranulfi de, 1819.
——Hen. f. Galfridi de, 1821.
——Hen. f. Reg. de, 1818.
——Hen. f. Rog. de, 1820.
——Peter f. Haylwardi de, 1820.
——Ralph de, 134.
——Ralph f. Petri de, 1820.
Pexi, Henry, 730, 731.
Peygden, *al.* Pygden, Sir Rob., priest, 907.
Peyure, Thomas, 587.
Phelip, Will., chaplain, 1174.
Phelipot, John, 1652.
Phelype, George, 2253.
Philip, Abbot of Lavendon, 387.
——canon of Kenilworth, chaplain to the Dean of Lichfield, 179.
——clericus, 1953.
——clericus de Duffeld, 1113.
——clericus de Wirksworth, 2655.
——Decanus, 412.
——Decanus de Derebi, 1081.
——sacerdos, 880.
Philippa, Queen, 1843; *v.* also under England.
Phole, Tho. de la, de Assheburn, 60.
Phytun, *v.* Fitun.
Picard, Pecard, Pichard, Pikard, Pycard, Pychard, Pykard.
——Adam, 744, 2313.
——John f. Ade, of Neuton, 1757.
——Juliana, 1972.
——Nicholas, 1959, 1972.
——Rekewere w. of Ric., of Mapulton, 1641.
——Richard, 1641, 1643.
——William, 1758, 1759, 1958, 1962.
Picheford, Will. de, 1503.
Pichot, sacerdos de Suttunia, 530.
Pickworth, Pickeworth, Alan de, 191, 1552.
Picot, William, 538.
Pierpount, Perepont, Perepount, Perpound, Perpount, Perpunt, Pierpount, Pirpont.
——Hen., knt., 827, 840, 1344, 1601, 1896, 2316, 2317, 2475.
——Henry, 1317-1319, 1357, 1602, 1869, 2521, 2564.
——John, 2475.
Pigton, Ric., de, 673.
Pilcote, Pilkote, John de, 2101.
——Thomas de, 1365.
Pilkyngton, Pylkynton.
——Henry, 1256.
——Richard de, 2119.
——Thomas, knt., 2475.
Pillesley, Ric., of Chesterfield, 1384.
Pincerna, Reginald, 1940.
——Robert, 536.
——William, 534.

Pinel, Simon, 175.
Pipard, Pippard, Pypard, Pyppard,
Ralph, 928, 2180, 2386, 2741.
Pipe, Robert de, 1029, 2614.
Piper, Pyper.
———Alice, 1981.
———Laurence, chaplain of St.
Mary's Gild, Chesterfield,
872.
———Richard, 1981.
Pirpont, *v.* Pierpount.
Piru, Piro, Pyry.
———R—— de, 1390, 1391.
———Rob. de, dapifer, 238, 332, 532.
Pistor, Adam f. Joh., de Cesterfeld,
2308, 2309.
———Adam f. Ric., 912.
———Nich., of Cruch, 1888.
———*v.* also Baker.
Pite, Ric. f. Rog., of Ridding, 2192.
Plastowe, Plaustowe.
———Geoffrey de, 920, 1888.
———John de, 2628, 2630, 2631,
2632, 2635.
———Ric. f. Galfr. de, 1889.
———William de, 1887, 1888.
Pleasley, Pleselei, Pleseley, Pleslay.
———Adam de, 2291.
———Roger de, 1511.
———Serlo de, 1397.
———Tho. f. Hug. de, 1894.
———Tho. super grenam de, 1894.
Plesaunce, John, vicar of Sheffield, 1129.
Plessetis, John de, Earl of Warwick,
1555.
Plompton, William, 953.
Plumley, Plumleye, Plomley.
———John de, 1106, 2433.
———Robert, 207, 803, 830.
———Will., 127, 273, 274, 830, 2170.
Plummer, *al.* Plumer, John, 1282, 1284.
Poer, Poher, Pouer, Power.
———Ralph le, 1862.
———Ranulph le, 1862.
———Robert, 1552.
———Thomas le, 1337, 2171, 2172,
2176, 2177.
Pointon, Ralph de, rector of Willington,
2573.
Poklynkton, Roger, 802.
Pokoc, William, 393.
Pole, Poole.
———Alice, 1935.
———Edw. de la, 2304.
———German, 90, 960, 961, 1680,
1936, 2305, 2307.
———Hen. de la, 96, 161, 982, 1069,
1935, 2020, 2086.
———Hen., of Mogenton, 1526.
———Hen., s. of Peter de la, 1251.
———John de la, knt., 1692, 2415,
2416.
———John de la, 69, 72, 74, 403,
1588, 1616, 2133, 2134,
2598.
———John de la, de Assheburn, 340,
512, 2412-2414.
———John, of Hertyngton, 156-159,
1769, 2119.
———John, of Nuburthe, 1488.

Pole, etc., John, s. and h. of Rauff, of
Wakebruge, 923.
———Peter de la, 49, 1251, 1393,
1934.
———Ralph, 1543, 2362.
———Ralph de la, de Hertyndon, 67.
———Ralph de la, sergeant-at-law,
610, 2188.
———Ralph, s. of Peter de la, 1251.
———Rauf., of Wakebridge, 2489.
———Richard de la, 40, 1214.
———Robert, parson of Colwyk, 1181.
———Tho., of Wakbrigge, 1543, 1679.
———Will. de la, Marquis of Suffolk,
2461, 2467.
———Will. de la, 1724.
Poleson, Thomas, 81.
Pollesworth, Ric., vicar of Stapenhull,
2239.
Ponger, *v.* Pouger.
Ponte, Peter de, 2472.
Pontefract, prior of, 1696.
Pontem, John ad, de Thurvaston, 2323.
———Isabella w. of John de, 2323.
Ponynton, Will. de, 2093.
Poole, *v.* Pole.
Poore, Ric. le, Bp. of Durham, 910, 911.
Port, Porte.
———Johane w. of John, 1203-1205.
———Sir John, knt., King's Justice,
492, 960, 1813.
———John, of Etwall, 1001, 1004,
1203-1206, 1266, 1528, 1529,
1531.
———John s. and h. of John, 1605.
———Margery, 1001.
———Tho., LL.D., 1001.
Porteioye, Henry, 2101.
Porter, Agneta w. of Hugh le, 741.
———Hugh le, 741.
———John le, 15.
———John le, of Caldelowe, 2657.
———John s. of Ric., of Chesterfield,
817.
———Margery wid. of Will., 841.
———Nicholas, 2663.
———Richard le, 423, 430, 717, 2661.
———Ric., vicar of Chesterfield, 785.
———Dom. Ric., chaplain, 753, 771.
———Ric. le, of Caldelowe, 1474.
———Ric., of Chesterfield, 817.
———Robert, 824.
———Thomas, 2663, 2668.
———Tho. f. Nich. le, 1146.
———Will. le, 2661, 2664, 2665.
———Will. s. of Ric., clerk, 815.
Porton, Walter de, canon of Lichfield,
189.
Portyngton, John, Justice of the Com-
mon Bench, 1763.
Potloc, Potlock, Potlok.
———Marg. w. of Thos. de, 2584,
2586, 2588-2597.
———Rich. f. Th. de, 2596.
———Thomas f. Galfr. de, 2584.
2586, 2588-2597.
———William de, 1143.
Potter, Pottere, Elias, 2266, 2267.
———Eliz. w. of Tho., 1915.
———Thomas, 1915.

Potter, etc., Tho. f. Nich. de, 1141, 1145.
———William, 2266, 2267.
Pouer, *v.* Poer.
Pouger, Ponger.
———Alice w. of Will., of Wilsthorpe, 1337.
———Matilda f. Sim., 2178.
———Rob. f. Tho., 2208.
———Simon, de Wilsthorpe, 47.
———Simon f. et h. Will., 2177, 2178.
———Thos. f. Will., 2205, 2207.
———William, 1337, 1338.
———Will., of Wilkstorf, 2204, 2205-2207.
Poule, Margery, 2295.
Pountfret, Pontfreynt, Pountfreyt, Pountefreit.
———Richard de, 1572, 1630, 2321.
———Will. f. Ric. de, 1577.
Poutrel, Poutrell, Powtrell, Puterel, Putrel.
———Geoffrey, 2090.
———Robert, 2207.
———Roger, 134.
———Thomas, 1749-1751.
———William, 54.
Povay, Ralph, 2446.
Power, *v.* Poer.
Powte, Alice w. of Rob., 464.
———Rob., of Chestrefeld, 464.
Praers, Robert de, 119.
Pratellis, Engelram de, 171, 1419.
———John de, 171.
Pratt, Agnes, 1995.
———John, 1995, 1996.
Preers, Beatrix ux. Matth. de, 529.
———Matthew de, 529.
Prentys, Peter le, 979.
Prepositus, Ivo, 571.
Prest, Preest, Preste, Prust.
———Henry, 582, 584, 585, 591, 592.
———John, 1992.
———Matilda w. of Hen., 582.
———Ric., of Catton, 600.
———Thomas, 600.
———William, 1476, 1477.
Prestclif, Will. f. Rob. de, 1912, 1913.
Prestessone, Prustessone, John, 582, 584, 585.
———Matilda w. of John, 584, 585.
Prestwode, Prestwode, Nigel de, 879, 1346.
Preston, Dom. Gilbert de, Justice Itinerant, 399, 2582.
———John, Justice, 1806.
Prestwike, Adam de, 1472.
Prihe, Ric., of Chesterfield, 1384.
Prince, Prynce.
———Christopher, clerk, 87.
———Johanna, 2602.
———John, 2602.
———Katerine, 2602.
———Matilda w. of Rich., 2602.
———Richard, 2602.
Proctour, Hen., clerk, 1528, 1529, 1531.
Proudfot, Robert, 733, 734.
Prudhomme, Prodhom, Prodhomme, Prudhome, Purdhomme, Purdon.

Prudhomme, etc., Margaret w. of Ric., 1854, 1855, 1857, 1858.
———Ric., of Slefford, 1857, 1858.
———William, 2239, 2678.
———Will., merchant, 394.
———Will., of Burton-upon-Trent, 345.
Prust, *v.* Prest.
Prustessone, *v.* Prestessone.
Puis, Nigel des, 530.
Pulein, Unfridus, 1078.
Punt, Harry, 1004.
———Henry, of Ashburn, 2391.
Purchas, Tho. s. of Tho., of Langeley Mareys, 1455.
Purdon, *v.* Prudhomme.
Purley, John de, 2705.
Purseglowes, Will., vicar of Tyddeswell, 2360.
Putrel, *v.* Poutrel.
Pycard, Pychard, *v.* Picard.
Pye, John, 269, 271.
———Rob., of Tuxford-in-le-Cley, 272, 273.
Pygot, Cecily wid. of Will., 554.
———German, 552.
———Richard, 1250.
———Ric., of Hokelowe, 1440.
———William, 552.
Pyk, John, 618.
Pykard, *v.* Picard.
Pykryng, Will., of Thorneton, 2401.
Pylkyngton, *v.* Pilkyngton.
Pylle, John, of Smisby, 2124.
Pymme, Henry, 582.
———John, 581, 584.
Pynkeston, John de, 1866.
Pyper, *v.* Piper.
Pypard, Pyppard, *v.* Pipard.
Pypes, Pypys.
———John, chaplain, 466.
———John, of Normanton, 1885.
Pyrot, Ralph f. Reg., 578.
Pyrton, William, 827.
———Will., clerk, 1195.
Pyry, *v.* Piru.
Pyte, Will., 1896.

Q.

Quickeshull, Geoffrey de, 57.
Quyxley, John, 842.
Qwyt, Nicoll, 1409.

R.

R——, Bishop of Coventry, 1957.
———capellanus, 532.
———precentor of Lincoln, 2634.
———presbyter, 284.
———prior de Lenton, 2093.
———vicar of Radford, 186.
Rachel, Geoffrey, 2193.
———Ric., in Stanleg', 1632.

Radcliff, Radclyff, Raddecliff, Rade-
clive.
———John de, 759.
———John, clerk, 2455, 2456.
———Ric. de, knt., 1588, 1591, 1594.
———Ric. de, rector of Longford,
1874.
———Robert, 1256.
———Mag. Stephen de, 1544.
Radeford, Robert de, 1831.
Radissh, Hen., clerk, 1597-1599.
Radnoure, Radenouere, Peter de, Arch-
deacon of Salopesbir', 189, 1705.
Rage, Alice w. of Rog., 1273.
———Roger, 898, 1273.
———Tho., of Codnor, 1273.
———William, 2694.
Ragged, Raggedde, Raggede, Ragget,
Raggit.
———Matilda w. of Rob. le, 1794,
1795.
———Richard le, 1547, 2341, 2342,
2622.
———Rob. f. Ric. le, 1794.
———Rob. f. Ric. le, jun., 1795.
———Thomas le, 194, 552.
Rakestone, Robert de, 1752.
Ralph, Archdeacon of Chester, 182.
———capellanus, 2335.
———chaplain to Hugh, E. of
Chester, 535.
———chaplain of Ashover, 108, 934,
2284.
———clericus, 1081, 1945, 2027.
———clericus, de London, 175.
———clericus de Rollustone, 1292.
———clericus de Stapenhill, 284.
———persona de Ekenton, 1727,
1729, 2560.
———prior of Laund, 1078.
———[de Leicester], Treasurer of
Lincoln, 2634.
———Vicecomes de Valle Vire, 1942.
Ralston, John, 465.
Rampestone, Hugh de, 2094.
Rampton, Stephen de, 2023.
Rancekell, Ranckel, Ranckell, Rankel,
Rankell, Rankelle, Raunkell,
Renkel.
———Gervase, 1215, 1217.
———John, of Eyam, chaplain, 1226-
1228, 1230-1233, 1235-
1237, 1282-1284.
———John f. Gervasii, of Eyum,
1218.
———Thomas, 1217.
Ranulf, Earl of Chester, 486, 487, 528.
v. also Chester, Earls of.
———Vicecomes, 1397.
Rapendon, Rapenduna, *v.* Repton.
Rappoke, Thomas, 1497.
Rasur, Jordan, 535, 1939, 1945.
———Thomas, 1945.
Ratcliffe, Reginald, 1877.
Ratclyff, Tho., knt., master of Burton
St. Lazars, 613.
Raueneston, Goda f. Rad. de, 2029.
Raunckel, *v.* Rancekel.
Raunsley, John de, 250.

Rauson, Tho., clerk, Gardianus de
Tonge, 213.
Rawe, Will. del, 158.
Rawlyn, Rob., of Makkeney, 1627.
Rawlynson, Will., of Hegate, in Bow-
don, 460.
Raynburgh, John, of Collowe, 450.
Reddeford, Henry, chaplain, 2123.
Rede, Will. f. Ric. le, of Wyngerworth,
699.
Redfern, Reddefern.
———Edward, perpetual vicar of
Longford, 1359.
———Emmot w. of Will., 632.
———William, 632.
Rediman, Redimon, Redymone.
———John, chaplain, 2357.
———William, 2345, 2349, 2352.
Redser, Redesir, Redsyr.
———Giles, 2316.
———John, rector of Eyam, 1228,
1230, 1233, 1234, 1283.
Reedus, Thos., 2681.
Regge, Joan w. of John, 1192.
———John, de Walley, 1192.
Reginald, capellanus, 1197.
———capellanus de Rapindon, 2571.
———clericus, fil. Will. sac. de
Thicheal, 537.
———pincerna, 1940.
———prior of Repton, 1756.
———quondam vicarius B. Petri,
Derby, 329.
Regotte, Roger, 838.
Reinaldus, canon of Calk, 532.
Rempstone, Robert, 903, 904.
Repdone, John, de Ketilstone, 1505.
Repton, Priors of, *v.* Index of Places.
Repton, Rapendon, Rapenduna, Repen-
done, Repindon.
———Agnes ux. Rob. de, 1976.
———Edwin de, 2570.
———Milo de, capellanus, 2582.
———Ralph f. Galf. de, 1959, 1960.
———Reginald f. Alfwini de, 536.
———Rob. s. of Henry de, 1976.
Reresbi, Reresby, Rerisby, Rersby,
Rerysby.
———Dom. Adam de, 115, 117-119,
122, 2147.
———Deugya w. of Adam de, 115.
———Margery w. of Rad. de, 114,
115, 1815.
———Ralph de, 115-119, 122, 411,
697, 1102, 2144, 2418,
2702.
———Rob. f. Rad de, 114.
———Symon de, 110, 111.
Resintone, John de, 296.
Retherby, Peter de, capellanus, 2251.
Reve, Peter f. Bate dicti, de Stanle,
2193.
———Walter le, 294.
Revel, Reuel, Revell.
———Thomas, 526, 527, 550.
———William, 1946.
Reverewiche, Tho. de, 401.
Reveriis, Ric. de, 171.
Rey, John, Vicar of Scarcliffe, 2276.

Reyd, John, of Hartyll, 2482.
Reydon, Matthew de, 1396.
———Rob. f. Mathei de, 1396.
Reygate, John de, Justice Itinerant, 2013.
Reynald, Reynalde.
———Isabel w. of Thos., 2230.
———Thomas, 2230.
———Thos., LL.B., 2522.
Reynar, Reynare.
———Cecily w. of John, of Swanwyk, 484.
———Cecily w. of Ric., 2210.
———John, of Swanwyk, 484.
———John, s. and h. of Will., of Swanwyke, 2210.
Reyndon, Matthew de, 2762.
———Robert de, 191.
Ribef, Riboef, Ribuf, Rubef, Rybef, Rybof, Ryboffe, Ryboyf, Rybuf, Rybuff, Rybyf.
———Celestra wid. of Walter de, 517, 518.
———Isabel d. of Celestra de, 517, 518.
———Ric. de, Dom. de Etwell, 520, 521.
———Richard de, knt., 1487.
———Rob., of Assheover, 110, 126.
———Dom. Walter de, 114, 116, 517, 519, 697.
———Walter de, mil., 2418.
———Walter de, de Etwell, 2585, 2703.
———Walter f. Walteri de, 518.
———Will. le, of Etwall, 1199.
Rich, Ryche.
———Sir Ric., knt., Lord High Chancellor, 678, 1012.
———Thomas, 1039.
Richard II. of England, 776, 877, 1846. *v.* also under England.
Richard III. of England, 514.
Richard, capellanus, 1681.
———bercarius Alti Decani quondam Lincolniensis, 422.
———Bishop of Coventry, *v.* Peche, R.
———capellanus de Cesterfeld, 542.
———clericus, 532, 1945, 2243.
———clericus, de Aulneton, 1137.
———clericus de Findern, 1276.
———officialis Derbeiensis, 2385.
———prior of Tutbury, 1360.
———rector of Bingham, 1844.
———Thesaurarius Regis, 1080.
———uncle of Hugh, comes Cestrie, 535.
———vicar of Alstonefeld, 2184, 2185, 2355.
Richardson, Rychardson.
———Elias, 1884.
———William, 1886.
———John, of Pynkeston, 1885.
———Richard, 1875.
Richir, Will. f. Will., 710, 711.
Richmond, Margaret, Countess of, 599.
Ridefort, Frembalt de, 1942.
Ridel, Geoffrey, 1078, 1397.
———Geva, 536.

Ridel, Stephen, Chancellor to John, Earl of Morton, 175, 1419.
Rideware, Rydeware.
———John br. of Rog. de, 332.
———Philomena w. of Rog. de, 336.
———Roger de, 332, 338.
———Rog. f. Dom. de Boyleston, 335.
———Rog. s. of Will. de, 385.
———Tho. de, 296.
———Walter de, 331, 332.
———Walter f. Walteri de, 340.
———Walter s. of Will. de, 385.
———Will. de, senescallus, 51, 385, 1113, 1159.
———William de, 215, 1499.
Rigby, Robert, 1350.
Rigeway, Riggewaye, Riggewey, Ruggeweye, Rygeway, Ryggeway.
———John, capellanus, 689, 778, 791.
———Roger de, 735.
———William de, 308, 369, 370, 430, 717, 799.
Rippelay, Richard de, 788.
Riseley, Risele, Risleya, Ryseleghe, Rysley.
———Elias de, 485, 2195, 2196.
———Herbert de, 1337.
———Hugh de, 1998.
———William de, 1334, 2194.
Rissch, Risscher, Alice, relicta Ric. le, of Baslow, 760, 764.
Roard, Will. f. Ad. de, clerk, 2425.
Robert, Archdeacon of Shrewsbury, 1082.
———armiger, 2091.
———Bishop of Coventry and Lichfield, *v.* Stretton, R.
———Canon of Lichfield, 179.
———clericus, 1425, 2570, 2571, 2620, 2721.
———dapifer Com. Cestrie, 2022.
———frater Baldwini, 1726.
———nepos Ailwini f. Swani, 215.
———officialis of Derby, 2638.
———prepositus, 1565.
———prior of Repton, 1704.
———rector de Myldenhale, 332.
———rector of Stowe, 477.
———sacerdos, 2384.
———vicar of Winnefeud [Wingfield], 2605.
Robert, Robart, Robartte.
———Giles, of Birley, 278.
———John, of Birley, 274, 276-278.
———Thomas, 1648.
———William, 277.
Robinson, Robynson.
———Ellen w. of John Guylte, 323.
———Robert, 2705.
———William, 629.
Robyn, Nic., de Bradeburn, 389.
———Roger, 999.
———Thomas, of Nederthorp, 2259, 2260.
Roc, John le, de Bradelg', 136.
Rocheford, John de, 50, 522, 1918.
Rockfield, John, 2467.

Rodd, Christopher, of Haghe, 2263.
Rodde, Hugh, 1305.
Roddesley, Roddesleye, Roddisley.
———Michael f. Nich. de, 2016.
———Nich. f. Leticie de, 1144.
———Nich. f. Mich. de, 1145.
———Nich. f. Rog. de, 2018.
———Reg. f. Reg. de, 2001.
Rode, Philip de la, plaisterer, 2650, 2651.
Rodeheyth, Thos. f. Hen. de, 2657.
———Alice w. of Thos., 2657.
Rodemaretheyt, Rodmerthwayt, Hugh de, 1317, 1318, 1319, 1896.
Rodes, Rodys, Roedes, Roodes.
———Alice wid. of Will. del, de Thurleston, 1320.
———Christopher, de la Halgh in Staveley, 1513.
———John s. of Will. del, de Thurleston, 1320.
———John, of Nederthorp, 2259, 2261.
———John, of Staveley Wodethorpe, 1342, 1343, 2170.
———Robert, 2265, 2253.
———Thomas de, chaplain, 816.
———William, 902, 904.
———Will. s. of Will. del, de Thurleston, 1320.
Rodman, Rob. le, de Yoxhelle, 571.
Roger, Abbot of Beauchief, 131.
———Bishop of Chester, v. Clinton, Rog. de.
———Bishop of Coventry, etc., v. Longespee, Rog.
———capellanus, 531, 2576.
———capellanus, rector de Stapilford, 332.
———clericus, 173, 539, 2620.
———clericus et senescallus, 1727, 1729.
———clericus, fil. Rathnal de Derb', 537.
———dominus de Wendesleye, 290.
———fr. Alberti clerici, 530.
———seniscallus, 1276.
Roger, Rogger.
———John, 930.
———John, of Hanley, 1344.
———John, of Onston, 1069.
———Robert, 1344, 2558.
———Rob., of Hanley, 1128.
———Thomas, of Park Gate, 2558.
Rogers, John, 1186.
———William, 2078.
Rogerson, John, 1186.
Roges, John, 538.
Roland, Bishop of Coventry and Lichfield, v. Lee, Roland.
Roland, Rolande, Rolond, Rolund, Rouland, Roulond, Rowlande.
———Geoffrey de, 1238.
———Godfrey de, 549, 1701, 2082-2084.
———Henry de, 140.
———Johanna de, 1614.
———John de, 2082.
———Margaret d. and h. of Rog., 2084.

Roland, etc., Margery d. of Godfrey de, 2084.
———Oliver de, 140, 1520.
———Peter de, 191, 248, 1212, 1353, 1608, 1613, 2216, 2762.
———Stephen de, 2084.
———Thomas de, 1912.
Role, Henry de la, 1670.
Rollesby, Will., 2564.
Rollesley, Rollesle, Rolleslege, Roulesley, Roulislegh, Roulisleye, Rowleslege.
———Adam de, 2215.
———Dionisius de, 256.
———Joan w. of Nich. de, 2660.
———John de, 247, 249, 254, 951, 1670.
———John, jun., 1670.
———John, of Rollesley, jun., 868.
———John s. of Will., 868.
———Nicholas de, 2660.
Rolleston, Rolliston, Rolston.
———Alice w. of Hen., 1380.
———Arthur de, 345, 1919, 2390, 2391.
———Gervase, 1748.
———Godith w. of Hen., 2363.
———Henry, 2123, 2363, 2364, 2368, 2370, 2371.
———Hen. s. and h. of John, of Swerkeston, 1188, 1189.
———James, 127, 1749, 1750.
———John de, 1177, 1178, 1184.
———Margery de, 1919.
———Ralph de, knt., 338, 974.
———Ralph de, 2100.
———Richard de, 1178, 1184, 1188.
———Thomas de, 1174, 1175, 1180.
———Will. de, sen., 1278.
———Will. de, of La Lee, 1892.
Rolueston, Agnes f. Rob. de, 2611.
———Rob. de, capellanus, 2611.
Rondel, v. Roundel.
Rondithe, Emma ux. Will. de, 364.
———Will. de, quond. serviens Decani Lincolnie, 364.
Ronisleye, Rob. f. Sussanne de, 683.
Ronnesley, Adam de, 248.
Roodes, v. Rodes.
Rooper, Robert, 1119.
Roos, v. Rous.
Roper, Will., of Baslow, 761.
Roppelei, Robert de, 1939.
Ros, Walter de, clerk, 891.
———Will. de, Dom. de Ilkesdone, 1634.
Rose, Agnes, 2105.
———John, 2105.
Rosel, Roselle, Rossell.
———John, of Draycote, 1459.
———Patrick, 2091, 2545.
———William, 47.
———Will., of Dracot, 1030, 2601.
Rossinton, Rossyngton, Rosyngton.
———John de, of Tissinton, 392.
———Nich. de, of Knyveton, 392.
———Roger de, 801, 806.
———Simon de, 882.
———Thomas de, 403.
———Will., of Foston, 1316.

Rostlaston, Ralph de, capellanus, 2040.
Rotheram, Tho., Bishop of Lincoln, Chancellor of England, 1068.
Rothomago, Will. de, 1554.
Rotour, Nich., chaplain, 2184, 2185, 2355.
Rotur, Will., clericus, 556.
Roucester, Roucestre, Dom. John de, 339.
————John de, 882.
————John de, capellanus, 1146.
Roughton, Thomas, 2360.
Roulee, Gralam, 994, 995.
Roumelay, Giles de, 1738.
Roundel, Rondel, Roundell.
————Geoffrey, of Merston, 1364.
————Hugh, 1368.
————Reginald, de Stapenhell, 2618.
————William, 1367.
Rous, Roos, Rus.
————Agnes w. of Rog. le, 1212, 1214.
————John f. Rog. le, 1214, 1215.
————Roger le, 1212.
————Thomas, 323.
————Tho., 10th Lord Roos, 489, 490.
Rouworth, Anabilla, of Hope, 1439.
————Ric. de, of Hope, 1439.
Rowe, Ro, Roe, Roo, Rowhe.
————Henry, 2400, 2401.
————Humphrey, 878.
————John, 2391.
————John, chaplain, 1201.
————John le, of Bradale, 2702.
————Stephen del, clerk, 2110.
————Thomas le, 2741.
————William, 156.
Rowmley, William, 2443.
Ruane, Peter, 1948.
Rudde, Alice, w. of Tho., 1315.
————Hugh, 2103.
Rudyngh, Richard de, 2617.
Ruffus, Nicholas, 2384.
Rufus, Ralph, 27.
————Robert, 238.
Ruggeley, Ric. de, sen., 581.
Ruggeweye, *v.* Rigeway.
Rupheint, Cecily quond. ex. Will., 948.
————Ysabel f. Will., of Hackinhale, 948.
Rupill, Mag. Godfrey de, 1696.
Rus, *v.* Rous.
Russell, Russel.
————Alice w. of Ric., 1363.
————John, 844.
————Ralph, 1727.
————Richard, of Tutbury, 1363, 1366.
————Sir Tho., "rood-prest" of Assheburne, 91.
————Will., of Kyrkelongeleye, 1521.
Russhyndene, Alice w. of Will. de, 1104.
————Will. de, 1104.
Rusteng, Rog., Canon of Lichfield, 1546.
Rybef, Ryboyf, etc., *v.* Ribef.
Rych, *v.* Rich.
Rycher, Matilda, 1057.
————Tho., of Dronfeld, 1050.

Rydeware, *v.* Rideware.
Ryerway, Will. de, 718.
Ryley, Ralph, 2691.
————William, 1357, 1599, 1601.
Ryuall, Peter de, capicerius Pictavensis, 680.
Rypley, Tho., vicar of St. Michael, Derby, 1181.
Rypun, Hugh, 972.
Ryther, Idonia w. of Tho. de, 1103.
————Tho. de, of Netherlangwathe, 1103.
Ryseley, *v.* Riseley.

S.

S————, rector of Chesterfield, 685.
Sabaudia, Peter de, 1555.
Sacheverel, Sacheverell, Sacheverelle, Saucheverel, Saucheuerell, Sauchev-erelle, Saunzcheuerel, Sautcheuerel, Sautdecheuerel, Sawcheuerell, Say-cheuerell.
————Elizabeth, 1916.
————Elizabeth, w. of Ralph, 129.
————Sir Henry, of Morley, 43, 613, 2237.
————Henry, 1886.
————Henry s. and h. of Ralph, 13.
————Hen., of Ratclyf-upon-Sore, 283.
————Isabel w. of Sir Hen., 613.
————John, dominus de Morley, 957.
————John, Lord of Hopwell, 1914.
————John, 129, 1554, 1670, 2230.
————John, of Aston, 1184.
————John, s. and h. of Rauf, 26, 2234, 2235.
————Dom. Oliver de, 2570.
————Oliver de, 44, 326, 1160, 1207.
————Patrick de, 327.
————Rauf, 26, 129, 327, 957, 1189, 1479, 1480, 1672, 1886, 2234, 2235, 2690.
————Rauf, of Ratclif-upon-Sore, 1542.
————Richard, gent., 11.
————Richard, knt., 107, 491.
————Richard, 526, 527, 1916.
————Rob. de, Dom. de Bolton, 327, 328.
————Dom. Robert, 2289.
————Rob. mil., of Hopwell, 22, 1338, 2205.
————Robert, 1123, 1916, 2203.
————Thomas, 1882, 1885, 1886.
————Tho., of Cheuerell Hall, 283.
————Tho., of Kyrkby in Asshfeld, 21, 1460, 1884.
————Tho., of London, 1883.
————Tho., s. and h. of Will., 1481.
————Will., Dom. de Hopwell, 330.
————Will., knt., 1553.
————William, 47, 614, 1882, 1916, 2123, 2206, 2701.
————Will. s. of Sir. Hen., knt., 613.
————Will, of Hopwell, 2209.
Sadeworthe, Rob., of Murcaston, 1690.

Saer, Adam, of Chestrefeld, 838, 844.
———Thomas, 830.
Saghe, Roger de, 1913.
St. Albans, Archdeacon of, 1827.
Saint Andrew, John, 1123.
———Roger de, 1338.
St. David's, Bishop of, *v.* Beke, Thomas.
St. John of Jerusalem, Hospital of, 167,
  168, 1539, 1575, 1772-1774, 2380,
  2715, 2744, 2771.
———Priors. Garner de Neapoli
  [1189], 1539; Philip de
  Thame [1337], 1575;
  William Weston [1535],
  168.
St. John, Sir John, knt., 905.
Sais, Thomas de, 1078.
Sala, Sale.
———John de, 1277.
———Robert de la, 1141.
———Tho. f. Hug. de la, 1140.
Salcroft, Richard, 833.
———Thomas, 833.
Salford, Geoffrey de, 1156.
———Will. de, parson of Longford,
  1580.
Salisbury, William, Earl of *v.*
  Longespec, Will. de.
Sallicosa Mara, Geoffrey de, 940, 2093.
Salloe, Sallou, Sallowe.
———Osbert de, 2090.
———Robert de, 933, 1286, 1453,
  1635, 2201, 2207, 2741.
———William de, 77.
———Will de, of Stanton, 1488.
Salmoun, John, 2501.
Saluanus, Leonius, 1032.
Salvage, John, 2121.
Salvain, Salveyn.
———Augnes, 397.
———Marjory w. of Ralph, 1032.
———Ralph, of Thorp, 1032.
Salysbery, Edward, of Rythlond, 1823.
———Ralph, 1823.
Sampson, John, s. of Rob., of Pleseleye,
  1895.
———Ralph f. Will., de Pleseley,
  1894.
———Richard, 1895.
———Robert, 1895.
———Robert s. of Rob., 1895.
Samson, Abbot of Caen, 1753.
———camerarius Hug. de Bello
  Campo, 534.
Sancta Cruce, Alan de, 1539.
———Hugh de, 571.
———Isabel w. of Hugh de, 571.
Sancta Elena, William de, 1098.
Sancta Frideswida, David de, canon of
  Lincoln, 188.
Sancta Maria, Pagan de, 1397.
Sancto Amando, Alianora, wid. of
  Almaric de, 583, 587, 588.
———Dom. Almaric, 571, 578, 583.
———John de, knt., Dom. de Catton,
  575.
Sancto Botulfo, Henry de, 175.
Sancto Eadmundo, Will. de, 2025.

Sancto Edwardo, Lawrence de, Abbot
  of Burton, 1277, 1699.
Sancto Johanne, Will. de, 2199.
Sancto Mauro, Geoffrey de, 1726.
———Dom. Nich. de, 1166.
———Simon de, 52, 932, 1167, 1698,
  1726, 2383.
———Yseuda de, 1726.
Sancto Paulo, Mary de, Countess of
  Pembroke, 1982.
Sancto Petro, Dom. Brian de, 2154.
———Rob. de, 2642, 2643.
Sandale, John de, 661.
Sandford, Cicely, of Cryche, 286.
Sandiacre, Sancdiacre, Sandiakere,
  Saundiacre.
———Alan f. Walt. de, 2094.
———Athelina de, 2090.
———Baldwin, 2091.
———Geoffrey de, 1338, 2204.
———Mathew de, 1335.
———Peter de, 933, 936, 2090, 2091,
  2545.
———Peter f. Petri de, 2090, 2091.
———Richard de, 1160, 1334, 1335,
  2194.
———Ric. f. Petri de, 940, 941, 2093,
  2094.
———Rob. f. Petri de, clericus, 2093.
———Walter de, 2091.
———William de, 1334, 2094, 2194,
  2196, 2197.
———Will. f. Petri de, 1335.
Sanford, John, 2259.
Sany, John, 346.
Saperton, Sapertone, Sapreton, Sapur-
  ton, Sapurtone, Sapurtune.
———Eliz. w. of Rog. de, 342.
———Hamo de, 2151.
———Hamund de, 1561.
———John de, 341, 1298, 2383.
———Nicholas, 348.
———Robert, 348.
———Rog. de, sen., 341, 342.
———Rog. f. Rog. de, 342, 1306,
  1311, 1312.
———Thomas, 2089.
———Will., capellanus, 930.
Saule, John, of Essebure, 2011.
Saundebi, William de, 2161.
Saundeby, Walter f. Dom. Will. de,
  2154-2156, 2159.
Saunders, John, 1028.
Saunderson, Rob., 2507.
———Thos., of Thwathewaith, 2604.
Saundiacre, *v.* Sandiacre.
Saunfayle, Hugh, 378.
Savage, Sauuage, Sauvage, Sawvage.
———Alice w. of Sir John, 1028.
———Edmund, clerk, 1877, 1878,
  1882.
———Edward, rector of Heth, 1881.
———Lady Elizabeth, 1415.
———Geo., clerk, 645.
———Jacobus, de Lyndeby, 1878.
———John, knt., 870, 871, 997, 1028,
  1409, 1416, 1672, 2266,
  2267.
———John le, coroner of Derby, 1098.

Savage, etc., John le, 144, 145, 1099, 1739.
———John, of Eidale, 1449.
———John, de Hakenall, 1878.
———Margaret wid. of Sir John, 1410.
———Ralph, of Newsted, 1877, 1878, 1882.
———Richard, 525.
———Robert le, 2566.
———Tho., de le Spytell, in Castelton, 567-570, 655, 657.
Saveney, Saueney.
———John f. Rog., of Neuton Sulny, 1759.
———Robert, 1989.
———Roger, 1759.
———Thomas, 1759.
Sawere, Will. f. Thom. de, of Beghton, 270.
Saxton, John de, clerk, 2295.
Say, Avissia wid. of Rob. le, 1434.
———John le, 2423.
Scaiward, Richard, 1638.
Scalt', Richard de, 1082.
Scardeclive, Gregory de, 1080.
Scarleclive, William f. Gregorii de, 1084.
Scarleston, Peter, canon of Lichfield, 620.
Scha, v. Shaw.
Schakelok, v. Shakelock.
Schakersley, v. Shakersley.
Schaldeford, v. Shelford.
Scharf, v. Sharp.
Schatergod, Henry, 155.
Schath, John de, 1912.
Schatton, v. Shatton.
Schavinton, Schauinton, Schauynton, Schawenton.
———John de, 2161.
———Richard de, 2159, 2160.
———Ric. f. Mathei de, 2155.
Schaw, v. Shaw.
Schefeld, Rob. f. Ric. de, 691.
———Will. f. Ric. de, 691.
Schelford, v. Shelford.
Schemeld, Schemyld, v. Shemyld.
Schene, v. Shene.
Schenette, Will., of Pakynton, 2619.
Schentowe, John, 864.
Schepe, Schepeye, Schepye, v. Shepey.
Schepherde, v. Shepherd.
Schercroft, Ralph, of Eyton, 31, 32.
Scheret, v. Shiret.
Scherle, v. Shirley.
Scherston, John, 1192.
Scheyl, Scheylle, v. Shayle.
Schingull, v. Shingull.
Schirebroc, Scherbroke, v. Shirbroke.
Schiremer, Lambert f. Will. de, 434.
Schiret, v. Shiret.
Schirle, Schirlee, Schirley, v. Shirley.
Schobenhale, v. Scobenale.
Schryvenham, Laurence de, vicar of Tiddeswell, 1860.
Schwatwayt, Ric. f. Nich. de, 440.
Schyret, v. Shirret.
Schyrle, v. Shirley.
Scobenhal, Matthew de, 2615.
———Tho. f. Rad. de, 1502.

Scodley, Richard de, 2282.
Scorer, Anker, 1110.
Scortred, Margery w. of Tho., 1691.
———Nicholas, 2685.
———Thomas, 1691.
Scot, Scotte, Skotte.
———Agnes w. of Rob., 2080.
———Hen., chaplain, 2510.
———John, 510.
———John, of Brimington, 495.
———Margery, 2039.
———Richard, 2039, 2053.
———Robert, 2080.
———Will., de Rosliston, 913.
———Will. f. Ric., of Rosliston, 2039.
Scotard, Ric., 363, 713.
Scoth', Fr. Simon de, 1539.
Scriptor, John, de Derby, 1623.
Scrivenere, Will., of Derby, 511.
Scrop, Ric., Bishop of Coventry and Lichfield, 1761.
Scryschlaw, Rog., of Walton, 132.
Segeshale, Seggessale, Segissal, Segisshale.
———G— de, 1390, 1391.
———Rob. de, 2152, 2153, 2154, 2155, 2156.
———Will. s. of Hen. de, 2114.
Segrave, Sedgrave.
———Geoffrey s. of Thos., 2254.
———Gilbert de, 912, 2027.
———Joan w. of Geoffr., 2254.
———John de, Dom. de Segrave, 2035.
———John de, 1322.
———John s. and h. of Nich. de, 2028.
———Nicholas de, 2028.
———Stephen de, Justice, 487, 682, 909-911, 1160-1162, 1663, 1697, 1955, 2024-2026.
———Steph. f. Joh. de, 2035.
———Thomas, 2254.
Seil, Seile, Seille, Sele.
———Agatha de, 2760.
———Lucian de, 2760.
———Michael, 1268.
———Ralph de, constabularius, 532. 2621.
———Ralph, of Bonsall, 310.
Seka, Mag. Rob. de, 1544.
Seket, Adam, 497.
Seladon, Selladon.
———Ralph de, 1396.
———Thomas, 1070.
Selby, Robert, 1371.
Seldeford, v. Shelford.
Sele, v. Seil.
Seliock, Seliok, Selioke, Selyok. Selyoke, Sellyok.
———John s. of Rob. de, 1042.
———John, 1780, 1782, 1783, 2468. 2477.
———Richard, 2451, 2459, 2469.
———Robert, 1019, 1020, 1776.
———Rob. f. Tho. de, 1042.
———Thomas, 2471.
Selvein, Selveyn, Selven, Selveyn.
———Agnes f. Rad., 1034.

Selvein, etc., Geoffrey, 879.
———John, 1131, 1133, 1151, 1630, 2016.
———John, de Reggusley, 1157.
———John, of Winster, 290.
———Nicholas, 1147-1149, 1576, 1577.
———Nich. f. Joh., 2624.
———Ralph, 542.
———Robert, 1034.
———William, 661.
———*v.* also Salvain.
Sely, George, 1001.
Semper, John, of Asshe, 2395.
———Thomas, 2400.
Sempringham, Ralph de, Dean of Lichfield, 1705.
Senteney, Walter de, Abbot of Dale, 934, 1544, 2284.
Sergeant, Sergant, Sergeaunt, Seriand, Seriant, Seriaunt, Serjant, Serjaunt.
———Adam, 1051, 1062, 2461.
———Alice w. of Rob., 1062.
———Cecilia w. of Will le, 1029.
———John, 1051, 1060.
———Matthew le, of Haddon, 1706.
———Nicholas le, 1173, 1373.
———Richard le, 1170, 2114.
———Robert, 235, 1061, 1062.
———Rob., of Dronfield, 2458, 2460.
———William le, 1029, 1173.
———Will., of Bradwey, 1060.
Serlby, Serleby, Nicholas, 1513, 2259.
Serle, Thomas, 2137.
Seruelauedy, Will., of Derby, 970.
Sewal, 536.
Sewardsithe, Emma, w. of Rob. de, 1665.
———Rob. f. Walteri de, 1665.
Seylyn, Ranulf, of Rotinton, 1766.
Seymor, Dom. Nicholas de, 1754, 1757.
Seynpere, Ralph de, of Murcaston, 1691.
Seyntandrew, *v.* Saint Andrew.
Seyton, Mag. Rog. de, Justice, 1279.
Shahe, *v.* Shaw.
Shaille, *v.* Shayle, Isabel wid. of John, 2131.
Shakelock, Schakelok, Henry, 1372, 1375.
Shakere, Ric., warden of All Saints', Derby, 1002.
Shakerley, Shacurley.
———John, 2455.
———Rob., of Longsdon, 1617.
Shakersley, Schakersley.
———Geoffrey, 1616.
———John, 1616.
———Richard, 1616.
———Robert, 102, 103.
Shakulton, Henry, 1482.
Shalcross, Shalcros, Shalcrus.
———Agnes f. Benedicti de, 2161.
———Anthony, 657.
———John, 628.
———Leonard, 657.
Shanynton, Tho., of Farley, 1517.
Shardelawe, Shardelowe, Shardlowe.
———John de, 977, 1914.
———Ric. de, chaplain, 793.
Sharman, Robert, 2000.

Sharp, Scharp.
———Rich., chaplain, 2354, 2357.
———Tho., chaplain, 806.
Shatton, Schatton.
———Peter de, 2, 515.
———Will. f. Petri de, 1430.
Shaw, Scha, Schae, Schage, Schagh, Schaghe, Schaw, Schawe, Sha, Shaghe, Shahe, Shaugh, Shawe.
———Adam del, 433.
———Agnes w. of John, 2519.
———Christopher, 2531.
———*al.* Somersall, Elizabeth, w. of John, 1384.
———Gilbard, of Walton, 7.
———Jocosa wid. of Rog. del, of Elkeston, 1489.
———John, 447, 1072, 1856.
———*al.* Somersall, John, of Chesterfeld, 1384.
———John, of Doghole, 466.
———John, of Somersall, 454, 456, 2149, 2150.
———John s. and h. of John, of Somersale, 2519.
———John s. of Ric., of Brampton, 452, 454, 456.
———Margaret d. of Thos., 2150.
———Oliver, chaplain of Brampton, 167.
———Richard, 468, 470, 2294.
———Rob. f. Will. del., of Brampton, 433.
———Roger, 1817.
———Rog., of Brampton, 453.
———Thomas de, 1489.
———Thos., of Somersall, 2149, 2150.
———William de, 784, 2476.
———Will. s. of John, late of Chanderell, 458.
———Will de, sen., of Wadscholf, 446, 447.
Shayle, Shaille, Scheylle.
———Isabel w. of John, 2131.
———John, 1761.
———Nicholas de, 1181.
———Rob. de, of Elleford, 576.
Shead, Richard, 1812.
Sheldon, Hew, jun., of Monyashe, 1725.
Shelford, Schaldeford, Scheldeford, Schelford, Seldeford.
———Anabilia quondam ux. Rob. de, 1689.
———Henry, 1470.
———Hen. de, of Murcastone, 1691.
———Robert de, 1501, 1502, 1688, 2546.
Shelley, Will., knt., 1680.
Shemyld, Schemeld, Schemyld.
———Rob., 233, 1062, 2447, 2460, 2461, 2476.
———William, 1050, 1061.
Shemyng, Shymmyng, Will., 1064, 1065, 1453.
Shene, Schene, Thomas de 1645, 2130.
Shepey, Schepeye, Schepye.
———Agnes w. of John de, 541.
———John de, Dean of Lincoln, 1693.

Shepey, etc., John de, lord of Smythesby, 541.
———John de, 1980.
———Dom. Will de, knt., 2013.
———Will de, of Caldewal, 2061.
Shepherd, Schepherde, Shepard, Sheperde, Shepherde.
———Cecily w. of John, of Catton, 590.
———Elizabeth f. Petri le, 499.
———John, 2471.
———John, sythesmyth, 611.
———John, of Alshop, 42.
———John, of Catton, 591.
———John, of Marketon, 1653.
———John f. Joh., 2056.
———Robert, 1891.
———Thomas, 1625.
Shepiere, Philip, 583.
Sherard, Ralph, 636.
Shingull, Schingull, Shyngull, Shynggl.
———Adam, 1366.
———William, 1366-1368.
Shirbroke, Schirbroke, Schirebrok.
———Robert, 446.
———Tho. f. Joh. de, 1894, 1895.
Shiret, Scheret, Schirret, Schyret, Shirret, Shyret.
———Elizabeth, 1305, 1308.
———Rob., sen., 1290, 1310, 2100.
———Rob. f. Rob., 1298, 1310.
———Will. f. et her. Rob., de Foston, 1308-1310.
Shirley, Scherle, Schirle, Schirlee, Schirleg, Schirley, Schyrle, Shirle, Shirlee, Shirleye, Shyrle, Sirley, Sirly.
———Elias de, carpenter, 2650, 2651.
———Hugh f. Will. de, 2002.
———James, dom. de Shirley, 1629, 2002, 2004, 2006, 2008, 2720, 2723.
———James de, 1689, 2711.
———James f. Sewalli de, 2005.
———John de, 96, 297.
———Margaret w. of Ralph de, 67.
———Ralph, knt., 337-339, 1588, 1591, 2122.
———Ralph, 67, 879, 1592, 1594, 1597.
———Ric. f. Hen. de, 2299.
———Robert de, knt., 2014.
———William, 524.
———Will. de, chaplain, 2714.
Shorthose, Marragdus, 2669.
———William, 1190.
Shrewsbury, Earls of, v. Talbot.
Shropschyre, Alice w. of Regin. de, 2404.
———Regin. f. Rob. de, 2404, 2406.
———Robert de, 2405.
Shypley, Elizabeth w. of Tho., 1004.
———Tho., of London, 1004.
Shyrwode, Alice de, 1925.
———John de, 1925.
Sidenal, Sidenale, Sidenhale, Sydenale, Sydenhale.
———Ralph de, 1092, 2492, 2493.
———Roger de, 1893, 2282, 2566.

Siliott, William, 207.
Silvester, magister, 1081.
———vicar of Gt. Baddow, 1949.
Simon, Abbat of Darley, 1980.
———Abbot of Stanley, 1632.
———clericus, 1954.
———fr. Hen. Domini de Morsbur', 1727, 1729.
———nepos Comitisse Matilde, 1940.
———prepositus, 134.
———rector of Trusley, 2385, 2568.
Sippele, Matilda de, 28.
Sirley, Sirly, v. Shirley.
Skargille, Nicholas de, 1127.
Skeggeby, Thomas de, 732.
Skinner, Skynner, Skynnere.
———John, 222, 2318.
———Nicholas, 2318.
———Rob., de Baumforde, 221, 222.
———Rob., de Thornhyll, 2318.
———Roger, 2318.
———Rosa, w. of Rob., 221.
———Thomas, 809.
———William, 221, 222.
Skipwith, Skypewith.
———Margaret w. of Will. de, 1022.
———Will. de, 1022.
———Dom. Will. de, 1899.
Skyrbrok, Thomas de, 2121.
Skyres, John, 2259.
Slack, Adam, 2216.
Slayer, Henry, of Chaddesden, chaplain, 2183.
Sleford, Will. de, Dean of the King's Chapel at Westminster, 342.
Slegh, Hugh, 1525.
Slore, John, 342.
Smale, John, of Allerhampton, 865.
———Thomas, 865.
———William, 865.
Smallege, Ralph de, 972.
Smalley, Elena w. of John, 81.
———John, 81.
———Robert, 1183, 1393.
———Rob., of Alwaston, 1181.
———Will., parson of Morton, 1869.
Smetheley, Nicholas, 2233, 2236.
———William, vicar of Youlgrave, 303, 2235.
Smith, Smyth, Smythe.
———Adam le, of Bondishal, 312.
———Agnes w. of Tho., 1482.
———Alice wid. of John le, de Moniasch, 1717.
———Clement, knt., 1625.
———George, 1996.
———Henry, 838.
———Hen., of Dore, 1049.
———Hen. f. Joh., 1048.
———Hugh, 317, 318.
———Joan w. of Thos., 2059, 2067.
———Joan w. of Will., 2067.
———John, chaplain, 2357.
———John, 595, 1996, 2358, 2684, 2690.
———John le, of Birchovere, 297.
———John f. Ade, 502.
———Richard, 597, 2266, 2267.
———Richard, rector of Yrton, 2690.

Smith, etc., Ric., s. and h. of Tho., 1486.
———Robert, 156, 272, 315, 316, 1915, 2665.
———Rob., of Coventry, 1454.
———Rob., of Kyrk Yreton, 1485.
———Rob., of Warsop, 2554.
———Rob. s. of John, 2690.
———Roger, chaplain, 1994.
———Thomas, 601, 1482.
———Thos., of Medilton, 2691.
———Thomas, de Thorp, 2059, 2067.
———Tho. f. Joh., of Dronfeld, 1049.
———Thos. s. and h. of Thos., 2697.
———William, 597, 2535.
———Will., de Ekyngton, 1341.
———Will., of Morysburgh, 272, 275.
———Will. f. Joh., de Ascheford, 1238.
———Will. f. Tho., 2067.
———Will. son of Will., 272.
Smylter, John, 1715.
Snelleston, Geoffrey de, 135.
Snepston, Snipeston, Snypeston.
———Philip de, 1961.
———Robert le, 1960, 1969-1971.
———Warin de, 1726.
Sneterton, Snetirton, Sniterton, Snitertona, Snitertone, Snitterton, Snittertone, Snuterton, Snutertone, Snyterton, Snytertone.
———Cecily w. of Ranulph de, 2147.
———Dunyig de, 2144.
———John f. Ranulphi de, sen., 1476.
———Jordan de, 28, 135, 139, 926, 1609, 1726, 1820, 1821, 2640, 2641.
———Ralph f. Gilb., 2144.
———Ranulph de, 14, 15, 16, 293, 949, 1475, 1476, 1665, 2145-2148.
———Ranulph f. Ran. de, 15-17, 1475, 1491.
———Tho. s. of Ranulf de, 949.
Snow, John, 2671.
Soleny, Solney, etc., v. Sulney.
Solfuene, Sir Averey, 1286.
Somer, Margaret w. of Chrisopher, 1484, 1485.
———Roger, 2099.
———al. Somers, Tho. s. and h. of Christopher, 1484, 1486.
Somerbrige, Peter f. Hug. de, 2419.
Somercotes, Thomas, 2190.
Somerforde, John de, 1690.
Somerlesowe, Somerlese, Somerleson, Somerleso, Somerlesue.
———Adam de, 2424.
———John de, 1045.
———John f. Ade de, 1036.
———John s. of Rob., the clerk of, 810.
———Nich. f. Joh. de, 2436, 2437, 2460.
Somers, Hen., Chancellor of the Exchequer, 1873.
Somersal, Somersale, Somersall, Somersell.
———Hugh de, 417, 422.

Somersal, etc., John, v. Shawe, John.
———John, 468, 2163.
———Ric. f. Herberti de, 399.
———Robert de, 705.
———Stephen f. Hug., 429.
———Thomas de, 1044, 2498, 2500.
———Thos. f. Herberti, 399.
———Tho. f. Hug. de, 439.
———Tho. f. Marg. de, 2157, 2158.
———Tho. f. Rob. de, 431-433, 437, 439.
———Will. f. Alex. de, 2158.
———Will. f. Rob. de, 358.
Somersdeby, Gilbert de, 270.
Somervil, Somervile, Somervill, Somerville, Sumerville.
———Alan de, 2782, 2783.
———Alice de, 2763, 2764.
———Rodbert de, 215.
———Roger de, coroner for co. Derby, 201.
———Roger, 1034, 1102, 1956, 2030, 2325, 2328, 2418.
Somery, John de, chaplain, 2162.
Someter, Ric., de Neuton, 1758.
Sonde, William, rector of Blore, 2138.
Sondy, Will., 1655.
Sonyoure, John, 302.
Sotheron, Hugh le, 201.
Sotteby, Hugh de, canon of Lichfield, 189.
Sottewell, John de, 1626.
Souch, v. Zouch.
Souter, John le, 280, 313.
Southwell, Ric. de, chaplain, 770.
Sparewater, Ralph, 139, 335.
Spari, Ric. le, 130.
Spencer, Spenser.
———Adam le, 1039, 1046.
———Henry, le, 1891.
———John, 2512.
———John f. Ric., 2541.
———Roger, 1747.
———Walter, of Walton Grange, 2509.
———William, 1515.
Spendlove, Spendeloue, Spendeluve.
———Elen w. of Ric., 1377, 1379.
———Henry, 334.
———Johanna wid. of John, 1378, 1379.
———John, 1379.
———Richard, 1377, 1379.
———William, 404.
Spicer, Spycer.
———John, 1052, 1182.
———Richard, 1692.
———Ric., Bailiff of Ashbourne, 79.
———Ric., of Assheburn, 81, 883.
Spichfat, Simon, 2203.
Spondon, Hen. f. Nigelli de, 2171.
———John, chaplain, 1228, 1233, 1234.
Sprott, Tho., of Asshmerbroke, 602.
Stabeler, John, 2513.
Stadone, Richard de, 1244.
Stafford, Estafford, Staford, Staforth, Staforthe, Stafforth.
———Family of, 1269.

Stafford, etc., Alice w. of John, 1232, 1235, 1237.
———Alice w. of Sir Tho., 1867, 1872, 1873.
———Anthony s. of Humphrey, 1268.
———Edm. de, clerk, 2184, 2185.
———Edm. de, canon of Lichfield, 2355.
———Eliz. w. of Nich. de, 2185, 2355, 2357.
———Elizabeth, w. of Rob., 1259, 1260.
———Gundreda w. of Dom. Rob. de, 1169.
———Hen., rector of Treton, formerly "preceptor" of Halomeshire, 464.
———Hen., of Beley, 259-261.
———Hen. de, of Myddelton Clyff, 1245, 1247.
———Humfrey, of Eyam, 1725.
———Humphrey, Duke of Buckingham, 319, 489, 490.
———Humphrey de, 7th Earl of Stafford, 2392.
———Humphrey, 1266, 1268.
———Humphrey s. of Hum., 1268.
———Isabella w. of Ric., de, 1213.
———Isabella wid. of Will. de, 61.
———John, Archbishop of Canterbury, 490.
———John, Abbot of Burton-on-Trent, 1279.
———John de, 1712.
———John I. de, of Eyam, 549, 1219-1229, 1236, 1237, 1282, 1284, 1464, 1467, 1701, 1712, 2357.
———John. II., of Eyam, 623, 1195, 1237-1242, 1244, 1245, 1247, 1252, 1254, 1721, 2084-2087, 2736.
———John III., of Eyam, 1249, 1255, 2085, 2086.
———John, of Mydelton, 1250.
———John s. of Hen., of Eyam, 1242.
———John f. Rog. de, of Eyam, 1218.
———John s. of Will de, 57.
———Margaret w. of John, 1249, 1255, 1261, 2085-2087.
———Matilda w. of Will. de, 1219.
———Nich. de, knt., 76, 2184, 2185, 2354-2357.
———Nicholas, 1264.
———Nich., of Shrewsbury, 1263.
———Nich. f. Joh. de, 1466, 1467.
———Ric., lord of Clyfton, 74.
———Richard I., of Eyam, 1207.
———Ric. II. s. of Ric. de, 1207-1211, 1213.
———Richard III. de, 1231, 1232, 1235, 1236, 1805, 2085.
———Richard IV. de, 1261, 1285, 1724.
———Ric. s. and h. of John, 1264, 2087.
———Ric., cous. and heir of Rob., 1262.

Stafford, etc., Ric. de, of Highlowe, 1237.
———Dom. Rob. I. de, 1169, 1170, 2585.
———Robert II. de, 1248, 1253, 1257-1260, 1723, 1724, 2086-2324.
———Robert III., 550, 1285.
———Rob. s. of John, 1232, 1235, 1237.
———Roger de, 1216, 1324, 1463.
———Rog. s. of John, 1237.
———Rog. s. of Ric. de, 1209, 1210.
———Rog. f. Rog. de, 1211.
———Roland s. of Humphrey, 1268.
———Thomas, knt., 1867.
———Thomas de, 57.
———Thomas de, of Asschebourne, 37.
———William I. de, 57.
———Will. II. f. Will. de, 1219.
———William III. de, 1244.
Stainsby, Staynesby, Staynusby, Steinesby, Steynesby, Steynisby.
———Jocelin, 697, 1034, 1088, 1548, 2702.
———John de, 2329.
———Will., mil., 2282.
———Dom. William de, 426, 1896.
———William de, 114, 1317-1319.
Stake, Nich., de Swarkeston, 1683.
Staley, Staleys.
———Agnes w. of Nich., of Hope, 1446.
———Christofer, 1446.
———Elias, Elizeus, Ellys, etc., 564, 566-568, 655, 1449, 1450.
———Nich., of Hope, 629, 1446.
Stanclif, Stanclive, John de, 1640.
———Nicholas de, 173.
———Rob. de, diaconus, 948.
Standiche, Roger, 347.
Stanedon, John de, 1708.
Stanes, Mag. Ric. de, Justice, 1279.
Stanford, Staunford.
———Mag. A—— de, 182.
———Geoffrey de, steward, 920.
———Will. de, canon of Lichfield, 1427.
———Will. de, 2335.
Stanley, Stanle, Stanleg, Stanleye.
———Adam f. Bate de, 2193.
———Everard de, 1632, 2197.
———Humphrey, 2398.
———John, knt., 523, 2288.
———John, 985, 1111, 2392.
———Rob. s. of John, 1111.
———Thomas, Earl of Derby, 1603.
———Thomas, 594.
———Thos., scutifer, 2539-2541.
———William, knt., 523.
———William de, 1741.
———Will. f. Will. de, 2193.
Stanlowe, Adam de, 1819.
Stanop, Edward, 2120.
Stanshop, John f. Joh. de, 42.
Stanton, Stantone, Stantona, Stantun, Staunton, Staunthona, Stauntona.
———Adam de, 1610, 2733, 2775.

30

Stanton, etc., Adam f. Rob. de, 2212, 2213.
——Alex. s. of Rob. de, 2088.
——Clemencia w. of Tho., 2650, 2651.
——David de, 2545.
——Eliz. de, 1917, 1918.
——Geoffrey de, 1755, 1756.
——Hugh de, 2651.
——Hugh f. Rob. de, 2225, 2226.
——Isabella, 1917, 1918.
——John de, 46.
——John de, chaplain, 1920, 1922-1924, 1927, 1928.
——John del Lee f. Ric. de, 2217.
——Richard de, vicar of Melburn, 1961.
——Richard de, clerk, 2214.
——Richard de, 2218.
——Richard f. Ad. de, 2216, 2224.
——Rob. de, knt., 2654.
——Rob. de, 135, 173, 571, 662, 1208, 1274, 1757, 2130, 2214, 2735.
——Rob. f. Ad. de, 2212.
——Robert s. of Ralph de, 2088.
——Rob. f. Ric. de, 2221-2223.
——Rob. f. Walt. de, 2194.
——Simon de, 1939.
——Thomas de, 1917, 1918.
——Thomas f. et h. Hug. de, 2650, 2651.
Stantonleyis, Tho. f. Hen. de, 291, 292.
Stapenhill, Stapehull, Stapenhell, Stapenhall, Stapnhul, Stepenhull.
——John de, 540, 1754-1756, 2027, 2030, 2587.
——John de, seneschal of Burton, 2611.
——Ralph de, 1276.
——Ralph f. Will., clerici de, 2611.
——Robert de, 1197.
——Will. de, 1962.
Stapleford, Stapelford, Stapilford.
——Adam f. Rob. de, 2092.
——Hugh de, 548.
——Ric. f. Rob. de, 936.
——Rob. f. Will. de, 2092.
Stapleton, Isabel w. of Sir Bryan, 2518.
——Milo de, 2246.
——Nicholas de, 2608.
Stapulle, William de, 1497.
Starky, Sterky.
——Edmund, of Stretton-on-Dunsmore, 596.
——John f. Rog., 589.
——Will. f. Rog., of Northwich, 590.
Statham, Stathom, Stathum.
——Elizabeth w. of John, of Horsley, 524.
——German, of Tansley, 2307.
——Henry, lord of Morley, 2123.
——Henry, 1189, 1459, 1886, 2123.
——Hen., of Morley, 894.
——Hen., of Nottingham, 525.
——Joan w. of W. Zouch, 1916, 2123.

Statham, etc., John, 2362.
——John, of Gonerton, 525.
——John, of Tansley, 2307.
——John s. and h. of John, of Horseley, 524.
——Richard de, 987.
——Roland, of Tansley, 2307.
——Tho., knt., 1189, 2362.
Staveley, Hospitallers of, 228, 2242.
Staveley, Stafeleg, Staffelay, Staueleg.
——John, 557, 1442.
——Ralph de, knt., 1440.
——Richard de, 1080.
——Ric. nepos Pet. clerici de, 2248.
——Will. de, chaplain, 763.
——Will. de, rector of Tetwick, 780.
Stavensby, Alex. de, Bishop of Coventry and Lichfield, 178, 179, 182, 331, 935, 1953, 2385.
——Ric. de, Treasurer of Lichfield, 178, 179.
——Richard de, bro. of the Bp. of London, 1953.
Stayne, William de, 1899.
Staynton, Steynton.
——Elizabeth w. of Will., 102, 103.
——Thos., vicar of Trusley, 2396.
——Will de, 271.
——Will., of Peterboro', 102, 103.
Stedman, Stedeman.
——Jauin, 735.
——Roger, 557, 2118.
Steel, John, rector of Sudbury, 1354.
Stephen, capellanus, 2125.
——clericus de Rependona, 533, 537, 1940.
——clericus, fil. Osberti de Ticheam, 537.
——fr. Will. sacerdotis de Rapendon, 1945.
——persona de Cestirfeld, 412.
——sacerdos, 534.
——vicar of Brampton, 420.
Stepul, John de, 2664.
Ster, Stere, Sterre.
——Henry, 1769.
——Rob. le, de Calton, 1134.
——William, 70.
Sterky, v. Starky.
Stevenson, Stevynson.
——John, sen., of Brampton, 453.
——John, 473, 1655, 1656.
——Matilda w. of John, 1817.
——Richard, 1817, 2484.
——Rog., of Brampton, 449.
——Will., of Alfreton, 449.
Steverdale, John s. and h. of Will., 2233.
——Richard, 301.
Steynesby, etc., v. Stainsby.
Steynton, v. Staynton.
Stiveton, Hugh de, 2773.
——Sara de, 2773.
Stodle, Thomas de, 578.
Stoffyn, Stuffin, Stuffyn.
——Hugh, 1317-1319, 1894-1896, 2121.
——Richard, 499-501, 732, 738, 739, 2313.

Stok', Stoke.
———Avice w. of Gerebert de, 2776.
———Gerebert de, 2776.
———Hugh f. Gerberti de, 1790.
———John de, 2095.
———Rob. s. and h. of Tho., of Derby, 992.
———Seer de, 1942, 1945.
Stokeport, Rob. de, mil., 2536.
———Rob. de, 1274.
Stokes, William, 588.
Stolbaley, John de, clerk, 1017.
Stone, Johanna w. of Will. de, 258.
———Will. de, of Harewode, 258.
Stones, John del., of Ibul, 1477.
———William le, 316.
Stonore, John de, Justice, 2251.
Stonthacker, Stonethakker, Innocent, of Chastrefeld, 748, 815.
Store, Reginald, 2617.
Storer, Storar, Storor.
———Robert, 2690.
———Thomas, 324, 1484, 2684.
———William, 2671.
Stortrede, Henry, of Muggington, chaplain, 2693.
Stoteville, Stotvill, Stutevill, Stutevilla.
———John de, Dom. de Ekynton, 1095.
———John de, 1727.
———William de, 1198, 2247.
Stouerdale, Will., chaplain, 2369.
Stowe, John de, 783.
———Will. de, 1965.
Stownesby, Isabel de, 2201.
———Philip de, 2201.
Strandes, Rob. de, 2227.
Strangholf, Robert, 2560.
Strangways, James, 831.
———Jas., Justice of C. Pleas, 2457.
Stranley, Strenley.
———Hugh, knt., 537, 1983.
———Joan de, 1983.
———John de, knt., 1983.
Stratford, Ralph, Bp. of London, 1973.
Stratton, v. Stretton.
Strelley, Sterelly, Streddeley, Stredlega, Stredley, Stredleya, Strely, Streyleye.
———Alice w. of Phil. de, 204.
———Dom. Hugh de, 327, 2013.
———Hugh de, Ballivus de alto Pecco, 619.
———Hugh de, 2118.
———Joan f. Phil. de, 2734.
———John, 2120.
———John f. Nic. de, knt., 300.
———Nich., knt., 1873.
———Nich. de, 2734.
———Phil. f. Phil. de, 204.
———Robert, 2120.
———Dom. Will. de, 1464.
———Will. de, 2734.
Strenley, v. Stranley.
Strete, Ric., clerk, 1781.
———Tho., warden of Chaddesden Chantry, 611, 612.
Stretehay, John, 598, 600.
———Tho., 600.

Stretleye, Strethleg, Stretleg'.
———Nich. f. Hug. de, 662.
———Philip de, 2093.
———Sire Rob. de, lord of Chilewelle, 974.
Stretton, Stratton, Streton, Strton.
———Aline quond. ux. Herv. de, 2418.
———Elyas de, 1552.
———Henry de, 398.
———John, s. and h. of Walter de, 1170.
———Osbert f. Walt. de, 2285.
———Pavia de, 2285.
———Rich. de, mil., Dom. de Unstone, 2418-2421, 2426, 2434.
———Dom. Ric. de, 1396.
———Ric. fil. Herv. de, 1031.
———Ric. f. Ric. de, 2418, 2422, 2423.
———Robert, Bp. of Coventry, 609.
———Dom. Rog. de, 108, 109, 934, 2284.
———Tho. de, Dean of Lichfield, 208, 1441.
———Walter de, 48, 1170, 2023.
———Walter f. Will. de, 2285.
———Dom. Will. de, 398.
———William de, persona, 2023.
———Will. de, 2285, 2743.
Strindes, Stryndes.
———Richard del, 1798.
———Robert del, 1371.
Strongeshul, Rob. de, seneschal, 141, 152.
Strynger, Stryngar.
———John, of Derby, 999.
———Ric., of Derby, 994, 999.
Stryt, Adam del., 1477.
Stubbez, Thomas, 2320.
———William, 2320.
Stubbyng, Stubbinge, Stubbinges, Stubbynge, Stubbynges.
———Giles, of Hulme, 2518.
———Godfrey del, 117.
———Hawisia ux. Godefridi del, 119.
———Johanna ux. Sim. del, 118.
———John, 689, 2518, 2604.
———John de, chaplain, 774.
———Robert de, 2493.
———Rob. de la, 120.
———Simon f. Godefridi del, 118.
———William, 223.
Stubley, Stobbeleye, Stubleye.
———John de, 1035-1037, 2428.
———John, of Wodsmythes, 2443.
———Nicholas de, 1035.
———William de, 131.
Stuffin, v. Stoffyn.
Sturston, Hervy de, 2721.
Stuteville, v. Stoteville.
Stylton, Hen., 1383.
Suan, Herbert, 1622.
Sub-bosco, Rob. f. Rob. de, 2615.
Sub-monte, Nicholas, 226, 227.
Suckthorn, Will. de, 2780.
Sudbery, Ric. de, rector of Crofton, 1440.
———Thomas, 829.

Sudbury, John, Warden of Pembroke
    Coll., Cambridge, 1982.
Sudeley, Ralph, Lord, 489, 490.
Suein, 2242.
Suet, John, 47.
Suffolk, Earl and Marquis of, *v.* Pole.
Sugkenhull, Petronilla de, 2777.
———Robert de, 2777.
Sulby, James de, 1217.
———Robert de, 1222.
Sulghl', Geoffrey, clericus de, 1083.
Sulney, Solenei, Soleni, Solenneio,
    Soleny, Suleini, Sulene, Suleny,
    Sulign', Suligny, Sulne, Sulney,
    Sulni, Sulny.
———A— de, 486.
———Aldred, knt., 1376.
———Alfred de, 536.
———Alured I. de, 1753.
———Alured II. de, 1753.
———Dom. Alured III. de, Dom. de
        Neuton super Trentam,
        knt., 1758, 2585.
———Alured IV. de, knt., 1760, 1863-
        1866, 1869.
———Auered de, 1176.
———Dom. John de, 1470, 1661.
———John, knt., 1872.
———Norman de, Dom. de Neuton,
        1754-1757, 1954.
———Robert, 1759.
———Rob. f. Aluredi de, knt., 1759.
———Will. de, clerk, 1758.
Sumetal, Walter de, 239.
Super-le-Hal, William, 1971.
Sureys, Sures, Sureis.
———Matilda f. Will. le, 2653.
———Matthew le, 174, 177.
———Peter le, 2639.
———Peter f. Will. le, 2653.
———Will. le, 2630.
Surrey, Earl of, *v.* Warenne, John de.
Susanson, John, 102-104.
———*al.* Bryggesende, Tho., of Peter-
        boro', 104.
———Will., jun., 102-104.
Suthrone, Henry de, 202.
Suthworth, Tho., rector of Normanton,
    1885.
Sutton, Soton, Suttone, Suttonia.
———Adelicia w. of Gerard de, 1787.
———G— de, 1078.
———Dom. Gerard de, 1661, 1787,
        2144.
———Henry de, 2148, 2289.
———Hen. de, magister scolar. de
        Cestrefeld, 2499.
———Herui sacerdos de, 530.
———Johanna w. of John, 121.
———John de, 293, 949, 1665, 1666,
        2145, 2148.
———John de, of Nottingham, 778.
———John, of Wynster, 1478.
———John f. et h. Joh. de, 2146.
———John f. Ric. de, de Averham,
        121.
———Jordan de, 1896, 2703.
———Richard, 551, 1266, 1655, 1656,
        1982, 2246.

Sutton, etc., Dom. Rouland de, 1423,
    1425.
———Simon de, prior of Repton, 541.
———Thomas, 1331, 1924, 2148.
———Tho., "of the Kynge's medewe
        nighe Derby," 1015.
———Will., clerk, 820, 1386, 1387.
———Will. f. Tho. de, 1084.
Suttone-in-Dal, Avice f. Al. de, 2291.
Suyenell, Nicholas, 2747.
Swalo, Swaloe, Swalowe, Thomas, 827,
    839, 2316.
Swanne, Joan, 2076.
Swannyld, Henry, 1910.
Swanswyre, John, 978.
Swarkeston, Tho. f. Rog. de, 1683.
———Will. de, 1972.
Swathuyt, Matild. quond. ux. Nich. de,
    2494.
Swathweyt, Nich. f. Joh. de, 2493.
Sway, Thomas, 2247.
Swepston, Will. de, clericus, 1682.
Sweyn, Will., de Tanesley, 2302.
Swift, Swyffte.
———Gilbert, clerk, 1570.
———John, Abbot of Beauchief, 242.
Swillyngton, Dom. Rob. de, knt., 2607-
    2609.
Swynok, Elen w. of Tho., 1437.
———Tho., 1437.
Swynorton, Dom. Roger de, knt., 2017.
Sy . . . ., Ralph, knt., 1868.
Syatton, Peter de, 1422-1425.
Sydenale, Sydenhale, *v.* Sidenal.
Syerd, Richard de, 1424.
Sylverlok, John, 1445.
Sylvester, *v.* Silvester.
Syminel, Robert, 1956.
Symond, Hen. f. Joh., de Fostone, 1297,
    1299, 1303.
———John, 1315.
Sympson, Margaret, 848.
Symsone, James, clerk, 2294.
Syrefort, Rob. de, 2125.

T.

Tabbe, Robert, 1919.
Taddel', Taddeleg'.
———Ivo de, 53, 2740.
———Ric. f. Hen. de, 2740.
———Ric. fil. Rog. de, 53.
Tadinton, Tadigton, Tadygton, Tadyng-
    ton, Tadynton.
———Henry de, 1323, 1324.
———Henry f. Ivonis de, 2299.
———John, de Assheburne, chaplain,
        1620, 2164.
Tagg, Tagge, Will., of Matlock, 1673,
    1674, 1676, 1677.
Taillour, *v.* Taylor.
Talbot, Talebot, Thaleboth.
———Alice q. f. ux. Will., 2040, 2043.
———Cecily ux. Will., 2038.
———Francis, 5th Earl of Shrews-
        bury, 2280.
———George, 4th Earl of Shrews-
        bury, 237, 1348.
———Dom. John, 1165.

Talbot, etc., John, Lord Furnival and [1442] 1st Earl of Shrewsbury, 557, 1495, 1722, 1932, 2118, 2446.
———John, knt. [2nd Earl of Shrewsbury, 1453], 1722.
———John, 3rd Earl of Shrewsbury, 243, 550, 854.
———John, Lord Lisle, 489, 490.
———John f. Will., 2040.
———Ralph, of Roliston, 1422, 1423, 2022, 2031, 2032.
———Ralph f. Rad., 2029.
———Roger, 1753.
———Thomas, 1495.
———William I., 913, 2040, 2041.
———William II., 2036-2041.
———William III., 2040-2042.
———Will., de Rostelaston, 2537.
Tanesley, Tanysley.
———Geoffr. de, 2303.
———John f. Galfr. de, 2302.
———Ric. f. Rob. de, 2303.
———Rob. f. Galf. de, 2303.
———Thos. f. Rob. de, 2303.
Tanner, Tannator, Tanour.
———Hen. le, 1958, 1962.
———John f. Joh., de Cestrefeld, 726.
———Wymarc f. Ric., de Baucwell, 174.
Tapitur, John, 846.
———John s. of John, 846.
Tapton, Tappeton, Taptone, Taptona, Taptun.
———Adam f. Gilb. de, 2311.
———Adam f. Rog. de parva, 2312.
———Adam f. Tho. de, 2313.
———Ascer de, 410.
———Gilbert de, 494, 2311.
———Hen. s. and h. of Will. de, 719.
———John de, 775, 2312.
———John de, of Hemyngton, 990.
———John f. Alex. de, 699.
———Peter de, 362, 744, 749, 2557.
———Ralph de, 2308.
———Ric. f. Hen. de, 709.
———Ric. f. Joh. de, 739.
———Robert, 1052, 2310.
———Rob. s. and h. of Peter de, 818.
———Rob. s. of Ralph, 2472.
———Roger, 832, 839, 2515.
———Rog. f. Ad. de, 2429, 2430.
———Rog. f. Ric. de, 500.
———Thomas de, 699, 818, 819.
———William de, 493, 506.
———Will. f. Petri de, 719.
Taryngton, Will. de, chaplain, 1525.
Tas, Moses le, 1950.
Taweran, Margaret, 448.
Taylboys, John, of Stalyngburgh, 1988.
Taylor, Taillour, Tailur, Tavlliour, Tayllour, Taylour, Taylur, Taylyor.
———Alan le, 1614.
———Alice relicta Rob. le, de Folowe, 1283.
———Alice ux. Rob. le, of Fornmerk, 1969-1971.
———John, D.D., Dean of Lincoln, 1013.
———John, 1064, 2435.

Taylor, etc., John, of Balydene, 217.
———Margery, of Bretby, 1977.
———Nich. f. Rog. le, 150.
———Richard, 2501.
———Ric. f. Joh. de, 1144.
———Robert le, 553, 1569, 1972.
———Rob., of Balydene, 217.
———Robert le, de Fornewerke, 1969-1971.
———Rob. f. Rog. le, 759.
———Stephen, of Bretby, 1977.
———Thos., vicar of Tideswell, 2366.
———Tho. s. of Steph., 1977.
———Will., of Meynel Langley, 2137.
———Will. f. Rog. le, 2332.
Tebald, John, chaplain, 2601.
Telar, Robert, 52.
Tenerey, Hugh le, of Eyton, 485.
Terne, Ralph de, canon of Lichfield, 189.
Terricus, clericus, 1945.
Terry, John, 2128.
Ters, Robert, 2295.
Testard, Will., tunc archidiaconus, 538.
Tetlowe, Adam, 1046.
———Matilda w. of Adam, 1046.
———Richard, 2434, 2435.
Teuren, Laurence, Abbot of Dale, 2202.
Teveray, Teverey.
———Robert, 1123, 1124, 1321.
———William de, 1338, 2200.
Textor, James, 404.
———Robert, 404.
Thachet, Thos., chaplain, 2353.
Thacker, Thakker.
———Cristofer, 1006.
———Gilbert, 1012.
———Olyver, of Little Chester, 1014.
———Rob., vicar of Mackworth, 1625.
———Thos., of Highege, 1012.
Thaleboth, v. Talbot.
Thame, Philip de, Prior of the Hospital of St. John of Jerusalem in England, 1575.
Thamenhorn, Richard de, 2027.
Thasilharst, Thomas de, 130.
Thebirthis, Rob. f. Rog. de, 419.
Thirland, Thos., of Nottingham, 2516.
Thirmot, Rob., de Lynton, 2542.
Thoke, Humphrey de, 239.
Thokeby, Hugh de, 2127.
Thokes, Thokies, Thocus, Thokus, Tokes.
———Alice w. of Will. de, 2660.
———John de le, 389, 391.
———Margery f. Will. del, 393.
———Matilda f. Will. del, 393.
———Rob. de le, de Bradeburn, 389, 390, 391, 393.
———William de, 2660.
———Will. f. Rob. de, 392.
Tholi, 134.
Tholy, Dionisia, w. of Rob. f. Rob. f., 386.
———Rob. f. Rob. f., 386.
Thomas, Bishop of Durham, 2455, 2456.
———Abbot of Beauchief, 859.
———Abbot of Crokesden, 2383.
———capellanus fil. Rad. de Duniaton, 537.

Thomas, clericus, 1948, 2702.
———clericus de Apilcaol, 2425.
———clericus de Bakewell, 216.
———clericus de Luhteburht [Lough-
    borough], 1045.
———clericus de Wodehuses, 2374.
———dominus de Acouere, 153.
———foristarius dom. Will. de Strton,
    398.
———fr. Rodberti, 530.
———persona de Croxhale, 1500.
———precentor of Lichfield, 188, 189,
    2335.
———prior of Laund, 1356.
———prior of Trentham, 1489.
———rector of Asshover, 125.
———rector of Cubley, 2089.
Thomlynson, Thomlynsone.
———John, 319, 321.
———Ric., of Greveys, 259-261.
Thomson, Tomson.
———Alice d. of John, of Chattes-
    worthe, 255.
———John, 272.
———John, Alderman of St. Mary's
    Gild, Chesterfield, 2778.
———John, of Rygeway, 273, 274.
———Thomas, 1007-1009.
Thopton, v. Topton.
Thorley, Rob., of Leighes, co. Essex,
    1625.
———al. Draper, Will., of Mack-
    worth, 1625.
Thornhill, Thornhyl.
———Elias de, 1422-1425, 1430.
———Elyas f. Elye de, 1422-1425.
———Will. f. Phil. de, 1789-1791.
Thornworth, Richard de, 694.
Thorp, Thorpe, Torp.
———Adam de, 27.
———Emma, 2602.
———Henry de, 2127.
———John de, 27.
———Hugh de, 788.
———Nicholas de, 707.
———Ric. f. Rad. de, 27.
———Robert de, 27, 28, 134, 135,
    1636, 1820, 1821.
———Thomas de, 1134.
Thorsmon, Isabel w. of Will., 2720.
———Rich. f. Will., 2720.
———Rob. f. Will., 2720.
———Will., 2720.
———Will. f. Will., 2720.
Thorton, Rog. de, clericus, 182.
Threesse, John, 955.
Thurkelby, Thurkleby, Rog. de, Justice
    Itinerant, 1557, 1582.
Thurmeleye, Ric. de, vicar of Ashbourne,
    986.
Thurmeston, Thomas de, 35.
Thurmond, Thirmond, John, 2058.
———Roberto de Lynton, 2061.
Thurneweit, Herbert de, 2241.
———Robert de, 2241.
Thurvastone, Ric. f. Will. de, 2323.
Thurytf, Agnes w. of Will., 943.
———John s. of Will., 943.
———Rob. s. of Will., 943.
———William, 943.

Thwathewait, Nich. de, 2509.
Thwathweyt, Giles f. Anote de, 498.
Tibbesone, Tybbesone.
———Nicholas, 1667.
———Walter, de Longford, 1155,
    1157.
Tibshelf, Tibshylf, Tippeshelf, Tybe-
    schelf, Tybethilf, Tybschall, Tyb-
    schelfe.
———Hugh de, chaplain, 1042.
———Mary w. of Peter de, 351.
———Peter de, 351.
———Richard, 2333.
———Rob., clericus de, 1083.
———Rog. de, vicar of Bakewell, 207,
    209.
———Rog., chaplain, 1861, 2353.
———Sym. de, perpet. vicar of Tib-
    shelf, 2332.
———Will., of Skegby, 2333.
Tich', Adam de, 532.
Ticheam, Stephen f. Osberti de, cler.,
    537.
Tichenale, Tikehale, Tikenhall, Tykeh,
    Tykenh', Tykenhal.
———Alan de, 2778.
———Ralph de, 284, 326, 540, 1755,
    1756, 2579.
Tiddeswall, Tiddeswell, Tyddiswal,
    Tydeswelle.
———Henry de, 1224, 1464, 1468,
    2357.
———John de, 142.
———Rob. f. Rob. de, 2740.
———Thomas de, 55.
Tildesley, Hugh, 993.
———John, 993.
———Matilda w. of Hugh, 993.
Tilley, Will., of Hakunthorpe, 273.
Tillot, Robert, 1984, 1985.
Tinctor, Simon, 44.
———Symon s. of Walter, of Esse-
    burn, 970.
———Tho. f. Elie, of Chesterfield,
    1744.
———Walter s. of Will., of Esseburn,
    970.
———Ynga w. of Walter, of Esse-
    burn, 970.
Tissington, Ticent', Ticentona, Tys-
    tyngton.
———Herbert de, 134.
———Robert de, 55.
———Roger de, 38.
———William de, 1292, 1741.
———Will. de, clericus, 135.
Toc, Tocha, Tok, Toke, Tonk, Took,
    Tonka, Touke.
———John, 2107-2109, 2281.
———Jordan de, 51, 1346, 1786, 2716,
    2746.
———Peter de, 399, 2005, 2583, 2711,
    2723.
———Philip de, 936, 2092, 2383.
———Robert de, 1275, 1698, 1699,
    2574, 2591.
———Symon de, 1470.
Tochet, Toschet, etc., v. Tuschet.
Todd, Christopher, of Walton, 856.
Tokes, v. Thokes.

Toller, Richard le, 2628.
Tomas, John, 1656.
Tomes, Richard, 2515.
Tomson, *v.* Thomson.
Tonk, Tonka, *v.* Toc, etc.
Tonstedes, Tonstedus, *v.* Tunsted.
Tonyclyff, Nicholas, 613.
Toples, John, of Tyssyngton, 1647.
————Thomas, 2401.
Topton, Toptone, Thopton.
————Peter de, 356, 546.
————Rob. f. Tho. clerici de, 2409.
Torald, Adam, chaplain, 1864, 1865.
Torcard, Hawisa f. Roberti, 1084.
Torf, Rob. de, decanus, 538.
Torfinus, 216.
Torp, *v.* Thorp.
Toruardeston, Ralph de, 1159.
Totinley, Ric. f. Ade de, of Dore, 1017.
Toton, Ric. de Grey, Lord of, 974.
Toturdon, Will. de, 2391.
Toturhurst, Tho. s. of Gylbart de, 661.
Totynglay, Thomas de, 1039.
Touchet, James, Lord Audley, 951, 1616.
Touk, Touke, *v.* Toc.
Tounesenda, Tounhende, Tounende, Toyneshende, ad finem ville.
————Hen. de., 1550.
————Hen. atte, 2354, 2357.
————John atte, 2438-2440.
————Ralph, 2612.
————Thomas, 2436.
————Thurston, chaplain, 564.
Townerow, John, of Bolsover, 2276.
————Dom. Walter, capellanus, 127.
Trafford, Edmund, 1605.
————Edmund, knt., 1616.
————John, knt., 1601.
Traine, Rob., 539.
Tranger, Henry, 1966.
Trayhot, Will., 554.
Traynel, John, 2537.
Trech, Tho., of Moniassh, 1719.
Trees, Tho., 1456.
Trehanton, Ralph de, knt., 1487.
Trengeston, Robert de, 1726.
Trippett, Ric., of Atterclyffe, 1129.
Troche, Thomas, 2736.
Trote, Tho. s. and h. of John, of Folowe, 1285.
Trowell, Trewelle, Triwelle, Trouwelle.
————Geoffrey de, 2090-2092.
————Nich. de, of Derby, 975.
————Robert de, 180, 2193.
————Walter de, bailiff of Derby, 978, 979.
Trubaha, William, 2141.
Trusbutes, Trussebutte, Rob., knt., 1865, 1898.
Trusley, Trussele, Trusselege, Trusse-legh, Trusseley, Trusseleye.
————Hen. f. Hen. de, of Kyrke-longele, 520, 521.
————Johanna f. Will. de, 2389.
————Robert de, 238.
————Rob. f. Will. de, capellanus, 2389.
————Will. de, 1522-1524, 2389.
————Will. de, presbyter, 2381.

Trussebouz, Will., 402.
Trussell, Theobald, 1176.
Trusselove, Trosselove.
————John, 2652.
————Nicholas, 2649.
Truttok, Trucok, Tructok.
————John, of Brunnaldeston, 520, 521.
————Walter, 519, 520.
————Will., chaplain, 801, 806.
Trykett, Ralph, 564.
Tuderley, Will., 583.
Tunstead, Tonstedes, etc.
————John de, 1221, 1283, 2360, 2447, 2449, 2452-2455.
————Robert, 1389.
————Rob. f. Will. del, 2708.
————Rog. f. Rad. del, 2405.
Turberuile, John de, 239.
Turch', persona de Repton, 1939.
Turkeys, Hen., of Dubbruge, 1024.
Turnepeny, Robert, 2204.
Turner, Turnor, Turnour.
————Edmund, warden of All Saints', Derby, 1002.
————George, of Chaundrell, 473.
————John, 456, 2516, 2519.
————John, of Chaundrell, 473.
————John, of Chasterfeld, 473.
————John, of Woodthorpe, 2263.
————Peter, 2459, 2469.
————Ric., of Brampton, 103, 167.
————Ric. s. and h. of John, of Chaundrell, 473.
————Roger, 2260, 2263.
————Rog., of Staveley, 1128.
————Thomas, 2261.
————Dom. Will., capellanus, 127.
Turri, clericus, 531.
————John de, 1501, 1502.
Turvey, John, 2184.
Tuschet, Tochet, Tosch', Toschet, Tuscheth.
————Henry, 1504, 2091.
————John s. of John, 2667.
————Matthew de, 2382.
————Simon, 1499, 1554, 1948, 2091, 2382.
————Thomas, clerk, 986.
Tutbury, Totesbiri, Tutesbir', Tutes-biri, Tuttebury, Tuttebyri.
————John de, 1390.
————John f. Hen. f. Gode de, 2610.
————Ric. de, chaplain, 1177.
————Symon de, 55.
————Tho. de, bailiff of Derby, 975, 981.
————Thomas de, 1455.
————William de, 1455.
————Will., of Derby, 1176, 1177.
Tuxforde, Hugh de, 546.
Twyford, Tuiford, Twiford.
————Dom. John de, 520, 521, 1572.
————Dom. John de, knt., 2017, 2321.
————John de, vicar of Spondon, 2182, 2183, 2353.
————John de, 2179-2181.
————Margaret w. of John de, 2179.
————Margaret, wid. of Walter, 610, 2187, 2188.

Twyford, etc., Dom. Rob. de, 50.
——Rob., Dominus de Longley, 1505, 1930, 1931.
——Rob. de, knt., 1376, 1924, 1928, 1929, 2295.
——Robert, 1526.
——Rob., of Kirk Langley, 1694, 2187.
——Thomas, 2189.
——Tho., of Kirk Langley, 1527-1531.
——Walter, 1251.
Tybbesone, *v.* Tibbesone.
Tybeschelf, Tybethelf, Tybschall, etc., *v.* Tibshelf.
Tyddiswal, Tydeswelle, *v.* Tiddeswall.
Tydnesore, Hen. de, chaplain, 345.
Tyeys, John le, mil., 2536.
Tykeh', Tykenh', *v.* Tichenale.
Tykhill, Tykhull, Tykhulle.
——Henry, 1598.
——Robert, 611.
——Rob., of Stanley Grange, 281.
——Thomas, 2602.
Tyler, Sir Will., knt., 1193.
Tylly, Will., of Hakenethorpe, 1326.
Tym, Hen., of Castleton, 563.
——Oliver, s. and h. of Hen., of Castleton, 562.
Tymborhill, John, 898.
Tymorth, John de, 1175.
Tynet, John, 1776.
——Isabella, w. of John, 1776.
Tyneworth, John de, 1174.
Tyrry, John, of Cubley, 2287.
——Walter, of Snelston, 1768.
Tystyngton, *v.* Tissington.

U.

Ubbestoft, Rob. de, 118, 120.
Uftone, William de, 1099.
Ulecote, Joan de, 2785.
——Philip de, 2785.
Ulkerthorp, Ulkerthorpe, Ulkerthorppe.
——Hugh, of Assheover, 126.
——Peter de, 2629, 2632.
——Will., knt., 2452, 2455.
——William de, 255, 256, 258, 449.
Ulley, John, 1052.
Ulnot, Ric. fil., 351.
Ulster, Matilda w. of William de Burgh, Countess of, 1687.
Umfridus, miles, de Boneburi, 530.
Umuill, Ingilran de, 2566.
Underwode, Ric. fil. Ran. de, 53.
——Roger fil. Rob. de, 53.
Unwyn, Adam, 2466.
Upton, Will. f. Warini de, 909.
Urpe, John, 601.
Usgathorp, John, 589.
——Robert, 589.
Uttokeshal, John de, 1546.
Uttokishath, Rob. f. Hen. de, 2614.
"Uueraddon pollard," John de, 173.

V.

Vade, Will., chaplain, 315, 316.
Valence, Valance, Valens.
——John, 8, 9, 12.
——Katherine w. of John, 8, 9, 12.
——Richard, 12.
Valle Vire, Ralph, vicecomes de, 1942.
Vallibus, Dom. John de, Justice Itinerant, 1564.
Vavasour, Vavaseur, Vavassur, Vavasur, Vavesour.
——John, Justice of the Common Pleas, 640.
——Rob. de, vicecomes Nottingeham, 2195.
——Robert le, knt., 1487, 2633.
——Dom. Rob. le, 326.
——Rob. le, 940, 2093, 2094, 2637.
——Rob. f. Will. le, of Scippeleg', 1623.
Vawsone, Joan wid. of Rob., 2441.
Venables, Hugh, 348.
——Dom. Ric. de, 1166.
——Rog., parson of Routhstorn, 1588, 1591, 1594, 1868.
Venator, Le Venur.
——Richard, 108, 109, 934, 2284.
——Roger, 1159.
——William, 108, 109, 934, 2284.
Venella, Adam de, de Cestrefeld, 700, 724.
——Agnes w. of Adam de, of Cestrefeld, 724.
——Magota f. Ade de, of Cestrefeld, 724.
——Margery f. Ade de, of Cesetrefeld, 308.
Venur, Le, *v.* Venator.
Ver, Baldwin de, 487, 1955.
Verdon, Verdoun, Verdun.
——Aliz de, 1726.
——Bertram de, 2571.
——Elys de, 1286.
——Hawise de, 2777.
——Henry de, 2777.
——John de, 1428.
——Nich. de, mil., 1962, 1963, 2585.
——Richard de, 2759.
——William de, 1554, 1726, 2570.
Verne, Hugh de, 2585.
Verney, Vernay.
——John, 2081.
——John, of Eddrichesey, 1482.
——Robert, 1498.
Vernon, Vernone, Vernun.
——Edmund, 460, 1992, 2398.
——Fulk, 2678.
——Geo., of Haddon, 213, 1333.
——Guarin de, 486.
——Henry, knt., 303, 1383, 1481, 2073, 2692, 2694, 2730.
——Henry, 102, 103, 211, 460, 510, 633, 866, 1189, 1339, 1344, 1597, 2397, 2399, 2521.
——Hen., Steward, Master of the Peak Forest, 100, 1849.

Vernon, etc., Hen. s. of Will. of Harlaston, knt., 593.
——John, 2697.
——John s. of Sir Rich., 2394, 2398, 2399.
——Ralph, 181, 865, 866.
——Randolph, 104.
——Richard I. de, knt., 355, 2212, 2213, 2340.
——Richard II., knt., 677, 1861, 2228.
——Richard III., knt., 1394, 1494, 1496, 1620, 1621, 2119, 2394, 2452, 2455.
——Richard IV., vicar of Youlgrave, 2216.
——Richard, esquire, 2233.
——Rich., of Horlastone, scutifer, 2539.
——Richard de, 215.
——Richard, 781.
——Rich., of Hasulbache, 2403.
——Ric. s. of Sir Henry, 303.
——Roger, Bailiff of Wirksworth Manor, 2693.
——Thomas, 1723.
——Tho. s. of Hen., 303.
——Tho., s. of Sir Ric., 1721.
——Warin de, 1948.
——Will de, Justiciarius Cestrie, 1954, 1955, 2574.
——Will., knt., 594, 1187, 1596, 1616, 1620.
——William I. de, 487, 1274, 1346, 1544, 2001, 2023, 2577, 2578.
——William II., 456, 1182.
——Will. s. of John, 2398.
——Will. s. of Sir Ric. de, 1256.
Vicarius, Thomas, 1281.
Vicars, Tho., of Chesterfield, 1384.
Viene, Hugh de, 1114.
Vikeresson, John, 1434, 1435.
Vikerson, Will. f. John de, 1436.
Vildegos, v. Wildgos.
Vincent, capellanus, 2628, 2634.
——John, 1962.
Vinetarius, Adam, de Burthon, 2615.
Vow, Nich. le, 2246.
Vygley, v. Wigley.
Vynfeld, Robert de, 1102.

W.

Wace, John, 1293.
——John, of Sudbury, 2286.
——Matilda, of Foston, 1300.
——Thomas, of Mackley, 2158, 2286.
Waddisley, Rob. de, 388.
——Rob. f. Ade de, 292.
Wade, Alice, de Coton, 2065.
——John, rector of Legh, 1645, 2020.
——John f. Will., 2065.
——Thomas, 2190.
——Will., of Coton, 2065.

Wadshelf, Wadeself, Wadesself, Waldeschef, Waldeshelf, Walderschef, Waltesheff.
——Joan w. of Walter, 338, 1271.
——Margaret d. of Walter, 67.
——Ric. f. Thom. de, 417, 421.
——Thomas de, 419, 422, 2487.
——Walter, 67, 338, 339, 1271.
Wak, Wake.
——Hugh, 681.
——John, dominus de Lidel, et Chestrefeud, 698.
——Dom. Nicholas, 693.
——Dom. Thomas, 496.
Wakebridge, Wakbrig, Wakbrugge, Wakebrig, Wakebrige, Wakebrigge, Wakebrug, Wakebruge, Wakebrugg.
——Elizabeth w. of Will. de, 921, 1890.
——Emma de, 2780.
——Henry de, 2780.
——John de, 108, 934.
——Nicholas de, 1353.
——Peter de, 916, 920, 1887, 1888.
——Ranulph de, 2629, 2632, 2635, 2780.
——William de, 752, 758, 921, 1889-1891, 2082.
Wakelen, Wakelyn, Margery w. of Ric., 2075.
——Richard, 2075-2079.
Waket, Alan, 177.
Walchelin, monetarius, 2545.
Waldewich, Ingeram de, 2753.
——Quenilda de, 2753.
Waldo, Hugh de, 1726.
Waleden, Simon de, 1961.
Walensis, le Waleys.
——Agnes, de Walton, 2034.
——Simon, 1950, 1967.
——Sim. f. Sim., 1951.
——Thomas, 2538.
——Will., of Gt. Gransden, 1964-1966.
——Will., of Walton, 576, 2034.
Walerand, Wallerand.
——Geoffrey, 1962.
——Robert de, 1555.
Walesby, Philip de, 2506, 2508.
——Richard, chaplain at Normanton, 921.
Walet, William, 322.
Walker, Richard, vicar of Wybunbury, 322.
Walle, Hugh, of Repton, 1962.
Wallour, Henry, 883.
Walsshe, John de, Lord of Sheldesley, 1703.
Walter, Abbot of Dale, 108.
——Abbot of Darley, 2382.
——Bishop of Coventry, v. Durdent, W.
——capellanus, 1082.
——clericus, 1424, 1425, 1539.
——clericus Hugonis de Bello Campo, 533, 534.
——clericus de Cestirfeld, 683.
——diaconus, 537.
——homo Roberti, 1083.
——nepos Cuthberti, 1197.
——perpet. vicar of Walsall, 2199.

Walton, Waleton, Waletona, Walltun, Waltone, Waktun.
———Adam de, 1957.
———Alan f. Finiani de, 2487.
———Alice, ux. Rog. de, 438.
———Eliz. f. Ric. clerici de, 2500.
———Hugh de, 225.
———Hugh f. Rob. de, 1274.
———Isabella de, 1919.
———John, of Lissyngton, co. Linc., 1923.
———John de, of Radbourne, 240, 1922, 1923.
———Robert de, 228, 1023, 1862, 2242.
———Rob. de, chaplain, 1181.
———Roger de, 1545.
———Rog. f. Galfridi de, 710.
———Rouland de, 1919, 1925.
———Will. f. Ran. de, mil., 2492.
Walyshe, William le, 153.
Wandesleya, Ranulph de, 22.
Waplod, Avice w. of Rob. de, 788.
———Robert, 788, 809.
Ward, Warda, Warde.
———Adam le, 1803.
———Agnes w. of Adam le, 1803.
———Alice w. of Nic. le, 312, 314.
———Gilbert le, 1895.
———Henry le, 1524.
———John, 220.
———John le, 891, 892.
———John del, 2616.
———Margaret f. Joh. le, 891.
———Nic. le, of Bonsall, 313-315.
———Richard, 1442.
———Rob. de la, knt., 2033.
———Dom. Rob. de la, 571, 1699.
———Rob. de, 2574.
———Steph. le, 2036, 2039, 2040, 2043, 2044, 2049, 2051, 2065.
———William de, 2587.
———Will. le, of Hopwell, 1914.
———Will., of Coton, 1989, 2035, 2036, 2038, 2055, 2058, 2061.
Wardelowe, Wardlow.
———John de, 1233, 1234.
———John s. and h. of Nich., 1253.
———Nicholas de, of Eyam, 1224-1226, 1232, 1238.
———Ralph de, 2404.
———Robert de, 2218.
———Thos. f. Thos. de, 2407.
Wardington, Roger de, 138.
Warenne, Waren, Warenn, Wareyn, Waryn.
———John de, Earl of Surrey, 1853.
———John, 1517, 1646, 1977.
———Laurence, knt., 1594.
———Peter f. Ric., of Hatton, 1362.
———Robert, 269.
———William, 36.
Warner, John, of Elyngton, 2407.
Warploc, Adam, 2007, 2009.
Warsop, Warsope, Warsoppe, Warsup.
———John de, 371, 372, 715, 722, 2497.
———Thomas de, 741.
Warwick, Earl of, v. Plessetis, John de.

Warwyk, Warrewik.
———John, of Lanforth, 1773.
———Nicholas de, 1964.
———Will., of Normanton, 1773.
Waryn, v. Warenne.
Waryngton, William de, 930.
Was, Thomas, 341.
Wascelin, John, 1032.
Wasse, Rob., de Macley Wodhouses, 1621.
Wassenuill, Reginald de, 1419.
Wasteneis, Wasteneys.
———Amphelisa de, 1726.
———Philip de, 1726.
———Dom. Will. de, 912.
———Will. de, 2024.
Wate, John, of Thwathweyt, 379.
Watecroft, Robert de, 2780.
Watenhow, Robert de, 22.
Waterfal, William de, 68.
Waterhows, Thomas, 1195.
———Tho., of Duffeld, 1510.
Watford, Rob. de, Dean of St. Paul's, 1952.
Wath, Wathe, John de, 1019, 1040.
Watson, Watsun.
———John, Chamberlain of Derby, 1006.
———John, 1110.
———Thomas, 472.
Watte, William, 2295.
Wauere, Will. de, Abbot of Merivale, 2033.
Waundell, Waundelle, John, 279.
———John, of Eggynton, 1184.
———Tho., of Derby, 1000, 1007.
Wawden, John, bailiff of Codnor, 898.
Wayne, Ric., of Herthill, 301.
———Rog., of Alport, 303.
Waynflete, Will. de, Bp. of Winchester, 2069.
Waynwright, Will., vicar of Glossop, 633.
Waystolke, Ralph de, 2227.
Wayte, Gilbert le, 1429.
Webbe, John f. Petri, of Caldham, 2501.
Webster, Webbester.
———Adam, 892.
———John, 317, 325.
———Will., chaplain, 806, 812, 814, 816, 823, 827, 837, 838, 2510.
———Will., chaplain of St. Mary's Guild, Chesterfield, 841, 845, 848.
Wederhed, Weydurherd, Hen., vicar of Dronfield, 1069, 2475.
Wednesley, etc., v. Wensley.
Wedo, Will., clerk of the Abbot of Dale, 2186.
Welbeck, Abbots of: John, 1111; Thomas, 1093; William, 1086.
Welbeck, Welbeke, Wellebeke.
———Richard, 79, 86.
———Richard, 1646.
———Ric., of Campeden, chaplain, 883.
Weld, Welde.
———Joan w. of Will., 2663.
———Margery wid. of John de, 2663.
———Matilda f. Will., 2663.

Weld, etc., Nicholas de la, 1525.
———Nich. del, persona de Derley, 757.
———Will. de, 2663.
Weledon, Robert de, 1078.
Weledune, Serlo f. Ric. de, 2202.
Wele, John, of Cadyngton, 1437.
———John, chaplain, 1439.
———Robert, 503, 1977.
Well, Will. at the, 2513.
Wellewick, Wellewik, Wellewike.
———Ralph de, knt., 1018.
———Ralph s. and h. of Sir Ralph de, 1019, 1021.
———Rob. br. of Sir Simeon de, 1022.
———Sir Simeon de, 1022.
Welfis, Wellys.
———John, 1358, 2403.
———Thomas, 1358.
Wells, Hugh de, Bishop of Lincoln, 1697.
Welond, Tho., Justice, 1279.
Welton, Welletune.
———Adam, 2166.
———Joyce w. of Thomas, 1064.
———Robert de, 415.
———Thomas, sen., 1064.
———Thomas, 1403, 1406.
Weluet, Ric., capellanus, 1329.
Wennefelt, Ralph de, 2218.
Wensley, Wedenesley, Wedenisley, Wednesl', Wedneslegh, Wednesley, Wednisl', Wednislegh, Wednisley, Wendesley, Wennesley, Wentlesle, Wodnesle.
———Avice w. of Rog. de, 2544.
———Gerard de, 2148.
———Hugh de, de Mapilton, 1643.
———John, 275.
———John, br. of Rog. de, 1637, 1638, 1640-1643.
———John f. Gilb. de, 1642.
———Ric. f. Gilb. de, of Matlok, 1666.
———Robert de, 54, 138, 1821, 2144, 2316, 2410, 2604.
———Rog. de, dominus de Mapilton, 1636-1643.
———Roger, Dom. de, 290.
———Rog. de, 14, 28, 135, 142, 949, 1274, 1491, 1667, 1820, 1821, 2145, 2146, 2148.
———Rog. de, jun., 2544.
———Rog. f. Rob. de, 149.
———Sir Tho. de, knt., 803, 1701, 1924-1928.
———Thomas de, 549, 677, 2020, 2228.
———Will. s. of Ric. de, 1666.
Wentworth, William, 1123, 1321.
———Will., jun., 1124.
Wepur, Richard de, 1429.
Weregrave, Will. de, 662.
Werist——, Alan de, 1950.
Wermondiswrth, Wermundisworth, Wuormodisworthe.
———Hugh de, 2093, 2194.
———Martin de, 2206.
———Martin f. Nich. de, 1337.
———Nich. s. of Hugh de, 485.

Wescham, Rog. de, Bishop of Coventry and Lichfield, 182, 1125.
Weston, Westona, Westone.
———Adam f. Andr. de, 2546.
———Henry de, 2552, 2553.
———Hen. f. Rob. de, 1523, 2552.
———Hugh de, 174, 177.
———Mag. John de, 1520.
———John de, 1961, 2642.
———John f. Rob. de, jun., 1523.
———Matilda de, 2546.
———Mag. Nich. de, 175, 1420.
———Ranulf de, 2126.
———Rob. f. Ade de, 2546, 2548.
———Will., Prior of the Hospital of St. John of Jerusalem in England, 168.
———Will. f. Fulcheri de, 2552.
Wetenthon, v. Whittington.
Wether, Wethyr, Wyther, Wythir, Wythur.
———John s. and h. of Rauf, of Ilom, 952.
———Nich., de Thorp, 1637.
———Rob. f. Mich., of Longeforde Wodehouses, 1568.
———Thomas, 38.
———Will., 2672.
———Will., of Longeford Wodehousus, 1574.
Wetton, Elena w. of John de, 406, 1435, 1436.
———Henry de, 982.
———John de, 406, 1435, 1436.
———Richard de, 1435, 1436.
———Will. de, 1954.
Weye, William, 955.
Weyley, Will., chaplain of Youlgrave, 2737.
Weyteburgh, Whetteburgh.
———John de, 2325-2328, 2331.
Whalley, Ralph, of Bunney (?), co. Notts., 1008.
———Thomas, 2699.
Whatton, Richard de, 368.
———Rob. de, sub-prior of Welbeck, 1093.
Wheston, Alice w. of Th. del, 2347.
———Thos. f. Will. del, 2347.
———Will. de, 155.
Whetecroft, John de, 1889.
Whetteburgh, v. Weyteburgh.
Whilwright, Emma w. of Rob. le, 1666.
———Robert le, 1666.
White, Wite.
———Henry, 2732.
———Johanna w. of Tho., 864.
———John, 101.
———Nich. le, of Hatton, 1362, 1365.
———Robert, 2186.
———Thomas, 1469.
Whitehead, Whitehede, Whithed, Whyteheued, Whytheued, Witehed.
———Henry, 1918.
———John, 285.
———John, of Ashbourne, 2115.
———John, parson of Muggington, 2607, 2609.
———Richard, 1343.
———Richard, chaplain, 2259.

Whitehead, etc., Ric., of Staveley, 1342, 2257, 2261-2264.
——Robert, 2000.
Whiterock, John de, 400.
Whitewell, Whitwell, Rob. de, 783, 2251.
Whithalgh, Thomas, 2358.
Whiting, Whythynge, Whytynge, Wyting.
——Henry, 595.
——John, 592.
——Matilda q. f. ux. Hug., 1997.
Whittington, Wetenthon, Whitington, Whityngton, Whitynton, Whytington, Whytinton, Whytyngton, Witenton, Witinton, Witintona, Wthytinton, Wytinton, Wyttyngtone, Wytyntone.
——Akon de, 493.
——David f. Sim. de, 2432.
——Davit de, 1040.
——Elena wid. of David de, 2433.
——Herbert de, 798.
——John de, "ballivus Domini" of Chesterfield, 745.
——John de, Alderman of St. Mary's Gild, Chesterfield, 747.
——John de, 443, 736, 738, 740, 741, 746, 748-750, 752, 755, 758, 759, 761, 763, 764, 1106, 1746.
——John, of Derby, 279.
——Osbert de, 1420.
——Ranulph de, 2437.
——Robert, 279, 789, 791, 804, 811, 817, 820, 1534, 1535, 2315.
——Rob. s. of John de, 759.
——Roger de, 742.
——Simon f. Rob. de, 410.
——Swanus f. Hug. de, 494.
——Will., clericus de, 1534.
Whittlesey, Will., Abp. of Canterbury, 1845.
Whitword, Jacobus, 1875.
Whitworth, Rob., of Pynkeston, 1883.
Whyteheued, Whytheued, v. Whitehead.
Whythyll, Will, of Brampton, 167, 856.
Whythynge, Whytynge, v. Whiting.
Whytyngton, v. Whittington.
Widele, Adam de, 2620.
Wideson, Robert, 2604.
Wigfall, William, 276.
Wigley, Wiggelay, Wiggley, Wygeley, Wygely, Wygley, Wygleye, Wyggely, Wyggeley.
——Agnes d. of Rob., 2564.
——John de, 429, 437, 439, 440, 1019, 1100, 2498, 2679, 2680, 2693.
——John, of Middleton, 1676, 1677.
——John, of Wyrkesworth, 394.
——John f. Joh. de, 2291.
——Ralph s. of John, 2.
——Richard, 1673, 1675.
——Richard, of Middleton, 2698.
——Rich. s. of Rog. de, 2664.
——Robert, 2564.
——Roger de, 429, 443, 757, 1047, 1341, 2506.

Wigley, etc., Roger f. Will. de, 2563.
——William de, 229, 2252, 2498, 2500.
——Will. de, of Brampton, 437.
——Will., of Workesworth, 1677.
Wikkilwod, Wyklewode.
——Will. de, parson of Boyleston, 1271.
——Will. de, rector of Bromlegh, 339.
Wilchar, Agnes w. of Hen., 32.
——Hen., of Alsop, 32.
Wilcokson, Wilkokson, Wylkokson.
——John, of Frytcheley, 2691.
——Robert, 2688, 2690, 2691.
——Roger, 2691.
Wild, Wilde, Wyld, Wylde.
——Elizabeth w. of Tho., of Offorton, 1448.
——John, of Abbenay, 4, 1805, 1806.
——Ric., of Abenay, 1801, 1802.
——Tho., of Offorton, 1447, 1448, 1724, 1809, 1810.
——Thurstan, 1378, 1379.
——William, 2555, 2565.
Wildebof, Wildebuef, Ralph de, 2090, 2091.
Wildegos, Vildegos, Wyldegos.
——John, 1291, 1297-1300, 1302, 1303, 1311, 2102.
——John f. Rog., de Foston, 1133, 1134, 1136.
——John s. of Will, 1292.
——Nich. f. Rob., 1294.
——Robert, 1300, 1306, 1309, 1311, 1312, 1314, 2182.
——Roger, 1291, 1298, 2100.
——Rog., de Fostun, 1289, 1290.
——Rog. f. Gerardi, 1288, 1294.
——Rog. f. Hen., 1297.
——William, 141, 152, 1288, 1290, 1291, 1295-1297, 1303, 2101, 2102.
——Will. f. Gerardi, 1292.
——Will. f. Rob., 1293, 1294.
Wildy, Wyldi, John, 141, 152.
——Richard, 44.
William, Archbishop of Canterbury, 528.
——Abbot of Burton, 2756.
——Abbot of Darley, 2383.
——Abbot of Lilleshall, 531, 1939.
——cantor of Burton Abbey, 1197.
——capellanus, 52, 182, 1819, 1940.
——capellanus de Bramton, 435.
——clericus, 174, 177, 180, 1396.
——clericus de Bakewell, 2762.
——clericus de Barva, 536.
——clericus de Neubolt, 2425.
——cler. de Stanton-on-Trent, 537.
——clerk to Hugh, E. of Chester, 535.
——de Ecclesia S. Marie, Bishop of London, 1949, 1952.
——f. Umfr. militis de Boneburi, 530.
——persona de Seyla, 2023.
——prior of Burton Abbey, 1197.
——prior of St. Helen's, Derby, 2383.

William, rector of Stretton, 2285.
————rector of Sutton-en-Dale, 2291.
————rector de Plesileg', 1893.
————vicar of Youlgrave, 2732.
William ad-crucem, 480, 607.
Williams, Wyllyams, Hen., Dean of
   Lichfield, 214, 408, 1333, 1451,
   1452, 1519, 1816.
Willington, Wilenton, Wilentun, Wilin-
   ton, Wylenton, Wylington, Wylm-
   ton, Wyllyngton.
————John, of Repton, chaplain,
   1991.
————Margery f. Nich., 2582.
————Nicholas, Dominus de, 2568.
————Nicholas de, 1274, 1277, 2576,
   2587, 2756-2758, 2781, 2784.
————Nich. f. Nich. de, 1277, 2577-
   2579.
————Philip de, 1276.
————Rob., of Merston, 1364.
Willoughby, Wilheby, Willughby,
   Wilughby, Wyloby, Wylughby,
   Wylyby.
————Sir Henry, knt., 905, 1121,
   2120.
————Henry, 24.
————Hugh, 384.
————Hugh de, 1998, 1999.
————Hugh de, clerk, 1488.
————Isabel w. of Tho., 2000.
————John f. Dom. Joh. de, 1899.
————Philip de, Chancellor of the
   Exchequer, 966.
————Richard, Sheriff of Derby,
   1999.
————Dom. Ric. de, sen., 891.
————Dom. Ric. de, 47.
————Richard, 2362, 2567.
————Robert de, 1893.
————Thomas, sen., 2000.
————Thomas, jun., 2000.
Willus, Robert, 233.
Wilne, Wilna, Wylne.
————John, Prior of Repton, 489, 490.
————John, de Melburne, 1349.
————Reginald de, 1726.
Wilnes de Rysseley, Alan in le, 1997.
Wilson, Wilsone, Willeson, Willyson,
   Wylson.
————Agnes w. of Robert, 24.
————Hugh, 2360.
————James, 2738.
————John, 275, 2317.
————John, of Calveovere, 1261.
————Richard, 1648.
————Robert, 24.
————Roger, 1182, 1183.
————Thomas, 1326, 1471.
————Tho. f. Ric., of Litton, 1549.
Wimudham, Tho. de, precentor of
   Lichfield, 1705.
Wimundewald, Andrew de, 2090, 2091.
Winchester, Bishop of, *v.* Beaufort,
   Hen. de.
Windsor, *v.* Wyndesore.
Winefeld, Winfeld, Winnefeld, Wyne-
   feld, Wynfeld, Wynnefeld.
————Alice wid. of Hen. de, 752, 779.
————Cecelia, 2684.

Winefeld, etc., Matilda w. of Will. de,
   2670.
————Nicholas de, 1396.
————Ralph de, 180.
————Richard de, 677, 1861.
————Robert de, 117, 118, 120, 122,
   2214, 2226.
————Rob. f. Radulphi de, 2222.
————Rog. f. Rob. de, of Esseovere,
   122, 123, 125.
————William de, 111, 112, 1815,
   2668, 2670, 2671, 2684.
————Will. de, parson of Thorp
   Basset, 791, 797.
Wingerworth, *v.* Wyngerworth.
Winshill, Wineshull, Winsul, Wyneshul,
   Wynnushale, Wynnushule, Wyns-
   hul, Wynsul, Wynsull.
————Adam f. Will. de, 2612, 2613.
————Ambrose f. Eugenulfi de, 2611.
————Henry de, Deacon, 2613.
————John f. Will. de, chaplain, 2613.
————Nich. f. Rob. le, clerk, 2616.
————Rich. f. Swain de, 2610.
————Rob., clericus de, 1758.
————Stephen de, 2613.
————William de, 2613.
————Will. f. Rob. de, 2612.
Winster, Winestre, Wynster.
————Alan f. Reg. de, 2224.
————Hugh de, 1508, 2621.
————Lodewyc de, 2623.
————Rob. f. Hen. de, 2624.
————Rob. f. Rob. de, 2224.
————Thomas de, 1135.
Winter, Wynter, Wyntour.
————Henry, 2689.
————Joan w. of Ric., 849.
————Richard, 849.
Wirksworth, Wirkeswrth, Wyrkesworthe.
————Nich. f. Walt. de, 2640, 2653.
————Philip de, 2643.
————Rob. de, chaplain, 296.
————Rob. f. Gilberti de, 2631, 2653.
————Rob. f. Herwici de, 2653.
————Will. f. Bate de, 2649, 2655,
   2657.
Wirley, Richard, 1646.
Wisbech, Richard de, canon of Lincoln,
   2634.
Wishawe, Wyshawe, Mag. Hen. de,
   canon of Lichfield, 182, 188.
Wite, *v.* White.
Withet, Dom. Will., 2100.
Withloc, Adam, 556.
Witmisleye, Geo., Chancellor to the
   Bishop of Chester, 655.
Wiuerdestan, Geoffrey de, 908.
Wlfet, Rich., chaplain, 1912.
Wlnad, Wlnet, Ric. fil., 352, 494.
Wlveleia, Geoffrey, heir of Matildis de,
   1083.
————Matildis de, 1083.
Wlvet, Ralph, de Litton, 1546.
————Ralph, de Tydeswell, 2335.
Wodcok, Thurstan, 1678.
Woddeslege, Robert de, 2215.
Wode *v.* Wood.
Wodehalle, Herbert de, 1338.
Wodehalls, Thomas, 2450.

Wodehous, etc., *v.* Woodhouse.
Wodehow, John de, 1020.
Wodell, *v.* Odell.
Woderowe, Wodrofe, Woderofe, Wode-
    reue, Woderove, Woderowe.
——————Edmund s. of Oliver, 561.
——————Gervase, 1433-1436.
——————Robert, 1430, 1437.
——————Thomas, 2086.
——————Tho., of Hope, 5.
——————Will., 1438, 1440, 2447, 2449,
    2452-2454.
Wodesmethis, Will. f. Alani de, 1040.
Wodeward, Wodeuard, Wodhard, Wod-
    warde.
——————Henry le, 1667.
——————Henry, vicar of Dronfield, 2474.
——————Isabell w. of Tho., of Horseley,
    1886.
——————John, 2410, 2604.
——————John le, of Murcaston, 1691.
——————Tho., of Horseley, 1886.
Wodnesle, *v.* Wensley.
Wolhous, William, 2446.
Wolley, Wulley.
——————Agnes d. of Walter, 2677.
——————Elena d. of Walter, 2677.
——————Eliz. d. of Walter, 2677.
——————Joan d. of Walter, 2677.
——————Margery w. of Walter, 2674,
    2677.
——————Roger s. of Walter, 2677.
——————Walter, 1498, 2671, 2672, 2674,
    2675, 2677, 2681.
Wolseley, William de, 400.
Wolsey, Tho., Cardinal Archbishop of
    York, 1028.
Wolstoncroft, Dom. John de, chaplain,
    212.
——————Robert, 212.
——————William, 212.
Wombwell, Wombewell, Wombewelle.
——————Thome de, ballivus de Alto
    Pecco, 406.
——————Thomas de, 77, 660, 757, 773,
    1222, 2416.
Wood, Wodde, Wode, Woode, Wudde.
——————Alice w. of Rob., 968, 2140.
——————Geoffrey, 2684.
——————Isabella, 1935.
——————John, 504, 508, 1402, 2257,
    2316, 2317.
——————Peter del, 504.
——————Peter del, of Briminton, 2440.
——————Ralph, 838.
——————Robert, 1935.
——————Rob., of Kell, 968.
——————Roger, of Matlock, 2690.
——————Stephen at, of Rowmley, 223.
——————Thomas, 321.
——————Will. del, 450.
Woodhouse, Wodhause, Wodhous,
    Wodhouse, Wodhouses, Wodhowse,
    Wodehous, Wodehouse, Wode-
    houses, Wodehousis, Wodehus,
    Wodehuses, Wuddus.
——————Adam de, 663.
——————Cecilia w. of Tho. de, 1057.
——————Dionisia, 465.
——————Edward s. and h. of John, of
    Retford, 2479.

Woodhouse, etc., John, 994, 1018, 1045,
    2479.
——————John, clericus, 1703, 2599.
——————John, of Brampton, 167.
——————Nich., of London, pewterer,
    168, 169, 472.
——————Peter de, 131, 2426.
——————Richard de, 1035, 1038, 1043.
——————Ric., chaplain, 455.
——————Ric., of Brampton, 168.
——————Ric., of Rypley, 470.
——————Ric. f. Tho. de le, 1036.
——————Rob. s. and h. of Thos., 2483.
——————Roger de le, 54.
——————Tho. de, 130, 224, 1057, 1775,
    2428, 2451, 2459, 2462.
——————Tho. de, clerk, 1017.
——————William, 167.
——————Will. s. and h. of John, of
    Brampton, 470.
Wordisleye, Rob. de, 19.
Wormhill, Wormell, Wormehill, Roger,
    807, 951, 1195.
Worsley, William, 841.
Worteley, Wortteley.
——————Nicholas, Lord of, 2254.
——————Nicholas, 2259.
——————Richard, 557, 2118.
——————Sir Thos., knt., 2259.
Worth, Rob., "Baile" of Crich, 638.
Wortheye, John, chaplain, 466.
Worthinton, Symon de, 2615.
Woulf, Hugh, chaplain, 2440.
Wray, Ralph de, 1954.
Wrhynton, John de, 2617.
Wright, Writh, Wryght, Wryghte,
    Wryht, Wryth.
——————Adam le, 1048.
——————Adam, de Aston, 2439.
——————Adam le, de Moniassch, 1716.
——————Amicia w. of Adam le, of Mony-
    assch, 1715.
——————Catherine wid. of Hen. le, of
    Rolleston, 2110.
——————Joan w. of John le, 1224.
——————John, chaplain, 2239.
——————John le, 1224.
——————John, of Ashford, 2083.
——————John f. Joh. le, of Egynton,
    1180.
——————Ralph, chaplain of Duckman-
    ton, 1112.
——————Randall, 2738.
——————Richard, rector of Staveley,
    2260.
——————Roger, 1112.
——————Rog., of Herdycwall, 565.
——————Thomas, 768, 1129.
——————Will., of Stanley, 1879, 1880.
Wrigley, Wrygley.
——————Geoffrey, 106, 107.
——————Thomas, 105, 106.
Wrlyot, John f. of Joh. le, of Egynton,
    1175.
Wudeham, Ralph de, 1113.
Wulley, Walter, *v.* Wolley.
Wy, 2243.
Wyardeston, Wyardestone, Wyardiston.
——————Avice f. Hen. de, 1132.
——————Emma w. of Tho. de, 1132,
    1138.

Wyardeston, etc., Hen. f. Tho. de, 1132, 1138.
———John f. Tho. de, 1154.
———Margery f. Hen. de, 1132, 1138.
———Matilda, quondam ux. Hug. de Aula de, 881.
———Will. f. Hen. de, 1132, 1138, 1151.
Wychard, Henry, 1280.
———John, de Breslya, 540.
Wychegea, Hugh del, 1822.
Wychelles, Will. de, chaplain, 2665.
Wychyngham, Will de, 1845.
Wyggely, Wygley, etc., v. Wigley.
Wyght, Will., of Hopton, Public Notary, 2662.
Wygornia, W———, de, 1953.
Wyklewode, v. Wikkilwod.
Wylcokes, Tho., of Coventry, 1454.
Wyld, Wylde, v. Wild.
Wyldegos, v. Wildegos.
Wylenton, Wyllyngton, etc., v. Willington.
Wyley, Lesota wid. of Ric., 1784.
Wylkokson, v. Wilcokson.
Wylkynson, Thomas, 2060.
Wyllyams, v. Williams.
Wylne, v. Wilne.
Wylnebi, Rob. f. Dom. Rob. de, 116.
Wyloby, Wylughby, Wylyby, v. Willoughby.
Wylson, v. Wilson.
Wylte, Henry, 2556.
Wymbische, Wymbyssh.
———Nich., clerk, 1873.
———Thomas, 884.
Wymme, John, of Uttoxeter, 2114.
———Walter, of Uttoxeter, 2114.
Wymundham, Tho. de, Precentor of Lichfield, 1427.
Wyndeley, Peter de, 482.
Wyndesore, Andrew, knt., 1657.
Wyndeston, Adam de, 1149.
Wyne, Wine, Wyn.
———Adam le, 475.
———Dionisia le, Lady of Pynkeston, 1866.
———Joan relicta Rob. le, 2638.
———Nicholas le, 605.
———Nich. f. Rob. le, 1552.
———Ralph le, 1472.
———Robert le, 2629-2631, 2635, 2638.
———Rob. le, de Haddon, 1706.
———Rob. s. of Adam le, 1490, 1840, 2654.
———Rog. le, 2762.
———Will. de, chev., 1863.
———William le, 174, 177, 1396, 1707, 2178, 2179, 2762.
———Will. le, of Chaddesdon, 973.
———Will. f. Rob. le, 2658.
Wynefeld, Wynfeld, etc., v. Winefeld.
Wynemere, Winemer, Odo, 1163, 1168.
Wyneshul, Wynsull, etc., v. Winshill.
Wyngeby, Wymby.
———Alice de, of Nottingham, 2505.
———John s. and h. of Rob. de, 2504.
———John s. of Rob. de, 2505.
———Rob. de, 2506.

Wyngerworth, Wyngreworth, Wyngurworth.
———Hen. de, in Chesterfield, 369.
———Roger de, 815, 1505, 1930.
———Thomas de, 366.
Wynstanley, Peter, 1008, 1009.
Wynster, v. Winster.
Wynter, Wyntour, v. Winter.
Wynton, Robert de, 2243.
Wyrkes', v. Wirksworth.
Wyshawe, v. Wishawe.
Wysmon, William, 1224.
Wystowe, John, 2619.
Wyther, Wythir, Wythur, v. Wether.
Wythewolf, Alice w. of Hen., 618.
———Henry, 618.
Wythrne, Amabilia f. Phil. de, 912.
Wythur v. Wether.
Wyting, v. Whiting.
Wytintona, etc., v. Whittington.
Wyttlome, Ric., chaplain, 951.
Wytur, Will., sen., 2668.
Wytwalle, John, clericus de, 1511.
Wyuill, John de, Justice Itinerant, 1557.
Wyverton, Robert de, 1086, 1089.
Wyvile, Tho. de, of Stanton, 1767.

Y.

Yate, Rob. atte, de Berwardecote, 2599.
———Roger atte, 2162.
Ybol, Ybole.
———Nich. f. Galfridi de, 310.
———Nich. f. Ric. de, 1474.
———Rob. f. Nich. de, 1475.
———v. also Ibole, etc.
Yeph, Ric. le, 880.
Yerdeleye, Tho. de, de Derby, 977, 978, 983.
Yerlle, Wylliam, Chamberlain of Derby, 1005.
Yeveley, John, parson of Cubley, 2287.
———Richard de, 2710.
Yldresle, Robert de, 134.
———Swanus de, 134.
Ynce, Hen., of Spynkhill, 1513.
———John s. of Richard, 2279.
———Meriella, 2278.
———Richard, 2277-2279.
———Robert, 2277.
———v. also Ince.
Ynguareby, Nich. de, 1961.
Yoman, John, 2400.
Yonge, John, Prior of Repton, 1995.
Yorke, Robert, of Derby, 1006, 1010.
Yotton, John, Dean of Lichfield, 1617.
You, John, 1469.
Yoxhale, John, 583, 2538.
Ypestanes, William de, 2125.
Yrlond, Dulcissa, wid. of Rob., 2727.
———v. also Ireland.
Yrpe, William, 593.
Yrton, Yrtone.
———Rob. de, vicar of Wirksworth, 2662.
———Roger de, 1305.
———Ysola w. of Rog. de, 1305.
———v. also Ireton.

Ysaac, armiger, 530.
Yamay, William, 607.
Yve, John, of Chaddesdene, chaplain, 1670.
———*v.* also Ive.
Yvo, persona [de Holme?], 1396.

Z.

Zouch, Zouche.
———Dame Agnes la, 942.
———Elizabeth w. of Will. la, 942.

Zouch, etc., George, 907.
———Joan wid. of Will., of Morley, 1916, 2123.
———John, knt., 907.
———John, 905.
———William I. la, sen., 942.
———Will. II. la, 3rd Baron of Totness and Haringworth, 942, 1488.
———Will. III. la, Lord Zouche, 2360.
———Will. IV., of Morley, 1916, 2123.

INDEX OF MATTERS.

A.

Accompts, Bailiffs': Bakewell [1359], 205; Walton Manor, *temp*. Edw. I.-II., 2495; Wirksworth [1280], 2645.

Aids, subsidies, etc., 1974, 2242, 2402.

Aids from tenants, for the knighting of an eldest son and marriage of an eldest daughter of the lord, 1500.

Ashbourne, chantry of J. Bradburne at St. Oswald's altar in the church of, 1331.

B.

Bakewell, accompt-roll, 205; parochial visitations, 190; tithe rolls of wool, etc., 195, 196.

Barkhouses: at Beauchief, 242; at Wirksworth, 2692.

Barton Blount, charter witnessed by "omnis Halimot de Bartun," 238.

Boat, confirmation to Calk Abbey of the gift of a boat for the fishery of Chester, 536.

Boundaries: "le kirke styule" at Tansley, 2303; an ash tree at Wirksworth, 2655; oak trees at Yeldersley, 2717.

Bridges: at Chesterfield, 683, 684, 817, 829; "Kirkehouse bridge" over the Roder at Staveley, 2264; at Whatstandwell, 2555.

Burial rights: at Taddington, 2298; application for a burying-ground at Chaddesden, 606; at Chelmorton, 665.

C.

Calk Abbey, subject to Repton Priory, 1939, 1941.

Cambridge, part of Repton Manor held by Pembroke College at, 1982.

Chantries: at Ashbourn, 91, 1331; at Boylestone, 339; at Chaddesden, 609, 611, 612; at Chelmorton, 665; at Chesterfield, 774, 776; at Crich, 921; at Lichfield, 171; at Monyash, 2736; at Tideswell, 2354, 2357.

Chaplains, provision for: at Beeley, 262; at Calk, 537; at Chaddesden, 609; at Chesterfield, 765, 776, 872; at Tideswell, 2354, 2356.

Charter, laid on the Altar at Coventry, 1428.

Charters, twelfth century (transcribed in full): Atlow, 134, 135; Bakewell, 170, 171; Balledon, 215, 216; Barton Blount, 238, 239; Brushfield, 516; Calk, 528-534; Coton-in-the-Elms, 908; Dale Abbey, 933; Duckmanton, 1078-1081; Duffield, 1113; Etwall, 1197; Findern, 1274; Over Haddon, 1338; Hatton, 1360; Holmesfield, 1397; Hope, 1419, 1420; Kedleston, 1499, 1500; Linacre, 1539; Morley, 1726; Repton, 1939, 1940, 1942-1947; Sandiacre, 2090, 2091; Trusley, 2380-2382; Weston Underwood, 2545; Winster, 2620, 2621; Yeldersley, 2716.

Confraternity, admission to, at Beauchief Abbey, 244.

Crosses: Breadsall, 480, 481; Chesterfield, 797, 858; Derby (alba crux) and (Hedlecross), 988; Litton, 1546; Longford, 1556; Tideswell, 2340, 2348; Wadshelf, 244.

Council, held at London [1132], 528.

E.

Ecclesiastical matters: case of intrusion of a chaplain at Chapel-en-le-Frith, 620; church books, plate and vestments at Ashbourne, 91; Council at London [1132], 528; marriage fees, 48.

Education, 599, 867.

Enclosures: liberty to enclose woodland in Rosliston, 2033.

Estovers, quit-claim to Repton Priory of right to estovers in the Priory woods, 1980.

F.

Fishery rights: Chester, 536; Newton Solney, 1758; Sawley, 2097; Willington, 1954.

Fishponds: Atlow, 135; Bradley, 396, 2717; Burton Abbey, 1274, 1275; Rosliston, 2030; Yeldersley, 2718.
Fuel, grant of a one-horse wagon for carriage of fuel at Ticknall, 1954.

G.

Guilds: at Bakewell (Holy Cross), 210; at Chesterfield (Holy Cross), 378, 785, 808, 813, 849, 859—(of St. Mary), 375, 378, 747, 808, 810, 819, 841, 848, 872-877—(gilda fabrorum), 378; at Dronfield (of St. Mary), 1064, 1065; at Tideswell (of St. Mary), 2357.

H.

Hermits, Hermitage, etc.: at Ashover, 108, 117; at Stretton, 2284; "Ermite medowe" at Trusley, 2387.
Holy Land, resignation of lands on setting out for the, 970.
Horse, gift of a horse on granting land, 2620.
Husbote and Haibote, 1113, 2730.

J.

Justices at Westminster [A.D. 1187-8]: Ranulf de Glanuill, Hugh, Bishop of Durham; John, Bishop of Norwich; Geoffrey, Bishop of Ely; Godfr. de Luci, Gocelin, the Archdeacon, Richard, the King's Treasurer, 1080.
Justices Itinerant at Derby: [A.D. 1258] John, Abbot of Peterboro', Rog. de Thurkleby, Pet. de Percy, John de Wyvil, 1557; [A.D. 1269] Gilb. de Preston, 399; [A.D. 1277] John de Reygate, Will. de Norbury, 2013; [A.D. 1281], John de Vallibus, 1564.—at Nottingham: [A.D. 1198-1199] Hugh Bardolf, Rog. Arundel, Phil. f. Roberti, Geoffr. Haket, al. Haget, 1499, 1947; [A.D. 1202], John, Bishop of Norwich, Hugh de Bardolf, Rog. Arundell, John de Gestling, Hugh de Bobi, 2334; [A.D. 1226] Hugh, Bishop of Lincoln, Steph. de Segrave, Rob. de Lexinton, Will. f. Warin, Will. Basset, 682, 1697; [A.D. 1252], Silvester, Bishop of Carlisle, Rog. de Thurkelby, Gilb. de Preston, Ad. de Hilton, 2582.

K.

Knights Hospitallers, sale of the site of the Commandery of, at "Stede" in Yeaveley, 2715.
Knights' service, 1397, 1499, 2022, 2025, 2026.

L.

Lamps in churches, support of: Eyam, 1207, 1209; Repton, 1978; Spondon, 2171, 2173, 2174; Welbeck, 2244, Youlgrave, 2735.
Lead, Leadmine, 998; at Eyam, 1229; at Winster, 2621.
London, Council at [A.D. 1132], 528.

M.

Masses, 375, 853, 942.
Measures of land: the perch of 17 ft., 1113; the perch of 20 ft., 2717.
Mills: fulling mills at Sallowe, 2097; sythe mills at Derby, 1000, and at Staveley, 2260; walk mills at Beauchief, 242, and at Derby, 1015.
Mills, suit and rights at, 26, 137, 141, 150, 1951, 2425, 2568, 2577, 2578.
Money: unum aureum, 170; besants or gold besants, 239, 244, 2573.

N.

Nativi, grants of, 27, 1472, 1965, 2011, 2419, 2421, 2547, 2581, 2583, 2733.
Nottingham, dispute concerning toll at, 1487.

O.

Ovens, at Chesterfield, 745.

P.

Pannage, 2244.
Pardons, general, 2407, 2526.
Peter's Pence, 48.

Q.

Quarries, 531, 1938, 1948.

R.

Rent Tenures or Charges: an apple in autumn 424, 427; a barbed arrow, 53. Boots: a pair of boots every second year on St. Martin's Day, 414; due ocree cordewanine ad pentecosten annuatim, 2621. Capons: "duo capones," in Mayo, 1472. Corn: "sex denarios vel dimid. modium seglei omni anno vite sue," 529. Cumin: 1 lb., 110; 1 lb. at Easter, 2002; 2 lb. yearly, 2769. Gillyflowers: unum clavum gariofili at Midsummer, 361; unum clavum gilofre at Michaelmas, 2017; one clove of gillyflower at Christmas, 2205. Gloves: on St. James's Day [25 July], 28; yearly, 242, 2703, 2717; valued at one penny, yearly, 284;

white gloves or one penny, 396, 2577; white gloves at Easter, 2126, 2340. Hawks: unum nisum sorum, yearly, 1360; unum ruffum nisum in anno in seisone, 2620; a sparrow hawk or two shillings, 2765; a sparrow hawk, 2777. Pepper: unum semen piperis, 2204; 1 oz. pepper yearly, 2446; 1 lb. pepper yearly, 916; 1 lb. pepper on acquittance for services, 920; 1 lb. pepper, 2245; a peppercorn yearly, 153, 2740; "Roba competens" at Christmas, 2667. Roses: on F. of SS. Peter and Paul (29 June), 405, 2032; on St. John Baptist's Day (24 June), 1978, 2030, 2038, 2095, 2448, 2537, 2549, 2618, 2710, 2762; a red rose on St. James's Day (25 July), 2127. Gilt spurs: (or sixpence) at Easter, 2025; yearly, 2536; (or sixpence) at Christmas, 2418; two "toge," on acquittance for lands, 2520;—*v.* also Tenants' Services.

Repton Manor, chronicle of, twelfth to fifteenth cent., 1987.

Rouen, Archbishop of, present at Council in London [1132], 528.

S.

Schirrevestur, payment reserved "ad le Schirrevestur," 519.

Scutage, payment of 2s. 6d. reserved for scutage "quando currit," 519.

Sheep, seizure of, in Tideswell Church, 184, 2336.

Soul-alms, 529, 530, 532, 533, 535, 536, 921, 933, 1079, 1081, 1419, 1939, 1942, 1962, 2171, 2244, 2260, 2357.

Spondon Church, appropriation of, to Burton Lazars Hospital, 2175.

Subsidies *v.* Aids.

Sutton Bonnington, co. Notts., grant of the baptismalis ecclesia S. Anne at, 537.

T.

"Taberna depicta," 339.

Templars: at Temple Normanton, 167-169, 465, 470, 1772-1774; land at Brampton belonging to, 414; land at Hartshorn belonging to, 2759.

Tenants' Services: "an able horse and harnes for oone man to do the Kynge seruyce" when demanded, 43; "et preterea semel metet in autumpno ad cibum Rectoris eiusdem ecclesie" [*sc.* Bakewell], 173; metendo uno die in autumpno cum uno homine ad cibum Rectoris ecclesie (Bakewell), 180; "seruicio metendi in autumpno per vnum diem precii duorum denariorum," 515; one day's work with the sickle, 603; "salvo tantummodo servicio forinseco, scilicet tres denarios argenti per annum ad Tolnetum de Tutteburi, et tres denarios ad Le Schirrevestur et ad palefridum, et scutagium Domini Regis quando currit," 519.

————*v.* also Rent Tenures or Charges.

Tideswell, seizure of sheep and wool in the church, 184, 2336.

Timber, for repairs and for making wheels and carts, 2376.

U.

Unstone Manor, descent of, 2434.

W.

Wells or Springs [Fontes]: at Beauchief, 242; at Bradley, 2717; "Neuhalhewelle," at Repton, 536; at Spondon, 2181; Wyhitlakeswelle, in Stanton-by-Dale, 2195; the Abbot's well at Whatstandwell, 2555.

Wirksworth, grant by Edw. I. of a market and fair at, 2656; grant of the office of bailiff and beremaister of, 2689.

Wool, seizure of, in Tideswell Church, 2336.

Y.

Yeaveley, sale of the site of the late commandry of Yeaveley, otherwise called "Stede" (1542), 2715.

York, Archbishop of, present at a Council in London [1128-39], 528.

Z.

Zacheus, St., charter dated on the Feast of, 1255.

Index of Owners and Sources.

B.

BEMROSE, Sir H. H.: 45, 285, 337, 338, 394, 412, 488, 530-532, 551, 554, 559-562, 564-568, 813, 874, 907, 1119, 1265, 1267, 1320, 1326, 1327, 1355, 1449, 1450, 1482-1486, 1540, 1694, 1695, 1823, 1904, 1906, 1912, 1913, 1938, 1991, 1992, 2296, 2320, 2535, 2627, 2701.

BOWLES, C. E. B.: 7, 96, 616, 617-626, 628, 630-632, 634, 638, 646, 648, 650, 651, 653, 654, 658, 1210, 1213, 1214, 1220, 1221, 1224-1236, 1238-1241, 1248-1250, 1253, 1255, 1256, 1259, 1260, 1263, 1268, 1269, 1282-1285, 1396, 1430, 1463-1468, 1712, 1718, 1722-1724, 2324.

BURDETT, Sir F., Bart.: 535, 540, 1939-1941, 1944, 1948, 1954, 1956-1958, 1961-1963, 1968, 1980, 1982, 1985, 1986.

C.

COKE, Col. W. J., of Brookhill: 50, 213, 1243, 1323-1325, 1447, 1448, 1788-1803, 1805-1810, 1873, 1877-1886, 2020, 2721.

COKE, Hon. H. J., of Longford: 355, 356, 365, 368, 370, 376-378, 382, 383, 1357-1359, 1393-1395, 1554, 1556, 1557, 1559-1565, 1568-1578, 1580-1605, 1629-1631, 1762, 1764, 2322, 2409.

COKE, Gen. J. T., of Trusley: 280, 283, 511, 525, 1004, 1130-1158, 1457, 1458, 1481, 1606, 1875, 1876, 2007, 2008, 2014-2016, 2018, 2157, 2169, 2390, 2391, 2397-2401, 2599.

D.

DERBY MUNIMENTS: 999, 1005-1007, 1010, 1013-1015.

DE RODES, Miss: 1191, 1192.

[D. / right column]

DRURY, Charles, of Sheffield: 43, 57, 61, 68, 69, 77, 79, 81, 87-89, 286, 403, 880, 883, 952, 1025, 1372, 1647, 1747-1751.

DRURY LOWE, W., of Locko: 90, 956-964, 1121, 2171-2174, 2181-2183, 2190.

E.

EVERY, Sir E. O., Bart.: 1160-1173, 1175-1190, 1200-1202, 1380, 1690, 1753, 1756-1759, 1761, 1763, 1765, 1934, 2080.

F.

FITZHARDINGE, Lord, of Berkeley: 487, 490-492, 1663, 2069.

FOLJAMBE, Rt. Hon. F. J. S.: 23, 97-104, 126, 132, 133, 207, 209, 223, 231, 232, 234, 236, 242, 243, 269, 271-278, 308-325, 352-354, 357-359, 361-364, 366, 367, 371-374, 380, 381, 415-477, 421-423, 430, 431, 444, 448, 450, 456, 458, 460-464, 466-468, 474, 493-500, 502-510, 542, 543, 552, 553-556, 619, 621, 629, 660, 662-664, 677, 681, 683, 684, 686-694, 697-703, 706-712, 717, 719, 720, 723, 726-731, 733-739, 741-747, 749-751, 753-758, 760-764, 766, 768-770, 773-775, 777, 778, 780-784, 786, 788-793, 795-806, 808-812, 814, 816, 819-821, 823, 825-831, 833-835, 837-842, 844-851, 855-859, 862-872, 930, 931, 997, 1031-1039, 1041-1045, 1047-1061, 1066, 1068, 1070-1075, 1194-1196, 1215, 1262, 1287, 1329, 1330, 1339, 1344, 1345, 1351-1354, 1376, 1392, 1433-1436, 1439, 1440, 1442, 1443, 1445, 1456, 1461, 1491-1496, 1512, 1535-1538, 1547, 1608, 1610-1613, 1669, 1773, 1779, 1815, 1855, 1856, 1858, 1859-

1861, 1902, 1903, 1905, 1907-1911, 1915, 2019, 2099, 2117, 2121, 2128, 2129, 2228, 2245, 2252, 2255, 2256, 2308-2310, 2312-2317, 2325-2333, 2340-2342, 2344, 2347-2349, 2351-2353, 2358-2365, 2367-2371, 2410, 2433, 2460, 2486, 2491, 2494, 2496-2533, 2554, 2557, 2558, 2560, 2561, 2564, 2567, 2604, 2667, 2706.

G.

GREGORY, J.—110-112, 116, 118-120, 125.

GRESLEY, Sir R., Bart.—603, 604, 909-914, 1026-1028, 1322, 1682, 1683, 1784, 1955, 2022-2068, 2070-2079, 2537, 2542, 2618.

H.

HALLOWES, Rev. B.: 915, 954, 1370, 1371, 1374, 1375, 1473.

HOLLAND, W. R.: 28-42, 922, 2147, 2635.

HORTON: 571-577, 579-602, 2538-2541.

K.

KERRY, Rev. C.: 290, 294, 299-303, 563, 610, 1120, 1636, 1917-1933, 1936, 1983, 1988, 2176-2180, 2187-2189, 2580, 2583-2597, 2600, 2650, 2651, 2665, 2671, 2672, 2674-2678, 2681-2683, 2686, 2687, 2692, 2694.

L.

LICHFIELD: 92, 170, 171, 173-177, 179-182, 185, 188-193, 195-199, 203, 205, 208, 214, 407, 408, 530, 606, 615, 620, 627, 644, 647, 649, 665, 853, 944, 945, 1270, 1272, 1328, 1333, 1356-1359, 1410-1428, 1431, 1432, 1438, 1518, 1519, 1551, 1579, 1615, 1617, 1618, 1662, 1705, 1710, 1720, 1811, 1814, 1816, 1824-1839, 1841, 1842, 1847, 1848, 1850-1852, 2175, 2298-2301, 2335-2337, 2343, 2346, 2350, 2372, 2378, 2379, 2404, 2406, 2408, 2495.

M.

MUNDY, Mrs.: 613, 614, 1300, 1522, 1524-1531, 1625, 1651-1660, 1774, 2100-2103, 2715.

O.

OGSTON: 817.

OKEOVER, H. C., of Okeover: 27, 54, 55, 59, 60, 65, 67, 70, 75, 76, 78, 80, 84, 86, 93, 129, 135-166, 339, 386, 388-393, 395, 404, 512-514, 882, 973, 1118, 1280, 1517, 1637-1646, 1648-1650, 1702, 1768, 1769, 1771, 1820, 1821, 2125-2127, 2130, 2132-2139, 2141-2143, 2707, 2729, 2730.

P.

POLE-GELL, the late H. Chandos: 8-10, 12, 13, 105-107, 210, 212, 475-479, 938, 975, 986, 1007-1009, 1389, 1451, 1452, 1454, 1490, 1624, 1840, 2654, 2699.

R.

ROPER, S.: 537-539.

S.

SCARSDALE, Lord, of Kedleston: 1499-1505, 1741, 2545-2553.

W.

WILMOT, Sir R. H. S., Bart.: 480, 481, 605, 607-609, 611, 612, 977-979, 981, 983, 985, 988, 992-995, 1002, 1003, 1459, 1616, 2281, 2411.

Bemrose & Sons Limited, Printers, Derby and London.

Lightning Source UK Ltd.
Milton Keynes UK
UKHW020009101122
411940UK00005B/64

9 781358 978654